the
Ultimate
Book of
Non-League
Players
2002-03

Compiled by
Steve Whitney

Published by Baltic Publications Limited

Published in Great Britain by
Baltic Publications Limited
Tel: 0191 442 4001
Fax: 0191 442 4002

Front Cover photographs (top to bottom):
Yeovil Town's 'keeper Chris Weale, taken by Peter Barnes;
Whitley Bay's Ian Chandler - scorer of the winning goal in the
2002 Vase final - with his medal, taken by Eric Marsh;
Whitley Bay manager Andy Gowans with the FA Vase, taken by
Graham Brown; current England Internationals- Nick
Crittenden (Yeovil Town - left) and Simon Wormull (Stevenage
Borough - right), taken by Peter Barnes.

Printed in Great Britain by
The Creative Design and Print Company
Washington, Tyne and Wear.

ISBN: 0-9544091-0-8

PUBLISHER'S PREFACE

This book contains details on almost 8000 Non-League players. In compiling the book we have taken the view that it is best to supply as much information as possible about a player. There is a varying degree of information about each player but it is fair to say that, thanks to Steve Whitney, this book can certainly be described as *The ULTIMATE* Book of Non-League Players.

After working with Steve Whitney over the past two years on a number of Non League projects I have no doubt that the expanse of his knowledge of Non-League players is unequalled. However, due to the nature and structure of Non-League football, even Steve cannot guarantee the accuracy of every fact contained herein. Non-League players can (and do) change clubs every day.

The Ultimate Book of Non-League Players 2002-03 is the closest there is to a comprehensive record of Non-League players at a point in time. Should any reader be aware of omissions or come across information which is inaccurate you are encouraged to visit www.thenon-leaguepaper.com where you can submit players' details as they change on an on-going basis. This website is edited by Steve Whitney and provides the most comprehensive on-line source of Non-League Football information.

It is important for me to mention the sponsors of this book. All advertisers in this book are paying to demonstrate their support for Non-League football and in doing so they are recognising the importance of football at this level. You are asked to remember this the next time you are considering purchasing anything which could be supplied by these advertisers. Without the support of such companies not only would books like this not be published but Non-League Football as a whole would suffer financially.

Finally, thanks are owed to Tony Williams for his advice and assistance in putting this book together and, most importantly, thanks to you for buying.

Andy Mullen

FROM THE EDITOR

This is the fourth Non-League Players book that I have been involved in compiling, and this is without doubt the biggest and most comprehensive to date.

Included in this edition are detailed pen-pictures of thousands of players from all levels of the Non-League Pyramid plus previous club details on thousands of others.

As with the last edition in 1997, it has mainly been produced in pen-picture style as that is how most people prefer it. Compiling it in this way means that it is not only a useful source of information but also a more than handy companion for hard-working programme editors up and down the country.

The very nature of football at our level means that some of the players included in this book will already have moved on from the last club given. But we have left the production as late as possible so as to be as up-to-date as we can be.

The previous editions of the Non-League Players book have not only proved popular with supporters but also with scouts from Premiership and Football League clubs as well as the actual players themselves, who always like to see their names in print!

I should like to express my thanks to Andy Mullen for his work on getting this project up and running and for Baltic Publications Limited for their hard work in the production of the book.

I hope you enjoy the 2002-03 edition and find the information both interesting and informative.

Steve Whitney

THE NON-LEAGUE PAPER

ESSENTIAL READING FOR FOLLOWERS OF THE NATIONAL GAME

SHARE THE PASSION

THE NON-LEAGUE PAPER

Issue No 186 Sunday October 27, 2002

ESSENTIAL READING FOR FOLLOWERS OF THE NATIONAL GAME £1.00

FA CUP SPECIAL

COVERAGE OF ALL YESTERDAY'S GAMES – INSIDE

48 PAGES OF NON-STOP SOCCER ACTION

TIVVY SEND THEM DIZZY

BBC get score wrong as Shreeves suffers

THE NON-LEAGUE PAPER

Issue No 135 Sunday October 20, 2002

CONFERENCE & PYRAMID LEAGUES SOCCER £1.00

EXCLUSIVE: BORG
I paid £15,000 in paper bag to sign player

EXCLUSIVE: CHAPPLE
Death threat to my daughter made me want to walk out

48 PAGES OF NEWS, MATCH REPORTS, RESULTS & FIXTURES

HUDSON AT HIGH-SPEED

EVERY SUNDAY

A

ABBASI, KAMRAN — *Midfielder*

Current Club:
Birthplace: Oxford
Previous clubs include: Oxford C - December 2001, Witney T, Oxford C.

ABBEY, BEN — *Forward*

Current Club: Woking
D o B: 13/05/1978   *Birthplace: London*
Talented striker who signed for Conference side Woking in August 2002 from Dr Martens Premier outfit Crawley Town. Had originally joined Crawley from Maidenhead United in September 1997 and scored 46 times during a two-year spell. Went on to make 13 appearances for Oxford United (one goal to his name) before transferring to Aldershot. Southend United's leading marksmen during 2000/01 with 13 goals, he spent the opening part of the 2001/02 season abroad, playing in PFA-sponsored competitions. Trained with Leyton Orient upon his arrival back to the UK and made one appearance for Stevenage Borough before returning to Crawley in December 2001.

ABBOTT, GARY — *Forward*

Current Club: Grays Athletic
D o B: 07/11/1964   Birthplace: Catford
Honours won: England Semi-Pro Int.
One of the most prolific goalscorers currently playing Non-League football, Gary re-joined Welling United during the summer of 2001 from Aldershot Town before switching to Ryman Premier outfit Grays Athletic in August 2002. A former England semi-professional international and Golden Boot winner, Gary spent his formative years with Welling and has subsequently been sold twice (to Barnet and Enfield) and brought back twice. Also had a spell with Slough Town, Gary is one of the highest goalscorers in the history of the Conference and, of course, is Wellings record marksman.

ABBOTT, JIMMY — *Defender*

Current Club: Ware
Birthplace: Herts
Previous clubs include: Hertford T - September 2001, Ware.

ABBOTT, MARK — *Midfielder*

Current Club: Carshalton Athletic
Birthplace: Surrey
Mark joined Ryman Division One South side Carshalton Athletic during the 2001/02 season, having spent two years with Gloucester City in the Dr Martens League, where he made 56 first-team appearances. Mark is one of the most competitive and vociferous players. His ability to work tirelessly from box to box was integral to the clubs reserve success.

ABBOTT, PAUL — *Midfielder*

Current Club: Aberystwyth Town
Birthplace: Herts
Previous clubs include: Stevenage Borough - August 2002.

ABBOTT, STUART — *Forward*

Current Club: Erith & Belvedere
Birthplace: Kent
Joined Erith & Belvedere two years ago from Dartford. Started his career at Welling United. A talented right sided quick and versatile player.

ABBS, MARK — *Midfielder*

Current Club: Mildenhall Town
Birthplace: Cambridge
Previous clubs include: Histon - July 2001.

ABDOL, ALI — *Forward*

Current Club: Haverfordwest County
Birthplace: France
Previous clubs include: Albion Rovers - February 2002.

ABERCROMBIE, MATT — *Midfielder*

Current Club: Bedworth United
Birthplace: Coventry
From Youth team.

ABIODUN, AYODEJI — *Forward*

Current Club: Maidenhead United
Birthplace: London
Previous clubs include: Enfield - October 2001, Dulwich Hamlet.

ABOAGYE, RAY — *Midfielder*

Current Club: Whitstable Town
D o B: 23/07/1972   *Birthplace: Kent*
Previous clubs include: Herne Bay - July 2000, Erith & Belvedere, Furness.

ABRAHAM, GARETH — *Defender*

Current Club: Rhayader Town
D o B: 13/02/1969   *Birthplace: Merthyr Tydfil*
Signed from Merthyr Tydfil in July 2001. Has played in the football league for both Cardiff City and Hereford United. Very strong, commanding centre back, who is also the club captain.

ABRAHAM, MERVN — *Forward*

Current Club: Grays Athletic
D o B: 13/11/1980   *Birthplace: Forest Gate*
Very fit and fast forward who can give 100% for the whole game, he is a proven goalscorer, and saw service with Dulwich Hamlet before joining Grays last season.

ABRAHAMS, PAUL — *Forward*

Current Club: Heybridge Swifts
D o B: 31/10/1973   *Birthplace: Colchester*
Experienced striker latterly with Colchester United, who joined Heybridge Swifts from Wivenhoe during the summer of 2001. Cultured attacker, super skills on the ball and a proven goalscorer. Has also seen service with Brentford, Kettering Town, Canvey Island and Chesham United. Made over 150 League appearances.

ABRAHAMS, PAUL — *Midfielder*

Current Club: Hamble ASSC
Birthplace: Hampshire
Previous clubs include: Portsmouth RN - August 2001.

ABRAHART, LEE — *Defender*

Current Club: Stanway Rovers
Birthplace: Essex
Previous clubs include: Wivenhoe T - July 2001, Harwich & Parkeston, Wivenhoe T, Heybridge Swifts, Harwich & Parkeston, Brantham Ath.

ACHAMFUUR, NANA — *Forward*

Current Club: Aldershot Town
Teenage striker, highly-rated, who joined Aldershot in January 2000 from Division Two side Egham Town.

A

ACTON, DARREN — Goalkeeper

Current Club: Tamworth

D o B: 19/05/1973   Birthplace: Wolverhampton

An experienced goalkeeper, Darren began his career with Telford United and has also played for Burton Albion. He signed for Tamworth in June 1999 from Kidderminster Harriers and become a favourite with both the players and fans. He gained Southern League representative honours during the 2000/01 season.

ACTON, RICHARD — Goalkeeper

Current Club: Hyde United

D o B: 16/10/1979   Birthplace: Manchester

Previous clubs include: Runcorn - March 2001, Woodley Sports.

ADAMS, ADI — Forward

Current Club: Forest Green Rovers

D o B: 12/06/1984   Birthplace: Rinteln, Germany

A product of Conference side Forest Green Rovers Youth/College system, Adi is a highly-promising young centre forward. Played in Englands under-18s Schoolboy international squad during the 2001/02 season.

ADAMS, CARL — Midfielder

Current Club: Hednesford Town

D o B: 13/03/1974   Birthplace: Birmingham

An experienced left-sided midfielder who joined Dr Martens Premier side Hednesford Town in August 2002 after spending a season with Ryman Premier outfit Bedford Town. Began his career with Birmingham and then had spells with Weymouth and Stevenage Borough before enjoying a lengthy spell with Kettering Town, where he appeared in the FA Trophy final at Wembley.

ADAMS, CHRIS — Defender

Current Club: Altrincham

D o B: 10/10/1975   Birthplace: Manchester

Re-signed for Altrincham in June 2001 from Ashton United for whom he played 53 games during the 2000/01season. Originally signed at the start of 97-98 season from Congleton but had limited chances and moved on to neighbours Trafford and Nantwich before signing for Ashton United. Has also played for Droylsden, Northwich and started with Oldham Athletic.

ADAMS, DANNY — Midfielder

Current Club: Hemel Hempstead Town

D o B: 11/02/1975   Birthplace: Watford

Previous clubs include: Hertford T - October 2000, Hemel Hempstead, Enfield, Yeovil T, Hendon, Enfield, Walton & Hersham, St.Albans C, Enfield, St.Albans C, Watford (Trainee).

ADAMS, DARREN — Forward

Current Club: Erith & Belvedere

D o B: 12/01/1974   Birthplace: Bromley

Strong, quick centre forward. Played for Cardiff City, Welling United and Dover before signing for Erith & Belvedere in February 2001. Great goalscorer will get goals at any level.

ADAMS, DAVE — Forward

Current Club: Eastbourne Borough

Birthplace: Sussex

Signed from Hailsham Town (Sussex County League) during the close season. The subject of interest of several professional clubs and has recently had trials with Brighton and Hove Albion.

ADAMS, DYLAN — Midfielder

Current Club: Halesowen Harriers

Birthplace: Worcestershire

Previous clubs include: Sandwell Borough - July 1997, Lye T, Halesowen Harriers, Halesowen T.

ADAMS, GAVIN — Defender

Current Club: Halesowen Harriers

Birthplace: Worcestershire

Previous clubs include: Cradley T - July 2001, Willenhall T, Halesowen Harriers.

ADAMS, GLEN — Forward

Current Club: Cheshunt

Birthplace: Essex

Previous clubs include: Aveley - August 1999, Witham T, Billericay T, Braintree T, Enfield.

ADAMS, KIERAN — Midfielder

Current Club: Windsor & Eton

D o B: 20/10/1977   Birthplace: St.Ives

Very talented midfielder who signed for Windsor & Eton in January 2002 from Ryman Premier Division Purfleet. Started out at Barnet where he made a number of League appearances and has also gained experience with Billericay Town and Boreham Wood.

ADAMS, MARK — Midfielder

Current Club: Dereham Town

Birthplace: Norfolk

Product of the Youth set-up. Strong, tenacious and pacey wing back who has a keen eye for goal. Just a shame he never manages one!

ADAMS, RICHARD — Forward

Current Club: Haverfordwest County

D o B: 15/05/1979   Birthplace: Bristol

Previous clubs include: Milford Utd - December 2001.

ADAMS, TERRY — Defender

Current Club: Barking & East Ham United

From Youth team.

ADAMSON, CHRIS — Midfielder

Current Club: Newtown AFC

D o B: 03/05/1978   Birthplace: Liverpool

Honours won: British Universities Rep.

Young mid-field player who has had experience with British University teams. Joined the club at the start of last season from Conwy United, has already made his mark in the first team. Has good vision with an excellent turn of speed and the ability to pressure defenders.

ADAMSON, LEE — Forward

Current Club: Spennymoor United

D o B: 30/06/1971   Birthplace: Easington

Previous clubs include: Seaham Red Star - January 2002, Spennymoor Utd, Seaham Red Star, Gateshead, Seaham Red Star, Jarrow Roofing, Whitley Bay, Spennymoor Utd, Murton, Harrogate T, Whitby T, Murton.

ADCOCK, WAYNE — Forward

Current Club: Clacton Town

D o B: 14/07/1971   Birthplace: Essex

Previous clubs include: Heybridge Swifts - December 2000, Witham T, Braintree T, Chelmsford C, Eton Manor.

2   **The Ultimate Book of Non-League Players 2002-03**

ADDAI, KENNY — Goalkeeper
Current Club: Enfield
Previous clubs include: Beaconsfield SYCOB - January 2001, Haringey B, Chalfont St.Peter, Leyton Pennant, Chesham Utd, St.Albans C, Grays Ath., Leyton Pennant, Boreham Wood, Fisher Ath., Walton & Hersham, Sutton Utd.

ADDIS, DARRYL — Forward
Current Club: Cinderford Town
Birthplace: Gloucestershire
Local lad who first played Dr Martens League football as a 16-year-old. Re-joined Cinderford Town from Westfields during the early part of the 2000/01 season and is now attracting interest from many clubs. An exciting attacking prospect.

ADEBOWALE, ANDY — Midfielder
Current Club: Berkhamsted Town
Birthplace: Hertfordshire
Previous clubs include: St.Albans C - December 2000, Chesham Utd, Berkhamsted T, Gravesend, Gloucester C, Merthyr Tydfil, Chesham Utd, Bishops Stortford, Hertford T, Balls Park.

ADEDEJI, OLLIE — Defender
Current Club: Canvey Island
Birthplace: London
Ollie joined Canvey Island in June 2002 after being released by Ryman League rivals Aldershot Town towards the end of the 2001/02 season. Was a summer 1999 acquisition for the Shots from Bromley where he had played for the previous six seasons. A reliable and consistent centre half, Ollie progressed through the Shots reserves initially before making the centre half position his own. A former player of the year at Bromley, Ollie has also played for Finchley and Boreham Wood.

ADEOYE, KUNLE — Forward
Current Club: Clapton
D o B: 26/05/1983   *Birthplace: London*
Previous clubs include: Leyton Orient - July 2001, QPR (Junior).

ADES, MATT — Goalkeeper
Current Club: Whitehawk
Birthplace: Sussex
Goalkeeper: made his first-team debut for Whitehawk during 1999/2000 whilst still a member of their youth side: regular choice from August 2001 onwards.

ADEY, DAVE — Goalkeeper
Current Club: Evesham United
Birthplace: Worcestershire
Previous clubs include: Redditch Utd - February 2002, Solihull B, Redditch Utd, Sutton Coldfield T, Redditch Utd, Boldmere St.Michaels.

ADLINGTON, TOM — Defender
Current Club: Dartford
D o B: 29/01/1975   *Birthplace: Kent*
Previous clubs include: Ashford T - March 1999, Erith & Belvedere, Banstead Ath., Horsham, Maidstone Utd, West Ham Utd (Trainee).

ADOLPHE, PAUL — Midfielder
Current Club: Ford United
Birthplace: Essex
Honours won: Ryman League Div.One Winners
Utility player, capable of performing equally well in defence or midfield. Signed for Ford United in February 2002 from Harrow

Borough to strengthen the Motormens ultimately successful bid for the Ryman League Division One title. Originally with Enfield, he has also had spells with Leyton Pennant, St Albans City, Grays Athletic and Hendon.

AFANDIYEV, FARHAD — Goalkeeper
Current Club: Hinckley United
Birthplace: Azerbaijan
Honours won: Azerbaijan u-21 Int.
Farhad is an Azerbaijan national currently working as goalkeeping coach for Nuneaton Borough. He joined Hinckley in the 2001/02 season and made mostly local cup appearances, but did get some first-team action towards the end of the season. Farhad has played for the Azerbaijan under-21 national side.

AGER, ADRIAN — Defender
Current Club: Norwich United
D o B: 24/08/1983   *Birthplace: Norfolk*
Former youth team captain and young player of the year at Norwich United. Has established himself as a regular in the side in defence.

AGER, PAUL — Defender
Current Club: Felixstowe & Walton United
Birthplace: Suffolk
In in his third season at Dellwood Avenue having originally signed for Felixstowe P & T under Scott Clark. Reliable centre or left back.

AGGREY, JIMMY — Defender
Current Club: Dover Athletic
D o B: 26/10/1978   *Birthplace: London*
Previous clubs include: Torquay Utd - December 2001, Fulham, Chelsea.

AGNEW, STEVE — Midfielder
Current Club: Gateshead
D o B: 09/11/1965   *Birthplace: Shipley*
Vastly experienced midfielder who made over 250 League appearances in a 15-year period. He made his name at home-town club Barnsley before reaching his peak at Leicester City and Sunderland in the Premiership. Steve joined Gateshead in the summer of 2001 and instantly became the club captain and later player/assistant-manager.

AGOGO, JUNIOR — Forward
Current Club: Barnet
D o B: 01/08/1979   *Birthplace: Accra, Ghana*
A tall, 6ft 1ins tall consistent goalscorer who played for QPR on a non-contract basis at the end of the 2001/02 season when the club was in administration and made two first-team appearances in the Second Division. Rangers were keen to keep him, but Agogo opted to join Barnet in June 2002 on a longer contract and work again with head coach Peter Shreeves, who was at Wednesday when he was there. Ghanian Agogo has also played on loan from Wednesday at Oldham, Chesterfield, Lincoln City, and Chester City - were he scored 6 goals in 10 games. Agogos last club was San Jose Earthquakes in the USA Major League. Agogo - whose first name is Manuel but is known as Junior - was a schoolboy at Chelsea. He signed professional forms for Wednesday at 17 after being spotted playing at Willesden Hawkeye. He made four first-team appearances at Hillsborough. He joined the Major League as a junior international player when he moved to the USA and played for Chicago and Colorado before San Jose.

A

AGUDOSI, CHUK — Forward
Current Club: Egham Town
Birthplace: Nigeria
Previous clubs include: Windsor & Eton - August 2002, Croydon, Maidenhead Utd, Osterley.

AHMET, GANI — Midfielder
Current Club: Dorking
Birthplace: London
Previous clubs include: Whyteleafe - October 2000, Tooting & Mitcham Utd, Leatherhead, Carshalton Ath., Leatherhead, Tooting & Mitcham Utd, Hampton, Tooting & Mitcham Utd, Vandyke, Brentford (Junior).

AINSCOUGH, PHIL — Midfielder
Current Club: Curzon Ashton
Previous clubs include: Glossop North End - October 2000.

AINSLEY, JASON — Midfielder
Current Club: Spennymoor United
Previous clubs include: Bishop Auckland - October 2001, Barrow, Balestier (Singapore) Gateshead, Jurang (Singapore), Gateshead, Jurang (Singapore), Blyth Spartans, Spennymoor Utd, Hartlepool Utd, Spennymoor Utd, Bishop Auckland, Spennymoor Utd, Guisborough T.

AINSLIE, KEVIN — Midfielder
Current Club: Stamford
Birthplace: Lincolnshire
Previous clubs include: Bourne T - January 2002.

AIRDRIE, STEWART — Forward
Current Club: Hednesford Town
Birthplace: Bradford
Stewart is a talented forward who signed for Hednesford Town during the close season of 1999 from Guiseley. During his time at the club Stewart has gained great appreciation from the supporters, thanks to his pace, skill and wizardry when He's flying down the wing.

AJET, ADEWALE — Forward
Current Club: Altrincham
Birthplace: Nigeria
Pacey Nigerian-born striker who joined UniBond Premier side Altrincham in last August 2002 after a spell with Dr Martens Premier outfit Hednesford Town. First played in England with Chester City and then went north of the border to join Queens Park and Hamilton. Signed for the Pitmen in January 2002.

AKERS, LEE — Defender
Current Club: Dulwich Hamlet
D o B: 02/03/1966　　Birthplace: London
Veteran defender who returned to Dulwich Hamlet for an incredibl FIFTH time in December 2001from Carshalton Athletic, where he had also been twice before. Apart from over 400 appearances for Hamlet, Lee has also played for Bromley, Greenwich Borough, Malden Vale, Tonbridge and Croydon.

AKMENKALNS, DARREN — Midfielder
Current Club: Littlehampton Town
Birthplace: Sussex
Industrious midfielder, who really adds some steel to the side (also used as a defender during 2000/01 because of the number of injuries): Littlehamptons best young performer of 1999/2000 and outright player of the year last season.

AKUAMOAH, EDDIE — Forward
Current Club: Bromley
D o B: 20/11/1972　　Birthplace: London
Honours won: FA Trophy Winners, Ryman League Premier Div.Winners, British Universities Rep.
Striker who joined Ryman League Division One South club Bromley in July 2002 from Premier Division Sutton United. Had signed for Sutton during the summer of 2001 after eight seasons with Kingstonian, for whom he played over 300 games, featuring in the Ryman League triumph of 1998 and two subsequent FA Trophy victories, scoring twice in the 3-2 defeat of Kettering in the 1999/00 final at Wembley. He also scored the only goal of the victory at Southend during Kingstonians FA Cup run last season. Previously with Carshalton Athletic and Bedfont, he represented Great Britain in the 1996 World Student Games.

AKURANG, CLIFF — Forward
Current Club: Purfleet
D o B: 27/02/1981　　Birthplace: Ghana
Previous clubs include: Hitchin T - December 2001, Chesham Utd, Luton T (Junior), Chelsea (Junior).

ALDERY, MATTHEW — Forward
Current Club: Harrogate Town
Birthplace: Yorkshire
Honours won: UniBond League Div.One Winners
Promising young forward who signed for Harrogate Town over the summer of 2001 from Guiseley. He was on loan to Farsley Celtic from November to January this season.

ALBRIGHTON, MARK — Defender
Current Club: Doncaster Rovers
Birthplace: Coventry
Mark is regarded as one of the best defenders in the Conference. He began his career with Nuneaton but it was with neighbouring Atherstone United that he really started to come to the fore. Telford paid £15,000 for his services in 1999 and he formed a fine partnership with Neil Moore and Jim Bentley at the heart of the Lilywhites defence. Transferred to Doncaster just after the end of the 2001/2002 season.

ALDEN, DARREN — Goalkeeper
Current Club: Sutton Coldfield Town
Previous clubs include: Stourbridge - June 2001, Evesham Utd, Bromsgrove R, Paget R, Bromsgrove R, Tamworth, Burntwood.

ALDER, KEVIN — Goalkeeper
Current Club: North Leigh
D o B: 22/07/1964　　Birthplace: Oxford
Previous clubs include: Witney T - July 2001, Clanfield, Bicester T.

ALDERSON, RICHIE — Midfielder
Current Club: Spennymoor United
D o B: 15/12/1977　　Birthplace: Newcastle
Attacking midfielder who returned to UniBond First Division Spennymoor United in July 2002 from Premier Division Gateshead. Started his career as a trainee with Newcastle United and then had spells with Whitley Bay and Whickham before joining the Moors for the first time in 1995. His form was such that York gave him a second bite at League football, but he was soon back again on the Non-League scene with Whitby Town, Gateshead and Durham City, returning to Gateshead in February 2001.

ALDERSON, SIMON — Forward
Current Club: Mickleover Sports
Birthplace: Newcastle
Previous clubs include: Darlington - July 2000.

ALDIS, ROGER — Midfielder
Current Club: Stowmarket Town
Birthplace: Suffolk
Previous clubs include: Diss T - July 1999, Great Yarmouth T, Stowmarket T, Lowestoft T.

ALDRIDGE, IAN — Forward
Current Club: Cradley Town
Birthplace: Birmingham
Previous clubs include: Oldbury Utd - July 2001, Halesowen T, Cradley T.

ALDRIDGE, PAUL — Defender
Current Club: Berkhamsted Town
Birthplace: Berkhamsted
Previous clubs include: Tring T - February 2000, Hemel Hempstead, Tring T, Berkhamsted T, Tring T, Berkhamsted T.

ALEXANDER, ANDY — Midfielder
Current Club: Worthing
Birthplace: Sussex
Powerfully-built young midfielder: played for the reserves 1998/99 and was recalled into the first-team from Shoreham in September 2001: ended a Worthing goal-drought by scoring their first for 413 minutes against Tooting/Mitcham during January 2002 (lost 2-1).

ALEXANDER, TIM — Defender
Current Club: Total Network Solutions
D o B: 29/03/1974 Birthplace: Chertsey
Honours won: British Universities Rep.
A talented central defender and skipper of the British Universities team. Signed for TNS in July 1999 from Ryman Leaguers Carshalton Athletic, he has also enjoyed experience with Barnet, Woking, Walton & Hersham, Bromley, Dagenham & Redbridge and Brentford and also plyed in South Africa for Cape Town.

ALFORD, CARL — Forward
Current Club: Yeovil Town
D o B: 11/02/1972 Birthplace: Denton
Honours won: England Semi-Pro Int., FA Trophy Winners
One of the most prolific scorers in the Conference in recent years, Carl has been the leading marksman in the Conference on more than one occasion. Began his career with Rochdale, Stockport and Burnley but it wasn't until joining the Non-League ranks at Witton Albion and then Macclesfield Town that his career began to blossom. Switched to Kettering Town for £25,000 in 1994 and enjoyed a very productive couple of years at Rockingham Road. Moved to neighbouring Rushden & Diamonds in March 1996 for a Non-League record fee of £85,000 but, following a change of manager, Carl became unsettled at Nene Park and transferred to Stevenage Borough after two years on a Bosman. Found his goalscoring boots again and that pursuaded Doncaster to part with £55,000 to take him to Yorkshire in June 2000, and then to Yeovil a year later. Scored one of the goals that won the FA Trophy for the Glovers in May 2002.

ALGIERI, NICO — Forward
Current Club: Haverfordwest County
D o B: 16/09/1981 Birthplace: Wales
From Youth team.

ALI, ALTON — Forward
Current Club: Great Wakering Rovers
Birthplace: Southend
Previous clubs include: Southend Manor - March 2001.

ALICOCK, RICHARD — Forward
Current Club: Leatherhead
Birthplace: Surrey
Previous clubs include: Hampton & Richmond Borough - September 2001.

ALIGHIERI, DANTE — Forward
Current Club: Molesey
Birthplace: London
Previous clubs include: Sutton Utd - October 2001, Woking.

ALIMI, BASHIRU — Midfielder
Current Club: Kingstonian
D o B: 20/03/1982 Birthplace: London
Young midfielder thrust into the centre of the Kingstonian defence during an early season injury crisis, but proved so effective that he kept his place for the rest of the 2001/02 campaign. Works extremely hard and is tough in the tackle. Was previously on Millwalls books.

ALLAIN, CYRILLE — Midfielder
Current Club: Clapton
D o B: 23/03/1978 Birthplace: Paris, France
Previous clubs include: Auxerre (France) - July 2001.

ALLCOCK, JOHN — Defender
Current Club: Barwell
D o B: 14/01/1972 Birthplace: Yorkshire
Previous clubs include: Gresley Rovers - December 2001, Hucknall T, Hinckley Utd, Hucknall T, Alfreton T, Treeton Welfare, Rotherham Utd (Junior), Barnsley (Junior).

ALLEN, ADRIAN — Forward
Current Club: Maidenhead United
D o B: 25/06/1977 Birthplace: Islington
Signed for United in March 2000. At the time was leading scorer at Leyton Pennant with 17 goals to his name in al lcompetitions. Also saw action with Clapton.

ALLEN, ALEX — Defender
Current Club: Gainsborough Trinity
D o B: 10/02/1980 Birthplace: Doncaster
Previous clubs include: Brodsworth Welfare - December 1999, Norwich C.

ALLEN, CHRIS — Forward
Current Club: Aldershot Town
D o B: 18/11/1972 Birthplace: Oxford
Honours won: England u-21 Int.
Experienced winger signed from Dover Athletic in March 2002 having previously played for Oxford United, Nottingham Forest, Port Vale, Stockport County and Brighton & Hove Albion. Once commanded a half a million pound transfer fee, when he moved from Oxford to Forest. A former England under-21 international whose skillful play on the wing and his pacey, determined running with be a big asset to the Shots.

ALLEN, CHRIS — Midfielder
Current Club: Fairford Town
Birthplace: Wiltshire
From Youth team.

A

ALLEN, DANIEL — *Midfielder*
Current Club: Forest Green Rovers

D o B: 09/09/1983   *Birthplace: Swindon*
A product of Conference side Forest Green Rovers Youth/College system. Midfielder with good passing ability and a very promising future. Played in Englands under-18s Schoolboy international squad during the 2001/02 season.

ALLEN, DAVE — *Defender*
Current Club: Enfield Town (Essex)

Birthplace: Herts
With Harlow Town last season, where he made several first team appearances including two in the FA Trophy against eventual winners Canvey Island. Previously with Cockfosters, made his Enfield Town debut in September 2001.

ALLEN, DEAN — *Forward*
Current Club: Ford United

D o B: 09/05/1979   *Birthplace: Rush Green*
Striker who re-joined Ryman Premier newcomers Ford United from Barking & East Ham United in July 2002. Had signed for Barking from neighbours East Thurrock United in March 2002. A former Hornchurch and Grays Athletic player, Dean really came to the fore whilst in his first spell at Ford.

ALLEN, EBEN — *Forward*
Current Club: Dulwich Hamlet

Birthplace: London
Forward who is in his second spell with Dulwich Hamlet, rejoining from Croydon in October 2001. Has also played for Yeading, Molesey, Hampton, Staines Town, Marlow, Goldalming & Guildford and was on the books at both Arsenal and West Brom as a youngster. Has been a regular scorer in recent seasons.

ALLEN, GARY — *Forward*
Current Club: Whitstable Town

Birthplace: Kent
Honours won: Kent League Winners
Previous clubs include: Lordswood - July 1999, Herne Bay, Canterbury C, Sheppey Utd, Canterbury C, Sittingbourne.

ALLEN, GAVIN — *Forward*
Current Club: Aberystwyth Town

D o B: 17/06/1976   *Birthplace: Deiniolen*
Previous clubs include: Bangor C - July 2000, Aberystwyth T, Stockport Co., Tranmere R.

ALLEN, JASON — *Defender*
Current Club: Banbury United

Birthplace: Oxfordshire
Previous clubs include: Brackley T - February 2002, Bicester T, Brackley T, Buckingham T, Brackley T, Bicester T.

ALLEN, JASON — *Forward*
Current Club: Whitehawk

Birthplace: Sussex
Striker and Hawks player of the year in 1998/99. Sidelined with injury for the start of the following campaign and was signed by Three Bridges in February 2000, scoring five times before rejoining Whitehawk the following October. Out of form until striking both goals in the defeat of Ringmer on the opening day of the 2001/02 campaign.

ALLEN, LEE — *Forward*
Current Club: Gloucester City

Previous clubs include: Longlevens - July 2001.

ALLEN, LEE — *Midfielder*
Current Club: Purfleet

D o B: 12/03/1979   *Birthplace: Islington*
Former Leicester City attacking midfielder who joined Ryman Premier side Purfleet in the summer of 2002 from rivals Enfield. Started his career at Filbert Street and then had a spell on Wycombe Wanderers books before going Non-League with Walton & Hersham. Chesham United was his next port of call before switching to the Es in October 2000.

ALLEN, LEIGHTON — *Forward*
Current Club: Peacehaven & Telscombe

Birthplace: Sussex
Impressive forward, who started his football career with the likes of Wimbledon and Colchester: more recently spent three years with Saltdean (having joined from Ringmer) and was their leading scorer during 1999/2000 with 28 goals: subsequently had a brief spell with Lewes at the start of the following season before joining Peacehaven and contributed 18 goals towards the start of their promotion-winning campaign, including one in the Division Two Cup Final victory over Oving.

ALLEN, MARC — *Midfielder*
Current Club: Redhill

Birthplace: Sussex
Exciting midfielder, with a sharp eye for goal. Previously played at Horsham before having a spell on-loan with Redhill towards the end of 1999/2000: spent last season at Pease Pottage (Mid-Sussex League champions) and returned to Kiln Brow during the summer. Dealt a massive blow during Reds FA Cup replay at Oxford City. Marc fell awkwardly under a challenge and snapped his cruciate ligament. Has undergone two operations, one to replace the ligament, and has high hopes of returning to playing next season after his playing days looked over.

ALLEN, MARK — *Defender*
Current Club: Flexsys Cefn Druids

D o B: 02/09/1976   *Birthplace: Cheshire*
Previous clubs include: Bangor C - September 1999, Conwy Utd.

ALLEN, MATT — *Defender*
Current Club: Cheshunt

Birthplace: Herts
Previous clubs include: Potters Bar T - July 2002, Hertford T, Northwood, Hertford T, Sawbridgeworth T.

ALLEN, MATT — *Forward*
Current Club: Eastbourne Borough

Birthplace: Bristol
Previous clubs include: Mangotsfield Utd - March 2002.

ALLEN, MATT — *Forward*
Current Club: Paulton Rovers

Birthplace: Eastbourne
Signed from Lewes (Ryman League) during the 1998/99 season, having also played for Saltdean United (Sussex County League). Played for Sussex FA Representative teams at both youth and senior level.

ALLEN, PAUL — *Midfielder*
Current Club: Buxton

Birthplace: Sheffield
Previous clubs include: Staveley Miners Welfare - October 2001, Denaby Utd, Worksop T, Rotherham Utd.

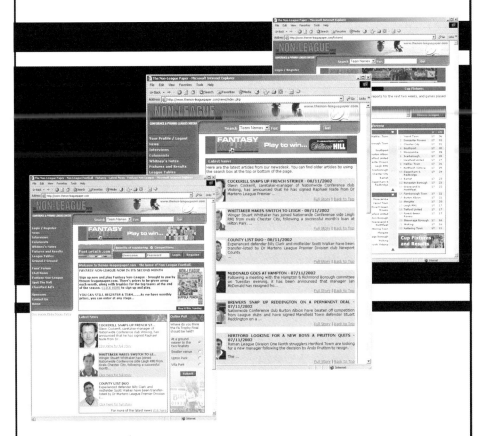

www.thenon-leaguepaper.com

ALLEN, ROY   *Forward*
Current Club: West Auckland Town
Birthplace: Co.Durham
From Youth team.

ALLER, ROSS   *Forward*
Current Club: Epsom And Ewell
Birthplace: Surrey
Previous clubs include: Maidenhead Utd - July 2001.

ALLEYNE, ANTHONY   *Forward*
Current Club: AFC Newbury
Birthplace: Berkshire
Forward who is capable of scoring a number of goals. Signed for
AFC Newbury in June 2002 from Ryman League Premier side
Maidenhead United. Originally with Newbury Town, he joined Dr
Martens outfit Burnham from local football at the start of the
2001/02 season and then switched to Maidenhead in January
2002.

ALLEYNE, DANNY   *Forward*
Current Club: Enfield Town (Essex)
Birthplace: Herts
Graduated from the Enfield FC Youth and reserve teams to make
66 first-team appearances, scoring 6 goals. Left the Es at the
start of this year and finished out the season playing for Yeading.
Made an immediate impact upon joining Enfield Town with two
goals on his debut against Saffron Walden Town.

ALLIS, ROB   *Midfielder*
Current Club: Mildenhall Town
Birthplace: Cambridge
Previous clubs include: Ely C - August 2001, Cambridge C,
Mildenahll T, Cambridge C.

ALLISON, CARL   *Midfielder*
Current Club: Bishops Stortford
Birthplace: Essex
A close season signing in the summer of 2001 from neighbours
and Essex Senior League side Saffron Walden. Carl is a fast and
compact player that stepped straight into the first team without
any problems. An injury has kept him out of the side recently and
his return is eagerly awaited.

ALLISON, MIKE   *Goalkeeper*
Current Club: Trafford
D o B: 17/03/1966   Birthplace: Johnstone
Previous clubs include: Rossendale Utd - March 2002, Trafford,
St.Helens T, Congleton T, St.Helens T, Droylsden, Leigh RMI,
Witton Alb., Morecambe, Chesterfield, Horwich RMI.

ALLISON, NEIL   *Defender*
Current Club: Gainsborough Trinity
D o B: 20/10/1973   Birthplace: Hull
Previous clubs include: Geylang Utd (New Zealand) - July 1999,
Guiseley, Chesterfield, Swindon T, Hull C.

ALLISON, RICHARD   *Forward*
Current Club: Garforth Town
D o B: 08/05/1981   Birthplace: Leeds
Now in his second season with Town, playing mostly with the
Reserves. Had a short spell in the First Team towards the latter
part of last season. Has now burst into the first team on a regular
basis due to his powerful, pacy runs down the right wing always
posing a danger to any defender. He is also good at tracking back
and making important tackles when required.

ALLISON, SAM   *Forward*
Current Club: Bath City
Birthplace: Chippenham
Re-joined Dr Martens League Premier Division club Bath City in
July 2002 after a spell at Western Division Clevedon Town. The
promising young striker had signed for Clevedon in October 2001
from Bath , where he scored 8 goals during the 2001/02 season.
Born in Chippenham, Sams only other senior club was
Cirencester Academy.

ALLMAN, JONATHAN   *Forward*
Current Club: Tonbridge Angels
D o B: 23/04/1983   Birthplace: London
Previous clubs include: Woking - December 2001, Charlton Ath.,
Tottenham Hotspur (Junior).

ALLMAN, NICK   *Midfielder*
Current Club: Shepshed Dynamo
D o B: 19/09/1978   Birthplace: Birmingham
Previous clubs include: Corby T - July 2001, Gresley R, Sutton
Coldfield T, Tamworth, Carlisle Utd.

ALLPRESS, TIM   *Defender*
Current Club: Hitchin Town
D o B: 27/01/1971   Birthplace: Hitchin
Experienced central defender who first joined Hitchin Town in
1995 after a Football League career with Luton, Preston and
Colchester United. His first period with the club was brief as he
moved to Hong Kong with the Enterprise club, but he is now in his
third spell with Hitchin after returning from St Albans City in
February 2000 and has now played more than 250 games for
the Canaries. Named Supporters Club Player of the Year in
2000/01.

ALLSOP, MICHAEL   *Defender*
Current Club: Belper Town
Previous clubs include: Burton Alb - May 2000.

ALMUNCHI, MARK   *Defender*
Current Club: Brodsworth Welfare
Birthplace: Doncaster
Previous clubs include: Rossington Main - December 1998,
Goole T, North Ferriby Utd, Bridlington T, Rossingtom Main,
Doncaster R (Trainee).

ALVITE, JOSE   *Forward*
Current Club: Beaconsfield SYCOB
Birthplace: Middlesex
Previous clubs include: Southall - July 2000.

AMANING, KWABENA   *Forward*
Current Club: Bromley
Birthplace: Kent
Has progressed this season from playing in Bromleys Reserve
team to the fringe of the first-team squad and has made his
appearances from the substitutes bench this season.

AMANUEL, GERMAIN   *Forward*
Current Club: Lewes
Birthplace: London
Previous clubs include: Redhill - December 2001, Ringmer,
Tooting & Mitcham Utd, Erith & Belvedere, Horsham, Bromley,
Beckenham T.

AMARTEIFIO, BILLY   *Defender*
Current Club: Wealdstone

D o B: 15/09/1982   Birthplace: London
Billy is a promising defender who joined Wealdstone in January 2001 after playing at the start of that season for Wembley. Suffered an injury in mid-season but returned to make a regluar place for himself in the senior side.

AMBRIDGE, GRANT   *Defender*
Current Club: Hanwell Town

D o B: 20/10/1977   Birthplace: Hammersmith
Previous clubs include: Bournemouth University - August 2001, Northwood.

AMES, DANNY   *Midfielder*
Current Club: Harrogate Railway

Birthplace: Harrogate
Previous clubs include: Farsley Celtic - December 1999, Harrogate RA, Harrogate T.

AMOOIE, DAVID   *Midfielder*
Current Club: Dawlishyde Town

D o B: 11/07/1979   Birthplace: Devon
Previous clubs include: Topsham T - July 2000, Alphington.

AMOS, CRAIG   *Defender*
Current Club: Feltham

Birthplace: Feltham
A regular member of the Reserve side, youngster Amos made his 1st team debut this season, mainly due to suspensions but has filled in admirably when required, returning some impressive performances way beyond his years. Known as Pup to his colleagues.

AMOS, DARREN   *Forward*
Current Club: Whitstable Town

Birthplace: Kent
Previous clubs include: Fisher Ath - July 1999, Faversham T, Nottingham Forest, Charlton Ath (Junior).

AMOS, GEOFF   *Midfielder*
Current Club: Stratford Town

Birthplace: Coventry
Previous clubs include: Racing Club Warwick - July 2000, Alveston, Kenilworth T, Stratford T.

AMOS, MIKE   *Forward*
Current Club: Ossett Town

Previous clubs include: Ossett Albion - August 2001, Selby T, Emley.

AMOS, NICK   *Midfielder*
Current Club: Solihull Borough

Birthplace: Essex
Signed from Conference side Hednesford Town during the summer of 2000. Essex born he has played for Hornchurch and Rainhan Town in the ICIS League as a teenager. He then moved to the Midlands and signed for Rushall Olympic. He then switched to the Conference to play for Bromsgrove Rovers in July 1995. He was awarded Managers Player of the season last season.

ANANE, DAVID   *Forward*
Current Club: Witton Albion

Previous clubs include: Cheadle Heath Nomads - November 1998, Altrincham, Sheffield Utd.

ANDERSON, CARL   *Forward*
Current Club: Stafford Town

Birthplace: Stafford
From Youth team.

ANDERSON, DALE   *Forward*
Current Club: Burton Albion

D o B: 10/11/1979   Birthplace: Birmingham
Dale Anderson was signed in March 1999 from Hednesford Town. He has an abundance of pace and is a constant menace to opposing defences. Dale started his career at Nottingham Forest where he was a member of the Forest youth side that won the League Championship. Dale has had a great season and his workmanlike performances and constant running have endeared him to the Eton Park faithful. Dale weighed in with 14 goals but created many with his surging runs.

ANDERSON, DALE   *Forward*
Current Club: West Auckland Town

Birthplace: Co.Durham
Previous clubs include: Evenwood T - July 2000, Darlington.

ANDERSON, DANNY   *Defender*
Current Club: Whitley Bay

Birthplace: Newcastle
A close season signing from Morpeth Town. Danny is a big strong no-nonsense defender who will strengthen up the defence.

ANDERSON, DAVE   *Midfielder*
Current Club: Whitby Town

D o B: 28/09/1979   Birthplace: Co.Durham
Tall, industrious midfielder who signed for UniBond Premier side Whitby Town from Albany Northern Leaguers Chester-le-Street in January 2002. Great distribution and comfortable on the ball, he can also play in defence. A former Sunderland youth player who has also had spells with Whitley Bay and South Shields.

ANDERSON, LEE   *Defender*
Current Club: Ashington

Birthplace: Northumberland
Previous clubs include: Newbiggin CW - July 1998.

ANDERSON, LUKE   *Midfielder*
Current Club: Welling United

D o B: 15/09/1974   Birthplace: London
Honours won: British Universities Rep.
Tall and elegant midfielder who switched from Crawley Town to Dr Martens rivals Welling United in June 2002 for an undisclosed fee. Had a spell on-loan at Crawley from Dulwich Hamlet prior to joining permanently in March 2000. Previously with Gravesend & Northfleet, he missed the start of 2001/02 as he was competing in the World Student Games in Beijing.

ANDERSON, MARK   *Forward*
Current Club: Gainsborough Trinity

Birthplace: Lincolnshire
Highly-promising young forward who joined UniBond Premier side Gainsborough Trinity in June 2002. Had been on Scunthorpe United's books through from schoolboy to young professional and made a handful of first-team appearances before being released at the end of the 2001/02 season.

ANDERSON, MARTIN — Defender

Current Club: Ashford Town

Birthplace: Kent

A young and highly-promising defender who uses the ball well. First played for Dr Martens Eastern side Ashford Town in April 2001 at Newport IOW. Came through the clubs youth ranks and spent much of the 2001/02 season on loan to Kent Leaguers Greenwich Borough.

ANDERSON, WAYNE — Midfielder

Current Club: Kings Lynn

Birthplace: Kings Lynn

Wayne is a battling midfielder who has made the successful move through the ranks at Kings Lynn. Beginning in Lynns under-18s, he went on to captain the Reserves. He was drafted into the first team squad and made his debut when coming on as a substitute during the 1999/00 season. He has since made an enormous impact in the side and has become a regular choice in the first-team midfield.

ANDERSON, WAYNE — Midfielder

Current Club: West Auckland Town

Birthplace: Co.Durham

Previous clubs include: Crook T - March 2001, West Auckland T, Willington, Washington, Derby Co.

ANDISON, GARY — Defender

Current Club: Chester-Le Street

Birthplace: Co.Durham

Signed for Chester-le-Street from Gretna during the close season of 2001. Well-travelled player who has also seen service with Sheffield United as a trainee, Whitley Bay, Spennymoor United, Bedlington Terriers, South Shields and Gretna. Has a great left foot.

ANDREWS, BEN — Defender

Current Club: Burgess Hill Town

Defender, who was once on the books of Brighton & Hove Albion: had been playing for West Chiltington (West Sussex League), until being called up as forward for Horsham YMCA in the John OHara League Cup Final during March 2002: Signed for County League Champions Burgess Hill in the 2002/2003 close season.

ANDREWS, GARY — Midfielder

Current Club: Atherton Laburnum Rovers

Birthplace: Wigan

Garry joined LR during the 1999/2000 season and, despite being in and out of the first team, he always impresses with his commitment. He is a very versatile player who always works hard for the team. Away from football, Garry is an electrical engineer.

ANDREWS, JIMMY — Midfielder

Current Club: Felixstowe & Walton United

Birthplace: Suffolk

Quickly established himself in the side at the start of last season having moved over from Walton United after the merger and is now maturing rapidly at Jewson League level despite his tender years.

ANDREWS, MARK — Defender

Current Club: Stowmarket Town

Birthplace: Suffolk

Previous clubs include: Haughley - July 2001, Bury T.

ANDREWS, MARK — Goalkeeper

Current Club: Rossendale United

Birthplace: Lancashire

Goalkeeper who joined Rossendale United in October 1999 from neighbours Chorley. Became recognised as one of the top keepers in the North West Counties League and played a major role in Dales promotion to the UniBond in 2000/01.

ANDREWS, NEIL — Midfielder

Current Club: Histon

Previous clubs include: Cambridge C - July 1997.

ANDREWS, NICKY — Defender

Current Club: Walton & Hersham

Birthplace: London

Nicky played for Fulham after coming through the youth side at Craven Cottage. Following a spell with near neighbours Molesey, Nicky made his debut for Swans in March 1999 after being a regular in the reserve side. A short spell with Leatherhead followed before he returned to Stompond Lane to be a regular in the first-team squad last season.

ANDREWS, PHIL — Forward

Current Club: Dorchester Town

D o B: 14/09/1976   Birthplace: Andover

Previous clubs include: Bashley - February 2001, Brighton.

ANDREWS, RICHARD — Forward

Current Club: Atherstone United

D o B: 26/03/1981   Birthplace: Warwickshire

Previous clubs include: Nuneaton Borough - August 2001, WBA, Walsall (Junior), Leicester C (Junior).

ANDREWS, RYAN — Midfielder

Current Club: Horsham

Birthplace: Sussex

Previous clubs include: Crawley T - July 2000, Broadbridge Heath.

ANDREWS, SHANE — Defender

Current Club: Chippenham Town

Birthplace: Wiltshire

Signed for Chippenham Town in October 1999 from Clevedon Town where he was in the side that won the Dr Martens Midlands Division Championship. Prior to that he was one of several Chippenham players who played for Calne Town. A tough-tackling defender. He played left back at Wembley in the FA Vase final. A builder by trade.

ANGEL, MARK — Midfielder

Current Club: Boston United

D o B: 23/08/1975   Birthplace: Newcastle

Boston United signed up Mark Angel from Darlington in June 2001. A skilful winger in the traditional mould, he had been on-loan at Queen of the South for much of the previous season.

ANGUS, TERRY — Defender

Current Club: Nuneaton Borough

D o B: 14/01/1966   Birthplace: Coventry

Terry can easily be described as one of the best central defenders in Non-League football. After starting his footballing life at VS Rugby he was soon snapped up by Northampton Town. He made 116 League appearances for The Cobblers. Terry then left Northampton Town to join Fulham. Again at Fulham he made numerous first-team appearances and was highly regarded by the Craven Cottage club. However he decided to leave Fulham and he joined Slough Town, despite the close attention of scouts at Nuneaton Borough. Eventually he was to look elsewhere and in July 1998 he signed with Nuneaton Borough.

ANI-OKOYE, IKEDI CALVIN   *Forward*
Current Club: Herne Bay
Birthplace: Chad
Previous clubs include: Addis - November 2001.

ANNAN, CHRISTIAN   *Forward*
Current Club: Ossett Town
Birthplace: Yorkshire
Arrived at Town in the pre-season of 1999/2000 from Frickley Athletic. Chris is a quick centre forward who has gained experience at a host of UniBond clubs including Bradford Park Avenue. Always amongst the goals and causes plenty of problems for defenders.

ANNIS, DARREN   *Forward*
Current Club: Wick
Birthplace: Sussex
Previous clubs include: Worthing - July 1999, Southwick.

ANNIS, PAUL   *Defender*
Current Club: St Margaretsbury
D o B: 06/05/1980   *Birthplace: Enfield*
Previous clubs include: Wodson Park - July 1999, Broxbourne, Leyton Orient (Junior).

ANNON, DARRON   *Midfielder*
Current Club: Farnborough Town
D o B: 17/02/1972   *Birthplace: London*
30-year-old midfielder who came through the ranks at Carshalton Athletic. Burst on to the Isthmian League scene with a bag and soon had the scouts flocking to Colston Avenue. Eventually moved to Brentford in March 1994 for a £20,000 fee and made 20 first-team appearances before returning to the Isthmian League in January 1996 with Kingstonian. Transferred to Enfield in October 1996 and then switched to Farnborough during the summer of 2000.

ANSBORO, GRANT   *Midfielder*
Current Club: Peacehaven & Telscombe
Birthplace: Sussex
Midfielder who was in good form for Lancing reserves during 2000/01 before returning to Whitehawk. Subsequently signed for Peacehaven in January 2002.

ANSELL, DARREN   *Midfielder*
Current Club: Pelsall Villa
Birthplace: Birmingham
Previous clubs include: Bridgnorth T - December 2001, Willenhall T, Rushall Olympic, Blakenall, Rocester, Chasetown, Rushall Olympic, Bilston T, Tamworth.

ANSELL, GARY   *Forward*
Current Club: Harlow Town
D o B: 08/11/1978   *Birthplace: London*
Striker who signed for Ryman Division One North side Harlow Town in August 2002 from neighbours St Albans City. Had joined City from Barnet in June 2000. Missed much of his first season due to a succession of injuries but still managed 11 goals in 23 appearances.

ANSON, ROBERT   *Defender*
Current Club: Flackwell Heath
Birthplace: Buckinghamshire
Previous clubs include: Marlow - January 2002, Flackwell Heath, Marlow, Flackwell Heath, Marlow.

ANSTEY, CRAIG   *Midfielder*
Current Club: Bashley
Birthplace: Hampshire
Previous clubs include: Havant & Waterlooville - January 2002, Waterlooville, Basingstoke T, Mansfield T, Basingstoke T.

ANSTISS, RICHARD   *Goalkeeper*
Current Club: Redditch United
Birthplace: Birmingham
Much-admired goalkeeper who has given sterling service to Hinckley Town, Racing Warwick, Bromsgrove Rovers and Paget Rangers and Solihull Borough. Transferred to Moor Green in October 2001 but then lost his first-team shirt to Adam Rachel and subsequently joined Redditch United in May 2002.

ANTHONY, GRAHAM   *Midfielder*
Current Club: Barrow
D o B: 09/08/1975   *Birthplace: South Shields*
Born in South Shields, Graham is a midfielder who began his career as a trainee with Sheffield United and went on to make three League appearances for the Blades before being released. Whilst he was with the Bramall Lane club, he also made two League appearances, on loan at Scarborough. He made three League appearances for Swindon Town and a further five League appearances for Plymouth Argyle before joining Carlisle United. He made a total of 69 League appearances for the United, scoring three times. He was released in the summer of 2000 and joined Barrow in August. He.

ANTHONY, PAUL   *Midfielder*
Current Club: Gateshead
D o B: 04/03/1982   *Birthplace: Carlisle*
Previous clubs include: Carlisle Utd - February 2002.

ANTHROBUS, STEVE   *Forward*
Current Club: Total Network Solutions
D o B: 10/11/1968   *Birthplace: Lewisham*
Well-known with League clubs as a strong target man, who can also adapt well to central defensive role. Signed for TNS in August 2001 from Oxford United, he made over 200 League appearances with the Us, Wimbledon, Shrewsbury, Millwall and Crewe.

ANTOINE, RICKY   *Midfielder*
Current Club: Enfield Town (Essex)
Birthplace: London
A member of the Enfield FC reserve team last season. Includes Bromley, Sutton and Stevenage among his previous Non-League clubs. Spent four years as a pro at Charlton and 18 months at Sheffield United.

ANTONIO, JOHN   *Forward*
Current Club: Clapton
D o B: 27/01/1980   *Birthplace: London*
From Local football - July 2001.

A

ANTROBUS, MARK   *Defender*

Current Club: Colwyn Bay

D o B: 09/07/1973   Birthplace: Liverpool
Previous clubs include: Caernarfon T - October 2001, Rhyl, Vauxhall Motors, Caernarfon T, Flint Town Utd, Bangor C.

APLIN, MATTY   *Midfielder*

Current Club: Didcot Town

Birthplace: Oxfordshire
Another player who has graduated through Didcots Youth system, Matty looks to be a strong contender in the Midfield. Scored one of the winning goals in the Final of the Jim Newman Trophy last year.

APPLEBY, STEVE   *Midfielder*

Current Club: Holbeach United

D o B: 24/05/1967   Birthplace: Lincoln
Honours won: Dr Martens League Premier Div.Winners
Previous clubs include: Gainsborough Trinity - August 2002, Holbeach Utd, Spalding Utd, Boston Utd, Bourne T, Boston Utd, Bourne T, Kettering T, Bourne T.

APPLETON, ANDY   *Defender*

Current Club: Wick

Birthplace: Sussex
Previous clubs include: East Preston - July 2001.

APPLETON, ARTHUR   *Forward*

Current Club: Paulton Rovers

Birthplace: Bristol
Previous clubs include: Mangotsfield Utd - July 2000, Yeovil T.

APPLETON, SCOTT   *Forward*

Current Club: Herne Bay

Birthplace: Kent
Previous clubs include: Dartford - July 2000, Deal T, Herne Bay, Tynham & Lynsted, Chatham T.

APPS, DARYL   *Forward*

Current Club: Erith & Belvedere

Birthplace: Kent
A striker who signed for Erith & Belvedere two years ago played in our first game at Park View Road, from local Club Dartford. A young promising striker.

ARANSIBA, ANDY   *Midfielder*

Current Club: Tiptree United

Birthplace: Essex
Previous clubs include: Ford Utd - March 2002, Barking, Ford Utd, Hornchurch.

ARANSIBIA, ANDY   *Forward*

Current Club: Ford United

Birthplace: Essex
Honours won: Ryman League Div.One Winners
Striker who is enjoying his football again. Broke his leg during the 2000/01 season, returned to figure strongly in Ford United's Ryman League First Division title win of 2001/02. Originally signed from Hornchurch during the 1996/97 season, his previous clubs include Enfield, Staines, Slough, Molesey, Grays, Hornchurch. A travel Consultant.

ARBER, MARK   *Defender*

Current Club: Barnet

D o B: 08/10/1977   Birthplace: Johannesburg
Moved to Barnet on a permanent basis in November 1998 after enjoying a successful two-month loan spell with the Bees. He was a product of Tottenham Hotspurs youth system and was transferred to Barnet in a deal worth around £75,000. A confident footballer and promising defender with an eye for goal.

ARCHBOLD, PHIL   *Defender*

Current Club: Kendal Town

Previous clubs include: Fleetwood Freeport - July 2001.

ARCHER, DALE   *Midfielder*

Current Club: Harlow Town

Birthplace: Scotland
Young striker who joined Harlow Town in December 2001 having started the season with Scottish First Division side Falkirk. Much is expected from this youngster in future seasons.

ARCHER, LEON   *Forward*

Current Club: Cheshunt

Birthplace: Herts
Previous clubs include: Potters Bar T - July 2002, Boreham Wood, Potters Bar T.

ARCHER, RICHARD   *Midfielder*

Current Club: Gloucester City

Birthplace: Gloucester
Previous clubs include: Chipping Norton T - November 2001.

ARIS, STEVE   *Defender*

Current Club: Fisher Athletic (London)

D o B: 27/04/1978   Birthplace: London
Previous clubs include: Millwall - July 1998.

ARKINS, STEVE   *Forward*

Current Club: Oxford City

D o B: 09/08/1980   Birthplace: Dublin
Previous clubs include: Maidenhead Utd - September 2001, Slough T, Basingtoke T, Reading.

ARKLE, PAUL   *Midfielder*

Current Club: Goole AFC

D o B: 05/11/1976   Birthplace: Yorkshire
Re-signed for Garforth from Ossett Albion during the 2001/2002 season, whom he had joined from Town at the beginning of the season. Spent 3 years at Barnsley as a YTS trainee followed by 1 year at Ossett Town. Pacey player, who is at home playing in midfield or in defence, a strong tackler. Moved to Goole in March 2002.

ARKWRIGHT, DANNY   *Defender*

Current Club: Sutton United

Birthplace: Surrey
Tall and promising centre back who joined Sutton United in the close season of 2001 after returning from a year in Australia. He has previously played for Epsom & Ewell and Whyteleafe.

ARMSTRONG, ADRIAN   *Midfielder*

Current Club: Harwich & Parkeston

Birthplace: Essex
Local player who was given a chance at Harwich earlier this season. Hard working and powerful, he grasped the opportunity enthusiastically and has established himself as an automatic first team choice.

ARMSTRONG, CARL — Defender
Current Club: Bideford

Birthplace: Devon
Carl is a quality centre half, who is in his second spell with us, having also been on the books of Holsworthy, Torrington & Appledore. He has made over 50 first team appearances.

ARMSTRONG, DAVE — Forward
Current Club: Clapton

D o B: 04/02/1978   *Birthplace: Essex*
Previous clubs include: Hornchurch - December 1998.

ARMSTRONG, DAVE — Midfielder
Current Club: Horsham YMCA

Birthplace: Sussex
Left-footed midfielder: former Three Bridges captain who joined YM early into 2001/02: rarely scores, but when he does its usually quite spectacular.

ARMSTRONG, IAN — Defender
Current Club: Gretna

Previous clubs include: Queen of the South - October 2000, Gretna, Queen of the South.

ARMSTRONG, JOEL — Goalkeeper
Current Club: Bradford Park Avenue

D o B: 25/09/1981   *Birthplace: Chesterfield*
Highly-promising young goalkeeper who joined UniBond Premier side Bradford Park Avenue on a permanent basis in July 2002 after being released by Chesterfield. Made a handful of League appearances for the Spireites and also had loan spells with both Avenue and Dr Martens side Ilkeston Town during the 2001/02 season.

ARMSTRONG, LEE — Defender
Current Club: Workington

Birthplace: Carlisle
Solid and reliable defender who re-signed for UniBond First Division side Workington from Gretna after the latters election into the Scottish League. Originally with Carlisle United, he had a spell in Scotland with Queen of the South as well as with Annan Athletic, joining Gretna in August 1999.

ARMSTRONG, PAUL — Forward
Current Club: Bishops Stortford

Birthplace: Herts
A product of Stevenage Borough's EFCO scheme, Paul is an exciting prospect, and his pace, and crosses have proved a major feature of his game. He had an impressive start and soon became a regular first-team squad player before trying his luck Ryman Premier outfit Bishops Stortford in July 2002 after turning down a move to Leagie of Wales side Aberystwyth Town.

ARNOLD, ANDY — Midfielder
Current Club: Arundel

Birthplace: Worthing
Midfielder: has been at Mill Road for four seasons, having previously played for Worthing Utd: sidelined for the first two months of 2001/02, and injured himself scoring a goal against Three Bridges in November.

ARNOLD, ARCHIE — Midfielder
Current Club: Hadleigh United

Birthplace: Suffolk
Tenacious hard working midfielder who doesnt know how to give less than 100%. Has remained loyal to Hadleigh United, despite many approaches. Eighth season with the Club.

ARNOLD, CHRIS — Forward
Current Club: Erith & Belvedere

Birthplace: Kent
Talented forward who joined Dr Martens Eastern side Erith & Belvedere from rivals and neighbours Dartford in August 2002. Had come up through the youth and reserve ranks with the Darts to become a valuable member of the first-team squad.

ARNOLD, IAN — Forward
Current Club: Morecambe

D o B: 04/07/1972   *Birthplace: Durham*
Honours won: England Semi-Pro Int.
Joined Morecambe from Conference neigbours Southport in the summer of 2001. Started out as a trainee at Middlesborough. Previous Clubs, Carlisle United, Kettering Town, Stalybridge Celtic, Kidderminster Harriers, Southport. Has represented England at semi pro level, playing against Holland.

ARNOLD, MICKY — Midfielder
Current Club: Thornaby on Tees

Birthplace: Cleveland
Previous clubs include: Billingham T - July 2001, Bishop Auckland, Billingham T, Middlesbrough (Trainee).

ARNOTT, ANDY — Defender
Current Club: Dover Athletic

D o B: 18/10/1973   *Birthplace: Chatham*
An experienced, versatile defender, Andy joined Dover Athletic in June 2002 after a spell out of the game through injury. Signed for Stevenage from Colchester at the start of the 2001/02 season after making 169 career League appearances. He slotted well into a solid defence before injury struck in October. Former clubs include Gillingham, Manchester United, Leyton Orient, Fulham, and Brighton.

ARSHAD, NARVEED — Forward
Current Club: Solihull Borough

D o B: 19/02/1983   *Birthplace: Birmingham*
Previous clubs include: Paget Rangers - August 2001.

ARTER, DAVE — Forward
Current Club: Maidstone United

Birthplace: Kent
Previous clubs include: Tonbridge Angels - October 2001, Folkestone Invicta, Gravesend, Ashford T, Sittingbourne, Hythe T, Ashford T, Tonbridge, Herne Bay, Ashford T.

ARTHUR, ALLAN — Forward
Current Club: Letchworth

Birthplace: Herts
Previous clubs include: Greenacres - July 2001, Hemel Hempstead.

ARTHUR, MARVIN — Defender
Current Club: Llanelli AFC

D o B: 25/09/1970   *Birthplace: Wales*
Previous clubs include: Bridgend T - March 2001, Llanelli, Llanelli Steel.

A

ARTHUR, STEVE — Forward
Current Club: Rhayader Town
D o B: 23/11/1979　Birthplace: Wales
Versatile player, can do a job upfront or in midfield. Good touch, brings people into the game well. Strong in the air.

ASH, GRAHAM — Defender
Current Club: Shildon
Birthplace: Newcastle
Previous clubs include: Walker Central - August 2001, Tow Law T.

ASHBY, NICK — Defender
Current Club: Stamford
D o B: 29/12/1970　Birthplace: Northampton
Honours won: England Semi-Pro Int., Dr Martens League Premier Div.Winners
Nick is an expierienced defender signed from Raunds Town. He was signed in 1999 and started out with Nottingham Forest before joining highflying Non-League teams, Rushden & Diamonds and Ayelsbury United.

ASHCROFT, JAMIE — Defender
Current Club: Withdean 2000
Birthplace: Sussex
Former Crawley reserve: joined Withdean during December 2001 from Tooting & Mitcham: had briefly appeared for Horsham towards the end of 2000/01.

ASHDOWN, ALLAN — Forward
Current Club: Peacehaven & Telscombe
Birthplace: Sussex
Forward who joined Peacehaven from Newhaven in February 2000 and scored 7 goals for the Tyes during 2000/01. Previously with Langney Sports.

ASHE, RYAN — Midfielder
Current Club: Maidenhead United
Birthplace: Middlesex
Midfielder or defender who joined Ryman Premier side Maidenhead United in july 2002 from Division One North outfit Northwood. Originally with Ruilsip Manor in the Spartan South Midlands League, Ryan then had spell with Chertsey Town before joining the Wood during the summer of 2001.

ASHER, ALISTAIR — Defender
Current Club: Halifax Town
D o B: 14/10/1980　Birthplace: Leicester
Young defender who was signed by Conference side Halfax Town in August 2002 after impressing in pre-season trials. Started his career with Mansfield as a trainee and went on to make ove 70 League appearances before being released at the end of the 2001/02 season.

ASHLEY, CRAIG — Midfielder
Current Club: Bridgnorth Town
Birthplace: Shropshire
Previous clubs include: Shifnal T - July 2001, Knighton T.

ASHLEY, STEVE — Defender
Current Club: Yeading
Birthplace: Middlesex
Strong centre-back who broke through from the reserve ranks to become club captain inside three seasons. Has suffered a number of injury set-backs, and has not featured for the first team since March. Now nearing full fitness again, his assurance in defence and regular goals are an asset to any side.

ASHMAN, HUGH — Forward
Current Club: Tilbury
Birthplace: Essex
Previous clubs include: Molesey - August 2001, Staines T, Southend Utd (Trainee), West Ham Utd (Junior).

ASHTON, CARL — Midfielder
Current Club: Cheshunt
Birthplace: Herts
Previous clubs include: Potters Bar T - July 2002.

ASHTON, DAVE — Defender
Current Club: Droylsden
Previous clubs include: Curzon Ashton - January 1997, Droylsden, Mossley, Caernarfon T, Glossop NE, Crewe Alexandra.

ASHTON, JON — Defender
Current Club: Hayes
D o B: 04/08/1979　Birthplace: Plymouth
Previous clubs include: Exeter C - August 2001, Plymouth Argyle.

ASHTON, LEE — Defender
Current Club: Frome Town
D o B: 08/11/1979　Birthplace: Somerset
Previous clubs include: Bristol C - July 1999, QPR.

ASHTON, MARK — Defender
Current Club: St.Helens Town
D o B: 02/01/1974　Birthplace: Liverpool
In his second season having joined Town from neighbours Warrington Town after previous spells with Runcorn and Curzon Ashton. Mark is a very adaptable player who can operate in most positions.

ASHTON, NICKY — Midfielder
Current Club: Tilbury
Birthplace: Essex
Previous clubs include: Witham T - August 2001, Tilbury.

ASHTON, RICHARD — Defender
Current Club: Stocksbridge Park Steels
Birthplace: Sheffield
Previous clubs include: Rotherham Utd (Junior) - July 1999.

ASHWELL, PAUL — Forward
Current Club: Buxton
Birthplace: Sheffield
Previous clubs include: Emley - September 2001.

ASHWELL, PAUL — Midfielder
Current Club: Hyde United
D o B: 26/06/1979　Birthplace: Manchester
Midfielder who signed for UniBond Premier side Hyde United from local football at start of 2001/02 season. Has also had experience in Mid-Cheshire League. Can play either in midfield or at the back.

ASKER, DAVE — Midfielder
Current Club: Eastleigh
Birthplace: Hampshire
Honours won: Jewson Wessex League Winners
Previous clubs include: Andover - May 2002, Basingstoke T, Chertsey T, Basingstoke T.

ASKEY, IAN — Midfielder
Current Club: North Ferriby United
Birthplace: Sheffield
Previous clubs include: Stocksbridge Park Steels - November 2001, Matlock T, Worksop T, Hallam, Worksop T, Alfreton T, Sheffield Aurora.

ASOMBANG, VICTOR — Forward
Current Club: Wealdstone
D o B: 07/10/1980
Previous clubs include: Hayes - August 2001, Hendon.

ASPIN, NEIL — Defender
Current Club: Harrogate Town
D o B: 12/04/1965   Birthplace: Gateshead
Honours won: UniBond League Div.One Winners
Vastly experienced defender who bagan his career at Leeds United, making over 300 appearances for the club, before moving to Port Vale, where he again made more than 300 appearances. Spells with Darlington and Hartlepool followed beforehe signed for Harrogate Town as player-coach in the summer of 2001.

ASPINALL, BRENDAN — Defender
Current Club: Ossett Town
D o B: 22/07/1975   Birthplace: Huddersfield
Ossett Town's record signing following an undisclosed 4-figure move from Hyde United in January 2001. An inspirational player who played 50 first team games for Mansfield Town, as well as appearing with Huddersfield Town and Coleraine in Ireland. Has captained Town on several occasions.

ASPINALL, MARTIN — Midfielder
Current Club: Clitheroe
Birthplace: Lancashire
Signed from Great Harwood at the start of last season - looked unbeatable in the first 10 games of the season. Found it harder going as the pitches got heavier but came good in the Spring.

ASPINALL, STEVE — Defender
Current Club: Runcorn FC Halton
Birthplace: Cheshire
Previous clubs include: Bamber Bridge - December 2001, Chorley, Winsford Utd, Caernarfon T, Macclesfield T, Poulton Victoria.

ASTLE, BROOK — Forward
Current Club: Kendal Town
Previous clubs include: Trafford - August 2001, Bolton Wanderers.

ASTON, DAVE — Forward
Current Club: Bedworth United
Birthplace: Coventry
Dave signed for Bedworth United from Nuneaton Griff, where he was a prolific scorer and very highly-rated. Has looked good alongside Chris Partridge and will settle into the Dr Martens Western style quickly. Had a spell wih Weymouth after being released by Birmingham City where he was a trainee.

ATHERTON, LEE — Defender
Current Club: Trafford
Birthplace: Cheshire
Defender who signed for UniBond First Division side Trafford August 2002 from Cammell Laird Gained previous UniBond experience with Winsford United.

ATKIN, RICHARD — Midfielder
Current Club: Borrowash Victoria
Birthplace: Nottingham
Previous clubs include: Long Eaton Utd - July 1998, Borrowash V, Grantham T, Borrowash V, Nuthall.

ATKINS, ANDY — Forward
Current Club: Eastbourne United
Birthplace: Sussex
Rejoined Sidley from Little Common Albion at the start of 2000/01: scored 4 times before returning to the East Sussex League a couple months later with Hooe Sports: had another stretch at Little Common during 2001/02, but then moved to Eastbourne United towards the end of the campaign.

ATKINS, MARK — Defender
Current Club: Soham Town Rangers
Birthplace: Cambridgeshire
Previous clubs include: Newmarket T - July 2000, Soham Town R.

ATKINSON, CRAIG — Midfielder
Current Club: Denaby United
D o B: 29/09/1977   Birthplace: Rotherham
Honours won: England Youth Int.
Previous clubs include: Alfreton T - November 2001, Worksop T, Frickley Ath., Ilkeston T, Nottingham Forest.

ATKINSON, GRAEME — Midfielder
Current Club: Lancaster City
D o B: 11/11/1971   Birthplace: Hull
Vastly experienced midfielder who joined UniBond Premier side Lancaster City in August 2002 after his release by Rochdale. Started his career with his home-town club Hull City and went on to make over 300 League appearances with Hull, Preston, Brighton, Scunthorpe, Scarborough and Rochdale. Follows in the line of a number of former Preston players to have joined the Dollies in recent years.

ATKINSON, PAUL — Defender
Current Club: Scarborough
D o B: 16/10/1981   Birthplace: Whitby
A third year scholarship student Paul is a product of the successful youth policy at Scarborough and was voted young player of the year for 2000/2001. A regular member of the reserve team he was also in the youth side which reached the quarter finals of the Youth Alliance Cup. After making a number of appearances as Sub. Paul commanded the right back position as his own in the second half of last season. A definite prospect for the future. From the age of 12 to 16 Paul never missed a single training session for the Centre of Excellence even trudging through snow to arrive on time a clear demonstration of his determination.

ATKINSON, PETER — Defender
Current Club: Guiseley
Birthplace: Yorkshire
Honours won: FA Vase Winners, UniBond League Div.One Winners
Well-respected defender who started his career with his home town club, Otley Town, before moving to Guiseley, for whom he made over 550 appearances in ten seasons, including two FA Vase finals at Wembley. He joined Harrogate Town in the summer of 1999 and helped the club to win the UniBond First Division title in 2001/02 before returning to Guiseley in the summer of 2002.

ATKINSON, PHIL   *Defender*
Current Club: Guiseley
From Youth team.

ATKINSON, ROSS   *Midfielder*
Current Club: Ashington
Birthplace: Northumberland
Previous clubs include: Queen of the South - August 2001, Ashington.

ATTUQUAYEFIA, GLENN   *Defender*
Current Club: Winsford United
Birthplace: Manchester
Full back with bags of pace, new signing from the local Manchester league.

AUGUSTE, ANDY   *Forward*
Current Club: Marlow
Birthplace: Berkshire
Local Marlow lad who was at Wycombe Wanderers and Oxford United as a youth player. A pacey attacker. Andy joined Marlow at the start of the 2000/01 season and forced his way into the first-team after impressing in the reserves.

AUSTIN, BEN   *Defender*
Current Club: Eastbourne Borough
Birthplace: Sussex
Moved to the club during the 2000 close season from neighbours Eastbourne Town (Sussex County League). Played for the Sussex FA Representative side, and was voted Supporters' Player of the Year in his first season at Priory Lane.

AUSTIN, SIMON   *Forward*
Current Club: Chatham Town
Previous clubs include: Gillingham - July 2000.

AVERY, MARK   *Defender*
Current Club: Thame United
D o B: 04/06/1979   *Birthplace: Oxford*
A young player who has progressed through Thame United's youth system after joining from Chinnor in 1999. A promising central defender who is determined to make a big impact.

AXCELL, LOUIS   *Forward*
Current Club: Spalding United
Birthplace: Lincolnshire
Previous clubs include: Denaby Utd - July 2001, Winterton R.

AYLING, JOHN   *Forward*
Current Club: Folkestone Invicta
D o B: 09/03/1982   *Birthplace: Kent*
Teenage striker who made a big impact after forcing his way into the Folkestone Invicta first team squad. Has great pace and first came to the fore towards the end of the 1997/98 season. John has scored a number of goals and has been watched by a lot of Football League scouts.

AYRES, JAMES   *Defender*
Current Club: Enfield
D o B: 18/09/1980   *Birthplace: Luton*
Previous clubs include: Kettering T - March 2001, Dagenham & Redbridge, Luton T.

AYRES, WARREN   *Goalkeeper*
Current Club: Stratford Town
Birthplace: Warwickshire
Previous clubs include: Racing Club Warwick - July 2000, Alveston.

AZZOPARDI, MICHAEL   *Defender*
Current Club: Tonbridge Angels
Birthplace: Surrey
Defender who signed for Dr Martens Eastern side Tonbridge Angels in July 2002 from Conference neighbours Margate. Had been with the Gate since February 2001 after arriving from Ryman Leaguers Dulwich Hamlet. Started out in the youth and reserve teams at Tooting & Mitcham United.

The Official Football Association
Non-League Club
Directory 2003
(25th Edition)
now available

Price £19.95
(free p&p)

Details of over 1000
Semi-Professional Clubs

Call 01823 490 080 for details
The Non-League Club Directory
Helland, North Curry
Taunton, Somerset, TA3 6DU
Fax: 01823 491 481
Email: TonyWilliams12@virgin.net

Special Discounts Available

BACK, ROBBIE   *Forward*
Current Club: Swaffham Town

Birthplace: Norfolk
Experienced striker whose pace is a problem for any defence. Formerly with Kings Lynn and Downham. Joined Swaffham in the summer of 2000.

BACON, CARL   *Defender*
Current Club: Oadby Town

Birthplace: Leicester
Previous clubs include: Hinckley Utd - November 2001, Eastwood T, Nuneaton B, Leicester C.

BADDAMS, ADRIAN   *Midfielder*
Current Club: Sutton Coldfield Town

D o B: 19/02/1972   Birthplace: Birmingham
Previous clubs include: Bilston T - January 2002, Moor Green, Solihull Borough, Tamworth, Stourbridge, Moor Green, Bedworth Utd, Tamworth, Atherstone Utd, Sandwell B, Torquay Utd, Walsall.

BADMAN, MARK   *Midfielder*
Current Club: Chippenham Town

D o B: 21/12/1979   Birthplace: Bath
Talented young midfielder who started his career with Bristol City. Didnt make the first-team with City and joined Clevedon Town in July 1999 where some impressive performances led to a move to his home-town club Bath City in October 2001. Transferred to newly-promoted Chippenham Town in May 2002.

BAFFOUR, CYRIL   *Midfielder*
Current Club: Leyton Pennant

Birthplace: London
From Local football - August 1997.

BAGLEY, ANDY   *Forward*
Current Club: Pelsall Villa

Birthplace: Birmingham
Previous clubs include: Bolehall Swifts - October 2001.

BAGNALL, JOHN   *Goalkeeper*
Current Club: Burscough

D o B: 23/11/1973   Birthplace: Southport
An experienced and much-admired goalkeeper who signed for UniBond Premier side Burscough in September 2000 from Winsford United. Also had spells with Southport, Chester City, Bury, Wigan Athletic and Preston North End.

BAGNALL, WARREN   *Forward*
Current Club: Crawley Town

Birthplace: Sussex
Former Lewes player who has also appeared in the County League for Selsey and Saltdean Utd (scored 25 times for the Tigers during 1999/2000): returned to the Dripping Pan during the 2000 close season and helped the Rooks gain promotion out of Ryman Division Three, as well as scoring both their goals in the Sussex Senior Cup Final victory over Bognor Regis: joined Crawley at the start of 2001/02.

BAGSHAW, NEIL   *Defender*
Current Club: Bradford Park Avenue

Birthplace: Yorkshire
Defender who signed for Bradford Park Avenue in January 1999 from Rotherham United and has impressed ever since with some commanding displays. Is surely destined for a higher level.

BAGSHAW, PAUL   *Midfielder*
Current Club: Ilkeston Town

D o B: 25/09/1979   Birthplace: Sheffield
Previous clubs include: Emley - January 2002, Hednesford T, Barnsley.

BAILEY, ALAN   *Forward*
Current Club: Marine

D o B: 01/11/1978   Birthplace: Macclesfield
Honours won: UniBond League Premier Div.Winners
Helped Burton Albion to win the UniBond Premier title in 2001/02 before moving to Marine in June 2002. A talented forward, he began his career with Manchester City but made his League bow whilst on-loan to his home-town club Macclesfield. Joined Stockport in July 1999 and played around 20 times for the Edgeley Park outfit before joining the Brewers.

BAILEY, CHRIS   *Midfielder*
Current Club: Leek Town

Birthplace: Nottingham
A talented young midfielder who has a good future in the game. Signed for Leek Town from the Hucknall Academy in July 2002.

BAILEY, DANNY   *Forward*
Current Club: Congleton Town

Birthplace: Staffs
Age 21. Forward. Played for Port Vale, Stockport County and local side Bollington Ath. Signed in summer 01.

BAILEY, DANNY   *Midfielder*
Current Club: Bath City

D o B: 21/05/1964   Birthplace: Leyton
Previous clubs include: Weston-Super-Mare - March 2002, Forest Green R, Telford Utd, Slough T, Exeter C, Reading, Exeter C, Wealdstone, Torquay Utd, Walthamstow Ave.

BAILEY, DENNIS   *Forward*
Current Club: Stafford Rangers

D o B: 13/11/1965   Birthplace: Lambeth
Vastly experienced forward who is still remembered as being the last man to score a hat-trick against Manchester United at Old Trafford whilst playing for Queens Park Rangers. Joined Dr Martens Premier side Stafford Rangers in August 2002 after a spell with Halesowen Town, whom he helped to win promotion from the Western Division. Originally with Barking and Farnborough Town, he went on to make over 250 League appearances with Crystal Palace, Bristol Rovers, Birmingham, QPR, Gillingham and Lincoln, Returned to the Non-League game with various clubs, including Cheltenham, Forest Green Rovers, Aberystwyth Town and Tamworth.

BAILEY, JERMAINE   *Defender*
Current Club: Hucknall Town

Previous clubs include: Eastwood T - July 2001, Ilkeston T.

BAILEY, JOHN   *Midfielder*
Current Club: Dorchester Town

D o B: 06/05/1969   Birthplace: London
Previous clubs include: Brockenhurst - March 2002, AFC Bournemouth, Enfield, Croydon, Dagenham.

BAILEY, JOHN-PAUL   *Defender*
Current Club: Didcot Town

Birthplace: Oxfordshire
Jon was an outstanding player in local youth football and is now maturing into a reliable midfield player of real quality with Didcot.

B

B

Made his debut in 1995 and has played more than 150 games for the Railwaymen. Deservedly clinched the Player of the Year trophy for some stunning displays at the back end of last season. Works as an Office Equipment Executive.

BAILEY, LINTON — Defender
Current Club: Sutton Coldfield Town
Birthplace: Birmingham
From Youth team.

BAILEY, MARK — Defender
Current Club: Woodbridge Town
Birthplace: Essex
Returned to Notcutts Park in July 1999, having spent five seasons with Town before he moved to Sudbury Town. A tough and versatile competitor and occasionally a reliable Goalkeeper who we originally signed from Hadleigh.

BAILEY, NICK — Forward
Current Club: Sutton United
Birthplace: Surrey
From Youth team.

BAILEY, RICHARD — Forward
Current Club: Stamford
D o B: 29/10/1974   Birthplace: Kettering
Richard is a forward or able midfielder who topped the Stamford scoring charts in season 1999/2000. Richard spent six years at Rushden & Diamonds before moving to Nuneaton Borough from where Steve Evans signed him in 1998 . He also scored Stamfords first ever DML goal.

BAILEY, SHANE — Midfielder
Current Club: Clacton Town
Birthplace: Braintree
Midfield player with great ball skill and vision. Previous clubs include Braintree and Chelmsford. Joined Clacton in season 2000/ 2001.

BAILLIE, LEWIS — Midfielder
Current Club: Heybridge Swifts
Birthplace: Cambridge
Strong and aggressive left-sided midfield player with a good touch on the ball and a great attitude. Signed for Heybridge Swifts in the summer of 2001 from Wivenhoe Town after previous service with Bishops Stortford and Cambridge City. Only young and with plenty of time to make the big impression that his potential deserves. Is a student at Essex University. Players' Player of the Season for 2001/02.

BAILY, NIEL — Midfielder
Current Club: Arnold Town
Birthplace: Nottingham
Previous clubs include: Gedling T - August 2001, Lincoln Utd, Hucknall T, Stamford, Grantham T, Lincoln Utd, Ilkeston T, Hucknall T, Dunkirk.

BAINBRIDGE, DANNY — Forward
Current Club: Leek Town
Birthplace: Nottingham
Moved to Leek Town in the close season from Hucknall Town. A highly-promising teenage striker with a good future ahead of him in the game.

BAINBRIDGE, DAVE — Defender
Current Club: Buxton
Birthplace: Derbyshire
Previous clubs include: Leek T - July 1992, Stalybridge Celtic, Buxton, Biggin Rovers.

BAINBRIDGE, RICKY — Midfielder
Current Club: Marine
Birthplace: Southport
Rick signed for Marine from local Southport football after moving to Merseyside from Derbyshire where he played for Buxton . Twice chosen by the supporters as Player of the Year, he is an attacking midfielder who scores some memorable goals.

BAINBRIDGE, TERRY — Defender
Current Club: Tow Law Town
Birthplace: Co.Durham
In his second spell with us having also been with Spennymoor, Evenwood and Hartlepool and had a period as Manager at Shotton Comrades.

BAINES, IAN — Defender
Current Club: Runcorn FC Halton
D o B: 05/03/1964   Birthplace: Liverpool
Honours won: UniBond League Premier Div. Winners
Ian signed for Runcorn during November 2001 after being released by Marine during pre-season. A good solid defender with a wealth of experience who is at the club primarily as cover.

BAINES, PAUL — Forward
Current Club: Croydon Athletic
Birthplace: Surrey
Previous clubs include: Walton & Hersham - July 1999, Croydon Ath., Sutton Utd.

BAIRSTOW, SCOTT — Defender
Current Club: Farsley Celtic
Birthplace: Bradford
Previous clubs include: Bradford Park Avenue - December 2001, Harrogate T, Lancaster C, Bradford PA, Gainsborough Trinity, Guiseley, Bradford C.

BAKER, DARREN — Defender
Current Club: Eastbourne Borough
Birthplace: Brighton
Has been a regular in the side since making his debut in 1992. Began his career with Brighton and Hove Albion, and Littlehampton Town Youth; and was a member of the Sussex Representative side that won the SW Counties championship in 1999/00. Holds the club record for the number of senior appearances, having played well over 400 games.

BAKER, DARREN — Forward
Current Club: Leek Town
Birthplace: Staffs
Darren is the son of former Leek manager Neil - now assistant boss at Crewe Alexandra. He was a member of Leek Town's reserve side during the Conference seasons but had few first team chances. A striker who has returned via Leek CSOB and Congleton Town for whom he has scored 11 goals this season.

BAKER, DAVID — Defender
Current Club: Billingham Synthonia
Birthplace: Cleveland
Previous clubs include: Middlesbrough - July 1997.

BAKER, DEAN — Forward
Current Club: Sutton Coldfield Town
Previous clubs include: Paget Rangers - January 2000, Holly Lane OB.

BAKER, JAMES — Goalkeeper
Current Club: Belper Town
Birthplace: Nottinghamshire
Previous clubs include: Ilkeston T - February 2002, Arnold T, Ilkeston T, Heanor T.

BAKER, JAMIE — Forward
Current Club: Chalfont St.Peter
Birthplace: Wycombe
Previous clubs include: Flackwell Heath - October 2001, Chalfont St.Peter.

BAKER, JOE — Forward
Current Club: Billericay Town
D o B: 19/04/1977   Birthplace: London
Joe made his debut on 8th January 2000 against Dagenham & Redbridge after joining Billericay from Sutton United. Earlier in his career, Joe played League football for Leyton Orient before playing for Welling. He can play on either wing or through the middle, and his great ability to beat his man with ease. He achieved the rare feat of scoring hattricks in consecutive matches, against Heybridge and Sutton, and also scored a remarkable goal from the half way line after coming on as a sub against Hendon.

BAKER, LEWIS — Midfielder
Current Club: Stourbridge
Birthplace: Birmingham
Previous clubs include: Birmingham C (Trainee) - February 2000.

BAKER, MARK — Midfielder
Current Club: Ely City
Birthplace: Cambridgeshire
Previous clubs include: Eynesbury Rovers - July 1997.

BAKER, MATT — Goalkeeper
Current Club: Hereford United
D o B: 18/12/1979   Birthplace: Harrogate
A young goalkeeper signed in August 2000 from Hull City. Baker turned professional in the summer of 1998 after graduating from the Hull City youth team and made his debut as a substitute in the 3-2 home defeat to Macclesfield, following Lee Braceys red card. His next showing came at Torquay as a substitute, and ten days later was thrown on against Liverpool at Anfield following another Bracey dismissal. In 2000, Baker was loaned out to Bradford Park Avenue to gain match experience. He was released at the end of the season and signed for United as reserve goalkeeper. The youngster has had just two chances to prove his worth to the side. He made his debut against Southport in a 1-1 draw, a game in which he played very competently. Since then, he has played just one match, a 1-0 home defeat by Woking. After Scott Cookseys unfortunate injury in the summer of 2001, Baker started 2001/02 as first goalkeeper.

BAKER, MATT — Midfielder
Current Club: Three Bridges
Birthplace: Sussex
Spent 13 years with Crawley Down, making 500+ appearances, before joining Three Bridges in December 2000: scored a total of 3 goals last season.

BAKER, NEIL — Defender
Current Club: Bracknell Town
D o B: 04/09/1979   Birthplace: Middlesex
Previous clubs include: Sutton Utd - August 2001, Boreham Wood, Aldershot T, Farnborough T, Wycombe Wanderers.

BAKER, NICK — Defender
Current Club: Garforth Town
D o B: 30/05/1968   Birthplace: Selby
Experienced centre half who joined the club last season to strengthen the defence. The powerfully built defender was previously at Beeston St Anthony in local football but has had successful years at Selby Town.

BAKER, PAUL — Forward
Current Club: Blyth Spartans
D o B: 05/01/1963   Birthplace: Newcastle
Previous clubs include: Durham C - November 2001, Bedlington Terriers, Carlisle Utd, Hartlepool Utd, Scunthorpe Utd, Torquay Utd, York C, Gillingham, Motherwell, Hartlepool Utd, Carlisle Utd, Southampton, Bishop Auckland.

BAKER, PETER — Forward
Current Club: St.Leonards
Birthplace: Sussex
Striker who has spent most of his career at St Leonards, but had a great season for Westfield in 1997/98 in the Sussex County League Division 3, scoring 36 times. Subsequently returned to The Firs and had 17 goals to his name in 2000/01 before signing for Sidley United in February 2001. Struggled with injury during the final part of that season, but was again amongst the goals in 2001/02, earning a third spell at St Leonards in July 2002.

BAKER, RYAN — Forward
Current Club: Caernarfon Town
D o B: 28/08/1980   Birthplace: Manchester
Previous clubs include: Flixton - January 2000, Trafford, Crewe Alexandra (Trainee).

BAKER, SHAUN — Midfielder
Current Club: Bridlington Town
Birthplace: Hull
Joined mid way through last season and was instrumental in Town's rise up the table. Links play well and manages to get in some great tackles. Will be looking to improve his scoring record this year after disappointing in front of goal.

BAKER, STEVE — Defender
Current Club: Scarborough
D o B: 08/09/1978   Birthplace: Pontefract
Perhaps Scarborough manager Russell Slades most influential signing of the 2001/02 season. The talented defender left Middlesbrough with several colleagues as their manager Steve McClaren sought to prune the large squad inherited from Bryan Robson. His strong performances were a major contribution to the tightening of Boros defence.

BAKER, STEVE — Midfielder
Current Club: Lincoln United
Birthplace: Lincoln
Steve is another player to progress through Lincoln United's youth ranks. A versatile midfield player who is not frightened to get his tackles in.

B

B

BAKHSHIAN, ELAS — Midfielder
Current Club: Leatherhead
Birthplace: Surrey
Previous clubs include: Hampton & Richmond Borough - September 2001.

BALCH, PAUL — Forward
Current Club: Sidley United
Birthplace: Sussex
Experienced, athletic player: top scorer for Stamco as far back as 1990/91: has also spent time at Hailsham, Bexhill and, more recently, Langney Sports (missed a large part of 1999/2000 due to work commitments): joined Sidley in September 2000 and had 11 goals to his name that season: sometimes plays as a centre-forward, although seems to be more effective as a winger.

BALDE, PAVIK CHRISTOVAO FERNANDES — Forward
Current Club: Yeading
Birthplace: Portugal
Portuguese Pav joined the Ding in October 2001 and made his debut as sub in the league win at Thame. Spent pre-season at Rotherham United after moving from his home country where he had featured in the successful under 18 sides of both Boavista and Benfica.

BALDWIN, STUART — Midfielder
Current Club: Goole AFC
D o B: 30/07/1975   Birthplace: Leeds
Previous clubs include: Garforth T - August 2001, Farsley Celtic, Garforth T, Beeston St.Anthonys.

BALE, CHRIS — Midfielder
Current Club: Cinderford Town
Birthplace: Cardiff
Very promising young midfielder who joined Cinderford Town from UWIC Inter Cardiff of the League of Wales at the start of the 2001/02 season. Previously gained Dr Martens League experience with Newport County.

BALFE, CHARLIE — Midfielder
Current Club: Bognor Regis Town
Birthplace: Southampton
Joined Bognor Regis Town from Jewson Wessex League side Eastleigh during the summer of 2001. Manager Jack Pearce considers Charlie to be a fine midfield prospect. Lives in Dibden, Southampton.

BALL, GREG — Forward
Current Club: Kingstonian
D o B: 31/08/1981   Birthplace: Surrey
Excellent prospect up front for Kingstonian. Made a rapid jump from the reserves to the first team in August 2001, making a quick impact when he scored a hat-trick in only his third start. Has the nack of being in the right place at the right time and has taken a lead in the goalscoring stakes.

BALL, JAMIE — Defender
Current Club: Rugby United
Birthplace: Coventry
Signed for Rugby United from West Bromwich Albion during the summer of 2001 after spending seven years at The Hawthorns. A strong young defender or wing back with a lot of potential, he played in all but five of Albions reserve team games prior to joining Rugby.

BALL, OWEN — Defender
Current Club: Sidley United
Birthplace: Sussex
Right wing-back: hard-working established member of the side, who scored five times during Sidleys 2000/01 best-ever season.

BALL, RICHARD — Forward
Current Club: Oldbury United
Birthplace: Birmingham
Previous clubs include: Bloxwich Utd - December 2001, Bromsgrove R, Paget R, Bromsgrove R, Weymouth, WBA.

BALL, STEFFAN — Forward
Current Club: Tonbridge Angels
Birthplace: Surrey
Previous clubs include: Leatherhead - January 2002, Dorking, Croydon.

BALL, STEVE — Defender
Current Club: Bilston Town
D o B: 22/11/1973   Birthplace: Leeds
Honours won: UniBond League Div.One Winners
Birthplace: Birmingham
Previous clubs include: Bridgnorth T - November 2001, Rushall Olympic, Willenhall T, Bilston T, Hednesford T.

BALL, STEVE — Defender
Current Club: Farsley Celtic
Defender who started his career as an apprentice at Leeds United before joining Darlington, for whom he played over 80 League games. He then moved over to Ireland, playing for Cork City, before returning to Yorkshire with spells at Farsley Celtic, Emley and Bradford Park Avenue. He joined Harrogate Town in February 2001 before returning to Farsley in the summer of 2002.

BALL, STEVE — Midfielder
Current Club: Stanway Rovers
D o B: 02/09/1969   Birthplace: Colchester
Previous clubs include: Heybridge Swifts - October 1998, Sudbury T, Colchester Utd, Cambridge Utd, Norwich C, Colchester Utd, Arsenal.

BALLARD, SCOTT — Midfielder
Current Club: Romford
Birthplace: Essex
Previous clubs include: Aveley - January 2001, Barking, Grays Ath., Ford Utd.

BALMER, WAYNE — Midfielder
Current Club: Tunbridge Wells
Birthplace: Kent
Previous clubs include: St.Leonards - July 2000, Tonbridge Angels.

BAMBROOK, SIMEON — Midfielder
Current Club: Wakefield & Emley
Birthplace: Leeds
In his second spell at Emley, rejoining in February 2000 from Garforth Town, the club he was signed from in 1998/99. That season he scored 12 goals for Emley after scoring 20 for Garforth.

BAMFORD, BARRY — *Defender*
Current Club: Uxbridge
Previous clubs include: Ashford T (Middx) - December 2000, Bedfont.

BAMFORD, GAVIN — *Defender*
Current Club: Uxbridge
D o B: 30/05/1977   *Birthplace: Middlesex*
A highly-talented player who graduated through Uxbridges ranks to the first-team squad having been outstanding in the Youth and Reserve sides. He made he first team debut in December 1995 and has made over 300 appearances. Besides being an excellent defender, Gavin is also a very capable midfield player as well.

BAMFORD, STUART — *Defender*
Current Club: Uxbridge
D o B: 08/01/1976   *Birthplace: Middlesex*
Stuart, an uncompromising defender, signed on Isthmian forms in August 1996 after having successfully progressed through the ranks at Uxbridge from the reserves and into the first-team squad. Also a regular representative for the Middlesex County FA. Older brother of Gavin and a former Players' Player of the year

BAMGBOLA, OLATUNJI — *Forward*
Current Club: Wealdstone
D o B: 22/08/1985   *Birthplace: London*
Young forward Tunji joined Wealdstones PASE Youth scheme at the begining of the 2001/02 season and soon became established in the first team squad. Formerly with Maidstone United and Southampton.

BAND, PETER — *Forward*
Current Club: Altrincham
D o B: 18/12/1973   *Birthplace: Lancashire*
Highly-rated attacker who signed for UniBond Premier side Altrincham in July 2002 from rivals Hyde United. Began his career in local football with Bollington United and then became a firm favourite with Tigers supporters after arriving at Ewen Fields in June 1998.

BANGER, NICKY — *Forward*
Current Club: Woking
D o B: 25/04/1971   *Birthplace: Southampton*
Vastly experienced forward with over 200 League games to his name. Began his career with Southampton and then had spells with Oldham, Oxford, Dundee and Plymouth. Signed for Dr Martens side Merthyr Tydfil after being released by Argyle during the 2001/02 season but then had another stab at League football with Torquay before re-joining the Martyrs in March 2002. Joined Conference side Woking in August 2002.

BANGURA, ALU — *Midfielder*
Current Club: Dunston Federation Brewery
Birthplace: Co.Durham
Previous clubs include: Jarrow Roofing - July 2001, Spennymoor Utd, Morpeth T, Lemington Social, South Shields, Washington.

BANGURA, CHRIS — *Forward*
Current Club: Aylesbury United
Birthplace: Sierra Leone
Previous clubs include: Tottenham Hotspur - July 2001.

BANGURA, KOLLIER — *Forward*
Current Club: Whyteleafe
Previous clubs include: Kingstonian - September 2001, Walton & Hersham.

BANHAM, NICK — *Goalkeeper*
Current Club: Great Yarmouth Town
D o B: 28/05/1970   *Birthplace: Norfolk*
Signed for Yarmouth from Anglian Combination club Mulbarton and now in his fourth season. Has missed very few games and is now one ot the strongest keepers in the league.

BANIM, JODY — *Forward*
Current Club: Radcliffe Borough
Birthplace: Manchester
Tricky forward who quickly became a favourite at Radcliffe Borough with his goalscoring exploits. Jody signed for Boro just before the start of the 2001/02 season from neighbours Rossendale United and ended the campaign as the clubs top scorer. Previously with Hyde United, Flixton, Altrincham and Trafford and was a trainee at Manchester United.

BANKS, ADAM — *Defender*
Current Club: Shepshed Dynamo
D o B: 21/03/1975   *Birthplace: Nuneaton*
Previous clubs include: Nuneaton Griff - August 2001, Sutton Coldfield T, Nuneaton B.

BANKS, ANDY — *Midfielder*
Current Club: Spennymoor United
D o B: 14/11/1971   *Birthplace: Middlesbrough*
Midfielder Andy joined Spennymoor United in November 2000 but struggled with the rest of the team. However, he was an inspiration the following campaign and his confidence has been at all time high as he exhibits superb ball skills and has scored several goals worthy of professional football this season. Originally with Ipswich Town, he has also served Billingham Synthonia, Bishop Auckland, Guisborough Town, Whitby Town and Dunston Federation, from whom he joined the Moors.

BANKS, IAN — *Defender*
Current Club: Newcastle Town
D o B: 11/10/1972   *Birthplace: Stoke*
Previous clubs include: Stafford Rangers - July 1998, Leek T, Port Vale.

BANKS, KINGSLEY — *Goalkeeper*
Current Club: Heybridge Swifts
D o B: 06/12/1968   *Birthplace: London*
Commanding goalkeeper who began his career as an apprentice at Tottenham Hotspur before moving into the Non-League scene with Dartford. Has also played for Barking, Enfield, Basildon United and had a brief spell at Gillingham. Joined Heybridge Swifts from Witham Town in July 1995, Kingsley is widely regarded as one of the best keepers outside the Football League and has been selected for the Ryman League representative side. Regular winner of player of the season awards, showing the esteem he is held in by supporters, managers and team-mates.

BANKS, STEVE — *Defender*
Current Club: Matlock Town
Previous clubs include: Doncaster Rovers - August 2000.

BANKS, STEVE — *Forward*
Current Club: Three Bridges
Birthplace: Sussex
Solid forward: top goalscorer for East Grinstead in both 1995/96 and 1996/97: had another great season for the Wasps in 1999/2000, registering 23 goals in 22 appearances: joined Three Bridges at the start of the following campaign, striking 23 times (also played for Sussex that year).

BANNATYNE, GRAHAM   *Goalkeeper*

Current Club: St.Leonards

Birthplace: Brighton

Graham signed for St Leonards as a goalkeeper from Ryman League side Lewes in January 2000. At the age of 39, he has a great deal of experience of the Sussex County football scene and has won various honours and trophies with a number of senior Sussex clubs, most notably Peacehaven & Telscombe, Lewes and Seaford.

BANNER, KEVIN   *Forward*

Current Club: Bromsgrove Rovers

Birthplace: Birmingham

Previous clubs include: Oldbury Utd - February 2001, Halesowen T.

BANNISTER, CHARLIE   *Midfielder*

Current Club: Arnold Town

Birthplace: Nottingham

Previous clubs include: Wollaton - July 2000.

BANTHORPE, ALEC   *Goalkeeper*

Current Club: Ely City

Birthplace: Suffolk

Previous clubs include: Newmarket T - December 2000, Histon, Haverhill R.

BANYA, SAM   *Forward*

Current Club: Maldon Town

Birthplace: Suffolk

Prolific goalscorer who joined Jewson Eastern Leaguers Maldon Town in August 2002 after originally agreeing to sign for Ryman Premier side Braintree Town a month earlier from champions AFC Sudbury. Felixstowe, Diss Town, Bedford Town and Kettering Town had the services of Sam before he signed for AFC Sudbury at the start of the 2001/02 season. He had already knocked in 40 goals by the turn of the year including three hat- tricks. His goalscoring attracted much local media interest, especially during a run of 10 consecutive scoring matches and setting a new club record.

BAPTISTE, ROCKY   *Forward*

Current Club: Farnborough Town

Birthplace: London

Rocky was one of Farnborough Town's chairman/manager Graham Westleys biggest signing in the 2001close season from Luton Town. His electric pace can frighten the best of defenders. Previously at Chelsea, Wealdstone and Hayes.

BARBER, DANNY   *Defender*

Current Club: Heybridge Swifts

Birthplace: Essex

Young full back who returned to Heybridge Swifts midway through the 2001/02 season after spells at Chelmsford City, Maldon Town and Clacton Town. Strong tackler with a highly cultured left foot. Has stacks of ability if he can get his mind set right.

BARBER, PAUL   *Goalkeeper*

Current Club: Histon

D o B: 30/08/1977   Birthplace: Burnley

Previous clubs include: Newmarket T - July 1999, Cambridge C, Sudbury T, Cambridge C, Norwich C.

BARBER, PHIL   *Midfielder*

Current Club: Redhill

D o B: 10/06/1965   Birthplace: Tring

Very experienced left-sided midfield player who joined Sussex County League side Redhill in August 2002 from Ryman Leaguers Croydon. Had signed for Croydon in October 2000 from Dulwich Hamlet. Started his career as a striker for Aylesbury United, before spending many years in the Football League, mainly with Crystal Palace, for whom he made some 250 appearances, including the 1990 FA Cup Final against Manchester United. Phil then went on to play for Millwall, Plymouth Argyle, Bristol City, Dover Athletic and Carshalton Athletic.

BARBER, WAYNE   *Defender*

Current Club: Tring Town

Birthplace: Tring

A very promising young defender who featured in the clubs youth team during 1998/99. Has played elsewhere since, but rejoined last season and is expected to feature strongly this season.

BARBROOK, MATTHEW   *Midfielder*

Current Club: Lowestoft Town

Birthplace: Great Yarmouth

Previous clubs include: Wroxham - August 2001, Lowestoft T, Scunthorpe Utd.

BARCLAY, DOMINIC   *Forward*

Current Club: Erith & Belvedere

D o B: 05/09/1976   Birthplace: Bristol

Dominic is a prolific forward who joined Dr Martens Eastern side Erith & Belvedere in the summer of 2002 from rivals St Leonards. Had originally signed for St Leonards in January 2001 from Croydon for the remainder of season 2000/01and scored a hat-trick on his debut against Folkestone. He re-signed for St Leonards In September 2001, and although he didnt repeat the feat of his original debut, he scored five in his next match away at Dartford. He is a graduate of Bristol City's training scheme, where he secured a full-time contract and went on to make some 24 first-team appearances before a move to Macclesfield. He moved into Non-League football with Nuneaton Borough and subsequently moved south. After moving back to play football in South London mid-way through the 2000/01 season, Dominic returned to the side for the game against Eastbourne Borough on 4th April to help in Saints battle against relegation. Dominic typically scored in his first game back at the club. He left the Saints in November 2001 after receiving a substantial financial offer to sign for Croydon, but returned again in April 2002 to make an impressive contribution towards Saints relegation battle.

BAREFIELD, DAVID   *Forward*

Current Club: Tiptree United

Birthplace: Essex

Previous clubs include: Braintree T - September 1999.

BARHAM, ANDY   *Defender*

Current Club: Wimborne Town

Birthplace: Bournemouth

Previous clubs include: Salisbury C - December 1997, Bournemouth FC, AFC Lymington.

BARHAM, LIAM   *Midfielder*

Current Club: St.Leonards

Birthplace: Brighton

Liam is a vastly experienced midfielder who signed for St Leonards from Eastbourne Borough in mid-November 2001, for whom he made 110 appearances. He has previously played for

St Leonards prior to the 1999/00 season, and has also played for Hastings Town (two spells), and spent periods with Hayes, Kingstonian, Dover Athletic and Veendam (Holland).

BARIMA, MICHAEL   Forward
Current Club: Harrow Borough
Birthplace: Berkshire
Previous clubs include: Hampton & Richmond Borough - October 2001, Beaconsfield SYCOB.

BARK, ADAM   Defender
Current Club: Denaby United
Birthplace: Sheffield
Previous clubs include: Hallam - August 2001.

BARKER, ALAN   Defender
Current Club: Ossett Town
D o B: 10/05/1977   *Birthplace: Leeds*
Talented left back or sweeper who joined Town from Carlton Athletic. Scored on his first team debut in 1999 and has impressed sufficiently enough in the Reserves over the past few seasons to be considered part of the first team squad. Was a key part of the Reserves cup-winning side last season

BARKER, DANNY   Defender
Current Club: Eastleigh
Birthplace: Hampshire
Honours won: Jewson Wessex League Winners
Previous clubs include: Andover - May 2002, Fleet T, Basingstoke T, Portsmouth.

BARKER, GLYN   Midfielder
Current Club: Stalybridge Celtic
D o B: 23/10/1983   *Birthplace: Manchester*
Glyn is a utility midfielder, brought in to strengthen the squad. He started playing as a youth for Stockport County, before joining the Rochdale trainees, and finally getting his senior debut for Celtic.

BARKER, IAN   Forward
Current Club: Chorley
Birthplace: Bolton
Previous clubs include: Mossley - November 2001, Chorley, Mossley, Leigh RMI.

BARKER, JAMIE   Forward
Current Club: Histon
Birthplace: Cambridge
From Youth team.

BARKER, JOHN   Defender
Current Club: St Margaretsbury
D o B: 06/07/1980   *Birthplace: Romford*
Previous clubs include: Harlow T - July 2001, Hitchin T, Colchester Utd.

BARKER, KEVIN   Defender
Current Club: Stowmarket Town
Birthplace: Suffolk
Previous clubs include: Stonham Aspal - July 1999, Stowmarket T.

BARKER, MICHAEL   Defender
Current Club: Bishop Auckland
Birthplace: Bishop Auckland
Drafted from the Bishop Auckland under-18 team and made his debut as a substitute v Whitby Town in the NPL Cup late in 2000. Excellent distribution with long balls from defence.

BARKER, NICKY   Midfielder
Current Club: Felixstowe & Walton United
Birthplace: Suffolk
Joined the club as an 18 year old some 13 years ago and gave over ten seasons service to the Seasiders before a spell at Ipswich Wanderers. Returned midway through last season and adds vital experience to a young squad.

BARKER, RORY   Midfielder
Current Club: Spennymoor United
Birthplace: Hartlepool
Previous clubs include: Seaham Red Star - January 2002, Brandon Utd, Durham C, Hartlepool Utd.

BARKER, STEWART   Defender
Current Club: Fakenham Town
Birthplace: Norfolk
Previous clubs include: Watton Utd - July 2000, Fakenham T.

BARLASS, LEE   Defender
Current Club: Mangotsfield United
D o B: 26/03/1968   *Birthplace: Bristol*
Signed for Mangotsfield United from Almondsbury Town in March 1998. Became team captain and won both the Supporters and Players' Player of the Year awards before signing for league rivals Clevedon Town in the of summer 2001, but returned to Mangotsfield in September 2001. A solid reliable defender.

BARLOW, BRETT   Defender
Current Club: Newcastle Town
D o B: 06/09/1977   *Birthplace: Stoke*
Previous clubs include: Stafford Rangers - March 1999, Barry T, Stafford R, Chester C.

BARLOW, GLEN   Forward
Current Club: Redhill
Birthplace: Surrey
Prolific goalscorer who joined Redhill early in Bill Tuckers reign at Kiln Brow. His signing was a major coup for the club. He left Hartley Wintney of the Combined Counties League with 14 goals in 15 games and his record at Redhill has bettered even that goals to games ratio. Has scored some spectacular goals and with his vast array of close ball skills has proved to be a real team player, setting up as many or more goals than his own for other players.

BARLOW, MARTIN   Midfielder
Current Club: Weymouth
D o B: 25/06/1971   *Birthplace: Barnstaple*
Something of a legend in Devon for his twelve-year spell with Plymouth Argyle where he totalled over 300 League appearances. Transferred to neighbours Exeter in the summer of 2001 and added a further 30-plus games to his tally before being released at the end of the 2001/02 season. Eventually signed for Dr Martens Premier side Weymouth after a number of clubs were interested in his services.

BARNABY, MATT   Defender
Current Club: Hertford Town
Birthplace: Herts
Previous clubs include: Ware - January 2001, Hertford T, Bishops Stortford, Ware, Baldock T, Bishops Stortford, Stevenage B.

BARNARD, DARREN — *Defender*

Current Club: Stowmarket Town

Birthplace: Suffolk

Previous clubs include: Needham Market - January 1999.

BARNARD, MARK — *Defender*

Current Club: Worksop Town

D o B: 27/11/1975   Birthplace: Sheffield

Experienced, Sheffield-born defender who started his career with Rotherham United as a trainee. Moved to Darlington in 1995 and became a forst-team regular at Feethams, making over 150 League appearances. Moved on to Doncaster Rovers in 1999 and then on to Northwich Victoria in October 2000. Transferred to Worksop Town in May 2002.

BARNARD, MARK — *Defender*

Current Club: Stowmarket Town

Birthplace: Suffolk

Previous clubs include: Soham Town Rangers - July 2000, Watton Utd, Stowmarket T, Bury T.

BARNARD, RICHARD — *Goalkeeper*

Current Club: Maidenhead United

D o B: 27/12/1980   Birthplace: Frimley

Previous clubs include: Millwall - August 2000.

BARNARD, SIMON — *Defender*

Current Club: Chichester City United

Birthplace: Portsmouth

Big defender: has bags of experience, having previously spent time at Portsmouth, Petersfield, Gloucester, Worcester, Havant/Waterlooville and Worthing: scored 3 goals in 12 matches during a brief stint at Oaklands Park early in 1998/99: rejoined in December 2000 from Sidlesham.

BARNES, CHRIS — *Midfielder*

Current Club: Epsom And Ewell

Birthplace: Surrey

Chris is one of the youngest players at Epsom. He captains Surreys under 18 (county) and scored in the Surrey cup to put Epsom through to the next round.

BARNES, DAVE — *Defender*

Current Club: Sidlesham

Birthplace: Sussex

Left-back: now in the veteran stage, having previously played for Selsey, Bosham, Chichester City and Portfield: mainly appeared for Sidlesham reserves until re-emerging for the first-team during 2001/02.

BARNES, GARETH — *Midfielder*

Current Club: Brockenhurst

D o B: 11/05/1978   Birthplace: Bournemouth

Previous clubs include: Wimborne T - July 2001, Lymington & New Milton, Bashley, Christchurch, Bournemouth FC, West Ham Utd (Trainee).

BARNES, KEVIN — *Forward*

Current Club: Kendal Town

D o B: 12/09/1975   Birthplace: Fleetwood

Previous clubs include: Fleetwood Freeport - October 2001, Lancaster C, Fleetwood Freeport, Blackpool, Lancaster C.

BARNES, PAUL — *Forward*

Current Club: Doncaster Rovers

D o B: 16/11/1967   Birthplace: Leeds

Experienced striker who began his career as an apprentice with Notts County and signed as a professional on his 18th birthday. Moved on to Stoke City in March 1990 for a £30,000 fee. Had a spell on loan at Chesterfield in November 1990 before joining York City in July 1992 for £50,000. Cost Birmingham City £350,000 in March 1996 but left for Burnley in September of that year for the same fee. In January 1998 he joined Huddersfield Town and moved on to Bury in March 1999 for £40,000. From March 2001 to the end of the season he was loaned out to Nuneaton Borough. Signed by Doncaster Rovers in the close season of 2001.

BARNES, PAUL — *Forward*

Current Club: Sidlesham

Birthplace: Sussex

Leading scorer for Bosham during 2000/01 with 8 goals: joined Sidlesham for the start of the following season.

BARNES, ROB — *Forward*

Current Club: Ossett Albion

From Youth team.

BARNES, ROGER — *Defender*

Current Club: Withdean 2000

D o B: 12/10/1965   Birthplace: London

Previous clubs include: Horsham - September 2001, Burgess Hill T, Faversham T, Horsham, Malden Vale, Croydon, Horsham, Croydon Ath.

BARNES, STEVE — *Midfielder*

Current Club: Welling United

D o B: 05/01/1976   Birthplace: Wembley

Previous clubs include: Chesham Utd - October 2001, Welling Utd, Harrow Borough, St.Albans C, Hayes, Barnet, Birmingham C, Welling Utd.

BARNETT, AARON — *Defender*

Current Club: Gravesend & Northfleet

Birthplace: Kent

Honours won: Ryman League Premier Div.Winners

Aaron signed for Gravesend in March 2000 from local rivals Erith & Belvedere having previously spent some time at Charlton Athletic. Aaron is a natural athlete and can play in almost any position on the football field. He never gives less than 100% and is particularly strong in the air. A player who could play at a higher level.

BARNETT, JASON — *Defender*

Current Club: Lincoln United

D o B: 21/04/1976   Birthplace: Shrewsbury

Defender who made over 200 League appearances for Lincoln City before joining UniBond First Division neighbours Lincoln United in July 2002. Started his career at Wolves but failed to make the senior side and moved to Sincil Bank in October 1995 for a bargain £5,000.

BARNETT, JONATHAN — *Forward*

Current Club: Hitchin Town

D o B: 07/09/1982   Birthplace: Herts

A teenage forward with an eye for goal. Played in Hitchin Town's successful PASE scheme under-19s side in season 2000-2001. Was previously with the Stevenage Borough EFCO scheme before transferring to the Hitchin Town PASE scheme.

BARNETT, PHIL   *Forward*
Current Club: Havant & Waterlooville
Birthplace: Portsmouth
Phil is a local lad released by Portsmouth at the end of last season. Picked up in August to provide support in the front line, tough competition for first team places has meant he has so far been unable to display his abilities.

BARNFIELD, MARTIN   *Midfielder*
Current Club: Parkgate
Birthplace: Chesterfield
Previous clubs include: Hallam - July 1999, South Normanton Ath., Parkgate, Worsbrough Bridge, Denaby Utd, Sheffield, Parkgate, Ashfield Utd, Denaby Utd, Ashfield Utd, Chesterfield (Junior).

BARNHOUSE, DAVID   *Defender*
Current Club: Carmarthen Town
D o B: 19/03/1975   *Birthplace: Swansea*
Honours won: Wales u-21 & Semi-Pro Int.
Previous clubs include: Merthyr Tydfil - July 1998, Swansea C.

BARNSBY, PETER   *Defender*
Current Club: Kingstonian
D o B: 24/05/1978   *Birthplace: London*
Young central defender who was Bill Williams first signing as Kingstonian manager in June 2001, for an undisclosed fee from local side Hampton & Richmond Borough. Made 96 appearances at the Beveree and was voted Newcomer of the Year there in 1998-99 after graduating from the Borough's successful Suburban League team. A former Crystal Palace youth team player.

BARNWELL, DARREN   *Midfielder*
Current Club: Shifnal Town
Birthplace: Birmingham
Previous clubs include: Sandwell Borough - July 2001, Paget R, Bloxwich T, Tividale, Redditch Utd, Atherstone Utd, Stapenhill, Armitage, Leicester Utd, Sandwell B, Atherstone Utd.

BARNWELL-EDINBURGH, JAMIE *Forward*
Current Club: Hall Road Rangers
D o B: 26/12/1975   *Birthplace: Hull*
Previous clubs include: Hinckley Utd - December 2001, Scarborough, Brigg T, Goole AFC, Brigg T, Denaby Utd, North Ferriby Utd, Gainsborough Trinity, North Ferriby Utd, Doncaster R, Goole AFC, Stevenage B, Cambridge Utd, Coventry C.

BARON, NEIL   *Defender*
Current Club: Great Harwood Town
Birthplace: Lancashire
Previous clubs include: Clitheroe - August 1998, Great Harwood T, Clitheroe, Great Harwood T.

BARR, HAMID   *Midfielder*
Current Club: St.Albans City
Birthplace: London
A latecomer into the full professional game when the attacking midfielder was signed by QPR in the summer of 2001 from Dr Martens Eastern side Fisher Athletic. Hamid had been on the books at Millwall and Crystal Palace as a youngster but then had spells with Welling United, Sutton United, Crockenhill and Erith & Belvedere before joining Fisher in October 1999 via a second stint at Crockenhill. Things didnt quite work out at QPR, and he was released at the end of the 2001/02 season. Signed for Ryman Premier side St Albans City in August 2002.

BARRANCE, TERRY   *Midfielder*
Current Club: Beaconsfield SYCOB
Birthplace: Middlesex
Previous clubs include: Hillingdon Borough - July 2000, Harefield Utd.

BARRASS, MARK   *Midfielder*
Current Club: Bridlington Town
Birthplace: Hull
Previous clubs include: North Ferriby Utd - July 2001, Hall Road R, Sculcoates Amateurs, Immingham T, Goole T.

BARRATT, GAVIN   *Defender*
Current Club: Redditch United
Birthplace: Redditch
Local Redditch-based defender who showed his qualities in his first season at Dr Martens League level in 2001/02. Aged just 23, he will now be looking to make his mark even more.

BARRETT, DANNY   *Defender*
Current Club: Matlock Town
D o B: 25/09/1980   *Birthplace: Bradford*
Previous clubs include: Chesterfield - January 2002.

BARRETT, DAVID   *Defender*
Current Club: Chertsey Town
Birthplace: Surrey
A defender who has made his way from the Chertsey Juniors side and who signed first team forms just after the start of this season.

BARRETT, GRAHAM   *Midfielder*
Current Club: Dereham Town
Birthplace: Norfolk
Holds the Norfolk County Youth record number of appearances. Quality act whose only fault is he won't stop talking! Product of the Youth set-up.

BARRICK, DEAN   *Defender*
Current Club: Doncaster Rovers
D o B: 30/09/1969   *Birthplace: Hemsworth*
Experienced defender who joined Sheffield Wednesday as a trainee, signing professional forms in May 1988. Cost Rotherham United £50,000 in September 1991 and moved on to Cambridge United for the same fee in August 1993. Transferred to Preston North End in September 1995 and on to Bury in July 1998. Had a loan period with Ayr United in February 1999 and joined Doncaster Rovers on loan from Bury in March 2001. Signed a permanent deal with Rovers at the end of the season.

BARRIE, JAMIE   *Defender*
Current Club: Leyton Pennant
Previous clubs include: St.Margeretsbury - August 2001, Hoddesdon T.

BARROW, LEE   *Defender*
Current Club: Stafford Rangers
D o B: 01/05/1973   *Birthplace: Belper*
Experienced defender who is capable of playing anywhere across the back line. Joined Stafford Rangers in June 2002 from Dr Martens Premier rivals Hednesford Town. Had been with the Pitmen since November 2001, signing from League of Wales outfit Aberyswyth Town. Originally with Notts County, he went on to make over 200 League appearnces with Scarborough and Torquay before joining another LoW side, Barry Town.

BARROW, PAUL — Defender
Current Club: Witton Albion
Birthplace: Manchester
Previous clubs include: Barnton - November 2001, Mossley, Cheadle T, Mossley, Cheadle T, Stockport Co.

BARROWCLIFF, PAUL — Midfielder
Current Club: Slough Town
D o B: 15/06/1969   Birthplace: Hillingdon
Honours won: Conference Winners
Paul joined the club after being signed by former Rebels boss Graham Roberts from his former club Chesham United. Barras is as popular with the players as he is with the fans. He has an excellent left foot and is a strong tackler. He is very much the same as Darron Wilkinson in his style of play - but left footed. Barras has played for 12 teams throughout his career such as Brentford and Wycombe. He made 11 league appearances for Brentford, but his time playing at Brentford was hampered by injury. Paul captained Stevenage Borough to the Conference title in the 1992/1993 season and was voted as their player of the season on that occasion. Later he moved to Brenford from Stevenage in what was thought to be a fee of around £50,000. Paul is a very committed player and wants to see Slough do well. His performances over the season Slough were relegated from the Ryman Premier League was one a a few bright spots in that season. Paul will have to work hard to keep his place in the Rebels side now though as there are now many midfield players at the club battling for that central position.

BARRS-JAMES, EMERSON — Forward
Current Club: Walton Casuals
Birthplace: Surrey
Strong natural goalscorer who joined from Raynes Park Vale in Aug 99, missed most of last season through injury, but still managed 8 goals in as many appearances. Emerson return briefly to Raynes Park before returning in October 2000. Previous clubs include Redhill and Hampton.

BARRY, DANIEL — Forward
Current Club: Marske United
Birthplace: Newcastle
An exciting young striker who signed for Albany Northern League side Marske United from York City towards the end of last season. Has a great deal of potential.

BARRY, PETER — Defender
Current Club: Atherstone United
D o B: 13/11/1979   Birthplace: Nuneaton
Previous clubs include: Hinckley Utd - October 2001, Nuneaton Borough.

BARSDELL, ADAM — Midfielder
Current Club: Newport Isle Of Wight
Previous clubs include: Cowes Sports - July 2001, Newport IOW.

BARTH, GARY — Midfielder
Current Club: Potters Bar Town
Birthplace: Herts
Previous clubs include: Welwyn Garden C - July 2000.

BARTLE, CARL — Midfielder
Current Club: Lincoln United
Birthplace: Lincoln
A product of Lincoln City's youth scheme but joined Lincoln United upon his release in 1997. Been in and out of the first team mainly due to injury but is now pressing for a regular first team spot.

BARTLETT, DARREN — Midfielder
Current Club: Brigg Town
Birthplace: Hull
Previous clubs include: Lincoln C (Junior) - July 1997.

BARTLETT, JUSTIN — Midfielder
Current Club: Hamble ASSC
Birthplace: Hampshire
Previous clubs include: BAT Sports - July 2000.

BARTLETT, NEAL — Defender
Current Club: Leverstock Green
Birthplace: Herts
Experienced defender who joined Spartan South Midlands side Leverstock Green from Ryman outfit Tring Town in July 2002. Was club captain at Tring, after signing in October 1999 from Chertsey Town. Previous clubs include Hendon, Chesham United, Dunstable, Wealdstone, Hemel Hempstead and Berkhamsted Town.

BARTLETT, NEAL — Forward
Current Club: Bath City
D o B: 07/04/1975   Birthplace: Southampton
Southampton-born, Neal is a talented attacking player who joined his home-town club as a trainee in August 1996. Went on to make 8 first team appearance for the Saints before a spell in Sweden preceeded a switch to Non-League football with Hampshire-based Dr Martens League side Bashley. Briefly returned to the professional game with Hereford United at the beginning of the 1996/97 season and then moved on to Newport AFC in January 1997. Neal is currently serving in the armed forces, based at Farnborough, and has to balance his football with Bath City, whom he join in August 2001, with his Army responsibilties.

BARTLETT, SCOTT — Defender
Current Club: Salisbury City
D o B: 30/05/1979   Birthplace: Wiltshire
Locally-based player who signed for Dr Martens Eastern side Slaisbury City from Cirencester Town in February 2000. Formerly with AFC Bournemouth, his versatility and pace make him an important member of the side.

BARTLEY, CARL — Forward
Current Club: Bromley
D o B: 06/10/1976   Birthplace: London
Forward in his second spell with Bromley. He holds the ball up and uses his build to put pressure on defenders. Signed from Bromley at the start of the 2001/02 season from Gravesend & Northfleet. He has also played for Dulwich Hamlet, Carshalton Athletic, Walton & Hersham and Hayes.

BARTLEY, KEVIN — Forward
Current Club: Port Talbot Town
D o B: 26/09/1975   Birthplace: Swansea
Previous clubs include: Pontardawe - July 1998, Briton Ferry Ath., Afan Lido, Cardiff C.

BARTLEY, MICHAEL — Forward
Current Club: Burnham
Birthplace: Berkshire
Re-signed for Dr Martens Eastern Division side Burnham from Ryman Division One North neighbours Slough Town in August 2002. Had joined Slough from their near rivals despite Burnhams best attempts to keep the player at the Gore when at Burnham this season Michael started the season in fine fashion - scoring five goals for the Blues in the opening few matches which

saw him up the top of the Dr Martens Eastern Division scoring charts. When Michael joined Slough he took while to settle in, but scored in two goals in successive games against Whyteleafe and Thame to open his account for the Rebels.

BARTLEY, SIMON — Goalkeeper
Current Club: Leighton Town
Birthplace: Herts
Goalkeeper who followed manager Paul Burgess to Ryman Division Two side Leighton Town from Tring Town in July 2002. Had signed for Tring in October 2000 from local side Sun Postal Sports and was first-choice keeper ever since.

BARTON, DANNY — Forward
Current Club: Colwyn Bay
D o B: 21/06/1974   Birthplace: Oswestry
Forward who signed for UniBond Premier side Colwyn Bay in the summer of 2002 from League of Wales outfit Caernarfon Town. Had spent the majority of his time in the LoW with spells at Welshpool Town, Total Network Solutions and Rhyl, joining Caernarfon in October 2001. Started his playing days at Oswestry Town.

BARTON, GARETH — Forward
Current Club: Haverfordwest County
Birthplace: Wales
Previous clubs include: Carmarthen T - December 2001, UWIC Inter Cardiff, Carmarthen T, Kiddderminster Harriers.

BARTON, JASON — Defender
Current Club: Tunbridge Wells
Birthplace: Kent
Previous clubs include: Tonbridge Angels - December 2000.

BARTON, MICHAEL — Goalkeeper
Current Club: Oswestry Town
D o B: 23/09/1973   Birthplace: Oswestry
A local lad who returned to his home town team from Rhayader during the close season having previously played for Oswestry in the Cymru Alliance. Previously had played for Newtown and Shrewsbury Town.

BARZEY, JOSH — Forward
Current Club: Great Yarmouth Town
Birthplace: Norfolk
Played a few games for Yarmouth at the end of last season before joining Diss Town in August, returning to the Wellesley at the end of October. Has also played for Fakenham and Gorleston.

BASFORD, LUKE — Defender
Current Club: Dulwich Hamlet
D o B: 06/01/1980   Birthplace: London
Honours won: FA Trophy Winners
Left back who joined Ryman Division One South side Dulwich Hamlet from rivals Whyteleafe in the summer of 2002. Had been with the Leafe since January 2002 after signing from Croydon, whom he had joined from Woking at the beginning of the 2001/02 season. He has played in the Nationwide League for Bristol Rovers, and has also played for Kingstonian for whom he made a substitute appearance in the 2000 FA Trophy Final.

BASHFORTH, RICHARD — Midfielder
Current Club: Frickley Athletic
From Youth team.

BASS, DAVID — Midfielder
Current Club: Hitchin Town
D o B: 29/11/1974   Birthplace: Frimley
Hitchin Town signed midfielder David from fellow Ryman Premier side Kingstonian in November 2001. He has had a long and varied career that has taken in Reading, Rotherham, Carlisle, Scarborough and Stevenage Borough, gaining plenty of League and Conference experience along the way.

BASS, SAM — Midfielder
Current Club: Aveley
Birthplace: Essex
Previous clubs include: Leyton Pennant - July 2000, Metropolitan Police, Aveley, Dagenham & Redbridge, St.Leonards, Dagenham & Redbridge.

BASSINDER, GAVIN — Midfielder
Current Club: Farsley Celtic
D o B: 24/09/1979   Birthplace: Mexborough
Previous clubs include: Gainsborough Trinity - December 2001, Mansfield T, Barnsley,

BASTABLE, ADAM — Defender
Current Club: Stourbridge
Birthplace: Wolverhampton
Previous clubs include: Bilston T - November 2001, Willenhall T, Stourbridge. Lye T.

BASTIAN, DAVE — Defender
Current Club: Horsham
Birthplace: Essex
Previous clubs include: Barking - August 1999, Wivenhoe T.

BASTOCK, PAUL — Goalkeeper
Current Club: Boston United
D o B: 19/05/1970   Birthplace: Leamington Spa
Paul is one of the most highly regarded goalkeepers in Non-League football and is now in his ninth season with the club after joining United from Kettering Town. It is not surprising that when he was younger he admired Peter Shilton and Neville Southall and one of his favourite players was Chris Woods, all great international goalkeepers in their time. During the earlier part of his career Paul spent six months playing football in Malaysia, which he enjoyed considerably. Had a testimonial last season.

BASTOW, IAN — Midfielder
Current Club: Taunton Town
D o B: 02/08/1971   Birthplace: Torquay
Honours won: FA Vase Winners
A talented midfielder with previous League experience at Torquay United, having made 25 League appearances. Comes from a family of footballers and has also played for Dawlish, from whom he re-joined Taunton Town in November 1999. Works for the Gas Board.

BATCHELOR, JAMES — Forward
Current Club: Frickley Athletic
D o B: 18/11/1980   Birthplace: Aylesbury
Highly-promising young forward who joined UniBond Premier side Frickley Athletic in August 2002 from Northern Counties East outfit Armthorpe Welfare. Was a junior with Doncaster Rovers and then had spells with Rossington Main and Hatfield Main before signing for Armthorpe in March 2002.

B

BATCHELOR, PAUL — Forward

Current Club: Holmer Green

Birthplace: Bucks
Previous clubs include: Chalfont St.Peter - July 2001, Holmer Green.

BATE, ROBBIE — Midfielder

Current Club: Witham Town

Previous clubs include: Heybridge Swifts - October 2001, Stanway Rovers, Needham Market, Whitton Utd.

BATE, ROSS — Goalkeeper

Current Club: Oldbury United

Birthplace: Birmingham
Previous clubs include: Bloxwich Utd - December 2001, Moor Green, Walsall.

BATES, IAN — Midfielder

Current Club: Wembley

Previous clubs include: Harrow Borough - September 2001, Wembley, Southall,. Wembley.

BATES, JAMIE — Defender

Current Club: Chorley

Birthplace: Manchester
Signed from Northwich V in February 2002. Started his career at Maine Road before teaming up with Runcorn, where he first caught the eye with some steady displays at Conference level.

BATES, JON-BARRIE — Midfielder

Current Club: Hendon

Birthplace: London
Experienced midfielder who joined Hendon during the summer of 2001. Spent most of his career at Wembley and Harrow Borough where he was skipper. Jon-Barrie also played for Hendon boss Dave Anderson at Southall a few years ago.

BATES, MICK — Midfielder

Current Club: Newcastle Town

D o B: 28/09/1968   Birthplace: Northern Ireland
Previous clubs include: Leek T (£2,000) - August 1997, Eastwood Hanley, Port Vale, Arsenal.

BATES, NICK — Goalkeeper

Current Club: Thornaby on Tees

Birthplace: Teesside
From Local football - July 1996.

BATES, PAUL — Midfielder

Current Club: Tonbridge Angels

Birthplace: Kent
Honours won: England Schools Rep.
Previous clubs include: Erith & Belvedere - July 1999, Furness.

BATES, PHIL — Defender

Current Club: Ludlow Town

Birthplace: Shropshire
Previous clubs include: Newtown - July 2001, Bridgnorth T, Welshpool, Stourbridge.

BATES, SCOTT — Forward

Current Club: Denaby United

Birthplace: Sheffield
Previous clubs include: Hallam - October 2001.

BATES, SIMON — Defender

Current Club: Gateshead

D o B: 02/10/1973   Birthplace: Newcastle
Joined Gateshead from Spennymoor United in February 2000 and was starting to impress at the back before picking up an injury which required an operation. The former Manchester United trainee recovered well, however, and featured in the first-team again towards the end of the 2001/02 season. Had a spell at Northern Leaguers Evenwood Town after being released from Old Trafford.

BATH, MATT — Goalkeeper

Current Club: Gloucester City

Birthplace: Gloucestershir
Became City's fifth goalkeeper of the season by November, but looks to have made the position his own with some confident handling and impressive saves. His move was initially on a trial basis but his form has been so assured that City did not move to renew Matt Taylors loan from Newport County. Bath had long been highly rated at County League side Whitminster but had to wait six seasons for a club in a higher division to give him an opportunity. He has not only managed to regularly produce top notch stops but has possibly impressed even more with his consistency and the often under rated ability to do the simple things well and without fuss. A vital factor in our recent run of form who has been slightly overshadowed by the return of Baylo up front, but according to rumour has not gone un-noticed by the scouts of local League sides. Works locally as an engineer and looks set to be offered a contract once the FA lift their ban.

BATHGATE, DAVID — Midfielder

Current Club: Dover Athletic

Birthplace: Dover
From Youth team.

BATHURST, ANTHONY — Midfielder

Current Club: Herne Bay

Birthplace: Kent
From Youth team.

BATTAMS, STEVE — Defender

Current Club: Staines Town

D o B: 02/02/1977   Birthplace: Middlesex
A member of Staines Town's youth side in 1994/95, he was added to the senior squad after a string of fine performances, notably in the FA Youth Cup tie at Luton. A Surrey Youth representative who has also played for Walton Casuals, he captained the reserves and was the maintstay of the defence. However, he was released and joined Carshalton Athletic in December 1998, returning in September 1999. Shared the Players' Player of the year award for 2001/02.

BATTELL, PHIL — Defender

Current Club: Tiptree United

Birthplace: Essex
Previous clubs include: Sudbury T - July 1998, Sudbury Ath.

BATTEN, IAN — Midfielder

Current Club: Metropolitan Police

Birthplace: London
Previous clubs include: Leyton Orient - July 1997.

BATTERSBY, RICHARD — Defender

Current Club: Radcliffe Borough

D o B: 13/06/1979   Birthplace: York
Richard joined Radcliffe Borough after being released by Oldham Athletic in October 1999. A very attacking full back who is always

keen to push forward, he looks to have a very bright future in the game.

BATTRAM, PAUL — Forward
Current Club: Brentwood
Birthplace: Essex
Former Billericay Town striker who was signed last season from Witham Town. An experienced player who was in excellent form during the championship season, scoring 14 goals.

BATTY, LAURENCE — Goalkeeper
Current Club: Walton & Hersham
D o B: 15/02/1964   *Birthplace: Westminster*
Honours won: England Semi-Pro Int., Ryman League Premier Div.Winners, FA Trophy Winners
Previous clubs include: Molesey - March 2002, Woking, Farense (Portugal), Brentford, Fulham, Maidenhead Utd.

BAULKHAM, LUKE — Forward
Current Club: Aveley
Birthplace: London
A former Tottenham Hotspur trainee who joined Ryman Premier side Boreham Wood in July 2002 from rivals Purfleet. Joined East Thurrock United after being released by Spurs in the summer of 1999.

BAURESS, GARY — Defender
Current Club: Southport
D o B: 19/01/1971   *Birthplace: Liverpool*
Honours won: UniBond League Premier Div.Winners
Gary moved to Southport along with manager Phil Wilson at the start of the 2001/02 summer following a highly successful spell with then UniBond Premier League champions Stalybridge Celtic. An established and accomplished midfielder, Gary enjoyed a spell with Tranmere Rovers where he made just the one first team appearance before moving on to have spells with Ashton United, Barrow and Leek Town. Gary is a double winner of the UniBond League championship and has considerable Conference experience.

BAVERSTOCK, STUART — Goalkeeper
Current Club: Woking
Birthplace: Surrey
From Youth team.

BAVESTER, MICHAEL — Goalkeeper
Current Club: Tiptree United
Birthplace: Essex
Previous clubs include: AFC Sudbury - March 2002, Halstead T, Haverhill R.

BAXENDALE, MARK — Forward
Current Club: Atherton Laburnum Rovers
Birthplace: Leigh
Mark joined LR from Castleton Gabriels during the close season. He is a very quick and tricky attacker who loves to run at defenders. Mark works as a surveyor and he enjoys snooker.

BAXTER, BRETT — Midfielder
Current Club: Rossendale United
Birthplace: Manchester
Midfielder who joined UniBond First Division side Rossendale United in August 2002 after a spell with Conference outfit Chester City. Started his playing days in Traffords youth side before spending time on Tranmere Rovers books. The played for Ashton United and Accrington Stanley before signing for City in October 2001.

BAXTER, MATTHEW — Defender
Current Club: Ely City
Birthplace: Cambridge
Previous clubs include: Chatteris T - September 1999, Ely C, Newmarket T.

BAYLES, DAVID — Midfielder
Current Club: Shildon
Birthplace: Bishop Auckland
Previous clubs include: Bishop Auckland - November 2001, Shildon, Consett, West Auckland T, Bishop Auckland.

BAYLEY, TOM — Defender
Current Club: Boldmere St.Michaels
Birthplace: Birmingham
Previous clubs include: Bloxwich T - June 2001, Chasetown, Pelsall Villa.

BAYLISS, KARL — Forward
Current Club: Gloucester City
D o B: 24/02/1968   *Birthplace: Gloucester*
Honours won: Dr Martens League Premier Div.Winners
Previous clubs include: Clevedon T - November 2001, Gloucester C, Newport Co., Forest Green R, Gloucester C, Stroud, Sharpness, Forest Green R, Cheltenham T.

BAYLISS, PHIL — Defender
Current Club: Ashton United
Birthplace: Manchester
Teenage defender, rated as a fine prospect, who joined newly-promoted UniBond Premier side Ashton United in July 2002 after a short spell with First Division Trafford. Had signed for Trafford during the 2001/02 season after being released by Crewe where he had been a trainee.

BAYLISS, WARREN — Forward
Current Club: Edgware Town
Birthplace: London
Previous clubs include: Chertsey T - November 2001, Yeading, Boreham Wood, Chertsey T, Windsor & Eton, Hampton, Manchester C (Trainee).

BEAGAN, NEIL — Forward
Current Club: Willenhall Town
Birthplace: Birmingham
Previous clubs include: Stratford T - December 2001, Redditch Utd, Sutton Coldfield T, Solihull B.

BEALE, JOHN — Defender
Current Club: Marlow
Birthplace: Nottingham
Honours won: England Schools Rep.
A former England Schools representative defender, John is a Nottingham lad who was on the books at nottingham Forest and Notts County before going Non-League with Ruddington, Netley Central and Arnold Town. Was reckoned to have a very bright future in the game until injury struck, but he came back well and after a return to Arnold he moved south through work commitments and played for Stotold in the United Counties league and then, from July 2001, Marlow in the Ryman League.

BEALE, OWEN — Midfielder
Current Club: Bishops Stortford
Birthplace: Essex
A promising youngster having made the transition from Blues youth to the first team squad. Made his debut for the senior side

at the end of the 2000/2001 season. Loan spells this season have gained valuable experience for Owen.

BEALE, RICHARD — Defender
Current Club: Stafford Rangers
Birthplace: Birmingham
Defender who joined Dr Martens Premier side Stafford Rangers on the eve of the 2002/03 season after a successful pre-season trial at Marston Road. Started his playing days in the Midland Combination with Knowle and then tasted Dr Martens football with Solihull Borough before becoming a regular at Western Division Redditch United after joining in January 2002.

BEALEY, TIM — Defender
Current Club: Erith & Belvedere
D o B: 03/03/1973   Birthplace: Kent
Reliable, strong player who is the longest serving player at Erith & Belvedere, having joined the club in August 1996 after previously playing for Tooting and Mitcham. A reliable, strong and confident who has had plenty of experience in the Ryman League. He was voted Players' Player of the year season in 2000.

BEALL, BILLY — Midfielder
Current Club: Cambridge City
D o B: 12/04/1977   Birthplace: Enfield
Talented midfielder who signed for Cambridge City mid-February 2002 from Leyton Orient. Billy Mathew Beall made over 80 League appearances for neighbours Cambridge United before following former Us manager Tommy Taylor to Orient, making over 60 appearances for the Brisbane Road outfit.

BEAMISH, ANTHONY — Defender
Current Club: Leighton Town
Birthplace: Herts
Tall central defender who can play in midfield and scores a number of goals with his head. Signed for Ryman Division Two side Leighton Town, following manager Paul Burgess from Tring Town, in July 2002. Previously played at Tring under Paul Burgess during season 1997/98, and rejoined in January 2000 from Leverstock Green. Has also played at Berkhamsted Town.

BEAN, DAVID — Defender
Current Club: Radcliffe Borough
D o B: 15/01/1973   Birthplace: Lancashire
Originally played for Radcliffe Borough's reserves before moving to Cheadle Town, David returned to Boro in July 1993. A cultured defender who can also play in midfield, he was voted as Supporters' Player of the year for 2000/01 and is a threat to opposition defences at set pieces from where he has scored several important goals. Had a testimonial game at the start of the 2002/03 season.

BEAN, GRANT — Forward
Current Club: Saltdean United
D o B: 12/12/1982   Birthplace: Brighton
Son of Steve Bean, the man responsible for bringing the new breed of youngsters into the Saltdean side during 2000/01: scored twice that season: also plays in the British Colleges Academy League for Brighton, and had trials for the English Colleges squad during the autumn 2001.

BEANEY, BUSTER — Forward
Current Club: Ashford Town
Birthplace: Kent
A teenage wing forward who was a very prominent youth team player with both Ashford Town and Welling United. Moved up into Dr Martens Eastern side Ashfords senior squad for 2002/03.

BEARD, MATTHEW — Midfielder
Current Club: Stourport Swifts
Birthplace: Worcestershire
Previous clubs include: Local football - February 2002, Bromsgrove R, Evesham Utd, Melville Utd (New Zealand), Kidderminster Harriers.

BEARD, ROBBIE — Forward
Current Club: Rugby United
Birthplace: Nuneaton
Previous clubs include: Bedworth Utd - July 2000.

BEARD, SIMON — Midfielder
Current Club: Margate
D o B: 08/09/1972   Birthplace: Bromley
Previous clubs include: Dover Ath - May 2001, Hastings T, Sittingbourne, West Ham Utd.

BEASLEY, CARL — Midfielder
Current Club: Spennymoor United
Previous clubs include: West Auckland T - August 2001, Spennymoor Utd, Evenwood T.

BEASLEY, SCOTT — Midfielder
Current Club: Congleton Town
Birthplace: Cheshire
Age 23. Midfield. Signed in summer 01. Previously at Crewe Alex, Stone Dominoes, Leek Town and Nantwich Town. Keele Classic winner in 1996 and voted Player of the Tournament.

BEATON, MICHAEL — Defender
Current Club: Dulwich Hamlet
Birthplace: Berkshire
Previous clubs include: Maidenhead Utd - March 2002.

BEATTIE, DAMIEN — Goalkeeper
Current Club: Shepshed Dynamo
D o B: 24/10/1978   Birthplace: Melbourne, Australia
Previous clubs include: Evesham Utd - February 2002, Hinckley Utd, Evesham Utd, Ilkeston T, Notts Co.

BEATTIE, SCOTT — Midfielder
Current Club: Cheshunt
Birthplace: Scotland
Previous clubs include: Wealdstone - October 2001, Ware, Pollok.

BEAUCHAMP, LUKE — Midfielder
Current Club: Abingdon Town
Birthplace: Oxford
Previous clubs include: Thame Utd - December 1999.

BEAUMONT, CHRIS — Midfielder
Current Club: Ossett Town
D o B: 05/12/1965   Birthplace: Sheffield
Vastly experienced player who joined Town this summer from Chesterfield. Made 450 professional appearances with the Spirerites, Stockport County and Rochdale after beginning his career with Denaby United and Sheffield FC. Also appeared in an FA Cup semi final whilst at Saltergate.

BEAVERS, PAUL — Forward
Current Club: Morpeth Town
D o B: 02/10/1978   Birthplace: Hastings
Previous clubs include: Oldham Ath - August 2001, Sunderland.

BEAVERSTOCK, NICK — *Defender*

Current Club: Swindon Supermarine

Birthplace: Wiltshire
Previous clubs include: Odd Down - November 2001, Chippenham T, Cinderford T, Calne T.

BEAZLEY, ADAM — *Defender*

Current Club: Oadby Town

Birthplace: Leicester
Previous clubs include: Atherstone Utd - March 2002, Oadby T, Barrow T, Telford Utd, Stafford R, VS Rugby, Bognor Regis T, Hinckley T, Leeds Utd (Trainee), Shepshed Charterhouse.

BECK, CHRIS — *Defender*

Current Club: Hanwell Town

D o B: 29/09/1968   Birthplace: Hammersmith
Previous clubs include: Old Actonians - July 2000, Yeading.

BECK, MARTIN — *Forward*

Current Club: Eastleigh

Birthplace: Hampshire
Previous clubs include: Winchester C - May 2002, Bashley.

BECK, TERRY — *Defender*

Current Club: Romford

Birthplace: Essex
Previous clubs include: Ford Utd - September 2001, Barking, Aveley, Ford Utd, Romford, Collier Row, Ford Utd, Barking, Rainham T, Basildon Utd, Dagenham.

BECKETT, ADAM — *Midfielder*

Current Club: Brackley Town

Birthplace: Banbury
From Youth team.

BECKETT, DARREN — *Defender*

Current Club: Brackley Town

Birthplace: Banbury
Previous clubs include: Abingdon T - October 2000, Brackley T.

BECKETT, DUANE — *Midfielder*

Current Club: Stocksbridge Park Steels

D o B: 31/05/1978   Birthplace: Sheffield
Previous clubs include: Frickley Ath - June 2001, Grantham T, Doncaster R, Barnsley.

BECKETT, GRANT — *Midfielder*

Current Club: Bromsgrove Rovers

Birthplace: Birmingham
Previous clubs include: Bloxwich Utd - December 2001, Bromsgrove Rovers, Sutton Coldield T, Telford Utd.

BECKETT, NATHAN — *Defender*

Current Club: Arlesey Town

D o B: 31/05/1975   Birthplace: Hertford
Honours won: England Youth Int., Ryman League Div.1,2 & 3 Winners
Born in Hertford, Nathan works in the Building trade. Widely acclaimed as a cultured defender who is more than capable in front of his opponents goal, Nathan is enjoying his second spell at Arlesey Town. He first made his debut at Croydon Ath on August 19th 2000. Former clubs include Leyton Orient, Enfield, Chesham United, Berkhamsted, Wealdstone and Ware. Was capped as an Enland Youth international.

BECKFORD, ANDY — *Forward*

Current Club: Borrowash Victoria

Birthplace: Nottingham
Previous clubs include: Grantham T - January 1998, Shepshed Alb., Hucknall T, Gedling T, Ilkeston T, Shepshed Alb., Eastwood T, Belper T, Leicester Utd, Ilkeston T, Shepshed Alb., Matlock T, Shepshed Alb., Crewe Alexandra, Shepshed Alb., Worksop T, Ilkeston T, Boston Utd, Leicester C, A.

BECKFORD, JERMAINE — *Forward*

Current Club: Wealdstone

D o B: 09/12/1983   Birthplace: London
A highly-promising teenage forward, Jermaine signed for Wealdstone after some impressive performances in the clubs youth team. He is still eligible for the youth side and is now on a first team contract.

BEDDARD, GAVIN — *Forward*

Current Club: Merthyr Tydfil

D o B: 14/08/1980   Birthplace: Wales
Striker who joined Dr Martens Western side Merthyr Tydfil in the summer of 2001 from League of Wales outfit UWIC Inter Cardiff. Gavin enjoyed a successful time at the university club and also impressed in a loan spell at League of Wales champions Barry Town but suffered from serious injury which hampered his progress during the 2001/02 season and joined Port Talbot Town for a while before returning to the Martyrs in the summer of 2002.

BEDDOES, NICK — *Defender*

Current Club: Caersws

D o B: 28/07/1973   Birthplace: Wales
From Youth team.

BEDDOWES, MARK — *Midfielder*

Current Club: Studley

Birthplace: Birmingham
Previous clubs include: Burmans - February 2002, Stourbridge, Sutton Coldfield T, Oldbury Utd, Evesham Utd, Paget R, Bromwgrove R, Kings Norton T, Paget R, Kings Norton T, Solihull B.

BEDWARD, SHAUN — *Forward*

Current Club: Racing Club Warwick

D o B: 19/01/1977   Birthplace: Birmingham
Well-travelled striker who can also play in midfield. Joined Racing Club Warwick in January 2002 following the demise of Bloxwich United. Has League of Wales experience with Rhayader Town and Aberystwyth Town and Dr Martens experience at Gresley Rovers, Bromsgrove Rovers, Sutton Coldfield Town and Hinckley United.

BEEBY, MATTHEW — *Defender*

Current Club: Kidsgrove Athletic

Birthplace: Stoke
Honours won: NWCL Winners
Solid defender who spent ten years at Leek Town before joining Kidsgrove in February 2002. Formerly with Macclesfield and Port Vale, he played in the Conference, UniBond Premier, Dr Martens Premier and UniBond Division One during his time at Leek.

BEECH, ANDREW — *Defender*

Current Club: Worthing

Birthplace: Brighton
Teenage defender: former Brighton & Hove Albion reserve team player who really impressed when appearing for Worthing during the last two months of 2000/01.

B

BEECH, SHAUN — *Midfielder*

Current Club: Newcastle Blue Star

D o B: 02/10/1979 — *Birthplace: Wallsend*

Previous clubs include: Wallsend Boys Club - December 1998.

BEECH, STEWART — *Forward*

Current Club: Farsley Celtic

Birthplace: Yorkshire

Previous clubs include: Glasshoughton Welfare - December 2001, Ossett T, Local football.

BEECH, TOM — *Forward*

Current Club: Trafford

Birthplace: London

Former Chelsea junior striker who signed for UniBond First Division side Trafford during the 2001/02 season from Leek Town and made his debut away at Chorley in March 2002. Previous clubs include Bromley, Crawley Town and Accrington Stanley.

BEECROFT, DANNY — *Forward*

Current Club: St.Leonards

D o B: 11/01/1988 — *Birthplace: Hastings*

Previous clubs include: Sidley Utd - August 2000, Hastings T, Brighton (Junior).

BEENEY, MARK — *Goalkeeper*

Current Club: Sittingbourne

D o B: 30/12/1967 — *Birthplace: Pembury*

Honours won: England Semi-Pro Int., Conference Winners

Appointed as manager of Sittingbourne midway through the 2001/2002 season, after making over 160 League appearances in his professional career for Gillingham, Maidstone, Aldershot, Leeds United and Doncaster. Born in Tunbridge Wells he was a strong reliable goalkeeper who started his career as a trainee with Gillingham, where he made his first team debut at eighteen before moving to Maidstone United. He made nearly eighty appearances, including a loan spell with Aldershot, before Brighton bought him for £30,000 in March, 1991. Two years later he transferred to Leeds United for £350,000. Spent much of his time at Elland Road as understudy to John Lukic and Nigel Martyn before moving to Doncaster Rovers. With nearly two hundred first team appearances to his credit he joined Dover Athletic. Has a UEFA B coaching badge and is goalkeeping coach to Chelseas under nineteen side.

BEER, JAMIE — *Defender*

Current Club: Leatherhead

Birthplace: London

Midfielder who was a Brentford trainee. After that he played for Chesham United, Chertsey Town, Walton & Hersham and Hayes before joining Hampton & Richmond Borough in 1998, and was a regular in their first Premier Division season. Signed for Ryman League side Leatherhead in August 2000 and is also the Club Captain.

BEESLEY, DARREN — *Defender*

Current Club: Worksop Town

D o B: 16/03/1981 — *Birthplace: Rotherham*

Defender who joined UniBond Premier side Worksop Town in August 2002 after being a member of Boston United's squad that won the Conference title. Had signed for the Pilgrims in January 2002 from Harrogate Town after spells with Airdrie, Kilmarnock and Rotherham.

BEESLEY, MARK — *Forward*

Current Club: Chester City

Birthplace: Lancaster

Preston Reserves top scorer in season 1999/00, scoring 20 goals. The striker was then signed by Conference side Chester City in the summer of 2000. Mark has been top scorer at the club ever since, making over 90 appearances and scoring 35 goals.

BEESTON, MARK — *Defender*

Current Club: Newcastle Town

Birthplace: Stoke

Previous clubs include: Hyde Utd - July 2001, Crewe Alexandra.

BEESTON, MATT — *Midfielder*

Current Club: Lewes

Birthplace: Sussex

Joined in July 2000 from Three Bridges. Although not always in the starting eleven last season, Matt saved his best performance for the Sussex Senior Cup final, when he was also instrumental in the move which led to the winning goal. A DT teacher when not playing football.

BEETON, LEE — *Midfielder*

Current Club: Garforth Town

D o B: 07/09/1980 — *Birthplace: Yorkshire*

Joined Garforth this season following a spell at Harrogate Town. A competent young midfielder who likes to play the pass and move style of role in middle linking the defence with the forwards. An ex-Leeds United trainee.

BEEVOR, STUART — *Midfielder*

Current Club: Hitchin Town

D o B: 23/04/1975 — *Birthplace: Herts*

Honours won: Conference Winners

Tough defender or midfielder who spent several seasons with Stevenage Borough. Was a member of Boros Conference-winning side but was released by the club at the end of the 1998/99 season. Joined Aylesbury United before moving to Hitchin Town in December 1999. Made captain of the side on the departure of Adam Parker to Aldershot in September 2001. Placed on the transfer list in November 2001 but returned to the side under new manager Robbie O`Keefe in December, underlying his worth to the team by scoring 2 goals in 2 games. Left to join St Albans City prior to the start of the 2002/03 season but before the season had started, he re-signed for the Canaries.

BEGGS, JOHN — *Midfielder*

Current Club: Stocksbridge Park Steels

Previous clubs include: Rotherham Utd - August 2001.

BEGLEY, KIERAN — *Defender*

Current Club: Hucknall Town

Birthplace: Nottingham

Strong, quick and committed defender who is good both in the air and on the deck. Arrived at UniBond Premier side Hucknall Town from local football in November 1993 and is now one of the clubs longest-serving players.

BEHAN, STEVE — *Defender*

Current Club: Boldmere St.Michaels

Previous clubs include: Sutton Coldfield T - November 2001, Baldock T, Lewes, Sutton Coldfield T, Hitchin T.

BEHARALL, STEVE — Midfielder
Current Club: Ashington
Birthplace: Newcastle
From Local football - July 2000.

BEJADA, LELE — Forward
Current Club: Ford United
Birthplace: Essex
Honours won: Ryman Leaguie Div.One Winners
Highly-rated young striker who was in good form as Ford United took the Ryman League Division One championship in 2001/02. Had re-joined the Motormen in the summer of 2001 after a spell with Grays Athletic. Had been with Barking and Barkingside prior to his first stint with Ford.

BELCHER, JASON — Midfielder
Current Club: Arnold Town
Birthplace: Nottingham
From Youth team.

BELCHER, MARK — Defender
Current Club: Cirencester Town
D o B: 25/11/1978   Birthplace: Swindon
Another product of the successful Cirencester Town Academy, Mark is a versatile player who has played in many positions for the past three seasons.

BELFORD, DALE — Goalkeeper
Current Club: Atherstone United
D o B: 11/07/1967   Birthplace: Birmingham
Previous clubs include: Sutton Coldfield T - July 2000, Atherstone Utd, Hinckley Utd, Sutton Coldfield T, Hinckley T, Tamworth, Nuneaton B, Tamworth, Sutton Coldfield T, Tamworth, Nuneaton B, VS Rugby, Notts Co., Sutton Coldfield T, Aston Villa.

BELL, DANNY — Forward
Current Club: Barnstaple Town
D o B: 19/09/1978   Birthplace: Devon
Previous clubs include: Torrington - July 1997, Bideford T, Exeter C.

BELL, DEREK — Midfielder
Current Club: Durham City
D o B: 19/12/1963   Birthplace: Newcastle
Previous clubs include: Lemington Social - July 2000, Durham C, Blyth Spartans, Whitley Bay, Berwick R, Bishop Auckland, Bridlington T, Gateshead, North Shields, Gateshead, Newcastle Utd.

BELL, KARL — Defender
Current Club: St.Helens Town
D o B: 14/05/1974   Birthplace: Liverpool
Highly-rated central defender who can also play in midfield. Joined from UniBond League outfit Accrington Stanley in November 2000. Lots of skill and bags of experience.

BELL, LEON — Midfielder
Current Club: Barnet
D o B: 19/12/1980   Birthplace: Hitchin
Industrious young player who has worked his way up through from the youth ranks at Barnet. He has a great work rate and an ability to ignite attacking moves with measured passes. Made a professional during the 1999/00 season, Leon made his first team debut against Hull City and is highly-rated by his fellow pros.

BELL, LEON — Midfielder
Current Club: Ipswich Wanderers
D o B: 23/09/1977   Birthplace: Ipswich
Honours won: England Schoolboy Int.
Previous clubs include: Woodbridge T - July 2001, Chelmsford C, Braintree T, Ipswich T.

BELL, MARTIN — Midfielder
Current Club: Newcastle Blue Star
Birthplace: Newcastle
Previous clubs include: Birtley T - July 2001, Whickham.

BELL, MICHAEL — Forward
Current Club: Penrith
Birthplace: Cumbria
From Local football - July 1997.

BELL, STEVE — Midfielder
Current Club: Spalding United
Birthplace: Newcastle
Previous clubs include: Guisborough T - January 2002, Bishop Auckland, North Shields.

BELL, STEVE — Midfielder
Current Club: Lincoln United
Previous clubs include: Winterton Rangers - September 2000, Louth Utd, Boston T, Gainsborough Trinity, Grimsby T (Trainee).

BELLAMY, DAVID — Defender
Current Club: Tow Law Town
Birthplace: Co.Durham
A Utility player who had a number of seasons with Crook after playing in minor football. Signed for the Lawyers last season.

BELLINGER, STUART — Defender
Current Club: Swindon Supermarine
Birthplace: Swindon
From Youth Academy.

BELLINGHAM, MARK — Forward
Current Club: Sutton Coldfield Town
Previous clubs include: West Midlands Police - March 2001, Halesowen T, Cheltenham T, Chelmsford C, Great Wakering R, Stambridge.

BELLINGHAM, ROB — Defender
Current Club: Wednesfield
Birthplace: Birmingham
Previous clubs include: Bloxwich T - July 1997.

BELLIS, DALE — Forward
Current Club: Redhill
Birthplace: Sussex
Another product of the Redhill Youth programme who has broken into the First Team and shows great promise.

BENBOW, STEVE — Goalkeeper
Current Club: Swindon Supermarine
D o B: 05/04/1982   Birthplace: Cheltenham
Previous clubs include: Cheltenham T - December 2001.

BENDELOW, JOHN — Defender
Current Club: Peterlee Newtown
Birthplace: Co.Durham
Previous clubs include: Easington Colliery - July 1998, Ryhope CA.

B

BENJAMIN, ALEX   *Forward*

Current Club: Bedlington Terriers

Birthplace: Newcastle

Alex is only 20 and is one of the hottest properties in the Northern League. Signed in the close season and scored a load of goals in pre-season games and impressed many along the way. Will push Willie Moat and Dean Gibb all the way to partner John Milner up front but this lad is definately one for the future. He also scored many goals for West Allotment Celtic last season and he joined the Terriers at the start of the 2001/2 campaign.

BENJAMIN, IAN   *Forward*

Current Club: Wisbech Town

D o B: 11/12/1961   *Birthplace: Nottingham*

Honours won: England Youth Int.

Previous clubs include: Soham Town Rangers - January 2002, Warboys T, Raunds T, Corby T, Chelmsford C, Kettering T, Ilkeston T, Bury T, Wigan Ath., Brentford, Luton T, Southend Utd, Exeter C, Chester C, Cambridge Utd, Northampton T, Peterborough Utd, Notts Co., WBA, Sheffield Utd.

BENN, WAYNE   *Midfielder*

Current Club: Bradford Park Avenue

D o B: 07/08/1976   *Birthplace: Pontefract*

Signed for Bradford Park Avenue in 1995 upon his release from Bradford City and has been a very consistent and creative performer whether as a sweeper or in central midfield. He had a spell away at Halifax before returning to Avenue in September 1996. Player of the season for 1998/9.

BENNETT, DARREN   *Defender*

Current Club: Tilbury

Birthplace: Essex

Previous clubs include: Aveley - March 2000.

BENNETT, DES   *Defender*

Current Club: Armthorpe Welfare

D o B: 30/10/1963   *Birthplace: Doncaster*

Previous clubs include: Denaby Utd - July 1996, Frickley Ath., Bridlington T, Frickley Ath., Armthorpe Welfare, Doncaster R.

BENNETT, FRANKIE   *Forward*

Current Club: Bath City

D o B: 13/01/1969   *Birthplace: Birmingham*

Pacey and experienced striker whose career began in Non-League football with Halesowen Town before becoming yet another export from The Grove into the professional game when he joined Southampton in 1993. Played a handful of Premiership games for the Saints and then went on to make over 100 appearances for Bristol Rovers and Exeter before signing for Conference side Forest Green Rovers. Followed manager Frank Gregan to League of Wales side Aberystwyth Town at the start of the 2001/02 season and then again to Dr Martens side Weston-Super-Mare in December 2001. Switched to Bath City in June 2002.

BENNETT, GARY   *Defender*

Current Club: Durham City

D o B: 04/12/1961   *Birthplace: Manchester*

Previous clubs include: Scarborough - December 2001, Worksop T, Darlington, Scarborough, Carlisle Utd, Sunderland, Cardiff C, Manchester C, Ashton Utd.

BENNETT, GARY   *Forward*

Current Club: AFC Sudbury

D o B: 02/06/1969   *Birthplace: Enfield*

Honours won: Conference Winners, FA Trophy Winners

Rejoined AFC Sudbury this season from Chelmsford City where he was their Player of the Year last term. An intelligent player who makes the game look easy and finishes with clinical precision. Former Conference and Trophy double winner with Colchester.

BENNETT, GARY   *Midfielder*

Current Club: Hertford Town

D o B: 30/06/1977   *Birthplace: Cheshunt*

Previous clubs include: Wormley Rovers - July 2001.

BENNETT, IAN   *Forward*

Current Club: Sutton Coldfield Town

D o B: 12/02/1972   *Birthplace: Birmingham*

Previous clubs include: Bilston T - November 2001, Redditch Utd, Blakenall, Solihull B, Stourbridge, Tamworth, Leicester Utd, Paget R, Armitage, Rushall Olympic, Armitage, Bilston T, Armitage, Bury.

BENNETT, JONATHAN   *Forward*

Current Club: Littlehampton Town

Birthplace: Sussex

Left-winger: made a handful of first-team appearances for Littlehampton during 2000/01 before establishing a regular place in the line-up for the following season: also a current member of the Sussex youth squad.

BENNETT, MICKEY   *Defender*

Current Club: Canvey Island

D o B: 27/07/1969   *Birthplace: Camberwell*

Honours won: England Youth Int., FA Trophy Winners

Mickey signed for Canvey Island from Brighton in August 1999 where he was player of the year. Strong, quick skilful player who is equally at home in midfield or defence, he has also played for Leyton Orient, Cambridge C, Cardiff C, Millwall, Charlton Athletic, Brentford and Wimbledon. Has represented England under-19s, touring Brazil.

BENNETT, NEIL   *Goalkeeper*

Current Club: Barrow

Birthplace: Dewsbury

Goalkeeper Neil began his career with Sheffield Wednesday as a trainee and graduated to their full-time ranks. He was released in the summer of 2000 without making a League appearance. He joined Ossett Town where he spent a season before joining Airdrieonians in the Scottish League. He made 11 appearances for them during the 2001/02 season. Joined UniBond Premier side Barrow in August 2002 and made his debut in the opening game of the season at home to Hucknall Town.

BENNETT, NIGEL   *Midfielder*

Current Club: Epsom And Ewell

D o B: 09/10/1971   *Birthplace: Surrey*

Epsoms longest serving, and probably most consistent player having joined at 15 and played for the club at all levels. Made his 500th 1st XI appearance against Chalfont St Peter on 3rd November 2001.

BENNETT, PAUL   *Goalkeeper*

Current Club: Newcastle Blue Star

D o B: 10/10/1974   *Birthplace: Newcastle*

Previous clubs include: Benfield Park - January 1997.

BENNETT, RICKY — Forward
Current Club: VCD Athletic
D o B: 29/07/1969   *Birthplace: Northumberland*
Previous clubs include: Deal T - July 2001, Erith & Belvedere, Swanley Furness, Dartford, Greenwich B, Beckenham T.

BENNETT, STEVE — Midfielder
Current Club: Egham Town
D o B: 29/03/1980
A recent signing from Gloucester City, previously with neighbours Cirencester Town. An accomplished player with a sweet left foot, not afraid to battle it out with the best. Currently playing wing-back but loves to get forward to support the forwards. An excellent crosser of the ball from outwide. He has played extremely well in the pre-season games since his signed and this was against some tough opposition.

BENNETT, STEVE — Midfielder
Current Club: Swindon Supermarine
Birthplace: Surrey
From Youth team.

BENNETT, TROY — Midfielder
Current Club: Barrow
D o B: 25/12/1975   *Birthplace: Barnsley*
Honours won: England Youth Int.
Born in Barnsley, Troy is a midfielder who began his career as a trainee with his home-town club and went on to make two League appearances for them before being released. Before his release, Troy had enjoyed a five League game loan spell with Scarborough, scoring once and Boro then signed him permanently. He went on to play 34 League games for them, scoring twice before he was released in the summer of 1998. He joined Gainsborough Trinity in August 1998 and over two seasons at the Northolme, he scored over 20 goals. He joined Barrow in July 2000 and made his debut in the opening home game of the season against Emley. He missed the second half of the 2000/01 season after sustaining a serious knee injury in the FA Cup tie with Leyton Orient but ws back in action for the following campaign.

BENNETTS, SCOTT — Midfielder
Current Club: Erith & Belvedere
Birthplace: Hampshire
Promising young midfielder who came through Farnborough Town's youth side. Became a regular first-team squad member during the 1999/2000 season but then drifted out of contention when manager Graham Westley began to sign former professionals upon gaining a place in the Conference. Moved on to Dr Martens Eastern side Erith & Belvedere in August 2002.

BENSON, DAVE — Defender
Current Club: Eastbourne United
Birthplace: Sussex
Defender, previously with Sidley United: scored 4 times for Rye Utd during 2000/01 before signing for Eastbourne United at the start of the following season.

BENSON, JOHN — Midfielder
Current Club: Prescot Cables
Birthplace: Liverpool
Previous clubs include: Runcorn FC Halton - September 2001, Marine.

BENSTOCK, DANNY — Defender
Current Club: Hornchurch
D o B: 10/07/1970   *Birthplace: Essex*
Honours won: Ryman League Div.One Winners
A now very experienced player who was originally a forward but is now more regularly seen in defence. Started his career at Gillingham and then played for Enfield and Barking before returning to League football with Leyton Orient in 1992. He played 21 League games for the Os before returning to the semi-pro game with Purfleet and Romford, where he was top scorer in their Essex Senior League title success. After a short spell with Bishops Stortford, Danny joined Ford United in December 1999 and played a major part in helping the club to promotion to the Premier Division of the Ryman League in 2001/02. Switched to Division One North club Hornchurch in June 2002.

BENT, DANIEL — Forward
Current Club: Doncaster Rovers
D o B: 22/02/1983   *Birthplace: Boston*
Lincolnshire-born Bent, had been with Lincoln City since 1995 when he played for the clubs under-12 side. He completed his third year of a scholarship within the Youth Academy set up at Sincil Bank. A regular in City's reserve side over the past two seasons, Bents only taste of first team experience in his career came in April 2000 when he was an unused substitute in City's 2-0 League defeat at Hartlepool United. Moved on to Doncaster Rovers in May 2002.

BENT, JAMIE — Forward
Current Club: Chesham United
D o B: 12/03/1980   *Birthplace: Cornwall*
Highly-rated young forward who joined Ryman League Premier side Chesham United in July 2002 after a short spell with Dr Martens Western outfit Chippenham Town. Had signed for Chippenham in January 002 and helped them to gain promotion to the Premier Division. Started out with Cornish side Penzance before joining Yeovil Town in the Conference. Made a number of first-team appearances for the Glovers and played under current Chesham boss Colin Lippiatt at Huish Park.

BENTLEY, CHRIS — Defender
Current Club: Maltby Main
Birthplace: Yorkshire
Previous clubs include: Parkgate - October 2001, Emley.

BENTLEY, ERNIE — Defender
Current Club: Clapton
Birthplace: Essex
Previous clubs include: Ilford - July 2001, Collier Row, Ilford, Rainham T.

BENTLEY, JIM — Defender
Current Club: Morecambe
D o B: 11/06/1976   *Birthplace: Liverpool*
A trainee with Manchester City, scouser Jim quickly made himself a fans favourite at Telford United. United fans need no reminding of his fathers exploits as record club goalscorer, but Jim established himself in his own right as one of the best central defenders in the league. Transferred to Morecambe in May 2002.

BENTLEY, MARK — Defender
Current Club: Pelsall Villa
Birthplace: Walsall
From Local football - December 1999, Pelsall Villa.

B

B

BENTLEY, MARK — Midfielder
Current Club: Gravesend & Northfleet
Birthplace: London
Very highly-rated midfield player who was the subject of much interest from League quarters in recent seasons. Signed for Aldershot Town during the summer of 1999 from Enfield where he had progressed through the ranks. Turned down an offer to sign for Barnet during the 1998/99 season and then joined Gravesend in May 2002.

BENTLEY, SCOTT — Goalkeeper
Current Club: Kidsgrove Athletic
Birthplace: Stoke
A key member of the 1997/8 squad that won the double; he saved seven consecutive penalties at one point in the season. Returns to Kidsgrove after spells at various clubs including Leek Town, Rocester and Newcastle Town.

BENTON, DAVID — Defender
Current Club: Stourbridge
D o B: 08/01/1971 — Birthplace: Birmingham
Previous clubs include: Bilston T - November 2001, Moor Green, Burton Alb., Worcester C, Kidderminster Harriers, Birmingham C.

BENTON, STEVE — Defender
Current Club: Newport County
D o B: 20/12/1974 — Birthplace: Bristol
Signed for Newport County from Hellenic League side Shortwood United in March 2000, Steve has extensive experience from a four-year period with Cheltenham Town for whom he made more than 120 appearances. The defender initially with Bristol City for four years without breaking into the first-team.

BERE, BRIAN — Defender
Current Club: Bracknell Town
Birthplace: Berkshire
Previous clubs include: Chalfont St.Peter - March 2000, Bracknell T, Egham T, Feltham, Hampton, Feltham, Windsor & Eton, Hampton, Staines T, Hounslow, Staines T.

BERE, KEVIN — Midfielder
Current Club: Chertsey Town
Birthplace: Middlesex
Joined the Curfews in the summer after a spell out of senior football. Plays in the midfield.

BERESFORD, JOHN — Defender
Current Club: Halifax Town
D o B: 04/09/1966 — Birthplace: Sheffield
Honours won: England Schoolboy, Youth & B Int.
Former England B international who enjoyed a successful professional career with Barnsley, Portsmouth and Newcastle United. Retired from the pro game whilst with Southampton in 2000 and signed UniBond forms for Ossett Town in the summer of 2001 and then joined Alfreton in January 2002. Switched to Conference side Halifax Town in the summer of 2002. Can operate at left back or in midfield.

BERESFORD, PAUL — Goalkeeper
Current Club: Rugby United
Birthplace: Essex
Paul is a tremendous shot-stopper and is rated as one of the best goalkeepers in the Dr Martens League Eastern Division. He joined Rugby United from Corby Town in August 1999, where he had a couple of spells. Started his career with Cambridge United and also turned out for Billericay Town, Rothwell Town and Stamford.

BERG, JOEL — Defender
Current Club: Wingate And Finchley
D o B: 29/10/1981 — Birthplace: London
Previous clubs include: Heath Park - July 2000, Hendon.

BERKLEY, AUSTIN — Forward
Current Club: Gravesend & Northfleet
D o B: 28/01/1973 — Birthplace: Dartford
Experienced forward or midfielder who joined Gravesend in June 2002 from Barnet following the Fleets promotion to the Conference. Started his career with Gillingham and then went on to make over 150 League appearances with Swindon, Shrewsbury and Carlisle, returning to Underhill after a short spell in Cumbria in October 2001.

BERKS, DAVID — Midfielder
Current Club: Stafford Rangers
Birthplace: Birmingham
After spending four years at Aston Villa, midfielder David joined Stafford Rangers in March 2002. He made his debut at Worcester at the begining of April to follow his twin brothers Peter and John who both played for the Rangers during the mid-nineties. Davids grandfather Reg was both manager and coach at Marston Road.

BERMINGHAM, CHRIS — Midfielder
Current Club: St.Helens Town
D o B: 20/01/1974 — Birthplace: Warrington
Much-travelled and vastly experienced midfield player. Chris is a quality left footed player whose skill can turn a game with one pass. Former clubs include Flixton, Tetley Walker and Warrington Town.

BERNARD, CURTIS — Forward
Current Club: Goole AFC
Birthplace: Yorkshire
Previous clubs include: Frickley Ath - August 2002, Barnsley.

BERRY, DEAN — Defender
Current Club: Hampton & Richmond
Birthplace: Surrey
Teenage right back or midfielder who started out with Notts County in their Academy before moving to Carshalton and then Ashford Town (Middx) during the 2001/02 season. Dean, who can play either in defence or midfield, joined Ryman Premier side Hampton & Richmond Borough in August 2002.

BERRY, GREG — Midfielder
Current Club: Purfleet
D o B: 05/03/1971 — Birthplace: Essex
Previous clubs include: Millwall - October 1997, Wimbledon, Leyton Orient, East Thurrock Utd.

BERRY, GWYNNE — Defender
Current Club: Corinthian Casuals
D o B: 18/12/1963 — Birthplace: Ystrad Mynach
Honours won: FA Trophy Winners, Ryman League Premier Div.Winners
Previous clubs include: Sutton Utd - December 2001, Dulwich Hamlet, Sutton Utd, Welling Utd, Sutton Utd, Woking, Sutton Utd, Whyteleafe, Sutton Utd.

BERRY, PAUL — Forward
Current Club: Leek Town

D o B: 06/12/1978   Birthplace: Warrington
Joined Leek Town from Chester City in February 2002 having joined them from Warrington Town. Also played for Rhyl in the League of Wales on loan during the early part of the 2001/02 season. Paul can play wide on the right or up front.

BERRY, STEVE — Midfielder
Current Club: Bedford Town

D o B: 04/04/1963   Birthplace: Gosport
Honours won: Conference Winners
Previous clubs include: Stevenage Borough - February 2001, Rushden & Diamonds, Stevenage B, Kettering T, Instant Dict (Hong Kong), Northampton T, Swindon T, Sunderand, Portsmouth.

BERRY, TOM — Defender
Current Club: Sittingbourne

Birthplace: Kent
Left-sided young defender who came to Sittingbourne from Kent League side Chatham Town in July 1998. A string of outstanding performances won him a regular first-team spot. Likes to attack down the flanks and is a good crosser of the ball.

BEST, STEVE — Defender
Current Club: Chatham Town

Honours won: FA Vase Winners
Previous clubs include: Ashford T - November 2000, Deal T, Herne Bay, Deal T, Chatham T.

BETSON, PAUL — Midfielder
Current Club: AFC Sudbury

Birthplace: Essex
Joined Sudbury in season 1999/2000 from Braintree. Composed and pacey player who scores the odd goal. Managers Club Player of The Year last season.

BETTERIDGE, TOM — Midfielder
Current Club: Mickleover Sports

Birthplace: Derby
Previous clubs include: Stamford - October 2001, Mickleover Sports, Newport IOW, Derby Co (Trainee).

BETTNEY, CHRIS — Forward
Current Club: Alfreton Town

D o B: 27/10/1977   Birthplace: Chesterfield
Made his Football League debut aged 19 as a trainee with Sheffield United in April 1997 as a sub in a 1-1 draw at Tranmere Rovers. Had a spell on loan at Hull City before signing for Chesterfield at the start of the 1999/00 season, moving on to Rochdale and Macclesfield before joining the Non-League game. In total Chris made 48 full appearances in the Football League and a further 23 as substitute. Has since turned out for South Normanton, Staveley MW, Worksop Town and Ilkeston Town and moved to UniBond First Division side Alfreton Town at the start of the 2002/03 season.

BETTS, ANDREW — Forward
Current Club: Frickley Athletic

Birthplace: Yorkshire
Previous clubs include: Yorkshire Main - October 2001, Frickley Ath.

BEVAN, JODY — Forward
Current Club: Weston-Super-Mare

D o B: 20/10/1978   Birthplace: Gloucester
Signed during last season from Cinderford Town, was previously with Trowbridge Town and Gloucester City. Voted Supporters' Player of the season last season after notching 21 league goals including hat-tricks in three successive games.

BEVAN, RICHARD — Defender
Current Club: Leek Town

Birthplace: Lancashire
Moved to Leek Town in July 2002 from Buxton. Talented defender who began his career at Plymouth Argyle and has also enjoyed spells at Stalybridge Celtic, Mossley and Curzon Ashton.

BEZHADI, BOBBY — Midfielder
Current Club: Yeading

Strong, determined player who joined the Ding in the summer and put in several impressive displays in midfield and at wing-back. Still only twenty years old but in recent seasons has seen action in the Conference for Heyes and prior to that had a spell at Stevenage Borough.

BIANCHINI, MATT — Forward
Current Club: Didcot Town

Birthplace: Oxfordshire
Summer 2001 signing for Didcot from near neighbours Abingdon United who has already shown enough to suggest that he will become vital in Didcots push for honours this season. Forms a potent strike partnership with Andy Marriott.

BICKERS, JOHN — Forward
Current Club: Felixstowe & Walton United

Birthplace: Suffolk
Joins the club from Division 1 side Needham Market. Former Ipswich Wanderers youth player who has represented Liverpool University in National competitions and has shown a cool head and clinical finishing in pre-season friendlies.

BICKLE, GAVIN — Forward
Current Club: Chichester City United

Birthplace: Sussex
Right-winger: former member of Chichester City's youth side, who also fleetingly featured for the first team during the latter part of 1999/2000: spent the following season at Pagham before moving to Church Road for the start of 2001/02.

BICKNELL, MARTYN — Defender
Current Club: Glapwell

Birthplace: Sheffield
Previous clubs include: Sheffield Utd - August 2001.

BICKNELL, MATTHEW — Defender
Current Club: Andover

Birthplace: Hampshire
Previous clubs include: Slough T - July 1999, Reading, Crystal Palace, Southampton (Junior).

BIDDLE, ANDY — Midfielder
Current Club: Studley

Birthplace: Worcestershire
Previous clubs include: Bromsgrove Rovers - March 2001, Alvechurch.

B

BIDDLE, MICK — Forward
Current Club: Biddulph Victoria
Birthplace: Stoke
Previous clubs include: Kidsgrove Ath - August 1997, Knypersley V, Congleton T, Eastwood Hanley, Witton Alb., Congleton T, Port Vale, Stoke C.

BIDWELL, DANNY — Midfielder
Current Club: Broxbourne Borough V&E
D o B: 19/06/1974   *Birthplace: Enfield*
Previous clubs include: Cheshunt - July 2000, Bedford T, Cheshunt.

BIGGINS, WAYNE — Forward
Current Club: Stocksbridge Park Steels
D o B: 20/11/1961   *Birthplace: Sheffield*
Previous clubs include: Leek T - July 1998, Wigan Ath., Oxford Utd, Stoke C, Glasgow Celtic, Barnsley, Stoke C, Manchester C, Norwich C, Burnley, Matlock T, Kings Lynn, Lincoln C.

BILLENNESS, GLEN — Midfielder
Current Club: Erith & Belvedere
Birthplace: Kent
A central midfield player who signed for Erith &Belvedere from Bromley in July 2001 after having previously been at Gravesend and Northfleet for 5 seasons, also had a short spell at Welling United. Honours include the Kent Youth League Southern Division winners, Kent Cup Winner and Kent Senior Cup finalist all with Gravesend and Northfleet.

BILLING, TOM — Midfielder
Current Club: Haverfordwest County
D o B: 05/01/1982   *Birthplace: Wales*
From Youth team.

BILLINGTON, DAVID — Defender
Current Club: Oxford City
D o B: 15/10/1980   *Birthplace: Oxford*
Previous clubs include: Sheffield Wednesday - September 2001, Peterborough Utd.

BINES, JON — Midfielder
Current Club: Selsey
Birthplace: Sussex
Wideman spent some time at Chichester City during 1998/99 before returning to Selsey for the start of the following season. Scored four times during 2000/01.

BINGHAM, LUKE — Midfielder
Current Club: Hamble ASSC
Birthplace: Hampshire
Previous clubs include: AFC Totton - July 1998, Andover.

BINKS, TOMMY — Defender
Current Club: Chatham Town
Previous clubs include: Ashford T - July 2001, Sittingbourne.

BINNS, DALE — Midfielder
Current Club: Hendon
Birthplace: London
Young but talented midfield player who has progressed through Hendons successful youth and reserve set-up making his debut against Boreham Wood in April 1999. Dale is now a regular member of the first-team squad with over 150 appearances to his credit. Leading scorer and both supporters and Players' Player of the season in 2000/01.

BIRCH, DAVID — Defender
Current Club: Curzon Ashton
Previous clubs include: Glossop North End - July 2001.

BIRCH, GARY — Midfielder
Current Club: Nuneaton Borough
D o B: 08/10/1981   *Birthplace: Birmingham*
Previous clubs include: Walsall - January 2002.

BIRCH, PETER — Defender
Current Club: Whitehawk
Birthplace: Sussex
Defender and long serving member of the side, who gained his first ever red card in the match against Eastbourne United during August 2001 - for an obscure incident that was only noticed by a linesman (the game ended 0-0 after the referee blew the final whistle as the ball flew into the back of the Whitehawk net). Has previous experience with Peacehaven.

BIRCH, RAY — Midfielder
Current Club: Burscough
Birthplace: Liverpool
Experienced midfielder who is one of the most-travelled players currently in Non-League football. Signed for UniBond Premier side Burscough from Congleton Town in January 1999 to begin his third spell with the club. Deep breath for his other clubs include - Tranmere Rovers, Warrington Town, Droylsden, Knowsley United, Accrington Stanley, Newtown, Bangor City, Caernarfon Town, Rhyl, Fleetwood, Morecambe, Colne Dynamoes, Kettering Town, Corby Town, Rushden Town, Stamford, Bradford City and Halifax!

BIRCHALL, CHRIS — Defender
Current Club: Ossett Town
D o B: 22/01/1983   *Birthplace: Wakefield*
Talented defender who can operate anywhere along the back line including right or left wing back. Arrived at the club in the summer from Halifax Town and was also on schoolboy forms at Barnsley.

BIRD, ALAN — Defender
Current Club: Brook House
D o B: 06/05/1967   *Birthplace: Wiltshire*
Defender who signed for Weston-Super-Mare in the summer of 1998. Previous clubs include Chippenham Town, Clevedon Town, Witney Town and Gloucester City.

BIRD, ALAN — Defender
Current Club: Weston-Super-Mare
Birthplace: Middlesex
Previous clubs include: Hayes - July 1997.

BIRD, DANNY — Defender
Current Club: Withdean 2000
Birthplace: Sussex
Played for Southwicks County League Division Two championship-winning side during 2000/01: switched to Withdean at the start of the following season.

BIRD, JAMES — Midfielder
Current Club: Horsham
Birthplace: Sussex
Originally a member of Horsham YMCAs youth team before going on to play for Broadbridge Heath and Burgess Hill: almost cost the Hillians the league title in 1999 when making an appearance for them whilst suspended: rejoined YM midway through

1999/2000: scored 8 times for them the following season and went next door to Horsham during the summer 2001.

BIRD, MATTHEW — Forward

Current Club: Aveley

D o B: 04/03/1978   Birthplace: Dagenham
Previous clubs include: Enfield - March 2001, Aveley, Dagenham & Redbridge, Leyton Orient.

BIRD, STEVE — Defender

Current Club: Holmer Green

D o B: 23/11/1975   Birthplace: Liverpool
One-time army man who played North West Counties League football for Warrington Tow whilst still a serving member. The Liverpool-born defender then had a spell in the League of Wales with Barry Town when stationed near there and then joined Rossendale United in September 2000 and helped the club to promotion to the UniBond League.

BIRD, STEVE — Defender

Current Club: Rossendale United

Birthplace: Bucks
Previous clubs include: Penn & Tylers Green - July 1996.

BIRDSEY, JAMES — Defender

Current Club: Witton Albion

Previous clubs include: Northwich Victoria - August 2001.

BIRKBY, DEAN — Forward

Current Club: Bath City

Birthplace: Bristol
Experienced forward who re-joined Dr Martens Premier side Bath City in August 2002, offering to play for nothing in order to ease the clubs financial pressure. Played in the League of Wales with Aberystwyth Town for part of the 2001/02 season and has also served the likes of Clevedon Town, Mangotsfield United, Gloucester City, Yate Town, Yeovil Town and Forest Green Rovers.

BIRMINGHAM, JACK — Midfielder

Current Club: Newtown AFC

Birthplace: Newtown
Local youngster who is well thought of. Great passing ability and capable of quality goal scoring.

BIRMINGHAM, MICHAEL — Midfielder

Current Club: Bognor Regis Town

Birthplace: Portsmouth
A highly-rated midfield player and a former professional with Portsmouth who actually started out in Bognor Regis Town's youth side. Has a tremendous engine always gives 110% and is a great favourite with the supporters. Re-joined Bognor in August 1995 after a spell with Dorchester Town. Lives in Portsmouth.

BISHOP, ADAM — Defender

Current Club: Port Talbot Town

D o B: 04/10/1981   Birthplace: Gwent
Signed for Port Talbot in the summer of 2000 after being released by Swansea City. A tall defender, who impressed early on and found an immediate place in the starting line-up.

BISHOP, DANNY — Forward

Current Club: Hertford Town

Birthplace: Hertford
Previous clubs include: Ware - March 2002, Yeading, Ware.

BISHOP, EDDIE — Forward

Current Club: Nantwich Town

D o B: 28/11/1962   Birthplace: Liverpool
Previous clubs include: Witton Alb - November 2001, Northwich Victoria, Chester C, Tranmere R, Runcorn, Altrincham, Northwich V, Winsford Utd.

BISHOP, GARY — Forward

Current Club: Gorleston

Birthplace: Norfolk
Previous clubs include: Acle - July 2000.

BISHOP, IAN — Midfielder

Current Club: Barry Town

D o B: 29/05/1965   Birthplace: Liverpool
Honours won: England B Int.
Vastly experienced midfielder with over 500 League appearances to his name, mostly at the top level. Joined League of Wales champions Barry Town in July 2002 after returning from the United States where he had been playing for Miami Fusion. Started his career with Everton and went on to play for Carlisle, Bournemouth, Manchester City and West Ham.

BISHOP, JOHN — Defender

Current Club: AFC Sudbury

Birthplace: Essex
Recent acquisition from Chelmsford City, John is a reliable and tough-tackling defender who reads the game with great intelligence. A real assett in the back line who has settled quickly at the club.

BISHOP, MATT — Defender

Current Club: Rhayader Town

D o B: 15/09/1973   Birthplace: Wales
Previous clubs include: CPD Penrhyncoch - January 2002.

BISHOP, NEIL — Midfielder

Current Club: Gateshead

Birthplace: Co Durham
Neil joined UniBond Premier side Gateshead for the start of the 2002/03 season from Albany Northern Leaguers Billingham Town. Possesses a real competitive streak and should be an acquisition that should add steel to the midfield and prove to be great at this level. Started as a junior with Middlesbrough.

BISHOP, SIMON — Goalkeeper

Current Club: Barrow

Birthplace: Middlesbrough
Honours won: England Schoolboy Int.
Born in Middlesbrough, Simon is a highly-rated goalkeeper who began his career as a junior with Newcastle United and won caps for England at under-17 level before starting his Non-League career in the Northern League with Guisborough Town. He featured in the same League for both Whitby Town and Northallerton Town before first sampling UniBond soccer in the Premier Division with Bishop Auckland. He remained with the Kingsway outfit until 1999 when he moved back to the Northern League with Dunston Federation. He joined Barrow in January 2000 and was an ever-present in the squad that won the Chairmans Cup and won the Player of the Year and Players' Player of the Year awards at the end of the 2000/01 season.

BISHOP, STEVE — Midfielder

Current Club: Gorleston

Birthplace: Norfolk
Previous clubs include: Great Yarmouth T - July 2000.

B

BLACK, NEIL — Forward

Current Club: Marine

Birthplace: Bootle

This speedy 20-year-old scored on his Marine debut at Guiseley in season 1999/00. Neil was YTS with Tranmere Rovers having played with various Rovers sides since the age of 12. From Bootle, he represented both Sefton Schools and Merseyside Schools and signed for Marine in March 2000. Neil is studying a Sports Studies course at Edge Hill University College, Ormskirk.

BLACK, RYAN (ZICO) — Midfielder

Current Club: Morecambe

Birthplace: Morecambe

Honours won: Northern Ireland Youth Int.

Northern Ireland under-18 squad forward. Has had frequent first-team appearances and the club management seem great future potential in Ryan as a player. Called Zico by his Dad who is a fan of the Great Brazilian player.

BLACK, SIMON — Forward

Current Club: Paget Rangers

D o B: 09/11/1976   Birthplace: Marston Green

Previous clubs include: Stourbridge - January 2002, Bedworth Utd, Halesowen T, Brierley Hill T, Doncaster R, Birmingham C.

BLACK, TONY — Forward

Current Club: Leigh RMI

D o B: 15/07/1969   Birthplace: Barrow

Honours won: UniBond Premier Winners

Previous clubs include: Chorley - March 1999, Accrington Stanley, Wigan Ath., Bamber Bridge, Burnley Utd.

BLACKBURN, CHRIS — Midfielder

Current Club: Chester City

D o B: 02/08/1982   Birthplace: Chester

Chris graduated from Conference club Chester City's youth squad to become a first-team regular. There was much speculation whether Chris would still be at The Deva as he went on trial at Manchester City at the start of the 2001/02 season. However, he remains an important part of Chesters midfield.

BLACKBURNE, ROB — Goalkeeper

Current Club: Kingsbury Town

Birthplace: London

Previous clubs include: Boreham Wood - December 2000, Kingsbury T.

BLACKETT, GRAEME — Midfielder

Current Club: Dunston Federation Brewery

Birthplace: Newcastle

Previous clubs include: Gretna - November 2000, Bedlington Terriers, Whitley Bay, Prudhoe T.

BLACKETT, LEE — Midfielder

Current Club: Workington

Previous clubs include: South Shields - September 2001, Seaham Red Star, Red House.

BLACKIE, JIMMY — Defender

Current Club: Cwmbran Town

D o B: 17/04/1963   Birthplace: Wales

Honours won: Wales Semi-Pro Int.

Previous clubs include: Ton Pentre - September 1996, Cwmbran T, Barry T, Bideford, Minehead, Barry T, Cardiff C.

BLACKLER, ADAM — Defender

Current Club: Frome Town

D o B: 19/04/1977   Birthplace: Somerset

From Youth team.

BLACKLER, MARTIN — Midfielder

Current Club: Cirencester Town

D o B: 14/06/1963   Birthplace: Swindon

Honours won: FA XI

Previous clubs include: Salisbury C - July 1995, Gloucester C, Moreton T, Bath C, Worcester C, Gloucester C, Cheltenham T, Swindon T.

BLACKMAN, DEAN — Defender

Current Club: Ely City

Birthplace: Cambridgeshire

Previous clubs include: Somersham T - July 2001.

BLACKMAN, GARFIELD — Midfielder

Current Club: Walton & Hersham

D o B: 30/07/1967   Birthplace: Berkshire

Hard working right-sided defender or midfielder who joined Walton & Hersham in the summer of 1996 from Slough Town where he had spent two seasons. Garfield was formerly regarded mainly as a forward and he scored over 100 times as a young player with his first club Northwood, from whom he moved on to Marlow. Voted Player of the Season for 1999-2000 and now the longest serving player at Swans, having passed 200 appearances. Missed a large part of last season through injury.

BLACKMORE, CLAYTON — Midfielder

Current Club: Bangor City

D o B: 23/09/1964   Birthplace: Neath

Honours won: Wales Schoolboy, Youth, u-21 & Full Int., FA Cup Winners, Premiership Winners, European Super Cup Winners

An experienced campaigner with Manchester United, Middlesboro and Notts County. Neath-born Clayton has 39 Wales caps and brought a wealth of experience to League of Wales side Bangor City when he arrived at Farrar Road in October 2000 after short stints at Leigh RMI and Castleton Gabriels.

BLACKSTONE, IAN — Forward

Current Club: Farsley Celtic

D o B: 07/08/1964   Birthplace: Harrogate

Vastly experienced striker whose career began at Non-League level with Harrogate Railway before he went on to make over 150 League appearances with York and Scarborough. Played Conference football with Southport before moving into the UniBond with Chorley, Guiseley, Blyth Spartans and Harrogate Town. Re-joined Farsley Celtic for a second time in June 2002.

BLACKWELL, OLLIE — Defender

Current Club: Heybridge Swifts

D o B: 15/10/1982   Birthplace: Colchester

Promising young defender who joined Ryman Premier side Heybridge Swifts in August 2002 after a short spell with rivals Billericay Town. Started his career at Colchester United, where he progressed through the ranks, but failed to make the senior side.

BLAIN, PETER — Goalkeeper

Current Club: Haverfordwest County

Birthplace: Wales

Previous clubs include: Carmarthen T - July 2000.

BLAIR, SCOTT — Defender
Current Club: Atherstone United
D o B: 24/11/1975   Birthplace: Nuneaton
Previous clubs include: Stoke C - February 1996.

BLAKE, ADRIAN — Goalkeeper
Current Club: Gravesend & Northfleet
D o B: 23/11/1964   Birthplace: Surrey
Previous clubs include: Kingstonian - December 2001, Walton & Hersham, Carshalton Ath., Crawley T, Carshalton Ath., Chertsey T, Kingstonian, Walton & Hersham, Kingstonian, Yeading, Feltham, Walton & Hersham.

BLAKE, DEAN — Midfielder
Current Club: Havant & Waterlooville
Birthplace: Hampshire
Dean started his career as an apprentice at Southampton before signing for Bognor Regis, from whom he signed for Havant & Waterlooville in August 2000. Dean very quickly proved his worth in the reserve team and has since become a regular first team member. The teams showboating expert, his ability to dance the ball through opponents defences has lead him to score several times. Not least in our League Cup game against Salisbury in 2000, where his goal in the 94th minute of play kept the Hawks in a match eventually won on penalties.

BLAKE, GARY — Forward
Current Club: Marlow
Birthplace: Berkshire
Previous clubs include: Wokingham T - December 2001, Marlow, Chalfont St.Peter, Marlow, Flackwell Heath, Egham T, Maidenhead Utd.

BLAKE, LEON — Midfielder
Current Club: Hinckley United
Birthplace: Birmingham
Previous clubs include: Stourbridge - February 2002, Solihull Borough.

BLAKE, MARVIN — Forward
Current Club: Bromsgrove Rovers
Birthplace: Coventry
Previous clubs include: Shepshed Dynamo - December 2001, Bromsgrove Rovers, Atherstone Utd, Nuneaton B.

BLAKE, RICHARD — Forward
Current Club: Edgware Town
Birthplace: London
Previous clubs include: Potters Bar T - July 2001, Basildon Utd, Bishops Stortford, Romford, Uxbridge, Bishops Stortford, St.Albans C, Saffron Walden T, Enfield, Harrow B, FC Bourges (France), Grimsby T, Peterborough Utd.

BLAKELEY, ANDY — Defender
Current Club: Ludlow Town
Birthplace: Shropshire
Previous clubs include: Halesowen Harriers - July 2001, Bridgnorth T, Worcester C, Walsall (Trainee).

BLAKEMAN, CHRIS — Defender
Current Club: Bamber Bridge
D o B: 03/06/1978   Birthplace: Southport
Central defender who joined Bamber Bridge in July 2002 from UniBond First Division rivals Chorley. A former junior at Liverpool, Chris then skippered Southports youth side before being given a chance at Conference level in 1995/96. Moved on to Accrington Stanley before returning to Port and then on to Burscough. Signed for Chorley in the summer of 2000.

BLAKEMORE, CHARLIE — Forward
Current Club: Chasetown FC
Birthplace: Shropshire
Previous clubs include: Ludlow T - June 2002, Bilston T, Bridgnorth T, Rushall Olympic, Chasetown, Stourbridge, Willenhall T, Halesowen Harriers, Wednesfield, Chasetown, Bridgnorth T, Bilston T, Shifnal T.

BLANCHARD, DAVE — Defender
Current Club: Brigg Town
Birthplace: Hull
Previous clubs include: North Ferriby Utd -September 2000, VS Rugby, Wokingham T, Hull C (Trainee). Leeds Utd (Junior).

BLAND, DARREN — Defender
Current Club: Ossett Albion
Birthplace: Sheffield
Previous clubs include: Stocksbridge Park Steels - November 2001, Parkgate, Hallam, Stocksbridge Park Steels, Parkgate, Maltby Main, Hallam, Sheffield, Matlock T, Chesterfield (Trainee).

BLAND, RICHARD — Defender
Current Club: Haverfordwest County
D o B: 28/05/1973   Birthplace: Wales
Previous clubs include: Milford Utd - November 2001.

BLANEY, STEVE — Midfielder
Current Club: Harlow Town
D o B: 24/03/1977   Birthplace: Orsett
Honours won: England Schoolboy & Wales u-21 Int.
Joined Harlow Town in March 2002 from Braintree Town. Midfielder who has previously played for West Ham, Billericay Town, Grays Athletic and St Albans City. A former England Schoolboy internationl who went on to win Wales under-21caps.

BLENCOWE, JON — Midfielder
Current Club: Brackley Town
Birthplace: Brackley
Previous clubs include: Abingdon T - July 2001, Banbury Utd, Witney T, Brackley T, Chesham Utd, Racing Club Warwick, Aylesbury Utd, Buckingham T, Worcester C, Buckingham T, Long Buckby, Brackley T, Leicester C (Trainee), Brackley T.

BLOCKLEY, ROSS — Midfielder
Current Club: Oadby Town
Birthplace: Leicester
From Youth team.

BLOOM, LEE — Defender
Current Club: Felixstowe & Walton United
Birthplace: Ipswich
Close season signing from SIL side Old Newton and at just 19 shows great composure and no little skill on an off the ball. Former Ipswich Wanderers Youth team player.

BLORE, DARREN — Defender
Current Club: Trafford
Birthplace: Oldham
Previous clubs include: Congleton T - February 2001, Flixton, Manchester C.

BLOUNT, MARK — Defender
Current Club: Burton Albion
D o B: 05/01/1974   Birthplace: Derby
Honours won: UniBond League Premier Div.Winners
Mark started his career at Derby County, but after failing to make an impact he joined Gresley Rovers. A series of impressive displays for Gresley saw Blount return to the pro-game with Sheffield United in February 1994. A move to Peterborough followed before Blount once again returned to the Moat Ground. Burton Albion signed the defender at the beginning of the 1997/98 season. Mark missed the latter part of the 2000/01 season through injury but bounced back to claim a place in the Brewers defence where he has performed so consistently over the years.

BLOW, DAVID — Defender
Current Club: Woodley Sports
Birthplace: Manchester
Previous clubs include: Glossop North End - July 2000, Droylsden, Mossley, Radcliffe B, Hyde Utd, Flixton, Hyde Utd, Glossop NE, Hyde Utd, Horwich RMI, Glossop NE, Bury, Oldham Ath (Junior).

BLOWER, ANDY — Defender
Current Club: Chester-Le Street
Birthplace: Co.Durham
Previous clubs include: Gretna - August 2001, Blyth Spartans, Whitley Bay, South Shields, Whitley Bay, Chester-le-Street.

BLOWER, DAVID — Goalkeeper
Current Club: Flexsys Cefn Druids
Birthplace: Wales
From Youth team.

BLOWERS, ROBBIE — Defender
Current Club: Stamford
Birthplace: Peterborough
Robbie is a defender who has returned for a second spell with the club from neighbouring Blackstones, in August 2001. He started his career with Peterborough United. He is currently studying his UEFA B coaching coarse after coaching the reserve and U19 teams.

BLUCK, IAN — Defender
Current Club: Gresley Rovers
D o B: 19/04/1978   Birthplace: Birmingham
Talented defender who joined Gresley Rovers during the summer of 1999 from Midland Alliance side Boldmere St Michaels. Originally with Kings Norton Town, he has been a regular at Moat Street since making his first-tem debut in August 1999.

BLUNDELL, GREGG — Forward
Current Club: Northwich Victoria
Birthplace: Liverpool
A prolific centre forward, Gregg joined Conference side Northwich Victoria in an £8,500 deal from Vauxhall Motors in January 2001 after scoring more than 100 goals in three seasons with the UniBond Leaguers. He began his career as a trainee with Tranmere Rovers and since his release from Prenton Park, has taken the eye of a number of clubs with his predatory instincts. Following the virtual retirement of manager Jimmy Quinn, Vics will be looking to Blundell to continue and even improve his goal scoring exploits.

BLUNDELL, KEVIN — Defender
Current Club: Skelmersdale United
Birthplace: Liverpool
Previous clubs include: Vauxhall Motors - February 2001.

BLUNT, JASON — Midfielder
Current Club: Scarborough
D o B: 16/08/1977   Birthplace: Penzance
Honours won: England Youth Int.
Jason signed for Scarborough during last season from Italian Club Grottaglie wanting to play his football in England. His previous clubs include Blackpool where he made 16 first team appearances, scoring a memorable goal in the 1998 FA Cup. He spent four years at Leeds United and appeared in the first team on several occasions. Jason has also played for England at under 18, 19 and 20 level A tenacious midfielder who holds the ball up well and has good distribution.

BLUNT, KEVIN — Forward
Current Club: Holmer Green
Birthplace: Bucks
From Youth team.

BLUNT, TONY — Defender
Current Club: Corinthian Casuals
Birthplace: Surrey
Tony is a solid and reliable defender who joined Corinthian Casuals in July 1996 having previously been with Sutton United. Tony has also played professionally in the USA where he regulary strapped on his boots next to the likes of Alexi Lalas.

BLYTH, JORDAN — Forward
Current Club: Norwich United
Birthplace: Norfolk
Recent new signing for Norwich United from Mulbarton United. Scored two goals on his debut against AFC Sudbury. Another skilful player, and a very good prospect for the future.

BLYTHE, MARK — Forward
Current Club: Frickley Athletic
Birthplace: Hull
Previous clubs include: North Ferriby Utd - August 2001, Hull C.

BOAD, STEVE — Midfielder
Current Club: Leighton Town
Birthplace: Herts
Signed for Leighton from Tring Town in February 2002, and has previous experience in Ryman Division One with Berkhamsted Town, whom he joined from local side Bedmond Sports.

BOARDMAN, CRAIG — Defender
Current Club: Ossett Town
D o B: 30/11/1970   Birthplace: Barnsley
Gary Brooks first signing as manager towards the end of 1998/99 season. Influential figure who has twice picked up the player of the year award. Began his career at Nottingham Forest and went on to play for Peterborough United and Scarborough, before winning the GMVC with Halifax Town.

BOARDMAN, JONATHAN — Defender
Current Club: Woking
D o B: 27/01/1981   Birthplace: Reading
A highly-rated defender or midfield player who joined Woking in March 2002 from Crystal Palace following a successful loan spell at Kingfield. Came through the ranks at Selhurst Park and was on the fringes of the first-team before moving to Woking.

BOATENG, DES — Midfielder

Current Club: St.Leonards

D o B: 05/06/1980   *Birthplace: Accra*

Des signed for St Leonards in October 2000 from Ryman League side Walton & Hersham. His impressive midfield work rate and goalscoring ability quickly made him a popular member of the side both with team-mates and supporters. He has also previously played for Egham Town, Crawley Town, Yeading and Woking.

BOATENG, PAUL — Midfielder

Current Club: Wingate And Finchley

Birthplace: London

Previous clubs include: Watford - July 2000, Luton T (Junior).

BODDY, ROBERT — Midfielder

Current Club: Saltdean United

D o B: 11/01/1984   *Birthplace: Brighton*

Previous clubs include: Lewes - December 2001.

BODEN, LIAM — Defender

Current Club: Atherton Laburnum Rovers

Birthplace: Oldham

Signed from Atherton Collieries during the last season, Liam is a quick and skilful defender with a positive attitude, which is shown in his captaincy of the team. He is a tough tackler and a clever passer of the ball. Away from the pitch Liam has a strong passion for golf.

BODLEY, MICK — Defender

Current Club: Canvey Island

D o B: 14/09/1967   *Birthplace: Hayes*

Honours won: FA Trophy Winners, Conference Winners, Ryman League Premier Div. Winners

Vastly expeienced defender who began his career as a schoolboy with Chelsea and progressed through to the first-team before joining Northampton Town. Had a three-year spell with Barnet, then followed Barry Fry to Southend United. Mick had loan spells with Gillingham and Birmingham City prior to joining Peterborough United, where he was club captain. Left the Posh in 1999, before joining St. Albans and then Dagenham & Redbridge at the start of the 1999/2000 season. Signed for Canvey Island in May 2000.

BOGAN, DARREN — Forward

Current Club: Arnold Town

Birthplace: Newcastle

Previous clubs include: Grantham T - January 2000, Scarborough, Grantham T, Arnold T, Grantham T, Billingham T.

BOGIE, IAN — Midfielder

Current Club: Bedlington Terriers

D o B: 06/12/1967   *Birthplace: Newcastle*

Ian is a vastly experienced player who signed for the Terriers in early October 2001 from Kidderminster. Ian came through the ranks at Newcastle United with a young Paul Gascoigne in the mid 80s. Spells at Port Vale and Kidderminster followed and was snapped up by the Terriers when he moved to the north east. A valuable player with a great eye for a pass.

BOLD, IAN — Defender

Current Club: Chorley

Birthplace: Liverpool

Honours won: UniBond League Premier Div. Winners

A competitive midfielder or defender who signed for Chorley in July 2002 from UniBond First Division rivals Leek Town. Had joined Leek in September 2001 from Witton Albion. Ian has also

played for Caernarfon Town, Chester City and Leigh RMI, whom he helped to win the UniBond League title.

BOLGER, MICHAEL — Goalkeeper

Current Club: Egham Town

Birthplace: Middlesex

Michael arrived at Ryman Division One South side Egham Town in the summer of 2002 from Dr Martens neighbours Burnham. Had signed for Burnham at the back end of the 99/00 season as back up goalkeeper but soon made the number 1 shirt his own.

BOLLAND, PHIL — Defender

Current Club: Chester City

D o B: 26/08/1976   *Birthplace: Liverpool*

Tall central defender was signed by Chester City in March 2002 for a £15,000 fee from Mark Wrights old club Oxford United having followed the ex-Liverpool and England star previously from Southport in June 2001. He formed a fine centre back partnership with Scott Guyett at Southport as they finished in the top four in the Conference in 2000/01. Tall and dominant, he attacks the ball and can read danger well, often sticking out one of his long legs to make a crucial tackle or inch-perfect...

BOLT, DANNY — Midfielder

Current Club: Sutton United

D o B: 05/02/1976   *Birthplace: Wandsworth*

Midfielder Danny started as a trainee with Fulham before making moves to Slough Town, Woking, Dover Athletic and Sutton Utd. Signed for Canvey Island in March 2002 on a free transfer from Kingstonian and then switched back to Sutton United in August 2002.

BOLTON, NIGEL — Forward

Current Club: Shildon

Birthplace: Bishop Auckland

Previous clubs include: Tow Law T - July 2001, Shildon, Darlington, Shildon.

BOLTON, TIM — Defender

Current Club: Sidley United

Birthplace: Sussex

Veteran defender: solid and reliable type who previously had spells with Hastings and Bexhill.

BOND, MARK — Goalkeeper

Current Club: Diss Town

Birthplace: Norwich

Previous clubs include: Blofield Utd - September 2001, Watton Utd, Diss T.

BOND, RICHIE — Forward

Current Club: Morpeth Town

D o B: 27/10/1965   *Birthplace: Newcastle*

Previous clubs include: Gretna - August 2001, Bedlington Terriers, Whitley Bay, Blyth Spartans, Bishop Auckland, Carlisle Utd, Blackpool, Blyth Spartans.

BONE, CHAD — Midfielder

Current Club: Chester-Le Street

Birthplace: Newcastle

Previous clubs include: Dunston Federation Brewery - December 2000, Chester-le-Street, Rothwell T, Desborough T, Wellingborough T, Bishop Auckland, Chester-le-Street, Newcastle Blue Star, Northampton T.

BONE, JON — Defender

Current Club: Hitchin Town

D o B: 06/11/1968   Birthplace: Luton

A former England Schoolboy international, Jon is in his third spell with Hitchin Town. He rejoined the club in the summer of 2000 and reminded everyone what a steady player he is. His Hitchin career has been interupted by sojourns to Baldock Town and Bedford Town, but since making his debut in 1986, he has played over 600 games for the Canaries.

BONE, LEE — Defender

Current Club: Hertford Town

D o B: 14/07/1980   Birthplace: Enfield

Previous clubs include: Wormley Rovers - July 2001, Cheshunt.

BONFIELD, DARREN — Goalkeeper

Current Club: Hemel Hempstead Town

Birthplace: London

Moved to Ryman Division One North side Hemel Hempstead Town in July 2002 from Farnborough Town. Darren was signed by Farnborough from Boreham Wood during the close season of 2001and has the makings of a fine goalkeeper. Started his playing days with Kingsbury Town and also has spells with Wealdstone and Hitchin Town.

BONHAM, SAM — Forward

Current Club: Brentwood

Birthplace: Essex

Another youth team product who has been appearing in the first team this season. Talented striker who loves to score goals, he is now the first choice partner for Paul Battram up front.

BONNINGTON, DARREN — Goalkeeper

Current Club: Sheffield FC

Birthplace: Derbyshire

Previous clubs include: Maltby Main - August 2000, Sheffield, Maltby Main, Worksop T, Ashfield Utd, Chesterfield (Junior).

BONSALL, SCOTT — Midfielder

Current Club: Harrogate Town

Birthplace: Nottingham

Honours won: UniBond League Div.One Winners

Midfielder who signed for Harrogate Town just before the start of the 2001/02 season from Hednesford Town. Scott began his career at Goole Town before moving to to Eastwood Town. He was then transfered to Hednesford, where he made 20 Conference appearances.

BONSER, JASON — Defender

Current Club: Eastwood Town

Previous clubs include: Parkgate - July 1999, Army.

BOOKER, ALEX — Defender

Current Club: Wokingham Town

Birthplace: Berkshire

Previous clubs include: Aldershot T - July 2000, Fleet T, Thatcham T, Wokingham T, Woking.

BOON, STEVE — Midfielder

Current Club: Bedlington Terriers

Birthplace: Newcastle

A former Sheffield United and Luton Town trainee Steve had his testimonial season at Bedlington last term. Has scored well over 100 goals for the Terriers in that time. Perhaps his nicknames of Mr Magic and The Artful Dodger sum up this little mans talents best. Has the knack of being able to produce the unexpected and has a fine somersault goal celebration in his repertoire. One of the jokers in the Bedlington pack with many a ready quip to hand. Suffered from injury last season but gradually getting back to his best.

BOOT, TONY — Forward

Current Club: Welling United

D o B: 08/09/1980   Birthplace: Essex

Previous clubs include: Windsor & Eton - March 2002, Harlow T, Southend Utd.

BOOTH, GREG — Midfielder

Current Club: Marske United

Birthplace: Cleveland

Previous clubs include: New Marske - July 2000.

BOOTH, LEE — Forward

Current Club: Redditch United

Birthplace: Worcestershire

Previous clubs include: Stourport Swifts - December 2001, Redditch Utd, Lye T, Stourbridge, Lye T, Oldbury Utd, Dudley T, Worcester C, Halesowen Harriers, Stourport Swifts.

BOOTH, NATHAN — Forward

Current Club: Glapwell

Birthplace: Mansfield

Previous clubs include: Shirebrook T - July 2001.

BOOTH, PAUL — Forward

Current Club: Gravesend & Northfleet

Birthplace: Kent

Honours won: Ryman League Premier Div.Winners

Paul signed for Maidstone United as a schoolboy before moving to Tonbridge Angels and then on to Tunbridge Wells. He is strong, quick and good in the air and it is these attributes that had led him to score 16 goals in eight games at The Wells before being snapped up for Gravesend by manager Andy Ford in the early part of the 1998/99 season. Paul travelled to Australia where he did some football coaching before moving back to rejoin the club at the beginning of the 2001/02 season, and he has the undoubted ability to become one of the top strikers at this level.

BOOTHE, CHRIS — Forward

Current Club: Enfield

Birthplace: London

Honours won: Dr Martens League Premier Div.Winners

Well-respected player, capable of filling a number of roles. Became renowned as a prolific striker with Hanwell Town and then Farnborough Town in the Conference before making a move to Hayes. Returned to Boro and helped them regain their place in the Conference before miving on again to Sutton United. Switched to Aylesbury United in December 2001 after a loan spell and played a major role in helping the Ducks to promotion to the Ryman Premier Division. Transferred to Enfield in June 2002.

BORDER, BEN — Midfielder

Current Club: Abingdon Town

Birthplace: Oxford

Previous clubs include: Oxford C - December 1998, Hitchin T, Abingdon T, Oxford Utd (Trainee).

BORG, PAUL — Goalkeeper
Current Club: Carshalton Athletic
D o B: 07/11/1981   *Birthplace: Surrey*
A promising young goalkeeper who worked his way through the youth and reserve ranks at Carshalton Athletic. Made a number of first-team appearances in 2001/02.

BORMAN, LEE — Forward
Current Club: Brigg Town
Birthplace: Hull
Previous clubs include: Pontefract Collieries - July 2000, Hull C.

BOSSU, BERTRAND — Goalkeeper
Current Club: Hayes
D o B: 14/10/1980   *Birthplace: Calais*
Previous clubs include: Barnet - July 2001.

BOSTOCK, JORDON — Defender
Current Club: Leyton Pennant
Previous clubs include: Waltham Abbey - August 2001.

BOSWELL, MATTHEW — Goalkeeper
Current Club: Colwyn Bay
D o B: 19/08/1977   *Birthplace: Shrewsbury*
Shrewsbury-born goalkeeper who signed for UniBond Premier side Colwyn Bay in the summer of 2002 after a spell with Dr Martens Western outfit Rocester. Started his career with Port Vale and then played in Ireland with Sligo Rovers and Scotland for Morton. Went Non-League with Kendal Town, Kidderminster Harriers and Bilston Town, joining Rocester in January 2002.

BOSWELL, STEVE — Defender
Current Club: Metropolitan Police
Birthplace: London
Previous clubs include: Whyteleafe - January 2000, Sutton Utd, Crystal Palace (Junior).

BOTHAM, GRAHAM — Midfielder
Current Club: North Ferriby United
D o B: 08/03/1979   *Birthplace: Hull*
Attacking midfielder who signed for North Ferriby United at the start of the 2000/01 season from local side Brighams, where he won an FA Sunday Cup winners medal. Adapted well to the higher level and became a first-team regular almost immediately.

BOTT, ANDY — Forward
Current Club: Stafford Rangers
D o B: 03/11/1975   *Birthplace: Stoke*
Prolific goalscorer who won the North West Counties Leagues Golden Boot for 2001/02, scoring 48 goals for Newcastle Town. Originally with Meir KA, Andy had a spell in the Dr Martens League with Rocester before signing for Newcastle in January 2001. Switched to Dr Martens Premier side Stafford Rangers in June 2002.

BOTT, STEVE — Forward
Current Club: Newcastle Town
Birthplace: Stoke
Previous clubs include: Leek T - March 2001, Meir KA, Rocester, Meir KA.

BOTTERILL, JAMIE — Defender
Current Club: Barwell
Birthplace: Leicester
Previous clubs include: Downes Sports - June 2002, Barwell.

BOUCHEZ, CHRIS — Goalkeeper
Current Club: Hampton & Richmond
Birthplace: Surrey
Goalkeeper who signed for Ryman Premier side Hampton & Richmond Borough in the summer of 2002 from Tooting & Mitcham United where Chris was reserve team keeper under new Hampton number two Matt Beard. Chris has also played at Carshalton Athletic and Chipstead.

BOUGHEY, DARREN — Defender
Current Club: Stafford Rangers
D o B: 30/11/1970   *Birthplace: Stoke*
Honours won: Dr Martens Legue Western Div.Winners
Darren is Stafford Rangers longest-serving current player with well over 450 appearances stretching back to the Conference days. He was recruited from Stoke City where he had gained first team experience and after loan spells at Wigan, Exeter and Macclesfield signed for Stafford Rangers during the 1992 close season. His first two games were the held over 1991/92 two-legged Staffs Senior Cup final which Rangers won and Darren was a member of the 1999/2000 Dr Martens League Western Division Championship side. Darren is a versatile player who has proved equally effective in defence, midfield and as a striker and has worn every outfield shirt from 2 to 14. 2000/01 was his Testimonial season and he was rewarded with a game against West Bromwich Albion in August 2001 in which he scored the opening goal after two minutes.

BOULTER, JON — Defender
Current Club: Arnold Town
Birthplace: Nottingham
Previous clubs include: Clifton - December 1996, Sandiacre T.

BOULTON, CHRIS — Forward
Current Club: Bangor City
D o B: 23/10/1981   *Birthplace: Wales*
Honours won: Wales Youth Int.
Tall, powerful striker who signed for League of Wales side Bangor City from Mold Alexandra in January 2002. Was with both Manchester City and Preston North End as a youngster before joining his home-town club. Scored a club record 52 goals in the 2000/01 season and had another 26 for Mold prior to his move to Farrar Road. Has represented Wales under-18 Schools and made a handful of LoW appearances as a teenager with Conwy United.

BOURNE, ANDREW — Forward
Current Club: Gresley Rovers
D o B: 03/02/1976   *Birthplace: Stafford*
Stafford-born forward who spent two years at Derby County's centre of excellence before going Non-League with Kidsgrove Athletic. Capable of playing at centre half or in attack, he then had a spell with Leek Town before joining Rocester in September 1999 before moving on to Gresley Rovers exactly two years later.

BOURNE, JASON — Midfielder
Current Club: Tunbridge Wells
Birthplace: Kent
Previous clubs include: St.Leonards - July 2000.

BOWATER, JASON — Defender
Current Club: Glapwell
Birthplace: Chesterfield
From Local football - July 2001, Glapwell, Blackwell MW, Chesterfield.

BOWDEN, ANTHONY   *Midfielder*

Current Club: Marine

Birthplace: Lancashire
Previous clubs include: Accrington Stanley - December 2001, Burnley.

BOWEN, ADAM   *Defender*

Current Club: Rocester

Birthplace: Burton
Previous clubs include: Burton Alb - June 2001.

BOWEN, JAMIE   *Midfielder*

Current Club: Llanelli AFC

D o B: 13/05/1978   Birthplace: Wales
Previous clubs include: Port Tywyn Suburbs - July 1999, Seaside.

BOWEN, JUSTIN   *Defender*

Current Club: Wealdstone

Birthplace: London
Another spell with Bishops Stortford was heralded when Justin signed from Bromley in late autumn 2001. Justins height and tenacity on the ball have won him many admirers and he can score a goal or two as well. Left the Blues again for Wealdstone in March 2002.

BOWEN, RYAN   *Defender*

Current Club: Burscough

Birthplace: Liverpool
Highly-rated left-sided defender now in his sixth season in UniBond Premier Division Burscoughs senior side. Came through from the clubs successful youth ranks and is now the longest serving player at Victoria Park.

BOWEN, SAM   *Forward*

Current Club: Bromsgrove Rovers

Birthplace: Worcestershire
Previous clubs include: Halesowen T - March 2001, Evesham Utd, Worcester C, Merthyr Tydfil, Westfields, Moor Green, Westfields.

BOWER, CRAIG   *Midfielder*

Current Club: Guiseley

Birthplace: Bradford
Previous clubs include: Liversedge - October 2001, Guiseley, Bradford C.

BOWER, DANNY   *Defender*

Current Club: Fisher Athletic (London)

D o B: 20/11/1976   Birthplace: Woolwich
Signed for Dr Martens Eastern side Fisher Athletic in August 2002 after a six-month spell with Ryman Premier outfit Grays Athletic, where he mainly featured in their Capital League side. The defender was previously at Croydon, where he was captain for two seasons, Carshalton Athletic, Leatherhead and Dulwich Hamlet. Began his career as a youngster at Fulham.

BOWER, MATTY   *Defender*

Current Club: Ashford Town

D o B: 10/12/1976   Birthplace: Kent
A versatile defensive player with a lot of energy, Matt re-signed for Ashford Town in May 2002 from Folkestone Invicta. Had moved to Invicta during the summer of 2001 from Welling United having started his career in local football with Bromley Green but was snapped up by Ashford Town, where he became a first team regular during the 1998/99 season.

BOWERS, TYRONE   *Midfielder*

Current Club: Salisbury City

Birthplace: Bournemouth
Tenacious midfield player who signed for Dr Martens Eastern side Salisbury City for a £3,500 fee from Fareham Town in July 1998. Former AFC Bournemouth player whose wholehearted and energetic displays make him a firm crowd favourite.

BOWES, ANDREW   *Defender*

Current Club: Peterlee Newtown

Birthplace: Co.Durham
Previous clubs include: Shildon - July 2000, Peterlee Newtown.

BOWES, ANDY   *Defender*

Current Club: Whitley Bay

Birthplace: Newcastle
Andy signed for the club from Bedlington Terriers last October via Soennymoor. He has impressed every one with his passing skills and also his tenacity in the tackle.

BOWES, MARK   *Defender*

Current Club: Harrogate Town

D o B: 17/02/1973   Birthplace: Bangour
Previous clubs include: Hamilton Academical - January 2002, Forfar Ath., Dunfermline Ath.

BOWES, TERRY   *Midfielder*

Current Club: Purfleet

D o B: 13/09/1979   Birthplace: London
Previous clubs include: Chesham Utd - December 2001, Wisbech T, Ipswich T, Arsenal.

BOWKER, TERRY   *Defender*

Current Club: Stalybridge Celtic

D o B: 18/01/1981   Birthplace: Manchester
A central defender who signed for Stalybridge Celtic in June 2002 from Bamber Bridge. Had joined Brig in September 2001 after re-joining Altrincham in December 2000 from Brig midway through last season having played just once for the Lancashire outfit. Has also appeared in the colours of Maine Road and Castleton Gabriels in the North West Counties League.

BOWLER, JASON   *Forward*

Current Club: Flackwell Heath

Birthplace: Nottingham
Honours won: England Youth Int.
A former England Youth international striker who was originally on the books at Notts County. Was out of the game for 18 months because of a serious illness but made a successful comeback with Ilkeston Town, Stamford, Belper Town and Wisbech Town before moving south through work commitments, joining Ryman Leaguers Marlow in October 2000. Switched to Division Two side Flackwell Heath in August 2002.

BOWLER, RICHARD   *Midfielder*

Current Club: Holmer Green

Birthplace: Bucks
Previous clubs include: Prestwood - July 2001, Holmer Green.

BOWLING, IAN   *Goalkeeper*

Current Club: Kettering Town

D o B: 27/07/1965   Birthplace: Sheffield
Honours won: Dr Martens League Premier Div.Winners
The experienced goalkeeper, with over 300 League games under his belt, arrived at Kettering Town shortly after the start of the 2000/01 season and has since become the Poppies first choice

keeper. Ians former clubs include Mansfield Town, Bradford and Lincoln. Missed the latter part of the 2001/02 season after suffering a serious head injury.

BOWMAN, DARREN — *Midfielder*
Current Club: Stalybridge Celtic
D o B: 04/11/1978   Birthplace: Abergavenny
Welsh-born midfielder who became one of a number of players to switch from North West Counties League side Ramsbottom United to Rossendale United during the summer of 2001 after Dale gained promotion to the UniBond League. Started his career with West Bromwich Albion and then had spells with Grantham Town, Radcliffe Borough and Leigh RMI before joining Rammy. Transferred to Premier Division side Stalybridge Celtic in the summer of 2002.

BOWMAN, ROB — *Defender*
Current Club: Gateshead
D o B: 21/11/1975   Birthplace: Durham
Honours won: England Youth Int.
Rob played in the same England under-18 team as Sol Campbell and Robbie Fowler and played several matches for Leeds United in the Premiership before joining Carlisle. A stong and confident defender, he then flew over to Ireland to play for Bohemians before returning to England in December 2000 and became an instant hit when he joined Gateshead.

BOWN, MATTY — *Forward*
Current Club: Paulton Rovers
Birthplace: Bristol
Previous clubs include: Melksham T - July 1999, Trowbridge T, Wimborne T, Trowbridge T, Poole T, Weymouth, Poole T, Yeovil T, Brighton.

BOWYER, GARY — *Midfielder*
Current Club: Molesey
Birthplace: Surrey
Previous clubs include: Whyteleafe - February 2002, Bromley, Croydon, Dulwich Hamlet, Carshalton Ath., Tooting & Mitcham Utd, Carshalton Ath., Kingstonian, Carshalton Ath., Bromley, Whyteleafe, Carshalton Ath., Crystal Palace.

BOXALL, PAUL — *Forward*
Current Club: Horsham YMCA
Birthplace: Sussex
Exciting striker: had extensive Ryman League experience before scoring 7 times for Burgess Hill during the early part of 1998/99: has only made limited appearances since (looked to be back to his best when scoring a hat-trick for Saltdean on the opening day of the 2000/01 season but was once again sidelined shortly afterwards): joined Horsham YMCA in August 2001.

BOYCE, MARK — *Defender*
Current Club: Enfield
D o B: 11/08/1980   Birthplace: Hammersmith
Defender or midfielder who joined Ryman Premier side Enfield in July 2002 from rivals Chesham United. Began his career at Watford and then had spells in the Conference with Hayes and Kingstonian before signing for Chesham in November 2001.

BOYD, CHARLIE — *Midfielder*
Current Club: St.Helens Town
D o B: 20/09/1969   Birthplace: Liverpool
Classy midfield player with bags of experience gained with Liverpool. An early season signing who is just starting to show his true form.

BOYLAN, LEE — *Forward*
Current Club: Canvey Island
D o B: 02/09/1978   Birthplace: Chelmsford
Lee previously played for West Ham, Trelleborg, Kingstonian, Exeter, Hayes and Heybridge Swifts. Signed for Caney Island in August 2001 after a highly impressive trial period and it proved to be a master stroke as he ended the season as the Ryman Leagues top scorer.

BOYLE, ANDY — *Defender*
Current Club: Tunbridge Wells
Birthplace: Kent
Previous clubs include: Tonbridge Angels - July 2000.

BOYLE, MARTIN — *Forward*
Current Club: Yate Town
Birthplace: Bristol
Previous clubs include: Mangotsfield Utd - July 2001, Paulton R, Forest Green R, Newport AFC, Cheltenham T, Bath C, Mangotsfield Utd, Trowbridge T, Bristol R.

BOYLE-RENNER, VICTOR — *Midfielder*
Current Club: Harlow Town
D o B: 18/04/1979   Birthplace: Sierra Leone
Hihgly-rated midfielder, born in Sierra Leone, whose career began at Wimbledon. Moved into the Non-League game with Gravesend and then spent three years with Chesham United before having a short stint at Ryman Premier rivals Purfleet. Switched to Harlow Town in March 2002.

BRABIN, GARY — *Midfielder*
Current Club: Total Network Solutions
D o B: 09/12/1970   Birthplace: Liverpool
Honours won: England Semi-Pro Int.
Very experienced, tough-tackling midfielder who signed for League of Wales side Total Network Solutions from Conference outfit Chester City in July 2002. A former England semi-professional international, he had signed for Chester from Torquay in January 2002 after appearing in over 200 League games for the Gulls, Hull, Blackpool, Bury and Doncaster Rovers. Had earlier been at Runcorn and Gateshead in the Conference.

BRACE, DERYN — *Midfielder*
Current Club: Haverfordwest County
D o B: 15/03/1975   Birthplace: Wales
Previous clubs include: Tenby Utd - February 2002.

BRACEY, LEE — *Goalkeeper*
Current Club: Ossett Town
D o B: 11/09/1968   Birthplace: Barking
Experienced keeper who signed on the eve of the current season after leaving Hull City. Has enjoyed an excellent professional career with Swansea City, Halifax Town, Bury and Ipswich Town where he was understudy to Richard Wright. Has proved to be an excellent signing.

BRACKLEY, PETER — *Forward*
Current Club: Lewes
Birthplace: Sussex
Re-joined the Rooks this summer after a spell at Worthing. Peter is a skilful winger who will undoubtedly also chip in with some goals this season.

B

BRADBURY, SHAUN — Forward
Current Club: Chasetown FC
D o B: 11/02/1974 — *Birthplace: Birmingham*
Previous clubs include: Blakenall - July 1997, Shifnal T, Hereford Utd, Chester C, Wolverhampton Wanderers.

BRADFORD, LEE — Defender
Current Club: Weymouth
Birthplace: Bournemouth
Defender who re-joined Dr Martens Premier side Weymouth in the summer of 2002 from relegated Newport Isle of Wight. Began his career with his home-town club AFC Bournemouth and then had spells with Poole Town and Dorchester Town before signing for the Terras for the first time in July 1995. Moved on to Salisbury City and then joined Newport in September 2001.

BRADLEY, ANDY — Defender
Current Club: Stourport Swifts
Birthplace: Birmingham
Previous clubs include: Redditch Utd - March 2002, Worcester C, Stafford R, Halesowen T, Tividale.

BRADLEY, CARL — Forward
Current Club: Bridgnorth Town
Birthplace: Staffordshire
Previous clubs include: Tividale - August 1998, Bridgnorth T, Halesowen Harriers, Blakenall, Halesowen Harriers, Stafford R,Tividale.

BRADLEY, JIM — Defender
Current Club: Marlow
Birthplace: Berkshire
Solid and reliable defender whose playing days began at Wokingham Town. Had a spell with Staines Town before returning to Wokingham and has since turned out for Burnham, Windsor & Eton, Bracknell Town and Egham Town before signing for Marlow in July 1998, where he was player of the year at the end of his first season with the club.

BRADLEY, LEE — Forward
Current Club: Goole AFC
Birthplace: Yorkshire
Previous clubs include: Ossett Alb - February 2002, Emley.

BRADSHAW, CARL — Defender
Current Club: Alfreton Town
D o B: 02/10/1968 — *Birthplace: Sheffield*
Honours won: England Youth Int.
Vastly experienced defender who became a real coup for UniBond First Diviion Alfreton Town when they signed him in July 2002 after he had been released by Scunthorpe. A former England Youth international, Carl made over 400 League appearances, many at the top level, and was once the subject of a £500,000 transfer when moving to Norwich from Sheffield United in 1994. Also played for Manchester City and Wigan and started out at Sheffield Wednesday.

BRADSHAW, CHARLIE — Forward
Current Club: Ossett Albion
Previous clubs include: Emley - August 2001, Droylsden, Ossett Alb., Emley, Altrincham, Emley, Accrington Stanley, Ossett T.

BRADSHAW, DARREN — Defender
Current Club: Worksop Town
Birthplace: Sheffield
Previous clubs include: Stevenage Borough - July 2001, Rushden & Diamonds, Blackpool, Peterborough Utd, Newcastle Utd, York C, Chesterfield, Matlock T.

BRADSHAW, MARK — Defender
Current Club: Mossley
D o B: 07/09/1969 — *Birthplace: Ashton*
Honours won: England Semi-Pro Int., Conference Winners
Vastly experienced former England semi-professional international defender who joined North West Counties League side Mossley in June 2002 from UniBond neighbours Droylsden. Consistent and effective left back who began his career with Blackpool where he made 42 League appearances. Was released at the end of the 1990/91 season and joined Stafford Rangers where he soon gained th reputation for being one of the best in his position in the Conference. Moved to Macclesfield in 1994/95 and went on to complete a Conference championship winning double with the Silkmen in 1995 and 97. Then moved to Halifax Town where he added to his League tally before signing for Droylsden at the start of the 2001/02 season.

BRADY, ANDY — Midfielder
Current Club: Tiptree United
Birthplace: Essex
Previous clubs include: Clacton T - July 1998, Tiptree Heath.

BRADY, JON — Midfielder
Current Club: Woking
D o B: 14/01/1975 — *Birthplace: Newcastle, Australia*
Honours won: Conference Winners
Left-sided midfielder who joined Conference side Woking just prior to the start of the 2002/03 season from Rushden & Diamonds. Had cost the Diamonds a £40,000 fee when signing from Hayes in May 1998. Australian-born, he has also had spells with Swansea, Wycombe and Brentford and spent a summer plying in Norway with Mjolner. Gained a Conference winners medal with Diamonds.

BRADY, MATT — Midfielder
Current Club: Windsor & Eton
D o B: 27/10/1977 — *Birthplace: London*
Previous clubs include: Boreham Wood - February 2002, Wycombe Wanderers, Boreham Wood, Barnet.

BRADY, MICHAEL — Defender
Current Club: Tooting & Mitcham United
Previous clubs include: Leatherhead - August 1999, Carshalton Ath., Leatherhead, Carshalton Ath.

BRAGG, JASON — Midfielder
Current Club: Whitstable Town
Birthplace: Kent
Previous clubs include: Sheppey Utd - July 1999, Cray Wanderers, Sheppey Utd, Dartford, Beckenham T, Furness, Purfleet, Chatham T.

BRAHAM, TROY — Midfielder
Current Club: Bishops Stortford
Birthplace: Essex
An exciting player to watch, Troy was a junior at Charlton Athletic having been spotted captaining the Newham Schoolboys side. From the Addicks, Troys first senior football was with Tilbury and he signed for The Blues from Romford in February 1999. A

regular in the first team and very popular with the supporters for his exciting style of play.

BRAIN, CHRIS — *Goalkeeper*
Current Club: Thame United
Birthplace: Oxfordshire
An outstanding young goalkeeping prospect who was thrown in at the deep end at the end of the 2000/01 season after progressing through the clubs youth team. Chris still has a lot to learn but is a superb shot-stopper as he showed in the Oxfordshire Senior Cup final when his display played a big part in Thame winning the Trophy.

BRAITHWAITE, LEON — *Forward*
Current Club: Margate
D o B: 17/12/1972   *Birthplace: London*
Previous clubs include: Welling Utd - May 2000, St.Patricks Ath., Charlton Ath., Exeter C, Bishops Stortford.

BRAKE, NIGEL — *Forward*
Current Club: Crawley Town
Birthplace: Sussex
Previously with Oakwood and Carshalton before joining Crawley from Redhill in 1999: fractured a cheekbone in the FA Cup tie with Fareham during October 2001.

BRANDT, MARK — *Forward*
Current Club: Haverhill Rovers
Birthplace: Suffolk
Has been at Haverhill on-and-off for seven years, and has had spells at Mildenhall Town, Halstead Town and West Wratting; likes to score goals. Top scorer last season.

BRANNAN, FRANK — *Midfielder*
Current Club: Chalfont St.Peter
Birthplace: Berkshire
Previous clubs include: Marlow - December 2001, Wycombe Wanderers (Trainee), Chelsea (Junior).

BRANT, JOHN — *Forward*
Current Club: Stratford Town
Birthplace: Stratford
Previous clubs include: Kenilworth T - February 2000, Stratford T.

BRASSART, OLIVIER — *Midfielder*
Current Club: Scarborough
D o B: 20/05/1977   Birthplace: Noisy-le-Sec, France
Midfielder Olivier joined Conference side Scarborough just before the start of the 2002/03 season from rivals Yeovil Town. A Frenchman, he played for The Glovers from January 2002, joining them from Stuttgart. Previous experience with Belgian sides RAEC Bergen, FC Denderleeuw and Royal Antwerp and French club Lens.

BRATT, WILLIAM — *Midfielder*
Current Club: Rocester
Birthplace: Stoke
Previous clubs include: Stone Dominoes - December 2001.

BRAY, NEIL — *Midfielder*
Current Club: Gainsborough Trinity
Birthplace: Nottinghamshire
Previous clubs include: Long Eaton Utd - February 2002, Eastwood T, Worksop T.

BRAYBROOK, DEAN — *Defender*
Current Club: Clacton Town
Birthplace: Essex
Solid dominant defender with great character and sportsmanship. Previous clubs include Braintree, Witham and Ford United before joining Clacton.

BRAYLEY, BERT — *Forward*
Current Club: Canvey Island
D o B: 05/09/1981   Birthplace: London
Bertie was a product of the West Ham Youth Scheme. A foward who can also play on the left wing, he has played along Hammers stars Joe Cole and Michael Carrick. Brayley starred for West Ham in their 1999 FA Youth Cup win over Coventry City, scoring three goals over the two-legged final. Berties previously played for QPR, Swindon and spent a day training with Southend United. Signed for Ryman Premier side Canvey Island on a free transfer in August 2002.

BRAZIER, PHIL — *Defender*
Current Club: Vauxhall Motors
D o B: 03/09/1977   Birthplace: Liverpool
Honours won: FA Youth Cup Winners
Captain of Liverpools FA Youth Cup-winning side of 1995, this cultured defender joined Vauxhall Motors in July 1998. Installed as captain, after leaving Anfield following ten years with the club Phil tried his luck with Tranmere, Notts County, Stockport and Rochdale before joining the Motormen. Has since settled into the heart of the defence and was named player of the year in 2000/01.

BRAZIL, DEREK — *Defender*
Current Club: Haverfordwest County
D o B: 14/12/1968   Birthplace: Dublin
Honours won: Republic of Ireland u-21 Int.
Previous clubs include: Inter Cardiff - December 1999, Newport AFC, Cardiff C, Manchester Utd, Rivermount.

BREEZE, KEVIN — *Defender*
Current Club: Flexsys Cefn Druids
Birthplace: Wales
Previous clubs include: Brymbo Broughton - March 2000, Flexsys Cefn Druids, Brickfield.

BRENNAN, DEAN — *Midfielder*
Current Club: Hitchin Town
Birthplace: Luton
Dynamic midfielder who joined Ryman Premier side Hitchin Town during the 2001/02 season on-loan and played a key role in the clubs excellent end to the campaign. Formerly with Luton Town, Bohemians and Sheffield Wednesday, Dean still hopes to make the grade as a full-time professional.

BRENNAN, GERRY — *Defender*
Current Club: Wembley
Birthplace: London
Previous clubs include: Wealdstone - August 2001, Wembley, Edgware T, Kingsbury T, Hemel Hempstead, Edgware T, Kingsbury T, Arsenal (Junior).

BRENNAN, KARL — *Midfielder*
Current Club: Halesowen Town
D o B: 19/03/1981   Birthplace: Leicester
Previous clubs include: Hinckley Utd - March 2002, Nuneaton Borough.

B

B

BRENNAN, MARK — Midfielder

Current Club: Accrington Stanley

D o B: 04/10/1965 — Birthplace: Rossendale
Honours won: England Youth & u-21 Int.

Mark signed for Billericay Town in June 2000 following two successful seasons wih Dagenham & Redbridge in the Conference. The experienced midfielder started at Ipswich, where he played nearly 170 first team games before being sold to Middlesborough for £600.000. After two years with Boro he moved on to Manchester City for a fee of £500,000 before ending his Football League career with Oldham Athletic. In total Mark made more than 400 League & Cup appearances. He also represented England 6 times at Under-21 level.

BRENNAN, MARK — Midfielder

Current Club: Billericay Town

Birthplace: Liverpool
Honours won: UniBond League Premier Div.Winners

Strong midfielder who originally signed for Accrington Stanley from Ashton United in the summer of 1999. Experienced player who has had spells at South Liverpool, Bootle, Morecambe, Southport, Chorley, Marine, Bangor and Bamber Bridge. Left for a brief spell as assistant-manager at St Helens before rejoining Stanley in February 2002.

BRENNAN, PEDRO — Midfielder

Current Club: Mossley

Birthplace: Stockport
Previous clubs include: Grove Utd - August 1997, Radcliffe B, Congleton T, Bramhall.

BRENNAN, SEAN — Midfielder

Current Club: Corby Town

D o B: 03/09/1982 — Birthplace: Corby
From Youth team.

BRESLIN, NEIL — Defender

Current Club: Chertsey Town

Birthplace: Surrey
A local player who has made significant progress after signing in the millennium summer. Has come through the years with Chertsey Juniors and is regularly selected for the Surrey County rep side.

BRETT, GRAHAM — Defender

Current Club: Bangor City

D o B: 27/11/1977 — Birthplace: Ireland
Irishman who has Irish League experience with UCD (Dublin) and Shelbourne. A composed defender who can play wingback or sweeper, Graham is a student at the Bangor University and joined Bangor City in July 1999. Had an outstanding match in the Welsh Cup Final success against Cwmbran at The Racecourse in May 2000.

BRETT, PAUL — Defender

Current Club: Burnham

Birthplace: Slough
Last seasons player of the year (and for a few other seasons), Paul has now been at the club for 12 seasons. Consistent and highly dependable, he is a great asset to the club.

BREWERTON, JAMES — Defender

Current Club: Rhyl

Birthplace: Rhyl
Previous clubs include: Llandudno - February 2000, Rhyl.

BREWINGTON, PAUL — Defender

Current Club: Brentwood

Birthplace: Essex
Strong left sided player who can play at the back or in midfield, became a first team regular three seasons ago and quickly established himself as one of Blues key players.

BRICE, JASON — Midfielder

Current Club: Bemerton Heath Harlequins

Birthplace: Wiltshire
Previous clubs include: AFC Bournemouth (Trainee) - July 1996.

BRIDDON, WAYNE — Midfielder

Current Club: Atherton Laburnum Rovers

Birthplace: Oldham
Wayne came to LR from Ramsbottom United in March 2001. He is a strong, competitive player in the middle of the park who always works hard in both defending and attacking. Wayne is an industrial roofer and his interests include skiing and scuba-diving.

BRIDGE, MARK — Forward

Current Club: Arlesey Town

Birthplace: Herts
Previous clubs include: Stevenage Borough - September 2001.

BRIDGE, PHIL — Forward

Current Club: Halesowen Harriers

Birthplace: Worcestershire
Previous clubs include: Lye T - July 1997.

BRIDGEMAN, GLEN — Forward

Current Club: Sidlesham

Birthplace: Sussex
Forward, who walks a tight line between sheer genius and madness: scored 34 times for Chichester City (1996/97 to 1998/99) before a brief stay at Portfield: began playing for Sidlesham in August 2001.

BRIDGES, JUSTIN — Defender

Current Club: Newtown AFC

Birthplace: Wales
Previous clubs include: Oswestry T - November 2001, Welshpool T - July 1997, Bridgnorth T.

BRIDGES, RONNIE — Midfielder

Current Club: Heybridge Swifts

Birthplace: Essex
Young man who has come through from Heybridge Swifts youth and Alliance sides. Versatile midfielder or defender who has all the attributes to go a long way in the game. Popular with his team-mates and anyone who has seen him play. Aggressive and hard-working with a great engine.

BRIDGEWATER, DAVID — Midfielder

Current Club: Total Network Solutions

D o B: 27/09/1980 — Birthplace: Stourbridge
A good passer of the ball, can keep it simple or produce match-winning passes as good as anyone. Works hard for the team - a box-to-box player. Joined TNS in the summer of 2001 from Conference club Telford United and was originally on the books at Preston.

BRIDLE, KRISTIAN — Midfielder

Current Club: Wick

Birthplace: Sussex
Previous clubs include: Storrington - July 2001.

BRIERLEY, PAUL   Defender
Current Club: Stanway Rovers

Birthplace: Essex
From Youth team.

BRIGGS, PERRY   Defender
Current Club: Dunston Federation Brewery

Birthplace: Newcastle
Previous clubs include: Whitley Bay - December 1997, Durham C, Whitley Bay, Durham C, Whitley Bay, Gateshead, Durham C, Bedlington Terriers.

BRIGGS, RYAN   Midfielder
Current Club: Tonbridge Angels

D o B: 06/04/1981   Birthplace: London
Previous clubs include: Dulwich Hamlet - December 2001, Bromley, Grays Ath, Folkestone Invicta, Chesham Utd, Dover Ath., West Ham Utd.

BRIGHT, DAVID   Forward
Current Club: Clevedon Town

Birthplace: Bristol
Previous clubs include: Chippenham T - February 2002, Brislington, Salisbury C, Clevedon T, Mangotsfield Utd, Clevedon T, Paulton R, Mangotsfield Utd, Stoke C.

BRIGHTON, STEWART   Defender
Current Club: Bromsgrove Rovers

D o B: 30/10/1966   Birthplace: Bromsgrove
Honours won: England Semi-Pro Int., Dr Martens Premier Div.Winners
Re-signed for Bromsgrove Rovers from Moor Green, where he had spent the past three seasons, in the summer of 2002. One of the best-known full-backs in Non-League football. Following three seasons at Crewe Alexandra, he then had a 14-year spell at Bromsgrove Rovers, playing around 450 matches. Honours include a Premier Division champions medal, a Conference runners-up medal, an England semi-professional cap and he has twice toured with the Middlesex Wanderers.

BRIGHTWELL, STUART   Forward
Current Club: Durham City

D o B: 31/01/1979   Birthplace: Easington
Honours won: England Schoolboy & Youth Int.
Previous clubs include: Bishop Auckland - July 2000, Hartlepool Utd, Manchester Utd.

BRIGNALL, PHIL   Midfielder
Current Club: Eastwood Town

Birthplace: Nottingham
Previous clubs include: Hucknall T - December 2001.

BRILL, RUSSELL   Defender
Current Club: Wingate And Finchley

D o B: 30/11/1975   Birthplace: London
From Youth team.

BRINDLEY, CHRIS   Defender
Current Club: Hednesford Town

D o B: 05/07/1969   Birthplace: Stoke
Honours won: Conference Winners, FA Trophy Winners, FA XI Rep.
Vastly experienced central defender who re-joined Hednesford Town in May 2002 from Stafford Rangers. His career started at Hednesford before moving to Wolverhampton Wanderers where he made seven League appearances. Then after moving to

Telford United, he played in their 1989 FA Trophy-winning side. Chris joined Kidderminster Harriers for £20,000 and was a member of their 1993/94 Conference-winning side before returning to Hednesford. Signed for Stafford at the start of the 2000/10 season.

BRINDLEY, DERRIN   Defender
Current Club: Haverhill Rovers

Birthplace: Suffolk
Has played at left back, centre back and even centre-forward. In his seventh season at Haverhill Rovers.

BRISCOE, GARY   Forward
Current Club: Borrowash Victoria

Birthplace: Derbyshire
Previous clubs include: Hucknall T - July 2000, Belper T, Sandiacre T.

BRISCOE, ROBBIE   Midfielder
Current Club: Mickleover Sports

D o B: 01/09/1969   Birthplace: Derby
Previous clubs include: Sandiacre T - July 1999, Heanor T, Mickleover Sports, Sandiacre T, Burton Alb., Gresley R, Derby Co.

BRISTOW, JASON   Defender
Current Club: Basingstoke Town

D o B: 23/04/1980   Birthplace: Basingstoke
Strong and dependable defender who signed for Basingstoke Town from Reading at the start of the 1999/2000 season where he was captain of their second team. Equally at home either on the right or at the heart of defence, Jasons long throw and good crossing abilities make him useful when the team is pushing forward. Jason recently gained FA XI recognition against the Combined Services and has also represented the South East Counties league.

BRITNELL, GARRY   Defender
Current Club: Canvey Island

D o B: 06/09/1964   Birthplace: Essex
Honours won: FA Trophy Winners
Previous clubs include: Enfield - July 1994, Dartford, Chelmsford C, Canvey Island.

BRIZZELL, JASON   Defender
Current Club: Hungerford Town

Birthplace: Hungerford
From Youth team.

BROAD, RAY   Midfielder
Current Club: Lordswood

Birthplace: Kent
From Youth team.

BROADHURST, NEIL   Defender
Current Club: Mickleover Sports

D o B: 22/10/1977   Birthplace: Derby
Previous clubs include: Belper T - July 2002, Gresley R, Hednesford T, Derby Co.

BROCKETT, LUKE   Midfielder
Current Club: Berkhamsted Town

Birthplace: London
Previous clubs include: Chalfont St.Peter - July 2000, Chesham Utd, Chelsea (Junior).

B

BROCKIE, VINCE — Midfielder
Current Club: Glasshoughton Welfare
D o B: 02/02/1969   Birthplace: Greenock
Previous clubs include: Farsley Celtic - January 2002, -Bardsey, North Ferriby Utd, Garforth T, Harrogate T, Bardsey, Hyde Utd, Guiseley, Goole T, Doncaster R, Leeds Utd.

BRODIE, STEVE — Forward
Current Club: Chester City
D o B: 14/01/1973   Birthplace: Sunderland
Exprienced goalscorer who joined Chester City in June 2002 after being released by Swansea City. Started his career with his home-town club Sunderland but made only one first-team start although he did have loan spells with Doncaster Rovers and Scarborough. Moved permanently to the Seadogs in February 1997 and suffered relegation from the Football League with them before transferring to Swansea in November 2001. Totalled over 200 League appearances.

BROMLEY, DANNY — Midfielder
Current Club: Willenhall Town
Birthplace: Wolverhampton
Summer signing from Darlaston, hoping to impress at the higher level, a Birmingham League cricketer.

BROOK, GARY — Forward
Current Club: Ossett Town
D o B: 09/05/1964   Birthplace: Dewsbury
Guided Town to the UniBond League following his appointment as player/manager in January 1999 and has built a squad that is more than capable of holding its own since. Arrived as a player in 1998 after winning the GMVC with Halifax and has had a solid pro career with Scarborough, Newport County and Blackpool. Still a feared striker at this level.

BROOKE, DAVID — Midfielder
Current Club: Glasshoughton Welfare
D o B: 23/11/1975   Birthplace: Barnsley
Previous clubs include: Pontefract Collieries - July 2001, Frickley Ath., Stocksbridge Park Steels, Scarborough, Barnsley.

BROOKER, DANNY — Defender
Current Club: Carshalton Athletic
D o B: 05/12/1975   Birthplace: London
Previous clubs include: Sutton Utd - January 2002, Kingstonian, Sutton Utd, Dorking, Wimbledon (Trainee).

BROOKES, ANDREW — Defender
Current Club: Stafford Rangers
D o B: 25/04/1984   Birthplace: Stafford
Teenage, Stafford born defender, Andrew was a member of the Stafford Rangers youth team and made his first-team debut against Rocester in January 2002. Highly-rated, much is expected from this youngster in the future.

BROOKES, CHRIS — Midfielder
Current Club: Rossendale United
Birthplace: Lancashire
Midfield player who spent the majority of his playing days in the North West Counties League with Daisy Hill and Ramsbottom United. Became renowned as one of the best in his position in the league before trying his luck at UniBond level with Rossendale United in October 2001.

BROOKES, DARREN — Defender
Current Club: Alfreton Town
D o B: 07/07/1978   Birthplace: Sheffield
Honours won: NCEL & Cup Winners
Vastly experienced centre back who returned to Alfreton Town in October 2001 for his second spell at North Street. Made 9 appearances for Doncaster Rovers in the Football League and has enjoyed spells with Grantham Town and Worksop Town (twice).

BROOKES, KEVIN — Forward
Current Club: Cradley Town
Birthplace: Birmingham
Previous clubs include: Stourbridge - March 2002, Sandwell Borough, Oldbury Utd, Stourbridge, Paget R, Stourbridge, Oldbury Utd.

BROOKES, MORGAN — Defender
Current Club: Bromsgrove Rovers
Birthplace: Birmingham
Previous clubs include: Blakenall - June 2001, Stourbridge, Blakenall, Dudley T, Brierley Hill T.

BROOKES, PAUL — Defender
Current Club: Borrowash Victoria
Birthplace: Heanor
Previous clubs include: Heanor T - July 1999.

BROOKES, TOM — Midfielder
Current Club: Hyde United
Birthplace: Yorkshire
Signed for UniBond Premier side Hyde United at the start of November 2001from rivals Frickley Athletic. A hard working midfield player formerly with Worksop Town.

BROOKS, BRYAN — Defender
Current Club: Thackley
Birthplace: Yorkshire
Previous clubs include: Harrogate T - August 2000, Guiseley.

BROOKS, LEYTON — Midfielder
Current Club: Uxbridge
Birthplace: Middlesex
Progressed from the Uxbridge reserve side, this talented player is equally at home in defence or midfield. Another former Brentford youth who had brief spells at Chertsey Town and Yeading before joining Uxbridge towards the end of the 1998/99 season.

BROOKS, NICKY — Midfielder
Current Club: Mangotsfield United
D o B: 23/06/1968   Birthplace: Bristol
Rejoined Mangotsfield United from Bath City in June 2000. First played for Mangotsfield when they won the Great Mills League Championship in 1990/91, then played for Clevedon Town and Bath City, who awarded him a testimonial match against Southampton in August 2000. He also had short spells at Newport County and Brislington. Experienced and influential member of the team, not scared to put his foot in, his experience has proved invaluable.

BROOKS, SCOTT — Defender
Current Club: Broxbourne Borough V&E
D o B: 07/05/1981   Birthplace: St Albans
Previous clubs include: Potters Bar T - July 2001.

BROOM, JASON — Midfielder
Current Club: Grays Athletic

D o B: 15/10/1969   Birthplace: Essex

Now an experienced midfielder who started his career with Eton Manor before joining the Dagenham & Redbridge for a four-figure fee from Billericay Town in 1991. Featured in the Isthmian League championship-winning team that year and gained FA representative honours in 1993 and 1995. A member of the 1997 FA Umbro Trophy final team, his career was dogged by injuries and he missed the majority of the 1997/98 season following an operation on a recurring shoulder problem. Celebrated his testimonial season with winning another Ryman League title and helped the Daggers to finish runners-up in the Conference in 2001/02 before switching to Grays Athletic in May 2002.

BROOME, DANNY — Defender
Current Club: Curzon Ashton

Birthplace: Manchester

Previous clubs include: Altrincham - November 2000.

BROOME, SIMON — Goalkeeper
Current Club: Bridgnorth Town

Birthplace: Bridgnorth

Previous clubs include: Bridgnorth Sports & Social - June 2001.

BROOMHALL, JASON — Midfielder
Current Club: Pagham

Birthplace: Sussex

Midfielder: scored once for Littlehampton during 1999/2000 and was also selected for the Sussex U-18 squad that season: began 2001/02 playing for East Preston reserves until signing for Pagham in December.

BROOMHEAD, ADAM — Midfielder
Current Club: Dorking

Birthplace: Surrey

Previous clubs include: Ashford Town (Middx) - August 2001.

BROOMHEAD, DANNY — Midfielder
Current Club: Oxford City

Birthplace: Sheffield

Previous clubs include: Denaby Utd - August 2001, Sheffield, Worksop T, Hallam, Staveley MW.

BROSTER, LEE — Goalkeeper
Current Club: Arnold Town

Birthplace: Nottingham

Previous clubs include: Gedling T - August 2001, Dunkirk, Nuthall, Dunkirk.

BROTHERS, MICHAEL — Midfielder
Current Club: Harwich & Parkeston

Birthplace: Essex

Formerly with Colchester United youth, this youngster is still only sixteen years old and is a tremendous prospect for the future at Harwich. Fast and hard working, he can only get better,.

BROTHERTON, BRADLEY — Defender
Current Club: Enfield Town (Essex)

Birthplace: Essex

Joined the club in the summer of 2001, having finished the previous season with St.Albans City after a spell at Hertford Town. Has also played for Harlow Town, Leyton Pennant and Romford. Started career with Enfield FC YTS scheme, going on to represent

the Es at all levels. Voted Enfield Supporters Club Reserve team player of the year 1995/6.

BROUGHTON, LEE — Midfielder
Current Club: Bedford Town

Birthplace: Milton Keynes

Signed for Bedford Town in May 2002, Lee is a hard-working midfielder who is full of running and is a good ball winner and creator. Spent the latter part of the 2000/01 season at Harrow Borough and rejoined Arlesey Town for the following campaign. Former clubs include Buckingham Athletic, Buckingham Town, Newport Pagnell and Milton Keynes City. During the day he works as a Data, Voice and Electrical Engineer.

BROWN, ANDY — Defender
Current Club: Salford City

Birthplace: Manchester

Honours won: English Universities Rep.

Previous clubs include: Trafford - July 2000, Radcliffe B, Leigh RMI, Radcliffe B, Salford C, Irlam T.

BROWN, ASHLEY — Defender
Current Club: Coalville Town

D o B: 15/08/1978   Birthplace: Leicestershire

Honours won: Leicestershire Senior League Winners

Previous clubs include: Thringstone - September 2001, Gresley R, Shepshed Dynamo, Halesowen T, Gresley R, Lutterworth T.

BROWN, BEN — Defender
Current Club: Lincoln United

Birthplace: Lincoln

Lincoln United's most consistent player during the turmoil of the 2000/01 season. It was this consistency which earned Ben the 2000/01 Supporters' Player of the Season award.

BROWN, CARL — Midfielder
Current Club: Leyton Pennant

Birthplace: Essex

Previous clubs include: Hendon - July 2001, Bishops Stortford, Dagenham & Redbridge.

BROWN, CHRIS — Defender
Current Club: Southwick

Birthplace: Sussex

Battle-hardened defender: previous experience with Burgess Hill, Wick and Ringmer: played for Whitehawk during 2000/01 (scored once): signed for Southwick at the start of the current season.

BROWN, CHRIS — Forward
Current Club: Bilston Town

Birthplace: Birmingham

Previous clubs include: Atherstone Utd - February 2002, Moor Green.

BROWN, CLIVE — Defender
Current Club: Hyde United

D o B: 05/03/1981   Birthplace: Manchester

Previous clubs include: Bangor C - July 2001, Curzon Ashton, Manchester C.

BROWN, DANNY — Forward
Current Club: Great Yarmouth Town

D o B: 05/03/1981   Birthplace: Norfolk

Signed for Yarmouth recently from Anglian Combination side St Andrews. Very forceful and committed striker.

B

BROWN, DANNY · Forward
Current Club: Hailsham Town
Birthplace: Sussex
Highly regarded teenage striker, who has apparently attracted interest from QPR: scored on his second senior appearance against Redhill in October 2001.

BROWN, DARREN · Defender
Current Club: Kendal Town
Birthplace: Preston
Previous clubs include: Bamber Bridge - July 2000, Great Harwood T, Preston NE.

BROWN, DARREN · Goalkeeper
Current Club: Mossley
Birthplace: Oldham
Previous clubs include: Oldham Ath - January 2002.

BROWN, DAVE · Defender
Current Club: Salford City
Birthplace: Manchester
Previous clubs include: Mossley - July 1999, Salford C, Mossley, Bacup Borough.

BROWN, DAVID · Forward
Current Club: Telford United
D o B: 02/10/1978 · Birthplace: Bolton
Former Manchester United striking product who signed for Conference side Telford United in August 2002 from rivals Chester City. Played League football for Hull City and Torquay United after being released from Old Trafford.

BROWN, DAVID · Midfielder
Current Club: Burnham
Birthplace: Wales
Previous clubs include: Castel Alan - August 2001.

BROWN, DERECK · Midfielder
Current Club: Yeading
D o B: 08/08/1963 · Birthplace: London
Honours won: England Semi-Pro Int.
Dereck joined Ryman Division One North club Yeading as player-coach in July 2001 after a three-year spell with Chesham United. Had signed for Chesham from Welling Utd in the summer of 1999, and has also played for Walton, Woking, Wembley and Hendon. A highly-rated midfield player who won 2 caps for the England semi-professional side in 1994 and is a former Non-League player of the year.

BROWN, DEREK · Defender
Current Club: St.Albans City
D o B: 08/01/1975 · Birthplace: Newport Pagnell
Solid centre-back who had three successful seasons at Baldock Town prior to a summer move to St.Albans City. Switched to Bedford Town in January 2002, but then returned to St Albans at the end of the season on a two-year contract.

BROWN, GARRY · Midfielder
Current Club: Hanwell Town
D o B: 13/02/1975 · Birthplace: Perivale
Previous clubs include: North Greenford Utd - July 1999.

BROWN, GAVIN · Defender
Current Club: Gorleston
Birthplace: Norfolk
Previous clubs include: Lowestoft T - July 1998, Great Yarmouth T, Gorleston.

BROWN, GRANT · Defender
Current Club: Telford United
D o B: 19/11/1969 · Birthplace: Sunderland
An experienced defender who made over 400 League appearances before joining Conference club Telford United in July 2002. Sunderland-born, Grant began his career with Leicester City but made the majority of his League appearances after joining Lincoln City in August 1989 for £60,000. Was an almost ever-present for the Imps before being released at the end of the 2001/02 season.

BROWN, GREG · Defender
Current Club: Morecambe
Birthplace: Wythenshawe
A defender previously borrowed on loan twice from Macclesfield Town, his home-town club. Signed permanently in January 2000.

BROWN, IAN · Forward
Current Club: Witham Town
D o B: 11/09/1965 · Birthplace: Ipswich
Previous clubs include: Ipswich Wanderers - December 2000, Braintree T, Felixstowe T, Cambridge C, Sudbury T, Northampton T, Bristol C, Chelmsford C, Harwich & Parkeston, Stowmarket T, Sudbury T, Felixstowe T, Colchester Utd, Birmingham C.

BROWN, IAN · Forward
Current Club: Littlehampton Town
Birthplace: Sussex
Had an eventual game during Littlehamptons 4-3 RUR Cup defeat at the hands of Second Division Broadbridge Heath in October 2001: came off the bench and gave away the ball that led to the third Bears goal, then missed a sitter from one yard before heading home a late consolation for the Golds.

BROWN, IAN · Midfielder
Current Club: Stafford Town
Birthplace: Stafford
Previous clubs include: Pelsall Villa - July 2000, Rocester, Pelsall Villa, Stafford R, Worcester C, Halesowen T, Burton Alb., Stafford R, Telford Utd, Stafford R.

BROWN, JAMES · Midfielder
Current Club: VCD Athletic
D o B: 22/11/1982 · Birthplace: Dartford
Previous clubs include: Phoenix Sports - July 2000.

BROWN, JAMIE · Midfielder
Current Club: Dorchester Town
Birthplace: Bournemouth
Previous clubs include: B.A.T. Sports - July 2001.

BROWN, JASON · Defender
Current Club: Rhayader Town
D o B: 12/08/1976 · Birthplace: Wales
Previous clubs include: Bridgend T - September 2001.

BROWN, JIMMY — Midfielder
Current Club: Sidlesham

Birthplace: Sussex
Left sided midfielder: former member of Richard Towers Chichester City youth side (which moved wholesale to Sidlesham in 1999): made several appearances for Chis first team in 1997/98 and 1998/99: also captain of the University College Chichester team, from whom Sidlesham draw upon several players: struck down by illness midway through 2001/02.

BROWN, JONATHAN — Defender
Current Club: Ossett Town

D o B: 08/09/1966   Birthplace: Barnsley
Experienced defender or midfielder who made almost 200 League appearances with Exeter and Halifax after being signed by the Grecians from Northern Counties East League side Denaby United in August 1990. Joined Nuneaton Borough in June 1999 and then signed for Stocksbridge Park Steels in the summer of 2000. Switched to UniBond First Division rivals Ossett Town in July 2002.

BROWN, JONATHAN — Defender
Current Club: Consett

Birthplace: Consett
Signed for club in 1992.

BROWN, KENNY — Defender
Current Club: Barry Town

D o B: 11/07/1967   Birthplace: Barking
Previous clubs include: Portadown - July 2000, Kingstonian, Gillingham, Millwall, Birmingham C, West Ham Utd, Plymouth Argyle, Norwich C.

BROWN, KEVAN — Defender
Current Club: Woking

D o B: 25/06/1968   Birthplace: Andover
Honours won: England Semi-Pro Int.
Previous clubs include: Yeovil T - March 2000, Woking, Aldershot, Brighton, Southampton.

BROWN, KEVIN — Defender
Current Club: Bracknell Town

Honours won: Combined Services Rep.
Previous clubs include: Beaconsfield SYCOB - July 2000, Windsor & Eton, Maidenhead Utd, Windsor & Eton, Wycombe Wanderers, Weymouth.

BROWN, LEE — Defender
Current Club: Great Yarmouth Town

D o B: 06/08/1983   Birthplace: Norwich
Defender or midfielder who signed for Yarmouth from Norwich City Youth, where he played for four years. Now playing in his second full season. Has 15 County Youth caps to his name.

BROWN, LEE — Defender
Current Club: Halesowen Harriers

Birthplace: Worcestershire
Previous clubs include: Causeway Utd - July 1998, Halesowen T.

BROWN, MALCOLM — Forward
Current Club: Glapwell

Birthplace: Mansfield
Previous clubs include: Shirebrook T - July 2001.

BROWN, MARTIN — Defender
Current Club: Oxford City

D o B: 10/11/1975   Birthplace: Reading
Defender who re-joined Oxford City from neighbouring Ryman Division One North side Thame United in July 2002. Was Thames club captain and inspirational figure at the heart of the defence, who led the club to promotion and FA Vase semi-finals in 1998. Has attracted the attention of several League clubs in the past. Signed for Thame from Oxford City in July 1998 and previously with Abingdon Town.

BROWN, MICKEY — Midfielder
Current Club: Chester City

D o B: 08/02/1968   Birthplace: Birmingham
Signed for Boston United from Shrewsbury Town at the start of the 2001/2 season after impressing in pre-season trials. An attacking midfielder with the speed and ability to beat defenders. He joined Shrewsbury Town as an apprentice in 1985 and broke into the first team a year later, he had spells with Bolton Wanderers, Preston North End and Rochdale, but in own case he returned to Shrewsbury to continue his footballing career. Overall he made 418 League appearances, scoring 36 goals. Transferred to Chester in May 2002 after helping Boston to lift the Conference championship.

BROWN, NEIL — Midfielder
Current Club: Herne Bay

Birthplace: Kent
Previous clubs include: Ramsgate - July 2000, Herne Bay, Ashford T, Ramsgate, Herne Bay.

BROWN, NIGEL — Defender
Current Club: Sutton Coldfield Town

Birthplace: Worcestershire
Previous clubs include: Redditch Ut - December 2001, Solihull B, Moor Green, Dudley T, Oldbury Utd, Halesowen T, Tamworth, Moor Green.

BROWN, PAUL — Defender
Current Club: Kendal Town

Birthplace: Preston
Previous clubs include: Fleetwood Freeport - August 2001, Bamber Bridge.

BROWN, PAUL — Defender
Current Club: Glasshoughton Welfare

Birthplace: Yorkshire
Previous clubs include: Pontefract Collieries - February 1997, Glasshoughton Welfare, Frickley Ath.

BROWN, PAUL — Midfielder
Current Club: Seaham Red Star

Birthplace: Newcastle
Previous clubs include: Easington Colliery - December 2001, Billingham Synthonia, Whitley Bay, Jarrow Roofing.

BROWN, PAUL — Midfielder
Current Club: Dunston Federation Brewery

Birthplace: Newcastle
Previous clubs include: South Shields - July 1999, Whitley Bay, Jarrow Roofing, South Shields.

B

BROWN, PHIL — Defender

Current Club: Frickley Athletic

Birthplace: Yorkshire

Previous clubs include: Brodsworth Welfare - October 2001, Frickley Ath., Brodsworth Welfare, Gainsborough Trinity, Brodsworth Welfare.

BROWN, PHIL — Forward

Current Club: Lancaster City

Birthplace: Lancashire

Signed for Lancaster City from Kendal Town lin December 2000, where he had been assistant-manager for a spell, Phil had a busy few months as cover for both midfielders and strikers as his first seasons multiple postponements led to fixture backlogs. Formerly with Bamber Bridge, Great Harwood and Leigh RMI.

BROWN, PHIL — Midfielder

Current Club: Matlock Town

D o B: 16/01/1966   Birthplace: Sheffield

Honours won: Conference Winners

vastly experienced attacking midfielder who joined UniBond First Division side Matlock Town in August 2002 from Premier side Gainsborough Trinity, linking up again with manager Ernie Moss, whom he had worked for previously at both Trinity and Kettering Town. After starting his career with Chesterfield, he then helped Lincoln City to win their place back in the League as Conference champions before enjoying a long spell with Kettering. Had stints at Boston United and Gainsborough before returning to the Poppies again. Re-joined Trinity in July 2001 and had a spell as caretaker boss in 2001/02.

BROWN, RICHARD — Midfielder

Current Club: Pagham

Birthplace: Sussex

Midfielder: originally featured for Oving reserves (came through the youth ranks in 1999/2000): squad member at Wick until joining Pagham during December 2001.

BROWN, RICKY — Midfielder

Current Club: Edgware Town

D o B: 12/02/1978   Birthplace: London

Previous clubs include: Wembley - August 2001, Yeading, Willesden Constantine, Hayes, Watford.

BROWN, RUSSELL — Defender

Current Club: Willenhall Town

Birthplace: Birmingham

Honours won: British Students Rep.

Rejoined Willenhall in summer 2000, after a couple of seasons at Rushall Olympic, former WBA junior. Has played representative football for English and British Students team helping England complete a hat-trick of Home Tournament wins. Always gives 110% and is a firm favourite with the crowd.

BROWN, SIMON — Defender

Current Club: Hucknall Town

Birthplace: Nottingham

Former captain of the British Universities side, Simon is a no-nonsense central defender who always gives 110%. Joined UniBond Premier side Hucknall Town in August 1995 after being released by Notts County.

BROWN, STEVE — Forward

Current Club: Purfleet

D o B: 06/12/1973   Birthplace: Rochford

Previous clubs include: Kingstonian - November 2001, Dover Ath., Macclesfield T, Lincoln C, Gillingham, Colchester Utd, Scunthorpe Utd, Southend Utd.

BROWN, STEVE — Forward

Current Club: Chippenham Town

Birthplace: Bristol

Signed for Chippenham Town in July 1998 from Calne Town, Steve is a very direct left winger who is superb at taking on defenders. Originally with Larkhall Athletic and Paulton Rovers, he played on the left wing at Wembley in the FA Vase final.

BROWN, STEVE — Midfielder

Current Club: Maidenhead United

31 year old now in his fifth season at York Road since moving from Feltham in August 1996. Influential midfielder with Middlesex County Honours. Missed much of last season through unavailability but has made a welcome return to the side with some strong performances. A knee injury in January ruled him out for the rest of the season.

BROWN, STUART — Forward

Current Club: Salisbury City

Birthplace: South Africa

South African-born striker who signed for Dr Martens Eastern side Salisbury City in August 2002. Has played for Amazulu and Jomo-Cosmos in his native country.

BROWN, TIM — Defender

Current Club: Chichester City United

Birthplace: Sussex

Midfielder: had spells with both Chichester City and Portfield prior to their merger in 2000: previously played for Fareham and Petersfield: can be temperamental (received two red cards during 2000/01): sidelined with injury during the opening month of the current campaign.

BROWN, TIM — Midfielder

Current Club: Burgess Hill Town

Birthplace: Sussex

Tall, left-footed midfielder: has previously played soccer in Australia but more recently featured in the lower divisions of the County League: transferred from Forest to Wealden during November 1999 before joining Burgess Hill for the start of 2001/02.

BROWN, TONY — Defender

Current Club: Arnold Town

Birthplace: Nottingham

Previous clubs include: Eastwood T - November 2000, Hucknall T, Ilkeston T.

BROWN, WAYNE — Defender

Current Club: Shifnal Town

Birthplace: Shropshire

Previous clubs include: Warley Rangers - July 2001.

BROWN, WAYNE — Defender

Current Club: Fisher Athletic (London)

D o B: 19/01/1970   Birthplace: Waterloo

Honours won: FA XI

Experienced central defender who joined Dr Martens Eastern side Fisher Athletic from Premier Division Welling United in August

2002. Was in his second spell with the Wings, with whom he began as a youngster, making numerous Conference appearances. Moves to Kingstonian, Enfield and Boreham Wood followed before he returned to Park View Road in the summer of 2001. Has represented the FA XI.

BROWN, WAYNE — *Goalkeeper*
Current Club: Chester City
D o B: 14/01/1977   *Birthplace: Southampton*
Honours won: England Semi-Pro Int.
Signed for Chester City at the start of the 1996-97 season from Non-League Weston-super-Mare. Has now established himself as the first choice keeper.

BROWNE, ALEX — *Defender*
Current Club: Weymouth
D o B: 05/04/1973   *Birthplace: Weymouth*
Honours won: England Youth Int.
Alex joined the club as a youth and was an England Youth Player and he has now been here 10 years. Alex is a strong defender who likes to attack He will be looking for a long run back in the side after having spent a year on the sidelines due to a ruptured cruciate ligament.

BROWNE, BEVAN — *Defender*
Current Club: Hinckley United
D o B: 29/03/1980   *Birthplace: Wellingborough*
Defender Bevan joined Hinckley United in the close season f 2001. He spent the previous season with Cambridge City, and was formerly with Chesham United, Leicester City and Nottingham Forest.

BROWNE, COREY — *Midfielder*
Current Club: Boreham Wood
D o B: 02/07/1970   *Birthplace: Edmonton*
Honours won: England Semi-Pro Int.
Corey is a vastly experienced midfield player who can also play as a forward. He joined Boreham Wood from Harlow Town and made his debut against Grays Athletic on New Year's Day 2002. Corey, born in Edmonton, is a former England semi-professional International who began his career at Kingsbury Town before moving on to play for Fulham, Haringey Borough, Exeter City, Wealdstone, Dover Athletic, Stevenage Borough, Slough Town, Aylesbury United, St. Albans City, Harrow Borough and Chesham United.

BROWNE, SIMON — *Defender*
Current Club: Weymouth
D o B: 02/04/1971   *Birthplace: Weymouth*
Weymouth-born Simon is the elder brother of Alex. Returned to the club in 1998 after 5 seasons with Salisbury City. Last season Simon fulfilled a lot of roles including spending a period of time in midfield. Will be looking to be consistently in the starting eleven.

BROWNE, STAFFORD — *Forward*
Current Club: Grays Athletic
D o B: 04/01/1972   *Birthplace: Hastings*
Prolific goalscorer who joined Grays Athletic in June 2002 from Ryman Premier rivals Aldershot Town, where he had been top scorer in 2001/02. A Hastings-born striker, his early playing days were spent in Sussex with Ringmer, Lewes, Horsham, Hastings Town and Brighton. He then had spells with Welling United, Billericay Town and Dagenham & Redbridge before joining the Shots in October 2000.

BROWNE, TONY — *Defender*
Current Club: Dover Athletic
D o B: 12/02/1977   *Birthplace: Sheppey*
Former West Ham apprentice who has had spells with Gravesend and Brighton. Joined Folkestone from Dover at the start of the 2001/2002 season but then returned to The Crabble in December 2001.

BROWNING, ROBERT — *Forward*
Current Club: Dartford
Birthplace: Kent
Previous clubs include: Tonbridge Angels - March 2002, Erith & Belvedere, Welling Utd, Fulham (Trainee).

BROWNRIGG, ANDY — *Defender*
Current Club: Gainsborough Trinity
D o B: 02/08/1976   *Birthplace: Sheffield*
Experienced and well-travelled defender who joined UniBond Premier side Gainsborough Trinity in June 2002 from Dr Martens Premier outfit Hednesford Town. Played League football with Hereford and Rotherham and also had a spell with Norwich before going Non-League with Stalybridge Celtic, Kidderminster Harriers, Yeovil Town and Northwich. Also played in Scotland for Morton.

BROWNRIGG, JOHN — *Defender*
Current Club: Skelmersdale United
Birthplace: Liverpool
Skelmersdales longest-serving player, having joined from neighbours St Helens Town in November 1999. A defender who has powerful shot, especially from free-kicks, and always enjoys the goals he scores.

BRUCE, MARCELLE — *Defender*
Current Club: Hemel Hempstead Town
D o B: 15/03/1971   *Birthplace: Detroit, USA*
Previous clubs include: Baldock T - July 1998, Colchester Utd, Tottenham Hotspur.

BRUCE, PAUL — *Midfielder*
Current Club: Dagenham & Redbridge
D o B: 18/02/1978   *Birthplace: London*
Midfielder who joined Conference club Dagenham & Redbridge in August 2002 from Queens Park Rangers. Came through the ranks at Loftus Road to make around 40 appearances for the Londoners. Also had a spell on-loan at Cambridge United during the 1998/99 season.

BRUMPTON, DAVID — *Midfielder*
Current Club: Shildon
Birthplace: Co.Durham
Previous clubs include: Billingham T - January 1999, Middlesbrough.

BRUMWELL, PHIL — *Defender*
Current Club: Blyth Spartans
D o B: 08/08/1975   *Birthplace: Darlington*
An experienced defender who signed for UniBond Premier side Blyth Spartans from Darlington in the summer of 2002. Started his career with Sunderland and then had his first spell with the Quakers, making over 150 League appearances. Left for Hull in August 2000 but then returned to Darlington less than four months later.

B

BRUNSKILL, DANNY — Forward
Current Club: Spennymoor United
Birthplace: Co.Durham
Previous clubs include: Bishop Auckland - March 2002, North Shields Ath, Marske Utd.

BRUNSKILL, IAIN — Defender
Current Club: St.Helens Town
D o B: 05/11/1976 — Birthplace: Ormskirk
Honours won: England Youth Int.
Experienced former England Youth international defender who joined North West Counties side St Helens Town from UniBond Premier outfit Droyslden in August 2002. Originally with Liverpool, he then played for Bury before spells in Non-League football with Leek Town, Hednesford Townand Runcorn, signing for the Bloods in October 2000.

BRUNTON, DANNY — Defender
Current Club: Bridlington Town
D o B: 13/12/1980 — Birthplace: Bridlington
Former Scarborough youth team player who graduated at the end of season 1999 with an initial one-year professional contract. Has since made a number of appearances in the first team after making his first start against Southport in September 2000. Season 2000/01 saw Danny establish himself as Boros first choice left back who, for a small built player, is very strong, determined and not easily shrugged off the ball. He is excellent coming forward and scored his first goal for Boro in the LDV Vans Trophy against Stoke. Switched to Northern Counties East League side Bridlington Town in August 2002.

BRUSH, DAVID — Forward
Current Club: Boldmere St.Michaels
Birthplace: Warwickshire
Previous clubs include: Coventry C (Trainee) - May 2002.

BRYAN, DEREK — Forward
Current Club: Welling United
D o B: 11/11/1974 — Birthplace: London
Previous clubs include: Gravesend & Northfleet - March 2002, Brentford, Hampton.

BRYAN, OWEN — Forward
Current Club: Bath City
Previous clubs include: Team Bath - August 2000.

BRYAN, SIMON — Goalkeeper
Current Club: Bilston Town
Birthplace: Shropshire
Previous clubs include: Bridgnorth T - November 2001, Telford Utd, Bridgnorth T, Telford Utd.

BRYANT, DANNY — Goalkeeper
Current Club: Eastwood Town
D o B: 16/08/1975 — Birthplace: Nottingham
Previous clubs include: Pelican - July 1998, Scarborough, Nottingham Forest.

BRYANT, JAMIE — Goalkeeper
Current Club: Ringmer
Birthplace: Sussex
Goalkeeper and one-time apprentice with Aldershot. Transferred from Worthing to East Preston at the end of 1998 and was playing for the reserves when Saltdean recruited him in October 1999 (occasionally acted as penalty taker). Signed for Ringmer at the start of the current season, but forced out of action after suffering a horrific leg injury in a match against Arundel during August.

BRYANT, MARK — Goalkeeper
Current Club: Weston-Super-Mare
Birthplace: Bristol
Signed in December 2001 from Aberystwyth Town. Previously with Chippenham Town and Brislington, and has also played in the USA.

BRYSON, PAUL — Midfielder
Current Club: Chester-Le Street
Birthplace: Co.Durham
Previous clubs include: Jarrow Roofing - July 1997, Eppleton CW, Dunston Federation Brewery, Spennymoor Utd.

BRYSON, TOMMY — Defender
Current Club: Wealdstone
D o B: 01/05/1980 — Birthplace: London
Previously with Hayes where he made six appearances in the Conference, Tom signed for Wealdstone during the summer of 2001. After agreement between the two clubs, the defender was released to join Ryman League rivals Wembley before returning in March 2002.

BUBB, ALVIN — Forward
Current Club: Billericay Town
D o B: 11/10/1980 — Birthplace: Paddington
Diminutive forward who signed for Ryman Premier side Billericay Town in August 2002 after being released by Bristol Rovers. Began his career with Queens Park Rangers. Made one first-team appearances before being transferred to Rovers in June 2001. Played 13 times in their League side before being released at the end of the 2001/02 season.

BUBB, BYRON — Midfielder
Current Club: Hendon
D o B: 17/12/1981 — Birthplace: Harrow
Joined Hendon at the beginning of October 2001from Millwall. This highly-talented young midfielder had previously played a couple of trial matches for the clubs reserves when he was an under-14 player! He has since gone on to make 8 Nationwide League appearances for the Lions before being released.

BUCKLE, ANTHONY — Forward
Current Club: Rocester
Birthplace: Stoke
Previous clubs include: Kidsgrove Ath - February 2002, Newcastle T, Nantwich T, Congleton T, Kidsgrove Ath., Eastwood Hanley.

BUCKLE, PAUL — Midfielder
Current Club: Aldershot Town
D o B: 16/12/1970 — Birthplace: Hatfield
Paul began his career in 1989 with Brentford. He enjoyed six years with the Bees, helping the Londoners gain promotion to the First Division. The central midfielder was made surplus to requirements and, in a bid for regular football, decided to drop the league ladder to join Torquay United. Paul, a regular fixture in the Gulls first team - opted to move onto brighter pastures after the Plainmoor side were narrowly defeated in a playoff final against Preston. In an exchange for Russell Coughlin, Paul embarked on his first spell with City in 1995. He appeared in every one of City's games until he sustained ligament damage in his return game at Torquay. The injury would keep him out for a large portion of the season, and after failing to agree terms with financially troubled Exeter, Paul joined Colchester United via short

spells with Northampton Town and Wycombe Wanderers the following season. He spent three seasons with the Us, helping them to two Wembley finals. Bucks won promotion with the club and spent a season in the Second Division, before making a return to Exeter on the Bosman free transfer ruling. His 100% commitment and endless work-rate made Paul a favourite amongst the St. James Park faithful, who were naturally disappointed to see him move on to Ryman League Aldershot Town in July 2002.

BUCKLEY, NEIL — Defender
Current Club: Hall Road Rangers
D o B: 29/05/1968   Birthplace: Hull
Honours won: FA Vase Winners
Previous clubs include: Brigg T - July 2001, North Ferriby Utd, Brigg T, Guiseley, Hull C, Burnley.

BUDGE, KEVIN — Forward
Current Club: Heybridge Swifts
D o B: 09/04/1976   Birthplace: Leicester
Uncomplicated, skilful striker with an appetite for hard work. Joined Heybridge Swifts from Braintree Town in October 2001 and after performing well in the reserves initially, joined the first-team squad and immediately made his mark with some crucial goals - and plenty of them. Now a contracted player, popular with team-mates and crowd alike for his ability and attitude, and his unique character and dress sense! Won both the Managers Player of the Season and Supporters' Player of the Season for the 2001/02 campaign. Leicester-born he has previously turned out for Ibstock Welfare, Corby Town, Shepshed Dynamo and Barrow Town in his home county.

BUFFON, JAMIE — Forward
Current Club: Tilbury
Birthplace: Essex
Previous clubs include: Leyton Pennant - August 2001, Romford.

BUFFONG, JONATHAN — Midfielder
Current Club: Grays Athletic
D o B: 02/03/1977   Birthplace: London
Very commanding forward with great pace determination and insight, he has a terrific long throw as well, beginning to establish himself in the team.

BUGDALE, NEIL — Midfielder
Current Club: Norwich United
D o B: 26/08/1981   Birthplace: Norfolk
A tough, hard-working player for Norwich United with an eye for goal. Formerly with Wroxham, and Norfolk county youth honours.

BUGG, PHIL — Defender
Current Club: Wroxham
D o B: 08/08/1974   Birthplace: Norwich
Honours won: FA Vase Winners
Returned to the club last season from Watton United. Excellent player who likes to get forward and has a good shot.

BUGGIE, LEE — Forward
Current Club: Accrington Stanley
D o B: 11/02/1981   Birthplace: Bury
Previous clubs include: Bury - March 2002.

BUGLIONE, MARTIN — Forward
Current Club: Purfleet
D o B: 19/06/1968   Birthplace: Essex
Previous clubs include: Ashford T - October 2000, Welling Utd, Boreham Wood, Hampton & Richmond B, Hayes, Margate,

Sittingbourne, St.Johnstone, Margate, Welling Utd, Tonbridge, Dagenham, Walthamstow Ave., Boreham Wood, Enfield.

BULGIN, PAUL — Midfielder
Current Club: Thackley
Birthplace: Yorkshire
Previous clubs include: Guiseley - July 2001, Eccleshill Utd, Thackley, Ossett T, Thackley, Farsley Celtic.

BULL, GARY — Forward
Current Club: Grantham Town
D o B: 12/06/1966   Birthplace: West Bromwich
Signed for Grantham Town from Scunthorpe for the start of the 2000/01season and picked up the Supporters' Player of the Year Award in his first season. Has scored over 50 goals for the Gingerbreads during his two seasons with the team. Started his career in Non-League football with Paget Rangers before going on to make over 250 League appearances with Southampton, Cambridge United, Barnet, Nottingham Forest, Brighton, Birmingham, York and Scunthorpe.

BULL, LIAM — Goalkeeper
Current Club: Swindon Supermarine
Birthplace: Bristol
Honours won: England Youth Int.
Previous clubs include: Bath C - January 2002.

BULL, NIKKI — Goalkeeper
Current Club: Aldershot Town
D o B: 02/10/1981   Birthplace: Hastings
Nikki is a highly-promising young goalkeeper who joined Queens Park Rangers from Aston Villas youth system. When Rangers released Lee Harper and Ludo Miklosko Nikki stepped up to become number two to Chris Day at Loftus Road. This was perhaps too early in his career for that to happen, and his form suffered as a consequence. However, he had a spell on-loan at Conference club Hayes and some outstanding displays led to Aldershot Town snapping up the 21-year-old when he was released by Rangers in May 2002.

BULLEN, KEVIN — Midfielder
Current Club: Oswestry Town
D o B: 06/12/1981   Birthplace: Manchester
Previous clubs include: Altrincham - March 2002.

BULLETT, ADY — Defender
Current Club: Soham Town Rangers
Birthplace: Suffolk
Previous clubs include: Bury T - July 1997, Soham Town R, Diss T, Sudbury Wanderers, Soham Town R.

BULLIMORE, JAMES — Forward
Current Club: Stafford Town
Birthplace: Staffordshire
Previous clubs include: Stone Dominoes - July 2001.

BULLIMORE, LEE — Forward
Current Club: Willenhall Town
Birthplace: Wolverhampton
Re-signed for Willnehall in February 2002 from Bilston Town. Now in his third spell at Noose Lane and always a prolific scorer in a Willenhall shirt.

BULLIMORE, WAYNE — Midfielder

Current Club: Barrow

D o B: 12/09/1970 — Birthplace: Mansfield

Wayne is an experienced midfielder who began his career as a trainee with Manchester United but made no League appearances for the Reds before being released. He joined Barnsley and made 35 League appearances for the Oakwell outfit scoring once before he joined Stockport County. He did not feature in County's League side. He then joined Scunthorpe United and he enjoyed success with the Irons making 67 League appearances for them, scoring eleven times before joining Bradford City. His spell at Valley Parade lasted just two League games before he joined Doncaster Rovers where he played four League games on loan. His next permanent move saw him join Peterborough United where he made 21 League appearances, scoring just once before he headed north to join Scarborough. He played 35 League games for Boro, scoring once before being released and, he began the1999/00 season with Dr Martens Premier Division outfit Grantham Town. He joined Barrow in September 1999.

BULLOCK, DARREN — Midfielder

Current Club: Evesham United

D o B: 12/02/1969 — Birthplace: Worcester

Vastly experienced, tough-tackling midfielder who joined Dr Martens Western side Evesham United in August 2002 after a very brief spell with UniBond outfit Hucknall Town. Had only signed for Hucknall in June 2002 after a short period out of the game. Originally with Worcester City, Darren had a spell with Nuneaton Borough and was then snapped up by Huddersfield in 1993. Went on to make over 250 League appearances with Huddersfield, Swindon and Bury before rejoining Worcester in October 2001. Other commitments forced him to leave St Georges Lane shortly after the New Year, but he relished the opportunity to make a comeback.

BULLOCK, MATTHEW — Midfielder

Current Club: Leek Town

D o B: 01/11/1980 — Birthplace: Stoke

Honours won: England Youth Int.

Midfielder snapped up by Leek Town following his release by Stoke City in January 2002. Matt has Football League experience and has put together a string of impressive displays as he looks to get back into the professional game. A former England youth international.

BUNCE, MARTIN — Goalkeeper

Current Club: Spalding United

Birthplace: Lincolnshire

Previous clubs include: Boston Utd - July 2001.

BUNCE, NATHAN — Defender

Current Club: Farnborough Town

D o B: 02/05/1975 — Birthplace: Hillingdon

Honours won: Ryman League Premier Div.Winners

Nathan was signed during the close season of 2001 after spells as captain at both Stevenage Borough and Hayes. Began his career at Brentford and also turned out for Yeading before joining Hayes, whom he helped to promotion to the Conference. Now rated as one of the best defenders in the Conference.

BUNTING, TREVOR — Goalkeeper

Current Club: Windsor & Eton

D o B: 22/05/1968 — Birthplace: Chalfont St.Giles

Signed for Windsor & Eton in March 1997. Previously played over 400 games for Slough Town having joined them from Wycombe Wanderers. A highly-rated goalkeeper who just seems to get

better each season. The 1998/99 Players' Player Of The Year and 1999/00 Supporters' Player Of The Year.

BUNYARD, NICK — Defender

Current Club: Frome Town

Birthplace: Somerset

Previous clubs include: Warminster T - July 2001, Bath C, AFC Lymington, Westbury Utd.

BURBRIDGE, RIKKI — Forward

Current Club: Tilbury

Birthplace: Essex

Previous clubs include: East Thurrock Utd - July 2001.

BURBY, LEE — Midfielder

Current Club: Swindon Supermarine

Birthplace: Gloucester

Previous clubs include: Worcester C - February 2002, Weston-Super-Mare, Cinderford T, Cheltenham T.

BURDEN, ANTHONY — Defender

Current Club: Abingdon Town

Birthplace: Oxford

Honours won: England Schoolboy Int.

Previous clubs include: Thame Utd - October 1999, Cheltenham T, Northampton T (Trainee).

BURDEN, GARY — Defender

Current Club: Bemerton Heath Harlequins

Birthplace: Wiltshire

Previous clubs include: Andover - July 1994.

BURDEN, NEIL — Defender

Current Club: Paget Rangers

Birthplace: Birmingham

Joined Paget in July 2000. Previous clubs include Birmingham City, where he played for three years as a YT, Tamworth and Solihull Borough. After leaving Birmingham City he attended university in USA before returning to play football in England.

BURDICK, CRAIG — Midfielder

Current Club: Bridlington Town

Birthplace: Hull

Previous clubs include: Goole AFC - November 2001, Bridlington T, Goole T, Bridlington T, Hall Road R, Kelvin Hall.

BURGESS, ADAM — Defender

Current Club: Oswestry Town

Birthplace: Wales

Been with the club since its re-birth 8 seasons ago, and has played for Town in the Welsh National League and Cymru Alliance as well as the League of Wales.

BURGESS, KENNY — Forward

Current Club: Bangor City

D o B: 08/02/1975 — Birthplace: Liverpool

Pacey winger who signed for League of Wales side Bangor City in August 2001 from West Cheshire side Cammell Lairds. Equally at home on left and right wings where his pace and close control catch the eye.

BURGESS, PAUL — Goalkeeper

Current Club: Ashford Town (Middx)

Birthplace: London

Goalkeeper, signed for Ashford Town (Middx) from Ruislip Manor in the summer of 1990. Has been a model of consistency for the club and has completed well over 300 senior games for the club.

Ashfords first ever contract player with full County and League honours to his name. Missed much of last two seasons, following a severe injury, but now back to his best. Aged 32.

BURGESS, RICHARD   *Forward*

Current Club: Bromsgrove Rovers

D o B: 01/08/1974   *Birthplace: Stourport*
On his day and exciting forward to watch, Richard re-joined Dr Martens Western side Bromsgrove Rovers in July 2002 after a spell with Conference outfit Nuneaton Borough. Had signed for Boro after a return to the professional game at Port Vale. Started his career with Aston Villa and also played for Stoke before joining Rovers via a stint at Worcester City.

BURGESS, STUART   *Forward*

Current Club: Thackley

Birthplace: Yorkshire
Previous clubs include: Bradford C (Trainee) - July 1996.

BURKE, CHRIS   *Defender*

Current Club: Congleton Town

Birthplace: Hampshire
Age 26. He is a versatile player who is happy on the left wing or in defence. He lives in St Helens and signed from Winsford in November 01. Previous teams include Portsmouth as a schoolboy, Tetley Walker and Eastleigh (Jewson League) where he won a Carlsberg Cup medal in the final at Wembley.

BURKE, GARY   *Defender*

Current Club: Droylsden

Birthplace: Ashton-under-Lyne
A tall central defender, Gary signed for UniBond Premier side Droylsden in the summer of 2002 from Conference outfit Northwich Victoria. Had joined the Vics from Runcorn in July 2000 after winning rave reviews at Canal Street. Born in Ashton-under-Lyne, he began his career with Woodley Sports.

BURKE, MARK   *Defender*

Current Club: Hitchin Town

D o B: 30/03/1967
Previous clubs include: Luton T - July 1985, QPR (Trainee).

BURKE, NICKY   *Forward*

Current Club: Barry Town

Birthplace: Leeds
Previous clubs include: Port Talbot T - February 2002, Llanelli, Barry T, Swindon T, Nottingham Forest, Leeds Utd.

BURKE, PAUL   *Forward*

Current Club: Frickley Athletic

D o B: 17/07/1981   *Birthplace: Doncaster*
Talented young attacker who joined Sheffield United as a trainee. Spent three years as a professional at Bramall Lane but failed to make the senior side and moved to Northern Counties East League neighbours Sheffield FC at the start of the 2001/02 season after a short period out of the game and made an immediate impression. Was signed by UniBond Premier side Hucknall Town in January 2002 and again impressed. Switched to Harrogate Town in June 2002 but then made a rapid move to rivals Frickley Athletic on the eve of the 2002/03 season.

BURKE, TERRY   *Goalkeeper*

Current Club: Bedlington Terriers

Birthplace: Newcastle
An excellent goalkeeper signed from Whitby Town. Terry had a short spell at Whitby after being first choice at Blyth for a number of years. Well respected keeper who commands his box well and

is an excellent shot stopper. Experienced in the higher leagues so should be a useful addition to the squad.

BURLEY, MIKE   *Goalkeeper*

Current Club: Hall Road Rangers

Birthplace: Hull
Previous clubs include: Brigg T - September 1997.

BURMAN, JASON   *Defender*

Current Club: Ipswich Wanderers

Birthplace: Essex
Previous clubs include: Felixstowe T - November 1999, Stowmarket T, Woodbridge T, Diss T, Bury T, Lowestoft T, Brantham Ath., Wivenhoe T, Bury T, Wivenhoe T, Hatfield T, Sudbury T, Clacton T, Colchester Utd.

BURN, CHRIS   *Defender*

Current Club: Chester-Le Street

Birthplace: Co.Durham
Signed for low Law at the beginning of this season from Durham an ex-County Junior player. Transferred to Chester-le-Street in February 2002.

BURN, NEIL   *Forward*

Current Club: Shildon

Birthplace: Newcastle
Previous clubs include: Chester-le-Street - March 2002, Morpeth T, Crook T.

BURNDRED, JOHN   *Forward*

Current Club: Biddulph Victoria

Birthplace: Stoke
Previous clubs include: Redgate Clayton - July 2001, Newcastle T, Stafford R, Port Vale, Knypersley V, Witton Alb., Knypersley V, Port Vale (Junior).

BURNDRED, KEVIN   *Defender*

Current Club: Biddulph Victoria

Birthplace: Stoke
Previous clubs include: Abbey Hucton - July 2000.

BURNHAM, JASON   *Defender*

Current Club: Halesowen Town

D o B: 08/05/1973   *Birthplace: Mansfield*
Honours won: Dr Martens Western Div.Winners
Jason, who signed for Halesowen Town in March 2001, has been captain at The Grove since joining the club. He started his career at Northampton Town making a couple of appearances for the Cobblers. Left Sixfields for St Georges Lane, Worcester in 1996. Was player of the year at Worcester City in the 1997/98 season, but left for £3,000 in 1999 for Boston United. Failed to make an impact at York street and left to join Atherstone United. Had a brief stint with the Adders to join Cambridge City. Returned to the Midlands again with Rugby United and later Halesowen Town in 2001. Usually a left back Burnham can play in the centre of defence.

BURNHAM, MARK   *Forward*

Current Club: Eccleshill United

Birthplace: Bradford
Previous clubs include: Thackley - October 2001, Harrogate T, Eccleshill Utd, Fields.

BURNHAM, TONY — Forward
Current Club: Hassocks
Birthplace: Sussex
Mainly used as a substitute so far during 2001/02, and came off the bench to score his first goal (in extra time) during the 5-3 Sussex Senior Cup victory over Saltdean in September.

BURNLEY, HARRY — Midfielder
Current Club: Cirencester Town
Previous clubs include: Witney T - July 2001.

BURNS, ANDY — Defender
Current Club: Winsford United
Birthplace: Cheshire
Last seasons Players' Player of the year. Central defender who was playing senior football at the age of fifteen. Returned to Winsford from Leigh RMI for his second spell at The Barton Stadium.

BURNS, BEN — Forward
Current Club: Redhill
Birthplace: Surrey
Quick skilful 20-year-old striker who joined in November 2001 from near neighbours East Grinstead Town. Scored a hatrick in the game at Saltdean early in December.

BURNS, CHRIS — Midfielder
Current Club: Gloucester City
D o B: 09/11/1967   Birthplace: Manchester
Previous clubs include: Forest Green Rovers - July 2001, Gloucester C, Northampton T, Swansea C, Portsmouth, Cheltenham T, Sharpness, Brockworth.

BURNS, LEE — Midfielder
Current Club: East Thurrock United
Birthplace: Essex
From Youth team.

BURNS, PAUL — Midfielder
Current Club: Accrington Stanley
D o B: 01/10/1967   Birthplace: Liverpool
Signed for Accrington Stanley on a free transfer from Morecambe after his contract run out at the end of the 1999/2000 season. He played 46 games for Stanley in the early 90s, scoring 14 goals, though his favoured playing role has since changed from a flying winger to a steady midfielder, and has even played as a full back since joining Stanley. He started his career with Grimsby Town, and has since played for Burscough, Prescott Cables, Caernarfon and Morecambe.

BURNS, ROBERT — Defender
Current Club: Paget Rangers
Birthplace: Birmingham
Recently signed from Bromsgrove Rovers whom he joined from Boldmere St Michaels. Previously with Birmingham City, but has suffered from injury problems which have held back his early promise.

BURNS, STEVE — Midfielder
Current Club: Witton Albion
Birthplace: Manchester
Previous clubs include: Mossley - March 2002, Trafford, Glossop NE, Ashton Utd, Stockport Co.

BURROUGHS, ADE — Defender
Current Club: Whitstable Town
Birthplace: Kent
Previous clubs include: Ramsgate - November 1998, Dover Ath., Millwall (Junior), Faversham T.

BURROW, DAVID — Defender
Current Club: Kendal Town
Birthplace: Preston
Previous clubs include: Bamber Bridge - July 1995, Horwich RMI, Preston NE (Trainee).

BURROW, MARC — Defender
Current Club: Worcester City
Birthplace: Worcester
Honours won: Represented England at Schoolboy level.
Talented defender who re-joined Worcester City from Bromsgrove Rovers in December 2000, having originally begun his career at St. Georges Lane. Made his first-team debut in 1996 before leaving to pursue a degree course, during which time he played for Inter Cardiff in the League of Wales.

BURROWS, DAVID — Defender
Current Club: Aberystwyth Town
Birthplace: Wales
Previous clubs include: Haverfordwest County - October 2001, Carmarthen T, Haverfordwest Co., Inter Cardiff, Briton Ferry Ath.

BURROWS, PAUL — Forward
Current Club: Haverfordwest County
D o B: 02/10/1967   Birthplace: Wales
Previous clubs include: Carmarthen T - February 2000, Haverfordwest Co., Inter Cardiff, Briton Ferry Ath., Barry T, Haverfordwest Co., Swansea C.

BURRY, SCOTT — Midfielder
Current Club: Fairford Town
Birthplace: Wiltshire
From Youth team.

BURSNELL, SHAUN — Midfielder
Current Club: Great Harwood Town
Birthplace: Lancashire
Previous clubs include: Rossendale Utd - October 2000, Great Harwood T, Clitheroe, Bamber Bridge, Great Harwood T, Rossendale Utd, Great Harwood T, Clitheroe, Accrington Stanley.

BURT, MARK — Midfielder
Current Club: Worthing
Birthplace: Sussex
Midfielder and captain: originally came through the youth team and returned to Woodside Road in 1997 after spells at Crawley, Southwick and Shoreham: has now made 300+ appearances for Worthing.

BURT, TONY — Defender
Current Club: Hastings United
D o B: 21/08/1968   Birthplace: Hastings
Honours won: Dr Martens League Southern Div.Winners
Good old-fashioned central defender who had spells with St Leonards and Langney Sports (during their 1999/2000 County League championship year) before returning to Hastings for the start of 2000/01: has now made 400+ appearances for the Arrows.

BURTON, ANDREW　　　　　*Forward*
Current Club: Brandon United
Birthplace: Middlesbrough
Young striker who made an instant impact when joining the club towards the end of last season from Middlesbrough, scoring a number of excellent goals. He's a hard working player with tremendous ability and vision. Hopefully he will pick up where he left off last season.

BURTON, DAN　　　　　*Goalkeeper*
Current Club: Hendon
Birthplace: London
Dan joined Ryman Premier side Hendon in the summer of 2002 from Poole Borough. Talented young goalkeeper who has formerly been on the books at both West Ham United and Fulham.

BURTON, NICK　　　　　*Defender*
Current Club: Gravesend & Northfleet
D o B. 09/10/1975　　　　*Birthplace: Bury St.Edmunds*
Nick signed for Gravesend & Northfleet in October 2001 from Hampton & Richmond Borough where he was club captain. He is a versatile defender who can play anywhere at the back but is probably at his best in a central position. Nick has good vision, is tough-tackling and is particularly strong in the air. He began his footballing career at Torquay United before moving into Non-League football with Yeovil Town and Aldershot Town.

BURTON, PAUL　　　　　*Midfielder*
Current Club: Lincoln United
Previous clubs include: Frickley Ath - June 2001, Matlock T, Scarborough, Sheffield Wednesday (Trainee).

BURTON, SIMON　　　　　*Forward*
Current Club: Witton Albion
Birthplace: Preston
Previous clubs include: Bamber Bridge - November 2001, Atherton LR, Darwen.

BURTON, TOM　　　　　*Defender*
Current Club: Eastbourne United
Birthplace: Sussex
Young defender who scored his first goal for Eastbourne United when coming on as a substitute in the 4-1 defeat at the hands of Ringmer in October 2001.

BURTON, WARREN　　　　　*Forward*
Current Club: Dulwich Hamlet
Birthplace: Surrey
Striker who returned to Dulwich Hamlet in March 2002 after a short spell with Corinthian Casuals. A regular goalscorer at Ryman League level, Warren has also seen service with Carshalton Athletic, Molesey, Banstead Athletic, Tooting & Mitcham United, Leatherhead and Sutton United.

BURVILL, GELNN　　　　　*Midfielder*
Current Club: Whitehawk
D o B: 26/10/1962　　　　*Birthplace: Canning Town*
Former professional, who was once a member of West Hams FA Youth Cup winning side Spent three years at the Hammers, but never played for the first team before going on to appear for Aldershot, Reading and Fulham. More recently featured in the County League for Newhaven, Peacehaven and Saltdean and took over as manager of the Tigers for the start of 1999/2000 and finished that season by winning the John OHara Cup. Resigned in January 2001 following a poor run of results, and subsequently rejoined Newhaven (also appeared for Lewes in the Sussex Senior Cup semi-final). Recruited by Whitehawk during the summer as player-coach.

BUSBY, CHRIS　　　　　*Forward*
Current Club: Boldmere St.Michaels
Birthplace: Birmingham
Previous clubs include: Atherstone Utd - March 2002, Boldmere St Michaels, Halesowen Harriers.

BUSH, CHRIS　　　　　*Midfielder*
Current Club: Tiptree United
Birthplace: Essex
Previous clubs include: AFC Sudbury - July 2001, Braintree T.

BUSH, GARY　　　　　*Defender*
Current Club: Swaffham Town
Birthplace: Norfolk
Promising young left back who is learning fast and will push hard for a starting spot in Swaffhams first-team.

BUSHELL, STEVE　　　　　*Midfielder*
Current Club: Halifax Town
D o B: 28/12/1972　　　　*Birthplace: Manchester*
Impressive and experienced midfielder or defender who was re-signed by Conference club Halifax Town in August 2002 after originally being released by the administrators at the end of the 2001/02 season. Began his career with York and then joined Blackpool in June 1998. Signed for Stalybridge Celtic at the start of the 2001/02 season before moving to the Shay in November 2001. Totalled almost 300 League appearances.

BUSS, WARREN　　　　　*Defender*
Current Club: Whitehawk
Birthplace: Sussex
Tough defender who suffered with a spine injury during 1999/2000. Scored twice for Whitehawk in the early part of the following season before transferring to Saltdean. Also represented the County that year and rejoined the Hawks at the start of the current campaign.

BUSSELL, HARVEY　　　　　*Defender*
Current Club: Rocester
Birthplace: Norwich
Previous clubs include: Leek T - October 2001, Rocester, Watton Utd.

BUTCHER, LEE　　　　　*Midfielder*
Current Club: Three Bridges
Birthplace: Sussex
Captain and penalty-taker: joined Horsham YMCA at the start of 1998/99 from Oakwood, having previously been at Ifield: described as a typical box to box performer and was voted YM managers player of the year in 1999/2000 (12 strikes to his name): represented Sussex during 2000/01, as well as scoring 13 times for his club: signed for Three Bridges at the start of the current campaign.

BUTCHER, MICHAEL　　　　　*Forward*
Current Club: Stowmarket Town
Birthplace: Suffolk
From Youth team.

BUTCHER, RICHARD — *Midfielder*

Current Club: Kettering Town

D o B: 22/01/1981   *Birthplace: Peterborough*
Honours won: Dr Martens League Premier Div.Winners
Highly-rated young midfield player who joined Kettering Town in October 2001 from neighbours Rushden & Diamonds. Immediately gained a first-team spot at Rockingham Road and enjoyed such a good campaign that he ended up as the clubs player of the year.

BUTLER, BRIAN — *Midfielder*

Current Club: Lancaster City

D o B: 04/07/1966   *Birthplace: Salford*
Honours won: England Semi-Pro Int.
A hugely influential player able to control a game from midfield on his day, Brian was formerly with Southport, and also played in the League with Halifax, Blackpool and Stockport. Then had spells in the Conference with Northwich Victoria and Leigh RMi before joining Lancaster City in July 2000. Played for the England semi-professional international side.

BUTLER, CRAIG — *Goalkeeper*

Current Club: Parkgate

Birthplace: Sheffield
Previous clubs include: Staveley Miners Welfare - July 1999, Club Roma (Canada), Parkgate, Belper T.

BUTLER, DANNY — *Defender*

Current Club: Northwood

Birthplace: Middlesex
Previous clubs include: Hayes - July 1999.

BUTLER, DAVE — *Defender*

Current Club: Weston-Super-Mare

Birthplace: Bristol
Made his debut for Weston-Super-Mare diring the 2000/01 season against Solihull Borough, as a replacement and the defender has never looked back after orginally being signed for the reserve side. He has also played for Welton Rovers, Keynsham Town and Larkhall Athletic.

BUTLER, DAVID — *Midfielder*

Current Club: Leighton Town

D o B: 25/03/1974   *Birthplace: Herts*
Experienced Non-League midfielder who followed manager Paul Burgess to Ryman Division Two side Leighton Town from Tring Town in July 2002. Had re-joined Tring at the start of the 2001/02 season from Hemel Hempstead and has previously seen services with Northwood and Berkhamsted Town.

BUTLER, DAVID — *Midfielder*

Current Club: Rushall Olympic

D o B: 19/07/1972   *Birthplace: Wolverhampton*
Previous clubs include: Willenhall T - December 2000, Bilston T, Atherstone Utd, Willenhall T,Tamworth, Stourport Swifts, Oldswinford, Chasetown, Wolverhampton Wanderers.

BUTLER, IAN — *Defender*

Current Club: Ossett Town

Birthplace: Yorkshire
Previous clubs include: Farsley Celtic - June 2002, Barnsley.

BUTLER, LEE — *Goalkeeper*

Current Club: Halifax Town

D o B: 30/05/1966   *Birthplace: Sheffield*
A vastly experienced goalkeeper, Lee began his League career back in 1986 with Lincoln City after starting out at Harworth CI and played ten games for Aston Villa in the old First Division, plus numerous games for Barnsley, Wigan Athletic, Dunfermline Athletic (where he played around 40 games in a years stint just a few years ago - twice playing in front of 50,000 and 60,000 at Celtic and Rangers) before a knee injury ended his full time career in December 2001 at Halifax Town after he had made 25 appearances. He moved on to Doncaster Rovers in january 2002 where he made 10 full and five substitute appearances in the Conference. Signed for Alfreton Town in May 2002, but two monhs later, without playing a game for Alfreton, Lee returned to Halifax as the clubs new assistant-manager.

BUTLER, MARK — *Forward*

Current Club: Staines Town

D o B: 23/05/1965   *Birthplace; Aldershot*
A prolific goalscorer wherever he has been, which has included Iongham, Egham Town, Wycombe Wanderers, Chesham United and particularly Aldershot Town. Signed for Staines Town during the summer of 1998 and has finished each season as the Swans top scorer.

BUTLER, NEIL — *Midfielder*

Current Club: Hitchin Town

D o B: 11/09/1975   *Birthplace: Luton*
Signed for Ryman Premier side Hitchin Town in the summer of 2002 after appearing for Rushden & Diamonds and Woking. A strong, combative player who can play in midfield or up front. Began his career with Luton Town and also appeared for Colchester United.

BUTLER, RICHARD — *Defender*

Current Club: Eastwood Town

Birthplace: Derby
Previous clubs include: Belper T - November 2001, King Lynn, Derby Co.

BUTLER, ROD — *Midfielder*

Current Club: Consett

Birthplace: Consett
Previous clubs include: Prudhoe - July 2000, Consett.

BUTLER, STEVE — *Forward*

Current Club: Tiptree United

Birthplace: Essex
Previous clubs include: Maldon T - July 2001.

BUTLER, STEVE — *Midfielder*

Current Club: Walton & Hersham

D o B: 27/01/1962   *Birthplace: Birmingham*
Honours won: England Semi-Pro Int., Conference Winners
Previous clubs include: Leicester C - October 2001, Gillingham, Peterborough Utd, Gillingham, Cambridge Utd, Watford, Maidstone Utd, Brentford, Windsor & Eton.

BUTLER, STEVE — *Midfielder*

Current Club: Maidstone United

Birthplace: Watford
Signed for Ryman Premier side Hendon in December 2001. Was at Berkhamsted Town where his father Roy was manager and has also previously been with Harrow Borough, St Albans City, Aylesbury United and Hemel Hempstead. He scored some

important goals for the Dons, especially the only goal in the semi-final of the Middlesex Senior Cup.

BUTLIN, JAMES — Forward
Current Club: Chichester City United
Birthplace: Sussex
Forward, known as Billy: originally with Chichester City several years ago and rejoined from Moneyfields in January 2001: finished last season with a tally of 7 goals.

BUTTERWORTH, DEAN — Forward
Current Club: Chorley
Birthplace: Lancashire
Talented striker who signed for Chorley in the deadline for the start of the 2002/03 season. Had trails with Crewe Alex and is one to watch for the future.

BUTTERWORTH, GARY — Midfielder
Current Club: Farnborough Town
D o B: 08/09/1969   Birthplace: Peterborough
Honours won: England Semi-Pro Int., Conference Winners, Dr Martens League Premier Div.Winners
One of the most experienced and respected midfield players around, Gary returned to the Conference with Farnborough Town in May 2002 after a season in the League with Rushden & Diamonds. Skippered Diamonds to the Conference title in 2000/01 and was a regular in the England semi-professional side, being captain on most of his nine appearances. Started his career with his home-town club Peterborough where he made 120 first-team appearances before joining Dagenham & Redbridge in 1992. Transferred to Diamonds in July 1994 for £20,000 which proved to be a bargain.

BUXTON, MARK — Defender
Current Club: Paulton Rovers
Birthplace: Bristol
Previous clubs include: Westbury Utd - July 1999.

BYRNE, GARY — Midfielder
Current Club: Oswestry Town
D o B: 15/06/1984   Birthplace: Shrewsbury
From Youth team.

BYRNE, JIMMY — Defender
Current Club: Congleton Town
Birthplace: Northern Ireland
Age 25. Left back. Signed in summer 01. Previously played for Kidderminster Harriers and Leek Town as well as experience in Gaelic Football. Set piece specialist with a ferocious left foot shot.

BYRNE, JOHN — Forward
Current Club: Whitehawk
D o B: 01/02/1961   Birthplace: Manchester
Honours won: Republic of Ireland Int.
Striker, now in his 40s, who is a former Republic of Ireland International. Previously played for Sunderland (appeared for them in the 1992 FA Cup Final), Oxford Utd, Queens Park Rangers, York City and Brighton & Hove Albion (made 110 appearances and scored 28 goals for the Seagulls). Drafted into the new-look Whitehawk team at the start of 2001/02, although his availability is restricted due to work commitments.

BYRNE, KEVIN — Midfielder
Current Club: Corby Town
Birthplace: Corby
Talented young midfielder who joined his home-town club Corby Town in July 2002. Represented Northants Youth and played United Counties League football with S & L Corby and Desborough Town before joining the Dr Martens Eastern side.

BYRNE, TOMMY — Defender
Current Club: Redditch United
D o B: 18/02/1974
Previous clubs include: Cape Cod Crusaders (USA) - January 2000, Blakenall, Stourbridge, Hednesford T, Leicester C (Trainee).

BYROM, DAVID — Defender
Current Club: Bashley
From Youth team.

BYTHEWAY, MATT — Defender
Current Club: Bilston Town
D o B: 11/03/1977   Birthplace: Birmingham
Previous clubs include: Bridgnorth T - December 2001, Bromsgrove R, Telford Utd, Aero Lucas, Willenhall T, Wolverhampton Wanderers.

B

CABLE, MARC — Defender

Current Club: Lewes

Birthplace: Sussex
Signed from Burgess Hill at the start of the 2000-1 season, he made a huge contribution despite missing a couple of months through injury. A real rock at the heart of the defence.

CADMAN, LUKE — Midfielder

Current Club: North Ferriby United

Birthplace: Hull
Highly-rated attacking midfielder who joined UniBond First Division side North Ferriby United from Northern Counties East League neighbours Brigg Town in the summer of 2002. Was a junior at Scunthorpe and then played local football before joining Brigg in July 2000.

CAFFREY, JOHN — Goalkeeper

Current Club: Whitley Bay

Birthplace: Co.Durham
A recent signing from South Shields this is Johns second spell at the club. For such a big keeper John is very agile and is an excellent handler of the ball. Has also been at Jarrow Roofing.

CAIN, BEN — Midfielder

Current Club: Edgware Town

Birthplace: London
Previous clubs include: Forest Utd - August 2001, Norwich C (Junior).

CAIN, DREW — Defender

Current Club: Mossley

Birthplace: Manchester
Previous clubs include: Flixton - August 1997, Maine Road.

CAIN, WESLEY — Midfielder

Current Club: Leatherhead

Birthplace: London
Tough midfielder who arrived at Ryman Division One South side Leatherhead from Hemel Hempsted in 2002. Immediately added some steel to the Tanners midfield. A quiet guy off the pitch, Wes makes his presence well known on it! Has also seen service with Romford, St Albans City, Chertsey Town and Bromley.

CALCUTT, DEAN — Midfielder

Current Club: Accrington Stanley

Birthplace: Yorkshire
Highly-rated right-sided midfielder who signed for UniBond Premier side Accrington Stanley from rivals Bradford Park Avenue for a £5,000 fee in August 2002. Joined Park Avenue in April 2000 from Emley in March 2000. Was originally spotted by Emley in the Huddersfield League in 1997 playing for Brackenhall United.

CALDICOTT, DANNY — Defender

Current Club: Stalybridge Celtic

Birthplace: Oldham
Danny signed for UniBond Premier side Stalybridge Celtic in August 2002 from North West Counties Leaguers Atherton LR. Joining LR in January 2001 from local football, Danny is a superb crosser of the ball with two good feet. He is a pacey player up and down the left flank and is not afraid to battle for the ball. Danny is an engineer by trade.

CALDWELL, BRIAN — Forward

Current Club: Gretna

D o B: 20/03/1981   *Birthplace: Glasgow*
Previous clubs include: Queen of the South - February 2001.

CALDWELL, MARTIN — Midfielder

Current Club: Warrington Town

Birthplace: Warrington
From Youth team.

CALLAGHAN, ANTHONY — Forward

Current Club: Curzon Ashton

Birthplace: Manchester
Previous clubs include: Droylsden - August 2001, Runcorn, Abbey Hey, Flixton.

CALLAN, AIDAN — Midfielder

Current Club: Kidsgrove Athletic

D o B: 08/10/1976   *Birthplace: Stoke*
Stoke-born midfielder who joined UniBond First Division side Kidsgrove Athletic in August 2002 following a short spell with Dr Martens Western outfit Gresley Rovers. Had signed for Gresley from UniBond Leaguers Leek Town in February 2002 and scored on his debut against Cirencester Town. Started out with his home-town club Stoke City before joining Leek in the summer of 1997.

CALLAND, DARREN — Midfielder

Current Club: Leigh RMI

D o B: 13/12/1982   *Birthplace: Billinge*
From Youth team.

CALLEAR, STEVE — Midfielder

Current Club: Leek Town

Birthplace: Leek
Signed for Leek Town from ground-sharers Leek CSOB in February 2002. Steve is an attacking midfielder who has also played for Congleton Town and Newcastle Town.

CALLENDER, LEON — Forward

Current Club: Beaconsfield SYCOB

Birthplace: Berkshire
Previous clubs include: Wembley - July 2000, Wycombe Wanderers (Junior).

CALLINAN, TOMMY — Midfielder

Current Club: Cinderford Town

Birthplace: Cheltenham
Former player-manager at Gloucester City and an ex-Forest Green Rovers regular. Signed for Cinderford Town in November 2001 from Clevedon Town. A vastly experienced midfielder who has also turned out for Dorchester Town and Cheltenham Town an is now in is second spell at Cinderford.

CALLINGHAM, GARY — Defender

Current Club: Burgess Hill Town

Birthplace: Eastbourne
Defender: formerly with Hailsham, Eastbourne Town and Langney Sports (captain of their reserve side for 2000/01): helped Sussex win the South-West Counties Championship during 1994/95: signed for Burgess Hill in August 2001.

CALVER, MARTIN — *Defender*
Current Club: Harwich & Parkeston
Birthplace: Essex
Another local lad who previously played for Little Oakley in the Border League. He stepped up to the Jewson League with Harwich two seasons ago to become a virtually ever present member of the squad. A strong defender who likes to get up at set pieces.

CALVERT, LEE — *Midfielder*
Current Club: Ashton United
Previous clubs include: Ossett Alb - January 2001, Local Football, Ossett Alb.

CAMBRIDGE, ADIE — *Forward*
Current Club: Histon
Birthplace: Cambridge
Previous clubs include: Cambridge C - January 2000, Histon, Cambridge C, Foxton, Cambridge C, Foxton.

CAMBRIDGE, IAN — *Forward*
Current Club: Histon
Birthplace: Cambridge
Gifted striker who plundered 31 goals for Chelmsford City in 1998/99, a tally that understandably brought him the Player of the Year award. He then returned to Cambridge City for a third time but came back to Essex, also for a third spell, just prior to the 2001/02 season despite strong interest from Dover Athletic. Left Chelmsford again to join Eastern Division Histon in July 2002. His other former clubs include Foxton and Kings Lynn.

CAMERON, DAVID — *Forward*
Current Club: Chester City
D o B: 24/08/1975   Birthplace: Wales
Began his career as a trainee at St. Mirren where he made ten appearances scoring two goals. Signed for Brighton in July 1999 making 22 appearances but by February his attitude was in doubt and Brighton gave him a free transfer. Brightons local Non-League neighbours Worthing signed Dave and he repaid they faith in him by scoring nine goals in nine games. That scoring rate drew attention and then Lincoln boss Phil Stant moved quickly to secure Daves signature, beating both Brentford and Rushden. The transfer was seen as gamble but as Dave had cost nothing it was a move which had potential. Unfortunately he had trouble breaking into the first team but finished the 2000/01 season as leading goalscorer for the reserves. Was released at the end of the 2001/02 season and joined Chester City.

CAMERON, MARK — *Defender*
Current Club: Whitley Bay
Birthplace: Whitley Bay
This is Marks third time at the club. He is vastly experienced and has been brought in by Manager Andy Gowens for his coaching skills. Mark joined us from Bedlington Terriers where in his first season as coach the Terriers reached the second round of the F.A.Cup beating Colchester United in the First Round and they also made it to the final of the F.A. Vase.

CAMMOCK, ROMI — *Forward*
Current Club: Atherstone United
D o B: 24/08/1983   Birthplace: Birmingham
Previous clubs include: Continental Star - July 2001, Alvechurch.

CAMPBELL, ANDY — *Defender*
Current Club: Sidlesham
Birthplace: Sussex
Defender, known as Bugsy: has been around since the 70s, having started off with Selsey: other previous clubs include Bognor Regis and Portfield: featured in Sidleshams 1999/2000 Division Two title-winning side, before mainly playing for the reserves the following season: first-team captain for 2001/02.

CAMPBELL, BEN — *Forward*
Current Club: Walton Casuals
Birthplace: Surrey
Ben is currently in his 3rd season at Franklyn Road. Last season was the Reserves league topscorer. this season Ben will looking to break into the First Team.

CAMPBELL, CARLTON — *Forward*
Current Club: Leyton Pennant
Birthplace: Essex
Previous clubs include: Waltham Abbey - August 2001, Leyton Pennant, Haringey B.

CAMPBELL, COLIN — *Forward*
Current Club: Egham Town
Birthplace: Berkshire
Previous clubs include: Windsor & Eton - August 2002, Maidenhead Utd.

CAMPBELL, COREY — *Defender*
Current Club: St.Albans City
D o B: 06/03/1979   Birthplace: London
23 year-old central defender now in his second season at Clarence Park, having signed in the summer of 2000 from Gravesend & Northfleet.

CAMPBELL, DANNY — *Forward*
Current Club: Hallam
Birthplace: Sheffield
Previous clubs include: Matlock T - August 2000, Hallam, Worksop T, Wombwell T, Sheffield Wednesday (Junior).

CAMPBELL, DAVID — *Goalkeeper*
Current Club: Gateshead
Birthplace: Durham
Honours won: FA Vase Winners
A former FA Vase winner with Whitby Town in 1997, David is a highly-rated goalkeeper who joined UniBond Premier side Gateshead in the summer of 2002 from relegated Bishop Auckland. Originally with Northern League sides South Bank and Guisborough, he then spent a number of years as Whitbys number one before moving to Spennymoor United. Re-joined Whitby in March 2000 before switching to Bishop Auckland at the start of the 2001/02 season.

CAMPBELL, DUDLEY — *Forward*
Current Club: Stevenage Borough
Birthplace: London
Signed for Stevenage from Chesham United at the end of the 2000/01 season, Dudley Junior has made an immediate impact at Broadhall Way. In his first game of the season he lived up to his potential and netted twice against Hayes. Has suffered with injury problems, but now looks to be on his way to full fitness again. Started his career as a trainee at Aston Villa before joining Queens Park Rangers.

CAMPBELL, JAMES　　　　　*Defender*
Current Club: Sittingbourne
D o B: 16/11/1979　　　　　　　　Birthplace: Kent
Released by Peterborough United at the end of the 2000/01 season where he completed 5 years, 2 years YTS and 3 years as full professional. Was in a successful FA Youth Cup run in 1998 in a side which included both Simon Davies and Matthew Etherington (now with Spurs) when they reached the semi-final. Had 2 loan periods with Spalding United and the second spell was curtailed when he ended up in hospital on Boxing Day 2000 when he smashed his foot badly in a tackle that put him out of football for about 4 months. Joined Tonbridge Angels after being released by the Posh and then signed for Kent neighbours Sittingbourne in February 2002.

CAMPBELL, JAMIE　　　　　*Defender*
Current Club: Stevenage Borough
D o B: 21/10/1972　　　　　　　Birthplace: Birmingham
Jamie joined Stevenage in March 2002 from Exeter City, where after winning their player of the year award, he decided he wanted to move closer to home. His former clubs include Luton, Mansfield, Cambridge, Barnet, and Brighton, and he has well in excess of 250 league games under his belt. He is described as a versatile player, at home in defence, or midfield, and can comfortably play in either central or left sided positions. He played for Cambridge when Boro famously knocked the Us out of the FA Cup, and he was infamously accredited with the first of Boros goals!

CAMPBELL, JAMIE　　　　　*Midfielder*
Current Club: Solihull Borough
Birthplace: Birmingham
Local youngster who has returned to the Solihull this season after joining Walsall 18 months ago on full time terms. Jamie is the son of ex -Birmingham midfield star Alan Campbell.

CAMPBELL, JASON　　　　　*Defender*
Current Club: Letchworth
Birthplace: Beds
Previous clubs include: Brache Sparta - July 2001, Toddington R, Brache Sparta, Toddington R.

CAMPBELL, MARK　　　　　*Defender*
Current Club: Edgware Town
Birthplace: Middlesex
Previous clubs include: Yeading - October 2001, Hampton & Richmond B, Wealdstone, Ashford T (Middx), Harefield Utd.

CAMPBELL, NEIL　　　　　*Forward*
Current Club: Scarborough
D o B: 26/01/1977　　　　　Birthplace: Middlesbrough
One of Scarborough manager Russell Slades summer 2002 signings from near neighbours Doncaster Rovers. Striker Neil signed on for a second spell at The McCain Stadium. He had previously played for Boro in their League days between 1997 and 1999. His career has also taken in stops at York, Telford and Southend.

CAMPBELL, NEIL　　　　　*Midfielder*
Current Club: Walton Casuals
Birthplace: Surrey
Neil is in his 3rd season at Franklyn Road, has claimed a first team spot through the Reserves, can play midfield or as a forward. Also a very keen cricketer.

CAMPBELL, NICKY　　　　　*Defender*
Current Club: Burnham
Birthplace: Cornwall
Joined the club this season after a spell with Wokingham Town. Born in Cornwall, he previously appeared for Saltash United, Falmouth Town and Tiverton Town.

CAMPBELL, PAUL　　　　　*Defender*
Current Club: Sittingbourne
Birthplace: Kent
Solid and reliable defender who returned to Sittingbourne in September 2002 for a second spell from Kent neighbours Erith & Belvedere. Experienced player whose career began at Charlton and has since given service to Bromley, Bishops Stortford, Dagenham & Redbridge, Berkhamsted Town and Chelmsford City.

CAMPBELL, SEAN　　　　　*Defender*
Current Club: St. Leonards
D o B: 07/04/1976　　　　　　Birthplace: Pembury
Previous clubs include: Cobham - July 2001

CAMPBELL, SEAN　　　　　*Forward*
Current Club: Clacton Town
D o B: 31/12/1974　　　　　　Birthplace: Bristol
Previous clubs include: Wivenhoe T - August 2001, Chelmsford C, Clacton T, Wivenhoe T, Peterborough Utd, Chelmsford C, Harwich & Parkeston, Chelmsford C, Colchester Utd.

CAMPBELL, STEVE　　　　　*Midfielder*
Current Club: Mangotsfield United
Birthplace: Wiltshire
Joined Mangotsfield United in July 2001 from Cinderford Town. Previously with Forest Green Rovers, he is an attacking midfielder who scored 9 goals for Cinderford in their end of season run which saw them avoid relegation.

CAMPBELL, STUART　　　　　*Midfielder*
Current Club: Pagham
Birthplace: Sussex
Midfielder: originally at Pagham before having a brief spell with Selsey in 1999: signed from Eastergate during December 2001.

CAMPION, SEAN　　　　　*Defender*
Current Club: Bromsgrove Rovers
Birthplace: Birmingham
Previous clubs include: Swindon T - August 2001.

CANAVAN, MICHAEL　　　　　*Forward*
Current Club: Durham City
D o B: 17/09/1980　　　　　Birthplace: South Shields
Previous clubs include: Middlesbrough - July 2000.

CANN, MATT　　　　　*Defender*
Current Club: Bideford
Birthplace: Devon
Matt is a promising young wing back who has graduated up through the ranks from our youth set up.

CANNIE, SCOTT　　　　　*Defender*
Current Club: Wimborne Town
Birthplace: Dorset
Previous clubs include: Dorchester T - July 2001, Poole T, Flight Refueling.

CANNIE, STUART — Forward

Current Club: Wimborne Town

Birthplace: Bournemouth
Previous clubs include: Bournemouth FC - July 1999.

CANNING, LEON — Forward

Current Club: Leatherhead

Birthplace: London
Previous clubs include: Hampton & Richmond Borough - September 2001.

CANNON, DAVE — Midfielder

Current Club: Aveley

Birthplace: Essex
Previous clubs include: Romford - July 2001, Aveley, East Thurrock Utd.

CANNON, NEIL — Defender

Current Club: Aveley

Birthplace: Essex
Previous clubs include: East Thurrock Utd - February 2002.

CANOVILLE, DEAN — Forward

Current Club: Molesey

D o B: 30/11/1978 Birthplace: Perivale
A striker who signed for Ryman Division One South side Molesey from Chertsey Town in July 2002. Had joined Chertsey after injury at Plymouth Argyle forced him out of the full-time game. Prior to his spell at Home Park, Dean had spells with Welling United, Chesham United, Hampton, St Albans City and Walton & Hersham.

CAPE-MELBOURNE, DAVE — Forward

Current Club: Hall Road Rangers

Birthplace: Hull
From Local football - July 2001.

CAPLETON, MELVIN — Goalkeeper

Current Club: Grays Athletic

D o B: 24/10/1973 Birthplace: London
Recent re-aquisition from Southend United, he previously played for Grays Athletic then was transfered to Us, he returned this season firstly on loan, then as a permanent team member.

CAPONE, JULIAN — Forward

Current Club: Chesham United

D o B: 03/06/1972 Birthplace: Northampton
Winger who has played for Rushden and Diamonds, Boreham Wood, Bedford Town and Enfield. Compares himself to a Jan Molby style winger. Signed for Ryman Premier side Chesham United in August 2002.

CAPPER, DAVID — Defender

Current Club: Sheffield FC

D o B: 08/09/1978 Birthplace: Stoke
Previous clubs include: Denaby Utd - December 1999, Worksop T, Northwich V, Dundalk, Sheffield Utd.

CAPPER, STEVE — Defender

Current Club: Northwich Victoria

Birthplace: Manchester
From Youth team.

CAPUANO, JULIAN — Midfielder

Current Club: Matlock Town

Birthplace: Nottingham
A midfielder who signed for Matlock at the beginning of the season. Julian has had UniBond League experience with both Alfreton and Belper, and most recently he has been with Staveley in the Northern Counties (East) League.

CARDEN, PAUL — Midfielder

Current Club: Chester City

D o B: 29/03/1979 Birthplace: Liverpool
Back in his second spell at Chester following a £3,000 move from Doncaster Rovers in the summer of 2001.

CARDEN, SIMON — Midfielder

Current Club: Accrington Stanley

Birthplace: Lancashire
Young goalscroing midfielder who signed for Accrington Stanley on 6th December 2000 from Radcliffe Borough for a £5,000 fee. Scored 22 goals for Radcliffe in the 1999/2000 season. Made his Stanley debut on 9th December, 2000 at home against Colwyn Bay.

CARDY, JON — Goalkeeper

Current Club: Witham Town

Birthplace: Essex
Previous clubs include: Wivenhoe T - August 2001, Clacton T, Sudbury T, Kirby Utd, Norwich C.

CARE, DAVID — Defender

Current Club: Racing Club Warwick

Birthplace: Coventry
Previous clubs include: Paget Rangers - August 2001, Solihull B, Racing Club Warwick, Southam Utd.

CAREY, DAVID — Forward

Current Club: Sidley United

Birthplace: Sussex
Forward: prolific goalscorer for Sidleys U-18 side during 1998/99: only briefly featured for the first-team in 2000/01 (named as a substitute a few times): promoted from the reserves early on in 2001/02.

CAREY, SHAUN — Midfielder

Current Club: Chester City

D o B: 13/05/1976 Birthplace: Kettering
Honours won: Conference Winners
Classy midfielder with good vision and a good passer of the ball. Played over 50 games for Norwich City before joining Rushden & Diamonds, but struggled to make the first team after they gained promotion. Had a short loan spell at Stevenage Borough on-loan before joining Conference rivals Chester City in February 2002.

CARFOOT, JAMIE — Defender

Current Club: Brandon United

Birthplace: Co.Durham
A hard-tackling player who joined the club last season from Consett, having previously had spells with Middlesbrough and Darlington.

CARGILL, ALEX — Defender

Current Club: Clapton

D o B: 16/09/1976 Birthplace: London
Previous clubs include: Hanwell T - August 2001.

CARMICHAEL, MATT — Forward
Current Club: Wivenhoe Town

Birthplace: Essex
Previous clubs include: Harwich & Parkeston - December 2001, Little Oakley.

CARMODY, MIKE — Midfielder
Current Club: Ashton United

D o B: 09/02/1966   Birthplace: Huddersfield
Previous clubs include: Altrincham - July 2000, Emley, Tranmere R, Huddersfield T.

CARNEY, ANDY — Goalkeeper
Current Club: Ossett Albion

Birthplace: Sheffield
Based in Rotherham. A Former Stocksbridge Park Steels, Frickley Athletic and Hadnesford Town player. A very commanding goalkeeper and an excellent shot stopper.

CARNEY, LEE — Midfielder
Current Club: Horsham

Birthplace: Sussex
Teenage midfielder who amazingly scored five times for Broadbridge Heath on his full debut against Worthing United in April 2000: struck 20 goals for the Bears during the following season and had trials with Millwall: began 2001/02 with Pease Pottage (Sussex County League Division Three) before being snapped up by Horsham a couple of months into the campaign.

CARR, ASHLEY — Forward
Current Club: Burgess Hill Town

Birthplace: Sussex
Extremely popular forward, who became something of a celebrity after The Sun newspaper chronicled Burgess Hills FA Cup exploits in 1999: principal goalscorer for the club during their three championship winning years in 1997/98/99: leading Hillians marksman during 2000/01 with 18 strikes: has also played for Whitehawk and Shoreham in the past: seemed to be on the verge of retirement a couple of years ago, but is still going as strong as ever: also plays for the County.

CARR, CHRISTIAN — Midfielder
Current Club: Fleet Town

Birthplace: Hampshire
Previous clubs include: Hartley Wintney - July 2001.

CARR, DARREN — Defender
Current Club: Bath City

D o B: 04/09/1968   Birthplace: Bristol
Vastly experience defender who made more than 300 Football League appearances. He signed for Dr Martens Premier side Bath City in July 2002 after a brief trial period at Rushden & Diamonds. Joined Dover Athletic in October 2001 from Brighton after previously serving Bristol Rovers, Newport County, Sheffield United, Crewe, Chesterfield and Gillingham.

CARR, DAVID — Midfielder
Current Club: Whitley Bay

Birthplace: Newcastle
Starting his second season at the club, David is an excellent utility player who can play in defence or midfield. Signed from Morpeth Town.

CARR, GERALD — Defender
Current Club: Stratford Town

Birthplace: Coventry
Honours won: Republic of Ireland Youth Int.
Previous clubs include: Bedworth Utd - August 2001, Evesham Utd, Shepshed Dynamo, Hinckley Utd, Hinckley Ath., Bedworth Utd, VS Rugby, Nuneaton B, Sligo R, Coventry C.

CARR, GRAEME — Defender
Current Club: Workington

D o B: 28/10/1978   Birthplace: Chester-le-Street
Talented defender who joined the club from Scarborough in November 1999, taking over the captaincy soon after his arrival. Scored several goals from the penalty spot, including one in the clubs Cumberland Cup Final success.

CARR, JAMIE — Defender
Current Club: Woodbridge Town

Birthplace: Essex
Central defender signed by the new Team Manager Paul Leech midway through last season from Leiston St Margarets. Made his First Team debut at Brightlingsea in February 2001 and looks to be a tremendous prospect.

CARRAGHER, STEVE — Defender
Current Club: Runcorn FC Halton

Birthplace: Liverpool
Steve signed for Runcorn for the second time in his career from Accrington Stanley during pre-season before the 2001/2002 season. Is extremely fast down the right hand wing, and can deliver a pin-point cross at pace for the attackers in the box. Caz is also an excellent tackler when called upon, and is a firm fans favourite with his 100 per cent commitment.

CARRINGTON, BEN — Forward
Current Club: Worthing

Birthplace: London
Forward: previously with Welling before joining Worthing from Eastbourne Town for 1998/99 (scored 23 times that season): struggled with a groin injury throughout 2000/01: a great favourite at Woodside Road.

CARR-LAWTON, COLIN — Forward
Current Club: Morpeth Town

D o B: 05/09/1978   Birthplace: South Shields
Previous clubs include: Whitby T - July 2000, Berwick Rangers, Barrow, Burnley.

CARROLL, DANNY — Midfielder
Current Club: Farnborough Town

Birthplace: Surrey
Previously with Whyteleafe and Bromley, Danny was leading scorer for Dulwich Hamlet before joining Crawley during the 2000 close season. Developed into one of the most highly-rated midfielders in the Dr Martens League before transferring to Farnborough in May 2002.

CARROLL, DAVID — Midfielder
Current Club: Aldershot Town

D o B: 20/09/1966   Birthplace: Paisley
Honours won: England Youth Int., Conference Winners, FA Trophy Winners
Previous clubs include: Wycombe Wanderers - March 2002, Ruislip Manor, Wembley, Fulham.

CARROLL, LEE — Goalkeeper
Current Club: Marlow
D o B: 06/04/1977   Birthplace: London
Highly-rated goalkeeper who made a record number of appearances in Chelseas youth yeam where he spent five years and made the bench for a European game. He was subsequently released and joined Northwood in September 1995. Soent four years with the Wood before switching to Marlow at the start of the 1999/00 season and was voted as player of the year at the end of his first campaign with the club.

CARROLL, MARK — Midfielder
Current Club: Bridlington Town
Birthplace: Hull
Former Hull City youngster who contributed well in the early part of the season. Bobbys well flighted free kicks and corners create many scoring chances. Missed a few games towards the end of last season but will hopefully be able to concentrate on regaining his place.

CARROLL, MIKE — Defender
Current Club: Connahs Quay Nomads
D o B: 01/12/1970   Birthplace: Wales
From Local football - October 1992.

CARROLL, TONY — Forward
Current Club: Salford City
Birthplace: Manchester
Previous clubs include: Droylsden - July 2000, Radcliffe B, Northwich V, Hyde Utd, Bamber Bridge, Radcliffe B.

CARRUTHERS, MATT — Forward
Current Club: Dover Athletic
D o B: 22/07/1976   Birthplace: Dover
Matts versatility has seen him play as a forward, a right wing-back and on the right side of midfield. Currently in his second spell at Dover Athletic following his return from Newport IOW in December 1998. Following his work with the Parachute Regiment, Carruthers was given a contract. Matt was originally a forward in the 1999/00 season, but found himself third choice and was given an opportunity on the right wing. But in addition, the 2000/01 season saw Carruthers used as a right wing back in a 5-3-2 formation. Originally with Dover, he also had a spell with Ashford Town and Folkestone Invicta.

CARTER, ADIE — Midfielder
Current Club: Glapwell
Birthplace: Chesterfield
Previous clubs include: Shirebrook T - July 2001, Glapwell.

CARTER, ALFIE — Forward
Current Club: Evesham United
D o B: 13/08/1980   Birthplace: Birmingham
Previous clubs include: Newport Co - February 2002, Halesowen T, Bromsgrove R, Walsall.

CARTER, ANDY — Goalkeeper
Current Club: Wealdstone
D o B: 31/01/1972   Birthplace: London
Goalkeeper Andy was previously at Edgware Town and Haringey Borough. He joined Wealdstone during the close season of 2001/2 from Hemel Hempstead Town.

CARTER, BEN — Midfielder
Current Club: Wisbech Town
D o B: 01/12/1978
Previous clubs include: Fisher Ath - July 2001, Concord R, Norwich C.

CARTER, CHARLEY — Forward
Current Club: Staines Town
D o B: 15/04/1979   Birthplace: Middlesex
Joined Staines Town originally as a junior in 1995 after previously being at Brentford, Isleworth and Osterley. Made his first-team debut in 1997 and has been a regular scorer ever since.

CARTER, DANNY — Midfielder
Current Club: Merthyr Tydfil
D o B: 29/06/1969   Birthplace: Hackney
Vastly experienced midfielder who was recruited for Merthyr Tydfil in August 1999 from League of Wales Champions Barry Town. Started his League career with Leyton Orient after he was discovered playing for Billericay Town. Stayed at Brisbane Road for seven seasons accumulating 188 first team appearances while scoring 22 goals. A £25,000 transfer took him to Peterborough United in June 1995 but his stay at London Road lasted only two seasons, making 45 appearances and scoring 1 goal.

CARTER, GRAEME — Defender
Current Club: Brandon United
Birthplace: Newcastle
A very reliable defender who reads the game well. Longest serving player at the club, now in his seventh season. Previous clubs include Newcastle Utd and Newcastle Blue Star.

CARTER, JASON — Defender
Current Club: Wroxham
D o B: 07/03/1970   Birthplace: Essex
Honours won: FA Vase Winners
Signed from Cambridge City. Versatile defender who was in Diss Town's FA Vase winning side. Can play anywhere in the back line.

CARTER, JIMMY — Forward
Current Club: Cirencester Town
D o B: 11/02/1976   Birthplace: Bristol
A strong, speedy front runner who never stops working and consistently puts defenders under pressure. Jimmy joined Cirencester Town in July 1999 after previously playing for Bristols University side.

CARTER, MARTIN — Midfielder
Current Club: Aylesbury United
Birthplace: Middlesex
Former Watford attacking midfielder who signed for Ryman Premier side Aylesbury United from Division One North outfit Wealdstone in July 2002. After leaving Vicarage Road, Martin had spells with Hayes, Norwegian side Odda, Yeading, Chesham United, Chertsey Town and Hampton & Richmond Borough before joining the Stones in October 2001.

CARTER, MICHAEL — Defender
Current Club: Ossett Albion
Previous clubs include: Liversedge - August 2000, Pontefract Collieries, Worsbrough Bridge, Wakefield C.

CARTER, NICKY — Forward

Current Club: Bilston Town

D o B: 29/11/1981 — Birthplace: Stoke
Previous clubs include: Halesowen T - August 2001, Tamworth, Atherstone Utd, Stafford R, Nottingham Forest.

CARTER, NICKY — Midfielder

Current Club: Moor Green

D o B: 29/11/1981 — Birthplace: Stoke
Previous clubs include: Bloxwich Utd - December 2001, Halesowen T, Tamworth, Atherstone Utd, Stafford R, Nottingham Forest.

CARTER, RICHARD — Defender

Current Club: Cwmbran Town

D o B: 10/01/1972 — Birthplace: Wales
Previous clubs include: Cardiff Civil Service - August 1995, Lisvane.

CARTER, RICHARD — Midfielder

Current Club: Burgess Hill Town

Birthplace: Brighton
Big midfielder: went from Southwick to Lewes midway through 1999/2000, before being released in April that year: joined Shoreham at the end of that season but signed for Burgess Hill in September 2000: scored five times altogether last term.

CARTER, SIMON — Defender

Current Club: Willenhall Town

Birthplace: Shropshire
Signed for Willenhall in October 2001 from Shifnal Town. A solid defender who has improved with every game.

CARTER, STEVE — Defender

Current Club: East Thurrock United

Birthplace: Essex
Previous clubs include: Aveley - July 2000, East Thurrock Utd.

CARTER, STEVE — Midfielder

Current Club: Chester-le-Street

Birthplace: Co. Durham
Previous clubs include: Guisborough T - July 2000, Chester-le-Street, Bishop Auckland, Jarrow Roofing, Bishop Auckland, Durham C, Scarborough, Durham C, Northallerton T, North Shields, Scarborough, Manchester Utd.

CARTER, STEVE — Midfielder

Current Club: Brigg Town

Birthplace: Lincoln
Previous clubs include: Lincoln Utd - July 2001, Brigg T, Lincoln Utd, Brigg T, Lincoln C (Trainee).

CARTER, STUART — Defender

Current Club: Guisborough Town

Previous clubs include: Norton - July 2001.

CARTER, TOM — Defender

Current Club: Redhill

D o B: 20/01/1980 — Birthplace: Sussex
Defender joined Redhill from Horsham during the 2000 close season, but only made a few appearances last year due to being away at university. Now a regular at right back. Very calm on the ball with great passing abilities.

CARTER, WAYNE — Forward

Current Club: Northwood

Birthplace: Middlesex
Previous clubs include: Hayes - July 2001.

CARTHY, MARTIN — Midfielder

Current Club: Billericay Town

Birthplace: Kent
Martin joined Billericay from Purfleet in the summer of 2001, and made his debut in the first game of the season at home to Grays Athletic. He made over 250 appearances for the Ship Lane side, and was a regular goalscorer for them with over 50 goals to his name, including several against Billericay. A tall, powerful midfielder, Martin has formed a good partnership with Lee Williams in the center of the park, and his ability to arrive in the box and get goals is well known.

CARTLEDGE, STEVE — Defender

Current Club: Warrington Town

D o B: 26/09/1974 — Birthplace: Warrington
From Youth team.

CARTLIDGE, MARK — Midfielder

Current Club: Boreham Wood

Birthplace: Essex
Promising midfielder who joined Ryman Premier side Boreham Wood from rivals Billericay Town in July 2002. Began his playing days with East Thurrock United, where he had two spells, and has also turned out for Aveley and then Billericay.

CARTWRIGHT, MATT — Midfielder

Current Club: Pelsall Villa

Birthplace: Birmingham
Previous clubs include: Stourport Swifts - August 2000, Pelsall Villa, Rushall Olympic, Bloxwich T, Pelsall Villa, Manders.

CARTWRIGHT, NEIL — Defender

Current Club: Hinckley United

D o B: 25/06/1982 — Birthplace: Wrexham
Honours won: Dr Martens League Western Div.Winners
Neil progressed to the Hinckley United first-team through the reserves and the youth side. His father, Les, is a former Welsh international who plied his trade with Coventry City and Wrexham. Neil looks best on the right as a wingback, but is not out of place in a back four. A fans favourite because he tends to run his heart out all game. Won a Dr Martens Western Division championship Medal with Hinckley United in 2000/01.

CARTWRIGHT, NEIL — Midfielder

Current Club: Bromsgrove Rovers

D o B: 20/02/1971 — Birthplace: Stourbridge
Honours won: Conference Winners
Previous clubs include: Redditch Utd - January 2002, Bromsgrove R, Halesowen T, Telford Utd, Kidderminster Harriers, Sogndal (Norway), WBA.

CARTY, PAUL — Midfielder

Current Club: Worcester City

D o B: 22/10/1976 — Birthplace: Liverpool
Powerful midfielder, Paul began his career at Everton before moving into Non-League football. He had spells at Nuneaton Borough, VS Rugby and Bromsgrove Rovers before signing for Hednesford Town in 1994. After five seasons at Bromsgrove, Paul was released by the Pitmen and joined Worcester City for a fee in August 1999. Spent much of the 2001/02 season on the transfer list.

CARTY, PETER — Forward

Current Club: *Curzon Ashton*

Birthplace: Manchester
Previous clubs include: Ashton Utd - August 2001, Woodley Sports, Abbey Hey, Woodley Sports, Hyde Utd, Woodley Sports, Oldham T.

CARUS, JOSH — Defender

Current Club: *Wroxham*

Birthplace: Norfolk
From Youth team.

CARVELL, MATT — Defender

Current Club: *Wealdstone*

Birthplace: Derbyshire
Honours won: Dr Martens League Premier Div.Winners
Derbyshire-born defender who helped Grantham Town to gain promotion to the Dr Martens Premier Division in 2001/02 and then re-located to the London area in the summer whereupon he joined Ryman Division One North side Wealdstone. A very consistent performer, he began his playing days at Gresley Rovers.

CASE, JON — Defender

Current Club: *Hayes*

Birthplace: Hillingdon
From Youth team.

CASEY, KIM — Forward

Current Club: *Rushall Olympic*

D o B: 03/03/1961   Birthplace: Birmingham
Honours won: England Semi-Pro Int., Conference Winners, FA Trophy Winners
Previous clubs include: Moor Green - February 2002, Kidderminster Harriers, Solihull B, Wycombe Wanderers, Cheltenham T, Kidderminster Harriers, Gloucester C, AP Leamington, Sutton Coldfield T.

CASH, STUART — Defender

Current Club: *Aldershot Town*

D o B: 05/09/1965   Birthplace: Dudley
Honours won: FA Trophy Winners
Vastly experienced defender who has proved to be a great influence in the dressing room under his assistant managers role. A former professional with Nottingham Forest, Chesterfield, Rotherham and Brentford, Stuart actually began his playing days in Non-League football with Bilston Town, Stourbridge and Halesowen Town before joining Forest. Has since turned out for Stevenage Borough, Wycombe Wanderers, where he won an FA Trophy winners medal, Chertsey Town, Slough Town, Chesham United and Enfield. Joined the Shots in September 1997.

CASHA, STEVE — Forward

Current Club: *St Margaretsbury*

D o B: 08/07/1974   Birthplace: London
Previous clubs include: Ware - July 1999, Hertford T.

CASS, BRENDAN — Forward

Current Club: *Tonbridge Angels*

D o B: 19/07/1983   Birthplace: Kent
Progressed through Tonbridge Angels youth and reserve teams. Brendan is a highly-promising striker.

CASSON, KEVIN — Midfielder

Current Club: *Paget Rangers*

Birthplace: Birmingham
Previous clubs include: Stourbridge - January 2002, Atherstone Utd, Paget R, Bilston T, Paget R, Hendon, Boldmere St.Michaels, Moor Green, Kidderminster Harriers.

CASTLE, STEVE — Midfielder

Current Club: *St.Albans City*

D o B: 17/05/1966   Birthplace: Barking
An experienced central midfielder, he began his career at Orient in the 1984/85 season and went on to make 243 appearances for them before moving to Plymouth Argyle. Also appeared in the Football League for Birmingham City, Gillingham and Peterborough United making a total of almost 500 games and scoring over 100 goals, before stepping into Non-League at Stevenage Borough. Signed for Ryman Premier side St Albans City in June 2002.

CASTLEDINE, GARY — Midfielder

Current Club: *Eastwood Town*

D o B: 27/03/1970   Birthplace: Dumfries
Honours won: NCEL & Cup Winners
Very experienced and widely travelled midfielder who returned to UniBond First Division side Eastwood Town in the summer of 2002 after helping Alfreton Town to win the Northern Counties Easl League double. Originally with Shirebrook MW, Gary then played League football with Mansfield before having spells with Telford United, Gainsborough Trinity, Cork City, Gresley Rovers and Ilkeston Town before joining Eastwood for the first time. Left for Gedling Town and Hinckley United before returning again to the Badgers. Moved to Alfreton in October 2000.

CASTRECHINI, CARLO — Midfielder

Current Club: *Three Bridges*

Birthplace: Sussex
Slightly-built midfielder: former reserve for Crawley, who has had trials with Tottenham Hotspur and Millwall in the past: began the current season with Peacehaven before transferring to Three Bridges in September.

CASTRONOVO, CARLO — Defender

Current Club: *Walton Casuals*

Birthplace: Surrey
Joined Casuals last season from Molesey, recently has become a 1st team regular. Very quick and good in the air for his height of 5 5.

CASWELL, STEVE — Defender

Current Club: *Accrington Stanley*

D o B: 23/06/1972
Previous clubs include: Droylsden - November 1999, Ashton Utd, Glossop NE, Mossley, Hyde Utd, Ashton Utd, Glossop NE, Dukinfield T.

CATLEY, ANDY — Midfielder

Current Club: *Chippenham Town*

D o B: 29/05/1979   Birthplace: Bath
Previous clubs include: Weston-Super-Mare - November 2001, Welton Rovers, Forest Green R, Southampton, Exeter C.

CATLEY, PAUL — Goalkeeper

Current Club: *Braintree Town*

Previous clubs include: Chelmsford C - July 2001, Braintree T, Sudbury T, Bury T, Braintree T.

CATLIN, NEIL — *Midfielder*
Current Club: Flackwell Heath

D o B: 15/09/1972   *Birthplace: Amersham*
Previous clubs include: Windsor & Eton - January 2002, Flackwell Heath, Marlow, Harrow B, Aylesbury Utd, Chesham Utd, Hayes, Stevenage B, Slough T, Marlow, Maidenhead Utd, Marlow, Flackwell Heath, Thame Utd, Marlow.

CATLIN, PAUL — *Defender*
Current Club: Flackwell Heath

Birthplace: Wycombe
Previous clubs include: Marlow - December 1999, Flackwell Heath.

CATON, COLIN — *Defender*
Current Club: Colwyn Bay

D o B: 27/08/1970   *Birthplace: Wales*
Central defender, originally signed for Colwyn Bay from Rhyl. Now in his second spell at the club after returning from Witton Albion in October 1996, where he was transferred for a club record fee. Won Supporters' Player of the year two seasons running. Appointed player-manager at the start of the 2001/02 season, taking on the mammoth task of replacing the long-serving Bryn Jones.

CATON, SEAN — *Midfielder*
Current Club: Wivenhoe Town

Birthplace: Essex
Promising midfielder who re-signed for Ryman Division One North side Wivenhoe Town in August 2002 from Essex neighbours Heybridge Swifts. Had signed for the Swifts from Wivenhoe in March 1999 and made an immediate impression after gaining experience with loan spells with Barking and Chelmsford City to further his footballing education with some first-team football. Good engine, gets into some superb forward positions with an eye for goal. Started his career as a trainee at Tottenham Hotspur.

CATT, ANDY — *Defender*
Current Club: Arlesey Town

Birthplace: Bedfordshire
Honours won: Ryman League Div.3 Winners
Andy is a useful utility player who can fill in just about any position on the field. He is tall, quick, a hard worker and a good player to have around in a crisis. Joined Arlesey Town from Stotfold in the summer of 2000 and gained his first winners medal at the end of his first season, helping the Blues lift the Ryman League Division 3 title. He is a Loss Adjuster by trade.

CATTEN, JAMES — *Defender*
Current Club: Haverhill Rovers

Birthplace: Suffolk
Broke into the Haverhill first team three seasons ago. Strong with good vision, he reads the game well and delivers excellent crosses.

CATTERMOLE, DANNY — *Defender*
Current Club: Ipswich Wanderers

Birthplace: Suffolk
Previous clubs include: Needham Market - July 1998, Felixstowe T.

CAUDWELL, MATTHEW — *Midfielder*
Current Club: Worksop Town

D o B: 14/10/1979   *Birthplace: Chesterfield*
Previous clubs include: Doncaster Rovers - May 2002, Hallam.

CAVANAGH, ANDY — *Midfielder*
Current Club: Skelmersdale United

Birthplace: Southport
Previous clubs include: Vauxhall Motors - January 2001, Accrington Stanley, Marine, Burscough, Southport.

CAVANAGH, PETER — *Defender*
Current Club: Accrington Stanley

D o B: 14/10/1981   *Birthplace: Liverpool*
Signed for Accrington Stanley in August 2001. 21-year-old right back released by Liverpool at the end of the 200/01 season after ten years on the clubs books. Unfortunately a foot injury at the end of the 1999/2000 season interrupted his career, just as he had broken into the reserve side. He spent most of the next season playing with the Under 19s squad.

CAVE, MICHAEL — *Defender*
Current Club: Newcastle Blue Star

D o B: 12/11/1979   *Birthplace: Newcastle*
Previous clubs include: Newburn - July 2000.

CAWTHORN, PAUL — *Forward*
Current Club: Glasshoughton Welfare

D o B: 26/05/1975   *Birthplace: Yorkshire*
Previous clubs include: Tadcaster Alb - February 2000, Glasshoughton Welfare, Harrogate T, Frickley Ath., Guiseley, Farsley Celtic, Guiseley, Scarborough.

CECIL, DANNY — *Defender*
Current Club: Croydon Athletic

Birthplace: Surrey
Previous clubs include: Dulwich Hamlet - August 2001, Croydon MO, Whyteleafe.

CEGIELSKI, JAN — *Forward*
Current Club: Afan Lido

D o B: 25/01/1971   *Birthplace: Wales*
Signed last season from Port Talbot. Jan was previously with Llanelli, Haverfordwest and Treowen, and therefore has plenty of LoW experience. A fully committed player who can be a prolific goalscorer.

CERAOLO, MARK — *Forward*
Current Club: Accrington Stanley

D o B: 10/11/1975   *Birthplace: Birkenhead*
Previous clubs include: Ashton Utd - July 1999, Chorley, Morecambe, Crewe Alexandra.

CHADBOURNE, MARTYN — *Defender*
Current Club: Eastwood Town

Birthplace: Nottingham
Previous clubs include: Notts Co - July 1994.

CHADDERTON, DANNY — *Midfielder*
Current Club: Mossley

Birthplace: Oldham
Previous clubs include: Oldham Ath - January 2002.

CHADWICK, GARETH — *Midfielder*
Current Club: Warrington Town

Birthplace: Cheshire
Previous clubs include: Nantwich T - July 2001, Winsford Utd, Newtown, Crewe Alexandra.

CHALK, IAN — Midfielder
Current Club: Bemerton Heath Harlequins
Birthplace: Wiltshire
Previous clubs include: Salisbury C - July 2001, Warminnster T, Bemerton Ath., Swindon T, Peterborough Utd, Wrexham.

CHALKLEY, MATT — Forward
Current Club: Potters Bar Town
Birthplace: Herts
Previous clubs include: Welwyn Garden C - July 2000, Hatfield T.

CHALLENDER, GREG — Defender
Current Club: Ashton United
D o B: 05/02/1973   Birthplace: Rochdale
Previous clubs include: Leek T - January 2002, Northwich Victoria, Chorley, Droylsden, Finn Harps, Droylsden, Barrow, Winsford Utd, Accrington Stanley, Stalybridge Celtic, Altrincham, Bath C, Southport, Preston NE, Mossley, Horwich RMI, Oldham Ath.

CHALLINOR, JON — Midfielder
Current Club: St.Albans City
D o B: 02/12/1970   Birthplace: Northampton
Very highly-rated midfielder who started his career with Rushden & Diamonds. Moved to Stamford at the start of the 2000/01 season in search of first-team football and impressed so much that he earned a moved into the Dr Martens League Premier Division with Cambridge City in February 2001. Was one of the successes of the 2001/02 season at Milton Road, but then moved to St Albans City in August 2002 after a spell in America with Kalamazoo Kingdom.

CHALLINOR, PAUL — Defender
Current Club: Hyde United
D o B: 06/04/1976   Birthplace: Newcastle-under-Lyme
Experienced defender who joined UniBond Premier side Hyde United in July 2002 after a short spell out of the game. Began his career with Birmingham and then had a short spell with Lincoln. He then turned out for Baldock Town, Telford United and League of Wales side Aberystwyth before having a brief return to League football with Bury. Returned to the Non-League scene with Ilkeston Town in the summer of 2000.

CHAMBERLAIN, BEN — Midfielder
Current Club: Newtown AFC
D o B: 05/06/1982   Birthplace: Lancashire
Previous clubs include: Chester C - February 2002, Blackburn R.

CHAMBERLAIN, DEAN — Midfielder
Current Club: Rye & Iden United
Birthplace: Sussex
Young midfielder who is a former Gillingham trainee. Played for Hastings reserves during 1999/2000 and switched to Hailsham the following season. Transferred to Rye early into the latest campaign.

CHAMBERLIN, TERRY — Midfielder
Current Club: Ruislip Manor
D o B: 27/09/1982   Birthplace: London
Previous clubs include: Wealdstone - March 2002, Boreham Wood, Wembley.

CHAMBERS, DAVID — Forward
Current Club: Sheffield FC
Birthplace: Nottingham
Previous clubs include: Staveley Miners Welfare - January 2002, Eastwood T, Hull C.

CHAMBERS, LEROY — Forward
Current Club: Belper Town
D o B: 25/10/1972   Birthplace: Sheffield
Well-travelled and prolific goalscorer who joined UniBond First Division side Belper Town in August 2002 for a four-figure fee from Premier Division Frickley Athletic. Made almost 100 League appearances with Sheffield Wednesday, Chester City, and Chesterfield. Then went Non-League with Boston United before returning to the full-time game with Macclesfield. Spells with Altrincham, Hucknall Town and Bradford Park Avenue followed before he joined Frickley in January 2002.

CHAMBERS, PAUL — Midfielder
Current Club: Folkestone Invicta
D o B: 19/03/1972   Birthplace: Kent
Having returned to Folkestone Invicta during the summer of 2002 for a sixth spell, Paul started the season as the clubs record appearance holder and goalscorer in senior football. He loves to get forward and is always at the hub of things. Paul first joined Invicta from Lydd Town for the 1994/95 season and has also had spells at Dover Athletic, Ashford Town and Tonbridge Angels. Scored the clubs first ever goal in the Dr Martens Premier Division when he was captain and top goalscorer during the 2000/01 season.

CHAMP, DAVE — Defender
Current Club: Oxford City
Previous clubs include: Thame Utd - August 2001.

CHAMP, PAUL — Defender
Current Club: Clacton Town
Birthplace: Colchester
Previous clubs include: Halstead T - July 2000, Gas Recreation, Halstead T, Witham T, Clacton T, Colchester Utd (Trainee).

CHAMPION, NEIL — Midfielder
Current Club: Havant & Waterlooville
D o B: 05/11/1975   Birthplace: Hampshire
Signed for Havant & Waterlooville from Ryman League Aldershot Town in August 2000, for whom he made 111 appearances in three seasons. Neil started as an apprentice at Bournemouth. He has also played for Havant Town and Fareham Town. A positive asset to the team, Neil made his 50th appearance at the beginning of this season.

CHAMPION, TOBY — Defender
Current Club: Chichester City United
Birthplace: Hampshire
Former Havant &Waterlooville defender who played a handful of times for Chichester City at the start of 1998/99; spent the latter half of the next season with Sidlesham (Division Two champions); transferred to Chi in October 2000.

CHANDLER, DEAN — Defender
Current Club: Purfleet
D o B: 05/06/1976   Birthplace: London
Previous clubs include: Woking - November 2001, Slough T, Yeovil T, Lincoln C, Torquay Utd, Charlton Ath.

CHANDLER, IAN — Forward
Current Club: Whitley Bay
D o B: 20/03/1968   Birthplace: Sunderland
Honours won: England Schoolboy Int.
Ian has just resigned for the club. He left in 1995 after six years in which he made 260 appearances scoring 120 goals making him third in Whitleys all time scoring charts. Ian is just at home in the centre of defence or as sweeper but it his goalscoring prowess which puts fear into many opposition defences.

CHANDLER, MARTIN — Midfielder
Current Club: Folkestone Invicta
D o B: 09/01/1983   Birthplace: Kent
Teenager who originally progressed through Folkestone Invictas youth ranks before being signed by West Ham United. A creative midfield player, Martin rejoined from the Hammers in February 2001.

CHANDLER, SHAYNE — Defender
Current Club: Cheshunt
D o B: 29/09/1972
Previous clubs include: Wealdstone - October 2001, Enfield, Edgware T, Cheshunt, Beaconsfield SYCOB, Burnham, Fisher Ath., Finchley.

CHANDLER, STUART — Midfielder
Current Club: Chichester City United
Birthplace: Sussex
Stealth-like attacking midfielder: originally joined Chichester City in 1996: had a poor disciplinary record during 1999/2000, and ended that campaign at Bognor Regis after serving a lengthy ban: principally played for Moneyfields (Wessex League) last season, but also scored four Chichester goals: capable of producing some really skilful touches and is also a great free-kick taker.

CHANG, SIMON — Goalkeeper
Current Club: Yeading
Birthplace: Stevenage
Previous clubs include: Edgware T - January 2002, Stevenage B.

CHANNELL, LEE — Forward
Current Club: Maidenhead United
D o B: 18/09/1971   Birthplace: Hillingdon
Previous clubs include: Feltham - July 1999, Hillingdon B.

CHAPMAN, ALAN — Defender
Current Club: Bideford
Birthplace: Devon
Honours won: FA Vase Winners
Alan joined us for a third time this summer, from League Champions Taunton Town, and played in their F.A Vase winning side last season. He is an uncompromising wingback, who has also played for Barnstaple Town, Clevedon & Torrington. He has also played for Devon.

CHAPMAN, ANDY — Forward
Current Club: Penrith
Birthplace: Cumbria
Previous clubs include: Kirkby Stephen - July 1997, Stokes Valley (New Zealand), Kirkby Stephen.

CHAPMAN, ANTHONY — Midfielder
Current Club: Bedlington Terriers
Birthplace: Newcastle
A youngster who caught the eye of the Bedlington management with his displays against the Terriers last season for Easington.

Eventually the Terriers swooped and Chappy became a Bedlington player in August 2000. Plays mainly on the right hand side of midfield and has electric pace, good crossing ability and an eye for goal. Formerly with Gateshead who may yet regret letting him go. Rumoured to have many a scout casting an eye over him.

CHAPMAN, DANNY — Defender
Current Club: Tonbridge Angels
D o B: 19/04/1981   Birthplace: London
A defender who was with Barnet before moving to Welling. Joined Folkestone at the start of the season and then switched to Tonbridge in December 2001.

CHAPMAN, DANNY G. — Midfielder
Current Club: Dover Athletic
D o B: 21/11/1974   Birthplace: Greenwich
Played for Leyton Orient (78 appearances), Millwall (12), Hastings Town, Welling United and Dover Athletic before joining Folkestone Invicta in August 2001. A battling midfield player who captained the Dr Martens League X1 against the FA X1 at Crawley in November 2001, he returned to Dover in June 2002.

CHAPMAN, GARY — Forward
Current Club: Pickering Town
D o B: 01/05/1964   Birthplace: Bradford
Previous clubs include: Harrogate T - July 2000, Farsley Celtic, Harrogate T, Hatfield Main, Bradford PA, Farsley Celtic, Emley, Darlington, Torquay Utd, Exeter C, Notts Co., Mansfield T, Notts Co., Bradford C, Farsley Celtic, Harrogate RA.

CHAPMAN, IAN — Defender
Current Club: Whitehawk
D o B: 31/05/1970   Birthplace: Brighton
Ex-professional with Brighton & Hove Albion and Gillingham, appointed Whitehawk manager for the start of the 2001/02 season. Evidently well-connected and has assembled a variety of talent at East Brighton Park still makes occasional appearances on the pitch, performing as sweeper.

CHAPMAN, JAMES — Midfielder
Current Club: Thornaby on Tees
Birthplace: Newcastle
Previous clubs include: Billingham T - December 2001, Spennymoor Utd, Billingham T, Crook T.

CHAPMAN, JIMMY — Goalkeeper
Current Club: Ford United
Birthplace: Essex
Honours won: Ryman League Div.One Winners
Veteran goalkeeper who also had the honour of guiding Ford United to the Ryman League Division One title as chairman s well as keeper! Started his days at Watford before moving into the Non-League scene with Rainham Town, Purfleet, Aveley, Collier Row, East Thurrock Unitedand Barking. Returned to Ford in September 1996 to begin his third spell with the club.

CHAPMAN, PAUL — Defender
Current Club: Borrowash Victoria
Birthplace: Derbyshire
Previous clubs include: Heanor T - July 1998.

CHAPPELL, GRAHAM — Defender
Current Club: Epsom And Ewell
Birthplace: Surrey
Joined Epsom in 1999-2000 from Merstham, where he played in the youth side. Since making his first team debut in November

1999, he made the righ-back slot his own until picking up a knee injury in December.

CHAPPLE, SHAUN — *Midfielder*

Current Club: Carmarthen Town

D o B: 14/02/1973   *Birthplace: Swansea*
Honours won: Wales u-21 & B Int.
Previous clubs include: Newport Co - March 2001, Forest Green R, Merthyr Tydfil, Swansea C.

CHARIE, DAMIEN — *Midfielder*

Current Club: Hednesford Town

Birthplace: Birmingham
A highly-promising young attacking midfielder who is another player who has progressed to the first team from Dr Martens Premier side Hednesford Town's successful youth set-up. Has only a handful of first team appearances to his name, but is already creating quite an impression.

CHARITY, SIMON — *Midfielder*

Current Club: Chippenham Town

Birthplace: Bristol
Signed for Dr Martens Premier side Chippenham Town from Paulton Rovers in July 1998. He is a very talented midfield player who possesses as superb engine. He has been a vital member of the team in both of the clubs recent promotions as well as playing in all four of the clubs recent cup finals, including Wembley where he played in central midfield in the FA Vase final. Along with Steve Brown he is the longest-serving member of the team and the club were delighted when he agreed to stay for another season. Has also seen service with Odd Down, Mangotsfield United, Gloucester City and Bristol Rovers, where he was a trainee.

CHARLERY, KEN — *Forward*

Current Club: Farnborough Town

D o B: 28/11/1964   *Birthplace: Stepney*
Honours won: England Semi-Pro Int.
Ken signed for Farnborough Town in May 2002 after helping Dagenham & Redbridge to the runners-up spot in the Conference. He joined the Daggers on a free transfer in October 2000 from Boston United and has also played for Peterborough United, Watford, Birmingham City, Southend United, Stockport County and Barnet. He joined Boston United in September 2000 from Barnet for £25,000 having finished the previous year as the Bees top goalscorer. It didnt take him long to settle in at York Street and he scored 16 goals from 34 starts in the Conference last season. He broke into the England semi-professional team, scoring on his debut in Holland.

CHARLES, ANTHONY — *Defender*

Current Club: Aldershot Town

D o B: 11/03/1981   *Birthplace: Isleworth*
Impressive central defender who joined Ryman Premier side Aldershot Town in July 2002 from Hayes. Started his career with Spartan Leaguers Brook House and was then snapped up by Crewe for £5,000 in June 2000. Couldnt quite make the breakthrough into League football but, following a successful loan spell in the Conference with Hayes, joined the Missioners on a permanent basis in October 2001.

CHARLES, JAMIE — *Midfielder*

Current Club: Flackwell Heath

Birthplace: Berkshire
Previous clubs include: Marlow - October 2001, Flackwell Heath, Maidenhead Utd.

CHARLES, LEE — *Forward*

Current Club: Aldershot Town

D o B: 20/08/1971   *Birthplace: Hillingdon*
Honours won: England Semi-Pro Int.
Former England semi-professional international striker who signed for Ryman Premier side Aldershot Town in July 2002 from Conference outfit Nuneaton Borough. Had signed for Nuneaton from Hayes in June under the Bosman ruling. Hillingdon-born, Lee was a member of the England semi-professional international squad throughout the 2000/01 season although he made his debut against Italy in March 1999. He scored 38 times in 103 appearances for Hayes following his arrival from Queens Park Rangers. He also had a short stint at Barnet where he was a first team regular scoring 19 goals in 51 games.

CHARLES, STEVE — *Midfielder*

Current Club: Matlock Town

D o B: 10/05/1960   *Birthplace: Sheffield*
42-year-old Steve is a vastly-experienced midfielder who joined the Gladiators in pre-season. Formerly with Sheffield United, he spent time as a player under Ernie Moss at Boston United and Gainsborough Trinity. He has impressed with his knowledge, fitness and performances since his arrival.

CHARLTON, ASA — *Defender*

Current Club: Stourport Swifts

Previous clubs include: Rushall Olympic - July 2001, Sandwell B, Willenhall T, Telford Utd, Willenhall T, Kidderminster Harriers.

CHARLTON, DANNY — *Forward*

Current Club: Peterlee Newtown

Birthplace: Co.Durham
From Local football - July 2001.

CHARLTON, STEVE — *Midfielder*

Current Club: Shifnal Town

Birthplace: Shropshire
Previous clubs include: Chasetown - October 2001,Rushall Olympic, Sandwell B, Willenhall T, Ettingshall HT.

CHARMAN, GARY — *Forward*

Current Club: Horsham

Birthplace: Sussex
Began as a Horsham youth team player in 1996: scored 22 goals for the club during 2000/01, including one against Yeovil in the final qualifying round of the FA Cup (drew 1-1 before losing the replay 0-2).

CHARMAN, PAUL — *Defender*

Current Club: Horsham YMCA

Birthplace: Sussex
Defender: previously with Horsham (brother of Hornets winger Gary Charman) before having a spell at Redhill: joined YM in November 2001.

CHARTERS, ROSS — *Goalkeeper*

Current Club: Felixstowe & Walton United

Birthplace: Suffolk
Joined the club in the close season from Suffolk & Ipswich League side Ransomes, having had previous Jewson League experience with Stowmarket Town. Ross is any ever present in the side and an excellent shot stopper.

CHATER, JIMMY — *Defender*

Current Club: Eastbourne United

Birthplace: Sussex

Real heavyweight defender who re-signed for United from neighbours Eastbourne Town in October 1999: only made limited appearances during the latter half of 2000/01, due to a combination of injuries and suspensions (suffers from a recurring hip problem): continued to be sidelined during the autumn 2001 after fracturing his jaw.

CHATFIELD, IAN — *Goalkeeper*

Current Club: Horsham

D o B: 10/11/1972   Birthplace: Sussex

Highly-rated goalkeeper and one-time Chelsea youth. Joined Horsham from Redhill during the 2000 close season and has since made 100+appearances for the Hornets: had previously spent time at Crawley as well as playing for Sussex.

CHATTOE, RICHARD — *Defender*

Current Club: Guiseley

Birthplace: Bristol

Previous clubs include: Thackley - February 2002, Histon, Baldock T, Cambridge C, Baldock T, Weston-Super-Mare, Bristol R.

CHEAL, MARK — *Forward*

Current Club: Kendal Town

Birthplace: Lancaster

Previous clubs include: Lancaster C - August 2001.

CHEESMAN, GARY — *Midfielder*

Current Club: Staines Town

D o B: 18/01/1974   Birthplace: Hampshire

A versatile player, equally at home in either full back position or anywhere across the midfield. Gary joined Staines Town in the summer of 2000 from Farnborough Town and previously played for Aldershot Town.

CHEETHAM, ANDY — *Defender*

Current Club: Gresley Rovers

Birthplace: Derby

Talented defender who was on the books at Derby County as a youngster. The had spells with Stapenhill and Burton Albion before joining Gresley Rovers in March 1999. The son of former Gresley player Keith Cheetham, Ady was promoted from the reserve team during the 2000/01 season after being voted as reserve team managers Player of the Year.

CHEETHAM, CAINE — *Forward*

Current Club: Belper Town

Birthplace: Sheffield

Previous clubs include: Alfreton T - March 2002, Maltby Main, Buxton, Matlock T, Alfreton T, Matlock T, Hatfield Main.

CHEETHAM, MICHAEL — *Midfielder*

Current Club: AFC Sudbury

D o B: 30/06/1967   Birthplace: Amsterdam, Holland

Another greatly experienced player having played for Ipswich Town, Cambridge United and Chesterfield. An inspiration to those around him, he assists AFC Sudbury manager Keith Martin in coaching the squad.

CHENERY, BEN — *Defender*

Current Club: Canvey Island

D o B: 28/01/1977   Birthplace: Ipswich

Honours won: FA Trophy Winners

Solid defender who started his career at Luton Town where he made two League appearances. Joined Cambridge United in July 1997. Ben made 96 appearances for the Us, scoring 2 goals, before joining Kettering Town in July 2000. He joined Canvey Island in December 2000.

CHENERY, CARL — *Midfielder*

Current Club: Lowestoft Town

Birthplace: Great Yarmouth

Previous clubs include: Leiston - February 2000.

CHENOWETH, PAUL — *Midfielder*

Current Club: Tiverton Town

D o B: 05/02/1973   Birthplace: Bristol

An all action midfield dynamo who is just as hyperactive off the pitch as he is on it. Has the ability to piece together quick passing movements and provide the forward impetus to get out of trouble. Provides a vital fluid link between defence and attack, and makes the sort of runs from midfield beyond the forwards that keep defenders awake at night. Left Gloucester City for Merthyr when the then manager was sacked in March 2000, but never took to the Welsh valleys and returned to Meadow Park on another free in July 2000. Pauls career started with Bristol Rovers, earning a pro contract at the Gas before really making his name in local football in four seasons in the Conference with Bath. He moved to Cheltenham for £15,000 where his goal scoring form attracted League clubs to watch him. He then moved on to Worcester City in 1998 but failed to settle at St. Georges Lane. Paul was quickly signed by Tiverton Town in March 2001.

CHESSEL, COURTNEY — *Midfielder*

Current Club: Fairford Town

Birthplace: Gloucestershire

Previous clubs include: Purton - July 2001.

CHESTER, ADAM — *Forward*

Current Club: Cradley Town

Birthplace: Birmingham

Previous clubs include: Willenhall T - July 2000, Oldbury Utd.

CHESTER, DEREK — *Defender*

Current Club: Selsey

Birthplace: Sussex

Versatile performer, generally recognized as a defender. Introduced into the Littlehampton side at the start of 1999/2000 (scored 9 times that year). Vastly improved the following season and built a reputation for being a real utility man. Has a habit of appearing from nowhere to score goals (struck 10 times during 2000/01). Signed for Selsey in October 2001.

CHESTER, STEVE — *Defender*

Current Club: Tiptree United

Birthplace: Essex

Previous clubs include: Harwich & Parkeston - July 1999, Tiptree Utd.

CHESTERFIELD, GAVIN — *Defender*

Current Club: Llanelli AFC

D o B: 18/08/1979   Birthplace: Neath

Previous clubs include: Rhayader T - July 2000, Merthyr Tydfil, Exeter C.

CHESTERS, BEN — Midfielder

Current Club: Leighton Town

Birthplace: Tring

Honours won: English Public Schools Rep.

Former English Public Schools representative midfielder who followed manager Paul Burgess to Ryman Division Two side Leighton Town from Tring Town in July 2002. Had signed for Tring from neighbours Tring Athletic at the start of the 2001/02 season.

CHEWINS, JASON — Defender

Current Club: Aldershot Town

A left back who has proved popular with the supporters and is now the longest-serving player at the club. Is one of only three players to make 250-plus appearances for the club and has Mark Butlers record of 303 matches firmly in his sights. Joined in July 1994 after serving Alton Town, Basingstoke Town and Wealdstone.

CHEWTER, CHRIS — Forward

Current Club: Hamble ASSC

Birthplace: Hampshire

Previous clubs include: Sarisbury Green - July 2000.

CHILLINGSWORTH, CARL — Forward

Current Club: Bishop Auckland

Birthplace: Co Durham

Former Whitby Town forward who signed for Bishop Auckland in pre-season 2001 following the departure of Danny Mellanby to Darlington. Scored in his first four games for the club, and lead the goalscoring charts for the 2001/02 season. Formerly with Irish side Coleraine and Guisborough Town.

CHIN, TONY — Defender

Current Club: Dulwich Hamlet

Birthplace: London

Highly-rated central defender who had joined Croydon during the summer of 2001 from local rivals Dulwich Hamlet. A former West Ham and Fulham junior, Tony had been with Dulwich since youth team days, making around 200 first-team appearances in that time. Returned home to Dulwich in March 2002.

CHINNERY, JON — Midfielder

Current Club: Hadleigh United

Birthplace: Suffolk

Busy, aggressive midfielder who can also play up front. Played an important role in Hadleighs Reserves promotion last term and now looking to establish himself as regular part of the first team set up. Second full season with the Club.

CHISHOLM, MARK — Defender

Current Club: Holmer Green

Birthplace: Bucks

Previous clubs include: Stokenchurch - July 1993, Chesham Utd, Burnham, Amersham T.

CHIVERS, DAVID — Forward

Current Club: Whitley Bay

Birthplace: Ashington

Another recent signing, David shown in our friendlies that he has a great left foot and is an excellent crosser of the ball. Has also played at Ashington, South Shields and Morpeth Town.

CHIVERTON, ESTON — Defender

Current Club: Haverfordwest County

D o B: 22/12/1971   Birthplace: Bristol

Previous clubs include: Cinderford T - December 2001, Weston-Super-Mare, Cwmbran T, Merthyr Tydfil, Ebbw Vale, Evesham Utd, Cinderford T, Bath C, Cinderford T, Inter Cardiff, Ton Pentre, Newport AFC, Merthyr Tydfil, Cardiff Civil Service.

CHORLEY, KEVIN — Midfielder

Current Club: Bridgwater Town

D o B: 13/07/1983   Birthplace: Somerset

Previous clubs include: Plymouth Argyle (Junior) - July 2000.

CHRISTIE, OLLIE — Midfielder

Current Club: Dereham Town

Birthplace: Norfolk

Ex-Fakenham Town and Diss Town. Terrorises defenders with his pace and skill downthe left-hand flank.

CHRISTIE, TINIO — Midfielder

Current Club: Basingstoke Town

Birthplace: New Zealand

Honours won: New Zealand Int.

Previous clubs include: Bisley Sports - February 2002, North Shore (New Zealand).

CHRISTISON, JOSH — Midfielder

Current Club: Whitehawk

Birthplace: Australia

Australian midfielder who joined Whitehawk during the summer of 2001, and had previously been with Croydon Kings in his home country. Said to possess ability to read and anticipate play before opponents.

CHRISTOPHE, STEVE — Forward

Current Club: Feltham

Birthplace: Leytonstone

Ex-QPR Youth player Christophe played in Felthams successful youth side of 1993/1994 when they reached the FA Youth Cup 2nd Round. Since then Steve has been in & out of the side, due to injury and suspension. When fit Steve was a 1st team regular, playing right midfield or as wingback. Two seasons ago and now established as a striker, Steve joined local rivals Walton Casuals and finished as their top scorer. Christophe rejoined Feltham during the summer of 1998/1999 and hit 38 goals in his first season. Last season after hitting 18 goals in as many games a recurring hamstring injury ruled him out for the final three months of the season.

CHRISTOPHER, JON — Defender

Current Club: Wokingham Town

Birthplace: Berkshire

From Youth team.

CHUDY, LEE — Forward

Current Club: Staines Town

D o B: 06/08/1980   Birthplace: Reading

Left-winger or striker who was on schoolboy forms with Crystal Palace, Nottingham Forest and Reading. Moved to Wokingham Town and from there to Basingstoke Town. Joined Staines Town on-loan in September 2001 and the move was made permanent two months later.

CHURCH, DANNY — Defender
Current Club: Romford
Birthplace: Essex
Previous clubs include: Aveley - January 2001.

CHURCHILL, PHIL — Forward
Current Club: Burgess Hill Town
D o B: 19/10/1973   Birthplace: Sussex
Predatory striker: top scorer for Broadbridge Heath in 1994/95 before moving to Horsham YMCA: headed YMs goal charts too for the next two seasons prior to a spell with Wick: overall leading marksman in the County League Division One when returning to YM during 1998/99 (also represented Sussex): spent a brief period with East Preston at the start of the following campaign before once again going back to Gorings Mead (November 2000): strong as ever in 2000/01, when regaining his crown as the leagues leading scorer with a tally of 36: has built a reputation for goals that strike right through the net - had one of these disallowed in an FA Cup match against Cowes in September 2000 (scored five others that did count), and repeated the trick in a Sussex Senior Cup match at Shoreham in March 2001 (goal was allowed to stand that time): joined Burgess Hill in September 2001.

CHURCHILL-BROWNE, KEVIN — Defender
Current Club: Marlow
Birthplace: Berkshire
Previous clubs include: Maidenhead Utd - August 2000, Slough T.

CIRCUIT, STEVE — Midfielder
Current Club: Alfreton Town
D o B: 11/04/1972   Birthplace: Sheffield
Honours won: NCEL & Cup Winners
Steve was released as part of Gainsborough Trinitys cost-cutting exercise in January 2002, but their loss was certainly Alfreton Town's gain. Steve plays in midfield but can also play just as comfortably in the right back position. His former clubs include Leek Town, Macclesfield Town, Boston United, Stalybridge Celtic and Scarborough. His wealth of experience helped Town to promotion back to the UniBond League.

CLANDON, MICHAEL — Defender
Current Club: St.Helens Town
Birthplace: Liverpool
Previous clubs include: Burscough - March 2002.

CLARE, DARYL — Forward
Current Club: Boston United
D o B: 01/08/1978   Birthplace: Jersey
Honours won: Republic of Ireland u-21 Int.
Boston United signed up Republic of Ireland under-21 International Daryl Clare from Grimsby Town in the summer Of 2001. He had two loan spells with Northampton Town and one with Cheltenham Town during his time with Grimsby. Overall made 118 League appearances, scoring 13 goals.

CLARIDGE, ROB — Forward
Current Club: Mangotsfield United
D o B: 13/03/1980   Birthplace: Bristol
Promising young striker who signed for Mangotsfield United from Weston Super Mare in June 2000. Previously with Bristol Rovers, he had previous Dr Martens League experience with Yate Town and Clevedon Town. Hard-working player who gives everything week in week out, his work rate has made him popular with the supporters, he will never give anything less than 100% committment.

CLARK, BILLY — Defender
Current Club: Newport County
D o B: 19/05/1967   Birthplace: Christchurch
Vastly experienced defender with a Football League experience that encompassed ten years at Bristol Rovers, four years at Bournemouth and 18 months at Exeter. Signed for Newport County in June 2001 from Conference club Forest Green Rovers for whom he made almost a century of appearances in a two-year spell.

C

CLARK, CRAIG — Defender
Current Club: Kings Lynn
Birthplace: Nottingham
Craig signed for Kings Lynn from Stamford in November 1998. He was one of former Linnets boss Gary Mills players at Grantham Town during their Dr Martens League Midland Division championship season. He started off in and out of the side when he first arrived, but then become a regular starter in defence. Previously with Arnold Town, Ilkeston Town and Nottingham sides Dunkirk and Radcliffe Olympic.

CLARK, DEAN — Midfielder
Current Club: Hayes
D o B: 31/03/1980   Birthplace: Hillingdon
Previous clubs include: Uxbridge - August 2001, Brentford.

CLARK, JOE — Midfielder
Current Club: Lewes
Birthplace: Sussex
Signed from Horsham at the start of this season, Joe has begun to show us his best form, and scored his first goal for the Rooks at Molesey.

CLARK, KENNY — Forward
Current Club: Parkgate
Birthplace: Sheffield
Previous clubs include: Maltby Main - October 2001, Worksop T, Matlock T, Worksop T, Alfreton T, Worksop T, Kiveton Park.

CLARK, LEE — Goalkeeper
Current Club: Wembley
Birthplace: London
Previous clubs include: Farnborough T - August 2001, Chalfont St.Peter, St.Albans C.

CLARK, LEE — Midfielder
Current Club: Fairford Town
Birthplace: Gloucestershire
Previous clubs include: Cirencester Utd - July 2001, Fairford T.

CLARK, MARTIN — Defender
Current Club: Southport
Birthplace: Accrington
Martin can play at full-back or sweeper and is currently in his second spell at the club. Martin Southport joined from Rotherham where he had moved to from the Port along with manager Ronnie Moore. Martin has now played more games for the club than any other currently on the books.

CLARK, MICK — Goalkeeper
Current Club: Ossett Town
D o B: 02/03/1974   Birthplace: Leeds
A popular figure at Ingfield and has served the club well over the past three years. Began locally with Lower Hopton before helping Ossett Albion to the NCEL championship in 1999 before

switching to Town the following year. Has missed 9 months with a broken arm between March - December 2001.

CLARK, PETER — Defender

Current Club: AFC Totton

Birthplace: Hampshire
Previous clubs include: BAT Sports - May 2002.

CLARK, RICHARD — Defender

Current Club: Evesham United

Previous clubs include: Tamworth - March 2001, Evesham Utd, Cheltenham T, Forest Green R, Moreton T, Cheltenham T, Port Vale, Cheltenham T.

CLARK, SIMON — Goalkeeper

Current Club: Billingham Town

D o B: 12/11/1978   *Birthplace: Co.Durham*
Previous clubs include: Spennymoor Utd - July 2000, Billingham T, Northallerton T, South Bank, Dormans Ath, Wolviston.

CLARK, STEVE — Forward

Current Club: Aylesbury United

D o B: 04/02/1964   *Birthplace: Essex*
Previous clubs include: Canvey Island - August 2001, St.Albans C, Wivenhoe T, Saffron Walden T, Stansted.

CLARK, STEVE — Forward

Current Club: Tunbridge Wells

Birthplace: Kent
Previous clubs include: Sheppey Utd - July 1999, Tonbridge Angels, Canterbury C, Tunbridge Wells, Tonbridge.

CLARK, TIM — Midfielder

Current Club: Croydon

Birthplace: Surrey
A skilful hard-working midfield player who first joined Croydon in 1994, playing some 150+ games for the Trams, before retiring in 1998, after a number of injury problems. Fully recovered now, Tim re-joined the club in the summer of 2000 and and broke back into the first team towards the end of the season. Formerly a junior with Crystal Palace for whom he picked up an FA Youth Cup runners-up medal.

CLARK, TOBY — Defender

Current Club: Cirencester Town

Birthplace: Swindon
A young defender who was brought into the Cirencester Town first-team squad during the 2001/02 season. Another product of Cirencesters highly-successful Academy.

CLARKE, ADRIAN — Forward

Current Club: Stevenage Borough

D o B: 28/09/1974   *Birthplace: Cambridge*
Honours won: England Schoolboy Int.
Adrian joined Stevenage in the summer of 2000 on trial after being released by Southend, and was awarded a contract soon afterwards following some tremendous performances. The attacking midfielder started his career at Arsenal where he was part of a successful FA Youth cup winning side. Has made the left sided midfield role his own, and has proven himself a handy goalscorer. Also had loan spells at Carlisle and Rotherham, and has 120 league games behind him.

CLARKE, ALEX — Defender

Current Club: Haverhill Rovers

Birthplace: Suffolk
25-year-old sweeper/central midfield player. A former Ipswich Town Schoolboy player, is in his second spell at Haverhill Rovers, has had experience at Mildenhall Town and Histon.

CLARKE, ANDY — Defender

Current Club: Oadby Town

Birthplace: Leicester
Honours won: Combined Services Rep.
Previous clubs include: Kibworth T - July 1997.

CLARKE, CHRIS — Goalkeeper

Current Club: Marine

D o B: 01/05/1974   *Birthplace: Barnsley*
Goalkeeper who signed for Marine from Chorley in September 1998. Started at Bolton and then played in the League for Rochdale before a bad injury brought his League career to an end. Whilst with Dale he played at Anfield in the FA Cup 3rd round losing 1-7 to a rampant Liverpool. Now in his fourth season at Marine he has established himself as the number one choice rarely missing a game. Chris is a policeman.

CLARKE, DANNY — Forward

Current Club: Enfield Town (Essex)

Birthplace: Midlesex
Joined the club during the summer of 2001 from Barking. Yet another product of the Enfield FC reserve and Youth team set-up. Made 33 first team appearances at Enfield, scoring 1 goal. Currently leads both club and League goal-scoring charts.

CLARKE, DAVE — Defender

Current Club: Pelsall Villa

Birthplace: Wolverhampton
Previous clubs include: Bloxwich T - August 2000, Stapenhill, Pelsall Villa, Wednesfield, Bilston T.

CLARKE, DAVID — Midfielder

Current Club: Kingstonian

D o B: 20/09/1971   *Birthplace: Nottingham*
Fast and determined midfield player who signed for Kingstonian from Dover Athletic in June 2001. Began his career with Notts County and also played for Eastwood Town before moving south to join Harrow Borough. Moved to Dover in February 1998, where he was on the verge of the England semi-professional side in 1999.

CLARKE, DEAN — Midfielder

Current Club: Merthyr Tydfil

D o B: 28/07/1977   *Birthplace: Hereford*
Returned to Merthyr Tydfil in February 2000 as part of a player-exchange deal that took Garry Shephard to Newport County plus £3,000. In his previous spell at the club under Colin Addison, the midfielder made over 50 appearances scoring on 2 occasions when the team finished runners-up to Forest Green Rovers. Dean has previously played for Hereford United and Cheltenham Town.

CLARKE, DWAIN — pos###
Midield Current Club: Aylesbury United

Previous clubs include: Yeading - February 2001, Wealdstone, Yeading, St.Albans C, Harrow B, Leighton T, Harrow B, Luton T.

CLARKE, GARY　　　　　*Forward*
Current Club: Chester-Le Street
Birthplace: Co.Durham
Previous clubs include: Brandon Utd - September 2001, Consett, Middlesbrough.

CLARKE, HUGH　　　　　*Defender*
Current Club: Caersws
D o B: 15/06/1971　　　　　Birthplace: Wales
Previous clubs include: Rhayader T - July 1998, Caersws.

CLARKE, IAN　　　　　*Midfielder*
Current Club: Matlock Town
Birthplace: Chesterfield
A midfielder who was recommended to Ernie Moss by his current assistant Sean ONeill, before the Irishman was appointed as number two. Formerly with Staveley and Dagenham, much is expected from Ian this season.

CLARKE, JAMIE　　　　　*Forward*
Current Club: Grantham Town
D o B: 07/03/1982　　　　　Birthplace: Nottingham
Striker Jamie signed for Grantham Town in May 2002 from Kings Lynn. He had arrived at Lynn from Ilkeston Town in May 2001. He is seen as a highly-promising youngster who broke into the Robins first team during the 1999/00 season after a prolific scoring record in their reserve side. He possesses electric pace and has bags of ability and a good future.

CLARKE, KEVIN　　　　　*Forward*
Current Club: Romford
Birthplace: Essex
Previous clubs include: Tilbury - August 2001.

CLARKE, LEE　　　　　*Defender*
Current Club: Lordswood
Birthplace: Kent
From Local football - July 1992.

CLARKE, MARK　　　　　*Forward*
Current Club: Halesowen Harriers
Birthplace: Worcestershire
Previous clubs include: Brierley Hill T - July 1997.

CLARKE, MARK　　　　　*Midfielder*
Current Club: Eastwood Town
Birthplace: Nottingham
Previous clubs include: Gedling T - September 2001, Borrowash V, Hucknall T, Arnold T, Ilkeston T, Eastwood T, Arnold T, Ilkeston T, Arnold T, Eastwood T, Gedling T, Alfreton T, Eastwood T, Grimsby T.

CLARKE, MATTHEW　　　　　*Defender*
Current Club: Windsor & Eton
Birthplace: Berkshire
Previous clubs include: Marlow - March 2002, Windsor & Eton, Slough T, Burnham, Windsor & Eton, Eton Wick, Burnham.

CLARKE, MATTHEW　　　　　*Defender*
Current Club: Hereford United
Birthplace: Derbyshire
Previous clubs include: Hallam - October 2000, Maltby Main, Parkgate, Killamarsh, Chesterfield (Junior).

CLARKE, MATTHEW　　　　　*Defender*
Current Club: Denaby United
Birthplace: Cardiff
Honours won: British Universities Rep.
United's current player of the year signed from Kidderminster three years ago. A pacy full-back who likes to get forward.

CLARKE, PAUL　　　　　*Defender*
Current Club: Oldbury United
Birthplace: Birmingham
Previous clubs include: Stratford T - February 1999.

CLARKE, RICHARD　　　　　*Defender*
Current Club: Harrow Borough
Joined Harrow Borough in the summer of 2001 from Jewson Eastern League side Stanway Rovers. Previously with Luton Town and Scunthorpe United. Is a student.

CLARKE, ROB　　　　　*Goalkeeper*
Current Club: Mangotsfield United
Birthplace: Bristol
Honours won: England Schoolboy Int
Joined Mangotsfield United in February 2002 from Hellenic League side Hallen. A former England Schoolboy international, Rob was also a trainee at Bristol City, he has also played for Paulton Rovers and Chippenham Town in the Screwfix League and Almondsbury in the Hellenic League. Rob has excellent agility and has made a promising start to his career at Mangotsfield. Is a Marketing Executive.

CLARKE, ROB　　　　　*Goalkeeper*
Current Club: Stourport Swifts
Previous clubs include: Boldmere St.Michaels - August 1999, Northfield T.

CLARKE, ROY　　　　　*Defender*
Current Club: Sittingbourne
Birthplace: Kent
Previous clubs include: Fisher Ath - January 2000, Sittingbourne, Gravesend, Gillingham.

CLARKE, SIMON　　　　　*Defender*
Current Club: Chelmsford City
D o B: 23/09/1971　　　　　Birthplace: Chelmsford
Was Hendons longest-serving player with almost 400 appearances to his credit before signing for Dr Martens League side Chelmsford City in June 2002 after moving to the Essex area to live and work. A stylish and talented defender, he signed for Hendon at the start of the 1995/96 season from Kettering Town, but previously he had made 3 Football League appearances for West Ham United, making his debut in the away fixture at Manchester City. Supporters' Player of the Year 1996/97.

CLARKE, STUART　　　　　*Defender*
Current Club: Matlock Town
Birthplace: Sheffield
Previous clubs include: Hucknall T - March 2002, Sheffield Utd.

CLARKE, TIM　　　　　*Goalkeeper*
Current Club: Halesowen Town
D o B: 19/09/1968　　　　　Birthplace: Stourbridge
Honours won: Conference Winners, Dr Martens Western Div.Winners
Tim started his career with Halesowen back in the late eighties. The big goalkeeper was influential in the clubs promotion from the Dr Martens Midland Division back in the 1989/90 season. In

October 1990 he made a move to Coventry City for £25,000 but failed to make his mark at the club due to the popularity of Steve Ogrizovic. Huddersfield Town signed Tim for £15,000 in July 1991 and made over 80 appearances for the Beagles before returning to Halesowen Town on a free transfer in July 1993. However his stay was short as he left for Shrewsbury Town in October of that year. Later he joined Scunthorpe and then in 1999 joined Conference outfit Kidderminster Harriers. Made numerous appearances in the League for Harriers but lost his place to Stuart Brock and was released in the summer of 2001 when he joined Halesowen Town. Tim had an eventful 2001/02 season. First he got through to the Masters Finals with Coventry in July and joined up with Barry Town on loan for their two Champions League ties with the Azerjabani champions and FC Porto. Then, of course, he won the Western Division title with the Yeltz in May 2002.

CLARKE, TOM   Forward
Current Club: Diss Town
Birthplace: Norwich
From Youth team.

CLARKSON, ANDY   Defender
Current Club: Great Harwood Town
Birthplace: Bradford
Previous clubs include: Accrington Stanley - July 1996, Guiseley, Bradford C.

CLARKSON, GARY   Defender
Current Club: Peterlee Newtown
Birthplace: Co.Durham
Previous clubs include: Jarrow Roofing - July 1998, Harrogate T, Seaham Red Star, Shotton Comrades.

CLARKSON, PHIL   Midfielder
Current Club: Halifax Town
D o B: 13/11/1968   *Birthplace: Hambleton*
An experienced midfielder who was signed by Conference side Halifax Town in August 2002. Began his career in Non-League football with Fleetwood Town, then members of the Northern Premier League. before being signed by Crewe for £22,500 in October 1991. Went on to make over 300 League appearances for Crewe, Scunthorpe and Blackpool before being released by the latter at the end of the 2001/02 season.

CLARRY, ADAM   Midfielder
Current Club: Hemel Hempstead Town
D o B: 04/05/1978   *Birthplace: Watford*
Previous clubs include: Chalfont St.Peter - August 2001, Aylesbury Utd, London Colney, Sutton Utd, St.Albans C.

CLASSEY, ANDREW   Defender
Current Club: Walton Casuals
Birthplace: Surrey
Currently in his first season with Casuals, Andy is a left sided defender who joined from Chobham & Ottershaw.

CLAYDON, ANDREW   Forward
Current Club: AFC Sudbury
Birthplace: Suffolk
Joined AFC Sudbury at the beginning of last season from Newmarket Town. Porky is strong, pacey and finishes well in addition to being an unselfish provider of goals for others.

CLAYTON, LEE   Forward
Current Club: Selby Town
Birthplace: Selby
From Youth team.

CLEARY, JAMIE   Midfielder
Current Club: Uxbridge
D o B: 06/11/1974   *Birthplace: Middlesex*
A former Uxbridge youth player who has progressed through the ranks. Now an important member of the team and yet another success story from the clubs youth policy. He has made over 350 appearances in midfield.

CLEARY, KEVIN   Defender
Current Club: Uxbridge
D o B: 07/09/1976   *Birthplace: Middlesex*
Rejoined Uxbridge in January 1999 from Chertsey Town, whom he had left in the summer of 98. This classy defender was at Brentford as a youth and was the Uxbridge Supporters' Player of the year in 1997/98. Has now made over 200 appearances.

CLEGG, BRADLEY   Defender
Current Club: Witton Albion
Birthplace: Manchester
Previous clubs include: Mossley - August 2002, Manchester Utd (Junior).

CLEGG, CHRIS   Defender
Current Club: Armthorpe Welfare
Birthplace: Doncaster
Previous clubs include: Harrogate T - August 2001, Hatfield Main, Goole T, Hatfield Main.

CLEGG, ROSS   Midfielder
Current Club: Witton Albion
Birthplace: Manchester
Previous clubs include: Mossley - November 2001, Curzon Ashton, Bury, Manchester C (Junior).

CLEMENTS, MATTY   Forward
Current Club: Cambridge City
D o B: 17/09/1977   *Birthplace: Birmingham*
Striker who signed for Kings Lynn originally on loan from Cambridge United in December 2001 and then made the move permanent in February 2002. He began his career as a trainee at West Ham United and was offered a professional contract but declined, opting instead to pursue a career in athletics as he was being touted as a future world-beater over the 110m hurdles. Injury prevented this promise from being fulfilled so he turned his attentions back to football. He has a reputation for terrorising defences with his pace. Transferred to home-town club Cambridge City in May 2002.

CLEVERLEY, WAYNE   Midfielder
Current Club: Bath City
Previous clubs include: Swindon T (Trainee) - August 2000.

CLEWLEY, JASON   Defender
Current Club: Clacton Town
Birthplace: Essex
A strong, no-nonsense super centre half with great ability and confidence on the ball. Previous clubs include Wivenhoe Town.

CLEWLEY, JIMMY — Midfielder
Current Club: Clacton Town
Birthplace: Essex
Very Strong player with good skill and top finishing. Joined Clacton from Wivenhoe in December 2000.

CLIFF, STUART — Midfielder
Current Club: Kendal Town
Previous clubs include: Fleetwood Freeport - July 2001, Bamber Bridge, Great Harwood T, Accrington Stanley.

CLIFFORD, KEVIN — Defender
Current Club: Maidstone United
Birthplace: Kent
Previous clubs include: Ramsgate - July 2001, Lewes, Ramsgate, St.Leonards, Ramsgate, Hythe Utd, Folkestone Invicta, Gillingham (Trainee).

CLIFFORD, PETER — Defender
Current Club: Berkhamsted Town
Birthplace: Berkshire
Previous clubs include: Aylesbury Utd - December 2001, Berkhamsted T, Bishops Stortford, Berkhamsted T, Chesham Utd, Beaconsfield SYCOB.

CLIFFORD, STEVE — Forward
Current Club: Bridgnorth Town
D o B: 13/07/1973   Birthplace: Wales
Previous clubs include: Oswestry T - November 2001, Shifnal T, Newtown, Welshpool T, Stafford R, Mount Maunganui (New Zealand), Bay of Plenty (New Zealand), Shifnal T, Bridgnorth T, Llansantffraid, Bristol C.

CLIFTON, MARK — Defender
Current Club: Evesham United
Birthplace: Wolverhampton
Previous clubs include: Bilston T - November 2001, Blakenall, Bilston T, Redditch Utd, Dudley T, Stourport Swifts, Dudley Sports, Wolverhampton Wanderers.

CLITHEROE, LEE — Midfielder
Current Club: Lancaster City
D o B: 18/11/1978   Birthplace: Chorley
Lee signed for UniBond Premier side Lancaster City in January 2000 after being released by Oldham, and soon played in a League Cup Final win followed by a season as a regular on the left of midfield. He impressed in that role considerably with his general play. Looked likely to join Stalybridge Celtic in the summer of 2002 but decided to stay with the Dollies.

CLITHEROE, STEWART — Defender
Current Club: Lancaster City
Previous clubs include: Port Vale - August 2000.

CLOKE, CRAIG — Defender
Current Club: Dover Athletic
Birthplace: Dover
From Youth team.

CLOSE, JAMIE — Midfielder
Current Club: Kendal Town
Birthplace: Preston
Previous clubs include: Gretna - August 1998, Netherfield, Ilkeston T, Netherfield, Morecambe, Preston NE (Trainee).

CLOSE, RICHARD — Defender
Current Club: Kendal Town
Birthplace: Netherfield
Previous clubs include: Gretna - November 2001, Kendal T, Gretna, Netherfield, Ilkeston T, Netherfield, Morecambe, Netherfield.

C

CLOUGH, MICHAEL — Forward
Current Club: Glasshoughton Welfare
Birthplace: Yorkshire
Previous clubs include: Pontefract Collieries - July 1997, Glasshoughton Welfare, Pontefract Collieries.

CLOUGH, NIGEL — Midfielder
Current Club: Burton Albion
D o B: 19/03/1966   Birthplace: Sunderland
Honours won: England u-21, B & Full Int.
Nigel Clough was appointed manager of Burton Albion in October 1998, his appointment attracting wide media attention for the club and town of Burton on Trent. Nigel had an illustrious career and played at the very peak of his profession. Nigel began his playing career under the management of father Brian at Nottingham Forest in 1984. He made 311 appearances for the club, scoring 101 goals before joining Liverpool in June 1993 for £2.3 million. An injury hit three years at Anfield saw Nigel move to Manchester City. Injury forced him to retire from the full time game and his desire to get into management saw him acquire the hot seat at Burton Albion. The Sunderland born midfielder also won 14 full England caps to add to those earned at Under-21 and B level. As a manager Nigel has improved each season with two runners-up placings and a some superb cup runs which has seen the Brewers pick up the League Cup and Birmingham Senior Cup in recent years.

CLOUT, GENE — Midfielder
Current Club: Chatham Town
Previous clubs include: Tonbridge - August 2001, Sittingbourne, Herne Bay, Dorking, Whitstable T, Tonbridge, Canterbury C, Tonbridge, Gillingham (Trainee).

CLOWES, PAUL — Defender
Current Club: Leek Town
Birthplace: Stoke
Originally joined Leek Town in April 1987 following his release by Port Vale. Played in the 1990 FA Trophy final against Barrow and went on to play over 350 games for the club. Left for Ashton United in July 1994 for whom he made 263 appearances before returning to Harrison Park in August 2001. A commanding central defender who is also dangerous from set pieces.

CLUXTON, NEIL — Midfielder
Current Club: Sheffield FC
Birthplace: Nottinghamshire
Previous clubs include: Staveley Miners Welfare - July 2000, Eastwood T, Staveley MW, Worksop T.

CLYDE, DARRON — Defender
Current Club: Stamford
D o B: 26/03/1976   Birthplace: Northern Ireland
Darron is Stamfords skipper who joined the Daniels at the start of the 1999 / 2000 season. He was voted Players' Player of the season at the end of his first season after a run of fantastic performances. Darron started his career at Barnsley and turned out for Emley, Gateshead and Boston United.

COATES, DANNY — Defender
Current Club: Rushall Olympic
Birthplace: Birmingham
Previous clubs include: Bilston T - February 2002, Bridgnorth T, Bilston T, Oldbury Utd, Blakenall, Willenhall T, Rushall Olympic, Willenhall T, Stourbridge, Blakenall, Halesowen T, Hednesford T.

COATES, SCOTT — Defender
Current Club: Brandon United
Birthplace: Co.Durham
Strong, no-nonsense defender, who re-joined the club at the start of this season. Had previous experience with Ipswich, Sunderland, Berwick and Consett. Will be a valuable addition to the squad when he regains full fitness.

COATES, STEVE — Midfielder
Current Club: Ilkeston Town
D o B: 10/01/1977 — Birthplace: Leicester
Honours won: England Schoolboy Int.
Steve was an Ilkeston Town recruit from Gresley Rovers, for whom he played nearly 100 appearances and was voted Player of the Year in 2000/01, in March 2002. A cultured midfield performer, he started at Stoke City before turning out for Rothwell Town, VS Rugby, Leicester United and Hinckley United. Steve is a very highly-rated player and was once an England Schoolboy international.

COATHAM, STEVE — Defender
Current Club: Maidstone United
Birthplace: Kent
Previous clubs include: Erith & Belvedere - July 2001, Ashford T, Ramsgate, VCD Ath., Dartford, Welling Utd.

COATHUP, LEE — Defender
Current Club: Rhyl
D o B: 02/05/1967 — Birthplace: Singapore
Previous clubs include: Total Network Solutions - November 2001, Winsford Utd, Stalybridge Celtic, Barrow, Stalybridge Celtic, Witton Alb., Stalybridge Celtic, Vauxhall GM, Newtown, Everton.

COBB, NATHAN — Goalkeeper
Current Club: Wealdstone
D o B: 23/06/1978 — Birthplace: London
Nathan is a former Portsmouth Universities goalkeeper who had completed his studies and moved to the Harrow area, joining Wealdstone during the summer of 2001/02. Now back fit again after a nasty knee injury.

COBB, PAUL — Forward
Current Club: Canvey Island
D o B: 13/12/1972 — Birthplace: Essex
A diminutive but extremely lively striker who has been a prolific scorer in recent seasons. Began his playing career with Purfleet before joining Leyton Orient in 1990. Played five times in the League for the Os before returning to Purfleet in 1992. Then had a spell at Enfield before re-joining the Ship Lane outfit again in February 1996. Became the Fleets record goalscorer before transferring to Dagenham & Redbridge in July 1997 for £14,000, where he continued to be a prolific marksman. Switched to Canvey Island in the summer of 2001.

COBBY, LEE — Goalkeeper
Current Club: Bracknell Town
Birthplace: Bracknell
From Youth team.

COBURN, NEIL — Defender
Current Club: Histon
Birthplace: Ipswich
Previous clubs include: Cambridge C - February 2001, Chelmsford C, Ipswich T.

COBURN, STUART — Goalkeeper
Current Club: Leigh RMI
D o B: 05/05/1975 — Birthplace: Manchester
Originally signed for Altrincham from Trafford in March 1997 after playing a major part in their promotion to the UniBond 1st Division and played a major part in Altrinchams return to the Conference with 23 clean sheets in all competitions. Stuart missed two thirds of season 1999/00 due to injury but came back as good as ever. Supporters' Player of the year in season 98/99, he previously played for Maine Road and Irlam Town. Transferred to Leigh RMI in May 2002.

COCHRANE, GARY — Defender
Current Club: Lincoln United
Birthplace: Lincoln
Previous clubs include: Lincoln Moorlands - March 2002, Lincoln C, Lincoln Utd.

COCHRANE, JAMES — Defender
Current Club: Chalfont St.Peter
Birthplace: Wycombe
Previous clubs include: Flackwell Heath - October 2001, Chalfont St.Peter, Martin Baker.

COCHRANE, KARL — Forward
Current Club: Eccleshill United
Birthplace: Leeds
Previous clubs include: Thackley - August 2001, Eccleshill Utd, Ossett Alb., Halifax T, Brighouse T.

COCKBURN, ROBBIE — Forward
Current Club: Bedlington Terriers
Birthplace: Northumberland
Robbie joined the club from Alnwick Town in February 2001 after impressing against the Terriers in the Northumberland Senior Cup-ties. Equally at home in either wide position where his searing pace and close ball skills are a problem for most defenders. Prior to joining Bedlington has spent his entire career with Alnwick where he started in the u-10 side and progressed through the ranks to the 1st team. Did have a trial with Norwich City but didnt make the grade. Their loss, Bedlingtons gain as he has settled well and is showing he knows where the goal is.

COCKERILL, GARY — Goalkeeper
Current Club: Marlow
Birthplace: Berkshire
Previous clubs include: Chalfont St.Peter - July 2000, Marlow, Chalfont St.Peter, Flackwell Heath, Beaconsfield Utd.

COCKINGS, ROBERT — Defender
Current Club: Port Talbot Town
D o B: 26/02/1976 — Birthplace: Neath
Signed for Port Talbot in the summer of 1999 from Trefelin, Robert is a defender who established himself in the side during the 1999/00 campaign and was an ever-present towards the end of that successful season, where he made 31 appearances.

COCKRILL, DARREN — Defender

Current Club: Gorleston

Birthplace: Cambridge
Previous clubs include: Diss T - November 1999, Cambridge C.

CODDINGTON, MATT — Goalkeeper

Current Club: Billingham Synthonia

D o B: 17/09/1969   *Birthplace: Cleveland*
Previous clubs include: Guisborough T - August 2001, Whitby T, Darlington, Middlesbrough.

CODNER, ROBERT — Midfielder

Current Club: Banstead Athletic

D o B: 23/01/1965   *Birthplace: Walthamstow*
Vastly experienced midfielder with a tremendous predigree. Joined Ryman Division One South side Banstead Athletic in August 2002 from rivals Chertsey Town. Began his career with Spurs and then had a short spell with Leicester before making his name at Dagenham and then Barnet. His form with Barry Frys Bees earned him a then record £125,000 transfer to Brighton as he embarked on a professional career that took in over 350 League appearances with the likes of Reading, Peterborough, Barnet again, Southend and Cardiff. Played Conference football again for Kettering Town in 2000/01 and briefly for Dover the following season before joining Chertsey via Chesham United in january 2001.

COE, JUDD — Forward

Current Club: Maldon Town

Birthplace: Essex
Previous clubs include: Tiptree Utd - July 1996, Braintree T.

COE, PAUL — Forward

Current Club: Soham Town Rangers

Birthplace: Cambridgeshire
Previous clubs include: Watton Utd - July 2000, Soham Town R, Histon, Cambridge C, Rushden & Diamonds, Cambridge C, Sudbury T, Newmarket T.

COE, WAYNE — Midfielder

Current Club: Fakenham Town

Birthplace: Norfolk
Previous clubs include: Diss T - July 1994, Wroxham.

COGGER, NEIL — Forward

Current Club: Haverhill Rovers

Birthplace: Suffolk
Came back to Haverhill Rovers after a four year stint at Cambridge City and travelling abroad. A great left footed midfielder or striker with an eye for goal and a very professional attitude.

COHEN, TERRY — Defender

Current Club: Fisher Athletic (London)

From Youth team.

COKE, STUART — Forward

Current Club: Arnold Town

Birthplace: Nottingham
From Youth team.

COLBOURNE, GRAHAM — Forward

Current Club: Paulton Rovers

Birthplace: Bristol
Previous clubs include: Welton Rovers - November 2001, Bath C, Paulton R, Radstock T.

COLBRAN, SIMON — Midfielder

Current Club: Rye & Iden United

Birthplace: Sussex
Utility player: joined Langney Sports for a second time during the summer 1999, having previously spent time at Tonbridge Angels and Crowborough Ath (where he was player-manager): one of numerous quality performers to be introduced into the Rye line-up at the start of 2001/02, sparking off rumours that the club had substantial financial backing in an attempt to gain league promotion for the second year running.

C

COLCLOUGH, ANDY — Defender

Current Club: Rocester

Birthplace: Stoke
Previous clubs include: Goldenhill Wanderers - January 2002.

COLCLOUGH, STEVE — Defender

Current Club: Newcastle Town

Birthplace: Stoke
Previous clubs include: Kidsgrove Ath - September 2001, Eastwood Hanley, Newcastle T.

COLCOMBE, SCOTT — Defender

Current Club: Willenhall Town

D o B: 15/12/1971   *Birthplace: West Bromwich*
Skilful midfielder signed for Willenhall from Redditch, previously with WBA, Torquay Utd., Doncaster Rovers, Stourbridge and Stafford Rangers.

COLDRAKE, ROBBIE — Defender

Current Club: Brook House

Birthplace: Middlesex
Previous clubs include: Ruislip Manor - July 2000, Harefield Utd.

COLE, ANDY — Midfielder

Current Club: Thornaby on Tees

Birthplace: Cleveland
From Youth team.

COLE, BEN — Goalkeeper

Current Club: Brandon United

D o B: 23/10/1977   *Birthplace: Co.Durham*
A young keeper who joined Northern League side Brandon United in July 1998 from Gateshead. Has proved very reliable and played a major role in last two seasons successful teams. He was ever present last season. Previous clubs include Middlesbrough.

COLE, JAMIE — Defender

Current Club: Carterton Town

Birthplace: Oxford
Previous clubs include: Witney T - July 2000, Oxford C.

COLE, LEIGH — Midfielder

Current Club: Newport Isle Of Wight

Previous clubs include: Havant T - July 1997.

COLE, NEIL — Forward

Current Club: Bemerton Heath Harlequins

Birthplace: Wiltshire
Previous clubs include: Andover - July 1998, Trowbridge T, Bemerton Heath Harlequins, Downton.

COLE, TIM — Defender

Current Club: Dagenham & Redbridge

Birthplace: London

Highly-rated defender who is also capable of playing in midfield. Tim started his playing days with Walthamstow Pennant but had to wait until September 1995 for his debut due to an injury. Dagenham & Redbridge signed him in March 1997 from Leyton Pennant for a four-figure fee after being watched by many Football League scouts. Named the clubs player of the year in 1997/98, he has also represented the Ryman League.

COLEANO, RUDI — Forward

Current Club: Wakefield & Emley

Previous clubs include: Garforth T - August 2001, Guiseley, Barnsley.

COLEBY, PAUL — Forward

Current Club: Thornaby on Tees

Birthplace: Cleveland

From Youth team.

COLEMAN, ANDY — Defender

Current Club: Wisbech Town

Birthplace: Cambridgeshire

Previous clubs include: Soham Town Rangers - January 2002, Warboys T.

COLEMAN, JOHN — Forward

Current Club: Accrington Stanley

D o B: 12/10/1962 — *Birthplace: Liverpool*

Honours won: England Semi-Pro Int.

Previous clubs include: Ashton Utd - June 1999, Lancaster C, Morecambe, Witton Alb., Rhyl, Macclesfield T, Runcorn, Southport, Marine, Burscough, Kirkby T.

COLEMAN, OMARI — Midfielder

Current Club: Dulwich Hamlet

Birthplace: London

An exciting prospect, Omari is a fast and powerful attacking midfielder, who can also play on the left. A former Millwall junior, Omari joined Croydon two seasons ago, before breaking into the first team last season. Switched to Dulwich in January 2002.

COLEMAN, SIMON — Defender

Current Club: Ilkeston Town

D o B: 13/03/1968 — *Birthplace: Worksop*

A very experienced defender with over 400 League games under his belt. Signed for Dr Martens Premier side Ilkeston Town in August 2002, re-uniting with manager John McGinlay with whom he played at Bolton. Became a much-sought after player amongst Non-League sides after being released by Rochdale at the end of the 2001/02 season. Cost over £1.3 million in transfer fees moving from Mansfield to Middlesbrough and then Derby, Sheffield Wednesday, Bolton, Southend and Rochdale.

COLES, FRANK — Midfielder

Current Club: Cray Wanderers

D o B: 05/12/1964 — *Birthplace: London*

Previous clubs include: Bromley - March 2001, Enfield, Leyton-Wingate, Leytonstone & Ilford, Dagenham, Leytonstone & Ilford, Charlton Ath.

COLES, KEVIN — Midfielder

Current Club: Fairford Town

Birthplace: Gloucestershire

Previous clubs include: Mangotsfield Utd - July 2001.

COLES, NEIL — Defender

Current Club: Pelsall Villa

Birthplace: Birmingham

Previous clubs include: Rushall Olympic - September 1998, Pelsall Villa.

COLEY, JOHN — Forward

Current Club: Harlow Town

Birthplace: Hertfordshire

Joined Harlow Town in the summer of 2000 from Spartan South Midlands League side Letchworth. Scored 16 goals in 36 appearances in his first season and became a firm favourite with the Harlow crowd. Previously played for Stotfold, Barton Rovers and Hitchin Town.

COLKIN, LEE — Defender

Current Club: Morecambe

D o B: 15/07/1974 — *Birthplace: Nuneaton*

Signed for Morecambe from Hednesford Town during the summer of 2001. Started out as a trainee at Northampton Town. Played at Hednesford on loan before joining them in the summer of 1999.

COLL, OWEN — Defender

Current Club: Grays Athletic

D o B: 09/04/1976 — *Birthplace: Donegal*

Honours won: Republic of Ireland u-21 Int.

A former Tottenham Hotspur apprentice, Owen made his Football League debut for Bournemouth in March 1996 and made 24 appearances for the south coast club before joining Aldershot Town via a brief spell at Stevenage Borough. Owen, who has also represented the Republic of Ireland at junior and under-21 level, is a commanding central defender who is also comfortable at full back. Switched to Grays Athletic in May 2002.

COLLEY, CHAD — Midfielder

Current Club: Stocksbridge Park Steels

Birthplace: Yorkshire

Wide midfielder who returned to the UniBond League in August 2002 with Stocksbridge Park Steels after a spell with Northern Counties East Leaguers Goole AFC. Started out at Worksop Town and then played for Hallam, Alfreton Town and Denaby United, signing for Goole in November 2000.

COLLEY, NICK — Midfielder

Current Club: Tamworth

D o B: 04/09/1974 — *Birthplace: Birmingham*

Nick was voted Supporters' Player of the Year at Tamworth for the 2000/01 season after some tremendous performances wide on the right of midfield. He also gained representative honours with the Dr Martens League after coming back into the side after a dreadful knee injury which saw him miss the 1998/99 season. He signed for Tamworth in July 1998 after being with Telford United. He began his career with Wolverhampton Wanderers and has also played for Halesowen Town and Chasetown.

COLLIER, DARREN — Goalkeeper

Current Club: Billingham Town

D o B: 01/12/1967 — *Birthplace: Stockton*

Darren has been a great acquisition to Town having played pro football with Middlesbrough, Blackburn Rovers, Darlington, Sing Tao (Hong Kong) and Berwick Rangers. Darren commands his box and is an excellent shot stopper.

C

COLLIER, LEE — Midfielder
Current Club: Bath City
Birthplace: Bristol
Yet another Twerton Park old boy who has returned to Bath City during the 2001/02 campaign, although Lee made just one appearance under Paul Bodin at the end of the 1998/99 season. Originally a reserve team player at Yeovil Town, he left Huish Park after finding his first team opportunities limited. A back injury meant he made just one outing for City and although he featured in a number of friendlies during the 1999/00 pre-season campaign he failed to earn a contract. Went on to play for Larkhall Athletic in the Western League and then Chippenham Town.

COLLIER, PETER — Forward
Current Club: Selby Town
Birthplace: Selby
Previous clubs include: Pontefract Collieries - July 1998, Selby T, Pickering T, Harrogate T, Bridlington T, Pickering T, Goole T, Selby T.

COLLINGS, LEE — Defender
Current Club: Shildon
Birthplace: Co.Durham
Previous clubs include: Morpeth T - August 2001, South Shields, Brandon Utd, Blyth Spartans, Middlesbrough.

COLLINS, CHRIS — Defender
Current Club: Woking
D o B: 26/09/1979   *Birthplace: Chatham*
Highly-rated defender who joined Conference side Woking in May 2002 for an undisclosed fee from Dr Martens League side Newport Isle of Wight. Started his career with Southampton but the Chatham-born six-footer was released without playing a Premiership game for the Saints. Had a short spell with Stevenage Borough before joining Newport in August 2000.

COLLINS, DANNY — Midfielder
Current Club: Chester City
Birthplace: Flintshire
Previous clubs include: Buckley T - December 2001.

COLLINS, DARREN — Forward
Current Club: Cambridge City
D o B: 24/05/1967   *Birthplace: Winchester*
Honours won: England Semi-Pro Int., Dr Martens League Premier Div.Winners (2)
Experienced former England semi-professional international striker who joined Dr Martens Premier side Cambridge City in June 2002 from league champions Kettering Town. Had joined Kettering in November 2000 from local neighbours Rushden & Diamonds for a £25,000 fee - equalling the clubs record transfer fee. Had six years at Diamonds, scoring 153 goals and becoming their all-time record goalscorer. Played Leageu football for Northampton Town and has also seen service with Petersfield, Aylesbury United and Enfield. Skippered the Poppies to the Dr Martens title.

COLLINS, DAVID — Forward
Current Club: Trafford
Birthplace: Lancashire
Originally with Burnley, Dave is a young forward who joined UniBond First Division side Trafford in August 2002 from rivals Radcliffe Borough. Had signed for Radcliffe exactly two years earlier from Altrincham. A skilful player who also has an eye for goal.

COLLINS, JIMMY — Midfielder
Current Club: Vauxhall Motors
D o B: 28/05/1978   *Birthplace: Liverpool*
Talented, Liverpool-born midfielder who joined UniBond Premier side Vauxhall Motors in the summer of 2002 after a spell with Conference outfit Northwich Victoria. Began his career with Crewe Alexandra, for whom he made 24 League appearances. Had loan stints in the Conference with Kidderminster and Northwich before joining the Vivs on a permanent basis in September 2001.

COLLINS, JOE — Midfielder
Current Club: Bath City
Previous clubs include: Paulton Rovers - July 2001.

COLLINS, KEIRON — Defender
Current Club: VCD Athletic
Birthplace: Dartford
From Youth team.

COLLINS, LEE — Defender
Current Club: Halesowen Town
D o B: 10/09/1977   *Birthplace: Birmingham*
Honours won: Dr Martens Western Div.Winners
Lee joined Halesowen Town in the summer of 2001 from Nationwide Division 2 outfit Stoke City. Lee, Rosss older brother started his career in the same youth team as Lee Hendrie at Aston Villa. Stoke City requested his services but the reluctant Villa stated that they would have a percentage of his selling on fee. Collins very rarely made a first-team appearances for the Potters and moved to Moor Green on loan for the back end of the 2000/01 season. Brendan Phillips signed him in July and made him club captain and he has forged a good partnership with former Redditch United defender Lee Knight.

COLLINS, LIAM — Midfielder
Current Club: Kingstonian
D o B: 10/06/1982   *Birthplace: Surrey*
Exciting young talent on the right wing. Previously with Walton and Hersham, he impressed at Kingstonian during the pre-season of 2001 and was rewarded with a place in the first team squad.

COLLINS, MARTIN — Defender
Current Club: Herne Bay
Birthplace: Kent
Previous clubs include: Dover Ath - July 1997.

COLLINS, PHIL — Forward
Current Club: Margate
D o B: 03/07/1972   *Birthplace: Kent*
Honours won: Dr Martens League Premier Div.Winners
Had a terrific goalscoring season when helping Margate win the Dr Martens League and gain promotion to the Conference in 2000/01. Plundered many goals in the Kent League for Sheppey United and Cray Wanderers and then in the Dr Martens for Dartford before joining Margate in the summer of 1998.

COLLINS, ROBBIE — Forward
Current Club: Crawley Town
Birthplace: Sussex
Originally with Three Bridges: took a year out but re-emerged in 1999/2000, scoring 6 times for Redhill: subsequently graduated through Crawleys reserve side: made a handful of first-team appearances during 2000/01 before putting in some impressive performances this term: believed to have attracted interest from several other clubs, including Millwall and Charlton.

COLLINS, ROSS — Defender

Current Club: Halesowen Town

Birthplace: Birmingham
Honours won: Dr Martens Western Div.Winners

Ross is Lees younger brother and started his career at Halesowen Town playing in the now defunct youth team. Started making first-team appearances during the 1997/98 season but had a fair run in the side in the 1998/99 season due to injuries. Only made a handful of appearances in the 1999/00 season but made himself a first team regular the following campaign, playing in a variety of positions outside his natural defensive role.

COLLINS, SIMON — Defender

Current Club: Harrogate Town

D o B: 17/08/1983   Birthplace: York

Burst onto the scene with Garforth having arrived from College football in York. Talented young full back who loves to get forward on the overlap. A sharp short passer of the ball with a good turn of pace. Transferred to Harrogate in March 2002.

COLLINS, SIMON — Midfielder

Current Club: Belper Town

D o B: 16/12/1973   Birthplace: Pontefract

Highly-rated midfielder who joined UniBond First Division side Belper Town from Premier Division Frickley Athletic in August 2002 for a four-figure fee. Made over 150 League appearances for Huddersfield, Plymouth and Macclesfield before joining Frickley at the start of the 2001/02 season.

COLLINS, TONY — Defender

Current Club: Chasetown FC

Birthplace: Birmingham
Previous clubs include: Oldbury Utd - August 2001, Sandwell B.

COLLINS, TREVOR — Midfielder

Current Club: Bury Town

Birthplace: Suffolk
Previous clubs include: Mildenhall T - July 2000, Soham Town R, Histon, Bury T, Ely C, Cornard Utd, Dulwich Hamlet, Wivenhoe T, Bury T, Stowmarket T, Bury T, Colchester Utd (Junior).

COLLINSON, GARETH — Forward

Current Club: Brodsworth Welfare

Birthplace: Doncaster
Previous clubs include: Sheffield - October 2001, Gainsborough Trinity, Rossington Main.

COLLINSON, MATT — Defender

Current Club: Stratford Town

Birthplace: Stratford
From Youth team.

COLLIS, DAVE — Midfielder

Current Club: Grays Athletic

Birthplace: Essex
Young and highly-promising midfielder who came through the ranks at Charlton Athletic. Was a regular in the reserve side at The Valley but was released at the end of the 2001/02 season and joined Ryman Premier Division side Grays Athletic.

COLLISTER, PHIL — Goalkeeper

Current Club: Connahs Quay Nomads

D o B: 19/02/1965   Birthplace: Wales

Phil is a veteran goalkeeper with 235 LoW appearances to his name. He is a reassuring presence at the back, and gives confidence to the young defensive unit in front of him. Made his

debut for Connahs Quay in 1992 against Afan Lido in the inaugural LoW fixture.

COLVIN, DAVID — Forward

Current Club: Gateshead

D o B: 06/08/1982   Birthplace: Newcastle

Young, highly-promising attacker who signed for UniBond Premier side Gateshead in August 2002 after being somewhat unluckily released by Nationwide First Division club Sheffield United.

COLWELL, RICHARD — Defender

Current Club: Halesowen Town

D o B: 14/08/1980   Birthplace: Kettering
Honours won: Dr Martens Western Div.Winners

Skilful right-back who re-signed for Halesowen Town from Midland Alliance neighbours Halesowen Harriers in the summer of 2001. Made his first appearance in a Yeltz shirt in a pre-season friendly in 1999 after being released from Coventry City. Committed and reliable, Richard has rightly earned his place in the starting eleven.

COMERFORD, TONY — Midfielder

Current Club: Ware

Birthplace: London
Previous clubs include: Hertford T - August 2001, Bishops Stortford, Harlow T, Bishops Stortford, Sawbridgeworth T, Bishops Stortford, West Ham Utd (Trainee).

COMMANDER, ANDY — Defender

Current Club: Rugby United

D o B: 17/10/1978   Birthplace: Coventry
Previous clubs include: Shepshed Dynamo - August 2002, Port Vale.

COMPTON, PAUL — Midfielder

Current Club: Witton Albion

Birthplace: Lancashire
Previous clubs include: Fleetwood Freeport - January 2002, Kendal T, Lancaster C, Leigh RMI, Wigan Ath.

CONCANNON, IAN — Forward

Current Club: Didcot Town

Birthplace: Oxfordshire
Ian moved to Didcot in September 2001 after a short spell at Abingdon Town. Ian has a proven goalscoring record with AFC Wallingford, Oxford City and Thame United and could be a vital signing if we are to improve on last season.

CONKIE, MATTHEW — Goalkeeper

Current Club: Witton Albion

Previous clubs include: Winsford Utd - August 2001, Chester C.

CONLON, SCOTT — Midfielder

Current Club: Harrogate Town

Birthplace: Yorkshire
Honours won: UniBond League Div.One Winners

Midfielder who signed for Harrogate Town in August 2001 from Canberra Cosmos of the Australian Premier League. Only made available for selection from December 2001, he was formerly with Cheadle Town.

CONNELL, CRAIG — Midfielder

Current Club: Corby Town

Birthplace: Milton Keynes
Previous clubs include: Newport Pagnell T - December 2001, Potton Utd.

CONNELL, DARREN — *Forward*

Current Club: Gainsborough Trinity

D o B: 03/02/1982 — Birthplace: Blackpool
Previous clubs include: Scarborough - March 2002, Macclesfield T, Blackpool.

CONNELLY, JAMES — *Defender*

Current Club: Southport

Previous clubs include: Preston NE - July 1999.

CONNELLY, MICHAEL — *Midfielder*

Current Club: Afan Lido

D o B: 20/11/1974 — Birthplace: Wales
Previous clubs include: Port Talbot Ath - February 2001.

CONNELLY, PETER — *Midfielder*

Current Club: Leigh RMI

D o B: 08/08/1983 — Birthplace: Vancouver, Canada
From Youth team.

CONNOLLY, GARY — *Defender*

Current Club: Havant & Waterlooville

Birthplace: Portsmouth
Gary joined Havant & Waterloville initially on loan from Portsmouth at the end of the 1999/00 season, where he had been a first year professional, and impressed enough to be offered a contact in the close season. Moving from left defence to wing back, he has been responsible for setting up numerous goals with his ability to place extremely accurate crosses.

CONNOR, ASHLEY — *Goalkeeper*

Current Club: Harrogate Town

Birthplace: Yorkshire
Honours won: UniBond League Div.One Winners
Goalkeeper who spent two years at Rotherham United as an apprentice, followed by a year as a professional. He was Rotherhams reserve goalkeeper before he signed for Harrogate Town in the close season of 2001.

CONNOR, BRIAN — *Defender*

Current Club: Maidenhead United

D o B: 24/03/1969 — Birthplace: Taplow
Honours won: Ishtmian League Winners
Experienced player with service at Marlow, St Albans City, Windsor & Eton, Yeading, CheshamUnited and Slough Town where he won an Isthmian Championship medal. Locally born 32 year old who started his career on the books of QPR. Made his 200th appearance for the Magpies in September 2000. Signed for United in December 1996. Injury has restricted his appearances towards the end of this season.

CONNOR, DAVID — *Forward*

Current Club: Marske United

Birthplace: Co.Durham
Previous clubs include: Billingham Synthonia - February 2002, Gateshead, Billingham Synthonia, Nunthorpe.

CONNOR, JON — *Midfielder*

Current Club: Pickering Town

Birthplace: Scarborough
Previous clubs include: Scarborough (Trainee) - July 1997.

CONNOR, LEE — *Defender*

Current Club: Ashton United

Birthplace: Yorkshire
Defender who was signed by Ashton United in the summer of 2002 from Farsley Celtic after gaining promotion to the UniBond Premier Division. Started out at Northern Counties East League sides Eccleshill United, Hatfield Main and Liversedge before signing for Bradford Park Avenue. Joined Farsley in August 1999 and became recognised as one of the most consistent defenders in the UniBond First Division.

CONROY, NICKY — *Goalkeeper*

Current Club: Boston United

D o B: 09/04/2000 — Birthplace: Peterborough
Nick Conroy signed for Boston United in December 2000 from United Counties League side Yaxley as goalkeeping cover following Kevin Martins departure. He made his first-team debut for the Pilgrims in the Lincolnshire Senior Cup Final against former club Stamford - but it was not a happy debut as Boston were beaten 2-1. He made his Conference debut in April 2001 when he was brought on at the end of the first half in the match at Hednesford Town following the dismissal of Paul Bastock. He showed little sign of nerves and this time he finished on the winning side as Boston romped home 4-2.

CONSTABLE, DEAN — *Defender*

Current Club: Rye & Iden United

Birthplace: Hastings
Defender who returned to action during the latest season following a serious knee problem.

CONSTABLE, SHAUN — *Midfielder*

Current Club: Ossett Town

D o B: 21/03/1968 — Birthplace: Yorkshire
Honours won: British Universities Rep.
Strong midfield player now in his fourth season at the club after signing from Harrogate Town. Experienced player who has represented the British Universities as well as playing for Altrincham and Emley. Has also managed Town's Reserves and Under 19s in his time at Ingfield.

CONWAY, GREG — *Defender*

Current Club: Pagham

Birthplace: Sussex
Centre-half: played for Oving in recent seasons before having a brief spell at Sidlesham at the start of 2001/02: signed for Wick in October until switching to Pagham at the start of February.

CONWAY, JIM — *Defender*

Current Club: Stratford Town

Birthplace: Birmingham
Previous clubs include: Stourbridge - June 2002, Rushall Olympic, Stourport Swifts, Oldbury Utd, West Midlands Police.

COOGAN, MARC — *Defender*

Current Club: Bilston Town

Birthplace: Birmingham
Previous clubs include: Moor Green - March 2002, Blakenall, Atherstone Utd, Sutton Coldfield T, Solihull B, Sutton Coldfield T, Solihull B, Sherwood Celtic, Barry T, Kidderminster Harriers, Birmingham.

COOK, AARON — *Defender*

Current Club: Bashley

D o B: 06/12/1979 — Birthplace: Caerphilly
Previous clubs include: Havant & Waterlooville - January 2002, Swansea C, Crystal Palace, Portsmouth.

C

COOK, ANDY — Defender
Current Club: Salisbury City

D o B: 10/08/1969   Birthplace: Romsey

Signed for Dr Martens Easter side Salisbury City from Milwall in October 1999. Started his League career with his home-town club Southampton, where he made 16 appearances, scoring once in the old First Division. Totalled 146 Football League appearances and one goal in spells with Swansea City, Exeter City, Portsmouth and Millwall. Currently the clubs full time Football in the Community Officer. Good professional whose experience and ability in defence benefits those around him.

COOK, ANDY — Midfielder
Current Club: Maidenhead United

Birthplace: Herts

One-time Watford trainee who joined the Army after being released from Vicarage Road. Then signed for Ryman Leaguers Northwood in December 2000 and developed into one of the best in his position in the division. Came as no surprise when he moved into the Ryman Premier with Maidenhead United in June 2002.

COOK, DANNY — Midfielder
Current Club: Three Bridges

Birthplace: Sussex

Key midfielder: established member of the side, who has made around 250 appearances: scored four times in 1999/2000.

COOK, DAVE — Defender
Current Club: Harlow Town

Birthplace: Hertfordshire

One of former Harlow Town manager Ian Allinsons first signings, joining the club in February 2000 from Barton Rovers. Previously played for Stevenage Borough and Stotfold.

COOK, GARY — Forward
Current Club: Whitley Bay

Birthplace: Seaton Delaval

First season at the club, having signed from Seaton Delaval Amateurs of the Northern Alliance League. Another player with a great left foot who also can put over some superb crosses.

COOK, GLENN — Defender
Current Club: Tonbridge Angels

Birthplace: Kent

Defender who joined Dr Martens Eastern Division side Tonbridge Angels in the summer of 2002 from neighbours and rivals Chatham Town. Had been with the Chats since July 1997 after signing from Lordswood.

COOK, JAMIE — Midfielder
Current Club: Boston United

D o B: 02/08/1979   Birthplace: Oxford

Jamie Cook was one of three players signed by Boston United from Oxford United on free transfers in February 2001. A tricky striker who is capable of wriggling his way through opposition defences. He opened his goalscoring account in the final game of the season against Hereford United with a pair of goals, one of which was a spectacular long-range volley. Whilst at Oxford he made 92 League appearances, scoring seven goals.

COOK, JON — Defender
Current Club: Letchworth

Birthplace: Beds

Previous clubs include: Brache Sparta - July 2001, Toddington R.

COOK, MICHAEL — Defender
Current Club: Afan Lido

D o B: 29/05/1965   Birthplace: Wales

Veteran defender, brother of Stephen, who has spent much of his football playing life at the Lido. Strong in the air.

COOK, MIKE — Midfielder
Current Club: Gloucester City

D o B: 18/10/1968   Birthplace: Stroud

Vastly experienced and highly respected creative midfielder who joined Meadow Park to resume his playing career having spent a spell concentrating on his coaching. Is reported to be looking forward to linking up again with fellow Stroud man and former Coventry team-mate Gary Marshall. Cook will add some expertise to the City side, having considerable experience in this league with many seasons at Corby and Cambridge. Works at old club Cheltenham Town as their Community Officer having held a similar post at Cambridge United. Cook will bring some good contacts to Meadow Park as well as his own skill on the pitch. Has a UEFA coaching badge and his knowledge will doubtless also be an asset to Burns and Godfrey, although his return to playing from a coaching position at Cinch shows his determination to get his boots back on.

COOK, ROB — Midfielder
Current Club: Forest Green Rovers

D o B: 28/03/1970   Birthplace: Stroud

Honours won: Dr Martens League Premier Div. Winners

Talented midfielder who re-joined Conference side Forest Green Rovers in August 2002 after a two-year spell with Ryman Leaguers Basingstoke Town. Helped Rovers to win promotion to the Conference in the first of his three spells with the club. Has also served Shortwood United and Cinderford Town.

COOK, STEPHEN — Defender
Current Club: Afan Lido

D o B: 29/09/1963   Birthplace: Wales

Brother of Michael and another long term servant of the club. Stephen has played in both the centre of defence and at right-back.

COOK, TIM — Midfielder
Current Club: Marlow

D o B: 03/08/1969   Birthplace: Wycombe

Was captain and a highly- influential player with Maidenhead Unirted, winning the Player of the Year Award on three occasions after signing in 1994 from Burnham. Left for a brief spell with Thame United in 1997 and played over 350 games for the Magpies before leaving for Chesham in February 2002. Only three months later Tim was on his way to Marlow.

COOK, TONY — Midfielder
Current Club: Tring Town

D o B: 17/09/1976   Birthplace: Hemel Hempstead

Previous clubs include: Berkhamsted T - October 2000, Hemel Hempstead, Chelmsford C, Hemel Hempstead, Berkhamsted T, Wivenhoe T, Colchester Utd.

COOKE, DAVID — Midfielder
Current Club: Guiseley

Birthplace: Bradford

Honours won: British Universities Rep.

From Local Football - July 1998, Bradford C.

THE NON-LEAGUE PAPER

ESSENTIAL READING FOR FOLLOWERS OF THE NATIONAL GAME

SHARE THE PASSION

EVERY SUNDAY

COOKE, PAUL   *Defender*

Current Club: Chester-Le Street

Birthplace: Co.Durham
Previous clubs include: Willington - August 1997, Dunston Federation Brewery.

COOKSEY, ERNIE   *Midfielder*

Current Club: Crawley Town

Birthplace: Essex
Utility player, capable of performing in defence or midfield. He joined Dr Martens Premier side Crawley Town in July 2002 after a spell at Ryman Premier outfit Chesham United. Had signed for Chesham in November 2000 from Bromley and also appeared in the coloursof Colchester, Heybridge Swifts and Bishops Stortford.

COOKSLEY, GRAEME   *Midfielder*

Current Club: Walton Casuals

Birthplace: Surrey
Graeme is in his second spell with us , having re-joined from Hersham RBL in the summer. Club Captain and recently made his 100th appearances.

COOMBE, MARK   *Goalkeeper*

Current Club: Bideford

D o B: 17/09/1968   Birthplace: Torquay
Mark is a goalkeeper with pedigree, who joined us from Taunton Town. He has previously been on the books of Bournemouth, Bristol City, Carlisle, Colchester, Dorchester, Elmore & Minehead, Salisbury & Torquay. He has made over 50 first team appearances.

COOMBS, PAUL   *Forward*

Current Club: Slough Town

D o B: 04/09/1970   Birthplace: Bristol
Signed for a four-figure fee from Purflee, Paul is a hard working strong forward, who links up play well and is very capable of scoring many goals. The striker joined Purfleet on loan from Basingstoke Town, a move which became permanent. He joined Basingstoke in October 1991 from Farnborough Town. At Basingstoke scored over 150 goals in more than 300 appearances. He continued that goalscoring form at Purfleet where he struck up an excellent partnership with Cypriot striker George Georgiou and scored nearly 1 in every 2 games for Purfleet. He signed for Purfleet for £3,500 In the 1999/2000 season, Coombs finished off as 4th top scorer in the Ryman league. He scored 15 goals in the league, 5 in the Ryman Cup and 7 in the Full Members Cup. When Paul initially joined Slough he did tend to struggle. He was struggling to make chances, and when he did was denied, either by excellent goalkeeping or defending. When Paul did eventually open his account against Farnborough, everyone was delighted. Paul celebrated by jumping on about 20 Rebels fans and going mad! He scored once again against Carshalton in the same season. This season Rebels fans and players alike hope Coombs can recapture the previous form he has shown for other Ryman Division Clubs.

COONAN, JAMES   *Midfielder*

Current Club: Great Harwood Town

Birthplace: Lancashire
Previous clubs include: Bamber Bridge - July 2001.

COONEY, PHIL   *Midfielder*

Current Club: Ashton United

Birthplace: Liverpool
Highly-rated midfielder who joined UniBond Premier side Ashton United in the summer of 2002 after their promotion via the play-offs. Phil arrived at Hurst Cross from North West Counties League

club Skelmersdale United, where he had been for one season after spells at St Helens Town and Ashton Town.

COOPER, ADAM   *Defender*

Current Club: Nuneaton Borough

D o B: 30/09/1982   Birthplace: Coventry
Adam is a strong centre back with a big future ahead of him. Graduated from Nuneaton Borough's youth side where he was captain in 2000/01. Spent a brief loan spell with Bedworth United but was recalled to Boros first team.

COOPER, ADRIAN   *Midfielder*

Current Club: Stourport Swifts

Previous clubs include: Halesowen T - June 2000, Dudley T, Stourbridge, Halesowen T, Dudley T, Haloesowen Harriers.

COOPER, ANDY   *Defender*

Current Club: Didcot Town

Birthplace: Oxfordshire
Player-coach Andy joined Didcot two summers ago from local rivals Oxford City and has a wealth of experience with City and Thame United. He constantly attracts interest from other clubs requiring his services. Second top scorer at the club in his first season at the club, and already finding the net this year too. A Distribution Manager.

COOPER, BARRY   *Midfielder*

Current Club: Eastwood Town

Birthplace: Glasgow
Previous clubs include: Glasgow Celtic - December 2001.

COOPER, DALE   *Defender*

Current Club: Norwich United

D o B: 15/05/1976   Birthplace: Norfolk
Stylish defender who rejoined Norwich United during the 2001/02 season from Great Yarmouth. Very popular player.

COOPER, DANNY   *Midfielder*

Current Club: Liversedge

Birthplace: Yorkshire
From Youth team.

COOPER, GRANT   *Defender*

Current Club: Chesham United

D o B: 16/09/1977   Birthplace: London
Highly-talented defender who progressed through Enfields youth and reserve sides to become a first-team regular. Stayed loyal to the Es through some troubled times in recent years and remained one of the most respected defenders in the Ryman League. Transferred to Chesham United in May 2002.

COOPER, IAN   *Midfielder*

Current Club: Solihull Borough

Birthplace: Walsall
Walsall-born Ian signed in the summer of 2001 from Blakenall. He joined them in December 1999 from Bromsgrove Rovers. He is also a former Walsall trainee.

COOPER, JIMMY   *Midfielder*

Current Club: Metropolitan Police

Birthplace: Essex
Previous clubs include: Aveley - July 1996, Hornchurch, Barking, Dagenham, Leytonstone & Ilford, Barking.

COOPER, KEVIN — Forward

Current Club: Hertford Town

D o B: 05/06/1978 — *Birthplace: Barnet*

Kevin made a few appearances for Ryman Division One North side Hertford Town at the end of the 2000/01season after scoring a hatful of goals for Elliott Star in the Herts Senior League. His first appearances were mostly as sub, but his impact later was sensational, being second highest goalscorer in all Ryman divisions with 36 league goals, and 38 senior goals in all. Has also played for Spartan South Midland outfit Leverstock Green.

COOPER, LEE — Forward

Current Club: Bamber Bridge

Birthplace: Liverpool

Prolific scorer who makes goals out of nothing. Terrific work-rate and an excellent finisher. Has had spells with Southport, Burscough, Barrow and Droylsden. Currently in his second spell with Brig. Last season scored 29 goals for the St.Helens Town.

COOPER, MARK — Defender

Current Club: Hendon

Birthplace: Berkshire

Signed for Hendon in October 2001 from Windsor & Eton, Mark is an accomplished defender who had only left Harrow Borough in the summer of 2001 for Windsor. Has also appeared for Chalfont St Peter, Marlow and Flackwell Heath.

COOPER, MARK — Midfielder

Current Club: Tamworth

D o B: 18/12/1968 — *Birthplace: Wakefield*

Mark is an experienced midfielder, who has vast experience, both in Non-League and the Football League. His previous clubs include Birmingham City, Exeter, Wycombe, Southend, Hartlepool, Macclesfield, Fulham and Rushden & Diamonds. Joined Forest Green Rovers in March 2001 from Hednesford Town and then transferred to Tamworth in May 2002.

COOPER, MICHAEL — Defender

Current Club: Salisbury City

Birthplace: Somerset

Started his career at Yeovil Town playing at Youth and Reserve team level. Joined Exeter City in July 1997 as a YTS player and after completing his two year YTS he was given a 12 month pro contract in July 1999. Michael played for Weston Super Mare on loan in the 1999/2000 season. Signed for Yeovil Town for the second time on his release from Exeter City in July 2000. Joined Salisbury in February 2002 from Yeovil Town.

COOPER, NICK — Defender

Current Club: Kingsbury Town

Birthplace: London
From Youth team.

COOPER, SAM — Midfielder

Current Club: Grays Athletic

D o B: 23/06/1977 — *Birthplace: London*

Tremendously pacy utility player loves to run at defenders, and can score goals. He was signed from Canvey Island last season. He has been at Orient and Peterborough as a professional.

COOPER, SEAN — Defender

Current Club: Peacehaven & Telscombe

Birthplace: Sussex

Defender, who was part of Peacehavens championship-winning side of the mid-90s. Returned to the club at the start of

2000/01, after a spell with Newquay in the South-Western League. Previous experience with Saltdean and Withdean.

COOPER, SEAN — Goalkeeper

Current Club: Gorleston

Birthplace: Norfolk
Honours won: Combined Services Rep.

Previous clubs include: Soham Town Rangers - July 2000, Diss T, Mildenhall T, Bury T, Wroxham, RAF.

COOPER, STEVE — Defender

Current Club: Stratford Town

D o B: 10/12/1979 — *Birthplace: Wales*

A former Wrexham player, Steve is son of referee chief, Keith Cooper. The versatile defender, who can also figure in midfield, joined League of Wales side Bangor City in September 2000 from rivals Rhyl.

COOPER, STEVE — Defender

Current Club: Bangor City

Birthplace: Birmingham

Previous clubs include: Paget Rangers - August 2001.

COOPER, STUART — Forward

Current Club: Bashley

From Youth team.

COOTE, ANDREW — Forward

Current Club: Woodbridge Town

Birthplace: Suffolk

Speedy and skilful young striker who made the move up to Jewson League level during the close season, having previously played for Achilles in the SIL. Made an instant impression by scoring seven goals in the pre-season friendlies.

COPE, MATTHEW — Goalkeeper

Current Club: Arlesey Town

Birthplace: Bishops Stortford

Goalkeeper born in Bishops Stortford, Matthew signed for Ryman Division One orth side Arlesey Town in the close season of 2002. Former clubs include Watford (trainee), Stansted, Harrow Borough, Ware, Wembley and Wivenhoe Town.

COPLEY, CHRIS — Defender

Current Club: Sidley United

Birthplace: Sussex

Big, tough-tackling member of Sidleys back four. Returned to County League action in 2000 after a two-year break and scored six times last season.

COPPARD, DEAN — Midfielder

Current Club: Enfield

Birthplace: Middlesex

Promising young central defender who joined Ryman League Premier Division side Enfield in July 2002. Came up through the ranks at Hayes and made a number of Conference appearances before being released following relegation.

COPPIN, MATT — Forward

Current Club: Bromsgrove Rovers

Birthplace: Birmingham

Previous clubs include: Blakenall - June 2001, Evesham Utd, Stourbridge, Redditch Utd, Solihull B, Upton T, Worcester C, Bromsgrove R, Derby Co.

C

CORBETT, JOHN — Midfielder
Current Club: Brigg Town
Birthplace: Scunthorpe
Previous clubs include: Scunthorpe Utd - July 2001.

CORBETT, JON — Midfielder
Current Club: Banbury United
D o B: 13/10/1968   Birthplace: Buckingham
Experienced fierce tackling ball-winner. Made his debut for
Banbury United at Harrow Hill after joining in September 1998,
and has also played for Dunstable, Hitchin Town, Wycombe
Wanderers, Boreham Wood, Buckingham Town, Bedford Town
and Brackley Town. Competitive midfielder and club captain.

CORBETT, SCOTT — Midfielder
Current Club: Farnborough Town
Birthplace: London
A solid, clever all-round midfield player who began his playing
days with Hampton before joining Kingstonian in August 1996.
Progressed through the Ks reserve side to become a regular in
the senior squad. Was a member of their 1999 FA Umbro Trophy
winning squad before moving to Farnborough the following
summer.

CORBETT, SCOTT — Midfielder
Current Club: Sutton United
Birthplace: Surrey
Honours won: FA Trophy Winners, Ryman League Premier
Div.Winners
Midfielder who began his career with Chelsea and then had a
spell at Hampton before joining Kingstonian, where he won a
Ryman League championship medal in 1998 and an FA Trophy
winners medal a year later. He then moved to Farnborough Town,
where he picked up a second championship last term before
joining Sutton during the summer of 2001.

CORBETT, SIMON — Defender
Current Club: Guisborough Town
Birthplace: Co.Durham
Previous clubs include: Seaham Red Star - February 2002,
Peterlee Newtown.

CORBETT, STEVE — Goalkeeper
Current Club: Bilston Town
Birthplace: Worcestershire
Previous clubs include: Pelsall Villa - March 2002, Willenhall T,
Bilston T, Worcester C, Evesham Utd.

CORBOULD, MATT — Midfielder
Current Club: Arlesey Town
Birthplace: Hertfordshire
Matt helped strengthen the Arlesey Town defence considerably
after joining In October 2001 from Edgware Town. Previously with
Boreham Wood, Potters Bar Town, Molesey and Edgeware, he
describes himself as tall, clumsy and slow who can head a ball
further than he can kick it!

CORCORAN, DAMIAN — Midfielder
Current Club: Kendal Town
Birthplace: Preston
Midfielder who joined UniBond First Division side Kendal Town in
August 2002 from rivals Chorley. Began his career as a trainee
with Preston and then played for Bamber Bridge before joining
Chorley in the summer of 1999.

CORCORAN, KEIRAN — Defender
Current Club: Chesham United
Birthplace: Berkshire
Started as a recruit for Chesham United's reserves after originally
joining from Tring Town. Aged 21, he re-joined Chesham in March
2001 after a brief spell at Aylesbury United. A solid defender who
likes to go forward.

CORDEN, PAUL — Midfielder
Current Club: Racing Club Warwick
Birthplace: Coventry
Previous clubs include: Stourbridge - October 2001, Bedworth
Utd, Hinckley Utd, Jet Blades, Bedworth Utd, Jet Blades.

CORDEN, STEVE — Midfielder
Current Club: Guisborough Town
Birthplace: Middlesbrough
Previous clubs include: Spennymoor Utd - March 2001,
Guisborough T, Whitby T, Brandon Utd, Middlesbrough.

CORDICE, TERRY — Defender
Current Club: Maidstone United
Birthplace: Kent
Previous clubs include: Sheppey Utd - July 2000, Chatham T,
Margate, Purfleet, Chelmsford C, Dover Ath., Gravesend,
Folkestone, Chatham T, Tonbridge, Gravesend, Charlton Ath.

CORDY, PAUL — Midfielder
Current Club: Mildenhall Town
Birthplace: Cambridge
Previous clubs include: Diss T - July 2000, Histon.

CORKAIN, GLEN — Midfielder
Current Club: Billingham Synthonia
Birthplace: Cleveland
Previous clubs include: Spennymoor Utd - July 1995, Billingham
T.

CORLETT, STUART — Defender
Current Club: Ringmer
Birthplace: Sussex
Experienced defender, once on the books of Crystal Palace.
Spent five years at Saltdean, having previously played for Bognor
Regis, Peacehaven and Langney Sports. Held back by injuries in
recent years, one of several players to defect from Hill Park to
Ringmer during the 2001 close season.

CORMACK, DAN — Midfielder
Current Club: Tooting & Mitcham United
Birthplace: Surrey
From Local football - July 2000.

CORMACK, LEE — Forward
Current Club: Whyteleafe
Birthplace: Hampshire
Honours won: England Youth Int.
Previous clubs include: Metropolitan Police - January 2002,
Whyeleafe, Carshalton Ath., Wokingham T, Worthing, Bognor
Regis T, Fareham T, Newport IOW, Waterlooville, Basingstoke T,
Bognor Regis T, Fisher Ath., Brighton, Southampton.

CORNELIUS, TONY — Defender
Current Club: St.Leonards
D o B: 25/03/1981   Birthplace: Hastings
Tony is a former member of the St Leonards youth team which
reached the final of the Sussex Youth Cup in 1999. He made a

number of Southern League and other league appearances as a teenager. A regular member of the reserves, he has not disappointed when given an opportunity at senior level. Unlike his club chairman father John, who was a flying winger for the club over twenty seasons, he is a strong-tackling defender.

CORNELLY, CHRIS   *Forward*
Current Club: Ashton United

Previous clubs include: Ossett Alb - November 1999, Lower Hopton.

CORNISH, RICKY   *Defender*
Current Club: AFC Sudbury

Birthplace: Suffolk
Previous clubs include: Bury T - May 2000, Sudbury Wanderers, Halstead T, Cornard Utd, Halstead T, Chelmsford C, St.Albans C, Aldershot, Cambridge Utd, Bury T.

CORREIA, ARTUR   *Midfielder*
Current Club: Lewes

Birthplace: Angola
Previous clubs include: Greenoak Merton January 2002, Charlton Ath., Wimbledon.

CORRIE, GEORGE   *Midfielder*
Current Club: Workington

Birthplace: Cumbria
Previous clubs include: Wilmington Hammerheads - December 2001, Gretna, Workington, Windscale Utd.

CORRY, STEVE   *Goalkeeper*
Current Club: Kings Lynn

Birthplace: Lincs
Highly-rated goalkeeper who signed for Kings Lynn from Stamford in June 2002. Had joined the Daniels at the beginning of the 2000/01 season from Wisbech Town. Started his career with Rushden & Diamonds and was on the bench for Rushdens FA Cup tie with Leeds United.

CORT, RICHARD   *Midfielder*
Current Club: Brockenhurst

Birthplace: Bournemouth
Previous clubs include: Lymington & New Milton - July 2001, AFC Bournemouth (Junior).

CORT, WAYNE   *Forward*
Current Club: Dulwich Hamlet

Birthplace: Southwark
Prolific striker who signed for Dulwich Hamlet in July 2002 from Thame United. Had joined Thame from Harlow Town in March 2000 after a short loan spell. Wayne was soon amongst the goals as he had been at his previous clubs Fisher Athletic and Erith & Belvedere. Brother of Newcastle United's Carl Cort.

CORY, DAVID   *Forward*
Current Club: Hampton & Richmond

Birthplace: Kent
David is a tireless, front-runner who first played for Margate as a 16-year-old. Moved to Ryman League side Walton & Hersham in July 1999, becoming a regular for the promotion-winning reserve side for whom he finished overall leading scorer in the Suburban League, averaging over a goal a game. Established a first-team spot the following season, ending as leading scorer and being named Player of the Year by both supporters and players. Transferred to Premier Division Hampton & Richmond Borough in August 2002.

COSSEVELLA, ALAN   *Midfielder*
Current Club: Thornaby on Tees

Birthplace: Cleveland
From Youth team.

COSTELLO, IAN   *Forward*
Current Club: Peacehaven & Telscombe

Birthplace: Sussex
Forward who emerged at the end of 1999/2000 when scoring twice for Saltdean as a substitute. Struck five times for the Tigers during the following season and was also a member of the Sussex under-18 squad. Subsequently improved further and scored 7 goals in the opening two months of 2001/02 before being picked up by Peacehaven in October.

COSTELLO, MARK   *Defender*
Current Club: Carshalton Athletic

D o B: 01/10/1971   *Birthplace: Kingston*
A former Sutton United defender, Mark joined Carshalton Athletic in the summer of 2001 after spending five years with Staines Town.

COSTELLO, PETER   *Midfielder*
Current Club: Boston United

Birthplace: Halifax
Signed after returning from a spell in Hong Kong. Has made over 100 League appearances, scoring 19 goals. His most memorable match was when he played for Bradford City against Leeds United at Elland Road in March 1989. The match, in the old Second Division, was played in front of a crowd of 33,325. It ended in a 3-3 draw and Peter scored the second Bradford goal with a stunning 25-yard volley. When he has finished playing he hopes to stay in the game, either as a coach or a manager, he is currently taking his UEFA B. Badge.

COTTERILL, CRAIG   *Goalkeeper*
Current Club: Blyth Spartans

Birthplace: Co.Durham
Craig has come up through the youth team at Blyth Spartans, and although not a regular first team choice, he is excellent cover. Craig is still learning and developing, and is one to watch for the future.

COTTON, KEVIN   *Defender*
Current Club: Beaconsfield SYCOB

Birthplace: Berkshire
From Youth team.

COTTRELL, NATHAN   *Defender*
Current Club: Barry Town

D o B: 15/12/1976   *Birthplace: Wales*
Previous clubs include: Cwmbran T - June 2002, Rhayader T, Bridgend T, Caerau Ely.

COTTRILL, IAN   *Midfielder*
Current Club: Worcester City

D o B: 12/02/1969   *Birthplace: Worcester*
Worcester City's most experienced player, Ian has played in excess of 400 games for City, having joined as a Youth Team player in the mid-1980s. The midfielder had one spell away from St. Georges Lane, completing a three year stay at Nuneaton Borough before rejoining home in 1994. Ian was rewarded with a testimonial in 2001/02.

C

COUBROUGH, JAMES — Forward
Current Club: Eccleshill United
D o B: 04/10/1980 — Birthplace: Bradford
Previous clubs include: Thackley - February 2001, Harrogate T, Sheffield Wednesday.

COUPE, MATTHEW — Defender
Current Club: Forest Green Rovers
D o B: 07/10/1978 — Birthplace: St.Asaph
Honours won: England Schoolboy Int., Dr Martens Leaguei Premier Div.Winners
Defender Matthew is now in his second spell at Conference club Forest Green Rovers after previously helping the side to reach the final of the FA Trophy in 1999. Also won Southern League championship honours whilst with Forest Green in season 1997/98. Matthew rejoined Rovers from League of Wales outfit Aberystwyth Town in January 2002. Originally on the books at Bristol City, the former England Schoolboy international has also seen service with Gloucester City, Clevedon Town and Bath City.

COUPLAND, PETER — Forward
Current Club: Chatham Town
Previous clubs include: Deal T - July 1999, Herne Bay, Cray Wanderers, Herne Bay, Slade Green, Erith & Belvedere, Crockenhill.

COURT, IAN — Forward
Current Club: Maidstone United
Birthplace: Kent
Previous clubs include: Ramsgate - July 2001, Margate.

COURT, TONY — Goalkeeper
Current Club: Yate Town
Birthplace: Bristol
Previous clubs include: Mangotsfield Utd - July 2001, Almondsbury T, Yate T, Almondsbury T, Yate T, Bristol R.

COURTNAGE, JAMES — Goalkeeper
Current Club: Hemel Hempstead Town
Previous clubs include: Aylesbury Utd - August 2001, Hampton & Richmond B, Watford (Trainee).

COURTNAGE, ROB — Defender
Current Club: Wealdstone
Birthplace: Hertfordshire
Rob joined Wealdstone during the pre-season of 2001 and quickly became a fans favourite with his hard tackling style and attacking capability. Now establishing himself in the first team. Formerly with Dulwich Hamlet. Previous clubs include: Hemel Hempstead T - December 2001.

COURTNEY, GED — Forward
Current Club: Stalybridge Celtic
Birthplace: Liverpool
Gerrad is a terrific youg striker from Marine. He was Marines top scorer in the 2000/01 season with 11. Marine signed him from Kendal Town, and before that he played for Accrington Stanley, Crawfords, and Southport. He has a proven strike rate at several levels of Non-League football. He was born in 1977.

COUSINS, CLIFF — Defender
Current Club: Brackley Town
Birthplace: Oxfordshire
Previous clubs include: Banbury Utd - July 1999, Brackley T, Racing Club Warwick, VS Rugby, Racing Club Warwick, Buckingham T, Witney T, Banbury Utd, Easington Sports, Aylesbury Utd, Buckingham T, Brackley T, Banbury Utd, AP Leamington, Banbury Utd, Swindon T.

COUSINS, IAN — Defender
Current Club: Chelmsford City
Birthplace: Essex
Summer 2000 capture for Chelmsford City from Burnham Ramblers. His early time with City though was wrecked by injury following a string of marvellous displays at left-back that alerted several League clubs. Was on Spurs books as a youngster where he enjoyed considerable success within their youth set-up. He returned to action during the opening stages of the 2001/02 season, and was a target for Dover Athletic in the summer of 2001 but chose to stay with City.

COUSINS, JASON — Defender
Current Club: Aldershot Town
D o B: 14/10/1970 — Birthplace: Hayes
Honours won: Third Div.Winners, Conference Winners, FA Trophy Winners
Highly-experienced defender who started his career with Brentford, where he made 21 first-team appearances. However, it was after joining Wycombe that his career really took off. Won numerous honours with the Chairboys, including a Conference and FA Trophy double and a Third Division championship. Made over 300 appearances for Wycombe and was their longest-serving player before being released at the end of the 2001/02 season. Was snapped up by Aldershot Town in June 2002.

COUSINS, ROB — Defender
Current Club: Tiverton Town
D o B: 09/02/1971 — Birthplace: Bristol
Honours won: England Semi-Pro Int.
Experienced defender, who spent seven years at Bath City, four years at Yeovil Town and a couple at Forest Green Rovers, all in the Conference. Over 400 Conference league games, and won three England semi-professional international caps. Transferred to Tiverton Town in May 2002.

COUTHARD, JORDAN — Defender
Current Club: Workington
Previous clubs include: Carlisle C - August 2000.

COVE, BILLY — Forward
Current Club: Leyton Pennant
Birthplace: Essex
Previous clubs include: Ford Utd - August 2001, Maidenhead Utd, Leyton Pennant, Bishops Stortford, Leyton Pennant, Walthamstow Pennant.

COVINGTON, PAUL — Defender
Current Club: Bedford Town
D o B: 28/04/1970 — Birthplace: Luton
Signed for Ryman Premier side Bedford Town from Buckingham Town in February 1996 and scored 25 goals in the Eagles Division Two title success in 1998/99. He then went back to his preferred position at centre half. Suffered a knee ligament injury which kept him out from November to the end of the 2001/02 season. Previous clubs include Shenley & Loughton, Buckingham Town and Dunstable before joining the Eagles in February 1996. Has now made over 300 appearances for the club.

COWAN, GAVIN — Defender
Current Club: Braintree Town
From Youth team.

COWAN, MICHAEL — *Midfielder*
Current Club: Newcastle Blue Star
D o B: 12/11/1979   Birthplace: Newcastle
Previous clubs include: Ponteland Utd - July 2000.

COWAP, STEVE — *Midfielder*
Current Club: Flexsys Cefn Druids
D o B: 05/08/1977   Birthplace: Wales
From Local football - September 2001.

COWARD, RONELL — *Forward*
Current Club: Molesey
Birthplace: Surrey
Previous clubs include: Whyteleafe - February 2002, Woking.

COWE, STEVE — *Forward*
Current Club: Newport County
D o B: 29/09/1974   Birthplace: Gloucester
Steve was with Aston Villa for five seasons including an initial period as a trainee and, despite not making a senior appearance, was the subject of a £100,000 transfer to Swindon Town. Played almost 100 times for Swindon despite suffering injury in February 2000. Signed for Newport County during the summer of 2001.

COWIE, PAUL — *Defender*
Current Club: Chichester City United
Birthplace: Sussex
No-nonsense defender/midfielder, who lets his chewing gum do the talking: originates from the Portfield side of the merger (joined them in 1997/98) and had previously played for Selsey, Fareham, Petersfield and Moneyfields.

COWKING, ANDY — *Defender*
Current Club: Clitheroe
Birthplace: Lancashire
A changed player last season. From the first few games onwards, particularly at Rossendale, he mixed aggression with skill and we saw the real Cowks in action.

COWLEY, ALAN — *Forward*
Current Club: Trafford
Birthplace: Liverpool
Forward who joined UniBond First Division side Trafford in July 2002 from Premier Division Runcorn FC Halton. Alan had been at Runcorn for three years after impressing the club whilst playing against them in the Isle of Man tournament. What he lacks in height, he makes up for in speed and skill, and he is an excellent finisher of the ball. Spent the start of the 2001/02 season building up first- team experience on loan at several clubs including Trafford and Skelmersdale United.

COWLEY, ALEX — *Forward*
Current Club: Redditch United
Birthplace: Birmingham
Highly-rated young forward who finally moved to Dr Martens Western side Redditch United from rivals and neighbours Stourport Swifts in August 2002 after a transfer tribunal set the deal at £750 with a further £250 after 25 first-team appearances. Started out as a trainee with West Bromwich Albion before joining Swifts in the summer of 2000. Showed tremendous form in 2001/02 which prompted a number of offers for him.

COWLEY, DANNY — *Midfielder*
Current Club: Harlow Town
Birthplace: Essex
Joined Harlow Town in March 1998 after impressing with his former club Barking. Still only 22, Danny has also played for Hornchurch and has become a regular member of the first team.

COWLEY, NICK — *Midfielder*
Current Club: Harlow Town
Birthplace: Essex
Younger brother of Danny who joined Harlow Town in March 2002 from Romford. Midfielder previously with Purfleet and Witham Town.

COWLING, BEN — *Forward*
Current Club: Haverhill Rovers
Birthplace: Suffolk
A forward in his third season at Haverhill. Previously with Steeple Bumpstead, and has had trials at Cambridge United and Norwich City.

COWLING, LEE — *Defender*
Current Club: Kings Lynn
D o B: 22/09/1977   Birthplace: Doncaster
Honours won: Dr Martens League Premier Div.Winners
Left-sided defender who signed for Kings Lynn in June 2002 from Kettering Town. Had joined the Poppies from Mansfield in July 1999 and helped the club to regain their place in the Conferemce. Previously a trainee with Nottingham Forest, Lee is following in his fathers footsteps as he was a professional for over 20 years. Became a regular in the Poppies line-up during the 2000/01 season after suffering from a spate of injuries.

COX, DARRELL — *Forward*
Current Club: Cheshunt
Birthplace: Herts
Previous clubs include: St Margaretsbury - January 1998.

COX, GAVIN — *Forward*
Current Club: Dartford
Birthplace: Leicester
Previous clubs include: Corby T - July 2001, Friar Lane OB.

COX, IAN — *Forward*
Current Club: Rhyl
D o B: 01/09/1981   Birthplace: Wales
Previous clubs include: Wrexham - August 2001, Total Network Solutions.

COX, JIMMY — *Forward*
Current Club: Gloucester City
D o B: 11/04/1980   Birthplace: Gloucester
Striker who re-joined Dr Martens Western side Gloucester City from rivals Weston-super-Mare for a £5,000 fee in August 2002. Signed for Weston from Gloucester during the summer of 2001. Has first-team experiance at Luton Town and has previously appeared for Bath City, scored 23 goals for Gloucester City in his previous spell at Meadow Park.

COX, KEVIN — *Defender*
Current Club: Hassocks
Birthplace: Sussex
Came to prominence whilst playing for the Hassocks U-18 side during 1998/99: first-team regular from November 2000 onwards.

COX, KEVIN — Forward

Current Club: Didcot Town

Birthplace: Oxfordshire

Kevin is another promising youngster who broke into the Didcot First Team set-up during the 2001/02 season. Has scored consistently for the Reserves after coming through the Didcot Youth ranks.

COX, LEE — Defender

Current Club: Worthing

Birthplace: Sussex

Previous clubs include: Shoreham - December 1996, Peacehaven & Telscombe, Lewes, Southwick, Peacehaven & Telscombe, Horsham, Shoreham.

COX, LEE — Defender

Current Club: Ringmer

Birthplace: Sussex

Veteran defender who made some 200 appearances for Worthing after joining them from Shoreham in December 1996. Had previously spent time at Lewes, Horsham, Peacehaven and Southwick and was recruited to Ringmer in September 2001 as player-coach.

COX, LEE — Midfielder

Current Club: Witton Albion

D o B: 16/10/1978 — Birthplace: Liverpool

Previous clubs include: Radcliffe Borough - February 1999, Altrincham, Crewe Alexandra.

COX, MATTHEW — Midfielder

Current Club: Histon

Birthplace: Cambridge

Previous clubs include: Ipswich T - March 2002.

COX, MICK — Defender

Current Club: Stafford Town

Birthplace: Stafford

Previous clubs include: Penkridge T - July 1999, Rocester, Stafford SE.

COX, PAUL — Defender

Current Club: Curzon Ashton

D o B: 06/01/1972 — Birthplace: Nottingham

Former professional at Notts County in four Wembley finals. Joined Leek Town as player/assistant-manager in May 2002 after a spell with Hucknall Town. Previously on the books at Kettering Town, Ilkeston Town and Gresley Rovers.

COX, PAUL — Defender

Current Club: Leek Town

Birthplace: Manchester

Previous clubs include: Atherton Colleries - November 2000, Hyde Utd, Altrincham, Bramhall, Sale Utd.

COX, RYAN — Midfielder

Current Club: Clapton

D o B: 05/03/1984 — Birthplace: Kent

Previous clubs include: Gravesend & Northfleet - July 2001, Gillingham (Junior).

COXALL, PHIL — Defender

Current Club: Gretna

Previous clubs include: Blyth Spartans - August 2000, Durham C, Whitley Bay, Seaham Red Star.

COYLE, JAMIE — Midfielder

Current Club: Gravesend & Northfleet

Birthplace: Kent

Jamie is the first player to have graduated into Gravesend & Northfleets first-team squad through the clubs PASE scheme. He is a talented youngster who has acquitted himself well whenever he has been given an opportunity in the senior side. He is a great passer of the ball and extremely comfortable in possession. Certainly one for the future.

COYLE, MARK — Forward

Current Club: Dulwich Hamlet

Birthplace: London

Teenage forward who was top scorer for Dulwich Hamlets reserve side in 2000/01. Made his first-team debut in September 2000 and was a regular member of the squad for 2001/02.

COYLE, NICK — Defender

Current Club: Morecambe

Birthplace: Morecambe

Honours won: England Schoolboy Int.

From Youth team.

COYLE, STEVE — Forward

Current Club: Dorking

Birthplace: Isle of Wight

Previous clubs include: Newport IOW - August 2001.

CRABB, MATT — Forward

Current Club: Eastbourne Borough

Birthplace: Eastbourne

Moved to Priory Lane from Eastbourne United (Sussex County League) in July 2000, having been voted Player of the Year at the Oval.

CRABBE, STEVE — Midfielder

Current Club: Llanelli AFC

D o B: 25/12/1984 — Birthplace: Wales

From Academy.

CRACE, RICCI — Forward

Current Club: Hendon

Birthplace: Hertfordshire

Young striker who arrived at Hendon in July 2001 from Division 3 side Ware, for whom he scored 24 Ryman League goals during the 2000/01 season. Ricci has terrific pace and has taken to the higher level with ease. Rated as a great prospect for the future.

CRACKNELL, TONY — Forward

Current Club: Hadleigh United

Birthplace: Suffolk

Strong uncompromising target man who loves scoring goals. Top goalscorer for Hadleighs first-team again last season. Deservedly won the Players' Player and Supporters' Player of the Year awards last season. Now in his seventh season with the Club.

CRAKER, LEWIS — Defender

Current Club: Oxford City

D o B: 02/05/1979 — Birthplace: Wycombe

Previous clubs include: Windsor & Eton - February 2002, Maidenhead Utd, Walton & Hersham, Molesey, Marlow, Yeading, Chesham Utd, Marlow, Wycombe Wanderers, Marlow.

CRAMMAN, KENNY — Midfielder
Current Club: Durham City
D o B: 17/08/1969   Birthplace: Gateshead
Honours won: England Semi-Pro Int.
Previous clubs include: Whitby T - September 2001, Gateshead, Boston Utd, Rushden & Diamonds, Gateshead, Bishop Auckland, Hartlepool Utd.

CRAMPSIE, NIGEL — Defender
Current Club: Letchworth
Birthplace: Herts
Previous clubs include: Brache Sparta - July 1999, Shillington, Ashcroft, Arlesey T, Dunstable, Caddington.

CRANDON, JAMIE — Forward
Current Club: Bath City
D o B: 24/03/1977   Birthplace: Bristol
Arrived at Bath City during the 2001 close season, utility man Jamie followed manager Alan Pridham from Western League Paulton Rovers. His career has closely mirrored that of the City boss after he first came to his attention playing for Somerset Senior League side Westlands in 1996. Spells with Dr Martens League sides Clevedon Town and Weston-Super-Mare followed before he once again joined up with Pridham at Backwell United during the 1997/98 season. When Pridham moved on to Paulton Rovers it was no surprise when the tough-tackling Crandon was amongst his first signings. Despite suffering a knee injury for a part of the 2000/01 season, Jamie had two successful years at Winterfield Road before becoming one of Pridhams first signings after his move to City.

CRANE, GAVIN — Forward
Current Club: Stanway Rovers
Birthplace: Ipswich
Previous clubs include: Woodbridge T - December 2000, Chelmsford C, Braintree T, Whitton Utd, Ipswich T.

CRANEY, IAN — Midfielder
Current Club: Altrincham
D o B: 21/07/1982   Birthplace: Liverpool
Ian is a skilful, young and very promising midfielder, who was formerly at Runcorn. He made his Altrincham debut against Emley in September, 2000. Ian is strong on the ball and has a powerful long-range shot in his armoury but his first goal for the first-team, against Spennymoor, was a skilful chip from outside the penalty area. Ian has attracted a number of scouts from clubs which included Manchester City.

CRANFIELD, MARK — Defender
Current Club: Maldon Town
D o B: 04/02/1971   Birthplace: Essex
Signed for Jewson Eastern Leaguers Maldon Town in July 2002 from Ryman Premier neighbours Heybridge Swifts. Made his Swifts debut in August 1995 having signed from Braintree Town and was a regular choice ever since, mainly at right back or central defence but in his younger days also operated in midfield. Strong-tackling and committed player, he began his career with Colchester United before moving on to Brightlingsea. Solid, reliable, uncomplicated defender.

CRANN, TIM — Defender
Current Club: Shifnal Town
Birthplace: Shropshire
Previous clubs include: Star - July 2002.

CRATE, DAVE — Defender
Current Club: Hertford Town
D o B: 27/01/1973   Birthplace: Hitchin
Previous clubs include: Royston T - December 1999, Hertford T, Bishops Stortford, Ware, Hertford T, Ware.

CRAVEN, DEAN — Midfielder
Current Club: Bridgnorth Town
D o B: 17/02/1979   Birthplace: Shrewsbury
Dean joined Midland Alliance club Bridgnorth Town in June 2002 from Dr Martens side Hednesford Town. Had signed for the Pitmen from local rivals Stafford Rangers part way through the 2000/01 campaign. His competitive midfielde style of play endeared him to the fans at Keys Park. Started his career at West Brom and also had spells with Shrewsbury, Merthyr Tydfil and Newtown in the League of Wales.

CRAVEN, GLEN — Goalkeeper
Current Club: Salisbury City
Birthplace: Wiltshire
Former Salisbury City youth team goalkeeper who signed as cover for the Eastern Division club in August 2002. Has had spells with AFC Bournemouth and Swindon Supermarine since leaving City.

CRAWFORD, MICHAEL — Midfielder
Current Club: Stourbridge
Birthplace: Birmingham
Honours won: St.Kitts & Nevis Int.
Previous clubs include: Halesowen T - March 2002, Bromsgrove R, Moor Green, Workington, Moor Green, Bohemians, Tamworth.

CRAWFORD, STUART — Defender
Current Club: Felixstowe & Walton United
Birthplace: Suffolk
Close season signing from Hadleigh United., his signature was much sought after by many clubs, very talented and able defender who is a former Lincoln City Youth Player.

CRAWFORD, TOMMY — Defender
Current Club: Bury Town
Birthplace: Suffolk
Previous clubs include: Newmarket T - February 2001, Mildenhall T, Newmarket T.

CRAWLEY, MITCHELL — Midfielder
Current Club: Dartford
Birthplace: Kent
Previous clubs include: Chesham Utd - December 2001, Tonbridge Angels, Gravesend, Dartford.

CRAWSHAW, GARY — Forward
Current Club: St.Albans City
D o B: 04/02/1971   Birthplace: Reading
Honours won: Conference Winners, Isthmian League Winners (2)
Striker with a proven record at Non-League level. Started his career at Luton and spent eight years at Kenilworth Road before being released to join Wycombe Wanderers in 1991. Then had successful spells with Staines Town and Hendon before playing a major part in Stevenage Borough's rise, winning Isthmian League and Conference championship medals as well as starring for Borough in their infamous FA Cup runs. Transferred to Aylesbury United in July 1998 and then to Farnborough Town two years later. Returned to the Ryman Premier in August 2002 with a move to St Albans City.

CRAWSHAW, STEVE   *Defender*
Current Club: Swaffham Town

Birthplace: Norfolk
Great skill for a big lad and a great personality in Swaffhams dressing room.

CREER, LEIGHTON   *Defender*
Current Club: Abingdon Town

Birthplace: Oxford
Previous clubs include: Oxford C - August 2001.

CREIGHTON, MARK   *Defender*
Current Club: Willenhall Town

Birthplace: Birmingham
Signed for Willenhall in January 2002 from Bromsgrove Rovers. A real scoop for Willenhall, a solid, dependable player who always gives 100%, played at Redditch and Halesowen Town.

CREIGHTON, MICKY   *Forward*
Current Club: Maidenhead United

D o B: 22/02/1968   *Birthplace: Windsor*
Popular and long serving player originally signing for the Magpies in 1991 from Windsor & Eton having started his career with home-town team Slough Town and with Chertsey Town. Left for spells with Uxbridge and back at Windsor before returning to York Road in July 1996. A serious back injury has restricted his appearances in recent seasons.

CRETTON, SCOTT   *Defender*
Current Club: Hitchin Town

D o B: 13/07/1976   *Birthplace: Herts*
Central defender who joined Hitchin Town from Stevenage Borough in July 1999. Played a key role in Hitchins promotion back to the Ryman Premier Division, but has seen the last couple of campaigns disrupted by injury. Is a close friend of Sunderland and England striker Kevin Phillips.

CRISP, MARK   *Midfielder*
Current Club: Moor Green

D o B: 15/09/1964   *Birthplace: Birmingham*
Honours won: Dr Martens League Premier Div.Winners
A hugely experienced player who was in theBromsgrove Rovers side that won promotion to the Conference. Has also played for Smethwick, Alvechurch, Redditch and Macclesfield.

CRISP, RICHARD   *Midfielder*
Current Club: Stourport Swifts

D o B: 23/05/1972   *Birthplace: Birmingham*
Previous clubs include: Halesowen T - March 2002, Telford Utd, Aston Villa.

CRITCHLEY, ADAM   *Defender*
Current Club: Kendal Town

Birthplace: Preston
Defender who joined UniBond First Division side Kendal Town in August 2002 from Chorley. Began his career as a trainee with Preston and then had his first spell at Chorley. Moved on to Mossley and Witton Albion before returning to Victory Park in the summer of 1997.

CRITCHLEY, NEIL   *Midfielder*
Current Club: Hyde United

D o B: 18/10/1978   *Birthplace: Crewe*
Previous clubs include: Leigh RMI - July 2001, Crewe Alexandra.

CRITTENDEN, ADAM   *Midfielder*
Current Club: Bracknell Town

Birthplace: Bracknell
Previous clubs include: Windsor & Eton - August 2001, Wycombe Wanderers.

CRITTENDEN, NICK   *Defender*
Current Club: Yeovil Town

D o B: 11/11/1978   *Birthplace: Ascot*
Honours won: FA Trophy Winners
Former Chelsea midfielder who was signed by Yeovil Town in August 2000. Two years ago he was named young player of the year at Stamford Bridge, where he made two League appearances as substitute. Also played League football whilst on loan at Plymouth.

CROAD, NIGEL   *Midfielder*
Current Club: Selby Town

Birthplace: Hambleton
Previous clubs include: Monk Fryston - July 1998, Halifax T.

CROCKETT, DANNY   *Defender*
Current Club: Paget Rangers

Birthplace: Birmingham
Joined the Club in pre-season. Cultured left foot gives a reassuring presence on the left hand side. Previously with Tamworth.

CROFT, PETER   *Midfielder*
Current Club: Chester-Le Street

Birthplace: Co.Durham
Previous clubs include: Tow Law T - July 2001, Spennymoor Utd.

CROME, MARC   *Defender*
Current Club: Banstead Athletic

Birthplace: Surrey
Solid left-sided defender who came up through Croydons youth team ranks to earn a regular first-team place toward the end of the 1996/97 season, at the expense of a certain Kenny Sansom! Made nearly 200 appearances for the Surrey club, and spent a brief spell on loan to Bromley before switching to Ryman Division One South rivals Banstead Athletic in August 2002.

CROMPTON, PAUL   *Midfielder*
Current Club: Kendal Town

Previous clubs include: Bamber Bridge - September 2001, Lancaster C, Leigh RMI, Wigan Ath.

CROOK, ALEX   *Midfielder*
Current Club: Bideford

Birthplace: Devon
Alex is the hub of our midfield and club captain. He is both playmaker, & skilful ball winner, who motivates the team around him. He joined us from Minehead, and has also played for Torquay United, Barnstaple Town, Dartmouth and Taunton Town. Alex has made over 50 first team appearances.

CROOK, DARREN   *Forward*
Current Club: Salisbury City

Birthplace: Salisbury
Local lad, a tall and pacey striker who has progressed from Dr Martens Eastern club Salisbury City's youth and reserve teams. Now a regular member of the senior side.

CROOK, GLEN — Midfielder
Current Club: Barton Rovers

Birthplace: Luton
Previous clubs include: Kempston Rovers - December 2000, Bognor Regis T, Kempston R, Barton R, Potton Utd, Biggleswade T, Peterborough Utd, Colchester Utd.

CROOK, WAYNE — Defender
Current Club: Paget Rangers

Birthplace: Birmingham
Joined the club during the close season. Previously with Sutton Coldfield Town and Tamworth. A competitive player whose battling qualities add to his undoubted ability.

CROOKES, DOMINIC — Defender
Current Club: Hyde United

D o B: 07/12/1974   Birthplace: Nottingham
Honours won: UniBond League Winners
Dominic is a Nottingham lad who signed for Stalybridge Celtic from Northwich Victoria, where he had played for nine years. He had spells at Dagenham and Redbridge, Telford United and Mansfield Town. Switched to Hyde United in January 2002.

CROOKES, PETER — Goalkeeper
Current Club: Hyde United

D o B: 07/06/1982   Birthplace: Liverpool
Young goalkeeper who was signed by UniBond Premier side Hyde United in August 2002. A former Liverpool apprentice, he has also played for Halifax Town, where he made one League appearance in their relegation season of 2001/02.

CROPLEY, BRENDAN — Goalkeeper
Current Club: Merthyr Tydfil

D o B: 24/11/1979   Birthplace: Norwich
Honours won: English Universities Rep.
Joined Dr Martens Western side Merthyr Tydfil during the summer of 2002 after moving to the South Wales area. Spent a number of seasons at Norwich City before being released by the Canaries and then played for Hinckley United whilst attending Loughborough University. Has represented the English Universities.

CROSBY, LEE — Defender
Current Club: Peterlee Newtown

Birthplace: Co.Durham
Previous clubs include: Durham C - September 2001.

CROSS, DAVID — Forward
Current Club: Hampton & Richmond

D o B: 07/09/1982   Birthplace: Bromley
Attacking midfielder or forward who was released from Notts County at the end of the 2001/02 season. Made one first-team appearance for County and then signed for Ryman Premier side Hampton & Richmond Borough in August 2002.

CROSS, GARRY — Defender
Current Club: Chelmsford City

D o B: 07/10/1980   Birthplace: Chelmsford
Chelmsford-born full back who spent the latter part of the 2000/01 season with Slough Town after being released by Southend United January 2001. Made around 20 League appearances for the Roots Hall club and signed for the Chelmsford in July 2001.

CROSS, JON — Midfielder
Current Club: Colwyn Bay

D o B: 02/03/1975   Birthplace: Wallasey
Previous clubs include: Chester C - August 2000, Wrexham.

CROSS, KEIRAN — Midfielder
Current Club: Studley

Birthplace: Worcester
Previous clubs include: Worcester C - September 2001.

CROSS, MATTHEW — Defender
Current Club: Rhyl

D o B: 25/09/1980   Birthplace: Bury
Previous clubs include: Rhayader T - July 2001, Bangor C, Hereford Utd, Barnsley.

CROSS, MICKEY — Midfielder
Current Club: Bedlington Terriers

Birthplace: Newcastle
Micky is a Bedlington lad through and through and one of the most loyal servants of the club. A real workhorse in the midfield he is one of the fittest players around. His box to box work has been a feature of many a good Bedlington performance.

CROSS, NICKY — Forward
Current Club: Studley

D o B: 07/02/1961   Birthplace: Birmingham
Previous clubs include: Sutton Coldfield T - February 2002, Redditch Utd, Solihull B, Hereford Utd, Port Vale, Leicester C, Walsall, WBA.

CROSS, RYAN — Defender
Current Club: Weston-Super-Mare

D o B: 11/10/1972   Birthplace: Plymouth
Former Dorchester Town defender, Ryan joined Weston-Super-Mare in May 2002 from Weymouth. Had arrived at the Wessex Stadium during the close season of 2000/01after making a total of 105 appearances during three years with the Magpies. Played League football for Plymouth, Hartlepool and Bury and also had a spell in Irish football with Sligo Rovers.

CROSS, STEVE — Forward
Current Club: Studley

Birthplace: Birmingham
Previous clubs include: Feckenham - June 2002, Redditch Utd.

CROSSLEY, MATT — Defender
Current Club: Andover

D o B: 18/03/1968   Birthplace: Basingstoke
Honours won: Conference Winners, Ryman League Premier Div.Winners, FA Trophy Winners
Previous clubs include: Aldershot T - July 2001, Kingstonian, Wycombe Wanderers, Overton Utd.

CROSSLEY, RYAN — Defender
Current Club: Wakefield & Emley

D o B: 23/07/1980   Birthplace: Halifax
Previous clubs include: Bury - October 2000, Huddersfield T.

CROSSLEY, RYAN — Defender
Current Club: Stevenage Borough

D o B: 12/11/1980   Birthplace: Huddersfield
Replaced the long-serving Simon Jones as Emleys left full back during the 2000-01 season and now full established in that position. Formerly with Bury and Huddersfield.

CROUCH, WESLEY — Forward
Current Club: Ware
Birthplace: Hertford
Previous clubs include: Hertford T - July 2000.

CROUCHER, DARREN — Goalkeeper
Current Club: Potters Bar Town
Birthplace: Hertfordshire
Previous clubs include: Hertford T - July 2001.

CROWE, MARK — Defender
Current Club: Lowestoft Town
D o B: 21/01/1965   Birthplace: Southwold
Previous clubs include: Wroxham - August 1999, Bury T, Cambridge Utd, Torquay Utd, Norwich C.

CROWFOOT, BEN — Defender
Current Club: Wisbech Town
D o B: 19/10/1980
Previous clubs include: Lincoln C - July 2001.

CROWLEY, DAVE — Midfielder
Current Club: Hinckley United
Birthplace: Coventry
Highly-experienced midfielder who joined Hinckley United from Nuneaton Borough in June 2002. Had signed for Boro from Stafford Rangers back in July 1995 and made over 250 first-team appearance for the Boro. He has played vital role in steadying the Boros midfield, and his hard work and energy made him an almost certain choice for inclusion in any Boro XI.

CROWLEY, JON — Defender
Current Club: Mangotsfield United
Birthplace: Bristol
Signed for Mangotsfield United in November 2000 from Bristol Rovers and gradually established himself in the side as the season progressed. Steady in defence and can also play in a midfield role, is rarely flustered.

CROWLEY, MARTIN — Defender
Current Club: Stratford Town
Birthplace: Coventry
Previous clubs include: Bedworth Utd - March 2002, Nuneaton B.

CROWN, JAMES — Defender
Current Club: Bury Town
Birthplace: Suffolk
Previous clubs include: Needham Market - July 2000, Thetford T, Bury T, Soham Town R, Bury T, Leyton Orient (Junior).

CROXFORD, STEVE — Defender
Current Club: Maidenhead United
D o B: 14/12/1971   Birthplace: Taplow
Returned to York Road in the summer of 1999 from Hampton & Richmond for his third spell. Steve, a local lad born in Maidenhead, is a product of the United youth team, making his debut at 17. Spent a couple of seasons at Walton & Hersham, Camberley Town, Kingstonian, Windsor & Eton and Wokingham Town.

CROXTON, LIAM — Midfielder
Current Club: Vauxhall Motors
D o B: 05/09/1980   Birthplace: Cheshire
Signed for Vauxhall Motors in March 2001 from Radcliffe Borough, Liam was soon vying for a midfield slot in the side

having impressed in pre-season matches. Had two spells with Droylsden and also turned out for Skelmersdale United.

CRUMP, ANDY — Defender
Current Club: Felixstowe & Walton United
Birthplace: Suffolk
At 16, Andy is the youngest member of the squad and has the distinction of becoming, at 15, the youngest player ever to represent the club at Jewson League level. A player with a great future in the game if he continues to progress at the same rate as he has done over the past twelve months.

CRUMPLIN, JOHN — Defender
Current Club: Three Bridges
D o B: 26/05/1967   Birthplace: Bath
Honours won: FA Trophy Winners
Ex-professional, who played 247 times for Brighton & Hove Albion (scored 9 goals) before a knee injury finished his professional career in 1995: went on to feature in Wokings FA Trophy-winning side as well having a spell with Crawley: more recently played (and managed) Selsey before moving to East Preston early in 1999: took over as player-manager at Three Bridges for the start of the 1999/2000 campaign, but quit after two seasons: began 2001/02 with St Leonards before being released in October when the club ran into financial difficulties: reinstated almost immediately, and was a contender to be manager at The Firs when Micky Taylor got the sack in November: returned to Three Bridges instead (injured in his first game back): has also appeared for the County over the last two years and apparently is Fatboy Slims all-time favourite player.

CRUST, NEIL — Defender
Current Club: Chatham Town
Previous clubs include: Lordswood - July 1999.

CRUTCHER, WAYNE — Defender
Current Club: Dorchester Town
Birthplace: Bournemouth
Previous clubs include: Peterborough Utd - February 2002, AFC Bournemouth.

CRUTE, NEIL — Midfielder
Current Club: Chester-Le Street
Birthplace: Newcastle
Previous clubs include: Bedlington Terriers - December 2001, Seaham Red Star, Peterlee Newtown, Jarrow Roofing, Murton, Esh Winning, Jarrow Roofing.

CRYER, LEE — Forward
Current Club: Clitheroe
Birthplace: Lancashire
Most unassuming centre forward around. Deadly in front of goal, brain several moves ahead of everyone else, the man was a revelation.

CUBITT, SAM — Defender
Current Club: Gorleston
Birthplace: Norfolk
Previous clubs include: Diss T - July 2000.

CUGGY, STEVE — Forward
Current Club: Whitley Bay
D o B: 18/03/1971   Birthplace: Wallsend
Now in his third season at Whitley Bay, Steve has been excellent acquisition for the club having been last seasons top scorer. Has played professionally for Maidstone as well as Dover in the

Conference and also Hastings United. Signed from Bedlington Terriers.

CULHAM, LEE   *Midfielder*
Current Club: Brook House

Birthplace: Middlesex
Previous clubs include: Ruislip Manor - July 2000, Uxbridge, Swansae C (Trainee).

CULLEN, TONY   *Midfielder*
Current Club: Salford City

D o B: 30/09/1969   *Birthplace: Newcastle*
Previous clubs include: Radcliffe Borough - July 2000, Blackburn R, Aston Villa, Sunderland, Newcastle Utd.

CULLIFORD, ANDY   *Midfielder*
Current Club: Bashley

Birthplace: Dorset
Previous clubs include: Poole T - December 2001.

CULSHAW, TOM   *Defender*
Current Club: Witton Albion

D o B: 10/10/1978   *Birthplace: Liverpool*
Honours won: England Schoolboy Int.
Previous clubs include: Leigh RMI - August 2001, Nuneaton B, Liverpool.

CULVERHOUSE, DAVE   *Defender*
Current Club: Heybridge Swifts

D o B: 09/09/1973   *Birthplace: London*
Experienced former Spurs defender who joined Ryman Premier side Heybridge Swifts in July 2002 from rivals Braintree Town. Spent a number of years with Dagenham & Redbridge after leaving White Hart Lane and then signed for Billericay Town in October 1999. Switched to Braintree in March 2001.

CUMISKEY, PETER   *Forward*
Current Club: Vauxhall Motors

D o B: 15/04/1974   *Birthplace: Liverpool*
Signed for Vauxhall Motors in the autumn of 2000 from Conference club Leigh RMI, having previously made his mark at Prescot Cables. A prolific scorer with Cables, Peter struggled to make his mark at Conference level but he soon showed that he had the ability to enhance the Motormens fire power. Has also seen service with Bootle and Maghull.

CUMMINGS, FRED   *Defender*
Current Club: Brook House

Birthplace: Middlesex
Previous clubs include: Ruislip Manor - July 2000, Wembley, Chalfont St Peter, Uxbridge, Hillingdon B.

CUNDY, DARREN   *Forward*
Current Club: Spalding United

Birthplace: Lincolnshire
Previous clubs include: Wisbech T - July 2001, Spalding Utd, Holbeach Utd, Spalding Utd.

CUNNINGHAM, ANDY   *Midfielder*
Current Club: Newcastle Blue Star

Birthplace: Middlesbrough
Previous clubs include: Brandon Utd - July 2001, Middlesbrough.

CUNNINGHAM, CARL   *Forward*
Current Club: Mickleover Sports

Birthplace: Derby
Previous clubs include: Belpr T - July 2002, Grantham T, Alfreton T, Gresley R, Derby Co.

CUNNINGHAM, CLIFF   *Midfielder*
Current Club: Sittingbourne

D o B: 20/07/1979   *Birthplace: Kent*
Another young midfielder to have come up through the various Sittingbourne teams. Has proved to be an able substitute when called on. Had spells away at Gravesend and Tonbridge before re-joining Sittingbourne in the summer of 2001.

CUNNINGHAM, HARVEY   *Midfielder*
Current Club: Droylsden

D o B: 11/09/1968   *Birthplace: Manchester*
Previous clubs include: Chorley - February 2002, Droylsden, Mossley, Hyde Utd, Droylsden, Doncaster R, Droylsden, Flixton, Southport, Halifax T, Witton Alb., Winsford Utd, Accrington Stanley, Mossley, Ashton Utd.

CUNNINGHAM, MICKY   *Forward*
Current Club: Brandon United

Birthplace: Co.Durham
A great all action striker who will always score and make goals. Always gives 110% and never knows when to give up. Now in his fourth season with the club, having signed from Jarrow Roofing. Another player who has demonstrated his commitment to Brandon, by rejecting offers from other clubs.

CUNNINGHAM, STEVE   *Forward*
Current Club: Witton Albion

Birthplace: Lancashire
Previous clubs include: Rossendale Utd - February 2002, Atherton LR.

CUNNINGTON, SHAUN   *Midfielder*
Current Club: Evesham United

D o B: 04/01/1966   *Birthplace: Bourne*
Previous clubs include: Kidderminster Harriers - November 2001, Notts Co., WBA, Sunderland, Grimsby T, Wrexham.

CURLEY, SCOTT   *Midfielder*
Current Club: Leyton

D o B: 22/08/1979   *Birthplace: Essex*
Midfielder who joined Leyton in the summer of 2001 from Romford and helped them to gain promotion to the Ryman League at the end of the season. Formerly with Braintree Town and Barkingside.

CURNOW, JULIAN   *Defender*
Current Club: Lewes

Birthplace: Sussex
Previous clubs include: Pagham - November 2001, Wick, Bognor Regis T, Littlehampton T, Bognor Regis T.

CURRAN, DANNY   *Forward*
Current Club: Aveley

D o B: 13/06/1981   *Birthplace: Essex*
Previous clubs include: East Thurrock Utd - March 2002, Aveley, Purfleet, Leyton Orient.

CURRAN, DANNY — Midfielder
Current Club: Thame United
Birthplace: Oxfordshire
A product of Thame United's youth system who has made the step into the senior side. An industrious midfield player who is a great competitor and one with a bright future.

CURRIE, CHRIS — Defender
Current Club: Welling United
Previous clubs include: Gravesend - July 2001, Croydon, Carshalton Ath., Hampton & Richmond B, Brentford.

CURRIE, MICHAEL — Forward
Current Club: Harrow Borough
D o B: 19/10/1979   Birthplace: Westminster
Joined Harrow Borough from Ryman Division 1 neighbours Northwood just before the transfer deadline at the end of March 2002, having previously played this season in the Nationwide Conference for Hayes. Formerly with Queens Park Rangers.

CURRIER, DAMIAN — Forward
Current Club: Stourbridge
D o B: 23/06/1976   Birthplace: Shropshire
Previous clubs include: Rushall Olympic - March 2002, Wednesfield, Rhyl, Witton Alb., Total Network Solutions.

CURRY, IAN — Defender
Current Club: Armthorpe Welfare
Birthplace: Sheffield
Previous clubs include: Denaby Utd - July 1998, Selby T, Armthorpe Welfare, Alfreton T, Bridlington T, Sheffield Wednesday (Trainee).

CURRY, NICK — Forward
Current Club: Penrith
Birthplace: Cumbria
Previous clubs include: Ullswater - July 1998, Wetheriggs.

CURRY, STEVE — Goalkeeper
Current Club: Matlock Town
Birthplace: Yorkshire
Previous clubs include: Lincoln Utd - March 2002, Gainsborough Trinity, Hatfield Main, Goole T, Hatfield Main, Bridlington T.

CURSON, MARC — Midfielder
Current Club: Swaffham Town
Birthplace: Norfolk
Former Downham favorite who really make things tick for Swaffham in midfield. Unselfish player who gets the best from those around him.

CURTIS, DARREN — Defender
Current Club: Eastleigh
Birthplace: Wiltshire
Previous clubs include: Salisbury C - July 2001, Fulham.

CURTIS, MARTIN — Forward
Current Club: Stanway Rovers
Birthplace: Essex
Previous clubs include: Tolleshunt Knights - August 2000.

CURTIS, MATTHEW — Forward
Current Club: Rothwell Town
Birthplace: Kettering
Previous clubs include: Burton Park Wanderers - July 2002.

CURTIS, SHAUN — Forward
Current Club: Woodbridge Town
Birthplace: Suffolk
Signed in October 1999, having previously played Jewson football for Felixstowe and Diss. Right-sided midfielder or front runner who made an immediate impact by scoring with his first touch in Woodbridge colours.

CURTIS, WAYNE — Forward
Current Club: Morecambe
Birthplace: Barrow
Forward player, who signed for Morecambe towards the end of the 1997/98 season after an extended trail, from the Barrow area where he played for a local side Holker Old Boys. Proving to have been one of manager Jim Harveys most astute signings.

CURTISS, GARY — Defender
Current Club: Colwyn Bay
D o B: 07/09/1970   Birthplace: Liverpool
A well-travelled defender who re-signed for Colwyn Bay in November 2001 from League of Wales outfit Rhyl. Began his career as a trainee with Grimsby and then sampled Conference football with Northwich Victoria before moving between the League of Wales and the UniBond through spells at Newtown, Radcliffe Borough, TNS, Colwyn Bay and Rhyl.

CUSS, PAUL — Goalkeeper
Current Club: Wakefield & Emley
D o B: 19/04/1979   Birthplace: Hanover
New young goalkeeper who joined Emley in the summer of 2000, after being released by Huddersfield Town. Emley have a tradition of quality keepers and are hoping Paul will follow in their footsteps. Paul was a professional at Huddersfield for three years though he never made his league debut.

CUSSONS, NEIL — Forward
Current Club: Braintree Town
Birthplace: Essex
Forward who joined Ryman Premier side Braintree Town in July 2002 from Jewson Eastern Leaguers Maldon Town. Started his playing days in the Essex Senior eague with Burnham Ramblers before signing for Maldon at the start of the 2001/02 season.

CUSWORTH, BRIAN — Forward
Current Club: Maltby Main
Birthplace: Yorkshire
Previous clubs include: Parkgate - October 2001, Frickley Ath., Parkgate, Rossington Main, Parkgate, Denaby Utd.

CUTHBERTSON, ANDY — Midfielder
Current Club: Brandon United
Birthplace: Middlesbrough
Young, extremely talented player who always appears to have time and plays the simple ball. Loves to get forward and score some spectacular goals. In his third season, having previously been with Middlesbrough.

CUTTICA, JAMIE — Midfielder
Current Club: Hanwell Town
D o B: 09/11/1968   Birthplace: London
Previous clubs include: Viking Greenford - July 2000, New Hanford.

STANNO

Sportswear

Our
new
2002/2003 catagloue
is now available!

Tel: 01332 799910
mail: stannosportsuk@hotmail.com

DACK, JIMMY   *Midfielder*
Current Club: Tooting & Mitcham United
D o B: 02/06/1972   *Birthplace: London*
Talented midfielder who joined Ryman League Tooting & Mitcham United in July 2002 from Dr Martens League side Crawley Town. Had returned to Crawley at the start of 2001/02, having played for Ryman champions Farnborough the previous season. Priginally left the Reds rather abruptly back in 1994, before moving on to Sutton United and Aldershot.

DADSON, PAUL   *Midfielder*
Current Club: Fleet Town
D o B: 15/11/1971   *Birthplace: Berkshire*
Previous clubs include: Bracknell T - November 1999, Windsor & Eton, Maidenhead Utd, Wokingham T, Farnborough T, Coventry C.

DAHL, PAUL   *Goalkeeper*
Current Club: Prescot Cables
Birthplace: Liverpool
Previous clubs include: Maghull - July 2000.

DAISH, LIAM   *Defender*
Current Club: Havant & Waterlooville
D o B: 23/09/1968   *Birthplace: Portsmouth*
Honours won: Republic of Ireland u-21, B & Full Int.
Liam was Billy Gilberts most prized signing or Havant & Waterlooville prior to the clubs first Premier Division season. Having retired from professional football through injury Liam has brought considerable experience to the team, echoed now in his managerial position. He has previously played for Birmingham City, Coventry City and has made international appearances for Ireland. Daishys commanding presence is never more felt than in the opponents goal mouth, from where he has scored more than his fair share of goals.

DAKIN, SIMON   *Defender*
Current Club: Hinckley United
D o B: 30/11/1974   *Birthplace: Nottingham*
Joined Dr Martens Premier side Hinckley United in August 2002 from Kings Lynn. Had signed for the Linnets from Grantham Town during the summer of 1999. Simon is one of the many players from Grantham Town's successful Midland Division championship-winning side. A dedicated defender with bags of energy who likes to go forward at every opportunity, he was on the books at Hull and Derby as a youngster and also turned out for Arnold Town.

DALE, ANDY   *Forward*
Current Club: Stourbridge
Birthplace: Birmingham
Previous clubs include: Sutton Coldfield T - March 2000, Bedworth Utd, Sutton Coldfield T, Rushall Olympic, Dudley T, Bromsgrove R, Dudley T, Sutton Coldfield T, Moor Green, Birmingham C.

DALEY, RYAN   *Midfielder*
Current Club: Bilston Town
Birthplace: Wolverhampton
Previous clubs include: Bridgnorth T - November 2001, Bromsgrove R, Telford Utd, Wednesfield.

DALEY, TONY   *Forward*
Current Club: Forest Green Rovers
D o B: 18/10/1967   *Birthplace: Birmingham*
Honours won: England Int.
Was signed after being released from Walsall. Previously with Aston Villa, Wolves and Watford. Played seven times for England and represented his country in the European Championships in 1992.

DALGARNO, TOM   *Defender*
Current Club: East Thurrock United
Birthplace: Essex
Previous clubs include: Great Wakering Rovers - July 2001, Ford Utd, Basildon Utd, Southend Manor, Stansted, Harlow T, Stambridge, Southend Utd.

DALLAWAY, STEVE   *Forward*
Current Club: Eastbourne Borough
Birthplace: Eastbourne
Previous clubs include: Eastbourne T - July 2001.

DALORTO, GEORGE   *Forward*
Current Club: Barking & East Ham United
Birthplace: London
Previous clubs include: Clapton - August 2001, Barking, Collier Row, East Thurrock Utd, Clapton, Dagenham, Enfield, Chelmsford C, Dagenham, Clapton, Colchester Utd, Fulham.

DALTON, CHRIS   *Defender*
Current Club: Atherton Loburnum Rovers
Birthplace: Bury
Coming to LR from local football, Chris is a talented young player who has easily slotted into central defence. Always reliable, he never fails to impress on the pitch. Chris is an insurance underwriter and enjoys playing snooker in his spare time.

DALTON, PAUL   *Forward*
Current Club: Billingham Town
D o B: 25/04/1967   *Birthplace: Middlesbrough*
Signed from Dunston Federation. Paul has played pro football for Manchester United, Hartlepool and Carlisle, a good acquisition to the squad.

DALY, IAN   *Midfielder*
Current Club: Maldon Town
Birthplace: Essex
Previous clubs include: Brightlingsea Utd - July 2000.

DALY, JON   *Midfielder*
Current Club: Metropolitan Police
Previous clubs include: Hendon - July 2001, St.Albans C, Kingstonian, Hendon, Dulwich Hamlet, Whyteleafe, Croydon, Tooting & Mitcham Utd, Croydon, Crystal Palace (Junior).

DALY, MATTHEW   *Defender*
Current Club: Bradford Park Avenue
D o B: 08/10/1976   *Birthplace: Derby*
Honours won: British Universities Rep.
An experienced defender who was signed by Bradford Park Avenue from Guiseley in March 2002. Was originally with Sheffield Wednesday and also played in Ireland with Sligo Rovers before going Non-League with Stalybridge Celtic. Has also been at Barrow and was in his second spell at Guiseley prior to joining Avenue. Has represented the British Universities.

DALY, SEAN   *Defender*
Current Club: Carshalton Athletic
D o B: 18/11/1974   *Birthplace: London*
Honours won: England Schoolboy Int.
Previous clubs include: Sutton Utd - July 1998, Carshalton Ath., Sutton Utd, Croydon, Fulham, Crystal Palace.

DALY, STEVE — Defender

Current Club: Slough Town

Birthplace: London

Joined the club for a four figure fee from fellow Ryman league club Boreham Wood during the latter part of the 1998/99 season. Made his Slough debut against Purfleet in a 4-0 win at Ship lane. His performance that day was of a high standard and he has continued be play to high standards to the current day for STFC. Steve is the club captain and is a hugely respected member of the squad by players and fans alike. He is one of the best defenders in the Ryman League, and Slough miss him when he does not play. During the end of the 2000/2001 season Daly played on for the Rebels despite suffering from a hamstring injury. Ultimately his efforts were unrewarded as Slough were relegated. Steve would not look out of place in the Conference and hopefully one day, although it looks a long way off, he will get his chance with Slough. Steve did tend to suffer with injuries in the past, but we hope that his injuries are well behind him now. Formed an excellent partnership with Keith McPherson in the 2000/2001 season.

DALY, STEVE — Midfielder

Current Club: Tiptree United

Birthplace: Essex

Previous clubs include: Brightlingsea Utd - November 1999, Sudbury T.

DAMEN, GLEN — Defender

Current Club: Andover

Birthplace: Berkshire

Previous clubs include: AFC Newbury - July 2000, Thatcham T.

DANBY, COLIN — Forward

Current Club: Gorleston

Birthplace: Norfolk

Previous clubs include: Lowestoft T - October 1999, Wroxham, Gorleston, Diss T.

DANBY, NIGEL — Defender

Current Club: Harrogate Railway

Birthplace: Yorkshire

Previous clubs include: Eccleshill Utd - July 2001, Thackley, Garforth T, Ossett T, Selby T, Goole T, Selby T, Harrogate T, Farsley Celtic, Garforth T.

DANCER, MARK — Midfielder

Current Club: Wimborne Town

Birthplace: Bournemouth

Previous clubs include: Brockenhurst - July 2001.

DANIEL, WAYNE — Defender

Current Club: Stafford Rangers

Birthplace: Birmingham

Wayne had signed for Midland Alliance side Boldmere St Michaels in May 2002 after he had been at Paget Rangers since October 200 after arriving from local Sunday team St Gerards. However, a month later a chance to join Dr Martens Premier side Stafford Rangers arrived and he wa quick to take the opportunity. A towering physical presence adds to his ability in organising his defensive colleagues.

DANIELS, SCOTT — Defender

Current Club: Folkestone Invicta

D o B: 22/11/1969 — Birthplace: Benfleet

Commanding centre half who is good in the air. Scott joined Folkestone Invicta during the summer of 2000 from Conference neighbours Dover Athletic, where he was once club captain and made 115 appearances. Previously Scott made 136 league appearances for Colchester United, 150 for Exeter City and 10 for Northampton Town. He is now the clubs coach and assisted Neil Cugley in the running of the Dr Martens League X1 against the FA X1 at Crawley in November 2001.

DANKS, PAUL — Forward

Current Club: Bromsgrove Rovers

D o B: 19/11/1979 — Birthplace: Worcestershire

Talented young striker who signed for Bromsgrove Rovers in May 2002 from neighbours Redditch United. Originally with Walsall as a trainee, Paul, moved into Non-League football with Stourbridge where he began to catch the eye. Transferred to Reddich in November 1999 and his keen eye for goal made him a great favourite with the fans.

DANN, CRAIG — Midfielder

Current Club: Barnstaple Town

D o B: 14/12/1977 — Birthplace: Plymouth

Previous clubs include: Weston-Super-Mare - July 2001, Plymouth Argyle.

DANYLYK, ANTHONY — Midfielder

Current Club: Leek Town

Birthplace: Stoke

A promising young midfielder who signed for Leek Town in March 2002 from Stone Dominoes. Previously on the books at Stoke City.

DANZEY, MICHAEL — Defender

Current Club: Woking

D o B: 08/02/1971 — Birthplace: Widnes

Honours won: England Semi-Pro Int.

Previous clubs include: Aylesbury Utd (£15,000) - October 1997, Cambridge Utd, St.Albans C, Peterborough Utd, Nottingham Forest.

DARBY, ALAN — Defender

Current Club: Great Yarmouth Town

D o B: 25/11/1983 — Birthplace: Norfolk

Former Yarmouth youth team player but is very well-built so looks older. Either partners Mark Vincent in the centre of defence or slays at right back.

DARK, JULIAN — Defender

Current Club: Oxford City

Birthplace: Oxford

Previous clubs include: Abigndon T - November 1997, Thame Utd, Banbury Utd, Abingdon T, Oxford C.

DARK, MICHAEL — Defender

Current Club: Walton Casuals

Birthplace: Surrey

Michael has progressed through the Youth side, very comfortable on the ball, and will pressing for a regular 1st Team place this season.

DARLINGTON, STEVE — Forward

Current Club: Carshalton Athletic

D o B: 16/10/1973 — Birthplace: London

A powerful striker who has always scored goals. Began at Hounslow and then turned out for Chalfont St.Peter, Windsor & Eton, Staines Town and Wokingham Town before being involved in big-money moves to Kingstonian and then Enfield. Transferred to Farnborough in July 1999 and played a major part in Boros promotion to the Conference. Switched to Chesham in November 2001but then moved on to rivals Billericay Town a month later. In February 2002 he was on his travels again, this time to Carshalton Athletic.

DARLINGTON, STEVE — Midfielder

Current Club: Racing Club Warwick

Birthplace: Birmingham
Previous clubs include: Solihull Borough - November 2001.

DARLOW, KEIRAN — Midfielder

Current Club: Frickley Athletic

Birthplace: York
Young midfielder who joined UniBond Premier side Frickley Athletic from rivals Harrogate Town in August 2002. Had signed for Harrogate from York City in May 2002 after being with the Third Division outfit since school and progressed through to make 5 League appearances, making his debut against Scunthorpe in November 2001.

DARNTON, ANDY — Defender

Current Club: Bashley

Previous clubs include: Fleet T - September 1999, Worthing, Newport IOW, Gosport B, Waterlooville, Follands Sports.

DARROCH, SCOTT — Forward

Current Club: Stratford Town

Birthplace: Coventry
Previous clubs include: Redditch Utd - March 2001, Bedworth Utd, Halesowen T, Stratford T, Bedworth Utd, Nuneaton B, Bedworth Utd.

DARTON, SCOTT — Defender

Current Club: Ipswich Wanderers

D o B: 27/03/1975   Birthplace: Ipswich
Previous clubs include: Chelmsford C - July 2001, St.Albans C, Heybridge Swifts, Cambridge C, Ipswich W, Kings Lynn, Blackpool, WBA.

DARWENT, DARREN — Defender

Current Club: Tow Law Town

Birthplace: Newcastle
Has had something like 11 seasons with the Lawyers. Also has had spell in America. Has spent most of his time with the Lawyers playing as left back but now plays as a central defender. An integral part of the teams which won the League Championship in 94/95 and the 97/98 FA Vase squad.

DAURIA, DAVID — Midfielder

Current Club: Newport County

D o B: 26/03/1970   Birthplace: Swansea
Experienced midfielder who joined Dr Martens Premier side Newport County in last August 2002 after being released by Chesterfield. David, who totalled over 270 League appearances, signed for Chesterfield from Hull City for a fee of £50,000 in November 1999 after being one of Hulls most influential and important players. Unfortunately for Dai his first few months at the club were hampered by injuries but since his return he looked an extremely good player. Formerly with Scunthorpe, Scarborough and Swansea, he is no stranger to Non-League football, having poreviously had spells with both Barry Town and Merthyr Tydfil after being released by the Swans.

DAVENPORT, DEAN — Defender

Current Club: Croydon Athletic

Birthplace: Surrey
Previous clubs include: Whyteleafe - July 1999.

DAVENPORT, RICHARD — Midfielder

Current Club: Sheffield FC

Birthplace: Sheffield
Previous clubs include: A.B.M. - July 1998.

DAVEY, MARTIN — Forward

Current Club: Barnstaple Town

D o B: 04/03/1984   Birthplace: Devon
Previous clubs include: Exeter C - July 2001.

DAVEY, NEIL — Forward

Current Club: Maidstone United

Birthplace: Kent
Previous clubs include: Ramsgate - July 2001, Deal T, Herne Bay, Canterbury C, Whitstable T.

DAVEY, PETER — Defender

Current Club: Arnold Town

Birthplace: Nottingham
From Youth team.

DAVEY, SIMON — Goalkeeper

Current Club: Littlehampton Town

Birthplace: Sussex
Goalkeeper, known as Rodders: originally the reserve choice at Wick, but was a first-team regular during 1999/2000 thanks to plenty of comings and goings at Crabtree Park: recruited by Langney Sports for their first season in the Doc Martens League (2000/01) as a stand-in for the injury-prone Dean Lightwood: briefly featured for Eastbourne United at the start of the latest campaign, before joining Littlehampton: gave a poor impression in his second appearance for the Marigolds (against Whitehawk in September), when punching an easy back-pass delivery into his own net: conceded another howler at Chichester the following month, when passing the ball straight to an opponent.

DAVEY, STEVE — Forward

Current Club: Harrogate Railway

Birthplace: Harrogate
Previous clubs include: Harrogate T - September 1998.

DAVID, CARL — Midfielder

Current Club: Woodbridge Town

Birthplace: Essex
Arrived from Hadleigh at the beginning of the 1995/96 season previously with Wivenhoe. Carl is a strong and skilful player whose commitment and loyalty to the Club is a fine example to others. Supporters' Player of the season in 2000/01.

DAVID, PAUL — Midfielder

Current Club: Wakefield & Emley

Birthplace: Leeds
Paul has been at Emley since 1992 when he was signed from Bradley Rangers. Paul has been player of the year and despite not being a striker was leading scorer in the 1998/99 season. Scored Emleys first goal of this campaign and the goal against West Ham in the glorious FA Cup run.

DAVID, RICHARD — Defender

Current Club: Cwmbran Town

D o B: 15/12/1976   Birthplace: Wales
Previous clubs include: Inter Cardiff - December 1999, UWIC, Merthyr Tydfil, Aberaman.

DAVIDS, MARIO — Forward

Current Club: Great Yarmouth Town

D o B: 06/06/1978 *Birthplace: Namibia*
Honours won: Namibian u-23 Int.

Signed for Yarmouth last season from Anglian Combination club Acle United but previous to that he was playing semi-professionally for Tigers FC in the Namibian National League. Has played at youth and Under 23 level for that country. Now a student in Norwich.

DAVIDSON, CRAIG — Defender

Current Club: Canvey Island

D o B: 02/05/1974 *Birthplace: Essex*

Defender who originally signed for Canvey Island in July 1999/00. He is a solid left back who loves to go forward. Previous clubs include Aldershot Town, Southend United, Chelmsford City and Dagenham & Redbridge. Re-signed for Canvey July 2002 after a seasons spell at Braintree Town. Craig is currently a Tutor at SEEVIC College.

DAVIDSON, DANNY — Forward

Current Club: Stafford Rangers

Birthplace: Staffordshire

Tall, former Leek Town front man who signed for Dr Martens Premier side Stafford Rangers in July 2001 from Conference outfit Hereford United. Had joined the Bulls on a part-time contract in August 2001 so that he could continue his other career as a trainee accounting technician. Previous experience with Rocester and Burton Albion.

DAVIDSON, ELLIOTT — Midfielder

Current Club: Aveley

Birthplace: Essex

Previous clubs include: Grays Ath - March 2001, Romford, Great Wakering R, Gravesend, Aveley, Barking, Dagenham & Redbridge, Grays Ath., Leatherhead, Barking, Romford, Leatherhead, Cheshunt, Wivenhoe T, Rainham T, Grays Ath.

DAVIDSON, ROSS — Defender

Current Club: Ashford Town (Middx)

D o B: 13/11/1973 *Birthplace: Chertesy*

Previous clubs include: Shrewsbury T - November 2001, Barnet, Chester C, Sheffield Utd, Walton & Hersham.

DAVIES, ALAN — Defender

Current Club: Rhayader Town

D o B: 12/07/1968 *Birthplace: Wales*

Left sided defender starting his third season at the club. Strong in the tackle and always gives 100%.

DAVIES, ALLAN — Defender

Current Club: Worcester City

Birthplace: Burton

Experienced right-back who signed for Worcester City in the summer of 2001 from Burton Albion, having spent three months at St Georges Lane on loan from the Brewers. Began his career as a trainee at Manchester City before moving to Burton in 1991.

DAVIES, ANDREW — Forward

Current Club: Afan Lido

D o B: 28/03/1974 *Birthplace: Wales*

Recent signing from PT Athletic. Has fitted well into the team as a striker, but also plays on the left of midfield.

DAVIES, ANDREW — Midfielder

Current Club: Flexsys Cefn Druids

D o B: 13/09/1978 *Birthplace: Wales*

Previous clubs include: Flint Town Utd - July 1999, Wrexham.

DAVIES, ANDY — Defender

Current Club: Eastwood Town

Previous clubs include: Notts Co - July 2000.

DAVIES, ANDY — Forward

Current Club: Caersws

D o B: 30/10/1979 *Birthplace: Wales*

From Youth team.

DAVIES, ANTHONY — Defender

Current Club: Oldbury United

Birthplace: Worcestershire

Previous clubs include: Stourbridge - Jan 2002, Stourport Swifts, Oldbury Utd, Stourport Swifts, Stourbridge, Stourport Swifts, Stourbridge, Blakenall, Sandwell B, Gornal Ath., Pronces End Utd, Dudley T.

DAVIES, BEN — Midfielder

Current Club: Chester City

D o B: 27/05/1981 *Birthplace: Birmingham*

A product of Kidderminster Harriers youth system, Ben was highly-rated by former boss Jan Molby, who demonstrated his faith in the midfielder by including him on a pre-season tour of Denmark. Davies was not intimidated by his elevation to the first team, performing with composure and maturity and opening his goalscoring account with a powerfully struck shot from 20 yards in the 2-1 win over Vordingborg. Formerly with Walsall, he was released by Harriers after Molby departed for Hull and joined Chester in May 2002.

DAVIES, BILLY — Goalkeeper

Current Club: Tring Town

Birthplace: Herts

Previous clubs include: Leverstock Green - July 2000, Berkhamsted T, Leverstock Green, Aylesbury Utd.

DAVIES, DARREN — Defender

Current Club: Dover Athletic

D o B: 13/08/1978 *Birthplace: Port Talbot*

Darren was an apprentice at Tottenham before he became a Morton player via a short spell back in his native Wales with Barry Town in the League of Wales. Signed for Dover Athletic in September 2001 and after originally being used as a left-back, Darren switched to a defensive midfield role, and instantly made an impression.

DAVIES, DAVID — Defender

Current Club: Stourport Swifts

Previous clubs include: Oldbury Utd - July 2001, Bridgnorth T, Paget R, Solihull B, Kidderminster Harriers, WBA (Trainee).

DAVIES, GARETH — Defender

Current Club: Chippenham Town

D o B: 11/12/1973 *Birthplace: Hereford*
Honours won: Wales u-21 Int.

Signed for Dr Martens Premier side Chippenham Town in March 2002 from Swindon Town. Dai is a former Welsh under-21 and B international. He started his playing career at Hereford United before moving to Crystal Palace for £250,000. Whilst at Palace he played under both Steve Coppell and Attilio Lombardo before leaving to join Reading and then to Swindon Town where he was forced to retire with a serious knee injury. His arrival at Chippenham was just perfect with the club going for promotion from the Western Division, and he soon showed his undoubted quality and big things are expected from him in rthe Premier.

DAVIES, GARETH   *Forward*
Current Club: Fairford Town
Birthplace: Wiltshire
From Youth team.

DAVIES, GARETH   *Midfielder*
Current Club: Buxton
Birthplace: Sheffield
Previous clubs include: Sheffield Utd - October 2000.

DAVIES, GARY   *Defender*
Current Club: Port Talbot Town
D o B: 09/09/1979   *Birthplace: Wales*
Joined Port Talbot Town in July 2001 after spells with Oxford United, Carmarthen Town & Llanelli. A hard, rugged & determined defender.

DAVIES, GLENN   *Defender*
Current Club: Ringmer
D o B: 20/02/1976   *Birthplace: Brighton*
Central defender and a former professional who made 52 appearances for Hartlepool. Played alongside Glen Geard at Worthing and Saltdean before joining Burgess Hill in November 1999. Transferred to Ringmer during the 2000 close season and scored five times last year, and also served a five week ban without missing a single game due to poor weather.

DAVIES, IAN   *Defender*
Current Club: Carmarthen Town
Birthplace: Wales
From Youth team.

DAVIES, JAMIE   *Midfielder*
Current Club: Caersws
D o B: 18/04/1984   *Birthplace: Wales*
From Youth team.

DAVIES, JAY   *Forward*
Current Club: Flexsys Cefn Druids
D o B: 21/07/1980   *Birthplace: Wales*
From Youth team.

DAVIES, KENNY   *Midfielder*
Current Club: Billingham Synthonia
D o B: 22/12/1970   *Birthplace: Stockton*
Previous clubs include: Stockport Co - July 1992, Gateshead, Hartlepool Utd.

DAVIES, KEVIN   *Defender*
Current Club: Telford United
D o B: 15/11/1978   *Birthplace: Sheffield*
Previous clubs include: Sheffield Utd - July 2000.

DAVIES, LEE   *Defender*
Current Club: Newtown AFC
D o B: 30/09/1977   *Birthplace: Wales*
From Youth team.

DAVIES, MARTIN   *Goalkeeper*
Current Club: Cambridge City
D o B: 28/06/1974   *Birthplace: Swansea*
Honours won: Wales u-21 Int.
Goalkeeper who has played for several Nationwide Conference clubs. After moving back to his native Wales at the beginning of the 2001/02 season he rejoined Cambridge City in Decembe 01 From Llanelli. Martin originally joined City from Dover Athletic and before that had spent five years at Coventry City. He originates from Swansea and has represented Wales at under-21 level.

DAVIES, MATT   *Defender*
Current Club: Salisbury CIty
D o B: 02/01/1982   *Birthplace: Wiltshire*
Honours won: England Schoolboy Int.
Formerly with Southampton. where he captained the Academy under-19 side, Matt has represented England at under-16 and under-17 levels. Signed for Dr Martens Eastern side Salsibury City in August 2001 from Woking, Matt has impressed with his ability and dedication Captained the side during the second half of the 2001/023 season. Has the attitude and ability to return to the full-time game.

DAVIES, MATTIE   *Forward*
Current Club: Cwmbran Town
D o B: 08/01/1976   *Birthplace: Cardiff*
Previous clubs include: Barry T - December 2001, Cwmbran T, Cardiff Institute of HE, Cardiff Civil Service.

DAVIES, MIKE   *Forward*
Current Club: Flexsys Cefn Druids
D o B: 09/12/1970   *Birthplace: Wales*
Previous clubs include: TNS Llansantfraid - July 1997.

DAVIES, NATHAN   *Midfielder*
Current Club: Newport County
D o B: 26/05/1982   *Birthplace: Pontypool*
Honours won: Wales Youth Int.
An eight-times capped Welsh under-18 international and a product of the Newport Schools Football Academy. He made his Dr Martens League debut for Newport County against Atherstone United in January 2000 and has now made over almost 100 first-team appearances. The highly-rated midfielder has been under close scrutiny from League clubs.

DAVIES, PAUL   *Defender*
Current Club: Warrington Town
Birthplace: Cheshire
Previous clubs include: Witton Alb - January 2000.

DAVIES, PAUL   *Forward*
Current Club: Evesham United
D o B: 09/10/1960   *Birthplace: Kidderminster*
Honours won: England Semi-Pro Int., Conference Winners, FA Trophy Winners, FA XI
Previous clubs include: Worcester C - January 2000, Kidderminster Harriers, SC Hercules (Holland), Trowbridge T, Cardiff C.

DAVIES, SHANE   *Defender*
Current Club: Sittingbourne
Birthplace: Kent
From Youth team.

DAVIES, SIMON   *Midfielder*
Current Club: Bangor City
D o B: 23/04/1974   *Birthplace: Winsford*
Honours won: Wales Int.
Skilful midfielder who made 11 Premiership appearances for Manchester United where he gained a full Welsh international cap before joining Luton Town for £150,000 in 1997. Joined League of Wales side Bangor City from Rochdale in July 2001 having also had a spell at Macclesfield.

DAVIES, STEVE   *Defender*
Current Club: Leyton Pennant
Birthplace: Essex
Previous clubs include: Barking & East Ham Utd - November 2001.

DAVIES, STEVE　　　　　　　　*Forward*
Current Club: Littlehampton Town
Birthplace: Sussex
Exciting young forward with plenty of promise: originally played for Rustington Otters youth team: made a real splash in the County League during 2000/01 when netting his first goal in October and, seven days later, came off the bench (against Whitehawk) to score twice and earn a 2-2 draw for Littlehampton: frustratingly held back after receiving a knee injury in a game with Pagham during January: a Sussex U-18 squad member during 2001/02 and has attracted interest from several Football League clubs: also a top class basketball player.

DAVIES, STEVE　　　　　　*Midfielder*
Current Club: Kidsgrove Athletic
Birthplace: Stoke
Usually found in midfield nowadays, but his versatility played a major part in the success of the 1997/8 season. Previous clubs include Barnton and Witton Albion.

DAVIES, TERRY　　　　　　*Midfielder*
Current Club: Flackwell Heath
Birthplace: Berkshire
Previous clubs include: Egham T - March 2002, Chertsey T, Bracknell T.

DAVIES, WILL　　　　　　　*Forward*
Current Club: Matlock Town
D o B: 27/09/1975　　　　　*Birthplace: Derby*
Will can operate as either a central defender or as a central striker. The popular local lad began his career with Derby County, before having spells in Ireland and Iceland. He eventually joined Gresley Rovers, before moving to Causeway Lane at the start of the 1998/99 season.

DAVIS, ADAM　　　　　　　*Defender*
Current Club: Selsey
Birthplace: Brighton
Full back/winger and captain of Brightons U-19 team in 1999/2000 and also played for Albions reserves (gained the curious nickname of Lipstick). A really useful additional to the Selsey line-up when joining in March 2001.

DAVIS, CRAIG　　　　　　*Midfielder*
Current Club: Bashley
Previous clubs include: Cardiff C - August 2000, Bashley.

DAVIS, DANNY　　　　　　*Midfielder*
Current Club: Lewes
D o B: 03/10/1980　　　　*Birthplace: Brighton*
Robust midfielder, previously with Brighton & Hove Albion: briefly figured at Lewes during 2000/01 (scored twice) after being released by the Seagulls, before joining St Albans: signed by Worthing during the summer 2001: picked up a shoulder injury in the match with Tooting & Mitcham during September returned to action in January and then transferred back to Lewes in March 2002.

DAVIS, DWAYNE　　　　　　*Forward*
Current Club: Southwick
Birthplace: Sussex
Former Worthing player under Sammy Donnelly: joined Southwick from Whyteleafe in December 2001 when Donnelly switched clubs.

DAVIS, GARY　　　　　　　*Defender*
Current Club: Mangotsfield United
Birthplace: Bristol
Previous clubs include: Almonsbury T - July 1999, Yate T, Almondsbury T, Yate T.

DAVIS, JAMES　　　　　　　*Defender*
Current Club: Horsham YMCA
Birthplace: Sussex
Signed from Steyning during the 2001 close season: son of former YM striker, Mark Davis.

DAVIS, KORI　　　　　　　*Defender*
Current Club: Soham Town Rangers
D o B: 19/02/1979　　　　*Birthplace: Wegburg*
Previous clubs include: Yeading - September 1999, Farnborough T, Norwich C.

DAVIS, LEIGH　　　　　　　*Forward*
Current Club: Saltdean United
Birthplace: Sussex
Brother of former Brighton & Hove Albion player Danny Davis: started out in the Saltdean youth team before joining Ansty Rangers: returned to Hill Park towards the end of 2000/01.

DAVIS, MIKE　　　　　　　*Forward*
Current Club: Mangotsfield United
D o B: 19/10/1974　　　　*Birthplace: Bristol*
Strong front runner who joined Dr Martens Western side Mangotsfield United in July 2002 from Ryman Premier Basingstoke Town. Began his career with Yate Town before moving into the League with Bristol Rovers in 1992. Went on to make around 17 first-team appearances for Rovers before being released and joining Bath City in July 1996. Spent five years at Twerton Park before moving to Stoke in the summer of 2001.

DAVIS, NEIL　　　　　　　*Forward*
Current Club: Newport County
D o B: 15/08/1973　　　　*Birthplace: Bloxwich*
Respected forward who signed for Dr Martens Premier side Newport County in August 2002 from Hednesford Town. Had joined Hednesford Town in September 1998. He started his career with Redditch United before moving on to Aston Villa and then to Wycombe Wanderers. He became a firm favourite with the Pitmen fans thanks to his regular goalscoring and was top goalscorer at the club for the past four seasons.

DAVIS, NEIL　　　　　　　*Midfielder*
Current Club: Havant & Waterlooville
Birthplace: Southampton
Joining Havant & Waterlooville for the 2001/02 campaign from Southampton, Neil sat on the bench for much of the first half of the season. He has however recently become a first-team regular and is gaining a reputation for his crunching midfield tackling. Started life with Southamptons youth side.

DAVIS, NICK　　　　　　　*Defender*
Current Club: VCD Athletic
D o B: 25/12/1981　　　　*Birthplace: Greenwich*
From Youth team.

DAVIS, RICHARD　　　　　　*Defender*
Current Club: Sidlesham
Birthplace: Surrey
Wing-back: previously with Godalming/Guildford (Combined Counties League): moved to Sussex as a student and signed for

Pagham at the start of 2001/02 (had a reputation for being a prolific goalscorer): out of action after being involved in a car crash and started in the Lions reserves before making his first-team debut in October 2001: switched to Sidlesham in December: also plays for University College Chichester.

DAVIS, RYAN — Defender
Current Club: Worksop Town

D o B: 16/11/1979   Birthplace: Stoke
Previous clubs include: Luton T - September 1999, Sheffield Wednesday.

DAVIS, STEVE — Defender
Current Club: Northwich Victoria

D o B: 26/07/1965   Birthplace: Birmingham
Honours won: England Youth Int.
Steve was appointed assistant-manager to Jimmy Quinn at Conference club Northwich Victoria in July 2001. He is a vastly-experienced central defender who started his career with Vics Cheshire neighbours Crewe Alexandra and went on to make 145 appearances for the Railwaymen. After leaving Gresty Road, he moved on to Burnley and Barnsley, playing more than 100 League games for both. Following a brief loan spell at York City, Steve teamed up with Oxford United before joining the Greens in August 2000. Now 36, Steve also coaches youngsters at Vics new school of excellence at Mid-Cheshire College.

DAVIS, STEVE — Defender
Current Club: Swindon Supermarine

Birthplace: Swindon
Steve played a few games at the end of the 1998/99 season and performed very well, and the following last season demonstrated that he was a very capable player who never let the side down when called upon. Expectations were high last season for him to become a regular in the first team. That was fulfilled with some excellent performances and great goals along the way. A few injuries have reduced his availability at times but his form saw him gain representative honours for the Wiltshire FA at U-21 level last season. Possesses an excellent left foot, is good in the air and his distribution out of defence is exceptional at times. A young player with a very bright future in football.

DAVIS, TONY — Goalkeeper
Current Club: Hanwell Town

D o B: 08/11/1972   Birthplace: Hammersmith
Previous clubs include: Old Actonians - July 2001, Yeading.

DAVISON, CRAIG — Defender
Current Club: Pelsall Villa

Birthplace: Birmingham
Previous clubs include: Rushall Olympic - July 2000, Stourbridge, Rushall Olympic, Wednesfield, Bloxwich T, Willenhall T, Bloxwich T, Bloxwich Strollers, Pelsall Villa.

DAVISON, IAN — Defender
Current Club: Consett

Birthplace: Newcastle
Previous clubs include: Prudhoe T - September 2001, Chester-le-Street, Consett, Durham C, Whickham, Ashington.

DAVY, JASON — Midfielder
Current Club: St.Leonards

D o B: 20/04/1976   Birthplace: Balham
Previous clubs include: Oxford C - July 2001, Croydon, Crawley T, Tooting & Mitcham Utd, Kingstonian, Walton & Hersham, Carshalton Ath., Millwall, Crystal Palace (Junior), Wimbledon (Junior).

DAVY, MICHAEL — Midfielder
Current Club: Glapwell

Birthplace: Nottinghamshire
Previous clubs include: Worksop T - July 2001.

DAWBER, MARK — Midfielder
Current Club: Berkhamsted Town

Birthplace: Surrey
Previous clubs include: Egham T - March 2001, Windsor & Eton, Chesham Utd, Hendon, Chertsey T, Sutton Utd, Chesham Utd, Staines T, Wycombe Wanderers, Woking, Virginia Water.

DAWSON, DOUGIE — Midfielder
Current Club: Nantwich Town

Birthplace: Cheshire
Previous clubs include: Trafford - July 1998, Nantwich T, Stafford R, Nantwich T, Crewe Alexandra.

DAWSON, MICHAEL — Midfielder
Current Club: Durham City

Birthplace: Newcastle
Previous clubs include: Darlington - July 2000, Middlesbrough, Newcastle Utd (Junior).

DAWSON, PHIL — Defender
Current Club: Whyteleafe

D o B: 09/08/1965   Birthplace: Hooley
Previous clubs include: Carshalton Ath - July 1997, Chipstead, Molesey, Carshalton Ath., Woking, Carshalton Ath., Sutton Utd, Chipstead.

DAWSON, STUART — Goalkeeper
Current Club: Blyth Spartans

D o B: 04/12/1968   Birthplace: Hartlepool
Previous clubs include: Spennymoor Utd - March 2002, Whitby T, Tow Law T, Durham C, Peterlee Newtown, Hartlepool Utd.

DAY, ADAM — Defender
Current Club: Fisher Athletic (London)

Birthplace: Kent
Previous clubs include: Welling Utd - August 2002.

DAY, ADAM — Midfielder
Current Club: Sidley United

Birthplace: Sussex
Midfielder: son of the chairman and once described as a creative magician: key member of Sidleys Division Two league-and-cup winning side of 1999: joined St Leonards in August 2000 before returning to Sidley three months later: scored two of the goals in the Blues 3-2 victory over Sidlesham in last seasons John OHara Cup Final.

DAY, ALAN — Forward
Current Club: Wivenhoe Town

Birthplace: Essex
Previous clubs include: Clacton T - September 1996, Stanway R.

DAY, DANNY — Forward
Current Club: Wakefield & Emley

Birthplace: Yorkshire
Emleys leading scorer in 1999/2000, his first with the club. The previous season he scored 42 goals for Ossett Albion, where they won the NCE championship and West Riding Cup. Scored in a pre-season friendly against Leeds United.

DAY, JAMIE — *Midfielder*

Current Club: Dover Athletic

D o B: 13/09/1979   *Birthplace: Sidcup*
Honours won: England Schoolboy & Youth Int.

Jamie is a promising midfielder who graduated in the England School of Excellence at Lilleshall alongside famous players such as Wes Brown and Michael Owen. During his youth days, Jamie was in the Arsenal youth squad and won caps for England at under-16, under-17 and under-18 levels. He signed for Bournemouth for a £20,000 fee in 1999, and then switched to Dover Athletic at the start of the 2001/02 season.

DAY, JUSTIN — *Forward*

Current Club: Bracknell Town

D o B: 02/02/1972   *Birthplace: Berkshire*
Previous clubs include: Egham T - July 1993, Bracknell T.

DAY, LEO — *Midfielder*

Current Club: Burgess Hill Town

Birthplace: Burgess Hill Town
Honours won: Sussex County League Div 2 (Southwick), Floodlit Cup, Norman Wingate Trophy and RUR Cup (all three with Burgess Hill Town)

Midfielder: originally a youth team player at Burgess Hill before having a spell with Crawley reserves: returned to Leylands Park in November 1999: was set to play for Withdean starting from August 2000 onwards, but was re-routed to Southwick when plans to compete in the Combined Counties League were thwarted by an FA ruling: a member of the relaunched Withdean squad from the start of 2001/02: Joined Burgess Hill in the close season of 2002/2003.

DAY, STEVE — *Midfielder*

Current Club: AFC Sudbury

Birthplace: Suffolk
Attacking midfielder with AFC Sudbury who played for Sudbury Wanderers for several seasons. Can score some great goals.

DE BONT, ANDY — *Goalkeeper*

Current Club: Stourbridge

D o B: 07/01/1974   *Birthplace: Wolverhampton*
Previous clubs include: Bilston T - November 2001, Moor Green, Stourbridge, Hereford Utd, Wolverhampton Wanderers.

DE LUCA, PAUL — *Forward*

Current Club: Walton & Hersham

Birthplace: London
Previous clubs include: Hampton & Richmond Borough - February 2002, Egham T.

DE SOUZA, MIGUEL — *Forward*

Current Club: St.Albans City

D o B: 11/02/1970   *Birthplace: Newham*
Highly-experienced striker who signed for Ryman Premier side St Albans City in August 2002. Began his career in the Football League at Birmingham City and then had successful spells at both Wycombe Wanderers and Peterborough United. Spent the 2001/02 season at Farnborough Town following earlier Conference stints at Rushden & Diamonds and Boston United.

DEADMAN, JOHN — *Midfielder*

Current Club: Wealdstone

D o B: 03/09/1972   *Birthplace: London*
Previous clubs include: Enfield - March 2001, Kingstonian, Purfleet, Hendon, Grays Ath.

DEAN, MICHAEL — *Midfielder*

Current Club: Weymouth

D o B: 09/03/1978   *Birthplace: Bournemouth*
Michael signed from AFC Bournemouth in July 2000. Had a poor start at Weymouth, but had the attitude and resilience to battle back and prove that he was good enough to be in the team. He went on to put in some impressive displays and won over the Weymouth faithful.

DEAN, PAUL — *Forward*

Current Club: Atherton Laburnum Rovers

Birthplace: Manchester
Paul is in his first season with Atherton LR following a spell at Atherton Collieries. He is a superb target man with the capability to beat defenders and is a big threat with his aerial ability. Paul is a civil engineer and he enjoys darts, snooker and camping.

DEAN, PHIL — *Forward*

Current Club: Arlesey Town

Birthplace: London
London-born Phil was a 2002 close season signing for Ryman Division One North side Arlesey Town from Edgware Town. Formerly with Welwyn Garden City, Stevenage Borough, Boreham Wood, Hitchin Town and Molesey Sustained a serious knee injury whilst with Edgware. His brave, bustling approach is sure to make him a favourite among the Arlesey supporters.

DEANER, ANDREW — *Forward*

Current Club: Slough Town

Birthplace: Berkshire
A powerfully built front runner who is another Slough player, who spent time with Reading football club. Andrew unfortunately failed to make the grade at Reading and drifted into the Non-League game. He had a successful spell with Newbury Town and a brief spell with Wokingham Town before joining the Rebels on a free transfer. By Andrews standards, his first season was not one of his best, but he scored some very important goals for Slough against Crawley (2 goals) in the FA Trophy in a 3-2 win and a goal in a 2-2 FA Cup draw against Macclesfield Town. In his second season at Slough, he could not have started the season better, scoring nine times in the early part of the season. Scored one goal in only a handful of appearances last season against Sutton United.

DEAR, CHRIS — *Defender*

Current Club: Wisbech Town

D o B: 25/05/1978
Previous clubs include: Spalding Utd - January 2001, Wisbech T, Norwich C.

DEARLOVE, MARK — *Defender*

Current Club: Stourport Swifts

Previous clubs include: Redditch Utd - January 2000, Bridgnorth T, Kidderminster Harriers.

DEARSLEY, STEVE — *Midfielder*

Current Club: Woodbridge Town

Birthplace: Suffolk
Signed Jewson forms in the 1997/98 season, and was made First Team captain for the 2000/01 season. His range of skills continue to greatly enhance our midfield, as well as providing us with the occasional spectacular goal.

DEASY, RICKY   *Midfielder*
Current Club: Felixstowe & Walton United
Birthplace: Suffolk
Signed as a striker early last season from SIL Achilles, but forced into midfield through injury to other players, now able to operate in a variety of roles when required. Bubbly character with loads of enthusiasm and effort.

DEATH, FREDDIE   *Midfielder*
Current Club: Mildenhall Town
Birthplace: Cambridgeshire
Previous clubs include: Peterborough Utd - November 2001.

DEEKS, CARL   *Forward*
Current Club: Bury Town
Birthplace: Suffolk
Previous clubs include: Walsham Le Willows - July 1999.

DEER, ANTHONY   *Goalkeeper*
Current Club: Herne Bay
Birthplace: Kent
Previous clubs include: Walmer Rovers - July 1996.

DEFOE, GINO   *Midfielder*
Current Club: Heybridge Swifts
Previous clubs include: Witham T - January 2001, Heybridge Swifts, Witham T, Braintree T, Witham T.

DeGARIS, SCOTT   *Midfielder*
Current Club: Leyton Pennant
Birthplace: Essex
Previous clubs include: Waltham Abbey - August 2001, Ilford.

DEGUTIS, ADRIAN   *Defender*
Current Club: Great Wakering Rovers
Birthplace: Southend
From Youth team.

DELANEY, KIERAN   *Forward*
Current Club: Curzon Ashton
Birthplace: Oldham
Previous clubs include: Oldham T - October 2000.

DELEA, GRANT   *Midfielder*
Current Club: Brentwood
Birthplace: Essex
After missing most of the last two seasons with a serious shoulder injury, Grant is fit again and will strengthen the Blues midfield this season.

DELEON, ANDRE   *Forward*
Current Club: Erith & Belvedere
Birthplace: London
Joined Erith & Belvedere in October 2001. Previous clubs include Boreham Wood, Grays and St. Albans. A very quick wing back or wide front man.

DELICATA, JULIAN   *Midfielder*
Current Club: Fakenham Town
Birthplace: Norfolk
Previous clubs include: Watton Utd - August 1999, Kings Lynn, Tottenham Hotspur (Trainee).

DELISSER, ANDRE   *Midfielder*
Current Club: Boreham Wood
Birthplace: London
Andre is an attacking wing forward who can also operate as a striker. He began his career at Southall, before moving on to Northwood and Yeading. He spent most of the 1998/99 Season with Hayes in the Nationwide Conference, and joined Boreham Wood during the 1999 summer, making his first-team debut against Dulwich Hamlet on the 14 August 1999. Andre suffered a bad injury, when he broke a leg on the opening day of the 2001/02 season.

DELL, STEVE   *Defender*
Current Club: Brook House
Birthplace: Middlesex
Previous clubs include: Ruislip Manor - July 2001.

DELLAR, BARRY   *Midfielder*
Current Club: Arlesey Town
Birthplace: Luton
Barry is an industrious attacking midfield player who covers a lot of ground during a game. A good tackler and retriever of the ball, he is also an excellent distributor from the middle of the park. Has played for Baldock and Hitchin Town, where he won Herts Senior Cup Medals with each club, and was in the Arlesey side that won the South Midlands League Premier Division in 1995/96. He is an assistant Building Surveyor.

DELLER-SMITH, ADAM   *Forward*
Current Club: Fleet Town
Birthplace: Hampshire
From Youth team.

DELVES, NICK   *Defender*
Current Club: Gloucester City
Previous clubs include: Brockworth - July 2001.

DEMAINE, PAUL   *Midfielder*
Current Club: Great Harwood Town
Birthplace: Lancashire
From Local football - July 2001.

DEMATTEO, RUSSELL   *Forward*
Current Club: Rocester
Birthplace: Stafford
Previous clubs include: Stafford T - July 2001.

DEMBA, ABDOUTAI   *Forward*
Current Club: Yeovil Town
D o B: 02/11/1976   *Birthplace: Mali*
Honours won: Mali Int.
Big Mali-born striker who joined Yeovil Town in June 2002. First came to prominence with the El Kahlij club in the United Arab Emirates but then began to attract attention through his goals for KV Ostende in the Belgian First Division.

DEMPSEY, MARK   *Midfielder*
Current Club: Radcliffe Borough
D o B: 10/12/1972   *Birthplace: Dublin*
Honours won: Republic of Ireland Youth & u-21 Int.
A very experienced midfielder, Mark still has a tremendous appetite for the game, despite now being in the veteran class. A skilful and hard-working player who began his career at Manchester United and enjoyed a long League career with Sheffield United and Rotherham. Signed for Radcliffe Borough in July 1998 from Alfreton Town where he was player-manager, and

has also served the likes of Gainsborough Trinity, Frickley Athletic, Buxton, Altrincham and Macclesfield. A former Republic of Ireland Youth and under-21 international, Mark is also now on the coaching staff at Old Trafford wher he coaches the youngsters.

DEMPSEY, PAUL   *Defender*
Current Club: Yate Town
Birthplace: Bristol
Previous clubs include: Mangotsfield Utd - July 2001, Brislington, Yate T, Clevedon T, Yate T.

DENHAM, CHRIS   *Forward*
Current Club: Stalybridge Celtic
Birthplace: Lancashire
Chris started life knocking goals in for fun at Prestwich Heys. Soon moved up the Pyramid to Stand Athletic for their 2001/2 season, where he scored 29 goals, despite spending a two month loan spell at Bamber Bridge in October and November to shake off a hamstring injury. He is tenacious and accurate with bags of pace.

DENNETT, CHRIS   *Forward*
Current Club: Hadleigh United
Birthplace: Suffolk
Talented and skilful youngster who again broke into the Hadleigh squad at the end of last season and proved his potential. Comfortable on the ball and extremely quick. Progressed with the Club from the youth teams.

DENNEY, ANDREW   *Defender*
Current Club: Bishops Stortford
Birthplace: Essex
Andrew is a product of the Blues Youth team and on the verge of breaking into the senior side.

DENNEY, PHIL   *Forward*
Current Club: Ashton United
Previous clubs include: Bradford PA (£2,500) - August 2001, Harrogate T, Bury.

DENNIS, CRAIG   *Defender*
Current Club: Great Wakering Rovers
Birthplace: Essex
Highly-rated young central defender who joined Ryman Division One North side Great Wakering Rovers from Essex league rivals Tilbury in July 2002. Began his playing days with Saffron Walden Tpown and also had a spell with Bishops Stortford before signing for Tilbury in January 2001.

DENNIS, MARCEL   *Forward*
Current Club: Horsham
Birthplace: Kent
Previous clubs include: Banstead Ath - July 2001, Bromley.

DENNY, STEVE   *Forward*
Current Club: Clitheroe
Birthplace: Lancashire
Previous clubs include: Cheadle T - Dec 1999, Squires Gate.

DENT, LEE   *Forward*
Current Club: Newport Isle Of Wight
Previous clubs include: Cowes Sports - July 1999.

DENT, NICKY   *Forward*
Current Club: Dover Athletic
D o B: 30/12/1967   *Birthplace: Bristol*
Flamboyant striker who re-signed for Dover Athletic in June 2002 from Kent neighbours Folkestone Invicta. Had joined Invicta from Hastings Town for a club record fee of £4,500 during the autumn of 1998. Nicky swept the board when he was voted Supporters, Players and the Player of the Year after finishing as the clubs top goalscorer with 30 goals in all competitions during the 2000/01 season. After a short spell as a professional at Bristol City he has played for Yeovil, Poole Town, Dover and Ashford Town, as well as enjoying a spell with Sing Tao in Hong Kong. Is always capable of producing something special.

DENTON, EDDIE   *Midfielder*
Current Club: Slough Town
D o B: 18/05/1970   *Birthplace: Oxford*
Signed for Slough following his release by Aylesbury United. Eddie is one of the most popular figures at the club. He is the assistant maager to Steve Browne, but also is manager of the Slough Town reserve side. Denton only made a handful of appearances for Slough last season. But most Slough fans believe Eddie can still do a good job for Slough at this level. Eddie has played league football for Oxford United and even played for Oxford in a cup match against Manchester United. He also has appeared for the Town's other side - Oxford City.

DENTON, LUKE   *Midfielder*
Current Club: Eastbourne Borough
Birthplace: Sussex
Signed from Eastbourne Town during the 2001 close-season. Has progressed to the first team squad following eye-catching performances for the Reserves this season.

DERBY, JAMIE   *Forward*
Current Club: Metropolitan Police
Birthplace: London
Previous clubs include: None - July 1997.

DERRY, SHAUN   *Forward*
Current Club: Bromsgrove Rovers
Birthplace: Birmingham
Previous clubs include: Chasetown - October 2001, Sandwell B, Pelsall Villa, Bolehall Swifts.

DESBOROUGH, MICKY   *Goalkeeper*
Current Club: Bishops Stortford
D o B: 28/11/1969   *Birthplace: Essex*
Experienced keeper signed from Grays Athletic in January 2001. Micky started his career with Clapton before moving onto Chelmsford City, Purfleet, Gravesend, Braintree, Canvey Island. In 1993/4 season, Micky played in the Football League helping out Colchester Utd. Micky was awarded the Ryman League safe hands award in August/September 2001.

DEVEREUX, BRIAN   *Forward*
Current Club: AFC Sudbury
Birthplace: Suffolk
Previous clubs include: Sudbury Wanderers - July 1999, Braintree T, Halstead T, Cornard Utd.

DEVEREUX, JAY   *Defender*
Current Club: Ford United
Birthplace: Essex
Honours won: *Ryman League Div.One Winners*
A talented defender who originally came through Dagenham & Redbridges ranks to make the fringes of the senior side at Victoria Road. Moved to Ford United in search of regular first-team football

and impressed enough to be given a chance at Ryman Premier Division level with Enfield in the summer of 2000 following four years with Ford. Re-joined Ford in August 2001 and played a major part in helping them win the Ryman Division One title.

DEVEREUX, ROBBIE — *Midfielder*
Current Club: AFC Sudbury
D o B: 31/01/1971   Birthplace: Bury St.Edmunds
Vastly experienced player who has tasted European football. A crowd pleaser who AFC Sudbury joined at the start of 2000/ 01 after spells with Southport, Irish side St Patricks and Ipswich.

DEVINE, RICHARD — *Defender*
Current Club: St.Leonards
D o B: 30/12/1980   Birthplace: Hastings
Richard is a defender and former member of St Leonards successful youth side. He has been a stalwart of the second eleven for the past three seasons and spent the summer of 2000 coaching in the USA.

DEVLIN, MARK — *Midfielder*
Current Club: Northwich Victoria
Birthplace: Irvine
A skilful midfielder who signed for Conference side Nortwhich Victoria in January 1999 from Exeter City. Marks pinpoint passing and creativity make him a focal point for many of the Greens attacks and is role in the team will assume even greater importance following the summer departures of Steve Walters and Val Owen. Scotland-born Mark has previously seen service with Stoke City as well as the Grecians.

DEVONALD, STEVE — *Midfielder*
Current Club: Llanelli AFC
Birthplace: Wales
From Youth team.

DEWEY, KEVIN — *Forward*
Current Club: Selsey
Birthplace: Sussex
Small striker who left Pagham to join Oving in March 2000, and scored 8 times for the Vikings during 2000/01 (missed the end of that campaign due to work commitments). In good form when returning to Nyetimber Lane for the start of the following season and signed for Selsey in December 2001, shortly after appearing for Sussex in their victory over the Navy.

DEWHURST, ROB — *Defender*
Current Club: North Ferriby United
D o B: 10/09/1971   Birthplace: Keighley
Experienced ex-professional defender who turned out for Blackburn rovers, Hull City, Exeter City and Scunthorpe United and made almost 200 League appearances. Signed for North Ferriby United in September 2000 following a spell with UniBond Premier side Gainsborough Trinity.

DEWS, LEE — *Forward*
Current Club: Denaby United
Birthplace: Sheffield
From Local football - August 2001.

DI BATTISTA, SUNTINE — *Defender*
Current Club: Llanelli AFC
Previous clubs include: Swansea C - July 2001, Oxford Utd.

DIACZUK, LEON — *Midfielder*
Current Club: Trafford
D o B: 09/08/1981   Birthplace: Manchester
Previous clubs include: Flixton - July 2000, Stockport Co., Manchester C (Junior).

DIALLO, CHERIF — *Forward*
Current Club: Hayes
Birthplace: Senegal
Previous clubs include: Exeter C - February 2002, Scarborough, Brighton, Draguignan (France).

DIBBLE, JAMIE — *Midfielder*
Current Club: Almondsbury Town
Birthplace: Bristol
Previous clubs include: Hallen - January 2002.

DICK, ALEX — *Midfielder*
Current Club: Hayes
D o B: 02/09/1982   Birthplace: Paddington
Previous clubs include: QPR - August 2001.

DICK, JIMMY — *Midfielder*
Current Club: Boston United
Birthplace: Scotland
A tenacious, hard tackling, central midfielder. Signed up from Airdrieonians in the close season.

DICKEN, DARRELL — *Midfielder*
Current Club: Witton Albion
Birthplace: Manchester
Honours won: NWCL Winners
Attacking midfielder who joined UniBond First Division side Witton Albion in August 2002 from Kidsgrove Athletic,whom he helped to promotion in 2001/02 . Had signed for Kidsgrove from North West Counties League rivals Mossley in October 2001, for whom he scored 33 goals in 150 appearances, and was NWCL player of the year in 1998/9. Prior to that he played for Winsford United, Congleton Town and Grove United.

DICKER, CHRIS — *Midfielder*
Current Club: St.Leonards
Birthplace: Sussex
Joined Lewes from Langney Sports (now Eastbourne Borough) in December 1999. Chris is a policeman with a fantastic left foot and an eye for goal which is reflected in an excellent scoring record for the Rooks. Transferred to St Leonards in February 2002.

DICKER, PHIL — *Defender*
Current Club: Aylesbury United
Birthplace: London
Vastly experienced Non-League defender who joined Aylesbury United in July 2002 from Ryman Premier rivals Hampton & Richmond Borough. Had re-signed for Hampton in October 2001 after previously serving Yeading, Harrow and Wealdstone. Was on the books at Brentford as a youngster.

DICKERSON, KARL — *Defender*
Current Club: Fakenham Town
Birthplace: Norfolk
Previous clubs include: Dereham T - July 2001, Watton Utd, Bury T, Watton Utd, Kings Lynn.

DICKESON, MARK   *Forward*

Current Club: Newport County

D o B: 20/10/1974   *Birthplace: Wales*

Honours won: Wales Semi-Professional Int.

Mark transferred from League of Wales side Llanelli to Dr Martens League Premier Division Newport County in May 2002. He started his career playing for Trostre Sports in the Carmarthenshire League and joined Llanelli in the 1992/93 season, playing mainly as a midfielder. Plagued with injuries over the years, he has had at least two lengthy layoffs, and also had a brief loan spell at Carmarthen Town. However, following Llanellis promotion-winning season in 1998/99, Mark established himself as first choice striker and made a huge impact, ranking as the League of Wales Presented with the Most Improved Player award at Stebonheath for the 1999-2000 season, and Player of the Season for 2000/01, he was also one of the heroes for Wales in their UniBond Four Nations success in May 2002.

DICKIE, JAMES   *Forward*

Current Club: Potters Bar Town

Birthplace: Herts

Previous clubs include: Watford (Junior) - July 2000.

DICKINSON, DAVE   *Forward*

Current Club: Glasshoughton Welfare

Birthplace: Yorkshire

Previous clubs include: Frickley Ath - March 1999.

DICKINSON, MARK   *Defender*

Current Club: Whyteleafe

Birthplace: Newcastle

A very influential central defender and occasional striker, Mark re-joined Whyteleafe in the summer of 2002 from Croydon. Had returned to Croydon in November 1994 after a brief spell with the club in season 1993/94. He was previously with Crawley Town, and made over 300 appearances for Croydon. Geordie, as he is known, changed his mind about retiring in 1998 and that decision has been fully vindicated ashe was rewarded in 2000 with a clean sweep of Player of the Year awards at Croydon.

DICKINSON, STEVE   *Defender*

Current Club: Aveley

Birthplace: London

Steve joined Ryman Division One North side Aveley in August 2002 from Premier Division Billericay Town. Had signed for Billericay from Grays Athletic in January 2001, making his debut against Dulwich Hamlet on the 6th of that month. He had to wait until March to establish himself in the side as he was cup-tied for Town's FA Trophy campaign. He can play at either sweeper or right back, and his reading of the game and his distribution add a touch of class to his defensive capabilities. As well as Billericay and Grays, Steve has played for Canvey Island, Purfleet and QPR.

DICKINSON, STEVE   *Goalkeeper*

Current Club: Southport

Birthplace: Bradford

Steve moved to Conference side Soutport at the start of the 1999/2000 season after an outstanding campaign at UniBond League Premier Division side Guiseley. Formerly with Bradford City, he has grown in confidence as a Conference keeper.

DICKS, GRANTLEY   *Defender*

Current Club: Clevedon Town

Birthplace: Bristol

Very experienced defender and brother of former West Ham and Liverpools Julian. Played for Western League sides Clandown and Paulton Rovers before moving into the Dr Martens scene with Bath City, Trowbridge Town, Forest Green Rovers and Newport County. Returned briefly to the Western League with Brislington before having spells with Weston-super-Mare, Gloucester City and Chippenham Town, whom he helped to promotion to the Premier Division of the Dr Martens before switching to Clevedon Town in July 2002.

DICKSON, CHRIS   *Midfielder*

Current Club: Croydon Athletic

Birthplace: London

Honours won: Scottish Youth Int.

Hard-working left-sided midfield player who joined Ryman Division One South side Croydon Athletic in August 2002 from near-neighbours Croydon. Originally signed for Croydon in July 1994 from Dulwich, spending three seasons with the club before moving onto Tooting & Mitcham United. Re-joined Croydon in October 1998 and made over 250 appearances for the club. Chris was formerly a junior at Tottenham, Fulham, Wimbledon and Brentford, and has won Scottish U-19 international caps.

DICKSON, PAUL   *Defender*

Current Club: Buxton

Birthplace: Sheffield

Previous clubs include: Hallam - October 2001.

DIDCOCK, TRISTAN   *Midfielder*

Current Club: Abingdon Town

Birthplace: Oxford

Previous clubs include: Carterton T - October 2001, Abingdon T, Witney T, Carterton T, Oxford Utd (Trainee).

DIGGLE, MARTIN   *Defender*

Current Club: Worksop Town

Birthplace: Yorkshire

Previous clubs include: Hallam - August 2001.

DILLNUT, JAMES   *Defender*

Current Club: Arlesey Town

Birthplace: Stevenage

Has been a real success since joining Arlesey Town in August 2001. He scored on his debut and looks good in defence and going forward. Has previously played for Stevenage and Hitchin Town and played for Boro in both FA Cup ties against Newcastle United. He works as a Gardener.

DILLON, LEON   *Forward*

Current Club: Whyteleafe

Previous clubs include: Bromley - July 2001, Whyteleafe, Crawley T, Netherne, Baldock T, Croydon, Crystal Palace (Trainee).

DILLON, NEIL   *Midfielder*

Current Club: Liversedge

Birthplace: Sheffield

Previous clubs include: Ossett Alb - November 2000, Liversedge, Sheffield Wednesday (Junior).

DILLON, PAUL   *Defender*

Current Club: Alfreton Town

D o B: 22/10/1978   *Birthplace: Limerick*

Republic of Ireland Youth and under-21 international defender who joined UniBond First Division Alfreton Town in July 2002. Born in Limerick, Paul came over to England and signed for Rotherham United, where he went on to make over 70 League appearances before being somewhat surprisingly released at the end of the 2001/02 season.

DILLON, STEVE — Forward

Current Club: Glapwell

Birthplace: Nottinghamshire
Previous clubs include: Clipstone Welfare - July 2001.

DIMASCIO, CHRISTIAN — Midfielder

Current Club: Gorleston

Birthplace: Norfolk
Previous clubs include: Great Yarmouth T - July 2001, Gorleston.

DIMICHELE, SANDRO — Midfielder

Current Club: Sidlesham

Birthplace: Sussex
Former Portfield reserve who went on to feature in Sidlesham's 2nd XI: got a call up to the injury-hit first-team on a few occasions during 2001/02 and scored from the penalty spot against Shinewater in October: another University College Chichester player.

DIMMOCK, RICHARD — Forward

Current Club: VCD Athletic

D o B: 27/03/1979   *Birthplace: Woolwich*
Previous clubs include: Erith & Belvedere - July 2001, VCD Ath., Bishops Stortford, Gravesend, Welling Utd.

DINEEN, JACK — Midfielder

Current Club: Southwick

D o B: 29/09/1970   *Birthplace: Brighton*
One time Burgess Hill and Crawley player: long serving member of the Southwick side, although he did have a brief spell away at Lewes midway through 1999/2000: scored 5 times for the Wickers during their Division Two championship season of 2000/01.

DIPPER, GUY — Defender

Current Club: Brockenhurst

Birthplace: Dorset
Previous clubs include: Wimborne T - July 2001, Weymouth, Christchurch.

DISNEY, LEE — Forward

Current Club: Havant & Waterlooville

Birthplace: Hampshire
From Youth team.

DIXON, BEN — Defender

Current Club: Whitby Town

D o B: 16/09/1974   *Birthplace: Lincoln*
Classy, left-sided defender who signed for Whitby Town in November 1998 from Singapore club Woodlands Wellington. His former clubs being Lincoln City and Blackpool. Another experienced player in the Whitby ranks.

DIXON, GARY — Forward

Current Club: Boreham Wood

Birthplace: Hertfordshire
Gary is a striker who joined Boreham Wood from Hitchin Town in March 2001. Whilst at Hitchin Town he proved to be a prolific goalscorer. He made his first-team debut for Boreham Wood against Braintree Town on the 24 March 2001 and scored a goal in the 3-0 victory. Gary began his career at Hemel Hempstead Town before moving on to Stevenage Borough and then Hitchin Town.

DIXON, IAN — Midfielder

Current Club: Gateshead

Birthplace: Durham
Honours won: FA Vase Winners
Despite having a bit of a reputation as a hot-head Ian is a classy midfielder who knows his role in the side and plays it well in competitive manor. Signed for UniBond Premier side Gateshead from Albany Northern Leaguers Whitley Bay, where he won an FA Vase winners medal, in the summer of 2002 and was previously with Blyth Spartans and Durham City.

DIXON, JOHN — Forward

Current Club: Broxbourne Borough V&E

Birthplace: London
Previous clubs include: Potters Bar T - September 2001.

DIXON, MATTHEW — Forward

Current Club: AFC Sudbury

Birthplace: Sudbury
Previous clubs include: Ipswich T - August 1999, Sudbury W.

DJELASSI, KARIM — Midfielder

Current Club: Whitehawk

Birthplace: Sussex
Midfielder who joined Ringmer from Peacehaven during the 2000 close season and has really come to prominence since signing for Whitehawk in August 2001.

DOBBS, SEAN — Midfielder

Current Club: Pagham

Birthplace: Sussex
Midfielder: named as a substitute several times for Pagham during the early part of 2001/02: made his full debut in November following the mass exodus of first-team regulars.

DOBBYN, DAMION — Midfielder

Current Club: Ringmer

Birthplace: Sussex
Midfielder and an established member of the successful Saltdean side in recent years Struck 11 goals during 1999/2000 (including in the John OHara League Cup Final) and also had the distinction of scoring after only three seconds in a Sussex Sunday League game for Park View that year. One of numerous players to leave Hill Park midway through 2000/01, and ended that season at Lewes. Signed for Ringmer at the start of the current season.

DOBIE, MARK — Forward

Current Club: Gretna

D o B: 08/11/1963   *Birthplace: Carlisle*
Previous clubs include: Barrow - August 1999, Gretna, Lancaster C, Workington, Queen of the South, Barrow, Gretna, Darlington, Torquay Utd, Cambridge Utd, Gretna, Workington.

DOBINSON, KEVIN — Midfielder

Current Club: Canvey Island

Birthplace: Ipswich
Midfielder who switched to Ryman Premier side Canvey Island from Dr Martens Premier outfit Chelmsford City in August 2002. Was a crowd favourite at Chelmsford and began his career at Ipswich Town before being released by the Premiership outfit, with Chelmsford being the fortunate club to gain his signature. Made significant progress in the youth team to gain a regular midfield place in the first-team some six years ago and made almost 200 appearances for the club.

DOBSON, JOFF — Midfielder
Current Club: *Royston Town*
Birthplace: Herts
From Youth team.

DOBSON, RICHARD — Defender
Current Club: *Glasshoughton Welfare*
Birthplace: Leeds
Previous clubs include: Garforth T - January 2002, Carlton.

DOBSON, SIMON — Goalkeeper
Current Club: *Royston Town*
Birthplace: Herts
From Youth team.

DOBSON, TONY — Defender
Current Club: *Rugby United*
D o B: 05/02/1969   *Birthplace: Coventry*
Previous clubs include: Forest Green Rovers - February 2001, Northampton T, Gillingham, WBA, Portsmouth, Blackburn R, Coventry C.

DOCKING, NEAL — Forward
Current Club: *Soham Town Rangers*
D o B: 14/06/1975   *Birthplace: Essex*
Previous clubs include: Braintree T - September 1999, Soham Town R, Heybridge Swifts, Chelmsford C, Saffron Walden T.

DOCTOR, NEIL — Midfielder
Current Club: *Hertford Town*
Birthplace: Herts
Talented midfielder whose playing days began in the Spartan South Midlands League with Welwyn Garden City. Moved to London Colney in July 1998 with his father Malcolm where he won a championship medal. Moved into the Ryman League with Hertford Town in June 2002.

DODD, ALAN — Defender
Current Club: *Leek Town*
Birthplace: Stoke
Previous clubs include: Leek CSOB - November 2000, Leek T.

DODD, GARETH — Defender
Current Club: *Ossett Albion*
Birthplace: Barnsley
Previous clubs include: Ossett T - October 2000.

DODD, GRAHAM — Forward
Current Club: *Skelmersdale United*
Birthplace: Liverpool
Previous clubs include: Congleton T - July 2001, Salford C, Ashton T, Warrington T, Stantondale, Warrington T, Atherton Collieries, Skelmersdale Utd, Stockport Co (Junior).

DODD, RUSSELL — Defender
Current Club: *Sutton Coldfield Town*
Birthplace: Worcestershire
Vastly experienced and much-travelled defender ho joined Sutton Coldfield Town in May 2002 after a brief spell with Midland Alliance side Oldbury United. Started the 2001/02 season in the Alliance with Stourbridge before being signed by Dr Martens Premier Division Hednesford Town in November 2001. Started his playing days with Kidderminster Harriers and has also seen service with Tamworth, Solihull Borough, Hinckley Athletic, Blakenall, Bloxwich, Evesham United and Bromsgrove Rovers.

DODDS, KARK — Defender
Current Club: *Carterton Town*
Birthplace: Oxfordshire
From Youth team.

DODDS, WARREN — Defender
Current Club: *Hassocks*
Birthplace: Sussex
Veteran defender, who has been at the club for almost 20 years: recalled into the side from the beginning of 2001/02.

DODSWORTH, ANDY — Midfielder
Current Club: *Ossett Albion*
Previous clubs include: Liversedge - July 2000.

DOEL, DAVE — Midfielder
Current Club: *Brentwood*
Birthplace: Essex
A real grafter in the middle of the park, Dave is another youngster who has been with the club for a number of years and is now looking for a regular first team spot.

DOGBE, STEVE — Midfielder
Current Club: *Chesham United*
D o B: 14/10/1982   *Birthplace: Berkshire*
Midfielder who joined Ryman Premier side Chesham United from Luton Town's reserves in the summer of 2002 and his strengths are running and tackling. His footballing hero is Pele and his best moment in his career was signing a scholarship with Luton when he was 16 years old. When not at Chesham he is part of the coaching team at Luton.

DOHERTY, GED — Goalkeeper
Current Club: *Total Network Solutions*
D o B: 24/08/1981   *Birthplace: Derry*
Honours won: Republic of Ireland Youth Int.
Former Derby County and Republic of Ireland Youth international goalkeeper, Ged signed for TNS in November 2001. Although still young, he has vast experience and an excellent acquisition to the squad. Originally with Derry City.

DOHERTY, LEE — Defender
Current Club: *Tooting & Mitcham United*
D o B: 06/02/1980   *Birthplace: Camden Town*
Hard-tackling defender who joined Ryman Division One South side Tooting & Mitcham United in August 2002 following a second spell with Dr Martens outfit Crawley Town. Originally played for Crawley towards the end of the 1999/00 season after signing from Chesham United and subsequently had a spell with Grays Athletic before returning to the Reds late in 2000/01. Rated as a much improved performer, he has also seen service with Arsenal, Charlton and Brighton as a youngster.

DOHERTY, MARTIN — Midfielder
Current Club: *Hyde United*
D o B: 17/10/1978   *Birthplace: Urmston*
Previous clubs include: Leek T - July 2001, Northwich V, Altrincham, Bolton Wanderers.

DOLAN, FRANCIS — Defender
Current Club: *Walton & Hersham*
Birthplace: Surrey
Formerly with Egham Town, Francis is a versatile defender who made several senior appearances for Swans towards the end of 1999-2000, securing a regular first team place last season.

DOLAN, WILL — *Midfielder*
Current Club: Marine
D o B: 08/12/1984   *Birthplace: Merseyside*
Highly-promising midfielder who is still only18. Was on Marines coaching course for under-11s and then went on to be with Liverpool as a boy. Came into the Mariners first-team squad via the youth team and has already been to Middlesbrough for trials.

DOLBY, CHRIS — *Midfielder*
Current Club: Alfreton Town
D o B: 04/09/1974   *Birthplace: Dewsbury*
Honours won: Northern Counties East League Winners
Talented left winger who returned to UniBond First Division side Alfreton Town for a second spell in February 2001 from Bradford Park Avenue. Started his career with Rotherham United before moving to Bradford City. Has also played for Matlock Town, Denaby United, Stocksbridge Park Steels, Stalybridge Celtic and Hyde United.

DOLBY, PAUL — *Defender*
Current Club: Glapwell
Birthplace: Chesterfield
From Local football - July 1997.

DOLBY, TONY — *Defender*
Current Club: Fisher Athletic (London)
D o B: 16/04/1974   *Birthplace: Greenwich*
Previous clubs include: Welling Utd - July 2001, Fisher Ath., Gravesend, Welling Utd, Millwall.

DOLPHIN, WES — *Forward*
Current Club: Witton Albion
Birthplace: Manchester
Previous clubs include: Macclesfield T - August 2002.

DOMINGO, ANDRE — *Midfielder*
Current Club: Croydon
Birthplace: Surrey
Young right-sided midfield player who has come up through Croydons youth ranks. Some impressive performances in the youth and reserve teams this season earned AndrÈ a first-team debut in November 2001.

DOMINIQUE, JERMAINE — *Midfielder*
Current Club: Barking & East Ham United
Birthplace: Essex
Previous clubs include: Purfleet - December 2001.

DONALD, WARREN — *Defender*
Current Club: Stamford
D o B: 07/10/1964   *Birthplace: Hillingdon*
Honours won: England Schoolboy Int., Division Four Winners, FA Trophy Winners, Conference Winners
Warren is a vastly experienced central midfielder who was recruited from Daventry and played in the 1st Division for West Ham. He was also a 4th Division Championship winner with Northampton and later helped Colchester to FA Trophy and coference success before spells with Kettering, Nuneaten and Raunds.

DONALDSON, CRAIG — *Forward*
Current Club: Stamford
Previous clubs include: Somersham T - July 1999, Rushden & Diamonds.

DONALDSON, DAVID — *Midfielder*
Current Club: Harrogate Town
D o B: 17/12/1978   *Birthplace: Gravesend*
Honours won: UniBond League Div.One Winners
Midfielder who began his career as a trainee and then as a professional at Arsenal, before joining Bradford City, where he made a dozen first-team appearances. Then joined UniBond neighbours Bradford Park Avenue and also had a short spell in the Dr Martens with Gresley Rovers before signing for Harrogate Town in the summer of 2001.

DONN, ROBERT — *Midfielder*
Current Club: Wingate And Finchley
D o B: 19/10/1977   *Birthplace: London*
Previous clubs include: Marshside - July 1999.

DONNELLY, MARK — *Midfielder*
Current Club: Leek Town
D o B: 22/12/1979   *Birthplace: Leeds*
A wide midfield player who signedfor Leek Town in September 2001 from Gainsborough Trinity. Appeared mainly as a substitute after joining Leek. Previously with Doncaster Rovers, Bury, Whitby Town and Congleton Town.

DONNELLY, MARK — *Midfielder*
Current Club: Ashford Town (Middx)
Birthplace: Middlesex
Previous clubs include: Hillingdon Borough - July 2001.

DONNELLY, PAUL — *Midfielder*
Current Club: Swindon Supermarine
Birthplace: Gloucestershire
Previous clubs include: Clevedon T - November 2001, Swindon Supermarine, Cirencester T, Cinderford T, Hungerford T, Cinderford T, Purton.

DONNELY, PAUL — *Defender*
Current Club: Barton Rovers
Birthplace: Luton
Previous clubs include: Totternhoe - July 2000.

DONOGHUE, MICKY — *Defender*
Current Club: Saltdean United
Birthplace: London
One of the London-based players to be brought into the line-up during Mick Fords short-lived reign in the autumn 2001: signed from Chessington & Hook.

DONOVAN, JASON — *Defender*
Current Club: Cinderford Town
Birthplace: Cardiff
Signed for Cinderford Town from Newport County, where he played over 200 games, in the summer of 2001. Talented and now experienced defender who has also played for Cardiff City, Ebbw Vale and Llanwern.

DONOVAN, MILES — *Midfielder*
Current Club: Hadleigh United
Birthplace: Suffolk
Tall ball-winning midfield anchor man with superb distribution, whose height causes problems for defences at set pieces and corners. Re-joined Hadleigh last season, having played for the youth and reserve teams in the past.

DONOVAN, ROSS — *Midfielder*
Current Club: Stafford Town
Birthplace: Staffordshire
Previous clubs include: Chasetown - July 2000.

DONOVAN, WAYNE — *Goalkeeper*
Current Club: Hadleigh United
Birthplace: Suffolk
Immensely talented keeper whose presence has a positive effect on the performance of the whole Hadleigh United team. Has the confidence and ability (and all other goalkeeping attributes) necessary to succeed at this level and higher. Holds full County Cap for Suffolk. Second full season with the Club.

DOOLAN, GARY — *Midfielder*
Current Club: London Colney
Birthplace: Herts
Previous clubs include: Welwyn Garden C - July 1999.

DOOLAN, JOHN — *Midfielder*
Current Club: Accrington Stanley
D o B: 10/11/1968   Birthplace: South Liverpool
Previous clubs include: Ashton Utd - August 1999, Marine, Barrow, Wigan Ath., Knowsley Utd.

DOOLAN, JOHN — *Midfielder*
Current Club: Barnet
D o B: 07/05/1974   Birthplace: Liverpool
Tenacious player who signed for Barnet from Mansfield Town in January 1998. Started at Everton before transferring to the Stags where he made over 100 League appearances. Inspirational in the Barnet midfield, with the ability to play the ball both short and long.

DOOLEY, JAMES — *Midfielder*
Current Club: Eastwood Town
Previous clubs include: Chesterfield - August 2000.

DOOLEY, LEE — *Defender*
Current Club: Epsom And Ewell
Birthplace: Surrey
Previous clubs include: Croydon Ath - March 2002, Carshalton Ath., Epsom & Ewell, Dulwich Hamlet, Sutton Utd, Fisher Ath., Dulwich Hamlet.

DOONER, GARY — *Defender*
Current Club: Congleton Town
Birthplace: Liverpool
Previous clubs include: St.Helens T - January 2002, Beeches, Garswood Utd, Stockport Co.

DOOTSON, CRAIG — *Goalkeeper*
Current Club: Stalybridge Celtic
D o B: 23/05/1979   Birthplace: Preston
Honours won: British Universities Rep.
Highly-rated young goalkeeper who signed for Leigh RMI pre-season 2000 from Bamber Bridge for an undisclosed fee. Made his league debut against Southport at Haig Avenue winning the MOM vote for an outstanding performance to help RMI to their first ever Conference points. Craig went on to establish himself as RMIs first choice keeper, keeping out Welsh legend Dave Felgate until an injury sustained at Hereford kept him out of the team. Represented the British Universities in the World Student Games in 2001, and then transferred to Stalybridge Celtic in May 2002.

DORIAN, MATTHEW — *Midfielder*
Current Club: Shepshed Dynamo
D o B: 03/10/1976   Birthplace: Guernsey
Matthew is one of the few practising doctors playing football. Guernsey-born, the midfielder has played at some varied places, including Yorkshire Amateurs and Farsley Celtic, whilst studying in Leeds, and Dalwish Town. Has represented the North of England universities.

DORMAN, LAWRENCE — *Midfielder*
Current Club: Eastbourne United
Birthplace: Sussex
Attacking midfielder who had a successful season playing for the reserves in 1999/2000: made an impressive start to the last campaign, scoring four times in the opening month before moving to Essex to take up a teaching job: returned to score a hat-trick in the 8-1 thrashing of East Preston in March.

DORMER, JAMIE — *Midfielder*
Current Club: Barking & East Ham United
Birthplace: Essex
Joined Barking from East ???? neighbours Leyton Pennant in October 2001. Shows great promise at left back and is reckoned to be a terrific prospect for the future. A former Spurs junior, Jamie has also had spells with Hertford Town, Romford and Grays Athletic.

DORMER, JASON — *Forward*
Current Club: Ashton United
Birthplace: Manchester
Previous clubs include: Hyde Utd (£500) - October 2001, Curzon Ashton.

DORRELL, GRAHAM — *Forward*
Current Club: Great Wakering Rovers
Birthplace: Essex
Previous clubs include: Purfleet - August 2000, Burnham Ramblers, Great Wakering R, Southend Manor.

DORRIAN, CHRIS — *Defender*
Current Club: Harlow Town
D o B: 03/04/1982   Birthplace: London
Promising young defender wo signed for Ryman Division One North side Harlow Town in August 2002 after being released by Leyton Orient. Played five times in the League for Orient and also had a three-month spell on-loan at then Conference side Dover Athletic during the 2001/02 season.

DORRIAN, FRANK — *Forward*
Current Club: Brackley Town
Birthplace: Oxfordshire
Previous clubs include: Banbuy Utd - July 2001, Brackley T, Wantage T.

DORRIAN, ROD — *Midfielder*
Current Club: Didcot Town
Birthplace: Oxfordshire
Rod has over 600 appearances for Didcot, and has proved to be a major influence again this season. Unfortunately, he suffered a double fracture to his right leg in February 2001 is still on the road to recovery. Probably the most under-rated player at the club whose absence from the side last campaign coincided with a downturn in fortunes. A Dry-lining Manager.

DORRIAN, RYAN — Midfielder
Current Club: Merthyr Tydfil
Birthplace: Wales
Honours won: Wales Youth Int.
Impressive young midfielder who joined Dr Martens Western side Merthyr Tydfil in July 2002 from rivals Clevedon Town. Ryan came through the youth team at Newport County to reach the first team, winning Gwent Schoolboy and Wales under-18 honours on the way. After a loan spell at League of Wales club Rhayader Town, he signed for Clevedon in November 2001.

DOUBLE, LEE — Midfielder
Current Club: Bishops Stortford
Birthplace: Essex
Signed in the Autumn of 2001 from East Thurrock Utd. Lee is equally at home in the heart of the midfield as well as the defence. A player with many qualities recognised by manager Martin Hayes and has been a regular in the first team since his arrival. Debut for The Blues was at Walton & Hersham in October 2001.

DOUGAL, BRAD — Midfielder
Current Club: Saltdean United
Birthplace: Sussex
Former youth-reserve member at Crawley, who signed for Whitehawk in December 1999: scored 5 times before going to Tonbridge Angels ten months later: returned to County League action in September 2001 when joining Saltdean.

DOUGHTY, ADRIAN — Forward
Current Club: Gresley Rovers
D o B: 28/12/1973   Birthplace: Staffs
Powerful forward who joined Gresley Rovers in August 2000 from neighbouring Hinckley United. Originally with Burton Albion, he played Southern League football with Rocester, Shepshed and Hinckley and also turned ut in the Midland Alliance with Stapenhill. The son of a former Gresley goalkeeper, Andy has also spent time out on loan at Mickleover Sports.

DOUGHTY, LEON — Midfielder
Current Club: Hinckley United
Birthplace: Leicester
Highly-rated young attacking midfielder who joined Dr Martens Premier side Hinckley United in August 2002 from Western Division Atherstone United. Leicester-born, he started out with Friar Lane OB and then had his first taste of Dr Martens football with Corby Town before signing for the Adders in November 2000.

DOUGLAS, ANDY — Forward
Current Club: Grays Athletic
D o B: 07/02/1980   Birthplace: Edmonton
Pacy young forward who hits lots of goals his previous clubs have been Sheffield Wednesday, and Arsenal. Mssed most of the 2001/2002 season through a horrendous stabbing injury.

DOUGLAS, JOHN — Forward
Current Club: Rugby United
Birthplace: Warwickshire
From Youth team.

DOUGLAS, MICHAEL — Midfielder
Current Club: Marine
Birthplace: Liverpool
Versatile young midfielder who joined Marine in August 1998 from Ashville, Was with Tranmere Rovers as a schoolboy. Student at John Moores University, Liverpool.

DOWD, DAVID — Midfielder
Current Club: Guisborough Town
Previous clubs include: Wolviston - July 2001.

DOWELL, ADAM — Goalkeeper
Current Club: Whitby Town
D o B: 06/12/1982   Birthplace: Gateshead
Adam is a promising former Sunderland goalkeeper, with excellent all-round ability. After rising through the Black Cats youth ranks, he spent three months on loan at Rushden & Diamonds before joining UniBond Premier side Whitby Town in July 2002, where he quickly challenged Phil Naisbett for the number one shirt.

DOWLEY, JOE — Defender
Current Club: Chatham Town
Previous clubs include: Sittingbourne - July 2001.

DOWLING, JOE — Forward
Current Club: Stratford Town
Birthplace: Birmingham
Previous clubs include: Redditch Utd - December 2001, Paget R, Solihull B, Sandwell B, Sherwood Celtic, Barry T, Sherwood Celtic, Moor Green.

DOWLING, LUKE — Defender
Current Club: Kingstonian
Birthplace: Reading
Previous clubs include: Lewes - December 2001, Walton & Hersham, Kingstonian, Maidenhead Utd, Reading.

DOWN, DANNY — Defender
Current Club: Hertford Town
Birthplace: Hertford
From Youth team.

DOWN, IAN — Midfielder
Current Club: Bideford
Birthplace: Devon
Honours won: FA Vase Winners
Ian is a former Torquay United midfielder who rejoined the club this summer from Taunton Town and was a member of their F.A. Vase winning side last season.

DOWNEY, ADRIAN — Midfielder
Current Club: Burgess Hill Town
Birthplace: Sussex
Strong midfielder who originally came through the youth team: rejoined from Ringmer during the 1999 close season: team captain.

DOWNEY, JASON — Midfielder
Current Club: Hemel Hempstead Town
Birthplace: Essex
Previous clubs include: Wivenhoe T - November 2000.

DOWNS, ROBBIE — Midfielder
Current Club: Salisbury City
Birthplace: Salisbury
Local lad who started his career at AFC Bournemouth and joined Dr Martens Eastern side Salisbury City's youth team in the 2001/02 season. His performances in the youth side quickly gained him a place in the senior side.

D

DOWSE, GARETH   *Defender*
Current Club: Aberystwyth Town
D o B: 18/08/1982   *Birthplace: Aberystwyth*
From Youth team.

DOWSON, ALAN   *Defender*
Current Club: Walton & Hersham
D o B: 17/06/1970   *Birthplace: Gateshead*
Alan, Walton & Hershams Football in the Community Officer, is a hard-tackling left-back or central defender who made his debut for the club on Boxing Day, 1996. After starting as a youth under George Graham at Millwall, Alan moved on to play for Fulham, Bradford City and Darlington, making 55 League appearances. Moved on to play Conference for Slough Town and his home town club, Gateshead and has now made over 200 appearances for Swans.

DOYLE, MAURICE   *Midfielder*
Current Club: Oswestry Town
D o B: 17/10/1969   *Birthplace: Ellesmere Port*
Another player with European experience with TNS last season who joined during the close season. Previously with Tranmere Rovers.

DOYLE, PAUL   *Midfielder*
Current Club: Corinthian Casuals
Birthplace: Surrey
From Youth team.

DOYLE, TOMMY   *Forward*
Current Club: Letchworth
Birthplace: Luton
Previous clubs include: Brache Sparta - July 2001, Toddington R, Barton R, Shillington, Vauxhall Motors.

DOZGIC, DINO   *Forward*
Current Club: Eastbourne United
Birthplace: Bosnia
Bosnian youngster who was a prolific goalscorer for Eastbourne United's under-18 side in 1999/2000 and also found the net on his first-team debut against East Preston that season.

DOZZELL, JASON   *Midfielder*
Current Club: Canvey Island
D o B: 09/12/1967   *Birthplace: Ipswich*
Honours won: England Youth & u-21 Int
Former England Youth and under-21international midfielder who started his career with Ipswich Town at the age of 16. He cost Spurs £1,900,000 in 1993 before moving to Northampton and Colchester United. Jason holds the record as the youngest player to score in top flight English football. (4th February 1984 against Coventry City aged 16). Signed for Ryman Premier side Canvey August 2002 after a pre-season trial.

DRAGE, PAT   *Defender*
Current Club: Fleet Town
Birthplace: Hampshire
From Youth team.

DRAPER, ANDY   *Defender*
Current Club: Hertford Town
Birthplace: Enfield
Previous clubs include: Northwood - August 2001, Leighton T, Bedford T, Boreham Wood, Tottenham Hotspur (Junior).

DRAPER, RYAN   *Goalkeeper*
Current Club: Taunton Town
D o B: 09/02/1975   *Birthplace: Barnstaple*
Honours won: FA Vase Winners
Experienced goalkeeper who has played for many clubs amongst whom are Plymouth Argyle as a trainee, Exeter City, Weymouth, Bath City, Oakland Pioneers in the USA and Barnstaple Town. Signed for Taunton Town from Ilfracombe Town in August 2000. Is employed by a Devon Newspapers as a Sales Consultant.

DRAY, ROB   *Defender*
Current Club: Bridgwater Town
D o B: 11/08/1969   *Birthplace: Somerset*
Previous clubs include: Minehead - July 1993, Spaxton.

DRAYTON, SIMON   *Midfielder*
Current Club: Brigg Town
Birthplace: Lincolnshire
Previous clubs include: Gainsborough Trinity - July 2001, Limestone Rovers.

DREW, CARL   *Forward*
Current Club: Hitchin Town
Birthplace: Luton
Striker who signed for Hitchin Town from Boreham Wood in November 20001. Carl has also played for Bedford Town, Barton Rovers, Harlow Town, Luton OB and Harpenden Town. Has established himself as a hard-working player with a keen eye for goal.

DREW, JASON   *Defender*
Current Club: Woodbridge Town
Birthplace: Suffolk
Versatile defender or midfield player who was another of Paul Leechs signings in the summer. SIL experience with Leiston and Leiston St.Margarets, he reads the game well and has made an immediate breakthrough into the First Team squad.

DREW, NICK   *Defender*
Current Club: Sutton United
Birthplace: Surrey
Previous clubs include: Fulham (Junior) - July 2000.

DREWETT, GARY   *Forward*
Current Club: Bromley
Birthplace: Surrey
Joined Bromley in October 2001 from Ryman League Premier Division and local rivals Sutton United. He was previously at Kingstonian and he made a handful appearances in their Conference side. Manager McIntyre, rates this player as the best right hand side midfielders in the Ryman League First Division.

DREWITT, IAN   *Midfielder*
Current Club: Bedworth United
Birthplace: Swansea
Appointed as player-manager of Bedworth United after the resignation of Gary Bradder and Dave Grundy. Highly-popular, Ian is hoping to take the Greenbacks onto the next step. One of the youngest managers in the league, he has vast experience in on-League football having had spells with Merthyr Tydfil, Stafford Rangers, Hinckley United and Welsh club Ton Pentre. Joined Bedworth from Dr Martens Western Division rivals Sutton Coldfield Town in November 1999.

DREYER, JOHN — *Defender*

Current Club: Stevenage Borough

D o B: 11/06/1963   *Birthplace: Alnwick*

A late summer 2001 addition to Stevenage Borough's squad. John adds a wealth of experience to Boros defence. Previous clubs include Cambridge, Stoke, Luton and Oxford, whilst he also played 17 times in the Premiership very recently with Bradford City. He spent his entire professional career playing in the top two divisions of the football league, but has adapted very well to life in the Conference.

DRINKALL, JAMES — *Midfielder*

Current Club: Lincoln United

Birthplace: Lincoln

Joined Lincoln United from Tadcaster Albion and has also had a spell at York City. A solid performer with a big future in the game.

DRISCOLL, DANNY — *Defender*

Current Club: Arlesey Town

Previous clubs include: Toddington Rovers - July 1999, Arlesey T, Barton R, Leighton T, Barton R, Vauxhall Motors (Luton), Barton R, Hitchin T, Letchworth GC, Barton R, Sandviken IF (Sweden), Luton T.

DRISCOLL, MARTIN — *Defender*

Current Club: Erith & Belvedere

Birthplace: Kent

A young promising defender with plenty of ability and skill. Won Erith & Belvederes Players' Player and Supporters' Player of the year last season.

DRISCOLL, MICHAEL — *Defender*

Current Club: Thornaby on Tees

Birthplace: Middlesbrough

Previous clubs include: Guisborough T - February 2002, Bishop Auckland, Norton, Easington Colliery, Guisborough T, Doncaster R, Middlesbrough (Junior).

DRIVER, GLEN — *Forward*

Current Club: Witham Town

Birthplace: Essex

Previous clubs include: Whitton Utd - September 2000, Witham T, Harwich & Parkeston, Needham Market, BS Fonnereau, Harwich & Parkeston.

DROZARIO, DAVID — *Forward*

Current Club: Walton Casuals

Birthplace: Surrey

Dave was on Charltons books at youth level and has honour of scoring our first ever FA Cup goal at Ashford Town. Dave also scored on his debut at Cobham last season. Previous clubs include Leatherhead.

DRUCE, MARK — *Forward*

Current Club: Oxford City

D o B: 03/03/1974   *Birthplace: Oxford*

Honours won: Conference Winners

Previous clubs include: Woking - December 2000, Kidderminster Harriers, Hereford Utd, Rotherham Utd, Oxford Utd.

DRUMMOND, STUART — *Midfielder*

Current Club: Morecambe

D o B: 11/12/1975   *Birthplace: Preston*

Honours won: England Semi-Pro Int.

From Preston, has progressed through the youth ranks and become a tireless, very skillful member of the midfield. Now a regular in the England semi-professional squad.

DRURY, ANDREW — *Midfielder*

Current Club: Sittingbourne

D o B: 28/11/1983   *Birthplace: Kent*

Andrew was introduced to Sittingbournes first-team via the clubs youth and reserve teams. The young midfielder is very skilful on the ball and one who the club expects great things off.

DRYDEN, JAMES — *Forward*

Current Club: Folkestone Invicta

D o B: 04/02/1980   *Birthplace: Kent*

James is a skilful forward player who progressed into the Folkestone Invicta first team squad from the reserves during the 1999/00 season. He scored on his full Southern League debut at Burnham during December 1999 and then again in the next home match against Fleet Town. He has attracted the attention of Football League scouts.

DRYDEN, RICHARD — *Defender*

Current Club: Scarborough

D o B: 14/06/1969   *Birthplace: Stroud*

Honours won: Division Four Winners

Vastly experienced defender who joined Conference club Scarborough in July 2002 from Luton Town. Had a successful three-month loan spell with the Seadogs in 2001/02 after amassing more than 300 League appearances with Bristol City and Rovers, Exeter, where he won a Division Four championship medal, Notts County, Birmingham, Southampton and Luton.

DRYSDALE, JASON — *Defender*

Current Club: Bath City

D o B: 17/11/1970   *Birthplace: Bristol*

Honours won: England Youth Int.

Talented left-sided player, Jason began his career as a trainee with Watford in 1988 before progressing through the ranks at the Vicarage Road side, going on to make nearly 150 appearances for the Hornets. In Augst 1994 he made a move to the Premiership with Newcastle United in a £425,000 deal but failed to make an impression at St James Park and moved onto Swindon Town less than a year later. Bristol-born Jason spent three years at Swindon but injury restricted his outings and, following a short spell at Northampton Town toward the end of the 1997/98 season, moved into Non-League football with Forest Green Rovers. Followed manager Frank Gregan to Aberystwyth Town in the summer of 2001 but when this move didnt work out headed to Bath City at the beginning of December.

DSANE, ROSCOE — *Forward*

Current Club: Aldershot Town

Birthplace: London

Highly-promising young forward who joined Aldershot Town in May 2002 from Conference club Woking. Originally on the books at Crystal Palace, Roscoe played a couple of times in the League for Southend before having a short spell with Slough Town. Joined Woking in December 2001.

DUBLIN, KEITH   *Defender*
Current Club: Carshalton Athletic
D o B: 29/01/1966   Birthplace: Brent
Honours won: England Youth Int.
Vastly experienced defender who spent six years with Chelsea and made over 50 first-team appearances before transferring to Brighton in 1987. Then played for Watford and Southend United and totalled more than 530 League appearances before joining Farnborough in August 1999. Turned down possible moves to Port Vale and Plymouth to join Farnborough Town in July 1999. The former England Youth international then took up the offer to become player-coach at Ryman League Carshalton Athletic in June 2002.

DUCILLE, ANDREW   *Midfielder*
Current Club: Eastbourne Borough
Birthplace: Hastings
Brownie signed from St. Leonards in March 1997. In recent seasons has proved to be something of a utility player. Another to have played for the Sussex Representative team.

DUCKETT, MARK   *Defender*
Current Club: Aberystwyth Town
Birthplace: Herts
Previous clubs include: Hitchin T - July 2002, Hemel Hempstead T, Stevenage B.

DUCKWORTH, KEVIN   *Forward*
Current Club: Tadcaster Albion
Birthplace: Yorkshire
Previous clubs include: Glasshoughton Welfare - July 2001, Tadcaster Alb.

DUDLEY, CRAIG   *Forward*
Current Club: Burton Albion
D o B: 12/09/1979   Birthplace: Newark
Honours won: England Youth Int.
Craig signed for Burton Albion in May 2002 after being released by Oldham Athletic. A striker, he had joined the Latics from Notts County in March 1999 for what was described at the time as a nominal sum. Still only 21, Craig had made 13 starts for his former club, scoring 4 goals during which time he spent loan spells at Hull City and Shrewsbury Town. He made a total of 7 starts for those 2 clubs, scoring 2 goals, before returning to County. Limited first team opportunities at Meadow Lane led Craig to put in a transfer request and Ritchie stepped in to secure his signature on deadline day 1999. Craigs first job as a Latics player was to represent his country at international level in the World Youth Championships in Nigeria. Craig appeared in all three of Englands group matches but retired injured in the last game to see England eliminated in the first round.

DUDLEY, DEREK   *Goalkeeper*
Current Club: Stourport Swifts
D o B: 02/02/1970   Birthplace: Birmingham
Previous clubs include: Romulus - November 2001, Stourport Swifts, Halesowen T, Chasetown, Pershore T, Bromsgrove R, Nuneaton B, Bromsgrove R, Telford Utd, Halesowen T, WBA, VS Rugby, Worcester C, Stourbridge, Sutton Coldfield T, Aston Villa.

DUERDAN, IAN   *Forward*
Current Club: Altrincham
D o B: 27/03/1978   Birthplace: Burnley
Started his career at Burnley, where he was signed a professional contract on his 18th birthday. Following a spell at Halifax Town, he moved onto Doncaster Rovers in 1998, where he was an instant hit. He scored 18 goals in his first season there and was

voted young player of the season. After losing his place through injury, he went to Kingstonian for a loan spell and made such an impression that he was eventually signed up by them in time for their 2001 FA Cup game against Bristol City. He was released by the Ks after they were relegated from the Nationwide Conference at the end of season 2000/2001, before joining Barrow in mid-July. Switched to Hucknall in February 2002 and, after a brief but productive spell at Watnall Road, moved to Altrincham in June 2002.

DUFF, GLEN   *Defender*
Current Club: Bideford
Birthplace: Devon
Glen is a former Bristol City player, who has also been on the books of Dawlish Town. He is a classy central defender, who can also play as a sweeper. Glen has made over 100 first team appearances.

DUFFELL, CRAIG   *Forward*
Current Club: Leatherhead
Birthplace: Surrey
Craig joined Leatherhead over the summer of 2001 from Dorking. He has had trials with Southampton, Charlton and Millwall and was the youngest player at age 15 to don a Dorking shirt since they joined the Isthmian League over 20 years ago.

DUFFIELD, MATT   *Defender*
Current Club: Horsham YMCA
Birthplace: Sussex
Dangerous wing-back: leading goalscorer for East Grinstead in 1997/98: subsequently had a spell at Three Bridges before returning to East Court: joined Redhill towards the end of 1998/99 and scored four times for them during the following season: signed up by Horsham YMCA at the start of 2000/01 (struck 11 times) and also represented Sussex that year.

DUFFTY, GARY   *Forward*
Current Club: Frickley Athletic
Previous clubs include: Matlock T - August 1998, Frickley Ath., Rotherham Utd.

DUFFUS, CRAIG   *Defender*
Current Club: Shifnal Town
Birthplace: Shropshire
Previous clubs include: Warley Rangers July 2001, Pelsall Villa.

DUFFY, CHRIS   *Midfielder*
Current Club: Canvey Island
D o B: 31/10/1973   Birthplace: Manchester
Honours won: FA Trophy Winners
A tall, athletic and skilful midfield player who possesses boundless energy. Became Canvey Islands record signing when joining from Conference side Northwich Victoria for £5,000 in July 1999. Played in the 1996 FA Umbro Trophy final for the Vics and repeated that with Canvy in 2001. Has has also seen service with Crewe and Wigan.

DUFFY, GARY   *Defender*
Current Club: Windsor & Eton
D o B: 10/02/1979   Birthplace: Kingston
Previous clubs include: Bracknell T - August 1999, Slough T, Hampton, Brentford, Bayer Leverkusen (Germany).

DUFTON, TOM — Defender

Current Club: Garforth Town

D o B: 03/09/1980   *Birthplace: Yorkshire*
Following a solid season in the Reserves, Tom has progressed into fighting for the regular left back position. Plays a more traditional full back role. A strong tackler with an aggressive but controlled attitude.

DUGDALE, ANDREW — Defender

Current Club: Egham Town

Birthplace: Berkshire
Honours won: British Universities Rep.
Defender who joined Ryman Division One South side Egham Town from Dr Martens neighbours Burnham in August 2002. Andrew spent the 2000/01 season at Henley Town before joining the Blues. Has represented British Universities.

DUGDALE, ANDREW — Defender

Current Club: Whitley Bay

Birthplace: Newcastle
Just signed for the club from Morpeth Town. A hard tackling full back, Andrew is seen as one of the brightest young prospects in the area.

DUIK, WAYNE — Midfielder

Current Club: Kettering Town

D o B: 26/05/1980   *Birthplace: Nottingham*
Honours won: Dr Martens League Premier Div.Winners
A talented young player who is capable of performing equally as well in midfield or as a full back. Has been highly-impressive since joining Kettering Town from Northern Counties East League side Gedling Town in 1999. Formerly with Notts County, Wayne looks to have a bright future ahead of him.

DUKE, JAMES — Midfielder

Current Club: Haverhill Rovers

Birthplace: Suffolk
Has had trials with Cambridge United, and in his sixth year at Rovers. A central midfielder. Grafts well. Reserve team captain.

DUKE, MATTHEW — Goalkeeper

Current Club: Burton Albion

Birthplace: Derby
Honours won: UniBond League Premier Div.Winners
Matt signed for Burton Albion from Sheffield United, the team he followed as a boy. Matt was formerly with Matlock Town and was second choice goalkeeper at Bramall Lane, until Nigel Clough persuaded the six foot, five inch custodian to join the Brewers. A great shot stopper, Matt turned in several match winning performances as the Brewers gained promotion to the Conference for the first time.

DUKU, FRANCIS — Defender

Current Club: Gravesend & Northfleet

Birthplace: London
Honours won: Ryman League Premier Div.Winners
Francis joined Gravesend in August 2000, having played for Dulwich Hamlet. He began his career with Reading as a youngster before moving into the Ryman League with Collier Row & Romford and Maidenhead United. A strong, uncompromising and highly influential defender, he has attracted interest from a number of Football League clubs.

DUMBRILL, JASON — Goalkeeper

Current Club: Horsham YMCA

Birthplace: Sussex
Goalkeeper who is now in his eighth year at the club, having played over 300 times. Recognized as one of the best stoppers in the league and is the usual first choice for the Sussex representative side: out of action for a few games during the autumn 2001.

D

DUNCAN, IAIN — Defender

Current Club: Hendon

D o B: 31/07/1972   *Birthplace: Berkshire*
Experienced defender who joined Hendon from Aylesbury United at the start of the 2000/01season. Iains former residences include Leicester City, Thatcham Town, Basingstoke Town, Wealdstone, Windsor & Eton, Wokingham Town and Hayes. Scored his first goal for Hendon in the FA Trophy match against Tonbridge Angels in early November 2000. Injury has kept him out for a good deal of the 01/02 season, but he made an unexpectedly early comeback against Braintree Town in April 2002.

DUNCAN, STEVE — Midfielder

Current Club: Studley

Birthplace: Worcestershire
Previous clubs include: Paget Rangers - February 2001, Kings Norton T, Evesham Utd, Studley BKL.

DUNDAS, CRAIG — Midfielder

Current Club: Croydon

Birthplace: Surrey
A powerful and tenacious 21-year-old midfield player or striker who joined the club in 1998 from local football. Broke through into the first-team ranks towards the end of the 1998-99 season, and is close to reaching 100 appearances for the club. A glut of goals during pre-season suggests that Craig will soon improve his current career tally of 6 goals.

DUNDAS, SCOTT — Midfielder

Current Club: Ilkeston Town

D o B: 31/12/1973   *Birthplace: Stoke*
Honours won: Dr Martens League Western Div.Winners
Goalscoring midfielder Scott joined Stafford Rangers in December 1999 from Leek Town. He began his career with Norton United and then played for Kidsgrove Athletic where he enjoyed a memorable 1997/78 season as they reached the FA Vase semi-final and won the North West Counties League. Scott was the Leagues leading scorer that season with 53 goals. Scott finished as Rangers leading scorer in 2000/01 and voted Supporters' Player of the Season. Switched to Ilkeston Town in May 2002.

DUNDERDALE, ROB — Defender

Current Club: Ossett Albion

Previous clubs include: Liversedge - August 2000, Worsbrough Bridge, Pontefract Colliery, Wakefield C.

DUNKLEY, ROY — Forward

Current Club: Nuneaton Borough

Birthplace: Coventry
From Youth team.

DUNN, ANDY — Midfielder

Current Club: Shepshed Dynamo

D o B: 06/10/1977   *Birthplace: Burton-upon-Trent*
Back with Dr Martens Western side Shepshed Dynamo for a second time- re-joining in the summer of 2002 from Midland Alliance outfit Boldmere St Michaels. The midfielder, a fitness

manager, had a spell at Nuneaton Borough early in his career and also represented Exeter University.

DUNN, IAIN — Forward
Current Club: Harrogate Town
D o B: 01/04/1970 — Birthplace: Derwent
Honours won: England Schoolboy Int., UniBond League Div.One Winners
Vastly experienced midfielder or striker who made 77 appearances for York City before moving on to Chesterfield, for whom he made a further 31 appearances. His final League club was Huddersfield Town where he made 120 appearances. He joined Town in the summer of 1999 from Gainsborough Trinity and made his 100th appearanc for the club during the 2001/02 season. A former England Schoolboy international.

DUNN, LEE — Midfielder
Current Club: St.Helens Town
Birthplace: Liverpool
Strong-tackling midfield player who hit some vital goals last season for Town. Picked after impressing during a pre-season fixture at Maghull last term. Scored some vital goals already this term.

DUNN, THOMAS — Defender
Current Club: Bishop Auckland
D o B: 21/12/1979 — Birthplace: Hartlepool
Young full back who originally signed for Bishop Auckland from Middlesbrough at the start of the 1999/00 season. Left to play Northern League football with Peterlee Newtown in 2001, but re-signed in February 2002.

DUNN, TOMMY — Goalkeeper
Current Club: Sutton United
Birthplace: Surrey
The regular goalkeeper in Sutton United's successful reserve side during the 2000/01 season having graduated from the youth team, he made his senior debut in September 2000 and had an extended run at the end of the season, impressing enough to earn a regular place in the senior side from then on.

DUNN, WILLIE — Midfielder
Current Club: Stourport Swifts
Previous clubs include: Oldbury Utd - July 2001, Kings Norton T, Solihull B, Northfield T.

DUNNE, NICKY — Defender
Current Club: Oldbury United
Birthplace: Stafford
Previous clubs include: Bloxwich Utd - December 2001, Stafford T, Blakenall, Stafford T, Blakenall, Stafford T, Stafford R.

DUNNING, RICHARD — Forward
Current Club: Whitby Town
D o B: 08/01/1981 — Birthplace: Scarborough
Richard signed for UniBond Premier side Whitby Town in September 2001 from Blackburn Rovers. He instantly established himself as a classy midfielder with an eye for goal, scoring on his debut against Accrington Stanley and becoming an instant crowd hit.

DUNSBY, ADAM — Midfielder
Current Club: Wokingham Town
Birthplace: Berkshire
Previous clubs include: Hampton & Richmond Borough - February 2002, Yeading.

DUNTON, DOMINIC — Defender
Current Club: Gloucester City
Birthplace: Cheltenham
Previous clubs include: Cirencester Academy - August 2001, Witney T, Cirencester T.

DUNWELL, CHRIS — Defender
Current Club: Guisborough Town
Previous clubs include: Seaham Red Star - July 2001.

DUNWELL, MIKE — Forward
Current Club: Durham City
D o B: 06/01/1980 — Birthplace: Stockton
Previous clubs include: Bishop Auckland - January 2001, Hartlepool Utd.

DUPORTE, TROY — Forward
Current Club: Hadleigh United
Birthplace: Suffolk
A new signing for Hadleigh this season, having been recommended by Bury Football Academy. Extremely quick front runner who holds the ball up well and shows a good touch. Looking to establish himself at this level.

DUPREE, CHRIS — Defender
Current Club: Fleet Town
Birthplace: Hampshire
From Youth team.

DURKIN, MICKY — Forward
Current Club: Burnham
Birthplace: Berkshire
Forward who signed from Hemel Hempstead in January 2001. Previously at Hungerford Town.

DURKIN, NEIL — Defender
Current Club: Leigh RMI
D o B: 01/07/1976 — Birthplace: Darwen
Talented defender who joined Leigh RMI at the beginning of season 2000/1 from North West Counties League outfit Darwen, where he played for 3 years. Neil was previously in the West Lancashire League with Feniscowles and then Padiham.

DURRANT, ADAM — Defender
Current Club: Egham Town
D o B: 20/10/1981 — Birthplace: Wycombe
Highly-rated young defender who came up through Maidenhead United's ranks to become a regular in the senior squad. Switched to Ryman Division One South side Egham Town in August 2002.

DURRANT, LEE — Midfielder
Current Club: Lowestoft Town
D o B: 18/12/1973 — Birthplace: Great Yarmouth
Previous clubs include: Harwich & Parkeston - July 1997, Ipswich T.

DURRANT, MARTIN — Midfielder
Current Club: Sidlesham
Birthplace: Sussex
Midfielder: played for Pagham U-18s and Sidlesham U-18s before progressing through the reserves and into the first-team: sidelined with an ankle ligament injury during 2001/02.

DURRANT, PETER — Defender
Current Club: Southwick
Birthplace: Sussex
Long serving defender for Horsham YMCA (made some 400 appearances in a 10 year stint) and had previously won a Sussex Senior Cup winners medal with Steyning: joined Peacehaven for the start of 2001/02: sent off in a match against his old club during November: reported to have retired shortly afterwards, but re-emerged at Southwick in January 2002.

DURU, KELECHI — Forward
Current Club: Yeading
Birthplace: London
Previous clubs include: Chesham Utd - December 2001, Harrow Borough, St.Albans C, Harrow B, Beaconsfield SYCOB, Kingsbury T, Willesden.

DUTTON, CRAIG — Goalkeeper
Current Club: Racing Club Warwick
Birthplace: Warwickshire
Well-respected goalkeeper who joined Racing Club Warwick in December 2000 from Midland Alliance side Chasetown. Started his playing days with Nuneaton Borough's second string.

DUTTON, CRAIG — Midfielder
Current Club: Solihull Borough
Birthplace: Coventry
Coventry-based Craig is now in his second season with Solihull after signing from Halesowen Town in September 2000. He played for Sutton Coldfield Town in the 1999/2000 season, making over 80 appearances, after signing from Bedworth United in October 1998. Has represented the Dr Martens League side and also played for Hinckley Town and Stratford Town.

DWYER, CARL — Forward
Current Club: Shifnal Town
Birthplace: Birmingham
Previous clubs include: Boldmere St Michaels - July 2002, Willenhall T, Rushall Olympic, Chasetown, Willenhall T, Chasetown, Rushall Olympic, Sutton Coldfield T, Rushall Olympic, Blakenall, Pelsall Villa, Rushal Olympic, Rovaniemi (Finland), Blakenall, Sutton Coldfield T, Wolverhampt.

DYE, DARREN — Defender
Current Club: Grantham Town
Birthplace: Lincoln
Previous clubs include: Lincoln Utd - July 2000, Worksop T, Grantham T, Lincoln Utd, Nettleham, Lincoln Moorlands.

DYER, DANIEL — Forward
Current Club: Harrow Borough
Birthplace: London
Forward who joined Harrow Borough in August from Wembley. Previously played in the Tottenham Youth Team. Impressed in the Capital League side last season.

DYER, JASON — Defender
Current Club: Rushall Olympic
Birthplace: Worcestershire
Previous clubs include: Kings Norton T - February 2000, Monica Star, Redditch Utd, Olton Royale, Oldbury Utd, Alvechurch, Paget R, Alvechurch.

DYER, KENDRICK — Defender
Current Club: Edgware Town
Birthplace: Middlesex
Previous clubs include: Wembley - March 2002, Leighton T, Ruislip Manor, Hayes.

DYER, MAX — Defender
Current Club: Eastbourne United
Birthplace: Sussex
Former Langney Sports youth player who ended up with a broken nose following a post-match incident with a Chichester player in October 2000.

D

DYER, WAYNE — Midfielder
Current Club: Sutton Coldfield Town
D o B: 24/11/1977   Birthplace: Birmingham
Honours won: Montserrat Int.
A Montserrat full international midfielder who returned to his native Midlands to join Dr Martens Western side Sutton Coldfield Town in August 2002 after a spell with Ryman Premier outfit Bedford Town. After starting out as a professional with Birmingham, Wayne has since had a well-travelled career that has taken in stops at Moor Green, a return to the full-time game at Oxford and Walsall, Hereford United, Bedworth United, Chesham United, Kettering Town, Stourbridge, Solihull Borough and Stevenage Borough.

DYKE, SHAUN — Forward
Current Club: Windsor & Eton
Birthplace: Hampshire
Talented young striker who joined Ryman league Division One South side Windsor & Eton in July 2002 after helping Andover to win the Jewson Wessex League. Originally on the books at Aldershot Town, Shaun then had spells with AFC Newbury and a brief one at Reading before joining Andover in the summer of 2000.

DYSON, IAIN — Defender
Current Club: Congleton Town
Birthplace: St. Helens
Age 26. Central defender. Signed from Winsford United in December 01 to team up again with Kevin Langley. He hails from St Helens and previously played for Everton Schoolboys, Chorley, St Helens Town.

DYSON, JAMES — Defender
Current Club: Bromsgrove Rovers
D o B: 20/04/1979   Birthplace: Wordsley
Tall, promising young defender who joined Dr Martens Western side Bromsgrove Rovers in the summer of 2002 from Premier Division Hednesford Town. Began his playing career on the books at Birmingham City, where he progressed through the ranks to become a professional before signing for the Pitmen in November 2001.

DYSON, LEE — Defender
Current Club: Folkestone Invicta
D o B: 16/10/1973   Birthplace: Wiltshire
An Army PTI teacher whose work with the club helped to improve the players fitness. He initially joined Folkestone Invicta during the summer of 2001 after spending a year in Cyprus, but a pre-season injury prevented him from establishing a first-team place and he subsequently joined Chatham Town. He re-joined Invicta during the summer of 2002. Lee has played in Wales, Ireland and Germany and whilst playing for Cwmbran Town had the honour of playing against Celtic in a televised UEFA Cup tie where he marked Eyal Berkovic, now of Manchester City. Other former clubs include Salisbury City.

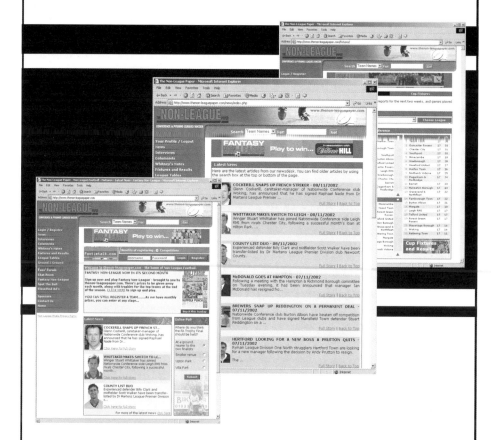

EADES, STUART — Defender
Current Club: Willenhall Town
Birthplace: Birmingham
Signed for Willenhall in January 2002. Former Kidderminster Hariers YTS, has settled in well and is a solid player and another great prospect for the future.

EADY, ANDY — Defender
Current Club: Bury Town
Birthplace: Suffolk
Previous clubs include: Newmarket T - August 2001, West Watting.

EAGLE, DARYL — Defender
Current Club: Harwich & Parkeston
Birthplace: Essex
Recently returned to Harwich from Brightlingsea United, he has had previous spells in the Reserves. A much improved defender who now looks faly at ease at Jewson League level.

EARLY, DEAN — Midfielder
Current Club: Skelmersdale United
Birthplace: Liverpool
Previous clubs include: St Helens T - July 2001, Flint Town Utd, Stantondale.

EASLEY, DUNACN — Midfielder
Current Club: Royston Town
Birthplace: Herts
Previous clubs include: Standon & Puckridge - July 2000, Ware, Royston T.

EASTEL, ANDREW — Midfielder
Current Club: Stamford
Andy is a midfielder who was recruited in August 2001. He is a former professional and has played for Plymouth Argyle, Drogheda, Spalding, Rothwell and Nuneaton.

EASTLAND, ROB — Midfielder
Current Club: Hamble ASSC
Birthplace: Hampshire
Previous clubs include: Bognor Regis T - July 2001, AFC Bournemouth.

EASTWOOD, PHIL — Forward
Current Club: Stalybridge Celtic
D o B: 06/04/1978 *Birthplace: Whalley*
A former YTS trainee with Burnley, where Phil won a Pontins League First Division Championship medal. Upon his release from Burnley Phil wanted to stay in the north-west and Morecambe were the quickest to sign him. He already had Conference experience with loan spells at both Telford and Kettering. Phil is a proven goalscorer with both his head and a sharp right foot. Transferred to Southport in October 2001and then switched to UniBond Premier side Stalybridge Celtic in August 2002.

EATOCK, DAVID — Forward
Current Club: Chorley
D o B: 11/11/1976 *Birthplace: Wigan*
Previous clubs include: Lancaster C - August 2000, Northwich V, Leigh RMI, Newcastle Utd, Chorley.

EATON, GEORGE — Defender
Current Club: Warrington Town
Birthplace: Cheshire
Previous clubs include: Lincoln C - July 2001.

EATON, GRANT — Defender
Current Club: Egham Town
D o B: 04/01/1978 *Birthplace: Berkshire*
Previous clubs include: Burnham - August 2002, Windsor & Eton, Yeading, Slough T.

EATON, JAMIE — Defender
Current Club: Eastwood Town
D o B: 27/10/1977 *Birthplace: Nottingham*
Nottingham-born Jamie is a cultured and stylish performer who re-joined Eastwood Town from Ilkeston Town in September 2001. Jamie started his career as a trainee at Notts County and despite showing great potential failed to break into the Magpies first team. Spent some time on loan at his previous club Eastwood towards thc cnd of last season but then signed for Ilkeston in January 2000.

EATON, JASON — Forward
Current Club: Bath City
D o B: 29/01/1969 *Birthplace: Bristol*
Lively, hard-working forward who is one of the rare breed to have made League appearances for both Bristol clubs. Signed for Bath City in July 2002 after a spell with Ryman League Basingstoke Town. After leaving Bristol City, Jason turned out for Gloucester City, Cheltenham Tow, who paid £15,000 for his services in 1992, Yeovil Town, Newport County and Forest Green Rovers.

EBANKS, MICHAEL — Defender
Current Club: Lewes
Birthplace: London
Previous clubs include: Dulwich Hamlet - March 2002.

ECCLES, MARC — Midfielder
Current Club: Tow Law Town
Birthplace: Cleveland
Spent many years with the Middlesbrough Academy and signed last season for Tow Law from Crook. Former County Junior and during last season had a brief spell at Whitby but returned at the end of last season.

ECCLESTON, MARK — Forward
Current Club: Glapwell
Birthplace: Derbyshire
Previous clubs include: Matlock T - July 2000.

ECCLESTON, STEVE — Defender
Current Club: Bridgnorth Town
D o B: 17/01/1967 *Birthplace: Bridgnorth*
Previous clubs include: Oswestry T - November 2001, Shifnal T, Newtown, Bridgnorth T, Wednesfield, Hednesford T, Atherstone Utd, Tamworth, Bridgnorth T, Welshpool T, GKN Sankey.

ECCLESTON, TONY — Forward
Current Club: Stafford Rangers
D o B: 28/06/1971 *Birthplace: Birmingham*
Honours won: Dr Martens League Western Div.Winners
Tony joined Stafford Rangers during summer of 1998 from Hednesford Town. A popular player with the fans, he was voted Supporters' Player of the Year at the end of his first season for his goalscoring and goal-making abilities. His other previous clubs are Wolverhampton United, Tamworth and Bloxwich Town.

E

ECKHARDT, JEFF — Defender
Current Club: Newport County

D o B: 07/10/1965   Birthplace: Sheffield

Vastly experienced defender who joined Newport County in July 2001 having spent five seasons with Nationwide League neighbours Cardiff City. His career has seen him play well over 500 Football League games, commencing with Sheffield United before moving to Fulham and Stockport County.

EDE, MICK — Defender
Current Club: Rocester

Birthplace: Stoke

Previous clubs include: Armitage - July 1994, Rocester, Burton Alb., Stoke C (Junior).

EDE, PAUL — Defender
Current Club: Rocester

D o B: 03/08/1968   Birthplace: Stoke

Previous clubs include: Chasetown - March 2001, Rocester, Burton Alb., Rocester, Port Vale, Stoke C (Trainee).

EDEN, MATTHEW — Forward
Current Club: Ely City

Birthplace: Cambridgeshire

Previous clubs include: Watton Utd - February 2000, Histon, Ely C, Newmarket T.

EDEN, PAUL — Forward
Current Club: Racing Club Warwick

Birthplace: Coventry

Highly-rated forward or midfielder who rejoined Racing Club Warwick in February 2002 after spells with Leamington and Rugby United. Started out at Hinckley Athletic and also played for Southam United prior to his first spell at Warwick.

EDENSON, JOHN — Goalkeeper
Current Club: Rocester

Birthplace: Stafford

Previous clubs include: Stafford T - February 2001.

EDESON, MATTY — Forward
Current Club: Goole AFC

D o B: 11/08/1976   Birthplace: Beverley

Previous clubs include: Bridlington T - November 2001, Alfreton T, Goole AFC, Bridlington T, Pontefract Collieries, Matlock T, North Ferriby Utd, Hall Road Rangers, Worksop T, North Ferriby Utd, Winterton R, Guiseley, Hull C.

EDGAR, SCOTT — Forward
Current Club: Walton & Hersham

D o B: 10/06/1976   Birthplace: Glasgow

After playing for several clubs in the Scottish League, including Queens Park and Stranraer, Scott has moved south, signing for Swans in August.

EDGCUMBE, WAYNE — Forward
Current Club: Bishop Auckland

D o B: 19/12/1970   Birthplace: Durham

Returned to Bishop Auckland in March 2002 from Spennymoor United to bolster the forward line in their relegation struggle. A well-travelled striker who has scored goals for virtually every club he has appeared for, and they include Crook Town, Gateshead, Tow Law Town and Blyth Spartans.

EDGE, CHRIS — Midfielder
Current Club: Rhyl

D o B: 19/11/1979   Birthplace: Birkenhead

Previous clubs include: Total Network Solutions - June 2002, Connahs Quay Nomads, Tranmere R.

EDGE, IAN — Defender
Current Club: Bedford Town

D o B: 10/01/1979   Birthplace: Gateshead

Ian signed for Ryman Premier side Bedford Town from Unibond Premier outfit Emley in October 2001. Ian moved to the Bedford area and was signed after impressive performances in the reserves. Can play on the right or left hand side of midfield. Previous clubs include Frickley Athletic Sheffield FC and Raunds Town.

EDGHILL, LUKE — Forward
Current Club: Dulwich Hamlet

Birthplace: London

Very skilful forward who signed for Dulwich Hamlet in the summer of 2001 following spells with Watford and Woking. Gradually became a key member of the Hamlet side with some highly-impressive performances and was one of the clubs leading goalscorers until sidelined by injury in January 2002.

EDGHILL, PAUL — Forward
Current Club: Feltham

Birthplace: Greenford

Paul returned to Feltham last season following a spell of two years away from the game. Edghill first came to prominence back in the 1995/96 season in which he scored over 30 goals and grabbed a hatful the following season as well. Personal problems meant Edghill could not play regularly over the next couple of seasons but there are signs that the prolific goalscorer is back to his best.

EDGINGTON, KURT — Goalkeeper
Current Club: Flixton

Birthplace: Manchester

Previous clubs include: Altrincham - February 2002, Hyde Utd, Flixton.

EDMONDS, ANDY — Defender
Current Club: Ware

Birthplace: London

Previous clubs include: Harlow T - September 1998, Wealdstone, Harlow T, Bishops Stortford, Dagenham, Hendon, Enfield, Tottenham Hotspur.

EDRIDGE, RUSSELL — Defender
Current Club: St.Leonards

Birthplace: Hastings

Defender who played for Hastings Town's reserves during 2000/01 and was also selected for the Sussex under-18 squad that season. Joined Sidley United during the autumn of 2001 and impressed everyone with his ability. Signed for Dr Martens Eastern side St Leonards in July 2002.

EDWARDS, BILLY — Defender
Current Club: Margate

D o B: 12/05/1975

Previous clubs include: Sutton Utd - July 1996, Tooting & Mitcham Utd, Sutton Utd, Fisher Ath.

EDWARDS, CHRISTIAN   *Midfielder*
Current Club: Burnham
Birthplace: Berkshire
Spent a brief spell at the club after leaving Bristol Rovers. Returned to the club from Thatcham Town.

EDWARDS, CRAIG   *Midfielder*
Current Club: Grays Athletic
D o B: 08/07/1982   *Birthplace: London*
Joined Grays at the start of the season from Southend United. Superb and very controlled midfield player.

EDWARDS, DARREN   *Forward*
Current Club: Mangotsfield United
Birthplace: Bristol
Highly-rated forward who signed for Mangotsfield United from Bristol Manor Farm in 1998. Leading scorer in his first two seasons, he is also the clubs substitute goalkeeper! He has been attracting the interest of League teams over the last two seasons.

EDWARDS, IAN   *Midfielder*
Current Club: Merthyr Tydfil
D o B: 06/09/1970   *Birthplace: Cardiff*
Right-sided midfielder who joined Merthyr Tydfil from Welsh League side Maesteg Park during the early part of the 2001/02 season. Showed signs of becoming a very good Dr Martens League player before suffering a bad injury which almost caused him to pack the game in. Recovered both from his injury and hurt pride to make a comeback near the end of the 2001/02 season.

EDWARDS, JAMIE   *Midfielder*
Current Club: Three Bridges
Birthplace: Dorset
One-time player with Bridport (Western League): joined Three Bridges during the summer 2000 and scored 4 goals last season.

EDWARDS, JULIAN   *Forward*
Current Club: Romford
Birthplace: Essex
Previous clubs include: Barry T - March 2002, Romford, Purfleet, Southend Utd (Trainee).

EDWARDS, LEE   *Goalkeeper*
Current Club: Molesey
Birthplace: Berkshire
Previous clubs include: Chertsey T - March 2002, Egham T, Chertsey T, Bracknell T, Farnborough T.

EDWARDS, MARK   *Defender*
Current Club: Caernarfon Town
D o B: 18/03/1967
Previous clubs include: Rhyl - August 1998, Bangor C, Conwy Utd, Rhyl.

EDWARDS, MATT   *Forward*
Current Club: Yeading
Birthplace: Nottingham
Top scorer for the past two seasons, Northerner joined the Ding in August 1999 from Hucknall Town after an impressive pre-season. He made an immediate impact, with three goals in his first three competitive matches. Has also previously played for AFC Trent.

EDWARDS, NATHAN   *Forward*
Current Club: Hendon
From Youth team.

EDWARDS, PAUL   *Defender*
Current Club: Taunton Town
D o B: 11/03/1969   *Birthplace: Devon*
Right wing-back who won two Western League titles with Taunton Town. Re-joined the club in June 2001 after a season with Millbrook. Previously with Plymouth Argyle, Saltash United and Tiverton Town.

EDWARDS, PAUL   *Goalkeeper*
Current Club: Tiverton Town
D o B: 26/02/1967   *Birthplace: Taunton*
Honours won: FA Vase Winners
One of the best goalkeepers in the Dr Martens League, he has been a regular at Tiverton Town for the past five seasons. Formally with Taunton Town, Bideford and Paulton Rovers. Since joining Tivvy in 1996 his all round game has improved. He is commanding in the box, good on crosses and an excellent shot stopper. To mark his appearances at Wembley in the FA Vase final he first had the Twin Towers tattooed on his bottom and the following year he dyed his hair yellow!

EDWARDS, PAUL   *Goalkeeper*
Current Club: Telford United
D o B: 22/02/1967   *Birthplace: Liverpool*
Previous clubs include: Shrewsbury T - August 2001, Crewe Alexandra, Leek T.

EDWARDS, RHYS   *Forward*
Current Club: Rhayader Town
D o B: 13/02/1983   *Birthplace: Newport*
Previous clubs include: Newport Co - October 2001.

EDWARDS, ROSS   *Defender*
Current Club: Maidstone United
Birthplace: London
Tall central defender re-joined Croydon at the beginning of 2001/2002 season. Originally joined the Trams on loan from Gravesend in February 2000, before making a permanent move at the beginning of last season. Left after a few months to join Ashford Town and then Welling United in the Dr Martens League. Switched to Maidstone in January 2002.

EDWARDS, RUSSELL   *Defender*
Current Club: Welling United
D o B: 21/12/1973   *Birthplace: London*
Tall and commanding central defender who began his career with Crystal Palace. Then had spells with Barnet and Dulwich Hamlet before moving to Welling United during the summer of 1999. Now an experienced performer, very little gets past Russell.

EDWARDS, SEAN   *Defender*
Current Club: Burgess Hill Town
D o B: 08/03/1974   *Birthplace: Brighton*
Experienced full back: previous clubs include Brighton & Hove Albion, Crawley, Horsham and Hythe: kept out of senior football due to work commitments in Hong Kong until joining Burgess Hill in 1999 (had previously been playing for Upper Beeding): reportedly thrown out of the side in December 2000 for not turning up for a match, but was subsequently reinstated: also acts as club coach.

EDWARDS, TIM   *Defender*
Current Club: Colwyn Bay
D o B: 24/04/1972   *Birthplace: Wrexham*
Previous clubs include: Total Network Solutions - December 2001, Rhyl, Bangor C, Rhyl.

E

EELES, TONY — Midfielder
Current Club: Ashford Town
D o B: 15/11/1970 — Birthplace: Chatham
Previous clubs include: Welling Utd - August 2001, Ashford T, Sittingbourne, Dover Ath., Gillingham.

EGAN, MIKE — Forward
Current Club: Ely City
Birthplace: Cambridge
Previous clubs include: Somersham T - July 2001, Ely C, Mildenhall T, Cambridge C, Somersham T.

EGAN, PAUL — Goalkeeper
Current Club: Folkestone Invicta
D o B: 13/12/1982 — Birthplace: Kent
Teenage goalkeeper who made his Dr Martens League debut for Folkestone Invicta away to Newport County in April 2002. The son of former Folkestone goalkeeper Cliff Egan.

EGGINGTON, ANTHONY — Forward
Current Club: Ashford Town (Middx)
Birthplace: Middlesex
Another player who came through Ashford Town (Middx)s youth set up. Aged 24, he averages almost a goal a game.

EIVORS, GERALD — Midfielder
Current Club: Boldmere St.Michaels
Birthplace: Birmingham
From Youth team.

EJIOFOR, EMEKA — Forward
Current Club: Sutton Coldfield Town
Birthplace: Nigeria
Nigerian-born striker who signed for Dr Martens Western side Sutton Coldfield Town in August 2002 from rivals Atherstone United. Originally with Burton Albion as a youngster, he then had spells with Moor Green and Rocester before joining the Adders in the summer of 2001. Spent part of the 2001/02 campaign on-loan at Shepshed Dynamo.

EKOKU, NKO — Midfielder
Current Club: Bracknell Town
Birthplace: Manchester
Previous clubs include: Hampton & Richmond Borough - January 2002, Chesham Utd, Sutton Utd, Harrow B, Hampton, Malden Vale, Sutton Utd.

EL MGARYEF, RAGIAB — Midfielder
Current Club: Whitby Town
Birthplace: Libya
Honours won: Libya u-21 Int.
Libyan striker who has had a loan spell at Oldham Athletic and has represented his country at under-21 level. Played for the AHLI club in his homeland and joined UniBond Premier side Whitby Town in February 2002. Rayjab will hopefully give the Blues some much needed firepower.

ELAM, BRAD — Defender
Current Club: Alfreton Town
Birthplace: Bradford
Honours won: NCEL & Cup Winners
Defender who was on the books at Bradford City as a trainee before joining Stocksbridge Park Steels where he won a NCEL championship medal in 1995. Also played for Matlock Town and Maltby before joining Alfreton Town in the summer of 1998. Brad

has been unfortunate to be left out of the side during the NCEL title run-in in favour of the experienced John Beresford.

ELAM, LEE — Midfielder
Current Club: Morecambe
D o B: 24/09/1976 — Birthplace: Bradford
Lee joined Conference side Morecambe from neighbours Southport on th eve of the 2002/03 season. Had signed for Port November 1998 from UniBond League outfit Guiseley. Capable of playing on either the left or right hand flank, he has a healthy goal return including a number of spectacular solo goals and is a great provider too, creating numerous chances for colleagues.

ELDER, MATT — Forward
Current Club: Hanwell Town
D o B: 18/06/1973 — Birthplace: Newmarket
Previous clubs include: Mickleover Sports - July 2000, Belper T.

ELDING, ANTHONY — Forward
Current Club: Boston United
D o B: 16/04/1982 — Birthplace: Boston
His impressive goal scoring with Boston United Reserves soon resulted in a call up to the first team squad. He finally made his full debut for the first team in a Nationwide Variety Club Trophy match against Nuneaton in September 2000, and what a start it was, he headed home the opening goal after just 32 seconds of the match. With strong competition for forward places he only managed to start one more first team match in the season, but he was often on the subs bench, sometimes being brought on for the last few minutes to pick up vital experience. With strength and an eye for goal, one to watch for the future. He has also scored nine goals in five games when playing for the Lincolnshire FA Under 18 side. Anthony says that it is all down to Chris Cook that he is at Boston United. He is also pleased that Steve Evans is taking an interest in the young players at the club, giving them an opportunity to succeed.

ELDRET, PHIL — Midfielder
Current Club: Hassocks
Birthplace: Sussex
Member of the Sussex U-18 squad back in 1998/1999: proved to be one of the best newcomers to emerge in the County League during 2000/01, scoring 13 times: typical quality product of the Hassocks youth system.

ELDRIDGE, JOHN — Midfielder
Current Club: Wroxham
Birthplace: Norwich
From Youth team.

ELDRIDGE, MARTIN — Defender
Current Club: Hastings United
D o B: 27/11/1980 — Birthplace: Boston
Left-footed defender: joined Hastings from Kings Lynn midway through 2001/02 after moving to Sussex as a student.

ELDRIDGE, PAUL — Midfielder
Current Club: VCD Athletic
D o B: 27/04/1976 — Birthplace: Dartford
Previous clubs include: Slade Green - July 2000, Crockenhill, Furness, Fleetdown Utd.

ELDRIDGE, RUSSELL — Defender
Current Club: Hastings United
Birthplace: Hastings
From Youth team.

ELEKES, STEFAN — Defender

Current Club: Feltham

Birthplace: Feltham

Club captain Elekes joined Feltham for his 2nd spell in the summer of 2000 from former CCL champions Ashford Town. Stef as he is known to his team-mates is very strong in the tackle and commanding in the air. A former YTS apprentice at Northampton Town, he lists Jimmy-Floyd Hasselbaink as his favourite player and admires team-mate Steve Tomkins skills, especially his first touch.

ELLENDER, PAUL — Defender

Current Club: Boston United

D o B: 21/10/1974 *Birthplace: Scunthorpe*

the club from Scarborough one day before the start of the 2001/2 season. He joined Scunthorpe United on leaving school but was released at the end of the 93/4 season. He was snapped up by Gainsborough Trinity where he was a great success. Moves to Altrincham and Scarborough followed, and at each club he has played at he has become an instant hero with the fans for his commanding displays.

ELLEY, SIMON — Defender

Current Club: Brockenhurst

Birthplace: Portsmouth

Previous clubs include: Bashley - July 2001, Havant & Waterlooville, Aldershot T, Havant T, Waterlooville, Havant T, Waterlooville, Havant T, Portsmouth.

ELLINGTON, LEE — Forward

Current Club: Gainsborough Trinity

D o B: 03/07/1980 *Birthplace: Bradford*

Previous clubs include: Exeter C - October 2000, Hull C.

ELLIOT, JOHN — Midfielder

Current Club: Dover Athletic

D o B: 04/07/1980 *Birthplace: Scotland*

Honours won: Scotland Youth Int.

Previous clubs include: Airdrie - August 2001, Dundee.

ELLIOTT, ANDY — Forward

Current Club: Dunston Federation Brewery

D o B: 02/05/1974 *Birthplace: Newcastle*

Previous clubs include: Gateshead - July 1999, Dunston Federation, Spennymoor Utd, Hartlepool Utd, Spennymoor Utd, Dunston Federation.

ELLIOTT, ANDY — Midfielder

Current Club: Consett

Birthplace: Consett

From Youth team.

ELLIOTT, CRAIG — Forward

Current Club: Harrogate Town

Birthplace: Doncaster

Honours won: UniBond League Div.One Winners

Prolific goalscorer who was a trainee at Doncaster Rovers before signing for Guiseley. He had a short spell at Stocksbridge Park Steels before signing for Farsley Celtic in the summer of 2000, although he played most of his football for Glasshoughton Welfare in the Northern Counties East League. He signed for Harrogate Town in November 2000.

ELLIOTT, DES — Goalkeeper

Current Club: Corby Town

D o B: 07/01/1970 *Birthplace: Corby*

Previous clubs include: Desborough T - December 2000, Stewarts & Lloyds, Desborough T, Corby T.

ELLIOTT, EAMONN — Midfielder

Current Club: Radcliffe Borough

Birthplace: Carlisle

A vastly experienced midfielder who signed for Radcliffe Borough in the summer of 2001 from Ossett Town. Previously with the likes of Workington, Harrogate Town and Ashton United, Eamonn is a tireless worker who has also contributed several goals from midfield.

ELLIOTT, GARETH — Defender

Current Club: Merthyr Tydfil

Birthplace: Merthyr

Gareth is a local lad from Focrhiw who came through Merthyr Tydfils youth system, and it is reckoned he will be a cornerstone of the sides defence in the next few years. With 31 appearances at centre half to his name and at only 19, he has been watched by a few First Division and Premiership teams already. Was called into the Wales under-19 squad during the 2001/02 season only to be withdrawn by the club due to injuries in the squad for a game at Havant. His reward was a broken collar bone and a season of injuries.

ELLIOTT, GARY — Defender

Current Club: Carshalton Athletic

D o B: 22/06/1974 *Birthplace: Surrey*

Re-joined Carshalton Athletic from Whyteleafe in October 2001 An experienced defender who was previously with Sutton United where he played Conference football.

ELLIOTT, JAMES — Defender

Current Club: Alfreton Town

Birthplace: Yorkshire

Previous clubs include: Emley - January 2001.

ELLIOTT, LEA — Forward

Current Club: Saltdean United

Birthplace: Sussex

Youngster, who is a relative old stager at crisis-hit Saltdean, having played for the reserves since 1998/99: became a first-team regular after Glenn Burvill quit as manager midway through 2000/01: scored once that season.

ELLIOTT, LEE — Defender

Current Club: Flackwell Heath

Birthplace: Wycombe

Previous clubs include: Marlow - October 1998, Flackwell Heath.

ELLIOTT, SIMON — Midfielder

Current Club: Ashford Town

Birthplace: Kent

Attacking midfielder who joined Dr Martens Eastern side Ashford Town midway through the 2001/02 season from rivals Tonbridge Angels. A former Gillingham junior who has also played Conference football with Dover Athletic and has also served Gravesend and Maidstone Invicta.

ELLIOTT, STUART   *Defender*
Current Club: Halifax Town

D o B: 27/08/1977   *Birthplace: London*
Well-travelled defender who joined Conference club Halifax Town in August 2002 after a short spell at Exeter. Started his career with Newcastle United and has gone on to make around 100 League appearances with Plymouth, Darlington, Carlisle and Exeter but has also had loan spells with the likes of Hull, Swindon, Gillingham, Hartlepool, Bournemouth, Wrexham and Stockport. Played for Durham Cirty briefly before signing for Scarborough in October 2001 and then on to Exeter in February 02.

ELLIS, JAMES   *Forward*
Current Club: Chatham Town

Previous clubs include: Bly Spartans (Kent) - July 2001.

ELLIS, PETER   *Defender*
Current Club: Runcorn FC Halton

D o B: 15/01/1973   *Birthplace: Liverpool*
Peter is in his seventh season with Runcorn after joining from Knowsley United. Ello has struggled over the last two years with injuries, but he is now back to full fitness and back to being a real handful for opposing attackers. Peter is very strong in the tackle, and is a firm favourite with the fans.

ELLIS, ROB   *Midfielder*
Current Club: Wembley

Birthplace: London
Previous clubs include: Harrow Borough - February 2002, Enfield, Wealdstone, Borough Road College.

ELLIS, STEVE   *Goalkeeper*
Current Club: Holmer Green

Birthplace: Bucks
Previous clubs include: Chalfont St.Peter - July 1998, Marlow.

ELLIS, TOMMY   *Forward*
Current Club: Dorking

Birthplace: Surrey
Previous clubs include: Aldershot T - March 2002.

ELLIS, TONY   *Forward*
Current Club: Leigh RMI

D o B: 20/10/1964   *Birthplace: Salford*
Well-travelled and vastly experienced forward who signed for Conference club Leigh RMI in August 2002 after being released by First Division Burnley. Made over 500 League appearances and netted more than 200 goals during a successful professional career with Oldham, Preston, Stoke, Blackpool, Bury, Rochdale and Burnley. Tony is back where it all began some 18 years ago, as Leighs predecessors, Horwich RMI, were his first club.

ELLISON, JASON   *Goalkeeper*
Current Club: Peacehaven & Telscombe

Birthplace: Sussex
Big goalkeeper who briefly featured in Burgess Hills first-team during 1997/98 before joining Withdean (when they were still a Sussex County League club). Moved, with the rest of the side, to Southwick in September 2001 before Withdean were finally admitted into the Combined Counties League at the start of 2001/02. Missed part of that season with a knee injury and subsequently joined Peacehaven during the spring 2002.

ELLISON, LEE   *Forward*
Current Club: Spennymoor United

D o B: 13/01/1973   *Birthplace: Bishop Auckland*
Previous clubs include: Barrow - March 2002, West Auckland T, Bishop Auckland, Gateshead, Barrow, Southport, Darlington, Bishop Auckland, Halifax T, Mansfield T, Hereford Utd, Crewe Alexandra, Leicester C, Darlington, Bishop Auckland.

ELM, DAVID   *Goalkeeper*
Current Club: Dorchester Town

Birthplace: Dorset
Previous clubs include: Swanage T - August 2000.

ELMES, ROB   *Forward*
Current Club: Halesowen Town

D o B: 29/03/1970   *Birthplace: Poole*
Striker Rob returned to Halesowen Town in May 2002 after a three-year spell in the Conference with Hereford United. Was the Bulls leading scorer in 2000/01 and combines his football career with teaching German at a school in Sutton Coldfield. Prior to his first spell with the Yeltz, Rob turned out for Northfield Town, Boldmere St Michaels and Bromsgrove Rovers.

ELSEGOOD, CHRIS   *Defender*
Current Club: Maidenhead United

Birthplace: London
Chris was released by Crystal Palace in the summer of 2002 and subsequently joined Ryman Premier side Maidenhead United. The sweeper, who played in the Palace reserve and under-19 teams, has impressed everyone since arriving at York Road.

ELSEY, DAVE   *Defender*
Current Club: Mangotsfield United

D o B: 19/11/1975   *Birthplace: Swindon*
Honours won: Wales Youth & u-21 Int.
Former Welsh under-21 international who signed for Mangotsfield United from Bath City in August 1999. Has also played for Swindon Town, Cheltenham Town and Gloucester City. Can also operate in a midfield role. Supporters' Player of the Year in 1999/00. Despite having work committments in London Dave still travels back to play for the club every weekend.

ELVERSON, MATT   *Defender*
Current Club: Kingstonian

Birthplace: London
Previous clubs include: Basingstoke T - March 2002, Hayes, Basingstoke T, Carshalton Ath, Walton & Hersham, Kingstonian, Walton & Hersham.

ELVIDGE, DAVE   *Forward*
Current Club: Eccleshill United

Birthplace: Yorkshire
Previous clubs include: Thackley - January 1999, Dudley Hill Ath., Guiseley.

ELVIN, KEVIN   *Defender*
Current Club: Racing Club Warwick

Previous clubs include: Stratford T - March 2001, Sutton Coldfield T, Atherstone Utd, Nuneaton B.

EMBLETON, DANNY   *Goalkeeper*
Current Club: Total Network Solutions

D o B: 27/03/1975   *Birthplace: Liverpool*
Previous clubs include: Caernarfon T - December 2001, UWIC Inter Cardiff, Colwyn Bay, Rhyl, Conwy Utd, Marine, Flint Town

Utd, Bamber Bridge, Holywell T, Chasetown, VS Rugby, Walsall, Northwich V, Liverpool.

EMERICK, KARL   *Defender*
Current Club: Erith & Belvedere

Birthplace: Kent
A strong central defender or midfielder who served apprenticeship with Gillingham and had several seasons with Margate before joining Erith & Belvedere in September 1999. Has won Dr Martens League Cup, Kent Senior Cup and promotion to the Dr Martens Premier Division whilst with Margate.

EMERSON, SCOTT   *Forward*
Current Club: Blyth Spartans

Birthplace: Newcastle
Aged 19, Scott signed for UniBond League Premier side Blyth Spartans at the start of the 2002/03 season from York City. A very promising young striker.

EMMERSON, CHRIS   *Midfielder*
Current Club: Durham City

Birthplace: Newcastle
Previous clubs include: Shildon - October 1998, Esh Winning.

EMMERSON, JAMES   *Midfielder*
Current Club: Withdean 2000

Birthplace: Sussex
Previous clubs include: Hassocks - August 2001.

EMMETT, DARREN   *Forward*
Current Club: Chorley

D o B: 13/10/1973   *Birthplace: Wales*
Previous clubs include: Trafford - March 2002, Caernarfon T, Conwy Utd, Trafford, Netherfield, Northwich V, Altrincham, Flint Town Utd, Witton Alb., Rossendale Utd, Mount Maunganui (New Zealand), Bury, Everton (Junior).

EMMS, ROGER   *Defender*
Current Club: Salisbury City

D o B: 04/03/1967   *Birthplace: Wiltshire*
Now in his elevnth season with Dr Martens Eastern side Salisbury City, having joined from Andover in July 1992. Strong, dominant defender well respected on the Non-League circuit. Re-appointed as captain in March 2001. As a reward for his loyalty to the club, Roger was granted a Testimonial in 2001/02.

EMSDEN, NIGEL   *Midfielder*
Current Club: Oxford City

Previous clubs include: Thame Utd - July 2000, Oxford C, Basingstoke T, Oxford Utd.

ENDERSBY, LEE   *Forward*
Current Club: Dulwich Hamlet

Birthplace: London
Honours won: England Semi-Pro Int.
Previous clubs include: Hitchin T - September 2001, Bishops Stortford, Yeading, Carshalton Ath., Farnborough T, Slough T, Aldershot T, Enfield, Harrow B, Wembley, Brimsdown R.

ENGWELL, MICKY   *Defender*
Current Club: Boreham Wood

D o B: 20/09/1966   *Birthplace: Grays*
Micky is an experienced left-sided player who began his career as a striker and successfully converted into a left back. He started at Southend United and had a Loan spell at Crewe Alexandra, before joining Chelmsford City in 1986. He then moved to

Barking before returning to Chelmsford City for a second spell. Micky then enjoyed spells with Chesham United, Harrow Borough, Enfield and Grays Athletic before moving to Yeovil Town for a small fee in July 1995, where he became an important member of their championship-winning side in 1996/97. He then returned to Chesham United for a second spell and also played for Slough Town, Hertford Town and Purfleet, from whom he joined Boreham Wood in February 2001, making his debut against Walton & Hersham on the 15 February 2001. Following the resignation of Tommy Sampson in November 2001, Micky was appointed as joint caretaker manager with Lee Harvey for the remainder of the 2001/02 season and then manager at the end of the campaign.

EPISCOPO, ANTHONY   *Midfielder*
Current Club: Rugby United

Previous clubs include: Blackburn Rovers - January 2001.

ERRINGTON, CHRIS   *Goalkeeper*
Current Club: Chester-Le Street

Birthplace: Co.Durham
Previous clubs include: Prudhoe T - February 2002, Spennymoor Utd, Shotton Comrades.

ERRINGTON, MARK   *Defender*
Current Club: Chester-Le Street

Birthplace: Co.Durham
Previous clubs include: Easington Colliery - August 1999, Hebburn.

ESDAILLE, DARREN   *Defender*
Current Club: Droylsden

D o B: 01/01/1976   *Birthplace: Manchester*
Previous clubs include: Cheadle T - July 2001, Hyde Utd, Doncaster R, Hyde Utd, Knowsley Utd, Flixton.

ESHELBY, PAUL   *Forward*
Current Club: Worksop Town

Birthplace: Sheffield
Previous clubs include: Northwich Victoria - July 2001, Ilkeston T, Alfreton T (£7,000), Scarborough, Exeter C, Endcliffe Utd.

ESSANDOH, ROY   *Forward*
Current Club: Bishops Stortford

D o B: 17/02/1976   *Birthplace: Belfast*
Striker who began as a junior at Cumbernauld United before joining Motherwell, locking horns with both Celtic and Rangers in that time. Spells at East Fife, VPS Vaasa (Finland), ST Polten (Austria) and Rushden & Diamonds followed before he famously scored the winner for Wycombe in the FA Cup quarter final tie at Leicester City, after answering a Teletext appeal for a striker by Wanderers manager Laurie Sanchez. He left Wycombe and after some unsuccessful trial periods with a handful of Nationwide League sides he settled at Conference side Barnet. Moved onto Dr Martens Premier side Cambridge City in December 2001, and then switched to Ryman Premier Bishops Stortford in August 2002.

ESSEX, MARK   *Midfielder*
Current Club: Banbury United

Birthplace: Banbury
Promising young defender who can also play in midfied or in attack. Progressed through Banbury United's youth side, he was voted young player of the year for 2000/01, and has achieved the unique double of representing both Oxfordshire and Northamptonshire Youth. Tremendous prospect who became a

regular first-team player during the 2001/02 season. Plenty of pace and has a great attitude.

ETHERIDGE, NEIL — Goalkeeper
Current Club: Glapwell
Birthplace: Chesterfield
Previous clubs include: Rainworth MW - July 1997.

ETUMNUN, ANAYO — Defender
Current Club: Enfield Town (Essex)
Birthplace: Essex
A former Norwich City and Reading reserve team player. Joined Enfield Town after impressing in a friendly fixture against the RAF in January 2002. Previous clubs also include Harrow Borough and Flackwell Heath.

EUSTACE, SCOTT — Defender
Current Club: Hinckley United
D o B: 13/06/1975 *Birthplace: Leicester*
Scott joined Hinckley United in September 2001 from Conference club Stevenage Borough. Experienced at Football League and Conference level, his former League Clubs include Leicester City, Mansfield Town, Chesterfield, Cambridge United and Lincoln City. His League career only came to an end when he was dismissed from Lincoln City following off the field events. After a successful 2001/02 season Scott was rewarded with a trial at Northampton Town.

EVANS, ALUN — Forward
Current Club: Colwyn Bay
D o B: 02/05/1973 *Birthplace: Wales*
Striker who joined Colwyn Bay from Ebbw Vale in December 1997. Alun is a consistent marksman and can play in any position. Previously played for Flint Town United and Bangor City.

EVANS, ANDY — Forward
Current Club: Frickley Athletic
D o B: 25/11/1975 *Birthplace: Aberystwyth*
Born in November in 1975 in Aberystwyth, Andy (real name David) naturally started his football career at Cardiff city before moving back to his home town to play for Aberystwyth Town in 1997 when Cardiff City released him. Having made a huge impact at the Welsh club, he was snapped up by Barnsley in 1999 for a paltry £15,000, forcing him to quit his part-time job as a postman. He made only two first team appearances for being sent on loan to Mansfield Town in March-April of 2000, and then August-September at Chester City, where he made a huge impact with the club as they signed him on, but rarely played him.

EVANS, CHRIS — Forward
Current Club: Dorchester Town
Birthplace: Weymouth
Previous clubs include: Bridport - July 2001, Weymouth, Bridport, Dorcheser T, Weymouth.

EVANS, CHRIS — Midfielder
Current Club: Wokingham Town
Birthplace: Surrey
Previous clubs include: Camberley T - March 2002, Wokingham T, Camberley T, Molesey.

EVANS, CRAIG — Midfielder
Current Club: Haverfordwest County
D o B: 04/03/1971 *Birthplace: Wales*
Previous clubs include: Carmarthen T - March 2002, Merthyr Tydfil, Ebbw Vale, Barry T, Newport AFC, Aberbargoed, Salisbury C, Army, Luton T.

EVANS, DANNY — Defender
Current Club: Dartford
Birthplace: Kent
Previous clubs include: Thamesmead T - July 1995.

EVANS, DARREN — Defender
Current Club: Rushall Olympic
D o B: 30/09/1974 *Birthplace: Wolverhampton*
Previous clubs include: Wednesfield - July 2001, Bilston T, Bridgnorth T, Wednesfield, Redditch Utd, Newport AFC, Bilston T, Hereford Utd, Aston Villa.

EVANS, DAVE — Midfielder
Current Club: Rushall Olympic
Birthplace: Worcestershire
Previous clubs include: Halesowen Harriers - May 2002, Lye T, Halesowen Harriers.

EVANS, GARETH — Defender
Current Club: Newtown AFC
D o B: 03/08/1977 *Birthplace: Wales*
Ex-Manchester City youngster who re-joined the club at the start of the 2000/2001 season. Exciting attacking left sided defender who won the Supporters' Player of the Year Award last season. Excellent passing qualities and always creates good attacking moves.

EVANS, GRAHAM — Forward
Current Club: Caersws
D o B: 16/06/1980 *Birthplace: Wales*
Honours won: Wales Schoolboy & Semi-Pro Int.
From Youth team.

EVANS, JAMIE — Midfielder
Current Club: Croydon Athletic
D o B: 03/10/1978 *Birthplace: Epsom*
Previous clubs include: Bristol C - July 1999, Tottenham Hotspur.

EVANS, JASON — Goalkeeper
Current Club: Ipswich Wanderers
Birthplace: Suffolk
Previous clubs include: Bury T - November 2000, Needham Market, Woodbridge T.

EVANS, JON — Defender
Current Club: Kidsgrove Athletic
Birthplace: Stoke
Left-sided player, capable of producing excellent crosses. Useful going forward. Signed from Congleton Town.

EVANS, KEITH — Forward
Current Club: Salford City
D o B: 08/12/1969 *Birthplace: Manchester*
Previous clubs include: Chorley - July 2001, Mossley, Salford C, Chorley, Leigh RMI, Hyde Utd, Ashton Utd, Curzon Ashton, Irlam T, Preston NE (Trainee).

EVANS, LEE — Defender
Current Club: Port Talbot Town
D o B: 28/06/1972 *Birthplace: Swansea*
Previous clubs include: Maesteg Park - January 2001, Swansea C.

EVANS, LEE — Forward
Current Club: Hyde United

D o B: 30/11/1981   Birthplace: Manchester

Former Stockport County player who has a reputation for scoring goals wherever he has played. Joined UniBond Premier side Hyde United in August 2002 from League of Wales outfit Caernarfon Town after a spell wiht Finnish club Euran Pallo. Rated as an excellent prospect.

EVANS, LOUIS — Forward
Current Club: Cambridge City

Birthplace: Peterborough

Former Peterborough United youth team star who signed for Cambridge City at the end of January 2002. The winger had been with Kings Lynn earlier that season after leaving London Road but failed to win a regular place with The Linnets. Joined City after his contract was cancelled by the Norfolk side.

EVANS, LUKE — Defender
Current Club: Marlow

Birthplace: London

Honours won: Wales Youth Int.

Talented defender who won under-18 honours for Wales when he was with Brentford. Moved to Hayes and Maidenhead United before joining Windsor & Eton in July 1999. Transferred to neighbouring Marlow at the start of the following season.

EVANS, MARK — Defender
Current Club: Port Talbot Town

D o B: 23/11/1971   Birthplace: Cardiff

Honours won: Wales Youth Int., Wales Universities Rep.

Previous clubs include: Llanelli - November 2001, Gloucester C, Merthyr Tydfil, Swansea C.

EVANS, NICK — Midfielder
Current Club: Spennymoor United

D o B: 12/05/1980   Birthplace: Carmarthen

Previous clubs include: North Shields - August 2001, Blyth Spartans, Hartlepool Utd.

EVANS, NIGEL — Defender
Current Club: Portland United

Birthplace: Weymouth

Previous clubs include: Bridport - July 2000.

EVANS, NIGEL — Forward
Current Club: Droylsden

Previous clubs include: Stalybridge Celtic - July 2001, Curzon Ashton, Droylsden, Hyde Utd, Droyslden.

EVANS, OLLIE — Forward
Current Club: Great Wakering Rovers

Birthplace: Southend

From Youth team.

EVANS, PAUL — Midfielder
Current Club: Afan Lido

D o B: 21/11/1973   Birthplace: Wales

Team captain with a strong will and a ferocious tackle. A traditional anchor man - consistent and committed with an eye for goal.

EVANS, PHIL — Defender
Current Club: Haverfordwest County

D o B: 01/03/1971   Birthplace: Wales

Honours won: Wales Semi-Pro Int.

Previous clubs include: Carmarthen T - September 1996, Briton Ferry Ath., Llanelli, Maesteg Park, Llanelli, Merthyr Tydfil, Swansea C.

EVANS, RICHARD — Defender
Current Club: Boldmere St.Michaels

Birthplace: Birmingham

From Youth team.

EVANS, RICHARD — Goalkeeper
Current Club: St Margaretsbury

D o B: 24/07/1976   Birthplace: Enfield

Previous clubs include: Welwyn Garden C - August 2001, Hoddesdon T, Cockfosters, Potters Bar T.

EVANS, RICHARD — Midfielder
Current Club: St.Albans City

D o B: 21/11/1977   Birthplace: London

Former Barnet youngster now into the second season of his second spell with Ryman Premier side St Albans City. Spent two seasons with Chertsey Town, and is equally effective in midfield or the centre of defence.

EVANS, RICHARD — Midfielder
Current Club: Caernarfon Town

D o B: 12/12/1979   Birthplace: Wales

From Youth team.

EVANS, RICKY — Midfielder
Current Club: Total Network Solutions

D o B: 24/09/1976   Birthplace: Wales

An exciting midfield player who joined TNS from Oldham Athletic after spending three years with the club. Specialises in tough tackling and long-range goals. One of the best midfielders in the league.

EVANS, ROBBIE — Forward
Current Club: Carmarthen Town

D o B: 07/02/1977   Birthplace: Wales

From Youth team.

EVANS, ROSS — Forward
Current Club: Woodbridge Town

Birthplace: Suffolk

Another of our exciting Under 18s prospects, Ross made a sensational First Team debut by scoring less than 20 minutes after coming on as substitute at Diss. Has the undoubted ability to make a neam for himself in the game.

EVANS, STEVE — Defender
Current Club: Parkgate

Birthplace: Sheffield

Previous clubs include: Maltby Main - July 1999, Denaby Utd, Maltby MW, Harworth Cl, North Ferriby Utd, Harworth Cl, Spalding Utd, New Stubbin.

EVANS, STEVE — Defender
Current Club: Total Network Solutions

D o B: 26/02/1979   Birthplace: Wrexham

A tough-tackling defender, who also proves to be reliable whereever he plays. A great header of the ball, and has good footwork for a big lad! Joined TNS in February 2000 fron Crewe Alexandra after starting out with West Bromwich Albion.

EVANS, STEVE — Midfielder
Current Club: Burton Albion
Steve Evans was another of Nigel Cloughs summer trialists who caught the eye in pre-season before being offered a two year contract. Steve came to the Brewers from Aston Villa where on occasions he was on the fringes of first team football. A tough tackling midfield player who can also run at the opposition, Steve joined Villa at the age of nine and developed through the youth and then reserve sides. Aged only 20, he has played at many top venues, Anfield being his favourite. His goal in the pre-season friendly against Sheffield United at Eton Park demonstrated why Nigel Clough was keen to secure the 20 year olds signature.

EVANS, STEWART — Defender
Current Club: Parkgate
D o B: 15/11/1960   *Birthplace: Sheffield*
Previous clubs include: Maltby Main - July 1999, Denaby Utd, Crewe Alexandra, Rotherham Utd, Plymouth Argyle, WBA, Wimbledon, Sheffield Utd, Gainsborough Trinity, Rotherham Utd.

EVANS, STUART — Defender
Current Club: Gresley Rovers
D o B: 01/03/1972   *Birthplace: Birmingham*
Strong and dominant central defender who re-joined Gresley Rovers in August 2001 from Hednesford Town, with whom he played Conference football. Also appeared in the Conference with Hereford United after joining the Bulls from Halesowen Town. Left Gresley for the Yeltz in October 1996 and started his playing days as a youngster with Wolves.

EVERETT, PHIL — Forward
Current Club: Tiverton Town
D o B: 09/08/1968   *Birthplace: Cyprus*
Honours won: FA Vase Winners, Non-League Footballer of the Year - 1998/99
Previous clubs include: Dawlish - July 1992, Lyme Regis, Uplyme.

EVERITT, ADAM — Defender
Current Club: Harrow Borough
Birthplace: London
Defender who rejoined Ryman Premier side Hrarow Borough in October 2001 after a spell with Luton Town. Has made a big impression during his short career at Earlsmead. Originally signed for Boro from Hemel Hempstead in the summer of 2000.

EVERITT, DAVE — Midfielder
Current Club: Staines Town
Birthplace: London
Well-travelled midfielder, Dave is also capable of playing in defence when required. Re-joined Staines Town in July 2002 after joining them Conference club Hayes from the Wheatsheaf Lane outfit in March 2001. Started out at Walton & Hersham and then had a spell on Leyton Orients books. Returned to the Non-League game with Sutton United, Chesham United and Banstead Athletic, originally joining Staines in October 1999.

EVERITT, JOHN — Midfielder
Current Club: Enfield Town (Essex)
Birthplace: Hertfordshire
Another recent signing. Joined the club from East Thurrock United, making his debut against Brentwood in October. Previous clubs include Hertford Town and Wingate & Finchley.

EVERITT, LEIGH — Defender
Current Club: Bedworth United
D o B: 09/09/1970   *Birthplace: Nuneaton*
Honours won: Dr Martens League Premier & Western Div.Winners
Defender Leigh joined Bedworth United in June 2002 from Dr Martens Premier side Stafford Rangers. He had signed for Rangers at the end of October 1999 from Nuneaton Borough having previously played for Evesham United and Atherstone United. He was a member of Rangers 1999/00 Dr Martens Western Division championship side and Nuneatons Premier Division title-winning team.

EVERITT, MICHAEL — Midfielder
Current Club: Folkestone Invicta
D o B: 16/10/1982   *Birthplace: Kent*
Michael has forced his way into the Folkestone Invicta first team squad after being a member of the successful youth side which reached the 2nd Round of the FA Youth Cup before going out to Millwall at the New Den. Michael is a busy midfield player who never stops running. He has had trials at both West Ham and Southampton and has represented Kent at youth level. Spent part of the 2001/02 season on-loan at Sittingbourne.

EWART, JOHN — Midfielder
Current Club: Brandon United
Birthplace: Co.Durham
A very tricky, left-sided midfield player with dazzling ability, which can turn defences inside out. John is now in his fourth season after leaving briefly for Whitby at the start of last season, but thankfully soon returned.

EWERS, GARY — Midfielder
Current Club: Great Wakering Rovers
Birthplace: Southend
Previous clubs include: East Thurrock Utd - August 2001, Great Wakering R, Burnham Ramblers, Hullbridge Sports.

EWING, CHRIS — Midfielder
Current Club: Halesowen Harriers
Birthplace: Worcestershire
Previous clubs include: Lye T - February 2000.

EYRE, PETER — Midfielder
Current Club: Hamble ASSC
Birthplace: Hampshire
Previous clubs include: Portsmouth RN - July 2001, Gosport B, Fareham T.

EYRE, RICHARD — Midfielder
Current Club: Hyde United
D o B: 15/09/1976   *Birthplace: Stockport*
Signed for UniBond Premier side Hyde United in August 2002 fron newly-promoted First Division outfit Kidsgrove Athletic. A midfield player who was previously with Macclesfield Town and Port Vale, making almost 50 League appearances.

FAGAN, TYRONE — Forward
Current Club: Bilston Town
Birthplace: Ireland
Previous clubs include: Congleton T - March 2002, Ballymena Utd, Congleton T, Leek T, Northwich V.

FAHEY, MARK — Defender
Current Club: Kendal Town
Birthplace: Blackpool
Previous clubs include: Blackpool - July 2000.

FAHEY, RYAN — Midfielder
Current Club: Cwmbran Town
D o B: 02/02/1984   Birthplace: Wales
From Academy.

FAIRBROTHER, JASON — Midfielder
Current Club: Brentwood
Birthplace: Essex
Manager Paul Delea recruited Jason from Intermediate football. A skilful wide midfield player, Jason has also played as a forward and is regularly among the goalscorers.

FAIRBROTHER, MARK — Goalkeeper
Current Club: Wivenhoe Town
Birthplace: Essex
Previous clubs include: Stanway Rovers - December 2001, Wivenhoe T.

FAIRCLOUGH, WAYNE — Defender
Current Club: Matlock Town
D o B: 27/04/1968   Birthplace: Nottingham
Previous clubs include: Hucknall T - February 2002, Ilkeston T, Grantham T, Northwich V, Chesterfield, Mansfield T, Notts Co.

FAIRHOLM, BRETT — Defender
Current Club: Ely City
Birthplace: Cambridge
Previous clubs include: St.Neots T - November 2001, Ely C, Eynesbury R, Diss T, St.Neots T, Eynesbury R, Ely C, St.Neots T, Soham Town R, Newmarket T, Soham Town R, Notts Co.

FAIRHURST, BRIAN — Midfielder
Current Club: Shildon
Previous clubs include: Peterlee Newtown - July 2001, Whitby T, Shotton Comrades, Spennymoor Utd, Shotton Comrades, Blyth Spartans, Shotton Comrades.

FAIRHURST, JAMIE — Defender
Current Club: Oswestry Town
D o B: 13/05/1975   Birthplace: Lancashire
Honours won: British Universities Rep.
Previous clubs include: Colwyn Bay - August 2001, Total Network Solutions, Rhyl, Bamber Bridge, Hednesford T, Preston NE.

FALANA, WADE — Forward
Current Club: Carshalton Athletic
Birthplace: London
Much-travelled and prolific striker who signed for Carshalton Athletic in the pre-season of 2001 from Tonbridge Angels. Previous clubs include Harlow Town, Romford, Braintree Town, Fisher Athletic, Erith & Belvedere, Heybridge Swifts, Sheffield United, Chesterfield, Scarborough, Doncaster Rovers, Tooting & Mitcham Utd, Leytonstone & Ilford and Millwall.

FALLA, STEFF — Defender
Current Club: Wivenhoe Town
Birthplace: Essex
A young defender who broke through from Clacton's Reserves, after enjoying a spell with Ipswich Youth. Steff, a fast strong centre half has a great future, and switched to Ryman Division One North side Wivenhoe Town in August 2002.

FALLON, DAVE — Defender
Current Club: Littlehampton Town
Birthplace: Sussex
Experienced left back: one of many players to have switched from East Preston to Littlehampton in 1998 when the two clubs swapped managers: missed the opening stages of 2001/02 through injury.

FANNON, CARL — Midfielder
Current Club: Bishops Stortford
Birthplace: Essex
A second spell for Bishops Stortford was heralded when Carl signed for the Club again from Romford. His strength in midfield is a useful tool for the squad and Carl has been a regular in the first team this season. Previous Clubs include Leyton Pennant, Aveley and Grays Athletic. Carl started his playing career in the Essex Senior league with Basildon Utd and Bowers Utd.

FARADAY, MARK — Defender
Current Club: Holmer Green
Birthplace: Bucks
Previous clubs include: Penn & Tylers Green - July 1999.

FARLEY, ADAM — Defender
Current Club: Droylsden
D o B: 12/01/1980   Birthplace: Liverpool
Previous clubs include: Altrincham - August 2001, Everton.

FARLEY, CRAIG — Defender
Current Club: Oxford City
Previous clubs include: Chesham Utd - March 2001, Barnet, Colchester Utd, Watford.

FARLEY, JOHN — Defender
Current Club: Fisher Athletic (London)
D o B: 18/02/1973   Birthplace: Greenwich
Previous clubs include: Welling Utd - July 2001, Lewisham Elms.

FARLEY, PAUL — Midfielder
Current Club: North Ferriby United
D o B: 25/12/1976   Birthplace: Hull
Defensive Midfielder who, after an early spell with North Ferriby United, played for Lincoln United and Matlock Town before returning to become a popular member of the squad with fans and players alike in August 2000. Can play in most positions and started his career as a trainee with Hull City.

FARLIE, NEIL — Midfielder
Current Club: Tiptree United
Birthplace: Essex
Previous clubs include: Halstead T - July 1999, Haverhill R, Sudbury T, Saffron Walden T.

FARMER, STEVE — Defender
Current Club: Witham Town
Birthplace: Essex
From Youth team.

FARMER, STEVE — Defender
Current Club: Sutton Coldfield Town
Birthplace: Coventry
Previous clubs include: Atherstone Utd - August 2001.

FARRELL, ANDY — Defender
Current Club: Leigh RMI
D o B: 07/10/1965 — Birthplace: Colchester
Andy joined Leigh RMI beginning of 2000/01 season from Conference team Morecambe. Andy played in the Football League for 17 years with Colchester United, Burnley, Wigan Athletic and Rochdale. He made over 600 Football League appearances playing at Wembley in 1988 when Burnley were runners-up in the Sherpa Van Final. Andy was also at Burnley when they won Division Four in 1992 and when they were Division Two play-off winners.

FARRELL, ANDY — Forward
Current Club: Halifax Town
D o B: 21/12/1983 — Birthplace: Easington
Andy signed as a YTS player wih Halifax Town in July 2000 and was a regular in both the Youth Team and in the Reserves. He was handed a first team chance in March 2002 and was on the bench for the game against Rochdale. Rated as a hot prospect who could make and immediate impact as an attacker.

FARRELL, MATTHEW — Defender
Current Club: St.Helens Town
Birthplace: Liverpool
Full back or centre half signed from Burscough were he established himself as a regular in the Unibond side. At only 21 he's a great future ahead of him.

FARRELLY, STEVE — Goalkeeper
Current Club: Woking
D o B: 27/03/1965 — Birthplace: Liverpool
Honours won: England Semi-Pro Int., FA Trophy Winners
Steve was signed by Hampton & Richmond Borough in July 2002 after a spell with Farnborough Town in the Conference. However, less than a month later he was given the opportunity to return to the Conference with Woking, which he took. Steve had joined Farnborough from Kingstonian just before the start of the 2001/02 season after rejecting new terms at the Surrey club. Originally with Chester, he then had spells with Macclesfield, where he won an FA Trophy winners medal, Rotherham and Barrow before joining Kingstonian. Steve has the reputation of being one of the best keepers outside the Football League and has won England semi-professional honours and an FA Trophy winners medal.

FARREY, MICHAEL — Defender
Current Club: Dunston Federation Brewery
D o B: 17/08/1965 — Birthplace: Gateshead
Previous clubs include: Blyth Spartans - July 2000, Gateshead, Chester-le-Street, Whickham.

FARRIER, WAYNE — Defender
Current Club: Sidley United
Birthplace: Hastings
Team captain, known as The Iceman: recognized as one of the top defenders in Sussex: steered Sidley to an amazing league and John OHara Cup double in 2000/01, which included a run of 26 First Division matches unbeaten: fittingly scored one of the goals in the victory over Selsey in May which clinched the title: had joined the Blues from Langney Sports during the 2000 close season (ironically missed their championship year after picking up an injury in a pre-season friendly): had previously enjoyed

success with St Leonards, making some 300 appearances for them between 1992 and 1997: reportedly turned down a lucrative offer to join Rye Utd at the start of 2001/02: described by The Times as a defensive rock: has missed a large part of the current season due to the reoccurrence of an old knee injury.

FARRINGTON, LOUIE — Defender
Current Club: Histon
Previous clubs include: Baldock T - July 2001, Ipswich T.

FARROW, PETER — Defender
Current Club: Swindon Supermarine
D o B: 02/03/1972 — Birthplace: Wrexham
Honours won: England Schoolboy & Youth Int.
A popular defender who joined the club in July 1995 and it wasn't long before he earned the respect of his team-mateswith some excellent performances. These performances are still evident today ashe played extremely well last season. A very committed player who always giveshis all. Powerful in the air, he is a danger at both ends of the field and when he does score it's usually one for the scrapbook. He has played for England U-18's and Schoolboys and has also represented the Hellenic League and Wiltshire FA Seniors XI.

FARTHING, DANNY — Midfielder
Current Club: Hucknall Town
Birthplace: Yorkshire
Highly-promising young midfielder who joined Harrogate Town from Northern Counties East League neighbours Pickering Town in June 2002. Had only signed for the Pikes at the start of the 2001/02 season from junior football and created quite an impression during the Yorkshire sides succesful campaign.

FARTHING, MARK — Forward
Current Club: Clacton Town
Birthplace: Colchester
Strong, experienced player with great character. Played at Braintree and in Finland. Been with Clacton for 4 Seasons.

FAULKNER, DAVID — Defender
Current Club: Sheffield FC
D o B: 08/10/1975 — Birthplace: Sheffield
Honours won: England Schoolboy & Youth Int.
Previous clubs include: Gresley Rovers - July 1999, Waterford, Hallam, Alfreton T, Gainsborough Trinity, Darlington, Sheffield Wednesday.

FAULKNER, WES — Defender
Current Club: Aveley
Birthplace: Essex
Previous clubs include: East Thurrock Utd - March 2002, Basildon Utd.

FAWCETT, CHRIS — Defender
Current Club: Billingham Synthonia
Birthplace: Cleveland
Previous clubs include: Norton & Stockton - December 1999.

FAYENUWO, VICTOR — Forward
Current Club: Billericay Town
Birthplace: Essex
Previous clubs include: Sheffield Utd - March 2002.

FAYERS, LUKE — Forward
Current Club: Carmarthen Town
Birthplace: Wales
From Youth team.

FEALEY, NATHAN — Midfielder

Current Club: Fleet Town

Birthplace: Hampshire

Previous clubs include: Egham T - March 1997, Cove, Aldershot T, Reading.

FEAR, PETER — Midfielder

Current Club: Crawley Town

D o B: 10/09/1973 — Birthplace: Sutton

Honours won: England u-21 Int., Dr Martens League Premier Div.Winners

Strong, hard-tackling midfielder who joined Crawley Town in June 2002 from Dr Martens League champions Kettering Town. Had signed for the Poppies just prior to the start of the 2001/02 season after being released by Oxford United. Made over 150 League appearances for Oxford and Wimbledon, with whom he played in the Premiership. Represented England at under-21 international level on three occasions.

FEARNS, TERRY — Forward

Current Club: Vauxhall Motors

D o B: 24/10/1977 — Birthplace: Liverpool

Striker snapped up by Vauxhall Motors from St Helens Town in the summer of 2001, having scored almost 40 goals the previous season in the North West Counties League. Previously with Wigan Athletic and Marine, he struck a hat-trick on his UniBond League debut and followed that with many more to finish the campaign as the clubs leading scorer.

FEARON, DEAN — Defender

Current Club: Stocksbridge Park Steels

D o B: 09/01/1976 — Birthplace: Barnsley

Previous clubs include: Ilkeston T - August 2000, Emley, Rotherham Utd, Barnsley.

FEATHERSTONE, JAMES — Forward

Current Club: Ossett Town

D o B: 12/11/1979 — Birthplace: Wharfedale

Re-joined the Town this season from North Ferriby United with whom he had spent 4 months. Began his career at Blackburn Rovers and Scunthorpe United before being forced into the Non-League game through injury. Has also played for Emley, Whitby Town and Harrogate Town.

FELGATE, DAVID — Goalkeeper

Current Club: Radcliffe Borough

D o B: 04/03/1960 — Birthplace: Blaenau Ffestiniog

Honours won: Wales Int.

Dave signed for UniBond First Division club Radcliffe Borough in July 2002 from Conference outfit Leigh RMI. Had joined Leigh at start of season 1996/97 from Crewe Alexandra. Made over 700 Football League appearances with Bolton Wanderers and Lincoln City and has also represented Wales at Full and Schoolboy levels. Season 1997/98 & 1998/99 Dave won both the Players' Player award and the Supporters' Player of the Year.

FELSTEAD, LEE — Defender

Current Club: Brentwood

Birthplace: Essex

Lee has been a first team member for eight seasons, usually at right back, but can also play centre back or in midfield. Team penalty taker.

FENNELL, ADAM — Forward

Current Club: Walton & Hersham

Birthplace: Surrey

Adam is a local lad who first played at Walton & Hersham in the youth side. After some impressive displays for the reserves last season forced his way in to the senior side to become a regular.

FENSOME, ANDY — Defender

Current Club: Lancaster City

D o B: 18/02/1969 — Birthplace: Northampton

An experienced defender, he joined UniBond Premier side Lancaster City in July 2002 from Conference neighbours Morecambe. Had signed for the Shrimps in March 1999 from Barrow. Won Third Division honours with both Cambridge United and Preston North End. Andy has also played for Norwich City and was virtually ever-present for Rochdale before joining Morecambe.

FENSOME, JAMES — Defender

Current Club: Saltdean United

Birthplace: Sussex

Another youth team player to be thrown into Saltdeans senior side during the latter half of 2000/01: selected for the Sussex U-21 squad the following season.

FENTON, ANTHONY — Defender

Current Club: Bangor City

D o B: 23/11/1979 — Birthplace: Preston

Defender who joined League of Wales side Bangor City briefly in November 2001 before playing the remainder of the season with Newtown. Re-signed in August 2002 after completing a spell with Notts County. Began his career with Manchester City and also had a period with Portsmouth, where had made one League appearance.

FENTON, SPENCER — Defender

Current Club: Wingate And Finchley

D o B: 17/03/1967 — Birthplace: London

From Local football - July 1998.

FENWICK, MIKE — Forward

Current Club: Whitley Bay

Birthplace: Seaton Delaval

Another player recruited from Seaton Delaval. Although only a youngster but shows great awareness in front of goal.

FERDINAND, CHRIS — Midfielder

Current Club: Egham Town

D o B: 11/03/1973 — Birthplace: Reading

Returned to Ryman First Division North side Oxford City in the summer of 2002 from Premier Division Maidenhead United. However, after only a matter of weeks, he switched to Division One South outfit Egham Town as he was finding the travelling to Oxford difficult. Previously at Abington Town as a striker and was top scorer for the Oxfordshire outfit in the 1997/98 season. Chris also had spells at Titcham Town, Newbury Town and Hemel Hempstead. Proved himself at playing in most roles while at York Road. Is the cousin of Englands Rio and Les Ferdinand. Spent several years at Southampton before being released and has also seen action playing for Kitchee FC in Hong Kong.

FERGUSON, COLIN — Defender

Current Club: Windsor & Eton

D o B: 21/11/1966 — Birthplace: Reading

Previous clubs include: Marlow - Chesham Utd, Marlow, Burnham, Maidenhead Utd, Reading (Junior).

FERGUSON, GARY — Forward
Current Club: Hertford Town
Birthplace: Herts
Previous clubs include: Edgware T - August 2001, Harlow T, Arlesey T, Potters Bar T, Baldock T, Boreham Wood, Potters Bar T, Wormley Rovers, Hemel Hempstead, London Colney.

FERGUSON, LUKE — Defender
Current Club: Tooting & Mitcham United
Birthplace: Surrey
Previous clubs include: Croydon Ath - July 1999, Tooting & Mitcham Utd.

FERGUSON, NATHAN — Forward
Current Club: Diss Town
Birthplace: Norwich
Previous clubs include: Dereham T - September 2001.

FERGUSON, STEVE — Midfielder
Current Club: St.Leonards
Birthplace: Hastings
Honours won: Dr Martens League Eastern Div.Winners
Tenacious midfielder who re-joined Dr Martens Eastern side St Leonards from neighbours Hastings United in July 2002. Helped Hastings to win promotion to the Premier Division in 2001/02 after signing from Langney Sports in the summer of 2000.

FERGUSSON, STEVE — Defender
Current Club: Stratford Town
Birthplace: Worcestershire
Previous clubs include: Gloucester C - March 2000, Worcester C, Telford Utd, Gloucester C, Worcester C, Redditch Utd, Alvechurch, Redditch Utd, Bromsgrove R.

FERNANDEZ, NILTON — Defender
Current Club: Edgware Town
Birthplace: London
Previous clubs include: Chertsey T - November 2001.

FERRABY, NEIL — Goalkeeper
Current Club: Sheffield FC
Birthplace: Sheffield
Previous clubs include: Dinnington T - February 2001.

FERREIRA, JERMAINE — Midfielder
Current Club: Oxford City
Previous clubs include: Witney T - July 2000, Oxford Utd (Junior).

FERRETT, CHRIS — Defender
Current Club: Havant & Waterlooville
D o B: 10/02/1977   Birthplace: Poole
Chris signed for Havant & Waterlooville in June 2001 from relegated Dorchester Town and has already shown himself to be an excellent ball crosser, setting up several goals already this season. He started his footballing career as a YTS trainee at AFC Bournemouth and spent two years there before moving to Portsmouth as a non-contracted player. His Non-League career started at Fleet Town and Chris also played at Basingstoke before moving to Dorchester in 1998 via a short stay at Salisbury. During his tenure in Dorset he made around 100 appearances for the club and scored in last seasons Senior Cup win over neighbours Weymouth.

FERRIS, BEN — Defender
Current Club: Hampton & Richmond
Birthplace: Surrey
Central defender and a product of Tooting & Mitcham United's Reserve side who joined Ryman Premier side Hampton & Richmond Borough in August 20002. Also played at Carshalton Athletic and Dorking.

FERRY, RICKY — Forward
Current Club: Whyteleafe
Previous clubs include: Addington - September 2001.

FEVRIER, ISAAC — Defender
Current Club: Letchworth
Birthplace: Beds
Previous clubs include: Brache Sparta - July 2001, Ampthill T.

FEWELL, KEVIN — Goalkeeper
Current Club: Chatham Town
From Youth team.

FEWINGS, PAUL — Forward
Current Club: Billericay Town
D o B: 18/02/1978   Birthplace: Hull
Paul signed for Billericay Town in June 2002 from Ryman Premier rivals Chesham United. Had joined Chesham shortly before the start of the 2001/02 season from Boston United. A strong-running forward, he started his career at Hull City as a 17-year-old YTS and then became their youngest player ever to get a three-year contract. He then went to Hereford United where he was their top scorer in 1999, including a goal against Leicester City in the FA Cup, before going on to Boston.

FEY, RICHARD — Goalkeeper
Current Club: Clevedon Town
Birthplace: Bristol
Goalkeeper who has made a number of appearances for Clevedon as well as appearing for Bristol Manor Farm, Bitton and Torrington in the Screwfix League.

FICKLING, ASHLEY — Defender
Current Club: Scarborough
D o B: 15/11/1972   Birthplace: Sheffield
Previous clubs include: Scunthorpe Utd - July 2001, Grimsby T, Sheffield Utd.

FIDDES, ALEX — Midfielder
Current Club: Grays Athletic
D o B: 04/03/1977   Birthplace: Shoeburyness
He has been on Grays books for almost 2 seasons now, and is a very fit utility player who has the knack of scoring vitall goals. He joined from Heybridge Swifts.

FIELD, ADRIAN — Midfielder
Current Club: Abingdon Town
Birthplace: Oxfordshire
Previous clubs include: Bicester T - July 2001.

FIELD, LEWIS — Forward
Current Club: Wokingham Town
Birthplace: Hampshire
Previous clubs include: Fleet T - August 2001, Sandhurst T, Fleet T, Farnborough T.

FIELD, RICHARD — Midfielder
Current Club: Redditch United
D o B: 14/04/1975   *Birthplace: Birmingham*
Strong, dynamic midfielder who can also fill in the back four. Signed from for Redditch United from Kings Norton Town in July 2000, he has also had spells with Sandwell Borough and Paget Rangers.

FIELDER, COLIN — Midfielder
Current Club: Staines Town
D o B: 05/01/1964   *Birthplace: Winchester*
Honours won: FA Trophy Winners, Dr Martens League Premier Div.Winners
Vastly experienced midfielder who joined Staines Town in September 2001 from Chertsey Town. Colin first made a name for himself with 88 League games for Aldershot. He then helped Farnborough Town into the Conference before Slough Town paid £18,000 for him. After moving on to Woking, Colin helped the Cards to win the Isthmian League and went on to gain two FA Trophy winners medals, scoring the winning goal in the 1995 final. He then signed for Yeovil Town where he took on some coaching duties and continued this arrangement when he signed for Aldershot Town

FIELDING, JOHN — Defender
Current Club: Harrogate Town
D o B: 07/04/1982   *Birthplace: Billingham*
Promising young defender who joined newly-promoted UniBond Premier side Harrogate Town in July 2002 after being released by York City. Injuries forced his inclusion into the York first-team at the start of the 2001/02 season but the first year pro coped admirably and looked one for the future. However, injuries curtailed his involvement thereafter and with an abundance of centre-backs he was not offered a new contract for 2002/03 at Bootham Crescent.

FIELDS, DEREK — Midfielder
Current Club: Taunton Town
D o B: 21/06/1977   *Birthplace: Newton Abbot*
Honours won: FA Vase Winners
A tricky young midfielder who went to Newton Abbot from Liverton Athletic in the summer of 1999 before joining Tiverton Town shortly afterwards. A great prospect, he scored the opening goal in the FA Carlsberg Vase final of 2000.

FILLERY, NEIL — Midfielder
Current Club: Great Wakering Rovers
Birthplace: Essex
Previous clubs include: Romford - March 2002, Purfleet.

FINLAY, GARY — Defender
Current Club: Aberystwyth Town
D o B: 14/11/1970   *Birthplace: Liverpool*
Previous clubs include: Conwy Utd - November 1999, Hyde Utd, Netherfield, Doncaster R, Netherfield, Curzon Ashton, Warrington T, Vauxhall GM, Warrington T, Marine.

FINNEY, RICHARD — Midfielder
Current Club: Ludlow Town
Birthplace: Shropshire
Previous clubs include: Shifnal T - July 2001, Newport T, Shifnal T, Rhayader T.

FINNIE, WAYNE — Defender
Current Club: Banstead Athletic
Birthplace: Surrey
Previous clubs include: Raynes Park Vale - August 2000.

FINNIESTON, JOHN — Midfielder
Current Club: Bracknell Town
Birthplace: Berkshire
Previous clubs include: Chertsey T - August 2001, Bracknell T.

FINNING, RICKI — Forward
Current Club: East Thurrock United
Birthplace: Essex
Previous clubs include: Ford Utd - November 1999, Basildon Utd, Concord R, Aveley, East Thurrock Utd, Tilbury, East Thurrock Utd, Tilbury, Canvey Island, Hornchurch, Billericay T, Barking, Billericay T.

FIORE, MARK — Midfielder
Current Club: Flackwell Heath
D o B: 18/11/1969   *Birthplace: Southwark*
Signed for Ryman Division Two side Flackwell Heath in August 2002 after spending exactly two years with neighbours Windsor & Eton. Had joined Windsor from Chalfont St Peter after previous service with clubs including Wimbledon, Plymouth Argyle, Slough Town, Walton & Hersham, Chesham United and Chalfont St Peter. A vastly experienced midfield player whose knowledge is helping some of the younger players at Flackwell.

FIRTH, STUART — Midfielder
Current Club: Great Wakering Rovers
Birthplace: Essex
Previous clubs include: Witham T - August 2001.

FISH, DAVID — Goalkeeper
Current Club: Witton Albion
D o B: 04/08/1980   *Birthplace: Manchester*
David spent three years at Manchester United playing in front of Englands Wes Brown. He became idolised in Ireland where fans stole his gloves from his hotel room as a souvenir (they left cash, etc.) before he took a YTS at Stockport County having turned down numerous clubs including Everton, York City, Bury and Tranmere. He played mainly for the youth and reserve teams, but at the start of his 2nd year age 16 he played a couple of games with the first-team in Portugal and was in the first-team squad at the start of the season prior to County signing Eric Nixon. His goalkeeping coach rated him higher than Stephen Bywater who went to West Ham from Rochdale for a large amount of money. After one year as a pro, he was released as County cut their wage bill. His final game was the Pontins League Cup Final at Tranmere. With his confidence shattered, he turned down offers from a number of UniBond clubs and joined Woodley Sports in the North West Counties League with whom he excelled and was a vital member of the championship squad, playing in all but 1 game. Whilst playing for Woodley he won the North West Counties division Safe Hands two months running. David became an instant hit with the Stalybridge Celtic crowd after arriving at Bower Fold in August 2000, saving a penalty on his debut against Worksop Town. His nickname is predictably Fishy but he has also been labelled Billy after the Viz character. Transferred to First Division Witton Albion in July 2002.

FISH, IAN — Defender
Current Club: Tiptree United
Birthplace: Essex
Previous clubs include: Halstead T - August 1999, Haverhill R.

FISHER, ANDY — Goalkeeper
Current Club: Cinderford Town
Birthplace: Wales
Goalkeeper who signed for Cinderford Town from Newport County in January 2001. Andy played through injury to help in the

relegation fight that season. Has also played for Havant Town, Fareham Town, Carmarthen Town and Milford United.

FISHER, DAVE   Forward
Current Club: St.Leonards
Birthplace: Kent
Previous clubs include: Sittingbourne - January 2002, Erith & Belvedere, Furness, Fisher Ath., Erith & Belvedere.

FISHER, MATT   Midfielder
Current Club: Stevenage Borough
Birthplace: Mansfield
Another summer 2001 signing for Stevenage, this former Marine adds steal to the Boro midfield. Signed from Kettering where he was voted player of the year, he missed the start of the season whilst recovering from a knee-operation, but made his first start of the season in November at Dover, and has since shown his worth and is an important member of the Boro squad.

FISHER, NEIL   Midfielder
Current Club: Leigh RMI
D o B: 07/11/1970   *Birthplace: St.Helens*
Previous clubs include: Chester C - July 2001, Connahs Quay Nomads, Chester C, Bolton W.

FISHER, RICHARD   Midfielder
Current Club: Barton Rovers
Birthplace: Bedfordshire
Previous clubs include: St Neots T - July 1998, Bedford T, St Neots T, Bedford T, Stotfold, Hitchin T, Stevenage B, Arlesey T.

FISHER, STEVE   Defender
Current Club: North Ferriby United
D o B: 01/02/1975   *Birthplace: Hull*
Defender who now in his second spell with North Ferriby United following a season at Brigg Town. Previously with Hull City as a trainee and Goole Town.

FISHER, WARREN   Defender
Current Club: Newcastle Blue Star
D o B: 27/11/1972   *Birthplace: Newcastle*
Previous clubs include: Gosforth Bohemians - August 1996, Tow Law T, Berwick R.

FISHER-COOKE, JON   Forward
Current Club: Colwyn Bay
D o B: 13/05/1982   *Birthplace: Wales*
Highly-rated young forward who signed for UniBond Premier side Colwyn Bay during the summer of 2001 from League of Wales oufit Rhyl. Had made his LoW debut as a 17-year-old and created a great deal of interest.

FISHLOCK, MURRAY   Defender
Current Club: Chippenham Town
D o B: 23/09/1973   *Birthplace: Marlborough*
Honours won: England Semi-Pro Int.
Experienced defender who won one England semi-professional international cap in 1999 whilst with Yeovil Town. Joined Dr Martens Premier newcomers Chippenham Town in July 2002 after an injury-hit spell with Woking. Started his career with Swindon and also had spells with Gloucester City, Trowbridge Town and Hereford.

FISK, ANDY   Midfielder
Current Club: Hassocks
Birthplace: Sussex
Evergreen midfielder, who has been playing in the County League since the 1970s: key member of the Hassocks side for the last 10 years and has previous experience with Burgess Hill, Three Bridges and Haywards Heath.

FISK, ASHLEY   Defender
Current Club: Wingate And Finchley
Birthplace: London
Previous clubs include: Kingsbury T - July 2001, Wingate & Finchley.

FITCH, MARK   Forward
Current Club: Weymouth
Birthplace: Dorset
Previous clubs include: Portland Utd - February 2002.

FITKIN, CHRIS   Goalkeeper
Current Club: Hertford Town
D o B: 30/07/1977   *Birthplace: Barnet*
Chris joined Ryman Division One North side Hertford Town from Cheshunt at the start of the 2001/2 season and made the number one shirt his own, appearing in most games. He quickly became a crowd favourite and turned down an offer from Bishops Stortford to stay at Hertingfordbury Park. Has also seen service with Barnet, Avley and St Leonards.

FITT, SIMON   Midfielder
Current Club: Chichester City United
Birthplace: Sussex
Former Fareham midfielder who originally graduated through Bognors youth team in 1995/96: had been linked with a move to Chichester in the autumn 2000, but instead joined Pagham (from Gosport) in January 2001: ended that season on a poor note, receiving two red cards in the space of four days: signed for Chichester during the summer.

FITTON, MARK   Midfielder
Current Club: Atherton Laburnum Rovers
Birthplace: Prestwich
Alan Lords first signing for LR in December 2000, Mark came to Crilly Park from neighbours Atherton Collieries. He is an aggressive, hard-working player and a proven goalscorer who is very useful on either side of midfield. Mark works in the catering industry and likes music and going out.

FITZGERALD, GARY   Defender
Current Club: Hemel Hempstead Town
D o B: 27/10/1976   *Birthplace: Hampstead*
Tall and powerful central defender who signed for Hemel Hempstead Town in July 2002 from rivals Slough Town. Had joined the Rebels for a small fee form Hendon in the summer of 2001after he had put in two excellent performances against them when he played for Hendon. Gary is a former Watford trainee who nearly made the breakthrough to the first team before being released by the Vicarage Road club. Since then he joined Enfield, where he was a popular member of their successful side which claimed high finishes in the league. He eventually went on to join Hendon where he became a popular player. His good performances for Hendon at the LOOT stadium were rewarded last season back as Gary was appointed Hendon first team Captain, where he went on to make well over 100 appearances for the north London club. Still only 25, Gary has a bright and long future left in the game.

FITZGERALD, JEROME — Defender
Current Club: Stalybridge Celtic
Birthplace: Lancashire
Well-respected defender whose playing days began with Conference side Morecambes youth side. Played North West Counties League football with Darwen and then switched to Rossendale United in the summer of 1998 and helped them to promotion to the UniBond in 2000/01. Transferred to Premier Division Stalybridge Celtic in July 2002.

FITZGERALD, LEE — Midfielder
Current Club: Peterlee Newtown
Birthplace: Co.Durham
Previous clubs include: Gateshead - July 2001, Peterlee Newtown, Shotton Comrades, Spennymoor Utd, Shotton Comrades, Easington Colliery, Peterlee Newtown.

FITZGERALD, PHIL — Defender
Current Club: Horsham YMCA
Birthplace: Sussex
One-time Fulham youth who also has past experience with Crawley and Horsham: now in his fifth season at Horsham YMCA. Voluted for Gussell during 2000/01.

FITZGERALD, ROBERT — Goalkeeper
Current Club: Carmarthen Town
D o B: 28/12/1978   *Birthplace: Wales*
Previous clubs include: Garden Village - November 1998.

FITZGERALD, SCOTT — Midfielder
Current Club: Northwood
Birthplace: Middlesex
From Youth team.

FITZHENRY, NEIL — Defender
Current Club: Leigh RMI
D o B: 24/09/1978   *Birthplace: Wigan*
Defender who joined Conference side Leigh RMI in August 2002 from rivals Chester City. Began his career with his home-town club Wigan, where he made a handful of senior appearances before signing for Chester in the summer of 2000. Was a regular until Mark Wright arrived as manager at The Deva.

FITZHUGH, ADIE — Midfielder
Current Club: Stratford Town
Birthplace: Warwickshire
Previous clubs include: Bedworth Utd - July 2000, Shepshed Dynamo, Raunds T, Evesham Utd, Hinckley Utd, Atherstone Utd, Hinckley Ath, Willenhall T, Racing Club Warwick, VS Rugby.

FITZPATRICK, GARY — Midfielder
Current Club: Telford United
D o B: 05/08/1971   *Birthplace: Birmingham*
Honours won: Republic of Ireland Youth Int.
Former Hednesford man Gary Fitzpatrick has spent much of his time with United sidelined by injury. The skillful midfield playmaker is quite possibly the best passer of the ball in the league.

FITZPATRICK, IAN — Forward
Current Club: Halifax Town
D o B: 22/09/1980   *Birthplace: Manchester*
Impressive young forward who was re-signed by Conference side Halifax Town in August 2002 after originally being released by the administrators at the end of the 2001/02 season. Started his career with Manchester United and then had a spell in Germany

before joining the Shaymen in March 2000, making around 50 League appearances.

FITZPATRICK, JAMES — Defender
Current Club: Haverhill Rovers
Birthplace: Suffolk
Stalwart defender, a winner of the Cambs League and K.O. Cup with Steeple Bumpstead. In his fourth season with Haverhill.

FITZPATRICK, LEE — Midfielder
Current Club: Rossendale United
D o B: 31/10/1978   *Birthplace: Manchester*
Previous clubs include: Leigh RMI - December 2001, Hartlepool Utd, Blackburn R.

FITZSIMMONS, CHRIS — Defender
Current Club: Rossendale United
D o B: 04/04/1978   *Birthplace: Liverpool*
Liverpool-born defender who joined UniBond First Division side Rossendale United in August 2002 after a spell in the League of Wales with Aberystwyth Town. Began his playing days with Marine before singing for Abar in December 2001.

FITZSIMON, ROSS — Midfielder
Current Club: Harrow Borough
Birthplace: London
Promising young midfielder who joined Harrow Borough in January 2002 following his release by Norwich City. Previously on YTS forms with Tottenham Hotspurs. Is a student.

FLACK, PAUL — Forward
Current Club: Great Wakering Rovers
Birthplace: Essex
Previous clubs include: Burnham Ramblers - July 1998, Great Wakering R, Southend Manor, Basildon Utd.

FLAHERTY, TERRY — Midfielder
Current Club: Brook House
Birthplace: Middlesex
Previous clubs include: Ruislip Manor - July 2000, Chertsey T, Berkhamsted T, Yeading, Ruislip Manor.

FLAIN, STEVE — Forward
Current Club: Leyton Pennant
Birthplace: Luton
Previous clubs include: Edgware T - March 2002, Horsham, Canvey Island, Hitchin T, Bishops Stortford, Lewes, St.Albans C, Stevenage B, Luton T.

FLANAGAN, ADAM — Defender
Current Club: Hastings United
Previous clubs include: St.Leonards - August 2001, Dagenham & Redbridge, Gillingham (Trainee).

FLANAGAN, LEE — Forward
Current Club: Gateshead
Birthplace: Cleveland
Became one of the hottest properties in north-east Non-League football after topping the goalscorers chart for Albany Northern Leaguers Billingham Synthonia in 2001/02. UniBond Premier side Gateshead eventually won the race for his services in August 2002. Previously with Northallerton Town and Spennymoor United.

FLANNERY, JAY — Defender
Current Club: Accrington Stanley
Previous clubs include: Lancaster C - July 1999, Southport, Bamber Bridge.

FLANNIGAN, CRAIG — Forward
Current Club: Gretna
D o B: 11/02/1973   Birthplace: Dumfries
Previous clubs include: Queen of the South - July 2001, Albion R, Partick Thistle, Queen of the South, Clydebank.

FLANZ, SIMON — Midfielder
Current Club: Wisbech Town
Previous clubs include: Ely C - August 2001, Cambridge C, St.Neots T, Stamford, Yaxley, Bury T, Chatteris T, Kings Lynn.

FLAVELL, MICK — Midfielder
Current Club: Bridgnorth Town
Birthplace: Shropshire
Previous clubs include: Shifnal T - July 2001, Willenhall T, Shifnal T.

FLECK, ROBERT — Forward
Current Club: Gorleston
D o B: 11/08/1965   Birthplace: Glasgow
Honours won: Scotland Youth, u-21 & Full Int., Scottish Premier Div.Winners, Scottish League Cup Winners
Previous clubs include: Reading - February 1999, Norwich C, Chelsea, Norwich C, Glasgow Rangers, Possil YM.

FLEMING, JASON — Defender
Current Club: Southwick
Birthplace: Sussex
Defender/midfielder: once on the books of Crawley before suffering with a knee injury: had been playing for Rottingdean in the Brighton League before Whitehawk signed him in February 2000: joined Saltdean during the 2001 close season: changed to Southwick after only six games.

FLEMING, PAUL — Defender
Current Club: Ossett Town
D o B: 06/09/1967   Birthplace: Halifax
Vastly experienced defender who made over 200 League appearances with Halifax Town and Mansfield. Re-joined Halifax in the Conference before switching to Chorley in August 1995. Transferred to Runcorn two years later and then re-signed for Chorley in August 1999 after a spell with Lancaster City. Joined Ossett Town in June 2002.

FLEMING, ROSS — Midfielder
Current Club: Lincoln United
Birthplace: Lincoln
Has graduated from Lincoln United's youth team to their first following the departure to Grantham Town of the vast majority of then first team players in January 2000. Having grasped his opportunity Ross has shown enough determination and commitment to keep his first team place.

FLEMMING, DAVE — Forward
Current Club: Fisher Athletic (London)
Birthplace: London
Striker who began the 2001/02 season with Welling United before switching to Folkestone Invicta. Moved to Ryman Leaguers Horsham and instantly made an impression. Signed for Dr Martens Eastern side Fisher Athletic in August 2002. Has previous experience with Enfield, Carshalton Athletic, Romford,

Kingstonian, Bromley, Leyton Orient and French side Dunkirk amongst others.

FLETCHER, ANDY — Defender
Current Club: Caersws
D o B: 10/03/1977   Birthplace: Wales
From Youth team.

FLETCHER, ANDY — Forward
Current Club: Dunston Federation Brewery
D o B: 12/08/1971   Birthplace: Saltburn
Previous clubs include: Netherfield - November 1998, Whitby T, Billingham Synthonia, Bishop Auckland, Spennymoor Utd, Billingham Synthonia, Hartlepool Utd, Scarborough, Middlesbrough.

FLETCHER, DANIEL — Midfielder
Current Club: Fisher Athletic (London)
D o B: 13/01/1979   Birthplace: Westminster
Previous clubs include: St Leonards - August 2002, Fisher Ath.

FLETCHER, NATHAN — Defender
Current Club: Leek Town
Birthplace: Nottingham
Talented young defender who is very comfortable on the ball. Joined Leek Town in June 2002 from Northern Counties East League side Arnold Town. Had signed for Arnold in the summer of 2001 from Hucknall Town, whose former boss John Ramshaw then re-signed him for Leek.

FLETCHER, SPENCER — Defender
Current Club: Aveley
Birthplace: Essex
Previous clubs include: Leyton Pennant - July 2001, Hornchurch, East Thurrock Utd, Aveley, East Thurrock Utd, Tilbury, Purfleet, Dagenham, Arsenal.

FLEURY, CRAIG — Forward
Current Club: Ashton United
Birthplace: Manchester
Highly-regarded young forward who was signed by Ashton United in the summer of 2002 upon their promotion to the UniBond Premier Division. Craig arrived from Tameside neighbours Curzon Ashton, where he had become a great favourite after joining from North West Counties League rivals Woodley Sports in July 2000.

FLINT, JON — Defender
Current Club: Matlock Town
Birthplace: Sheffield
Previous clubs include: Alfreton T - October 2001, Hucknall T, Gedling T, Ashfield Utd, Heanor T, South Normanton Ath., Ashfield Utd, Arnold T, Hucknall T, Ashfield Utd, Sheffield Wednesday (Junior).

FLINT, MATTHEW — Defender
Current Club: Flackwell Heath
Birthplace: Berkshire
Defender who has regularly switched between rivals Ryman League Berkshir sides Windsor & Eton, Marlow and Flackwell Heath. Re-joined Flackwell for the third time in August 2002 from Marlow.

FLINT, NICK — Forward
Current Club: Horsham YMCA
Birthplace: Sussex
Prolific scorer for East Grinstead in the first half of the 1998/99 season (18 goals in 22 matches for the Second Division side)

before joining Redhill: signed for Crawley at the end of that term but was subsequently loaned out to Horsham: moved to Gorings Mead for the start of the 2000/01 and scored 20 times during that campaign: can really blast the ball, as demonstrated in a game at Chichester in November 2000 when he sent a shot straight through the windscreen of a car that was parked behind the goal: had a brief term at Three Bridges for the first few weeks of 2001/02, before returning to Horsham YMCA: has also represented the County.

FLITCROFT, STEVE   Defender
Current Club: Accrington Stanley
Birthplace: Lancashire
Defender who signed for Accrington Stanley at the in the summer of 2000 after he was released by Blackburn Rovers. Brother of Rovers captain Gary Flitcroft. Made his full debut in the first game of the 2001/02 season, scoring a penalty in Stanleys 5-2 defeat at Gainsborough.

FLITTON, RUSSELL   Defender
Current Club: Cambridge City
Birthplace: Cambridge
Russell is a highly-rated young defender who started out in Cambridge City's youth team and progressed through the reserves to win himself a contract. Had a spell at Jeson Eastern League side Mildenhall Town before returning to City in December 2001.

FLOMO, LUKE   Forward
Current Club: Hassocks
Birthplace: Sussex
Excellent forward, although not exactly robust: had England School trials in 1998 as well as playing for Sussex U-18s: broke into the Hassocks first team midway through 1998/99 and scored six times during 1999/2000: has attracted interest from Charlton and Aldershot in his time: 10 goals to his name last season: used to be called Luke Phipps.

FLOUNDERS, ANDY   Forward
Current Club: Hall Road Rangers
D o B: 13/12/1963   Birthplace: Hull
Honours won: FA Vase Winners
Previous clubs include: Goole AFC - July 2001, North Ferriby Utd, Brigg T, Guang Dong (China), Northampton T, Rochdale, Scunthorpe Utd, Hull C.

FLYNN, JIMMY   Midfielder
Current Club: Stocksbridge Park Steels
Birthplace: Sheffield
Previous clubs include: Matlock T - August 2000, Sheffield.

FLYNN, LEE   Defender
Current Club: Barnet
D o B: 04/09/1973   Birthplace: London
Attacking wing-back who became Tony Cottees first signing in managment when he sealed his move to Barnet from Conference club Hayes in January 2001. A player of proven quality, Lee has an excellent left foot and creates attacking options down the left hand side.

FLYNN, MATTHEW   Midfielder
Current Club: Liversedge
Birthplace: Yorkshire
Previous clubs include: Harrogate Railway - August 2001, Thackley, Yorkshire Amateur.

FOGARTY, RICHARD   Defender
Current Club: Clitheroe
Birthplace: Burnley
Foggy joins from near neighbours Great Harwood. Exciting on the ball and will be looking to establish himself in the first team.

FOLDS, LIAM   Defender
Current Club: Bedford Town
Birthplace: Bedford
21-year-old defender who signed for Ryman Premier side Bedford Town in July 2002. Liam had been with Aston Villa since he was 13. He has been through the schoolboy and youth ranks and spent two years as a professional, playing for the reserves on occasions. Liam, who can play either at centre half or right back, is the son of former Bedford stalwart Bobby Folds.

FOLEY, BRENDAN   Defender
Current Club: Diss Town
Birthplace: Norfolk
Previous clubs include: Watton Utd - August 2000.

FOLEY, DEAN   Midfielder
Current Club: Rothwell Town
Birthplace: Corby
Previous clubs include: S & L Corby - March 1996, Desborough T, Raunds T, Corby T, Leicester C (Trainee).

FOLEY, PAUL   Defender
Current Club: Maidstone United
Birthplace: Kent
Previous clubs include: Ramsgate - July 2001, Greenwich B, Erith & Belvedere, Fisher Ath., Greenwich B.

FOLIGNO, JOANTHAN   Defender
Current Club: Aberystwyth Town
D o B: 26/08/1981   Birthplace: Aberystwyth
From Youth team.

FOLLAND, ROBERT   Forward
Current Club: Port Talbot Town
D o B: 16/09/1979   Birthplace: Swansea
Honours won: Wales U-21 Int.
Rob was a product of the Oxford United's youth team. He made his League debut against Ipswich Town in October 1997 and he is a Welsh under-21 international. He scored his first League goal in the 2-1 victory against Reading live on Sky TV in November 1999. Equally at home as a wing back or up front, he was released at the end of the 2001/02 season and returned to Wales to join League of Wales side Port Talbot Town.

FOLLETT, RICHARD   Midfielder
Current Club: Tamworth
D o B: 29/08/1979   Birthplace: Leamington Spa
Richard signed for Tamworth from Racing Club Warwick in February 2001. He began his career on a YTS at Nottingham Forest before signing as a full time professional for a further two years with them. He had a short loan spell with Bolton Wanderers and Kings Lynn before joing Warwick.

FOLWELL, JOHN   Defender
Current Club: Quorn
D o B: 22/10/1977   Birthplace: Leicester
Previous clubs include: Shepshed Dynamo - July 2002, Barrow T, Eastwood T, Notts Co.

FONTAINE, CHRIS — *Midfielder*
Current Club: Oxford City
Previous clubs include: Thame Utd - October 2001, Oxford C, Chesham Utd, Oxford C, Abingdon T, Oxford C, Abingdon Utd.

FONTANELLE, TONY — *Midfielder*
Current Club: Hitchin Town
Birthplace: London
Honours won: Ryman League Div.3 Winners
Tony is a tricky right winger who can cross the ball from practically any position. His pace and ball control is a threat to any defence and he showed excellent form after joining Arlesey Town from Barton Rovers in the summer of 2000, adopting a fuller role by getting back in defence as well. He is also a qualified referee but that doesnt stop him giving them a rough time! Has played for Exeter, Millwall, Luton, Brighton and Toddington Rovers. Transferred into the Ryman Premier ith Hitchin Town in June 2002. Is a Pensions Administrator.

FOOT, DANNY — *Defender*
Current Club: Bishops Stortford
D o B: 06/09/1975   *Birthplace: Edmonton*
Previous clubs include: Baldock T - October 1999, Boreham Wood, Bishops Stortford, Canvey Island, Romford, Crawley T, Southend Utd, Tottenham Hotspur.

FOOT, PAUL — *Defender*
Current Club: North Ferriby United
D o B: 31/03/1981   *Birthplace: Hull*
Central defender who has represented Humberside at all levels. Signed for North Ferriby United from Unibond Premier side Frickley Athletic in October 2001. Previously with Northern Counties East League sides Bridlington Town and Hall Road Rangers.

FORAN, MARK — *Defender*
Current Club: Telford United
D o B: 30/10/1973   *Birthplace: Aldershot*
A well experienced defender who joined Conference side Telford United in August 2002 after being released by Third Division Bristol Rovers at the end of the 2001/02 season. Started his career with Millwall and then went on to make over 150 League appearances with Sheffield United, Peterborough, Crewe at Bristol Rovers.

FORBES, DEAN — *Midfielder*
Current Club: Tooting & Mitcham United
Birthplace: Kent
Honours won: Guyana Int.
Became Tooting & Mitcham United's first-ever full international when he played for Guyana in the CONCACAF Cup competition in August 2002. Dean is a highly-rated defender who joined the Ryman Division One South side in October 2001 from Bromley. Has also appeared in the colours of Gravesend and Molesey.

FORBES, GARY — *Midfielder*
Current Club: Dunston Federation Brewery
Birthplace: Newcastle
Previous clubs include: Gretna - July 1996, Brandon Utd.

FORBES, SCOTT — *Midfielder*
Current Club: Canvey Island
D o B: 22/10/1976   *Birthplace: Essex*
Left-sided midfielder who has previously played for Saffron Waldon before having a trial with Canvey Island during the pre-season of 2000. Southend United then offered him a contract taking him from Park Lane. Forbes spent two years at Roots Hall after which he was released and re-joined Canvey Island in July 2002 on a two-year deal.

FORBES, STEVE — *Midfielder*
Current Club: Hendon
D o B: 24/12/1975   *Birthplace: Hackney*
Midfielder who joined Hendon from Dagenham & Redbridge in November 2001, having previously played for Sittingbourne, Millwall and Colchester United. Now an experienced midfielder with almost 100 League appearances to his name. Cost Millwall £45,000 when signing from Sittingbourne in 1994.

FORD, DANNY — *Defender*
Current Club: Saltdean United
Birthplace: Surrey
Chunky defender: son of Mick Ford (appointed Saltdean boss in October 2001) and signed for the Tigers from Cove, who lifted the 2000/01 Combined Counties League title: allegedly left in charge of picking the team whilst his father went away on holiday in November, during which time Saltdean lost 10-1 and 12-0.

FORD, IAN — *Forward*
Current Club: Selsey
Birthplace: Sussex
Spectacular forward, who has been at Selsey for four seasons (had previously played in the Wessex League for Hamble, Gosport and Portsmouth Royal Navy, as well as spells with Portfield and Bognor Regis). Scored 22 times during both 1999/2000 and 2000/01 and has also played for Hampshire. Once had trials with Exeter City.

FORD, JAMES — *Midfielder*
Current Club: Havant & Waterlooville
D o B: 23/10/1981   *Birthplace: Portsmouth*
James signed a two-year contract with Dr Martens Premier side Havant & Waterlooville in July 2002 after being released by AFC Bournemouth at the end of the previous season. Described as a diminutive midfielder, James started his career with a professional contract at Dean Court after rising through the youth ranks. He made several League appearances for the club, featured strongly as a defender in the reserve team, and also spent some time on loan with Dr Martens side Dorchester Town.

FORD, JON — *Defender*
Current Club: Bromsgrove Rovers
D o B: 12/04/1968   *Birthplace: Birmingham*
Previous clubs include: Evesham Utd - September 2001, Halesowen T, Telford Utd, Kidderminster Harriers, Barnet, Gillingham, Bradford C, Swansea C, Cradley T.

FORD, KEVIN — *Midfielder*
Current Club: Tiptree United
Birthplace: London
Previous clubs include: Burnham Ramblers - August 2001, Hillingdon Borough.

FORD, PAUL — *Defender*
Current Club: Peacehaven & Telscombe
Birthplace: Sussex
Defender who was captain of Saltdeans under-18 side during 2000/01, who looked fairly impressive when breaking into the Tigers first-team towards the back-end of that season. Signed for Peacehaven in December 2001.

FORD, RYAN — Midfielder
Current Club: Ilkeston Town
D o B: 03/09/1978   Birthplace: Worksop
Born in Worksop, Ryan started as a trainee at Manchester United. Left Old Trafford to join Notts County where he struggled with a string of niggling injuries. Spent a short spell on-loan at Gresley Rovers before joining Ilkeston Town towards the end of the 2001/02 season. Now his injury worries appear to be behind him, Ryan is starting to show why he was such a highly-rated prospect.

FORD, STUART — Goalkeeper
Current Club: Alfreton Town
D o B: 20/07/1971   Birthplace: Sheffield
Highly-rated goalkeeper who joined UniBond First Division side Alfreton Town in July 2002 from Dr Martens Premier outfit Ilkeston Town. Had signed for Ilkeston at the start of the 2001/02 season from Hednesford Town. Stuart was born in Sheffield and started his career at Rotherham. He made 5 League appearances for the Merry Millers before moving to Scarborough. After 22 League appearances for the Yorkshire club he had a short spell at Bury before joining Doncaster Rovers He then returned in Scarborough but soon ventured into Non-League football with Gresley Rovers. After a highy successful five-year spell at the Moat Ground he moved to Hednesford Town, who were then in the Conference.

FORDEN, BRETT — Midfielder
Current Club: Pagham
Birthplace: Sussex
Midfielder: Littlehampton youth team player during 1999/2000 (also selected for the Sussex U-18 squad); joined Pagham from East Preston reserves alongside Jason Broomhall, and scored on his debut in the surprise 4-2 victory over Three Bridges in December 2001.

FOREMAN, GEOFF — Midfielder
Current Club: Metropolitan Police
Birthplace: Surrey
Previous clubs include: Banstead Ath - July 1999, Carshalton Ath.

FOREMAN, JIMMY — Forward
Current Club: Corby Town
Birthplace: Leicester
Impressive forward who joined Corby Town in June 2002 from Dr Martens Eastern neighbours Stamford. Started his playing days in the Leicestershire Senior League with Holwell Sports and also had a spell in the Dr Martens with Rothwell Town.

FOREMAN, SHANE — Forward
Current Club: Stowmarket Town
Birthplace: Suffolk
Previous clubs include: Bury T - July 2001.

FORESTER, STEVE — Defender
Current Club: Carterton Town
Birthplace: Oxfordshire
Previous clubs include: RAF - July 1995.

FORINTON, HOWARD — Forward
Current Club: Yeovil Town
D o B: 18/09/1975   Birthplace: Boston
Former Yeovil Town favourite who returned to the West Country Conference side in August 2002 after a brief spell at Torquay. Began his career as a trainee with Oxford United and then played

for local Ryman sides Abingdon Town and Oxford City before beihg bought by Yeovil in August 1996. That was a good investment as his form for the Glovers earned them a £75,000 transfer fee when Howard joined Birmingham just over a year later. Although he made only a handful of first-team appearances for the Blues, they sold him on to Peterborough for £250,000 two years later, where he played over 60 times and netted around 20 goals. Had a two-month lopan spell back at Huish Park in 2000/01 before returning after suffering from his fair share of injury problems at London Road.

FORMBY, KEVIN — Defender
Current Club: Marine
D o B: 22/07/1971   Birthplace: Ormskirk
Defender /midfielderwho played in League for Rochdale and appeared for them in FA Cup at Anfield. Started with Burscough and then played for Southport in Conference and FA Trophy final.

FORREST, SHANE — Defender
Current Club: Selby Town
Birthplace: Leeds
Previous clubs include: Farsley Celtic - September 2001, Selby T, Dringhouses.

FORRESTER, MATT — Midfielder
Current Club: Cradley Town
Birthplace: Birmingham
Previous clubs include: Willenhall T - August 2001, Rushall Olympic, Sandwell B, Kings Norton T, Sandwell B, Oldbury Utd, Walsall.

FORRESTER, SCOTT — Forward
Current Club: Billericay Town
Birthplace: Surrey
Attcking midfielder or striker who joined Billericay Town from Ryman Premier rivals Aldershot Town in June 2002. Started his playing days with Sutton United where, once he graduated through the system to the senior side, attracted League attention. Switched to Dulwich Hamlet at the start of the 2000/01 season and then transferred to the Shots in March 2001.

FORSDICK, SIMON — Forward
Current Club: Stratford Town
Birthplace: Stratford
From Youth team.

FORSTER, RICHARD — Defender
Current Club: Blyth Spartans
D o B: 16/08/1981   Birthplace: Easington
Signed for Blyth Spartans during the summer 2000, from Hartlepool. Fozzy settled into the central defensive role, and is seen by many as the king pin of the defence. He is a very strong and skillful player. Voted Supporters & Players' Player of the Year 2000/01.

FORT, DAVID — Midfielder
Current Club: Brandon United
Birthplace: Co.Durham
Young local lad who is now in his second season at the club. He made quite an impact when given a run in the team towards the end of last season. Likes to play down the right and has fantastic ability. Will prove to be a tremendous asset to the club.

FORWARD, DAN — *Midfielder*
Current Club: Bridgwater Town
D o B: 05/02/1983   *Birthplace: Somerset*
Previous clubs include: Plymouth Argyle (Junior) - July 2000.

FORWELL, STEVE — *Forward*
Current Club: Wingate And Finchley
D o B: 17/01/1977   *Birthplace: London*
Previous clubs include: Cheshunt - February 2000, Wembley, Barnet, Colchester Utd.

FOSTER, ADRIAN — *Forward*
Current Club: Bath City
D o B: 19/03/1971   *Birthplace: Kidderminster*
Vastly experienced front man, Adrian arrived at Bath City in August 2001 from Conference side Forest Green Rovers. He began his career as a trainee with West Bromwich Albion back in 1989, making over 20 appearances for the Baggies before switching to Torquay United in the summer of 1992. During his two seasons at the Devon club he made nearly 100 appearances, scoring 28 goals in the process. Further spells at Gillingham, Exeter City and Hereford United followed before he moved into Non-League football, firstly with Rushden & Diamonds and then Yeovil Town. During this period he trialled for the England at semi-professional side before joining Forest Green Rovers at the beginning of the 2000/01 season. A knee injury restricted his opportunities at the Gloucestershire side, although he did gain some consolation for this disappointment, playing in the 2001 FA Umbro Trophy Final at Villa Park.

FOSTER, ALAN — *Goalkeeper*
Current Club: Thame United
Birthplace: Oxford
Honours won: English Universities Rep.
Signed for Thame United from local rivals Oxford City. Outstanding goalkeeper who is regarded as one of the best in the Ryman League. Winner of numerous Safe Hands awards. Previously with North Leigh and Witney Town. Has represented the English Universities.

FOSTER, ANTON — *Midfielder*
Current Club: Ilkeston Town
Birthplace: Nottingham
A highly-promising young midfielder who has made a good impression when called upon by Ilkeston Town so far. Spent some time at Alfreton Town on loan during the 2000/01 season but gained a more regular first-team spot with the Robins in 01/02.

FOSTER, DAVID — *Midfielder*
Current Club: Kendal Town
Birthplace: Carlisle
Previous clubs include: Carlisle Utd - July 1999.

FOSTER, JOHN — *Defender*
Current Club: Mossley
D o B: 19/09/1973   *Birthplace: Manchester*
Honours won: England Schoolboy Int.
Previous clubs include: Hyde Utd - February 2002, Bury, Carlisle Utd, Manchester C.

FOSTER, MARK — *Defender*
Current Club: Bishop Auckland
Birthplace: Bishop Auckland
Returned to the Bishop Auckland side during the 2000/01 season after two years out with injury. A product of the Bishop Auckland junior side. Filled in at left back and left midfield and played in over half of the games although never really a regular in

the side during 2000/1. Was almost ever present during the season 2001/02 and has been in consistent form throughout.

FOSTER, MARK — *Midfielder*
Current Club: Lincoln United
Birthplace: Lincoln
Previous clubs include: Grantham T - December 2001.

FOSTER, MARTIN — *Midfielder*
Current Club: Forest Green Rovers
D o B: 29/10/1977   *Birthplace: Rotherham*
Joined Conference side Forest Green Rovers at the end of January 2001, initially on-loan from Doncaster Rovers. Industrious midfield player who has settled well. Rated by many within the club as helping Rovers keep their Conference status during the 2000/01 season. Formerly with Leeds and Morton.

FOSTER, NEIL — *Midfielder*
Current Club: Caernarfon Town
D o B: 08/09/1974   *Birthplace: Wales*
Previous clubs include: Rhyl - July 1998.

FOSTER, STEVE — *Defender*
Current Club: Doncaster Rovers
D o B: 01/10/1979   *Birthplace: Mansfield*
Centre Half Steve was released by Bristol Rovers in the summer of 2002 after five years at the club. He had joined Rovers from Woking for £150,000 after only spending eight months with them. He had started his career at Mansfield Town as a youth player and also spent time as a professional before leaving with George Foster when he went to Conference side Telford United. He spent four years at Telford before his move to Woking. Signed for Doncaster Rovers in August 2002.

FOSTER, STEVE — *Forward*
Current Club: Hyde United
D o B: 30/12/1981   *Birthplace: Urmston*
Signed for UniBond Premier side Hyde United during the 2001/02 season having previously been with Blackburn Rovers. A strong striker who is expected to make a big impact at Ewen Fields.

FOSTER, TOM — *Defender*
Current Club: Basingstoke Town
Birthplace: Hampshire
A youngster who has progressed with his time with Basingstoke Town's youth and reserves to earn an introduction into first-team football during the 2001/02 season. Though predominantly playing in central defence in the reserves, Tom has been moved over to the right in the first-team. Not afraid to take players on, Tom has a good eye for the ball and has a sweet right foot for the long cross into the box.

FOTHERGILL, CARL — *Forward*
Current Club: Ossett Town
D o B: 26/05/1979   *Birthplace: Yorkshire*
Recent signing from Frickley Athletic and has already made a huge impression at the club with some fine displays. Began his career in the NCEL with Worsbrough Bridge and Pontefract Collieries before moving into the UniBond with Frickley and Gainsborough Trinity. Has also played Conference football with Kettering Town.

FOTHERINGHAM, DAVE   *Midfielder*
Current Club: Chesham United

D o B: 26/05/1985   Birthplace: Chesham

A promising young midfielder who was promoted from the ranks of Chesham United's youth squad and reserve team. A local Chesham Lad, Dave is a hard-working player with a good range of passing. He likes to get stuck in and is good with the ball at his feet. He is currently studying for his A Levels at a local 6th form school. His footballing hero is Gazza.

FOULKES, LUKE   *Defender*
Current Club: Holmer Green

Birthplace: Bucks

From Youth team.

FOWKES, GRAEME   *Midfielder*
Current Club: Borrowash Victoria

Birthplace: Nottingham

Previous clubs include: Gresley Rovers - July 2000, Weymouth, Birmingham C, Nottingham Forest (Junior),

FOWLER, DANNY   *Midfielder*
Current Club: Swaffham Town

Birthplace: Norfolk

Brother of Mark. Versatile and aggressive player who is keen to make his mark with Swaffham.

FOWLER, LEE   *Defender*
Current Club: Telford United

D o B: 21/06/1969   Birthplace: Eastwood

Previous clubs include: Halifax T - July 1995, Doncaster R, Preston NE, Stoke C.

FOWLER, MARK   *Goalkeeper*
Current Club: Wroxham

Birthplace: Norfolk

Joined in the close season from Cromer United. Looks a good prospect and highly rated by ex-Wroxham player and Cromer manager Terry Bea.

FOWLER, MARK   *Midfielder*
Current Club: Swaffham Town

Birthplace: Norfolk

Former Norfolk youth captain of whom great things are expected at Swaffham. Strong fast and with two good feet.

FOWLER, MATT   *Forward*
Current Club: Sutton United

Birthplace: Surrey

Honours won: Carshalton Ath - August 2001, Woking, Dulwich Hamlet, Carshalton Ath

Striker who signed for Sutton United just before the start of the 2001/02 season having scored nine goals during the pre-season campaign. A graduate of youth and reserve football with Carshalton Athletic, he joined Dulwich Hamlet at the start of the 2000/01 season and scored 17 goals in 23 games, the last six coming in one match at Bromley. After a spell with Woking, he rejoined Carshalton towards the end of that season and although his goals were unable to preserve their top flight status, he finished the season not only as their leading league scorer, but also as Dulwichs.

FOWLER, MICHAEL   *Midfielder*
Current Club: Newport County

Birthplace: Barry

Honours won: Wales Youth Int.

Previous clubs include: Woking - March 2002, Crystal Palace.

FOX, CARL   *Forward*
Current Club: Glasshoughton Welfare

D o B: 14/03/1976   Birthplace: Yorkshire

Previous clubs include: Garforth T - January 2002, Beeston St.Anthonys.

FOX, DARRELL   *Defender*
Current Club: Sheffield FC

Birthplace: Sheffield

Previous clubs include: Matlock T - July 2000, Gainsborough Trinity, Hallam, Harworth Cl, Hallam.

FOX, JOHN   *Goalkeeper*
Current Club: Dereham Town

Birthplace: Norfolk

Excellent shot stopper who has come through the clubs youth set-up to become the regular first team keeper. First played in first team football at the age of 17.

FOX, JUSTIN   *Forward*
Current Club: Wroxham

Birthplace: Suffolk

Previous clubs include: Diss T - July 2001, Wroxham, Ipswich T (Trainee).

FOX, MARTIN   *Defender*
Current Club: Hinckley United

D o B: 21/04/1979   Birthplace: Sutton-in-Ashfield

Highly-rated defender whose career began at Leicester City. Didnt manage to break into the senior side at Filbert Street and had spells with Grantham Town and Chesham United before joining Cambridge City at the start of the 2001/02 season. Became a firm favourite at Milton Road, but decided to move closer to home by signing for Dr Martens Premier Division rivals Hinckley United in May 2002.

FOX, MARTIN   *Defender*
Current Club: Ossett Albion

Previous clubs include: Frickley Ath - August 2001, Pontefract Collieries, Glasshoughton Welfare, Pontefract Collieries, Glasshoughton Welfare.

FOX, SHANE   *Forward*
Current Club: Brodsworth Welfare

Birthplace: Yorkshire

Previous clubs include: Hatfield Main - July 2000, Epsom & Ewell, Hallam, Brodsworth Welfare, Hallam, Frickley Ath., Sutton T.

FOX, SIMON   *Forward*
Current Club: St.Leonards

D o B: 28/08/1977   Birthplace: Basingstoke

imon is one of St Leonards most prolific strikers since joining in January 1999. He has previously played for both Brighton & Hove Albion, where he made his debut as the youngest ever player at the Goldstone, and Hastings Town. Simon has also gained two Sussex Senior Cup winners medals.

FOY, DAVID　　　　　　　　　*Defender*
Current Club: Worcester City

D o B: 20/10/1972　　　　Birthplace: Birmingham

Highly-impressive defender who started his career with hometown club Birmingham City. Had a spell with Scunthorpe and then a short stint at Stafford Rangers before joining Tamworth in October 1994. Soon became a firm favourite with the Lambs supporters, who were therefore disaapointed when he moved on to Dr Martens League rivals Worcester City in May 2002, shortly after helping Tamworth to the runners-up spot in the Premier Division.

FRAMPTON, KEVIN　　　　*Midfielder*
Current Club: Penrith

Birthplace: Cumbria

Previous clubs include: Workington - July 1999, Sunderland.

FRAMPTON, MARK　　　　　*Forward*
Current Club: Fleet Town

Birthplace: Hampshire

Previous clubs include: Aldershot T - July 1994, Fleet T, Farnborough T, Aldershot (Trainee).

FRANCE, DARREN　　　　　*Forward*
Current Club: Farsley Celtic

D o B: 08/08/1967　　　　　Birthplace: Hull

Previous clubs include: North Ferriby Utd - July 2001, Boston Utd, Voicelink (Hong Kong), Doncaster R, Hull C, Mouscron (Belgium), Bridlington T, Bridlington Trinity, North Ferriby Utd, Sheffield Utd (Trainee).

FRANCE, DUNCAN　　　　　*Defender*
Current Club: Pelsall Villa

Birthplace: Wolverhampton

Previous clubs include: Rushall Olympic - August 2000, Bloxwich T, Wednesfield, Bloxwich Strollers, Pelsall Villa, Blakenall, Willenhall T, Wolverhampton Utd.

FRANCE, PAUL　　　　　　*Defender*
Current Club: Ashton United

D o B: 10/09/1968　　　　Birthplace: Holmfirth

Previous clubs include: Stalybridge Celtic - July 1999, Altrincham, Burnley, Bristol C, Huddersfield T.

FRANCE, RYAN　　　　　　*Forward*
Current Club: Alfreton Town

Birthplace: Nottinghamshire

Honours won: NCEL & Cup Winners

A young right winger with excellent prospects of playing at a higher level in the game. Joined Alfreton Town at the start of the 1999/00 season rom local football and made a big impact at the Town Ground, where his skill and flair made him a favourite with the fans.

FRANCIS, ANTHONY　　　　*Forward*
Current Club: Hitchin Town

Birthplace: Hitchin

Strong and exciting forward who burst onto the scene during the 2001/02 season with his powerful approach to the game. A member of Hitchin Town's successful youth programme.

FRANCIS, DELTON　　　　　*Forward*
Current Club: Stourbridge

D o B: 12/03/1978　　　　Birthplace: Birmingham

Previous clubs include: Stafford Rangers - January 2002, Bedford T, Nuneaton Borough, Kingstonian, Halesowen T, Hednesford T, Birmingham C.

FRANCIS, JOE　　　　　　*Midfielder*
Current Club: Cray Wanderers

Birthplace: Kent

Previous clubs include: Ashford T - July 2000, Bromley, Kingstonian, Hayes, Enfield, Bromley, Welling Utd, Erith & Belvedere, Canterbury C, Dartford, Epsom & Ewell, Charlton Ath., Millwall.

FRANCIS, JOHN　　　　　　*Forward*
Current Club: Garforth Town

D o B: 21/11/1963　　　　Birthplace: Dewsbury

Ex-Burnley professional and much travelled striker who previous clubs include Emley, Farsley Celtic and Harrogate Town. Has joined Town to provide much-needed experience. A powerfully built striker who holds the ball up well and possess an explosive shot.

FRANCIS, KEVIN　　　　　*Forward*
Current Club: Hednesford Town

D o B: 06/12/1967　　　　Birthplace: Birmingham

Arrived at Dr Martens Premier side Hednesford Town during the pre-season of 2001 having played for Hull City the previous campaign. Kevin, being over 6 7 tall, is a nightmare for the average defender and he has scored goals at all of his previous clubs. He has played at Stockport Co., Oxford United and at Birmingham City and must surely become a prolific scorer at this level.

FRANCIS, MARK　　　　　　*Defender*
Current Club: Horsham YMCA

Birthplace: Sussex

Left sided player: made his Horsham YMCA debut in 1991, but since then has also spent time at Broadbridge Heath: scored twice during 2000/01.

FRANCIS, MARK　　　　　　*Midfielder*
Current Club: Hadleigh United

Birthplace: Suffolk

Very experienced, talented and capable midfielder, whose touch and ability is a big boost to the attacking capabilities of the side. Joined Hadleigh at the start of this season having played last term for Whitton United.

FRANCIS, MARTIN　　　　　*Defender*
Current Club: Ossett Albion

Birthplace: Sheffield

Previous clubs include: Denaby Utd - January 2002, Goole AFC, Alfreton T, Matlock T, Alfreton T, Hallam, Worksop T.

FRANCIS, NEIL　　　　　　*Midfielder*
Current Club: Worthing

Birthplace: Brighton

Previous clubs include: Brighton - July 1999.

FRANCIS, REUBEN　　　　　*Forward*
Current Club: Borrowash Victoria

Birthplace: Derbyshire

Previous clubs include: Matlock T - March 2002, Rocester, Burton Alb.

FRANCIS, SAM   *Forward*
Current Club: Lewes
Birthplace: Sussex
Joined from Southwick in October 2000. A young player who with the close season departures of Hudson and Bagnall now finds himself with a big responsibility on his shoulders as the main goalscorer.

FRANKLAND, ROB   *Goalkeeper*
Current Club: Croydon Athletic
Birthplace: Surrey
Previous clubs include: Hampton & Richmond Borough - August 2000, Croydon Ath.

FRANKLIN, SHANE   *Forward*
Current Club: Saltdean United
Birthplace: Surrey
Ex-Tooting & Mitcham forward: helped Saltdean record their first victory of 2001/02 when scoring on his debut in the 2-1 success at Pagham in October (one of seven new players on show that day): one of three Saltdean players to be sent off during the humiliating 10-1 defeat at the hands of Whitehawk in November.

FRANKLIN, TOM   *Midfielder*
Current Club: Paget Rangers
D o B: 17/04/1984   *Birthplace: Birmingham*
First full season with the Bears after joining at the end of last season and still only seventeen. Recently called in to the Birmingham County FA U18 representative squad. Made his debut for the senior team in the FA Cup tie against Belper Town when coming on as sub. His full debut came in November at Pelsall. Captain of the youth team. Featured in both the West Midland Metropolitan Schools U19 representative team and Birmingham County FA U18 squad.

FRANKS, MARK   *Midfielder*
Current Club: Bracknell Town
D o B: 08/05/1961   *Birthplace: Windsor*
Previous clubs include: Windsor & Eton - February 2000, Bracknell T, Windsor & Eton, Woking, Windsor & Eton, Maidenhead Utd, Woking, Windsor & Eton.

FRANKUM, NOEL   *Midfielder*
Current Club: Tooting & Mitcham United
D o B: 30/01/1973   *Birthplace: Surrey*
Previous clubs include: Carshalton Ath - July 2000, Leatherhead, Molesey, Carshalton Ath., Leatherhead, Tooting & Mitcham Utd, Kingstonian, Burnley.

FRASER, ALAN   *Forward*
Current Club: Newcastle Town
Birthplace: Scotland
Previous clubs include: Glasgow Celtic - August 2001.

FRASER, JIMMY   *Midfielder*
Current Club: Basingstoke Town
D o B: 22/10/1976
Previous clubs include: Bath C - June 2001, Worcester C, Kidderminster Harriers, Cirencester T, Cinderford T, Bath C, Portsmouth.

FRASER, STEWART   *Defender*
Current Club: Cirencester Town
D o B: 16/02/1975   *Birthplace: Swindon*
A great defender with a determined attitude who was signed three seasons ago from the Hellenic League.

FRASER, STUART   *Defender*
Current Club: Stevenage Borough
D o B: 09/01/1980   *Birthplace: Edinburgh*
Honours won: Scotland u-21 Int.
Edinburgh-born Stuart signed for Conference side Stevenage Borough from Luton Town in March 2002, where he had been captain of their Youth side. He is a determined and combative left back, and impressed on his debut in the win at Morecambe. He played the majority of the 2000/01 season for the Hatters, but failed to establish himself there after Joe Kinnear took over, and made just the one appearance in the LDV Trophy defeat against Dagenham & Redbridge. Stuart is also a former Scottish U21 International.

FRECKLINGTON, DAVID   *Midfielder*
Current Club: Spalding United
Birthplace: Lincoln
Previous clubs include: Lincoln Utd - December 2001, Lincoln Moorlands, Spalding Utd, Lincoln Utd, Lincoln C.

FREDRIKSON, MIKE   *Forward*
Current Club: Uxbridge
D o B: 17/09/1966   *Birthplace: Middlesex*
Michael signed Ryman League forms for Uxbridge in November 1997 after impressing greatly in the Suburban League side, where he scored regularly. Previously with Northwood, his appearances have been hampered by work commitments.

FREEBOROUGH, MARK   *Defender*
Current Club: Epsom And Ewell
Birthplace: Surrey
Joined Epsom at the start of the 2000/2001 season from Corinthian Casuals. Previously withDorking.

FREEMAN, DARREN   *Forward*
Current Club: Margate
D o B: 22/08/1973   *Birthplace: Brighton*
Talented striker who joined Margate in June 2002 from Brighton. Started his career in nn-League football in Sussex with Horsham and Worthing before going on to make around 150 League appearances with Gillingham, Fulham, Brentford and Brighton.

FREEMAN, MATT   *Midfielder*
Current Club: Borrowash Victoria
Birthplace: Derby
Previous clubs include: Heanor T - July 2000, Stapenhill, Borrowash V, Burton Alb.

FREEMAN, PAUL   *Defender*
Current Club: Andover
Birthplace: Reading
Previous clubs include: Thame Utd - July 2000, Reading.

FREESTONE, CHRIS   *Forward*
Current Club: Leek Town
D o B: 04/09/1971   *Birthplace: Nottingham*
Joined UniBond First Division side Leek Town in August 2002 following short spells with both Kings Lynn Dundalk and Rugby United. Began his career with Arnold Town before being signed by Middlesborough for a £15,000 fee. He has also played at Hartlepool United, who paid £75,000 for his services, Northampton Town, Shrewsbury Town and Forest Green Rovers and has enjoyed loan spells at Carlisle United and Cheltenham Town.

FRENCH, ADAM — Midfielder
Current Club: East Thurrock United
Birthplace: Essex
Previous clubs include: Great Wakering Rovers - August 2001, Purfleet, Boreham Wood, Basildon Utd, Grays Ath., Barnet, Southend Utd.

FRENCH, EDDIE — Defender
Current Club: Horsham
Birthplace: Sussex
Tall, impressive defender: previously with Hassocks and was captain of the Sussex side that reached the final of the FA County Youth Cup in 1999: ironically scored the goal that gave the Robins a shock victory over Horsham in the FA Cup during 1999/2000: moved to Queen Street in the summer 2001.

FRENCH, JONATHAN — Forward
Current Club: Barry Town
D o B: 25/09/1976   Birthplace: Bristol
Previous clubs include: Hull C -July 2000, Bristol R.

FRENCH, LENNIE — Goalkeeper
Current Club: Chester-Le Street
Birthplace: Durham
Previous clubs include: Hartlepool T - July 1995, Eppleton CW.

FRENCH, ROB — Midfielder
Current Club: Bishops Stortford
Birthplace: Berkshire
Impressive midfielder who joined Ryman Premier side Bishops Stortford in July 2002 from Dulwich Hamlet. Had signed for Dulwich in the summer of 2001 following a spell with Chertsey Town. Originally a trainee at Swindon Town, he then had a season in Finland with TP Seinjoki before returning to play for Hampton, Wokingham Town, Basingstoke Town, Bracknell Town and Chertsey. Was Dulwichs skipper for 2001/02.

FRENCH, SCOTT — Forward
Current Club: Hailsham Town
Birthplace: Sussex
Emerged through Hailshams youth team and was a prolific goalscorer during 1999/2000: scored six times the following season:.

FRENCH, TONY — Midfielder
Current Club: Tiptree United
Birthplace: Essex
Previous clubs include: Sudbury T - July 1999, Halstead T, Sudbury T, Brightlingsea Utd, Wivenhoe T, Sudbury T, Brightlingsea Utd, Coggeshall T.

FRETWELL, ADAM — Midfielder
Current Club: Alfreton Town
Birthplace: Sheffield
Honours won: NCEL & Cup Winners
Classy midfielder who quickly established himself in the Alfreton Town side after joining the club in November 1999 from NCEL Division One side Parkgate. Also played with Hallam and Maltby Main. One of the teams most consistent players missing only one game and finishing second highest goalscorer with 14 goals. A freak injury forced Adam to miss two months of the 2001/02 season, but he came back to help the club gain promotion back to the UniBond League.

FRIEND, JASON — Forward
Current Club: Barking & East Ham United
Birthplace: Essex
Experienced 32-year-old striker who joined Barking in October 2001 from Essex Ryman League neighbours Braintree Town. Has been around the Essex Non-League scene for some years.

FROGGATT, ADAM — Forward
Current Club: Glapwell
Birthplace: Chesterfield
From Youth team.

FROGGATT, JONATHAN — Forward
Current Club: Hallam
Birthplace: Sheffield
Previous clubs include: Ossett Alb - February 2001.

FROST, ANDY — Forward
Current Club: Ashford Town (Middx)
Birthplace: Middlesex
Winger and a product of the Ashford Town (Middx)youth set up. Aged 22 with exceptional pace, balance and confidence and with an eye for goal.

FROST, DEAN — Midfielder
Current Club: Bromley
D o B: 26/07/1976   Birthplace: Camberwell
London Taxi Driver who lives in Welling. He has played for Welling United, VCD Athletic, Fisher Athletic, Erith & Belvedere and joined Bromley from Dartford in October 2001.

FROST, STEVE — Defender
Current Club: Bromsgrove Rovers
Birthplace: Worcester
Previous clubs include: Redditch Utd - December 2001, Bromsgrove R, Worcester C, Pershore T, Worcester C.

FRUIN, RICHARD — Defender
Current Club: Gorleston
Birthplace: Norfolk
Previous clubs include: Great Yarmouth T - December 1998, Gorleston, Acle.

FRY, CHRIS — Forward
Current Club: Llanelli AFC
D o B: 23/10/1969   Birthplace: Cardiff
Previous clubs include: Haverfordwest County - July 2001, Barry T, Exeter C, Colchester Utd, Hereford Utd, Cardiff C.

FRY, TONY — Midfielder
Current Club: Trafford
D o B: 30/03/1980   Birthplace: Birkenhead
Previous clubs include: New Brighton - August 2001, Southport.

FUFF, GLENN — Defender
Current Club: Kings Lynn
Birthplace: Northampton
Glenn was signed by Kings Lynn during pre-season 1998. He had previously played for Rushden & Diamonds. A physically imposing centre back who makes life very difficult for opposing forwards. Highly-rated by opponents, he has been voted as player of the season at The Walks.

FULLER, ADY — Defender
Current Club: Banbury United

Birthplace: Oxfordshire
Honours won: England Schoolboy Int.

Signed for Banbury United from Ford Sports Daventry in July 1998 and made his debut at Cirencester Academy. Former England Schoolboy international, and an ex-Watford YTS player. Very dependable and reliable defender who always gives a solid performance. Free-kick specialist.

FULLER, CHRIS — Midfielder
Current Club: Billingham Synthonia

Birthplace: Cleveland

Previous clubs include: Guisborough T - October 2001.

FULLER, DAVE — Defender
Current Club: Leatherhead

Birthplace: Surrey

Left-sided defender who signed for Ryman Division One South side Leatherhead from neighbours Bookham, Dave missed a good deal of the 2001/02 season due to ankle and pelvis injuries.

FULLER, WARREN — Forward
Current Club: Swindon Supermarine

Birthplace: Swindon

Highly-rated young striker whose form in the Hellenic League with Highworth Town created a great deal of attention from higher grade teams in the south-west. The race to sign the prolific scorer was eventually won by Swindon Supermarine boss John Murphy in July 2002.

FULLING, LEE — Forward
Current Club: Aveley

Birthplace: Essex

Previous clubs include: Sawbridgeworth T - August 2000, Barking, Romford, Dagenham & Redbridge, Collier Row, Cheshunt, Wivenhoe T, Purfleet, Wivenhoe T, Boreham Wood, Billericay T, Redbridge Forest, Tottenham Hotspur (Trainee).

FUNNELL, GARY — Midfielder
Current Club: Salisbury City

Birthplace: Southampton

A left sided midfield player who signed for Dr Martens Eastern side Salisbury City in August 2002 from rivals Bashley. After a spell as a YTS player at AFC Bournemouth, he joined Weymouth before moving to Bashley in August 2001 for a £2,000 fee set at a tribunal hearing. Son of former Southampton forward Tony Funnell.

FUNNELL, SIMON — Forward
Current Club: Bognor Regis Town

D o B: 08/08/1974   *Birthplace: Shoreham*

Previous clubs include: Worthing - June 2001, Shoreham, Worthing, Shoreham, Brighton.

FURBER, JAMES — Defender
Current Club: Hailsham Town

Birthplace: Sussex

Left wing-back: graduated through Hailshams youth and reserve sides: broke into the first-team in 2001/02.

FURLONG, CARL — Forward
Current Club: Colwyn Bay

D o B: 18/10/1976   *Birthplace: Liverpool*

Signed for Colwyn Bay just before the transfer deadline of 2002 from League of Wales side Rhyl. Carl is a powerful centre forward who has previously played for Altrincham, Droylsden, Cammell Laird, Netherfield Kendal, Total Network Solutions and has Football League experience with Wigan Athletic.

FURLONG, LEE — Forward
Current Club: Burscough

Birthplace: Liverpool

Lee is a talented striker who was signed by UniBond Premier side Burscough in June 2001 from Conference outfit Southport. Had made over 100 first-team appearances for Port after coming through their own ranks.

FURNELL, ANDY — Forward
Current Club: Wisbech Town

D o B: 13/02/1977   *Birthplace: Peterborough*
Honours won: England Youth Int.

Previous clubs include: Grantham T - June 2001, Wisbech T, Stamford, Nuneaton B, Rushden & Diamonds, Peterborough Utd.

FUTCHER, SIMON — Forward
Current Club: Forest Green Rovers

Birthplace: Swindon

Plays his game wide left and signed for Conference side Forest Green Rovers during the close season of 2001 after a successful period with the champions of the Hellenic League, Swindon Supermarine. Enjoyed an excellent first season at the higher level.

FUTCHER, STEVE — Midfielder
Current Club: Rhyl

D o B: 24/10/1976   *Birthplace: Chester*

Previous clubs include: Connahs Quay Nomads - July 2001, Cwmbran T, Connahs Quay Nomads, Gresley R, Sligo R, Wrexham.

THE NON-LEAGUE PAPER

ESSENTIAL READING FOR FOLLOWERS OF THE NATIONAL GAME

SHARE THE PASSION

THE NON-LEAGUE PAPER

ESSENTIAL READING FOR FOLLOWERS OF THE NATIONAL GAME £1.00

Issue No 86 Sunday October 27, 2002

FA CUP SPECIAL

COVERAGE OF ALL YESTERDAY'S GAMES – INSIDE

48 PAGES OF NON-STOP SOCCER ACTION

TIVVY SEND THEM DIZZY

BBC get score wrong as Shreeves suffers

HUDSON AT HIGH-SPEED

THE NON-LEAGUE PAPER

CONFERENCE & PYRAMID LEAGUES SOCCER £1.00

Issue No 135 Sunday October 20, 2002

EXCLUSIVE: BORG I paid £15,000 in paper bag to sign player

EXCLUSIVE: CHAPPLE Death threat to my daughter made me want to walk out

48 PAGES OF NEWS, MATCH REPORTS, RESULTS & FIXTURES

EVERY SUNDAY

GABBIDON, NORE — Goalkeeper
Current Club: Uxbridge
Birthplace: Birmingham
Previous clubs include: Sutton Coldfield T - January 2002, Bromsgrove R.

GADSBY, MICK — Forward
Current Club: Arnold Town
Birthplace: Nottingham
Previous clubs include: Gedling T - August 2000, Dunkirk, Kimberley T.

GAFFEY, TONY — Defender
Current Club: Mossley
Birthplace: Manchester
Previous clubs include: Abbey Hey - August 2001.

GALE, RICHARD — Defender
Current Club: Oadby Town
Birthplace: Leicester
Previous clubs include: Lutterworth T - July 1993.

GALE, SHAUN — Defender
Current Club: Havant & Waterlooville
D o B: 08/10/1969   *Birthplace: Reading*
Signed for Havant & Waterlooville in August 2000 from Exeter City, Shaun has also played for Barnet and is a very experienced defender. Making 49 appearances for the team in his first season alone, Shaun has quickly become a stalwart member of the club. Away from the pitch he works for Portsmouth Football Club co-managing their football in the community programme.

GALE, STEVE — Midfielder
Current Club: Windsor & Eton
D o B: 22/04/1976   *Birthplace: London*
Signed for Windsor & Eton in March 2001 from Kingstonian. Spent two seasons out of the game due to a broken leg whilst playing at Kingstonian. Midfielder previously with Fulham.

GALLAGHER, BEN — Midfielder
Current Club: Farsley Celtic
D o B: 12/10/1978   *Birthplace: Rugby*
Previous clubs include: Guiseley - December 2001, Manchester C.

GALLAGHER, DAVID — Midfielder
Current Club: Billingham Town
Previous clubs include: Bishop Auckland - November 2001, Guisborough T, Marske Utd, Mannion Park, Dormans Ath.

GALLAGHER, JASON — Midfielder
Current Club: Altrincham
D o B: 25/03/1972   *Birthplace: Cheshire*
Jason signed for Altrincham from Hyde United as a right back but has spent most of the last four seasons on the right side of midfield. Pacey and hard-working, Jason always impresses with his commitment and stamina. Started his career with Marine before playing for Ternia (Belgium), Witton Albion, Northwich Victoria, Runcorn and Caernarfon.

GALLAGHER, KIERAN — Midfielder
Current Club: Hendon
Birthplace: London
Right-sided defender or midfielder who signed for Hendon in June 2002 from Slough Town. Had joined the Rebels on a free transfer from Dagenham & Redbridge in October 2001. Kieran is a

hardworking player who has good skill on the ball. He has an excellent workrate and is not afraid to get stuck in. Started his career as a youth team player at Chelseas before moving onto Barnet where he made some league appearances for the Bees at Underhill. He was the released and moved to Aylesbury United where he spent six successful seasons. During that time Kirean helped the Ducks win the Berks & Bucks Cup and also claim a second place finish in the Ryman Premier league. Sadly while at Aylesbury Kieran broke his leg while playing for the Ducks against St.Albans City Fotball club. He fully recovered from that injury and several months later he made his comeback. He impressed immediately and he soon joined Dagenham & Redbridge for a four-figure fee. Despite a handful of appearances in the Conference for the Daggers, Kieran did make a good impression with their fans. He scored the winning penalty in last seasons Essex Cup final against Canvey Island to secure Dagenham the trophy. Earlier that season Kieran spent a successful loan period at Boreham Wood before joining Slough.

G

GALLAGHER, RYAN — Defender
Current Club: Stratford Town
Birthplace: Coventry
Previous clubs include: Marconi - August 2001.

GALLAGHER, TOMMY — Defender
Current Club: Hucknall Town
D o B: 25/08/1974   *Birthplace: Nottingham*
Previous clubs include: Hinckley Utd - July 2001, Loughborough University, Tampa Bay Rowdies (USA), Notts Co.

GALLEN, BRENDAN — Defender
Current Club: Hayes
Birthplace: London
From Youth team.

GALLEN, STEVE — Defender
Current Club: Leighton Town
D o B: 21/11/1973   *Birthplace: Acton*
Previous clubs include: Hemel Hempstead - January 2002, Aylesbury Utd, Hemel Hempstead, Aylesbury Utd, Dundalk, Doncaster R, QPR.

GALLOWAY, ALAN — Midfielder
Current Club: Brook House
D o B: 24/05/1970   *Birthplace: Middlesex*
Previous clubs include: Southall - July 2000, Wealdstone, Epsom & Ewell, Southall, Uxbridge, Brook House, Hayes, Hanwell T, Woking.

GAMBLE, DAVID — Midfielder
Current Club: Runcorn FC Halton
D o B: 23/03/1971   *Birthplace: Liverpool*
Honours won: UniBond League Premier Div.Winners
Dave signed for Runcorn from Marine during pre-season before the 2001/2002 season. An excellent dead ball specialist who has the ability to punish teams who give away free kicks around the edge of their box. However, Gambo has a tendency to become anonymous during games and frequently gives the ball away to the opposition. Another weakness is his heading of the ball and his tackling during matches, which are very rare indeed, but when he does deliver a telling pass, it normally puts the Linnets attackers clean through on goal.

GAMMON, MARK — Defender
Current Club: Taunton Town
D o B: 23/11/1972   *Birthplace: Cornwall*
Previous clubs include: Weymouth - July 2001, Truro C.

GANNON, PAT — Goalkeeper

Current Club: Burgess Hill Town

D o B: 03/09/1980   Birthplace: Sussex

Goalkeeper: a member of the Sussex youth side in 1998/99 whilst with St Francis, and joined Burgess Hill during November 2000: became a first-team regular at the start of the current season (due to Richard Waters being injured), and has grabbed plenty of attention with some superb performances.

GANNON, TREVOR — Defender

Current Club: Norwich United

D o B: 03/02/1976   Birthplace: Norfolk

New signing for Norwich United from Attleborough Town in the summer of 2001. A skilful defender or midfielder who is good on the ball and will always give 100%.

GANT, ADAM — Midfielder

Current Club: Enfield

Previous clubs include: Witham T - August 2001, Enfield.

GARBUTT, JORDAN — Defender

Current Club: Farsley Celtic

Birthplace: Yorkshire

Previous clubs include: Garforth T - November 2001, Ossett T.

GARDINER, AARON — Midfielder

Current Club: AFC Sudbury

Birthplace: Suffolk

Has had spells at Diss Town, Braintree as well as both Sudbury clubs before their merger. A real 100% man who also has loads of natural skill. Last seasons Supporters and Players' Player of The Year.

GARDINER, GARETH — Midfielder

Current Club: Rossendale United

Birthplace: Lancashire

Midfield player whose playing days began at Ramsbottom United in the North West Counties League. Switched to neighbours Rossendale United in October 2000 and played a major part in Dales promotion to the UniBond.

GARDINER, MARK — Defender

Current Club: Nantwich Town

D o B: 25/12/1966   Birthplace: Cirencester

Previous clubs include: Middlewich T - February 2001, Leek T, Northwich V, Macclesfield T, Chester C, Crewe Alexandra, Torquay Utd, Swindon T.

GARDINER, MATT — Defender

Current Club: Evesham United

D o B: 28/03/1974   Birthplace: Birmingham

Well-travelled defender who joined Dr Martens Western side Evesham United from rivals Redditch United on the eve of the 2002/03 season. Started his career with Torquay before going Non-League with Moor Green, Stourbridge, Halesowen Town, Hereford United and Worcester City.

GARDNER, ADAM — Defender

Current Club: Clitheroe

Birthplace: Lancashire

Although Im not sure what plucked from junior football means, he was. Has made the full back position his own and gives the supporters on the top side great value for money with his surges forward. Rarely beaten - a great asset.

GARDNER, ADAM — Midfielder

Current Club: Holmer Green

Birthplace: Bucks

From Youth team.

GARDNER, DUDLEY — Midfielder

Current Club: Hampton & Richmond

Birthplace: Reading

Midfielder back with Ryman Premier side Hampton & Richmond Borough for his third spell at the club, re-joining from Egham Town in October 2001, after originally arriving under previous manager Chic Botley in early 1999. Started out with Reading before playing for AFC Newbury and Slough Town. A crowd favourite for his 100% commitment on the field.

GARDNER, JIM — Defender

Current Club: Farnborough Town

D o B: 26/10/1978   Birthplace: Beckenham

Previous clubs include: Exeter C - July 1999, Wimbledon.

GARDNER, JON — Defender

Current Club: Thame United

Birthplace: Oxfordshire

Previous clubs include: Abingdon T - February 2002.

GARDNER, JON — Midfielder

Current Club: Didcot Town

Birthplace: Oxfordshire

Jon staked a claim for the First Team last year with a series of gritty displays pre-season and in August/September 2001. Jon is yet another lad who progressed through Didcots Youth set-up and has already made over 130 appearances.

GARDNER, LEE — Defender

Current Club: Stocksbridge Park Steels

D o B: 18/05/1978   Birthplace: Doncaster

Previous clubs include: Frickley Ath - August 2001, Birmingham C.

GARDNER, RAY — Defender

Current Club: Boldmere St.Michaels

Birthplace: Birmingham

From Youth team.

GARDNER, RICHARD — Midfielder

Current Club: Stourport Swifts

D o B: 27/11/1975   Birthplace: Birmingham

Previous clubs include: Sutton Coldfield T - February 2002, Gresley Rovers, Blakanall, Merthyr Tydfil, Blakanall, Atherstone Utd, Worcester C, Nuneaton B, Bromsgrove R.

GAREY, STEVE — Midfielder

Current Club: Paget Rangers

D o B: 14/12/1982   Birthplace: Birmingham

From Youth team.

GARFIELD, DARREN — Forward

Current Club: Woodley Sports

Birthplace: Manchester

Previous clubs include: Abbey Hey - February 2001.

GARFORTH, KEVIN — Forward

Current Club: Prescot Cables

Birthplace: Liverpool

Previous clubs include: Burscough - March 2000, Witton Alb., Congleton T, Skelmersdale Utd.

GARLAND, MARK — Defender
Current Club: Whyteleafe

Birthplace: Croydon

Previous clubs include: Bromley - September 2001, Dulwich Hamlet, Crawley T, Kingtonian, Crystal Palace (Trainee).

GARLAND, PETER — Forward
Current Club: Whyteleafe

D o B: 20/01/1971   *Birthplace: Croydon*

Honours won: England Youth Int.

Experienced midfield player who signed for Ryman Division One South side Whyteleafe in August 2002 from neighbours Croydon. Had joined Croydon in December 2000, 14 years after his debut for the clubs youth team! His few appearances in 1986 earned him a Southern Youth League Cup winners medal, and preceded a long career in the professional game with Tottenham, Newcastle, Charlton, Wycombe and Orient. Peter has since had spells with Crawley Town and Dulwich Hamlet before joining Croydon.

GARMAN, LIAM — Defender
Current Club: Kingstonian

Birthplace: Surrey

Previous clubs include: Walton & Hersham - October 2001.

GARNER, ANDY — Forward
Current Club: Burton Albion

D o B: 08/03/1966   *Birthplace: Stonebroom*

Honours won: UniBond League Premier Div.Winners

Signed for Burton Albion from neighbours Gresley Rovers whilst assistant manager at the Derbyshire club. A player with vast experience, Andy made 230 league appearances scoring 54 league goals along the way whilst wearing the colours of Derby County and later in his career Blackpool. Although not a first-team regular any more, Andys contribution to the squad is invaluable as he coaches and guides the clubs younger players.

GARNHAM, DEAN — Goalkeeper
Current Club: Woodbridge Town

Birthplace: Ipswich

Re-joined Town in August 1997, following a lengthy period with injury. Dean was Sudbury Town's Wembley goalkeeper in the 1989 Vase Final, and he was both the supporters and the Players' Player of the season for 1998/99.

GARRARD, LUKE — Goalkeeper
Current Club: Walton & Hersham

Birthplace: London

Luke is a young goalkeeper who joined the Swans and made his debut in December 2000, several impressive displays making him regular first-choice by the end of the season. Numbers Leatherhead among previous clubs.

GARRAWAY, SAM — Forward
Current Club: Ware

Birthplace: Herts

Previous clubs include: Hertford T - October 2001.

GARRETT, ANDY — Defender
Current Club: Tunbridge Wells

Birthplace: Kent

Honours won: English Fire Service Rep.

Previous clubs include: Tonbridge Angels - July 1999.

GARRETT, PAUL — Defender
Current Club: Redhill

Birthplace: Kent

Tower of strength at the heart of the Redhill defence. Another to join Reds from the Kent League leaders VCD Athletic and has formed a formidable partnership with Steve Roberts.

GARRETT, SCOTT — Defender
Current Club: Jarrow Roofing & Boldon Ca

D o B: 09/01/1974   *Birthplace: Gateshead*

Previous clubs include: Blyth Spartans - July 2000, South Shields, Bedlington Terriers, Hebburn, Bishop Auckland, Blyth Spartans, Hartlepool Utd.

GARROD, STUART — Defender
Current Club: Wick

Birthplace: Sussex

Previous clubs include: Shoreham - July 1999, Southwick.

GARROOD, STEVE — Defender
Current Club: Leatherhead

D o B: 17/07/1967   *Birthplace: Surrey*

Signed for Ryman Division One South side Leatherhead from Egham Town in January 2001and was pitched straight into the first team. Started out as a junior for Fulham and since then has had three spells with Egham Town, two with Camberley Town and one with Staines Town.

GARSIDE, MIKE — Midfielder
Current Club: Trafford

Birthplace: Manchester

Previous clubs include: Mossley - December 2001, Trafford, Curzon Ashton, Wilmslow Alb., Curzon Ashton, Trafford, Caernarfon T, Netherfield, Salford C, Irlam T, Altrincham.

GARVEY, PAUL — Forward
Current Club: Ashton United

Previous clubs include: Flixton - August 2001, Radcliffe B, Cheadle T, Flixton.

GARVEY, STEVE — Forward
Current Club: Northwich Victoria

D o B: 22/11/1973   *Birthplace: Stalybridge*

Steve signed for Conference side Northwich Victoria from Blackpool in August 2001. He can play as an out-and-out winger or in a more orthodox midfield role. Steve began his career at Crewe Alexandra, where he played more than 100 Football League games, before making the switch to the seaside with Blackpool. A tricky right-sided player, the 28-year-old also has an ability for scoring spectacular goals.

GASTON, JAMES — Defender
Current Club: Hadleigh United

Birthplace: Suffolk

Exceptionally fast, skilful player who always gives 100%. Loves to get forward and pose problems for the opposition defence. Sixth season with the Hadleigh, broken only by a 12 month spell with Bury Town.

GASTON, RICHIE — Midfielder
Current Club: Billingham Town

Birthplace: Cleveland

Previous clubs include: South Bank - July 1998.

GATES, JOHN — Midfielder
Current Club: Wisbech Town
D o B: 23/01/1979
Previous clubs include: Cambridge C - July 2001.

GAUGHAN, STEVE — Midfielder
Current Club: Barrow
D o B: 14/04/1970 — Birthplace: Doncaster
Previous clubs include: Halifax T - August 2001, Darlington, Chesterfield, Darlington, Sunderland, Doncaster R, Hatfield Main.

GAUNT, CRAIG — Defender
Current Club: Hucknall Town
D o B: 31/03/1973 — Birthplace: Nottingham
Experienced central defender who was a product of the FAs Centre of Excellence. Was then on Arsenals books, and although he also had a spell at Scarborough as a professional, it has been at Non-League level that Craig has made his name. Played Conference football for Bromsgrove Rovers and Kettering Town and then more latterly Chester City. Also played in the Far East with Woodlands Wellington of Singapore and joined UniBond Premier side Hucknall Town in February 2002 after a short spell at Moor Green in the Dr Martens Premier.

GAUNTLETT, IAN — Defender
Current Club: Caernarfon Town
D o B: 25/11/1979 — Birthplace: Liverpool
Previous clubs include: Southport - April 2002.

GAUTREY, DANNY — Goalkeeper
Current Club: Garforth Town
Birthplace: Leeds
From Youth team.

GAUTREY, JON — Defender
Current Club: Marine
D o B: 19/01/1966 — Birthplace: Liverpool
Jon has now completed 16 years for Marine, having previously played for Southport and Bolton Wanderers. A tenacious tackler, Jon is also an excellent header of the ball. Expert penalty-taker, having taken around 70 for Marine and missed less than half a dozen. Won the Players' Player of the Year Trophy in 1999-2000.

GAVIN, PAT — Forward
Current Club: Harrow Borough
D o B: 05/06/1967 — Birthplace: Hammersmith
Re-joined Ryman Premier side Harrow Borough during the summer of 1997 from Conference side Farnborough Town. During an illustrious career he has played for Leicester City, Barnet, Peterborough Utd, Northampton, Wigan Athletic, Crewe Alexander, Hayes and Aylesbury.

GAWTHROP, STEVE — Defender
Current Club: Mildenhall Town
Birthplace: Cambridge
Previous clubs include: Cambridge C - July 2001, Mildenhall T, Cambridge C.

GAYLE, ANDY — Forward
Current Club: Mossley
D o B: 19/09/1970 — Birthplace: Manchester
Previous clubs include: St.Helens T - November 2000, Rossendale Utd, Nantwich T, Oldham T, Chorley, Witton Alb., Flixton, Ashton Utd, Horwich RMI, Accrington Stanley, Stalybridge Celtic, Horwich RMI, Naxxar Lions (Malta), Horwich RMI, Bury, Crewe Alexandra, Oldham Ath.

GAYLE, BRIAN — Defender
Current Club: Telford United
D o B: 03/09/1965 — Birthplace: Kingston
Previous clubs include: Shrewsbury T - March 2000, Bristol R, Exeter C, Sheffield Utd, Ipswich T, Manchester C, Wimbledon.

GAYLE, JOHN — Forward
Current Club: Moor Green
D o B: 30/07/1964 — Birthplace: Birmingham
Honours won: Leyland Daf Trophy Winners
Signed for Moor Green in August 2001 after a long and eventful career. Played for a number of Non-League sides before joining Wimbledon for £175,000. Later became part of Birmingham City folklore by scoring two of the goals that beat Tranmere 3-2 in the Leyland DAF trophy final in 1991. Moved on to play for Stoke, Shrewsbury and Torquay United.

GAYLE, MARK — Goalkeeper
Current Club: Hednesford Town
D o B: 21/10/1969 — Birthplace: Bromsgrove
Mark is an experienced keeper who signed for Hednesford Town just before the start of the 2000/01 season from Chesterfield. In the 2000/01 season Mark was chosen as the Supporters, Supporters Club and Travel Clubs Player of the Season. Previously with Blackpool, Walsall, Rushden & Diamonds, Crewe, Worcester City and Leicester City.

GAZILLO, DUNCAN — Forward
Current Club: Shifnal Town
D o B: 10/06/1976 — Birthplace: Shropshire
Previous clubs include: Rhayader T - July 2002, Shifnal T, Rhayader T, Welshpool T, Pershore T, Knighton T.

GEALL, JASON — Defender
Current Club: Pagham
Birthplace: Sussex
Defender: reserve player for Pagham before transferring to Arundel during the 2001 close season: returned to his old club in December.

GEARD, MATT — Forward
Current Club: Ringmer
Birthplace: Brighton
Tiny attacker, who made his Ringmer debut during 2000/01. Son of the manager who scored one of the goals in the Blues courageous 5-4 Sussex Senior Cup exit at the hands of Langney Sports in January. Also represented Sussex in the English Schools U-16 Trophy and played for Brighton & Hove Albion U-17s that season. Subsequently won a scholarship placing with the Seagulls, but returned to Ringmer in September 2001.

GEARING, DARREN — Defender
Current Club: Withdean 2000
Birthplace: Brighton
Experienced defender, who was an apprentice with Brighton & Hove Albion in his younger days: returned to Sussex in February 2000 and was snapped up by Saltdean (had previously been playing for Sudbury in the Eastern Counties League): looked set to join Withdean before the FA outlawed them from competing in August 2000: subsequently formed part of the mass transfer to Southwick (2000/01 County League Division Two champions): one of several players to appear for both the Wickers and Withdean during 2001/02 (appearances restricted by work commitments).

GEARING, LEE — Forward

Current Club: Newport Isle Of Width

Birthplace: Hampshire

Promising young striker who joined Dr Martens Eastern side Newport Isle of Wight in July 2002 from Island neighbours East Cowes Vics. Was a prolific scorer at Jewson Wessex League level.

GEARY, DANNY — Midfielder

Current Club: Rothwell Town

Birthplace: Leicester

Previous clubs include: Leicester YMCA - November 2001, Oadby T, Leicester YMCA.

GEDDES, GAVIN — Forward

Current Club: Horsham

D o B: 07/10/1972   *Birthplace: Brighton*

Goal-hungry forward, who came to prominence when shining for Sussex County League side Wick in 1992/93. Made 15 appearances for Brighton & Hove Albion before being released in 1994. Has had a high strike-rate in Sussex football over the years, but never seems to settle at one club for long. Has had spells at Crawley, Clough, Worthing, Horsham and Saltdean before being top scorer for Burgess Hill during their 1998/99 County League championship campaign. Consequently had another brief stay at Crawley until returning to Wick. Then signed for Horsham in January 2000 and was leading scorer with 35 goals during 2000/01, but was axed after failing to show up for a game at the end of the season. Subsequently joined Worthing for the start of 2001/02 and also briefly appeared for Eastbourne Borough in November before returning. Re-joined Horsham in August 2002.

GEDLING, LUKE — Midfielder

Current Club: Lewes

Birthplace: Brighton

Former Southampton youth midfielder who re-joined Lewes in July 2002 from Ryman Division One South rivals Horsham. Played for Worthing reserves during 1998/99 and had a spell at Horsham when Russell Mason was in charge before going to Lewes in October 1999. Brought into the Ringmer side by Mason for the last three months of that campaign, and scored a hat-trick in the vital defeat of Shoreham (a match which virtually decided which club got relegated from County League Division One that season). Again played under Mason during 2000/01, this time with Redhill, before returning to the Hornets at the start of the 2001/02 season.

GEE, DAVE — Defender

Current Club: Cirencester Town

D o B: 25/12/1976   *Birthplace: Swindon*

A speedly left-sided player, who signed for Cirencester Town at the start of the 2000/01 season from Hungerford Town. Originally on the books at Swindon Town and Reading, Dave also had a short spell at Barnet.

GEE, GRAEME — Midfielder

Current Club: Bashley

Birthplace: Portsmouth

Previous clubs include: Brockenhurst - January 2002, Bashley, Newport IOW, Weymouth, Portsmouth Civil Service.

GEE, RUSSELL — Defender

Current Club: Tiverton Town

Birthplace: Devon

Previous clubs include: Exeter C - August 2000.

GELL, CHRIS — Midfielder

Current Club: Northwood

D o B: 08/12/1975

Previous clubs include: Wycombe Wanderers - October 1994.

GELL, RICHARD — Midfielder

Current Club: Aldershot Town

An attacking midfield player who commenced his career on the books of Chelsea and Wycombe Wanderers. In 1995 he joined Yeading and spent three seasons with the Middlesex club before moving to Chesham United in June 1998. Switched to the Recreation Ground in the summer of 1999.

GELLING, STUART — Midfielder

Current Club: Marine

D o B: 08/09/1973   *Birthplace: Liverpool*

Signed for Marine from Colwyn Bay in August 2001, Stuart is a defender or midfielder who has. also played for Lancaster City, Accrington Stanley, Fleetwood Town and Knowsley United. Is a community coach with Liverpool wher he had begun his playing career.

GENNARD, SCOTT — Forward

Current Club: Rushall Olympic

Birthplace: Birmingham

Previous clubs include: Cradley T - May 2002, Willenhall T, Bromsgrove R, Halesowen T, Stourbridge, Old Hill T, Stoke C (Trainee).

GENTLE, DOMINIC — Forward

Current Club: Heybridge Swifts

D o B: 06/06/1974   *Birthplace: Herts*

Experienced striker who returned to Heybridge Swifts in November 2001 from Slough Town for a second spell at the club after playing for numerous other Non-League sides, including Grays Athletic, Purfleet, Hendon, Enfield, Billericay Town, St Albans City and Boreham Wood. His ability to hold the ball and bring others into the game plus an eye for goal have made him such a success at this level.

GENTLE, JUSTIN — Forward

Current Club: Harlow Town

D o B: 06/06/1974   *Birthplace: London*

Very experienced and much-travelled attacking midfielder who joined Harlow Town in February 2002. Previous clubs included Enfield, St Albans City, Dagenham & Redbridge, Chesham United and Billericay Town.

GEORGE, BOBBY — Forward

Current Club: Banstead Athletic

Birthplace: Kent

Previous clubs include: Dulwich Hamlet - November 2000, Whyteleafe, Molesey, Enfield, Whyteleafe, Faversham T.

GEORGE, DANNY — Defender

Current Club: Grantham Town

D o B: 22/10/1978   *Birthplace: Lincoln*

Signed for Grantham Town during the close season of 2001 from Hinckley United were he helped the Leicestershire club to win promotion to the Dr Martens Premier. Recovered from a early season injury to regain his place during the later part of the season and help the Gingerbreads into the Premier. Originally on the books at Nottingham Forest, the defender also had spells with Doncaster Rovers and Burton Albion.

GEORGE, JUNIOR — Forward
Current Club: Letchworth
Birthplace: Luton
Previous clubs include: Brache Sparta - July 2001, Arlesey T, Shillington, Brache Sparta, Luton OB.

GEORGE, MICKY — Defender
Current Club: Haverfordwest County
D o B: 17/09/1965   *Birthplace: Wales*
Previous clubs include: Carmarthen T - July 1995, Briton Ferry Ath., Haverfordwest Co., Port Talbot, Tamworth, Ton Pentre.

GEORGE, ROBERT — Midfielder
Current Club: Great Yarmouth Town
D o B: 02/10/1981   *Birthplace: Norwich*
Signed for Yarmouth in the summer of 2000 from Norwich City where he played in the Youth and Reserve teams. Also has County Youth appearances to his credit. Leading scorer and First XI Player of the Year for 2000/01.

GEORGIOU, CHRIS — Defender
Current Club: Southwick
Birthplace: Sussex
Defender/midfielder: played several times for Worthing reserves during 1998/99 before joining Shoreham at the start of the following season: subsequently had a spell at Southwick: started 2001/02 with Wick until moving back to Old Barn Way in November.

GEORGIOU, GEORGE — Forward
Current Club: Purfleet
D o B: 19/08/1972   *Birthplace: Camden*
Prolific scorer who has played League football with Leyton Orient and Fulham and has also had a spell in Cyprus with Paralimon. Re-joined Purfleet in July 2002 from fellow Ryman Premier side Enfield, whom he had joined in March 2001. Has also seen service with Dagenham.

GEORGIOU, JUSTIN — Forward
Current Club: Corinthian Casuals
Birthplace: Surrey
Previous clubs include: Banstead Ath - March 2002, Tooting & Mitcham Utd, Yeading, Brook House.

GERAGHTY, JASON — Midfielder
Current Club: Harlow Town
Birthplace: Essex
Honours won: England Youth Int.
Joined Harlow Town in February 2002 from Ford United. Highly-rated midfielder who was previously with Leyton Pennant and Enfield. A former England Youth international who started his career at West Ham.

GERBER, ARMADO — Defender
Current Club: Clapton
Birthplace: London
Previous clubs include: Tooting & Mitcham Utd - July 2001.

GERMAN, DAVID — Defender
Current Club: Stalybridge Celtic
D o B: 16/10/1973   *Birthplace: Sheffield*
Defender Dave played for Sheffield Boys before joining Sheffield Wednesday as a Schoolboy. In 1990 he joined Halifax Town in the Football League. This was followed by one season with Macclesfield Town in the Conference. He then spent three and a half years with Winsford United in the UniBond Premier Division before signing for Leigh RMI in July 1999. Switched to Stalybridge Celtic in July 2002. Switched to Stalybridge Celtic in

the summer of 2001 before moving onto UniBond First Division outfit Rossendale United in August 2002.

GIBB, DEAN — Forward
Current Club: Bedlington Terriers
D o B: 26/10/1966   *Birthplace: Newcastle*
Has emerged over the four seasons he has spent at Bedlington as one of the most fearsome strikers around and one that no defender looks forward to playing against. In recent times has also turned out in midfield and at full back. Before his switch to Bedlington he was at Brandon United and Durham City as well as having seen league action with Hartlepool United. When leaving Durham for the Terriers he brought the floodlights with him ! A real terrace favourite at Welfare Park where his all action style, goal scoring exploits and colourful character has made him a cult her.

GIBBIN, CRAIG — Defender
Current Club: Marske United
Birthplace: Cleveland
Previous clubs include: Guisborough T - July 2000, Marske Utd, Guisborough T.

GIBBONS, DANNY — Forward
Current Club: Newport Isle Of Wight
Previous clubs include: Weston-Super-Mare (£4,000) - December 1999, Poole T.

GIBBONS, STEVE — Forward
Current Club: Tunbridge Wells
Birthplace: Kent
Previous clubs include: Tonbridge Angels - July 1998.

GIBBS, DANNY — Midfielder
Current Club: Wealdstone
D o B: 08/12/1983
Previous clubs include: Edgware T - August 2001, Ware.

GIBBS, IAN — Defender
Current Club: Ashford Town
Birthplace: Kent
Central defender who can also play in midfield. Signed for Dr Martens Eastern side Ashford Town from rivans and neighbours Tonbridge Angels in December 2001. Experienced player whose other clubs include Gravesend & Northfleet.

GIBBS, WARREN — Defender
Current Club: Bangor City
D o B: 21/11/1977   *Birthplace: Bangor*
Locally-based central defender who had previous League of Wales experience with Caernarfon Town. Joined Bangor City from Porthmadog in August 2001. A tall, commanding defender who has also served Cemaes Bay.

GIBILIRU, JOE — Midfielder
Current Club: Witton Albion
Birthplace: Liverpool
Previous clubs include: Prescot Cables - August 2001.

GIBSON, ALEX — Defender
Current Club: Stafford Rangers
Birthplace: Plymouth
Plymouth-born, defender Alex grew up in Stafford and was signed on schoolboy forms by Stoke City. As first-team opportunities at the Brittania Stadium were limited, he moved to Port Vale during the 2002 close season and made his Football League debut for them in October 2001. Alex was one of Phil Robinsons summer signings for Dr Martens Premier side Stafford Rangers.

G

GIBSON, BARRY   *Defender*
Current Club: Erith & Belvedere
Birthplace: Kent
A young player that has progressed through from Erith & Belvederes youth team, has a promising future and can play in the midfield or as a defender.

GIBSON, CHRIS   *Defender*
Current Club: Tring Town
Birthplace: Hemel Hempstead
Previous clubs include: Leverstock Green - September 2000, Hemel Hempstead, Tring T.

GIBSON, CHRIS   *Goalkeeper*
Current Club: Tamworth
Birthplace: Birmingham
Former Mansfield Town trainee, who signed for Tamworth in November 2001. He started that season on the books of Midland Combination side Cadbury Athletic. Very promising young goalkeeper.

GIBSON, GEORGE   *Midfielder*
Current Club: Dulwich Hamlet
Birthplace: London
Previous clubs include: Bromley - March 2002, Dulwich Hamlet, Fisher Ath.

GIBSON, JAMIE   *Defender*
Current Club: Croydon Athletic
Birthplace: London
Previous clubs include: Egham T - September 1999, Carshalton Ath., Crawley T, Welling Utd.

GIBSON, JOE   *Defender*
Current Club: Tring Town
Birthplace: Hemel Hempstead
Previous clubs include: Leverstock Green - July 2000.

GIBSON, NEIL   *Midfielder*
Current Club: Southport
D o B: 10/10/1979   Birthplace: St Asaph
Welsh-born defender who joined Conference club Southport in August 2002 after being released by Sheffield Wednesday. Began his career with Tranmere Rovers, where he came up through the ranks at Prenton Park and made one League appearance. Transferred to Wednesday in January 2001 but failed to mae thr breakthrough at Hillsborough.

GIBSON, PAUL   *Goalkeeper*
Current Club: Northwich Victoria
D o B: 01/11/1976   Birthplace: Sheffield
Paul is a former Manchester United trainee who signed a one-year deal with Conference side Northwich Victoria in August 2001. Paul joined Notts County after his release from Old Trafford and played around 20 Football League games on loan at Mansfield Town and Hull City and also appeared in the County first team.

GIBSON, ROBERT   *Forward*
Current Club: Marlow
Previous clubs include: Windsor & Eton - October 2001, Marlow, Flackwell Heath, Windsor & Eton, Chertsey T, Walton & Hersham, Brentford (Trainee), Marlow.

GIBSON, ROBIN   *Forward*
Current Club: Stafford Rangers
D o B: 15/11/1979   Birthplace: Crewe
A fans favourite at previous club Wrexham, Robin joined Dr Martens Premier side Stafford Rangers during the summer of 2002. The forward made over 100 appearances for Wrexham and was twice named their Young Player of the Year. Amongst the highlights of his three year spell at the Racecourse Ground were scoring in Wrexhams 1999/00 FA Cup Third Round victory over Middlesbrough and being a member of their Welsh Premier Cup winning side the following year.

GIBSON, STUART   *Midfielder*
Current Club: Hamble ASSC
Birthplace: Hampshire
Previous clubs include: Hamble Club - July 2000, Hamble.

GIDDINGS, KERRY   *Forward*
Current Club: Stourport Swifts
Birthplace: Worcestershire
Previous clubs include: Halesowen T - December 2001, Halesowen Utd, Stourport Swifts, Redditch Utd, Bridgnorth T, Redditch Utd, Evesham Utd, Stourport Swifts.

GIERKE, LEON   *Forward*
Current Club: Caernarfon Town
D o B: 29/02/1980   Birthplace: Wales
Previous clubs include: Total Network Solutions - July 2001, Rhyl, Llandudno, Burnley (Trainee).

GIGGS, RHODRI   *Forward*
Current Club: Aberystwyth Town
D o B: 02/04/1977   Birthplace: Cardiff
Previous clubs include: Bangor C - January 2002, Salford C, Stockport Co.

GILBERT, ADAM   *Defender*
Current Club: Lincoln United
Birthplace: Lincoln
Adam has progressed through the youth ranks at Lincoln United and is now a first team regular. Tough tackler and good passer of the ball.

GILBERT, DAMIEN   *Defender*
Current Club: Woodbridge Town
Birthplace: Essex
Made his debut at the beginning of the 1996/97 campaign, and spent for seasons at Notcutts Park before leaving for a brief spell at Stanway. Speedy right-sided player who made a welcome return in October 2000.

GILBERT, DAVE   *Midfielder*
Current Club: Grantham Town
D o B: 22/06/1963   Birthplace: Lincoln
Returned to Grantham Town during the second half of the 2000/01 season and had an immediate impact on the team. A former manager of the Gingerbreads, he played a major part in Granthams promotion campaign and was voted Supporters' Player of the Year. Played over 500 League games for Scunthorpe, Northampton, West Brom and Grimsby.

GILBEY, CLIVE   *Defender*
Current Club: Chasetown FC
Birthplace: Staffordshire
Previous clubs include: Brereton Social - August 1999.

G

GILDEA, ALEX — Midfielder

Current Club: Whitby Town

D o B: 15/09/1980 — Birthplace: Scarborough

Alex is a talented young performer who signed for UniBond Premier side Whitby Town from local rivals Scarborough at the start of the 2001/02 season. Can play in midfield or on the left, he is a tough-tackler with good ball skills. Scored the opener against Plymouth in the FA Cup First Round.

GILDERDALE, JAMIE — Defender

Current Club: Haverfordwest County

D o B: 05/12/1978 — Birthplace: Wales

Previous clubs include: Carmarthen T - July 1999.

GILDERDALE, SIMON — Defender

Current Club: Haverfordwest County

D o B: 22/01/1984 — Birthplace: Wales

From Local football - July 2001.

GILDERSLEVE, LEE — Forward

Current Club: Broxbourne Borough V&E

D o B: 09/09/1978 — Birthplace: Edmonton

Previous clubs include: Ware - July 2001, Leyton Pennant, Ware.

GILES, CHRIS — Forward

Current Club: Yeovil Town

D o B: 16/04/1982 — Birthplace: Milborne Port

Honours won: FA Trophy Winners

Chris lives in Milborne Port and has previously played for Sherborne. Chris was the top scorer for the Yeovil Town youth team in their SWEB South-West Counties Youth League championship winning 1999/00 season, and was voted Youth Player Of The Season that same year. He made his first team debut away to Morecambe in the final game of the 1999/00 season, coming on as a late substitute. He followed that up this season with his debut first team goal, scoring the second goal in a 2-0 win over Wellington in the Somerset Premier Cup. During the 2000/01 season, he graduated into being the key striker in the clubs Screwfix Direct League Reserve side, and with time on his side, and made the step up to the first -team on a more frequent basis the following campaign.

GILES, DAVID — Defender

Current Club: Fleet Town

Birthplace: Hampshire

Previous clubs include: Camberley T - January 2001.

GILKES, MICHAEL — Midfielder

Current Club: Slough Town

D o B: 20/07/1965 — Birthplace: Hackney

Honours won: Division Two Winners, Football League XI

Joined Slough following his release by former Nationwide division two champions Milwall. Michael, now 35, has had a long and distinguished career in the professional game. His face will not be unfamiliar to Slough players, as he has played in the same side as Keith McPherson and Steve Mautone before while at Reading. While at Reading he didnt become a regular in the team until 1987/88, and although Reading were relegated, Gilkes was most remembered for the Simod Cup success which saw the Royals beat five First Division sides, including Luton Town by 4-1 in the Wembley final, where he scored the first goal He continued to play for the Royals for another ten seasons, sometimes as a mercurial striker, sometimes as a speedy and penetrating left wing-back, and he never failed to disappoint supporters in his massive total of 487 first team matches, during which he scored 52 goals. He won a Division Two championship medal in 1993/94. Since playing for Reading Gilkes has played for

Wolverhapton Wanderers in Nationwide Division One where he played in a left wing back role.

GILKS, DAVID — Defender

Current Club: Tadcaster Albion

Birthplace: Yorkshire

Previous clubs include: Rawdon - July 2000, Farsley Celtic.

GILKS, KEVIN — Defender

Current Club: Tadcaster Albion

Birthplace: Yorkshire

Previous clubs include: Thackley - November 1999.

GILL, DARREN — Midfielder

Current Club: Wroxham

Birthplace: Norwich

Previous clubs include: Fakenham T - July 1995, Norwich C.

GILL, KEVIN — Forward

Current Club: Lymington & New Milton

Birthplace: Dorset

Previous clubs include: Wimborne T - May 2002, Portland Utd.

GILL, ROBERT — Forward

Current Club: Doncaster Rovers

D o B: 10/02/1982 — Birthplace: Nottingham

Spent three years with Nottingham Forest as a trainee. Joined the Rovers Youth team in the summer of 2000 and was a prolific scorer in their successful season of 2000-01. Joined the professional staff at the end of season.

GILL, STEVE — Forward

Current Club: Barrow

Birthplace: Barrow

Steve is a promising young striker who joined Barrow from Barrow Celtic and progressed through the A team and the reserves to make his debut as a substitute in an ATS Trophy tie at Southport in February 1998. He subsequently left the club and last season featured for Kendal Town in the UniBond First Division. He then played for Barrow Rangers in the West Lancashire League before rejoining the club in September 2000.

GILLARD, CHRIS — Defender

Current Club: Moor Green

D o B: 30/09/1973

Previous clubs include: Port Vale - July 1993.

GILLESPIE, ADAM — Midfielder

Current Club: Braintree Town

Birthplace: Chelmsford

Local Essex lad, popular with all, who progressed from Heybridge Swifts reserves and battled against all comers to win a regular spot in the midfield. Scorer of a number of spectacular and crucial goals, has allied workrate and positional sense to his undoubted ability on the ball and in the air. Suffered a severe break of his left ankle in the Ryman League Cup semi-final at Northwood in 2000/01, and has astounded everyone with his rapid progress to return to the first-team squad. Had a loan spell at Tiptree United, featuring in their FA Carlsberg Vase final squad. Moved on to Braintree Town in July 2002.

GILLESPIE, RICHARD — Forward

Current Club: Bashley

Birthplace: Hampshire

From Youth team.

GILLHAM, BRAD — Goalkeeper
Current Club: Barton Rovers
Birthplace: Luton
Previous clubs include: Stotfold - July 1998, Baldock T, Langford, Hitchin T, Stotfold, Letchworth GC, Sunderland.

GILLICK, DEAN — Defender
Current Club: Newcastle Town
Birthplace: Stoke
Previous clubs include: Eastwood Hanley - July 1992, Newcastle T.

GILLIGAN, CRAIG — Forward
Current Club: Leigh RMI
D o B: 02/10/1983   *Birthplace: Stockport*
From Youth team.

GILMAN, LEE — Midfielder
Current Club: Diss Town
D o B: 11/09/1981   *Birthplace: Norwich*
Previous clubs include: Norwich C - August 2001.

GILMORE, MICK — Midfielder
Current Club: Skelmersdale United
Birthplace: Liverpool
Previous clubs include: Prescot Cables - November 2000, St Helens T, Bootle.

GILMORE, PAUL — Goalkeeper
Current Club: Blyth Spartans
Birthplace: Newcastle
Established himself as first choice keeper after some excellent performances in nets, to help Blyth reach the Presidents cup final 2000-2001. Very agile, and has one hell of a kick from an off the floor/stationary ball. Was brought into the team originally as cover from Northern League Seaham.

GINDRE, NICK — Goalkeeper
Current Club: Walton Casuals
Birthplace: Surrey
Nick is our 1st choice Keeper, as well as being Youth Team keeper, good shot stopper and very agile, without doubt a player for the future.

GIRDLER, STUART — Midfielder
Current Club: Basingstoke Town
Birthplace: London
Honours won: England Schoolboy Int.
Stuart signed for Basingstoke Town from Woking in June 2000 after a loan spell with the club. The midfielder has excellent vision and great passing skills. A former England Schoolboy international, he was previously a youth team player with Fulham.

GIRLING, BRETT — Defender
Current Club: Braintree Town
Previous clubs include: Chelmsford C - July 2001, Sudbury T, Woodbridge T.

GIRLING, JOHN — Defender
Current Club: Histon
D o B: 19/02/1974   *Birthplace: Essex*
Central defender who joined Histon in May 2002 from Chelmsford City. Had returned to Chelmsford for a second spell in January 2002 after leaving for Cambridge City in the summer of 2000 Has also briefly been with Dagenham & Redbridge and Cheshunt, this after being on West Hams books as a teenager.

GIRVAN, RONNIE — Defender
Current Club: Hampton & Richmond
Birthplace: London
Young left-sided defender who broke into the Hampton & Richmond Borough first-team squad after impressive displays for the Youth and Reserve sides. Previously spent eight years in Chelseas junior system.

GIVENS, WARREN — Midfielder
Current Club: Solihull Borough
Birthplace: Birmingham
Previous clubs include: Paget Rangers - August 2001, Moor Green, Cardiff C.

GLADMAN, DANNY — Goalkeeper
Current Club: Harrow Borough
Birthplace: London
Goalkeeper who joined Ryman Premier side Harrow Borough in the summer of 2002 from Northwood. Previously with Barnet, Arsenal, Wembley and Brook House. A Channel Marketing Executive.

GLADWELL, RICHARD — Midfielder
Current Club: Selby Town
Birthplace: Selby
Previous clubs include: Pontefract Collieries - February 1998, Selby T.

GLASGOW, BYRON — Midfielder
Current Club: Carshalton Athletic
D o B: 18/02/1979   *Birthplace: London*
Signed for Carshalton Athletic in March 2001 from St Albans. A talented midfielder who was previously with Walton & Hersham and Reading.

GLASS, DAVID — Midfielder
Current Club: Corby Town
D o B: 17/10/1983   *Birthplace: Corby*
Previous clubs include: Rushden & Diamonds - July 2000.

GLASSER, NEIL — Midfielder
Current Club: Burton Albion
D o B: 17/10/1974   *Birthplace: Nottingham*
Neil Glasser, a 26 year old signed from Grantham in May 1999. Neil is a great favourite with the crowd and last season won the goal of the season award for a brilliant individual goal that brought him his hat trick in the game against Dorchester, Like Darren Stride, Neil is a tough tackling midfielder who revels in midfield battles. Admired by the management and fellow players, Neil picked up the Supporters Away Player of the Season award as well as the Players' Player Runner-up trophy.

GLASSON, JAMIE — Forward
Current Club: Bemerton Heath Harlequins
Birthplace: Wiltshire
From Youth team.

GLASSUP, ELLIS — Goalkeeper
Current Club: Forest Green Rovers
Birthplace: Cornwall
Signed for Conference club Forest Green Rovers from St. Austell, where he received rave reviews. He is a tremendous goalkeeping prospect for the future and he is keen to learn his trade under the watchful eye of his current manager Nigel Spink, who achieved so much as a goalkeeper.

GLEAVE, ANDY — Defender

Current Club: Fakenham Town

Birthplace: Norfolk
Previous clubs include: Wisbech T - July 2001, Kings Lynn.

GLEDHILL, CHRIS — Midfielder

Current Club: Flackwell Heath

Birthplace: London
Previous clubs include: Kingsbury T - July 2000.

GLEDHILL, LEE — Midfielder

Current Club: Barnet

D o B: 07/11/1980   Birthplace: Bury
A promising defender, Lee is a former youth team captain at Barnet and is now showing great maturity Lee has been with Barnet since August 1998 when he signed as a trainee. Has since broken into the first-team squad on a regular basis.

GLEGHORN, NIGEL — Midfielder

Current Club: Nantwich Town

D o B: 12/08/1962   Birthplace: Seaham
Previous clubs include: Witton Alb - November 2001, Altrincham, Burnley, Stoke C, Birmingham C, Manchester C, Ipswich T, Seaham Red Star.

GLENDENNING, JAMES — Defender

Current Club: Droylsden

Previous clubs include: St.Helens T - August 2001, Altrincham, Kendal T, Ashton Utd.

GLENNERSTER, STUART — Defender

Current Club: Holmer Green

Birthplace: Australia
From Youth team.

GLOVER, ALAN — Defender

Current Club: Skelmersdale United

Birthplace: Liverpool
Honours won: British Universities Rep.
Previous clubs include: St Helens T - March 2001, Congleton T, Bamber Bridge, Southport, Liverpool (Junior).

GLOVER, GUY — Defender

Current Club: Sheffield FC

Birthplace: Sheffield
Previous clubs include: Hallam - November 2000, Oughtibridge.

GLOVER, JASON — Midfielder

Current Club: Liversedge

Birthplace: Yorkshire
Previous clubs include: Ossett Alb - March 2002, Liversedge.

GLOVER, SIMON — Forward

Current Club: Dover Athletic

Birthplace: Kent
On his day an exciting winger who joined Dover Athletic in March 2002 following a successful loan spell from Kent Dr Martens Premier neighbours Welling United. Originally on the books at Wycombe, he spent a season or so with Ashford Town prior to joining Welling.

GLYNN, JAMES — Forward

Current Club: Bracknell Town

Birthplace: Wycombe
Honours won: England Schoolboy Int.
Previous clubs include: Yeading - August 2001, Staines T, Farnborough T, Wycombe Wanderers.

GLYNN, MATTHEW — Midfielder

Current Club: Maidenhead United

D o B: 14/07/1979   Birthplace: Wycombe
Previous clubs include: Windsor & Eton - July 2000, Flackwell Heath.

GODBEHERE, STEVE — Defender

Current Club: Sheffield FC

Birthplace: Nottinghamshire
Previous clubs include: Staveley Miners Welfare - March 2001.

GODBER, MICK — Forward

Current Club: Alfreton Town

Birthplace: Sheffield
Honours won: NCEL & Cup Winners
Powerful and prolific goalscorer who signed from Ossett Albion in December 2001 after being with fellow NCEL club Sheffield FC Prior to joining Sheffield Mick scored 43 league goals in two seasons for Staveley MW and continued this success at Sheffield to become the NCEL top scorer in 1999/00 scoring 36 goals - 22 in the league. Was again leading scorer as he helped Town back into the UniBond League.

GODBOLD, JAMIE — Midfielder

Current Club: Lowestoft Town

D o B: 10/01/1980   Birthplace: Great Yarmouth
Previous clubs include: Stoke C - July 2000.

GODDARD, MICK — Midfielder

Current Club: Alfreton Town

Birthplace: Sheffield
Honours won: NCEL & Cup Winners
Prolific goalscorer who joined Alfreton Town from UniBond League side Worksop Town in November 2001 for a small fee. Joined Worksop from NCEL side Hallam where he was top scorer. Now fully recovered from a serious injury, Micks goals helped take Alfreton back into the UniBond League.

GODDARD, RICHARD — Defender

Current Club: Harrow Borough

D o B: 31/03/1978   Birthplace: Burnt Oak
Signed for Ryman Premier side Harrow Borough in August 2002 from rivals Chesham United. Had joined Chesham in September 2001 from St Albans City. A powerful central defender, Richard has previously been at Woking, Brentford and Arsenal, where he began as a trainee.

GODDARD, WAYNE — Midfielder

Current Club: Histon

Previous clubs include: Cambridge C - July 1999, Soham Town R, Histon, Chelmsford C, Cambridge C, Soham Town R, Rushden & Diamonds, Cambridge C, Histon.

GODDEN, NATHAN — Defender

Current Club: Eastbourne Borough

Birthplace: Hastings
oined the club from Sidley United (Sussex County League) in July 2000. Previous experience with Westfield, Rye United, Bexhill Town, and Stamco (now St. Leonards FC). Another player in the squad who has played for the Sussex Representative side.

GODDEN, ROY — *Forward*
Current Club: Dover Athletic

D o B: 17/02/1977   *Birthplace: Ashford*
Striker Roy returned to Dover Athletic towards the end of the 2001/02 season from Dr Martens Eastern side St Leonards. Had arrived at St Leonards on a permanent basis in December 2001 after a gap of nearly two seasons. Whilst with Dover, Roy moved on loan to St Leonards, then Folkestone Invicta, Tonbridge Angels and Dartford. Rated as an highly-talented striker who perhaps is yet to live up to his full potential.

GODFREY, ADAM — *Forward*
Current Club: Chertsey Town

Birthplace: Surrey
Signed senior forms in the summer after progressing through the youth sides with Chertsey Juniors.

GODFREY, DAVID — *Goalkeeper*
Current Club: Wealdstone

D o B: 30/01/1984   *Birthplace: London*
David is still a teenager, and after impressing in goal in Wealdstone's youth team has now signed a first team contract. Made his debut at home to Aylesbury in March 2002.

GODLEY, DAVE — *Forward*
Current Club: Cirencester Town

D o B: 25/05/1979   *Birthplace: Swindon*
Previous clubs include: Chippenham T - August 2001, Cirencester T, Swindon T, Bristol R (Junior).

GOGGIN, WESLEY — *Defender*
Current Club: Walton & Hersham

Birthplace: Surrey
Wes is a promising young, left-sided defender and another product of Swans youth and reserve sides to make the senior squad for this season.

GOLDFINCH, MARK — *Defender*
Current Club: Ipswich Wanderers

Birthplace: Ipswich
From Youth team.

GOLDING, PHIL — *Defender*
Current Club: Holmer Green

Birthplace: Bucks
Previous clubs include: Thame Utd - July 1993, Marlow.

GOLDSTONE, BILLY — *Defender*
Current Club: Aveley

Birthplace: Essex
Previous clubs include: Bromley - July 2000, Billericay T, Grays Ath., Purfleet, Hendon, Enfield, Grays Ath., Chelmsford C, Barking, East Ham Utd, Woodford T, Barking.

GOLLEY, NIGEL — *Defender*
Current Club: Whyteleafe

D o B: 19/05/1961   *Birthplace: Crystal Palace*
Previous clubs include: Sutton Utd - October 1996, Whyteleafe.

GOMERSALL, JOHN — *Forward*
Current Club: Stafford Town

Birthplace: Hampshire
Previous clubs include: AFC Newbury - July 2000, Andover, Newbury T.

GOMM, RICHARD — *Defender*
Current Club: Bideford

Birthplace: Devon
Richard is a skilful wingback, who can also play in midfield and likes to get forward. He is in his second spell at the club, having also played for Torquay United, & Vospers. He was ever present in the team last season and has made over 50 first team appearances.

GONSALVES, LEWIS — *Defender*
Current Club: Sutton United

Birthplace: Surrey
From Youth team.

GOOD, STEVE — *Forward*
Current Club: Braintree Town

D o B: 08/11/1979   *Birthplace: Essex*
Previous clubs include: Romford - January 2002, Hertford T, Romford, Billericay T, Romford, Billericay T.

GOODALL, ALAN — *Midfielder*
Current Club: Bangor City

D o B: 02/12/1981   *Birthplace: Liverpool*
Young left back who signed for League of Wales side Bangor City from Cammell Laird after a trial period with Tranmere Rovers. Can also operate in midfield.

GOODALL, DARREN — *Midfielder*
Current Club: Willenhall Town

Birthplace: Birmingham
Rejoined Willenhall after a spell at Bridgnorth. A skilful player who enjoys running at defences. Former WBA and Hereford.

GOODALL, GRANT — *Defender*
Current Club: Marlow

Birthplace: Oxford
Defender who joined Marlow in August 1995 after spending a season with Abingdon Town following his release by Oxford United. Now one of Marlows longest-serving players, he has twice been voted as player of the year and is team captain.

GOODCHILD, DAVID — *Defender*
Current Club: Gateshead

D o B: 15/08/1975   *Birthplace: Yorkshire*
Honours won: FA Vase Winners
A stylish central defender who signed for UniBond Premier side Gateshead from rivals Whitby Town in August 2002. A great favourite at Whitby, whom he had signed for from North Ormesby in March 1995. He quickly established himself in the side and won an FA Vase winners medal in 1997. UniBond First Division Championship medal 97/98. Season 99-00 was an exceptional season for Goochy becoming the seasons leading goalscorer with 17 goals taking his tally to 53 in just over 250 appearances. H He was also voted the seasons Runner-up Player of the Year.

GOODERICK, MATTY — *Forward*
Current Club: Banbury United

Birthplace: Derby
Very bright young striking prospect. Was top scorer for Oxford City reserves during the 1998/99 season and was high on Banbury United managers wanted list when he signed for United at the start of the 1999/00 season. Had a brief spell at Derby County and was reserve player of the year at Burton Albion. Scored a remarkable 41 goals in 56 games during United's promotion season and won the Hellenic League Golden Boot Award. Top goalscorer again during the 2000/01 and 01/02 seasons and has attracted League scouts.

G

GOODFELLOW, MARK — Midfielder
Current Club: Purfleet
From Youth team.

GOODHAND, PAUL — Midfielder
Current Club: Spalding United
D o B: 04/12/1980   Birthplace: Lincolnshire
Previous clubs include: Wisbech T - December 2001, Spalding Utd, Grimsby T.

GOODHIND, WARREN — Defender
Current Club: Barnet
D o B: 16/08/1977   Birthplace: Johannesburg
Warren is Barnets longest- serving player coming through the ranks of the youth and reserve teams. Became the youngest ever Bees captain at the age of 21, after showing his versatility with impressive displays in defence and midfield. Then tragedy struck when he sustained a broken leg in an FA Cup game at Hednesford in November 1998. Back in action with the first team again and his future looks bright.

GOODING, CLINT — Midfielder
Current Club: Sittingbourne
D o B: 19/07/1976   Birthplace: Ashford
Clint signed for Sittingbourne from Kent League side Lordswood in the close season of 2001. The midfielder is one of the most experienced players in the Sittingbourne side having previously played for Gravesend & Northfleet, Tonbridge Angels and Ashford Town.

GOODLIFFE, JASON — Defender
Current Club: Stevenage Borough
D o B: 07/03/1974   Birthplace: Hillingdon
Honours won: England Semi-Pro Int.
Another 2001 summer signing for Stevenage Borough, Jason signed from Hayes where he had made 335 appearances. Started his career at Brentford, and made his debut for the England Semi-Professional side during the 2000/.02 season. Jason is one of the most respected defenders in Non-League football. He has recently taken over the skippers armband, and was included in the National Game XI squad for the recent game with the USA.

GOODMAN, CHRIS — Midfielder
Current Club: Bedworth United
Birthplace: Coventry
Chris is now with Bedworth United for a second time. He is a very skillful player in the middle of the park, and since manager Ian Drewitt brought him back he made a superb impact. Chris moved to Rugby United and then teamed-up at Racing Club Warwick with ex-Bedworth manager Billy Hollywood before returning to Bedworth in November 2001.

GOODMAN, JAMES — Goalkeeper
Current Club: Wingate And Finchley
D o B: 13/01/1974   Birthplace: Blackburn
Honours won: Scottish Universities Rep.
Previous clubs include: Edware T - July 2000, Clitheroe.

GOODMAN, LEE — Forward
Current Club: Worcester City
Birthplace: Worcester
A former top scorer for Worcester City's youth team who now has some useful experience on the bench in first-team games. Made his debut at Belper Tow in the FA Cup and looks to have a good futire in the game.

GOODRIDGE, WAYNE — Midfielder
Current Club: Cwmbran Town
D o B: 26/05/1965   Birthplace: Wales
Previous clubs include: Port Talbot T - January 2002, Cwmbran T, Briton Ferry Ath, Barry T, Cwmbran T.

GOODWIN, CRAIG — Forward
Current Club: Flexsys Cefn Druids
Birthplace: Wales
Previous clubs include: Oswestry T - July 2001, Brymbo Broughton.

GOODWIN, LEE — Midfielder
Current Club: Dagenham & Redbridge
D o B: 05/09/1978   Birthplace: Stepney
Joined the Daggers during the 1998 close season from West Ham United, where he served an apprenticeship. He suffered a bad injury at Aylesbury, causing him to miss a large part of that season. However, he returned to the senior side fully fit to play a major part in the clubs Ryman League championship success as a defender.

GOODWIN, MARK — Forward
Current Club: Eastbourne Borough
Birthplace: Sussex
Another youngster to have joined Dr Martens Eastern side Eastbourne Borough from neighbours Eastbourne Town in the summer of 2001. Scored a fine goal against Chatham Town on his league debut in February 2002, and hit a memorable winner against Lewes in the 2001/02 Sussex Senior Cup Final. Rated as an outstanding striking prospect.

GOODWIN, MATT — Defender
Current Club: Cirencester Town
Birthplace: Swindon
Previous clubs include: Highworth T - January 2002.

GOODWIN, SCOTT — Midfielder
Current Club: Kettering Town
D o B: 13/09/1978   Birthplace: Hull
Scott signed for Conference side Kettering Town on the eve of the 2002/03 season after being released by Hereford United. Had joined the Bulls from Hednesford Town in May 2001 after previously serving Grantham Town, Shepshed Dynamo and Coventry City. Scott is equally at home in left-side defence or midfield.

GOODWIN, TOMMY — Defender
Current Club: Shepshed Dynamo
D o B: 08/11/1979   Birthplace: Leicester
Former Leicester City defender who still works for the Foxes in their commercial department. Played for Leicestershire Senior League side Anstey Nomads after being released by City and then joined Dr Martens Western Division outfit Shepshed Dynamo in the summer of 2001.

GOODYEAR, CRAIG — Midfielder
Current Club: Ossett Albion
D o B: 07/11/1980   Birthplace: Barnsley
Previous clubs include: Barnsley - September 2001.

GORDON, ALBERT — Forward
Current Club: Clapton
Birthplace: London
From Local football - July 2001.

GORDON, DANNY — Defender
Current Club: Aylesbury United
From Youth team.

GORDON, JERMAINE — Forward
Current Club: Hinckley United
D o B: 16/07/1980 — Birthplace: Leicester
Previous clubs include: Downes Sports - July 2001, Corby T, VS Rugby, Holwell Sports.

GORDON, NEVILLE — Midfielder
Current Club: Whitstable Town
D o B: 15/11/1975 — Birthplace: Greenwich
Previous clubs include: Fisher Ath - July 2000, Faversham T, Welling Utd, HJK Helsinki (Finland), Reading, Millwall.

GORDON, PETERJAN — Forward
Current Club: Bedworth United
Birthplace: Coventry
Previous clubs include: Coventry Marconi - February 2002.

GORE, IAN — Defender
Current Club: Gainsborough Trinity
D o B: 10/01/1968 — Birthplace: Liverpool
Previous clubs include: Boreham Wood - September 1999, Doncaster R, Torquay Utd, Blackpool, Southport, Birmingham C.

GOREHAM, MATTHEW — Defender
Current Club: Dereham Town
Birthplace: Norfolk
Skilful central defender who forms a formidable central partnership with Bob. Another to have played over 300 first team games.

GORMAN, MICHAEL — Midfielder
Current Club: Maidenhead United
Birthplace: London
Signed for Maidenhead in February 2002 after a second spell Yeading. Has also seen service at Hendon, Carshalton, Edgware and Wembley.

GORMAN, SEAN — Forward
Current Club: Basingstoke Town
Birthplace: London
Top scorer for 2000/01 and 01/02, Sean signed for Basingstoke Town from Allied Counties side Guildford & Godalming, where he scored over 100 goals, in the closing months of 1999. Was with Doncaster Rovers as a schoolboy and has represented the Combined Counties League. Previous clubs include Bromley and West Ewell.

GOSLING, JAMIE — Midfielder
Current Club: Bath City
Birthplace: Bristol
Talented midfielder, Jamie made the short journey to Bath City from Screwfix Direct Western League side Team Bath in September 2000. Had made an impression at the Bath University-based side during their debut Western League campaign, leading the goalscoring charts, but when his studies did not work out his availability came to the attention of City's reserve team boss Dave Hobbs. Having known the 19-year old from his Bath Arsenal days, Hobbs brought the former Bristol Rovers schoolboy to Twerton Park and he continued his impressive form for City's second string. A number of first-team substitute appearances, including his debut against Witney Town in the Dr Martens Cup, followed before he deservedly earned a starting slot for City and he looks set to continue his progress under manager Alan Pridham. He has also been the target of a number of League clubs and a move into the professional game looks a strong possibility in the near future.

GOTHARD, PAUL — Goalkeeper
Current Club: Dagenham & Redbridge
D o B: 24/06/1974 — Birthplace: Essex
Honours won: England Semi-Pro Int.
Paul returned to the Daggers in the close season after a 2 year spell at Hayes. Paul originally joined the Club in December 1994 having previously played for Grays Athletic and Colchester United. He was named as man-of-the-match in the Daggers 1997 FA Trophy final defeat at Wembley and won three England Semi-Professional caps.

GOUCK, ANDY — Midfielder
Current Club: Morecambe
D o B: 08/06/1972 — Birthplace: Blackpool
Previous clubs include: Southport - July 2001, Rochdale, Blackpool.

GOUGH, NEIL — Forward
Current Club: Hereford United
D o B: 01/09/1981 — Birthplace: Harlow
Young forward who joined Conference side Hereford United in August 2002. Started his career with Leyton Orient, where he progressed through the ranks to make around a dozen senior appearances. Had a spell on-loan at Dr Martens side Chelmsford City in the 2001/02 season before signing for Ryman Leaguers Hampton & Richmond Borough in March 02.

GOUGH, ROBERT — Midfielder
Current Club: Bideford
D o B: 24/04/1976 — Birthplace: Devon
Honours won: England Schoolboy Int.
Also back with us for his second spell at the club, Robbie rejoined us from Barnstaple Town. Robbie is an experienced forward, who is also a class act when he drops back into midfield. Robbie has represented his country at Schoolboy level and has also played for Devon, as well as also having been on the books of Newport County and Saltash. He has made over 100 appearances for the club.

GOUGH, SIMON — Defender
Current Club: Guiseley
Birthplace: Lancashire
Honours won: England Youth Int.
Previous clubs include: Accrington Stanley - August 2000, Guiseley, Clitheroe, Blackburn R (Trainee).

GOULBORN, MARK — Forward
Current Club: Hadleigh United
Birthplace: Suffolk
Enthusiastic front runner with impressive pace, work rate and ability. Former Suffolk County Under-18 player who returned to Hadleigh last season having played for the club as a youth.

GOULD, COLIN — Forward
Current Club: Chertsey Town
Birthplace: Surrey
Signed in October from Walton & Hersham, primarily as a defender but has since made a transistion to the forward line.

GOULD, DARREN — Goalkeeper
Current Club: Clacton Town
Birthplace: Essex
Dedicated player and one of the best shot-stoppers in the Jewson Eastern League. Big strong and very agile, he signed for Clacton Town in February 2000 from Harwich & Parkeston after previous service with Wivenhoe. Now in his third spell with the Seasiders.

GOULD, JAMIE — Midfielder
Current Club: Boston United
D o B: 15/01/1982   Birthplace: Northampton
A product of the Cobblers youth side, signed up for Boston United in June 2001 after being released by Northampton Town.

GOULD, PAUL — Defender
Current Club: Eastwood Town
Previous clubs include: Ashfield Utd - January 1997, Glapwell, Oakham Utd, Biwater.

GOULD, ROB — Defender
Current Club: St.Albans City
D o B: 07/07/1975   Birthplace: Northampton
Rob joined St Albans City in May 2002 from Dr Martens Premier side Tamworth. He had joined Tamworth in July 2001 from Ilkeston Town where he was leading goalscorer for the 2000/01 season, netting 14 times. A tall, classy defender or midfielder, he has also played for Rothwell, Raunds Town and Racing Club Warwick.

GOULD, TOM — Defender
Current Club: Chippenham Town
Birthplace: Bristol
22-year-old centre-back, who has recently finished an HND in sports performance at the University of Bath. Joined Chippenham Town in May 2002 from Screwfix Western League side Team Bath but is no stranger to the Dr Martens Premier Division. After a short spell at Odd Down he broke into the Bath City first team three years ago before joining Team Bath.

GOULDING, GRAHAM — Forward
Current Club: Workington
Birthplace: Cumbria
Talented player who excites the fans as soon as he is in possession of the ball. Attracted the interest of Newcastle United. Another discovery from local football.

GOULDING, JEFF — Midfielder
Current Club: Croydon
Birthplace: Surrey
Previous clubs include: Molesey - August 2002.

GOVE, SCOTT — Defender
Current Club: Clacton Town
Birthplace: Clacton
Promising young defender who has come through Jewson Eastern League club Clacton Town's Youth Development. Reads the game well.

GOWEN, CHRIS — Defender
Current Club: Frickley Athletic
Previous clubs include: York C - August 2001.

GOWER, DANNY — Forward
Current Club: Ludlow Town
Birthplace: Shropshire
From Youth team.

GOWER, MARK — Midfielder
Current Club: Barnet
D o B: 05/10/1978   Birthplace: Edmonton
Honours won: England Schoolboy, Youth & Semi-Pro Int.
An attacking midfielder who signed for Barnet in January 2001 from North London Premiership neighbours Tottenham Hotspur for £32,500. Mark was Tony Cottees second signing and in the few games he has played for the Bees looks to be a very

promising acquisition. Had been capped by England at Schoolboy and Youth level and then won semi-professional honours in the 2002 UniBond Four Nations tournament.

GOWER, PAUL — Defender
Current Club: Bracknell Town
Birthplace: Middlesex
Previous clubs include: Egham T - January 2002, Chertsey T, Molesey, Hampton.

GOWSHALL, JOBY — Defender
Current Club: Kings Lynn
D o B: 07/08/1975   Birthplace: Louth
Honours won: Dr Martens League Premier Div.Winners
Louth-born defender who started his career with Grimsby Town and also had a spell as a professional with Lincoln City before joining Boston United. Played a major part in helping the Pilgrims win the Dr Martens League and gain promotion back to the Conference before moving to Gainsborough Trinity in June 2001. Switched to Kings Lynn a year later.

GOZZARD, PAUL — Midfielder
Current Club: Racing Club Warwick
D o B: 29/11/1980   Birthplace: Sutton Coldfield
Former Walsall trainee midfielder who has since packed in a good deal of experience at Non-League level, despite his age. After leaving Walsall, Paul turned out for Mile Oak, Tamworth, Atherstone United and Bloxwich United before joining Racing Club Warwick from Oldbury United in November 2001.

GRAHAM, ANDY — Midfielder
Current Club: Didcot Town
Birthplace: Scotland
Scottish Andy is enjoying a new lease of life at Didcot following his 1998 transfer from Abingdon United. Has the knack of scoring vital goals and his League goal at North Leigh in August was breathtaking. An Accountant by profession.

GRAHAM, CHRISTIAN — Midfielder
Current Club: Bedlington Terriers
Birthplace: Newcastle
Christian was released by Middlesborough in the summer of 1999 and found himself at Northern Alliance outfit West Allotment. A good display in the Northumberland Senior Cup against the Terriers saw him snapped up by Bedlington in October of the same year. An attack minded youngster with good close ball skills he is comfortable anywhere in the midfield and is now an integral part of the Terriers squad where he is beginning to find his scoring touch. Has a great chance to become a significant player in the Northern League.

GRAHAM, DENIOL — Forward
Current Club: Colwyn Bay
D o B: 04/10/1969   Birthplace: Cannock
Honours won: Wales u-21 & Semi-Pro Int.
An experienced and well-respeted striker who as represented Wales at under-21 and semi-professional level. Started at Manchester United where he played four first team games and scored one goal before going to Barnsley (38 appearances - 2 goals), Preston North End (8 apps), Carlisle United (2 apps - 1 goal), Stockport County (11 apps - 2 goals), Scunthorpe United (3 apps - 1 goal). He then went to Halifax, Dagenham & Redbridge and signed for Colwyn Bay from UniBond Premier rivals Emley. Scored 29 goals for the Bay in the 1998/99 season and went to Cwmbran Town for a season. Rejoined Bay at the start of the 2000/01 season.

GRAHAM, GARETH — *Midfielder*
Current Club: Whyteleafe
D o B: 06/12/1978   *Birthplace: Belfast*
Honours won: Northern Ireland u-21 Int.
Former Northern Ireland under-21 international midfielder who signed for Ryman Division One South side Whyteleafe in August 2002 following a spell in Iceland with IVB. Started his career with Crystal Palace, where he made one League appearances before being transferred to Brentford in October 1999 after a successful spell on-loan at Griffin Park. Played 16 times for Brentford before joining Conference outfit Margate in October 2001, leaving for Iceland in June 02.

GRAHAM, GLEN — *Midfielder*
Current Club: Colwyn Bay
D o B: 01/03/1974   *Birthplace: Wales*
Signed for Colwyn Bay as a defender from then League of Wales side Flint Town United at the start of the 1995/96 season. Formerly with Holywell Town and Mostyn, Glen has been playing in midfield with great success in more recent seasons.

GRAHAM, JAMIE — *Midfielder*
Current Club: Hassocks
Birthplace: Sussex
Signed by Horsham at the start of 2000/01 (generally used as a substitute), before joining Hassocks the end of that season.

GRAHAM, JIMMY — *Defender*
Current Club: Lancaster City
D o B: 05/11/1969   *Birthplace: Glasgow*
Having signed for Lancaster City in February 1997, Jimmy is now the clubs longest-serving player. He took over the left back berth and has steadily become one of the most popular players among the fans for his whole hearted play. Before coming to City, he played in the League with Bradford, Rochdale and Hull, before being forced out of the full time game by knee injury and then joining Guiseley.

GRAHAM, KEVIN — *Defender*
Current Club: Whitby Town
D o B: 31/05/1978   *Birthplace: York*
Kevin signed for UniBond Premier side Whitby Town from Rowntrees York in March 2000. Made the two division jump seemlessly and quickly established himself as a valued member of the side. A stylish young defender with a promising future.

GRAHAM, MARK — *Midfielder*
Current Club: Billericay Town
D o B: 24/10/1974   *Birthplace: Newry*
Previous clubs include: Aldershot T - April 2002, Barry T, Stevenage B, Cambridge Utd, QPR.

GRAHAM, RICHARD — *Midfielder*
Current Club: Billericay Town
D o B: 05/08/1979   *Birthplace: Newry*
Honours won: Northern Ireland Youth & u-21 Int.
Former Northern Ireland Youth and under-21 international midfielder who joined Ryman Premier side Billericay Town from rivals Chesham United in July 2002. Began his career with QPR and then made a number of League appearances for Barnet before signing for Chesham in September 2001.

GRAHAM, RICKY — *Midfielder*
Current Club: Workington
Birthplace: Carlisle
Previous clubs include: Carlisle Utd - March 2001.

GRAHAM, ROLY — *Midfielder*
Current Club: Chatham Town
Honours won: FA Vase Winners
Previous clubs include: Ashford T - March 2001, Deal T, Herne Bay, Faversham T, Tonbridge, Gravesend.

GRAHAM, STEVE — *Midfielder*
Current Club: Hailsham Town
Birthplace: Sussex
Teenage midfielder: scored a great goal on his debut against Whitehawk during September.

GRAINGE, ANDY — *Defender*
Current Club: Cirencester Town
D o B: 06/11/1981   *Birthplace: Swindon*
A promising strong young defender, who was promoted into the first team squad last season from the Academy.

GRANT, JOHN — *Forward*
Current Club: Hereford United
D o B: 09/08/1981   *Birthplace: Manchester*
John made his way through the youth ranks at Crewe Alexandra and he really made an impression in the 1999/00 pre-season, scoring a couple of goals and supporters noted his excellent attacking ability. Before joining the senior side, Grant had been one of the most prolific strikers in the Alexs under-19s and with Crewe having a lack of strikers at the start of the 1999/00 season, John was drafted in against Crystal Palace in the opening game. Big and strong and a prolific scorer in the academy under-19 side, he gained further experience through loan spells with Hyde United in the UniBond and Northwich Victoria in the Conference before being snapped up by Hereford United in June 2002.

GRANT, KIM — *Forward*
Current Club: Yeovil Town
D o B: 25/09/1972   *Birthplace: Ghana*
Honours won: Ghana Int.
Kim arrived at Yeovil Town, initially on a trial basis in October 2001, after his release from Nationwide League side Scunthorpe United. He made his debut for Yeovil as a substitute on 16th October 2001 in an LDV Vans Trophy tie against Queens Park Rangers, scoring within minutes of his arrival on the field as the Glovers defeated Rangers 3-0. Kim has been capped 14 times by the Ghana full international side, and started his professional career in 1991 at Charlton Athletic. He made 155 appearances over the course of four years at The Valley before a £250,000 move took him to Luton Town where he spent two years. Kim also spent two years at Millwall along with a further two at Belgian League side Lommel and along with brief sessions at Notts County and Scunthorpe United has amassed over 270 appearances for Nationwide League clubs. Capable of playing as an orthadox striker, or as an attacking midfielder, Kim signed on the dotted line for Yeovil in January 2002, committing himself to the club until the end of the 2003 season. Kim is beginning to prove himself as an all-round striker.

GRANT, LEIGH — *Defender*
Current Club: Spennymoor United
Previous clubs include: Whitby T - February 2001, Gainsborough Trinity, Scarborough.

GRANT, STEVE — *Forward*
Current Club: Barking & East Ham United
Previous clubs include: East Ham Utd - July 2001.

GRANT, WAYNE — Midfielder
Current Club: Leyton Pennant
Birthplace: Essex
Previous clubs include: Dulwich Hamlet - January 2002.

GRANVILLE, PHIL — Defender
Current Club: Uxbridge
D o B: 02/01/1973   Birthplace: Middlesex
Phil signed Ryman League forms for Uxbridge in March 1995 after performing consistently well in defence for the reserves in the Suburban League. Phil has also been honoured to be selected for the Middlesex County Representative side and since breaking into the first team has made well over 300 appearances. Never fails to give less than 100 per cent.

GRASSBY, DARREN — Defender
Current Club: Shepshed Dynamo
D o B: 29/01/1976   Birthplace: Nuneaton
Much-travelled defender who joined Dr Martens Western side Shepshed Dynamo in July 2002 from Midland Alliance neighbours Barwell. A former trainee with Blackburn, he has had a number of spells with both Hinckley Athletic and United and has also seen service with Bedworth United, Nuneaton Borough and Stratford Town.

GRAVES, LEE — Defender
Current Club: Hemel Hempstead Town
D o B: 26/11/1972   Birthplace: Hertfordshire
Previous clubs include: Baldock T - September 1997, Gravesend, Brentford (Junior), Watford (Junior).

GRAVES, STUART — Midfielder
Current Club: Total Network Solutions
D o B: 04/06/1980   Birthplace: Bebbington
Previous clubs include: Rhyl - July 2001, Total Network Solutions, Poulton V, Southport, Stockport Co., Tranmere R.

GRAVES, TOM — Midfielder
Current Club: Withdean 2000
Birthplace: Sussex
Burgess Hill youth team player during 1998/99 who joined Whitehawk the following season: transferred to Southwick during January 2001 and was part of the reformed Withdean side that entered the Combined Counties League in August 2001.

GRAY, ADAM — Defender
Current Club: Ossett Town
D o B: 10/11/1978   Birthplace: Yorkshire
Younger brother of Ryan who arrived at the same time following three years with Burnley. Injury has hampered his career, which at one stage saw him on the verge of England Youth honours, but he has returned in fine form this year to win his first team place at left back.

GRAY, ADAM — Defender
Current Club: Molesey
D o B: 26/09/1978   Birthplace: Surrey
Previous clubs include: Kingstonian - February 1998.

GRAY, ANDY — Forward
Current Club: Worksop Town
D o B: 08/08/1975   Birthplace: Sheffield
Previous clubs include: Grantham T - November 2000, Lincoln Utd, Boston Utd.

GRAY, BRIAN — Forward
Current Club: Stourbridge
D o B: 25/11/1972   Birthplace: Birmingham
Previous clubs include: Solihull Borough - August 2001, Tamworth, Worcester C, Telford Utd, Bromsgrove R, Birmingham C.

GRAY, CHRIS — Midfielder
Current Club: Gresley Rovers
D o B: 14/11/1976   Birthplace: Leicestershire
Talented midfield player who joined Gresley Rovers during the summer of 2001 from Leicestershire Senior League side Coalville Town. Had a previous spell in the Dr Martens League with Shepshed Dynamo after being spotted playing for local side Bardon Hill.

GRAY, DANIEL — Forward
Current Club: Aylesbury United
From Youth team.

GRAY, DAVID — Defender
Current Club: Consett
Previous clubs include: Workington - July 1995.

GRAY, DAVID — Forward
Current Club: Accrington Stanley
D o B: 19/01/1980   Birthplace: Rossendale
Highly-regarded forward whose career started at Rochdale. Moved into the North West Counties League with Atherton Collieries and Rossendale United. Then tried his luck in the Conference with Northwich Victoria, but things didnt quite work out and he returned to Rossendale in the summer of 2000 and played a major part in Dales promotion to the UniBond League. Showed good form in the First Division in 2001/02 and earned a step up into the Premier with neighbouring Accrington Stanley in July 2002.

GRAY, DAVID — Midfielder
Current Club: Stanway Rovers
Birthplace: Essex
Previous clubs include: Clacton T - July 2000, Harwich & Parkeston, Wivenhoe T, Worthing, Wivenhoe T, Brightlingsea Utd, Clacton T, Wivenhoe T, Ipswich T.

GRAY, DAVID — Midfielder
Current Club: Harlow Town
Birthplace: Kent
Joined Harlow Town in January 2001 from Bromley. Now an experienced defender having gained Ryman Premier Division experience after breaking into the Kent sides first team from the reserves in 1996-97. Appointed captain of Harlow at the start of the 2001/02 season.

GRAY, EDDIE — Midfielder
Current Club: Egham Town
D o B: 04/09/1980   Birthplace: Berkshire
Previous clubs include: Windsor & Eton - March 2002, Wycombe Wanderers, West Ham Utd (Trainee).

GRAY, JULIAN — Goalkeeper
Current Club: Dorking
Birthplace: Surrey
Previous clubs include: Croydon - July 2001, Camberley T, Walton & Hersham, Woking.

GRAY, LIAM — Midfielder
Current Club: Harrogate Railway
Birthplace: Harrogate
Previous clubs include: Farsley Celtic - July 2001, Harrogate Railway, Harrogate T, Harrogate Railway.

GRAY, MARTIN — Midfielder
Current Club: Whitby Town
D o B: 17/08/1971   Birthplace: Stockton-on-Tees
Became a real coup signing for UniBond Premier side Whitby Town when they acquired this vastly experienced midfielder in August 2002 after his release from Darlington. Began his career with Sunderland, where he made around 60 League appearances. Moved on to Oxford United for £100,000 in March 1996 and played over 120 times for the Manor Ground outfit. Transferred back to the north-east to Darlington in May 1999 and was a regular until his release.

GRAY, MATT — Forward
Current Club: Sutton United
Birthplace: Surrey
A promising striker who scored prolifically at reserve and youth level for Sutton United, scoring four reserve team hat-tricks including one on his debut. He then became the youngest player for 24 years to play for the senior side when he made his debut at Farnborough in January 2000, the day before his 17th birthday, and at the end of the season became the first winner of the Ralph Carr Memorial Trophy for the Young Player of the Year.

GRAY, MICHAEL — Midfielder
Current Club: Sutton Coldfield Town
Birthplace: Birmingham
Honours won: Dr Martens Western Div.Winners
Michael joined Dr Martens Western Division side Sutton Coldfield Town in July 2002 after helping Halesowen Town to win the title the previous season. Signed for Halesowen having been released by Tamworth during the summer of 2001. A left-sided midfielder, he started his career with Premiership Leicester City. He then moved to Sheffield Wednesday. A successful period at Bromsgrove Rovers followed before being snapped up by Rushden & Diamonds.

GRAY, NICKY — Forward
Current Club: Chester-Le Street
Previous clubs include: West Allotment Celtic - July 2001, Morpeth T, Chester-le-Street, South Shields, Bedlington Terriers.

GRAY, PHIL — Forward
Current Club: Chelmsford City
D o B: 02/10/1968   Birthplace: Belfast
Honours won: Northern Ireland Int.
Vastly experienced striker with over 300 League appearances, 100 goals and 26 caps for Northern Ireland to his name. Joined Dr Martens Premier side Chelmsford City in July 2002 after being released by Oxford United. Started his career with Tottenham and went on to have spells with Luton, Sunderland, Burnley, Oxford and Dutch side Fortuna Sittard.

GRAY, RYAN — Defender
Current Club: Whyteleafe
Birthplace: London
Talented defender who joined Ryman Division One South side Whyteleafe in August 2002 after returning from a spell in the USA wher he turned out for Louisiana Outlaws. Originally with Fulham, he has also had spells with Sutton United and Dulwich Hamlet.

GRAY, RYAN — Midfielder
Current Club: Ossett Town
D o B: 28/08/1974   Birthplace: Halifax
Arrived from local club Dewsbury Moor back in 1998. Previously with Barnsley, Halifax Town and Gainsborough Trinity, injury wrecked his first season at Ingfield as he spent 6 months on the treatment table. Returned in style last season however as he walked off with the player of the year award.

GRAY, SIMON — Midfielder
Current Club: Clacton Town
Birthplace: Essex
Previous clubs include: Witham T - August 2001, Wivenhoe T, Clacton T, WoodbridgeT, Wivenhoe T, Felixstowe T, Woodbridge T, Harwich & Parkeston, Wivenhoe T, Colchester Utd, Ipswich T (Trainee).

GRAY, STEVEN — Defender
Current Club: Oxford City
Previous clubs include: Quarry Nomads - August 2001.

GRAYBURN, MARLON — Defender
Current Club: Romford
D o B: 14/11/1972   Birthplace: Essex
Previous clubs include: East Thurrock Utd - August 2001, Romford, Basildon Utd, Aveley, Tilbury, Hornchurch, Dover Ath., Southend Utd (Trainee).

GRAYSON, JOHN — Forward
Current Club: Harwich & Parkeston
Birthplace: Essex
A Harwich favourite who has recently returned to the fold after a spell at Brightlingsea. A hard grafter who will always score goals.

GRAYSON, NEIL — Forward
Current Club: Forest Green Rovers
D o B: 01/11/1964   Birthplace: York
Honours won: England Semi-Pro Int., Conference Winners
Former England semi-professional international forward who joined Conference club Forest Green Rovers in July 2002 after being released by Cheltenham Town. Became a living legend at Whaddon Road where Neil won all three player of the year awards in the season the club won promotion to the Football League. Fittingly, he scored Cheltenhams first ever Football League goal and finished as top scorer for the third season running. A strong, fit player whose appetite for the game shows no sign of dimming with age, Neil joined Doncaster Rovers from local football in Yorkshire and went on to play for Boston United, Chesterfield, York City, Northampton Town and Hereford United before joining Cheltenham in March 1998. He battled back from a broken ankle to lead the forward line last season and claimed the fifth hat-trick of his professional career in the 3-1 win over Cardiff City.

GRAYSTON, NEIL — Defender
Current Club: Halifax Town
Birthplace: Keighley
Defender who signed for Conference side Halifax Town in August 2002 after impressing in pre-season trials. Neil had joined Southport in the summer of 1999 from Bradford Park Avenue and enjoyed a utility role, playing in defence and midfield. He had former Football League experience with Bradford City.

GRAYSTONE, DANNY — Midfielder
Current Club: Witton Albion
Previous clubs include: AFC Zeneca - July 1999, Barton R, Harpenden T, Hitchin T.

GREARS, PAUL — Goalkeeper
Current Club: Barwell
D o B: 23/08/1980   Birthplace: Nuneaton
Highly-rated goalkeeper who joined Midland Alliance side Barwell in the summer of 2000. Previously with Nuneaton Griff and Atherstone United, he was named as Supporters' Player of the year for both 2000/01 and 2001/02.

GREATHOLDER, CHRIS — Forward
Current Club: Stafford Town
Birthplace: Stafford
From Local football - July 2001.

GREATOREX, ADIE — Defender
Current Club: Shepshed Dynamo
D o B: 01/10/1974   Birthplace: Rugby
Previous clubs include: Barwell - August 2002, Rugby T, Barwell, Bedworth Utd, Nuneaton B.

GREATOREX, MARK — Forward
Current Club; Tonbridge Angels
D o B: 04/10/1973   Birthplace: Kent
Previous clubs include: Margate - July 2001, Tonbridge, Chelmsford C, Dartford, Thamesmead T, Sheppey Utd.

GREAVES, PAUL — Defender
Current Club: Staines Town
D o B: 20/03/1981   Birthplace: Middlesex
A fine defensive prospect who joined Staines Town in November 2001 after a short spell in the Spartan South Midlands League with Brook House. Began his playing days with Hillingdon Borough and then made a number of appearances for Uxbridge in the Ryman League as a teenager.

GREDLEY, IAN — Defender
Current Club: Aveley
Birthplace: Essex
Previous clubs include: Grays Ath - July 2001, Purfleet, Hornchurch.

GREEN, ALEX — Midfielder
Current Club: Buxton
D o B: 04/01/1980   Birthplace: Bolton
Previous clubs include: Ashton Utd - August 2002, Gresley R, Stalybridge Celtic, Hallam, Buxton, Bury.

GREEN, ANDY — Defender
Current Club: Racing Club Warwick
Birthplace: Birmingham
Previous clubs include: Shepshed Dynamo - December 2000, Massey Ferguson, Racing Club Warwick, Nuneaton B, Birmingham C (Trainee).

GREEN, ANDY — Forward
Current Club: Rhyl
D o B: 23/08/1969   Birthplace: Liverpool
Previous clubs include: Droylsden - December 2001, Barrow, Altrincham, Knowsley Utd, Morecambe, Macclesfield T, Binche (Belgium), South Liverpool, Bootle.

GREEN, ANTHONY — Forward
Current Club: Peterlee Newtown
Birthplace: Co.Durham
Previous clubs include: Bishop Auckland - July 2000.

GREEN, DARREN — Midfielder
Current Club: Hanwell Town
D o B: 24/11/1978   Birthplace: Langley Wood
Previous clubs include: Hillingdon Borough - July 2000, Yeading, Brentford (Junior).

GREEN, DEAN — Forward
Current Club: Farnborough Town
Birthplace: London
Very promising young striker whose career began at Fulham. Was released and resurrected his career in Non-League football with the likes of Waltham Abbey, Dulwich Hamlet, Crawley Town and Leyton Pennant. Started to become noticed again after joining Hampton & Richmond Borough and his form led to a move into the Conference with Farnborough Town in October 2001.

GREEN, GARETH — Midfielder
Current Club: Lewes
Birthplace: Sussex
Signed for Ryman League Division One South side Lewes from Bognor neighbours Bognor Regis Town in July 2002. Had joined Bognor Regis from Sussex Country League side Wick in January 2002. Previous clubs include Southwick, Steyning and Shoreham Town. A talented midfielder who lives in Shoreham.

GREEN, KIM — Forward
Current Club: Racing Club Warwick
D o B: 01/02/1965   Birthplace: London
Previous clubs include: Atherstone Utd - July 2000, VS Rugby, Solihull B, Hednesford T, VS Rugby, Atherstone Utd, Nuneaton B, VS Rugby, Coventry Sporting, MSA.

GREEN, LEON — Forward
Current Club: Harlow Town
Birthplace: London
Young forward who joined Harlow Town in January 2002 after being released by Leyton Orient. A hihgly-promising player of whom much is expected.

GREEN, MARC — Defender
Current Club: Workington
Birthplace: Carlisle
Arrived at Borough Park mid-way through the 1998-99 season from Bamber Bridge, having spent time with Carlisle United's youth set up. Won the Supporters' Player of the Year award for 1999/2000 and should achieve his ambition of playing at a higher level in the game.

GREEN, MATTHEW — Midfielder
Current Club: Stamford
D o B: 22/10/1975   Birthplace: Northampton
Matt Green is a strong and physically-minded central midfielder. Matt was recruited in 1999 and was a one time Derby apprentice who has also worn Cogenoe, Rothwell and Irish club Larne, shirts.

GREEN, NEIL — Midfielder
Current Club: Haverhill Rovers
Birthplace: Suffolk
Midfielder in his third season at Haverhill. A three-times championship winner with Castle Camps, had a trial at the Norwich City School of Excellence.

GREEN, PAUL — Midfielder
Current Club: Doncaster Rovers
D o B: 10/04/1983   *Birthplace: Sheffield*
Began with Sheffield Wednesday Juniors and joined the Rovers Youth team in the summer of 1999. Has played a big part in the success of the Youth team over the last two seasons.

GREEN, RICHARD — Defender
Current Club: Barnstaple Town
D o B: 25/11/1979   *Birthplace: Devon*
Previous clubs include: Clyst Rovers - July 2000, Cheltenham T.

GREEN, RONNIE — Forward
Current Club: Kingstonian
D o B: 02/12/1981   *Birthplace: London*
Honours won: FA Trophy Winners
The young striker is now the longest-serving player at Kingstonian. A product of the youth side who made his debut against Woking in a Surrey Senior Cup tie in March 2000. Pacey and skillful, he continues to add to his game and enjoyed an outstanding game in the 2000 FA Umbro Trophy Final.

GREEN, RUSSELL — Defender
Current Club: Stocksbridge Park Steels
D o B: 06/10/1970   *Birthplace: Barnsley*
Previous clubs include: Bradford PA - August 2001, Frickley Ath., Farsley Celtic, Emley, Altrincham, Emley, Burnley.

GREEN, TERRY — Midfielder
Current Club: Newtown AFC
Birthplace: Hereford
Signed from Hellenic League side Pegasus, he is a highly rated and competitive mid-field player. Keen to progress in the game and has already impressed the home fans with his strong running and attacking qualities. Has scored some vital goals and has started well in the new season.

GREENALL, COLIN — Defender
Current Club: Rossendale United
D o B: 30/12/1963   *Birthplace: Billinge*
Previous clubs include: Wigan Ath - November 2001, Lincoln C, Chester C, Preston NE, Bury, Oxford Utd, Gillingham, Blackpool.

GREENAWAY, JAY — Midfielder
Current Club: Beaconsfield SYCOB
Birthplace: Berkshire
From Youth team.

GREENAWAY, JULIAN — Midfielder
Current Club: Banstead Athletic
Birthplace: Surrey
Previous clubs include: Charlton Ath - August 2001, Banstead Ath.

GREENE, DENNIS — Forward
Current Club: Windsor & Eton
D o B: 14/04/1965   *Birthplace: Essex*
Vastly experienced and much-travelled striker who was appointed as player-manager of Windsor & Eton in November 2001. First signed for the Royalists in September 1998 from RIPS of Riihimaki (Finland) where he won a Division Two championship medal. Previously with Harlow Town, Dagenham & Redbridge, Wycombe Wanderers, Chelmsford City, Wealdstone, Hemel Hempstead Town and Heybridge Swifts amongst others.

GREENGRASS, MARK — Defender
Current Club: Dereham Town
Birthplace: Norfolk
Suffered a serious head injury at the end of the 1998/99 season. Returned to first team action towards the end of the following season. Ex-Watton United.

GREENHILL, ROSS — Forward
Current Club: Newcastle Blue Star
D o B: 14/09/1979   *Birthplace: Newcastle*
Previous clubs include: Gretna - December 1998, Derby Co.

GREENLEY, MATT — Goalkeeper
Current Club: Wivenhoe Town
Birthplace: Essex
Young goalkeeper and former star of Heybridge Swifts successful under-18 side having joined the youth set up from Colchester United. Developed well in the reserves and made a number of first-team appearances in 2001/02, impressing everyone. Moved on to Ryman Division One North side Wivenhoe Town in the summer of 2002 in search of more regular first-team football.

GREENO, MICK — Forward
Current Club: Portland United
Birthplace: Weymouth
Previous clubs include: Weymouth - July 1999, Bridport, Havant T, Fareham T, Dorchester T, Weymouth, Dorchester T, Floriana (Australia), Dorchester T, Weymouth, Dorchester T.

GREENSMITH, ANDY — Defender
Current Club: Rothwell Town
Birthplace: Kettering
Previous clubs include: Rothwell Corinthians - July 2001.

GREENWOOD, CARL — Midfielder
Current Club: Clitheroe
Birthplace: Lancashire
Initially fell foul of the if he's better looking than me then he must be crap police. Turned in his best year last term and added extra bite to his distribution quality.

GREGORIO, GEORGE — Forward
Current Club: Enfield
Previous clubs include: Cheshunt - February 2001.

GREGORY, ANDY — Defender
Current Club: Frickley Athletic
D o B: 08/10/1976   *Birthplace: Barnsley*
Previous clubs include: Emley - January 2001, Barnsley.

GREGORY, DAVID — Defender
Current Club: Canvey Island
D o B: 23/01/1970   *Birthplace: Colchester*
Experienced defender or midfielder who joined Ryman Premier side Canvey Island from Colchester in July 2002. Played over 250 League appearances with Ipswich, Peterborough and Colchester and joins brother Neil at Canvey.

GREGORY, JUSTIN — Defender
Current Club: Farnborough Town
Birthplace: Sussex
An experienced Non-League defender who joined Farnborough Town in February 2000 from rivals Dulwich Hamlet, whom he had joined in July 1999. Had earlier spent the majority of his playing days in Sussex with Shoreham, Worthing, Hastings Town and Crawley Town, with whom he enjoyed two spells.

GREGORY, NEIL　　　　　　Forward
Current Club: Canvey Island
D o B: 07/10/1972　　　　　Birthplace: Zambia
Honours won: FA Trophy Winners
Signed for Canvey Island from Colchester United in February 2000. Previous clubs include Ipswich Town, Peterborough (loan) and Torquay (loan). Transferred to Colchester for £50,000 on 26th March 98. In the summer of 99 he was on loan to the Boston Bulldogs. After a two month loan period Neil, signed for Canvey on a free transfer for a three-year contract period. Made 119 football league appearances and scored 29 goals.

GREGSON, LYNDON　　　　Midfielder
Current Club: Aberystwyth Town
Birthplace: Carmarthen
Previous clubs include: Swansea C - July 2001.

GREIG, NEIL　　　　　　　Midfielder
Current Club: Abingdon Town
Previous clubs include: Thame Utd - October 2001, Oxford C, Abingdon T, Oxford Utd (Trainee).

GREYGOOSE, DEAN　　　　Goalkeeper
Current Club: Canvey Island
D o B: 18/12/1964　　　　　Birthplace: Thetford
Honours won: England Youth Int.
Vastly experienced goalkeeper who signed for Ryman Premier side Canvey Island in August 2002 after being released by Conference outfit Stevenage Borough. Dean joined Stevenage in the summer of 2001from Witton Albion, and was a valued member of the squad. Played all his football in the North West with previous clubs Chester, Northwich, Altrincham and Crewe after starting out at Crystal Palace, Leyton Orient and Cambridge United.

GRICE, NEIL　　　　　　　Midfielder
Current Club: Witham Town
Birthplace: Essex
Previous clubs include: Heybridge Swifts - February 2000, Sudbury W, Braintree T, Heybridge Swifts, Sudbury T, Saffron Walden T, Braintree T, Bayswater (Australia), Braintree T, Witham T, Fisher Ath., Braintree T, Chelmsford C, Braintree T, Ipswich T.

GRICE, SHAUN　　　　　　Forward
Current Club: Ringmer
Birthplace: Sussex
Goal-hungry young striker who scored 13 times for Burgess Hill in 1998/99. Signed for Crawley at the start of the following campaign, but went to Saltdean a few months later. Joined Ringmer in March 2001 and struck a total of 17 goals last season.

GRIDELET, PHIL　　　　　　Midfielder
Current Club: Harrow Borough
D o B: 17/09/1971　　　　　Birthplace: Hendon
Honours won: England Semi-Pro Int.
Vastly experienced defender or midfielder who joined Ryman Premier side Harrow Borough from Bishops Stortford in October 2001. Previous clubs include Hendon, Barnsley, Barnet, Rotherham, Southend, Woking and Canvey Island. A former England semi-professional international.

GRIEVES, DARREN　　　　　Forward
Current Club: Hemel Hempstead Town
D o B: 15/04/1977　　　　　Birthplace: Watford
Previous clubs include: Maidenhead Utd - October 2001, Boreham Wood, Aylesbury Utd, Yeading, Watford (Trainee).

GRIFFIN, CHARLIE　　　　　Forward
Current Club: Woking
D o B: 25/06/1979　　　　　Birthplace: Bath
An exciting striker on his day, Charlie joined Woking for a £25,000 fee in November 2000 from Swindon Town after an impressive spell on loan, during which he scored the winning goal at Dagenham & Redbridge on his debut. He began his career with Melksham Town and has also played for Chippenham Town.

GRIFFIN, COREY　　　　　　Forward
Current Club: Sittingbourne
Birthplace: Kent
Forward who takes a pride in keeping himself fit. Made his debut for Sittingbourne during the 1999/2000 season after impressing in the reserves. A product of Bourne youth team.

GRIFFIN, MICHAEL　　　　　Midfielder
Current Club: Chertsey Town
Birthplace: Surrey
Joined in the past close season and was in local football last season but has also played at youth level with Crystal Palace and Sutton United. Plays in the midfield.

GRIFFIN, SCOTT　　　　　　Midfielder
Current Club: Cinderford Town
Birthplace: Gloucestershire
Joined Dr Martens Western Division Cinderford Town in July 2002 from Eastern Division Salisbury City. The attacking midfielder had signed for City in December 2001 from Clevedon Town. Previously with Newport County and Cirencester Town. Highly-rated product of the Cirencester Academy.

GRIFFITH, ADAM　　　　　　Midfielder
Current Club: Peacehaven & Telscombe
Birthplace: Sussex
Previous clubs include: Yeading - August 2001.

GRIFFITH, IAN　　　　　　　Midfielder
Current Club: Peacehaven & Telscombe
Birthplace: Sussex
Midfielder/all-rounder who was formerly with Lewes and Wick.

GRIFFITHS, ANDY　　　　　Midfielder
Current Club: Connahs Quay Nomads
Birthplace: Wales
From Youth team.

GRIFFITHS, ANTONY　　　　Defender
Current Club: Caersws
D o B: 23/07/1968　　　　　Birthplace: Wales
From Youth team.

GRIFFITHS, BRYAN　　　　　Midfielder
Current Club: Congleton Town
D o B: 26/01/1965　　　　　Birthplace: St.Helens
Assistant to Kevin Langley. He lives in St Helens and had good playing career with Wigan Athletic, Blackpool and Southport. Treasures his memory of scoring for Wigan against Liverpool at Anfield. Loves golf and snooker and being bossy at training sessions.

GRIFFITHS, HUW　　　　　　Defender
Current Club: Bangor City
D o B: 09/02/1977　　　　　Birthplace: Wales
Centre back whose consistent, powerful performances for Cefn Druids caught they eye during the 2000-01season. Joined League of Wales side Bangor City in the summer of 2001 and

established himself as a firm favourite with the Farrar Road faithful. Also had a spell with Newtown.

GRIFFITHS, JUSTIN — *Forward*
Current Club: *Arlesey Town*
Birthplace: Bedford
Promising young striker who signed for Ryman Division One North side Arlesey Town in the close season of 2002 from Bedford Town. Formerly at United Counties League outfit Stotfold.

GRIFFITHS, KENNY — *Goalkeeper*
Current Club: *Hereford United*
Birthplace: Devon
Joined Conference side Hereford United as a goalkeeper on a one-year deal in the close season of 2002 after his release from Third Division Torquay United. The promising youngster had spent most of the summer on trial with Leicester City and arrived at Edgar Street with glowing references from The Foxes and he will be pushing for a place in the first-team.

GRIFFITHS, LEROY — *Forward*
Current Club: *Farnborough Town*
Birthplace: Surrey
Striker who started out with the likes of Sutton United, Banstead Athletic and Corinthian Casuals before signing for Hampton & Richmond Borough in February 2000. Had barely a season with the Beavers before making a surprise switch to Queens Park Rangers in June 2001. Played 23 times for the Rangers before being released at the end of the 2001/02 season and joined Fanborough Town in August 2002.

GRIFFITHS, MARTYN — *Midfielder*
Current Club: *Caersws*
D o B: 07/11/1969   *Birthplace: Wales*
Previous clubs include: Aberystwyth T - July 2001, Llanidloes T, Aberystwyth T.

GRIFFITHS, MATTHEW — *Goalkeeper*
Current Club: *Caersws*
D o B: 16/04/1972   *Birthplace: Wales*
Previous clubs include: Oswestry T - July 1996.

GRIFFITHS, MICHAEL — *Forward*
Current Club: *Rushall Olympic*
Birthplace: Birmingham
Previous clubs include: Paget Rangers - September 2001, Sutton Coldfield T, Halesowen T, Torquay Utd, Boldmere St.Michaels, Worcester C, Sutton Coldfield T, Boldmere St.Michaels.

GRIFFITHS, NEIL — *Defender*
Current Club: *Gloucester City*
Birthplace: Gloucester
From Youth team.

GRIFFITHS, PETER — *Midfielder*
Current Club: *Aberystwyth Town*
D o B: 01/12/1978   *Birthplace: Aberystwyth*
Previous clubs include: Penrhyncoch - July 1998.

GRIFFITHS, STEVE — *Defender*
Current Club: *Biddulph Victoria*
Birthplace: Stoke
Previous clubs include: Meir KA - June 1999, Knypersley V, Kidsgrove Ath., Knypersley V, Newcastle T, Knypersley V, Newcastle T, Eastwood Hanley, Ball Haye Green.

GRIFFITHS, STEVE — *Defender*
Current Club: *Yeading*
Birthplace: Middlesex
Strong young defender who first broke into the first team at the end of 2000. Calm and confident in his approach to the game and a great prospect for the club. Scored his first senior goal for the club against Worthing in March 2001.

GRIFFITHS, TOM — *Defender*
Current Club: *Hednesford Town*
Birthplace: Birmingham
Tom is a young left-sided defender who can also play in midfield. He signed for the Pitmen as a youth team player and was one of that sides most consistent performers. Already gained valuable first team experience during the ill-fated 2000/2001 Conference campaign, Tom is one to watch for the future.

GRIGGS, DANNY — *Forward*
Current Club: *Northwich Victoria*
Birthplace: Cheshire
Danny is a 21-year old player who spent his early years under the wing of Dario Gradi at Crewe and subsequently played over 100 games for Nantwich Town before signing for Mossley during the 2001/02 season. Prior to that, however, Danny had made his debut for Conference side Northwich Victoria in October against Doncaster Rovers before returning to Nantwich. He is a tricky and skilful wide player possessing excellent crossing ability.

GRIME, DOMINIC — *Defender*
Current Club: *Boreham Wood*
Birthplace: Hertfordshire
Dominic can play either in defence or midfield. He joined Boreham Wood from Hitchin Town and made his debut on 18 October 1997 and scored a goal against Purfleet. His twin brother Nick who was with him at Boreham Wood, now plays for Hitchin Town. Previously Dominic played for Stevenage Borough. He won a Herts Senior Challenge Cup Winners medal with Boreham Wood in 1998/99.

GRIME, NICK — *Defender*
Current Club: *Hitchin Town*
D o B: 17/05/1977   *Birthplace: Herts*
Left Back who joined Hitchin Town initially in August 1997 on loan from Stevenage Borough but a cruciate ligament injury halted his Top Field career. Moved to Boreham Wood, but returned in December 1999 and in 2000/01 was named Players' Player of the year.

GRIMM, ENRICO — *Forward*
Current Club: *Hampton & Richmond*
Birthplace: Surrey
Teenage forward who has progressed from Ryman Premier side Hampton & Richmond Borough's successful under -18 side into the first-team squad. Enrico made his debut coming on as substitute at Bedford Town during the latter part of the 2001/02 season.

GRIMSDELL, DANNY — *Midfielder*
Current Club: *Arlesey Town*
Birthplace: London
Previous clubs include: Harrow Borough - March 2002, Arlesey T, Aveley, Leyton Orient.

GRIMSHAW, STEVE — Midfielder
Current Club: Frome Town

D o B: 30/09/1981 — Birthplace: Yeovil
Previous clubs include: Yeovil T - August 2001, Southampton (Junior).

GRIST, NEIL — Defender
Current Club: Eccleshill United

Birthplace: Yorkshire
Previous clubs include: Liversedge - July 2001, Eccleshill Utd, Thackley.

GROCUTT, DAMIAN — Defender
Current Club: Rocester

Birthplace: Stafford
Previous clubs include: Meir KA - July 1998, Nantwich T, Leek T.

GROCUTT, DARREN — Defender
Current Club: Tamworth

D o B: 05/09/1969 — Birthplace: Birmingham
Darren is a talented and experienced midfielder or defender who brings a calm assurance to the team. He joined Tamworth in March 1999 from Burton Albion and was so impressive that he was made club captain for the 1999/00 season. He completed a second spell at Burton before joining the Lambs having previously been with Bromsgrove Rovers in the Conference. He has also played for Evesham United and Moor Green.

GROGAN, GARY — Forward
Current Club: Ely City

Birthplace: Cambridge
Previous clubs include: Chatteris T - July 1999, Ely C, Chatteris T, Ely C, Soham Town R, Cambridge C, Barnstaple T, Cambridge C, Soham Town R, Cambridge C.

GROSE, CHRIS — Midfielder
Current Club: Ashton United

From Youth team.

GROSS, MARCUS — Defender
Current Club: Tiverton Town

Birthplace: Exeter
Previous clubs include: Exeter C - November 2001.

GROSVENOR, STUART — Forward
Current Club: Willenhall Town

Birthplace: Birmingham
Previous clubs include: Redditch Utd - July 2002, Bilston T, Oldbury Utd, Willenhall T, Stourport Swifts, Blakenall, Oldbury Utd, Lye T, Halesowen Harriers, Dudley T, Redditch Utd, Halesowen T.

GROVE, ROB — Defender
Current Club: Arundel

D o B: 26/06/1981 — Birthplace: Chichester
Left wing-back: reserve player until breaking into the first team during February 2001: described by the Arundel website as being a bit of a loose cannon.

GROVER, DUNCAN — Defender
Current Club: Romford

Birthplace: Essex
Previous clubs include: Aveley - August 2001, Concord R, Tilbury, East Thurrock Utd.

GROVES, MATTHEW — Forward
Current Club: Dorchester Town

D o B: 17/04/1980 — Birthplace: Bournemouth
Previous clubs include: Portsmouth - November 1998.

GROVES, STEVE — Midfielder
Current Club: Tring Town

Birthplace: Buckinghamshire
Previous clubs include: Amersham T - September 1999.

GRUAR, DANNY — Defender
Current Club: Edgware Town

Birthplace: London
Previous clubs include: Boreham Wood - November 2001.

GUEST, JOHN — Defender
Current Club: Sittingbourne

D o B: 07/01/1982 — Birthplace: Kent
An exciting prospect who grabbed his first-team chance when injuries hit Sittingbournes squad and is now a regular member of the first-team in the centre of defence. Strong in the air, he came through Sittingbournes own youth and reserve ranks.

GUEST, MARK — Forward
Current Club: Gainsborough Trinity

Previous clubs include: Dinnington - September 2001, Barnsley (Junior).

GUILE, NEIL — Goalkeeper
Current Club: Newport Isle Of Wight

Birthplace: Hampshire
Previous clubs include: East Cowes Vics - July 2002, Havant T, Portsmouth (Trainee).

GUILLE, DES — Defender
Current Club: Burgess Hill Town

Birthplace: Sussex
Versatile type, who usually plays in defence: previous experience with Worthing Utd and Southwick before joining Burgess Hill from Lancing during the 2000 close season: primarily featured for the reserves before winning a regular first-team spot: has appeared for Sussex this term.

GUINAN, STEVE — Forward
Current Club: Hereford United

D o B: 24/12/1975 — Birthplace: Birmingham
Forward who joined Conference side Hereford United just prior to the start of the 2002/03 season after being released by Shrewsbury. Began his career with Nottingham Forest, where he made a handful of senior appearance and also spent time out on-loan at various clubs, including Burnley, Crewe, Scunthorpe and Plymouth. Moved on to Cambridge United in December 1999 and then on to Plymouth before joining the Shrews in March 2002.

GUIVER, LEE — Forward
Current Club: Dartford

Previous clubs include: Witham T - July 1999, Chelmsford C, Billericay T, Chelmsford C.

GUIVER, ROY — Forward
Current Club: Ashford Town

D o B: 03/06/1983 — Birthplace: Kent
Previous clubs include: Folkestone Invicta - August 2001.

GUMMER, SEAN — Forward
Current Club: Burton Albion
D o B: 14/04/1981 — Birthplace: Derby
Sean arrived at Conference club Burton Albion from Belper Town in the summer of 2002. He started his career with Derby County and also had a short spell with Mandal in the Norweigan First Division. His successful time at Belper Town resulted in him being voted Supporters' Player of the Year in 2000/01.

GUNN, BRYN — Defender
Current Club: Arnold Town
D o B: 21/08/1958 — Birthplace: Corby
Honours won: Euuropean Cup Winners, Football League Div. 1 Winners
Previous clubs include: Dunkirk - August 1996, Ilkeston T, Hednesford T, Corby T, Chesterfield, Peterborough Utd., Nottingham Forest.

GUSTARD, KEVIN — Forward
Current Club: Whitley Bay
Birthplace: Newcastle
Another youngster snapped up from New Hartley Juniors, He has taken the step up in his stride and is another one for the future.

OUTZMORE, LEON — Forward
Current Club: Cambridge City
D o B: 30/10/1976 — Birthplace: London
Leon arrived at Cambridge City just before Christmas 2001 from Ryman Premier outfit Braintree Town. Born in London, his career began with neighbouring Cambridge United as a youngster. When things didnt work he moved to Billericay Town where he was a prolific striker. At the end of 1998 Aldershot Town parted with £11,000 for his services and this was followed about a year later by a £6,000 move to Bedford Town, from where he eventually moved to Braintree.

GUY, NICKY — Midfielder
Current Club: Ludlow Town
Birthplace: Shropshire
Previous clubs include: Shifnal T - July 2001, Rhayader T, Knighton T.

GUYETT, SCOTT — Defender
Current Club: Chester City
D o B: 20/01/1976 — Birthplace: Ascot
Scott was signed by Chester City in August 2002 from Oxford United. He was another to play for Southport and followed manager Mark Wright, who was keen to secure his signature for Oxford and has re-signed him again. A strong centre half, who likes to get forward, Scott had a good understanding with Phil Bolland at both Southport and Oxford and they should bolster the City defence.

GWILLIAM, GARETH — Forward
Current Club: Ashford Town
Birthplace: Kent
Previous clubs include: Crystal Palace - March 2002, Welling Utd.

GWINNETT, MARTIN — Midfielder
Current Club: Winsford United
Birthplace: Wigan
Signed from Wigan Athletic. Has quickly settled in to establish a regular place in midfield.

GYNN, MICKY — Midfielder
Current Club: Wisbech Town
D o B: 19/08/1961 — Birthplace: Peterborough
Honours won: FA Cup Winners
Previous clubs include: Stratford T - February 2002, Soham Town Rangers, Warboys T, Stafford R, Corby T, Stamford, Kings Lynn, Kettering T, Hednesford T, Stoke C, Coventry C, Peterborough Utd.

GYOURY, NICKY — Defender
Current Club: Chelmsford City
Birthplace: Essex
Highly-promising young central defender who joined Chelmsford City in June 2002 after spending a season in the Ryman League with Enfield. Was originally on the books at Colchester United.

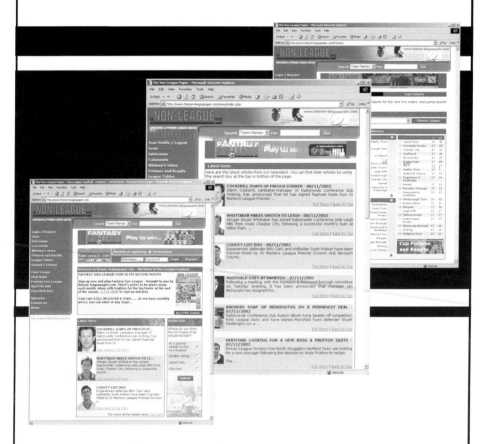

HAAG, KELLY   *Forward*
Current Club: Ware
D o B: 06/10/1970   *Birthplace: Enfield*
From Local football - July 2001, Fisher Ath., Aylesbury Utd, Baldock T, St.Albans C, Dagenham & Redbridge, Sutton Utd, Leyton Orient, Barnet, Fulham, Brentford.

HAARHOFF, JIMMY   *Forward*
Current Club: Droylsden
D o B: 27/05/1981   *Birthplace: Lusaka, Zambia*
Tricky winger who joined UniBond League Premier Division side Droylsden in August 2002 from Chester City. Had signed for the Conference outfit in January 2001 from Birmingham City initially on loan, but signed full time in the summer of 2001.

HABBERSHAW, MARK   *Forward*
Current Club: Stourbridge
Birthplace: Birmingham
Previous clubs include: Bilston T - January 2002.

HACK, STUART   *Defender*
Current Club: St.Leonards
Birthplace: Sussex
A former stalwart of Lewes who made well over 150 appearances for the Rooks. Impressive in the air at both ends of the pitch and never less than totally commited to the cause, he thoroughly deserved his 2000-1 Players' Player of the Season award. Transferred to St Leonards in February 2002.

HACKETT, BRENDAN   *Midfielder*
Current Club: Redditch United
D o B: 02/03/1966   *Birthplace: Wolverhampton*
Previous clubs include: Stourport Swifts - November 2001, Stourbridge, Gloucester C, Burton Alb., Rushden & Diamonds, Hednesford T, Telford Utd, Gloucester C, Worcester C, Dudley T, Stourbridge, Redditch Utd, Bilston T.

HACKETT, MEKEL   *Forward*
Current Club: Harrow Borough
Birthplace: London
Young midfielder or striker who rejoined Ryman Premier side Hrarow Boough in the summer of 2002 from Ford United. Previously with Chelsea, Millwall, Brentford and Woking as a youth.

HACKETT, RYAN   *Midfielder*
Current Club: Redhill
Birthplace: Kent
Former Horsham utility man, described by former Redhill manager Russell Mason as the new Paul Madeley: began playing for Redhill in September 2000 after losing his first-team place at Bromley. Went on to join Lewes before suffering a serious injury. Fought his way back to fitness and then rejoined Redhill in January 2002.

HACKETT, WARREN   *Defender*
Current Club: Ford United
D o B: 16/12/1971   *Birthplace: Plaistow*
Honours won: Ryman League Div.One Winners
It was quite a coup when Ford United managed to persuade Warren to join their Ryman League Division One title race, which ultimately proved successful, in January 2002. After starting his career with Spurs, the defender went on to make over 280 League appearances with Leyton Orient, Doncaster Rovers, Mansfield and Barnet. Had a three-month spell at Grays Athletic prior to joining the Motormen.

HACKNEY, ROB   *Goalkeeper*
Current Club: Droylsden
Birthplace: Stoke
Previous clubs include: Mossley - March 2002, Leek CSOB, Stone Dominoes, Port Vale (Junior).

HADDAWAY, PAUL   *Defender*
Current Club: Chasetown FC
Birthplace: Staffs
Previous clubs include: Brocton - July 1996.

HADDOW, PAUL   *Midfielder*
Current Club: Lancaster City
Birthplace: Blackpool
A summer 1999 signing for Lancaster City from Barrow who has established a great reputation with City fans despite never holding down an established position. Prefers midfield, but can play full back, but is best noted for his knack of scoring vital goals. Has also been with Morecambe and Blackpoool as a youngster

HADDRELL, MATT   *Defender*
Current Club: Vauxhall Motors
D o B: 19/03/1981   *Birthplace: Staffordshire*
Strong young player captured by Vauxhall Motors from Newcastle Town in January 2001 for a fee of around £2,300. Matt is a versatile player who became an instant hit with Motors. Previously with Nantwich Town and Kidsgrove Athletic, he can operate in several positions but excels in the heart of the defence an has popped up with a number of important goals.

HADJATO, GEZA   *Midfielder*
Current Club: Port Talbot Town
D o B: 23/10/1981   *Birthplace: Cardiff*
Previous clubs include: Cardiff C - July 2001.

HADJ-LAKEHAL, LYAZID   *Defender*
Current Club: Feltham
Birthplace: Algiers
One of the foreign contingent - Yazz, as he known at Feltham joined the side in 1995/1996 after playing in a friendly game at the Arena before a Feltham midweek match. Yazz asked if he could come training and the rest as they say is history. Now in his 6th season at Feltham, Yazz has become an established regular in the first XI. Voted Managements Player of the Year in 1999/2000.

HADLAND, GUY   *Defender*
Current Club: Hinckley United
D o B: 23/01/1979   *Birthplace: Nuneaton*
Honours won: Dr Martens League Western Div.Winners
Guy was on the books of Aston Villa and has played for their reserve team on a number of occasions. A transfer to Northampton Town was shelved after he sustained a knee injury that kept him out of the game for 3 years. Signed for Hinckley United in January 2000. A Midfield utility player, he often plays at the back of midfield. Won a Dr Martens Western Division championship medal with Hinckley United in 2000-01. Left to join Evesham on loan during the 2001/02 season but returned within months to fight his way back into the first-team and was a regular for the rest of that season.

HADLEY, STEWART — Forward

Current Club: Worcester City

D o B: 30/12/1973   *Birthplace: Dudley*

Honours won: Conference Winners

Signed for Worcester City in January 2002 from Kidderminster Harriers after a successful loan spell. Stewart, 28, began his career at Derby County before making over 100 appearances for Mansfield Town and 50+ for Harriers. Started his career in Non-League football with Halesowen Town and has a Conference winners medal to his name whilst with Kidderminster.

HAFNER, STEVE — Midfielder

Current Club: Folkestone Invicta

D o B: 24/08/1983   *Birthplace: Kent*

Steve joined Folkestone Invicta in the summer of 2002 from Kent neighbours Margate, for whom he played in the Nationwide Conference. Full of running, Steve started his career as a youth team player at Gillingham.

HAGAN, DAVID — Defender

Current Club: Consett

Birthplace: Middlesbrough

Previous clubs include: Dunston Federation Brewery - July 1999 Consett, Winlaton Hallgarth, Middlesbrough.

HAGER-HAMMOND, LOUIS — Forward

Current Club: Pagham

Birthplace: Sussex

Teenager: scored twice on his debut during the 3-2 defeat of Ringmer in November 2001.

HAIGH, RYAN — Forward

Current Club: Garforth Town

D o B: 05/02/1979   *Birthplace: Yorkshire*

After an excellent season in the Reserves, Ryan has been rewarded with promotion to the 1st team squad. This tricky winger loves to take players on. One of the most gifted players with the ball at his feet at the club.

HAINES, DANNY — Defender

Current Club: Tiverton Town

Birthplace: Bristol

Previous clubs include: Merthyr Tydfil - May 2002, Clevedon T, Evesham Utd, Cheltenham T, Bristol C.

HAINES, PAUL — Goalkeeper

Current Club: Hungerford Town

Birthplace: Wiltshire

Previous clubs include: Swindon Supermarine - August 2002, Melksham T.

HAINSWORTH, LEE — Midfielder

Current Club: Shildon

Birthplace: Co.Durham

Previous clubs include: Billingham T - October 1998, Billingham Synthonia.

HAKKI, VELI — Midfielder

Current Club: Slough Town

Birthplace: London

Signed for a £1,000 fee from Dulwich Hamlet and few would argue that he is Steve Brownes best signing to date. Since signing for the Rebels Veli has proved what a capable young player he is. He has constantly been the best player in a Slough shirt in many matches this season and at 22 and with Velis ability and talent, it will surely not be too long until league clubs come

sniffing round the popular midfielder. Before joining Slough Hakki was best remembered as one of the Dulwich players which played in the two sides 2-2 draw at Champion Hill last season - a game which both Rebels fans and Dulwich fans will never forget. One of Velis plus points is that he never gives up. He is strong in the tackle, and although sometimes he can be a little over-eager he is one of those players who gives 100% commitment every game. While at Dulwich Veli made over 100 appearances. At Slough he has now settled into a right-sided midfield role which he has fitted into very well, but is also equally capable, or if not better in a more central role in the midfield.

HALE, JOHN — Midfielder

Current Club: Tow Law Town

Birthplace: Co.Durham

Previous clubs include: Morpeth T - July 2001.

HALE, MATTHEW — Defender

Current Club: Mangotsfield United

D o B: 02/02/1979   *Birthplace: Bristol*

Matthew signed for Dr Martens Western side Mangotsfield United in July 2002 from Premier Division Weymouth - representing quite a coup for the Bristol based club. He had rejoined Weymouth in August 2000 after a short spell with Yeovil Town in the Conference. Before that, he was with Bristol City. He is a diminutive player who always gives 100% for the side and has a great role on the left side of the field.

HALE, STEVE — Forward

Current Club: Slough Town

Birthplace: Middlesex

Prolific and much-travelled goalscorer who joined Slough Town in May 2002 from Hayes. Had joined the Missioners in February 2002 from Northwood in an attempt to help them stay in the Conference. Originally with Uxbridge, Steve has had spells with Egham Town, Chalfont St Peter, Ruislip Manor, Brook House, Tring Town and Beaconsfield SYCOB.

HALES, LEIGH — Forward

Current Club: Sittingbourne

D o B: 01/05/1981   *Birthplace: Gillingham*

Previous clubs include: Dover Ath - September 2001, Charlton Ath.

HALFORD, JOHN — Midfielder

Current Club: Stratford Town

Birthplace: Birmingham

Previous clubs include: Rugby Utd - August 2001, Bedworth Utd, Racing Club Warwick, Tamworth, Weymouth, VS Rugby, Hinckley Ath., Birmingham C.

HALFORD, STEVE — Defender

Current Club: Accrington Stanley

D o B: 21/09/1980   *Birthplace: Bury*

Previous clubs include: Chester C - January 2002, Bury.

HALL, ANDY — Goalkeeper

Current Club: Enfield Town (Essex)

Birthplace: Enfield

A product of the Enfield FC reserve and Youth team set-up. Graduated to the Es first team, making 42 appearances, before joining Barking. One of the first players to join Enfield Town during the formative months of the clubs existence.

HALL, ANTHONY   *Defender*
Current Club: Barrow
Birthplace: Middlesbrough
Born on Billingham, Tony is a well-travelled defender who began his career as a junior with Middlesborough before joining Northern League Billingham Town. He moved, briefly to Tranmere Rovers and made a single League appearance for them before returning to the north east and joining Hartlepool United. He made a single League appearance for them, also before heading north of the border and joining East Fife in the Scottish League. He first joined Gateshead in late 1990 and featured for the Tynesiders in the Conference. He returned for a spell with East Fife before having two seasons with Berwick Rangers. He moved to Ireland and featured for Ballymena United for a season before moving into the League of Ireland featuring for Waterford United after which he joined Kilkenny City. He returned to Gateshead and went on to complete over 150 first team appearances for them. He joined Barrow in December 2000 and made his debut on Boxing Day in the draw at Lancaster City.

HALL, BEN   *Forward*
Current Club: Peterlee Newtown
Birthplace: Hartlepool
Previous clubs include: Hartlepool Utd - July 2001.

HALL, CHRIS   *Defender*
Current Club: Bognor Regis Town
Birthplace: Surrey
Signed for Ryman Division One South side Bognor Regis Town during the close season of 2002 from rivals Leatherhead. He was previously with Conference outfit Woking A very promising young defender.

HALL, DANNY   *Defender*
Current Club: Rugby United
D o B: 29/12/1981   *Birthplace: Rugby*
Honours won: England Schoolboy Int.
Signed for Rugby United in August 2001 after spending five years with Coventry City where he was a regular in the reserve side at Highfield Road. Having played for England at Schoolboy level, Danny has a very good football brain and is an excellent passer of the ball who is capable of filling a defensive or midfield role.

HALL, DEREK   *Forward*
Current Club: Solihull Borough
Birthplace: Birmingham
Signed in the summer of 2001 from Moor Green. Derek finished top goalscorer for them in the last two seasons including last season in the Premier Division. Finishing with 57 goals in the Moor Green promotion year of 1999/2000. He previously played for Highgate United.

HALL, DEREK   *Midfielder*
Current Club: Curzon Ashton
D o B: 05/01/1965   *Birthplace: Manchester*
Previous clubs include: Woodley Sports - July 2000, Curzon Ashton, Stalybridge Celtic, Buxton, Hyde Utd, Rochdale, Hereford Utd, Halifax T, Southend Utd, Swindon T, Torquay Utd, Coventry C.

HALL, DREW   *Midfielder*
Current Club: Sheffield FC
Birthplace: Birmingham
Previous clubs include: Solihull Borough - January 2002.

HALL, GARETH   *Defender*
Current Club: Havant & Waterlooville
D o B: 20/03/1969   *Birthplace: Croydon*
Honours won: England Schoolboy & Wales u-21 & Full Int.
Gareth arrived at Havant & Waterloville two games into the 2001/02 season to provide extra support in our defensive line. His extensive League football history is sure to bring considerable experience. Gareth started his career as an apprentice at Chelsea in 1986. During a ten-year life with the club he made 172 appearances in all. He moved to Sunderland in January 1996 for £300,000 where he made a further 54 appearances up to the end of the 97/98 season. Signing for Swindon in May 1998 he played 97 games for them over three seasons before retiring at the age of 32 from full time football to the Non-League.

HALL, GARETH   *Midfielder*
Current Club: Atherton Laburnum Rovers
Birthplace: Bolton
Although principally a reserve team player, Jasper has made a handful of appearances for the first team. He is a tall, quick-footed player who is also useful in both defence and attack. Besides football, he enjoys most other sports.

HALL, GRAEME   *Defender*
Current Club: Enfield Town (Essex)
Birthplace: Herts
Made his debut in December 2001 against Burnham Ramblers. Previously with Barnet and before that a YTS trainee at Arsenal under Pat Rice. Spotted playing Sunday football by an Enfield Town supporter and recommended to manager Jim Chandler.

HALL, JAMES   *Defender*
Current Club: Epsom And Ewell
Birthplace: Surrey
Joined Epsom at the start of 1998-99 from local side Croygas, was immediately named in the first team at centre half, and has never looked back. Recently made his 100th 1st XI appearance and had reserve team games for Reading last season. Player of the Year in 1998-99 & 1999-2000 who has the potential to play at a higher level.

HALL, JEFF   *Defender*
Current Club: Tow Law Town
Birthplace: Co.Durham
Part of the 97/98 squad which went to Wembley in the FA Vase. Joined Crook from local football before joining the Lawyers during the Vase season and then returned to Crook. Rejoined the Lawyers last season. Always noted as a fullback but currently playing well as a sweeper.

HALL, JESSE   *Midfielder*
Current Club: Yeading
Birthplace: London
Moved to the club near the end of pre-season 2001 and put in some impressive performances, teasing defenders down the left. Previous clubs include Harrow Borough, Southall, Hendon, Aldershot Town, Hampton and Wembley.

HALL, KIERON   *Defender*
Current Club: Bashley
From Youth team.

HALL, LEIGH   *Midfielder*
Current Club: Cinderford Town
D o B: 10/06/1975   *Birthplace: Hereford*
Signed for Cinderford Town from Newport County at the start of the 2001/02 season. Leigh can play in defence or midfield and gained some League experience with Hereford United and has also played for Worcester City and Ross Town.

HALL, LEON   *Forward*
Current Club: Enfield
Previous clubs include: Cheshunt - February 2001, Slough T, Colchester Utd.

HALL, LYNDON   *Defender*
Current Club: Nantwich Town
Birthplace: Stoke
Previous clubs include: Newcastle T - July 2001, Kidsgrove Ath., Nantwich T, Newcastle T.

HALL, MARK   *Midfielder*
Current Club: Chalfont St.Peter
Birthplace: Hertfordshire
Previous clubs include: Flackwell Heath - September 2001, Hemel Hempstead, Tring T.

HALL, MARTIN   *Goalkeeper*
Current Club: Bishop Auckland
Birthplace: Bishop Auckland
Signed for Bishop Auckland from Northern League neighbours West Auckland Town as cover in October 2000, making his debut against Worksop Town and filling in on a number of occasions towards the end of that season.

HALL, MARVIN   *Defender*
Current Club: Wembley
Birthplace: London
Previous clubs include: Edgware T - Jan 2002, Wealdstone, Harrow B.

HALL, MATTY   *Midfielder*
Current Club: Redditch United
Birthplace: Birmingham
A pacy right winger, Matty was originally an apprentice with Rotherham United he was released by The Millers at the end of the 1999/00 season and agreed terms with Western Division Redditch United. Snapped up by Brendan Phillips for Halesowen Town in the summer of 2001 but he spent the latter part of the 2001/02 season on-loan back at Redditch, whom he returned to on a permanent basis in May 2002.

HALL, NEIL   *Midfielder*
Current Club: Droylsden
D o B: 12/05/1972   Birthplace: Manchester
Previous clubs include: Hyde Utd - December 2001, Droylsden, Flixton, Witton Alb., Winsford Utd.

HALL, ROBERT   *Goalkeeper*
Current Club: Banstead Athletic
Birthplace: Surrey
Previous clubs include: Epsom & Ewell - November 2001, Leatherhead, Banstead Ath., Connahs Quay Nomads, Croydon Ath.

HALL, RUDI   *Midfielder*
Current Club: Enfield Town (Essex)
Birthplace: London
Signed in January 2002. Started his career in the West Ham youth set-up before joining Enfield, where he made several reserve and youth team appearances. Joined Hitchin Town, where he graduated to the first team, and then Hertford Town before the switch to East Thurrock United, from where he joined Enfield Town.

HALL, WAYNE   *Defender*
Current Club: Gainsborough Trinity
D o B: 25/10/1968   Birthplace: Rotherham
Previous clubs include: York C - August 2001, Hatfield Main, Darlington.

HALLAM, MARK   *Forward*
Current Club: Tamworth
D o B: 29/08/1967   Birthplace: Leicester
A prolific goalscorer, Mark won several Non-League awards for the 2000/01 season after becoming the leading scorer in the Dr Martens Premier Division. He was made Players' Player of the Year and was also joint Player of the Year in the local press. He signed for Tamworth in December 1998 from Forest Green Rovers. He began his career with Leicester United and has also played for Boston United, Ilkeston Town, Hednesford Town, Gloucester City and Worcester City.

HALLCRO, WAYNE   *Midfielder*
Current Club: Grantham Town
Birthplace: Peterborough
Previous clubs include: Kings Lynn - October 1999, Dunkirk, Grantham T, Dunkirk, Stamford, Cotgrave, Northampton T (Trainee).

HALLE, RICHARD   *Defender*
Current Club: Heybridge Swifts
D o B: 12/01/1982   Birthplace: Rochford
Young local Essex defender, who was previously with Southend United and Barking. Signed for Heybridge Swifts in July 2002 after spending the 2001/02 campaign with fellow Ryman Premier side Grays Athletic.

HALLET, PAUL   *Midfielder*
Current Club: Ashford Town
D o B: 08/10/1982
Previous clubs include: Greenwich Borough - August 2001, Fisher Ath., Cambridge Utd (Junior).

HALLETT, DANNY   *Defender*
Current Club: Mangotsfield United
Birthplace: Bristol
Signed from Cadbury Heath during the summer of 1999 although he had played for Mangotsfield the previous season. Tough-tackling defender who likes to get forward whenever possible, and is dangerous with his long range attempts at goal. Previously with Bristol Rovers.

HALLETT, WES   *Goalkeeper*
Current Club: Pagham
Birthplace: Sussex
Stocky goalkeeper, who has spent five seasons at the club (previously a youth team player with Bognor, Graduated from the reserves to the first team in 1999: picked up an injury whilst playing cricket towards the end of last season and sidelined again from October 2001 onwards: played for Sussex during the latest season.

HALLIWELL, WILL   *Midfielder*
Current Club: Chippenham Town
Previous clubs include: Southampton - August 2001.

HALLOWS, MARCUS   *Forward*
Current Club: Stalybridge Celtic
D o B: 07/07/1975   Birthplace: Bolton
Highly-rated forward who joined Stalybridge Celtic in June 2002 from Conference club Leigh RMI. Actually started his playing career with Leigh before enjoying a professional career with Stockport and then Irish sides Sligo Rovers and St Patricks Athletic. Rejoined Leigh at the start of the 2001/02 season.

HALLWORTH, JON — Goalkeeper
Current Club: Newport County

D o B: 26/10/1965 *Birthplace: Stockport*
Previous clubs include: Cardiff C - March 2002, Oldham Ath., Ipswich T.

HAMBI, ALEX — Midfielder
Current Club: Edgware Town

Birthplace: London
Previous clubs include: Northwood - September 2001.

HAMBLEY, TIM — Midfielder
Current Club: Havant & Waterlooville

Birthplace: London
Signed for Havant & Waterlooville from rival Southern Division team Fisher Athletic in February 1999, Tim brought a commanding presence to the midfield during the challenge for the championship. A regular goalscorer, Tims accomplishments have been crowned by being selected for the Southern League XI representative squad two seasons in sucession. Tim is the team captain and a member of the elite group of players to have made over 100 league appearances for Havant and Waterlooville.

HAMER, ROB — Midfielder
Current Club: Caersws

D o B: 25/07/1972 *Birthplace: Wales*
From Youth team.

HAMILTON, JIMMY — Midfielder
Current Club: Abingdon Town

Birthplace: Oxfordshire
Previous clubs include: Bicester T - August 2001, Witney T, Carterton T, Marlow, Buckingham T, Thame Utd, Burnham, Oxford C, Thame Utd.

HAMILTON, LEON — Forward
Current Club: Droylsden

Birthplace: Manchester
Previous clubs include: Curzon Ashton - December 2001, Abbey Hey, East Manchester, Reddish WMC, Old Chorltonians.

HAMILTON, PAUL — Defender
Current Club: Holmer Green

Birthplace: Bucks
From Youth team.

HAMLET, ALAN — Defender
Current Club: Northwood

Birthplace: London
Previous clubs include: Uxbridge - December 2001, Boreham Wood, Chertsey T, Boreham Wood, Barnet.

HAMLET, GARETH — Forward
Current Club: Ashton United

Previous clubs include: Emley - July 2000, Barrow, Halifax T.

HAMMATT, BRYAN — Midfielder
Current Club: Hemel Hempstead Town

D o B: 25/01/1973 *Birthplace: London*
Well-travelled attacking midfielder who signed for Hemel Hempstead in July 2002 following a second spell at Wealdstone. Started out at Hertford Town and has also seen service at Boreham Wood, Northwood, Cheshunt, Wembley, Chesham United, Hayes and Slough Town.

HAMMICK, PAUL — Midfielder
Current Club: Leyton Pennant

Birthplace: Essex
Previous clubs include: Waltham Abbey - August 2001.

HAMMOND, ANDY — Forward
Current Club: Denaby United

Birthplace: Yorkshire
Previous clubs include: Buxton - Dec 2000, Armthorpe Welfare, Maltby Main, Goole AFC, Hatfield Main, Stalybridge Celtic, Doncaster R.

HAMMOND, CHRIS — Midfielder
Current Club: Aberystwyth Town

D o B: 18/09/1979 *Birthplace: Atherstone*
Previous clubs include: Racing Club Warwick - July 1999.

HAMMOND, LEE — Midfielder
Current Club: Pagham

Birthplace: Sussex
Attacking midfielder: first-team regular for Pagham until Richie Reynolds took charge midway through 1999/2000: laid off with injury before returning to the side in January 2002.

HAMMOND, MARK — Forward
Current Club: Bromley

D o B: 03/10/1978 *Birthplace: Sidcup*
Former Millwall forward who had spells with Conference club and Welling United and with Dover Athletic before joining Kent Leaguers Cray Wanderers in July 1999. Showed great form in 2001/02 and was snapped up by Ryman League Bromley in June 2002.

HAMMOND, NEIL — Defender
Current Club: Haverhill Rovers

Birthplace: Suffolk
19 year old, former captain of Haverhill Academy. Has had trials with Cambridge United and Colchester United. His second season at the club and is doing well.

HAMMOND, PHIL — Midfielder
Current Club: Haverhill Rovers

Birthplace: Suffolk
Tremendously improved midfielder, previously at Steeple Bumpstead and in his fourth season with Haverhill.

HAMMOND, TIM — Forward
Current Club: Congleton Town

Birthplace: Cheshire
Age 22. Forward. Signed summer 01. Played for local sides Astra Zeneca (Sats) and IAS (Suns). Finished leading goal scorer and Players' Player of the Year for both.

HAMMONDS, JAMIE — Midfielder
Current Club: Cinderford Town

Birthplace: Newport
Left sided player with great ball skills. Signed for League of Wales side Rhayader Town from Newport County during August 2001. Tricky player who has bags of potential who switched to Dr Martens Western outfit Cinderford Town in the summer of 2002.

HAMMONDS, STUART — Defender
Current Club: Bracknell Town

D o B: 25/07/1978 *Birthplace: Nottingham*
Dominant central defender who joined Sutton at the start of the 2000/2001 season from UniBond League side Lincoln United after re-locating to the area. Played in the Northern Counties East

League with Arnold Town previously, and is a rising star at The Non-League Paper. Transferred to Bracknell Town in May 2002.

HAMODU, FLOYD — *Forward*
Current Club: Pagham
Birthplace: Nigeria
Little-known youngster from Nigeria, who featured for Pagham during the early part of 2001/02: evidently highly-rated, and scored four times in five starts (mainly used as a substitute).

HAMPSHIRE, MARK — *Forward*
Current Club: Great Wakering Rovers
Birthplace: Southend
Previous clubs include: Grays Ath - August 1998, Southend Manor, Inter Cardiff, Old Southendians.

HAMPTON, PAUL — *Goalkeeper*
Current Club: Stourbridge
Birthplace: Wolverhampton
Previous clubs include: Lye T - June 2002.

HAMS, NEIL — *Midfielder*
Current Club: Walton & Hersham
Birthplace: Surrey
A former Chelsea Youth, Neil joined Walton & Hersham at the end of January from Tooting & Mitcham United after playing in their Division Two championship side last season.

HAMSHER, JOHN — *Defender*
Current Club: Carshalton Athletic
D o B: 14/01/1978   *Birthplace: Lambeth*
John signed for Carshalton Athletic in June 2002 from Stevenage Borough. He had joined Stevenage in January 2001, and made his debut against his former club Rushden and Diamonds. He made the right back position his own with several hard-working displays and also established himself as a penalty taker of note. Started his career as a trainee at Fulham.

HANBY, ROB — *Defender*
Current Club: Goole AFC
D o B: 24/12/1974   *Birthplace: Pontefract*
Talented defender who was on the books at Barnsley as a trainee before moving to Scarborough. Joined Gainsborough Trinity and became renowned as being amongst the best in his position in the UniBond League. Injuries affected his progress and he eventually moved to Frickley Athletic in September 1999. Switched to Northern Counties East League side Goole AFC in May 2002.

HANCOCK, ADAM — *Forward*
Current Club: Stamford
Birthplace: Northampton
Previous clubs include: Bedford T - Aug 2001, Rushden & Diamonds.

HANCOCK, DAVE — *Midfielder*
Current Club: Biddulph Victoria
Birthplace: Stoke
From Youth team.

HANCOCK, MARK — *Defender*
Current Club: Frickley Athletic
Birthplace: Yorkshire
Very experienced, competitive defender who re-signed for UniBond Premier side Frickley Athletic in the summer of 2002 as player/assistant-manager after a four-year spell with Bradford Park Avenue. Had joined Bradford Park Avenue from Frickley in July 1999. Had been with Frickley for the previous twelve seasons

after serving local sides Wharncliffe Arms and Grimethorpe Miners Welfare, and has represented the UniBond League.

HAND, STEVE — *Forward*
Current Club: Beaconsfield SYCOB
Birthplace: Berkshire
Previous clubs include: Edgware T - July 2001, Tottenham Hotspur (Junior).

HANDBURY, LEE — *Defender*
Current Club: Matlock Town
Birthplace: Sheffield
Lee is a highly-rated defender who started his career with Rotherham United, where he progressed through from schoolboy to YTS forms. Upon his release in October 1994 he joined UniBond side Matlock Town and spent six years at The Causeway before switching to Belper Town in the summer of 2000. Returned to Matlock in August 2002.

HANDS, STEVE — *Midfielder*
Current Club: Studley
Birthplace: Worcestershire
Previous clubs include: Evesham Utd - July 2000, Pershore T, Feckenham.

HANFORD, CRAIG — *Defender*
Current Club: Port Talbot Town
Birthplace: Neath
From Youth team.

HANMER, GARETH — *Defender*
Current Club: Telford United
D o B: 12/10/1973   *Birthplace: Shrewsbury*
A free transfer from local rivals Shrewsbury Town, Gareth began his playing career with Jake King at Newtown. He later moved to first division West Bromwich Albion where he enjoyed a successful four year spell, commanding a regular place in the first team. Subject to a successful £10,000 bid from Shrewsbury, he moved to rejoin his former manager at the Gay Meadow before following Jake once again to Telford having fallen out of favour with current Shrews manager Kevin Ratcliffe. A pacy left wing-back who can cross the ball well and also operate admirably in defence.

HANN, MATTHEW — *Forward*
Current Club: Dorchester Town
D o B: 06/09/1980   *Birthplace: Saffron Walden*
A very talented wide attacker, Matt signed for Dr Martens Eastern side Dorchester Town from Premier Division Cambridge City in August 2002 after moving to the area to study. Had joined Cambridge during February 2001 from Peterborough United after a successful loan spell at the club. He made around a dozen first-team appearances for the Posh after joining them from Cambridge United at the age of 17.

HANNA, FADI — *Midfielder*
Current Club: Trafford
Birthplace: Liverpool
Very experienced midfield player who joined UniBond First Division side Trafford in August 2002. Previous clubs include Vauxhall Motors, Witton Albion and Cammell Laird.

HANNIGAN, AL-JAMES — *Defender*
Current Club: Bishops Stortford
D o B: 26/01/1971   *Birthplace: London*
Honours won: Northern Ireland B int., Dr Martens League

Premier Div.Winners
Signed from Dulwich Hamlet at the end of 2001, Al is a vastly experienced player and former Arsenal Junior. Previous clubs include Barnet, Harwich & Parkeston, Harlow Town, Marlow and Enfield. From there, Rushden & Diamonds paid £5,000 for his services. Spells afterwards with Enfield, Yeovil and Stevenage Borough.

HANNIVER, MATT — Midfielder
Current Club: Histon
Birthplace: Cambridge
Previous clubs include: Cambridge Utd - March 2001.

HANNON, STUART — Forward
Current Club: VCD Athletic
D o B: 09/11/1981 — Birthplace: London
From Youth team.

HANOVER, JACQUES — Defender
Current Club: Wingate And Finchley
D o B: 12/04/1981 — Birthplace: London
Previous clubs include: Heath Park - July 2000, Hendon, Colchester Utd (Junior), Ipswich T (Junior).

HANSEN, PETER — Midfielder
Current Club: Ramsgate
Birthplace: Kent
Previous clubs include: Margate - July 1996, Ramsgate, Herne Bay, Ramsgate.

HANSON, JON — Forward
Current Club: Rushall Olympic
Birthplace: Birmingham
Previous clubs include: Boldmere St.Michaels - August 2001, Pelsall Villa, Bridgnorth T, Bilston T, Armitage, Chasetown, Tamworth, Stourbridge, Tamworth, Kidderminster Harriers, WBA, Stoke C (Trainee).

HANSON, LEE — Midfielder
Current Club: Three Bridges
Birthplace: Sussex
Transferred from Crawley Down to Three Bridges during the 2000 close season: last terms club player of the year.

HANSON, NEIL — Defender
Current Club: Burscough
Birthplace: Liverpool
Now in his seventh season at UniBond Premier side Burscough, where he has made over 350 appearances. A solid and reliable defender, he signed iin July 1995 from Bootle and also had spells with Formby and Marine.

HAPGOOD, LEON — Midfielder
Current Club: Taunton Town
D o B: 07/08/1979 — Birthplace: Torbay
Honours won: FA Vase Winners
Previous clubs include: Merthyr Tydfil - March 2002, Taunton T, Yeovil T, Plymouth Argyle, Torquay Utd.

HARAN, MARK — Defender
Current Club: Kettering Town
D o B: 21/01/1977 — Birthplace: Rotherham
Signed for the Conference side Kettering Town in July 2002 after a successful pre-season trial period. Joined Hednesford Town during the pre-season of 2000-2001 from Emley, but the powerful, highly-rated central defender couldnt prevent the Pitmen losing their Conference status, although he was voted as

the Players' Player of the Season for 2000/01. Previously with Rotherham and Eastwood Town.

HARBOTTLE, DAVE — Midfielder
Current Club: Barwell
Birthplace: Nottingham
Previous clubs include: Gedling T - June 2002, Stamford, Grantham T, Lincoln Utd, Ilkeston T, Gedling T, Sutton T, Dunkirk, Notts Co, Scarborough.

HARBOTTLE, MARK — Midfielder
Current Club: Barwell
D o B: 29/06/1968 — Birthplace: Nottingham
Honours won: England Youth Int.
Previous clubs include: Hucknall T - January 2002, Shepshed Dynamo, Grantham T, Kings Lynn, Hinckley Utd, Stamford, Grantham T, Tamworth, Ilkeston T, Tamworth, Ilkeston T, Leicester Utd, Shepshed Dynamo, Ilkeston T, Burton Alb., Shepshed Alb., Ilkeston T, Burton Alb., Shepshed Charter.

HARBUT, ROBBIE — Midfielder
Current Club: Salisbury City
Birthplace: Hampshire
Rejoined the club in the close season. Originally signed from Bashley in June 1995. Talented player with a good goalscoring record from a midfield berth. After recovering from a long-term injury, left the club in January 2001, regaining his fitness during short spells with Bashley and Poole Town.

HARDCASTLE, JOHN — Midfielder
Current Club: Great Yarmouth Town
D o B: 04/05/1968 — Birthplace: Yarmouth
Experienced midfield campaigner with Yarmouth and a mainstay of the Reserves in recent seasons.

HARDING, ALEX — Forward
Current Club: Chertsey Town
Birthplace: Surrey
Previous clubs include: Banstead Ath - December 2001, Southall, Dorking, Leatherhead.

HARDING, DAVID — Defender
Current Club: Paget Rangers
D o B: 14/01/1981 — Birthplace: Birmingham
University student who is only available outside of term dates. Previously with Aston Villa as a YT and after leaving the professional game he joined Tamworth. Linked up with Paget in the close season and started the season as a regular fixture.

HARDING, DEAN — Defender
Current Club: Arlesey Town
Birthplace: London
Honours won: Ryman League Div.3 Winners
Dean is a zippy player whos abilities at wing back have earned him many man of the match awards. Absolutely tireless and gives everything, runs well with the ball and can cross with awsome accuracy. Started his career at Tottenham and then had spells with Ware and Hemel Hempstead before joining Arlesey Town in October 2000. Is a Payroll Clerk.

HARDING, DEAN — Midfielder
Current Club: Romford
Birthplace: Essex
Previous clubs include: Southend Utd (Junior) - July 2001.

HARDING, JOEL — Goalkeeper

Current Club: Hassocks

Birthplace: Sussex

Teenage goalkeeper: son of the late Chelsea vice-chairman Matthew Harding: first-team regular from August 2001 onwards following the retirement of Paul John: selected for the Sussex U-21 side during 2001/02.

HARDING, PAT — Forward

Current Club: Hassocks

Birthplace: Sussex

Twin brother of the goalkeeper: incredibly scored all five goals for Sussex in their FA County Youth Cup victory over Hertfordshire during September 2001, including a hat-trick within seven minutes: predominantly plays for the Hassocks U-18 side, but has also made some first-team appearances and is clearly an outstanding prospect.

HARDING, RICKY — Midfielder

Current Club: Edgware Town

Birthplace: Stevenage

Previous clubs include: Hoddesdon T - August 2001, Stevenage B.

HARDINGHAM, MARK — Goalkeeper

Current Club: Tilbury

Birthplace: Essex

Previous clubs include: Bowers Utd - September 1999, Brentwood.

HARDMAN, LUKE — Midfielder

Current Club: Atherton Laburnum Rovers

Birthplace: Radcliffe

Luke joined LR in February 2001, having previously been with Ramsbottom United and Atherton Collieries. He is a tireless worker in midfield and always gives his all for the team. Young and accomplished, Luke has all the makings of a superb player. He works as a lab technician and enjoys clubbing.

HARDY, ANDY — Midfielder

Current Club: Goole AFC

Birthplace: Yorkshire

Previous clubs include: Pontefract Collieries - January 2002.

HARDY, DAVID — Forward

Current Club: Ilkeston Town

Birthplace: Nottingham

David is a strong, quick and powerfull striker who is reckoned to be a real asset to the club. A number of scouts have been watching his progress.

HARDY, NEIL — Midfielder

Current Club: Radcliffe Borough

D o B: 03/12/1977 — Birthplace: Bury

Goalscoring midfielder who returned to UniBond First Division Radcliffe Borough in July 2002 after a season in Division One with Stockport County. Had cost County a £15,000 fee but made only a dozen or so League appearances during a troubled campaign at Edgeley Park. Started out at Bolton and Crewe and then played Conference football with Nortwhich Victoria, Altrincham and Morecambe before joining Boro for the first time in July 2000.

HARDY, STUART — Defender

Current Club: Horsham

Birthplace: Sussex

Full-back and captain: scored 9 times for East Grinstead during the first half of 2000/01, having joined them from Lingfield in the summer of 1999: signing for Horsham in January 2001: one of four players (two from each side) to receive a red card in the FA Cup victory over Tonbridge Angels during September 2001.

HARE, EDDIE — Midfielder

Current Club: Rhayader Town

D o B: 19/07/1981 — Birthplace: Rhayader

Local lad starting his third season at the club. Strong player with a good engine. Looking to prove his ability this season. Current reserve team player of the yea.

HARE, MATTHEW — Defender

Current Club: Bideford

D o B: 26/12/1976 — Birthplace: Barnstaple

Matt rejoined us in the summer from Weymouth Town; he is a strong Central defender, who has also been on the books of Exeter City and Sligo Rovers.

HARE, RUDI — Defender

Current Club: Norwich United

D o B: 10/10/1978 — Birthplace: Norfolk

Currently the longest serving player at Norwich United. Former Stockport County trainee having his best season so far.

HAREWOOD, JERMAINE — Defender

Current Club: Ipswich Wanderers

Birthplace: Ipswich

From Youth team.

HAREWOOD, MARK — Defender

Current Club: Wembley

Birthplace: Berkshire

Previous clubs include: Bracknell T - July 1999, Egham T, Maidenhead Utd.

HAREWOOD, WINSTON — Forward

Current Club: Ipswich Wanderers

Birthplace: Ipswich

From Youth team.

HARFORD, PAUL — Midfielder

Current Club: Bracknell Town

Birthplace: Lancashire

Son of former Blackburn boss Ray Harford, Paul is a talented midfielder who joined Bracknell Town from Ryman Premier Division side Aldershot Town in May 2002. Started his career with his dad at Blackburn and then played in the Conference with Farnborough Town and Welling United. Arrived at Aldershot for a £4,000 fee from Sutton United in May 2001.

HARGREAVES, ANTHONY — Forward

Current Club: Hyde United

Birthplace: Manchester

Signed by UniBond Premier side Hyde United in August 2002 from relegated Bamber Bridge. He is a young striker who can also play in midfield. Was formerly with Altrincham and Maine Road.

HARGREAVES, DANNY   *Midfielder*
Current Club: *Lincoln United*
Birthplace: Lincoln
One of the fans favourites as his pace can create the openings to turn matches around. Joined Lincoln United from local junior football.

HARKIN, MAURICE   *Forward*
Current Club: *Crawley Town*
D o B: 16/08/1979   *Birthplace: Derry*
Honours won: Northern Ireland Youth & u-21 Int.
Talented former Northern Ireland Youth and under-21 international forward who joined Crawley Town in June 2002 from Conference club Nuneaton Borough. Derry-born, Maurice joined Wycombe Wanderers and made a number of League appearances for the Chairboys and then Carlisle United before signing for Aldershot Town during the early part of the 2001/02 season. Switched to Nuneaton in January 2002 before moving back south to Crawley.

HARKNESS, PAUL   *Forward*
Current Club: *Walton & Hersham*
Birthplace: Surrey
Paul is a quick, left-sided player who has returned to Stompond Lane this season after leaving in 1999 for spells with Camberley Town, Basingstoke Town, Leatherhead and North Shore United in New Zealand. Originally made his Swans debut in April 1999 after joining from Camberley.

HARKNESS, STEVE   *Defender*
Current Club: *Chester City*
D o B: 27/08/1971   *Birthplace: Carlisle*
Honours won: England Youth Int.
Former England Youth international defender with bags of experience at the highest level. Joined Conference club Chester City in July 2002 following an injury-hit two years at Sheffield Wednesday. Started his career with his home-town club Carlisle and made only 13 appearances before being signed by Liverpool for £75,000 in 1989. Played over 100 games for the Reds, many alongside his new boss Mark Wright, before joining another former Liverpool legend, Graeme Souness at Portugese giants Benfica for £750,000 in 1999. A short spell at Blackburn followed before he signed for Wednesday in September 2000.

HARLOW, DAVID   *Midfielder*
Current Club: *Crawley Town*
D o B: 02/11/1967   *Birthplace: London*
Honours won: England Semi-Pro Int.
Attacking midfielder: prolific goalscorer for many seasons, having spent six years with Kingstonian before joining Farnborough: signed for Crawley from Sutton United during the 2001 close season: appeared for the Southern League representative side in November 2001.

HARMISON, JAMES   *Defender*
Current Club: *Bedlington Terriers*
Birthplace: Ashington
James was signed from Ashington towards the end of the 1999/2000 season and immediately impressed with his mature displays in the right back position despite his young age. Member of the famous Harmison sporting family. Brother Steve is making a name for himself in cricketing circles with Durham and England and father James is a well known former Northern League player. Can also fill in at centre half where many a pundit believes he will eventually end up on a regular basis. James also had a trial with Fulham at the end of last season and is also attracting interest from other league clubs.

HARNETT, PAUL   *Defender*
Current Club: *Bishop Auckland*
Birthplace: Co.Durham
Previous clubs include: West Auckland T - January 2002, Crook T.

HARNEY, MICHAEL   *Defender*
Current Club: *Bromley*
Birthplace: Kent
First joined Bromley in the summer of 1998 when Bromley went top of the Ryman Premier Division. A long-term injury restricted appearances before he joined Welling United one year later. He was relegated with both teams. Was a regular in their Conference side before rejoining Bromley last December on loan. Made the return permanent in March 2001. His father Dave, also played for Bromley.

HARPER, GRAHAM   *Midfielder*
Current Club: *Lewes*
Birthplace: London
A hard-working right-sided midfield player who joined Ryman Division One South side Lewes from rivals Croydon in August 2002. Had been with Croydon since the summer of 1999 when arriving from neighbouring Croydon Athletic. A former Portsmouth junior, Graham is a good crosser of the ball, and also scores goals. Made over 150 appearance for Croydon, and has also played for Carshalton Athletic.

HARPER, LEE   *Defender*
Current Club: *Bridlington Town*
Birthplace: Yorkshire
Club Captain Lee led by example last year and got amongst the goals. Inspires the side with regular outstanding displays. Former Scarborough and North Ferriby player who scooped the awards at last Mays presentation evening.

HARPER, MARTIN   *Forward*
Current Club: *Hamble ASSC*
Birthplace: Hampshire
Previous clubs include: Gosport Borough - July 2001.

HARPER, STEVE   *Forward*
Current Club: *Burgess Hill Town*
Birthplace: Sussex
Forward: joined Burgess Hill from Tonbridge Angels in March 2001: didnt look particularly special, despite scoring three times in a handful of appearances that season: vastly improved, and set his stall out by claiming a goal in the opening minute of the first match of the current campaign (Hillians 2-1 defeat at the hands of Sidley in the Norman Wingate Trophy): also chosen for the Sussex U-21 squad this year.

HARRIMAN, LEE   *Midfielder*
Current Club: *Coalville Town*
Birthplace: Leicester
Honours won: Leicestershire Senior League Winners
Previous clubs include: Thringstone - June 2001, Highfield R, Gresley R, VS Rugby, Corby T, Shepshed Dynamo, Hinckley Ath., Corby T, Barwell, Atherstone Utd, Hinckley T, Grantham T, VS Rugby, Hinckley T, Houghton R, Hinckley Ath., Highfield R, Lutterworth T.

HARRINGTON, MARK   *Midfielder*
Current Club: *Chippenham Town*
Birthplace: Bristol
Signed for Chippenham Town in July 2001 from Bath City where he spent the previous six years. An experienced midfielder with a great deal of talent, he started his career as a trainee with Bristol Rovers and also had a spell at Paulton Rovers prior to joining Bath.

HARRINGTON, SHAUN — Midfielder
Current Club: Histon
Birthplace: Cambridge
Previous clubs include: Cambridge C - July 1996, Newmarket T, Eynesbury R, Cambridge C, Cambridge Utd.

HARRIS, ADIE — Defender
Current Club: Gloucester City
Birthplace: Wales
An experienced left-sided forward with extensive Dr Martens League experience following spells with Gloucester City and Trowbridge Town. Made over 250 appearances for Trowbridge and re-joined Cinderford in July 1998 and passed the 250 game-mark before switching back to Gloucester in July 2002.

HARRIS, ADRIAN — Forward
Current Club: Llanelli AFC
D o B: 21/02/1982   Birthplace: Wales
Previous clubs include: Merthyr Tydfil - March 2001, Cardiff C.

HARRIS, ANDY — Forward
Current Club: Dorchester Town
D o B: 18/01/1974   Birthplace: Weymouth
Previous clubs include: Weymouth - September 1996, Bridport, Dorchester T, Bridport.

HARRIS, BOBBY — Goalkeeper
Current Club: Accrington Stanley
Birthplace: Lancashire
Young goalkeeper signed for Accrington Stanley from Padiham at the start of the 2000-2001 season. Plays for the Reserves most weeks but has covered for Jamie Speare when the regular goalkeeper has not been available for selection.

HARRIS, CARL — Defender
Current Club: Eastbourne United
Birthplace: Sussex
Left-back who has come through Eastbourne United's youth ranks and developed into a first-team regular during 1999/2000. Former Sussex under-18 squad member.

HARRIS, CRAIG — Midfielder
Current Club: Bilston Town
Previous clubs include: Rushall Olympic - August 2001, Oldbury Utd, Willenhall T, Oldbury Utd.

HARRIS, DANNY — Defender
Current Club: Barnstaple Town
D o B: 18/12/1979   Birthplace: Devon
Previous clubs include: Heavitree Utd - July 2001, Clyst Rovers, Exeter C.

HARRIS, DAVID — Forward
Current Club: Eastbourne United
Birthplace: Eastbourne
Right-winger who is an exciting teenage prospect. Gained a super-sub reputation during 1999/2000 when he struck 11 times and also scored twice for Park College in their 2000/01 Sussex Schools League play-off victory: made a couple of appearances for Langney Sports towards the end of that campaign: played several more times for the re-named Eastbourne Borough side during the latest season as well as being a member of the Sussex under-21 squad.

HARRIS, GILES — Midfielder
Current Club: Chippenham Town
D o B: 13/04/1981   Birthplace: Swindon
A tenacious skilful midfielder, who never stops running. Promoted from the Cirencester Academy, Giles finished as Cirencesters top scorer last season and was their joint highest scorer. Giles also won the Managers Player of the Year for 2000/02. Switched to Weston in January 2002 and then moved on to Chippenham Town in July 2002.

HARRIS, JASON — Forward
Current Club: Nuneaton Borough
D o B: 24/11/1976   Birthplace: Sutton
Jason is a pacy stiker who has made a big impression since joining Conference side Nuneaton Borough in February 2002 from Harrogate Town. Has strength, skill and good agility and is keen to help Boro push for promotion to the Football League. Jason has previously played with Hull City, Crystal Palace, Leyton Orient, Preston North End and Southend United.

HARRIS, JUSTIN — Midfielder
Current Club: Lewes
Birthplace: Sussex
The undisputed hard man of the team, but also an excellent footballer who is an essential part of the midfield. It is amazing how few opposing midfielders come back for more after one 50-50 challenge with him!

HARRIS, MARK — Defender
Current Club: Bromley
D o B: 15/07/1963   Birthplace: Reading
Honours won: FA Trophy Winners
Very experienced player who joined Bromley in October 2001 making his Bromley debut in Stuart McIntyres first game in charge. Has had a long career with several clubs which include Cardiff City, Gillingham, Swansea City, and up until last season was captain of Kingstonian leading them to two FA Trophy Finals. Lives and works in Reading, Berkshire as a Sales Rep for a Tool Hire Company.

HARRIS, MATT — Defender
Current Club: Frome Town
Birthplace: Somerset
Previous clubs include: Street - July 2001.

HARRIS, MATTHEW — Goalkeeper
Current Club: Paget Rangers
D o B: 18/10/1983   Birthplace: Birmingham
Joined the youth team towards the end of last season and quickly established himself as first team keeper. Very agile, brave and quick. Still eligible for youth football, an outstanding prospect. \Member of the Birmingham County FA U18 representative team. Previously with Birmingham City and Kidderminster Harriers where he won Worcester County FA representative honours.

HARRIS, PAUL — Midfielder
Current Club: Newcastle Town
Birthplace: Stoke
Previous clubs include: Stafford Rangers - February 2002, Rocester, Leek T, Crewe Alexandra.

HARRIS, RICHARD — Midfielder
Current Club: Mossley
D o B: 12/07/1967   Birthplace: Mottram
Honours won: UniBond Premier Div. Winners
Previous clubs include: Rossendale Utd - February 2002, Leigh RMI, Altrincham, Hyde Utd, Runcorn, Hyde Utd, Altrincham, Ashton Utd.

HARRIS, RYAN　　　　　　*Defender*

Current Club: Leyton Pennant

Birthplace: Hertfordshire
Previous clubs include: Edgware T - December 2001, Potters Bar T, Cheshunt, Boreham Wood, Cheshunt.

HARRIS, SCOTT　　　　　*Midfielder*

Current Club: Walton & Hersham

Birthplace: Surrey
Scott is a clever, young midfielder who has progressed through Swans youth and reserve sides. Skipper of the Suburban League side last season.

HARRIS, TOMMY　　　　　*Midfielder*

Current Club: Bilston Town

Birthplace: Birmingham
Previous clubs include: Bridgnorth T - December 2001.

HARRISON, ASHLEY　　　*Goalkeeper*

Current Club: Canvey Island

Birthplace: Southend
Honours won: FA Trophy Winners, British Universities Rep.
Promising young goalkeeper who rejoined Canvey Island in July 1999 after a spell with Dover Athletic. Previously played for Southend Manor and Basildon United. He has represented Great Britain Universities and his most memorable matches include playing for Basildon United in the FA Youth Cup against Chelsea winning 3-1 and the 2001 FA Trophy success at Villa Park with Canvey.

HARRISON, GARRY　　　　*Midfielder*

Current Club: Banbury United

D o B: 12/03/1975　　　　Birthplace: Birmingham
Formerly with Raunds Town, this experienced player signed for Banbury at the beginning of the 2000/01 season and proved to be a useful addition to the squad. Has Football League experience with Northampton Town after starting his career at Aston Villa. Suffered with injuries shortly after joining but has still managed a good strike rate.

HARRISON, GAVIN　　　　*Midfielder*

Current Club: Croydon Athletic

Birthplace: London
Previous clubs include: Staines T - August 2000, Sutton Utd, Chelsea (Trainee).

HARRISON, GERRY　　　　*Midfielder*

Current Club: Leigh RMI

D o B: 15/04/1972　　　　Birthplace: Lambeth
Previous clubs include: Prestwich Heys - November 2001, Halifax T, Sunderland, Burnley, Huddersfield T, Bristol C, Watford.

HARRISON, GRANT　　　　*Defender*

Current Club: Eastbourne Borough

Birthplace: Sussex
Honours won: English Universities Rep.
Signed in September 2000 from Eastbourne United (Sussex County League). Previously with Billericay Town (Ryman League) and Hastings Town. Represented England Universities in 2000/01.

HARRISON, JODY　　　　　*Defender*

Current Club: Great Yarmouth Town

D o B: 22/07/1977　　　　Birthplace: Norfolk
Has been with Yarmouth a number of years and played at all levels within the club, though now, mostly in defence for the Reserves.

HARRISON, LEE　　　　　*Goalkeeper*

Current Club: Barnet

D o B: 12/09/1971　　　　Birthplace: Billericay
Ranks amongst the most highly-rated players in the Barnets history, winning the Player of the Year award in three successive years. Rarely puts a foot wrong in goal, his close range shot stopping is second to none. Lost his place in the team to Danny Naisbett after injury but regained his position and is looking to stay as first-choice for the rest of the season. Signed from Fulham in March 1997 and formerly with Charlton.

HARRISON, RICHARD　　　*Midfielder*

Current Club: Bridlington Town

Birthplace: Hull
Richard made his debut last year and performed well. Tasted NCEL action last season and is ready for more. Another Hull based youngster with a bright future.

HARRISON, ROSS　　　　　*Forward*

Current Club: Bedford Town

D o B: 28/12/1979　　　　Birthplace: Leamington Spa
Striker or midfielder who re-joined Ryman League Premier side Bedford Town from Dr Martens Western outfit Bedworth United in July 2002. Ross had signed for Bedworth from Western Division rivals Solihull Borough shortly after the departure of Adam Webster to Worcester City in January 2002. He is a powerful forward who holds the ball up well and can create opportunities. Fierce striker of the ball and he is not afraid to make a tackle. Started his career at Reading and then played Conference football for Stevenage Borough and Ryman football with Bedford Town.

HARRISON, STEVE　　　　*Midfielder*

Current Club: Tilbury

Birthplace: Essex
From Youth team.

HARRISON, STUART　　　　*Midfielder*

Current Club: Sittingbourne

Birthplace: Kent
Previous clubs include: Ashford T - July 1999, Dover Ath., Gillingham.

HARROLD, MATTIE　　　　*Forward*

Current Club: Wingate And Finchley

Birthplace: Essex
Young, pacy forward who joined Ryman League side Wingate & Finchley in August 2002 from Premier Division Grays Athletic. Broke into the Grays first-team after hitting many goals for the reserves in the Capital League during the 2001/02 season.

HARROLD, MATTIE　　　　*Midfielder*

Current Club: Aveley

Birthplace: Leyton
Previous clubs include: Grays Ath - December 2001, Southend Utd.

HART, ADAM — Goalkeeper
Current Club: Erith & Belvedere
Previous clubs include: Billericay T - September 2001, Bishops Stortford, Tilbury, Grays Ath., East Thurrock Utd, Grays Ath., Aldershot T, Lincoln C.

HART, ADAM — Midfielder
Current Club: Rugby United
Birthplace: Leicester
Previous clubs include: Atherstone Utd - February 2002, St.Andrews.

HART, BARRIE — Defender
Current Club: Accrington Stanley
Birthplace: Scotland
The former Clitheroe captain signed a 2-year contract with Accrington Stanley at the start of November 2001. The 24-year-old defender was on Oldham Athletics books after leaving school and had a spell at Radcliffe Borough before joining Clitheroe and the Stanley.

HART, GAVIN — Midfielder
Current Club: Northwood
Previous clubs include: Tring T - August 1999, Ruislip Manor, Wealdstone, Harrow B, Hanwell T, Rayners Lane.

HART, IAN — Midfielder
Current Club: Harrogate Railway
Birthplace: Cheshire
Previous clubs include: Dunnington - July 1999, Harrogate T, Guiseley, Halifax T, Crewe Alexandra, Manchester Utd (Trainee).

HART, IAN — Midfielder
Current Club: Ware
Birthplace: Hertford
Previous clubs include: Yeading - July 1999, Hertford T, Ware, Hertford T.

HART, JAKE — Midfielder
Current Club: Marske United
Birthplace: Middlesbrough
Signed for Albany Northern League side Marske United from Darlington in the summer of 2002. Jake is still only a teenager but is an exciting midfield prospect for the future.

HART, JAMIE — Forward
Current Club: Stourport Swifts
Previous clubs include: Evesham Utd - July 2000, Redditch Utd.

HART, MICHAEL — Midfielder
Current Club: Tilbury
Birthplace: Essex
Previous clubs include: East Thurrock Utd - November 1997.

HART, PAUL — Forward
Current Club: Vauxhall Motors
Birthplace: Liverpool
A diminutive striker with a huge appetite and improving all the time. Joined Vauxhall Motors from Altrincham in September 2000, and the club have high hopes of this youngster.

HARTE, STEWART — Defender
Current Club: Bracknell Town
D o B: 12/12/1977   Birthplace: Basingstoke
Previous clubs include: Staines T - August 2001, Aldershot T, Farnborough T, Bristol R.

HARTIGAN, NATHAN — Midfielder
Current Club: Molesey
Birthplace: Surrey
Previous clubs include: Dorking - March 2002, Banstead Ath.

HARTLE, PAUL — Defender
Current Club: Wroxham
D o B: 22/07/1961   Birthplace: Norfolk
Honours won: FA Vase Winners
Experienced player signed from Gorleston but previously with Diss and Norwich United. Won a Vase medal at Diss.

HARTLEY, STEVE — Defender
Current Club: Harrogate Railway
Birthplace: Harrogate
Previous clubs include: Harrogate T - July 1999.

HARVEY, CHRIS — Goalkeeper
Current Club: Ford United
Birthplace: Essex
Another member of Ford United's successful youth programme. Played at the beginning of the 2001/02 season in the senior side with great success whilst veteran goalkeeper Jimmy Chapman was injured. Laid the foundations for a very successful season all round.

HARVEY, GARY — Defender
Current Club: Harwich & Parkeston
Birthplace: Essex
A Harwich regular for many years and Club Captain, he played in almost every match last season. Brave and totally committed he would command a place in any defence at this level. Club Player of the Year for the past two seasons.

HARVEY, IAIN — Midfielder
Current Club: Bath City
D o B: 05/09/1977   Birthplace: Bristol
One of a number of players in their second spell at Btah City, midfielder Iain first appeared for City during the 1996/97 Conference campaign under the management of Steve Millard. He only made three full starts during that season, spending a spell on loan at Western League Odd Down, where Alan Pridham was in charge, before making the switch to Clevedon Town in the summer of 1997. The former Swindon Town apprentice was soon named captain at the Seasiders and lead the side to promotion to the Dr Martens Premier Division in 1999. However, Clevedons return to the Western Division saw Harvey look to end his four-year spell the Hand Stadium, and when Pridham came in for him he took the opportunity to join up again with his former boss in July 2001.

HARVEY, JUSTIN — Forward
Current Club: Stowmarket Town
Birthplace: Suffolk
Previous clubs include: Walsham-le-Willows - November 1998.

HARVEY, KEVIN — Midfielder
Current Club: Barking & East Ham United
Previous clubs include: East Ham Utd - July 2001.

HARVEY, LEE — Defender
Current Club: Bedford Town
D o B: 21/12/1966   Birthplace: Harlow
Signed for Ryman Premier side Bedford Town in August 2001 from Stevenage Borough. Lee is a very experienced defender who has played at League level. Made over 34 appearances for

Conference side Stevenage Borough in two years and was also at Brentford for over four years, making 130 appearances for the club. Other clubs include Nottingham Forest and Leyton Orient where he started as an apprentice. Lee was voted Players' Player of the year after putting in some very consistent performances during the 2001/02 campaign.

HARVEY, LEE — Defender
Current Club: Boreham Wood
D o B: 03/10/1969   Birthplace: Watford
Lee is a vastly experienced central defender who originally joined Boreham Wood on a temporary transfer during the 1999/00 season, making his debut against Enfield on the 1st April 2000. After a spell on loan at Enfield Lee finally joined Boreham Wood permanently from St. Albans City in November 2000. He has also played for Watford as a junior, Edgware Town, Berkhamsted Town, Chertsey Town, Hemel Hempstead, Aylesbury United, Slough Town, Yeovil Town and Aylesbury United. Lee was appointed captain in November 2001, and later that month, joint caretaker manager with Micky Engwell for the remainder of the 2001/02 season.

HARVEY, NATHAN — Forward
Current Club: Oldbury United
Previous clubs include: Stourport Swifts - October 2001, Moor Green, Sandwell Borough, Causeway Green, Halesowen T.

HARWOOD, DANNY — Goalkeeper
Current Club: Bromley
D o B: 22/06/1979   Birthplace: Kent
Danny signed for Bromley way back in February 1999 from Dr Martens League side Erith & Belvedere. Has also played for Coney Hall and was in the Dulwich Hamlet squad at the age of 16. He has seen many changes at Hayes Lane and has played under Frank Coles, Dave Garland, Alan Seamons and Stuart McIntyre. Danny was voted Player of the Year last season, and is a loyal clubman.

HARWOOD, RUSSELL — Forward
Current Club: Horsham YMCA
Birthplace: Sussex
Emerged through YMs youth team and was a key member of the reserve league-and-cup double winning side of 2000/01: fulfilled his promise when scoring 10 goals in 37 days for the first-team during the autumn 2001.

HASLER, JIMMY — Midfielder
Current Club: Arundel
Birthplace: Sussex
Attacking midfielder: originally with Pagham before enjoying great success at Oving: scored 35 times during their Division Three championship winning year in 1998/99: claimed 19 strikes the following season and scored 14 during 2000/01: signed for Arundel at the start of the current campaign.

HASSALL, JAMES — Goalkeeper
Current Club: Harlow Town
Birthplace: Hertfordshire
Young custodian who first came to the club in October 2000 from Stevenage Borough, having gained Conference experience with Boro. Signed a two year contract with Stevenage during the summer, but has been loaned to Harlow for the current season.

HASSALL, JON — Defender
Current Club: Leek Town
D o B: 15/04/1975   Birthplace: Stoke
Left back who likes to get forward. Jon was a trainee at Bolton Wanderers and has also played for Brighton & Hove Albion. He had a brief spell at Leek Town in 1998, but left to join Witton Albion. Returned via Hinckley United prior to the start of the 2001/02 season.

HASSETT, DAVID — Forward
Current Club: Ashford Town
Birthplace: Kent
Forward who signed for Dr Martens Eastern side Ashford Town from East London team Metro Gas in the summer of 2001. Hard-running and enthusiastic player, he was the Nuts & Bolts leading marksman in the 2001/02 season. Holds the player of the year award.

HASWELL, MICHAEL — Defender
Current Club: Grays Athletic
D o B: 23/08/1983   Birthplace: Whitechapel
Was on Southend United's books he is a powerfull defender with plenty of pace.

HATCH, LIAM — Forward
Current Club: Gravesend & Northfleet
Birthplace: Kent
Honours won: Ryman League Premier Div.Winners
Liam joined Gravesend & Northfleet at the beginning of season 2001/02 from Kent League side Herne Bay where in his first full season he notched 23 goals and was the Leagues top scorer. His goalscoring ability alerted many Kent-based clubs and he chose to join The Fleet. Liam is a real handful for defenders and his all-action style has already made him a firm favourite with the supporters. He broke into the first-team0 on a regular basis during the latter stages of the Fleets Ryman League title-winning season of 2001/02, making a big impact and scoring some crucial goals in the championship race.

HATCH, PAUL — Defender
Current Club: Grays Athletic
D o B: 27/12/1981   Birthplace: Forest Gate
Previous clubs include: Barking - July 2001, Southend Utd, Leyton Orient.

HATCHER, ADRIAN — Defender
Current Club: Tunbridge Wells
Birthplace: Kent
Previous clubs include: Tonbridge Angels - July 1999.

HATCHETT, DAVE — Defender
Current Club: Arlesey Town
Birthplace: London
Honours won: Ryman League Div. 1 & Div.3 Winners
Dave has been the cornerstone of the Arlesey Town's defence and one of manager Nicky Irontons first and best aquisitions in July 2000. Formerly with Enfield and Boreham Wood where he established a record number of appearances. Has numerous medals for the Ryman League Cup, Ryman League Division One and Three winners, London Senior Cup and Herts Senior Cup. Works as a Software Development Manager.

HATELEY, GARY — Goalkeeper
Current Club: Solihull Borough
Birthplace: Coventry
Promising young goalkeeper who joined Solihull Borough in May 2002 following a short spell with Telford United in the

Conference. Started his career with Crystal Palace where he progressed through the ranks to become second choice for a time. Was released during the 2001/02 season and returned to his native Midlands and joined Bedworth United briefly before being snapped up by Telford in March 2002.

HATFIELD, ASA   Forward
Current Club: Liversedge
Birthplace: Yorkshire
Previous clubs include: Ossett Alb - December 2000.

HATHAWAY, JOHN   Midfielder
Current Club: Fairford Town
Birthplace: Wiltshire
From Youth team.

HATHERLEY, ALAN   Defender
Current Club: Ware
Birthplace: Herts
Previous clubs include: Hertford T - September 2000, Ware, St.Albans C, Peterborough Utd (Trainee).

HATCWELL, WAYNE   Defender
Current Club: Chester City
D o B: 08/02/1975   Birthplace: Swindon
Wayne signed for Chester City in May 2002 from Oxford United. He had joined Oxford United for £35,000 from Conference club Forest Green Rovers in December 2000 and after making his League debut from the subs bench at Oldham, he soon established himself as a first-team regular. A big, strong, left-footed defender, he has also apppeared in the colours of Cinderford Town and Witney Town prior to joining Forest Green.

HATTO, GARY   Midfielder
Current Club: Wakefield & Emley
Birthplace: Huddersfield
Signed during the summer of 2000 from Frickley Athletic where he spent several seasons, broken by a spell at Ossett Town. Gary was Frickleys player of the year in 1999 and was their top scorer in 1995-96 despite playing at full-back.

HATTON, BRIAN   Forward
Current Club: Congleton Town
D o B: 12/02/1971   Birthplace: Liverpool
Previous clubs include: Skelmersdale Utd - January 2002, Burscough, St.Helens T, Netherfield, Rhyl, Netherfield, St.Helens T, Stockport Co (Junior).

HATTON, PAUL   Defender
Current Club: Tamworth
D o B: 02/01/1978   Birthplace: Birmingham
Honours won: England u-17 Int.
A quick and calm centre back it came as no surprise when he gained Southern League representative honours during the 2000/01 season. However, his season ended somewhat prematurely after a serious injury at Kings Lynn. Paul was previously with Birmingham City and Hednesford before joining Tamworth in 1998. He has represented England at under-17 level.

HATTON, SIMON   Forward
Current Club: Epsom And Ewell
D o B: 06/02/1980   Birthplace: Kingston
Rejoined Epsom at the start of the season after spells with Croydon Athletic and Leatherhead.

HAUGHTON, WARREN   Forward
Current Club: Havant & Waterlooville
Birthplace: Birmingham
Striker who joined Dr Martens Premier side Havant & Waterlooville from Conference outfit Woking in August 2002. Had signed for Woking in June 2001 from Tamworth and his tricky skills and pace led him to score over 20 goals in his first season at Conference level. He joined Tamworth in November 1997 from Sutton Coldfield having started his career with Leicester City. He has also had spells with Stourbridge, VS Rugby and Stafford Rangers.

HAULE, DAVIS   Forward
Current Club: Harrow Borough
Birthplace: London
Midfielder or striker who joined Ryman Premier side Harrow Borough in February 2002 from rivalsHendon, where he had been a prominent member of the side for 3 seasons. Previously played for Jacksonville Cyclones (USA A-League), Vidir FC (Iceland), Birmingham City, Wembley, Wimbledon and Hemel Hempstead (on-loan).

HAUXWELL, BRIAN   Midfielder
Current Club: Arundel
Birthplace: Sussex
Honours won: England Schoolboy Int.
Midfielder: former English U-16 and U-18 Schools International (some 12 years ago), who once scored a goal at Wembley: subsequently spent three years on the books of Bradford City: has more recently had spells in the County League with Chichester City, Littlehampton, East Preston and Pagham before joining Arundel during the 1999 close season: missed the opening month of the current campaign through injury.

HAVERMANS, MICKY   Forward
Current Club: Bracknell Town
Birthplace: Berkshire
Previous clubs include: Egham T - July 1999, Binfield, Bracknell T, Binfield, Cove, Fleet T, Bracknell T, Fleet T, Binfield.

HAWES, STEVE   Midfielder
Current Club: Worksop Town
D o B: 17/07/1978   Birthplace: High Wycombe
Started his career at Sheffield United as a central midfield player, where he made 4 League appearances. Subsequently went initially, on loan and eventually joining Doncaster Rovers where he made another 10 League appearances. On his release he joined Hull City, making a further 19 appearances. Appointed club captain after joining Altrincham in November 1999 before a spell out of the game, Steve then moved to Worksop Town in May 2002.

HAWKE, DAVID   Defender
Current Club: Denaby United
Birthplace: Sheffield
Previous clubs include: Parkgate - July 2001, Maltby Main, Parkgate.

HAWKES, MARC   Forward
Current Club: Biddulph Victoria
D o B: 22/09/1976   Birthplace: Stoke
Previous clubs include: Witton Alb - February 2002, Newcastle T, Winsford Utd, Witton Alb., Leek T, Stalybridge Celtic, Leek T, Stoke C.

HAWKESWORTH, DANNY — Defender
Current Club: Yeading
Birthplace: Middlesex

Twenty-three year old who made his debut for the Ding as a substitute in the opening game of season 2000/2001. Has since proven a mature and competent player playing on either flank and made himself a first team regular. Previous clubs include local rivals, Southall, Uxbridge and Northwood.

HAWKINGS, DARREN — Defender
Current Club: Taunton Town
D o B: 21/04/1975   Birthplace: Barnstaple
Honours won: FA Vase Winners

Played in various roles for Barnstaple Town where, until joining Taunton Town in the summer of 2000, he had been since the age of 11 years. Scored on his debut for Taunton Town and quickly took over the captains role. Is a handful on the ground. A tough-tackling defender who heads the ball well. Played a key role in Tauntons 2000 FA Vase-winning success.

HAWKINS, CHRIS — Midfielder
Current Club: Leek Town
Birthplace: Bristol

Previous clubs include: Brislington - January 2002.

HAWKINS, CRAIG — Forward
Current Club: Redditch United
Birthplace: Australia

Previous clubs include: Oldbury Utd - November 2001, Brisbane Utd (Australia).

HAWKINS, SIMON — Defender
Current Club: Wednesfield
Birthplace: Shropshire

Previous clubs include: Willenhall T - July 1998, Telford Utd.

HAWKRIDGE, BRETT — Defender
Current Club: Haverfordwest County
D o B: 03/02/1981   Birthplace: Wales

From Local football - November 2001.

HAWLEY, JON — Forward
Current Club: Grantham Town
D o B: 23/01/1978   Birthplace: Lincoln

Previous clubs include: Lincoln C - July 2000, Portsmouth.

HAWORTH, ROB — Forward
Current Club: Hendon
D o B: 21/11/1975   Birthplace: Edgware

Striker who joined Hendon from Ryman Premie rivals Sutton United in June 2002. Had signed for the Us in February 2001 following a successful month on loan from Dagenham & Redbridge, rejoining Sutton for a four-figure fee and finishing the season with 11 league goals to his credit in 23 games. He moved to Dagenham in the summer of 2000 after four seasons with St Albans City, and has also played for Kettering Town and Aylesbury United having had Football League experience with Fulham and Millwall.

HAWTHORN, JAMIE — Defender
Current Club: Corby Town
Birthplace: Aylesbury

Previous clubs include: Leighton T - July 2001, Kings Lynn, Corby T, Buckingham T, Baldock T, Kings Lynn,Corby T, Bedford T, Newport Pagnell T, Wootton Blue Cross, Wolverton T.

HAWTHORNE, MARK — Midfielder
Current Club: Slough Town
D o B: 31/10/1973   Birthplace: Glasgow

Now in his second spell at the club having re-signed from Crawley Town, who the Rebels sold him to for a four-figure fee last season. Mark re-joined the club having been released by Crawley at the end of last season - and manager Steve Browne quickly snapped up the popular playmaker. Mark is very much a favourite with the fans. He covers every blade of grass on the pitch and is capable of scoring goals from midfield. His former clubs in the football league include Sheffield United and Torquay United. Mark originally made his Slough Town debut in 1998 on the opening day of the season against St.Albans City. He scored the only goal in that game which the Rebels went on to win. Both fans and players alike are delighted to see Mark back in a Rebels shirt.

HAWTIN, DALE — Defender
Current Club: Kidsgrove Athletic
Birthplace: Crewe

Gained plenty of UniBond League experience through spells with Leek Town and Witton Albion before joining newly-promoted Kidsgrove Athletic in August 2002 after a season at Hyde United. The defender started his career with Crewe and also played in Ireland with Sligo Rovers.

HAY, ANDY — Forward
Current Club: Whitley Bay
D o B: 20/10/1980   Birthplace: Stockton

A close season signing from Blyth Spartans. Andy will cause defences all sorts of problems with his electrifying speed. Has also been at Hartlepool United.

HAY, DARRAN — Forward
Current Club: Stevenage Borough
D o B: 17/12/1969   Birthplace: Hitchin
Honours won: FA Trophy Winners

Former Stevenage boss Paul Fairclough finally got his man when he captured Darran from Conference rivals during the close season of 2000-01. He had tried on three previous occasions to sign the bustling striker, failing each time. Formerly of Cambridge, and Hitchin Town, he has been a thorn in Boros side for many years, scoring some important goals for the Cards, not least in the FA Trophy semi-final, which broke Boro hearts. Scored 16 times in only 30 games in 2000/2001.

HAY, GARY — Forward
Current Club: Willenhall Town
Birthplace: Birmingham

Signed for Willenhall from Alvechurch in March 2002. A lively striker who is an excellent battler, scores lots of goals and is a great investment for the future.

HAYDE, MICK — Midfielder
Current Club: Solihull Borough
D o B: 20/06/1971   Birthplace: Liverpool

Previous clubs include: Moor Green - October 2001, Worcester C, Altrincham, St.Helens T, Linfield, Chester C, Liverpool.

HAYDEN, JOHN — Defender
Current Club: Alfreton Town
D o B: 08/09/1981   Birthplace: Kilkenny

Previous clubs include: Forest Green Rovers - November 2001, Sheffield Utd.

H

HAYDER, TROY   *Forward*
Current Club: Flixton
Birthplace: Manchester
Previous clubs include: Rossendale Utd - March 2002, Droylsden, Leigh RMI, Winsford Utd, Flixton, Chorley, Rhyl, Curzon Ashton.

HAYDON, NICKY   *Defender*
Current Club: Heybridge Swifts
D o B: 10/08/1978   Birthplace: Barking
Cultured midfielder or sweeper, who has also performed at full back. Returned to Heybridge Swifts in September 2001 after a sojurn at Chelmsford City. Began his career at Colchester United and made over 40 League appearances. Now settled into the heart of the defence and is a key element of the attacking nature of the club with his prowess from dead ball situations. Has the ability also to bring the ball out from defence and create with either a short or long ball. Has also seen service with Leyton Orient and Kettering Town.

HAYES, ADIE   *Midfielder*
Current Club: Cambridge City
D o B: 22/05/1978   Birthplace: Norwich
Adie signed for Cambridge City in July 2002 after a couple of years with Dr Martens rivals Kings Lynn. Had joined Kings Lynn in October 2000 from Conference neighbours Boston United for a £2,000 fee. He is a hard-working midfielder who is comfortable on the ball and has good distribution. He began his career on the books of Cambridge United making 34 appearances before moving on to Kettering Town and Diss Town. Joined Boston United in their promotion season for a fee of £4,000.

HAYES, MARTIN   *Forward*
Current Club: Bishops Stortford
D o B: 21/03/1966   Birthplace: Walthamstow
Honours won: England B & u-21 Int.
Stylish player and quietly determined manager for The Blues since his appointment in November 1999. Martin has played at the highest level, winning a League Cup Final and a League Championship medal with Arsenal in 1989 and notching up over 100 appearances for the Gunners before moving north of the border and a spell with Scottish giants Glasgow Celtic. Martin had Wembley success again in the 1994 Autoglass Trophy Final and finished his Football League playing career at Swansea City. From there Martin played for Conference side Dover Athletic before completing his tour of Britain in Northern Ireland with Cliftonville. Back in England, he went on to play for Crawley Town, before joining Collier Row & Romford. Martin was the sides top scorer in the 1997/8 season and went on to manage this and the metamorphosed Romford FC, punctuated with a brief spell at Purfleet. A useful addition to the Blues squad, he continues to score goals alongside his managerial responsibilities. He took Bishops Stortford to 4th place in Division 1 in season 2000/2001 and is hoping for a promotion slot this time out.

HAYES, PETER   *Goalkeeper*
Current Club: Armthorpe Welfare
Birthplace: Yorkshire
Previous clubs include: Carcroft - July 1996, Brodsworth Welfare.

HAYFIELD, MATT   *Midfielder*
Current Club: Basingstoke Town
D o B: 08/08/1975   Birthplace: Bristol
Honours won: British Universities Rep.
Signed for Basingstoke Town in September 2001 from Woking. A tough-tackling midfielder who has a good touch on the ball. Formerly with Yeovil Town and Bristol Rovers, he has also represented the British Universities team.

HAYGREEN, JASON   *Goalkeeper*
Current Club: Tiptree United
Birthplace: Essex
Previous clubs include: Sudbury Wanderers - July 1999, Halstead T, Cornard Utd, Sudbury W.

HAYNES, JUNIOR   *Forward*
Current Club: Dulwich Hamlet
D o B: 16/04/1976   Birthplace: Croydon
Signed for Ryman Division One South side Dulwich Hamlet from Slough Town in August 2002. Had joined the Rebels from Carshalton Athletic on a free transfer in January 2000. Junior is someone who always gives 100% and gives a good performance in every game he plays. Started his career at the Tottenham youth side, but drifted out of the professional game and has had spells at Hayes, Sutton, Hendon and Carshalton before joining Slough. Junior is a left winger by trade, but is also capable at playing as a left back and a makeshift striker - which he did to good effect in large parts of the 2000/01 season. Junior does not have to beat players to get a cross in. He can deliver from any angle - which is one of his best attributes.

HAYTER, JONNY   *Midfielder*
Current Club: Carterton Town
Birthplace: Oxford
From Local football - July 2001, Carterton T, Oxford Utd.

HAYTER, ROBBIE   *Midfielder*
Current Club: Hertford Town
D o B: 20/04/1977   Birthplace: London
Previous clubs include: Wormley Rovers - July 2001, Stevenage B, WBA.

HAYTHORNE, CRAIG   *Midfielder*
Current Club: Maltby Main
Birthplace: Yorkshire
Previous clubs include: Rotherham Utd - July 2001.

HAYWARD, ANDY   *Forward*
Current Club: Bradford Park Avenue
D o B: 21/06/1970   Birthplace: Barnsley
Prolific striker who signed for Bradford Park Avenue from Frickley Athletic in September 2000, for whom he had scored 34 times the previous season. Previously with Hednesford Town, Doncaster Rovers and Barrow, Andy was second leading scorer in the UniBond in 1993/94 and this earned him a move to Rotherham United. Avenue faced stiff competition from other clubs for his signature.

HAYWARD, DANNY   *Defender*
Current Club: Staines Town
D o B: 19/09/1977   Birthplace: Hampshire
A former Southampton trainee who appeared in the Conference with Farnborough Town before joining Staines Town in July 1999. Midfielder Danny represented Surrey Schools and also gained a trial for the England Schools team. Was voted as Players' Player of the year for 2000/01.

HAYWARD, JUSTIN   *Midfielder*
Current Club: Cinderford Town
Birthplace: Hereford
Former Hereford United trainee, Justin is a very promising young midfielder who made several Dr League appearances for Cinderford Town since joining the club at the start of the 2000/01 season.

HAYWARD, MATT — *Defender*
Current Club: Oxford City

D o B: 31/12/1971   Birthplace: Oxford

Previous clubs include: Aylesbury Utd - July 1998, Thame Utd, Pitstone & Ivinghoe, Aylesbury Utd.

HAYWOOD, CRAIG — *Forward*
Current Club: Racing Club Warwick

Birthplace: Warwick

Striker who joined Racing Club Warwick for his first taste of Dr Martens football in December 2001 from local side Romulus. Previously played for Polesworth North Warwick.

HAYWOOD, DAVID — *Defender*
Current Club: Tamworth

D o B: 18/02/1978   Birthplace: Birmingham

Dave is a local lad who joined Tamworth in the summer of 2000 from Sutton Coldfield Town after also being with Bolehall Swifts. Talented defender who has the ability to go much further in the game.

HAYWOOD, PAUL — *Defender*
Current Club: Brodsworth Welfare

D o B: 04/10/1975   Birthplace: Barnsley

Previous clubs include: Frickley Ath - August 2000, Emley, Doncaster R, Nottingham Forest.

HAYWOOD, TRISTAN — *Midfielder*
Current Club: Flackwell Heath

Birthplace: Buckinghamshire

Previous clubs include: Tring T - November 2000, Flackwell Heath, Tring T.

HAZEL, CHRIS — *Defender*
Current Club: Littlehampton Town

Birthplace: Sussex

Enormous defender: made a handful of appearances for Littlehampton during January/February 2001: had a close encounter with the fist of Whitehawks Mark Sheriff during one of those matches - an incident which earned a red card for Sheriff, who then duly assaulted the referee, too!

HAZEL, IAN — *Midfielder*
Current Club: Tooting & Mitcham United

D o B: 01/12/1967   Birthplace: Merton

Previous clubs include: Chesham Utd - October 1998, Carshalton Ath., Aylesbury Utd, Slough T, Maidstone Utd, Bristol R, Wimbledon.

HAZEL, JULIAN — *Forward*
Current Club: Wivenhoe Town

Birthplace: Colchester

Previous clubs include: Heybridge Swifts - December 2001, Stanway R, Wivenhoe T, Bedford T, Wivenhoe T, Collier Row, Wivenhoe T, Harwich & Parkeston, Wivenhoe T, Halstead T, Brightlingsea Utd, Wivenhoe T, Chelmsford C, Colchester Utd.

HAZELDEN, DANNY — *Midfielder*
Current Club: Dagenham & Redbridge

Birthplace: Essex

Signed for Dagenham from Grays Athletic at the end of January. Danny has a bright future ahead of him after scoring at Woking and Morecambe last season.

HAZELDEN, SEAN — *Defender*
Current Club: Newtown AFC

D o B: 04/05/1981   Birthplace: Yorkshire

Currently a student at Bangor University, Sean signed for League of Wales side Newtown in August 2002 from rivals Bangor City. Had joined Bangor from UniBond League side Emley in the summer of 1999.

HEAD, BEN — *Midfielder*
Current Club: Mildenhall Town

Birthplace: Cambridge

Previous clubs include: Chatteris T - July 2001, Histon, Soham Town R, Cambridge C.

HEAD, REECE — *Defender*
Current Club: Lewes

Birthplace: Brighton

Used more as cover last season whilst still playing most of his football for Saltdean. However this season Reece appears likely to be a more regular fixture. A Spurs supporter who makes his living as a graphic art dealer.

HEADLEY, RUSSELL — *Midfielder*
Current Club: Mossley

Birthplace: Manchester

Previous clubs include: Woodley Sports - August 2001, Castleton Gabriels, Mossley, Radcliffe B, Curzon Ashton, Squires Gate.

HEALD, ANDY — *Midfielder*
Current Club: Leigh RMI

D o B: 26/07/1980   Birthplace: Manchester

A young winger from the Morecambe Academy with several first team appearances. Joined the club August 2001.

HEALD, GREG — *Defender*
Current Club: Barnet

D o B: 26/09/1971   Birthplace: London

Honours won: England Schoolboy Int.

Club captain at Barnet, Greg is an outstanding central defender and a great leader. Previously played under John Still at Peterborough, Heald was one of Stills first signings for Barnet when he arrived from London Road in a club record deal in July 1997. Has marshalled the Bees back line ever since and often pops up with powerful headed goals.

HEALER, ANTHONY — *Forward*
Current Club: Durham City

Birthplace: Durham

Previous clubs include: Dunston Federation Brewery - February 2002, Chester-le-Street, Durham C.

HEALEY, NATHAN — *Goalkeeper*
Current Club: Whyteleafe

Previous clubs include: Dorking - October 2000, Chipstead, Whyteleafe.

HEALY, BRETT — *Midfielder*
Current Club: Solihull Borough

D o B: 06/10/1977   Birthplace: Coventry

Now playing in his second season for Solihull. He signed from Conference side Nuneaton Borough in the summer of 2000. Spent three seasons with Nuneaton and was in the side that was promoted from the Premier Division in 98/99. He started his career with Coventry City.

HEALY, BRIAN — Midfielder
Current Club: Shildon
D o B: 27/12/1968   Birthplace: Glasgow
Previous clubs include: Darlington - January 2002, Torquay Utd, Morecambe, Spennymoor Utd, Gateshead, Bishop Auckland, Billingham T, West Auckland T.

HEANEY, CRAIG — Defender
Current Club: Rocester
Birthplace: South Africa
Previous clubs include: Cirencester T - December 2001.

HEAPY, JAMIE — Defender
Current Club: Didcot Town
Birthplace: Oxfordshire
Jamie has already made 150 appearances for Didcot and continues to mature into an exceptional defensive talent. Never loses his cool, possesses a brilliant attitude, Jamie has an exciting future ahead of him.

HEARMAN, GORDON — Goalkeeper
Current Club: Didcot Town
Birthplace: Oxfordshire
Gordon moved to Didcot from Wallingford in the summer of 2001 and immediately impressed with a string of good performances. Spent 5 years at Abingdon Town where he was Youth Player of the year.

HEARN, CLIFF — Midfielder
Current Club: Chatham Town
Previous clubs include: Whitstable T - July 1998, Sheppey Utd.

HEARN, STEVE — Forward
Current Club: Chatham Town
Previous clubs include: Whitstable T - July 1998, Sittingbourne, Chatham T, Tonbridge, Sheppey Utd, Corinthian.

HEARNE, DARREN — Goalkeeper
Current Club: Coalville Town
D o B: 06/01/1972   Birthplace: Leicester
Honours won: Leicestershire Senior League Winners
Previous clubs include: Oadby T, - September 2001, St Andrews, Holwell Sports, Lutterworth T.

HEATH, BILLY — Defender
Current Club: Bridlington Town
Birthplace: Hull
Tall and strong, he is a vastly experienced defender who has included spells at Hull and Lincoln as well as a number of Non-League sides. Previously at Alfreton Town as Assistant Manager. A good leader who will set the example at the heart of the defence.

HEATH, DOMINIC — Midfielder
Current Club: Rocester
D o B: 02/09/1978   Birthplace: Shropshire
Previous clubs include: Shifnal T - August 2002, Bloxwich Utd, Warley Rangers, Stafford R, Stone Dominoes, WBA.

HEATH, GARETH — Forward
Current Club: Harwich & Parkeston
Birthplace: Essex
Local lad who came through from Harwichs Reserves. Fast and skilful, he has a powerful shot. A genuinely two-footed player who is at home on either the left or the right.

HEATH, JAMIE — Midfielder
Current Club: Gretna
Previous clubs include: Penrith - July 2001.

HEATH, ROBERT — Midfielder
Current Club: Stafford Rangers
D o B: 31/08/1978   Birthplace: Stoke
Highly-rated midfielder, Robert joined Stafford Rangers in January 2002 following five years at Stoke City, where he made 19 League appearances. Was one of the first players to commit himself to the club for th 2002/03 season.

HEATH, STEVE — Defender
Current Club: Alfreton Town
D o B: 15/11/1977   Birthplace: Hull
Honours won: England Schoolboy Int., NCEL & Cup Winners
A former England Schoolboy International defender, who was on the books of Leeds United, Carlisle and Rotherham before joining the Non-League ranks with Stamford. Steve joined Alfreton Town in the summer of 2000 from Ilkeston Town and has also played for Matlock Town. His commitment and effort endeared him to the Town Ground supporters who voted him Player of the Year.

HEATON, PAUL — Defender
Current Club: Boldmere St.Michaels
Birthplace: Birmimgham
Previous clubs include: Tamworth - July 1991.

HEATON, SIMON — Midfielder
Current Club: Abbey Hey
Birthplace: Manchester
Previous clubs include: Glossop North End - July 2000, Ashton Utd, Droylsden, Glossop NE, Flixton, Buxton, Stalybridge Celtic, Droylsden, Mossley, Caernarfon T.

HEAVEY, PAUL — Forward
Current Club: St.Helens Town
Birthplace: Warrington
Centre forward who eventually arrived at Town after being part of Rossendale United's Championship winning squad last term. Paul has had Football League experience with Preston North End. A local lad whos previous clubs include Runcorn, Accrington Stanley and Prescot Cables.

HECKLEY, MICHAEL — Defender
Current Club: Bishop Auckland
Birthplace: Bishop Auckland
Drafted from the Bishop Auckland under-18 team and made his debut v Horden CW in the Durham Challenge Cup in December 2000. Tall and strong, excellent header of the ball. Returned to Bishops from Northern League Nissan to start his first game against Gateshead in October 2001.

HEDGES, GARRY — Midfielder
Current Club: Edgware Town
Birthplace: London
Previous clubs include: Wembley - January 2002.

HEELEY, CARL — Defender
Current Club: Worcester City
D o B: 17/10/1969   Birthplace: Birmingham
One of the most popular players of recent times at Worcester City, Carl won the Supporters' Player of the Year award for the third time in 2000/01. Joined City from Sutton Coldfield Town in 1994. Proved that he is still capable of playing equally well in midfield or in the centre of the defence.

HEEPS, JIMMY — Goalkeeper
Current Club: Bedford Town
D o B: 16/05/1971   Birthplace: Luton
Previous clubs include: Leighton T - June 1997, Baldock T, Cheltenham T, Swansea C.

HEEPS, STUART — Goalkeeper
Current Club: Nantwich Town
Birthplace: Cheshire
Previous clubs include: Congleton T - July 1999, Nantwich T, Caernarfon T, Nantwich T, Congleton T, Whitchurch Alport, Nantwich T.

HEFFER, JOHN — Defender
Current Club: Great Wakering Rovers
Birthplace: Southend
Previous clubs include: Southend Manor - March 1994, Barking, Billericay T, Grays Ath., Southend Utd, West Ham Utd (Junior).

HEFFER, STEVE — Midfielder
Current Club: Dagenham & Redbridge
D o B: 11/01/1973   Birthplace: London
Boxacca manager Garry Hill, worth signing, joining the Daggers from Boreham Wood for £5,000 during the summer of 1999. Began his career at West Ham, where his father Paul played during the early 1970s, and then went on to have spells with Southend, Swindon, Grays Athletic, Hendon and Boreham Wood.

HEFFERNAN, JASON — Forward
Current Club: Rossendale United
D o B: 01/06/1979   Birthplace: Burnley
Talented forward whose career started with his home-town club Burnley. Moved to Accrington Stanley upon his release from Turf Moor and then joined Rossendale United in January 1999. Played a key role in Dales promotion to the UniBond in 2000/01.

HEGGARTY, JOHN — Forward
Current Club: Chester-Le Street
Birthplace: Co.Durham
Previous clubs include: South Shields - July 2001, Walker Central.

HEGGS, CARL — Forward
Current Club: Forest Green Rovers
D o B: 11/10/1970   Birthplace: Leicester
Striker who was released by Carlisle United at the end of the 2000/01 season and signed for Conference side Forest Green Rovers as a front line striker on 9th August. Previous experience with West Bromwich Albion, Bristol Rovers and Swansea City. Joined Northampton Town for £40,000 and then moved to near neighbours Rushden & Diamonds.

HEGLEY, NICK — Midfielder
Current Club: Hastings United
Birthplace: Kent
Attacking midfielder who joined Hastings in February 2002. Previous experience with Carshalton and Gravesend.

HEIGHWAY, GREG — Midfielder
Current Club: Ford United
Birthplace: Essex
Honours won: Ryman League Div.One Winners
Midfielder who was originally on the books at Colchester United. After being released by the Layer Road outfit, Gary joined Purfleet where he gained plenty of Ryman Premier Division experience. Spells with Aveley and Grays Athletic followed before he joined Ford United in October 2001 and played his part in helping the club to win the Ryman Division One title.

HEIGHWAY, STEVE — Defender
Current Club: Glapwell
Birthplace: Derbyshire
Previous clubs include: Heanor T - January 2001, Mickleover Sports.

HEINMAN, NICKY — Defender
Current Club: Halifax Town
D o B: 04/01/1985   Birthplace: Bradford
Nicky is a young defender who impressed in Halifax Town's reserves and was consequently given a first team chance during the 2001/02 season. He can play at either left back or centre back and looks a promising player for the future.

HEIR, MARTIN — Defender
Current Club: Solihull Borough
Birthplace: Warwick
Previous clubs include: Bedworth Utd - February 2001, Sutton Coldfield T, Racing Club Warwick, Moor Green, Stratford T, Southam Utd, Stratford T.

HELLEN, RICHIE — Defender
Current Club: Littlehampton Town
Birthplace: Sussex
Commanding defender, known as The Rhino, who was captain of East Preston during 1999/2000: has been around the County League for some time, having played for Arundel, Wick and Pagham as well as a previous spell at Littlehampton: said to have retired in August 2001, but returned to action during the autumn.

HEMINGWAY, MARK — Midfielder
Current Club: Tring Town
Birthplace: Birmingham
Birmingham-born midfielder who re-joined Ryman Division Two side Tring Town in July 2002 after a short spell with rivals Edgware Town. Originally with Dr Martens outfit Solihull Borough, Mark signed for Tring in the summer of 2000 before switching to the Wares in February 2002.

HEMMINGS, TONY — Midfielder
Current Club: Tamworth
D o B: 21/09/1967   Birthplace: Burton-on-Trent
Honours won: England Semi-Pro Int., FA Trophy Winners
Tony joined Tamworth in December 2001 for a fee of around £7,500 from Dr Martens League rivals Ilkeston Town. He was in his second spell at the New Manor Ground having signed from Carlisle United at the start of the 2001/02 season. He started his career at home town club Burton Albion, and then joined Rocester where he came to the attention of Conference side Northwich Victoria. After one season at the Drill Field he was signed for £25,000 for Wycombe Wanderers where Tony made his League debut. Two years later he joined Macclesfield where he won a FA Trophy winners medal scoring in the final against former club Northwich and graduated to the England semi-professional team. Tony then joined Hednesford Town and spent three successful years there before joining Gloucester City. After a short spell at Altrincham he joined Ilkeston Town. A very popular player at the New Manor Ground it was a blow when Chester paid £10,000 to give Tony a second chance in League football.

HENDERSON, DAVID — Midfielder
Current Club: Scarborough
D o B: 28/09/1982   Birthplace: Newcastle
A product of Conference club Scarborough's renowned youth scheme, David is a promising midfielder who has now graduated to the first-team squad.

HENDERSON, MICKY — Defender
Current Club: Enfield Town (Essex)
Birthplace: Herts
With Hertford Town last season, having joined them as a 14 years old. Made his Enfield Town debut against Eton Manor in November 2001.

HENDERSON, PHIL — Defender
Current Club: St.Leonards
Birthplace: Northampton
Phil first played in the Football League for Northampton Town when he was only sixteen years old. Phil, who plays in defence, signed for St Leonards from Eastbourne Borough in January 2002, and has also previously played for Wivenhoe, Hastings Town and Eastbourne Town.

HENDY, SCOTT — Defender
Current Club: Mangotsfield United
Birthplace: Bristol
Rejoined Mangotsfield United in January 2000 after a short spell at Western League side Backwell United. Previously with Bristol Manor Farm. Supporters and Players' Player of the Year for 2000/01.

HENHAM, DAVID — Defender
Current Club: Hastings United
D o B: 03/01/1981   *Birthplace: Hastings*
Sweeper who came through the youth side at St Leonards and made several first-team appearances for them over the last few years. Had a brief spell at Hailsham early on into 2001/02 before returning to The Firs. Moved next door to Hastings in March.

HENMAN, MATTHEW — Midfielder
Current Club: Dereham Town
Birthplace: Norfolk
Skilful and influential skipper who on his day is worth the entrance fee alone. Yet another product of the clubs Youth set-up and member of the 300 plus brigade.

HENNESEY, SIMON — Midfielder
Current Club: Lincoln United
Previous clubs include: Collingham - August 2000, Alfreton T, Ilkeston T, Hull C (Trainee).

HENNESSEY, BRENDAN — Forward
Current Club: Warrington Town
Birthplace: Cheshire
Previous clubs include: Nantwich T - July 2001.

HENNESSEY, MARK — Defender
Current Club: Cwmbran Town
D o B: 20/04/1974   *Birthplace: Cardiff*
Previous clubs include: Cardiff Corinthians - December 2001.

HENNEY, MATT — Midfielder
Current Club: Gretna
Previous clubs include: Workington - July 2001, Windscale Utd.

HENNIGAN, GED — Midfielder
Current Club: Aberystwyth Town
D o B: 02/08/1977   *Birthplace: Liverpool*
Previous clubs include: Rhyl - February 2002, Burscough, St.Helens T, Droylsden, Barrow, Everton.

HENNIN, PAUL — Forward
Current Club: Nantwich Town
Birthplace: Cheshire
Previous clubs include: Witton Alb - January 2002, Barnton.

HENRIQUES, TUTU — Midfielder
Current Club: Carshalton Athletic
Birthplace: Paris
French-born midfielder who played for the University of Luton before signing for Ryman Division One South side Carshalton Athletic. Currently studying in Sports Fitness & Management.

HENRY, CARL — Forward
Current Club: Abingdon United
Birthplace: Suffolk
Previous clubs include: Witney T - January 2001, AFC Wallingford, Witney T, Wallingford T, Hungerford T, Thame Utd, Abingdon T, Bury T, Whitton Utd.

HENRY, DAVE — Forward
Current Club: Guiseley
D o B: 21/11/1979
Previous clubs include: Garforth T - December 2000, Burnley (Trainee).

HENRY, NICK — Midfielder
Current Club: Scarborough
D o B: 21/02/1969   *Birthplace: Liverpool*
Honours won: Division Two Winners
Liverpool-born Nick joined Conference club Scarborough in July 2002 following his release by Tranmere Rovers. Nick made his name at Oldham where he spent ten years and won a Division Two championship medal in 1991. A £500,000 move took him from Boundary Park to Sheffield United in February 1997 but he was dogged by a series of injuries that hindered his opportunities at Bramall Lane. After regaining fitness after a back operation, he made his first appearance for the Blades as a substitute, ironically against Rovers, and promptly sustained a broken hand. Unable to gain a permanent place and spending much of his time on the bench, Nick moved to Walsall in March 1999 on a short-term contract, where his keen tackling, energy, commitment and use of the ball showed up well. Despite clinching promotion to Division One with the Saddlers, he decided on a move to Prenton Park during summer of 1999, moving closer to his roots where John Aldridge was looking for a new leader in the midfield engine-room following the departure of Kenny Irons. Although not known as a regular goalscorer, the occasion seems to bring the best out of Henry. He struck two near-identical 30 yard goals against West Ham in the FA Cup and Bolton in the Worthington Cup showing that he is more than willing to chip in with goals from midfield. His 1999/00 season was brought to a premature end following injuries sustained in a car crash and he suffered further injury woe just two months into the 2000/01 season when he was diagnosed as suffering from a blood disorder which drained his energy during matches.

HENRY, TONY — Defender
Current Club: Folkestone Invicta
D o B: 13/09/1979   *Birthplace: London*
A classy defender who joined Folkestone Invicta in August 2001 and who is very comfortable on the ball. His previous clubs include West Ham United, where he spent two years as a professional, and Lincoln City, where he made 20 first team appearances. Anthonys only goal so far this season came for the Dr Martens League X1 against the FA X1 at Crawley in November 2001.

HENSHAW, BEN — Midfielder
Current Club: Telford United
Birthplace: Wolverhampton
Previous clubs include: Oxford U - July 1999.

HENSHAW, TERRY — Defender
Current Club: Burton Albion
D o B: 29/02/1980   Birthplace: Nottingham
Terry Henshaw joined the Brewers at the start of last season after captaining Notts County's reserve side. Terry is still only 21 years old and last season made the successful transition to the left full back position. He has continued in this position this season and his strong tackling and consistant displays have made him a firm favourite with the Burton crowd. Terry is an adaptable player and has filled in at centre-back and in midfield. He was given a two-year contract in the summer.

HENSON, CHRIS — Midfielder
Current Club: Borrowash Victoria
Birthplace: Derby
Previous clubs include: Eastwood T - July 2000, Borrowash V, Eastwood T, Dronfield v, R. Derby Co (trainee).

HENTY, GARY — Midfielder
Current Club: Billericay Town
Birthplace: London
Gary is one of the younger members of the Billericay Town squad, and one of the most improved since he signed in the summer of 1999. A former captain of Havering Schools, Gary spent 8 years at Wimbledon achieving reserve team status. Has played in Non-League football for Barking and Purfleet. Spent much of his first season at Billericay on the bench, after making his debut in the opening match of the 99/00 season, however he managed to score three goals, including a brace against Wembley in the league cup. After spending much of his first season on the bench, Gary forced his way into the first team reckoning with a good start to the season in 2000. A versatile player, he was often asked to fill in at various positions due to injury. He has played on both wings for Billericay as well as in defense, he has also had to play through the middle for a few games. Unfortunately missed the start of the 2001/02 season due to a long standing injury, but came back to force his way into the side.

HENTY, PAUL — Defender
Current Club: St.Leonards
D o B: 03/08/1983   Birthplace: Hastings
Paul is a defensive product of the St Leonards youth side who gained valuable experience with the reserves and has now progressed to the first-team squad.

HEPBURN, GLEN — Forward
Current Club: Clacton Town
Birthplace: Essex
Previous clubs include: Wivenhoe T - July 1998, Clacton T, Harwich & Parkeston, Clacton T.

HEPWORTH, RICHARD — Midfielder
Current Club: Goole AFC
Birthplace: Leeds
Well-travelled midfielder in the Yorkshire Non-League scene, Richard joined Northern Counties East Leaguers Goole AFC in May 2002 from UniBond League side Farsley Celtic. Started his career as a junior with Leeds United before spells with Glasshoughton Welfare, Armthorpe Welfare, Guiseley and Stocksbridge Park Steels followed. Joined Farsley in August 2001.

HERBERT, CRAIG — Defender
Current Club: Rugby United
D o B: 09/11/1975   Birthplace: Coventry
Coventry-born central defender who joined Rugby United originally in January 2001 after being released by Shrewsbury Town. Played around 100 times for Torquay, West Bromwich Albion and Shrewsbury before joining Rugby and also had a short spell in the Conference with Hayes during the 2000/01 campaign.

HERBERT, ROBERT — Midfielder
Current Club: Halifax Town
D o B: 19/08/1983   Birthplace: Durham
Robert has come through the youth system at Halifax Town and is the clubs youngster ever player, aged 16, to make his debut, which was against Brighton & Hove Albion during the 2000/01 season. Roberts appearances have been limited due to a number of little injuries, but he has a bright future ahead of him as a midfielder. One of the quickest players at the club, Robert will be hoping that this coming season he can make a name for himself.

HERBERT, SIMON — Defender
Current Club: Basingstoke Town
Birthplace: Basingstoke
Simon has progressed from Basingstoke Town's youth and reserve teams and made his senior debut during the first half of season 2001/02. Not afraid to take players on, Simon has a fine burst of speed and has impressed with his performances as a full back.

HERCULES, TYRONE — Midfielder
Current Club: Wealdstone
D o B: 05/05/1972   Birthplace: Essex
Midfielder or forward, Tyronne signed for Wealdstone from Bishops Stortford in January 2002. Suffered an injuury during the summer of 2002 which was expected to keep him out for some time. Formerly with Leyton Pennant, Braintree Town, Harlow Town, Boreham Wood and Enfield.

HERITAGE, PAUL — Goalkeeper
Current Club: Gretna
D o B: 17/04/1979   Birthplace: Sheffield
Previous clubs include: Barrow - December 2000, Carlisle Utd, Barnsley, Sheffield Utd.

HERITAGE, PETER — Forward
Current Club: Sidley United
Birthplace: Sussex
Hugely influential contributor to Sidleys incredible progress in recent years (originally came through their youth team): top goalscorer for Bexhill several seasons running in the early 80s: graduated from Hastings to playing in the Football League, and made 145 professional appearances (scoring 22 goals) during a career with Gillingham, Hereford, and Doncaster: has been back at Sidley for some time, having rejoined them from Margate, and was their leading marksmen in 1996/97: now in his 40s and took over the managers job from Dickie Day at the end of 2000/01: played regularly from November onwards that season, and was the clubs leading scorer with 12 goals (has a habit of coming on as a substitute and grabbing a late winner): also made the odd appearance for St Leonards during 2001/02.

HERMAN, ROBERT — Forward
Current Club: Newcastle Blue Star
D o B: 08/09/1969   Birthplace: Newcastle
Previous clubs include: Percy Main - August 2001.

HEROD, BEN — Midfielder
Current Club: St Margaretsbury
D o B: 01/03/1984   Birthplace: Chelmsford
Previous clubs include: Chelmsford C - July 2001.

HERVIN, MARK — Goalkeeper
Current Club: Bath City
Birthplace: Bristol
Mark returned to Bath City after two years away during the summer of 2001, becoming manager Alan Pridhams first signing in the process. His first spell at City began in the 1994 close season when he arrived from Forest Green Rovers as understudy to long-serving keeper Dave Mogg. During the first two years his first team opportunities where few and far between, making six appearances during the 1994/95 season including his debut in the 3-1 Bob Lord Trophy win over Welling United. The following season saw Mogg ever present but mid-way through the 1996/97 campaign an injury to the keeper gave Hervin his chance which he took with both hands. Went onto miss just one match in the following two years and his performanes soon lead to a number of league clubs following his progress. A move to Crewe Alexandra in May 1999 looked to be on the cards but this fell through and Mark found himself heading to Gloucester City Financial problems meant he soon moved on to Clevedon Town where he remained before returning to City. As a youngster Mark spent two years at Bristol Rovers as a youth trainee before switching to Yeovil Town. Made 16 appearances for the Somerset club before spells at Mangotsfield United, Frome Town and Forest Green preceeded his first move to City. As well as being an excellent shot-stopper Mark has also shown an appetite for penalty taking, scoring during a Somerset Cup victory over Wellington as well as twice converting successfully in penalty shoot-outs during the 1998/99 season.

HESKEY, DAMIEN — Forward
Current Club: Shepshed Dynamo
Birthplace: Leicester
Previous clubs include: Highfield Rangers - December 2000.

HESLOP, CHRIS — Defender
Current Club: Clitheroe
Birthplace: Burnley
Youth teams Player of the Year. 18-year-old with bags of pace and skill. Will frighten more than a few old-timers this season when given a chance.

HESSON, NEIL — Midfielder
Current Club: Oldbury United
Birthplace: Birmingham
Previous clubs include: Darlaston - July 1997, WBA (Trainee).

HETHERINGTON, KEITH — Forward
Current Club: Ipswich Wanderers
Birthplace: Ipswich
From Youth team.

HEVERIN, MIKE — Forward
Current Club: Warrington Town
D o B: 13/11/1969   Birthplace: Liverpool
Previous clubs include: Runcorn - October 2000, Northwich V, Leek T, Northwich V, Crewe Alexandra.

HEWITT, CHRIS — Defender
Current Club: Hassocks
Birthplace: Sussex
Reliable defender and captain: joined Hassocks seven years ago from Burgess Hill: usually referred to as Jack.

HEWITT, GARY — Defender
Current Club: Croydon Athletic
D o B: 21/08/1963   Birthplace: Kent
Previous clubs include: Dulwich Hamlet - August 2001, Erith & Belvedere, Bromley, Margate Bromley, Gravesend, Hendon, Dulwich Hamlet, Erith & Belvedere, Gateway.

HEWITT, WAYNE — Defender
Current Club: Llanelli AFC
Birthplace: Trelewis
Previous clubs include: Rhayader T - July 2001, Aberystwyth T, Inter Cardiff, Cwmbran T, Inter Cardiff, Cwmbran T, Yate T, Barry T, Newport AFC, Brecon Corinthians, Pontllanfraith, Trelewis.

HEY, NICK — Midfielder
Current Club: Guiseley
Birthplace: Bradford
Previous clubs include: Thackley - October 2001, Harrogate T, Bradford PA, Thackley, Bradford C (Trainee).

HEYS, DANNY — Forward
Current Club: Witton Albion
Birthplace: Lancashire
Previous clubs include: Rossendale Utd - December 2001, Morecambe.

HIBBERD, CHRIS — Defender
Current Club: Wick
Birthplace: Sussex
Previous clubs include: East Preston - July 2001.

HIBBERT, LEON — Midfielder
Current Club: Tring Town
Birthplace: Tring
From Youth team.

HIBBERT, STEVE — Defender
Current Club: Flixton
Birthplace: Manchester
Previous clubs include: Mossley - January 2002, Winsford Utd, Flixton, Droylsden, Flixton, Congleton T, Accrington Stanley, Flixton, Mossley, Glossop NE.

HIBBERT, TERRY — Midfielder
Current Club: Brook House
Birthplace: Middlesex
Previous clubs include: Northwood - July 1999, Wealdstone, Brook House, Yeading, Chelsea (Junior).

HIBBINS, JOHN — Midfielder
Current Club: Lincoln United
D o B: 17/11/1979   Birthplace: Sheffield
Previous clubs include: Worksop T - December 2000, Sheffield Wednesday.

HICKEY, TOM — Midfielder
Current Club: Maidenhead United
D o B: 25/04/1977   Birthplace: Hillingdon
Previous clubs include: Feltham - July 1999, Brentford (Junior).

HICKMAN, TOM — Midfielder
Current Club: Dover Athletic
Birthplace: Kent
From Youth team.

HICKS, BILLY — Midfielder
Current Club: Tadcaster Albion
Birthplace: Yorkshire
Previous clubs include: Kellingley Welfare - July 1999.

HICKS, GRAHAM — Defender
Current Club: Chorley
D o B: 17/02/1981   *Birthplace: Oldham*
Previous clubs include: Rochdale - October 2001.

HICKS, JOHN — Midfielder
Current Club: Hamble ASSC
Birthplace: Hampshire
Previous clubs include: AC Delco - September 2001, Hamble, Romsey T, Sholing Sports, Brockenhurst, Awbridge.

HICKS, MARTIN — Midfielder
Current Club: Tadcaster Albion
Birthplace: Yorkshire
Previous clubs include: Magnet Sports - July 1999.

HICKS, STUART — Defender
Current Club: Matlock Town
Birthplace: Peterborough
Previous clubs include: Mansfield T - March 2002, Chester C, Leyton Orient, Scarborough, Preston NE, Huddersfield T, Doncaster R, Scunthorpe Utd, Colchester Utd, Wisbech T, Peterborough Utd.

HICKS, STUART — Defender
Current Club: Hucknall Town
D o B: 30/05/1967   *Birthplace: Peterborough*
Vastly experienced, no-nonsense central defender who joined UniBond Premier side Hucknall Town from Mansfield in March 2002. Made over 500 League appearances with Peterborough, Colchester, Scunthorpe, Doncaster, Huddersfield, Scarborough and Leyton Orient.

HICKS, TIM — Forward
Current Club: Carmarthen Town
Birthplace: Wales
From Youth team.

HICKTON, NEVILLE — Defender
Current Club: Great Wakering Rovers
Birthplace: Essex
Previous clubs include: Southend Manor - August 1995, Dagenham, Leyton Orient.

HIDER, ALAN — Midfielder
Current Club: Ludlow Town
Birthplace: Shropshire
Previous clubs include: Bridgnorth T - July 2001, Birmingham C.

HIGGINBOTTOM, MATT — Defender
Current Club: Ossett Albion
Previous clubs include: Pickering T - January 2001, Garforth T, Emley.

HIGGINS, ALEX — Midfielder
Current Club: Wakefield & Emley
D o B: 22/07/1981   *Birthplace: Sheffield*
Alex started out at Hillsborough with Sheffield Wednesday (his hometown team) before moving on to join QPR in March of 2001. After making just one first team appearance in his 8 months with QPR (as a substitute for the final 10 minutes of a game against Wolves), he moved to Chester early in the 01/02 campaign on a free transfer. Though he was rated as a talented midfielder by Rangers, he was told that they could not offer him a contract at the end of the season due to financial constraints. Crewe were nterested in signing Alex, who can play either wide left or central midfield, but Chester offered him a better deal. When he failed to get into Chesters first team, he asked to be released in February 2002 and joined Stalybridge. However, just over a month later he returned to Yorkshire to join Emley.

HIGGINS, ANTHONY — Defender
Current Club: Billingham Town
Birthplace: Co.Durham
Previous clubs include: Northallerton T - July 1994.

HIGGINS, DEAN — Forward
Current Club: Bashley
Previous clubs include: Bournemouth Poppies - July 2001, Colden Common, Bashley, Torquay Utd, Bashley.

HIGGS, ANDY — Goalkeeper
Current Club: Stourbridge
Birthplace: Birmingham
Previous clubs include: Sutton Coldfield T - August 2001, Atherstone Utd, Birmingham C.

HIGGS, JOHN — Goalkeeper
Current Club: Swaffham Town
Birthplace: Norfolk
Impressive young goalkeeper who continues to develop having taken over the first team spot at Swaffham four seasons ago.

HIGHFIELD, MARK — Midfielder
Current Club: Alfreton Town
Birthplace: Sheffield
Honours won: NCEL & Cup Winners
A competitive and hard-working midfield player who re-joined Alfreton Town in the summer of 2001 from Hallam after spells with Stocksbridge Park Steels, Hyde United, Stalybridge Celtic, Matlock Town, Denaby United, Sheffield and Parkgate. First played for Alfreton in the 1994/95 season when he made a handful of first team appearances.

HILDRETH, PHIL — Defender
Current Club: Bedlington Terriers
Birthplace: Newcastle
Now in his third season at Bedlington having joined from Whitley Bay. This airport worker is now settled into the squad at Welfare Park. A consistent, hard working performer who is as reliable as they come. Usually to be found raiding up and down the line at right back he has also filled in well in the left back slot and across the midfield when required. A whole hearted committed player wherever he is asked to play.

HILL, ANDY — Defender
Current Club: Barrow
Birthplace: Lancaster
Born in Lancaster, Andy is a whole-hearted defender who joined Barrow in February 1999 from local West Lancashire League outfit Vickers SC. He previously played in the North West Counties League with Holker OB. He made his debut for the Bluebirds in a Conference game at Telford at the end of February 1999 as a substitute.

HILL, ANDY — Goalkeeper
Current Club: Bury Town
Birthplace: Suffolk
From Youth team.

HILL, ANDY — Midfielder
Current Club: Llanelli AFC
D o B: 18/10/1978   *Birthplace: Wales*
Honours won: Wales Youth Int., Wales Colleges Rep.
Previous clubs include: Pontardawe Ath - July 1999, Briton Ferry Ath.

HILL, BRAD — Midfielder
Current Club: Denaby United
Birthplace: Sheffield
From Local football - August 2001.

HILL, CHRIS — Goalkeeper
Current Club: Harrogate Town
Birthplace: Hull
Honours won: UniBond League Div.One Winners
Goalkeeper who joined Hull City as a junior and spent three years with the club playing at every level. His first taste of Non-League football came at North Ferriby United and he then went on to play for Whitby Town and Bridlington Town, before joining Harrogate Town at the start of the 2000/01 season.

HILL, DANNY — Midfielder
Current Club: Dagenham & Redbridge
D o B: 01/10/1974   *Birthplace: Enfield*
Honours won: England u-21 Int.
Danny began his career at White Hart Lane as a trainee and made his way through the ranks to become a full professional in 1992. He made his Premiership debut in 1992 against Birmingham City and went on to make 10 appearances for Spurs. He had loan spells at Birmingham City, Watford and Cardiff City before joining Oxford United in 1997. He only spent four months at the Manor Ground before Cardiff City snapped him up. After impressing this summer in pre-season friendlies, Garry Hill persuaded Danny to join the Daggers. He made his debut on the opening day of the season against Southport.

HILL, DARREN — Goalkeeper
Current Club: Walton Casuals
Birthplace: Surrey
Darren has recently joined Casuals from Carshalton Athletic, recently made his 1st team debut at home to AFC Wallingford.

HILL, GORDON — Midfielder
Current Club: Windsor & Eton
D o B: 16/10/1968   *Birthplace: Berkshire*
Gordon joined Windsor & Eton from local football to make his debut in January 1996 and scored 10 goals from sixteen appearances that season. Has been a regular goalscorer from midfield ever since and has become a very popular player at Stag Meadow.

HILL, KEITH — Defender
Current Club: Morecambe
D o B: 17/05/1969   *Birthplace: Bolton*
Former skipper of Blackburn Rovers who joined Conference side Morecambe in August 2002 after being released by Cheltenham Town. The experienced defender began his career with Blackburn, where he made over 100 appearances, before moving on to have spells with Plymouth, Rochdale and Cheltenham, totalling over 400 League games.

HILL, OWEN — Midfielder
Current Club: Peacehaven & Telscombe
Birthplace: Sussex
Exciting midfielder, who played under Jimmy Quinn at Wick and Lewes (left the latter club in January 2000 to visit Australia). Spent 2000/01 with East Preston (scored five times), but was held back by a toe injury. Fleetingly appeared for Wick again at the start of the 2001/2002 season until transferring to Peacehaven midway through the campaign.

HILL, PAUL — Defender
Current Club: Wisbech Town
D o B: 25/05/1973
Previous clubs include: Blackstone - July 2001, Wisbech T, Yaxley, Stamford, Raunds T, Holbeach Utd, Spalding Utd, Eynesbury R, Corby T, Peterborough Utd.

HILL, SAMMY — Midfielder
Current Club: Droylsden
Birthplace: Manchester
Previous clubs include: Chester C - November 2001, Witton Alb., Crewe Alexandra

HILL, SIMON — Midfielder
Current Club: Rothwell Town
Birthplace: Leicester
Previous clubs include: Holwell Sports - July 2000, Friar Lane OB, Shepshed Dynamo.

HILLAM, SIMON — Midfielder
Current Club: Thackley
Birthplace: Yorkshire
From Local football - August 1997.

HILLIER, DAVID — Midfielder
Current Club: Barnet
D o B: 19/12/1969   *Birthplace: Blackheath*
Honours won: England u-21 Int., (old) Division One Winners
Experienced former England under-21 international midfielder who signed for Conference side Barnet on the eve of the 2002/03 season after being released by Bristol Rovers. Began his career with Arsenal, where he made over 100 appearances and was a member of their 1991 title-winning squad. Joined Portsmouth for £250,000 in 1996 and then moved on to Rovers three years later. Totalled more than 250 League games in an injury-hampered professional career.

HILLIER, PAUL — Midfielder
Current Club: Clacton Town
Birthplace: Clacton
One of the most saluted players at Jewson Eastern League side Clacton Town. Has been with the Seasiders since a very young age and is always inspirational on the pitch. With one of the best first touches at this level, scores some breathtaking goals.

HILLIER, SEAN — Forward
Current Club: Clacton Town
D o B: 11/09/1981   *Birthplace: Clacton*
Striker Sean joined Jewson Eastern League side Clacton Town at the start of the 2001/02 season after being released from Colchester United. Has proved to be very skilful, fast, and is a proven goalscorer. Scooped just about every award at the 2001/02 seasons presentation evening.

HILLMAN, STEVE — Defender
Current Club: Stourbridge
Birthplace: Wolverhampton
Previous clubs include: Bilston T - November 2001, Bromsgrove Rovers, Blakanell, Worcester C, Bloxwich T, Bloxwich Strollers, Oxford Utd (Trainee).

HILLS, LUKE — Goalkeeper
Current Club: Tunbridge Wells
Birthplace: Kent
Previous clubs include: Tonbridge Angels - July 1999, Gravesend, Folkestone Invicta, Margate, Maidstone Utd.

HILTON, CHRIS — Defender
Current Club: Belper Town
D o B: 08/12/1975   Birthplace: Barnsley
Chris is a defender who started his career with Rotherham United. Joined UniBond Premier side Frickley Athletic in September 1995 and stayed at Westfield Lane for almost six years before transferring to Stocksbridge Park Steels in the summer of 2001. Switched to UniBond First Division rivals Belper Town in July 2002.

HILTON, DAMIEN — Forward
Current Club: Wroxham
D o B: 06/09/1977   Birthplace: Norwich
Previous clubs include: Watton Utd - July 1999, Kings Lynn, Brighton, Norwich C.

HILTON, STEVE — Goalkeeper
Current Club: Vauxhall Motors
D o B: 03/08/1977   Birthplace: Lancashire
Joined Vauxhall Motors in the spring of 1998 from Marine, Steve has previous goalkeeping experience with Doncaster Rovers and Wigan Athletic. He made the Motors number one shirt his own with some excellent displays which saw him claim the safe hands award in the UniBond League on three separate occasions.

HILTON, TIM — Forward
Current Club: Boldmere St.Michaels
Birthplace: Birmingham
Previous clubs include: Coleshill T - June 2001, Boldmere St.Michaels.

HINDLEY, RYAN — Forward
Current Club: Alfreton Town
Birthplace: Sheffield
Ryan has had more than his fair share of experience at the top level of the game having signed professional terms for Sheffield Wednesday. Whilst in their youth team he was on the losing side for the Owls in the FA Youth Cup. Ryan is a versatile winger who can play just as effectively on either wing. His previous clubs include spells at Kingdom, Rotherham United, Nottingham Forest, Sheffield Wednesday and Worksop Town, where the young winger made twenty first-team appearances in the UniBond Premier Division during the 2001/02 season before joining First Division Alfreton Town in the summer of 2002.

HINE, MARK — Midfielder
Current Club: Frickley Athletic
D o B: 18/05/1964   Birthplace: Middlesbrough
Honours won: England Semi-Pro Int., Division Four Winners, Conference Winners
Vastly experienced former England semi-professional international midfielder who joined UniBond Premier side Frickley Athletic as player-coach in August 2002 after a season with Northern Counties East outfit Armthorpe Welfare. Has Division Four and Conference winners medals to his name and over 220

League appearances through spells with Grimsby, Darlington, Peterborough, Scunthorpe, Gateshead, Stalybridge Celtic, Spennymoor United, Goole and Harrogate Town.

HINES, LES — Midfielder
Current Club: Halesowen Town
D o B: 07/01/1977   Birthplace: Iserlohn, Germany
Honours won: Conference Winners, Dr Martens Western Div.Winners
Signed for Halesowen Town in the summer of 2000 and quickly won over the fans who voted him player of the season in 2000/01. Les started his career at Aston villa and played alongside Lee Collins, Lee Hendrie, Darren Byfield and Gareth Farrelly. Sadly he failed to make an impact at Villa but sparked interest from Kidderminster Harriers who signed him in 1999. Played a small role in Kiddys promotion to the League. Released at the end of the 1999/00 season and was snapped up quickly by the Yetlz in August 2000. Ha shown great commitment to the club by travelling to and from Scunthorpe to play for Halesowen.

HINGLEY, ANDY — Forward
Current Club: Wealdstone
Previous clubs include Borough Road College - March 2001, Coventry C (Junior).

HINSHELWOOD, DANNY — Defender
Current Club: Selsey
D o B: 04/12/1975   Birthplace: Bromley
Honours won: England Youth Int.
Right back who had an impressive professional career including three years at Nottingham Forest (never actually appeared in their first eleven but was youth team captain). Also played for Portsmouth, Brighton and Torquay as well as collecting 16 England youth caps. More recently had spells at Bognor and Havant before becoming player-manager at Selsey midway through 1999/2000. Said to be the youngest ever boss in the history of the County League. Instantly produced positive results that have led to speculation over the possibility of him moving somewhere to a bigger club. Kept off the pitch during the middle part of 2001/02 with ligament problems.

HINSHELWOOD, MARC — Defender
Current Club: Selsey
Birthplace: Kent
Central defender and cousin of the manager and son of former pro Paul Hinshelwood (who played for Millwall and Crystal Palace). Scored 3 times in 2000/01 and played for Sussex during the latest season. Has previously spent time with Kent team, Lordswood.

HINSHELWOOD, SCOTT — Defender
Current Club: Selsey
Birthplace: Sussex
Defender and younger brother of the manager and one time member of Portsmouths youth squad. Played for Chichester City during 1998/99, but returned to his home village the following season and was voted Selseys player of the year. Sent off in a match against Burgess Hill during January 2001 and picked up a serious knee injury in the same incident. Returned to action towards the end of that campaign. Represented the County during 2001/02.

HINTON, DARREN — Defender
Current Club: Redhill
Birthplace: Sussex
Club Captain who leads by example totally cool and unflappable in the heart of the Redhill defence. Son of former Chelsea man Marvin Hinton, Darren joined Reds from East Preston in the

summer of 1999. Quickly proved to be a firm favourite with the home fans and was voted Supporters' Player of the Year at the end of his first season at Kiln Brow. A double groin injury has ruled Darren out for the most of the season. Still out but hopeful of a comeback in time for next season.

HINTON, PAUL *Forward*
Current Club: Peterlee Newtown
Birthplace: Co.Durham
Previous clubs include: South Shields - July 1999, Whitby T, Shotton Comrades, Peterlee Newtown.

HIPKINS, ADRIAN *Goalkeeper*
Current Club: Stourport Swifts
Previous clubs include: Bewdley T - July 2001.

HIPPERSON, ROSCOE *Defender*
Current Club: Histon
Previous clubs include: Spalding Utd - July 2000, Histon, Cambridge C, Kings Lynn, Thetford T, Diss T, Thetford T.

HIRONS, PAUL *Midfielder*
Current Club: Paulton Rovers
D o B: 06/03/1971   Birthplace: Bristol
Previous clubs include: Trowbridge T - July 1999, Bath C, Taunton T, Forest Green R, Yate T, Clevedon T, Cheltenham T, Westbury Utd, Bath C, Yeovil T, Torquay Utd, Bristol C (Trainee).

HIRST, ANDY *Midfielder*
Current Club: Spennymoor United
Birthplace: Newcastle
Previous clubs include: Whitby T - October 2001, Newcastle Blue Star, West Denton.

HITCHAM, MARK *Goalkeeper*
Current Club: Lowestoft Town
Birthplace: Great Yarmouth
From Youth team.

HITCHCROFT, ANDY *Defender*
Current Club: Chasetown FC
Birthplace: Shropshire
Previous clubs include: Shifnal T - July 1997, Darlaston, Shifnal T.

HIVES, PAUL *Midfielder*
Current Club: Warrington Town
D o B: 24/04/1983   Birthplace: Liverpool
Previous clubs include: Stoke C (Junior) - July 2000, Everton (Junior), Liverpool (Junior).

HO, KOHEI *Midfielder*
Current Club: Staines Town
D o B: 29/08/1977   Birthplace: Japan
Young midfield player who played for Rokko High School and Kyoto University in his native Japan before coming to England in 2001. He has subsequently played for Ashford Town (Middx), Buckfastleigh Rangers of the Devon League and Dr Martens side Bedworth United before signing for Staines Town in February 2002.

HOBBS, DARREN *Defender*
Current Club: Yate Town
Birthplace: Bristol
Previous clubs include: Chippenham T - July 2001, Yate T, Gloucester C, Clevedon T, Bristol C (Trainee).

HOBBS, PAUL *Defender*
Current Club: Ashford Town
Previous clubs include: Hastings T - October 2000, Gillingham (Trainee).

HOBBY, DANNY *Forward*
Current Club: Gresley Rovers
Birthplace: Stoke
Forward or right winger whose previous clubs include Port Vale, Newcastle Town and Kidsgrove Athletic. Signed for Dr Martens Western side Gresley Rovers in July 2002 from Leek Town. He joined Leek in July 1999 and was in his third spell at Harrison Park after returning from Kidsgrove Athletic in April 2002.

HOBSON, LEE *Defender*
Current Club: Alfreton Town
Birthplace: Sheffield
Honours won: NCEL & Cup Winners
A 2001 close season signing for Alfreton Town from NCEL rivals Hallam. Highly experienced and quality defender whose previous clubs include Worksop Town and Sheffield.

HOBSON, MICHAEL *Defender*
Current Club: Oswestry Town
Birthplace: Wales
Towering defender who has taken the step up to the LoW from local football.

HOCKTON, DANNY *Forward*
Current Club: Crawley Town
D o B: 07/02/1979   Birthplace: Barking
Strong-running attacker whose career began at Millwall. Made around 35 first-team appearnces for the Lions before joining Conference side Stevenange Borough for a £7,500 fee in 2000. Switched to Dover Athletic before joining Chelmsford City at the start of the 2001/02 season. Transferred to Dr Martens Premier Division rivals Crawley Town in May 2002.

HODDY, KEVIN *Midfielder*
Current Club: Ford United
D o B: 06/01/1968   Birthplace: Romford
Honours won: Ryman Legaue Div.One Winners
Very experienced midfielder who was with Fulham and Charlton Athletic, making around 30 League appearances, before spending time in Belgium with FC Roeselare. Upon his return to England, Kevin turned out for Welling United in the Conference and then Chelmsford City, Cheshunt and Barking before joining Ford United in the summer of 2000. Played a key role on the Motormens Ryman Division One title success of 2001/02.

HODGE, IAN *Forward*
Current Club: Hayes
Previous clubs include: St.Ives - August 2001.

HODGES, DANNY *Defender*
Current Club: Sutton United
D o B: 14/09/1976   Birthplace: Greenwich
Honours won: England Youth Int., Ryman League Premier Div.Winners
Former England Youth international defender who originally signed for Ryman Division One South side Tooting & Mitcham United from Premier Division Hampton & Richmond Borough in July 2002 but then switched to Sutton United less than a month later. Began his career with Wimbledon and then had spells with Sutton United and Farnborough Town, whom he helped gain promotion back to the Conference, before joining Hampton in October 2001.

HODGES, JEZ　　　　　*Midfielder*
Current Club: Holmer Green
Birthplace: Bucks
Previous clubs include: Flackwell Heath - July 1993, Amersham T, Burnham, Holmer Green.

HODGES, MARK　　　　　*Defender*
Current Club: Cradley Town
Birthplace: Birmingham
Previous clubs include: Chaddesley Corbett - July 2001, Cradley T.

HODGETTS, ANDY　　　　　*Forward*
Current Club: Sutton Coldfield Town
D o B: 05/03/1981　　　　　Birthplace: Birmingham
Previous clubs include: Evesham Utd - December 2001, Halesowen T, Evesham Utd, Kidderminster Harriers, Walsall.

HODGKINSON, GARY　　　　　*Midfielder*
Current Club: Buxton
Birthplace: Derbyshire
From Local football - July 1999, Buxton.

HODGKINSON, TIM　　　　　*Defender*
Current Club: Thornaby on Tees
Birthplace: Cleveland
Previous clubs include: Dormans Ath - July 1997.

HODGSON, CHRIS　　　　　*Forward*
Current Club: Consett
Birthplace: Consett
From Youth team.

HODGSON, NEIL　　　　　*Midfielder*
Current Club: Marske United
Birthplace: Cleveland
Honours won: FA Vase Winners
Previous clubs include: Whitby T - July 1999, Guisborough T.

HODGSON, PAUL　　　　　*Defender*
Current Club: Jarrow Roofing & Boldon Ca
Birthplace: Newcastle
Previous clubs include: Washington - July 1996.

HODGSON, PHIL　　　　　*Defender*
Current Club: Kendal Town
Birthplace: Morecambe
Previous clubs include: Morecambe - July 1995, Netherfield.

HODGSON, STEVE　　　　　*Goalkeeper*
Current Club: Nuneaton Borough
D o B: 23/12/1981　　　　　Birthplace: Macclesfield
Steve signed for Conference side Nuneaton Borough from Macclesfield Town in February 2002. Although he failed to make a first team impact during the 2001/02 season, Boro manager Steve Burr announced that the promising young goalkeeper will have a part to play in Boros first-team. Started out on Manchester City's books.

HODSON, BEN　　　　　*Midfielder*
Current Club: Hayes
D o B: 25/01/1976　　　　　Birthplace: Nottingham
Previous clubs include: Forest Green Rovers - September 1998, Wycombe Wanderers.

HODSON, MARK　　　　　*Defender*
Current Club: Racing Club Warwick
Birthplace: Birmingham
Experienced Non-League defender who joined Racing Club Warwick from Paget Rangers at the start of the 2000/01season. Started out with Sherwood Celtic and has since gained experience with the likes of Solihull Borough, Sutton Coldfield Town, Pelsall Villa and Bloxwich Town.

HODSON, MATT　　　　　*Goalkeeper*
Current Club: Yeading
Birthplace: Middlesex
In his second spell at the club after returning to The Warren at the beginning of season 2001/02. Began in the Wycombe Youth ranks before spells in the Ding reserve ranks and at Marlow before moving to Hayes, where he made numerous appearances between the sticks in the Nationwide Conference.

HOE, MICHAEL　　　　　*Forward*
Current Club: Ossett Albion
Birthplace: Sheffield
Previous clubs include: Parkgate - December 2001, Denaby Utd, Parkgate, Sheffield FC, Alfreton T, Stalybridge Celtic, Guiseley, Worksop T, Hereford Utd, Rotherham Utd (Trainee).

HOGAN, ANTHONY　　　　　*Midfielder*
Current Club: Chorley
D o B: 19/05/1974　　　　　Birthplace: Limerick
Irish-born midfielder who joined Chorley in June 2002 from UniBond rivals Trafford. Plays on the left hand side of the midfield, he signed for Trafford from neighbours Flixton in October 1999. Previously with Ashton United, Curzon Ashton and Maine Road.

HOGARTH, DANNY　　　　　*Midfielder*
Current Club: Welling United
Birthplace: Kent
From Youth team.

HOGG, ANTHONY　　　　　*Midfielder*
Current Club: Welling United
Birthplace: Kent
A central midfield player who started his career with Chelsea. Anthony graduated through Dovers youth ranks and had a spell in Scotland with Ayr United. He returned to Dover Athletic and had a spell on loan at St Leonards during which time he hit a cracking goal against Folkestone Invicta. He joined Invicta on loan in January 2001 and signed for the club after helping them to secure Premier Division safety. Switched to Welling in January 2002.

HOGG, CRAIG　　　　　*Defender*
Current Club: Colwyn Bay
D o B: 08/10/1981　　　　　Birthplace: Liverpool
Highly-promising six-foot central defender who joined Colwyn Bay after being released by Everton during the summer of 2001.

HOGG, GRAEME　　　　　*Defender*
Current Club: Bedlington Terriers
Birthplace: Blyth
A Blyth lad who eventually joined his hometown Spartans in the summer of 1999 after being released by Newcastle United where he was a YTS. Arrived at Welfare Park in September 2000. Graham possesses a sweet left foot and looks to be a fine signing for the Terriers. Can also play on the left side of midfield with equal effect. He suffered last season from a lack of games due to injuries and suspensions.

HOGG, MATT   *Forward*
Current Club: Alfreton Town
Birthplace: Mansfield
Came to UniBond First Division side Alfreton Town in 2000 when he joined the under-19 Academy side run in conjunction with West Notts Technical College. He has represented the British Colleges of Sport on a number of occasions including a tour to the West Indies. Matt impressed with the clubs reserve side last season and also had a spell on loan at Clipstone Welfare of the Central Midlands League and is now looking to stake his claim for a first-team place.

HOGG, MATTHEW   *Midfielder*
Current Club: Vauxhall Motors
Birthplace: Liverpool
Previous clubs include: Bamber Bridge - October 2001, Liverpool (Trainee).

HOGG, PAUL   *Defender*
Current Club: Dunston Federation Brewery
Birthplace: Newcastle
Previous clubs include: Blyth Spartans - August 2000, Dunston Federation, Ponteland Utd.

HOGG, STEVE   *Midfielder*
Current Club: Folkestone Invicta
D o B: 10/06/1981   *Birthplace: Kent*
Steve joined Folkestone Invicta during the summer of 2001 from Kent League neighbours Maidstone United, teaming up with elder brother Anthony, who was then in the first-team but is now at Welling United. Steve made his first stating appearance away to Merthyr Tydfil during April but needed both internal and external stitches after a nasty head injury at the end of the first-half, but he was back for the clubs next game in Wales away to Newport County just nine days later.

HOGGETH, GARY   *Goalkeeper*
Current Club: Workington
D o B: 07/10/1979   *Birthplace: South Shields*
Joined the club in December 1999, having previously been with Bury for two seasons. Actually made his debut in the Unibond league as an outfield substitute before establishing himself I his more accustomed position.

HOLBROOK, ADAM   *Midfielder*
Current Club: Newport Isle Of Wight
D o B: 17/10/1980   *Birthplace: Isle of Wight*
Previous clubs include: Portsmouth - December 2000.

HOLCROFT, PETER   *Midfielder*
Current Club: Kidsgrove Athletic
D o B: 03/01/1976   *Birthplace: Liverpool*
Honours won: NWCL Winners
Signed for Kidsgrove from Northwich Victoria, this skilful midfielder made an immediate impression with four goals in his first two games. Previous clubs include Everton, Swindon Town and Exeter City.

HOLCROFT, ROBBIE   *Goalkeeper*
Current Club: Skelmersdale United
Birthplace: Liverpool
Previous clubs include: Colwyn Bay - August 1996, Droylsden, Accrington Stanley, Colwyn Bay, Marine, Holywell T, Skelmersdale Utd, Stantondale, Liverpool.

HOLDCROFT, DANNY   *Goalkeeper*
Current Club: Caernarfon Town
D o B: 22/05/1978   *Birthplace: Chester*
Previous clubs include: Buckley T - March 2002.

HOLDCROFT, MARK   *Midfielder*
Current Club: Wednesfield
Birthplace: Wolverhampton
Previous clubs include: Blakenall - July 2001, Wednesfield, Rushall Olympic, Wednesfield, Rushall Olympic, Wednesfield, Bloxwich T, Stourbridge, Bloxwich T, Blakenall, Wolverhampton Utd.

HOLDCROFT, ROBBIE   *Defender*
Current Club: Wednesfield
Birthplace: Wolverhampton
Previous clubs include: Rushall Olympic - August 2000, Wednesfield.

HOLDEN, MICHAEL   *Midfielder*
Current Club: Sittingbourne
Birthplace: Kent
From Youth team.

HOLDEN, STEVE   *Defender*
Current Club: Cambridge City
D o B: 04/09/1972   *Birthplace: Luton*
Honours won: England Semi-Pro Int., Dr Martens Premier Winners
One of the most experienced nd respected central defenders in the Dr Martens League, Steve is a former England semi-professional international who joined Cambridge City in June 1998 from Conference club Stevenage Borough. Started his career with Leicester City, but made just one League appearance before being transferred to Carlisle United in 1992. Injuries blighted his time at Brunton Park and he eventually joined Kettering Town where his form earned him his England call-up. Moved to neighbouring Rushden & Diamonds and helped them into the Conference before joining City.

HOLDEN, TOM   *Defender*
Current Club: Peacehaven & Telscombe
Birthplace: Sussex
Defender who was red-carded twice for Ringmer during the early part of 2000/01 and subsequently received a lengthy suspension. Joined Peacehaven for the start of the following campaign.

HOLDEN, TONY   *Forward*
Current Club: Ringmer
Birthplace: Sussex
Superb striker: and a former Shoreham and Worthing player who joined Burgess Hill midway through 1999/2000 and finished that season as the clubs leading scorer with 22 goals. Transferred to Southwick in September 2000, and helped steer them to the Division Two title before joining Ringmer in October 2001, and subsequently went through a real purple patch (scored 11 goals in the space of three games midway through the season - including a five-timer against Oakwood). Known as Goalden Holden.

HOLDER, JORDEN   *Midfielder*
Current Club: Oxford City
D o B: 22/10/1982   *Birthplace: Oxford*
Previous clubs include: Oxford Utd - March 2002.

HOLDING, SCOTT — Forward

Current Club: Boreham Wood

Birthplace: Essex

Utility player who is capable of performing well in a number of positions on the field. Joined Ryman Premier side Boreham Wood in the summer of 2002 from neighbours and rivals St Albans City. Started out at Enfield and then had spells with Dagenham & Redbridge second string, Ford United and East Thurrock United, joining the Saints in March 2002.

HOLLAND, JAMIE — Forward

Current Club: Lymington & New Milton

Birthplace: Dorset

Previous clubs include: Poole T - May 2002.

HOLLAND, MARK — Defender

Current Club: Stafford Town

Birthplace: Staffordshire

Previous clubs include: Stourport Swifts - July 2001, Eccleshall.

HOLLENBACH, BECKETT — Defender

Current Club: St.Albans City

D o B: 17/02/1980   *Birthplace: United States*

Left-sided defender who signed for Ryman Premier side St Albans City in August 2002 after appearing against them for Northampton Town in a pre-season friendly. Appeared on the college circuit during a degree course in his native North America.

HOLLIDGE, KRIS — Midfielder

Current Club: Bromley

Birthplace: Kent

Youngster who joined Bromley at the commencement of last season but appearances have been limited. Kris spent a loan period at Kent League side Slade Green last season but is now a fringe member at Bromley. Played for Cambridge United and Luton Town before joining Welling United. Student lives in Bromley.

HOLLIER, PAUL — Forward

Current Club: Jarrow Roofing & Boldon Ca

D o B: 19/03/1980   *Birthplace: Newcastle*

Previous clubs include: Newcastle Blue Star - December 2001, Gretna, Newcastle Blue Star.

HOLLINGDALE, ROB — Midfielder

Current Club: Woking

Birthplace: London

Rob started out as a junior with Arsenal. He was signed by Woking for a £15,000 fee from Ryman League club Boreham Wood in late September 1998, the first signing by Brian McDermott. He was in the Boreham Wood sides that enjoyed good FA Cup runs in the previous two seasons. Rob has Ryman League honours and was on the 1998 Middlesex Wanderers tour to Brunei and Myanmar (Burma). Joint Supporters Club Player of the Year for 1998/99.

HOLLINGSWORTH, ORLANDO — Defender

Current Club: Carshalton Athletic

D o B: 09/10/1977   *Birthplace: London*

In his second spell with Carshalton Athletic after rejoining in February 2001 from neighbours Croydon. Originally a trainee at Arsenal, he then turned out for Egham Town before signing for Carshalton the first time.

HOLLINGWORTH, NATHAN — Defender

Current Club: Hucknall Town

Previous clubs include: Teversal - July 2001.

HOLLIS, DAVE — Midfielder

Current Club: Coalville Town

Birthplace: Leicester

Honours won: Leicestershire Senior League Winners

Previous clubs include: Corby T - July 2001, Friar Lane OB.

HOLLIS, SIMON — Forward

Current Club: Solihull Borough

Birthplace: Birmingham

A young player now actually in his fifth season with Solihull. He first appeared in the First team against Stamford in September 1998. He came through Solihulls Youth & reserve teams. Last season he won the Goal of the Season award for the second successive season.

HOLLIS, STEVE — Defender

Current Club: Accrington Stanley

D o B: 22/08/1972   *Birthplace: Liverpool*

Signed for Accrington Stanley from Ashton United at the start of the 1999/2000 season. Started out as a trainee with Liverpool before joining Wigan, playing one first team game. Also played with Fleetwood Town.

HOLLMAN, JAMES — Goalkeeper

Current Club: Ipswich Wanderers

Birthplace: Canterbury

Previous clubs include: Diss T - July 1999, Chelmsford C, Kings Lynn, Ipswich T.

HOLLOWAY, CHRIS — Midfielder

Current Club: Newport County

D o B: 05/02/1980   *Birthplace: Swansea*

Swansea-born midfielder who joined Dr Martens Premier side Newport County in last August 2002. Started his career with Exeter City, where he made over 60 League appearances. Then spent the 2001/02 season at Rotherham before being released at the end of the campaign. Spent much of the summer of 2002 on trial at Mansfield, who, in the end, decided they couldnt offer him a deal.

HOLLOWAY, GARY — Midfielder

Current Club: Farnborough Town

Birthplace: Surrey

Highly-rated midfielder who first came to the fore as a teenager in Ryman League Walton & Hershams first-team. Established himself at Stompond Lane and earned a move into the Premier Division with Hampton & Richmond Borough at the start of the 2000/01 season. Moved up the football ladder again in October 2001 by signing for Conference side Farnborough Town.

HOLLOWAY, JAMIE — Midfielder

Current Club: Barking & East Ham United

Previous clubs include: Leyton Pennant - July 2001, Barking, Ruislip Manor, Dover Ath., QPR, Millwall (Trainee).

HOLLOWAY, JON — Midfielder

Current Club: Worcester City

D o B: 11/02/1977   *Birthplace: Swindon*

Highly-rated midfield player who signed a two-year contract for Worcester City after leaving Bath City in May 2001. Jon works as a development officer with Swindon Town, where he started out as an apprentice. He spent three years at the County Ground, and then had a three-year stint at Gloucester City before moving onto Bath for two seasons.

HOLMES, BRIAN   Defender
Current Club: Prescot Cables
Birthplace: Liverpool
Previous clubs include: Burscough - July 2000, Droylsden, Congleton T, Skelmersdale Utd, Warrington T, Burscough.

HOLMES, BRIAN   Midfielder
Current Club: Haverhill Rovers
Birthplace: Suffolk
A Haverhill Rover through-and-through; in his twentieth season at Hamlet Croft; has picked up First Team Player of the Year, Supporters' Player of the Year, Reserve Team Player of the Year and Top Scorer awards for both sides in his time.

HOLMES, CARL   Midfielder
Current Club: Worksop Town
Birthplace: Manchester
Previous clubs include: Droylsden - December 2001, Buxton, Dove Holes, Buxton, Stockport Co.

HOLMES, CARL   Midfielder
Current Club: Kings Lynn
Birthplace: Northampton
Carl is a central midfielder who joined Kings Lynn from Stamford in June 2002. Had been with the Daniels since the start of the 2001/02 season after signing from Wealdstone where he was the highest scorer for 2 of his 3 seasons there. First started with United Counties League team Northampton Spencer where he was among the top scorers while still at the age of only 17.

HOLMES, CHRIS   Goalkeeper
Current Club: Kidsgrove Athletic
D o B: 13/09/1964   Birthplace: Staffordshire
Experienced Non-League goalkeeper who signed for Vauxhall Motors from Newcastle Town for a £2,000 fee in December 2000. Previously with Nantwich Town, Leek Town, Kidsgrove Athletic and Ashton United, Chris was a target for Motors earlier and once on board he quickly demonstrated his value with some match-winning performances. However, after helping the club to runners-up spot in 2001/02, Chris was involved in a swap deal that took him back nearer his home, joining UniBond First Division newvcomers Kidsgrove Athletic in August 2002.

HOLMES, DAMIEN   Defender
Current Club: Farsley Celtic
D o B: 27/10/1974   Birthplace: Leeds
Previous clubs include: Garforth T - July 2000, Leeds Utd (Trainee).

HOLMES, DARREN   Midfielder
Current Club: Gainsborough Trinity
Previous clubs include: Hallam - October 2000, Worsbrough Bridge, Tadcaster Alb., Glasshoughton Welfare, Ossett Alb., Emley.

HOLMES, DAVID   Forward
Current Club: Ilkeston Town
D o B: 22/11/1972   Birthplace: Derby
David had two loan spells at Ilkeston Town during the 2000/01season before signing on a more permanent basis at the start of the following campaign. He had League experience with Scarborough before joining Gresley Rovers. Moved to Gloucester City and then Burton Albion. David is a whole hearted striker who quickly became a fans favourite.

HOLMES, LAWRENCE   Forward
Current Club: Hanwell Town
D o B: 11/07/1961   Birthplace: London
Previous clubs include: Northwood - July 1999, Chesham Utd, Northwood, Hemel Hempstead, Kingsbury T, Boreham Wood, Hendon, Redbridge Forest, Harrow B, Harlow T, Edgware T.

HOLMES, MATTHEW   Midfielder
Current Club: Dorchester Town
D o B: 01/08/1969   Birthplace: Luton
Previous clubs include: Charlton Ath - June 2000, Blackburn R, West Ham Utd, AFC Bournemouth.

HOLMES, STEWART   Defender
Current Club: Crawley Town
Birthplace: Sussex
Defender: won two Sussex County League championships with Burgess Hill in the 90s: went from Bognor Regis to Lewes in October 1998 before signing for Saltdean at the start of the 1999/2000 season: one of numerous players to leave the Tigers midway through 2000/01, and subsequently joined Crawley.

HOLMES, TOMMY   Defender
Current Club: Total Network Solutions
D o B: 01/09/1979   Birthplace: Birkenhead
Solid central defender who can also cope as full-back. A handful for any forward to get past, and very good in the air. The Mr Reliable of the TNS side, whom he joined in July 2000 after being released by Tranmere Rovers.

HOLMSHAW, JAMIE   Goalkeeper
Current Club: Stocksbridge Park Steels
Birthplace: Sheffield
Exprienced Non-League goalkeeper who joined UniBond First Division Stocksbridge Park Steels in June 2002 from Premier Division Worksop Town. Had been with the Tigers since October 1995, when he joined from Gainsborough Trinity.

HOLMSHAW, RICHARD   Midfielder
Current Club: Ossett Albion
Birthplace: Sheffield
Previous clubs include: Matlock T - March 2002, Stocksbridge Park Steels, Denaby Utd, Alfreton T, Sheffield Wednesday (Trainee).

HOLNESS, CORIN   Defender
Current Club: Mickleover Sports
D o B: 13/01/1972   Birthplace: Derby
Previous clubs include: Belper T - July 1999, Gresley R, Belper T, Burton Alb., Derby Co (Junior).

HOLROYD, JASON   Midfielder
Current Club: Atherton Laburnum Rovers
Birthplace: Salford
A very experienced and confident player, Jason is also the assistant manager at LR whose commanding presence on the pitch is of great benefit. He joined LR from neighbours Atherton Collieries last season. Jason is a sales manager who enjoys reading.

HOLSGROVE, PAUL   Midfielder
Current Club: Hayes
D o B: 26/08/1969   Birthplace: Wellington
Previous clubs include: Slough T - October 2001, Barry T, Darlington, Hibernian, Brighton, Stoke C, Crewe Alexandra, Reading, Millwall, Heracles (Holland), Luton T, Wokingham T, Aldershot.

HOLSGROVE, PETER　　　*Midfielder*

Current Club: Hayes

Previous clubs include: Wycombe Wanderers - September 2001.

HOLT, GRANT　　　*Forward*

Current Club: Barrow

D o B: 12/04/1981　　　　*Birthplace: Carlisle*

Born in Carlisle, Grant is a striker who began his career with Workington and first made an impact during their North West Counties First Division title-winning campaign. He then moved to Halifax Town for a four-figure fee in the autumn of 1999. He made four League appearances for the Shaymen without scoring. He had a spell on loan with Barrow during March 2000. He made his debut at Spennymoor United and scored once in seven outings before returning to the Division Three outfit. During the early part of the current season, he had an extended loan spell with Workington in the UniBond First Division. He returned to Barrow, initially on loan at the end of February 2001 and made the move permanent the following July. Had a spell playing in Singapore with Sengkang Marine during the summer of 2002 before rejoining the Bluebirds in August 2002.

HOLT, MICHAEL　　　*Forward*

Current Club: Northwich Victoria

Birthplace: Barnoldswick

Previous clubs include: Rochdale - August 1999, Preston NE, Blackburn R.

HOLT, NATHAN　　　*Defender*

Current Club: Cirencester Town

D o B: 29/07/1973　　　　*Birthplace: Swindon*

A very gifted defender, who was signed by Cirencester Town from Hellenic League side Highworth Town in the summer of 2001. Started out with Swindon Supermarine.

HOLTOM, JAY　　　*Midfielder*

Current Club: Shepshed Dynamo

D o B: 15/12/1980　　　　*Birthplace: Nuneaton*

Previous clubs include: Nuneaton Borough - October 2001.

HOLTOM, ROSS　　　*Midfielder*

Current Club: Shepshed Dynamo

D o B: 25/03/1979　　　　*Birthplace: Nuneaton*

Midfielder who returned to England in the summer of 2002 after a spell in Australia, where he turned out for Swan IC. Joined Dr Martens Western side Shepshed Dynamo, where his brother Jay is also a squad member. Previously with Oswestry Town.

HOLTZMAN, GARY　　　*Forward*

Current Club: Bracknell Town

Birthplace: Berkshire

Previous clubs include: Reading - July 1999.

HOMER, CHRIS　　　*Defender*

Current Club: Redditch United

Birthplace: Worcestershire

Solid and reliable defender who signed for Redditch United in May 2002 from Midland Alliance outfit Rushall Olympic. Started out at Lye Town and also saw service at Sandwell Borough, Oldbury United and Willenhall Town.

HOMER, DANNY　　　*Midfielder*

Current Club: Hamble ASSC

Birthplace: Portsmouth

Previous clubs include: AFC Totton - July 2001.

HONE, ANDY　　　*Goalkeeper*

Current Club: Matlock Town

Previous clubs include: Staveley Miners Welfare - August 2001.

HONE, MARK　　　*Defender*

Current Club: Welling United

D o B: 31/03/1968　　　　*Birthplace: Croydon*

Honours won: England Semi-Pro Int.

Vastly experienced defender who has won five caps for the England semi-professional international side. Began his career with Crystal Palace but made just 3 first-team appearances for the Selhurst Park outfit before joining Welling United in 1990. His form not only attracted the England selectors but also the League scouts nd it came as little surprise when he was sold to Southend United in 1994. Went on to play over 120 times in the League for Southend and then Lincoln before returning to Welling via a spell at Kettering Town in July 1999.

HONEY, CHRIS　　　*Forward*

Current Club: Hastings United

Birthplace: Sussex

Young forward, previously on the books of Millwall. Joined Hastings in February 2000 and scored five times during the second-half of 2000/01.

HONEY, PAUL　　　*Midfielder*

Current Club: Sutton United

Birthplace: Surrey

Honours won: England Schoolboy Int.

A product of Sutton United's youth team and another to make an impact at first-team level after making his senior debut in December 2000. An impressive and highly-promising midfielder, he represented England Schoolboys during their tour of the Far East.

HONEYBALL, DANNY　　　*Defender*

Current Club: Leyton Pennant

D o B: 25/11/1977　　　　*Birthplace: London*

Full-back who can also operate in the wing-back role. Danny became one of the youngest managers in senior football when he was appointed as player boss of Ryman Division One side Leyton Pennant in July 2002. Was a summer 2001 signing for St Albans City from Aylesbury United after previous service with Barnet and Harlow Town.

HONEYBALL, SCOTT　　　*Defender*

Current Club: Aylesbury United

Previous clubs include: Gravesend & Northfleet - November 1999, Bishops Stortford, JKB (Finland), Gravesend, Leyton Orient.

HONOR, CHRIS　　　*Defender*

Current Club: Bath City

D o B: 05/06/1968　　　　*Birthplace: Bristol*

Honours won: Dr Martens League Premier Div. Winners

Vastly experienced defender who joined Dr Martens Premier side Bath City in July 2002 from Ryman Premier outfit Basingstoke Town. Had signed for Basingstoke from Forest Green Rovers in July 2000 after helping the Gloucestershire side to promotion to the Conference. Chris has experience at all levels and has played for Bristol City, Torquay and Swansea in the Football League and in Scotland for Partick Thistle and Airdrie, appearing for the latter in two cup finals.

HOOD, JOHN — Goalkeeper

Current Club: Goole AFC

Birthplace: Yorkshire

Previous clubs include: Glasshoughton Welfare - November 2001, Ossett Alb., Frickley Ath., Ossett Alb., Glasshoughton Welfare, Ossett Alb.

HOOK, CLAYTON — Midfielder

Current Club: Cinderford Town

Birthplace: Gloucestershire

Forest of Dean-based midfield player who has now played over 150 games for Cinderford Town. Re-signed for the club from Fairford Town in August 1999 and has also played for Cheltenham Town's reserves and for Harrow Hill in the Hellenic League.

HOOK, DAVID — Goalkeeper

Current Club: Hendon

Birthplace: London

Vastly experienced goalkeeper who signed for Hendon before the start of the 2001/02 season. David had previously given many years of service to Harrow Borough where he was a great favourite. Has also played for Hampton, Chesham United and was a junior at Reading.

HOOK, LEE — Goalkeeper

Current Club: Whitstable Town

Birthplace: Kent

Previous clubs include: Ramsgate - January 1999, Wolverhampton Wanderers (Junior).

HOOK, MARTIN — Forward

Current Club: Northwood

Previous clubs include: Boreham Wood - July 2000, Hayes, Chelsea (Trainee).

HOOK, STEVE — Defender

Current Club: Chorley

Previous clubs include: Guiseley - July 2000, Chorley, Bury, Goole T, Halifax T.

HOOPER, DEAN — Midfielder

Current Club: Aldershot Town

D o B: 13/04/1971   Birthplace: Harefield

Talented midfielder or wing back who joined Aldershot Town in May 2002 from Peterborough. Spent the latter part of the 2001/02 season on-loan at Dagenham & Redbridge and had previous experience in Non-League football before joining the Posh, where he made over 100 League appearances, in August 1998. Started his career as a junior at Brentford and then turned out for Marlow, Yeading and Chalfont St Peter before joining Hayes under current Shots boss Terry Brown in 1994. Moved to Kingstonian in August 1998 before joining Posh.

HOOPER, ELLIS — Defender

Current Club: Crawley Town

Birthplace: Crawley

Centre-back who re-joined Dr Martens League Premier Division side Crawley Town in July 2002 from Sussex County Leaguers Horsham YMCA. He came into the Horsham side late in 1999/00 after he had been playing for Crawleys reserve side and was previously at Ryman League neighbours Horsham in 1998/99. Capable of producing really classy performances, he was selected for the Sussex under-21 squad during 2001/02. Left YMCA in November 2001 to travel but then represented the county's senior side upon his return in March 2002.

HOOPER, NICK — Forward

Current Club: Staines Town

D o B: 12/11/1980   Birthplace: Surrey

Highly-rated young striker who originally joined Staines Town on-loan from Farnborough Town in August 2000 before making the move a permanent one two months later. His career as a youngster began with Portsmouth and he went on to have a short spell with Doncaster Rovers before spending two years with Farnborough. Has formed a terrific partnership with Mark Butler in the Staines attack.

HOPE, DANNY — Defender

Current Club: Brigg Town

Birthplace: Hull

Previous clubs include: Pontefract Collieries - July 2000.

HOPKINS, CRAIG — Midfielder

Current Club: Ossett Albion

Birthplace: Nottingham

Previous clubs include: Hednesford T - February 2002, Ilkeston T, Kettering T, Spalding Utd, Kings Lynn, Shirebrook T.

HOPKINS, FRED — Midfielder

Current Club: Bridgwater Town

D o B: 15/05/1983   Birthplace: Somerset

From Youth team.

HOPKINS, GARETH — Forward

Current Club: Cirencester Town

D o B: 14/06/1980   Birthplace: Cheltenham

Young striker who was top scorer for Cheltenham Town's reserve side in 2001/02. Featured 8 times in the senior side at Whaddon Road and also had loan spells wih Bath City and Forest Green Rovers. Looked like joining Conference side Kettering Town in the summer of 2002 after being released by the Robins, but opted to stay nearer home with Dr Martens Western outfit Cirencester Town instead.

HOPKINS, STEVE — Defender

Current Club: Connahs Quay Nomads

Birthplace: Wales

From Youth team.

HOPKINS, TONY — Defender

Current Club: Cinderford Town

Previous clubs include: UWIC Inter Cardiff - June 2001, Newport Co., UWIC, Merthyr Tydfil, Chesham Utd, Hendon, Aldershot T, Ebbw Vale, Merthyr Tydfil, Ebbw Vale, Bristol C (Trainee), Chelsea (Trainee).

HOPPER, GAVIN — Goalkeeper

Current Club: Sittingbourne

D o B: 28/09/1980   Birthplace: Kent

First-choice goalkeeper who signed for Sittinbourne in July 2001 from Dr Martens League rivals Fisher Athletic. Former Gillingham youth who has previous Non-League experience with Gravesend & Northfleet, Beckenham Town, Chertsey Town and Erith & Belvedere.

HOPPER, TONY — Midfielder

Current Club: Barrow

D o B: 31/05/1976   Birthplace: Carlisle

Midfielder Tony began his career with Carlisle United as a trainee and graduated to their full time ranks. He made his League debut in the 1992/93 season and by the end of the 2001/02 season had played over 100 games for the Cumbrians, scoring once before he was released. In March 1993, Tony had a month long spell with Barrow on loan, playing six times and scoring once. Tony re-joined the UniBond Premier club in August 2002.

HORGAN, GARY — *Midfielder*
Current Club: Bath City
D o B: 19/04/1977   *Birthplace: Swindon*
Signed for Dr Martens Premier side Bath City in July 2002 from Western Division neighbours Cirencester Town. Had joined Cirencester from Hungerford Town in July 2000, A versatile midfield player with a wealth of experience, Gary started his career with Swindon Town and then turned out for Swindon Supermarine for a number of years.

HORNE, ADRIAN — *Defender*
Current Club: Shifnal Town
Birthplace: Shropshire
Previous clubs include: Pelsall Villa - August 2001, Rushall Olympic, Pelsall Villa, Stourbridge, Pelsall Villa, Moor Green, Banbury Utd, Pelsall Villa, Rushall Olympic.

HORNE, BARRY — *Midfielder*
Current Club: Belper Town
D o B: 18/05/1962   *Birthplace: St Asaph*
Honours won: Wales Int., FA Cup Winners
Previous clubs include: Walsall - September 2001, Kidderminster Harriers, Sheffield Wednesday, Huddersfield T, Birmingham C, Everton, Southampton, Portsmouth, Wrexham, Rhyl.

HORNE, JAY — *Midfielder*
Current Club: Ossett Albion
Birthplace: Doncaster
Previous clubs include: Goole AFC - December 2000, North Ferriby Utd, Hatfield Main, Worsbrough Bridge, Goole T.

HORNE, STUART — *Goalkeeper*
Current Club: Romford
D o B: 05/03/1970   *Birthplace: Essex*
Previous clubs include: Barking - October 2000, Romford, Purfleet, Whyteleafe, Barking, Enfield.

HORNER, GLYN — *Midfielder*
Current Club: Oadby Town
D o B: 01/10/1971   *Birthplace: Sheffield*
Previous clubs include: Kirby Muxloe - August 2001, Gresley R, Corby T, Gresley R, Kirby Muxloe, Holwell Sports.

HORNER, RICHARD — *Defender*
Current Club: Aylesbury United
Birthplace: Liverpool
Experienced Liverpool-born defender whose playing days began with north-west Non-League sides Southport, Stalybridge Celtic and Droyslden. Moved south to join Wealdstone and then joined Farnborough Town in January 1999. A moves to Sutton United and Chesham United followed before he rejoined the Stones in November 2001. Transferred to Aylesbury United in May 2002.

HORRIGAN, IAN — *Defender*
Current Club: Vauxhall Motors
D o B: 28/03/1973   *Birthplace: Liverpool*
A former Everton trainee, Ian suffered a bad injury that kept him out of the game for over 18 months. A much-travelled defender, he has seen service with Prescot Cables, Knowsley United, Conwy United, Barrow, Morecambe, Altrincham, Droylsden, Stafford Rangers, Caernarfon Town and Rhyl, from whom he joined Vauxhall Motors in July 2000.

HORRILL, DANNY — *Defender*
Current Club: Newport Isle Of Wight
Birthplace: Sussex
Highly-rated young defender who spent one season at Portfield in1999/00) before moving to Pagham. Good enough to play in the Football League according to former Wick boss and current Newport Isle of Wight manager Richie Reynolds, and has had trials with Portsmouth, Charlton and Southampton. Missed two months early on in 2001/02 thanks to injury, and formed part of the mass exodus of players from Nyetimber Lane when Reynolds was sacked in November and joined Wick in February 2002. Reunited with Reynolds at Dr Martens side Newport in July 2002.

HORSLEY, JAMIE — *Midfielder*
Current Club: Ossett Albion
Birthplace: Halifax
Previous clubs include: Doncaster Rovers - February 2002, Huddersfield T.

HORSTED, JON — *Defender*
Current Club: Wokingham Town
Birthplace: Berkshire
Previous clubs include: Farnham T - September 2000, Aldershot T.

HOSKINS, ANDY — *Forward*
Current Club: Gloucester City
Birthplace: Gloucester
Previous clubs include: Brockworth - July 2001, Cinderford T, Gloucester C, Cinderford T, Forest Green R, Tuffley R.

HOSKINS, JASON — *Defender*
Current Club: Cinderford Town
Birthplace: Gloucestershire
Previous clubs include: Caldicot T - January 2002.

HOTCHKISS, JOHN — *Goalkeeper*
Current Club: Corinthian Casuals
Birthplace: Surrey
Signed for Corinthian Casuals from Carshalton Athletic in 1999. Joh is a reliable goalkeeper who has been in good form since his arrival, becoming a first-team regular. Was on the books at Peterborough United as a youngster.

HOTTE, MARK — *Defender*
Current Club: Scarborough
D o B: 27/09/1978   *Birthplace: Bradford*
Defender Mark was one of several players signed by Scarborough manager Russell Slade from Oldham during the 2001/02 season. Born in Bradford, he left Boundary Park in January last season appearing 17 times for his new club.

HOUGHTON, GARY — *Defender*
Current Club: Letchworth
Birthplace: Herts
Previous clubs include: Potton Utd - July 1998, Langford, Shefford.

HOUGHTON, MICHAEL — *Defender*
Current Club: Winsford United
Birthplace: Cheshire
Previous clubs include: Congleton T - December 2001.

H

HOUGHTON, SCOTT — Midfielder

Current Club: Stevenage Borough

D o B: 22/10/1971 — Birthplace: Hitchin
Honours won: England Schoolboy & Youth Int.
Wayne Turners first signing as manager of Stevenage, Scott joined the club in March 2002. Hitchin-born, he made over 250 league appearances, for a string of clubs including Tottenham, Ipswich, Charlton, Cambridge, Gillingham, Luton, Walsall, Peterborough, Southend, Orient and Halifax.

HOUGHTON, WAYNE — Defender

Current Club: Braintree Town

Birthplace: Essex
Impressive defender who joined Ryman Premier side Braintree Town in July 2002 after spending three years in the Jewson Eastern League with Tiptree United. Actually began his playing days with Tiptree before having a spell at Maldon Town. Played in the 2002 FA Carlsberg Vase final t Villa Park.

HOUSE, KENNY — Defender

Current Club: Congleton Town

Birthplace: Staffs
Defender/midfield. Age 23. Signed in summer 00 from local side Vale Juniors OB. Previously with Knypersley Vics and represented Macclesfield & District in the County Youth Cup. A,

HOUSHAM, STEVE — Midfielder

Current Club: Barrow

D o B: 24/02/1976 — Birthplace: Gainsborough
Born in Gainsborough, Steve is an attacking midfielder who joined Scunthorpe United as a trainee and had made 106 League appearances for them, scoring four times by the end of the 1998/99 season. He had a spell on loan with Gainsborough Trinity early in the 1999/00 season and joined Barrow on loan from the Irons in January 2000. He returned to Scunthorpe United in February and remained with them until the end of the season when he was released, after making 115 league appearances for them, scoring four times. He joined Barrow permanently in July 2000.

HOUSLEY, CRAIG — Forward

Current Club: Alfreton Town

Birthplace: Nottingham
Honours won: NCEL & Cup Winners
A Highly-promising young striker who joined Alfreton Town after being released by Notts County midway through the season 2000/01. Craig has shown his potential and is certainly a young man who will progress in the game at higher levels.

HOUSTON, TYRONE — Defender

Current Club: Slough Town

D o B: 15/09/1972 — Birthplace: London
Previous clubs include: Maidenhead Utd - November 2001, Chalfont St.Peter, Maidenhead Utd, Slough T.

HOWARD, ANTHONY — Defender

Current Club: Slough Town

Birthplace: London
Young central defender capable of playing in a number of positions. Signed from Hampton and Richmond Borough. Since joining Slough Anthony has made a good impression on the Wexham Park faithful. He scored on his debut against Bishops Stortford and followed that up but adding a second goal in two games against Harlow Town. He is a strong player who is equally good in the air as he is on the ground. He has appeared as a centre back and a right back for the Rebels this season and has looked very assured and composed in whatever position the

youngster has played in. Anthony started his career at Fulham where he was a regular member of their youth side. After his release he joined Hampton & Richmond, but did interest a number of league clubs before signing for the Beavers. He made a number of impressive appearances for the Beavers before joining Slough. Anthony is only eighteen years of age and has a bright future in the game. He is one of a number of promising youngsters that manager Steve Browne has brought into the side this season.

HOWARD, CRAIG — Defender

Current Club: Sutton United

Birthplace: Surrey
Another graduate of Sutton United's youth team who featured regularly for the reserves during the 2000/01 season and has impressed in defence after making his senior debut in February 01.

HOWARD, GARY — Defender

Current Club: Boreham Wood

Birthplace: Essex
An experienced defender who is also capable of performing in midfield. Joined Boreham Wood in June 2002 from Ryman Premier rivals Purfleet. Had arrived at Fleet in the summer of 1999 following a spell with Dagenham & Redbridge. Has also turned out for Great Wakering Rovers, Billericay Town, Chelmsford City and Grays Athletic.

HOWARD, JAMIE — Defender

Current Club: Penrith

Birthplace: Cumbria
Previous clubs include: Netherfield - July 1997.

HOWARD, JON — Defender

Current Club: Stafford Rangers

D o B: 02/04/1974 — Birthplace: Birmingham
Talented defender, Jon arrived at Stafford Rangers in February 2002 after a long spell with Tamworth. He joined the Lambs in 1994 and was a regular and popular player until injuries restricted his appearances in the last year at the club. Before joining Tamworth he was with Wolverhampton Wanderers.

HOWARD, JOSH — Midfielder

Current Club: Hyde United

D o B: 15/10/1980 — Birthplace: Manchester
Previous clubs include: Stalybridge Celtic - July 2001, Manchester Utd.

HOWARD, KENNY — Defender

Current Club: Gloucester City

Birthplace: Gloucestershire
Yet another signing from local league team Brockworth who was signed up on DML forms having impressed in several mid-season friendly and training games. Initially signed as cover he has apparently continued to impress and has forced his way into the first team squad, although appearances to date have been too brief to offer any judgement.

HOWARD, RICHARD — Forward

Current Club: St Margaretsbury

D o B: 06/06/1976 — Birthplace: Harlow
Previous clubs include: Hoddesdon T - July 1999, Cheshunt, St Margaretsbury, Brentford.

HOWARD, TERRY — *Defender*
Current Club: Great Wakering Rovers
D o B: 26/02/1966 — *Birthplace: Stepney*
Giant central defender with vast experience. Joined Ryman Division One North side Great Wakering Rovers in July 2002 from Premier Division Braintree Town. Had signed for the Iron in the summer of 2002 from Boreham Wood. Made over 400 League appearances for Chelsea, Leyton Orient and Wycombe before going Non-League with Yeovil Town, Woking and Aldershot Town.

HOWARTH, ANDY — *Defender*
Current Club: Coalville Town
Birthplace: Leicester
Honours won: Leicestershire Senior League Winners
Previous clubs include: Thringstone - July 2001, St Andrews, Leicester Utd.

HOWARTH, CARL — *Forward*
Current Club: Rossendale United
Birthplace: Lancashire
Forward whose career began at Everton as a youngster. Drifted into Non-League football after being released from Goodison Park and played for Nelson in the North West Counties League and then for Burscough in the UniBond before joining Rossendale United in November 2002. Became a regular goalscorer at UniBond First Division level with Dale.

HOWARTH, LEE — *Defender*
Current Club: Kettering Town
D o B: 03/01/1968 — *Birthplace: Bolton*
Honours won: Dr Martens League Premier Div.Winners
Vastly experienced central defender who joined Kettering Town from Boston United on a permanent basis during the early part of the 2001/02 season after a period on-loan at Rockingham Road. Made over 250 League appearances with Peterborough, Mansfield and Barnet after starting out at Chorley.

HOWARTH, PAUL — *Defender*
Current Club: Rossendale United
Birthplace: Lancashire
Defender whose career began at Shrewsbury Town, where he turned professional before being released in 1999/00. Returned to his native Lancashire and signed for Accrington Stanley where he became a regular in the UniBond League. Switched to neighbours Rossendale United in March 2002.

HOWDEN, HUGH — *Forward*
Current Club: Southwick
Birthplace: Sussex
Big experienced forward, having played for Chichester City and Bognor Regis in previous years: more recently spent time at Bosham until joining the new Withdean side for the start of 2001/02: also appeared for Southwick during the autumn.

HOWE, BOBBY — *Midfielder*
Current Club: Havant & Waterlooville
D o B: 06/01/1973 — *Birthplace: Annitsford*
Bobbys League career began with Newcastle United, before he moved as a trainee to Nottingham Forest in December 1990. He spent eight years with the then Premiership side and enjoyed a brief loan period at Ipswich Town in 1997 before moving to Swindon Town in January 1998 for a £30,000 fee. There he played four and a half seasons, notching up over one hundred appearances and eleven goals from his midfield position. In the 2001/02 season it was his 76th minute goal that settled Swindons FA Cup tie with Hereford United, putting the team into a fouth round match with Manchester City. Bobby signed for Dr

Martens Premier side Havant & Waterlooville two days before the start of the 2002/03 campaign.

HOWE, CHRIS — *Goalkeeper*
Current Club: Frickley Athletic
Birthplace: Doncaster
Previous clubs include: Rossington Main - December 2001.

HOWE, JAMIE — *Defender*
Current Club: AFC Sudbury
Birthplace: Sudbury
A solid and reliable defender with AFC Sudbury who is fearless in his tackling. Previously with Sudbury Wanderers for several seasons.

HOWE, STEVE — *Defender*
Current Club: Wivenhoe Town
Birthplace: Essex
Midfielder or defender, who had been with Clacton Town for 4 seasons before re-joining Ryman Division One North side Wivenhoe Town in August 2002. Steve is a no-nonsense tackler and very intelligent player who distributes the ball very well. Apart from three other spells with Wivenhoe, he has also turned out for Brightlingsea United, Harwich & Parkeston and Braintree Town.

HOWELL, AREN — *Midfielder*
Current Club: Ipswich Wanderers
Birthplace: Essex
Previous clubs include: Whitton Utd - July 1999, Ipswich W, Woodbridge T, Hadleigh Utd.

HOWELL, DARREN — *Forward*
Current Club: Hungerford Town
D o B: 28/01/1972 — *Birthplace: Chiswick*
Striker who was Hungerford Town's leading marksman in 2001/02 with 21 goals - a feat that saw him win both player and Players' Player of the year awards. Signed for the Ryman Division Two side from Egham Town in 2000 and has also seen service with Hounslow, Feltham, Northwood and Kingsbury Town.

HOWELL, DEAN — *Defender*
Current Club: Southport
Birthplace: Nottingham
Dean made his Southport debut on December 1st 2001, just a day after his 21st birthday. He is a left wing-back and had signed the day before that game from Crewe after starting his career as an apprentice with Notts County. Dean is a pacy player who has a rocket shot and an eye for goal.

HOWELL, GREG — *Midfielder*
Current Club: Tonbridge Angels
D o B: 26/03/1973 — *Birthplace: London*
Previous clubs include: Harlow T - July 2000, Dagenham & Redbridge, St.Albans C, Bromley, St.Albans C, Aylesbury Utd, Hemel Hempstead, St.Albans C, Enfield, Wellington (New Zealand), Barnet, Notts Co., Aston Villa, Tottenham Hotspur.

HOWELL, IAN — *Defender*
Current Club: Bath City
Previous clubs include: Cinderford T - July 2001, Wokingham T, Cinderford T, Salisbury C, Bashley, Gloucester C, Cheltenham T, Gloucester C, Trowbridge T, Hungerford T, Trowbridge T, Swindon Ath., Swindon T.

HOWELL, JAMIE — Midfielder

Current Club: Bognor Regis Town

D o B: 19/02/1977   Birthplace: Rustington
Honours won: England Schoolboy & Youth Int.
Midfield player with lots of experience for his age. A former England Schoolboy and Youth international, he started his career with Arsenal. Has since played for Torquay, Portsmouth and Brighton. Lives in Worthing and joined Bognor Regis Town in October 1997.

HOWELL, LEE — Defender

Current Club: Hungerford Town

D o B: 10/05/1973   Birthplace: Hounslow
Previous clubs include: Walton Casuals - July 2000, Egham T, Feltham, Hounslow B, Brentford (Junior).

HOWELL, PETER — Midfielder

Current Club: Pelsall Villa

Birthplace: Birmingham
Previous clubs include: Rushall Olympic - December 2000, Plymouth Argyle.

HOWELL, REUBEN — Forward

Current Club: Burnham

Birthplace: Berkshire
Reuben is a young forward with plenty of potential. Always likely to pop-up with the all important goal.

HOWELL, RICHARD — Midfielder

Current Club: Stevenage Borough

D o B: 29/08/1982   Birthplace: Hitchin
Richard is from Hitchin, and impressed Stevenage Borough boss Wayne Turner when he scored a cracking goal for Crystal Palace Reserves whilst being watched. He can play either right back, or in midfield. Stevenage had been tracking him for some time and was delighted to make the signing of a player he rates as a real prospect in March 2002. He impressed in his only start at Boston in April 2002, but was then diagnosed with a fractured bone in his foot.

HOWELLS, GARETH — Goalkeeper

Current Club: Aldershot Town

D o B: 13/06/1970   Birthplace: Guildford
Previous clubs include: Sutton Utd - July 2001, St.Albans C, Dorking, Hellenic (South Africa), Torquay Utd, Tottenham Hotspur.

HOWELLS, MARK — Defender

Current Club: Caersws

D o B: 16/03/1975   Birthplace: Wales
Previous clubs include: Newtown - July 1997.

HOWES, GLENN — Midfielder

Current Club: Basingstoke Town

Birthplace: Southampton
Young midfield player who joined Basingstoke Town in October 1999 from Eastleigh. Played all his schoolboy football at Southampton. Glenn has excellent dribbling abilities and has used them to great effect since arriving at the club.

HOWES, SEAN — Midfielder

Current Club: Guisborough Town

Previous clubs include: Thornaby - July 2001.

HOWES, SHAUN — Defender

Current Club: Wroxham

D o B: 07/11/1977   Birthplace: Essex
Robust young left sided player who was on Leyton Orients books until he suffered a serious knee injury. Took over from club stalwart Stu Larter and like Larter scores vital goals.

HOWEY, LEE — Defender

Current Club: Nuneaton Borough

D o B: 01/04/1969   Birthplace: Sunderland
33-year-old centre half, Lee started his career at Ipswich as a trainee before moving to Belgium for two years. He then joined Sunderland and made 100 appearances for them. After a spell at Burnley, Lee spent 3 years at Northampton before joining Forest Green towards the start of the 2001/2002 season, and then switched to Nuneaton in a player/exchange deal.

HOWLETT, CHRIS — Defender

Current Club: AFC Sudbury

Birthplace: Colchester
Joined AFC Sudbury in March 2001 from Diss Town and made an immediate impact. Good reader of the game and has great aerial strength.

HOWSE, IAN — Midfielder

Current Club: Yate Town

Birthplace: Bristol
From Youth team.

HOY, GARY — Defender

Current Club: Billericay Town

Birthplace: Hertfordshire
Previous clubs include: Enfield - March 2002, Arlesey T, Barton R, Enfield, Chesham Utd, Stotfold, Stevenage B, Gillingham (Junior).

HOYLE, COLIN — Defender

Current Club: Burton Albion

D o B: 15/01/1972   Birthplace: Derby
Honours won: Dr Martens Premier Div.Winners
Colin Hoyle was signed from Conference side Boston United on deadline day to boost the Brewers title challenge. Previously with Kings Lynn, a free transfer took him to Boston where he became part of their successful title winning side. Previously with Arsenal, Chesterfield, Barnsley, Bradford City, Notts County and Mansfield Town, Colin has made 73 Football League appearances, scoring 1 goal for Bradford City).

HUCKERBY, SCOTT — Forward

Current Club: Hucknall Town

Birthplace: Nottingham
Striker who joined Hucknall Town in June 2002 from Dr Martens side Hinckley United. Scott originally signed on loan for Hinckley during the middle of the 2001/02 season from Conference club Woking. Started his career at Ilkeston Town where he was bought by Telford United for £10,000. After suffering a knee injury he was released to Woking, following Telfords decision to revert to semi-professional status. Returned to Woking after a two-month loan period, and then signed permanent for Hinckley in March 2002. Scotts brother Darren plays for Manchester City.

HUCKLE, SIMON — Forward

Current Club: Epsom And Ewell

Birthplace: Surrey
Previous clubs include: Banstead Ath - July 2001.

HUDGELL, LEE — Forward
Current Club: Haverfordwest County
Birthplace: Wales
From Local football - July 2001.

HUDSON, CHRIS — Defender
Current Club: Arnold Town
Birthplace: Nottingham
Previous clubs include: Lincoln Utd - August 2001, Gedling T, Borrowash V, Gedling T.

HUDSON, CHRIS — Defender
Current Club: Harrogate Town
Birthplace: Yorkshire
Honours won: UniBond League Div.One Winners
Defender who signed for Harrogate Town from the UniBond Premier Division outfit Whitby Town in June 2000 and apart from a one-match suspension, was ever present in Town's line-up in his first season. He began his career at Pickering Town in the Northern Counties East League.

HUDSON, DAVE — Goalkeeper
Current Club: Great Wakering Rovers
D o B: 11/02/1972   Birthplace: London
Previous clubs include: Southend Manor - January 2001, Great Wakering R, Billericay T, Chesham Utd, Dulwich Hamlet, Molesey, Banstead Ath., Hendon, Malden Vale, Chalfont St.Peter, Wealdstone, Wimbledon (Trainee).

HUDSON, GARY — Defender
Current Club: Wivenhoe Town
Birthplace: Essex
Big, strong centre half who usually wins everything in the air. Gary had been with Clacton Town for the three years with a brief spell at Wivenhoe Town before re-joining the Ryman Division One North side for the fourth time in August 2002. Has also seen service with Harwich & Parkeston, Halstead Town and Sudbury Town.

HUDSON, LEE — Forward
Current Club: Kings Lynn
Birthplace: Peterborough
Lee Hudson re-joined Kings Lynn from Kettering Town for a second spell at The Walks in July 2001. His pace and endless running helped him become a favourite with the fans during his previous three seasons at Lynn. He was the clubs top scorer before joining former manager Peter Morris at Kettering Town in 1998. Started out at Boston Town.

HUDSON, MARC — Defender
Current Club: Dorking
Birthplace: Surrey
Previous clubs include: Croydon Ath - March 2000, Banstead Ath.

HUDSON, PAUL — Forward
Current Club: Wokingham Town
Birthplace: Berkshire
Previous clubs include: Camberley T - September 2001.

HUDSON, RICHARD — Defender
Current Club: Bognor Regis Town
Birthplace: Sussex
Impressed whilst playing for Lewes against Bognor Regis Town in the 2000/01 Sussex Senior Cup Final. Signed for Bognor in the summer of 2001. Previously with Worthing, the midfielder lives in Southwick.

HUDSON, RYAN — Midfielder
Current Club: Littlehampton Town
Birthplace: Sussex
Midfielder: struck twice for Wick during their crisis period towards the end of 1999/2000: transferred to Littlehampton in February 2001: was responsible for the Marigolds being disqualified in the Reserve Section League Cup last season, after he appeared in their quarter-final victory (having already played for Wick in an earlier round): scored a superb goal direct from a corner kick in the 2-0 FA Cup victory over Selsey during September 2001.

HUGGETT, SIMON — Defender
Current Club: Kingsbury Town
Birthplace: London
From Youth team.

HUGGINS, LEROY — Forward
Current Club: Fisher Athletic (London)
Birthplace: Kent
Previous clubs include: Crawley T - August 2001, Fisher Ath., Crockenhill, Erith & Belvedere, Crockenhill.

HUGGINS, STEVE — Midfielder
Current Club: Brandon United
Birthplace: Sunderland
Honours won: Voted Young Player of the Year in 2000-01.
Excellent young utility player, now in his second season with Brandon, having previously been with Middlesbrough and Sunderland. In his first season, he was voted Young Player of the Year and came very close to pulling off the senior awards. He has shown tremendous commitment to the club, not only on the field, and also rejected offers from clubs higher in the pyramid system.

HUGHES, ANDY — Midfielder
Current Club: Haverfordwest County
D o B: 25/02/1977   Birthplace: Wales
Previous clubs include: Ton Pentre - December 2000.

HUGHES, CLINT — Forward
Current Club: Bilston Town
Birthplace: Birmingham
Previous clubs include: Rushall Olympic - March 2002, Willenhall T, Halesowen Harriers, Stourbridge, Paget R, Oldbury Utd.

HUGHES, CRAIG — Forward
Current Club: Cwmbran Town
D o B: 18/12/1978   Birthplace: Wales
Previous clubs include: Rhayader T - July 2001, UWIC Inter Cardiff, Coventry C (Trainee).

HUGHES, DAVID — Midfielder
Current Club: Eastleigh
D o B: 30/12/1972   Birthplace: St Albans
Honours won: Wales u-21 Int., England Schoolboy Int.
Previous clubs include: Southampton - July 2001.

HUGHES, GARETH — Midfielder
Current Club: Newtown AFC
D o B: 08/01/1981   Birthplace: Rhayader
Gareth signed for Newtown in August 2002 from former League of Wales rivals Rhayader Town. Had joined his home-town team after two year spell at Aberystwyth Town, and was previously a trainee at Wrexham. Strong, very skillful player, comfortable in several positions. Enough ability to dominate games.

HUGHES, GARRY · Defender

Current Club: Kettering Town

D o B: 19/11/1979   *Birthplace: Birmingham*
Honours won: Dr Martens League Premier Div.Winners
Signed for Kettering Town in July 2001 after impressing in pre-season. Can play in the centre of defence or at right back where he performed well for neighbours Northampton Town in Division Two. Looks to have a promising future ahead of him.

HUGHES, GERAINT · Defender

Current Club: Llanelli AFC

Birthplace: Wales
Previous clubs include: Rhayader T - November 2001, Mold Alexandra.

HUGHES, GLYNDWR · Midfielder

Current Club: Aberystwyth Town

D o B: 04/09/1977   *Birthplace: Pontrhydfendigaid*
Previous clubs include: Pontrhydfendigaid - July 1996.

HUGHES, JASON · Defender

Current Club: Arundel

Birthplace: Sussex
Generally recognized as a right back or wing back, but is something of a utility player: scored six times during 2000/01, including two goals in an amazing 8-5 (after extra time) FA Vase victory over Chessington & Hook.

HUGHES, JOHN · Goalkeeper

Current Club: Rothwell Town

Birthplace: Wellingborough
Previous clubs include: Wisbech T - December 1998, Raunds T, Wellingborough T.

HUGHES, JOHN-PAUL · Midfielder

Current Club: Nantwich Town

Birthplace: Cheshire
Previous clubs include: Witton Alb - January 2002, Atherton LR.

HUGHES, KEVIN · Midfielder

Current Club: Beaconsfield SYCOB

Birthplace: Berkshire
From Youth team.

HUGHES, LEE · Forward

Current Club: Ludlow Town

Birthplace: Birmingham
Previous clubs include: Racing Club Warwick - November 2001, Bromsgrove R, Rugby Utd, Paget R, Bilston T, Bloxwich T, Blakenall, Valerengen (Norway), Birmingham C.

HUGHES, MARC · Midfielder

Current Club: Caersws

D o B: 19/03/1968   *Birthplace: Wales*
From Youth team.

HUGHES, PAUL · Midfielder

Current Club: Llanelli AFC

D o B: 17/08/1983   *Birthplace: Wales*
From Youth team.

HUGHES, ROB · Midfielder

Current Club: Bromley

Previous clubs include: Fulham - September 2001.

HUGHES, SIMON · Defender

Current Club: St. Helens Town

Birthplace: Liverpool
Centre half signed from Prescot Cables. Great competitor who will add a little steel and organisation to Town's back four. Simon was captain of Cables last term and brings to Town a wealth of experience.

HUGHES, STEFFAN · Defender

Current Club: Aberystwyth Town

D o B: 17/09/1983   *Birthplace: Llanarth*
From Youth team.

HULBERT, TATE · Forward

Current Club: Swindon Supermarine

Tate returned in October last year after a couple of seasons away and made his debut against Highworth Town in November. Picked up a second Championship last season as he was another member of our championship winning squad of 1997/98, also our leading goalscorer that season. A very direct and quick forward who likes nothing better than running at the oppositions defence. He possesses some wonderful skills and can easily win the game by himself. Since his return to the club he has gained Hellenic League Representative honours.

HULME, KEVIN · Midfielder

Current Club: Mossley

D o B: 07/12/1967   *Birthplace: Farnworth*
A highly competitive central midfielder with a decisive tackle. Kevin is a versatile player who is capable of performing effectively in just about any position. After moving from Radcliffe Borough in 1989 gained vast experience in League football with Bury (twice), Chester, Doncaster, Lincoln, Halifax and York City. Signed for Altrincham July 25th 2001and the moved onto North West Counties League side Mossley just over a year later.

HUME, MARK · Defender

Current Club: Barrow

D o B: 21/05/1978   *Birthplace: Barnsley*
Born in Barnsley, Mark is a highly-rated and versatile player who started his career with his hometown club as a trainee but failed to make a League appearance for them before he was released. He joined Doncaster Rovers in the summer of 1998 and featured during their first Conference season. In October 1999 he had a spell, on loan, with Gainsborough Trinity. He initially joined Barrow on a loan basis in November 1999 and made his debut in the home win over Spennymoor United. The move became permanent in January 2000 and he proved his versatility by featuring as a striker on occasion. A regular goalscorer from set plays. He won the Official Supporters Club Player of the Year award at the end of the 2000/01 season.

HUMPHREY, NICKY · Defender

Current Club: Dover Athletic

D o B: 20/09/1980   *Birthplace: Kent*
Very promising young defender who joined Dover Athletic from Dr Martens Eastern neighbours Tonbridge Angels in June 2002. Had progressed through Tonbridges youth set up to become a regular in the first-team during the 2000/01 season.

HUMPHREYS, IAN · Midfielder

Current Club: Curzon Ashton

Birthplace: Cheshire
Previous clubs include: Cheadle T - November 2000.

HUMPHREYS, LEE — *Midfielder*
Current Club: Great Yarmouth Town
D o B: 21/12/1975   *Birthplace: Norfolk*
Joined Yarmouth from Gorleston in October 1999. Player of the year 1999/2000, and has been promoted to team captain this season.

HUMPHRIES, PAUL — *Midfielder*
Current Club: Brodsworth Welfare
Birthplace: Yorkshire
Previous clubs include: Mexborough Main Street - July 1999.

HUNT, ADRIAN — *Midfielder*
Current Club: Haverhill Rovers
Birthplace: Suffolk
Former Academy player in his second spell at Haverhill Rovers. An attacking player with frightening pace.

HUNT, ANDY — *Goalkeeper*
Current Club: Fleet Town
Birthplace: Hampshire
Previous clubs include: Bromley - August 2001, Leatherhead, Fleet T, Farnborough T, Brentford.

HUNT, CARL — *Midfielder*
Current Club: Wealdstone
D o B: 03/09/1983   *Birthplace: London*
Carl signed for Wealdstone in October 2001, having previously been involved in the PASE Youth Scheme. His first club was Coventry City and he was subsequently at Ware before joining the Stones youth team in 2000.

HUNT, CLARK — *Goalkeeper*
Current Club: Chalfont St.Peter
Birthplace: London
Honours won: England Youth Int.
Previous clubs include: Canvey Island - February 2002, Gillingham.

HUNT, DANNY — *Defender*
Current Club: Weston-Super-Mare
Birthplace: Swindon
Defender who started his career with his home-town club Swindon Town. Upon his release he joined Newport County and became a regular in the Exiles Dr Martens League side. Moves to Gloucester City, Cinderford Town and Chippenham Town followed before he teamed up with Weston-Super-Mare in May 2002.

HUNT, DAVID — *Defender*
Current Club: Durham City
D o B: 05/03/1980   *Birthplace: Durham*
Previous clubs include: Darlington - July 2000.

HUNT, DAVID — *Defender*
Current Club: Barking & East Ham United
Birthplace: Essex
Highly-promising 20-year-old defender who joined Barking from Leyton Orient in December 2001. Presently a student, the club have high hopes of David.

HUNT, DAVID — *Defender*
Current Club: Weston-Super-Mare
Birthplace: Cardiff
Signed in September 2000 from Newport County. Previously on YTS forms at Cardiff City and has also played for local side Longlevens.

HUNT, MARCUS — *Midfielder*
Current Club: Haverhill Rovers
Birthplace: Suffolk
A utility player, aged just 20, had a trial at Cambridge United. In his fourth year at Haverhill having previously been with Kedington United.

HUNT, MATTHEW — *Midfielder*
Current Club: Woodbridge Town
Birthplace: Suffolk
Tenacious midfielder who has given excellent service to the Reserves for a number of seasons, and although his First Team appearances have been limited, he has not let the side down when called upon.

HUNT, OLIVER — *Defender*
Current Club: Tonbridge Angels
D o B: 05/09/1978   *Birthplace: London*
Previous clubs include: Dulwich Hamlet - December 2001.

HUNT, STUART — *Midfielder*
Current Club: Great Yarmouth Town
D o B: 04/01/1976   *Birthplace: Norfolk*
Joined the club last season from Mulbarton United. Highly-skilled in all aspects of play.

HUNTER, COLIN — *Midfielder*
Current Club: Harrogate Town
Birthplace: Harrogate
Honours won: UniBond League Div.One Winners
Talented wide midfielder who began his career with Harrogate Railway before moving to Guiseley. He then made 10 Conference appearances for Hednesford Town before moving to Morecambe, where he made a further 20 appearances. He signed for Harrogate Town prior to the start of the 2001/02 season.

HUNTER, JAMIE — *Midfielder*
Current Club: Flexsys Cefn Druids
Birthplace: Wales
Previous clubs include: Lex XI - July 2000.

HUNTER, JERMAINE — *Forward*
Current Club: Chesham United
Birthplace: London
Signed for Ryman Premier side Chesham United in August 2002 from rivals Harrow Borough, Jermaine is a left winger or centre forward who spent four years at Fulham before a spell at Leyton Orient. A pacy and agile attacking player.

HUNTER, LEE — *Defender*
Current Club: Clacton Town
D o B: 05/10/1969   *Birthplace: Colchester*
Honours won: Northern Ireladn Youth Int.
One of Clacton's major signings this season from Diss Town. Lee is simply a presence on the pitch, a great organiser and a very strong defender. Can also play in midfield.

HUNTER, LEON — *Defender*
Current Club: Heybridge Swifts
Birthplace: Essex
Signed for Ryman Premier side Heybridge Swifts in August 2002 from rivals Grays Athletic. Originally on the books at Southend, he chose to join Grays at the start of the 2001/02 season instead of Mansfield, A steady and influential defender with a real appetite for the game.

HUNTER, MARK — *Midfielder*
Current Club: Walton Casuals
Birthplace: Surrey
Joined in the summer of 1999 from Raynes Park Vale, shown promise over his period with the club as a hard working wide player with an eye for goal. Member of last seasons League Cup winning side.

HUNTER, PAUL — *Forward*
Current Club: Hinckley United
D o B: 14/02/1966   *Birthplace: Birmingham*
Honours won: Dr Martens League Western Div.Winners
Powerful stiker previously played at Conference level with Telford United. Other clubs include Tamworth, Blakenall, Inter Cardiff and Merthyr Tydfill. A strong physical presence often means he plays the support striking role, very good at holding the ball. He aquired the nickname Supersub after scoring many goals as a substitute in the 2000/01 season. Won a Dr Martens Western Division championship medal with Hinckley United in 2000/01. Was released December 2001 and spent a couple of months at Moor Green before returning to United in January 2002.

HUNTON, JAMIE — *Forward*
Current Club: Norwich United
D o B: 02/01/1977   *Birthplace: Norfolk*
Last seasons top goalscorer for Norwich United, a very quick player with bags of ability and an eye for goal. He joined the club from junior side Thorpe Rovers.

HURD, STEVE — *Midfielder*
Current Club: Potters Bar Town
Birthplace: Middlesex
Previous clubs include: Edgware T - July 1999, Ruislip Manor, Edgware T.

HURDLE, GUS — *Defender*
Current Club: Yeading
D o B: 14/10/1973   *Birthplace: Kensington*
Honours won: Barbados Int.
Joined the Ding in September 2001 and made his debut the following month in the away win at Thame. A class act whose ability has been recognised at international level by Barbados. Made over 80 appearances for Brentford in the Football League, during a four-year spell, but has also seen service at Plymouth, Fulham (as a trainee), Dorchester Town, Crawley Town, Dulwich Hamlet, St.Albans City, Basingstoke Town, Carshalton Athletic and Whyteleafe.

HURLEY, GREG — *Midfielder*
Current Club: Afan Lido
D o B: 24/04/1976   *Birthplace: Wales*
One of the clubs most skilful players, Greg plays most games on the right wing. Also used as a striker in many games, he is fast, creative and competitive.

HURLIN, RICHARD — *Forward*
Current Club: Llanelli AFC
D o B: 14/01/1984   *Birthplace: Wales*
From Youth team.

HURLOCK, JOHN — *Midfielder*
Current Club: Hertford Town
Birthplace: Manchester
Midfielder who signed for Ryman Division One North side Hertford Town just prior to the start of the 2002/03 season from Harrow Borough. Rejoined Boro in the summer of 1999 after a spell with Chesham United. John previously played for Stockport County, Altrincham, Bedworth, Nuneaton Borough and Droylesden. A Barrister by profession.

HURLSTONE, GARY — *Forward*
Current Club: Stocksbridge Park Steels
D o B: 25/04/1963   *Birthplace: Mexborough*
Previous clubs include: Hatfield Main - July 1996, Goole T, Buxton, Denaby Utd, Bishop Auckland, Gainsborough Trinity, Goole T, Bridlington T, York C, Hatfield Main, Worksop T, Gainsborough Trinity.

HURST, ANDY — *Midfielder*
Current Club: Tow Law Town
Birthplace: Newcastle
Previous clubs include: Newcastle Blue Star - February 2002, West Denton.

HURST, CHRIS — *Midfielder*
Current Club: Gainsborough Trinity
D o B: 03/10/1973   *Birthplace: Barnsley*
Previous clubs include: Frickley Ath - June 2001, Ilkeston T, Emley, Huddersfield T, Emley.

HURST, DANNY — *Goalkeeper*
Current Club: Radcliffe Borough
Birthplace: Cheshire
Talented goalkeeper who joined Radcliffe Borough in the summer of 2000 from Cheadle Town initially as cover. Quickly made the first-team slot his own and is rated as a tremendous prospect who hs trained with Manchester City and has attracted the attention of several other League clubs.

HURST, MATT — *Midfielder*
Current Club: Selsey
Birthplace: Sussex
Midfielder and established member of the side. Another one of the managers cousins, and is also son of the club chairman. Scored seven times during 1999/2000 and twice in 2000/01.

HURST, RICHARD — *Goalkeeper*
Current Club: Chelmsford City
D o B: 23/12/1976   *Birthplace: Hammersmith*
Goalkeeper who signed for Chelmsford City from St. Albans in July 2001 having started his career with Queens Park Rangers, with whom he spent six years. Has also played for Kingstonian.

HUSBANDS, DANNY — *Midfielder*
Current Club: Dulwich Hamlet
Birthplace: Hampshire
Industrious midfielder who joined Dulwich Hamlet in November 2001 after a spell out of the game through injury. Originally played in the Jewson Wessex League with Eastleigh and Brockenhurst and also gained Dr Martens experience with Newport Isle of Wight.

HUSSAIN, ABUL — *Midfielder*
Current Club: Clapton
D o B: 25/03/1982   *Birthplace: Essex*
Previous clubs include: Ilford - July 2001. Hendon.

HUSSEY, STEVE — *Midfielder*
Current Club: Burscough
Birthplace: Liverpool
Another player with UniBond Premier side Burscough to make a favourable impression after progressing from the clubs successful youth squad. The talented midfielder was on Evertons books as a junior.

HUSSEY, STUART — Forward
Current Club: Bashley
D o B: 04/12/1980   Birthplace: Southampton
Previous clubs include: Brockenhurst (£2,500) - August 2001, Bristol C, Portsmouth (Trainee).

HUSSIN, EDDIE — Midfielder
Current Club: Marine
D o B: 13/12/1977   Birthplace: Liverpool
Back in the Marine squad for 2001/02 after a serious illness stopped him playing for over a season. Experienced midfielder who was on Evertons books and has also played for Winsford United, Northwich Victori and Chorley. Rejoined Marine in August 2000.

HUSTWICK, MAX — Defender
Current Club: Kingstonian
D o B: 11/06/1982   Birthplace: Surrey
Young defender who can play in the centre of defence or at full back. Broke into the Kingstonian first-team at the beginning of the 2001/02 season after impressing hugely in pre-season following his move from Walton & Hersham.

HUTCHINGS, OTIS — Midfielder
Current Club: Yeading
Birthplace: London
Once ranked as one of the most promising youngsters in the Non-League game, Otis joined the Ding in the summer and finds himself as one of the elder statesmen of the squad at just thirty-years of age. Great ball-winner and motivator, Otis began his career as a Chelsea trainee and has since seen service with Boreham Wood, Aldershot Town, Walton & Hersham, Tooting & Mitcham, Molesey, Hampton, Dulwich Hamlet and Chesham United.

HUTCHINSON, ANDY — Goalkeeper
Current Club: Dunston Federation Brewery
Birthplace: Newcastle
Previous clubs include: Bishop Auckland - July 2000, Dunston Federation, Whickham, Blackpool.

HUTCHINSON, CRAIG — Midfielder
Current Club: Connahs Quay Nomads
D o B: 28/01/1973   Birthplace: Wales
Previous clubs include: Holywell T - June 1997.

HUTCHINSON, GRANT — Forward
Current Club: Banstead Athletic
Birthplace: London
Previous clubs include: Chertsey T - August 2000, Molesey, Marlow, Walton & Hersham, Staines T, Walton & Hersham, Woking, Aldershot, Fulham (Junior).

HUTCHINSON, IAN — Midfielder
Current Club: Weymouth
D o B: 07/11/1972   Birthplace: Stockton
Ian is another player who made the long journey south. Now in his 7th season with the club, Ian played is one of a trio of players in the squad who passed 250 games for the terras last season. Joined from Halifax Town.

HUTCHINSON, JAKE — Forward
Current Club: Redhill
Birthplace: Yorkshire
Team captain leading scorer for the Reds in 1997/98 but has his appearances limited over the last couple of seasons whilst away studying. Is now back full time with the Reds for the 2001/02 season and scored 11 goals before Christmas. Previously played for Guiseley in the Northern Premier League.

HUTCHINSON, SEAN — Midfielder
Current Club: Matlock Town
Birthplace: Sheffield
Powehouse Sean is equally at home in the centre of either the defence or midfield. His aggression and heart won over the Town fans following his signing from Harrogate Town in October 2000. Hutch also works as a coach with former boss Tommy Spencer at Sheffield United.

HUTCHINSON, STEVE — Midfielder
Current Club: Bishop Auckland
Birthplace: Gateshead
Previous clubs include: Durham C - February 2002, Gretna, Blyth Spartans, Gateshead.

HUTCHINSON, TOBY — Forward
Current Club: Southwick
Birthplace: Sussex
Forward, whose name is written all over the leagues goalscoring history books: played for Langney Sports in the late 80s/early 90s, and more recently was top scorer for Shoreham (1993/94), Eastbourne Town (1994/95) and Peacehaven (1998/99): began 2000/01 with Southwick before joining Eastbourne Utd a couple of months later (previously had a spell at The Oval in 1996/97): had a total of 14 goals to his name during 2000/01: returned to Old Barn Way in December 2001, following the appointment of Sammy Donnelly as boss.

HUTCHISON, DEAN — Forward
Current Club: Corby Town
Birthplace: Corby
Previous clubs include: Rothwell T - July 2002, Corby T.

HUTT, STEVE — Defender
Current Club: Spennymoor United
D o B: 19/02/1979   Birthplace: Middlesbrough
Previous clubs include: Bishop Auckland - March 2002, Hartlepool Utd.

HUTTLEY, CRAIG — Defender
Current Club: Maldon Town
Birthplace: Essex
Previous clubs include: Burnham Ramblers - July 2000, Basildon Utd.

HUTTON, JOHN — Defender
Current Club: Blyth Spartans
Birthplace: Newcastle
Signed for the club during summer 2001, from Darlington. Although a centre back, John has the ability to play in a variety of positions. Made his debut against Bamber Bridge, coming on as Sub to score his first goal for the club.

HYATT, DAVE — Goalkeeper
Current Club: Epsom And Ewell
D o B: 12/04/1967   Birthplace: Sussex
Previous clubs include: Tooting & Mitcham Utd - September 1995, Sutton Utd, Epsom & Ewell, Leatherhead, Horsham.

H

HYATT, FREDDIE *Midfielder*

Current Club: Bishops Stortford

D o B: 18/01/1968   *Birthplace: Middlesex*
Honours won: Isthmian League Premier Div.Winners
This useful and experienced player signed for The Blues pre-Christmas 2001 on loan from Chelmsford City. Freddie scored a superb goal on his debut in the Boxing day derby against Harlow Town and has proved a regular in the team since. Wokingham Town paid Burnham £5,000 for Freddies services in 1990. Other clubs include Ruislip Manor, Hayes and Hendon. Freddie signed permanant forms with the Blues in February 2002.

HYDE, JAMIE *Midfielder*

Current Club: Worcester City

From Youth team.

HYDE, LEE *Midfielder*

Current Club: Wisbech Town

D o B: 04/03/1982
From Youth team.

HYDE, NICKY *Defender*

Current Club: Stourbridge

Birthplace: Birmingham
Previous clubs include: Kings Norton T - July 2000.

HYDE, PAUL *Goalkeeper*

Current Club: Dover Athletic

D o B: 07/04/1963   *Birthplace: Hayes*
Honours won: Conference Winners, FA Trophy Winners
Paul joined Dover Athletic in the summer of 1999. A vastly experienced goalkeeper, he played a big role in Martin ONeills Wycombe side that won promotion into the Football League. Paul later followed ONeill to Leicester City before moving on to Leyton Orient. Has consistently performed well for Dover and has won a number of Supporters' Player of the year awards.

HYDE, SIMON pos###
Midield   **Current Club: AFC Sudbury**

Birthplace: Sudbury
Tall, hard-working and tough-tackling player who can also perform well in defence. Played for both Sudbury clubs prior to the merger.

HYDEN, SIMON *Defender*

Current Club: Chasetown FC

Birthplace: Staffs
Previous clubs include: Rushall Olympic - July 1996, Chasetown, Armitage, Hednesford T, Chasetown, Hednesford T.

HYNES, MARK *Forward*

Current Club: Whyteleafe

Birthplace: Surrey
Striker who re-signed for Ryman Division One South side Whyteleafe in August 2002 from neighbours Carshalton Athletic. Had signed for Carshalton pre-season 2001 from Crawley. Previous clubs include Welling United, Sutton United, Whyteleafe, Fisher Athletic, Croydon Athletic, Merstham, Croydon and Brentford, where he was a trainee.

HYSLOP, CHRISTIAN *Defender*

Current Club: Harrow Borough

D o B: 14/06/1972   *Birthplace: Watford*
Joined Boro from Baldock Town in March 2001. Previously with Southend United, Northampton Town, Colchester United, Chelmsford City, Billericay Town and Waterford United (Ireland).

HYSON, MATTHEW *Midfielder*

Current Club: Thornaby on Tees

D o B: 02/05/1976   *Birthplace: Stockton*
Previous clubs include: Spennymoor Utd - February 2002, Guisborough T, Blyth Spartans, Jurong Cobras (Singapore), Gateshead, Jurong Cobras (Singapore), Blyth Spartans, Jurong Cobras (Singapore), Durham C, Willington, Chester-le-Street, Hartlepool Utd.

HYSON, MATTY *Midfielder*

Current Club: Bishop Auckland

D o B: 02/05/1976   *Birthplace: Stockton*
Widely-travelled midfielder who joined UniBond First Division side Bishop Auckland in August 2002 from Albany Northern Leaguers Thornaby. Started his career at Hartlepool and has also had experience with Chester-le-Street, Willington, Durham City and Jurong Cobras in Singapore. In between stints with Jurong, Matty played for Gateshead, Blyth Spartans and Guisborough Town.

IGA, ANDREW — Goalkeeper
Current Club: Hampton & Richmond

D o B: 09/12/1977 — Birthplace: Kampala

Much-travelled goalkeeper who joined Ryman Premier side Hampton & Richmond Borough from Division One South side Whyteleafe in July 2002. Was a professional with Millwall, Gillingham and Watford and has since had spells of varying lengths with Chesham United, Hendon, Dover Athletic, Rushden & Diamonds, St Leonards and Carshalton Athletic, signing for the Leafe in December 2001.

ILLINGWORTH, JEREMY — Midfielder
Current Club: Stocksbridge Park Steels

D o B: 20/05/1977 — Birthplace: Huddersfield

Previous clubs include: Altrinchgam - October 2001, Ashton Utd, Wisbech T, Cambridge Utd, Huddersfield T.

IMBER, NOEL — Goalkeeper
Current Club: Boreham Wood

D o B: 04/12/1976 — Birthplace: London

Noel, is a 25-year-old goalkeeper who was born in London and joined Arsenal from school. He continued with them as a trainee and as a professional, before moving on to Chelsea. He gained further experience with Woking and Stevenage Borough before joining Slough Town in 1997. In recent years he has played for Wealdstone and St. Albans City, from whom he joined Boreham Wood during the summer of 2000. He made his first-team debut for Wood against Bognor Regis Town in the Ryman League on the 19th August 2000. Noel scored his first goal for the club direct from a free-kick in his own half in Woods 2-0 victory against Staines Town at home in 2000/01.

IMPEY, JAMIE — Defender
Current Club: Forest Green Rovers

D o B: 28/07/1977 — Birthplace: Bournemouth

Signed for Conference club Forest Green Rovers just prior to the start of the 2001/02 season from Dorchester Town. From a famous footballing family, he gained much of his experience playing in the League of Ireland.

INCE, ANDY — Midfielder
Current Club: Bury Town

Birthplace: Suffolk

Previous clubs include: Newmarket T - September 1999, Sudbury T, Halstead T, Haverhill R, Newmarket T.

INCE, JAMIE — Midfielder
Current Club: Cinderford Town

Birthplace: Birmingham

Exciting midfield player who started his career with West Bromwich Albion. Then became a regular at Barry Town in the League of Wales before joining Halesowen Town. Signed for Cinderford Town in August 2001.

INDGE, ANDY — Midfielder
Current Club: Hamble ASSC

Birthplace: Hampshire

Previous clubs include: Otterbourne - September 2001, Hedge End.

INGALL, ASA — Midfielder
Current Club: Eastwood Town

Previous clubs include: Staveley Miners Welfare - July 2001, Local Football, Staveley MW, Eastwood T.

INGHAM, GARY — Goalkeeper
Current Club: Belper Town

D o B: 09/10/1964 — Birthplace: Rotherham

Honours won: UniBond League Winners

Vastly experience goalkeeper who joined Belper Town in June 2002 as player-coach from UniBond Premier side Gainsborough Trinity. Had signed for Trinity for the third time in September 2001 after a spell at Stalybridge Celtic. Has also appeared for Leek Town, Stocksbridge Park Steels, Doncaster Rovers, where he played League football, Maltby MW, Goole Town, Bridlington Town nd Rotherham, where he began his career.

INGLE, DAVE — Defender
Current Club: Warrington Town

Birthplace: Warrington

From Youth team.

INGLEDOW, JAMIE — Midfielder
Current Club: Stocksbridge Park Steels

D o B: 23/08/1980 — Birthplace: Barnsley

Highly-promising young midfielder who joined UniBond First Division side Stocksbridge Park Steels in August 2002 after being released by Chesterfield. Started his career with Rotherham, where he made 25 League appearances. Transferred to Chesterfield in the summer of 2000 and figured over 40 times for their senior side. Certainly hasn't given up hope of a return to the full-time game.

INGLETHORPE, ALEX — Midfielder
Current Club: Leatherhead

D o B: 14/11/1971 — Birthplace: Epsom

Previous clubs include: Exeter C - June 2001, Leyton Orient, Watford.

INGRAM, CRAIG — Defender
Current Club: Hadleigh United

Birthplace: Suffolk

Hard tackling defender with Hadleigh who can play either at full-back or in the middle with equal capability. Loves to run with the ball and play out of trouble.

INGRAM, DAVE — Midfielder
Current Club: Bridlington Town

Birthplace: Hull

David is an attacking midfielder and scored on his debut at Dene Park for Town in a Wilkinson Cup tie. Previously with Humber Premier side Sculcoates Amateur.

INGRAM, DENNY — Defender
Current Club: Northwich Victoria

D o B: 27/06/1976 — Birthplace: Sunderland

Denny is a defender who signed for Conference side Northwich Victoris from rivals from Scarborough in October 2001. A quick defender who likes to play quality balls out of defence and he rarely wastes possession. He also possesses a handy long throw-in. Denny started his career with Hartlepool United and it was while on-loan at Scarborough during the 1999/00 season that he made a big impression with the Seadogs management.

INGRAM, MARK — Defender
Current Club: Gorleston

Birthplace: Norfolk

Previous clubs include: Ace - July 2000, Gorleston, Great Yarmouth T.

INMAN, NIALL — Forward

Current Club: Kettering Town

D o B: 06/02/1978   Birthplace: Wakefield
Honours won: Republic of Ireland Youth & u-21 Int., Dr
Martens League Premier Div.Winners
Former Republic of Ireland under-21 international who has been
unlucky with injuries in the past couple of seasons. Although
most at home wide on the right flank, he is capable of playing in
the centre of midfield and also as a right back. Spent most of the
2000/01 season on-loan with Kettering Town from Peterborough
United and then re-joined on a permanent basis during the early
part of the 2001/02 season after a short spell with Dover
Athletic.

INNES, GARY — Forward

Current Club: Blyth Spartans

D o B: 07/10/1977   Birthplace: Shotley Bridge
Honours won: England Youth Int.
Previous clubs include: Seaham Red Star - October 2000,
Gateshead, Durham C, West Auckland T, Gateshead, Darlington,
Sheffield Utd.

INNES, LEE — Forward

Current Club: Tow Law Town

D o B: 28/02/1976   Birthplace: Co.Durham
His previous clubs include West Auckland, Gateshead,
Spennymoor, Darlington and Sheffield United where he was
signed as a professional. Played professionally in New Zealand.
Also plays as a cricket professional in local league.

INNS, ALAN — Midfielder

Current Club: Wokingham Town

Birthplace: Berkshire
From Youth team.

IQBAL, AMJAD — Defender

Current Club: Thackley

Birthplace: Yorkshire
Previous clubs include: Farsley Celtic - July 2000.

IQBAL, MAZHAR — Defender

Current Club: Wednesfield

Birthplace: Birmingham
Previous clubs include: Warley Rangers - July 2001, Wednesfield,
Bloxwich T, Smethwick Rangers, Pelsall Villa.

IQBAL, ZAFFIR — Goalkeeper

Current Club: Wednesfield

Birthplace: Birmingham
Previous clubs include: Kings Norton T - November 2000.

IRELAND, SIMON — Midfielder

Current Club: Wisbech Town

D o B: 23/11/1971   Birthplace: Halifax
Honours won: England Schoolboy Int.
Previous clubs include: Guiseley - March 2001, Boreham Wood,
Doncaster R, Mansfield T, Blackburn R, Huddersfield T.

IRVINE, ALEX — Defender

Current Club: Spalding United

Birthplace: Scotland
Previous clubs include: Wisbech T - January 2001, Winterton R,
Shepshed Dynamo, Racing Club Warwick, Shepshed Dynamo,
Wisbech T, Hinckley Utd, Hinckley Ath., Westfields, Altrincham.

IRVINE, STUART — Forward

Current Club: Durham City

D o B: 01/03/1979   Birthplace: Hartlepool
Previous clubs include: Whitby T - July 2000, Bishop Auckland,
Hartlepool Utd.

IRVING, CRAIG — Forward

Current Club: Gretna

D o B: 19/04/1978   Birthplace: Dumfries
Previous clubs include: Queen of the South - January 2001.

IRVING, IAN — Defender

Current Club: Blyth Spartans

Birthplace: Newcastle
Previous clubs include: Morpeth T - March 2002, Whitley Bay,
Blyth Spartans, Lynn University (USA).

IRWIN, BILLY — Defender

Current Club: Dunston Federation Brewery

Birthplace: Newcastle
Previous clubs include: Durham C - July 1998, North Shields.

ISAAC, LEE — Midfielder

Current Club: Burgess Hill Town

Birthplace: Sussex
Attacking right-winger, who was originally at Burgess Hill several
years ago (their leading scorer in 1993/94): spent four seasons
playing professional football for Inter Turku (in Finland) before
returning to the UK and signing for Langney Sports in August
2000: moved to Leylands Park a couple of months later: a quiet
individual, who is capable of producing flashes of brilliance:
scored 9 times for the Hillians last season, despite being
suspended during the latter stages: also plays for the County.

ISAACS, JOHN — Midfielder

Current Club: Marlow

Birthplace: Berkshire
Quality left-sided midfield player with a good deal of potential.
John came through the youth system at Flackwell Heath before
signing for Marlow in December 2000. Soon won a place in the
first-team and has become a vital member of the side.

ISTED, KEVIN — Defender

Current Club: Hailsham Town

Birthplace: Sussex
Strong tackling centre back and captain: joined Hailsham from
Eastbourne Utd in October 1999: has previous experience with
Lewes.

IVERS, DAVID — Defender

Current Club: Holmer Green

Birthplace: Bucks
From Local football - July 1998.

JACK, MATT — *Midfielder*
Current Club: Hungerford Town
Birthplace: Swindon
Previous clubs include: Swindon Supermarine - July 2001.

JACK, MATTHEW — *Defender*
Current Club: Swindon Supermarine
D o B: 03/07/1979 *Birthplace: Luton*
Matty joined the club at the start of the 1990/00 season from Cirencester Town where he came through their Academy set-up and was part of their successful National College championship winning side. A versatile and talented player who is equally at home in defence or midfield, well-balanced and a very intelligent player, a great asset to the team. His form this season has been exceptional and it has gained him both Wiltshire FA Senior and Under-21 honours.

JACKMAN, STEVE — *Defender*
Current Club: Bedford Town
D o B: 27/05/1985 *Birthplace: Aylesbury*
Steve is still a teenager and was signed by Ryman Premier side Bedford Town from Eagle Bitter United Counties League outfit Raunds Town in the summer of 2001. He spent three years at the Northampton Town centre of excellence. A player who is comfortable with the ball and his distribution is first class. Steve was the managers young player of the season for 2001/02.

JACKSON, ALLAN — *Midfielder*
Current Club: Kendal Town
Birthplace: Lancashire
Previous clubs include: Fleetwood Freeport - December 2001.

JACKSON, ANDY — *Midfielder*
Current Club: Brodsworth Welfare
Birthplace: Hull
Previous clubs include: Parkgate - January 2002, Brodsworth Welfare, Denaby Utd, North Ferriby Utd.

JACKSON, CHRIS — *Defender*
Current Club: Brackley Town
Birthplace: Banbury
Previous clubs include: Banbury Utd - July 2001.

JACKSON, DARREN — *Defender*
Current Club: West Auckland Town
Birthplace: Co.Durham
Previous clubs include: Cockfield - July 1997.

JACKSON, DAVID — *Defender*
Current Club: Racing Club Warwick
Birthplace: Birmingham
Utility player capable of performing in defence or midfield. Joined Racing Club Warwick for his first taste of Dr Martens football in October 2001 after being in the Midland Alliance with Cradley Town and Oldbury United.

JACKSON, DUNCAN — *Defender*
Current Club: Stanway Rovers
Birthplace: Essex
From Youth team.

JACKSON, ELLIOTT — *Goalkeeper*
Current Club: Hungerford Town
D o B: 27/08/1977 *Birthplace: Swindon*
Previous clubs include: Swindon Supermarine - November 2001, Cirencester T, Bath C, Oxford Utd.

JACKSON, GARY — *Forward*
Current Club: Clitheroe
Birthplace: Lancashire
Another young local lad who has progressed through the ranks. Scored 6 goals in his few appearances last season and will be hoping for more this season.

JACKSON, JIMMY — *Midfielder*
Current Club: Gravesend & Northfleet
Birthplace: Kent
Honours won: Ryman League Premier Div.Winners
Joined Gravesend in July 1994 when released by Charlton Athletic after spending three years at the Valley as a trainee. Local lad Jimmy soon adapted to life in Non-League football and has become a key member of the side, often attracting the attention of Football League scouts. The clubs free kick specialist and can play anywhere on the left side of the park, Jimmy is one of the most consistent players at the club and is a firm favourite with the crowd. He has now made almost 400 appearance for the Fleet.

JACKSON, JUSTIN — *Forward*
Current Club: Doncaster Rovers
D o B: 26/06/1975 *Birthplace: Nottingham*
Honours won: England Semi-Pro Int., Conference Winners, FA Trophy Winners
Began his career at Bolton Wanderers but was released at the end of season 1993-94. Moved to Scotland to play for Ayr United in 1994-95. In the close season 1995 he joined Penrith, then in October that year moved on to Ilkeston Town. In March 1996 he was transferred to Morecambe where his goalscoring exploits prompted Woking to splash out a club record fee of £30,000 in January 1997. A move back to the Football League followed in September 1997 when Notts County came in with £30,000 for his registration. He was loaned out to Rotherham United in January 1999 but was recalled in February to sign for Halifax Town for a fee of £30,000. In September he was transferred to Morecambe and netted 27 goals in 37 Conference games. This feat brought Rushden & Diamonds on the scene and he moved in the summer of 2000 for a fee of £180,000, a new record for the Non-League scene. Having helped them to win the Conference and promotion to the Football League, he moved to Doncaster Rovers in September 2001 for a reputed fee of £150,000.

JACKSON, KIRK — *Forward*
Current Club: Stevenage Borough
D o B: 16/10/1976 *Birthplace: Barnsley*
Honours won: England Semi-Pro Int.
Kirk joined Stevenage in January 2002 from Darlington, and made an immediate impact with two goals in his first start against Dover in the Trophy. He also scored on his debut for Darlington in March 2001. Darlington signed him from Worksop Town, after hed netted 40 times in his last season there, but with first team opportunities at a premium, he failed to settle. His signature ended a long chase for Paul Fairclough, who had been trying to land his man for over a year. Kirk was called into the National Game XI for the game with the USA in March 2002.

JACKSON, LEE — *Defender*
Current Club: Kendal Town
Previous clubs include: Fleetwood Freeport - July 2001.

JACKSON, LEE — *Defender*
Current Club: Bridlington Town
Birthplace: Hull
Recent transfer from the local Humber Premier League. Caught the eye while playing for Hull side Chisholms and should help strengthen the defensive unit along side the likes of Lee Harper and Billy Heath.

JACKSON, LEON   *Forward*

Current Club: Bilston Town

Birthplace: Wolverhampton

Previous clubs include: Redditch Utd - July 2001, Blakenall, Bromsgrove R, Bilston T, Bloxwich T, Bilston CC, Port Vale (Trainee).

JACKSON, LEON   *Midfielder*

Current Club: Worcester City

Birthplace: Birmingham

Leon, 23, is the nephew of former Worcester City legend Joe Jackson. His all-action displays in the centre of midfield for Bilston Town earned him rave reviews, and City fans were soon able to see why manager John Barton parted with a substantial fee for Jackson in December 2001 after an impressive debut against Newport County.

JACKSON, MARK   *Defender*

Current Club: Newtown AFC

Birthplace: Wrexham

Young Wrexham based player and a welcome addition to the squad. Right-sided defender. Keen to establish himself in the team.

JACKSON, MARK   *Forward*

Current Club: Bognor Regis Town

Birthplace: Brighton

Highly-promising teenage striker who joined Ryman Division One South side Bognor Regis Town from Brighton & Hove Albion in the summer of 2002. He had spent the previous three years with the Seagulls. Lives in Portslade.

JACKSON, MARK   *Midfielder*

Current Club: Ramsgate

Birthplace: Kent

Previous clubs include: Whitstable T - July 2000.

JACKSON, MICHAEL   *Defender*

Current Club: Rhyl

Birthplace: Liverpool

Previous clubs include: Southport - August 2001.

JACKSON, RUSELL   *Midfielder*

Current Club: Tiptree United

Birthplace: Essex

Previous clubs include: Halstead T - July 2001, Clacton T, Saffron Walden T, Bishops Stortford, Chelmsford C.

JACKSON, SCOTT   *Forward*

Current Club: Harrogate Town

D o B: 06/01/1977   Birthplace: Bradford

A prolific striker who finished top scorer in Ossett Town's first UniBond campaign following a transfer from Emley. Had previously played with Bradford City, Bradford PA and Farsley Celtic. Transferred to UniBond First Division champions Harrogate Town in July 2002.

JACKSON, STUART   *Defender*

Current Club: Billingham Town

Birthplace: Cleveland

Previous clubs include: Guisborough T - July 2000.

JACKSON, TOBY   *Defender*

Current Club: Swindon Supermarine

D o B: 24/02/1971   Birthplace: Bath

Previous clubs include: Chippenham T - December 2001, Newport AFC, Salisbury C, Forest Green R, Witney T, Clevedon T, Gloucester C, Trowbridge T, Bath C, Larkhall Ath.

JAGGARD, GAVIN   *Forward*

Current Club: Leighton Town

Birthplace: Luton

Previous clubs include: Hitchin T - November 2001, Leighton T, Bedford T, Leighton T, Luton T.

JAGO, MICHAEL   *Goalkeeper*

Current Club: Chester City

Birthplace: Liverpool

Previous clubs include: Liverpool (Trainee) - August 2001.

JAMES, CHRIS   *Defender*

Current Club: Matlock Town

D o B: 16/01/1969   Birthplace: Sheffield

Now in his second spell at Causeway Lane, after also serving in the Football League with Scarborough, as well as spells at Bridlington, Workson, Boston, Gainsborough and Leek. He has used his experience and knowledge of the game to the full to shine in the Town defence, where he can operate either at full-back or in the middle.

JAMES, CHRISTIAN   *Defender*

Current Club: Hereford United

Previous clubs include: Swansea C - August 2001.

JAMES, CLEMENT   *Forward*

Current Club: Slough Town

Birthplace: London

Now forced his way into the Slough first team squad having played for the Rebels reserve side for much of last season. Clement is an exciting left winger who is also capable of playing as a striker. He is probably the most skilful player at the club. On his day he will frighten any Ryman League right back in this league. After a spell on loan at Burnham last season CJ has been a major plus point in the Rebels start to the season leaving many supporters wondering why James was not involved in last seasons campaign. With Junior Haynes and Michael Gilkes as competition for the left-sided position CJ faces a battle to stay in the team. At only 21 years of age, it is still possible for the youngster to return to League football after being released by Brentford two seasons ago.

JAMES, KRISTIAN   *Midfielder*

Current Club: Dover Athletic

D o B: 24/05/1980   Birthplace: Neath

Rated as a real midfield talent for the future, Kristian was signed by Dover Athletic by former boss Neville Southall, who spotted him playing in South Wales with Port Talbot. Originally on the books at Swansea.

JAMES, LUTEL   *Forward*

Current Club: Accrington Stanley

D o B: 02/06/1972   Birthplace: Manchesrter

Honours won: St Kitts & Nevis Int.

Experienced striker who signed for Accrington Stanley after being released from Bury just before the start of the 2001/02 season. Had an impressive Bury debut against Manchester United in the 1998 League Cup before a knee injury hampered his career. Has played International football with St Kitts & Nevis. Quickly became a crowd favourite after scoring 9 goals in his first 9 league games for the club!

JAMES, MARK — Defender
Current Club: Spennymoor United
Birthplace: Co.Durham
Previous clubs include: Marske Utd - January 2002.

JAMES, MARTIN — Defender
Current Club: Bradford Park Avenue
D o B: 18/05/1971   *Birthplace: Formby*
Defender who signed for Bradford Park Avenue in July 1999 from Winsford United. Played 250 Football League matches with Rotherham United, Stockport County and Preston before injury cut short his League career. Has also played for Accrington Stanley and Leigh RMI.

JAMES, MATTHEW — Midfielder
Current Club: Windsor & Eton
D o B: 03/08/1981   *Birthplace: Berkshire*
Midfielder who signed for Windsor & Eton in July 2000 from Bracknell Town. Spent two years on YTS forms at Wycombe Wanderers where he was put forward for trials for England under-16s. Joined Farnborough Town before moving to Bracknell.

JAMES, OWEN — Defender
Current Club: Gresley Rovers
D o B: 01/09/1978   *Birthplace: Derby*
Derby-bron defender who was originally on the books at Sheffield United. Decided to undertake a university degree and attended Loughborough University, and whilst there played one game for Gresley Rovers against Tamworth during the 1997/98 season. Had a spell with Shepshed Dynamo before re-joining Gresley in March 2002.

JAMES, PAUL — Forward
Current Club: Biddulph Victoria
Birthplace: Stoke
Previous clubs include: Rocester - July 2001, Knypersley V, Goldenhill Wanderers, Knypersley V, Goldenhill Wanderers, Kidsgrove Ath., Newcastle T.

JAMES, PHIL — Midfielder
Current Club: Cwmbran Town
D o B: 24/10/1974   *Birthplace: Wales*
Honours won: Wales Youth Int.
Previous clubs include: Inter Cardiff - July 1997, Grange Quins, Cardiff C (Trainee).

JAMES, SEAN — Defender
Current Club: Harrow Borough
Birthplace: London
Defender or midfielder who rejoined Ryman Premier side Harrow Borough in July 2002 having moved back to the area. Helped Halesowen Town to win the Dr Martens Western Division in 2001/02. Also played for Bedfont and St Albans City and has made over 200 appearances for Boro.

JAMES, SIMON — Defender
Current Club: Bognor Regis Town
Birthplace: Hampshire
Previous clubs include: Worthing - December 2001, Bashley, Worthing, Havant & Waterlooville, Waterlooville, Havant T, Petersfield Utd.

JAMES, STUART — Midfielder
Current Club: Newport County
D o B: 12/09/1975   *Birthplace: Bristol*
Signed for Newport County from Bath City in the summer of 2000, Stuart played over 200 games for the Twerton Park club over five seasons, two of them in the Conference. Originally with Swindon on YTS and then as a first year professional, Stuart has been a regular in County's defence ever since.

JAMES, TONY — Defender
Current Club: Hereford United
Birthplace: Birmingham
A Welsh boy from near Cardiff, Tony joined West Bromwich Albion as a YTS straight from school. After completing his YTS he was offered a one-year professional contract which was not renewed. He joined the Bulls in May 1998 having played a number of games in the West Brom reserve side. A versatile defender with quite a lot of pace.

JANNEY, MARK — Midfielder
Current Club: Dagenham & Redbridge
D o B: 02/12/1977   *Birthplace: Romford*
Was released by Tottenham Hotspur in September 1997 and joined the Daggers. After making a big impression in the reserves, Mark broke into the first-team on a regular basis. Spent two months on loan to Braintree Town at the start of the 1999/2000, returning to play a major role in the clubs title success from midfield.

JANSEN, NICKY — Forward
Current Club: Staines Town
Birthplace: Hampshire
Previous clubs include: Farnborough T - July 1999, Southampton (Trainee).

JARDINE, JAMIE — Defender
Current Club: Colwyn Bay
D o B: 01/02/1977   *Birthplace: Liverpool*
Central defender who signed for Colwyn Bay from League of Wales side Bangor City in March 2001. Previously at Tranmere Rovers as a professional and also had two spells in the LoW with Connahs Quay Nomads.

JARDINE, STEVE — Defender
Current Club: Nantwich Town
Birthplace: Cheshire
From Youth team.

JARMAN, LEE — Defender
Current Club: Barry Town
D o B: 16/12/1977   *Birthplace: Cardiff*
Honours won: Wales u-21 Int.
Previous clubs include: Merthyr Tydfil - October 2001, Oxford Utd, Exeter C, Cardiff C.

JARRETT, MICKY — Forward
Current Club: Arlesey Town
Birthplace: Hertfordshire
Micky is a very quick striker, who isnt afraid to take defenders on and go for goal. He has good vision and creates as many goals as he scores. Signed from Hertford Town in the summer of 2001 and has also seen service with Harlow Town and Ware and is in his second spell with Arlesey. He works as a roofer.

J

JARVAND, RAMIN — Forward
Current Club: Horsham YMCA
Birthplace: Sussex
Youthful-looking forward: played for the reserves during 2000/01 before showing some outstanding form in the opening weeks of the latest campaign (scored on his debut against Hassocks in August).

JARVIS, JAMIE — Midfielder
Current Club: Hayes
Birthplace: Slough
An experienced and well-travelled midfielder who was signed by Ryman Premier side Hayes in the summer of 2002 from Maidenhead United to add some bite in the middle of the park. Has played the majority of his football in the Berkshire area with spells at Windsor & Eton, Slough Town, Burnham, Beaconsfield SYCOB, Uxbridge and Maidenhead.

JARVIS, LEE — Midfielder
Current Club: Edgware Town
Previous clubs include: Yeading - October 2001, Chesham Utd.

JARVIS, STUART — Defender
Current Club: Maldon Town
Birthplace: Essex
Previous clubs include: Tiptree Utd - July 2000.

JAY, GARY — Defender
Current Club: Woodbridge Town
Birthplace: Ipswich
Signed from Bury Town in time for the beginning of the current season, having spent six seasons at the West Suffolk club. A strong and consistent player who will undoubtedly enhance our defensive unit.

JEANNE, LEON — Forward
Current Club: Newport County
D o B: 17/11/1980   *Birthplace: Cardiff*
Pacey young striker who joined Dr Martens Premier side Newport County in last August 2002. Cardiff-born, his career began at Queens Park Rangers, where he progressed through the ranks to make over a dozen senior appearances. Moved to his home-town club in the summer of 2001 but played only a couple of times in the first-team before being released.

JEAN-ZEPHERIN, DOMINIQUE — Goalkeeper
Current Club: Slough Town
Birthplace: France
French-born goalkeeper originally signed by Ryman Division One North side Slough Town as cover for regular keeper Steve Mautone. He signed permanently in August 2002 following his release from Hampton and Richmond Borough. Zepherin looks comfortable in goal with his quick distribution of the ball one of his best features. Another of his good features is his kick. He is able to get long distance, which sets Sloughs attacks up well.

JEFFERIES, LEE — Defender
Current Club: Clevedon Town
D o B: 16/03/1973   *Birthplace: Bristol*
Lee joined Clevedon in January 1996, for the then Dr Martens side Yate Town, after spells with both Almonsbury Town and Shortwood United. Lee appeared in every match of our championship side of 1998 - 1999. Lee is our longest serving player.

JEFFERSON, MIKE — Defender
Current Club: Ashton United
From Youth team.

JEFFERY, ORLANDO — Defender
Current Club: Maidenhead United
Birthplace: Berkshire
Orlando Jeffrey arrived at Burnham from Thatcham Town in December 2000 and immediately secured a place in the heart of the defence. Transferred to Ryman League neighbours Maidenhead in December 2001.

JEFFREY, ANDY — Defender
Current Club: Histon
D o B: 15/01/1972   *Birthplace: Bellshill*
Previous clubs include: Cambridge C - July 1998, Cambridge Utd, Cambridge C, Leicester C.

JEFFREY, STUART — Goalkeeper
Current Club: Garforth Town
D o B: 29/11/1980   *Birthplace: Yorkshire*
Promising young keeper who has earned a regular First Team place with a string of consistent performances. A good shot stopper and safe handler of the ball. What he lacks in height, he makes up for by his excellent agility.

JEFFRIES, ALEX — Forward
Current Club: Flackwell Heath
D o B: 11/12/1981   *Birthplace: Berkshire*
Previous clubs include: Windsor & Eton - March 2002, Reading.

JEFFRIES, BARRY — Midfielder
Current Club: Maidstone United
Birthplace: Kent
Previous clubs include: Herne Bay - August 2001.

JEFFRIES, ROSS — Forward
Current Club: Colwyn Bay
D o B: 05/08/1979   *Birthplace: Wales*
Talented forward who moved into the UniBond League with Colwyn Bay in July 2002 from League of Wales outfit Flexsys Cefn Druids. Played for local sides Gresford United, Castell Alun and Rhydymwyn before joining Cefn Druids for the first time. Switched to Oswestry Town and then returned to Druids at the start of the 2001/02 season.

JEFFS, MARTIN — Defender
Current Club: Rushall Olympic
Birthplace: Worcestershire
Previous clubs include: Halesowen Harriers - May 2002, Stourbridge, Halesowen Harriers, Lye T.

JEHU, SEAN — Defender
Current Club: Caersws
D o B: 22/05/1975   *Birthplace: Wales*
From Youth team.

JEMMOTT, DURRAND — Forward
Current Club: Tooting & Mitcham United
Birthplace: Surrey
From Youth team.

JENKIN, PAUL — Midfielder
Current Club: Haverhill Rovers
Birthplace: Suffolk
An unsung hero who came to Haverhill from Wickhambrook. In his fourth season.

JENKINS, ADAM — Goalkeeper
Current Club: Hednesford Town

Birthplace: Birmingham
Adam is a product of Hednesford Town's Youth Development programme, having joined the club as a 13 year old. Still only 16, Adam has already featured in the first team, making three substitute goalkeeper appearances in the 2000/2001 season. He regularly features in reserve and youth team level and is viewed as a genuine prospect for the future.

JENKINS, DAVID — Defender
Current Club: Clapton

D o B: 23/09/1976   Birthplace: Essex
Previous clubs include: Hornchurch - August 1998.

JENKINS, IAIN — Defender
Current Club: Chester City

D o B: 24/11/1972   Birthplace: Whiston
Honours won: Northern Ireland Int.
Vastly experienced and popular defender now in his second spell at Chester. Has been capped for Northern Ireland.

JENKINS, JAMIE — Midfielder
Current Club: Barry Town

D o B: 01/01/1979   Birthplace: Pontypool
Previous clubs include: AFC Bournemouth - July 1999.

JENKINS, JODY — Forward
Current Club: Cwmbran Town

D o B: 12/12/1979   Birthplace: Cwmbran
Very skilful and pacy midfielder who can turn defence into attack very quickly. Re-joined Cwmbran Town from League of Wales rivals TNS in July 2002 having signed from Cwmbran the previous summer. He gained league honours with Barry Town after starting his career with AFC Bournemouth.

JENKINS, MARK — Defender
Current Club: Wisbech Town

D o B: 20/11/1978
Previous clubs include: Aveley - July 2001, Leyton Orient, West Ham Utd.

JENKINS, NIGEL — Forward
Current Club: Brackley Town

Birthplace: Banbury
From Local football - July 1998.

JENKINS, RICHARD — Midfielder
Current Club: Llanelli AFC

D o B: 15/01/1985   Birthplace: Wales
From Academy.

JENKINS, STEVE — Defender
Current Club: Forest Green Rovers

D o B: 02/01/1980   Birthplace: Bristol
Honours won: Wales Int.
Having earned 14 full caps playing for Wales and with a wealth of Football League experience the move by Conference side Forest Green Rovers manager Nigel Spink to sign him in August 2001 was fully vindicated as he enjoyed an excellent first season with the club. Started his career with Southampton and also played for Brentford.

JENKINS, STEVE — Defender
Current Club: Frome Town

Birthplace: Bristol
Previous clubs include: Welton Rovers - January 2002.

JENKINS, STEVE — Forward
Current Club: Banbury United

D o B: 04/08/1968   Birthplace: Oxford
Previous clubs include: Brackley T - July 1998, Oxford C, Brackley T, Abingdon T, Witney T, Oxford C, Wallingford T, Newbury T, Buckingham T, Wealdstone, Witney T, Cheltenham T, Oxford C, Limerick C, Varberg (Sweden), Oxford C, Oxford Utd.

JENKINS, STEVE — Midfielder
Current Club: Gloucester City

Birthplace: Gloucester
Previous clubs include: Cirencester T - March 2000, Gloucester C.

JENKINS, WILL — Defender
Current Club: Leatherhead

D o B: 27/04/1983   Birthplace: Sussex
In his second spell at Leatherhead after rejoining from Dorking. The centre-back started his career at Three Bridges.

JENKINSON, LEIGH — Forward
Current Club: Goole AFC

D o B: 09/07/1969   Birthplace: Thorne
Previous clubs include: Barrow - August 2001, Macclesfield T, Hearts, Wigan Ath., St.Johnstone, Coventry C, Hull C.

JERMYN, MARK — Defender
Current Club: Dorchester Town

Birthplace: Devon
Previous clubs include: Torquay Utd - August 2000.

JESSOP, SHANE — Midfielder
Current Club: Kendal Town

Birthplace: Preston
Previous clubs include: Bamber Bridge - January 2002, Lancaster C, Squires Gate, Rossendale Utd, Bamber Bridge.

JEWELL, ADAM — Midfielder
Current Club: Whitby Town

D o B: 17/09/1981   Birthplace: South Africa
Adam was a graduate of the Scarborough youth system and completed his third year scholarship and was then offered a one-year professional contract. A regular member of the reserve team he has been on the first team bench a number of times, making one appearance as sub in the LDV Vans Trophy versus Stoke. Transferred to Whitby in March 2002.

JEWSON, ANTHONY — Forward
Current Club: Peterlee Newtown

Birthplace: Hartlepool
Previous clubs include: Horden CW - July 2000, Peterlee Newtown, Chester-le-Street, Easington Colliery, Hartlepool T, Hartlepool Utd (Junior).

JEWSON, STUART — Forward
Current Club: Peterlee Newtown

Birthplace: Hartlepool
Previous clubs include: Chester-le-Street - March 2001, Bishop Auckland, Tow Law T, Inglewood Falcons (Australia), Middlesbrough (Junior).

JIMMY, KIERAN   *Goalkeeper*

Current Club: Yeading

Birthplace: Middlesex

Young keeper signed in September 2001 as cover for Matt Hodson. Previously with North Greenford United. Thrown in at the deep end with a debut in the FA Cup 4th Qualifying Round against Aylesbury United. Bounced back from that disappointing scoreline with a clean sheet in the following league game.

JIMSON, DARREN   *Forward*

Current Club: Wisbech Town

D o B: 24/10/1980

Previous clubs include: Outwell Swifts - July 2001.

JIMSON, MARK   *Midfielder*

Current Club: Wisbech Town

D o B: 16/06/1976

Previous clubs include: Outwell Swifts - August 2000, Wisbech T.

JJUNJO, MOSES   *Forward*

Current Club: Carshalton Athletic

Birthplace: London

Previous clubs include: Bromley - January 2002.

JOBLING, KEVIN   *Midfielder*

Current Club: Telford United

Birthplace: Sunderland

Previous clubs include: (Player/Assistant-Manager) Shrewsbury T - June 2000, Grimsby T, Leicester C.

JOE, RONNIE   *Midfielder*

Current Club: Aylesbury United

Previous clubs include: Thame Utd - July 2000, Hayes.

JOHN, JEROME   *Goalkeeper*

Current Club: Billericay Town

Birthplace: Essex

Previous clubs include: Grays Ath - February 2002, Enfield, Kingstonian, Altrincham, Dulwich Hamlet, West Ham Utd.

JOHN, RAY   *Defender*

Current Club: Llanelli AFC

D o B: 08/11/1964   Birthplace: Cardiff

Previous clubs include: Rhayader T - July 2001, Inter Cardiff, Cwmbran T, Merthyr Tydfil, Inter Cardiff, Ebbw Vale, Newport AFC, Inter Cardiff, Barry T, Ton Pentre, Happy Valley (Hong Kong), Plymouth Argyle, Cardiff Corinthians.

JOHN, VINNIE   *Forward*

Current Club: Bishops Stortford

D o B: 08/09/1975   Birthplace: London

A serial goalscorer, Vinnie has been selected and scored for the Rymans representative X1. One of the top goalscorers in the League for the last 2 seasons Vinnie has certainly gained hero status amongst the Bishops Stortford faithfull since signing for a club record fee of £5,000 from Grays Athletic in August 1999. A former Wimbledon junior, other clubs include Romford and Dagenham & Redbridge. Vinnie racked up 38 goals in the 2000/2001 season and is on track to better that this time out.

JOHNS, STEPHEN   *Midfielder*

Current Club: Tonbridge Angels

Birthplace: Kent

Previous clubs include: Dartford - February 2002.

JOHNSON, AARON   *Defender*

Current Club: Burton Albion

D o B: 01/11/1981   Birthplace: Derby

Aaron signed for Conferenece club Burton Albion after impressing the management in the pre-season of 2002. A former Doncaster Rovers schoolboy, Aaron moved to Borrowash Victoria in the Northern Counties East League where he gained a championship medal as the Vics took the First Division title. Another good prospect for the future, Aaron is an attacking full back who likes to get forward.

JOHNSON, ANDY   *Midfielder*

Current Club: Lewes

Birthplace: Brighton

Previous clubs include: Wick - June 2001, Lewes, Watford, Lewes.

JOHNSON, BEN   *Midfielder*

Current Club: Sidlesham

Birthplace: Sussex

Midfielder: former Chichester reserve player who switched to the Sidlesham squad during the 1999 close season: held back by injury and began 2001/02 with Emsworth (West Sussex League) until gaining a place in the Sids first-team midway through the season.

JOHNSON, BRIAN   *Defender*

Current Club: Tring Town

Birthplace: Herts

Previous clubs include: RAF - July 2000.

JOHNSON, CAMERON   *Midfielder*

Current Club: Peacehaven & Telscombe

Birthplace: Sussex

Began a second spell at the club in July 2000. A very steady presence for much of last season until an injury forced him to miss the last few glorious weeks. Cameron, a painter and decorator by trade, moved to Peacehaven in March 2002.

JOHNSON, CARL   *Goalkeeper*

Current Club: Warrington Town

Birthplace: Liverpool

Previous clubs include: Bamber Bridge - January 2002.

JOHNSON, CHRIS   *Midfielder*

Current Club: Ringmer

D o B: 25/01/1979   Birthplace: Brighton

Midfielder and brother of Lewes player Andy Johnson. Played once for Watford, but was thrown out of the club for disciplinary reasons but had a great season for Lewes in 1998/99, before leaving the club on acrimonious terms the following year. Consequently had a brief spell at Wick midway through 1999/2000 and joined Saltdean in February 2000, but picked up a thigh injury on his debut and wasn't seen out for again for ages. Rejoined the Rooks at the start of 2001/02 before signing for Ringmer in December.

JOHNSON, CHRIS   *Midfielder*

Current Club: Oxford City

Previous clubs include: Bicester T - August 2001, Abingdon T, Thame Utd, Northampton T (Junior).

JOHNSON, COLIN   *Goalkeeper*

Current Club: Oadby Town

Birthplace: Leicester

Previous clubs include: Corby T - July 2001, Rugby Utd.

JOHNSON, DAVID   *Defender*
Current Club: Brandon United
Birthplace: Co.Durham
Attacking lef-sided player now in his fourth season at the club after signing from Blyth Spartans, having also played for Darlington and Gateshead.

JOHNSON, DEAN   *Midfielder*
Current Club: Carmarthen Town
D o B: 09/05/1978   Birthplace: Wales
Honours won: Wales Colleges Rep.
Previous clubs include: Afan Lido - August 2001.

JOHNSON, DEAN   *Midfielder*
Current Club: Ashton United
Previous clubs include: Ossett Alb - November 1999, Marsden, Ossett Alb.

JOHNSON, GLEN   *Goalkeeper*
Current Club: Canvey Island
D o B: 19/09/1985   Birthplace: Essex
Highly-promising young goalkeeper who came through Canvey Islands under-18s and reserves and has made the substitutes honoh for several cup games with the senior side. He made his first-team debut in December 2001 against Bishops Stortford. Glen has represented Essex County Schoolboys for the past three years and has a very bright future at the club and one to look out for in the near future.

JOHNSON, IAN   *Midfielder*
Current Club: Ashington
D o B: 01/09/1975   Birthplace: Sunderland
Previous clubs include: Durham C - July 2001, Middlesbrough.

JOHNSON, LEE   *Defender*
Current Club: Leighton Town
Birthplace: Herts
Defender who followed manager Paul Burgess to Ryman Division Two side Leighton Town from Tring Town in July 2002. Had been with Tring since the summer of 2000, joining from local side Bedmond Sports.

JOHNSON, LEE   *Forward*
Current Club: Yeading
Birthplace: Middlesex
Young, pacy strikerin his earky twenties who linked up with the Ding during pre-season 2001. Made his debut v Dulwich Hamlet.

JOHNSON, LEE   *Midfielder*
Current Club: Yeovil Town
D o B: 07/06/1981   Birthplace: Newmarket
Honours won: FA Trophy Winners
Lee started his career with Watford as a trainee, as part of their Youth Academy, under Gary Johnson, then the Watford Youth Academy Director. Lee is manager Garys son, and he turned down the possibility of playing football in Denmark to come to Huish Park and work under his father. After he left Watford, Lee joined Brighton and Hove Albion where he made a handful of first team appearances, scoring on his debut in December 2000 against Cardiff City. Lee spent the last few months of the 2000/01 season as a non-contract player at Brentford but left them over the summer. Lee joined Yeovil in July 2001and made his debut for the club against Northwich Victoria on Saturday 18th August 2001. He has blended into the team as a regular in the centre of midfield and scored his debut goal against Scarborough just one month later on Saturday 15th September 2001.

JOHNSON, LEON   *Defender*
Current Club: Croydon Athletic
Birthplace: Croydon
From Youth team.

JOHNSON, MATTHEW   *Goalkeeper*
Current Club: Leek Town
Birthplace: Derby
Highly-rated goalkeeper who joined Leek Town in June 2002 after a long spell with Northern Counties East League side Buxton. Started his career as a junior at Derby County and then played local football with Cote Heath before joining Buxton in July 1997. Became a firm favourite with the Bucks supporters.

JOHNSON, MICHAEL   *Midfielder*
Current Club: Carshalton Athletic
D o B: 22/05/1982   Birthplace: Surrey
A left-sided midfielder who joined Ryman Division One South side Carshalton Athletic from Croydon during the 2001/02 season. Previously with Fulham Youth and has also played for Sutton United's reserve side.

JOHNSON, PAUL   *Defender*
Current Club: Staines Town
D o B: 10/06/1982   Birthplace: London
Defender Paul joined Staines Town in November 2001 following a very brief spell with Edgware Town. Had spent the foregoing year with Hendon after gaining first-team experience with Wycombe. Began in junior soccer with Wimbledon, Chelsea and QPR and represented Middlesex Youth.

JOHNSON, PAUL   *Midfielder*
Current Club: Fairford Town
Birthplace: Wiltshire
Previous clubs include: Wanborough - September 2001.

JOHNSON, PETER   *Forward*
Current Club: Harwich & Parkeston
Birthplace: Essex
Probably the most improved player at Harwich last season, Peter has a knack of scoring vital goals. Skilful on the ball he always gives 100 plus and his never-say-die attitude has quickly established him as a Royal Oak favourite.

JOHNSON, PHIL   *Midfielder*
Current Club: Oswestry Town
D o B: 07/04/1975   Birthplace: Liverpool
Another close season arrival with a wealth of League of Wales experience. Previously played for Barry, Aberystwyth, Cwmbran, Bangor and Rhayader.

JOHNSON, PHIL   *Midfielder*
Current Club: Harrow Borough
Birthplace: Liverpool
Previous clubs include: Runcorn FC Halton - October 2001, Real Madrid (Spain).

JOHNSON, ROSS   *Defender*
Current Club: Dagenham & Redbridge
D o B: 02/01/1976   Birthplace: Brighton
Defender who joined Conference side Dagenham & Redbridge in August 2002 from Colchester United. Born in Brighton, he signed for his home-town club and went on to make over 150 appearances for the Seagulls before moving to Colchester, iniitally on-loan, in February 2000.

JOHNSON, SCOTT — Defender

Current Club: Ely City

Birthplace: Cambridgeshire

Previous clubs include: Chatteris T - July 1999.

JOHNSON, SIMON — Forward

Current Club: Armthorpe Welfare

D o B: 27/06/1971   Birthplace: Doncaster

Previous clubs include: Worthing - July 1997, Eastwood T, Halifax T, Armthorpe Welfare.

JOHNSON, STEVE — Midfielder

Current Club: Alfreton Town

Birthplace: Nottingham

Honours won: NCEL & Cup Winners

Tenacious midfielder who rejoined Alfreton Town in November 2001 following spells at Worksop Town and Eastwood Town. In his previous three-year spell at North Street Steve scored 40 goals in 171 appearances and showed that he has not lost the scoring touch. He has also played for Buxton and Matlock Town.

JOHNSON, STEVE — Midfielder

Current Club: Wroxham

Birthplace: Norfolk

Previous clubs include: Watton Utd - January 1998.

JOHNSON, WAYNE — Defender

Current Club: Workington

From Youth team.

JOHNSON, WAYNE — Defender

Current Club: Leek Town

Birthplace: Stoke

Tough-tackling central defender who has good distribution. Signed for Leek Town from Congleton Town in February 2001 and has previously seen service with Witton Albion, Newcastle Town and Ball Haye Green.

JOHNSTON, ANDY — Goalkeeper

Current Club: Ashton United

D o B: 09/11/1967

Honours won: FA Vase Winners

Previous clubs include: Great Harwood T - July 1999, Atherton LR, Radcliffe B, Barrow, Knowsley Utd, St.Helens T, Barrow.

JOHNSTON, EDDIE — Defender

Current Club: St.Helens Town

D o B: 08/01/1960   Birthplace: Liverpool

Veteran defender who joined Town earlier this season from Droylsden. Has played for numerous clubs throughout a lengthy semi-professional career. Solid at the centre of defence, where he makes his calmness and experience count.

JOHNSTON, MICHAEL — Goalkeeper

Current Club: Consett

Previous clubs include: Annan Athletic - July 2001.

JOHNSTON, RAY — Goalkeeper

Current Club: Bath City

D o B: 05/05/1981   Birthplace: Bristol

Previous clubs include: Bishop Sutton - January 2002, Bristol R.

JOLLY, LUKE — Midfielder

Current Club: Molesey

Birthplace: Surrey

Tenacious midfield/flank player who joined Molesey after spells with Leatherhead, Fleet Town and Ashford Town (Middx). A member of Ashfords original junior side in the early 90s.

JONES, AARON — Midfielder

Current Club: Oswestry Town

Birthplace: Shropshire

Formerly a Birmingham City trainee, Aaron also had a spell with Telford United before joining Town in the summer. The coaching squad see a lot of promise in him.

JONES, ALED — Midfielder

Current Club: Bangor City

D o B: 08/02/1984   Birthplace: Wales

From Youth team.

JONES, ALLAN — Midfielder

Current Club: Rhyl

D o B: 24/12/1978   Birthplace: Wales

Previous clubs include: Llandudno - August 2001

JONES, ALYN — Forward

Current Club: Port Talbot Town

Birthplace: Swansea

Previous clubs include: Maesteg Park - June 2002.

JONES, ANDY — Forward

Current Club: Halesowen Town

Birthplace: Birmingham

Honours won: Dr Martens Western Div.Winners

Andy is an energetic forward who didnt feature much for Halesowen Town during the early part of the season due to injury and holiday commitments. However, once fit he became a vital member of the squad that lifted the Dr Martens Western Division championship. Signed from neighbouring Midland Alliance side Halesowen Harriers in the summer of 2001, Andy was previously with Kidderminster Harriers and originally at Crewe Alexander.

JONES, ANDY — Forward

Current Club: Lymington & New Milton

Birthplace: Essex

Honours won: FA Trophy Winners

Previous clubs include: Billericay T - July 1992, Rainham T, Billericay T, Purfleet, Basildon Utd.

JONES, ANDY — Forward

Current Club: Canvey Island

Birthplace: Cardiff

Previous clubs include: Brockenhurst - May 2002, Wimborne T, Ringwood T, Poole T, Cwmbran T, UWIC.

JONES, ANDY — Midfielder

Current Club: Colwyn Bay

Birthplace: Wales

Midfielder who joined UniBond Premier Colwyn Bay in June 2002 from League of Wales neighbours Rhyl. Spent some time in the United States before joining Rhyl. An enthusiastic squad member who was signed by Rhyl from Wrexhams Academy at the start of the 2001/02 season.

JONES, ANTHONY   *Defender*
Current Club: East Thurrock United
Birthplace: Essex
Previous clubs include: Purfleet - December 2001, Concord Rangers, Hornchurch, Billericay T, Colchester Utd, Southend Utd (Trainee).

JONES, ARWEL   *Defender*
Current Club: Flexsys Cefn Druids
D o B: 07/03/1970   *Birthplace: Wales*
Previous clubs include: Total Network Solutions - July 2001, Bangor C, Llansantfraid, Bangor C, CPD Porthmadog, Flint Town Utd, Wrexham (Trainee).

JONES, ASHLEY   *Midfielder*
Current Club: Peacehaven & Telscombe
Birthplace: Sussex
Midfielder who graduated through Peacehavens youth team: scored once during 2000/01. Sidelined with a broken collar bone for the early part of 2001/02.

JONES, BARRY   *Defender*
Current Club: Southport
D o B: 20/06/1970   *Birthplace: Prescot*
Previous clubs include: York C - August 2001, Wrexham, Liverpool, Prescot.

JONES, BEN   *Forward*
Current Club: Horsham
Birthplace: Sussex
Forward (better known as an ABA boxer): leading scorer for Redhill in 1999/2000 after joining them from Three Bridges: scored twice during a spell for Burgess Hill early the following season: returned to Sussex football when signing for Horsham from Whyteleafe in the autumn 2001.

JONES, BEN   *Midfielder*
Current Club: Worthing
Birthplace: Sussex
Previous clubs include: Whyteleafe - September 2001, Horsham.

JONES, BILLY   *Midfielder*
Current Club: Feltham
Birthplace: Feltham
Billy joined Feltham at the start of this season following in the footsteps of his brother Johnny. Billy has made the left side position his own with a string of sterling performances. Unfortunatley his season has been cut short following an injury against Ash United where after completing 45 minutes it turned out he had broken his foot.

JONES, BOBBY   *Midfielder*
Current Club: Trafford
D o B: 12/02/1976   *Birthplace: Manchester*
Previous clubs include: Flixton - July 2000, Salford C, Castleton Gabriels.

JONES, BRADLEY   *Forward*
Current Club: Leyton Pennant
Birthplace: Essex
Previous clubs include: Eton Manor - August 2001.

JONES, BRIAN   *Midfielder*
Current Club: Boreham Wood
Birthplace: London
Brian is an exciting wing forward who began his career with Yeading and then Bedfont, before joining Harrow Borough, where he had considerable success. He then made the short transfer to Wealdstone and had been a regular and popular member of their side in recent seasons. Brian joined Boreham Wood in May 2001, and made his first-team debut against Bedford Town on 18th August 2001.

JONES, BRYNMOR   *Defender*
Current Club: Aberystwyth Town
D o B: 03/11/1982   *Birthplace: Lledrod*
Previous clubs include: Oxford Utd - January 2002.

JONES, CARWYN   *Midfielder*
Current Club: Llanelli AFC
D o B: 10/10/1979   *Birthplace: Wales*
From Youth team.

JONES, CRAIG   *Goalkeeper*
Current Club: Telford United
Birthplace: Birmingham
Highly-promising young goalkeeper who was signed by Conference side Telford United on the eve of the 2002/03 season after being released by First Division Walsall. Was a regular in the Saddlers reserve side.

JONES, DALE   *Forward*
Current Club: Ludlow Town
Birthplace: Shropshire
Previous clubs include: Shifnal T - July 2000, Newport T.

JONES, DANNY   *Forward*
Current Club: Farnborough Town
Birthplace: London
Highly-promising young forward who is a product of Enfields youth system. Became a first-team regular during the 1999/00 season and then transferred into the Conference with Farnborough Town at the start of the 2001/02 season.

JONES, DAVID   *Forward*
Current Club: Frickley Athletic
D o B: 17/11/1978   *Birthplace: Goole*
Was a product of Goole Town when he earned a move into the League with Blackpool in the summer of 1998. Couldnt quite make the breakthrough into the senior side at Bloomfield Road, although he did suffer from his fair share of injury problems. Moved on to Doncaster Rovers and then had a second spell with Goole before joining Northern Counties East side Armthorpe Welfare at the start of the 2001/02 season. Transferred to UniBond Premier side Frickley Athletic in August 2002.

JONES, DEAN   *Defender*
Current Club: Belper Town
D o B: 01/01/1979   *Birthplace: Barnsley*
A highly-rated defender who became one of number of players to join UniBond First Division side Belper Town from Premier Division Frickley Athletic in the summer of 2002. Started his career with his home-town club Barnsley and then had his first spell with Frickley. Moved into the Dr Martens League with Ilkeston Town before returning to Frickley in December 2000.

JONES, DEAN — Forward
Current Club: Leatherhead

D o B: 04/12/1982 — *Birthplace: Surrey*
Formerly with both Wimbledon and Fulham Youth Academies, the forward is now a student and came to Leatherhead via Dorking Youth and Horsley Youth.

JONES, EIFION — Defender
Current Club: Bangor City

D o B: 28/09/1980 — *Birthplace: Llanrug*
Honours won: Wales u-21 Int.
Young centreback who spent three years with Liverpool and then three more at Blackpool where he was a member of the first team squad, making 8 League appearances. Joined League of Wales side Bangor City in August 2002. Is a Welsh under-21 international.

JONES, FRANCIS — Midfielder
Current Club: Tow Law Town

Birthplace: Co.Durham
Former Hartlepool YTS player who has been with the Lawyers for three seasons and has a very promising boxing career.

JONES, GARETH — Forward
Current Club: Barrow

Birthplace: Barrow
Barrow-born, Gareth joined his home-town club in February 2001 after scoring regularly for Dalton United in the West Lancashire League and helping them to the Lancashire Amateur Shield Final. He made his debut in the UniBond Cup tie against Gretna in February 2001 and scored on his debut.

JONES, GARY — Forward
Current Club: Nuneaton Borough

D o B: 06/04/1969 — *Birthplace: Huddersfield*
Much-travelled striker who joined Nuneaton Borough in July 2002 after being released by Halifax Town upon their relegation back to the Conference. Started his career with Rossington Main in the Northern Counties East League and then played a dozen times in the League for Doncaster before joining Kettering Town for £8,500 from Grantham in August 1990. Spells with Boston United, Southend, Notts County, Hartlepool and Halifax followed and he totalled more than 350 League games before joining Boro.

JONES, GAVIN — Defender
Current Club: Burnham

Birthplace: Slough
Youngster arrived from local football and made his debut at the start of the 00/01 season. Player with lots of potential.

JONES, GAVIN — Forward
Current Club: Worthing

Birthplace: Sussex
Exciting young forward: leading scorer for Worthing Utd during 2000/01 with 24 goals, before joining the Rebels at the start of the following season.

JONES, HUW — Forward
Current Club: Aberystwyth Town

D o B: 07/04/1982 — *Birthplace: Wales*
From Youth team.

JONES, IAN — Goalkeeper
Current Club: Chippenham Town

Previous clubs include: Mangotsfield Utd - November 1998, Yate T, Mangotsfield Utd.

JONES, IAN — Midfielder
Current Club: Paget Rangers

Birthplace: Birmingham
Previous clubs include: Stourbridge - January 2002, Paget R, Bedworth Utd, Evesham Utd, Kidderminster Harriers, Bedworth Utd, Bromsgrove R, Doncaster R, Birmingham C.

JONES, JASON — Forward
Current Club: Clitheroe

Birthplace: Lancashire
Started last season as a young reserve player looking for a break and ended the season as a regular who would run all day and score you vital goals. If he continues to make the massive improvements he did last season, there is no doubt he will be watched.

JONES, JASON — Midfielder
Current Club: Colwyn Bay

Previous clubs include: Oswestry T - July 2001, Rhydymwyn.

JONES, JEREMY — Midfielder
Current Club: Leatherhead

D o B: 13/03/1972 — *Birthplace: London*
Exciting left-sided player who can play at fullback or winger. Signed for Ryman Division One South side Leatherhead from Yeading in September 2000, Jeremy was previously with Harrow Borough, Walton & Hersham, Molesey, Whyteleafe, Tooting & Mitcham United, Dulwich Hamlet and Chelsea. He works as a residential social worker.

JONES, JOHN — Midfielder
Current Club: Hanwell Town

D o B: 16/11/1977 — *Birthplace: Perivale*
Previous clubs include: Uxbridge - July 1997.

JONES, JOHNNY — Midfielder
Current Club: Feltham

Birthplace: Chertsey
Johnny joined Feltham in the summer of 2001 from Ryman League side Leatherhead and has quickly made the wide right position his own. Not reknowned for his goalscoring ability Jones has still chipped in with some goals this season including a couple of beauties so far.

JONES, JONATHAN — Forward
Current Club: Oswestry Town

D o B: 27/10/1978 — *Birthplace: Wrexham*
Formerly with Chester City and TNS, Jonathon proved in Town's first LoW season that he is a pacey player who can find the back of the net.

JONES, JONATHAN — Midfielder
Current Club: Glasshoughton Welfare

Birthplace: Yorkshire
Previous clubs include: Bradford Park Avenue - July 1999, Glasshoughton Welfare, Ossett Alb.

JONES, JUSTIN — Midfielder
Current Club: Croydon Athletic

Birthplace: Surrey
Previous clubs include: Carshalton Ath - August 2001, Redhill.

JONES, KEITH — Defender
Current Club: Edgware Town
Birthplace: London
From Youth team.

JONES, KIERON — Midfielder
Current Club: St Margaretsbury
D o B: 06/07/1986   Birthplace: Harlow
From Youth team.

JONES, KRISTIAN — Forward
Current Club: Spalding United
Birthplace: Suffolk
Previous clubs include: Kings Lynn - March 2002, Hayes, Wisbech T, Ipswich T (Junior).

JONES, LEE — Forward
Current Club: Herne Bay
Birthplace: Kent
Previous clubs include: Canterbury C - November 1999.

JONES, LEE — Midfielder
Current Club: Dartford
Birthplace: Kent
Previous clubs include: Faversham T - September 1996, Dartford.

JONES, LEIGHTON — Defender
Current Club: Afan Lido
D o B: 13/07/1978   Birthplace: Wales
Youth team product who made his first team debut in 1996, and is now a reliable central defender and first team regular.

JONES, LUKE — Forward
Current Club: Paget Rangers
D o B: 13/12/1979   Birthplace: Birmingham
Previous clubs include: Boldmere St.Michaels - September 2001, Sutton Coldfield T, Paget R, Walsall Wood, Rushall Olympic.

JONES, MARK — Defender
Current Club: Kingstonian
D o B: 04/09/1981   Birthplace: London
The young defender has shown bursts of exciting potential and commitment in the Kingstonian side since joining from Wimbledon. Has progressed from the reserves, and made his first-team debut in November 2000.

JONES, MARK — Defender
Current Club: Stourbridge
Birthplace: Birmingham
Previous clubs include: Oldbury Utd - June 2001.

JONES, MARK — Defender
Current Club: Witton Albion
D o B: 16/09/1960   Birthplace: Liverpool
Previous clubs include: Bamber Bridge - August 2001, Chorley, Witton Alb., Winsford Utd, Hyde Utd, Northwich V, Southport, Preston NE, Runcorn.

JONES, MARK — Defender
Current Club: Workington
Birthplace: Carlisle
Began his carer with Carlisle United before arriving at Borough Park three years ago. Another member of the championship winning squad who missed several games through injury last season. Appeared to be back to his best in the pre-season programme.

JONES, MARK — Defender
Current Club: Braintree Town
Previous clubs include: Romford - February 2000, Billericay T, Romford, Burnham Ramblers.

JONES, MARK — Defender
Current Club: Llanelli AFC
D o B: 18/08/1985   Birthplace: Wales
From Youth team.

JONES, MARK — Goalkeeper
Current Club: Bedworth United
Birthplace: Derbyshire
Previous clubs include: Burton Alb - December 2001.

JONES, MARK — Goalkeeper
Current Club: Newtown AFC
D o B: 03/08/1962   Birthplace: Chirk
Vast experience in the game and is a highly-rated goalkeeper signed from Hereford United. He will be a great asset to the defence. Known to his friends as Jonah. Has great experience in the Conference and comes from a footballing family with brother Paul the present Southampton and Wales keeper, while another brother Andy played in our first season in the league.

JONES, MARK — Midfielder
Current Club: Atherton Laburnum Rovers
Birthplace: Stockport
Mark came to LR in March 2001 from Atherton Collieries. He is a quick, attacking winger with plenty of skill who can cross the ball with either foot. Mark works for the Post Office and in his spare time he enjoys reading.

JONES, MARK — Midfielder
Current Club: Bashley
Previous clubs include: Brockenhurst - August 2001.

JONES, MARK — Midfielder
Current Club: Thame United
Birthplace: Hertfordshire
Returned to Ryman Division One North side Thame United from rivals Arlesey Town in July 2002. A solid and reliable midfielder, he had played for Arlesey from Aylesbury United in February 2002. Began at Watford and also had spells with Rushden & Diamonds and Harrow Borough as well as two with Thame and Aylesbury.

JONES, MARK — Midfielder
Current Club: Hednesford Town
D o B: 07/09/1979   Birthplace: Walsall
Young, attacking midfielder who returned to the Midlands to join Dr Martens Premier side Hednesford Town in July 2002 after a spell in Scotland with Raith Rovers. Originally with Wolves, where he made a handful of substitute appearances, he then had sixteen months with Chesterfield, where he played in 9 League games before moving north.

JONES, MATT — Goalkeeper
Current Club: Racing Club Warwick
Birthplace: Birmingham
Previous clubs include: Redditch Utd - January 2002, Solihull Borough.

JONES, MATT — Midfielder

Current Club: Bashley

Previous clubs include: Eastleigh - September 2001, Havant &Waterlooville, B.A.T., Waterlooville, Havant T.

JONES, MATT — Midfielder

Current Club: Canvey Island

D o B: 09/10/1970   *Birthplace: Chiswick*

Honours won: England Schoolboy Int.

Tough-tackling midfielder who moved to Ryman Premier side Canvey Island in June 2002 from Conference outfit Dagenham & Redbridge. Had followed manager Garry Hill from Heybridge Swifts to St Albans towards the end of the 1997/98 season. Spent over four years at Heybridge having joined the Essex club from neighbouring Chelmsford City with whom he played for three seasons. A former England Schoolboy international, he made a handful of League appearances for Southend United ten years ago. Matt joined the Daggers and Garry Hill again from the Saints in the 1999 close season and played over 150 games for the club before moving to Ryman League Premier side Canvey Island in June 2002.

JONES, MICK — Midfielder

Current Club: Oswestry Town

D o B: 00/00/1965   *Birthplace: Wales*

Previous clubs include: Rhyl - February 2002, Local football.

JONES, NICKY — Defender

Current Club: Afan Lido

Birthplace: Wales

Honours won: Wales Youth Int.

Signed from Merthyr pre-season, Nicky is a quick, talented wing-back, whilst also being able to adapt to a midfield role. His exploits earned him a call-up to the Welsh Under 18 team earlier this season. Bright future prospect, who has interseted several professional clubs.

JONES, PAUL — Defender

Current Club: Colwyn Bay

D o B: 02/10/1976   *Birthplace: Wales*

Can play at full back or in central defence, Paul started his career at Wrexham. He then had a spell at Bangor City and signed for Colwyn Bay during the summer of 2000 from League of Wales neighbours Connahs Quay Nomads.

JONES, PAUL — Forward

Current Club: Welling United

Birthplace: Kent

Honours won: Dr Martens League Eastern Div.Winners

Highly-rated forward who joined Dr Martens Premier side Welling United from Hastings United in July 2002. Had signed for Hastings in August 1998 and helped them to win promotion to the Premier Division during 2001/02. Was previously with Gillingham.

JONES, PAUL — Midfielder

Current Club: Ossett Town

D o B: 22/05/1978   *Birthplace: Douglas*

Signed for the club in September 2001 from Farsley Celtic. Talented midfielder who is excellent on the ball and was previously with Stalybridge Celtic and Southport in the Conference before injury hampered his progress. Started with Stockport County.

JONES, PHIL — Midfielder

Current Club: Tow Law Town

Birthplace: Co.Durham

Another ex-County Junior, also at Sheffield Wednesday who had a brief time with Horden before joining the Lawyers last season.

JONES, RICHARD — Defender

Current Club: Shifnal Town

Birthplace: Shropshire

Previous clubs include: Telford Utd - July 2002.

JONES, RICHARD — Midfielder

Current Club: Haverfordwest County

D o B: 29/04/1969   *Birthplace: Usk*

Honours won: Wales u-21 Int.

Previous clubs include: Merthyr Tydfil - December 2001, Barry T, Swansea C, Hereford Utd, Newport Co.

JONES, RICKY — Defender

Current Club: Fleet Town

Birthplace: Hampshire

Previous clubs include: Sandhurst T - July 2000, Fleet T, Bracknell T, Fleet T, Cove, Newbury T, Cove, Petersfield Utd, Farnborough T, Reading.

JONES, ROBERT — Defender

Current Club: Gateshead

D o B: 03/11/1979   *Birthplace: Yorkshire*

Rob plays with a maturity that belies his lack of years. A towering central defender who is strong in the air in the tackle, he joined Gateshead at the start of the 2001/02 season from Spennymoor United. Originally a professional with York, he also saw service with Whitby Town and Northallerton Town before joining the Moors.

JONES, STEVE — Forward

Current Club: Hornchurch

D o B: 17/03/1970   *Birthplace: Cambridge*

Experienced striker whose signature for Ryman League Hornchurch in June 2002 was deemed as something of a coup. Steve began his career in Non-League football with Billericay Town before moving to West Ham in 1992. Spells with Bournemouth, West Ham again, Charlton and Bristol City followed, making over 200 League appearances and scoring more than 60 goals. He made a dramatic come-back to first-team action at Ashton Gate after an unhappy first two years at the club. Signed from Charlton Athletic in September 1999 for £425,000, rising to £500,000 depending on goals scored, he was loaned out to Brentford, Southend United and Wycombe Wanderers, before an ankle injury ruled him out of the 2000/01 season. Joined the Urchins as player-coach.

JONES, STEVE — Forward

Current Club: Bishop Auckland

Birthplace: Co.Durham

Previous clubs include: Harrogate Railway - January 2002, Bishop Auckland, Gateshead.

JONES, STEVE — Forward

Current Club: Maidstone United

Birthplace: Kent

Previous clubs include: Ramsgate - August 2001, Chatham T, Dover Ath., Folkestone Invicta.

JONES, STEVE — Forward

Current Club: Colwyn Bay

D o B: 19/07/1967

Previous clubs include: Rhyl - August 2001, Caernarfon T, Rhyl, Colwyn Bay, Rhyl, Flint Town Utd, Colwyn Bay, Conwy Utd., Rhyl, Colwyn Bay, Bangor C, Conwy Utd, Colwyn Bay, Rhyl, Bethesda Utd.

JONES, STEVE — Goalkeeper
Current Club: Thornaby on Tees
D o B: 31/01/1974   Birthplace: Stockton
Previous clubs include: Thornaby - October 2001, Bishop Auckland, Gateshead, Blyth Spartans, Bishop Auckland, Billingham T, Hartlepool Utd.

JONES, STEVE — Midfielder
Current Club: Kidsgrove Athletic
D o B: 11/11/1970   Birthplace: Stoke
Honours won: Dr Martens League Western Div. Winners, NWCL Winners
Joined Kidsgrove during the 2001/02 season from Stafford Rangers. Has played for Stoke City, Ashton United, Eastwood Hanley and Leek Town. A goalscoring midfielder who added a NWCL winners medal to the Dr Martens Western Division winners medal gained whilst with Stafford.

JONES, STEVE — Midfielder
Current Club: Southport
Birthplace: Stoke
Previous clubs include: Stalybridge Celtic - July 2001, Leek T, Eastwood Hanley, Stafford R, Stoke C.

JONES, STEWART — Midfielder
Current Club: Ware
Birthplace: Hertford
Previous clubs include: Hertford T - March 1999, Wealdstone, Hertford T.

JONES, STUART — Goalkeeper
Current Club: Weston-Super-Mare
D o B: 24/10/1977   Birthplace: Bristol
Born in Bristol and started his goalkeeping career as a trainee with Reading. After being released, he moved to Weston-Super-Mare, from where he joined Sheffield Wednesday. Unable to break into the Wednesday side, he moved on loan to Crewe Alexandra and then to Torquay United, for whom he made more than 30 appearances as first choice keeper last season. He moved to Chester City in December, but found himself a victim of the merry-go-round managerial system at the Deva and was released and subsequently joined Barry. Returned to Weston in July 2002.

JONES, TOM — Midfielder
Current Club: Stocksbridge Park Steels
Birthplace: Nottinghamshire
Previous clubs include: Denaby Utd - November 2001, Worksop T, Selston.

JONES, TOM — Midfielder
Current Club: Swindon Supermarine
D o B: 07/10/1964   Birthplace: Aldershot
Honours won: England Semi-Pro Int., Dr Martens League Premier Div. Winners
Tom joined the club in September 1999 and quickly showed that he hadnt lost the ability to pass the ball around the park. The same ability he demonstrated playing for Aberdeen in the Scottish Premier Division and Swindon Town in the Football League. Three years ago he was part of theForest Green Rovers side that won the Dr Martens Premier Division Championship. Tom returned to playing in September 1999 and we were delighted he decided to sign for Supermarine. A fully qualified UEFA coach and with his vast experience and knowledge he has undoubtedly helped our younger players and will continueto do so. Became director of the New College Academy this season.

JONES, WAYNE — Defender
Current Club: Carmarthen Town
D o B: 26/07/1979   Birthplace: Carmarthen
From Youth team.

JOPLING, STUART — Midfielder
Current Club: Stowmarket Town
Birthplace: Suffolk
Previous clubs include: Needham Market - January 2001, Witham T, Needham Market, Diss T, Soham Town R, Lowestoft T.

JORDAN, ALAN — Defender
Current Club: Egham Town
D o B: 25/01/1977   Birthplace: Dorset
Previous clubs include: Windsor & Eton - February 2002, Bridport, Dorchester T, Poole T, Dorchester T, Colchester Utd (Trainee), AFC Bournemouth (Trainee).

JORDAN, DANIEL — Defender
Current Club: Saltdean United
D o B: 23/04/1984   Birthplace: Woolwich
Joined Saltdean from Lewes during the 2001 close season.

JORDAN, KEVIN — Defender
Current Club: Aveley
Birthplace: London
Previous clubs include: Billericay T - March 2002, Bishops Stortford, Southend Utd, Tottenham Hotspur.

JORDAN, MARK — Midfielder
Current Club: Cirencester Town
Birthplace: Swindon
A midfielder with great skill, who returned to Cirencester Town after a spell with Hungerford Town in the summer of 2001. Was originally a product of Cirencesters successful Academy.

JORDAN, NEIL — Midfielder
Current Club: Hertford Town
Birthplace: Aylesbury
Previous clubs include: Potters Bar T - August 2001, Boreham Wood, Potters Bar T, Boreham Wood, Watford (Junior).

JORDAN, PAUL — Defender
Current Club: Ely City
Birthplace: Cambridgeshire
Previous clubs include: Soham Town Rangers - September 1998, Ely C, Chatteris T.

JORDAN, PAUL — Forward
Current Club: Hertford Town
D o B: 23/09/1974   Birthplace: Aylesbury
Previous clubs include: Potters Bar T - July 2001, Boreham Wood, Potters Bar T, Boreham Wood, Watford (Junior).

JORDAN, SCOTT — Midfielder
Current Club: Scarborough
D o B: 19/07/1975   Birthplace: Newcastle
Scott was born in Newcastle and signed on as a trainee with York City. After a successful spell at York he left Bootham Crescent to join Conference side Scarborough in March 2001 and made 25 appearances for the Seadogs in 2001/02.

JORDAN, STEVE — Goalkeeper
Current Club: Brigg Town
Birthplace: Hull
From Local football - July 2000, Rochdale (Junior).

JORDAN, STEVE — Midfielder
Current Club: Woodley Sports
Birthplace: Manchester
Previous clubs include: Mossley - July 1998, Ashton Utd, Congleton T, Grove Utd.

JOSEPHS, ROBBIE — Midfielder
Current Club: Pagham
Birthplace: Sussex
Midfielder: once had trials with Brighton & Hove Albion: a former Pagham player who has also previously spent time at Portfield and Oving: joined Arundel during the 2001 close season, but returned to Nyetimber Lane in December when Paul Gilbert was appointed manager.

JOSHUA, LEE — Goalkeeper
Current Club: Oxford City
Previous clubs include: Quarry Rovers - August 2001.

JOSLIN, MATT — Forward
Current Club: Bideford
Birthplace: Devon
Matt is a very promising forward, who has progressed up through our youth system and has also played for Torrington

JOYCE, SEAN — Midfielder
Current Club: Bideford
D o B: 15/02/1967   *Birthplace: Doncaster*
Sean is our Manager, who has seen League action for various clubs, Cambridge United, Doncaster Rovers, Exeter City & Torquay United. He has also played in the Western League for Elmore and Taunton Town. Sean stepped up from player to Manager, in very difficult times, but his skill and professionalism shone through and he has led the side from strength to strength.

JOYCE, SHAUN — Midfielder
Current Club: Ossett Albion
Previous clubs include: Ashton Utd - February 2001, Ossett Alb., Stocksbridge Park Steels, Ossett Alb., Bradley Rangers, Emley, Huddersfield T (Trainee).

JOYCE, TONY — Defender
Current Club: Thame United
D o B: 24/09/1971   *Birthplace: Wembley*
Previous clubs include: Banbury Utd - January 2002, Wealdstone, Hemel Hempstead, Bedford T, Boreham Wood, Stevenage B, Staines T, Woking, Aldershot, QPR.

JOYCE, TONY — Midfielder
Current Club: Swindon Supermarine
Birthplace: Swindon
Started the 1999/00 pre-season with Supermarine before joining Cirencester Academy on the opening day of the season. He returned to the club in December 1999 after some excellent performances for the Academy. He quickly settled into the side and showed he was very skilful on the ball with good balance and movement. A hard working player who likes nothing better than to attack the opposition's defence. Another young player at the club with a bright future ahead of him. His form last season saw him gain both Wiltshire FA - Under 21 and Hellenic League representative honours.

JOYCE, WES — Forward
Current Club: Moor Green
Birthplace: Worcestershire
Previous clubs include: Malvern T - March 2002, Moor Green, Worcester C.

JOYNSON, MATTHEW — Defender
Current Club: Diss Town
D o B: 21/03/1981   *Birthplace: Liverpool*
Honours won: England Youth Int.
Previous clubs include: Wroxham - August 2001, Norwich C.

JUDD, ROBIN — Midfielder
Current Club: Willenhall Town
D o B: 17/11/1967   *Birthplace: Birmingham*
Joined December 2001, looked classy on his debut. Experienced midfielder previously with Highgate United and Sutton Coldfield.

JUDD, STEVE — Goalkeeper
Current Club: Sidlesham
Birthplace: Sussex
Veteran goalkeeper: Pagham first-team regular until forced out by injury in 1999: featured for Selsey from time-to-time in 2000/01, having also appeared for Chichester Hospitals (West Sussex League): joined Sidlesham in November 2001.

JUDGE, BEN — Defender
Current Club: Crawley Town
Birthplace: London
Ultra-consistent defender: has had trials with Wolves, Cambridge, Oxford and Torquay: signed from Croydon in November 2001.

JUDGE, LEE — Midfielder
Current Club: St Margaretsbury
D o B: 28/08/1967   *Birthplace: Wimbledon*
Previous clubs include: Cheshunt - July 1999, St Margaretsbury, Ware.

JUKES, NATHAN — Defender
Current Club: Worcester City
D o B: 10/04/1979   *Birthplace: Worcester*
Previous clubs include: Dorchester T - February 1999, Portsmouth.

JULES, MARK — Defender
Current Club: Alfreton Town
D o B: 05/09/1971   *Birthplace: Bradford*
An experienced defender who joined Alfreton Town in June 2002 after being released by Halifax Town upon their relegation to the Conference. Started his career with home-town club Bradford City but moved on to Scarborough in August 1991 without having made the senior side at Valley Parade. However, Mark went on to play over 300 League games with Scarborough, Chesterfield and Halifax before joining the Reds.

JULIAN, STEVE — Defender
Current Club: Oadby Town
Birthplace: Corby
Previous clubs include: Corby T - July 2001.

JUPP, ANTHONY — Defender
Current Club: Dorking
Birthplace: Surrey
Previous clubs include: Croydon Ath - March 2002, Merstham.

JUPP, NATHAN — Midfielder
Current Club: Dorking
Birthplace: Surrey
Previous clubs include: Croydon Ath - January 2002, Merstham.

SEAGRAVE HAULAGE

are proud to support The Ultimate Book of Non-League Players 2002-03

Tel: 0208 991 2772

KADI, JUNIOR — *Midfielder*

Current Club: Dulwich Hamlet

D o B: 16/08/1979   *Birthplace: London*
Honours won: FA Trophy winners

Creative midfielder who signed for Dulwich Hamlet just before the 2002 transfer deadline from Slough Town. A member of Kingstonians FA Trophy-winning side at Wembley in 2000, he began his career in Coventry City's youth side and has also ha spells with Whyteleafe and Woking.

KADI, MO — *Forward*

Current Club: Whitstable Town

Birthplace: Kent

Previous clubs include: Greenwich Borough - July 2000, Faversham T, Arsenal (Junior).

KALLI, DANIEL — *Forward*

Current Club: Molesey

D o B: 27/11/1982   *Birthplace: Surrey*
From Youth team.

KALLI, MICHAEL — *Goalkeeper*

Current Club: Enfield

D o B: 24/06/1980   *Birthplace: London*
Honours won: English Universities Rep.

Previous clubs include: Wingate & Finchley - December 2001, Haringey Borough, Southend Utd (Junior), Watford (Junior).

KANDOL, TRESOR — *Forward*

Current Club: Heybridge Swifts

D o B: 30/08/1981   *Birthplace: Banga, Zaire*
Previous clubs include: Cambridge Utd - September 2001, Luton T.

KANE, CONRAD — *Midfielder*

Current Club: Tooting & Mitcham United

D o B: 25/07/1963   *Birthplace: Surrey*
Previous clubs include: Crawley T - September 1997, Bromley, Dulwich Hamlet, Kingstonian, Carshalton Ath., Dulwich Hamlet, Bromley, Dulwich Hamlet, Merstham.

KARAISKOS, ANDREAS — *Midfielder*

Current Club: Edgware Town

Birthplace: London

Previous clubs include: Millwall - August 2001.

KARAMOKO, KEITA — *Goalkeeper*

Current Club: Harrow Borough

Birthplace: Mali
Honours won: Mali Int.

Goalkeeper who joined Ryman Premier side Harrow Borough from Wembley in August 2001. Has also played for Yeading. Works in the pharmaceutical industry. He is the current second choice keeper for his country, Mali and played in the recent African Nations Cup.

KASONALI, SIMON — *Midfielder*

Current Club: Newcastle Blue Star

Birthplace: Newcastle

Previous clubs include: Spennymoor Utd - January 2002, Marske Utd, Guisborough T, Marske Utd.

KAVANAGH, JASON — *Defender*

Current Club: Burton Albion

D o B: 23/11/1971   *Birthplace: Birmingham*
Honours won: England Schholboy & Youth Int.

Jason Kavanagh, a former England Youth International, likes to get forward and hit the target several times earlier this season. Thirty year old Jason had spells with Derby County, Wycombe Wanderers and Stoke City before joining Cambridge. He made 99 appearances for Derby County and was part of the squad that got promoted to the Carling Premiership. He now combines football with his new career as a financial consultant.

KAVANAGH, RICHIE — *Midfielder*

Current Club: Stratford Town

Birthplace: Birmingham

Previous clubs include: Bromsgrove Rovers - February 2002, Studley BKL.

KAY, SIMON — *Defender*

Current Club: Radcliffe Borough

Birthplace: Oldham

Experienced defender who joined Radcliffe Borough in July 2000 from UniBond First Division rivals Chorley. Started out as a trainee at Oldham and then had spells with Mossley and Leigh RMI before signing for Chorley in August 1999.

KEAN, ROBBIE — *Midfielder*

Current Club: St.Albans City

D o B: 03/06/1978   *Birthplace: Luton*

Midfielder who signed for Ryman Premier side St Albans City from neighbours and rivals Hitchin Town in November 2001. Marked his debut against Braintree Town with a goal after coming on as a substitute. Formerly on the books at Luton Town and Stevenage Borough.

KEARN, STEWART — *Goalkeeper*

Current Club: Lymington & New Milton

D o B: 12/12/1975   *Birthplace: Bournemouth*

Previous clubs include: Basingstoke T - September 1999, Dorchester T, Bashley, Bournemouth FC, Wimborne T, Sheffield Wednesday (Junior).

KEARNS, ANDY — *Defender*

Current Club: Fisher Athletic (London)

Birthplace: Kent

Previous clubs include: Erith & Belvedere - March 2002, Fisher Ath, Tonbridge Angels, Erith & Belvedere, Gravesend, Sittingbourne.

KEDDLE, PAUL — *Midfielder*

Current Club: Merthyr Tydfil

Birthplace: Wales

The youngest member of the current Merthyr Tydfil squad. Joined the Martyrs during the close-season of 2002 form League of Wales outfit Rhayader Town after impressing during the pre-season friendly programme.

KEDWELL, DANNY — *Forward*

Current Club: Tonbridge Angels

Birthplace: Kent

Promising young striker who joined Tonbridge Angels in July 2002 from Kent and Dr Martens Eastern rivals Chatham Town. Had progressed through the Chats youth side and helped the club gain promotion from the Kent League.

KEEBLE, IAN — Midfielder
Current Club: Stowmarket Town
Birthplace: Suffolk
Previous clubs include: Debenham - July 2001, Stowmarket T, Framlingham T.

KEEBLE, JAMES — Midfielder
Current Club: Tiptree United
Birthplace: Essex
Previous clubs include: Maldon T - March 2002, Halstead T, Norwich C (Trainee).

KEEGAN, JOHN — Defender
Current Club: Hucknall Town
D o B: 05/08/1981   Birthplace: Liverpool
Previous clubs include: Rossendale Utd - March 2002, Scarborough, York C.

KEEGAN, JUSTIN — Midfielder
Current Club: Blyth Spartans
Birthplace: Darlington
Signed for UniBond Premier side Blyth Spartans in August 2000 from Darlington. Made his debut against Gainsborough Trinity on 19th August 2000. Scored his first goal for the club at Worksop Town.

KEEGANS, CHRIS — Midfielder
Current Club: Dunston Federation Brewery
Birthplace: Cleveland
Previous clubs include: New Marske - July 1999.

KEELER, JUSTIN — Forward
Current Club: Dorchester Town
D o B: 17/04/1978   Birthplace: Hillingdon
Previous clubs include: AFC Bournemouth - March 2001, Christchurch C.

KEELEY, BARRIE — Midfielder
Current Club: Staines Town
D o B: 18/12/1974   Birthplace: Hampshire
Central midfielder who started his playing days with Farnborough Town. Moved to Basingstoke Town and then switched to Leatherhead in January 2001. Signed for Staines Town in the summer of 2001 but then embarked on a world tour!

KEELING, BARRIE — Midfielder
Current Club: Radcliffe Borough
D o B: 20/08/1977   Birthplace: Oldham
Strong-running midfield player who has previously been on the books at Morecambe and Bamber Bridge. Signed for Radcliffe Borough in January 2002 upon his return from a spell playing in the Singapore League.

KEELING, JON — Midfielder
Current Club: Purfleet
Previous clubs include: Tilbury - February 1998, Concord R.

KEEN, DANIEL — Forward
Current Club: Thame United
Birthplace: Ofordshire
An exciting product of Thame United's youth set-up, Danny has a good eye for goal and is developing into a good all round player. Made his debut during the 2000/01 pre-season in a 0-0 draw with Brentford an became a first-team regular in 2001/02.

KEEN, MARK — Defender
Current Club: Chelmsford City
D o B: 23/07/1964   Birthplace: Essex
Previous clubs include: Dagenham & Redbridge - July 2001, Heybridge Swifts, Braintree T, St.Albans C, Heybridge Swifts, Chelmsford C, Enfield, Dartford, Witham T.

KEEPENCE, ANDY — Defender
Current Club: Bishops Stortford
Birthplace: Hertford
Talented defender who made the step up from Ryman Division Two with Ware to the Premier with Bishops Stortford in August 2002. Started out on Stevenage Borough's books and then had his first spell with Ware. Returned to Woodspring Park in September 1999 after a stint with neighbours Hertford Town.

KEEPER, ALAN — Defender
Current Club: Grays Athletic
Birthplace: Essex
Experienced central defender, previously with Hornchurch and Braintree Town.

KEEVILL, SAM — Midfielder
Current Club: Chelmsford City
D o B: 08/05/1981   Birthplace: Lewisham
Former Fulham midfielder who signed for Dr Martens Premier side Chelmsford City in the summer of 2002 following a brief spell with Eastern Division outfit Dartford. Began his career at Craven Cottage and then played in the Scottish Premier League with Kilmarnock before returning south of the border. Spells with Sutton United, Slough Town and Basingstoke Town followed before he joined the Darts in March 2002.

KEIGHT, MARTIN — Defender
Current Club: Studley
Birthplace: Worcestershire
Previous clubs include: Alvechurch - July 2001, Kings Norton T, Redditch Utd, Fairfield Villa.

KEISTER, JOHN — Midfielder
Current Club: Margate
D o B: 11/11/1970   Birthplace: Manchester
Honours won: Sierra Leone Int.
Sierra Leone international midfielder who joined Conference side Margate in March 2001 after a short spell with rivals Stevenage Borough. Began his career in England with Walsall, where he made over 100 League appearances. Moved on to Chester City and Shrewsbury before going Non-League.

KEITA, TIEMOKO — Forward
Current Club: Windsor & Eton
D o B: 31/05/1975
Previous clubs include: Slough T - October 2001.

KEITH, JAMES — Defender
Current Club: Ashford Town (Middx)
Birthplace: Surrey
Central defender, signed for Ashford Town (Middx) last season from Bedfont. Has also seen service with Epsom & Ewell and Farnborough Town. Aged 21.

KELLY, DEAN — Defender
Current Club: Witham Town
Birthplace: Essex
Previous clubs include: Braintree T - March 2001, Maldon T, Witham T, Billericay T.

KELLY, EAMONN — Midfielder

Current Club: Radcliffe Borough

Birthplace: Burnley

A competitive midfielder, Eamonn joined Radcliffe Borough during the 2000/01 season having been previously been a trainee with Burnley. He has developed well and could have a big future in the game.

KELLY, GAVIN — Goalkeeper

Current Club: Bridlington Town

D o B: 29/09/1968   *Birthplace: Beverley*

Previous clubs include: Bradford Park Avenue - December 2001, Whitby T, Harrogate T, North Ferriby Utd, Golden (Hong Kong), Scarborough, Bristol R, Hull C.

KELLY, JIMMY — Midfielder

Current Club: Chester City

D o B: 14/02/1973   *Birthplace: Liverpool*

Very experienced midfield player who made around 70 League appearances for Wrexham and Wolves before joining Hednesford Town in 1997/98. The Liverpool-born player had a major influence on the Pitmens fortunes before making a £15,000 transfer to Doncaster in June 2000. Transferred to Chester in May 2002.

KELLY, KEVIN — Midfielder

Current Club: Brodsworth Welfare

Birthplace: Yorkshire

Previous clubs include: Denaby Utd - August 2001, Matlock T, Frickley Ath., Goole T, Huddersfield T (Trainee).

KELLY, LEON — Forward

Current Club: Ilkeston Town

Birthplace: Birmingham

Joined Ilkeston from Cambridge United in May 2002. He had signed for Cambridge from Dr Martens League Western Division club Atherstone United for a reported £15,000 in July 2001. Leon is a strong, pacy young striker, who spent the majority of the season out on loan at the likes of Stalybridge Celtic and Dover and then joined Ilkeston at the end of the campaign.

KELLY, PAUL — Midfielder

Current Club: Maidenhead United

D o B: 24/02/1974   *Birthplace: Hillingdon*

Previous clubs include: Boreham Wood - August 2001, Chesham Utd, Gravesend, Chertsey T, Hendon, Chertsey T, Chesham Utd, Fulham.

KELLY, SIMON — Forward

Current Club: Didcot Town

Birthplace: Oxfordshire

Big Simon is equally at home in defence or attack, and his physical presence rewarded him with a steady stream of goals for Didcot last season. A Freight Manager.

KELLY, SIMON — Midfielder

Current Club: Radcliffe Borough

Birthplace: Radcliffe

Simon is an excellent prospect who is in his fourth season in Radcliffe Borough's senior side having graduated through the clubs junior and reserve teams. A classy central defender who has attracted the attention of several League clubs and has the ability to go far in the game.

KELLY, TOM — Midfielder

Current Club: Taunton Town

D o B: 28/03/1964   *Birthplace: Bellshill*

Honours won: FA Vase Winners

A very experienced Scottish mifielder who has played in the Scottish Premier League with Hibernian. Has also been at Queen of the South, Hartlepool, York City, Torquay and Exeter. Has made over 400 Professional League appearances. Joined Taunton Town from Ilfracombe in 1997 and is now the clubs player/assistant-manager.

KELLY, TONY — Midfielder

Current Club: Hemel Hempstead Town

D o B: 06/10/1963   *Birthplace: Middlesex*

Previous clubs include: Berkhamsted T - December 2001, Hemel Hempstead, Hendon, Hayes, Wealdstone, Hayes, Harefield Utd, Hillingdon B, Wealdstone.

KELLY, WARREN — Defender

Current Club: Hendon

D o B: 18/04/1968   *Birthplace: Watford*

Honours won: Ryman League Premier Div.Winners

Warren started season 2001/02 as player-coach at Hendon under Dave Anderson. Signed in January 2000 from St Albans City, Warren spent most of his career with Hayes (nine seasons) and helped them to the Ryman Premier Division championship. During his time at Hayes he also won a Player of the Year award. This experienced defender has previously played Conference football with Stevenage Borough and Rushden & Diamonds.

KEMBER, PAUL — Midfielder

Current Club: Whyteleafe

Birthplace: Surrey

From Youth team.

KEMBER, ROBERT — Midfielder

Current Club: Woking

D o B: 21/08/1981   *Birthplace: Wimbledon*

Promising young midfielder who signed for Conference side Woking on the eve of the 2002/03 season after being released by Crystal Palace. Had joined Palace, where his father Steve is a coach, at an early age and was on the verge of the senior side.

KEMP, BRENDAN — Midfielder

Current Club: Tunbridge Wells

Birthplace: Kent

Honours won: English Universities Rep.

Previous clubs include: Liverpool University - July 2001, Crystal Palace (Junior), Tottenham Hotspur (Junior).

KEMP, GARY — Defender

Current Club: Bath City

D o B: 25/05/1969   *Birthplace: Thornbury*

Gary arrived at Bath City along with team-mate Gary Thorne from Newport County in July 2001. Originally with Hellinic League side Almondsbury, Gary moved to Gloucester City in 1992 and spent eight years at Meadow Park making over 300 appearances during his time there, including an FA Trophy semi-final in 1997. A excellent centre-back who is very comfortable on the ball, he joined Newport in September 1999 following the Tigers relegation before an influx of new players for the Welsh side saw him head across the Severn bridge to City.

KEMP, GRAHAM — *Defender*
Current Club: Lymington & New Milton
Birthplace: Dorset
Previous clubs include: Brockenhurst - July 1995, Weymouth Sports, Bashley, AFC Lymington, Portland Utd, Dorchester T, Weymouth.

KEMP, GRAHAM — *Midfielder*
Current Club: Slough Town
D o B: 21/06/1968   *Birthplace: Berkshire*
Now the longest serving Rebels player to date and has made over 100 appearances for the club. Graham joined the club in 1998. He is one of only three players to remain at Slough after a side was patched together after the Rebels were demoted from the Conference after finishing 8th. Kempy can play in a number of positions. He is by trade a midfielder, but due to the many midfielders the club has on its books - Graham has to play in other roles. He has appeared for Slough in a sweeper position and at right back, which is arguably his best position. Graham is a former Shrewsbury Town player who made a number of appearances in the League. He also captained Yeovil and Chesham.Then under former Slough manager Graham Roberts. Graham may not get into the side as much as he likes, but he is still an important part of the club and helps Steve Browne out with coaching the players.

KEMPSTER, JAMIE — *Midfielder*
Current Club: Maidstone United
Birthplace: Kent
Honours won: FA Vase Winners
Previous clubs include: Erith & Belvedere - July 2001, Deal T, Greenwich B, Bromley, Fisher Ath., Erith & Belvedere, Cray Wanderers, Erith & Belvedere, Dulwich Hamlet, Croydon.

KEMPSTER, JODIE — *Midfielder*
Current Club: Maidstone United
Birthplace: Kent
Previous clubs include: Ramsgate - July 2001, Greenwich B, Fisher Ath.

KENDAL, PAUL — *Defender*
Current Club: Broxbourne Borough V&E
D o B: 19/03/1973   *Birthplace: Welwyn Garden City*
Previous clubs include: Potters Bar T - July 2001, Welwyn Garden C, Potters Bar T, Welwyn Garden C.

KENNA, WARREN — *Midfielder*
Current Club: Eastleigh
D o B: 18/05/1980   *Birthplace: Southampton*
Previous clubs include: Bemerton Heath Harlequins - May 2002, Cambridge C, Peterborough Utd.

KENNEDY, ALLAN — *Forward*
Current Club: Andover
Birthplace: Hampshire
Previous clubs include: Forest Green Rovers - July 1997, Andover.

KENNEDY, GARY — *Defender*
Current Club: Corby Town
D o B: 24/10/1975   *Birthplace: Corby*
Previous clubs include: Desborough T - June 2000, Stewarts & Lloyds, Corby T.

KENNEDY, JOHN — *Midfielder*
Current Club: Canvey Island
D o B: 19/08/1978   *Birthplace: Newmarket*
Honours won: FA Trophy Winners
A former Ipswich Town midfielder, who has come up through the youth system at the Suffolk club, playing six games for the first-team at Portman Road and making 2 appearances as a substitute. He signed for Canvey Island in August 2000 and was a member of the clubs 2001 FA Umbro Trophy-winning side.

KENNEDY, JOHN — *Midfielder*
Current Club: Croydon
Previous clubs include: Croydon Ath - August 2001, Tooting & Mitcham Utd, Croydon Ath., Swindon T.

KENNEDY, NEIL — *Defender*
Current Club: Great Harwood Town
Birthplace: Lancashire
Previous clubs include: Clitheroe - October 1999, Bamber Bridge, Great Harwood T, Bamber Bridge.

KENNEDY, NEIL — *Forward*
Current Club: Histon
Previous clubs include: Newmarket T - September 1999, Histon, Mildenhall T, Newmarket T.

KENNEDY, RICHARD — *Midfielder*
Current Club: Barry Town
D o B: 28/08/1978   *Birthplace: Waterford*
Previous clubs include: Brentford - March 2001, Crystal Palace.

KENNEDY, STEVE — *Defender*
Current Club: Belper Town
Previous clubs include: Worksop T - October 1994, Sheffield Utd (Trainee).

KENNERDALE, NICK — *Forward*
Current Club: Hucknall Town
Previous clubs include: Nuneaton Borough - October 2001, Eastwood T (4-fig fee), Shepshed Dynamo, Leicester Utd, Armitage, Doncaster R.

KENNETT, PAUL — *Midfielder*
Current Club: Worthing
Birthplace: Sussex
Midfielder: spent time at Brighton & Hove Albion as a teenager before joining Worthing in 1997: has made 200+ appearances for the Rebels.

KENNY, SEAN — *Forward*
Current Club: Taunton Town
Birthplace: Watchett
Great young striking prospect from Watchet. Previously played for Taunton Town's reserves and then played for Minehead in the Western Leagues Premier Division and was their top scorer. Returned to Taunton during the 2001/02 season.

KENT, SIMON — *Goalkeeper*
Current Club: Ashford Town (Middx)
Birthplace: Middlesex
Goalkeeper, son of Ashford Town (Middx) manager Dave Kent. Well over 6 feet and now with over 100 appearances. A dedicated club man who displays both confidance and agility when called upon. Aged 22.

KENTEBE, WINSTON   *Forward*
Current Club: Chertsey Town

Birthplace: Surrey

Previous clubs include: Romford - January 2002, Egham T.

KENWAY, MARK   *Defender*
Current Club: Weymouth

Birthplace: Dorset

Defender who returned to the club where his playing days started, Dr Martens Premier side Weymouth, in the summer of 2002 after a second spell with Jewson Wessex outfit Portland United. Had returned to Portland in July 2001 from Dorchester Town.

KENWORTHY, JON   *Midfielder*
Current Club: Connahs Quay Nomads

D o B: 18/08/1974   *Birthplace: Wales*
Honours won: Wales u-21 Int.

Previous clubs include: Tranmere Rovers - July 1997.

KERR, AARON   *Goalkeeper*
Current Club: Havant & Waterlooville

D o B: 08/12/1982   *Birthplace: Carrickfergus*

Aaron joined Dr Martens Premier side Havant & Waterlooville in August 2001 to replace outgoing goalkeeper Paul Nicholls. Still only a teenager, he started his career at the age of 16 as an Academy player at Wolverhampton Wanderers and progressed to a professional contract there before leaving the side in March 2001.

KERR, ADAM   *Defender*
Current Club: Gretna

Birthplace: Dumfries

Previous clubs include: Queen of the South - January 2000.

KERR, DAVID   *Midfielder*
Current Club: Droylsden

D o B: 06/09/1974   *Birthplace: Dumfries*

Strong tackler who joined Chester in July 2000 after being released by Mansfield Town. Switched to Droylsden in December 2001.

KERR, PADDY   *Goalkeeper*
Current Club: Liversedge

Birthplace: Yorkshire

Previous clubs include: Ashton Utd - July 2001, Liversedge.

KERRIGAN, STEVE   *Forward*
Current Club: Halifax Town

D o B: 09/10/1972   *Birthplace: Bailleston*

Scottish-born striker who was re-signed by Conference club Halifax Town in August 2002 after originally being released by the administrators at the end of the 2001/02 season. Played in Scottish football with Albion Rovers, Clydebank, Stranraer and Ayr United before joining Shrewsbury in January 1998. Switched to The Shay in March 2000 and totalled more than 150 League appearances.

KERRY, NATHAN   *Midfielder*
Current Club: Alfreton Town

Birthplace: Sheffield

Previous clubs include: Denaby Utd - July 1999, Worksop T.

KERSHAW, IAN   *Defender*
Current Club: Witham Town

Birthplace: Essex

Previous clubs include: Wivenhoe T - January 2002, Brightlingsea Utd, Wivenhoe T.

KESSACK, STEVE   *Defender*
Current Club: Broxbourne Borough V&E

D o B: 10/09/1975   *Birthplace: Singapore*

Previous clubs include: Potters Bar T - July 2001, Cheshunt, Chertsey T, Wingate & Finchley.

KESSELL, TOM   *Goalkeeper*
Current Club: Hastings United

Birthplace: Kent

Previous clubs include: Dartford - March 2002, Hastings T, Brighton, Charlton Ath.

KEVAN, ALEX   *Midfielder*
Current Club: Lancaster City

D o B: 23/02/1981   *Birthplace: Liverpool*

Midfielder who signed for Lancaster City in March 2002 from Hereford United. Originally on the books at Burnley, he also had a spell with Kidderminster Harriers before joining the Bulls.

KEVERAN, ANDY   *Forward*
Current Club: Cirencester Town

Previous clubs include: Witney T - August 2001, Harrow Hill.

KEY, ANDY   *Forward*
Current Club: Diss Town

Birthplace: Ipswich

Previous clubs include: Ipswich Wanderers - July 1999.

KEY, LANCE   *Goalkeeper*
Current Club: Kingstonian

D o B: 13/05/1968   *Birthplace: Kettering*

Outstanding goalkeeper who signed for Kingstonian from Northwich Victoria in June 2001. Arrived at the Drill Field from Rochdale in December 1998 as cover for an injury, but his form impressed the manager so much, he signed a contract for the club. Previously with York City, Oldham Athletic, Portsmouth, Oxford United, Lincoln City, Hartlepool United, Rochdale, Sheffield Wednesday, Sheffield United and Dundee United.

KEYWOOD, GRANT   *Midfielder*
Current Club: Walton Casuals

Birthplace: Surrey

Grant is a left sided midfielder, very quick, tricky and strong, signed from Walton & Hersham. Previous clubs include Camberley Town.

KIBBLEWHITE, DANNY   *Defender*
Current Club: Oswestry Town

D o B: 12/07/1983   *Birthplace: Shropshire*
From Youth team.

KIDD, STEVE   *Defender*
Current Club: Taunton Town

Birthplace: Devon

Centre-back who appeared finished after suffering a bad injury playing for Taunton in the 1995/96 championship season. Came back with Bideford then Barnstaple within 18 months. Re-signed with Taunton from Minehead at the start of the 2001/02 season.

KIELTY, GED   Midfielder
Current Club: Leigh RMI
D o B: 01/09/1976   Birthplace: Manchester
A competitive midfield player, Ged joined Manchester City for three years straight from school before spending one season with Cobh Rangers in Southern Ireland. He then moved to Southport in the Conference for one season, playing in the F.A. Trophy Final at Wembley. Ged was then with Barrow for eight months also in the Conference before having most of last season with Altrincham. For the last few weeks of the 1999/2000 season he was a loan player with Leigh RMI, making it a permanent move for the 2000/01 campaign.

KIELY, PAUL   Forward
Current Club: Ilkeston Town
D o B: 06/06/1974   Birthplace: Stoke
Honours won: Dr Martens League Western Div.Winners
Paul joined Stafford Rangers at the end of March 2000 for £5,000 from Leek Town where he was leading goalscorer. In just seven appearances he scored five vital goals in Rangers 1999/00 Dr Martens Western Division championship run-in. He was both voted Supporters and Players' Player of the Season in 2001/02 and also won the Dr Martens League Golden Boot as leading scorer. Previously with Kidsgrove Athletic and Eastwood Hanley, Paul switched to Ilkeston Town in May 2002.

KIERNAN, MICK   Defender
Current Club: Bridgnorth Town
Birthplace: Shropshire
Previous clubs include: Shifnal T - July 2001, Newport T.

KIFFIN, TERRY   Defender
Current Club: Clapton
D o B: 17/08/1978   Birthplace: London
Previous clubs include: Croydon Ath - July 2001.

KIKULUIE, KENNY   Forward
Current Club: Clapton
D o B: 20/01/1984   Birthplace: London
From Local football - July 2001.

KILBANE, FARRELL   Defender
Current Club: Lancaster City
D o B: 21/10/1974   Birthplace: Preston
Signed for Lancaster City in the summer of 1999 from Stafford Rangers, Farrell is the brother of Irish international Kevin Kilbane. Plays right-back and centre-back and has previously played for Preston and Cambridge United.

KILBY, RAY   Defender
Current Club: Hemel Hempstead Town
Birthplace: Hatfield
Previous clubs include: Baldock T - September 2001, Hatfield T.

KILGANNON, WES   Forward
Current Club: Caernarfon Town
D o B: 08/04/1982   Birthplace: Chester
Previous clubs include: Chester C - February 2002.

KILGOUR, MIKE   Defender
Current Club: Weston-Super-Mare
D o B: 25/05/1965   Birthplace: Dartford
Honours won: Dr Martens League Premier Div.Winners
Signed in January 2001 from Forest Green Rovers. His numerous clubs include Bath City, Sailsbury City, Gloucester City and Dorchester Town. Played in Forest Greens FA Trophy final appearance at Wembley in May 2000.

KILPARTRICK, DARIN   Defender
Current Club: Burgess Hill Town
Birthplace: Sussex
Former Worthing and Worthing Utd defender, who signed for Bognor Regis in 1995/96: resumed playing for Wick in 2000/01 after spending two years away travelling: signed for Burgess Hill during September 2001: current member of the Sussex representative side.

KIMBLE, GARRY   Defender
Current Club: Ford United
D o B: 06/08/1966   Birthplace: Poole
Honours won: Ryman League Div.One Winners
Vastly experienced player who joined Ford United in February 2002 from Harlow Town. Gained a wealth of Football League experience with the likes of Cambridge United, Peterborough United, Doncaster Rovers and Gillingham. Since moving into the Non-League game Garry has played for Dagenham & Redbridge, Hendon, Aylesbury, Enfield, Grays Athletic and Bishops Stortford.

KIMMINS, GED   Forward
Current Club: Salford City
Birthplace: Manchester
Honours won: England Semi-Pro Int.
Previous clubs include: Northwich Victoria - October 2000, Hednesford T, Hyde Utd, Salford C.

KINCH, SCOTT   Midfielder
Current Club: Carshalton Athletic
Birthplace: Surrey
A Carshalton Athletic youth product who became a regular first-team player during the 2001/02 season. A very promising young midfielder who is renowned for his highly charged playing style, competitive nature and wicked sense of humour!

KINDER, ADAM   Forward
Current Club: Racing Club Warwick
Birthplace: Coventry
Promising young striker who joined Racing Club Warwick from Dr Martens Western rivals Bedworth United in March 2002. Had previously played his football with Coventry Jet Blades.

KING, AARON   Goalkeeper
Current Club: Romford
Birthplace: Essex
Previous clubs include: Heybridge Swifts - August 2000, Aveley.

KING, DAVE   Goalkeeper
Current Club: Hastings United
Birthplace: Kent
Goalkeeper, rated one of the best goalkeepers in Kent when playing for Thamesmead during 2000/01. Joined Hastings for the start of the 2001/02 season.

KING, GAVIN   Goalkeeper
Current Club: Harlow Town
Birthplace: Herts
Gavin signed for Ryman Division One North side Harlow Town in August 2002 from Premier Division Billericay Town. Joined Billericay before the start of the 1999/00 season from Bishops Stortford, for whom he made nearly 350 appearances. Despite keeping 18 clean sheets from 55 appearances in his first season, the arrival of Paul Newell meant that his future with the club seemed uncertain. However he remained at Billericay and

won back the number one slot, and made over 150 appearances before switching to Harlow.

KING, HERVE — *Midfielder*
Current Club: Redhill
Birthplace: Surrey
Powerful midfielder, who joined Redhill from Croydon Athletic in January 2002. Has added a great deal more bite to the centre of the park, has a lot of pace and is an excellent crosser of the ball.

KING, JON — *Forward*
Current Club: Spennymoor United
D o B: 18/12/1968
Previous clubs include: Whitley Bay - September 2000, Easington Colliery, Whitley Bay, Durham C, Whitley Bay, Hartlepool Utd, Notts Co.

KING, JORDAN — *Midfielder*
Current Club: Telford United
Birthplace: Telford
Local lad Jordan King is a product of the Telford United youth scheme and has impressed so far in his first season with the first team pool. An excellent passer of the ball, Jordan picks out a nice pass and shows classy first touch.

KING, KEIRAN — *Midfielder*
Current Club: Paget Rangers
D o B: 10/09/1982   *Birthplace: Birmingham*
From Youth team.

KING, RICKY — *Forward*
Current Club: Carterton Town
Birthplace: Oxfordshire
From Local football - July 2001.

KING, RYAN — *Forward*
Current Club: Salisbury City
D o B: 17/03/1976   *Birthplace: Bristol*
A skillful player with the ball, Bristol-born Ryan also has an eye for goal. He was a YTS player on Bristol City's books, and has had spells with Weston-Super- Mare and Backwell United, from whom he joined Dr Martens Eastern side Salisbury City in November 2001.

KING, SIMON — *Midfielder*
Current Club: Berkhamsted Town
Birthplace: Essex
Previous clubs include: Leighton T - August 2001, Barton R, Totternhoe, Langford, Great Wakering R.

KING, STUART — *Defender*
Current Club: Dereham Town
Birthplace: Norfolk
Ex-professional with Cambridge United. Although small in stature, strong both on the ground and in the air. Last seasons Player of the Year.

KING, TYRONE — *Midfielder*
Current Club: Sittingbourne
D o B: 04/10/1977   *Birthplace: Kent*
Left-footed striker or winger who started his career at Sittingbourne in the youth team and made his debut in the 1994/95 season. Left in 1996 to play for Welling and also played for Deal and Dartford before returning to the Brickies in July 1999.

KINGSFORD, BARRY — *Midfielder*
Current Club: Croydon Athletic
Birthplace: Surrey
A hard-working midfield player or full-back who joined Croydon Athletic from neighbours and Ryman Division One South rivals Croydon in July 2002. Had signed for Croydon in August 1999 from Premier Division Carshalton Athletic, with whom he had been with since youth team days. Injury problems restricted his appearances in recent seasons, and he was on loan to St Leonards for much of the 2000/01 season.

KINNAIR, MICHAEL — *Defender*
Current Club: Marske United
Birthplace: Cleveland
Previous clubs include: Rotherham Utd (Trainee) - July 1997.

KINNEAR, TONY — *Defender*
Current Club: East Thurrock United
Birthplace: Essex
Previous clubs include: Romford - February 2001, Basildon Utd, Concord R, Canvey Island, Biggleswade T, Southend Utd (Trainee).

KINNEY, WEG — *Forward*
Current Club: Runcorn FC Halton
Birthplace: Liverpool
Skilful attacker who moved to UniBond Premier side Runcorn FC Halton in August 2002 from rivals Droylsden. Began his career as a trainee at Liverpool and then had spells with Knowsley United, Droylsden and Rhyl before rejoining the Bloods in September 2001.

KINSELLA, MIKE — *Goalkeeper*
Current Club: Aberystwyth Town
D o B: 02/10/1977   *Birthplace: Liverpool*
Previous clubs include: Kendal T - January 2002, Prescot Cables, Droylsden, Bamber Bridge, Conwy Utd, Bootle.

KINSLEY, ALEX — *Forward*
Current Club: Tring Town
Birthplace: Tring
From Youth team.

KIRBY, JOHN — *Defender*
Current Club: Horsham
Birthplace: Sussex
Giant defender, capable of making some really crunching tackles: scored six times for Horsham in 2000/01: also used as a forward during the latest season.

KIRBY, RYAN — *Defender*
Current Club: Harlow Town
D o B: 06/09/1974   *Birthplace: Chingford*
Impressive midfielder who is also capable of paying in midfield. Switched to Ryman Division One North side Harlow Town in July 2002 from Premier Division Aldershot Town. Had skippered the Shots in 2001/02 having joined in March 2001 from Stevenage Borough. Started his career with Arsenal and went on to make around 80 League appearances with Doncaster Rovers, Preston, Crewe, Wigan and Northampton.

KIRK, TONY — *Defender*
Current Club: Biddulph Victoria
Birthplace: Congleton
Previous clubs include: Congleton T - January 2002, Congleton Vale Juniors OB.

KIRKBY, MARTIN — Defender

Current Club: Bedlington Terriers

Birthplace: Cumbria

This former Penrith and Workington defender joined the Terriers in the summer of 1999 and has quickly established himself as a favourite with the fans winning the Supporters Club player of the season for 99/00. Excellent in the air for his size and one of the most comfortable defenders on the ball you will see in Non-League football. Played little football last season due to a nasty wrist injury.

KIRKUP, ANDKY — Midfielder

Current Club: Cambridge City

D o B: 17/10/1964   Birthplace: Hartlepool
Honours won: Dr Martens Premier & Midland Division Winners
Previous clubs include: Nuneaton Borough - July 1999, Raunds T, Rothwell T, Gloucester C, Rushden & Diamonds, Wellingborough T, Rushden T, Corby T, Rushden T.

KIRKWOOD, GLENN — Forward

Current Club: Burton Albion

D o B: 03/12/1976   Birthplace: Chesterfield
Glenn started his career at Eastwood Town where he gained rave reviews. Eventually he signed for Doncaster Rovers in the Vauxhall Conference. After two seasons at Belle Vue he joined Ilkeston Town at the start of the 2000/01 campaign, although he has been plagued by injury since joining the Robins. A talented striker who has yet to fulfil his undoubted potential, he moved on to UniBond League champions Burton Albion in May 2002.

KISSOCK, LEE — Forward

Current Club: Colwyn Bay

Birthplace: Lancashire

Joined Radcliffe Borough during the early part of the 2000/01 season from Tranmere Rovers where he was a trainee. A combative forward who settled in quickly and has scored some vital goals in the last season and a half. Transferred to UniBond Premier side Colwyn Bay in August 2002.

KITAMBIE, JOE — Forward

Current Club: Peacehaven & Telscombe

Birthplace: Sussex

Rangy teenage winger who joined Peacehaven from Lewes early on in 2001/02.

KITCHEN, ROBBIE — Forward

Current Club: Hassocks

Birthplace: Sussex

Top Hassocks marksman for five consecutive years (1993/94 to 1997/98): only makes rare appearances these days, but scored 5 times during 2000/01.

KITCHEN, SAM — Defender

Current Club: Durham City

D o B: 11/06/1967   Birthplace: Rintein
Sam returned to Gateshead in late November 2001 after a spell with Bishop Auckland before switching to Albany Northern League side Durham City in August 2002. He had been captain of Gateshead before leaving and was known to be one of the best central defenders seen at the club for many years. A cool, calm player, he knows how to handle difficult situations. Born in Germany, Sam started his playing days with Yorkshire Main before having spell with Goole, Stafford Rangers and Frickley Atlhletic. Played League football with Leyton Orient and Doncaster Rovers prior to his first spell at the International Stadium.

KITCHING, NEIL — Forward

Current Club: Sutton Coldfield Town

Birthplace: Birmingham

Previous clubs include: Gresley Rovers - November 2001, Boldmere St.Michaels, Highgate Utd, Paget R, Tamworth.

KNAPPER, JOHN — Midfielder

Current Club: Alfreton Town

Birthplace: Nottingham

John joined UniBond First Division newcomers Alfreton Town in July 2002 from Dr Martens Premier neighbours Ilkeston Town. Had signed for Ilkeston from UniBond side Eastwood Town just before Christmas 1996 for £4,000. A stylish performer, he became a regular in the Robins side and an excellent record as Ilkestons penalty taker. Had spells as captain and was one of the the clubs longest-serving players before his departure.

KNEE, MARK — Defender

Current Club: Worthing

Birthplace: Sussex

Full-back/utility player: joined Worthing from Lewes in 1997 (previously with Steyning): has some 150 appearances for the club to his name. Broke his leg in a match against Braintree (December 1999) and made his comeback during 2001.

KNIGHT, ALAN — Goalkeeper

Current Club: Havant & Waterlooville

D o B: 07/03/1961   Birthplace: Balham
Honours won: England Youth & u-21 Int., Division Three Winners
A man who needs no introduction, Alan has played his entire 21 year career with Portsmouth FC clocking up over 800 appearances and is now the clubs goalkeeping coach. He signed to play with Havant & Waterlooville in December 2001 to help out during a period in which first team keeper Paul Nicholls was injured.

KNIGHT, GARY — Defender

Current Club: Solihull Borough

Birthplace: Worcestershire

Swept the board at last seasons awards night. Gary picked up the Players' Player of the season and Supporters' Player of the Year as well as Supporters Most Consistent Player. He signed in the summer of 1999 from Paget Rangers. He was the skipper at Paget and spent three seasons with them. He previously played for Halesowen Harriers.

KNIGHT, GLENN — Goalkeeper

Current Club: Welling United

Birthplace: London

Highly-rated goalkeeper who was with Millwall and Leyton Orient before moving to Welling United for the first time in 1996. Had spells with Harrow Borough, Basingstoke Town, Farnborough Town, Gravesend, Boreham Wood and in South Africa before returning to Park View Road at the start of the 2000/01 season.

KNIGHT, JASON — Midfielder

Current Club: Barwell

D o B: 16/09/1974   Birthplace: Adelaide, Australia
Previous clubs include: Shepshed Dynamo - June 2002, Oadby T, Hinckley Utd, Shepshed Dynamo, Hinckley Ath., Doncaster R, Hinckley Ath., West Ham Utd (Trainee).

KNIGHT, KEIRAN *Midfielder*

Current Club: Aylesbury United

Birthplace: Middlesex
Previous clubs include: Northwood - March 2002, Southall, Chertsey T, Southall.

KNIGHT, KEITH *Midfielder*

Current Club: Cirencester Town

D o B: 16/02/1969   Birthplace: Cheltenham
Honours won: England Schoolboy Int.
Previous clubs include: Swindon Supermarine - February 2002, Clevedon T, Witney T, Worcester C, Cheltenham T, Halesowen T, Gloucester C, Trowbridge T, Yeovil T, Trowbridge T, Gloucester C, VV Veendam (Holland), Reading, Cheltenham T.

KNIGHT, LEE *Defender*

Current Club: Redditch United

Birthplace: Birmingham
Previous clubs include: Halesowen T - November 2001, Redditch Utd, Blakenall, Hednesford T, WBA.

KNIGHT, MARK *Defender*

Current Club: Berkhamsted Town

Birthplace: Berkhamsted
Previous clubs include: Hemel Hempstead - July 1999, Berkhamsted T, Chesham Utd, Berkhamsted T.

KNIGHT, MATT *Goalkeeper*

Current Club: Boldmere St.Michaels

Birthplace: Birmingham
Previous clubs include: Bloxwich T - June 2001, Darlaston.

KNIGHT, RICHARD *Defender*

Current Club: Rocester

D o B: 21/08/1974   Birthplace: Burton
Re-joined Dr Martens Western side Rocester in the summer of 2002 from UniBond outfit Leek Town. Had signed for Leek at the start of the 2001/02 season from Rocester. Made 30 appearances for Walsall in the Football League. An attacking full back, Richard has also played for Armitage, Leicester United, Bromsgrove Rovers and Atherstone United.

KNIGHT, ROSS *Midfielder*

Current Club: Studley

D o B: 07/06/1969   Birthplace: Worcestershire
Previous clubs include: Stourport Swifts - December 2001, Evesham Utd, Redditch Utd, Stourbridge, Sutton Coldfield T, Blakenall, Ebbw Vale, Merthyr Tydfil, Sandwell B, Halesowen T, Barry T, Evesham Utd, Barry T, Inter Cardiff, Evesham Utd, Barry T, Northfield T.

KNIGHT, SPENCER *Forward*

Current Club: Canvey Island

Birthplace: Herts
Highly-rated attacking midfielder who signed for Canvei Island from Harrow Borough in November 2001. Previous clubs include St.Albans City, Arlesey, Hoddensdon Town and Luton Town's reserve side.

KNIGHT, TONY *Midfielder*

Current Club: Brook House

D o B: 11/04/1964   Birthplace: Middlesex
Previous clubs include: Beaconsfield SYCOB - July 1999, Wealdstone, Hayes, Staines T, Uxbridge, Hayes, Uxbridge.

KNIGHTON, ANDY *Defender*

Current Club: Brockenhurst

Birthplace: Hampshire
Previous clubs include: Lymington & New Milton - July 2000, New Milton.

KNIGHTON, DAVE *Defender*

Current Club: Brockenhurst

Birthplace: Hampshire
Previous clubs include: Lymington & New Milton - July 2000, New Milton.

KNIGHTS, KARL *Defender*

Current Club: Felixstowe & Walton United

Birthplace: Suffolk
Former Felixstowe youth team player who has played for Felixstowe Town and Walton United prior to the merger. Excellent athlete who gives 100% for 90 minutes dogged by injury last season but now back to his best.

KNOTT, RICHARD *Goalkeeper*

Current Club: Halesowen Harriers

Birthplace: Birmingham
Previous clubs include: Causeway Utd - July 2000.

KNOWLES, BILLY *Midfielder*

Current Club: St.Helens Town

Birthplace: Liverpool
Experienced midfielder who re-signed for North West Counties outfit St Helens Town in August 2002 from UniBond Premier side Burscough. Had joined Burscough from St Helens in the summer of 1995. Also saw service with another North West Counties League outfit, Bootle.

KNOWLES, CHRIS *Goalkeeper*

Current Club: Staines Town

D o B: 04/02/1978   Birthplace: Stone
Highly-rated goalkeeper who started his career with Peterborough and then played in the League with Chester City. Spells with Hereford United, Northampton and Stalybridge Celtic followed before he went over to Canada to play for Edmonton Drillers. Returned in 2001 and turned out for Tamworth and then spent the first month of the 2001/02 seaon at Aldershot Town before signing for Staines Town.

KNOWLES, DARREN *Defender*

Current Club: Gainsborough Trinity

D o B: 08/10/1970   Birthplace: Sheffield
Very experienced defender who joined Gainsborough Trinity from Conference side Northwich Victoria in June 2002. Made over 300 League appearances with Sheffield United, Stockport, Scarborough and Hartlepool before joining Vics at the start of the 2001/02 season.

KNOWLES, JAMES *Midfielder*

Current Club: Harrogate Town

D o B: 21/05/1983   Birthplace: Leeds
Broke into the Garforth team squad initially 2 years ago at full back but was given the chance to show his immense talent in midfield. Shows great vision and maturity for someone so young. Transferred to Hrarogate in March 2002.

KNOWLES, MATT *Defender*

Current Club: Rossendale United

Birthplace: Rossendale
From Youth team.

KNOWLES, MICHAEL   *Midfielder*
Current Club: Morecambe

D o B: 03/03/1974   *Birthplace: Morecambe*
From Youth team.

KNOX, CHRIS   *Defender*
Current Club: Newcastle Blue Star

D o B: 16/02/1981   *Birthplace: Newcastle*
From Youth team.

KNOX, RICHARD   *Midfielder*
Current Club: Swindon Supermarine

Birthplace: Swindon
From Youth team.

KODRA, ELIS   *Defender*
Current Club: Hayes

Birthplace: Kosovo
Elis is a left sided utility player in his early twenties, who joined Boreham Wood earlier in the 2001/02 season, having been released by Watford, where he had been a Trainee. Transferred to Hayes in February 2002.

KORDUA, DEREK   *Midfielder*
Current Club: Stourbridge

Birthplace: Birmingham
Previous clubs include: Hinckley Utd - January 2000, Bedworth Utd, Stratford T, Knowle, Redditch Utd, Tamworth, Redditch Utd, Birmingham C (Trainee).

KORKMAZ, TUNCAY   *Midfielder*
Current Club: Soham Town Rangers

Birthplace: Turkey
Honours won: Turkey Youth Int.
Previous clubs include: Wisbech T - December 2001, Stamford, Soham Town R, Wisbech T, Spalding Utd, Stamford, Rushden & Diamonds, Spalding Utd.

KOROL, AARON   *Midfielder*
Current Club: Lincoln United

Birthplace: Lincoln
Brought to Lincoln United from neighbouring Lincoln Moorlands when manager Garry Goddard returned to Ashby Avenue in January 2002. Has a high work rate and can cross the ball with good effect.

KOTYLO, KRYSTOF   *Midfielder*
Current Club: Worksop Town

Birthplace: Sheffield
Previous clubs include: Nuneaton Borough - July 2001, Sheffield Wednesday.

KOULAMANOU, MIKE   *Forward*
Current Club: Enfield

Previous clubs include: Wembley - August 2001, Cheshunt.

KOZAK, ROB   *Forward*
Current Club: Rhayader Town

Birthplace: Wales
Very talented youngster. Left footed and posseses a deadly cross. Has a good first touch, but needs to work on his strength, so he isnt bullied out of games. Ability to go far but needs to keep working hard. One for the future.

KREYLING, DAVE   *Midfielder*
Current Club: Braintree Town

Birthplace: Essex
Previous clubs include: Heybridge Swifts - January 2002, Billericay T, Hullbridge Sports.

KURILA, ALAN   *Defender*
Current Club: Oldbury United

D o B: 16/09/1961   *Birthplace: Northampton*
Honours won: Southern League Premier Div.Winners, FA XI
Previous clubs include: Moor Green - August 1998, Solihull B, Rushden & Diamonds, Burton Alb., Kidderminster Harriers, Stafford R, Burton Alb., Bromsgrove R, Bedford T, Birmingham C.

KWASHI, TOSTOA   *Midfielder*
Current Club: Fisher Athletic (London)

Previous clubs include: Redhill - July 2001.

KYLE, TONY   *Defender*
Current Club: Dartford

Birthplace: Dartford
Locally-born defender who has progressed through Dartfords youth set up to become a valuable member of the senior side.

KYRIACOU, LOUIS   *Defender*
Current Club: Hertford Town

Birthplace: Hertford
From Youth team.

KYRIACOU, PAUL   *Defender*
Current Club: Enfield

Birthplace: Leicester
Previous clubs include: Bishops Stortford - March 2002, Rushden & Diamonds.

K

LACEY, NEIL — Defender
Current Club: Bradford Park Avenue
Previous clubs include: Emley - December 2000, Stocksbridge Park Steels, Gainsborough Trinity, Emley, Frickley Ath., Gateshead, Frickley Ath., Goole T, Denaby Utd.

LAFFERTY, MARK — Defender
Current Club: Ossett Albion
Previous clubs include: Frickley Ath - August 2001, Hull C.

LAIDLAW, JAMIE — Forward
Current Club: Bognor Regis Town
Birthplace: Sussex
Son of former pro (and current Chichester coach) Joe Laidlaw Spent three years as an apprentice with Swindon and has also played in the Conference with Yeovil and Farnborough. Joined Chichester from Newport IoW during the 2000 close season and had a superb first term at Church Road, striking 32 goals. Switched to Bognor Regis in March 2002.

LAIGHT, ELLIS — Forward
Current Club: Taunton Town
D o B: 30/06/1976   Birthplace: Birmingham
Honours won: FA Vase Winners
Prolific striker who played over 60 League games for Torquay and then joined Bath City on his release during the 1996-97 season. A flurry of Western League goals for Bideford earned a move to Dr Martens side Dorchester Town. Joined Taunton in June 1998 and scored the winning goal in the 2000 FA Vase final at Villa Park.

LAING, JAMES — Forward
Current Club: Hassocks
Birthplace: Sussex
Leading scorer for St Francis two years running before joining Hassocks during the 1999 close season: in great form during his first term at The Beacon with 22 goals: had another successful campaign during 2000/01, scoring 24 times as well as representing the County.

LAINTON, LEE — Forward
Current Club: Kidsgrove Athletic
Birthplace: Stoke
Previous clubs include: Stone Dominoes - July 2001.

LAIRD, CRAIG — Defender
Current Club: Bridgwater Town
D o B: 18/07/1963   Birthplace: Somerset
Previous clubs include: Taunton T - September 1977, Minehead, Bristol C.

LAIRD, JAMES — Midfielder
Current Club: Bridgwater Town
D o B: 13/09/1983   Birthplace: Somerset
Previous clubs include: Plymouth Argyle (Junior) - July 2000.

LAKE, CARL — Midfielder
Current Club: Rothwell Town
Birthplace: Kettering
Previous clubs include: Kettering T - July 2002.

LAKE, CRAIG — Defender
Current Club: Bishop Auckland
D o B: 10/02/1980   Birthplace: Stockton
Defender who returned to UniBond First Division side Bishop Auckland in the summer of 2002 after a season with Albany Northern League neighbours Durham City. Started his career with Hartlepool United before signing for Bishops for the first time in July 2000.

LAKE, DARREN — Midfielder
Current Club: Feltham
Birthplace: Ashford, Middx
Former Youth player Lake returned to the Arena last season after an unsuccessful spell with local Ryman League side Uxbridge. A strong well built midfielder with excellent vision and passing capabilities. Lake is a vital cog in the Feltham midfield engine room and is often the inspiration in the center of Felthams midfield.

LAKE, STUART — Midfielder
Current Club: Hednesford Town
Birthplace: Stone
Stuart joined Hednesford Town from Walsall FC in the 1994/95 season and as such is Hednesford Town's longest serving player. Lakey is a tough-tackling player in defence or midfield who likes nothing better than to strike at goal when he gets half a chance.

LAKER, BARRY — Defender
Current Club: Farnborough Town
Birthplace: London
An experienced defender who was orginally with Wimbledon. Was released and joined Banstead Athletic in 1995 and hius performances soon attracted attention. Moved to Sutton United in July 1996 and helped the Us to promotion back into the Conference in 1998/99. Switched to Farnborough in June 2000.

LAKIN, BARRY — Midfielder
Current Club: Chelmsford City
D o B: 19/09/1973   Birthplace: Dartford
Former Leyton Orient playmaker who is now with Dr Martens Premier side Chelmsford City for a second time, having also appeared for Stevenage Borough, Welling United and Erith & Belvedere. Is employed full-time by City as the clubs Youth Development Officer. Made some 70 appearances for the Brisbane Road club as a professional.

LALLY, ANTON — Midfielder
Current Club: Marine
Birthplace: Merseyside
Midfielder who joined Marine in December 2000 from Kendal Town after previously being with Southport. Represented Merseyside Schools and Knowsley Borough in a youth tournament in America. Strong player who is only 21 and full of promise.

LAMB, ANDY — Forward
Current Club: Farsley Celtic
Birthplace: Leeds
Previous clubs include: Horsforth St Margarets - July 2001.

LAMB, DARREN — Defender
Current Club: Great Yarmouth Town
D o B: 28/01/1984   Birthplace: Norfolk
Youth team player at Yarmouth who entered into the first team picture this season and could make the right back berth his own Previously with Caister Roma U16s and Caister United.

LAMB, JEFF — Midfielder
Current Club: Marlow
Previous clubs include: Wycombe Wanderers - July 1998.

LAMB, PAUL — Defender

Current Club: Margate

D o B: 19/04/1973 — Birthplace: Kent

Previous clubs include: Gravesend - July 1997, Ramsgate, Margate, Dartford, Ramsgate.

LAMB, PAUL — Defender

Current Club: Hemel Hempstead Town

D o B: 12/09/1974 — Birthplace: Northampton

Paul is a defensive midfield player or defender who joined Ryman Division One North club Hemel Hempstead Town in July 2002 from Premier Division Boreham Wood. Had signed for Wood from Wealdstone in December 2001 and made his first-team debut for the club against Sutton United in December 2001. Hisre pvious clubs include Northampton Town, Dunstable Town, Buckingham Town (two spells), Bedworth United and Wealdstone.

LAMBERT, MARK — Midfielder

Current Club: Ossett Town

D o B: 06/06/1981 — Birthplace: Ossett

A product of Town's youth set up who finally established himself in the first team last year. Stylish midfielder who is comfortable in position, can pass and is strong in the tackle. Also chips in with some important goals.

LAMEY, NATHAN — Forward

Current Club: Moor Green

D o B: 14/10/1980 — Birthplace: Leeds

Signed for Moor Green in the summer of 2001 from Hitchin Town. Former Wolves and Aston Villa trainee before signing for Cambridge United. Joined Hitchin in 2000, but wanted a move nearer his Birmingham home.

LAMONT, CLAY — Midfielder

Current Club: Withdean 2000

Birthplace: Sussex

Much-travelled player, having been on the books of Mile Oak, the original Withdean side and Ringmer before joining Whitehawk towards the end of 1999/2000: moved to Burgess Hill in October 2000 and went to Southwick month later: scored a total of six goals during 2000/01: switched to Combined Counties League action at the start of the following season.

LAMONT, JUNIOR — Forward

Current Club: Southwick

Birthplace: Sussex

Striker, who seems to move around clubs in the Brighton area on a regular basis: has made appearances for Mile Oak, Withdean, Ringmer, Southwick, Burgess Hill and Peacehaven over the last couple of years: had five goals to his name in 2000/01: began the latest season back at Mile Oak (scored twice) and returned to Southwick during October.

LAMPARD, SAMMY — Forward

Current Club: Molesey

Birthplace: Surrey

From Youth team.

LANCASHIRE, GRAHAM — Forward

Current Club: Hednesford Town

D o B: 19/10/1972 — Birthplace: Blackpool

Signed for Dr Martens Premier side Hednesford Town during the 2001 close season from Rochdale. Graham has extensive Football League experience which will be invaluable as Hednesford start the climb back to the Nationwide Conference.

LANCASTER, MARTIN — Defender

Current Club: Chester City

D o B: 10/11/1980 — Birthplace: Wigan

A product of Chester City's youth set-up Martyn had an impressive start to last season before fading. Will be looking to regain a regular spot in the side this time round. Spent a period on trial at Aston Villa last season.

LANDON, RICHARD — Forward

Current Club: Radcliffe Borough

D o B: 22/03/1970 — Birthplace: Worthing

Tall and experienced centre forward who signed for Radcliffe Borough during the summer of 2001 from Altrincham. Started his career in Non-League football with Bedworth United before going on to enjoy well over 150 League games with Plymouth, Stockport and Macclesfield,.

LANE, CHRIS — Midfielder

Current Club: Southport

D o B: 24/05/1979 — Birthplace: Liverpool

Chris signed for Conference club Southport at the start of January 2001 from rivals Hereford United and made an impressive debut, netting after just 10 minutes against Rushden & Diamonds. A right wing-back, Chris joined for an undisclosed five-figure transfer fee. Originally on the books at Everton.

LANE, IAN — Defender

Current Club: Shifnal Town

Birthplace: Shropshire

From Local football - December 2001, Shifnal T, Newport T.

LANG, IAN — Defender

Current Club: Kendal Town

Previous clubs include: Fleetwood Freeport - July 2001, Clitheroe, Lancaster C, Clitheroe, Great Harwood T, Nelson.

LANGAN, KEVIN — Defender

Current Club: Forest Green Rovers

D o B: 07/04/1978 — Birthplace: Jersey

Joined Conference club Forest Green Rovers from Team Bath of the Western League in October 2001. A former Bristol City trainee, the defender enjoyed an excellent first campaign at Conference level.

LANGER, TIM — Midfielder

Current Club: Bishops Stortford

Birthplace: Essex

A product of the Blues Youth set-up, Tim is an emerging player of considerable talent and versatility. Season 2000/1 saw sporadic appearances in the first team and loan spells at the start of season 2001/2 kept him away from Woodside Park. With that experience now under his belt, Tim is once again pushing for a first team place and certainly is one to watch for the not too distant future.

LANGFORD, BARRY — Defender

Current Club: Banstead Athletic

Birthplace: London

Previous clubs include: Tooting & Mitcham Utd - July 2000, Banstead Ath., Dulwich Hamlet, Crystal Palace.

LANGFORD, TIM — Forward
Current Club: Stourport Swifts

D o B: 12/09/1965   Birthplace: Kingswinford
Honours won: Conference Winners
Appointed as player-manager of Dr Martens Western side Stourport Swifts at the beginning of the 2001/02 season. Tim is an experienced striker who won the Conference title with Wycombe Wanderers. Originally with Halesowen Town, he made his name at Conference level with Telford United before joining Wycombe. He later returned to both Telford and Halesowen as well as Bromsgrove Rovers before signing for Swifts via a short stint at Halesowen Harriers in December 2000.

LANGHAM, OLLIE — Midfielder
Current Club: Stowmarket Town

Birthplace: Essex
Previous clubs include: Woodbridge T - July 2001, Whitton Utd, Chelmsford C, Stowmarket T, Chelmsford C, Colchester Utd.

LANGLEY, LES — Forward
Current Club: Shildon

Birthplace: Bishop Auckland
Previous clubs include: Crook T - November 1999, South Shields

LANGLEY, SIMON — Midfielder
Current Club: Chertsey Town

Birthplace: Surrey
A midfield player who signed in the past close season. Was previously with Carshalton Athletic and Bromley but spent a longer four year spell with Kingstonian.

LANGMEAD, SIMON — Defender
Current Club: Bideford

Birthplace: Devon
Simon is in his second spell as a Bideford player, having Re-joined from Barnstaple Town. Simon is the original utility player, who more often than not is to be found in the left side of midfield, putting in a gritty performance. He has slotted into almost every position on the park for the Robins with the exception of between the sticks, & in the process he has clocked up over 150 games for us and represented Devon.

LANGSTON, DAVE — Midfielder
Current Club: Stafford Town

Birthplace: Staffordshire
Previous clubs include: Chasetown - September 2001, Rocester, Bromsgrove R, Rocester, Ilkeston T, Blakenall, Sutton Coldfield T, Leicester Utd, Armitage, Chasetown.

LANNING, DAVE — Goalkeeper
Current Club: Shildon

Birthplace: Newcastle
Previous clubs include: Prudhoe T - July 2001.

LARKIN, ANDY — Defender
Current Club: Chatham Town

D o B: 24/09/1977   Birthplace: London
Central defender who signed for Dr Martens Eastern Division side Chatham Town in July 2002 from Premier Division neighbours Folkestone Invicta. Had joinedFolkestone from Hastings Town during the summer of 1998. Andy started his career at Charlton Athletic, including one year as a full-time professional. Supporters' Player of the Year and joint winner of the Players' Player of the Year Poll for the 1998/99 season, he made over 100 appearances for Folkestone.

LARKIN, DAN — Defender
Current Club: Folkestone Invicta

D o B: 02/12/1982   Birthplace: Kent
The teenage brother of Andy, Dan joined Folkestone Invicta during the summer of 2001 when he played at both full back and centre half in the clubs pre-season friendlies. A product of the Chatham Town youth system.

LATHOM, STEVE — Midfielder
Current Club: Warrington Town

Birthplace: Cheshire
Previous clubs include: Runcorn - July 2001.

LATTER, MATTHEW — Defender
Current Club: Sidlesham

Birthplace: Sussex
Defender: previously with Wick and Storrington before joining Sidlesham during the autumn 2001.

LATTIE, AEON — Defender
Current Club: Droylsden

Previous clubs include: Flixton - November 1996, Droylsden, Nova, Flixton, Irlam T, Droylsden.

LATUSKE, STEVE — Defender
Current Club: Southwick

Birthplace: Surrey
Former Epsom defender/midfielder: signed for Eastbourne Utd midway through 2000/01 after moving to the area: transferred to Southwick twelve months later: had previously played in the County League for Redhill some years ago.

LAVENDER, DANNY — Defender
Current Club: Leatherhead

D o B: 26/05/1976   Birthplace: London
Tough-tackling centre-half, arrived back at Ryman Division One South side Leatherhead from Molesey in March 2002. Good in the air and on the ground and a commanding yet calm influence on his team-mates. Previousy with Kingstonian and Hampton & Richmond Borough.

LAVERY, RICHARD — Midfielder
Current Club: Nuneaton Borough

D o B: 28/05/1977   Birthplace: Coventry
Previous clubs include: Hinckley Utd - July 2001, Tamworth, Atherstone Utd, Sutton Coldfield T, Massey Ferguson, Stratford T, Nuneaton B, Hinckley Ath., Bedworth Utd.

LAVIN, RICHARD — Goalkeeper
Current Club: Corby Town

Birthplace: Corby
Although on the small side for a goalkeeper, Richard was rated as one of the best in the United Counties League. Played for S & L Corby , Bourne Town and Desborough Town before joining his home-town side Corby Town in the Dr Martens Eastern in July 2002.

LAWFORD, CRAIG — Midfielder
Current Club: Liversedge

D o B: 25/11/1972   Birthplace: Dewsbury
Previous clubs include: Hull C - July 1997, Bradford C.

L

LAWFORD, JOHN — Forward

Current Club: Harrow Borough

Birthplace: London

Experienced striker who re-joined Ryman Premier side Harrow Borough in November 2001 from Boreham Wood. Previously with Luton Town, Bishops Stortford, Hayes, Aylesbury United, Wokingham Town, Berkhamsted Town and Chesham United. A prolific goalscorer.

LAWLESS, JOHN — Forward

Current Club: Burscough

Birthplace: Liverpool

Another highly-promising young player to have come up through UniBond Premier side Burscoughs successful youth ranks. Made his senior debut in the final game of the 1999/00 season and enjoyed a particularly fruitful 2001/02 season in front of goal. Has been the subject of interest from a number of League clubs.

LAWLEY, EDDIE — Defender

Current Club: Bedford Town

D o B: 10/11/1975 Birthplace: Nottingham

Plays wide on the left and is an excellent crosser of the ball. Previous clubs include Buckingham Town and Notts County. Signed for Ryman Premier side Bedford Town in 1996 and he has since made over 300 appearances for the Eagles.

LAWRENCE, CARL — Defender

Current Club: Shepshed Dynamo

D o B: 14/11/1979 Birthplace: Leicester

Well-travelled defender who re-joined Dr Martens Western side Shepshed Dynamo in the summer of 2001 from Leicestershire Senior Leaguers Highfield Rangers. Was on the books at Leicester City, Luton and Lincoln City as a youngster and then had spells with Telford United, Ilkeston Town, Nuneaton Borough, Racing Club Warwick and Corby Town before having his first stint at Shepshed.

LAWRENCE, DAVID — Forward

Current Club: Great Yarmouth Town

D o B: 11/02/1984 Birthplace: Norfolk

Player for the Youth team where he partners Darren Lamb up front and is that teams leading scorer. Very skilful with the ball. Came from Caister Roma U16s.

LAWRENCE, MARTYN — Forward

Current Club: Purfleet

Previous clubs include: Concord Rangers - July 1997, Maldon T, Billericay T, Southend Manor, Barking, Southend Utd (Trainee).

LAWRENCE-JONES, BARNEY — Forward

Current Club: Ashford Town (Middx)

Birthplace: Surrey

Striker aged 22. Signed for Ashford Town (Middx) this season from Hellenic League Club Englefield Green and has been elevated to the 1st Team squad after scoring 7 goals in his opening 3 reserve matches.

LAWS, DAVID — Forward

Current Club: Weymouth

D o B: 13/11/1968 Birthplace: Sunderland

David is now in his 7th season with the club after signing from Bishop Auckland. David has been the club's top scorer in each of his 6 previous seasons.

LAWS, MICHAEL — Defender

Current Club: Whitby Town

Birthplace: Yorkshire

Competitive young defender who signed for UniBond Premier side Whitby Town from Albany Northern Leaguers Northallerton Town in the summer of 2002. He battles hard on the ground and is strong in the air and is another of the Blues talented array of defenders.

LAWSON, ALEX — Midfielder

Current Club: Gateshead

Birthplace: Northumberland

Previous clubs include: Ashington - January 2002, Newbiggin CW, Morpeth T.

LAWSON, STEVE — Defender

Current Club: Tooting & Mitcham United

Birthplace: Surrey

Previous clubs include: Leatherhead - August 2000, Croydon, Carshalton Ath.

LAWTON, CRAIG — Midfielder

Current Club: Colwyn Bay

D o B: 03/01/1972 Birthplace: Mancot

Honours won: Wales Youth & u-21 Int.

Started at Manchester United where he was a regular reserve team player. Then played four games for Port Vale but moved to Holywell Town after an injury ended his full-time career. Signed for Colwyn Bay in November 1996 and is now in his sixth season. A skilful midfielder, Craig is a Welsh Youth an under-21 international and has twice been Player of the Year at Llanellian Road.

LAWTON, DANNY — Midfielder

Current Club: Didcot Town

Birthplace: Oxfordshire

Danny rejoined Didcot two seasons ago following a round the world trip and has really staked a claim in the side this season. With an average of a goal every 3 games, Danny has an excellent strike rate for a midfielder.

LAWTON, ROBBIE — Midfielder

Current Club: Vauxhall Motors

D o B: 14/06/1979 Birthplace: Liverpool

A skilful young winger who has come on leaps and bounds in the last year or so. Joined Vauxhall Motors from Marine in the spring of 1999. Originally signed from Marine, Robbie has also tried his luck with Caernarfon Town in the League of Wales before re-joining the Motormen. Can operate on either flank and has earned a great deal of admirers following a string of excellent displays.

LAZIC, VLADIMIR — Defender

Current Club: Bromley

Birthplace: London

Defender Vladimir returned to Bromley after spending time studying. He has played for Chelsea and Kingstonian as well as having a spell at Northwood when he was at Chelsea. Returned to Bromley in March 2002.

LE BIHAN, NEIL — Midfielder

Current Club: Crawley Town

D o B: 14/03/1976 Birthplace: Croydon

Honours won: British Universities Rep.

Neil was an apprentice at Tottenham before joining Dover Athletic in the summer of 1997. Neil, who had more than 50 League appearances to his name, immediately made an impact at The Crabble by scoring on his debut and provided much entertainment for Dover fans, by blasting the ball into the back of the net from long-range on several occasions with his left foot. Neil plays either on the left or centre of midfield and received the Player of the Year Award for the 1998/99 season, and has featured for Britain in the World Student Championships. Transferred to Crawley Town in June 2002.

LE FOUVRE, RUSSELL — Defender

Current Club: Horsham YMCA

Birthplace: Channel Islands
Played for Chelsea Academicals (Eastbourne League) before signing for Horsham YMCA midway through 2001/02.

LE GEYT, SINCLAIR — Midfielder

Current Club: Croydon

D o B: 10/07/1980   Birthplace: Port Elizabeth (S. Africa)
Honours won: English Independent Schools Rep.
22-year-old attacking midfield player who joined Croydon in February 2001 from Wimbledon. South African-born Sinclair previously spent two seasons at Derby County, helping Derbys second string to the Premier Reserves League title. Has also represented England Independent Schools.

LEA, MATTHEW — Midfielder

Current Club: Workington

Previous clubs include: Gretna - October 2001, Penrith, Netherfield Kendal, Penrith.

LEACH, MARC — Defender

Current Club: Chesham United

D o B: 12/07/1983   Birthplace: Berkshire
Young central defender who was released by Wycombe Wanderers at the end of the 2001/02 season and signed for Ryman Premier side Chesham United in August 2002. Previously on the books at Watford and Arsenal, Marc is an enthusiastic and hard-working player who has a good attitude. His footballing hero is Tony Adams and career highlight to date was playing in the Nationwide 2nd Division last season. He is in Computer Aided Design.

LEACH, NICK — Defender

Current Club: Dulwich Hamlet

Birthplace: Berkshire
Cultured young defender who was a trainee and later professional at Wycombe Wanderers, making six appearances in Division Two for the Chairboys. Joined Dulwich Hamlet during the summer of 2001 after spells with Aylesbury United and Hemel Hempstead.

LEACH, PAUL — Midfielder

Current Club: Thornaby on Tees

Birthplace: Cleveland
From Youth team.

LEACOCK, ALEX — Defender

Current Club: Wokingham Town

Birthplace: Berkshire
Previous clubs include: Bracknell T - August 2000, Wokingham T, Burnham, Binfield.

LEADBEATER, KEVIN — Forward

Current Club: Runcorn FC Halton

Birthplace: Liverpool
Previous clubs include: Southport (£5,000) - January 2002, Skelmersdale Utd.

LEADBEATER, RICHARD — Forward

Current Club: Halesowen Town

D o B: 21/10/1977   Birthplace: Dudley
Highly-rated striker who joined Halesowen Town in July 2002 after an injury-ravaged season with Nuneaton Borough. Started his career with Wolves and also played League football with Hereford United. The had spells in the Conference with Stevenage Borough, Hednesford Town and Nuneaton before joining the Yeltz.

LEADBETTER, MARTIN — Midfielder

Current Club: Rocester

Previous clubs include: Rushall Olympic - October 2001, Chasetown, Rushall Olympic, Chasetown, Lichfield C.

LEADBITTER, STEVE — Midfielder

Current Club: Spennymoor United

Birthplace: Co.Durham
Previous clubs include: Chester-le-Street - January 2002, Local football.

LEAH, JOHN — Midfielder

Current Club: Total Network Solutions

D o B: 03/08/1978   Birthplace: Shrewsbury
Excellent with or without the ball, and can adapt between midfield and upfront with ease, also excels in going forward with link-up play a speciality. Joined TNS from Newtown in November 2001 from LoW rivals Newtown, where he had begun his career. Had a spell with Darlington sandwiched between.

LEAHEY, STEVE — Midfielder

Current Club: St.Helens Town

Birthplace: Liverpool
Signed for North West Counties League side St Helens Town in August 2002 from Burscough. Was a graduate from Burscoughs highly-successful youth team. Steve is a talented young midfielder who made first-team debut for Burscough in October 2000 and was a regular in the senior side.

LEAHY, MARK — Defender

Current Club: Banstead Athletic

Birthplace: Kent
Previous clubs include: Crawley T - October 1999, Banstead Ath., Gravesend, Hitchin T, Bishops Stortford, Gravesend, Gillingham, Ashford T.

LEAROYD, STEVE — Defender

Current Club: Farsley Celtic

D o B: 23/04/1966   Birthplace: Leeds
Previous clubs include: Emley - July 1994, Harrogate T, Alrincham, Harrogate T, Bishop Auckland, Harrogate RA, Farsley Celtic.

LEARY, CHARLIE — Goalkeeper

Current Club: Kingsbury Town

D o B: 20/12/1982
Previous clubs include: Wealdstone - October 2001.

LEARY, TONY — Forward

Current Club: Aveley

Birthplace: Essex
Previous clubs include: Barking - July 2001, Grays Ath., Romford, Bishops Stortford.

LEATHER, IAN — Defender
Current Club: Chorley
Previous clubs include: Garswood Utd - September 1998.

LEAVER, DAVE — Midfielder
Current Club: Bamber Bridge
Birthplace: Preston
Honours won: UniBond League Premier Div. Winners
Preston-born experienced midfielder who re-joined UniBond First Division side Bamber Bridge for the third time from Chorley in July 2002. Originally with Leyland Daf, David then spent seven successful years with Brig which culminated in winning a UniBond Premier Division championship medal in 1995/96. A hard-working, left-sided player, he then had spells with Morecambe and Accrington Stanley before joining Chorley via a second spell at Brig in November 2001.

LEAVER, DAVID — Goalkeeper
Current Club: Selsey
Birthplace: Sussex
Plucky little goalkeeper who was actually playing for Selseys third XI at the beginning of 1999/2000, before becoming a first team regular. Former member of the Sussex U-18 squad and even played for Brighton & Hove Albion in an FA Youth Cup match during December 2000.

LEAVER, PAUL — Defender
Current Club: Three Bridges
Birthplace: Sussex
Long serving left-back: has been at the club for 10+ years (spent one season away at Whyteleafe, Oakwood and Ifield): has over 400 club appearances to his name: voted Three Bridges Players' Player of the year in 2000/01 for the second successive time.

LEBERL, JAKE — Defender
Current Club: Dover Athletic
D o B: 02/04/1977   *Birthplace: Manchester*
Talented and established member of the Dover Athletic side, who is equally comfortable in central defence or midfield. Signed from Crewe, he was voted as Players' Player of the year for 1999/00.

LEDGER, SAM — Defender
Current Club: Cheshunt
D o B: 04/01/1980   *Birthplace: Lewisham*
Previous clubs include: Broxbourne Borough V&E - August 2002, Potters Bar T, St Albans C.

LEE, ANTHONY — Midfielder
Current Club: Spennymoor United
Birthplace: Newcastle
Previous clubs include: Bishop Auckland - February 2002, North Shields Ath, Bishop Auckland, Guisborough T, Whitby T, Bishop Auckland, Ferryhill Ath., Northallerton T, Newcastle Utd (Trainee).

LEE, CHRISTIAN — Forward
Current Club: Farnborough Town
D o B: 08/10/1976   *Birthplace: Aylesbury*
Tall, yet skilful striker whose career began at Doncaster Rovers. Dint make the senior side at Belle Vue but went on to make League appearances for Northampton, Gillingham, Rochdale and Bristol Rovers. Joined Farnborough Town in September 2001 but then left for brief spells at Rushden & Diamonds and Eastwood Town before returning to Farnborough in February 2002.

LEE, DEAN — Goalkeeper
Current Club: Erith & Belvedere
Birthplace: Kent
Joined Erith & Belvedere in 1999 from Deal Town, also played for Slade Green and Charlton. A very promising young keeper who was voted Supporters' Player of the year season 1999/2000.

LEE, DWANE — Midfielder
Current Club: Yeading
Birthplace: Middlesex
Product of the young reserve side who in recent seasons has become a regular first teamer. Still only twenty-one, Dwane enjoys running at defenders and has an excellent right foot from dead ball situations.

LEE, GILES — Defender
Current Club: Fleet Town
Birthplace: Berks
Previous clubs include: Egham T - March 1997, Wokingham T, Basingstoke T, Fleet T, Chalfont St.Peter, Hampton, Wokingham T, Aldershot,

LEE, GRANT — Goalkeeper
Current Club: East Thurrock United
Birthplace: Essex
Previous clubs include: Hornchurch - November 1999, Basildon Utd, Aveley, East Thurrock Utd, Tilbury, East Thurrock Utd, Tilbury, Canvey Island.

LEE, JORDAN — Forward
Current Club: Bilston Town
Birthplace: Wolverhampton
From Youth team.

LEE, JUSTIN — Midfielder
Current Club: Oxford City
D o B: 19/09/1973   *Birthplace: Hereford*
Honours won: England Schoolboy Int.
Talented midfielder who signed for Thame United at the start of the 2000/01 season from Oxford City, Justin added a wealth of experience to the side for one so young. A former Arsenal and England Schoolboy international, he is a good organiser in the middle of the field with a cultured left foot. Previously with Abingdon Town, he re-joined Oxford City in July 2002.

LEE, KRIS — Forward
Current Club: Chelmsford City
Birthplace: Essex
Club record signing for Chelmsford City who was joint top scorer in the Ryman League in the 2000/01 season, netting some 30 goals for Heybridge Swifts. Switched to Chelmsford in a £15,000 deal despite strong interest from both Stevenage Borough and Farnborough Town. Had trials with Cambridge United and Colchester United in the 2001 pre-season but City's perseverance finally paid off in September 2001. Initially made a name for himself in the Jewson League with Tiptree United.

LEE, MARK — Forward
Current Club: Paget Rangers
Birthplace: Wolverhampton
From Local football - October 2001, Clyde, Wolverhampton Wanderers (Trainee).

LEE, MARK — *Midfielder*
Current Club: Selsey
Birthplace: Sussex
Midfielder and cousin of Paul Lee. Product of the reserve side who put in some eyecatching performances for the first team during 2000/01 (voted the clubs young player of the year).

LEE, MATTHEW — *Defender*
Current Club: Gravesend & Northfleet
D o B: 13/05/1979   *Birthplace: Farnborough*
Honours won: Ryman League Premier Div.Winners
Matt began his career as a YTS player at Charlton Athletic and was subsequently offered a two year full-time professional contract at The Valley. He joined Gravesend & Northfleet during the 1999/00 season before leaving the club to travel and then having a brief spell at Sutton United. He rejoined the club at the start of the 2000/01 season and rapidly built himself a reputation as a quality defender.

LEE, MATTHEW — *Forward*
Current Club: Curzon Ashton
Birthplace: Oldham
From Youth team,

LEE, PAUL — *Forward*
Current Club: Selsey
Birthplace: Sussex
Free-scoring Selsey striker for many years, he had 28 goals to his name in 1997/1998, and 25 in 1999/2000 even though he missed three months of the season whilst recovering from a leg operation. In equally fine form during the following campaign (29 goals), until being given the responsibility of taking a last-minute penalty against Sidley in May 2001 - his shot hit the woodwork, thus securing the title for United.

LEE, TOMMY — *Forward*
Current Club: Aveley
D o B: 24/04/1975   *Birthplace: Essex*
Previous clubs include: Leyton Pennant - November 2001, Romford, Ford Utd, East Thurrock Utd, Tilbury, Aveley.

LEECH, GARETH — *Defender*
Current Club: Curzon Ashton
Birthplace: Manchester
Previous clubs include: Woodley Sports - November 2000.

LEECH, JAMIE — *Midfielder*
Current Club: Brigg Town
Birthplace: Hull
Previous clubs include: Bridlington T - November 2001.

LEEDING, STUART — *Defender*
Current Club: Stourbridge
D o B: 06/01/1972   *Birthplace: Wolverhampton*
Previous clubs include: Bilston T - November 2001, Stafford Rangers, Stourbridge, Bilston T, Worcester C, Dudley T, Telford Utd, Wolverhampton Wanderers.

LEEKE, JOSH — *Defender*
Current Club: Heybridge Swifts
Birthplace: Essex
Joined Heybridge Swifts in September 2001 from Braintree Town having previously been with Maldon Town. Has performed well in the centre of defence or full back and is a strong tackler. Having impressed in the reserves, Josh is now very part of the first-team squad.

LEEKS, SHANE — *Midfielder*
Current Club: Hadleigh United
Birthplace: Suffolk
Talented and skilful player who is now an established member of the Hadleigh side. Clinical left foot used to good effect on corners and set pieces. Involved with the Club since youth football.

LEENDERS, ASHLEY — *Forward*
Current Club: Yeading
Birthplace: London
Previous clubs include: Windsor & Eton - March 2002, Harrow B, Edgware T, Yeading, Wealdstone, Hampton & Richmond B.

LEGG, STEVE — *Forward*
Current Club: Dorchester Town
Birthplace: Dorset
Previous clubs include: Wareham Rangers - July 2002.

LEGGATT, PHIL — *Midfielder*
Current Club: Arlesey Town
Birthplace: London
Phil is a talented utility player, capable of playing in defence or midfield, who joined Arlesey Town from Heybridge Swifts in November 2001. He was formerly with Southend United, Harlow Town and Heybridge Swifts. He is a Job Recruitment Consultant.

LEGGETT, KEVIN — *Forward*
Current Club: Wisbech Town
D o B: 24/02/1971
Previous clubs include: Downham T - July 2001, Fakenham T, Downham T.

LEIGH, JONATHAN — *Midfielder*
Current Club: Wingate And Finchley
D o B: 11/11/1982   *Birthplace: London*
From Youth team.

LEIGH, STEVE — *Midfielder*
Current Club: Newport Isle Of Wight
Previous clubs include: Havant T - July 1997.

LEMPRIERE, MARTIN — *Defender*
Current Club: Horsham
D o B: 08/03/1974   *Birthplace: London*
Long-serving defender/midfielder, who originally joined as a teenager in 1992: had a brief spell with Whyteleafe before returning to Horsham during Mark Dunks reign as manager: subsequently lost his place in the side when Sam Chapman and Steve Breach took joint command: back in favour under Russell Mason, becoming into an established member of the side: on the long-term injury list for the second half of 2001/02.

LENAGH, STEVE — *Midfielder*
Current Club: Hucknall Town
D o B: 21/03/1979   *Birthplace: Durham*
Honours won: Dr Martens League Premier Div.Winners
Steve is a midfielder who is also more than capable of playing in attack. Signed for Dr Martens Premier side Ilkeston Town in August 2002 after helping Kettering Town to win that division the previous season, but then quickly switched to UniBond Premier side Hucknall Town. Had signed for Kettering from Rochdale in the summer of 2000. He possesses quick feet for someone of 6 4 and played a handful of games in League football for Chesterfield and Rochdale after starting out as a trainee with Sheffield Wednesday.

LENCHNER, PAUL　　　　　　　*Forward*
Current Club: Wingate And Finchley
D o B: 30/12/1974　　　　　*Birthplace: London*
Previous clubs include: Shades - July 2000, Purfleet.

LENNON, MICK　　　　　　　*Forward*
Current Club: Newcastle Town
D o B: 27/07/1981　　　　　*Birthplace: Staffs*
Previous clubs include: Spennymoor Utd - August 2001, Colwyn Bay, Conwy Utd, Alasagar MWU.

LENTON, JAMIE　　　　　　*Midfielder*
Current Club: Hinckley United
D o B: 06/01/1977　　　　　*Birthplace: Nuneaton*
Previous clubs include: VS Rugby - June 1999, Solihull B, Racing Club Warwick, Nuneaton B, VS Rugby.

LEONARD, CHRIS　　　　　　*Defender*
Current Club: Spennymoor United
D o B: 09/01/1982　　　　　*Birthplace: Co Durham*
Chris joined Spennymoor United during the close season of 1999/00 after being released by Macclesfield Town. Previous to Macclesfield he was on schoolboy terms at Nottingham Forest where he started his career. He is now an established defender comfortable either in a central or left flank role, getting forward and assisting in the attack whenever possible.

LESLIE, KENNY　　　　　　　*Forward*
Current Club: Aveley
Birthplace: Essex
Previous clubs include: Grays Ath - July 1999, Purfleet.

LESTER, JAMIE　　　　　　*Defender*
Current Club: Atherton Laburnum Rovers
Birthplace: Grimsby
In his first season with LR, Jamie is a solid defender with bags of pace and energy. Previously with Atherton Collieries, he quickly established himself in the centre of defence and shows his enthusiasm in every game. Jamie is a hod carrier by trade and he likes swimming and clubbing.

LESTER, MICHAEL　　　　　*Midfielder*
Current Club: Bromley
Birthplace: Surrey
Lives in Fulham and is a Postman. Rejoined Bromley in November 2001 having made a handful of appearances last season. Was with Kingstonian when they were in the Nationwide Conference. He has also played for Carshalton Athletic.

LESTER, STEVE　　　　　　*Midfielder*
Current Club: Tiverton Town
D o B: 14/09/1965　　　*Birthplace: Weston-Super-Mare*
Previous clubs include: Gloucester C - March 1996, Trowbridge T, Mangotsfield Utd, Trowbridge T, Backwell Utd, Frome T.

LEVACK, ALEX　　　　　　*Defender*
Current Club: Wingate And Finchley
D o B: 28/07/1979　　　　　*Birthplace: London*
From Youth team.

LEVENDIS, ANDY　　　　　*Defender*
Current Club: Abbey Hey
Birthplace: Cheshire
Previous clubs include: Glossop North End - July 2001, Stalybridge Celtic, Witton Alb., Caernarfon T.

LEVENE, CARL　　　　　　　*Forward*
Current Club: Egham Town
Birthplace: London
Forward who signed for Ryman Division One South side Egham Town in August 2002 from Premier outfit Maidenhead United. Had joined the Magpies from Harrow Borough in December 2001 after spells with Yeading, Boreham Wood, Wembley, Northwood and Kingsbury Town.

LEVITT, TOM　　　　　　　*Forward*
Current Club: Burgess Hill Town
Birthplace: Sussex
Forward: progressed through the Burgess Hill youth ranks (also spent some time at Ansty Rangers): a member of the Sussex U-18 squad during 2000/01: broke into the first-team at Leylands Park this season and has put in some really eyecatching displays, usually starting on the bench.

LEWINGTON, STEVE　　　　*Forward*
Current Club: Thame United
Birthplace: London
Steve joined Thame United in August 2001 after spells in the Ryman Premier with Dulwich Hamlet and Hampton & Richmond Borough. A livewire front player with a good touch who should prove to be a real asset.

LEWIS, BEN　　　　　　　*Defender*
Current Club: Grays Athletic
D o B: 22/06/1977　　　　*Birthplace: Chelmsford*
Commanding central defender who joined Grays from Chelmsford City in May 2002. Originally with Heybridge Swifts as a youth before having spells with Colchester and Southend where he made a round of around 20 League appearances before rejoining Swifts. A spell at Welling preceded a third stint at Scraley Road before Ben signed for Chelmsford in March 2000.

LEWIS, CARL　　　　　　*Midfielder*
Current Club: Afan Lido
Birthplace: Wales
Plucked from the youth set-up earlier this season, Carl is certainly a future regular in the Lido team.

LEWIS, CRAIG　　　　　　*Midfielder*
Current Club: Wroxham
Birthplace: Norwich
Previous clubs include: Gorleston - August 2000, Great Yarmouth T, Norwich C.

LEWIS, DWAYNE　　　　　　*Forward*
Current Club: Enfield
Previous clubs include: Harrow Borough - August 2001.

LEWIS, GARI　　　　　　*Defender*
Current Club: Aberystwyth Town
D o B: 20/07/1974　　　　*Birthplace: Penryhncoch*
Honours won: Wales Youth Int.
Previous clubs include: Penryhncoch - July 1996, Aberystwyth T.

LEWIS, GARY　　　　　　　*Forward*
Current Club: Ramsbottom United
Birthplace: Lancashire
Previous clubs include: Colwyn Bay - February 2002, Clitheroe, Accrington Stanley.

LEWIS, GARY   *Forward*
Current Club: Frome Town
D o B: 23/08/1971   *Birthplace: Wiltshire*
Previous clubs include: Chippenham T - July 2000, Melksham T, Andover, Warminster T, Westbury Utd, Forest Green R, Salisbury C.

LEWIS, GERAINT   *Midfielder*
Current Club: Caersws
D o B: 20/12/1975   *Birthplace: Wales*
Previous clubs include: Oswestry T - July 1997.

LEWIS, GRAHAM   *Forward*
Current Club: Frickley Athletic
D o B: 15/02/1982   *Birthplace: Reading*
Previous clubs include: Northwich Victoria - August 2001, Lincoln C.

LEWIS, KEVIN   *Midfielder*
Current Club: Carterton Town
Birthplace: Oxfordshire
From Youth team.

LEWIS, MARK   *Defender*
Current Club: Chertsey Town
Birthplace: Surrey
A left sided defender who signed in the past close season from Feltham.

LEWIS, MARK   *Midfielder*
Current Club: Caersws
D o B: 09/05/1973   *Birthplace: Wales*
From Youth team.

LEWIS, MICKEY   *Midfielder*
Current Club: Oxford City
D o B: 15/02/1965   *Birthplace: Birmingham*
Honours won: England Youth Int.
Previous clubs include: Oxford Utd - November 2000, Derby Co., WBA.

LEWIS, STEFAN   *Defender*
Current Club: Bury Town
Birthplace: Suffolk
From Local football - July 2001.

LEWIS, STEVE   *Goalkeeper*
Current Club: Fakenham Town
Birthplace: Norfolk
Previous clubs include: Kings Lynn - November 1998, Cambridge Utd.

LEWIS, STUART   *Midfielder*
Current Club: Hailsham Town
Birthplace: Sussex
Midfielder: has been in and out of the first-team after coming through the youth side a few seasons ago.

LEWIS, TOM   *Midfielder*
Current Club: Mangotsfield United
Birthplace: Bristol
Promising youngster who has progressed through Mangotsfield Uiteds youth and reserve teams. Midfielder to watch for in the future.

LEWIS, VINCE   *Forward*
Current Club: Port Talbot Town
D o B: 23/07/1967   *Birthplace: Neath*
Previous clubs include: Maesteg Park - July 1995, Afan Lido, Port Talbot Ath.

LEWIS, WAYNE   *Defender*
Current Club: Bridlington Town
Birthplace: Bridlington
Previous clubs include: Hall Road Rangers - July 2001, North Ferriby Utd, Hall Road R, Bridlington T, Bridlington Trinity.

LEWORTHY, DAVID   *Forward*
Current Club: Havant & Waterlooville
D o B: 22/10/1962   *Birthplace: Portsmouth*
Honours won: England Semi-Pro Int., FA Trophy Winners, Ryman League Premier Div.Winners
David signed for Havant & Waterlooville in August 2000 and brings with him considerable experience from a lengthy career. Having played for Tottenham Hotspur and Oxford United in the 1980s he moved to the Non-League via Reading, signing for Farnborough Town. He has also played for Dover Athletic (for whom he signed for a record £50,000 in 1993), Rushden and Diamonds and came to Havant from Kingstonian with whom he won the FA Trophy in 2000. David was granted a testimonial match in 2000 when he scored for Kingstonian against Spurs at Kingsmeadow. Last season David was the Hawks top scorer with 14 league and 3 cup goals.

LEYS, CHRIS   *Midfielder*
Current Club: Hadleigh United
Birthplace: Suffolk
Strong, skilful, aggressive mid-fielder with an excellent left foot. Looking to establish a regular First Team spot after a number of appearances last season. Progressed through Hadleighs youth teams. County Under-16 player.

LIBURD, MARC   *Forward*
Current Club: Hemel Hempstead Town
Birthplace: Watford
Previous clubs include: Aylesbury Utd - August 1998, Boreham Wood, Peterborough Utd, Watford (Trainee).

LICATA, JOE   *Midfielder*
Current Club: Bromsgrove Rovers
Birthplace: Worcestershire
Previous clubs include: Bishops Cleeve - September 2001, Evesham Utd, Clevedon T, Cirencester T, Clevedon T, Pershore T, Evesham Utd, Cheltenham T, Bristol C.

LIDDLE, SIMON   *Forward*
Current Club: Croydon Athletic
Birthplace: Surrey
Previous clubs include: Carshalton Ath - August 2001, Croydon, Corinthian Casuals, Canvey Island, Dulwich Hamlet, Banstead Ath., Corinthian Casuals, Whyteleafe, Dulwich Hamlet, Wimbledon (Junior), Charlton Ath (Junior).

LIDDON, PAUL   *Defender*
Current Club: Bashley
Previous clubs include: Salisbury C - September 1999, Southampton.

LIGHTBODY, NATHAN　　　　　*Forward*

Current Club: Forest Green Rovers

D o B: 22/12/1981　　　　　*Birthplace: Swindon*
One of the first of many to come through Conference club Forest Green Rovers Youth/College set up. The youngster has a bright future in the game as a striker, although he has adapted well to a wide right position.

LIGHTBOWN, GRAHAM　　　　*Forward*

Current Club: Great Harwood Town

Birthplace: Lancashire
Previous clubs include: Bamber Bridge - July 2000, Great Harwood T.

LIGHTFOOT, CHRIS　　　　*Defender*

Current Club: Runcorn FC Halton

D o B: 01/04/1970　　　　　*Birthplace: Penketh*
Midfielder or defender with loads of experience. Signed for UniBond Premier side Runcorn FC Halton in July 2002 from Morecambe. Had joined the Conference club from Crewe Alexandra in the summer of 2001. Previous clubs include Chester City, (when in the Football League) and Wigan Athletic. Made a Wembley appearance in a play-off final with Crewe. Nearly 500 Football League appearances during 10 goals.

LIGHTWOOD, DEAN　　　　*Goalkeeper*

Current Club: Eastbourne Borough

Birthplace: Sussex
Arrived at Priory Lane during the 1999/00 Sussex County League championship-winning season from Saltdean United (Sussex County League). Previously with Newhaven, Shoreham and Ringmer (all Sussex County League), and Lewes.

LILLIS, ADAM　　　　*Forward*

Current Club: Witton Albion

Birthplace: Manchester
Previous clubs include: Caernarfon T - January 2002, Stockport Co.

LILLIS, JASON　　　　*Forward*

Current Club: Horsham

D o B: 01/10/1969　　　　　*Birthplace: Chatham*
Extensive Football League experience with Gillingham, Cambridge and Maidstone as well as playing for Dover, Sittingbourne, Chatham and Maidstone Invicta (also acted as manager for the last-named club): has additionally spent time in Finland and Hungary: joined Horsham in August 2001.

LIMA, CRAIG　　　　*Midfielder*

Current Club: Merthyr Tydfil

Birthplace: Wales
Honours won: Wales Semi-Pro Int.
Originally signed for Merthyr Tydfil from Maesteg Park before leaving to join Newport County. Returned to Penydarren Park from Newport County in September 1999 for a fee of £5,000. Talented midfielder who is a Welsh semi-professional international.

LIMBER, NICKY　　　　*Defender*

Current Club: Frickley Athletic

D o B: 23/01/1974　　　　　*Birthplace: Doncaster*
Previous clubs include: Gainsborough Trinity - July 2001, Weymouth, Doncaster R, Manchester C, Doncaster R.

LIMBERT, MARC　　　　*Midfielder*

Current Club: Colwyn Bay

D o B: 03/10/1973　　　　　*Birthplace: Liverpool*
Old fashioned-type winger who was signed from Altrincham in July 1997 after previously being with League of Wales outfit Connahs Quay Nomads. He started his career as a trainee at Everton and then played 14 League games for Chester City prior to joining Connahs Quay.

LIN, PAUL　　　　*Defender*

Current Club: Hyde United

Birthplace: Preston
Fast and skilful left back who signed for UniBond Premier side in August 2002 from relegated Bamber Bridge. Had been with Brig since the summer of 2000 after being released by Preston.

LINDEGAARD, ANDY　　　　*Midfielder*

Current Club: Yeovil Town

D o B: 10/09/1980　　　　　*Birthplace: Yeovil*
Honours won: FA Trophy Winners
Andys early career was spent as either a wing back or a full back, but since being drafted into the Yeovil Town first team by fomer manager Dave Webb in the latter half of the 2000/01 season he proved equally adept as a wide midfielder. He is a product of the clubs youth team development and is currently the only Yeovil-born player in the first team squad. He was part of the reserve team squad that lifted the Les Phillips Cup in May 1999, and will be remembered by all who travelled to Paulton for collecting a golf-ball sized bruise on his forehead following a collision during the game. Andy is a student and a keen cricketer who represented the club with the bat and ball in the summer of 1999, as part of an Erection 2000 fund-raising day. He made his full Conference debut for Yeovil against Doncaster at Belle Vue on March 18th 2000, and has immediately cemented a regular place within the team, providing many assists from his pin-point corners and right-wing crosses.

LINDLEY, JAMES　　　　*Goalkeeper*

Current Club: Gresley Rovers

D o B: 23/07/1981　　　　　*Birthplace: Sutton-in-Ashfield*
A highly-promising goalkeeper, James came on a months loan to Gresley Rovers from Notts County in February 2001 which was extended until the end of the season. Unfortunately, James got injured against Cirencester which ended his season. However he returned to Rovers to fight for the first team jersey. Signed permanently in August 2001 after being released by Notts County, but again suffered from injury.

LINDLEY, PHIL　　　　*Midfielder*

Current Club: Bradford Park Avenue

Birthplace: Doncaster
Promising young midfield player who signed for UniBond Premier side Bradford Park Avenue from local football in Doncaster early in the 2000/01 season. Has spent time away on-loan but is now considered a first-team regular at PA.

LINDSAY, ALISTAIR　　　　*Defender*

Current Club: Leigh RMI

D o B: 11/12/1982　　　　　*Birthplace: Wigan*
From Youth team.

LINDSAY, DALE　　　　*Forward*

Current Club: Redhill

Birthplace: Sussex
Diminutive player who has broken into the first team this season. His size deceives opponents into thinking he won't be too hard to handle. But has a extensive array of tricks up his sleeve and has already caused concerns for some experienced defenders.

LINDSAY, STUART — Goalkeeper
Current Club: Trafford
D o B: 05/08/1980 — Birthplace: Lanark
Previous clubs include: Abbey Hey - January 2000, Flixton, Ashton Utd.

LINDSEY, SCOTT — Midfielder
Current Club: Folkestone Invicta
D o B: 04/05/1972 — Birthplace: Walsall
An experienced and well-travelled midfielder who joined Dr Martens Premier side Folkestone Invicta from Kent neighbours Welling United in July 2002. Played League football with Scunthorpe and Gillingham and Conference football with Stafford Rangers. Has also seen service with Bridlington Town, Sutton Coldfield Town, Tamworth, Burton Albion, Goole Town, Canvey Island, Ashford Town and Gravesend.

LINE, PAUL — Midfielder
Current Club: Bridgnorth Town
D o B: 25/05/1975 — Birthplace: Bridgnorth
Previous clubs include: Oswestry T - November 2001, Newtown, Stafford R, Farmingville (USA), Stafford R, Bridgnorth T.

LING, ANDY — Defender
Current Club: Sutton Coldfield Town
Previous clubs include: Wolverhampton Wanderers - July 1988, Leicester C (Trainee).

LING, MARTIN — Midfielder
Current Club: Purfleet
D o B: 15/07/1966 — Birthplace: West Ham
Previous clubs include: Leyton Orient - December 2000, Brighton, Leyton Orient, Swindon T, Mansfield T, Southend Utd, Swindon T, Exeter C.

LING, RUSSELL — Goalkeeper
Current Club: Cheshunt
Birthplace: Essex
Previous clubs include: Leyton Pennant - August 2002, Potters Bar T, Boreham Wood, Potters Bar T, Cheshunt, Harlow T.

LINGER, PAUL — Midfielder
Current Club: Purfleet
D o B: 20/12/1974 — Birthplace: Stepney
Previous clubs include: Billericay T - July 2001, Welling Utd, Brighton, Leyton Orient, Charlton Ath.

LINIGHAN, BRIAN — Defender
Current Club: Worksop Town
D o B: 02/11/1973 — Birthplace: Hartlepool
Previous clubs include: Gainsborough Trinity - December 2001, Hallam, Bury, Sheffield Wednesday.

LINTON, PAUL — Forward
Current Club: Halesowen Harriers
Birthplace: Worcestershire
Previous clubs include: Feckenham T - December 2000.

LIPPIATT, MARK — Defender
Current Club: Almondsbury Town
Birthplace: Bristol
Previous clubs include: Hallen - January 2002, Oldland, Yate T, Paulton R, Yate T.

LISK, MARK — Defender
Current Club: Bashley
D o B: 27/04/1973 — Birthplace: Hampshire
A wing-back, Mark has a great engine with endless energy which enables him to get up and down the left side at will. Good in the tackle and has the ability to deliver good crosses. Re-joined Dr Martens Eastern Division club Bashley in July 2002 from Basingstoke Town. Had signed for the Ryman Leaguers in the summer of 1998 from Dorchester Town, and he previously played for Eastleigh and AFC Lymington.

LISS, KARL — Midfielder
Current Club: Newport Isle Of Wight
Previous clubs include: Gosport Borough - July 1998.

LITCHFIELD, ADAM — Midfielder
Current Club: Shepshed Dynamo
D o B: 07/11/1980 — Birthplace: Leicester
Leicester-born midfielder who came through Dr Martens Western club Bedworth United's youth ranks. Switched to rivals Shepshed Dynamo in the summer of 2001 and became a regular in the senior side.

LITTLE, ANDY — Goalkeeper
Current Club: Crawley Town
Birthplace: London
Previously with Sutton United and made his Crawley debut in October 1999: also represented the Southern League in their 3-3 draw with an FA XI during November 2001.

LITTLE, JAMIE — Defender
Current Club: Garforth Town
D o B: 12/06/1976 — Birthplace: Yorkshire
Joined last season after several successful years at Yorkshire Amateurs and previously Farsley Celtic. His leadership qualities have elevated him to 1st Team captain. Fine defensive player who reads the game well. Very good on the ball.

LITTLE, PADDY — Defender
Current Club: Blyth Spartans
Birthplace: Newcastle
Signed for Blyth Spartans during summer of 2000, from Jarrow Roofing. Previous clubs include Leeds Utd, Cambridge Utd, Seaham. Paddy has become a free kick specialist, finding the net on a number of occasions.

LITTLEWOOD, GLEN — Midfielder
Current Club: Tadcaster Albion
Birthplace: Yorkshire
Previous clubs include: Selby T - July 2001, Tadcaster Alb.

LIVERMORE, DENIS — Midfielder
Current Club: Whitley Bay
Birthplace: Newcastle
Previous clubs include: Percy Main - July 1999.

LIVERMORE, ROB — Midfielder
Current Club: Whitley Bay
Birthplace: Newcastle
Brother of Denis, Rob was also signed from Percy Main. Like Denis he also doesnt know when to give up. Has great skill on the ball.

L

LIVETT, SIMON — Midfielder
Current Club: Ford United
D o B: 08/01/1969 — Birthplace: Newham
Honours won: Ryman League Div.One Winners
Experienced midfielder who started his career with West Ham and had spells with Leyton Orient and Cambridge United before joining Southend in July 1999 where he finally made his League debut. Played 23 times in the League before Conference stints at Dover Athletic and Boston United followed. Had a short spell in the USA before signing for Ford United in December 2001 and helping the club to win the Ryman Division One title.

LLOYD, ANDREW — Midfielder
Current Club: Carmarthen Town
D o B: 15/04/1984 — Birthplace: Wales
From Youth team.

LLOYD, CARL — Midfielder
Current Club: Littlehampton Town
Birthplace: Sussex
Former Bognor youth performer: hard-working midfielder who is something of a set piece specialist: joined Littlehampton from East Preston in 1999: signed for Wick during the 2001 close season before returning to the Marigolds in October.

LLOYD, DAVID — Defender
Current Club: Winsford United
Birthplace: Cheshire
Defender who joined the Blues after being released by Chester City. Dangerous in dead ball situations.

LLOYD, GARY — Defender
Current Club: Barry Town
D o B: 26/03/1972 — Birthplace: Llanelli
Honours won: Wales u-21 & B Int.
Previous clubs include: Llanelli - July 1995, Inter Cardiff.

LLOYD, PAUL — Defender
Current Club: Bromsgrove Rovers
Birthplace: Worcestershire
From Youth team.

LLOYD, SPENCER — Midfielder
Current Club: Hednesford Town
Birthplace: Birmingham
Another product of Hednesford Town's youth programme, Spenner is a tough-tackling midfielder that always gives 100%. Spencer was a well respected team captain during the clubs first season in the Nationwide Conference PASE league.

LLOYD-WILLIAMS, MARC — Forward
Current Club: Southport
D o B: 08/02/1973 — Birthplace: Bangor
Honours won: Wales B & Semi-Pro Int.
Wales B and semi-pro international striker who joined Conference club Southport in July 2002 from League of Wales side Bangor City. Had returned to Bangor in January 2001 after League spells with Halifax and York. The talented striker has also played for Stockport, was a Welsh Cup winner in his last spell with City in 1998 and helped Wales to win the UniBond Four Nations tournament in May 2002.

LOCK, DEAN — Midfielder
Current Club: Whyteleafe
Previous clubs include: Addington - July 2000.

LOCK, KEVIN — Forward
Current Club: Banstead Athletic
D o B: 29/05/1982 — Birthplace: Surrey
A leading goalscorer for Whyteleafe youth where his form took him to Fulham under-17s for a season. Joined Carshalton Athletic in July 1998 where he played in the youth, reserves and first teams while only 17. Became an established member of the Robins senior squad before switching to rival Ryman Division One South side Banstead Athletic in August 2002.

LOCK, TONY — Forward
Current Club: Grays Athletic
D o B: 03/09/1976 — Birthplace: Harlow
Powerful full of running attacker, he joined from Dagenham following a successful loan spell. Has also played for Colchester United.

LOCKE, CLIVE — Defender
Current Club: Warrington Town
Birthplace: Cheshire
Previous clubs include: Squires Gate - July 2001.

LOCKE, STUART — Defender
Current Club: Droylsden
Birthplace: Manchester
Honours won: Conference Winners
Experienced defender who has a Conference winners medal to his name. Signed for UniBond Premier side Droylsden in August 2002 from rivals Accrington Stanley. Started out at Manchester City and then played for many years in the Conference with Northwich Victoria, Stalybridge Celtic, Macclesfield, where he won his winners medal, and Leigh RMI. Joined Stanley after a second spell at Stalybridge in September 2001.

LOCKER, STEVE — Defender
Current Club: Whitley Bay
D o B: 05/11/1970 — Birthplace: Ashington
This is Steves second spell at the club. A very experienced player he signed from Bedlington Terriers. Has also played at Blyth Spartans.

LOCKEY, RICHARD — Goalkeeper
Current Club: Holmer Green
Birthplace: Bucks
Previous clubs include: Penn & Tylers Green - July 1996, Holmer Green, Chalfont St.Peter, Windsor & Eton.

LOCKHART, JON — Forward
Current Club: Peacehaven & Telscombe
Birthplace: Brighton
Excellent striker who was originally on the books of Brighton & Hove Albion. Leading scorer for Peacehaven in 1996/97 and 1997/98. Top marksman for Lewes in 1998/99 before returning to his old club the following season (struck 15 times).

LOCKHART, STEVE — Midfielder
Current Club: Burnham
Birthplace: Slough
Steve has recently returned after a brief spell away from senior football. Local lad whose creative skills in midfield are an asset to the team.

LOCKIER, MARCUS   *Defender*
Current Club: Newtown AFC

Birthplace: Wales

Young defender who has joined the club from Shawbury. Is keen to establish himself in the starting line-up. has shown good maturity in pre-season gamesand the initial league fixtures. Son of Dereck Lockier who was an influential player in the Mid-Wales League with Welshpool and then the Robins.

LOCKWOOD, ADAM   *Defender*
Current Club: Yeovil Town

D o B: 26/10/1981   Birthplace: Wakefield
Honours won: England Semi-Pro Int., FA Trophy Winners
Adam joined Yeovil Town in Tuesday September 2001, initially on a one month loan deal from Nationwide League side Reading. The right-back, who is also equally happy as a central defender, spent his schoolboy years as part of the Leeds United Academy set-up but in March 1999 was offered a professional contract with Reading. The six foot tall defender worked under former Glovers Kevin Dillon and Alan Pardew at the Berkshire club, but could not force a place in the first team. As a result he went on loan to Conference side Forest Green Rovers and was part of their team who played in the FA Trophy Final in the 2000/01 season. Following a successful one month loan with the Glovers, which saw him make his Jubal at Edgar Street against Hereford United on 18th September 2001, Adam signed a two and a half year deal at Huish Park on Monday 15th October 2001. His early form has seen him grab the right-back slot on a near permanent basis and settle quickly into Yeovil Town's back-four line-up. Gained international recognition in the UniBond Four Nations tournament in May 2002.

LODGE, ANDY   *Defender*
Current Club: Boston United

Birthplace: Whittlesey
Signed in January 2000 from Stamford AFC. The player he most admires is Ryan Giggs. Away from football he likes playing snooker and pool and watching boxing.

LODGE, DAVE   *Defender*
Current Club: Tiptree United

Birthplace: Essex
Previous clubs include: Marconi - July 1999, East London University.

LOFT, SHAUN   *Forward*
Current Club: Dartford

Birthplace: Hastings
Leading marksman for Rye & Iden United during their 2000/01 Division Three championship-winning season, scoring 16 goals after joining them midway through the campaign from St Leonards (for whom he had struck 5 times), and was again top marksman in 2001/02. Had spent the previous year at Hastings Town, having played for Sidley United earlier in his career. Switched to Dr Martens Eastern side Dartford in July 2002.

LOGAN, DAVID   *Defender*
Current Club: Whitby Town

D o B: 05/12/1963   Birthplace: Middlesbrough
Honours won: FA Vase Winners
Vastly experienced defender who returned to Whitby Town after originally starting his career with the club in 1982 before joining Mansfield Town. Previous clubs include Northampton, Halifax, Stockport County, Scarborough, Northallerton and Bishop Auckland. Scorer of the opening goal in the FA Vase final. Vase winners medal 96/97. Voted Players' Player of the Year & Supporters' Player of the Year for 1996/97. UniBond First Division Championship medal 97/98. Season 99-00 saw David voted both Players' Player of the Year and Supporters' Player of the Year & as well as contributing 15 goals. He gets better with age.

LOMAS, COLIN   *Midfielder*
Current Club: Atherton Laburnum Rovers

Birthplace: Manchester
Colin came to LR in February 2001 and wasted no time finding the net, scoring twice on his debut. He is a terrific player in the centre of the park and is not afraid to have a shot at goal.

LOMAS, JAMES   *Midfielder*
Current Club: Matlock Town

D o B: 18/10/1977   Birthplace: Chesterfield
Previous clubs include: Mansfield T - August 2001, Chesterfield.

LONEY, BEN   *Midfielder*
Current Club: Walton & Hersham

Birthplace: Surrey
Talented young midfield player who joined Ryman Division One South side Walton & Hersham from rivals Molesey in August 2002. Began his playing days with Leatherhead before switching to the Moles in March 2000.

LONG, VINNIE   *Forward*
Current Club: Mildenhall Town

Birthplace: Cambridgeshire
Previous clubs include: Newmarket T - July 2001.

LONGDEN, ADAM   *Midfielder*
Current Club: Stocksbridge Park Steels

Previous clubs include: Denaby Utd - December 1999, Worksop T, Canvey Island, Leyton Orient, Thetford T, Bury T, Thetford T, RAF, Cambridge Utd.

LONGDIN, GRAHAM   *Defender*
Current Club: Hamble ASSC

Birthplace: Hampshire
Previous clubs include: AFC Totton - July 1999, BAT Sports, Bashley.

LONGHURST, RON   *Defender*
Current Club: Eastbourne Borough

Birthplace: London
Defender who signed for Dr Martens Eastern side Eastbourne Borough in April 2002 from Sussex County League side Wealdon who he had joined following a brief spell out of the game. A former YTS trainee with Brentford, Rob has Ryman Premier Divison experience with Hampton & Richmond Borough and was also on the books of Walton & Hersham.

LONGLEY, DARREN   *Forward*
Current Club: Ringmer

Birthplace: Sussex
Veteran striker and top scorer for Crowborough in 1993/94 and 1994/95. Has also played for Lewes in his time. Left Ringmer during September 1999 to join Saltdean but returned to Crowborough in February 2001 (scored 9 times, but was unable to save them from relegation to Division Three). Came back to Ringmer in August 2001.

LONNEN, MATT   *Midfielder*
Current Club: Dorchester Town

D o B: 30/01/1977   Birthplace: Bournemouth
Previous clubs include: Bournemouth Poppies - July 2000, Dorchester T.

LOOMES, JODY — Forward

Current Club: Enfield

Previous clubs include: Cheshunt - August 2001, Harlow T, Cambridge Utd, Leyton Orient (Trainee).

LOPEZ, WES — Midfielder

Current Club: Worthing

Birthplace: Sussex

Highly promising left sided midfielder: played for Glen Geard at Steyning (1999/2000) and Ringmer (2000/01, scored five times): also represented Sussex Schools U-19 B team that year and a member of the Sussex U-21 squad for 2001/02 : signed for Worthing in November 2001 and struck on his debut against Carshalton.

LORAM, MARK — Midfielder

Current Club: Taunton Town

D o B: 13/08/1967   Birthplace: Paignton

Honours won: FA Vase Winners

Previous clubs include: Elmore - July 1997, Mangotsfield Utd, Yate T, Minehead, Torquay Utd, Yate T, Torquay Utd, QPR, Torquay Utd, Brixham Villa.

LORD, MARK — Midfielder

Current Club: Barking & East Ham United

D o B: 05/12/1966   Birthplace: Nahuuli

Vastly experienced left-sided midfield player who is in his second spell with Barking having re-joined in February 2001 from Ford United. Has played for most of the senior Essex Non-League sides, including East Thurrock United, Aveley, Collier Row and Leyton. Is also assistant-manager at Barking & East Ham United.

LORMOR, TONY — Forward

Current Club: Telford United

D o B: 29/10/1970   Birthplace: Ashington

Big, strong and much-travelled centre forward who signed for Conference side Telford United on the eve of the 2002/03 season after being released by Hartlepool. Played over 350 League games and scored more than 120 times during a professional career that started at Newcastle and included spells at Lincoln, Peterborough, Chesterfield, Preston, Mansfield and Hartlepool.

LORRAINE, PAUL — Defender

Current Club: Welling United

Birthplace: Kent

Highly-promising central defender or full back who is a product of Welling United's successful youth system. Signed a professional contract during the 2000/01 season at the age of 17 after breaking into the first-team squad.

LOSS, COLIN — Midfielder

Current Club: Rhayader Town

D o B: 15/08/1973   Birthplace: Brentwood

Experienced Midfielder signed from Merthyr Tydfil in August 2001. Previously a trainee with Norwich City before spells at Derby County, Gresley Rovers and Bristol City. Classy midfield playmaker, superb distribution and shooting. Not afraid to put his foot in.

LOVATT, CRAIG — Midfielder

Current Club: Stafford Rangers

D o B: 16/11/1978   Birthplace: Stoke

A highly-rated attacking midfield player, Craig joined Stafford Rangers in October 2000, having previously played for three other Staffordshire clubs Kidsgrove, Leek and Hanford. At Kidsgrove he was a member of their successful 1997/98 side.

LOVE, JOHN — Defender

Current Club: Ramsgate

Birthplace: Kent

Previous clubs include: Margate - July 1995, Ramsgate, Herne Bay, Thanet Utd, Ramsgate.

LOVE, MICKEY — Defender

Current Club: Nuneaton Borough

Birthplace: Stockport

A left sided player who has the ability to operate as a wing back or even in a deeper role. Mickey came to Nuneaton Borough as the first pre-season signing Of 2000 under the Bosman ruling from Stevenage Borough. With Football League experience with Wigan Athletic, the Burbage-based player began his career at Hinckley Town.

LOVELL, DANNY — Defender

Current Club: Romford

Birthplace: Essex

Previous clubs include: Aveley - August 2001, Barkingside.

LOVELL, DAVID — Goalkeeper

Current Club: Aylesbury United

Previous clubs include: Barnet - November 2000, Tottenham Hotspur.

LOVELOCK, ANDY — Forward

Current Club: Solihull Borough

D o B: 20/12/1976   Birthplace: Swindon

Swindon-born Andy signed from then-Conference side Altrincham in the summer of 2000 after playing for them in the 1999/2000 season. He was one of the first players to be taken on at Lilleshall and spent 3 years at Coventry City as a trainee he has also played for Crewe Alexandra.

LOVERIDGE, LEE — Defender

Current Club: VCD Athletic

D o B: 03/01/1980   Birthplace: Orpington

From Youth team.

LOVETT, MATTHEW — Goalkeeper

Current Club: Staines Town

D o B: 05/09/1979   Birthplace: Middlesex

Highly-rated goalkeeper who became the first ever Staines Town player to work his way right through the junior system in which he started as an 8-year-old. Played his first senior game against Bognor Regis Town in April 1996 and in 1997 secured a unique double by gaining Middlesex Senior Cup and Middlesex Youth Cup winners medals in the same season. He has attracted the attention of clubs at a higher level and has made over 600 appearances at all levels for the club. Collected two player of the year awards for 2001/02.

LOVETT, NICK — Midfielder

Current Club: Pelsall Villa

Birthplace: Birmingham

Previous clubs include: Wednesfield - July 1998, Pelsall Villa, Rushall Olympic, Pelsall Villa.

LOW, ASHLEY — Defender

Current Club: Hassocks

Birthplace: Sussex

Quiet man of the team who lets his performances on the pitch do the talking: at home in any position across the back four: returned as a regular member of the starting line-up in March 2001, having only made limited appearances for the previous five months.

LOW, STEVE — *Midfielder*
Current Club: Mildenhall Town

Birthplace: Cambridge
Previous clubs include: Soham Town Rangers - July 1997, Cambridge C.

LOWE, DEAN — *Goalkeeper*
Current Club: Borrowash Victoria

Birthplace: Nottingham
Previous clubs include: Matlock T - July 1998, Borrowash V, Heanor T, Borrowash V, Priory Eastwood.

LOWE, MARC — *Defender*
Current Club: Ipswich Wanderers

Birthplace: Suffolk
Previous clubs include: East Bergholt - August 2000.

LOWE, MATTHEW — *Goalkeeper*
Current Club: Bromsgrove Rovers

D o B: 25/02/1974   Birthplace: Birmingham
Previous clubs include: Blakenall - June 2001, Stourbridge, Worcester C, Torquay Utd.

LOWE, PAUL — *Defender*
Current Club: Berkhamsted Town

Birthplace: Wycombe
Previous clubs include: Hemel Hempstead - July 1993, St.Albans C, Chesham Utd.

LOWERY, DARREN — *Midfielder*
Current Club: Selsey

Birthplace: Sussex
Strong, admirable type who signed from Portsmouth Royal Navy during Mick Marshs spell in charge of Selsey during 1999. Previous clubs include Gosport, Fareham and Eastleigh, he can either play in a central position or up front (scored 19 times during 1999/2000 and six the year after). Sidelined with injury throughout the first half of 2001/02.

LOWES, BRENDAN — *Midfielder*
Current Club: Thornaby on Tees

Birthplace: Co.Durham
Previous clubs include: Billingham Synthonia - December 2001.

LOWRIE, TONY — *Midfielder*
Current Club: Morpeth Town

Birthplace: Newcastle
Previous clubs include: Walker Central - July 1998.

LOWTHORPE, ADAM — *Defender*
Current Club: North Ferriby United

D o B: 07/08/1975   Birthplace: Hull
Released as a professional by Hull City in 1998, Adam is a solid and reliable defender who signed for North Ferriby United from Gainsborough Trinity in March 1999.

LOYDEN, EDDIE — *Forward*
Current Club: Glasshoughton Welfare

Birthplace: Yorkshire
Previous clubs include: Pontefract Collieries - February 2001, Goole AFC, Pontefract Collieries, Goole T, Glasshoughton Welfare, Hatfield Main, Ossett T, Glasshoughton Welfare, Ossett T, Grimethorpe MW, Pontefract Collieries, Ossett Alb., Woolley MW.

LOYDEN, GARETH — *Midfielder*
Current Club: Mangotsfield United

D o B: 23/03/1978   Birthplace: Hereford
Honours won: Wales Youth Int.
Ex-Bristol City professional and Welsh under-19 international who signed for Mangotsfield United from Bath City during the 1998/99 season. The engine room of the side, he was the Players' Player of the Year in 1999/00. Another dead ball expert.

LUCAS, ANDY — *Forward*
Current Club: Hinckley United

D o B: 12/09/1972   Birthplace: Nuneaton
Honours won: Dr Martens League Western Div.Winners
Andy joined Hinckley United in the summer of 2000 from Shepshed Dynamo. He was previously with Barwell where his prolific goalscoring earned him the Midland Alliance Golden Boot in 1998-99. Carried on this goalscoring run keeping his strike rate above 50% for the season 2000-01. He was also the unofficial top scorer in the FA Cup for 2000/01with 9 goals. Though, they were all scored before the First Round Proper and so are not recorded as Official. Won a Dr Martens Western Division championship medal with Hinckley United in 2000/01.

LUCAS, RICHARD — *Defender*
Current Club: Hednesford Town

D o B: 22/09/1970   Birthplace: Sheffield
A left sided defender or midfielder, Richard signed for Boston United from Halifax Town in the close season of 2000. Since starting out as a trainee with Sheffield United, he has made over 200 League appearances, for a variety of clubs, scoring 23 goals. Switched to Hednesford in June 2001.

LUCAS, TREVOR — *Midfielder*
Current Club: Walton Casuals

Birthplace: Surrey
Trevor rejoined Casuals in January 2002 for his second spell at the club, part of our League Cup winning squad. Previous clubs include Staines, Chessington & Hook and Feltham.

LUCKETT, COLIN — *Defender*
Current Club: Bromley

D o B: 19/01/1976   Birthplace: London
Honours won: FA Trophy Winners, Ryman League Premier Div.Winners
Very experienced midfielder who has an FA Trophy and Ryman League winners medals to his name whilst with Kingstonian. Joined Bromley in June 2002 after a spell with Dr Martens Eastern side Fisher Athletic, whom he has signed for in December 2001 following a stint at Stevenage Borough. Began his career with Millwall.

LUCKHURST, DAVID — *Midfielder*
Current Club: Diss Town

Birthplace: Norwich
Previous clubs include: Attleborough T - July 2000.

LUDDEN, DOMINIC — *Defender*
Current Club: Leigh RMI

D o B: 30/03/1974   Birthplace: Basildon
Honours won: England Schoolboy Int.
Basildon-born defender who represented England Schoolboys whilst at Leyton Orient. Went on to make around 60 first-team appearances at Brisbane Road before being signed by Watford for £100,000 in August 1994. Spells at Preston and Halifax followed before he signed for Conference side Leigh RMI in August 2002.

LUDLAM, CRAIG   *Defender*

Current Club: Stocksbridge Park Steels

D o B: 08/11/1976   Birthplace: Sheffield

Previous clubs include: Stafford Rangers - August 2001, Hucknall T, Ilkeston T, Matlock T, Sheffield Wednesday.

LUDLAM, RYAN   *Defender*

Current Club: Worksop Town

D o B: 12/05/1979   Birthplace: Carlisle

Previous clubs include: Sheffield Utd - July 1999.

LUDLOW, LEE   *Forward*

Current Club: Durham City

D o B: 14/03/1976   Birthplace: Newcastle

Previous clubs include: Whitby T - July 2001, Bedlington Terriers, RTM Newcastle, Whitley Bay, Spennymoor Utd, Berwick R, Halifax T, Notts Co.

LUKE, PAUL   *Defender*

Current Club: Haverfordwest County

D o B: 06/11/1982   Birthplace: Wales

From Youth team.

LUKIC, JAMES   *Defender*

Current Club: Matlock Town

Birthplace: Sheffield

Still only 20-year-old, James is in his fourth season at Matlock. A stylish, accomplished defender who should go far in the game. His uncle is former Arsenal and Leeds goalkeeper John Lukic.

LUNAN, JAMES   *Goalkeeper*

Current Club: Grays Athletic

Birthplace: Essex

Young keeper signed this season from Southend United, he is a steady custodian with a huge kick and bets have been laid as to if he will score a goal this season.

LUND, NICOLAJ   *Midfielder*

Current Club: Harrow Borough

D o B: 04/10/1976   Birthplace: Fodselsdato, Denmark

Previous clubs include: Gombak Utd (Singapore) - February 2002, FC Fredericia (Denmark), Harrow B, Trelde (Denmark), Fredericia KFUM (Denmark).

LUNN, STEVE   *Forward*

Current Club: Dorking

Birthplace: Surrey

Previous clubs include: Whyteleafe - August 2001, Leatherhead, Whyteleafe, Carshalton Ath., Dorking, Sutton Utd, Dorking, Walton & Hersham, Dorking, Leatherhead.

LUNT, GARY   *Midfielder*

Current Club: Runcorn FC Halton

Birthplace: Liverpool

Joined the Linnets during the 2000/2001 season after being released by Crewe Alexandra. Preferred as a midfielder by the Runcorn management, although fans think that he is more of an out and out striker. Lunty scored some memorable goals towards the end of last season, and hit his first hat-trick for Runcorn this season in the 4-2 FA Cup win at Gateshead.

LUNT, IAN   *Forward*

Current Club: Kendal Town

D o B: 25/09/1963   Birthplace: Manchester

Previous clubs include: Radcliffe Borough - March 2002, Salford C, Radcliffe B, Stalybridge Celtic, Radcliffe B, Curzon Ashton, Droylsden, Curzon Ashton, Winsford Utd, Witton Alb., Altrincham.

LUSH, DARREN   *Defender*

Current Club: Bemerton Heath Harlequins

Birthplace: Hampshire

Previous clubs include: Salisbury C - July 2001, Havant & Waterlooville, Trowbridge T, Bemerton Heath Harlequins, Salisbury C, Hereford Utd, AFC Bournemouth.

LUTWYCHE, ANDY   *Defender*

Current Club: Burgess Hill Town

Birthplace: Sussex

Solid workhorse defender: joined from Shoreham in 1999 and had previously played for Worthing: member of the Sussex representative team in both 1999/2000 and 2000/01: also a Sussex League cricketer.

LUTZ, STEVE   *Forward*

Current Club: Evesham United

Previous clubs include: Worcester C - July 2001, Pershore T, Worcester C, Hednesford T, Birmingham C.

LWANDO, BRUCE   *Forward*

Current Club: Atherstone United

Birthplace: Wolverhampton

Previous clubs include: Fulham - October 2001.

LYDON, JOHN   *Midfielder*

Current Club: Bishop Auckland

Birthplace: Bishop Auckland

Wide midfielder who made his Bishop Auckland debut as an impressive substitute at Bradford Park Avenue in September. Signed from West Auckland.

LYE, DANNY   *Midfielder*

Current Club: Gravesend & Northfleet

Birthplace: Kent

Danny was plucked from local football at Bearsted by Gravesend & Northfleet manager Andy Ford at the beginning of the 2001/02 season. He proved a real success story with a regular first-team place and performances befitting a seasoned Non-League player. He plays the game easily, has vision and is very comfortable with the ball.

LYNCH, ANDY   *Forward*

Current Club: Eastbourne United

Birthplace: Sussex

Forward who signed for Eastbourne United from Bexhill in August 2001: impressed for the reserves before scoring his first-team debut in the RUR Cup defeat of Storrington during August 2001.

LYNCH, ANTHONY   *Forward*

Current Club: Tiverton Town

D o B: 28/08/1975   Birthplace: Devon

Honours won: FA Vase Winners

Joined Tiverton Town from Taunton Town in May 2001. A prolific goalscorer i the Western League with over a 180 in three seasons, he settled very well since his move and proved, after a slow start, that he could score goals at the higher level. Won a FA Vase winners medal with Taunton before joining Tivvy.

LYNCH, CHRIS — *Defender*

Current Club: Spennymoor United

D o B: 18/11/1974   *Birthplace: Middlesbrough*
Previous clubs include: Gateshead - August 2001, Bishop Auckland, Hartlepool Utd, Halifax T.

LYNCH, GORDON — *Defender*

Current Club: Bromsgrove Rovers

Birthplace: Birmingham
Previous clubs include: Stourbridge - August 2001, Willenhall T, Solihull B.

LYNCH, KEVIN — *Midfielder*

Current Club: Vauxhall Motors

D o B: 01/07/1975   *Birthplace: Liverpool*
A midfielder who has never heard of a lost cause. Can also operate to good effect as a central defender. Previously with Prescot Cables, his versatility makes Kevin a very useful player to have on the books as he can operate with equal effectiveness in midfield or defence. Scored a number of important goals for the club since joining in May 2000.

LYNCH, PAUL — *Defender*

Current Club: Rossendale United

Birthplace: Lancashire
An experienced Non-League defender who has been around the Lancashire scene for a number of years. Started out at Darwen and then had spells with Clitheroe, Great Harwood Town, Accrington Stanley and Kendal Town before joining Rossendale United in the summer of 2000 and he helped the club to promotion to the UniBond at the end of that season.

LYNN, MATT — *Midfielder*

Current Club: Brook House

Birthplace: Middlesex
Previous clubs include: Ruislip Manor - July 2000.

LYONS, ANDY — *Midfielder*

Current Club: Lancaster City

D o B: 19/10/1966   *Birthplace: Blackpool*
Left-sided player Andy eventually joined Lancaster City, who tried to sign him as early as 1990, at the start of the 2001/02 season. Originally with Morecambe, he then had spells with Fleetwood Town, Crewe and Wigan, where he played League football, Scottish sides Partick Thistle and Ayr United and then in the Conference with Morecambe again before joining City.

LYONS, MICKEY — *Forward*

Current Club: Mickleover Sports

D o B: 24/06/1981   *Birthplace: Derby*
Honours won: England Schoolboy Int.
Previous clubs include: Shepshed Dynamo - March 2002, Loughborough University, Derby Co.

LYONS, PAT — *Midfielder*

Current Club: Worcester City

Birthplace: Derby
Midfielder Pat was previously with Derby County who joined Burton Albion in 1996/97 and made over 150 first team outings for the Brewers. A full time football coach at Derby County, he made his debut for the Brewers at Sudbury Town in April 1997. A consistent performer, he actually signed for Burton after a short spell at West Brom and helped the Eton Park club to lift the UniBond League championship before transferring to Worcester City in May 2002.

LYONS, STEVE — *Midfielder*

Current Club: Stafford Town

Birthplace: Stafford
Previous clubs include: Pelsall Villa - July 2000, Newcastle T, Stafford T.

LYTASSIA, KOLBASSIA — *Defender*

Current Club: Herne Bay

Birthplace: France
Previous clubs include: Addis - November 2001.

LYTOLLIS, PETER — *Forward*

Current Club: Brigg Town

Birthplace: Hull
From Local football - July 2000.

LYTTLE, CLIVE — *Goalkeeper*

Current Club: Basingstoke Town

Previous clubs include: Reading (Junior) - July 1998.

LYWARD, ELLIOTT — *Forward*

Current Club: Dorking

Birthplace: Surrey
Previous clubs include: Croydon Ath - January 2002.

L

THE NON-LEAGUE PAPER

ESSENTIAL READING FOR FOLLOWERS OF THE NATIONAL GAME

SHARE THE PASSION

EVERY SUNDAY

FOOTBALLER'S
N E W S L E T T E R

Autumn 2002

 ## Mulderrigs Achieve Lexcel

We are delighted to announce that Mulderrigs were awarded the Law Society's Practice Management Lexcel in July. The award is recognition of our commitment to consistently deliver a high quality service to all of our clients. We are proud of it because we are the first firm of our size in the whole of the North West to be recognised. We hope you'll notice an improvement... but we'll let you be the judge!

 ## Problems for Roy Keane

It hasn't been possible to open the sports pages over the last few weeks without reading about the infamous "Keane challenge" on Alfie Haaland. We can't comment on that case - it will be for the courts to decide the rights and wrongs of the matter, if it ever goes that far. However, here at Mulderrigs we have seen many examples of the devastation caused by deliberate dangerous challenges and wherever that kind of behaviour is proved, whether at professional or amateur level we believe the football authorities should act as swiftly and as firmly as possible.

 ## Recent Football Injury Cases at Mulderrigs

Mr G is a young professional player. He suffered a badly broken leg as a result of a foul challenge during a 1st Round FA Cup match. The incident was captured on video, which we were able to use and the other player eventually admitted that he had made a late, high challenge with studs showing; he agreed that it was a "last lunge". After all that, his insurers agreed to pay our client substantial compensation in respect of his injuries. There is also another happy ending to the story... after a long period out of the game Mr G has now been able to resume his career.

Mr M suffered a broken leg as a result of a foul challenge during a Sunday league game; he had broken through and was "one-on-one" with the keeper when he was kicked by a chasing defender who had no chance of getting the ball. The insurers for the other player refused to admit he was to blame and we had to take the case to court where our client won his case.

Mr J was asked to play in a five-a-side competition during his employers, annual "Fun Day". Unfortunately, it wasn't much fun for our client - an opponent (another employee) kicked him "up in the air" and broke his leg. The other player was sent off and because it was a company event, the employer was legally responsible and has now agreed to pay compensation to our client. All we have to do now is work out how much it should be!

Enjoy your football! - Paul Mulderrig

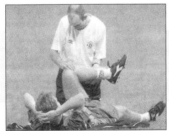

MAAMRIA, NOUREDDINE   *Forward*
Current Club: Leigh RMI

D o B: 18/02/1974   *Birthplace: Tunisia*
Honours won: Tunisia u-21 Int.

Tunisian under-21 international forward who joined Conference side Leigh RMI from rivals Southport in the summer of 2001. Played in Ireland for Glentoran and in Scotland with Ayr United before joining Doncaster Rovers in August 1998, making around 40 League appearances and then turning out in the Conference after their relegation. Switched to Southport in the summer of 2000 and he became hot property after scoring 15 times in 2001/02.

MACAULEY, CARL   *Defender*
Current Club: Burscough

Birthplace: Liverpool
Experienced defender who joined UniBond Premier side Burscough after a two-year spell with Conference outfit Southport. Started out as a youngster with Manchester City and then played for Witton Albion, Vauxhall Motors, Prescot Cables and Telford United before joining Port in the summer of 2000.

MACAULEY, DEAN   *Defender*
Current Club: Pickering Town

D o B: 20/04/1978   *Birthplace: Scarborough*
Previous clubs include: Whitby T - July 2000, Pickering T, Evesham Utd, Scarborough (Trainee).

MacDIARMID, PHIL   *Midfielder*
Current Club: Trafford

Birthplace: Liverpool
Previous clubs include: Rhyl - August 2002, Marine, Southport.

MacDONALD, CHARLIE   *Forward*
Current Club: Margate

D o B: 13/02/1981   *Birthplace: Southwark*
Promising young forward who joined Conference side Margate just after the start of the 2002/03 season from Charlton Athletic. Had come up through the ranks at The Valley and made a handful of first-team appearances in the Premiership. Also had loan spells at Cheltenham, Torquay and Colchester adding to his experience.

MACIAK, JASON   *Defender*
Current Club: Abingdon United

Birthplace: Oxford
Previous clubs include: Thame Utd - July 2000, Burnham, Witney T, Oxford Utd (Trainee).

MacINTOSH, STEWART   *Midfielder*
Current Club: Pagham

Birthplace: Sussex
Right-sided defender/midfielder: promoted to Paul Gilberts Oving team from the reserves towards the end of 1999/2000: scored 7 times for the Vikings the following season before transferring to Sidlesham for the start of 2001/02: recruited to the new-look Pagham side in December 2001.

MACKAIL-SMITH, CRAIG   *Midfielder*
Current Club: St.Albans City

D o B: 25/02/1984   *Birthplace: Hertfordshire*
A product of Ryman Premier club St Albans City's highly-successful midweek youth team. A promising young midfielder, he made his senior debut at the end of the 2000/01 season.

MACKAY, GRAHAM   *Midfielder*
Current Club: Horsham

Birthplace: Scotland
Joined Lewes in September 2001 from Three Bridges, and annouced his arrival with two goals on his debut at Romford. Transferred to St Leonards in February 2002 but then returned to Horsham a month later.

MACKAY, SCOTT   *Midfielder*
Current Club: Barwell

Birthplace: Leicester
Previous clubs include: Leicester Utd - July 1996, Lutterworth T, Luton T (Junior).

MACKENZIE, CHRIS   *Goalkeeper*
Current Club: Nuneaton Borough

D o B: 14/05/1972   *Birthplace: Northampton*
Chris is a talented goalkeeper who began his career with Corby Town before moving to Hereford United where he spent three seasons. He made more then 60 appearances for the Bulls before joining Leyton Orient two seasons ago. He was released from the Os at the end of the 1998/99 season and signed for Nuneaton Borough where he has been a model of consistency.

MACKENZIE, JAMES   *Forward*
Current Club: Oswestry Town

Birthplace: Wales
At 17, the youngest member of the squad. Formerly with Wolverhampton Wanderers, the coaching staff regard James as an exciting prospect.

MACKENZIE, STUART   *Goalkeeper*
Current Club: Hampton & Richmond

D o B: 21/03/1965   *Birthplace: London*
Honours won: FA Vase Winners, Ryman League Winners

Highly-experienced goalkeeper who joined Hampton & Richmond Borough from Farnborough Town in the summer of 2001. Stuart played in the Conference for the Hampshire side and helped them to win the Ryman League title in 2000. Has also played for Yeading and won an FA Vase winners medal way back in 1990, having appeared in a losing final four years earlier with Southall.

MACKLIN, PETER   *Forward*
Current Club: Swindon Supermarine

Birthplace: Wiltshire
Previous clubs include: Bath C - November 2001.

MacKRORY, DAVE   *Forward*
Current Club: Tiptree United

Birthplace: Essex
Previous clubs include: Heybridge Swifts - July 2000, Halstead T.

MACLEAN, GRAHAM   *Forward*
Current Club: Bath City

D o B: 07/10/1981   *Birthplace: Ontario, Canada*
Honours won: Canadian Youth Int.

Former Canadian Youth international front-runner, Graham returned to Bath City during the close season of 2001 following a short spell at Clevedon Town. First made an impression at City as part of the Youth set-up during the 1999/00 season where he scored over 20 goals and also made a handful of appearances for the first team during that campaign. The Canadian-born attacker arrived in Bristol in 1999 and following a call to reserve team manager Dave Hobbs at Bath. Five goals in City's 2000 pre-season matches looked set to push Graham into a regular first team place but, despite continuing this form in the early part of the season, he found further openings limited as then former manager Paul Bodin stuck with his front line partnership of Martin Paul and Graham Colbourne. Frustrated at this disappointment he made the short switch to Clevedon Town in February 2001. However, that move didnt work out as the Bristol-based side were relegated and he jumped at the chance of moving back to City.

MACLEAN, JEFF   *Midfielder*
Current Club: Llanelli AFC
D o B: 18/07/1978   *Birthplace: Canada*
Previous clubs include: Haverfordwest Co - March 2002, Bath C, Barry T, Mangotsfield Utd, Dorchester T, Yeovil T, Backwell Utd.

MacMAHON, JOHN   *Forward*
Current Club: Oxford City
Birthplace: Oxford
Previous clubs include: Quarry Rovers - July 1998, Oxford Utd (Junior).

MacMILLAN, AARON   *Forward*
Current Club: Peacehaven & Telscombe
Birthplace: Sussex
Right-winger who graduated from Saltdeans youth side to the first-team in 2000/01 (scored 4 times that season). Made a spectacle of himself during the infamous 10-1 defeat against Whitehawk in November 2001, by demonstrating a one-man strike and refusing to play when asked to go on as a substitute. Joined Peacehaven shortly afterwards.

MacPHERSON, DAVE   *Forward*
Current Club: Leek Town
Birthplace: Stoke
A talented midfield player who joined Leek Town mid-way through the 2000/01 season from Stone Dominoes. Possesses an excellent shot.

MacPHERSON, GAVIN   *Midfielder*
Current Club: Metropolitan Police
Birthplace: Berkshire
Previous clubs include: Windsor & Eton - July 1997, Northwood, Yeading, Chesham Utd, Boreham Wood, Windsor & Eton, Aylesbury Utd, Slough T, Barnet, St.Albans C, Nottingham Forest.

MADDISON, CRAIG   *Midfielder*
Current Club: Arnold Town
Birthplace: Nottingham
Previous clubs include: Hucknall T - November 1999, Grantham T, Ilkeston T, Arnold T, Grimsby T, GPT Plessey.

MADDOCK, WAYNE   *Defender*
Current Club: Kendal Town
Previous clubs include: Accrington Stanley - July 2001, Bamber Bridge, Morecambe , Barrow, Netherfield, Marine, BAC Preston, Leyland Motors.

MADDOX, MARK   *Defender*
Current Club: Altrincham
D o B: 11/03/1973   *Birthplace: Liverpool*
Originally signed for Altrincham in August 1996 from Sunday League football, after starting his career as a trainee at Tranmere Rovers. Joined Barrow at the start of 1998/99 season but rejoined the Robins in December 1998 after being unable to establish himself in the Barrow 1st team. A consistent and reliable defender at centre back. Currently Altrinchams longest serving player.

MADDOX, ROB   *Midfielder*
Current Club: Corby Town
Birthplace: Corby
Industrious midfielder who is also capable of playing in defence. Began his playing career on the books at Northampton and then spent a period in the Eagle Bitter United Counties League with Desborough Town, then managed by his father Derek. Had a spell in the Dr Martens with Corby Town before returning to the Steelmen, his home-town club, via a second stint at Desborough.

MADGWICK, BEN   *Midfielder*
Current Club: Salisbury City
Birthplace: Merthyr Tydfil
Honours won: Wales Schoolboy & Youth Int.
Merthyr Tydfil-born 20-year-old signed in August 2001. Previously with Southampton. Represented Wales at under 15 and under 18 levels.

MADIN, LEE   *Forward*
Current Club: Hyde United
Birthplace: Liverpool
Released by Preston North End and signed for UniBond Premier side Hyde United at the end of February 2002. Very promising yung forward with an eye for goal.

MAGNUS, IAN   *Goalkeeper*
Current Club: Soham Town Rangers
Birthplace: Cambridgeshire
Previous clubs include: Somersham T - December 2001, Soham Town R, Somersham T.

MAGONA, STEVE   *Defender*
Current Club: Arlesey Town
Birthplace: Hertfordshire
Defender who re-joined Ryman Division One North side Arlesey Town in the summer of 2002 after a spell with Premier Division Enfield. Originally joined Arlesey from Ware and then played for Boreham Wood before signing for the Es in November 2000.

MAGUIRE, GARY   *Goalkeeper*
Current Club: Burscough
Birthplace: Manchester
Young goalkeeper who signed for UniBond Premier side Burscough in August 2002. Gary spent one year on a YTS with Manchester City before moving to Stockport County where he signed as a professional, twice gaining a place in the first team squad.

MAGUIRE, LEE   *Midfielder*
Current Club: Tadcaster Albion
D o B: 09/09/1977   *Birthplace: Yorkshire*
Previous clubs include: Thackley - January 2000, Tadcaster Alb., Ossett T, Churwell.

MAGUIRE, NEIL   *Forward*
Current Club: Dereham Town
Birthplace: Norfolk
Ex-Norwich United and Wroxham. Pacey and skilful striker who finished last season as the clubs leading goalscorer.

MAHONEY, DEAN   *Goalkeeper*
Current Club: Maldon Town
Birthplace: Essex
Previous clubs include: Grays Ath - October 2001, Braintree T, Maldon T, Great Wakering R, Canvey Island, Tilbury, Aveley, Great Wakering R.

MAHONEY-JOHNSON, MICHAEL
Midfielder
Current Club: Ashford Town (Middx)

D o B: 06/11/1976   Birthplace: Paddington
Forward, who signed for Ashford Town (Middx) in March 2001. Played professionally for QPR, Wycombe Wanderers and Brighton, making 12 Football League appearances. Was previously at Sutton United before spending some time with Portadown in Ireland.

MAIN, JOHN   Midfielder
Current Club: Ashington

Birthplace: Newcastle
Previous clubs include: Newcastle Blue Star - July 2001, Washington, Jarrow Roofing, Prudhoe T, Newcastle Utd.

MAINWARING, ANDY   Forward
Current Club: Merthyr Tydfil

Birthplace: Wales
Honours won: Wales Youth Int.
Signed for Merthyr Tydfil in the close season of 2001, Andy came from Clevedon Town with an impressive 20-plus goal haul. A broken collar bone severely disrupted his 2001/02 season but he did finish the season on a high, getting back amounst the goals. Andy started his career at Everton and has also had spells with Inter Cardiff, Cwmbran Town, Bromsgrove Rovers, Gloucester City and Newport County and is a former Welsh Youth international.

MAINWARING, CARL   Midfielder
Current Club: Llanelli AFC

D o B: 15/03/1980   Birthplace: Wales
Previous clubs include: Haverfordwest County - November 2001, Inter Cardiff, Swansea C.

MAIRS, KEVIN   Midfielder
Current Club: Altrincham

D o B: 27/03/1981   Birthplace: Manchester
Keith is a young midfielder who made the bench for one Conference game in 1999/00 and then was an unused first-team sub against Burscough (6 January 2001). He made an impressive first-team debut in the UniBond Cup match at home to Ashton United in January 2001 and appeared again as sub at Ossett Town the following week. A product of the Altrincham youth set-up, he made his league starting debut at Gateshead (January 2001). Keith captained the reserves and towards the end of 2001/02 began to figure regularly in the first-team squad.

MAKINGS, ANDREW   Midfielder
Current Club: Ossett Town

Birthplace: Leeds
Previous clubs include: Ponte Prida (Brazil) - November 2001.

MALCOLM, NOEL   Forward
Current Club: Willenhall Town

Birthplace: Birmingham
Son of former Willenhall favourite Marcus, a young, very pacey player with an eye for goals, who impressed in pre-season friendlies.

MALE, CHRIS   Forward
Current Club: Chichester City United

Birthplace: Hampshire
Previous clubs include: Portfield - July 2000, Salisbury C, Newport IOW, Weymouth, Waterlooville, Stoke C, Portsmouth.

MALE, PHIL   Defender
Current Club: Oldbury United

Birthplace: Birmingham
Previous clubs include: Bloxwich Utd - December 2001.

MALESSA, TIM   Goalkeeper
Current Club: Taunton Town

Birthplace: Somerset
Previous clubs include: Weston-Super-Mare - December 2000, Bognor Regis T, Cheltenham T, Weston-Super-Mare.

MALKIN, CHRIS   Forward
Current Club: Total Network Solutions

D o B: 04/06/1967   Birthplace: Hoylake
Experienced forward who joined League of Wales side Total Network Solutions in July 2002 from Conference outfit Chester City. Made over 200 League appearances with Tranmere, Millwall and Blackpool before signing for Telford United. Moved to Chester in the summer of 2001.

MALLINSON, STEVE   Defender
Current Club: Witton Albion

Birthplace: Manchester
Previous clubs include: Rhyl - November 2001, Mossley, Cheadle T, Warrington T, Manchester C (Junior).

MALLON, SCOTT   Midfielder
Current Club: East Thurrock United

Birthplace: Essex
Previous clubs include: Tilbury - June 1999, Witham T, East Thurrock Utd, Tilbury, Concord R.

MALONE, PAUL   Defender
Current Club: Molesey

D o B: 20/03/1980   Birthplace: Surrey
Previous clubs include: Walton & Hersham - October 2000.

MALONEY, MIKE   Defender
Current Club: Oswestry Town

D o B: 11/09/1973
A close season signing who has had experience with Conwy United and local rivals T.N.S. Whilst with the Llansantffraid club obtained European experience.

MALONEY, TOMMY   Defender
Current Club: Chertsey Town

Birthplace: Surrey
Assistant first team manager. A summer signing who also plays in defence when required. Previous clubs include Dorking, Staines, Hampton and Molesey. Was on the youth books at Millwall.

MANCHESTER, GAVIN   Forward
Current Club: Penrith

Birthplace: Cumbria
Previous clubs include: Workington - February 2001, Penrith.

MANDERSON, LEE   Goalkeeper
Current Club: Maltby Main

Birthplace: Yorkshire
Previous clubs include: Parkgate - July 2001.

MANDEVILLE, GLYN   Forward
Current Club: Corinthian Casuals

Birthplace: Aldershot
Previous clubs include: Leatherhead - October 2000, Croydon Ath., Molesey, Aldershot T, Egham T, Aldershot T.

M

MANDRY, JAMES   *Midfielder*
Current Club: Pagham
Birthplace: Sussex
Midfielder: another former Oving player (had joined them from West Sussex League side Newtown Villa), who began 2001/02 with Sidlesham: briefly returned to the Vikings before signing for Pagham in January.

MANN, KEVIN   *Defender*
Current Club: Harwich & Parkeston
Birthplace: Essex
A strong and fast defender who signed for Harwich from Mistley United in the summer of 1998. He made an immediate impression at Jewson League level and has established himself as an ever present member of the defence.

MANNERS, JERMAINE   *Midfielder*
Current Club: Goole AFC
Birthplace: Leeds
Previous clubs include: Guiseley - November 2001, Ossett T, Yorkshire Amateurs, Hatfield Main, Farsley Celtic.

MANNERS, WAYNE   *Forward*
Current Club: Arnold Town
Birthplace: Nottingham
Previous clubs include: Gedling T - November 2000, Hinckley Utd, Gedling T, Ilkeston T, Dunkirk, Ilkeston T, Ruddington, Heanor T, Greenwood Meadows, Grantham T, Sutton T, Alfreton T, Stanton, Halifax T (Trainee).

MANNING, LEE   *Forward*
Current Club: Wimborne Town
Birthplace: Bournemouth
Previous clubs include: Westover Bournemouth - July 2001.

MANNING, PAUL   *Midfielder*
Current Club: Wimborne Town
Previous clubs include: Havant & Waterlooville - August 2000, Tonbridge, Folkestone Invicta, Dover Ath, Margate, Slough T, Millwall.

MANNING, PAUL   *Midfielder*
Current Club: Fisher Athletic (London)
Birthplace: Bournemouth
Previous clubs include: Inter Cardiff - July 2001, Blackburn R, AFC Bournemouth.

MANSFIELD, ALAN   *Goalkeeper*
Current Club: Three Bridges
Birthplace: Sussex
Highly regarded goalkeeper, who stepped up to the first-team following Matt Heasmans departure in December 2000: Three Bridges young player of the year: also made an appearance in the Youth Alliance for Brighton & Hove Albion U-19s during last season: hit with injury midway through 2001/02.

MANTHORPE, GAVIN   *Goalkeeper*
Current Club: Saltdean United
Birthplace: Sussex
Saltdean reserve goalkeeper: made a few first-team appearances during the autumn 1999 after Dean Lightwood left the club: recalled to First Division action on several occasions at the start of 2001/02.

MANTON, NEIL   *Defender*
Current Club: Redditch United
Birthplace: Birmingham
Experienced and well-travelled defender around the Midlands Non-League scene, Neil started out with Bilston Town, where he had a couple of stints. He then had spells with Knowle, Sutton Coldfield Town, Rushall Olympic and Redditch United before rejoining Sutton Coldfield in July 2001. Returned to Redditch in May 2002.

MANUEL, BILLY   *Midfielder*
Current Club: Bromley
D o B: 28/06/1969   *Birthplace: Hackney*
Experienced midfielder who joined Bromley in March 2002 from Dr Martens League side Tonbridge Angels. Started his career at Tottenham Hotspur before moving on to Gillingham, Brentford, Peterborough United, Cambridge United, Peterborough United, Gillingham and Barnet before moving into the Non-League game with Folkestone Invicta, Horsham, Grays Athletic and Tonbridge Angels.

MAPES, CHARLIE   *Midfielder*
Current Club: Wealdstone
D o B: 04/07/1982   *Birthplace: Middlesex*
Midfielder Charlie joined during pre-season of 2002 having impressed the previous season while playing for Edgware Town. Charlie has also played for Hayes.

MAPLE, KEVIN   *Midfielder*
Current Club: Bemerton Heath Harlequins
Birthplace: Wiltshire
From Local football - July 1996.

MARAGH, KIRK   *Forward*
Current Club: Sutton Coldfield Town
Previous clubs include: Paget Rangers - June 2001, Blakenall, Sutton Coldfield T.

MARCELLE, CLINT   *Forward*
Current Club: Harrogate Town
D o B: 09/11/1968   *Birthplace: Port of Spain*
Honours won: Trinidad & Tobago Int.
Signed for UniBond Premier side Harrogate Town in the close season of 2002 from Darlington. He is a Trinidad & Tobago full international, and began his careerwith Vitoria Setubal before moving to Barnsley. He also made over 125 League appearances while playing for Scunthorpe United, Hull City and Darlington.

MARCH, JAMIE   *Defender*
Current Club: Hinckley United
D o B: 21/03/1976   *Birthplace: Leicester*
Tough-tackling left-sided utility player, Jamie signed for Hinckley United in June 2002 from Kings Lynn. Had joined Lynn from Burton Albion in June 2000. Can operate in midfield or defence, he has had Conference experience with Kettering Town, Leek Town and was in the Stevenage Borough side which took Newcastle United to an FA Cup Third Round replay two seasons ago.

MARCH, RICHARD   *Defender*
Current Club: Sheffield FC
Birthplace: Leicester
Previous clubs include: Stocksbridge Park Steels - October 1999, Buxton, Leicester Utd, Shepshed Dynamo, Leicester C (Trainee).

M

MARCH, STEVE — Midfielder
Current Club: Hailsham Town
Birthplace: Sussex
Hailsham stalwart, who was a member of the side when they reached the last sixteen of the FA Vase in 1989: returned in 1999 after spells at Eastbourne Town and Langney Sports: picked up ankle injury in the match with Arundel during September: known as Bomber.

MARCHANT, GILES — Defender
Current Club: Bracknell Town
Birthplace: Berkshire
Previous clubs include: Wokingham T - August 2000, Sutton Utd, Walton & Hersham, Wimbledon (Junior).

MARCHANT, PETER — Defender
Current Club: Tonbridge Angels
Birthplace: Kent
From Youth team.

MARCHANT, RICHARD — Midfielder
Current Club: Goole AFC
Birthplace: Yorkshire
Previous clubs include: Glasshoughton Welfare - February 2002, Pontefract Colleries.

MARDENBOROUGH, STEVE — Midfielder
Current Club: Port Talbot Town
D o B: 11/09/1964   Birthplace: Birmingham
Vastly experienced and much-travelled midfielder who signed for League of Wales side Port Talbot Town from Rhayader Town following the latters relegation. Had plenty of League experience to call upon through spells at Newport County, Cardiff City, Hereford United, Darlington, Lincoln and Scarborough. Also played in Norway for Ostersund and has more recently been at Gloucester City, Merthyr Tydfil, Aberystwyth Town and Haverfordwest County.

MARFELL, ANDREW — Forward
Current Club: Caersws
D o B: 20/02/1982   Birthplace: Birmingham
Previous clubs include: Aston Villa - October 2001.

MARGINSON, KARL — Forward
Current Club: Salford City
D o B: 11/11/1970   Birthplace: Manchester
Previous clubs include: Hyde Utd - September 2000, Stalybridge Celtic, Barrow, Chorley, Macclesfield T, Rotherham Utd, Ashton Utd, Droylsden, Curzon Ashton, Blackpool, Stockport Co (Trainee).

MARKER, NICKY — Defender
Current Club: Tiverton Town
D o B: 03/05/1965   Birthplace: Exeter
Exeter-born, Nicky began his career with his home-town club making 202 appearances for the Grecians. He moved on to neighbours Plymouth Argyle and made another 202 appearances for the Pilgrims. Blackburn Rovers for £500,000 was Nickys next port of call, and he made 54 appearances for the Ewood Park championship-winning squad and also played in Europe before turning out 61 times for Sheffield United and 4 more for Plymouth whilst on loan. Joined Tiverton Town in January 2000 after a short spell with Cheltenham Town.

MARKHAM, STEVE — Defender
Current Club: Barwell
Birthplace: Leicester
Previous clubs include: Hinckley Ath - July 1996, Desford Colliery.

MARKS, CHRIS — Midfielder
Current Club: Alfreton Town
Birthplace: Derbyshire
An exciting young midfield prospect who has progressed from Alfreton Town's Centre of Excellence side and made a handful of first team appearances during the 2000/01 season. Prior to joining Alfreton, Chris was on the books at Gresley Rovers and the club have high hopes of the player for the future.

MARLOW, DANNY — Midfielder
Current Club: Corby Town
Birthplace: Desborough
Previous clubs include: Desborough T - July 2002, Rugby Utd, Desborough T, Rothwell T, Desborough T, Rothwell T, Northampton T (Trainee).

MARLOWE, ANDY — Defender
Current Club: Atherstone United
D o B: 25/09/1973   Birthplace: London
Honours won: England Youth Int.
Previous clubs include: Heath Hayes - August 2000, Blakenall, Telford Utd, Burton Alb., Moor Green, Bromsgrove R, Hednesford T, Bromsgrove R, Leyton Orient, Tottenham Hotspur.

MARNEY, DEAN — Defender
Current Club: Harrow Borough
Birthplace: London
Promising young defender, who joined Ryman Premier side Harrow Borough in January 2002. Previously played with Kent League outfit Greenwich Borough. A sales assistant, he soon became a first-team regular after joining.

MARPLES, SIMON — Defender
Current Club: Doncaster Rovers
Birthplace: Sheffield
Honours won: England Semi-Pro Int.
Highly rated young defender who was on the books at both Sheffield Wednesday and Rotherham as a youngster before joining Stocksbridge Park Steels, then of the Northern Counties East League, in July 1995. Immediately made a big impression, helping the Steels to promotion to the UniBond League, before being signed by Doncaster in August 1999 for a £12,000 fee. Gained England semi-professional international recognition in his first season as a Conference player.

MARQUIS, PAUL — Defender
Current Club: Frickley Athletic
D o B: 29/08/1972   Birthplace: Enfield
Former West Ham United trainee defender who joined UniBond Premier side Frickley Athletic in August 2002 after a short spell out of the game. After leaving Upton Park, Paul made over 30 League appearances for Doncaster Rovers before having spells with St Albans City, Gateshead, Gainsborough Trinity and then Bradford Park Avenue, whom he joined in July 1999.

MARRINER, STEVE — Midfielder
Current Club: Dartford
Birthplace: Farnborough, Kent
Born in Farnborough, Kent, Steve is a talented midfielder who was educated in the United States and played for Louisburg College where he was voted as Most Valuable Player for 1999/2000. He was also Region 10 player of the year and played for All-Southern State Select XI. At senior level, Steve played for Nashville Metros in the A League before returning to England an linking up with Dartford during the early part of the 2001/02 season.

MARRIOTT, ANDY　　　　*Forward*
Current Club: Didcot Town
Birthplace: Oxfordshire
Leading scorer for Didcot during the last 3 years and out in front again this season. Over 300 appearances and 80 goals to his credit in the Red and White. A great first touch and a ferocious shot. A Dairy Executive.

MARRON, TOMMY　　　　*Defender*
Current Club: Billingham Synthonia
Birthplace: Cleveland
From Local football - July 1999.

MARROW, JAMES　　　　*Forward*
Current Club: Leek Town
Birthplace: Stoke
A forward now in his second spell at Leek Town having returned to Harrison Park in March 2002. Started his career at Crewe Alexandra before moving to Leek for the first time in August 2000. He was then snapped up by League of Ireland outfit Finn Harps before getting a trial at Oldham. Eventually joined Biddulph Victoria (then known as Knypersley Victoria) for much of the 2001/02 season.

MARSDEN, TONY　　　　*Midfielder*
Current Club: Mickleover Sports
D o B: 03/12/1969　　　　*Birthplace: Derby*
Honours won: Dr Martens Premier Div.Winners
Previous clubs include: Kings Lynn - December 2000, Gresley R, Burton Alb., Gresley R, Grantham T, Belper T, Burton Alb.

MARSH, ASHLEY　　　　*Defender*
Current Club: Ford United
D o B: 25/02/1972　　　　*Birthplace: Brentwood*
Honours won: Ryman League Div.One Winners
A very experience Non-League defender who re-joined Ford United in February 2002 in time to help the club to achieve promotion to the Premier Division of the Ryman League for the first time. Played all his football with Essex sides, including spells at Collier Row, Clapton, Barking, Barkingside and Basildon United.

MARSH, CRAIG　　　　*Forward*
Current Club: Frickley Athletic
Previous clubs include: Matlock T - November 2000, Scunthorpe Utd.

MARSH, KIERON　　　　*Midfielder*
Current Club: Sittingbourne
Birthplace: Kent
Previous clubs include: Gillingham - December 2001.

MARSH, MIKE　　　　*Midfielder*
Current Club: Accrington Stanley
D o B: 21/07/1969　　　　*Birthplace: Liverpool*
Honours won: Football League Diviion One Winners, FA Cup Winners, Conference Winners
One of the most experienced and decorated players currently in Non-League football, Mike won honours galore whilst with Liverpool, whom he joined from local side Kirby Town in August 1987. Won League championship and FA Cup medals and went on to win a Conference winners medal with Kidderminster. Joined Boston United at the start of the 2001/02 season but was injured and semi-retired until accepting Accrington Stanleys offer to make a comeback in May 2002.

MARSH, SIMON　　　　*Forward*
Current Club: Stourport Swifts
Previous clubs include: Redditch Utd - June 1999, Stourport Swifts, Redditch Utd, Stourport Swifts.

MARSH, SIMON　　　　*Goalkeeper*
Current Club: Chorley
D o B: 18/12/1972　　　　*Birthplace: Blackpool*
Previous clubs include: Hyde Utd - July 1995, Blackpool (Trainee).

MARSH, TONY　　　　*Defender*
Current Club: Kingsbury Town
Birthplace: Essex
Previous clubs include: Clapton - July 2001, Leyton Pennant, Clapton, Tring T, Clapton, Collier Row, Barkingside, Collier Row, Chelsea (Junior).

MARSHALL, DWIGHT　　　　*Forward*
Current Club: Aylesbury United
D o B: 03/10/1965　　　　*Birthplace: Jamaica*
Previous clubs include: Slough T - July 2001, Kingstonian, Plymouth Argyle, Luton T, Plymouth Argyle, Grays Ath.

MARSHALL, GARY　　　　*Midfielder*
Current Club: Gloucester City
D o B: 09/08/1969　　　　*Birthplace: Stroud*
Honours won: FA Youth Cup Winners
Previous clubs include: Cirencester T - July 2000, Newport Co., Cirencester T, Uplands Utd, Melksham T, Yate T, Forest Green R, Shortwood Utd, Cambridge Utd, Swindon T, Coventry C.

MARSHALL, KEIRAN　　　　*Midfielder*
Current Club: Glapwell
Birthplace: Nottinghmshire
Previous clubs include: Forest Town Welfare - July 2001.

MARSHALL, LEE　　　　*Midfielder*
Current Club: Grantham Town
D o B: 01/08/1975　　　　*Birthplace: Nottingham*
Returned to play for Grantham Town after being released by Scunthorpe in July 2000. Originally played a few games on loan from Nottingham Forest under Warren Wards management. Played an influential role in midfield during the last two seasons.

MARSHALL, RICHARD　　　　*Defender*
Current Club: Harrogate Railway
Birthplace: Yorkshire
Previous clubs include: Harrogate T - July 2001, RTM Newcastle, Harrogate T.

MARSHALL, SHAUN　　　　*Forward*
Current Club: Hitchin Town
D o B: 24/10/1971　　　　*Birthplace: Herts*
One of the most consistent goalscorers in Ryman League football over the past decade. Shaun has averaged a goal every two games for most clubs, and has maintained his impressive ratio despite being hampered by injury for much of the past year or so. Started his playing days at Stevenage Borough and has also had spells with Enfield and Boreham Wood, from whom he rejoined Hitchin Town in November 1999.

M

MARSHALL, STEVE   *Forward*
Current Club: Maidstone United
Birthplace: Kent
Honours won: FA Vase Winners
Previous clubs include: Purfleet - January 2002, Margate, Ashford T, Deal T, Purfleet, Sheppey Utd, Cray Wanderers, Sheppey Utd, Spalding Utd.

MARSHALL, TIM   *Forward*
Current Club: Burgess Hill Town
Birthplace: Sussex
One time Lewes forward: played for relegated Shoreham in 1999/2000 and had the distinction of scoring the first goal conceded by Langney Sports in 537 minutes during February of that year: signed up by Burgess Hill in November 2000: scored 9 goals in total that season, but broke his ankle in the match against East Preston during March.

MARTIN, AENGUS   *Midfielder*
Current Club: Halesowen Town
Honours won: Northern Ireland Youth Int.
Previous clubs include: Solihull Borough - August 2001, Birmingham University.

MARTIN, ALLAN   *Midfielder*
Current Club: Peterlee Newtown
Birthplace: Co. Durham
Previous clubs include: Dunston Federation Brewery - July 2000, Bishop Auckland, Whitby T, Easington Colliery.

MARTIN, ANDY   *Defender*
Current Club: Blyth Spartans
Birthplace: Newcastle
Re-signed for Blyth Spartans in October 2000, after venturing over the border to play for Queen of the South in Scottish Div 2. Andy was voted club and Supporters' Player of the year for season 1999-2000. Andy is a rock solid defender with a good knowledge of the game. He isnt afraid to go forward and have a shot on goal. On many occasions putting the ball in the back of the net.

MARTIN, ANDY   *Defender*
Current Club: Potters Bar Town
Birthplace: Herts
Previous clubs include: Boreham Wood - July 1996.

MARTIN, BRUCE   *Midfielder*
Current Club: Corinthian Casuals
Birthplace: Surrey
Previous clubs include: Dorking - July 1996, Banstead Ath., Corinthian Casuals.

MARTIN, CHRIS   *Defender*
Current Club: Buxton
Birthplace: Derbyshire
Previous clubs include: Curzon Ashton - October 2000, Buxton, Flixton, Buxton, Dove Holes.

MARTIN, CRAIG   *Forward*
Current Club: Racing Club Warwick
Birthplace: Coventry
Previous clubs include: Stratford T - August 2001, Bedworth Utd, Sutton Coldfield T, Hinckley Utd, Hinckley Ath., Stratford T, Wellesbourne, Bedworth Utd, Wellesbourne.

MARTIN, CRAIG   *Midfielder*
Current Club: Afan Lido
D o B: 27/07/1984   *Birthplace: Wales*
From Youth team.

MARTIN, DANNY   *Forward*
Current Club: Atherstone United
Previous clubs include: Nuneaton Borough - November 1996, VS Rugby, Nuneaton B, Stoke C (Trainee).

MARTIN, DEAN   *Midfielder*
Current Club: Bradford Park Avenue
D o B: 09/09/1967   *Birthplace: Halifax*
Experienced midfielder who signed for Bradford Park Avenue from Lancaster City in March 2002. Made over 300 Football League appearances with Halifax Town, Scunthorpe United, and Rochdale. Also played for Stalybridge Celtic.

MARTIN, ELIOT   *Midfielder*
Current Club: Gravesend & Northfleet
Birthplace: Kent
A left-sided wing back who began his career at Gillingham where he made more than 50 first-team appearances. He had loan spells with Welling United, Chelmsford City and Margate before signing permanently for the Gate in 1995. He was a valued member of the side that won promotion to the Conference in 2000/01 before signing for Gravesend & Northfleet at the start of season 2001/02. Proved a very influential player for the team until his season was unfortunately curtailed by injury. Eliot has also taken on the role of reserve team manager for the 2002/03 season.

MARTIN, GUY   *Defender*
Current Club: Feltham
Birthplace: Feltham
The original Pikey joined Feltham last summer and started off playing for the reserve XI, but some outstanding performances led to his elevation to the first XI. Guy carried on where he had left off in the reserves and come the end of the season won both the 1st Team Player of the Year awards. Courier man Martin is known as the local nutter but always gives 100% on the field and is a very valuable addition to the back four.

MARTIN, JAE   *Forward*
Current Club: Moor Green
D o B: 05/02/1976   *Birthplace: London*
Signed for Moor Green in October 2000 from Woking. An experienced striker who started his career at Southend, before spells at Birmingham City, Lincoln (who paid £25,000 for him in Nov 96), and Peterborough. Scored within five minutes on his Moor Green debut.

MARTIN, KEITH   *Forward*
Current Club: Aveley
Birthplace: Essex
Previous clubs include: Purfleet - March 2002, Tilbury.

MARTIN, MATT   *Goalkeeper*
Current Club: Croydon
Birthplace: Surrey
Goalkeeper signed from Whyteleafe in September 2001. Injuries immediately gave Matt a chance in the first team, and a string of solid performances has cemented his place as first choice keeper. A former Millwall junior, Matts previous clubs include Dulwich Hamlet, Croydon Athletic and Chipstead.

MARTIN, SHAUN · Forward
Current Club: Holmer Green

Birthplace: Bucks
From Youth team.

MARTIN, SIMON · Forward
Current Club: St.Albans City

D o B: 08/07/1979   Birthplace: London
Exciting striker who cost Ryman Premier side St Albans City a tribunal-set £5,000 fee in the summer of 2001 when re-joining from UniBond outfit Hucknall Town. Began his playing days in the Saints youth side and eventually made a number of first-team appearances before moving north, firstly with Lincoln United and then Hucknall.

MARTINDALE, GARY · Forward
Current Club: Burscough

D o B: 24/06/1971   Birthplace: Liverpool
Re-joined UniBond Premier side Burscough in August 2002 from Conference outfit Telford United. Originally transferred from Burscough in March 1994 for a £10,000 fee to Bolton Wanderers. Moved on to Peterborough United before being transferred to Notts County for £175,000 in March 1996 where he went on to score a stunning goal that took County to the Second Division play-off final at Wembley. Also won the Golden Boot as the Divisions leading scorer. After a short loan spell with Mansfield Town moved on to Rotherham United before joining Telford in March 2000.

MARTINI, CHUCK · Goalkeeper
Current Club: Bromley

D o B: 23/02/1970   Birthplace: Maknes, Morocco
Honours won: Moroccan Youth, u-21 & Full Int.
Moroccan under-21 and full international goalkeeper who joined Ryman Division One South club Bromley in August 2002 after a spell with Dr Martens Eastern side Dartford. Originally with Wimbledon, Chuck (then known as Moussadic) made his name at Wycombe before having further spells at Barnet, Connecticut Wolves in America, Kings Lynn, Sutton United and, briefly, Folkestone Invicta before ending the 2001/02 season with the Darts.

MARVELL, DALE · Forward
Current Club: Epsom And Ewell

Birthplace: Surrey
From Youth team.

MARWA, RAM · Midfielder
Current Club: Erith & Belvedere

Birthplace: Norway
Honours won: Norway Youth Int.
Quality midfield player who originally signed for Erith & Belvedere from Leyton Orient two seasons ago. Had a spell away at Ilford before rejoining in Jnauary 2000. Great potential in the non - League scene and hoping to make it back to the pro game. Also Former Norwegian under-18 International.

MARWOOD, STEVE · Midfielder
Current Club: Salisbury City

Birthplace: Wiltshire
Younger brother of former Salisbury City player Chris Marwood and son of another ex-White Brian. Steve is a former youth team player with Dr Martens Eastern club Salisbury. Now being given an opportunity to claim a midfield place in the first-team squad.

MAS, BARTHOLOME · Defender
Current Club: Aveley

D o B: 08/01/1974   Birthplace: Essex
Previous clubs include: Purfleet - September 2000, Grays Ath., Dagenham & Redbridge, Billericay T, Barking, Dagenham & Redbridge, Maidstone Utd.

MASKELL, CRAIG · Forward
Current Club: Aylesbury United

D o B: 10/04/1968   Birthplace: Aldershot
Joined Aylesbury United as player-coach in May 2002, Craig is a very experienced striker who had moved into the Non-League game in September 1999 with Hampton & Richmond Borough after being released by Leyton Orient. Very experienced League professional with Southampton, Huddersfield, Reading, Swindon and Brighton, and scorer of over 130 league goals.

MASKELL, GARY · Forward
Current Club: North Ferriby United

D o B: 18/10/1975   Birthplace: Berkshire
Honours won: Combined Services Rep.
Previous clubs include: Army - July 2001, Forest Green R, Reading (Junior).

MASON, ANDY · Forward
Current Club: Chorley

Birthplace: Bolton
Previous clubs include: Leigh RMI - July 2001, Stalybridge Celtic, Kettering T, Macclesfield T, Chesterfield, Hull C, Bolton W.

MASON, ANDY · Midfielder
Current Club: Weston-Super-Mare

D o B: 26/10/1966   Birthplace: Manchester
Andy signed for Weston-Super-Mare in June 2002 as player-coach. Joined Weymouth from Thame United in August 1996 and was appointed team manager after the deaparture of Fred Davies in October 99. Formerly with Manchester City as a junior, Crewe as a trainee and Wallingford, he was somewhat surprisingly released from his contract at Weymouth towards the end of the 2001/02 season.

MASON, LEE · Defender
Current Club: Shildon

Birthplace: Bishop Auckland
Previous clubs include: Bishop Auckland - September 1997.

MASON, MICHAEL · Forward
Current Club: Bilston Town

D o B: 07/08/1979   Birthplace: Walsall
Previous clubs include: Halesowen T - August 2001, Macclesfield T.

MASON, PHIL · Midfielder
Current Club: Banbury United

D o B: 03/12/1971   Birthplace: Newcastle
Phil is a midfield player who has gained a vast amount of experience in football. He began his career with Newcastle United, and has subsequently played for Blyth Spartans, Kettering Town, Worcester City (two spells), Spennymoor United, Brackley Town, Oxford City and Aylesbury United, where he was club captain. He joined Boreham Wood in May 2001, making his debut against Bedford Town in August 2001, and then returned to Oxfordshire to join Banbury United in June 2002.

MASON, RICHARD — Midfielder
Current Club: Buxton

D o B: 05/06/1977 — Birthplace: Sheffield

Previous clubs include: Worksop T - June 2002, Boston Utd, Hednesford T, Boston Utd, Sheffield Wednesday.

MASON, STEVE — Midfielder
Current Club: Dunston Federation Brewery

Birthplace: Newcastle

Previous clubs include: Ponteland Utd - August 2001.

MASSARO, PAT — Forward
Current Club: Three Bridges

Birthplace: Sussex

Small striker: leading scorer for Oakwood in 1999/2000 before moving to Three Bridges at the start of the following season: kept on the sidelines for the whole of the winter with a hamstring injury before returning to form in the final stages of the campaign: has realised his full potential this year and has been putting in some excellent performances.

MASSEY, BARRY — Forward
Current Club: Atherton Laburnum Rovers

Birthplace: Salford

Barry joined LR at the start of last season after impressing during a loan spell at the end of the 1999/2000 season and he ended his first season at LR as top scorer. He is a big, strong front man who can open up defences and is capable of scoring some superb goals. Barry works on the railways and likes to play golf.

MASSEY, STUART — Midfielder
Current Club: Whyteleafe

D o B: 17/11/1964 — Birthplace: Crawley

Previous clubs include: Carshalton Ath - January 2002, Whyteleafe, Oxford Utd, Crystal Palace, Sutton Utd, Walton & Hersham, Carshalton Ath., Sutton Utd, Chipstead.

MASSINGHAM, DARREN — Defender
Current Club: Sutton Coldfield Town

Birthplace: Hull

Talented young defender who hails from Humberside. Was originally with Barton Old Boys before joining Brigg Town, where he became a first-team regular. Moved to the Midlands to study and joined Racing Club Warwick in the summer of 2001. Switched to Sutton Coldfield Town in May 2002.

MASSON, ALEC — Defender
Current Club: Havant & Waterlooville

Birthplace: Sussex

Honours won: Cayman Island Int.

Alec made a single appearance for Dr Martens Premier side Havant & Waterlooville in 1999 before signing for Bognor Regis Town. He made an extremely good impression on that occasion though and transferred to the team in August 2000. Hampered by a broken arm sustained in a reserve team match against Croydon in August 2000, Alec failed to gain a foothold in the first team and eventually left to concentrate on studying while playing less demanding football in the Sussex County league with Selsey and then Wick. Returning to the Hawks late in the 2001/02 season, his skill is evident, and he will certainly be one to watch in future. Alec has also played for the Cayman Islands National team and as a youth played for Bath City.

MASTER, KIRK — Forward
Current Club: Shepshed Dynamo

D o B: 24/11/1973 — Birthplace: Leicester

Became one of the most wanted players around the Dr Martens scene after topping the goalscoring charts for Western Division side Shepshed Dynamo in 2001/02. Started out with Shepshed and then had spells with North Kilworth, Hinckley Town, Rothwell Town, Leicester Nirvana, Highfield Rangers, Gresley Rovers, where he won a Premier Division championship medal, and Corby Town, re-joining Shepshed in the summer of 2001.

MASTERTON, PAUL — Forward
Current Club: Selby Town

Birthplace: Leeds

Previous clubs include: Whitkirk Wanderers - July 2001, Beeston St.Anthonys, Bardsey, Carlton.

MATHIESON, DAVE — Goalkeeper
Current Club: Gretna

D o B: 18/01/1978 — Birthplace: Dumfries

Previous clubs include: Queen of the South - August 2001, St.Johnstone.

MATTHEWS, COLIN — Goalkeeper
Current Club: Eastleigh

Birthplace: Sussex

Giant goalkeeper who is very highly-rated. Became the subject of the biggest fee ever paid by a Jewson Wessex League club when Eastleigh paid Dr Martens Eastern side £10,000 for his services in July 2002. Started out at local Sussex outfit Paulsgrove before joining Ryman Leaguers Bognor Regis Town, where he built his reputation. Signed for the Islanders for £5,000 in June 2000 and became recognised as one of the best keepers in the league. Eastleigh beat several clubs to his signature.

MATTHEWS, DAMIEN — Defender
Current Club: Arlesey Town

Birthplace: Bedford

Bedford-born Damien was a 2002 close season signing for Ryman Division One North side Arlesey Town. Played in the Ryman League Division Two for Leighton Town a couple of seasons ago and has also seen service with Wootton Blue Cross.

MATTHEWS, JASON — Goalkeeper
Current Club: Weymouth

Birthplace: Bristol

Jason is a former Mangotsfield United , Taunton Town, Westbury United, Welton Rovers and Exeter City keeper who signed for Dr Martens Premier side Weymouth in August 2002 after impressing in pre-season trials. Had joined Western Division outfit Clevedon Town from League of Wales side Aberystwyth Town in June 2001. Best known for his cameo performance as a substitute appearance for Exeter City in a televised FA Cup tie against Everton.

MATTHEWS, LEE — Defender
Current Club: Dagenham & Redbridge

Birthplace: Southend

Joined the Daggers for a £3,000 fee in January 1998 from near neighbours Purfleet. A former Southend United trainee who moved to Purfleet in July 1991, going on to make over 250 appearances at the back for the club.

M

MATTHEWS, LEE — Forward
Current Club: Hyde United
D o B: 14/07/1979   *Birthplace: Manchester*
Previous clubs include: Curzon Ashton - August 2001, Trafford, Salford C, Castleton Gabriels, Altrincham, Rochdale.

MATTHEWS, LEE — Midfielder
Current Club: Llanelli AFC
D o B: 26/09/1979   *Birthplace: Wales*
Previous clubs include: Rhayader T - July 2001, Bridgend T, Barry T, Cwmbran T.

MATTHEWS, MARTIN — Midfielder
Current Club: Kettering Town
D o B: 22/12/1975   *Birthplace: Peterborough*
Honours won: Dr Martens League Premier Div.Winners
Martin was a YTS player at Derby County for two years before getting a one-year contract. He joined Kettering Town from Kings Lynn in July 1998 and his footballing career shows a wealth of experience for his age. Missed all of the 1999/00 season through injury but made a successful comeback and showed impressive form in the sweeper role as the Poppies won the Dr Martens League title.

MATTHEWS, NEIL — Forward
Current Club: Swindon Supermarine
D o B: 11/11/1974   *Birthplace: Swindon*
Previous Clubs: Hungerford Town, Swindon Town, Highworth Town
Neil is in his second spell at Supermarine having returned to the club from Hungerford Town at the start of the 1999/00 season. An excellent target man with good heading ability. He holds the ball up well and always looks to bring his midfield colleagues into play.In his second season back Neil found it hard to regularly find the net but did play a number of games as the lone target man. Our pattern of play changed last season and whilst he is not scoring prolifically he has played exceptionally well in leading the line.

MATTHEWS, ROB — Midfielder
Current Club: Northwich Victoria
D o B: 14/10/1970   *Birthplace: Slough*
Rob is a vastly experienced left-sided midfield man who can also play in attack. He joined Northwich Victoria from Hull City in July 2002. He played under Neil Warnock at Notts. County and has also seen service with Stockport County, Halifax,Blackpool, Bury, (where he enjoyed back to back promotions), York and Luton Town. Rob played over 250 league game and scored over 40 goals.

MATTHEWS, ROBBIE — Forward
Current Club: Eastleigh
Birthplace: Wiltshire
Previous clubs include: Bemerton Heath Harlequins - May 2002, Salisbury C.

MATTINGLEY, CHRIS — Defender
Current Club: Walton Casuals
Birthplace: Surrey
Strong, skillful central defender, Chris is a good squad player and is probably the fittest player at the club, who is currently training to become a fire fighter.

MAUGHAN, PETER — Midfielder
Current Club: Tow Law Town
Birthplace: Co.Durham
The Docs captain from his days at Evenwood where he had spent many seasons after being signed from West Auckland.

MAUNDER, ADAM — Forward
Current Club: Redhill
Birthplace: London
Pacy striker, who was formerly with Barnet and Sheffield Utd. Family business meant a break from the game and linked up with Redhill.

MAUTONE, STEVE — Goalkeeper
Current Club: Slough Town
D o B: 10/08/1970   *Birthplace: Myrtlford, Australia*
Honours won: Australian u-21 Int.
Signed for Slough Town after a spell with Barry Town while playing for the Welsh club in the European Cup qualifying rounds in July of 1999. Steve first came to English football after former West Ham boss Harry Redknapp spotted him playing for a club in Australia. While at West Ham, Mauts appearances were limited and he found himself on the bench. Reading eventually moved in for the Aussie keeper and signed him for £250,000. During his time at Reading Mauts made himself a hero with the fans. During this impressive spell at the Royals he was once linked with a £1million + move to Premiership side Coventry City. But a bad spell of injuries saw Steve eventually be replaced as the Reading number one. He then had brief spells at Crystal Palace and Gillingham before drifting out of League football. When Steve arrived at Slough he found himself with a battle for the keepers jersey with Danny Honey. He eventually made himself a clear number one keeper at the club. Last season Steve produced save after save, but despite this fact, the Rebels were still relegated. He did however pick up the Supporters' Player of the year trophy and official website player of the year in his first season at the club. Overall Steve is a very confident and agile keeper and has made himself a firm favorite with the fans at Wexham Park.

MAW, DAMIAN — Forward
Current Club: Workington
Previous clubs include: Chester-le-Street - July 2001, Ryhope CA.

MAWSON, CRAIG — Goalkeeper
Current Club: Morecambe
D o B: 16/05/1979   *Birthplace: Keighley*
Goalkeeper who signed for Conference club Morcambe from Halifax Town in August 2001. Previously with Burnley, he made his debut v Nuneaton and kept clean sheet in a 1-0 victory and went on to make 39 appearances in 01/02.

MAWSON, DAVE — Forward
Current Club: Gretna
Birthplace: Sunderland
Previous clubs include: Durham C - February 2000, Chester-le-Street, Whitley Bay, Harrogate T, Bishop Auckland, South Shields, Whitley Bay, Spennymoor Utd, South Shields, Sunderland.

MAXFIELD, SCOTT — Midfielder
Current Club: Barrow
D o B: 13/07/1976   *Birthplace: Doncaster*
Born in Doncaster, Scott is a defender or midfielder who began his career with his home-town club as a trainee when they were still a Football League outfit. He made 29 League appearances for them, scoring once before he made the short journey to join Hull City. He made 35 League appearances for the Tigers without scoring before he was released in the summer of 1998. He returned to Doncaster Rovers in time for their first season in the Conference and over the last two seasons he has been a regular in their side. He was released in the summer and joined Barrow in July 2000 and made his debut in the opening home game of that season against Emley.

M

MAX-GRANT, REUBEN   *Forward*
Current Club: Barton Rovers
Birthplace: Buckinghamshire
Previous clubs include: Buckingham T - September 2001, Bletchley T.

MAXWELL, JASON   *Forward*
Current Club: Bradford Park Avenue
D o B: 01/09/1972   *Birthplace: Lincoln*
Striker who joined Bradford Park Avenue from Gainsborough Trinity in October 1998. Began his career with Scunthorpe United and has also played for Grantham and Buxton. Highly-committed to the cause, Jason was named player of the year for the 2000/01 season.

MAY, LEROY   *Forward*
Current Club: Evesham United
D o B: 12/08/1969   *Birthplace: London*
Honours won: England Semi-Pro Int., Dr Martens Western Div.Winners
A powerful striker, Leroy started his career with Ryman League side Enfield. His previous clubs include Kidderminster, Walsall, Hereford United and Stafford Rangers. A 2001 summer signing for Halesowen Town, Leroy regained some of the form during the Yetzs Dr Martens Western Division title-winning season that led him to winning England semi professional International recognition whilst at Stafford. Switched to Western Division outfit Evesham United in August 2002.

MAY, MATTHEW   *Goalkeeper*
Current Club: Worthing
Birthplace: Sussex
Previous clubs include: Lewes - July 1998, Brighton (Junior).

MAY, ROBBIE   *Midfielder*
Current Club: Wivenhoe Town
Birthplace: Essex
Previous clubs include: Harwich & Parkeston   December 2001, Heybridge Swifts, Wivenhoe T, Harwich & Parkeston, Wivenhoe T, Felixstowe T, Harwich & Parkeston, Felixstowe T, Ipswich T.

MAY, SEAN   *Midfielder*
Current Club: Burnham
Birthplace: Berkshire
Sean is another close season signing who suffered an injury that kept him out of action for fourteen months. Previous clubs AFC Bournemouth and AFC Newbury.

MAYERS, KENNY   *Midfielder*
Current Club: Stalybridge Celtic
D o B: 14/07/1970   *Birthplace: Lancashire*
Spent much of the 2000/01 season in central defence, but is more usually found in midfield or up front, and has been outstanding in all positions. Joined Lancaster City in the summer 1999 from Morecambe and was previously with Bamber Bridge and Horwich RMI. Has represented the UniBond League on a number of occasions. Switched to UniBond Premier rivals Stalybridge Celtic in July 2002.

MAYES, BOBBY   *Midfielder*
Current Club: Clacton Town
D o B: 18/12/1967   *Birthplace: Ipswich*
Honours won: England Semi-Pro Int.
Another major new signing for Clacton this season. Bobby is a natural goalscorer and holds the ball superbly. Typically plays as attacking midfield. Former England semi-pro international.

MAYES, DAVID   *Midfielder*
Current Club: Trafford
Birthplace: Cheshire
Skillfull central midfielder who signed for UniBond League First Division side Trafford in August 2002 from North West Counties Leaguers Winsford United. Was is in his second spell with the Blues with a stint at Bamber Bridge sandwiched between.

MAYNARD, PETER   *Defender*
Current Club: Leatherhead
D o B: 17/03/1983   *Birthplace: London*
Formerly with Wimbledon schoolboys and Horsley, the left-back/midfielder is a junior trader with Dutch bank, ABN AMRO.

MAYNARD, STUART   *Midfielder*
Current Club: Enfield
Birthplace: Herts
Talented midfielder whose career began at Watford where he was a trainee. Joined the Non-League circuit with St Albans City, where he had two spells with a period at Wealdstone and Aylesbury United sandwiched between. Transferred from the Ducks to Enfield in May 2002.

MAYO, ADAM   *Midfielder*
Current Club: Cirencester Town
D o B: 11/03/1983   *Birthplace: Cheltenham*
A strong young midfielder player who was promoted into the Cirencester Town first-team squad during the 2000/01 season. Originally with Cheltenham Town, Adam also had a spell on the books at Cardiff City before joining Ciren.

MAYS, ROSS   *Forward*
Current Club: Belper Town
Previous clubs include: Burton Alb - February 1999, Sheffield Utd (Trainee).

MAZZARELLA, PAUL   *Midfielder*
Current Club: Connahs Quay Nomads
D o B: 08/08/1980   *Birthplace: Wales*
Previous clubs include: Wrexham - July 1999.

MBALLA, IVAN   *Forward*
Current Club: Aldershot Town
Birthplace: France
Previous clubs include: Raith Rovers - September 2001, ASFC Vindelle (France).

MBALLA, PHILLIPPE   *Forward*
Current Club: Haverfordwest County
Birthplace: France
Previous clubs include: Caerleon - February 2002.

McALINDEN, GARETH   *Forward*
Current Club: Gateshead
D o B: 06/04/1977   *Birthplace: Hexham*
Gareth joined Gateshead in July 2000 from Scarborough. An impressive midfielder who is an expert at set pieces, he started his career with Newcastle United before going on to make over 50 League appearances for Carlisle.

McALLISTER, CRAIG   *Forward*
Current Club: Basingstoke Town
Birthplace: Hampshire
Exciting prospect who signed for Basingstoke Town from Eastleigh in March 2002 after scoring two goals in a trial against Brentford. Craig possesses terrifying pace which has enabled him to score some vital goals for Basingstoke.

McALLISTER, JOHN — *Forward*
Current Club: Skelmersdale United

Birthplace: Liverpool
Previous clubs include: Runcorn FC Halton - September 2001, Prescot Cables.

McANDREW, NEIL — *Forward*
Current Club: Bury Town

Birthplace: Suffolk
Previous clubs include: Soham Town Rangers - November 2000, Thetford T, Bury T.

McARTHUR, DUNCAN — *Midfielder*
Current Club: Hastings United

D o B: 06/05/1981　　　*Birthplace: Brighton*
Classy midfielder who joined Hastings in August 1999 from Brighton & Hove Albion. Scored 12 times during 2000/01 and had a trial with Aston Villa.

McAULEY, SEAN — *Defender*
Current Club: Halifax Town

D o B: 23/06/1972　　　*Birthplace: Sheffield*
Honours inns Scotland u 21 Int
Former Scottish under-21 international defender who joined Conference side Halifax Town in August 2002 after a spell in America with Portland Timbers. Started his career with Manchester United before signing for Scottish outfit St Johnstone in April 1992. Returned to England to have spells with Hartlepool, Scunthorpe and Rochdale, totalling over 200 League appearances.

McCABE, GRAEME — *Defender*
Current Club: Ashington

Birthplace: Newcastle
Previous clubs include: South Shields - July 2000, RTM Newcastle, Bedlington Terriers, Ashington, Whitley Bay.

McCALLUM, MARK — *Defender*
Current Club: Lewes

Birthplace: Sussex
The third member of a defence which conceded fewer goals than any other Ryman League team last season. Joined Lewes at the same time as Stuart Hack, and is an unsung hero who will be much missed should his new-found profession as a policeman prevent him from playing as much as in previous seasons.

McCANN, CHRISTIAN — *Midfielder*
Current Club: Barking & East Ham United

Previous clubs include: Cambridge C - August 2001, Baldock T, Chelmsford C, Welling Utd, Chelsea.

McCANN, GARY — *Goalkeeper*
Current Club: Aylesbury United

D o B: 25/07/1972　　　*Birthplace: London*
Experienced goalkeeper who joined Aylesbury United in May 2002 from Hendon. Had been a firm favourite with Hendon supporters since signing from Dulwich Hamlet towards the end of the 1996/97 season. Gary made over 180 appearances for the club, an injury slowing down the proceedings over the past year or so. Unfortunately Gary underwent further surgery which delayed the 2001/02 season. His other clubs include Sutton United, Chesham United and Enfield.

McCANN, JOHN — *Midfielder*
Current Club: Buxton

Birthplace: Sheffield
From Local football - February 2000.

McCANN, PETER — *Defender*
Current Club: Folkestone Invicta

D o B: 27/06/1982　　　*Birthplace: Paisley*
Promising young defender who joined Folkestone Invicta in June 2002 after being released by Conference side Barnet. Had been at Underhill from a young age, making a number of senior appearances, and also had a loan spell with Folkestone during the 2001/02 season.

McCARTAN, STEVE — *Midfielder*
Current Club: Rushall Olympic

Birthplace: Birmingham
Previous clubs include: Evesham Utd - February 2002, Bloxwich T, Blakenall, Boldmere St.Michaels, Sutton Coldfield T.

McCARTHY, ANDY — *Goalkeeper*
Current Club: Arundel

D o B: 16/12/1971　　　*Birthplace: Shoreham*
Goalkeeper: played for Rustington (1999/2000 West Sussex League champions) before transferring to Arundel in August 2000: vastly improved during the course of his first season at Mill Road and was voted the clubs player of the year.

McCARTHY, BILLY — *Defender*
Current Club: Whitstable Town

Birthplace: Kent
Previous clubs include: Beckenham T - July 2000, Cray Wanderers, Corinthian, Chatham T, Erith & Belvedere, Welling Utd, QPR (Trainee).

McCARTHY, DAVE — *Goalkeeper*
Current Club: Worksop Town

Birthplace: Nottingham
Previous clubs include: Hucknall T - February 2002, Oakham Utd, Ashfield Utd, Matlock T, Sutton T, AFC Bournemouth, Chesterfield.

McCARTHY, JAMES — *Defender*
Current Club: Rhayader Town

D o B: 10/02/1977　　　*Birthplace: Cardiff*
Previous clubs include: Cardiff Corinthians - October 2001.

McCARTHY, PAUL — *Forward*
Current Club: Deal Town

Birthplace: Kent
Previous clubs include: St Albans C - January 2002, Chelmsford C, Baldock T, Dartford, Cray Wanderers, Thamesmead T, Beckenham T, Erith & Belvedere, Cray Wanderers.

McCARTNEY, BILLY — *Defender*
Current Club: Chorley

D o B: 16/04/1976　　　*Birthplace: Manchester*
Previous clubs include: Ramsbottom Utd - March 2002, Trafford, Stalybridge Celtic, Trafford, Ramsbottom Utd, Castleton Gabriels, Macclesfield T, Rochdale.

McCLUSKEY, DARREN — Defender

Current Club: Gloucester City

Birthplace: Swindon

Previous clubs include: Swindon Supermarine - October 2001, Chippenham T, Cinderford T, Witney T, Cinderford T,Salisbury C, Cinderford T, Yate T, Trowbridge T, Fairford T, Gloucester C.

McCLUSKEY, RYAN — Midfielder

Current Club: Workington

D o B: 02/06/1981   *Birthplace: Ireland*

Previous clubs include: Sligo Rovers - November 2001, Cliftonville, Ballinamallard Utd.

McCOLGAN, PAUL — Midfielder

Current Club: Cradley Town

Birthplace: Birmingham

Previous clubs include: Bromsgrove Rovers - July 2001, Paget R, Cradley T, Oldbury Utd.

McCOMBIE, NIGEL — Goalkeeper

Current Club: Penrith

Birthplace: Cumbria

Previous clubs include: Wetheriggs - July 1998.

McCONNELL, DARREN — Midfielder

Current Club: Abbey Hey

Birthplace: Manchester

Previous clubs include: Hyde Utd - August 2001, Stockport County.

McCONNELL, MIKE — Defender

Current Club: Corby Town

D o B: 08/06/1973   *Birthplace: Belfast*

Previous clubs include: Desborough T - July 2001, Corby T, Raunds T, Stewarts & Lloyds, Corby T.

McCONNELL, PETER — Defender

Current Club: St.Leonards

Birthplace: Kent

Previous clubs include: Coventry C - January 2002, Norwich C.

McCORMACK, CONRAD — Midfielder

Current Club: Guisborough Town

From Local football - July 2001.

McCORMACK, FRANK — Midfielder

Current Club: Aylesbury United

Birthplace: London

Previous clubs include: Sutton Utd - August 2001, Harrow B, St.Albans C, Harrow B, Harwich & Parkeston, Colchester Utd, Wimbledon, Chelsea (Junior).

McCORMACK, JOE — Goalkeeper

Current Club: Newport Isle Of Wight

Birthplace: Isle of Wight

Previous clubs include: Cowes Sports - July 2000, Newport IOW.

McCORMACK, NEIL — Goalkeeper

Current Club: Warrington Town

D o B: 16/11/1976   *Birthplace: Warrington*

Previous clubs include: Tetley Walker - July 2001.

McCORMICK, STEPHEN — Forward

Current Club: Newtown AFC

D o B: 14/08/1969   *Birthplace: Scotland*

Previous clubs include: Clydebank - October 2000, Airdrie, Dundee, Stirling Alb., Queens Park.

McCOY, BARRY — Midfielder

Current Club: Wokingham Town

D o B: 12/10/1980   *Birthplace: Ascot*

Previous clubs include: Bracknell T - March 2002, Wokingham T, Aldershot T, Farnborough T, Wycombe Wanderers.

McCRACKEN, GARY — Defender

Current Club: Hampton & Richmond

Birthplace: Northern Ireland

Honours won: Northern Ireland u-19 Int.

Central defender who started out with Fulham making one appearance on the bench for a Worthington Cup tie. After a brief, unsuccessful spell at Cambridge, Gary moved on to play for Linfield in Northern Ireland. He has also represented Northern Ireland at under-19 level. Signed for Ryman Premier side Hampton & Richmond Borough in August 2002.

McCRAE, NICK — Defender

Current Club: Oxford City

Previous clubs include: Banbury Utd - August 2001, Cirencester Academy.

McCREADIE, STEWART — Midfielder

Current Club: Horsham YMCA

Birthplace: Sussex

Experienced, influential midfielder, who previously played for Lewes and Wick in addition to a past spell at Horsham YMCA: spent a couple of months at East Preston (joined them from Forest) before returning to YM in March 2001.

McDAID, BRENDAN — Midfielder

Current Club: Grantham Town

Birthplace: Lincoln

Signed for Grantham Town as one of the five players who moved from Lincoln United in December 1999. Now in his second spell with Grantham, Brendon scored an impressive 18 goals for the team from midfield during the Dr Martens Eastern Division promotion-winning season of 2001/02 to finish as the clubs second highest scorer.

McDERMOTT, DANNY — Defender

Current Club: Shepshed Dynamo

Birthplace: Leicester

Previous clubs include: Christ The King - February 1999.

McDERMOTT, WAYNE — Defender

Current Club: Vauxhall Motors

D o B: 30/10/1979   *Birthplace: Liverpool*

A former Evertonian who signed for Vauxhall Motors in the summer of 2001 from Leek Town. A natural left back who was previously with Northwich Victoria, Runcorn and Leek, he has impressed everyone at Rivacre Park since gaining a place in the starting line-up.

McDIARMID, DAVID — Midfielder

Current Club: Skelmersdale United

Birthplace: Liverpool

Previous clubs include: Vuaxhall Motors - July 2001, Caernarfon T, Prescot Cables, Marine.

McDONAGH, RICHARD — Midfielder
Current Club: Hemel Hempstead Town
D o B: 06/11/1973 — Birthplace: Middlesex
Previous clubs include: Wealdstone - January 2002, Hemel Hempstead, Boreham Wood, Hemel Hempstead, Chertsey T, Chesham Utd, Berkhamsted T, Ruislip Manor.

McDONALD, ANDY — Midfielder
Current Club: Altrincham
Birthplace: Manchester
Andy is a skilful central midfielder who signed for UniBond Premier side Altrincham from First Division Witton Albion in late July 2002. He had previously played for Ashton United, Woodley Sports, Winsford United and Abbey Hey. He scored his first goal for Altrincham in the friendly match against his old club Abbey Hey on 20 July 2002.

McDONALD, DAVID — Defender
Current Club: Billericay Town
D o B: 02/01/1971 — Birthplace: Dublin
Honours won: Republic of Ireland Youth & u-21 Int.
David is an experienced defender who joined Billericay Town in June 2002 from Ryman Premier rivals Boreham Wood. Had signed for Wood at the start of the 2001/02 season after a short spell at Enfield. He began his career as a trainee at Tottenham Hotspur in 1989 and went on to play for Gillingham, Bradford City, Reading, Peterborough United and Barnet, making a total of 155 League appearances. He is a Republic of Ireland International at Youth, under-21 and B level.

McDONALD, GRAEME — Forward
Current Club: Newcastle Blue Star
Birthplace: Newcastle
Previous clubs include: Brandon Utd - October 2000, Langley Park, South Shields, North Shields, Chester-le-Street, Blyth Spartans, Annfield Plain.

McDONALD, MARCUS — Midfielder
Current Club: Paget Rangers
Birthplace: Birmingham
Previous clubs include: Bromsgrove Rovers - August 2001, Paget R.

McDONALD, NICK — Midfielder
Current Club: Hornchurch
Birthplace: Essex
Previous clubs include: East Thurrock Utd - September 2001.

McDONALD, PHIL — Defender
Current Club: Goole AFC
Birthplace: Halifax
Previous clubs include: Glasshoughton Welfare - December 2001, Pontefract Collieries, Emley, Halifax T.

McDONALD, SCOTT — Forward
Current Club: Eastbourne United
Birthplace: Sussex
Forward who was leading scorer for Sidley United during 1999/2000 with 16 goals: switched to Little Common Albion (his previous club) early into the following season: drafted into the Eastbourne United side in March 2002 in an attempt to save the club from relegation.

McDONALD, STEVE — Forward
Current Club: Accrington Stanley
Birthplace: Burnley
Signed for Accrington Stanley in January 2001 from the Reserves, where he was the leading scorer with ten goals in eleven matches. He was also the Youth Team Player of the Season for the previous two years. Still plays most of his football with the Reserves, for whom he has become something of a prolific goalscorer.

McDONNELL, DANNY — Goalkeeper
Current Club: Worcester City
D o B: 07/09/1973 — Birthplace: Worcestershire
Now in the second year of a three-year contract at Worcester City after signing on a free transfer from Halesowen Town under the Bosman ruling in May 2001. Proved his reputation as one of the best goalkeepers in the Dr Martens Premier. Has also played for Lye Town and Stourbridge.

McDONNELL, NIC — Forward
Current Club: Crawley Town
Birthplace: Surrey
A very sharp and exciting young striker who joined Dr Martens Premier side Crawley Town in July 2002 from Ryman Leaguers Croydon. Had signed for Croydon in the spring of 1999 after being released by Farnborough Town. A glut of goals for the youth team and reserves earned Nic some early opportunities, and during the 2000/01 season he become a first-team regular, finishing up as leading goalscorer for 2000/01 and 01/02 and claiming the Player of the Year awards for 2001. Nic has had trials with a number of Nationwide League clubs in the past and is rated highly.

McDOUGALD, JUNIOR — Forward
Current Club: Dagenham & Redbridge
D o B: 12/01/1975 — Birthplace: Big Spring
Very talented forward who joined the Daggers during the summer of 1999 from Leyton Orient. Began his career with Tottenham Hotspur but had to wait until moving to Brighton in 1994 for his League debut. Went on to make around 114 League appearances for the Seagulls, Rotherham, Millwall and Leyton Orient and also had spells with Toulon in France and with Cambridge City.

McELROY, DEAN — Defender
Current Club: Hitchin Town
Birthplace: Hitchin
Young defender who made his debut for Ryman Premier side Hitchin Town in the 2000/01 season but had to wait until the latter part of the 2001/02 season to be given an extended run. Has shown plenty of composure in the heart of defence. A product of the Hitchin PASE scheme.

McEVOY, IAN — Defender
Current Club: Peterlee Newtown
Birthplace: Co.Durham
Previous clubs include: Easington Colliery - August 2001, Horden CW.

McFARLANE, DWAINE — Midfielder
Current Club: Worcester City
Birthplace: Birmingham
Previous clubs include: WBA - August 2001.

McFARLANE, JIM — Defender

Current Club: Purfleet

Previous clubs include: Concord Rangers - July 1997, Purfleet, Clapton, Millwall Wanderers.

McFEE, CHRIS — Forward

Current Club: Guisborough Town

Previous clubs include: Billingham Synthonia - December 2000, Guisborough T.

McFLYNN, TERRY — Midfielder

Current Club: Margate

D o B: 27/03/1981   Birthplace: Magherafelt
Previous clubs include: Woking - January 2002, QPR, Manchester Utd.

McGARRIGLE, KEVIN — Defender

Current Club: Spennymoor United

D o B: 09/04/1977   Birthplace: Newcastle
Previous clubs include: Tow Law T - August 2001, Blyth Spartans, Spennymoor Utd, Brighton.

McGAVIN, STEVE — Forward

Current Club: Dagenham & Redbridge

D o B: 24/01/1969   Birthplace: North Walsham
Honours won: Conference Winners, FA Trophy Winners
Steve has played over 250 Football League games for Birmingham, Wycombe Wanderers, Southend United, Northampton Town and Sudbury Town. He began his career at Ipswich Town as a youth but first came to light playing for Sudbury Town from where Colchester United snapped him up for a bargain £10,000. Steve brought instant success to the Us and by the end of the season had won the Conference and FA Trophy double. His performances brought him a move eighteen months later to Birmingham City, commanding a £150,000 transfer. Due to the size of Barry Frys squad, first team appearances at St Andrews were limited to only 20 but a year later Wycombe Wanderers paid £175,000 for his services and he became a huge hit with the Adams Park fans. The next two seasons he starred for Colchester United in the Second Division but rejected the new deal offered to him during the summer by Steve Whitton, deciding to join the Daggers in August 2001 instead. He made his debut on the opening day of the season against Southport.

McGEE, GARY — Forward

Current Club: Lowestoft Town

Birthplace: Great Yarmouth
Previous clubs include: Wroxham - July 2000, Gorleston, Oulton Broad.

McGEE, MARTYN — Midfielder

Current Club: Fakenham Town

Birthplace: Norfolk
Previous clubs include: Gorleston - July 2000, Fakenham T.

McGHEE, DEAN — Midfielder

Current Club: Billingham Synthonia

D o B: 07/08/1975   Birthplace: Cleveland
Previous clubs include: Bishop Auckland - July 2000, Whitby T, Billingham T, Guisborough T, Sunderland (Trainee).

McGIBBON, MARK — Defender

Current Club: Bishops Stortford

Birthplace: London
Signed for Blues in February 2002 from Tooting & Mitcham. Right-sided defender. Previous clubs include Dulwich Hamlet. Division 2 champion with Tooting, Mark is destined for the Premier and made his debut for blues in early March against Thame.

McGINLAY, JOHN — Forward

Current Club: Ilkeston Town

D o B: 08/04/1964   Birthplace: Inverness
Honours won: Scottish Int., Division One Winners, Isthmian League Premier Div.Winners
Vastly experienced former Scottish international striker who became manager of Ilkeston Town in April 2002. Played Non-League football for Yeovil Town and Elgin City before moving into the professional game with Shrewsbury in 1989 and went on to win a number of honours with the likes of Bury, Millwall, Bolton, Bradford City and Oldham before taking over as player-manager of Dr Martens League Western Division Gresley Rovers in December 2000. Won 9 full caps for Scotland.

McGINLAY, KIERAN — Midfielder

Current Club: Spennymoor United

Previous clubs include: Consett - August 2001, Esh Winning.

McGINN, CHRIS — Forward

Current Club: Rhyl

Birthplace: Liverpool
Previous clubs include: Cammell Laird - June 2002.

McGINN, CHRIS — Midfielder

Current Club: Consett

Birthplace: Consett
From Youth team.

McGINTY, DANNY — Goalkeeper

Current Club: Liversedge

Birthplace: Bradford
Previous clubs include: Dudley Hill Ath - July 2000, Bradford C.

McGINTY, STEVE — Midfielder

Current Club: Mickleover Sports

Birthplace: Derby
Previous clubs include: Kings Lynn - August 2000, Blakenall, Stapenhill, Gresley R, Stapenhill, Heanor T, Stapenhill, Sandiacre T, Mickleover RBL, Kilburn MW, Derby Co (Junior).

McGLASHAN, ANDY — Defender

Current Club: Salisbury City

D o B: 28/12/1982   Birthplace: Wiltshire
A young player who progressed from Dr Martens League club Salisbury City's youth team and was a regular reserve team member before joining the senior squad in 2001/02. Defender Andy has had short spells with Fareham Youth and Chichester School of Excellence.

McGLINCHEY, LEE — Forward

Current Club: Shepshed Dynamo

D o B: 24/09/1971   Birthplace: Leicester
Striker who has had five separate spells with Dr Martens Western side Shepshed Dynamo and now holds club appearance and goalscoring records. Originally on the books at Scunthorpe as a youngster, and apart from Shepshed, he has also turned out for Friar Lane Old Boys, Leicester United, Hinckley United and Hucknall Town, re-joining Dynamo again in September 2001.

McGOONA, DANNY — Forward

Current Club: Caernarfon Town

D o B: 16/06/1974   Birthplace: Liverpool
Previous clubs include: Colwyn Bay - July 2000, Connahs Quay Nomads, Conwy Utd, Bangor C, Altrincham, Connahs Quay Nomads, Colwyn Bay.

McGORRY, BRIAN   *Midfielder*
Current Club: Tamworth
D o B: 16/04/1970   *Birthplace: Liverpool*
Brian signed for Dr Martens Premier side Tamworth from Chester City in August 2002. He has a wealth of experience at previous clubs including Southport, Telford, Torquay, Hereford, Cardiff, Wycombe Wanderers, Peterborough, AFC Bournemouth and Weymouth.

McGOSH, GARY   *Defender*
Current Club: Connahs Quay Nomads
D o B: 27/07/1972   *Birthplace: Wales*
Previous clubs include: Rhyl - February 2001, Colwyn Bay, Flint Town Utd, Caernarfon T, Colwyn Bay.

McGOVERN, PAUL   *Midfielder*
Current Club: Kingsbury Town
Birthplace: London
Previous clubs include: Brook House - August 2000.

McGOVERN, ROB   *Midfielder*
Current Club: Mickleover Sports
Birthplace: Derby
Previous clubs include: Borrowash Victoria - October 2000, Heanor T, Stapenhill.

McGOWAN, GAVIN   *Defender*
Current Club: Bromley
D o B: 16/01/1976   *Birthplace: Blackheath*
Honours won: England Schoolboy Int.
A former England Schoolboy International who joined Bromley at the end of 2001 from Ryman League Second Division side Horsham. Gavin signed for Arsenal in 1992 at the age of 16 and made his first team debut for the Gunners in 1993. He left Highbury to sign for Luton Town in 1998 where he spent three years before being released in April 2001.

McGRATH, TONY   *Midfielder*
Current Club: Hall Road Rangers
Birthplace: Hull
Previous clubs include: Winterton Rangers - August 2001.

McGREGOR, BILLY   *Defender*
Current Club: Mildenhall Town
Birthplace: Cambridgeshire
Previous clubs include: Soham Town Rangers - July 2000, Mildenhall T.

McGREGOR, MARC   *Forward*
Current Club: Nuneaton Borough
D o B: 30/04/1978   *Birthplace: Southend*
Honours won: England Semi-Pro Int.
Marc was one of the hottest properties in the Conference before Boro swooped with a £35,000 transfer bid which took him from Forest Green Rovers to Manor Park last June. He netted 10 goals in the Conference last season and showed he had the potential to perform on a bigger stage. He joined Rovers from Hellenic League outfit Endsleigh at the start of the 1998-1999 campaign. Marc has previously had spells with Notts County and Oxford United.

McGREGOR, SCOTT   *Midfielder*
Current Club: Bedworth United
Birthplace: Coventry
Very attacking minded, Scott can play on the right of midfield or Wing back. Joined Bedworth United in the summer of 2001 from Midland Alliance side Stratford Town. Previously with Coventry City as a trainee, he has also had spells with Hinckley United, Coventry Sphinx and Shepshed Dynamo.

McGUCKIN, IAN   *Defender*
Current Club: Barrow
D o B: 24/04/1973   *Birthplace: Middlesbrough*
Previous clubs include: Oxford Utd - November 2001, Fulham, Hartlepool Utd.

McGUIRE, MARK   *Defender*
Current Club: Northwich Victoria
Birthplace: Cheshire
Mark is a promising teenager who joined Conference side Nortwhich Victoria in July 2002 from Nantwich Town. A talented fullback, Mark is the son of former Vics favourite Paul. He had trials with Glasgow Celtic during the 2000/01 campaign and it is believed that he has a bright future ahead of him.

McGUIRE, PAUL   *Defender*
Current Club: Hyde United
D o B: 17/11/1979   *Birthplace: Manchester*
Centre Back with great ball control and flare. Made several first-team appearances for Conference side Morecambe after progressing through the clubs adademy. Transferred to UniBond Premier outfit Hyde United in August 2002.

McHALE, KEVIN   *Midfielder*
Current Club: Skelmersdale United
Birthplace: Liverpool
Previous clubs include: Marine - September 2001, Tranmere R.

McHALE, KRIS   *Forward*
Current Club: Burscough
Birthplace: Liverpool
Young forward who signed for UniBond Premier side Burscough in the close season of 2002 from rivals Marine. Began as a junior with Tranmere Rovers. Also had a spell with Leigh RMI during the 2001/02 season.

McHUGH, FRAZER   *Defender*
Current Club: Tamworth
D o B: 14/07/1981   *Birthplace: Nottingham*
Frazer signed for Tamworth in November 2001 from Bromsgrove Rovers and made an immediate impact by scoring in his debut against Worcester City and picked up the man of the match award. Previously a full time professional at Swindon Town where he made 14 Football League appearances. Very talented young defender.

McHUGH, STEVE   *Defender*
Current Club: Ware
Birthplace: Hertford
Previous clubs include: St.Margaretsbury - December 2000.

McILVOGUE, JAMES   *Forward*
Current Club: Colwyn Bay
D o B: 16/10/1974   *Birthplace: Wales*
Strong centre-forward who signed for UniBond Premier side Colwyn Bay from League of Wales neighbours Conwy United in July 1999. Gilly was the Bays top marksman in his first season with 17 goals and scooped up all the player of the season awards for that season. Has also played for Llandudno and Crossville.

McINDOE, MICHAEL   *Midfielder*
Current Club: Yeovil Town
D o B: 02/12/1979   *Birthplace: Edinburgh*
Honours won: FA Trophy Winners
Michael was signed by Yeovil Town in February 2001 for a club record transfer fee of £25,000 from Conference side Hereford

United. Michael made his debut three days later in the home match against Boston United and had a dream start, netting Yeovils opening goal in a 2-1 win. He quickly settled into the side in the left wing position and established a reputation as an excellent crosser of the ball - particularly from dead ball situations. This reputation was enhanced when he set up no less than four goals in the home match against Leigh RMI when he was a key part of a side that handed out a 6-1 thrashing. Prior to joining Yeovil Town, Michael was picked up by Hereford on a free transfer from Luton Town during the summer of 2000. During his two years at Luton, he made just short of 50 appearances for the Nationwide League side. Michael is also capable of playing in the centre of the field, which has certainly given extra Yeovil options.

McINTOSH, KELVIN   Defender
Current Club: Oxford City
Birthplace: Oxford
Previous clubs include: Oxford Utd - March 2002.

McINTOSH, SCOTT   Forward
Current Club: Norwich United
D o B: 12/10/1967   *Birthplace: Norfolk*
A very experienced Jewson League player. Signed for Norwich United this season from Great Yarmouth Town. With his experience he has lots to offer the young players in the squad. A major signing.

McINTYRE, KEVIN   Midfielder
Current Club: Chester City
D o B: 23/12/1977   *Birthplace: Liverpool*
Honours won: England Semi-Pro Int.
Began with Tranmere Rovers as a trainee, signing professional in 1996. He was loaned out to Doncaster Rovers in August 1998 and had a spell on loan at Barrow in November the same year. Was then signed by Rovers in January 1999 for £10,000. An England semi-professional international, he transferred to Chester in May 2002.

McKAY, DAMIAN   Midfielder
Current Club: Great Harwood Town
Birthplace: Lancashire
From Local football - July 2000.

McKAY, JODY   Forward
Current Club: Banbury United
Birthplace: Banbury
Midfielder who prefers to play as an attacking left winger. Graduated from Banbury United's youth team and made his debut against Headington Amateurs in October 1991. Has scored over 150 goas in just over 450 appearances for United and, apart from a short spell at Brackley Town, has played all his football for Banbury. Firm favourite with the supporters.

McKAY, PAUL   Midfielder
Current Club: Leatherhead
D o B: 28/01/1971   *Birthplace: Berkshire*
Experienced midfielder spent ten years at Burnley and has also played for Slough Town, Chesham United and Harrow Borough. While at Turf Morr he played twelve Football League games in Claret and Blue. Signed for Ryman Division One South side Leatherhead from Wealdstone in July 2000.

McKAY, PAUL   Midfielder
Current Club: Whyteleafe
Previous clubs include: Chipstead - July 1999, Croydon, Molesey, Chipstead, Crystal Palace (Trainee).

McKEARNEY, DAVE   Defender
Current Club: Morecambe
D o B: 20/06/1968   *Birthplace: Liverpool*
Can play in a number of positions, though mainly he fills a defensive roll in the team. He has proved to be a wholehearted player with his 101% commitment to the team. Dave hails from Liverpool, he came to Morecambe from Chorley and has also played for Prescot Cables, Bolton Wanderers, Crewe Alexandra and Wigan Athletic.

McKECHNIE, MIKE   Midfielder
Current Club: Kendal Town
Birthplace: Barrow
Barrow-born, Mike, who is equally at home in defence or midfield, began his career with Carlisle United as a trainee but was released without making a League appearance. He had trials with both Hereford United and Doncaster Rovers without making his League bow and joined Barrow for the first time in October 1994. He made his debut the following month in a Cup-tie against Atherton LR. He left the club shortly after and following a spell with Stirling Albion, he sampled soccer in Iceland and Norway. He rejoined Barrow in October 1999 from local outfit Barrow Rangers who play in the West Lancashire League. Switched to UniBond First Division side Kendal Town in August 2002.

McKENNA, ANDY   Forward
Current Club: Tow Law Town
Birthplace: Co.Durham
Signed from Easington last season having scored over 30 goals a season for Easington in his last two seasons there. Had a short spell at Bishop Auckland and came out of the Hartlepool League.

McKENNA, GARETH   Defender
Current Club: Consett
Birthplace: Co.Durham
Previous clubs include: Whickham - September 2001.

McKENNA, IAN   Forward
Current Club: Tamworth
Birthplace: Birmingham
A series of impressive displays for Tamworths Youth and Reserve teams led to Ian being offered a contract in 2001. He broke through into the first-team towards the end of the 2000-01 season, but a nasty leg break in a pre-season friendly against Aston Villa meant that he missed the first half of the 2001/02 season. A highly-rated forward of whom much is expected.

McKENNA, KEVIN   Midfielder
Current Club: Harrow Borough
Birthplace: London
Age 23. Joined Harrow in March 2002 from Hillingdon Borough. Made his debut in the Capital League home fixture against Stevenage Borough. A PE Teacher.

McKENNA, RUSS   Midfielder
Current Club: Morecambe
Birthplace: Morecambe
A young midfield battler and another Academy graduate now joining the top ranks within the club.

McKENZIE, CALLUM   Midfielder
Current Club: Newtown AFC
D o B: 09/10/1966   *Birthplace: Wales*
Previous clubs include: Newtown - September 2001, Rhayader T.

McKENZIE, DENVA — *Forward*
Current Club: Whyteleafe

Birthplace: Surrey
Previous clubs include: Gravesend & Northfleet - February 2002, Carshalton Ath.

McKENZIE, MATT — *Defender*
Current Club: Ilkeston Town

D o B: 03/04/1979 — Birthplace: Sheffield
Signed for Ilkeston from Grimsby Town towards the end of the 1999-2000 season. Started his career at Dunkirk before attracting the attention of a number of league clubs. A very strong and fast defender he was originally plagued by injuries on joining the Robins but in the games he has played has won the admiration of the Ilkeston fans with his cool performances in the centre of defence.

McKENZIE, NEHRU — *Forward*
Current Club: Hyde United

D o B: 26/04/1982 — Birthplace: Manchester
Previous clubs include: Moss Side - July 2001.

McKENZIE, ROGER — *Forward*
Current Club: Denaby United

D o B: 27/01/1973 — Birthplace: Sheffield
Previous clubs include: Sheffield - August 2001, Matlock T, Sheffield, Maltby Main, Stocksbridge Park Steels, Matlock T, Mossley, Boston Utd, Northampton T, Scarborough, Doncaster R.

McKEY, JOHN — *Forward*
Current Club: Redhill

Birthplace: Essex
Appearances have been limited due to work commitments but has scored 4 goals in three games to date, including two as a sub in the amazing 4-4 draw with Eastbourne United. Joined from Ryman League side Aveley.

McKIMM, STEVE — *Midfielder*
Current Club: Gravesend & Northfleet

D o B: 30/07/1975 — Birthplace: London
Honours won: Ryman League Premier Div. Winners
Signed for Gravesend & Northfleet from Ryman League Kingstonian in October 2001. He has a wealth of experience at the highest level of Non-League football, having played for Kingstonian, Hayes and Farnborough in the Conference. Steve is totally committed to the cause and is the cornerstone in midfield. Although perhaps not known for his goalscoring ability, he does have the knack of getting into the right place at the right time and scoring crucial goals.

McKINLAY, JACK — *Defender*
Current Club: Egham Town

Birthplace: Berkshire
Previous clubs include: Staines T - March 2002, Egham T, Chertsey T, Hampton & Richmond B, Bedford College Academy.

McKINNEY, SCOTT — *Forward*
Current Club: Great Yarmouth Town

D o B: 18/06/1977 — Birthplace: Norfolk
Recent signing for Yarmouth from Sprowston Athletic of the Anglian Combination. May lack height but not courage or enthusiasm.

McLEAN, IAN — *Defender*
Current Club: Guiseley

D o B: 13/09/1978 — Birthplace: Leeds
Previous clubs include: Harrogate Railway - November 2001, Harrogate T, Gainsborough Trinity, Oldham Ath., Bradford C.

McLEAN, STEVE — *Defender*
Current Club: Guisborough Town

Previous clubs include: Seaham Red Star - July 2001, Hartlepool Utd.

McLEOD, COLIN — *Forward*
Current Club: Consett

Birthplace: Co.Durham
Previous clubs include: Whitley Bay - July 1991, Consett Spennymoor Utd.

McLOUD, ALAN — *Defender*
Current Club: Grays Athletic

Birthplace: London
Powerful defender now an essential part of the Grays rearguard, he joined last season.

McLOUGHLIN, ALAN — *Midfielder*
Current Club: Forest Green Rovers

D o B: 20/04/1967 — Birthplace: Manchester
Honours won: Republic of Ireland Int.
Hugely experienced midfield player who joined Conference club Forest Green Rovers in July 2002 after a six-month spell with Rochdale. Began his career as an apprentice with Manchester United and then went on to make over 500 League appearances with Swindon, Southampton, Portsmouth, Wigan and Rochdale. Capped 42 times by the Republic of Ireland, Alans signing is a real coup for Rovers.

McLOUGHLIN, DANIEL — *Forward*
Current Club: Arundel

Birthplace: Sussex
Under-18s left-winger for East Preston during 2000/01, who also scored twice after breaking into first-team midway through that season: joined Arundel in February 2002.

McMAHON, ADAM — *Defender*
Current Club: Guisborough Town

Previous clubs include: Middlesbrough - July 2001.

McMAHON, DAVID — *Forward*
Current Club: Blyth Spartans

David is a striker who made his debut for UniBond Premier side Blyth Spartans at Burton Albion in February 2002. Only 21-years-old he has previously played for both Newcastle United and Queen of the South.

McMAHON, FRANCIS — *Midfielder*
Current Club: Runcorn FC Halton

Birthplace: Liverpool
Franny joined the team pre-season before the current season after being released by Wigan Athletic. Has already made the left back role his own with skillful defending and accurate passing. Franny has also shown his attacking side in several matches this season, and he has the skill to take on and beat opposition defenders and get in a decent cross.

McMAHON, JOHN — Forward
Current Club: Abingdon Town
Birthplace: Oxfordshire
Previous clubs include: Carterton T - January 2002, Oxford C.

McMAHON, PAUL — Forward
Current Club: Stafford Town
Birthplace: Stafford
Previous clubs include: Walsall Wood - July 2001, Chasetown, Stafford T.

McMAHON, RYAN — Goalkeeper
Current Club: Trafford
Birthplace: Manchester
Signed for UniBond First Division side Trafford during the 2001/02 season from Altrincham. Other clubs include Prescot Cables and Runcorn. Made his first-team debut at Shawe View against Radcliffe Borough last April.

McMAHON, SAM — Midfielder
Current Club: Stevenage Borough
D o B: 10/02/1976   Birthplace: Newark
Sam joined Stevenage in the summer of 1999, and made a tremendous impact in his first couple of months. A horrific freak knee injury though at Hereford in October 1999 tragically ended his season prematurely. He recovered well however, making the midfield role his own. Newark-born, he spent seven years at Leicester after joining as a 16 year-old. Made five appearances, scoring against Port Vale on his debut and played one game in the Premiership, against Wimbledon. He joined Cambridge United in March 1999 and made three League appearances for the Us.

McMENAMIN, CHRIS — Midfielder
Current Club: Hitchin Town
D o B: 27/12/1973   Birthplace: Donegal
Rejoined Hitchin Town in September 2001 frok Boreham Wood. Chris left the Canaries to join Coventry City in 1997 and then went on to play for Peterborough United. Has also had spells at St Albans City and Luton OB. Highly-rated midfielder.

McMILLAN, ANTHONY — Defender
Current Club: Runcorn FC Halton
Birthplace: Wigan
Signed late on in the 2000/2001 season from Wigan Athletic, Tony gave some impressive performances in goal in the few appearances he had. He has a very quick mind and can set up counter attacks with his long throws. Unfortunatly for Tony, he suffered an injury during pre-season and has had to settle for the reserve keepers jersey, but he is definately one for the future, and an excellent substitute when called upon.

McMILLAN, STUART — Defender
Current Club: Atherstone United
D o B: 21/12/1975   Birthplace: Coventry
Previous clubs include: Folly Lane OB - February 2002, Coventry Sphinx, Shrewsbury T (Junior), Birmingham C (Junior).

McMILLAN, STUART — Forward
Current Club: Buxton
Birthplace: Sheffield
From Local football - October 2001.

McMULLEN, ANDY — Defender
Current Club: Vauxhall Motors
Birthplace: Liverpool
Signed for UniBond Premier side Vauxhall Motors in July 2002 from rivals Burscough. Had joined Burscough in July 1998 from North West Counties Leaguers Prescot Cables. Andy is a respected defender or midfielder who was Burscoughs Players' Player and Supporters' Player of the Year for 2000/01. Has also had spells with Maghull and Witton Albion.

McNAB, JOE — Midfielder
Current Club: Newport Isle Of Wight
D o B: 29/10/1980   Birthplace: Brighton
Previous clubs include: Utah Blitz (USA) - September 2001, Portsmouth, Manchester C (Trainee).

McNAB, NEIL — Midfielder
Current Club: Newport Isle Of Wight
D o B: 29/10/1980   Birthplace: Brighton
Previous clubs include: Utah Blitz (USA) - September 2001, Portsmouth, Manchester C (Trainee).

McNALLY, PAUL — Midfielder
Current Club: Marine
D o B: 20/10/1968   Birthplace: Liverpool
Rejoined Marine from UniBond League rivals Runcorn FC Halton in May 2002. He had joined Runcorn from the Mariners during the 1997/98 season, and notched up 20 goals in his first season. Good in the air, and totally committed to the cause, Macca has also played in defence, although returning a very healthy goal rate. The 2001/02 season saw McNally finish as the Linnets top scorer. Has also seen service with Warrington, Stalybridge, Runcorn and Oswestry.

McNALLY, TONY — Defender
Current Club: Harlow Town
Birthplace: Luton
Signed for Harlow Town in August 2000 from Barton Rovers where he had made over 500 appearances. A solid defender who has also played for Hemel Hempstead and is the son of former Luton star Brendan.

McNAMARA, BRETT — Forward
Current Club: Kings Lynn
D o B: 08/07/1972   Birthplace: Newark
Previous clubs include: Matlock T - Mar 2002, Bedford T, Gainsborough Trinity, Kettering T, Kings Lynn, Northampton T, Stamford.

McNAMARA, DARREN — Midfielder
Current Club: Didcot Town
Birthplace: Oxfordshire
29 year old midfielder who moved to Didcot from Brackley Town in January 2002. Has a wealth of experience with spells at Oxford City, Marlow, Thame, Abingdon Town, Witney Town and Chesham. Was part of the Marlow side that reached the 3rd Round of the FA Cup, and he also claims to have been Man of the Match in the defeat of Oxford United in the First Round of that campaign.

McNAUGHTON, MIKE — Defender
Current Club: Harrogate Town
D o B: 29/01/1980   Birthplace: Blackpool
Honours won: UniBond League Div.One Winners
Defender who started his career as a trainee at Scarborough when they were a Football League club. He went on to make around 30 appearances in the Third Division, and a further ten in the Nationwide Conference for the Seasiders before having a short spell at Northwich Victoria and Frickley Athletic. He joined Harrogate Town in January 2001.

McNEIL, MATTHEW — Forward
Current Club: Runcorn FC Halton
Birthplace: Manchester
Previous clubs include: Stalybridge Celtic January 2002, Woking, Stalybridge Celtic, Woodley Sports, Altrincham, Curzon Ashton, Burnley.

McNEIL, ROSS — Forward
Current Club: Kings Lynn
Birthplace: Kings Lynn
Ross is a student at King Edward VII School in Lynn, and he played for Downham Market and The Woottons in the Nar Valley Youth League before progressing to Kings Lynns under-18s and the Reserves. He has shown a great deal of promise as an attacker and has made a more regular spot as a first teamer during the 2001/02 season.

McNICHOLAS, DAVE — Defender
Current Club: Matlock Town
Birthplace: Barnsley
A consistent defender now in his third spell at the club, he scored on his debut at Goole in September 1992 before winning NPL runners-up medals in both the First and Premier Divisions with Worksop. He rejoined the Gladiators in January 2000.

McNIVEN, DAVID — Forward
Current Club: Northwich Victoria
D o B: 27/05/1978   *Birthplace: Leeds*
Striker who joined Conference club Northwich Victoria in July 2002 after a spell in Scottish football with Hamilton. Played almost 100 times in the League with Oldham and York and also played Conference football with Chester City and Southport.

McPHEE, DYLAN — Midfielder
Current Club: Newtown AFC
D o B: 10/03/1976   *Birthplace: Rhayader*
Joined Newtown in August 2002 from former League of Wales rivals Rhayader Town. Had signed for his home- town club after successful spell at Carmarthen Town where he featured in the Intertoto cup. Fit midfielder who covers every blade of grass. Strikes the ball well and scores his fair share of goals.

McPHERSON, DANNY — Forward
Current Club: Wisbech Town
Birthplace: Cambridgeshire
Previous clubs include: Spalding Utd - March 2002.

McPHERSON, KEITH — Defender
Current Club: Slough Town
D o B: 11/09/1963   *Birthplace: Greenwich*
Signed for Slough from Brighton and immediately looked assured and confident in the Slough defence. Maccas best attribute is that he reads the game so well. He looks unorthodox in his technique sometimes, but he is very effective. McPherson is one of a number of former Reading players at the club. He made well over 350 appearances for the Royals over a number of years and is still respected by their fans to the present day - and it is not hard to see why. Keiths performances during the 2000/2001 season were one of the few bright spots in a miserable campaign for the Rebels. He kept Ryman strikers at bay with his excellent defending and even scored a few goals for Slough himself, most notably a 87th minute header against Hendon at home. Keith turned down a move to Dover in order to join the Rebels and was subject to some interest from Hayes as well, but has remained loyal to the Rebels cause. Keith wants to do well for himself and the club. A good example of this being when he punctured a lung against Hitchin. It was diagnosed that Keith would be out for three months, but five weeks later, he was back in the Rebels

defence. Keith is very much a fans favorite at the club and was an excellent signing for Slough Town Football Club.

McQUADE, SCOTT — Midfielder
Current Club: Gretna
Birthplace: Scotland
Previous clubs include: Cowdenbeath - February 2002.

McROBERT, LEE — Forward
Current Club: Ashford Town
D o B: 04/10/1972   *Birthplace: Bromley*
Lee re-joined Dr Martens Eastern side Ashford Town in August 2002 from Folkestone Invicta. Had signed for Folkestone from Hastings Town in January 2002. He started his career under manager Neil Cugley at Ashford before signing for Sittingbourne for £20,000 in 1993, still a record fee for both clubs. He then joined Millwall for £35,000, where he made 23 Football League appearances, scoring one goal. After leaving the New Den, Lee joined Hastings Town before returning to Ashford Town and then having a spell in the Conference with Dover Athletic before re-joining Hastings.

McSHERRY, DAVE — Forward
Current Club: Whyteleafe
Previous clubs include: Chipstead - July 1997.

McSTEA, ANTHONY — Defender
Current Club: Brandon United
Birthplace: Middlesbrough
Tremendously talented right-sided player, who signed during the close season from Middlesbrough. A player who will prove to be a major asset to the club.

McTAGGART, GLENN — Forward
Current Club: Thamesmead Town
Birthplace: Kent
Previous clubs include: Dartford - November 2001.

McVARISH, IAN — Forward
Current Club: Redditch United
Birthplace: Coventry
Striker who joined Redditch United from Dr Martens Western rivals Rugby United in July 2002. A former Coventry and West Brom junior, Ian had spells with Racing Club Warwick and Burton Albion before signing for Rugby in August 2001.

McVEY, DANNY — Defender
Current Club: Nantwich Town
Birthplace: Liverpool
Previous clubs include: Prescot Cables - July 2001, Kidsgrove Ath., Nantwich T, Burscough.

McWILLIAMS, JAMIE — Defender
Current Club: Racing Club Warwick
Birthplace: Birmingham
Previous clubs include: Redditch Utd — December 2001, Paget R, Bromsgrove R, Racing Club Warwick, Kings Norton T, WBA.

MEACHAM, ROBBIE — Midfielder
Current Club: Hednesford Town
Birthplace: Birmingham
A skilful, left side midfield player who has progressed right through the youth team ranks at Hednesford Town FC. Rob has great ability and is always likely to get a goal. Definitely a player for the future, Rob is still young enough to play in the FA Youth Cup, but will undoubtedly also play at a more senior level this season.

MEAD, BILLY — Midfielder
Current Club: Hampton & Richmond

D o B: 07/01/1981   Birthplace: London

Tenacious midfielder who joined Ryman Premier side Hampton & Richmond Borough in July 2002 from rivals Kingstonian. Was signed by former manager Geoff Chapple for the Ks towards the end of the 2000/01 season. The midfielder famously forgot that hed already appeared in the Surrey Senior Cup, which meant that Ks were expelled from the competition when he played - and scored - against Tooting & Mitcham United in 2000/01. Originally on the books at Millwall.

MEAD, CRAIG — Midfielder
Current Club: Brentwood

Birthplace: Essex

Another utility player who can play in midfield or in defence. Played a key role in central midfield for last seasons successful side.

MEAD, GARETH — Midfielder
Current Club: Hamble ASSC

Birthplace: Hampshire

Previous clubs include: Colden Common - July 2000.

MEAD, STEVE — Goalkeeper
Current Club: Purfleet

Previous clubs include: Concord Rangers - August 1997.

MEAH, JAKE — Midfielder
Current Club: Arlesey Town

Birthplace: Stevenage

Jake joined Arlesey Town in August 2001 from Edgware Town and has also spent time at Baldock Town and Stevenage Borough. Proved to be a great asset in Arleseys midfield. He is a student and a fitness instructor.

MEAH, JERAN — Midfielder
Current Club: Boreham Wood

Birthplace: Hertfordshire

Jeran is a highly-rated attacking midfield player who joined Boreham Wood from Hitchin Town and made his debut for the club against Northwood on the 10 March 2001. He scored his first goal for the club on his second appearance against Romford. He began his career at Stevenage Borough and joined Hitchin Town in September 1998.

MEAKES, JON — Midfielder
Current Club: Potters Bar Town

Birthplace: Herts

Previous clubs include: Hertford T - January 2001, Northwood, Welwyn Garden C, Hertford T, Welwyn Garden C.

MEALOR, KEVIN — Forward
Current Club: Chesham United

D o B: 16/02/1984   Birthplace: Berkshire

Kevin is a young left winger who has progressed to the first-team from Ryman Premier side Chesham United's youth and reserve teams. He has a good fitness level and loves running at defenders. He is currently a student and his best moment in football was playing for Arsenal Youth.

MEARA, JAMES — Midfielder
Current Club: Leighton Town

D o B: 07/10/1972   Birthplace: Hammersmith

Previous clubs include: Hemel Hempstead T - February 2002, Aylesbury Utd, Doncaster R, Watford.

MEARS, SPENCER — Midfielder
Current Club: Ringmer

Birthplace: Sussex

One time Lewes, Whitehawk and Peacehaven midfielder who left Saltdean to play in Glen Geards Steyning side for the latter half of 1999/2000. Moved to Ringmer for the start of the following season and scored 9 times during 2000/0o. Went off to travel round the world in November 2001.

MEECHAN, ALEX — Forward
Current Club: Forest Green Rovers

D o B: 29/01/1980   Birthplace: Plymouth

Highly-rated striker who made an explosive start to the 2000/01 season, scoring seven goals in ten appearances whilst on-loan to Conference side Forest Green Rovers from Bristol City. Returned to the club with a full-time contract on 1st January 2001 and was top scorer for the next two campaigns. Started his career at Swindon Town.

MEHEW, DAVID — Forward
Current Club: Weston-Super-Mare

D o B: 29/10/1967   Birthplace: Camberley

Recently signed from Brislington. His football league appearance includes over 200 apearances for Bristol Rovers and spells at Exeter City and Walsall.

MEHMET, DANIEL — Defender
Current Club: Boreham Wood

Birthplace: Hertfordshire

Daniel is a nineteen year old defender who joined Boreham Wood in 2000/01, when he played for the Clubs Youth Team. He has progressed quickly and has been a member of the First Team Squad for much of the 2001/02 Season. He made his First Team debut against St. Margaretsbury (Away) in a Herts Senior Challenge Cup game on the 9 October 2001 and marked the occasion with a tremendous goal, scoring with a shot from forty yards.

MELLON, RICHARD — Defender
Current Club: Barwell

Birthplace: Nottingham

Previous clubs include: Gedling T - June 2002, Arnold T, Attenborough, Eastwood T, Norwich C (Trainee).

MELLON, SCOTT — Forward
Current Club: Denaby United

Birthplace: Sheffield

Previous clubs include: Maltby Main - January 2002, Parkgate, Chesterfield.

MELROSE, CRAIG — Defender
Current Club: Bedlington Terriers

Birthplace: Newcastle

Off the field he is as quiet as they come. On the field a true Terrier in every respect. Craig is a police officer by trade and has actually represented the force both at County and International level. A very powerful determined defender in the best traditions of centre halves Craig is in his third spell at the club after rejoining the Terriers from Blyth early in the 1999/00 season.

MELVIN, DAMIEN — Forward
Current Club: Liversedge

Birthplace: Yorkshire

Previous clubs include: Ossett T - December 2000.

MENSAH, EBOW — *Midfielder*
Current Club: Bromley

Birthplace: Surrey
Started his career with Kingstonian and worked with McIntyre from the age of 16 and worked his way up through the ranks at Kingsmeadow. He made some appearances for Bromley last season and played well on his return for Bromley at Aylesbury United in February 2002.

MERCER, JAMES — *Goalkeeper*
Current Club: Dulwich Hamlet

Birthplace: London
Very promising young goalkeeper who has been in outstanding form since joining Dulwich Hamlet at the start of the 2000/01 season and has attracted the attention of League scouts. Previously on the books of Cambridge United where he progressed to the fringes of the first-team.

MERCER, JASON — *Defender*
Current Club: Abingdon Town

Birthplace: Oxfordshire
Previous clubs include: Quarry Nomads - August 2001.

MEREDITH, SION — *Midfielder*
Current Club: Carmarthen Town

D o B: 18/01/1978   Birthplace: Wales
Honours won: Wales Universities Rep.
Previous clubs include: Pontrhydfendigaid - January 1999.

MEREDITH, TOM — *Midfielder*
Current Club: Hemel Hempstead Town

D o B: 27/10/1977   Birthplace: London
Previous clubs include: St.Albans C - September 2001, Bury T, Enfield, Stevenage B, Hendon, Peterborough Utd.

MERNAGH, GAVIN — *Forward*
Current Club: Flackwell Heath

D o B: 11/06/1978   Birthplace: Slough
Previous clubs include: Egham T- January 2002, Windsor & Eton, Enfield, Chertsey T, Beaconsfield SYCOB, Yeading, Maidenhead Utd, Chertsey T, Aldershot T, Enfield, Slough T, QPR.

MERRILL, ASHLEY — *Goalkeeper*
Current Club: Stocksbridge Park Steels

Birthplace: Sheffield
Ashley played for Sheffield Boys and South Yorkshire Boys at schoolboy level and was also on the books of Sheffield United before joining Stocksbridge Park Steels. Made his Steels debut in December 2001 when still only 18. Good build for a keeper, he is highly-promising and should go far if he keeps progressing.

MERRIMAN, TERRY — *Midfielder*
Current Club: Carterton Town

Birthplace: Oxford
Previous clubs include: Witney T - December 2000, Windsor & Eton, Cambridge Utd, Coventry C (Trainee).

MERRIS, DAVID — *Midfielder*
Current Club: Harrogate Town

Birthplace: Rotherham
Honours won: UniBond League Div.One Winners
Midfielder who started his career as a fourteen-year-old schoolboy at Rotherham United and then became a YTS player for two years. He moved on for a short time to Guiseley before signing for Harrogate Town early in the 1999/2000 season.

MERRITT, JUSTIN — *Midfielder*
Current Club: Thame United

Birthplace: Oxfordshire
Re-signed for Thame United in July 2000 from Witney Town, Justin added vast experience to the midfield. Formerly with Watford and Aylesbury United. Previously with Watford, Aylesbury United, Marlow, Windsor & Eton and Brackley Town.

MESHER, STEVE — *Forward*
Current Club: Fleet Town

Birthplace: Hampshire
Previous clubs include: Bournemouth FC - February 2001.

METCALFE, ANDY — *Midfielder*
Current Club: Soham Town Rangers

Birthplace: Cambridgeshire
Previous clubs include: Warboys T - July 2001.

METCALFE, CHRISTIAN — *Midfielder*
Current Club: Slough Town

D o B: 14/12/1974   Birthplace: London
Honours won: Ryman Premier Div.Winners
Experienced midfielder who joined Ryman Division One North side Slough Town in the summer of 2002 after spending a season with Premier Division St Albans City. Originally with Chelsea, Christian then had successful spells with Harrow Borough, Hayes, whom he helped to promorion to the Conference, Stevenage Borough and Woking, before signing for the Saints in August 2001.

METCALFE, STEVE — *Midfielder*
Current Club: Saltdean United

Birthplace: Sussex
Promising midfielder: recruited to the Saltdean first-team halfway through 2001/02: also a member of the Sussex U-18 squad.

METCALFE, WAYNE — *Midfielder*
Current Club: Thackley

Birthplace: Yorkshire
Previous clubs include: Farsley Celtic - July 2000.

METHERINGHAM, PAUL — *Forward*
Current Club: Yate Town

Birthplace: Bristol
Previous clubs include: Almondsbury T - July 2000, Yeovil T, Yate T.

MEYRICK, DEAN — *Forward*
Current Club: Studley

Birthplace: Wocestershire
Previous clubs include: Alvechurch - August 2001, Cradley T, Bromsgrove R.

MFONO, FRANCK-MICHEL — *Forward*
Current Club: Leek Town

Birthplace: France
Honours won: Cameroon under-21 Int.
Joined Leek Town in September 2001 from French club Croissant. Franck was born in France and has played in the French Second Division, as well as representing Cameroon at under-21 level. Has quickly assumed cult status amongst the Leek faithful with his all action style. His versatility has been shown in playing at left back, midfield and more recently as a striker.

MICCICHE, MARCO — Midfielder
Current Club: Bath City

Birthplace: Bristol

Former Bristol Rovers YTS player, Marco returned to Bath City from Clevedon Town during the summer of 2001. His first spell at Twerton Park came during the 1995/96 season, although injury restricted him to just 9 appearances during that campaign. Made the move to Clevedon in July 1996 and spent a number of successful seasons at the Hand Stadium. However, a serious cruciate knee ligament injury saw the tough-tackling midfielder miss most of the 2000/01 season but he regained his fitness following his switch to Bath.

MIDDLETON, CARL — Defender
Current Club: Barwell

D o B: 20/10/1978   *Birthplace: Leicester*

Previous clubs include: Gresley Rovers - February 2002, Burton Alb., Leicester C (Junior).

MIDDLETON, DARREN — Forward
Current Club: Worcester City

D o B: 28/12/1978   *Birthplace: Lichfield*

Former Aston Villa and Wolves attacker, who played for Stafford Rangers and Forest Green Rovers before joining Worcester City in August 2001. Earned a contract on the strength of some highly impressive pre-season performances.

MIDDLETON, GARRY — Defender
Current Club: Stocksbridge Park Steels

D o B: 01/04/1970   *Birthplace: Derbyshire*

Signed for Stocksbridge Park Steels in May 2002. Had joined Ilkeston from Arnold Town towards the end of the 1995/96 season after spells at Gainsborough Trinity, Matlock Town and Belper Town. A very reliable performer was Ilkestons longest-serving player with well over 200 appearances before his move to Steels.

MIDDLETON, GARY — Midfielder
Current Club: Whitley Bay

Birthplace: Newcastle

Experienced midfield player who is now in his third season with us after enjoying over 5 years of success at Bedlington Terriers. Club captain. Players' Player of the year last season.

MIDDLETON, JAMIE — Midfielder
Current Club: Thornaby on Tees

D o B: 02/10/1979   *Birthplace: Stockton*

Previous clubs include: Bishop Auckland - February 2002, Marske Utd, Whitby T, Middlesbrough.

MIDDLETON, KEITH — Forward
Current Club: Bashley

Birthplace: Dorset

Previous clubs include: Poole T - January 2002, Dorchester T, Hamworthy Utd, Poole T, Hamworthy Utd.

MIDDLETON, LEE — Midfielder
Current Club: Bedworth United

D o B: 11/09/1970   *Birthplace: Nuneaton*

Previous clubs include: Atherstone Utd - March 2002, Cambridge Utd, Swindon T, Coventry C.

MIDDLETON, LUKE — Defender
Current Club: Forest Green Rovers

Birthplace: Gloucester

Defender Luke joined Conference side Forest Green Rovers after being recommended by then Swansea boss John Hollins. He played at Southampton in their academy and after being released by the Saints, Luke earned a contract at Swansea where he made one first team appearance and numerous reserve team appearances Started out at local side Topsham Town.

MIDDLETON, MARK — Midfielder
Current Club: Edgware Town

Birthplace: Middlesex

Previous clubs include: Wembley - January 2002.

MIDDLETON, ROSS — Defender
Current Club: Barnstaple Town

D o B: 10/05/1981   *Birthplace: Devon*

Previous clubs include: Ilfracombe - July 2000.

MIDGLEY, CRAIG — Forward
Current Club: Halifax Town

D o B: 24/06/1976   *Birthplace: Bradford*

Pacey forward who was e-signed by Conference club Halifax Town in August 2002 after originally being released by the administrators at the end of the 2001/02 season. Began his career with his home-town club Bradford City, where he made a handful of first-team appearances. Also had loan spells with Scarborough and Darlington before moving to Hartlepool in March 1998. Switched to The Shay in the summer of 2001 and totalled around 150 League appearances, scoring over 30 times.

MIDGLEY, NEIL — Forward
Current Club: Barnet

D o B: 21/10/1978   *Birthplace: Cambridge*

A prolific goal-getter for Ipswich reserves, Neil had spells with both Luton and Kidderminster before joining Barnet in March 2001.

MIDSON, JACK — Forward
Current Club: Stevenage Borough

Birthplace: Herts

Jack made his first start for Stevenage Borough in April 2002 at Boston United, where he impressed in a goalless draw. A product of the EFCO scheme, he has shown tremendous potential. He scored for fun in the Youth team, but is still to net for the first team. Jack signed a new improved contract at the start of the 2002/03 season.

MIDWOOD, MICHAEL — Forward
Current Club: Farsley Celtic

D o B: 19/04/1976   *Birthplace: Huddersfield*

Previous clubs include: Ossett T - August 2001, Kuitan (Hong Kong), Doncaster R, Emley, Halifax T, Huddersfield T.

MIGHTY, PAUL — Forward
Current Club: Borrowash Victoria

Birthplace: Derbyshire

Previous clubs include: Mickleover Sports - March 2002, Mickleover RBL.

MILBOURNE, IAN — Forward
Current Club: Whitley Bay

D o B: 21/01/1979   *Birthplace: Hexham*

Ian is a pacey winger at home on either flank. Second season at the club having signed from Tow Law Town.

MILBURN, ELLIOTT — *Defender*
Current Club: Dunston Federation Brewery
Birthplace: Newcastle

Previous clubs include: Alnwick T - July 1994.

MILDENHALL, DEAN — *Midfielder*
Current Club: Hungerford Town
Birthplace: Berkshire

Previous clubs include: Kintbury Rangers - July 1997.

MILEHAM, IAN — *Midfielder*
Current Club: Hatfield Main
Birthplace: Hull

Previous clubs include: Parkgate - March 2002, Hatfield Main, Selby T, Goole T, Winterton R, Hatfield Main, Pontefract Collieries, Goole T, Denaby Utd, Selby T, Hull C.

MILES, ADIE — *Forward*
Current Club: Pagham
Birthplace: Sussex

Forward, now in his veteran days: scored a total of 104 goals for Bognor Regis since first playing for them in the 80s (spent 1999/2000 with their rivals, Worthing): famously struck two very late Rustie goals in their controversial 6-4 Sussex Senior Cup victory over Pagham in February 2001: signed for Wick at the start of 2001/02, but defected to the Lions (who he had played for some years ago) in February.

MILES, ANTHONY — *Defender*
Current Club: Wick
Birthplace: Sussex

Previous clubs include: Lancing - July 2001.

MILES, BEN — *Goalkeeper*
Current Club: Llanelli AFC
D o B: 13/04/1976   Birthplace: Middlesex

Previous clubs include: Haverfordwest County - November 2001, Wokingham T, Hampton & Richmond B, Wealdstone, Haverfordwest Co., Slough T, Swansea C, Southall.

MILES, IAN — *Defender*
Current Club: Ashford Town (Middx)
Birthplace: Middlesex

Defender whose only senior club has been Ashford Town (Middx). Aged 32 he is fast and tenacious and a vital member of Ashfords defence although he has played in a number of positions for the Club. Well on the way to 500 appearances for the club. Was voted Players' Player of the Year 2000 -01.

MILES, KEITH — *Forward*
Current Club: Rye & Iden United
D o B: 25/11/1967   Birthplace: Hastings

Experienced forward who spent seven years with St Leonards before joining Eastbourne Borough during the 2001 close season: turned down an offer to join Sidley when signing instead for Rye in November. Has also previously played for Hastings, Eastbourne Utd and Hailsham.

MILES, NICK — *Midfielder*
Current Club: Lymington & New Milton
D o B: 22/11/1976   Birthplace: Colchester
Honours won: England Schoolboy Int.

Previous clubs include: Salisbury C (£1,000) - October 2000, AFC Bournemouth.

MILES, PAUL — *Midfielder*
Current Club: Haverhill Rovers
Birthplace: Suffolk

Captain, has returned to Haverhill Rovers after spells at Kettering Town and Halstead Town. Midfielder with trials at Cambridge United and Ipswich Town under his belt. First team captain.

MILES, PHIL — *Defender*
Current Club: Chatham Town
Honours won: FA Vase Winners

Previous clubs include: Deal T - July 2000, Slade Green, Thamesmead T, Darenth Heathside, Welling Utd, Slade Green, Chatham T.

MILES, STEVE — *Forward*
Current Club: Chesham United
D o B: 08/11/1983   Birthplace: Maidenhead

Midfielder who has played for Brentford, Wycombe Wanderers, Luton and Marlow, signing for Ryman Premier side Chesham United in January 2002. He is a quick, hard-working and enthusiastic player. He is a student and his best moment in football was Cheshams replay game away to Hereford United during th 2001/02 season in the FA Trophy. His footballing hero is Roy Keane.

MILFORD, BEN — *Midfielder*
Current Club: Southwick
Birthplace: Sussex

Competitive midfielder: transferred from Shoreham to East Preston during the 1999 close season: followed boss Carl Stabler to Wick at the start of the following campaign (scored 12 times): moved to Southwick in January 2002.

MILLARD, PAUL — *Defender*
Current Club: Willenhall Town
Birthplace: Birmingham

Signed January 2001 from Tividale, former teams include Halesowen Harriers, Brierley Hill and Lye. Big, strong and awkward player who was the official Man of the Match in last seasons Invitation Cup final.

MILLARD, RICKY — *Goalkeeper*
Current Club: Enfield
D o B: 03/05/1984   Birthplace: London

Previous clubs include: Barnet - October 2001.

MILLER, ADAM — *Midfielder*
Current Club: Grays Athletic
Birthplace: Suffolk
Honours won: FA Trophy Winners

A very talented midfielder who signed for Ryman Premier side Grays Athletic in August 2002 from rivals Canvey Island involving a player/swap deal. Had joined Canvey in October 2000 from Ipswich Town's Youth Academy. Also had a trial with Southend United, and was offered a contract, but a change of management put paid to that. Enjoyed an outstanding 2001/02 season which saw him attract attention from League clubs again. Was a member of Canveys 2001 FA Trophy-winning side.

MILLER, ASHLEY — *Forward*
Current Club: Kidsgrove Athletic
Birthplace: Stoke

Young winger, who caused loads of problems for some of the better defences in the league last season. They usually resort to tripping him up inside the area, and on ocassions this has even led to a penalty being awarded. Hasn't really impressed so far this season.

M

MILLER, BARRY — Defender
Current Club: Doncaster Rovers
D o B: 29/03/1976   Birthplace: Ealing
Highly-rated defender who started out as a trainee with Brentford but moved on to Wokingham Town and then Farnborough Town. In August 1999 Gillingham signed him on a free transfer from Farnborough Town. He was loaned out to Woking in March 2000 and signed for Doncaster Rovers in October of that year.

MILLER, BEN — Midfielder
Current Club: Ipswich Wanderers
Birthplace: Ipswich
From Youth team.

MILLER, CHRIS — Forward
Current Club: Carmarthen Town
D o B: 20/05/1978   Birthplace: Wales
Previous clubs include: Haverfordwest County - November 2001, Pontardawe T.

MILLER, JAMES — Forward
Current Club: Oadby Town
Birthplace: Leicester
Previous clubs include: Corby T - November 2001, Friar Lane OB,

MILLER, JAMIE — Forward
Current Club: Ashton United
Previous clubs include: Liversedge - January 2000.

MILLER, JON — Defender
Current Club: Winsford United
Birthplace: Cheshire
Local youngster who has impressed in defence this season.

MILLER, JON — Defender
Current Club: Weston-Super-Mare
Birthplace: Somerset
Signed in December 2001 from Frome Town. Previous clubs include Yeovil Town, Street, Yate Town and Welton Rovers. Scored the very first goal in this seasons FA cup competition.

MILLER, JUSTIN — Forward
Current Club: Cirencester Town
D o B: 25/10/1976   Birthplace: Swindon
Signed for Cirencester Town from Hellenic League club Highworth Town in March 2001. Justin is a clever natural goalscorer, and has become a regular member of the first team. Started his playing days with Witney Town.

MILLER, KARL — Defender
Current Club: Havant & Waterlooville
Birthplace: Hampshire
Karl is the teams most recent signing, putting pen to paper in October 2001 on a contract that will keep him with the club until May 2003. A product of the youth team, Karl has this season been making waves in the reserve side and made his first team debut in the Senior Cup match against Moneyfields - scoring an excellent goal in the process.

MILLER, LEIGHTON — Defender
Current Club: Diss Town
Birthplace: Norwich
Previous clubs include: Gorleston - July 2001, Diss T.

MILLER, MATTHEW — Forward
Current Club: Yeading
Birthplace: London
Signed for the Ding during the summer having previously been with Hampton & Richmond Borough. Only twenty-one years old, Matt is skillful player who is not afraid of getting stuck in. Scored twice in the opening league game and win at Barking & East Ham United.

MILLER, NEIL — Defender
Current Club: Sittingbourne
Birthplace: Kent
A dependable defender who also likes going forward where he has scored many important goals. Very loyal player who has played for Sittingbourne since his youth team days.

MILLER, PAUL — Forward
Current Club: Lincoln United
D o B: 31/01/1968   Birthplace: Woking
Vastly experienced forward with over 300 League appearances to his name. Joined Wimbledon from Yeovil Town in August 1987 and then had spells with Bristol Rovers and Lincoln City. Signed for UniBond side Hucknall Town at the start of the 2001/02 season but played little due to other commitments. However, he joined UniBond First Division Lincoln United in July 2002.

MILLER, ROBBIE — Defender
Current Club: Bedford Town
D o B: 28/03/1980   Birthplace: Bedford
Signed for Ryman Premier side Bedford Town August 2001 from Conference outfit Stevenage Borough. Robbie made over 50 appearances with Stevenage prior to his arrival at the New Eyrie. Previous clubs include Cambridge United and Coventry City after starting his career at West Ham as a youth player. He has really made an impact at Bedford and has bags of ability.

MILLIGAN, DUNCAN — Midfielder
Current Club: Frickley Athletic
Birthplace: Yorkshire
Previous clubs include: Harrogate T - August 2002, Doncaster R.

MILLIGAN, ROSS — Defender
Current Club: Gretna
D o B: 02/06/1978   Birthplace: Dumfries
Previous clubs include: Carlisle Utd - October 1998, Glasgow Rangers, Maxwelton T.

MILLINGTON, LEWIS — Midfielder
Current Club: Boldmere St.Michaels
Birthplace: Birmingham
Previous clubs include: Oldbury Utd - November 2001, Sandwell B, Gresley R, Alvechurch, Chelmsley T.

MILLINGTON, SCOTT — Midfielder
Current Club: Caernarfon Town
D o B: 07/01/1974
Previous clubs include: Total Network Solutions - July 2001, Rhyl, Total Network Solutions, Rhyl.

MILLINS, MARTIN — Forward
Current Club: Tunbridge Wells
Birthplace: Kent
Previous clubs include: Tonbridge Angels - December 2000.

MILLS, DANNY — *Defender*

Current Club: Hanwell Town

D o B: 20/09/1976 — Birthplace: Ealing

Previous clubs include: North Greenford Utd - July 2000, Yeading, Millwall (Junior).

MILLS, PAUL — *Defender*

Current Club: Uxbridge

D o B: 22/10/1977 — Birthplace: Middlesex

Paul signed for Uxbridge in September 1996 and is an excellent defender, who can also play in midfield. Paul was previously with Brentford and briefly Woking. Paul is the clubs penalty taker and has now played over 250 games for the club. Won both the player of the year and Supporters' Player of the year awards in 1998/99.

MILLS, TOM — *Midfielder*

Current Club: Desborough Town

Birthplace: Rothwell

Previous clubs include: Rothwell T - August 2002.

MILNE, GARY — *Forward*

Current Club: Workington

Spent much of his career with Gretna before his arrival at Borough Park in the summer of 1999. Missed the entire pre season program because of a domestic accident but should prove a good asset to the squad. Scored on his full UniBond League debut.

MILNER, BEN — *Forward*

Current Club: Rugby United

Birthplace: Banbury

Tall, 63 striker who was a product of local football when he played for Banbury United's youth team. Played for Brackley Town where he was top goalscorer for 2000/01. Signed again for Banbury at the beginning of the 2001/02 season and made a big difference to Banburys attacking options. The former Witney & District representative then moved to Rugby United in July 2002.

MILNER, JOHN — *Forward*

Current Club: Bedlington Terriers

Birthplace: Newcastle

John started his career as a defender on apprentice forms with Newcastle United. After his release he ended up at Seaham Red Star where circumstances saw him switched to a front running role and he has never looked back. After joining Bedlington from Seaham he has become a goalscorer supreme. Three seasons ago his contribution to the Terriers success was 65 goals, he notched another 48 the next term and then scored 57 last season. More than just a goalscorer his leading of the line and all round forward play has seen him emerge as a possible target for several league and conference sides. 1999/2000 seasons Radio Newcastle Non-League player of the year.

MILNER, KARL — *Midfielder*

Current Club: Liversedge

Birthplace: Huddersfield

Previous clubs include: Brook Sports - July 1993, Huddersfield T (Junior).

MILROY, JONATHAN — *Forward*

Current Club: West Auckland Town

Birthplace: Co.Durham

Previous clubs include: Bishop Auckland - July 1998, West Auckland T, Blyth Spartans, Cockfield, Dunston Federation, Ferryhill Ath.

MILSOM, PAUL — *Forward*

Current Club: Bath City

D o B: 05/10/1974 — Birthplace: Bristol

Big target man Paul switched to Bath City from Clevedon Town in the summer of 2001. With the financial position of the club it had been nearly ten years since they had paid a transfer fee for a player but, with the assistance of the supporters club, an undisclosed fee (believed to be in the region of £3,000) was paid for the striker. Paul spent three seasons at the Hand Stadium, including their promotion campaign in 1999, but following the Seasiders relegation looked to get away from the Bristol-based club. Began his career as an apprentice at Bristol City, spending over three years at Ashton Gate before moving onto Cardiff City and Oxford United. Moved into Non-League in 1997 firstly with Trowbridge Town and, when they folded, Gloucester City. In his final year at Clevedon, Paul scored 13 goals in just 25 appearances as a number of injuries plagued his season, but it is his all round game that City required his services for.

MILTON, MICHAEL — *Defender*

Current Club: Leyton Pennant

Birthplace: Essex

Previous clubs include: Waltham Abbey - August 2001, Leyton Pennant, Romford, Chesham Utd, Collier Row, Walthamstow Pennant.

MINES, JASON — *Defender*

Current Club: Sidlesham

Birthplace: Sussex

Defender: has regularly played under Richard Towers during recent years in the U-18 sides at Chichester and Sidlesham: member of the reserves who was then promoted to the first-team in 2001/02: suffered with a hernia injury midway through the latest season.

MINETT, JASON — *Midfielder*

Current Club: Grantham Town

D o B: 12/08/1971 — Birthplace: Peterborough

Experienced midfielder who was signed towards the end of the 2001/02 season to boost Grantham Town's final promotion push. Joined from Kings Lynn after previously serving Norwich, Exeter, Lincoln City, Kettering Town, Doncaster Rovers and Boston United.

MINGS, ADIE — *Forward*

Current Club: Chippenham Town

Birthplace: Bristol

Very experienced wide attacker who joined Chippenham Town in July 2001 after a season with Basingstoke Town in the Ryman League. Originally with the club in their Western League days before joining Bath City in 1990 where he spent five years before joining Gloucester.

MINSHALL, MATTHEW — *Midfielder*

Current Club: Abbey Hey

Birthplace: Manchester

Previous clubs include: Glossop North End - July 2001.

MINTA, CHRIS — *Midfielder*

Current Club: Lincoln United

Birthplace: Lincoln

Chris is another player who has risen through Lincoln United's ranks to become a first team regular. He works tirelessly in the midfield and is likely to score spectacular goals.

M

MINTON, JEFF — Midfielder
Current Club: Canvey Island
D o B: 28/12/1973 Birthplace: Hackney
Very experienced midfielder who joined Ryman Premier side Grays Athletic in August 2002 after being released by Leyton Orient. However, after appearing twice for Grays, he switched to rivals Canvey Island in a player/exchange deal. Began his career with Spurs and went on to make over 250 League appearances with Brighton, Port Vale, Rotherham and Orient.

MINTURN, ANDY — Defender
Current Club: Bath City
D o B: 16/10/1974 Birthplace: Swindon
A versatile player who can play in defence or midfield, Andy joined Bath City in May 2002 from Dr Martens Western rivals Cirencester Town. Had returned to Cirencester Town in July 1999 following a spell in Germany. Has also seen service with the likes of Hungerford Town, Ferndale Athletic and Devizes Town in the past.

MINTUS, OSSIE — Defender
Current Club: Rothwell Town
Birthplace: Leicester
Previous clubs include: Corby T - December 2001, Phal Lane UB, Corby T, Leicester Utd, Hinckley T, Leicester Utd, Hinckley T, Hednesford T, Leicester Utd.

MINTUS, TYRONE — Defender
Current Club: Oadby Town
Birthplace: Leicester
Previous clubs include: Shepshed Dynamo - September 2001, Corby T, Stafford R, Shepshed Dynamo, Ilkeston T, VS Rugby, Shepshed Alb., Leicester Utd, Corby T, Leicester Utd, Barwell, Hinckley Ath., Hednesford T, Leicester Utd.

MIRANDA, LES — Forward
Current Club: Winsford United
Birthplace: Cheshire
Tireless front-runner who was signed from local football. Immediately impressed in pre-season friendlies.

MISON, MICHAEL — Midfielder
Current Club: Sutton United
D o B: 08/11/1975 Birthplace: London
Signed for Sutton United in August 2001 from St Albans City, although he spent much of the previous season out of the game through injury. He began his career with Fulham before spending three seasons with Rushden & Diamonds, making around 50 Conference appearances, and can play in midfield or at centre back.

MITCHELL, ADAM — Goalkeeper
Current Club: Harrogate Town
Birthplace: York
Previous clubs include: Pickering T - February 2002, York RI.

MITCHELL, ANDY — Defender
Current Club: Sheffield FC
D o B: 12/09/1976 Birthplace: Rotherham
Previous clubs include: Belper T - July 2000, Ilkeston T, Boston Utd, Chesterfield, Aston Villa.

MITCHELL, CARLTON — Midfielder
Current Club: Kingsbury Town
Birthplace: London
Joined Ryman Division Two side Kingsbury Town in August 2002 from Premier Division neighbours Harrow Borough. Had signed for Boro during the summer of 2001 having previously played for Hillingdon Borough, Windsor & Eton and Wembley. Works as a wire-worker.

MITCHELL, GRAHAM — Defender
Current Club: Bradford Park Avenue
D o B: 16/02/1968 Birthplace: Shipley
Very experienced defender with over 500 League appearances to his name in England and Scotland. Started his career with Huddersfield where he played for eight years and over 250 times. Spells with Bradford City, Raith Rovers, Cardiff and Halifax followed before he joined UniBond Premier side Bradford Park Avenue in July 2002.

MITCHELL, GRAHAM — Defender
Current Club: Selby Town
Birthplace: Selby
From Local football - July 2000.

MITCHELL, GRAHAM — Forward
Current Club: St.Helens Town
Birthplace: Liverpool
Young centre forward who joins from local football. Very intelligent player who looks full of goals. Recently returned to training following a hernia operation.

MITCHELL, IAN — Defender
Current Club: Studley
D o B: 30/06/1967 Birthplace: Birmingham
Previous clubs include: Redditch Utd - January 2002, Solihull Borough, Tamworth, Evesham Utd, Barry T, Solihull B, Telford Utd, Barry T, Solihull B, Banbury Utd, Kings Heath, Willenhall T, Nuneaton B, Highgate Utd, Moor Green, Solihull B.

MITCHELL, JAMIE — Forward
Current Club: Egham Town
Birthplace: Berkshire
Previous clubs include: Edgware T - November 2001.

MITCHELL, JOHN — Forward
Current Club: Oxford City
Previous clubs include: Thame Utd - August 2001, Chesham Utd.

MITCHELL, JUSTIN — Forward
Current Club: Walton & Hersham
Birthplace: Surrey
Justin has returned to Swans this season after playing for them from 1990-91 to 1995-96, making 225 appearances and scoring 78 goals. Was the leading scorer in Division One for season 1993-94, helping Swans to promotion. After leaving Stompond Lane he has played for Staines Town and Egham Town.

MITCHELL, LEON — Forward
Current Club: Sutton Coldfield Town
Previous clubs include: Rushall Olympic - March 2000, Tamworth.

MITCHELL, NEIL   *Midfielder*
Current Club: Chorley

D o B: 07/11/1974   *Birthplace: Lytham*
Honours won: England Youth Int.
Previous clubs include: Blackpool Rovers - September 1998, Morecambe, Macclesfield T, Blackpool.

MITCHELL, PAUL   *Midfielder*
Current Club: Hucknall Town

D o B: 08/11/1978   *Birthplace: Nottingham*
Previous clubs include: Arnold T - January 2002, Hucknall Rolls, Notts Co.

MITCHELL, RICHARD   *Forward*
Current Club: Hinckley United

D o B: 14/09/1973   *Birthplace: Stoke*
Honours won: NWCL Winners
Prolific Biddulph-based striker, who signed for Dr Martens Premier side Hinckley United for a £3,000 fee in June 2002. Had helped Kidsgrove Athletic to win the North West Counties League title in 2001/02 after joining from Northwich Victoria in October 2001. Previously with Stafford Rangers, where he scored 40 goals in a season in the Dr Martens League, Droylsden, Macclesfield, Southport and Port Vale.

MITCHELL, SHAWN   *Midfielder*
Current Club: Chatham Town

Previous clubs include: Lordswood - July 1999, Whitstable T, Chatham T.

MITTEN, CHARLIE   *Goalkeeper*
Current Club: Margate

D o B: 09/10/1974   *Birthplace: Woolwich*
Previous clubs include: Gillingham - July 2001, Dover Ath., Thamesmead T.

MOAN, GLEN   *Defender*
Current Club: Washington

Birthplace: Durham
Previous clubs include: Durham C - January 2002, Washington Nissan, Whitby T, Harrogate T, Tow Law T, South Shields, Ryhope CA.

MOAT, WILLIE   *Forward*
Current Club: Gateshead

Birthplace: Newcastle
Willie is an experienced striker well known in northern Non-League circles. He has a lovely first touch and a tremendous attitude to the game. Surprisingly released by Blyth Spartans in August 2000, where he was a huge favourite of the fans, he was quickly snapped up by the Bedlington Terriers management and settled in well at Welfare Park quickly getting amongst the goals. Another whose experience has served many clubs well and before his stint at Blyth he was previously with Spennymoor United and Brandon United amongst others. Returned to the UniBond Premier with Gateshead in the summer of 2002.

MOFFAT, STUART   *Forward*
Current Club: Workington

Previous clubs include: Motherwell - August 2001, Workington.

MOGG, DAVID   *Goalkeeper*
Current Club: Clevedon Town

D o B: 11/02/1962   *Birthplace: Bristol*
Honours won: England Schoolboy Int., FA XI
Re-joined Clevedon Town for a second spell in December 2001. Dave is a one of the most experienced goalkeepers in the Dr Martens League and has played for several clubs including Bath City, Weston-super-Mare, Salisbury City, Forest Green Rovers, Gloucester City, Bristol City and Cheltenham Town.

MOGG, LEWIS   *Midfielder*
Current Club: Rothwell Town

Birthplace: Leicester
Previous clubs include: Holwell Sports - July 2000, Hinckley Utd.

MOHAMMED, AARON   *Defender*
Current Club: Arnold Town

Birthplace: Nottingham
From Youth team.

MOHAN, JOHN   *Goalkeeper*
Current Club: Billingham Synthonia

Birthplace: Newcastle
Previous clubs include: Marske Utd - February 2002, Whitby T, Gateshead, Marske Utd.

MOHAN, NICKY   *Defender*
Current Club: Gateshead

D o B: 06/10/1970   *Birthplace: Middlesbrough*
Very experienced defender who made over 400 League appearances during a 15-year professional career that began with his home-town club Middlesbrough. Transferred to Leicester City in 1994 for £330,000 and then had spells with Bradford City, Wycombe, Stoke and Hull before joining UniBond Premier side Gateshead in August 2002.

MOLESEY, MARK   *Midfielder*
Current Club: Hayes

From Youth team.

MOLLOY, TOMMY   *Defender*
Current Club: Burscough

Birthplace: Liverpool
Very promising 20-year-old defender who graduated from UniBond Premier side Burscoughs successful side that did so well in the FA Youth Cup during 2000/01. Made debut at home to Hucknall Town in February 01 and became a regular the following season.

MOLYNEAUX, MARK   *Goalkeeper*
Current Club: Chorley

D o B: 28/10/1961   *Birthplace: Manchester*
Previous clubs include: Trafford - March 2002, Droylsden, Trafford, Salford C, Droylsden, Hyde Utd, Irlam T, Macclesfield T, Nottingham Forest.

MOLYNEUX, LEE   *Defender*
Current Club: Chorley

Birthplace: Blackpool
Previous clubs include: Daisy Hill - August 2001, Blackpool (Junior).

MOLYNEUX, MARVIN — Midfielder
Current Club: Burscough

Birthplace: Liverpool

Team captain at UniBond Premier side Burscough. Marvin progressed from the clubs highly-successful youth team and made his Unibond League debut against Bradford Park Avenue in October 1999. Has already made over 100 first team appearances.

MONINGTON, MARK — Defender
Current Club: Boston United

D o B: 21/10/1970   Birthplace: Mansfield

Vastly experienced defender who was signed by Boston United in June 2001 after being released by Rochdale.

MONK, IAN — Forward
Current Club: Leigh RMI

D o B: 30/06/1968   Birthplace: Burnley

Honours won: Conference Winners, UniBond Premier Winners

Signed pre-season 1998/99 from Morecambe. Began his playing career in the Lancs Amateur League before moving to Clitheroe for one season. This was followed by a period of just over one season at Ashton United in the Northern Premier Division One. Then moved to Macclesfield and was with the club when they won the Vauxhall Conference. From here, Ian moved to Morecambe and played at Christie Park for just over 2 years before joining RMI.

MONK, STEVE — Defender
Current Club: Hailsham Town

Birthplace: Sussex

Full back: scored twice for Hailsham during 2000/01: missed the middle part of the following season after travelling to Australia.

MONTEITH, DAVE — Defender
Current Club: Chatham Town

Honours won: FA Vase Winners

Previous clubs include: Ashford T - November 2000, Deal T, Herne Bay, Sheppey Utd, Welling Utd, Gravesend, Corinthian.

MONTGOMERY, ROBERT — Goalkeeper
Current Club: Bradford Park Avenue

Birthplace: Yorkshire

Goalkeeper who joined Bradford Park Avenue in December 2001 after spells with Harrogate Railway and Vauxhall Motors. Has also seen service with Witton Albion, Winsford United and Harrogate Town.

MOODY, ADRIAN — Defender
Current Club: Colwyn Bay

Birthplace: Wales

Young defender who joined UniBond Premier side Colwyn Bay in August 2002. Started his career as a trainee with Wrexham and progressed to make 3 League appearances before being released at the end of the 2001/02 season.

MOODY, DANNY — Defender
Current Club: Erith & Belvedere

D o B: 23/03/1973   Birthplace: Croydon

Danny is a former Surrey County youth player. He has matured into an experienced defender who signed for Erith & Belvedere from Dr Martens Eastern rival St Leonards in June 2002. He had joined St Leonards in October 2000 from Ryman League Premier side Croydon. His move ended a second spell with his local club having only returned the previous summer after a spell with Croydon United.

MOODY, PAUL — Forward
Current Club: Aldershot Town

D o B: 13/06/1967   Birthplace: Portsmouth

Big centre forward with an excellent goalscoring record who joined Ryman Premier side Aldershot Town in July 2002 from Oxford United. Actually started his career in Non-League football with then Southern League side Waterlooville before joining Southampton in July 1991 for £50,000. Went on to make over 280 League appearances and score more than 120 goals for the Saints, Oxford, Fulham and Millwall.

MOODY, STEWART — Midfielder
Current Club: Barking & East Ham United

Birthplace: Middlesex

Versatile player who can play in midfield or in attack. Joined Barking in August 2001 from Ryman League rivals Edgware Town after gaining previous experience with Enfield.

MOORE, ADAM — Midfielder
Current Club: Cwmbran Town

D o B: 11/12/1970   Birthplace: Wales

Previous clubs include: Afan Lido - July 1996, Hereford Utd, Newport Co.

MOORE, ANDY — Defender
Current Club: Spalding United

D o B: 14/11/1965   Birthplace: Lincoln

Honours won: Conference Winners

Previous clubs include: Lincoln Utd - August 2001, Brigg T, Fakenham T, Wisbech T, Gainsborough Trinity, Grantham T, Boston Utd, Western Suburbs (Australia), Lincoln C, Grimsby T.

MOORE, ANDY — Goalkeeper
Current Club: Altrincham

Birthplace: Lancashire

A talented young goalkeeper who signed for UniBond Premier side Altrincham on the eve of the 2002/03 season from North West Counties outfit Squires Gate. Made his debut against Gateshead on 26th August 2002.

MOORE, BARRY — Midfielder
Current Club: Woking

D o B: 04/02/1977   Birthplace: London

A talented midfielder, Barry joined Woking on a free transfer from Hayes, during the summer 2001. He spent three seasons with the London side, having been signed by them after helping Hampton gain promotion to the Ryman League Premier Division.

MOORE, CHRIS — Defender
Current Club: Billericay Town

Birthplace: Melbourne (Australia)

Now in his second spell with Billericay, Chris had a brief spell at Canvey at the beginning of the 1999/00 season, however a series of commanding defensive performances on his return to New Lodge won the supporters back on his side. He has now made over 250 appearances for the club, more than any other current player. His value to the managers he has played under can be gauged by the fact that in all his time with the club he has only been on the bench a handful of times times. Always dominant in the air he has scored 12 goals in his Billericay career.

MOORE, CHRIS — Forward
Current Club: Northwood

D o B: 13/01/1980   Birthplace: Middlesex

Previous clubs include: Uxbridge - March 2002, Hendon, Brentford (Junior).

MOORE, CHRISTIAN — Forward

Current Club: Burton Albion

D o B: 04/11/1972   *Birthplace: Derby*

Christian Moore was signed last season from Ilkeston Town; Christian started his career with Leicester City before moving to Stockport County. Christian had spells with both Gresley and Burton, but it was at New Manor Ground Ilkeston where he made his name, finishing top scorer during the 1997/98 campaign. His consistent battling displays and ability to find the net persuaded Brewers boss Nigel Clough to make Christian Moore Burton Albions record signing. Despite missing the early part of the season with injury, Christian still managed to find the net on no fewer than eighteen occasions.

MOORE, DANNY — Forward

Current Club: Carshalton Athletic

Birthplace: London

Previous clubs include: Dulwich Hamlet - October 2001.

MOORE, DAVID — Defender

Current Club: Workington

Previous clubs include: Bootle - August 2000.

MOORE, FERGUS — Defender

Current Club: Hemel Hempstead Town

D o B: 02/02/1972   *Birthplace: London*

A former captain at Wealdstone, Fergus left the Stones in 1998 to join Hemel Hempstead Town, returning during the summer of 2001. Originally at Brentford, he has also served Yeading, Staines Town and Uxbridge. The defender made over 200 appearances for Wealdstone before again leaving for Hemel in July 2002.

MOORE, JASON — Defender

Current Club: Dover Athletic

D o B: 16/02/1979   *Birthplace: London*

Previous clubs include: Ramsgate - July 2001, Dover Ath., Folkestone Invicta, Dover Ath., West Ham Utd.

MOORE, KEITH — Midfielder

Current Club: Wembley

Birthplace: Kent

Previous clubs include: Wealdstone - March 2002, Tonbridge Angels.

MOORE, KEVIN — Forward

Current Club: Sidlesham

Birthplace: Sussex

Striker: scored twice for Pagham early in 1999/2000 before playing for their reserve side: transferred to Sidlesham in November 2001.

MOORE, LUKE — Defender

Current Club: Mildenhall Town

Birthplace: Cambridge

Previous clubs include: Hemel Hempstead T - October 2001, Mildenhall T, Cambridge C.

MOORE, MICHAEL — Forward

Current Club: Caernarfon Town

D o B: 19/05/1978   *Birthplace: Liverpool*

Honours won: FA Youth Cup Winners

Previous clubs include: Droylsden - December 2001, Ashton Utd, Winsford Utd, Southport, Altrincham, Liverpool (Trainee).

MOORE, MICKY — Forward

Current Club: Stratford Town

D o B: 07/10/1973   *Birthplace: Derby*

Previous clubs include: Gresley Rovers - January 2002, Bromsgrove R, Stourbridge, Redditch Utd, Rothwell T, Stourbridge, Telford Utd, Moor Green, Stafford R, Cradley T, Swansea C, Derby Co.

MOORE, NEIL — Defender

Current Club: Harlow Town

Birthplace: Harlow

A local lad who is now in his eighth season with Harlow Town. Has made over 300 appearances for the club and won three consecutive Supporters' Player of the Year awards from 1998-2000. Missed much of the 2000/01 season through injury but was back for the following campaign.

MOORE, PAUL — Forward

Current Club: Telford United

Previous clubs include: Bromsgrove Rovers - September 2001, Stourport Swifts, Paget R, Redditch Utd, Bromsgrove R, Stourbridge, Bromsgrove R, Kidderminster Harriers, Walsall.

MOORE, ROGER — Forward

Current Club: Chichester City United

Birthplace: Hampshire

Prolific scorer for Hampshire League side Clanfield (some 150 goals in three years) until joining Chichester for the start of 2000/01, and had the distinction of registering the revamped clubs first-ever goal: scored 19 times for City that season, despite spending a three month spell back with his old club: the subject of many puns (licensed to score, etc) and also wears a distinctive pair of silver boots.

MOORE, STEVE — Goalkeeper

Current Club: Marske United

Birthplace: Cleveland

Previous clubs include: Northallerton T - July 1998, Whitby T, Northallerton T, Guisborough T.

MOORES, ANDY — Midfielder

Current Club: St.Helens Town

D o B: 10/06/1971   *Birthplace: Warrington*

Left-sided attacking midfield player who recently joined from neighbours Warrington Town. A player with lots of pace and skill that will trouble many defences. Will also score his fare share of goals.

MOORES, CHRIS — Forward

Current Club: Warrington Town

Birthplace: Liverpool

Previous clubs include: Castleton Gabriels - February 2001, Runcorn, Vauxhall Motors.

MOORES, JAMIE — Forward

Current Club: Wimborne Town

Birthplace: Dorset

Previous clubs include: Hamworthy Engineering - July 2000.

MOORHOUSE, TOM — Defender

Current Club: Camberley Town

Birthplace: Surrey

Previous clubs include: Dulwich Hamlet - December 2001, Corinthian Casuals.

M

MOORWOOD, BOB — Defender

Current Club: Sheffield FC

Birthplace: Derbyshire

Previous clubs include: Hallam - October 2000, Alfreton T, Denaby Utd, Alfreton T, Maltby Main, Matlock T, Parramore Sports.

MORAIS, GAVIN — Midfielder

Current Club: Norwich United

D o B: 04/07/1978 — Birthplace: Norfolk

New signing for Norwich United this season from Cromer United and previously with Great Yar- mouth Town. Speedy likes to play wide right but has also played as a central striker.

MORALEE, JAMIE — Forward

Current Club: Barry Town

D o B: 02/12/1971 — Birthplace: Wandsworth

Previous clubs include: Colchester Utd - July 2000, Brighton, Royal Antwerp (Belgium), Crewe Alexandra, Watford, Millwall, Crystal Palace.

MORAN, ANDY — Forward

Current Club: Rhyl

Birthplace: Cheshire

Previous clubs include: Bamber Bridge (£1,500) - December 2001, Total Network Solutions.

MORAN, DAMIAN — Defender

Current Club: Rossendale United

Birthplace: Lancashire

Defender who joined Rossendale United in Nov 2001. Played the majority of his previous football with Bacup Borough in the North West Counties League before trying his luck at UniBond level.

MORAN, NATHAN — Forward

Current Club: Sutton Coldfield Town

Birthplace: Birmingham

From Youth team.

MORAN, PAUL — Midfielder

Current Club: East Thurrock United

D o B: 22/05/1968 — Birthplace: Enfield

Previous clubs include: Hertford T - July 2001, Whitewebbs, Boreham Wood, Enfield, Peterborough Utd, Tottenham Hotspur.

MORAN, PAUL — Midfielder

Current Club: Edgware Town

Birthplace: London

Previous clubs include: Kingsbury T - January 2002.

MORAN, RYAN — Defender

Current Club: St.Albans City

D o B: 31/03/1982 — Birthplace: Luton

Defender who joined Ryman Premier side St Albans City from Luton Town during the 1999/00 campaign. Showed tremendous consistency, which culminated in him being named Supporters Club and Website player of the season.

MORBY, PAUL — Midfielder

Current Club: Newport Isle Of Wight

Birthplace: Sussex

Impressive utility player who joined Pagham from Portfield midway through the 1999/00 season, shortly after Richie Reynolds switched management jobs. Left Nyetimber Lane in November when Reynolds was sacked and signed for Wick two months later to be reunited with his old boss. Became reunited again when he moved to Dr Martens Eastern side Newport Isle of Wight in July 2002.

MORE, CLINTON — Forward

Current Club: Lewes

Birthplace: Sussex

Joined Eastbourne during the 2000 close season before switching to Lewes in February 2002. Began his career as an apprentice at Portsmouth, before going on to play for Bognor Regis Town (Ryman League); and Littlehampton Town, Wick, and East Preston (all Sussex County League).

MOREY, ALUN — Midfielder

Current Club: Selsey

Birthplace: Sussex

Classy midfielder who also appeared for Bognor Regis during 1999/2000, but played solely for Selsey the following season (club player of the year). Missed the first half of 2001/02 after recovering from a leg operation.

MOREY, GRAHAM — Defender

Current Club: Selsey

Birthplace: Sussex

Tenacious defender who began a spell with Chichester City in February 1998 before returning to Selsey a year later.

MOREY, STUART — Midfielder

Current Club: Selsey

Birthplace: Sussex

Midfielder who scored four times for Selsey during 1999/2000. Previously played for Sidlesham.

MORFITT, STEVE — Goalkeeper

Current Club: Stocksbridge Park Steels

Birthplace: Sheffield

Previous clubs include: Hallam - August 2001, Parkgate, Stocksbridge Park Steels, Hallam, Sheffield, Alfreton T, Maltby Main, Parkgate, Worsbrough Bridge, Woolley MW.

MORGAN, ALAN — Defender

Current Club: Doncaster Rovers

D o B: 02/11/1973 — Birthplace: Aberystwyth

Welsh-born defender who started his career with Wrexham and went on to make over 70 first-team appearances. Had a spell on-loan to Altrincham during the 1996/97 season and then joined Conference outfit Doncaster Rovers in July 2002.

MORGAN, BARI — Midfielder

Current Club: Aberystwyth Town

D o B: 13/08/1980 — Birthplace: Cilgerran

Previous clubs include: Swansea C - July 2001.

MORGAN, BRENDAN — Forward

Current Club: Belper Town

Birthplace: Derbyshire

Previous clubs include: Borrowash Victoria ñAugust 1983.

MORGAN, DAVID — Defender

Current Club: Gateshead

D o B: 09/12/1981 — Birthplace: Middlesbrough

David signed for UniBond Premier side Gateshead from Grimsby in the summer of 2002 after Paul Talbot left but has already proved himself as a worthy replacement. He has the best throw in the league, almost matching Tranmeres Dave Challinor in length. Originally with Sunderland, he is a good, talented defender with a wonderful future ahead of him.

MORGAN, FREDDIE — Midfielder

Current Club: Glapwell

Birthplace: Mansfield

Previous clubs include: Eastwood T - October 1999, Glapwell, Oakham Utd, Glapwell, Mansfield T.

MORGAN, IAN — Defender

Current Club: Port Talbot Town

D o B: 21/09/1981   Birthplace: Neath

Highly-rated former Swansea City apprentice who joined Port Talbot Town in the summer of 2000. Talented defender who had impressed since joining and has been a regular in the League of Wales.

MORGAN, JAMIE — Goalkeeper

Current Club: Lincoln United

Birthplace: Lincoln

Previous clubs include: Grantham T - January 2002, Lincoln Utd, Sleaford T, Boston T, Lincoln C (Trainee).

MORGAN, JAMIE — Midfielder

Current Club: Eastwood Town

Previous clubs include: Glapwell - August 2001, Heanor T, Ashfield Utd, Mansfield T (Junior).

MORGAN, JOE — Defender

Current Club: St.Helens Town

Birthplace: Liverpool

Another player in his second season in the Town ranks, Joe is a former Everton player who has also had spells with Southport, Marine and Ashton United. Can play in the centre of defence or at left back. Powerful striker of the ball, exceptional from dead ball situations.

MORGAN, JOHN — Forward

Current Club: Grays Athletic

Birthplace: London

Joined Grays this season from Stevenage Borough, he has a lot of natural ability and can split a defence with his running at them.

MORGAN, JOHN — Forward

Current Club: Marine

Birthplace: Merseyside

Back in the Marine squad after missing most of the 2000/01 season playing cricket in Australia. Was leading goalscorer for both seasons before that after joining from Southport. Elegant striker who scores some spectacular goals.

MORGAN, MARVIN — Forward

Current Club: Wealdstone

D o B: 13/04/1983

From Youth team.

MORGAN, MICHAEL — Forward

Current Club: Dartford

Birthplace: Kent

Previous clubs include: Welling Utd - June 2001, Tonbridge Angels.

MORGAN, NEIL — Forward

Current Club: Warrington Town

Birthplace: Liverpool

From Local football - July 2000.

MORGAN, NICKY — Midfielder

Current Club: Enfield Town (Essex)

Birthplace: Middlesex

Brother of ex-Enfield FC Youth team product John. His debut season at senior level, having joined during the summer of 2001 from local club Enfield Rangers.

MORGAN, RICHARD — Goalkeeper

Current Club: Aberystwyth Town

D o B: 28/01/1979   Birthplace: Wales

Re-signed for Aberystwyth Town in August 2002 from former League of Wales rivals Rhayader Town. Had joined Rhayader from Carmarthen Town during the previous summer, after being involved in the Intertoto Cup squad. Organizes the defence well, very commanding around the box.

MORGAN, SCOTT — Midfielder

Current Club: Barry Town

D o B: 22/03/1975   Birthplace: Bournemouth

Previous clubs include: Galway Utd - July 2001, Dorchester T, West Ham Utd.

MORGAN, STEVE — Defender

Current Club: Total Network Solutions

D o B: 19/09/1968   Birthplace: Oldham

One of TNS's many adaptable defenders at the club. Man to man marking is his speciality, although can also be used as sweeper or full-back if needed. Joined the club in February 2001 from Altrincham after previous experience with Blackpool, Plymouth, Coventry, Wigan, Burnley and Halifax.

MORGAN, TOM — Goalkeeper

Current Club: Guiseley

Previous clubs include: Halifax T - August 2001.

MORLEY, ANDY — Defender

Current Club: Maidenhead United

D o B: 21/12/1970   Birthplace: Derby

A play-anywhere defender signed just before the opening day of the 2000/2001 season from Basingstoke Town where he had spent five years following his move from Poole Town in 1995. Spent much of last season side-lined with injury.

MORLEY, DARREN — Defender

Current Club: Leyton

D o B: 01/09/1977   Birthplace: Essex

Previous clubs include: Romford - July 2001, Barking, Aveley, Wembley, Dagenham & Redbridge, Aveley, Barkingside, Dagenham & Redbridge.

MORLEY, DAVID — Defender

Current Club: Doncaster Rovers

D o B: 25/09/1977   Birthplace: St Helens

Powerful defender who joined Doncaster Rovers in June 2002 after his contract at Oxford United ended. Started his career with Manchester City but didnt make the senior side at Maine Road, although he did play first-team football for Ayr United whilst on-loan in 1998. Went on to make around 150 League appearances with Southend, Carlisle and Oxford before signing for Rovers.

MORLEY, DOMINIC — Midfielder

Current Club: Runcorn FC Halton

Birthplace: Liverpool

Dominic was signed from Droylsden about ten games into this season, and has shown himself to be a combative midfield player with a good first touch and a telling pass. Surprisingly, Dominic has yet to score for the Linnets.

M

MORLEY, NEIL — *Defender*

Current Club: Witton Albion

D o B: 16/11/1978   Birthplace: Warrington
Previous clubs include: Winsford Utd - July 2001, Manchester C.

MORRIS, ANDY — *Defender*

Current Club: Folkestone Invicta

D o B: 25/03/1972   Birthplace: Kent
Supporters' Player of the Year for 2000/01, Andy joined Folkestone Invicta in the summer of 1997 after a hugely successful spell at Ashford Town under manager Neil Cugley. He began his career with Folkestone in 1990 but moved to Ashford when the old club folded later that year. He spent the summer of 2001 playing for Manawatu in New Zealand. Has now made over 100 appearances for Invicta.

MORRIS, ANDY — *Midfielder*

Current Club: Runcorn FC Halton

D o B: 18/03/1982   Birthplace: Wigan
Andy was signed from Wigan Athletic about ten games into this season. Has only come on as substitute a few times up to yet, but he is a very skilful attacker who has got a wicked shot on him.

MORRIS, CHRIS — *Defender*

Current Club: Caersws

D o B: 25/04/1983   Birthplace: Welshpool
From Youth team.

MORRIS, DARRON — *Forward*

Current Club: Harrogate Railway

Birthplace: Yorkshire
Previous clubs include: Ossett Alb - February 2002, Glasshoughton Welfare, Farsley Celtic, North Ferriby Utd, Harrogate T, Ossett Alb., Bradford PA, Emley, Ossett Alb., Frickley Ath., Moor Green, Tamworth, Emley, Bradley Rangers.

MORRIS, DEAN — *Midfielder*

Current Club: Erith & Belvedere

Birthplace: Kent
Dean is a hard-working midfielder, with good distribution and tackling. He joined Dr Martens Eastern side Erith & Belvedere in August 2002 from Ryman Premier outfit Billericay Town. Had signed for Billericay in January 2001, making his debut against Waltham Abbey in the Essex Senior Cup on the 9th January. He joined after being released by Gillingham where he was a YTS trainee. A versatile player, he has featured both in the centre of midfield, and wide out on the wing, as well as being asked to play at right back on a few occasions.

MORRIS, GARETH — *Defender*

Current Club: Ashton United

From Youth team.

MORRIS, GRAHAM — *Defender*

Current Club: Epsom And Ewell

D o B: 27/10/1968   Birthplace: Surrey
Joined Epsom from Sutton United in 1990, previously with Maiden Vale as a Youth player. Whilst at Sutton was substitute in their FA Cup victory over Coventry City. Another model of consistency who made his 500th 1st XI appearance in the FA Carlsberg Vase 3rd Round tie against Marlow on 19th December 2000.

MORRIS, GRAHAM — *Forward*

Current Club: Sidley United

Birthplace: Sussex
Impressive forward: played for Hastings reserves in their 1999 Sussex Intermediate Cup final victory over Oving: made his debut for Eastbourne Utd in February 2000 and scored 14 times during 2000/01: signed for Hailsham at the start of the following season. Joined Sidley in December and marked his debut by scoring against Redhill.

MORRIS, JAMIE — *Midfielder*

Current Club: Enfield Town (Essex)

Birthplace: Herts
Began his career as a YTS trainee at Leyton Orient before joining Enfield, where he graduated through the ranks to make 65 first team appearances, scoring 9 goals. Finished last season with Ryman Premier club Hampton & Richmond Borough, who he joined from the Es in mid-season.

MORRIS, KEITH — *Forward*

Current Club: Barwell

Birthplace: Leicester
Previous clubs include: Hinckley T - July 1997.

MORRIS, LEE — *Forward*

Current Club: Frickley Athletic

Birthplace: Sheffield
Lee is a centre forward who scored 32 goals for Hallam during the 2001/02 season in the Northern Counties East League. Joined UniBond Premier side Frickley Athletic in the summer of 2002. Formerly with Denaby United.

MORRIS, MARK — *Defender*

Current Club: Dorchester Town

D o B: 26/09/1962   Birthplace: Morden
Previous clubs include: Hastings T - February 1999, Brighton, AFC Bournemouth, Sheffield Utd, Watford, Wimbledon.

MORRIS, PAUL — *Defender*

Current Club: Flexsys Cefn Druids

D o B: 22/08/1980   Birthplace: Cheshire
Previous clubs include: Llandudno - December 1998, Flexsys Cefn Druids.

MORRIS, PAUL — *Defender*

Current Club: Lymington & New Milton

Birthplace: Hampshire
Previous clubs include: New Milton - July 1995.

MORRIS, STEVE — *Goalkeeper*

Current Club: Woodley Sports

Birthplace: Ashton
Previous clubs include: Glossop North End - July 2001, Atherton Collieries, Woodley Sports, Glossop NE, Curzon Ashton.

MORRIS, STEVE — *Midfielder*

Current Club: Wokingham Town

Birthplace: Berkshire
From Local football - July 1992.

MORRISH, ADAM — *Midfielder*

Current Club: Dartford

D o B: 28/06/1980   Birthplace: Greenwich
Previous clubs include: Southend Utd - January 2000.

M

MORRISH, LUKE — Defender
Current Club: Welling United
D o B: 14/11/1977   Birthplace: Southend
Impessive defender who joined Dr Martens Premier side Welling United in July 2002 from Eastern Division neighbours Dartford. Started his career with Southend and then had spells with Carshalton Athletic, Dover Athletic and Canvey Island before signing for the Darts in August 1998.

MORSE, LEE — Midfielder
Current Club: Fairford Town
Birthplace: Gloucestershire
Previous clubs include: Highworth T - July 2001.

MORTIMER-JONES, JAMES — Midfielder
Current Club: Carterton Town
Birthplace: Oxfordshire
From Youth team.

MORTLEY, PETER — Defender
Current Club: Ashford Town
D o B: 17/10/1975   Birthplace: Gravesend
Experienced central defender who signed for Dr Martens Eastern side Ashford Town in November 2001. Previously with Tonbridge Angels, Gravesend & Northfleet and Sittingbourne. Started his career as a youngster at Ipswich.

MORTON, COLIN — Defender
Current Club: Blyth Spartans
D o B: 17/01/1981   Birthplace: Ashington
Signed for Blyth Spartans during the summer of 2001, from Hibernian and was originally with Derby. Displayed good defensive qualities during the pre-season games. As a result he established a first-team place.

MORTON, NEIL — Forward
Current Club: Lancaster City
D o B: 21/12/1968   Birthplace: Congleton
Previous clubs include: Morecambe - August 1999, Barrow, Altrincham, Wigan Ath., Chester C, Northwich V, Crewe Alexandra.

MORTON, RICHARD — Forward
Current Club: Newcastle Town
D o B: 20/12/1979   Birthplace: Pinner
Previous clubs include: Nothwood - September 1997, Watford.

MOSELEY, MIKE — Forward
Current Club: Witton Albion
Birthplace: Liverpool
Previous clubs include: Runcorn - August 2001.

MOSELEY, MIKE — Midfielder
Current Club: Willenhall Town
Birthplace: Wolverhampton
Previous clubs include: Wednesfield - June 2002, Bloxwich T, Rushall Olympic, Evesham Utd, Pelsall Villa, Bloxwich T, Bloxwich Strollers, Pelsall Villa.

MOSELY, STEVE — Defender
Current Club: Aveley
D o B: 26/11/1962   Birthplace: Rochford
Previous clubs include: Great Wakering Rovers - January 2001, Grays Ath., Purfleet, Dover Ath., Chelmsford C, Enfield, Dartford, Barking, Billericay T, Stambridge.

MOSES, ADRIAN — Midfielder
Current Club: Croydon Athletic
Birthplace: Surrey
Previous clubs include: Dorking - January 2002.

MOSES, JERRY — Midfielder
Current Club: Clapton
D o B: 23/11/1981   Birthplace: London
Previous clubs include: Luton T - July 2000.

MOSS, DEAN — Midfielder
Current Club: Carterton Town
Birthplace: Oxfordshire
Previous clubs include: Ardley Utd - July 2001.

MOSS, GLEN — Midfielder
Current Club: Heybridge Swifts
From Youth team.

MOSS, NEIL — Defender
Current Club: Maldon Town
Birthplace: Essex
Previous clubs include: Heybridge Swifts - July 2000.

MOSS, STEVE — Midfielder
Current Club: Hampton & Richmond
Birthplace: Southampton
Much-travelled and experienced midfielder who joined Hampton & Richmond Borough in July 2002 from Dr Martens outfit Newport IoW. Began his playing days as a youngster with Southampton and has since had spells in the Ryman and Dr Martens with the likes of Woking, Camberley, Worthing, Basingstoke, Carshalton, Crawley, Bishops Stortford, Walton & Hersham and Fisher.

MOTT, SHANE — Defender
Current Club: Chichester City United
Birthplace: Sussex
Right back: made over 100 appearances for the old Chichester City side (debuted in 1991): subsequently played for Littlehampton, Horsham YMCA and Broadbridge Heath until rejoining Adie Girdlers team during the 2000 close season: broke his leg in the FA Cup match at Hastings during September 2001.

MOTTON, MATTHEW — Defender
Current Club: East Thurrock United
D o B: 08/09/1977   Birthplace: London
Previous clubs include: Egham T - August 2002, Chertsey T, Maidenhead Utd, Windsor & Eton, Erith & Belvedere, Bromley, Chertsey T, Carshalton Ath., Chertsey T, QPR (Trainee).

MOTUM, PAUL — Goalkeeper
Current Club: Stafford Town
Birthplace: Stafford
Previous clubs include: Altrincham - July 2001, Stafford T.

MOTYKA, SIMON — Defender
Current Club: Maltby Main
Birthplace: Yorkshire
Previous clubs include: Denaby Utd - December 2001, Maltby Main, Denaby Utd, Maltby Main, Alfreton T, NCB Maltby.

MOULDING, JOHN — Defender
Current Club: Royston Town
Birthplace: Herts
From Youth team.

M

MOULT, STEVE — Defender
Current Club: Shepshed Dynamo
D o B: 12/12/1983   Birthplace: Loughborough
Previous clubs include: Loughborough Ath - August 2002, Hicnkley Utd, Qourn.

MOUNTAIN, PAT — Goalkeeper
Current Club: Newport County
D o B: 01/08/1976   Birthplace: Pontypridd
Honours won: Wales u-21 & Semi-Pro Int.
Goalkeeper who was with Cardiff City through his school years before progressing through YTS and having two years as a professional making eight first-team appearances for the Bluebirds. He represented Wales at four age levels up to and including under-21 and had European experience with Barry Town. Football Development Officer with the FA of Wales, he had six months experience with Yeovil Town after leaving Barry, followed by a similar period at Gloucester City immediately prior to joining Newport County two years ago. Added Wales semi-professional caps to his list of honours and was a member of their successful UniBond Four Nations squad in May 2002.

MOUNTFORD, PAUL — Defender
Current Club: Stourport Swifts
Previous clubs include: Oldbury Utd - June 1999, Lye T, Walsall.

MOUNTFORD, WAYNE — Defender
Current Club: Kidsgrove Athletic
Birthplace: Stoke
Honours won: NWCL Winners
Another key member of Kidsgroves double-winning side, has also played in midfield, and enjoys revisiting this role occasionally with forward charges of mixed success. Rejoined last season after a spell at Leek and has also seen service with Port Vale and Eastwood Hanley.

MOUSSI, JIMMY — Midfielder
Current Club: Feltham
Birthplace: Algeria
Moussi joined Feltham at the start of the 94/95 season under Tony Choules and broke in to the first team towards the end of the season and remained there ever since. Strong midfield player who played professionally in Algeria before moving to Auxerre in France and played for them in the French First Division. Has a fantastic strike on him and scores many spectacular goals from long range because of this.

MOWBRAY, ASHLEY — Defender
Current Club: Eastwood Town
Birthplace: Nottingham
Previous clubs include: Hucknall T - December 2001.

MOWBRAY, DARREN — Midfielder
Current Club: Spennymoor United
Previous clubs include: Guisborough T - November 2001, Northallerton T.

MOXHAM, GEOFF — Defender
Current Club: Wimborne Town
Birthplace: Dorset
Previous clubs include: Christchurch - July 2001, Wimborne T.

MOYE, ANDY — Forward
Current Club: Ely City
Birthplace: Cambridge
Previous clubs include: Soham Town Rangers - December 1999, Chatteris T, Wisbech T, Chatteris T.

MOYLES, DOMINIC — Midfielder
Current Club: Selby Town
Birthplace: Leeds
Previous clubs include: Whitkirk Wanderers - October 1996.

MTAMBARA, KEITH — Midfielder
Current Club: Peacehaven & Telscombe
Birthplace: Sussex
Midfielder who was a former member of Crawley Town's reserve side. Joined Peacehaven in August 2001.

MUCKLEBERG, TERRY — Defender
Current Club: Hook Norton
D o B: 29/09/1966   Birthplace: Oxford
Former Oxford United apprentice who signed professional forms for two years at The Manor. Made his Banbury United debut at Sutton Coldfield Town in November 1984 and has played over 200 times for Banbury in various spells. Transferred from Brackley Town to Banbury United in December 2000. Strong, classy defender, with lots of experience at this level having also played for Kettering Town, Buckingham Town, Worcester City and Marlow. Switched to Hellenic League side Hook Norton in July 2002.

MUDD, GAVIN — Midfielder
Current Club: Durham City
Birthplace: Newcastle
Previous clubs include: Brandon Utd - January 2000.

MUDGE, JAMES — Forward
Current Club: Tiverton Town
D o B: 25/03/1983   Birthplace: Exeter
Jamie joined Tiverton Town from Exeter City in November 2001. Having starred in Exeters under-19 side and been leading goalscorer, James was awarded a full contract in June 2001. He had made his first-team debut, whilst still a trainee at City, as a substitute in a game against Macclesfield Town in February 2001. He twice made the substitutes bench and impressed when called into action, none more so when he played a Man of the Match role in a friendly against Newcastle United at the end of the 2000/01 season.

MUIR, KARL — Defender
Current Club: Newcastle Blue Star
D o B: 04/09/1979   Birthplace: North Shields
Previous clubs include: Whitley Bay - August 2001, Blyth Spartans, Newcastle Utd.

MULDERS, JAN — Defender
Current Club: Stourport Swifts
Previous clubs include: Redditch Utd - February 2000, Solihull B, Bromsgrove R, Kidderminster Harriers, Malvern T.

MULDOWNEY, JOHN — Midfielder
Current Club: Fisher Athletic (London)
Birthplace: Kent
Previous clubs include: Greenwich Borough - August 2002.

MULHOLLAND, DENIS — Defender
Current Club: Moor Green
D o B: 28/09/1966   Birthplace: Birmingham
Career began as an apprentice at Grimsby Town. He originally joined Moor Green in the mid-80s from Kidderminster as a goal-scoring winger and was a key member of the treble-winning reserve side. He then went on to play for such clubs as Solihull, Paget, Sutton, Nuneaton, Redditch and Tamworth from where he returned to the Moors.

MULLEN, LEE   Defender
Current Club: Norwich United
D o B: 10/04/1981   Birthplace: Norfolk
Defender who progressed through Norwich Unitedfs ranks. Has established himself as a regular in the side.

MULLIN, LEE   Defender
Current Club: Marine
Birthplace: Crosby
Defender who came through the Marine youth team having been on Tranmere Rovers books as a youngster. Highly-promising Crosby lad who was signed on professional forms in February 2002.

MULLIN, PAUL   Forward
Current Club: Accrington Stanley
Birthplace: Lancashire
Forward signed for Accrington Stanley at the start of the 2000-2001 season from Radcliffe Borough where he had been the clubs top scorer and player of the year in the previous season.

MULLINER, ANDY   Goalkeeper
Current Club: Connahs Quay Nomads
D o B: 03/01/1971   Birthplace: Stoke
Honours won: Wales Youth & Semi-Pro Int.
Previous clubs include: Newtown - December 2001, Bangor C, Rhyl, Bangor C, Total Network Solutions, Ebbw Vale, Llansantffraid, Port Vale (Trainee).

MULLINS, ANDY   Midfielder
Current Club: Berkhamsted Town
Birthplace: Hertfordshire
Previous clubs include: Northchurch Agrevo Sports - October 1997.

MULLOCK, TIM   Goalkeeper
Current Club: Leek Town
Birthplace: Manchester
Honours won: England Youth Int.
Joined Leek Town in July 2002 from Kidsgrove Athletic. A former England Youth international goalkeeper, he has also played for the British Universities. Previously on the books at Leek CSOB, Newcastle Town, Rocester, Congleton Town and Mossley.

MULLY, KEVIN   Midfielder
Current Club: Tilbury
Birthplace: Essex
From Youth team.

MUNDAY, ADAM   Forward
Current Club: Racing Club Warwick
Birthplace: Warwick
Previous clubs include: Solihull Borough - (Re-signed - December 2001), VS Rugby, Sutton Coldfield T, Alveston, Bromsgrove R, Racing Club Warwick.

MUNDAY, MARK   Midfielder
Current Club: Margate
D o B: 17/01/1971   Birthplace: Kent
Honours won: Dr Martens Premier Div.Winners
Experienced midfielder who re-joined Margate in August 1997, helping them to gain promotion to the Conference. A goalscoring midfield player who began his playing days with Gate and also turned out for Ashford Town, Ramsgate, Herne Bay and Gravesend before returning to Hartsdown Park.

MUNDEN, MAURICE   Goalkeeper
Current Club: Dover Athletic
D o B: 08/11/1963   Birthplace: Kent
Vastly experienced goalkeeper who made a return to Dr Martens Premier side Dover Athletic in the summer of 2002 after spending three seasons with Fisher Athletic. After starting out at Charlton, Maurice served a number of Kent sides with distinction, including Folkestone, Welling United, Dover and Deal Town. Also had a spell in Hong Kong with Sing Tao.

MUNDY, RUSSELL   Defender
Current Club: Hanwell Town
D o B: 22/08/1974   Birthplace: Hammersmith
Previous clubs include: Brook House - July 1999.

MUNNS, PETER   Forward
Current Club: Histon
Previous clubs include: Wisbech T - October 2000, Chatteris T.

MUNRO, MICK   Defender
Current Club: Great Wakering Rovers
Birthplace: Essex
Previous clubs include: Basildon Utd - August 1999, Southend Manor, Ipswich T (Trainee).

MUNSON, NATHAN   Goalkeeper
Current Club: Stanway Rovers
Birthplace: Essex
Previous clubs include: Billericay T - July 1997, Wivenhoe T, Colchester Utd.

MUNT, LEE   Forward
Current Club: Hertford Town
D o B: 13/05/1977   Birthplace: Luton
Previous clubs include: Somersett & Ambury - July 2001, Welwyn Garden C, Wormley Rovers.

MURPHY, CARL   Midfielder
Current Club: Paget Rangers
Birthplace: Birmingham
Previous clubs include: Chelmsley T - October 2001.

MURPHY, CRAIG   Midfielder
Current Club: Skelmersdale United
Birthplace: Liverpool
Previous clubs include: Congleton T - July 1999, Melville Utd (New Zealand), Warrington T.

MURPHY, DANNY   Midfielder
Current Club: Altrincham
D o B: 10/05/1977
Speedy winger who is good in the air, Danny signed for Altrincham after an impressive performance for Mossley against the Robins in the FA Cup during the early part of the 2000/01 season. Scored on his Altrincham debut in a 1-1 draw with Leek Town. Danny impressed even though he was hampered with a hamstring problem for much of last season and Robins fans hope to see the best of him this year. Previous clubs include Wilmslow Albion, Mossley and Cheadle Town.

MURPHY, DANNY   Midfielder
Current Club: Brook House
Birthplace: Middlesex
Previous clubs include: Hayes - July 1998.

M

MURPHY, GARY   *Defender*

Current Club: North Leigh

D o B: 07/02/1970   *Birthplace: Oxford*

Previous clubs include: Witney T - July 2001, Oxford C, Witney T, Banbury Utd, Oxford C, Oxford Utd.

MURPHY, GED   *Defender*

Current Club: Droylsden

D o B: 19/12/1978   *Birthplace: Manchester*

Defender who started his career with Oldham Athletic before going Non-League with Barrow. Had a spell with Stafford Rangers before turning out for Nuneaton Borough, Leigh RMI and Stalybridge Celtic, who he helped gain a place in the Conference. Switched to Tameside UniBond neighbours Droylsden in August 2002.

MURPHY, GEZ   *Forward*

Current Club: Kettering Town

D o B: 19/12/1978   *Birthplace: Leicester*

Honours won: Conference Winners

Striker who joined Conference side Kettering Town in August 2002 after being released by 2001/02 champions Boston United. Boston signed up Gez in the summer of 2001 from Telford United, after he had been released by the Bucks at the end of the season. He had been Telfords top scorer in the 1999/2000 season with sixteen goals. Formerly with Crawley Rovers, Solihull Borough, VS Rugby and Atherstone United and was originally a trainee with Leicester City.

MURPHY, GREG   *Forward*

Current Club: Norwich United

D o B: 14/03/1978   *Birthplace: Norfolk*

A former Norfolk county youth player: coach Donny Pye has nick-named him the magician! A very skilful player who scores goals. Signed for Norwich United from neighbours Blofield United.

MURPHY, JAMIE   *Defender*

Current Club: Morecambe

D o B: 25/02/1973   *Birthplace: Manchester*

Central defender, a good stopper. Has played over 100 League game for Blackpool, Doncaster, and Halifax Town.

MURPHY, JOHN   *Defender*

Current Club: Fleet Town

Birthplace: Hampshire

Previous clubs include: Cove - July 1996.

MURPHY, JOHN   *Defender*

Current Club: Yeading

Birthplace: Middlesex

Another great product of the young Reserve side at The Warren. Jacko first broke into the first team last season, but has had limited chances since. A superb season so far in the Reserves has earned him another chance, and in his first full game back helped the Yeading defence keep a clean-sheet at home to Whyteleafe.

MURPHY, KEVIN   *Defender*

Current Club: Bognor Regis Town

Birthplace: Portsmouth

Signed for Bognor Regis Town from Dr Martens League side Waterlooville in the close season of 1996/97. Strong defender who has proved to be a good asset. Missed most of the 2000/01 season through injury but was back to his best for the following campaign. Lives in Portsmouth.

MURPHY, MICHAEL   *Defender*

Current Club: Windsor & Eton

D o B: 05/05/1977   *Birthplace: Slough*

Previous clubs include: RIPS Riihimaki (Finland) - February 2002, Windsor & Eton, RIPS Riihimaki (Finland), Slough T, Reading.

MURPHY, MITCHELL   *Forward*

Current Club: Aylesbury United

Birthplace: Middlesex

Previous clubs include: Edgware T - March 2002, Molesey, Wealdstone, Baldock T, Wealdstone.

MURPHY, NEIL   *Defender*

Current Club: Altrincham

D o B: 19/05/1980   *Birthplace: Liverpool*

Honours won: England Youth Int.

Neil is a right-back who made six starts for Blackpools firstteam in 2000/01 and one in 2001/02 before being released. He joined UniBond Premier side Altrincham during the 2002/03 pre-season and soon impressed. Neil was originally a trainee at Liverpool and has won England Youth honours.

MURPHY, SHAUN   *Midfielder*

Current Club: Borrowash Victoria

Birthplace: Derby

Previous clubs include: Alfreton T - January 1998, Derby Co.

MURRAY, CHAS   *Forward*

Current Club: Ford United

Birthplace: Essex

Honours won: Ryman League Div.One Winners

Promising young forward who came through the youth and reserve ranks at Ford United. Became a member of the senior squad during the 2000/01 season and played a part in helping the club to promotion to the Ryman League Premier Division for the first time in 2001/02.

MURRAY, JAMIE   *Midfielder*

Current Club: Port Talbot Town

D o B: 09/11/1975   *Birthplace: Cardiff*

Honours won: Wales Universities Rep.

Previous clubs include: Llanelli - November 2001, Maesteg Park, Inter Cardiff, Cardiff Civil Service.

MURRAY, JAY   *Forward*

Current Club: Barking & East Ham United

D o B: 23/09/1981   *Birthplace: Islington*

Highly-rated young forward who started his career as a trainee and then professional with Leyton Orient. Played a couple of times in Orients first-team and also had loan spells with Chelmsford City and Sutton United before joining Barking in February 2002.

MURRAY, JOE   *Midfielder*

Current Club: Chorley

D o B: 11/02/1977   *Birthplace: Wirral*

Honours won: New Zealand u-21 Int.

Previous clubs include: Weymouth - March 2002, Trafford, New Hampshire Phantoms (USA), Kendal T, Cammel Laird.

MURRAY, MARK   *Midfielder*

Current Club: Mossley

Birthplace: Cheshire

Previous clubs include: Caernarfon T - October 1997, Mossley, Ashton Utd, Macclesfield T, Blackpool.

MURRAY, NICK — *Forward*
Current Club: Barnstaple Town

D o B: 03/04/1981   *Birthplace: Devon*
Honours won: England Schoolboy Int.
Previous clubs include: Heavitree Utd - July 2000, Alphington.

MURRAY, ROB — *Midfielder*
Current Club: Dorchester Town

D o B: 31/10/1974   *Birthplace: Hammersmith*
Honours won: Scotland u-21 Int.
Previous clubs include: Richmond Kickers (USA) - November 1998, AFC Bournemouth.

MURRAY, SHAUN — *Midfielder*
Current Club: Kettering Town

D o B: 07/12/1970   *Birthplace: Newcastle*
Honours won: England Schoolboy & Youth Int., Dr Martens League Premier Div.Winners
Kicked off a promising career with Tottenham Hotspur before having spells with Scarborough, Bradford City, Portsmouth and Notts County, making over 250 League appearances. A highly-skilful midfielder, he won international honours for England at Schoolboy and Youth level. Joined Kettering Town on a permanent basis at the start of the 2001/02 season after an injury-hit period on-loan at the end of the previous campaign. Brings a touch of class and experience to the Poppies midfield.

MUSGROVE, NEIL — *Forward*
Current Club: Fleet Town

Birthplace: Hampshire
Previous clubs include: Molesey - July 2001, Fleet T, Aldershot T, Northampton T.

MUTCHELL, ROB — *Defender*
Current Club: Tamworth

D o B: 02/01/1974   *Birthplace: Solihull*
An outstanding full back, Rob joined Tamworth in March 1999. He was at Stevenage Borough and Kettering Town for the previous three seasons playing in the Conference, and was Player of the Year at both Kettering and Stevenage. His career began at Oxford United and then Barnet where he made 25 first-team appearances.

MUTTOCK, JON — *Defender*
Current Club: Abingdon Town

D o B: 23/12/1971   *Birthplace: Oxford*
Previous clubs include: Brackley T - July 2001, Witney T, Carterton T, Oxford C, Thame Utd, Carterton T, Oxford C, Wycombe Wanderers, Oxford Utd.

MUTTON, TOMMY — *Forward*
Current Club: Caernarfon Town

D o B: 17/01/1978   *Birthplace: Wales*
Previous clubs include: Rhyl - July 2001, Swansea C, Bangor C, Rhyl, Denbigh T.

MYALL, STUART — *Midfielder*
Current Club: Hastings United

D o B: 12/11/1974   *Birthplace: Eastbourne*
Utililty player and another former Brighton player who joined Hastings in January 1998 after being released by Brentford. Vastly experienced, he is mainly used as a midfielder by Hastings.

MYATT, JOHN — *Midfielder*
Current Club: Bromley

D o B: 09/07/1973   *Birthplace: Tooting*
Started his career at Crystal Palace in their youth and reserve teams from 1989-1991 and won the South East Counties

League Championship for the Eagles. Played for Tooting & Mitcham (1991-96), Croydon (1996-98), Banstead Athletic (1998-99) before joining the Hayes Lanc club in 1999. PE Teacher lives in Sidcup.

MYATT, ROB — *Defender*
Current Club: Rocester

Birthplace: Staffordshire
Previous clubs include: Newcastle T - June 2001, Rocester, Leek T.

MYERS, ANDREW — *Midfielder*
Current Club: Wingate And Finchley

D o B: 20/03/1972   *Birthplace: London*
Previous clubs include: Leeds University - July 1991.

MYERS, CHRIS — *Midfielder*
Current Club: Taunton Town

D o B: 01/04/1969   *Birthplace: Yeovil*
Honours won: FA Vase Winners
Previous clubs include: Dorchester T - July 1998, Exeter C, Scarborough, Wrexham, Dundee Utd, Torquay Utd, Barnstaple T, Dawlish T, Torquay Utd.

MYERS, MARTIN — *Midfielder*
Current Club: Moor Green

D o B: 10/01/1966   *Birthplace: Birmingham*
Honours won: FA Vase Winners
Signed for Moor Green in the summer of 2001 from Redditch United. Was at Birmingham City and Shrewsbury Town as a youngster, but made his mark at Tamworth, playing in the FA Vase Final at Wembley before enjoying six seasons in the Conference with Telford. Solihull Borough then signed him for £11,000 before his move to Redditch.

MYERS, PAUL — *Goalkeeper*
Current Club: Portland United

Birthplace: Northampton
Previous clubs include: Salisbury C - August 2000, Weymouth, Cogenhoe Utd, Northampton Spencer, Cambridge Utd (Trainee).

MYERS, PETER — *Midfielder*
Current Club: Frickley Athletic

Birthplace: Yorkshire
Pete is a young midfield player who signed initially for UniBond Premier side Frickley Athletic on-loan from Halifax Town during the 2001/02 season but has since signed permanently. He is a tall right-sided player who also has a bit of pace and the ability to unlock defences.

MYTON, TYRONE — *Midfielder*
Current Club: Croydon Athletic

Birthplace: Surrey
Previous clubs include: Carshalton Ath - March 2000, Sittingbourne, Dulwich Hamlet.

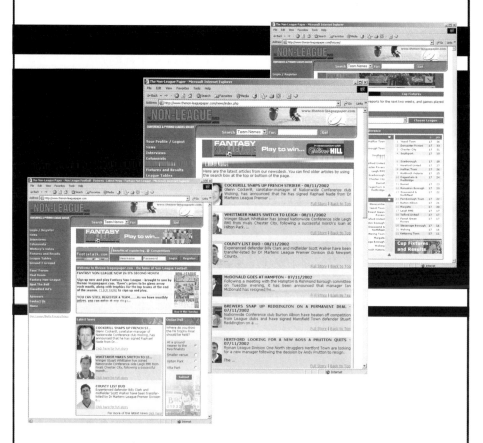

www.thenon-leaguepaper.com

NABIL, YOUNESS   *Forward*
Current Club: Tooting & Mitcham United
Birthplace: Morocco

Exceptionally quick front-runner who signed for Ryman Division One North side Tooting & Mitcham United from Premier Division St Albans City in July 2002. Had joined St Albans during the summer of 2001 from Boreham Wood having spent part of the season before in the Conference at Dagenham & Redbridge. Formerly with Chertsey Town and Chesham United. Transferred to Crawley in February 2002 but then returned to St Albans a month later.

NADE, RAPHAEL   *Forward*
Current Club: Welling United
Birthplace: Paris

French striker who signed for Dr Martens Premier side Welling United in July 2002 from Ryman Premier Hampton & Richmond Borough. Had joined Hampton from French side Troyes in August 2001. Attracted the attention of the club after playing against them in a pre-season friendly for QPR. Started his playing days with Le Havre.

NAISBETT, PHIL   *Goalkeeper*
Current Club: Whitby Town
D o B: 02/01/1979   *Birthplace: Easington*

Phil made a huge impact at UniBond Premier side Whitby Town after signing early in the 2001/02 season from Exeter. A superb shot-stopper, Phil had his best game against Plymouth in front of the Match of the Day cameras. Formerly with Sunderland and Scarborough, he was v oted Supporters' Player of the year 2001/02.

NAISBITT, DANNY   *Goalkeeper*
Current Club: Barnet
D o B: 25/11/1978   *Birthplace: Bishop Auckland*

Captured by Barnet from Walsall at the beginning of the 2000/01 season, Danny has continued to impress with some superb performances in goal. Got his chance when Lee Harrison was injured and has not looked back, impressing everyone who has watched him, which includes scouts from numerous big clubs.

NANCEKIVELL, KEVIN   *Midfielder*
Current Club: Tiverton Town
D o B: 22/10/1971   *Birthplace: Barnstaple*
Honours won: FA Vase Winners

The return of Kevin to Tiverton Town after a short spell at Plymouth Argyle was a massive boost for the club midway through the season 2000/01. He was the leading scorer the previous season and he won all the awards going at the end of season presentation, including Players' Player of the year and Supporters' Player of the year. Kevin is a human dynamo with boundless energy, very skillful and knows where the goal is. Started his playing days at Bideford.

NARAINE, GUY   *Midfielder*
Current Club: Boldmere St.Michaels
Birthplace: Birmimgham
Previous clubs include: Sutton FC - July 1996.

NARTEY, JOE   *Forward*
Current Club: Hemel Hempstead Town
D o B: 28/05/1976   *Birthplace: Ghana*
Previous clubs include: Hendon - January 2002, Enfield, Dulwich Hamlet, Maidenhead Utd, Sutton Utd, Chesham Utd, Aldershot T, Chertsey T, Hayes, Hillingdon B.

NARTEY, TONY   *Forward*
Current Club: Egham Town
Birthplace: London
Previous clubs include: Uxbridge - November 2001, Beaconsfield SYCOB, Yeading, Carshalton Ath., Uxbridge.

NASH, RYAN   *Forward*
Current Club: Rugby United
D o B: 16/03/1983   *Birthplace: Northampton*
Previous clubs include: Rothwell T - August 2002, Northampton T.

NAYLOR, CARL   *Defender*
Current Club: Metropolitan Police
Birthplace: Teeside
Previous clubs include: Sunderland Polytechnic - July 1986.

NAYLOR, DOMINIC   *Midfielder*
Current Club: Basingstoke Town
D o B: 12/08/1970   *Birthplace: Watford*
Honours won: Ryman League Premier Div. Winners

Experienced midfielder who is also capable of playing at the back. Signed for Basingstoke Town in November 2000 from Dagenham & Redbridge where he had helped the Essex side to win the Ryman League title. Gained League experience at Watford, Halifax, Barnet, Plymouth, Gillingham and Leyton Orient and also had a spell at Stevenage Borough.

NAYLOR, GAVIN   *Midfielder*
Current Club: Peterlee Newtown
Birthplace: Co.Durham
Previous clubs include: Easington Colliery - August 2001, Bishop Auckland.

NAYLOR, MARTYN   *Defender*
Current Club: Bilston Town
D o B: 02/08/1977   *Birthplace: Walsall*
Previous clubs include: Greenock Morton - September 2001, Telford Utd, Shrewsbury T, Telford Utd, Hereford Utd.

NAZHA, WAEL   *Forward*
Current Club: Ossett Town
D o B: 26/03/1974   *Birthplace: Lebanon*
Honours won: Lebanese Int.

Signed for Town just before Christmas from Bradford Park Avenue and has already become a firm favourite at the club. First emerged on the UniBond scene with Emley but has previously had huge success in his native Lebanon where he has been capped many times and played for the countrys largest club Nejmeh.

NDAH, JAMIE   *Forward*
Current Club: Croydon
D o B: 05/08/1971   *Birthplace: Camberwell*

Skilful 31-year-old striker who joined Croydon at the beginning in August 1998. Spent one and a half seasons with Torquay United making a number of league appearances, and has also appeared for Barnet, Rushden & Diamonds, Kingstonian and Dulwich Hamlet. His appearances for Croydon have been limited by work commitments, but scored a number of valuable goals during the championship winning campaign of 1999-2000.

N

NDEKWE, MALCOLM   Forward
Current Club: Stamford
Birthplace: Northampton
Malcolm is a striker who was first sent to Stamford on loan shortly after Billy started his management at the club. Injuries plagued Malcolm until he was released from Nene Park to wear Stamford colors again in 2000.

NEAL, ANDY   Midfielder
Current Club: Yate Town
Birthplace: Bristol
Previous clubs include: Brislington - July 2000, Yate T.

NEAL, JON   Midfielder
Current Club: Tonbridge Angels
Birthplace: Kent
Previous clubs include: Sittingbourne - November 2001, Folkestone Invicta, Gillingham (Trainee).

NEALE, LEE   Defender
Current Club: Harwich & Parkeston
Birthplace: Essex
Former Harwich favourite who returned to the fold in January 2002 after a spell with Brightlingsea United. He is a brave and hard tackling central defender who always gives 100 per cent.

NEDIMOVIC, ZAK   Midfielder
Current Club: Histon
Previous clubs include: Soham Town Rangers - January 2000, Walsall, Soham Town R, Newmarket T.

NEDIP, SENOL   Midfielder
Current Club: Molesey
D o B: 03/07/1980   Birthplace: Macedonia
Previous clubs include: Sloga Jugomaghat (Macedonia) - July 2001.

NEEDHAM, MARC   Defender
Current Club: Chalfont St.Peter
Birthplace: Wycombe
Previous clubs include: Marlow - November 2001, Flackwell Heath, Lewes, Wick, Lewes, Maidenhead Utd.

NEEDS, ADRIAN   Defender
Current Club: Merthyr Tydfil
Birthplace: Wales
Honours won: Wales Semi-Pro Int.
Adrian joined Merthyr Tydfil via Hong Kong, Swansea and Ebbw Vale. Normally plays left back, but is one of the finest sweepers in the area, although he regularly turns out for the Welsh semi-pro team in central midfield. Has been virtually ever present for the last three seasons. Other previous clubs include Swansea, Chesham United and Barry Town.

NEGUS, MATTHEW   Midfielder
Current Club: Enfield Town (Essex)
Birthplace: Herts
Joined the club from Hoddesdon, another product of the Enfield FC reserve and Youth set-up.

NEIL, CHRIS   Defender
Current Club: Whitley Bay
Birthplace: Co.Durham
Signed from Hebburn Town, Chris is a very accomplished defender good on the ground and strong in the air. Chris has had at least one Football League watching him this season.

Unfortunately a niggling knee injury may keep Chris out of football for most of the season.

NEIL, JIM   Defender
Current Club: Grantham Town
D o B: 28/02/1976   Birthplace: Bury St.Edmunds
Now in his second spell with the Grantham Town. Scorer of some great goals from free kick situations, he was Supporters' Player of the year 1999/00. Unfortunately missed much of the last two seasons through injury. Was originally on-loan with the Gingerbreads in 1996/97 from Scunthorpe after starting his career with Grimsby. Re-joined from Gainsborough Trinity in July 1999.

NEILL, TOM   Defender
Current Club: Chesham United
D o B: 13/11/1981   Birthplace: Harrow
Although still in his early twenties, Tom was a Watford player for 13 years before coming to Ryman Premier side Chesham United in July 2002. He has impressed as an attacking full back and has also played centre-half. in the past. He is hard-working and enthusiastic and describes himself as a perfectionist. His footballing hero is Nigel Gibbs and his best moment in football so far came when he signed his professional contract at Watford. He is a chief sales executive for a US fashion company.

NELSON, MICHAEL   Defender
Current Club: Harrogate Town
D o B: 15/03/1982   Birthplace: Gateshead
Defender who joined Harrogate Town in June 2002 after being released by Bury. Michael came to Bury initially on trial and impressed the management so much he was offered a contract after just two games. He played for Bishop Auckland in the UniBond League whilst employed as a window fitter in the North East after previous experience with Spennymoor United and South Shields. Such was his speed in grabbing a League game, he was fitting windows the day before his debut for Bury.

NELSON, STUART   Goalkeeper
Current Club: Doncaster Rovers
D o B: 17/09/1981   Birthplace: England
After starting his career with Cirencester Academy Stuart won three cup honours in two seasons and caped it of by winning player of the year. His talent didnt go unrecognised when he signed professionally for Millwall. Gaining experience and learning fast Stuart became one of the best keepers in the U19 Premier League. The young keepers contract was not renewed so he left for the States to join the Des Moines Menace, where they finished fourth in the PDL. On his return Stuart joined Oxford City where his talents didnt go unrecognised with a host of clubs taking an interest, QPR and Bristol Rovers to name a couple. Then, in March 2002, Stuart switched to Conference side Doncaster Rovers.

NELSON, TONY   Midfielder
Current Club: Dunston Federation Brewery
Birthplace: Newcastle
Previous clubs include: Tow Law T - August 2001, Queen of the South, Tow Law T, Penrith, Gretna, Newcastle Blue Star.

NENO, RICHARD   Defender
Current Club: Selsey
Birthplace: Sussex
Centre back and one time apprentice with Exeter City and Plymouth Argyle, who has been with Selsey for the last six seasons. Talented but wreckless performer, who has been absent on numerous occasions in recent times due to suspensions and other off-the-field problems.

NESBITT, CARL   *Midfielder*
Current Club: Vauxhall Motors
D o B: 31/01/1971   *Birthplace: Liverpool*
Long-serving battling midfielder who was previously on Liverpools books. Played West Cheshire football with Bromsborough Pool before coming to Vauxhall Motors for the first time. Captained the Motormen to the UniBond First Division title and is admired by many opposing managers. Rejoined Motors in July 1997 following spells with Curzon Ashton and Poulton Vics.

NESBITT, MARK   *Midfielder*
Current Club: Dunston Federation Brewery
Birthplace: Easington
Previous clubs include: Hartlepool Utd - July 2001.

NESOVIC, ALEX   *Forward*
Current Club: Barrow
D o B: 10/11/1972   *Birthplace: Bradford*
Alex began his career with Tadcaster Albion in the Northern Counties East League before having spells with Farsley Celtic and Eccleshill United. He then moved to Scotland and spent three years with Queen of the South before having brief stints at Albion Rovers and Partick Thistle. He played for Harrogate Town in the UniBond league during the 1999/00 season before moving to Ireland. He has played for Finn Harps, Bohemians and more latterly Dundalk in the League of Ireland. He joined UniBond Premier side Barrow in August 2002.

NESS, DAVID   *Defender*
Current Club: Runcorn FC Halton
Birthplace: Liverpool
Joined Runcorn Youth Team during the 1998/99 season, and has progressed through to the first team. Nessy is a calm and composed left back, and is an excellent passer of the ball. Nessy was firmly established as Runcorns left back until this season, and despite opening the Linnets goalscoring account after 17 seconds of the season, he has a battle on his hands with Franny McMahon to get his place back.

NESTOR, JAMES   *Midfielder*
Current Club: Eccleshill United
Birthplace: Bradford
Previous clubs include: Farsley Celtic - November 2001, Halifax T.

NESTOR, TERRY   *Midfielder*
Current Club: St.Helens Town
Birthplace: Liverpool
Signed from Warrington Town at the start of last season, Terry was a regular in the Liverpool Reserve side playing alongside Robbie Fowler and Steve McManaman before moving on to Runcorn and Warrington. Tough-tackling and excellent ball distribution from midfield. Another player arriving for a second spell at the club. Last seasons Players and Supporters' Player of the Year.

NETTLETON, JAMES   *Defender*
Current Club: Guiseley
Previous clubs include: Bradford C - July 1998.

NEUCHTERLIEN, STEVE   *Midfielder*
Current Club: Chasetown FC
Birthplace: Staffs
Previous clubs include: Brocton - July 1996.

NEUFVILLE, MARTIN   *Forward*
Current Club: Erith & Belvedere
Birthplace: London
Previous clubs include: Barking & East Ham Utd - October 2001, Sittingbourne, Braintree T, Canvey Island, Dagenham & Redbridge, Ford Utd, Bishops Stortford, Hitchin T, Charlton Ath (Trainee).

NEVILLE, BEN   *Forward*
Current Club: Fleet Town
Birthplace: Hampshire
Previous clubs include: Sandhurst T - July 2001.

NEVILLE, MARK   *Midfielder*
Current Club: Shifnal Town
Birthplace: Shropshire
Previous clubs include: Telford Utd - July 2002.

NEVIS, ROB   *Defender*
Current Club: Brigg Town
Birthplace: Hull
Previous clubs include: Harrogate T - July 2001, Goole AFC, Hall Road R, Goole T, Hall Road R, Winterton R.

NEWALL, GLEN   *Forward*
Current Club: Horsham YMCA
Birthplace: Sussex
Former Redhill player who signed for Horsham YMCA from Three Bridges in March 2000: scored 9 goals during 1999/2000 and 6 times the following season.

NEWALL, JOHN   *Defender*
Current Club: Atherstone United
Previous clubs include: QPR - August 2000.

NEWBERY, RICHARD   *Forward*
Current Club: Basingstoke Town
Honours won: FA Trophy Winners

Previous clubs include: Carshalton Athletic - July 2000, Gravesend, Wokingham T, Woking, Wokingham T, Hampton, Staines T, Farnborough T.

NEWBY, KEITH   *Midfielder*
Current Club: Yeading
Birthplace: London
Tenacious twenty-four year old who originally joined the Ding in March 2001 on loan from Harrow Borough, before a permanent move to The Warren in the summer. Newbs had joined Boro at the start of season 2000/1 from Chelmsford City. Has also gained experience at Cambridge City and Cambridge United.

NEWHAM, MARTIN   *Forward*
Current Club: Gainsborough Trinity
Birthplace: Nottingham
22-year-old right winger, considered one for the future after signing for Gainsborough Trinity from Central Midlands League outfit Long Eaton United in March 2002.

NEWLAND, JAMIE   *Midfielder*
Current Club: Atherstone United
D o B: 06/02/1985   *Birthplace: Leicester*
Previous clubs include: Nuneaton Borough - August 2001, Leicester C (Junior).

NEWMAN, CRAIG   *Midfielder*
Current Club: Maldon Town

Birthplace: Essex
Previous clubs include: Chelmsford C - July 2001, Basildon Utd, Chelmsford C.

NEWMAN, DAN   *Forward*
Current Club: Staines Town

D o B: 09/06/1975   *Birthplace: Bournemouth*
A tall, 6 3 striker who joined Staines Town in September 2001 from fellow Ryman Leaguers Wembley. He previously played for Bournemouth Poppies, Central United in New Zealand, Bashley, Lymington & New Milton, Kingstonian and Hampton & Richmond Borough. Won the British Universities championship with Birmingham.

NEWMAN, DAREN   *Defender*
Current Club: Burgess Hill Town

D o B: 14/01/1968   *Birthplace: Brighton*
Utility player and inspirational leader-type: once on the books of Brighton & Hove Albion: played a key role for Alan Pook in his championship winning sides at Peacehaven and Burgess Hill during the 90s (also had a spell with Newhaven): switched to Southwick in September 2000, and incredibly steered them from last to first place in the Second Division (scored 16 times): began the current campaign as player-manager of Withdean (Combined Counties League), but rejoined the Hillians in October: didnt waste much time, and marked his return by scoring two of the goals in the 5-1 thrashing of Whitehawk.

NEWMAN, GARY   *Forward*
Current Club: Bury Town

Birthplace: Suffolk
Previous clubs include: Walsham Le Willows - July 2000.

NEWMAN, GARY   *Midfielder*
Current Club: Saltdean United

D o B: 22/03/1981   *Birthplace: Brighton*
Previous clubs include: Peacehaven & Telscombe - November 2001.

NEWMAN, JOHN   *Midfielder*
Current Club: Trafford

Birthplace: Liverpool
Midfielder who signed for UniBond First Division side Trafford in August 2002 from North West Counties Leagures St. Helens Town. Previously with Southport, Burscough, Winsford United and Prescot Cables.

NEWMAN, LEE   *Forward*
Current Club: Lewes

Birthplace: Sussex
Joined from Saltdean over the summer. Lee has loads of skill and is an ideal weapon in the last twenty minutes against tiring defenders, although still too young and slight to be effective for the full ninety.

NEWMAN, TREVOR   *Midfielder*
Current Club: Bury Town

Birthplace: Suffolk
Previous clubs include: Walsham-le-Willows - July 2000, Bury T.

NEWSOME, PAUL   *Defender*
Current Club: Eccleshill United

Birthplace: Yorkshire
Previous clubs include: Thackley - July 1999, Otley T.

NEWSON, MARK   *Defender*
Current Club: Romford

D o B: 07/12/1960   *Birthplace: Stepney*
Honours won: England Semi-Pro Int., Football League Division Three Winners
Previous clubs include: Fisher Ath - September 2001, Gravesend, Aylesbury Utd, Oster (Sweden), Barnet, Fulham, AFC Bournemouth, Maidstone Utd, Charlton Ath.

NEWSTEAD, PETER   *Goalkeeper*
Current Club: St.Leonards

Birthplace: Sussex
Previous clubs include: Westfield - July 2002.

NEWTON, CHRIS   *Midfielder*
Current Club: Farsley Celtic

D o B: 05/11/1979   *Birthplace: Leeds*
Previous clubs include: Gainsborough Trinity - August 2001, Halifax T, Huddersfield T (Trainee).

NEWTON, PAUL   *Goalkeeper*
Current Club: Boston United

Birthplace: Yorkshire
Previous clubs include: Scarborough - December 2001.

NIBLETT, NIGEL   *Defender*
Current Club: Redditch United

D o B: 12/08/1967   *Birthplace: Stratford*
Honours won: FA XI
Strong, powerful central defender who in the time since joining Redditch United from Rugby United in January 2001, has shown why he has played at a higher level. Has represented the FA and played numerous games in the Conference with Telford United and Kidderminster Harriers. Has also had spells with Hednesford Town and Stratford Town.

NICHOLAS, MARK   *Midfielder*
Current Club: Whyteleafe

Birthplace: London
Previous clubs include: Bromley - January 2002.

NICHOLL, RYAN   *Midfielder*
Current Club: Arlesey Town

Birthplace: London
Talented midfielder, Ryan has had experaince at Watford Youth, Spurs Youth and Stevenage Borough Reserves. Had a Soccer Scholarship in the USA, and a third place in the World Youth Cup. Joined Arlesey Town in the summer of 2001. Is currently a student hoping to move into PE Teaching.

NICHOLLS, ADAM   *Midfielder*
Current Club: Stourport Swifts

Previous clubs include: Redditch Utd - June 2001, Kidderminster Harriers, Stourport Swifts, Halesowen Harriers.

NICHOLLS, JAMES   *Goalkeeper*
Current Club: Tilbury

Birthplace: Essex
Previous clubs include: East Thurrock Utd - July 2000, Tilbury, Southend Manor, Tilbury.

NICHOLLS, JAMIE   *Midfielder*
Current Club: Bilston Town

Birthplace: Birmingham
Previous clubs include: Oldbury Utd - March 2002.

NICHOLLS, JAY — Forward
Current Club: Belper Town
Birthplace: Nottingham
Big, powerfull striker who joined UniBond League side Belper Town from Ilkeston Town after failing to push his way in to the first team at the New Manor Ground.

NICHOLLS, MARK — Forward
Current Club: Maidenhead United
D o B: 30/05/1977   Birthplace: Hillingdon
Came into the Chelsea first-team as a teenager in 1996 and looked as though he was really going places. However, a combination of injuries and the influx of foreign players at Stamford Bridge stunted his progress. Spells with Partick Thistle, Torquay, Hamilton and Clydebank followed before he returned nearer home to join Ryman Premier side Chesham United in July 2002 but then switched to rivals Maidenhead United shortly afterwards.

NICHOLLS, MARTIN — Midfielder
Current Club: Mangotsfield United
Birthplace: Bristol
Martin is a product of Mangotsfield United's reserve side. Was formerly with Gloucester County League side Pucklechurch Sports. Martin has been involved with the first-team squad more often and is gaining valuable midfield experience all the time. One for the future.

NICHOLLS, PAUL — Goalkeeper
Current Club: Havant & Waterlooville
Birthplace: London
Signed for Havant & Waterlooville in August 2000 from Premiership team Chelsea. Paul is still eager to play professional football and has proved himself so far to be an invaluable addition to the team. Against Gloucester in the FA Cup in 2000 his 90th minute penalty save put the Hawks into the first round proper for the first time.

NICHOLLS, RYAN — Forward
Current Club: Carmarthen Town
D o B: 10/05/1973   Birthplace: Cardiff
Honours won: Wales u-21 & B Int.
Previous clubs include: Aberystwyth T - March 1999, Newport AFC, Merthyr Tydfil, Cardiff C, Leeds Utd.

NICHOLLS, STEVE — Midfielder
Current Club: Norwich United
D o B: 22/12/1974   Birthplace: Norfolk
A very good recent new signing for Norwich United. A tough-tackling player, who will always give you 100 per cent. Previously with Diss, Watton and Gorleston.

NICHOLLS, TIM — Midfielder
Current Club: Stourport Swifts
Previous clubs include: Bromsgrove Rovers - June 2001, Stourport Swifts, Willenhall T, Stourbridge, Cradley T, Blakenall.

NICHOLSON, JOHN — Midfielder
Current Club: Metropolitan Police
Birthplace: Cambridgeshire
Previous clubs include: Harlow T - December 2001, Dagenham & Redbridge, Romford, Metropolitan Police, Boreham Wood, Metropolitan Police, Wisbech T, March Town Utd, Huntingdon T.

NICHOLSON, MAX — Forward
Current Club: Gainsborough Trinity
D o B: 03/10/1971   Birthplace: Leeds
Experienced front runner who has spent the last five years or so switching to and from playing football in Singapore where he has represented Woodlands Wellington and Geyland United. Re-joined Gainsborough Trinity for the fourth time in July 2002. Made over 150 League appearances with Doncaster Rovers, Hereford United, Torquay and Scunthorpe before joining Trinity for the first time in July 1996.

NICHOLSON, SCOTT — Defender
Current Club: Tow Law Town
Birthplace: Co.Durham
Previous clubs include: Crook T

NICHOLSON, STEVE — Defender
Current Club: Wakefield & Emley
D o B: 20/10/1971   Birthplace: Leeds
Appointed captain in succession to Ian Banks. Steve joined Emley in 1994 from Farsley Celtic after previously spending four years with Leeds United.

NICHOLSON, STEVE — Goalkeeper
Current Club: Bilston Town
Birthplace: Wolverhampton
From Youth team.

NICKALLS, IAN — Defender
Current Club: Morpeth Town
Birthplace: Northumberland
From Youth team.

NICKLIN, RYAN — Forward
Current Club: Tunbridge Wells
Birthplace: Kent
From Local football - July 2000.

NIELSON, STUART — Midfielder
Current Club: Guisborough Town
Previous clubs include: Marske Utd - July 2001.

NIGHTINGALE, LEWIS — Forward
Current Club: Romford
Birthplace: Essex
Honours won: England Schools Rep.
Previous clubs include: Aveley - September 2001, Grays Ath, Fisher Ath., Millwall.

NIGHTINGALE, ROB — Midfielder
Current Club: Cambridge City
Birthplace: Cambridge
Rob came through from Cambridge City's successful youth set-up. He was converted from a striker to his current midfield position by former manager Chris Tovey.

NIGHTINGALE, TERRY — Midfielder
Current Club: Berkhamsted Town
Birthplace: Hitchin
Previous clubs include: Hitchin T - July 1994, Berkhamsted T, Hitchin T, Hertford T, St.Albans C, Hitchin T.

NIMMO, ANDY — Midfielder
Current Club: Epsom And Ewell
D o B: 15/03/1973   Birthplace: Surrey
Previous clubs include: Sutton Utd - July 1992, Epsom & Ewell, Sutton Utd, Brighton (Trainee).

NIVEN, STUART — Forward
Current Club: Barnet
D o B: 24/12/1978   Birthplace: Glasgow
Impressive Glaswegian youngster signed on a free from Ipswich Town in September 2000, Niven scored after just 44 seconds on his full debut away at Carlisle, and weighed in with another vital goal against Lincoln to spur a remarkable comeback. A confident and accurate passer of the ball, Niven links up well with John Doolan and provides a good link from defence to attack.

NIXON, ADAM — Defender
Current Club: Ossett Albion
Birthplace: Sheffield
Previous clubs include: Buxton - November 2001, Denaby Utd, Worksop T, Rotherham Utd.

NOAD, DARREN — Defender
Current Club: Walton Casuals
Birthplace: Surrey
Darren is currently in his third season at Casuals, part of our League Cup winning side. Previously with Staines Town and Egham.

NOAKES, STEVE — Defender
Current Club: Burnham
Birthplace: Berkshire
Young full back joined the club in November 2000 from AFC Newbury. His outstanding performances earned him young player of the year.

NOBES, SIMON — Goalkeeper
Current Club: Kings Lynn
Birthplace: Kings Lynn
Local goalkeeper Simon played for Heacham and Kings Lynn Youth teams before progressing to Lynns Reserves. A fine performance on his first team debut at Newport County during the 2000/01 season earned him a more permanent role in the senior side.

NOBLE, ANDY — Midfielder
Current Club: Shifnal Town
Birthplace: Shropshire
Previous clubs include: West Mildands Police - December 2001.

NOBLE, PAUL — Defender
Current Club: Didcot Town
Birthplace: Oxfordshire
Paul has almost legendary status at Didcot both on and off the field, and with over 500 appearances in 10 years its not difficult to see why. Unfortunately struck down with illness on the eve of the 2001/02 season, he showed his commitment to the club by jointly managing the reserve team as he battled back to full fitnes.

NOBLE, TOM — Forward
Current Club: Braintree Town
Previous clubs include: Maldon T - July 2000, Stanway R, Clacton T.

NOLAN, CARL — Defender
Current Club: Stratford Town
D o B: 07/03/1978   Birthplace: Coventry
Previous clubs include: Rugby Utd - August 2001, Shepshed Dynamo, Hinckley Utd, Coventry C.

NOLAN, DAVE — Midfielder
Current Club: Hyde United
D o B: 24/02/1968   Birthplace: Liverpool
Appointed as player-manager of UniBond Premier side Hyde United in September 2001. He was part of the successful Tigers team of the mid 1990s Moved to Runcorn and Droylsden before returning to Hyde. Has also turned out for Prescot Cables, Chester City and Barrow.

NOLAN, DAVE — Midfielder
Current Club: Northwood
D o B: 17/09/1970
Previous clubs include: Southall - July 1999, Chertsey T, Southall, Berkhamsted T, Chesham Utd, Enfield, Marlow, Northwood, Harrow B, Hendon.

NOLAN, GED — Defender
Current Club: St.Helens Town
Birthplace: Liverpool
Exprienced defender who was in his second spell with UniBond Premier side Burscough before switching to North West Counties outfit St Helens Town in August 2002. Ged acted as caretaker-manager for the latter end of the 2001/02 season following the departure of John Davison. Former clubs include Wrexham, Halifax Town, Southport, St Helens Town and Nantwich Town, Ged reached over 350 appearances for the Linnets.

NOLAN, JOHN — Midfielder
Current Club: Ashford Town
D o B: 30/11/1979   Birthplace: Irvine
Previous clubs include: Ayr Utd - July 2001, Dalry Thistle.

NOLAN, MATTHEW — Forward
Current Club: Hitchin Town
D o B: 25/02/1982   Birthplace: Hitchin
Highly-promising young striker who came up through the youth and reserve ranks at Hitchin Town. Became a first-team regular in 2000/01 and soon began to attract attention from League and Conference clubs. Is reckoned to have a big future in the game.

NOLAN, TERRY — Midfielder
Current Club: Ashford Town (Middx)
Birthplace: Slough
Arrived at Ashford Town (Middx) in 1999 as a central defender and ended up as top scorer with 43 goals after converting to striker. Experienced player who has seen service with both Hampton and Slough. Won Player of the Year and Players' Player of the Year in his first season. Aged 32 he is currently playing in midfield.

NOONE, MATT — Defender
Current Club: Stanway Rovers
Birthplace: Essex
From Youth team.

NORBURY, JAMIE — Forward
Current Club: Brodsworth Welfare
Birthplace: Yorkshire
Previous clubs include: Ossett Alb - January 2002, Brodsworth Welfare, Pontefract Collieries, Grimethorpe MW.

NORBURY, MIKE — Forward
Current Club: Stocksbridge Park Steels
D o B: 22/01/1969   *Birthplace: Hemsworth*
Much-travelled, aggressive forward. Joined UniBond First Division Stocksbridge Park Steels from Premier Division Wakefield Emley in June 2002. Had signed for Emley at the beginning of the 2001/02 season. Vastly experienced, he played League football with Cambridge United, Preston and Doncaster and Conference football with Telford United and Hednesford Town, from whom he joined Emley.

NORFOLK, LEE — Midfielder
Current Club: AFC Sudbury
D o B: 17/10/1975   *Birthplace: Dunedin, New Zealand*
Played for Sudbury Wanderers before the merger and is a reliable and unflappable performer. AFC Sudburys own Beckham-esk dead-ball specialist and a superb volleyer.

NORMAN, CRAIG — Defender
Current Club: Kettering Town
D o B: 21/03/1975   *Birthplace: Perivale*
Honours won; Dr Martens League Premier Div.Winners
Craig joined Kettering Town in October 1995 from Chelsea where he spent two years as a trainee and two as a professional. He has been voted as the Supporters' Player of the year on a couple of occasions and was the top goalscoring defender in the Conference in 1998/99. Something of a penalty expert, Craig is now the longest-serving player at the club.

NORMAN, DAVID — Defender
Current Club: Oswestry Town
D o B: 21/11/1973   *Birthplace: Wales*
Honours won: British Universities Rep.
Previous clubs include: Colwyn Bay - September 2000, Bangor C, Telford Utd, Colwyn Bay, Barry T, Macclesfield T, Northwich V, Llansantffraid, Rhyl.

NORMAN, JOHN — Forward
Current Club: Burscough
D o B: 26/06/1971   *Birthplace: Birkenhead*
An incisive, intelligent and highly creative forward. Signed for UniBond Premier side Burscough in July 2002 after a second spell at Morecambe. Went back to Christie Park after an abortive half season at Hednesford Town in March 2000. He was the Shrimps leading scorer in 1998/99 and again in 2001/02. Previous clubs include Tranmere, Heswall and Mold Alexandra.

NORMAN, PERRY — Defender
Current Club: Harrow Borough
Birthplace: Perivale
Defender or midfielder who rejoined Ryman Premier side Harrow Borough in February 202 from Chertsey Town. Previously with Nuneaton Borough, Cambridge City, Farnborough Town, Hayes, QPR and Wealdstone.

NORMAN, SEAN — Defender
Current Club: Lowestoft Town
D o B: 27/11/1966   *Birthplace: Lowestoft*
Previous clubs include: Walton & Hersham - August 1997, Chesham Utd, Lowestoft T, Chertsey T, Papatoetoe (New Zealand), Chesham Utd, Wealdstone, Wycombe Wanderers, Colchester Utd, Lowestoft T.

NORMAN, STEVE — Midfielder
Current Club: Dover Athletic
D o B: 30/01/1979   *Birthplace: Harold Wood*
Former Gillingham youth player who signed for Dover Athletic from St.Leonards in May 1999 after a period on loan at The Crabble. An attacking left-sided player who can play either as a winger or an attacking full back.

NORRIS, JON — Forward
Current Club: Egham Town
Birthplace: Berkshire
Forward who signed for Ryman Division One South side Egham Town in the summer of 2002 from Burnham. Jon arrived at Burnham in the previous close season from Thatcham Town. Equally comfortable in midfield or up front.

NORRIS, MATT — Forward
Current Club: VCD Athletic
D o B: 05/04/1970   *Birthplace: Sidcup*
Previous clubs include: Cray Wanderers - July 1999, Croydon, Dulwich Hamlet.

NORRIS, MICHAEL — Goalkeeper
Current Club: Shildon
Birthplace: Newcastle
Previous clubs include: Jarrow Roofing - February 2002, South Shields, Brandon Utd, York C.

NORRIS, RICHARD — Midfielder
Current Club: Northwich Victoria
D o B: 05/01/1978   *Birthplace: Birkenhead*
Richard is a talented midfielder whose performances for Marine prompted Crewe Alexandra to splash out £20,000 for his services in 1996. A succession of injuries prevented Richard from making the impact he would have liked at Gresty Road and he was released, joining Macclesfield. Richard is aiming to get his career back on track with Northwich Victoria after arriving in the summer of 2000 and became a vital part of the clubs midfield make-up during the 2001/02 season.

NORTH, ALAN — Midfielder
Current Club: Bury Town
Birthplace: Suffolk
Previous clubs include: Walsham Le Willows - August 1998.

NORTH, JOHN — Defender
Current Club: Lincoln United
Birthplace: Lincoln
Previous clubs include: Louth Utd - July 2000, Spalding Utd, Lincoln Utd.

NORTH, TIM — Defender
Current Club: Hungerford Town
D o B: 20/11/1963   *Birthplace: Marlborough*
Vastly experienced defender, now in the veteran stages of his career. Has been with Ryman Division Two side Hungerford Town since 1995 and has previously seen servicewith Kintbury Rangers and Lambourn.

NORTHERN, ANDREW — Midfielder
Current Club: Selby Town
Birthplace: Yorkshire
From Youth team.

NORTON, DAVE   *Midfielder*

Current Club: Tamworth

D o B: 03/03/1965   Birthplace: Cannock

Honours won: England Youth Int.

Vastly experienced midfielder who was appointed as player/assistant-manager of Dr Martens Premier side Tamworth in May 2002, leaving UniBond Premier Giansborough Trinity where he had been player-manager since November 2001. A former England Youth international, Dave started his career with Aston Villa and went on to make over 350 League appearances with Villa, Notts County, Hull, Northampton and Hereford before going Non-League with Cheltenham, Yeovil Town and Forest Green Rovers, where he was joint boss with Nigel Spink. He then joined Tamworth as a player at the start of the 2001/02 season before becoming manager at Gainsborough.

NORTON, MIKE   *Forward*

Current Club: Woodley Sports

Birthplace: Manchester
From Youth team.

NORTON, PAUL   *Goalkeeper*

Current Club: Denaby United

Birthplace: Sheffield
Previous clubs include: Armthorpe Welfare - February 2001, Denaby Utd, Frickley Ath., Alfreton T, Eastwood T, Ilkeston T, Alfreton T, Gainsborough Trinity, Worksop T, Bridlington T, Hartlepool Utd, Sheffield Utd.

NOTEMAN, KEVIN   *Forward*

Current Club: Matlock Town

D o B: 15/10/1969   Birthplace: Preston

Experienced midfielder or striker with a fierce shot, Kevin joined Matlock in January 2001 after spells in the full-time game with Mansfield Town and others. He has represented Ilkeston, Hucknall and Boston at Non-League level and fancies himself as the club comedian!

NOTEMAN, WAYNE   *Midfielder*

Current Club: Goole AFC

Birthplace: Harrogate
Previous clubs include: Farsley Celtic - September 2001, Bradford PA, Emley, Guiseley, Bishop Auckland, Bridlington T, Frickley Ath., Harrogate T, Farsley Celtic, Goole T, Harrogate T, Yorkshire Main.

NOTLEY, JAY   *Forward*

Current Club: Leyton Pennant

D o B: 04/12/1977   Birthplace: London

Previous clubs include: Charlton Ath - January 2000, Millwall (Trainee).

NOTT-MACAIRE, STEVE   *Forward*

Current Club: Chalfont St.Peter

Birthplace: Berkshire
Previous clubs include: Flackwell Heath - September 2001, Uxbridge, Marlow, Maidenhead Utd.

NOWER, BEN   *Goalkeeper*

Current Club: AFC Sudbury

Birthplace: Lincolnshire
Signed for Sudbury in December 2000 from Kings Lynn making his full debut at Great Yarmouth. A quality keeper who commands his area and has youth on his side.

NOZEDAR, PAUL   *Forward*

Current Club: Diss Town

Birthplace: Newcastle
Previous clubs include: West Auckland T - July 2001, Marske Utd, Brandon Utd.

NSUBUGA, ABBY   *Midfielder*

Current Club: Molesey

D o B: 09/09/1980   Birthplace: London

Previous clubs include: Fleet T - July 2001, Kingstonian.

NULTY, MARK   *Defender*

Current Club: St.Helens Town

Birthplace: Liverpool
Tall central defender who made the switch from UniBond outfit Marine earlier this season. Quality defender who excels in the air. Son of former Town captain, Newcastle United and Everton star Geoff Nulty.

NUNN, MARK   *Defender*

Current Club: Mildenhall Town

Birthplace: Cambridgeshire
Previous clubs include: Attleborough - July 2000.

NUNN, MICHAEL   *Forward*

Current Club: Bradford Park Avenue

Previous clubs include: Army - August 2001.

NUNN, MICKY   *Midfielder*

Current Club: Arlesey Town

Birthplace: Stevenage

Honours won: Ryman League Div.3 Winners

Mick is in his third spell at Arlesey Town, re-joining in July 1998, and in between times he has been at Stotfold, Bishops Stortford, Baldock, Hitchin and Stevenage. Experienced, no-nonsense midfield player who gets the job done. He has Cup Medals at County Senior and League levels and is a driving force. Works as a Interior Fitter and Builder.

NUNN, NICK   *Forward*

Current Club: Wivenhoe Town

Birthplace: Norway
Previous clubs include: Clacton T - December 2001.

NUNN, SIMON   *Goalkeeper*

Current Club: Stowmarket Town

Birthplace: Suffolk
From Youth team.

NURSE, MATT   *Goalkeeper*

Current Club: Cambridge City

Birthplace: Leicester
A newcomer to Cambridge City at the start of the 2001/02 season. Matt signed for City after being released by Premiership club Leicester City. He was a regular in the Reserves at Filbert Street. His form with City was o good that the goalkeeper became the attention of League scouts once again.

NUTTELL, MICKY   *Forward*

Current Club: Wisbech Town

D o B: 22/11/1968   Birthplace: Boston

Honours won: Dr Martens League Premier Div.Winners

Previous clubs include: Bedford T - December 2001, Wisbech T, Boston Utd, Kings Lynn, Kettering T, Burton Alb., Rushden & Diamonds, Dagenham & Redbridge, Kettering T, Boston U, Wycombe Wanderers, Cheltenham T, Peterborough U.

NUTTER, JOHN — *Defender*
Current Club: Aldershot Town
Previous clubs include: Wycombe Wanderers - May 2001, Blackburn R (Trainee).

NWADIKE, EMEKA — *Midfielder*
Current Club: Ilkeston Town
D o B: 09/08/1978   *Birthplace: Camberwell*
Emeka was John McGoverns only major signing as manager when he joined Ilkeston Town for £5,000 from Kings Lynn. He started out at Wolverhampton Wanderers but made his League debut at Shrewsbury. Joined Grantham Town and then moved on to Kings Lynn. Proved to be one of Ilkestons best signings for some time.

NWANGUMA, MEL — *Forward*
Current Club: Holmer Green
Birthplace: Bucks
Previous clubs include: Penn & Tylers Green - July 1999.

NWANZE, DANIEL — *Midfielder*
Current Club: Tooting & Mitcham United
Birthplace: Nigeria
Nigerian-born midfielder who re-joined Ryman Division One South side Tooting & Mitcham United from rivals Whyteleafe in the summer of 2002. Had began his playing days with Tooting before signing for the Leafe in August 2000.

NWOKEJI, MARK — *Forward*
Current Club: Chesham United
D o B: 30/01/1982   *Birthplace: London*
Mark has previously played for Charlton and Colchester at schoolboy level, Harlow Town, Leatherhead and the Protec football academy before signing for Ryman Premier side Chesham United in August 2002. He is a strong player with plenty of pace and is a sales executive. Used to be an athlete and was the 200m schoolboy level, all England champion.

NYAMAH, KOFI — *Defender*
Current Club: Boreham Wood
D o B: 20/06/1975   *Birthplace: Islington*
Kofi is a 27 year old Islington born left sided wing back or forward, who began his Career as a Trainee with Cambridge United, for whom he played from 1993/94 until 1996/97. He then had a spell with Kettering Town before joining Stoke City in 1996/97. He joined Boreham Wood early in 2002 and made his First Team debut for the Club against Harrow Borough (Home) on the 12 January 2002.

NYE, JULIAN — *Midfielder*
Current Club: Tunbridge Wells
Birthplace: Kent
Previous clubs include: Crowborough Ath - July 1995.

NYMAN, DEAN — *Forward*
Current Club: Wingate And Finchley
D o B: 12/09/1979   *Birthplace: London*
Previous clubs include: Enfield - March 1999, Wingate & Finchley, Leyton Orient, Charlton Ath., West Ham Utd.

N

The Official Football Association
Non-League Club
Directory 2003
(25th Edition)
now available

Price £19.95
(free p&p)

Details of over 1000
Semi-Professional Clubs

Call 01823 490 080 for details
The Non-League Club Directory
Helland, North Curry
Taunton, Somerset, TA3 6DU
Fax: 01823 491 481
Email: TonyWilliams12@virgin.net

Special Discounts Available

OAKES, DANIEL — *Defender*
Current Club: Hadleigh United
Birthplace: Suffolk
Strong, no nonsense, left-sided defender with great commitment and attitude. Fifth season with Hadleigh and a regular member of the First Team squad - despite travelling from his North London home for each game.

OAKES, DAVID — *Midfielder*
Current Club: Horsham YMCA
Birthplace: Sussex
Left-sided midfielder: signed from Eastbourne Town during the 2001 close season: missed the first six weeks of the campaign whilst suspended.

OAKES, SCOTT — *Midfielder*
Current Club: St.Albans City
D o B: 05/08/1972   Birthplace: Leicester
Honours won: England u-21 Int.
Experienced midfielder who began his career at home-town club Leicester City. Made his name during five successful seasons at Luton Town before a high profile transfer to Sheffield Wednesday in 1996. Has also appeared for Burnley and Leyton Orient. A former England under-21 international, he joined Ryman Premier side St Albans City in August 2002.

OBENG, STEVE — *Defender*
Current Club: Cheshunt
Birthplace: London
Previous clubs include: Edgware T - July 2001, Cheshunt, Kingsbury T.

OBILI, SHAUN — *Forward*
Current Club: Romford
Birthplace: Essex
Previous clubs include: Aveley - January 2002, Grays Ath.

OBONG, BEN — *Forward*
Current Club: Hyde United
Birthplace: Liverpool
Young striker who originally signed for UniBond Premier side Hyde United on loan from Conference outfit Southport. Made the move a permanent one in November 2001. Started out as a teenager with North West Counties Leaguers Bootle.

O'BRIEN, AIDAN — *Defender*
Current Club: Hampton & Richmond
Birthplace: London
Honours won: England Schoolboy Int.
Signed for Hampton in December 2001 from Harrow Borough. Previous clubs include Oxford University, Oxford United, Aylesbury United, South Shields, Barnet, Hayes, Welling United, Dulwich Hamlet and Newcastle United.

O'BRIEN, ALEX — *Midfielder*
Current Club: Tooting & Mitcham United
Birthplace: London
Previous clubs include: Leatherhead - July 2000, Walton & Hersham, Leatherhead, Hayes, Fulham.

O'BRIEN, BLAISE — *Forward*
Current Club: Yeading
Birthplace: Middlesex
Young pacy forward who has rattled in goals for the Reserves in recent seasons, earning a handful of appearances in the first team and at County level. Made his first team debut in September 1999.

O'BRIEN, CHRIS — *Defender*
Current Club: Chester City
D o B: 13/01/1982   Birthplace: Liverpool
Quick and calm defender who signed for City in January 2002 after a three month loan period at the Deva.

O'BRIEN, KIERON — *Defender*
Current Club: Ossett Town
Birthplace: Leeds
A talented defender, Kieron played for Leeds United's Centre of Excellence for 6 seasons (1990-1996) and then went to Hull City as an apprentice. He has since played for Harrogate Railway and Farsley Celtic. Spent season 1999/00 playing in the USA for Brescia University in Kentucky where he gained State honours. Signed for Bradford Park Avenue in January 2001 and then switched to UniBond First Division Ossett Town in July 2002.

O'BRIEN, LIAM — *Forward*
Current Club: Ringmer
Birthplace: Sussex
Beanpole left-winger who played for Saltdean during 2000/01, having graduated through their youth team. Impressed during the early part of this season and was recruited as a squad member by Lewes in September 2001. Signed for Ringmer in December and has also had trials for the English Colleges squad.

O'BRIEN, MICHAEL — *Midfielder*
Current Club: Chester City
D o B: 25/09/1979   Birthplace: Liverpool
Previous clubs include: Droylsden - October 2001, Torquay Utd, Everton.

O'BRIEN, NEIL — *Defender*
Current Club: Carmarthen Town
Birthplace: Llanelli
Honours won: Wales Semi-Pro Int.
Previous clubs include: Cwmbran T - July 2000, Merthyr Tydfil, Inter Cardiff, Aberystwyth T, Llanelli.

O'BRIEN, PAUL — *Defender*
Current Club: Rugby United
Birthplace: Coventry
Signed for Rugby United from Sutton Coldfield Town in July 2000, Paul is a sound defender with excellent distribution, hence his ability to also perform well in a midfield role when required. Player of the year for 2000/01, Paul started his career as a trainee with Coventry City and has also served the likes of Kidderminster Harriers, Hinckley Athletic, Stratford Town, Evesham United and Bedworth United.

O'BRIEN, ROY — *Midfielder*
Current Club: Yeovil Town
D o B: 27/11/1974   Birthplace: Cork
Honours won: Republic of Ireland Schholboy & Youth Int., FA Trophy Winners
Midfielder who comes from Cork City in Ireland. A hard-working player who is also very good in the air, he was signed by Yeovil Town from Dorchester Town in Augsut 2000 and has previously served Arsenal, Wigan and Bournemouh and won international honours for the Republic of Ireland at Schoolboy and Youth level.

O'BRIEN, SEAN — *Defender*
Current Club: Billingham Synthonia
Birthplace: Cleveland
Previous clubs include: Spennymoor Utd - July 1996, Billingham Synthonia, Gateshead, Billingham Synthonia, Billingham T, Norton.

O'BRIEN, SHANE — Midfielder
Current Club: Cheshunt
Birthplace: Essex
Previous clubs include: Leyton Pennant - March 2002, Ware, Hornchurch, Yeovil T, Enfield, Tottenham Hotspur (Junior).

O'BRIEN, STEVE — Midfielder
Current Club: Saltdean United
Birthplace: Sussex
Former Whitehawk youth team player who was then brought into the side at Hill Park when Paul Hubbard took charge midway through 2001/02: also happens to be a boxer.

OBWOYO-COO, WILLIAM — Midfielder
Current Club: Clapton
Birthplace: Essex
Previous clubs include: Wembley - January 2002, Harrow B, Holywell T, Uxbridge.

O'CALLAGHAN, BILLY — Forward
Current Club: St.Helens Town
Birthplace: Liverpool
Previous clubs include: Rhyl - January 2002, Prescot Cables, Accrington Stanley, Droylsden, Warrington T, Witton Alb., Skelmersdale Utd, Liverpool (Junior).

O'CALLAGHAN, MICK — Defender
Current Club: Rye & Iden United
D o B: 15/04/1974 — *Birthplace: Hastings*
Rejoined St Leonards from Rye United during the 2000 close season, but was released in December 2001 and subsequently returned to Rye. Previous experience with Bexhill, Hastings and Sidley Utd.

O'CARROLL, RYAN — Midfielder
Current Club: Hallam
Birthplace: Barnsley
Previous clubs include: Alfreton T - September 2000, Matlock T, Barnsley.

O'CONNELL, BRENDAN — Midfielder
Current Club: Rossendale United
D o B: 12/11/1966 — *Birthplace: Lambeth*
Very experienced midfielder whose career started at Portsmouth. Failed to make a first-team appearance at Fratton Park but went on to play over 500 League games with Exeter, Burnley, Barnsley, Charlton and Wigan. Joined Rossendale United in November 2001 whilst on the coaching staff at Wigan.

O'CONNELL, KEVIN — Forward
Current Club: Woodley Sports
Birthplace: Manchester
Previous clubs include: Glossop North End - December 2000, Mossley, Glossop NE, Winsford Utd, Glossop NE.

O'CONNELL, IAIN — Defender
Current Club: Margate
D o B: 09/10/1970 — *Birthplace: Southend*
Previous clubs include: Dover Ath. (£3,000) - August 1997, Southend Utd.

O'CONNOR, CRAIG — Midfielder
Current Club: Windsor & Eton
Birthplace: Slough
Craig is a local lad who made his debut for Dr Martens Eastern side Burnham during the 2000/01 season at Witney Town after joining from Spartan South Midlands Leaguers Beaconsfield SYCOB. His best position is as a wide midfielder, and thats where he was most impressive in 01/02. Transferred to Ryman Division One South side Windsor & Eton in July 2002.

O'CONNOR, DES — Forward
Current Club: Carterton Town
Birthplace: Oxfordshire
Previous clubs include: Bicester T - July 2001.

O'CONNOR, JOE — Forward
Current Club: Stafford Rangers
D o B: 20/10/1967 — *Birthplace: Wolverhampton*
Honours won: England Semi-Pro Int., Dr Martens League Premier Div.Winners
A prolific goalscorer, Joe returned to Stafford Rangers in October 2000 from Kingstonian, eleven years since signing for the first time. Winning a number of trophies as a schoolboy in the Walsall League and playing for the Wolves schoolboy team, he played senior football for Gornal Sports and then Lye Town. He joined Rangers for a reported £4,000 fee but after finding opportunities limited by a strikeforce of Chris Camden, Stan Collymore and Paul Cavell, Joe moved onto Hednesford Town. With the Cross Keys outfit, he was a member of their Welsh Cup Final side, Southern League Premier Division winning side and also hit the headlines during Hednesfords memorable FA Cup run. After a lengthy spell with Hednesford, Joe moved onto to Nuneaton Borough and then Kingstonian. Won two caps for the England semi-professional side.

O'CONNOR, LEE — Forward
Current Club: Cwmbran Town
D o B: 01/03/1984 — *Birthplace: Wales*
From Academy.

O'CONNOR, RICHARD — Midfielder
Current Club: Hampton & Richmond
D o B: 30/08/1978 — *Birthplace: Wandsworth*
Midfielder who signed for Hampton & Richmond Borough in the summer of 2001 from Leatherhead. Previously on the books at Wimbledon before joining Leatherhead. Has a thunderous shot.

O'CONNOR, SEAN — Goalkeeper
Current Club: Hayes
Birthplace: London
Goalkeeper who joined Ryman Premier side Hayes in June 2002 from Division One North club Berkhamsted Town. Played for Berko in the FA Carlsberg Vase final, having signed from Boreham Wood in February 2000. Originally on the books at QPR, Sean also had spell at Wealdstone.

O'CONNOR, TERRY — Midfielder
Current Club: Egham Town
Birthplace: Buckinghamshire
Previous clubs include: Beaconsfield SYCOB - July 2001.

O'CONNOR, TONY — Goalkeeper
Current Club: Ludlow Town
Birthplace: Shropshire
Previous clubs include: Shifnal T - July 2001, Lawson Mardon Star, Chasetown.

OCQUAYE, DAVID — Forward
Current Club: Molesey
Birthplace: London
Previous clubs include: Kingstonian - July 2001.

ODDY, ROB — *Defender*
Current Club: Bedworth United
Birthplace: Coventry
From Youth team.

ODEJAYI, KAYODE — *Forward*
Current Club: Forest Green Rovers
D o B: 21/02/1982   Birthplace: Ibadon, Nigeria
Big, pacey Nigerian-born striker who joined Conference side Forest Green Rovers on a permanent basis in August 2002 after being released by Bristol City. Made around half a dozen first-team appearances for City and spent a spell on-loan at Forest Green during the 2001/02 season.

ODEY, PAUL — *Forward*
Current Club: Andover
Birthplace: Hampshire
Previous clubs include: Wokingham T - August 2000, Andover, Havant T, Fareham T, Weymouth, Salisbury C, Basingstoke T, Andover, Newbury T, Andover.

ODGER, KEVIN — *Forward*
Current Club: Skelmersdale United
Birthplace: Liverpool
Previous clubs include: St Helens T - December 2001, Vauxhall Motors, Burscough, Vauxhall GM, Heswall.

ODLUM, GARY — *Midfielder*
Current Club: Whyteleafe
Previous clubs include: Dulwich Hamlet - August 2001, Wimbledon.

ODLUM, JOHN — *Goalkeeper*
Current Club: Erith & Belvedere
D o B: 19/02/1976   Birthplace: Croydon
John signed for Erith & Belvedere in June 2002 from Dr Martens Eastern rivals St Leonards. The goalkeeper was a 2001 close season signing for St Leonards from Ryman League side Dulwich Hamlet. Impressed with a number of excellent performances in goal. Was on the books at Wimbledon as a youngster and has also been at Tooting and Mitcham United.

O'DONNELL, JAMES — *Forward*
Current Club: Ossett Albion
Birthplace: Doncaster
Previous clubs include: Armthorpe Welfare - October 2001, Goole AFC, Frickley Ath., Matlock T, Emley, Hatfield Main, Armthorpe Welfare, Brodworth Welfare, Harworth CI, Doncaster R.

O'DONNELL, LEE — *Midfielder*
Current Club: Walton & Hersham
Birthplace: Surrey
Midfielder who signed for Ryman Division One South side Walton & Hersham in the summer of 2002 from rivals Windsor & Eton. Started out at Woking and then had a spell with Hendon before joining the Royalists in October 2001.

O'DONNELL, LEE — *Midfielder*
Current Club: Dorking
Birthplace: Surrey
Previous clubs include: Croydon Ath - August 2001.

O'DONOHUE, NEIL — *Defender*
Current Club: Mildenhall Town
Birthplace: Cambridge
Previous clubs include: Histon - September 2001, Watton Utd, Histon, Ely C, Cambridge C, St.Ives T, Eynesbury R, Cambridge C.

OFORI, EUGENE — *Forward*
Current Club: Hendon
Birthplace: Ghana
Honours won: Ghana u-21 Int.
Ghanian-born striker who made his debut against Canvey Island in September 2001. Having made a brief appearance during pre-season. Formerly with Liberty Porfessionals in his home country, Eugene looks to be a useful addition to the squad. Has represented Ghana at under-21 level.

OGELSBY, DAMIEN — *Midfielder*
Current Club: Didcot Town
Birthplace: Oxfordshire
Damien joined Didcot from Henley town in the summer and has impressed with his attitude and application. One of lifes fashion victims, he is already one of the most popular lads at the club.

OGILVIE, STUART — *Midfielder*
Current Club: Mildenhall Town
Birthplace: Cambridge
Previous clubs include: Foxton - July 1998, Littleover, Vangate, Cambridge C.

OGLEY, MARK — *Defender*
Current Club: Belper Town
D o B: 10/03/1967   Birthplace: Barnsley
A very experienced and well-travelled defender who joined UniBond First Division side Belper Town as player/assistant-manager in July 2002 after a spell with Frickley Athletic. Made over 120 League appearances with Burnley, Carlisle, Aldershot and York and then went Non-League with Altrincham, Stalybridge Celtic, Leek Town, Gainsborough Trinity and Emley. Joined Frickley in January 2001.

O'GORMAN, DAVE — *Defender*
Current Club: Billingham Synthonia
Birthplace: Cleveland
Previous clubs include: Wingate Mall - July 1993, Stockton.

O'GORMAN, DAVID — *Forward*
Current Club: Rhyl
D o B: 20/06/1972   Birthplace: Chester
Previous clubs include: Hellenic (Australia) - July 2001, Droylsden, Hellenic (Australia), Swansea C, Barry T, Northwich V, Hyde Utd, Wrexham.

O'HAGAN, DANNY — *Forward*
Current Club: Weston-Super-Mare
D o B: 24/04/1976   Birthplace: Truro
Highly-rated centre forward who has developed his own style. Re-joined Dr Martens Western side Weston-super-Mare in July 2002 from Eastern Division Dorchester Town. Started his career with Plymouth where he made a number of League appearances and then signed for Weston before being bought by Dorchester for £6,000 in May 1998.

O

O'HAGAN, PAT — Goalkeeper
Current Club: Cwmbran Town
D o B: 15/03/1971   *Birthplace: Wales*
Previous clubs include: Llanelli - December 2000, Cwmbran T, Ebbw Vale, Inter Cardiff, Briton Ferry Ath., Stroud, Cardiff C, Swansea C, Newport Co., Cwmbran T.

OHANDJANIAN, DAMIEN — Forward
Current Club: Woodley Sports
Birthplace: Manchester
From Youth team.

O'HARA, JOEL — Midfielder
Current Club: Horsham YMCA
Birthplace: Sussex
Another member of the successful reserve side of 2000/01 who has progressed into the first-team during the latest season.

O'HARA, MARK — Midfielder
Current Club: Abingdon United
Birthplace: Oxfordshire
Previous clubs include: Brackley T - December 2001, Abingdon Utd.

O'HARE, JOHN — Midfielder
Current Club: Mickleover Sports
Birthplace: Nottingham
Previous clubs include: Stapenhill - July 2001, Heanor T, Stapenhill, Leicester Utd, Grantham T, Nottingham Forest (Trainee).

O'HARE, PAUL — Forward
Current Club: Cirencester Town
Previous clubs include: Witney T - July 2001.

OJAPAH, SAMUEL — Defender
Current Club: Colwyn Bay
Birthplace: Nigeria
Nigerian-born, he signed for Colwyn Bay from Rhyl in January 2002 and made his debut against his former team in the North Wales Coast Cup game. Much is expected of this highly-promising young defender in the future.

OKAFOR, SAMMY — Midfielder
Current Club: Sittingbourne
D o B: 17/03/1982   *Birthplace: Xtiam, Nigeria*
Previous clubs include: Cambridge C - November 2001, Dover Ath., Colchester Utd.

OKITA, JEAN-MARIE — Forward
Current Club: Tilbury
Birthplace: Zaire
Previous clubs include: Enfield - October 2000, Haringey B.

OKORIE, KELECHI — Midfielder
Current Club: Workington
D o B: 08/10/1968   *Birthplace: Izomber, Nigeria*
Previous clubs include: Carlisle Utd - December 2001, Sarpsborg (Norway), Accrington Stanley, Bamber Bridge, Sarpsborg (Norway), Ashton Utd, Kalmar IF (Sweden), St.Mirren, Torquay Utd, Grimsby T.

OLALEYE, MOSES — Forward
Current Club: Aberystwyth Town
Birthplace: Hertfordshire
Signed for League of Wales side Aberystwyth Town in August 2002 from Ryman Division One North outfit Harlow Town. Had joined Harlow in November 2001 from Letchworth. A skilful young forward who has made an impressive start in the LoW.

OLD, JULIAN — Defender
Current Club: Chertsey Town
Birthplace: Herts
Previous clubs include: Dulwich Hamlet - February 2002, Leatherhead, Leighton T, Hitchin T, Baldock T.

OLDACRE, STEVE — Forward
Current Club: Rocester
Birthplace: Shropshire
Previous clubs include: Shifnal T - August 2002, Chasetown, Bloxwich T, Rushall Olympic, Chasetown, Sutton Coldfield T, Armitage, Burton Alb., Bromsgrove R, Armitage, Walsall.

OLDBURY, MARCUS — Defender
Current Club: Dorchester Town
D o B: 29/03/1976   *Birthplace: Bournemouth*
Previous clubs include: Lymington & New Milton - August 2000, Bashley, AFC Bournemouth, Norwich C.

OLDFIELD, CRAIG — Midfielder
Current Club: Woodbridge Town
D o B: 24/11/1963   *Birthplace: Wortley*
Has returned to Notcutts Park after a season at Felixstowe, before which he spent seven seasons with the Woodpeckers. His ability enables him to appear at home in any position, and his experience will be valuable assets.

OLDFIELD, NIGEL — Midfielder
Current Club: Selby Town
Birthplace: Selby
Previous clubs include: Pontefract Collieries - December 1997, Selby T, Eggborough.

OLDROYD, MARK — Goalkeeper
Current Club: Eastbourne United
Birthplace: Sussex
One-time Sussex youth goalkeeper who had a confidence-shattering season at Ringmer before being released from his contract in March 2000. Subsequently joined Eastbourne United, initially as a reserve: also called up (in an emergency) to play for Lewes in April that year: first-team regular at The Oval during 2000/01: began the latest campaign with Eastbourne Borough, mainly playing for the reserves but also making two Dr Martens League appearances: returned to Eastbourne United in October.

O'LEARY, AARON — Midfielder
Current Club: Ashford Town
Birthplace: Kent
Defender or midfielder with a sweet left foot. Moved up from Dr Martens Eastern side Ashford Town's reserve side and is a product of the clubs youth policy. Managers player of the year winner fo 2001/02.

O'LEARY, SHAUN — *Midfielder*
Current Club: Afan Lido

D o B: 10/04/1976 — Birthplace: Wales
Former Liverpool trialist. Shaun is a fantastic ambassador for the club and a consistent midfielder - also strong in the air and up front.

OLIPHANT, DANNY — *Midfielder*
Current Club: Bracknell Town

Birthplace: Berkshire
From Youth team.

OLIVER, JOHN — *Midfielder*
Current Club: Chichester City United

Birthplace: Sussex
Previous clubs include: Portfield - July 2000.

OLIVER, TONY — *Midfielder*
Current Club: Tring Town

Birthplace: Hemel Hempstead
Previous clubs include: Leverstock Green - November 1999.

OLLERTON, NEIL — *Midfielder*
Current Club: Clitheroe

Birthplace: Lancashire
Ex-Wigan and Chorley player in his second spell at Shawbridge after returning from Rossendale. Strong on the ball and a good supporting player.

OLNER, PAUL — *Midfielder*
Current Club: Atherstone United

D o B: 20/10/1965
Previous clubs include: Hinckley Utd - July 2001, Sutton Coldfield T, Atherstone Utd, Hinckley T, VS Rugby, Gloucester C, VS Rugby, Atherstone Utd.

OMAN, JON — *Defender*
Current Club: Bury Town

Birthplace: Suffolk
From Youth team.

OMEARA, LEE — *Defender*
Current Club: Brentwood

Birthplace: Essex
Skilful player who produced some impressive performances towards the end of last season and looks likely to establish himself in the first team squad this year.

O'NEILL, LIAM — *Midfielder*
Current Club: Banbury United

Birthplace: Coventry
Signed for Banbury United in the summer of 2001 from Ford Sports Daventry. Was a first season apprentice at Coventry City. Previous clubs include Mansfield Town, Cheltenham Town, Atherstone United, Bedworth United, VS Rugby and Racing Club Warwick. Has lots of experience at this level and has been a good addition to the squad.

O'NEILL, SHAUN — *Goalkeeper*
Current Club: Ware

Previous clubs include: Leyton Pennant - December 2000, Harlow T, Leyton Pennant, Enfield, Hoddesdon T, Aveley, Runcorn.

O'NEILL, STEVE — *Forward*
Current Club: Prescot Cables

Birthplace: Liverpool
Previous clubs include: St Helens T - July 2000, Runcorn, Bamber Bridge, Altrincham, Bootle, Marine.

ONIONS, DAVID — *Defender*
Current Club: Billingham Town

Birthplace: Cleveland
From Youth team.

ONIONS, LEE — *Defender*
Current Club: Cradley Town

Birthplace: West Midlands
Previous clubs include: Bloxwich T - July 2001, Lye T.

ONOCHIE, ELLIOT — *Forward*
Current Club: Tooting & Mitcham United

Birthplace: Surrey
Previous clubs include: Wimbledon - August 2001.

OPARA, KELECHI — *Forward*
Current Club: Enfield

D o B: 21/12/1981 — Birthplace: Oweri, Nigeria
Previous clubs include: Billericay T - March 2002, Leyton Orient, Colchester Utd.

OPINEL, SASHA — *Defender*
Current Club: Billericay Town

D o B: 09/04/1977 — Birthplace: Saint Maurice (France)
Honours won: France Schoolboy Int.
Previous clubs include: Aldershot T - October 2001, Leyton Orient, Plymouth Argyle, Raith Rovers, Partick Thistle, AS Cannes (France), Lille (France).

ORD, DEREK — *Defender*
Current Club: Dunston Federation Brewery

D o B: 18/01/1963 — Birthplace: Gateshead
Previous clubs include: Spennymoor Utd - August 1999, Gateshead, Gretna, Durham C, Bishop Auckland, Spennymoor Utd, Chester-le-Street, Gateshead, Blyth Spartans, North Shields.

ORD, RICHARD — *Defender*
Current Club: Durham City

D o B: 03/03/1970 — Birthplace: Easington
Honours won: England u-21 Int.
Previous clubs include: Queens Park Rangers - November 2000, Sunderland.

O'REAGAN, JOE — *Defender*
Current Club: Wealdstone

D o B: 20/01/1983 — Birthplace: London
Teenage defender Joe is another player to have progressed through from Wealdstones youth team, first breaking into the senior team at the end of the 2001/02 season. Joe is now establishing himself as a solid defender.

O'REILLY, ALEX — *Goalkeeper*
Current Club: Purfleet

D o B: 15/09/1979 — Birthplace: Epping
Honours won: Republic of Ireland Youth & u-21 Int.
Previous clubs include: Bristol Rovers - August 2001, West Ham Utd.

O'REILLY, JUSTIN — Forward

Current Club: Mickleover Sports

D o B: 29/06/1973 — Birthplace: Derby

Previous clubs include: Matlock T - August 2001, Gresley R, Newcastle T, Ilkeston T, Southport, Port Vale, Gresley R.

ORGAN, CHRIS — Defender

Current Club: Oxford City

Previous clubs include: Witney T - December 2000, Evesham Utd, Swindon T.

ORIOT, DANNY — Midfielder

Current Club: Edgware Town

Birthplace: London

Previous clubs include: Wealdstone - August 2001.

ORMEROD, ANTHONY — Midfielder

Current Club: Scarborough

D o B: 31/03/1979 — Birthplace: Middlesbrough

Honours won: England Youth Int.

It was quite a coup for Scarborough when they managed to acquire the services of Anthony from Premiership Middlesbrough in May 2002. A skilful midfielder, he made over 20 first-team appearances for Boro, but didn't feature after Bryan Robsons departure and had loan spells at Hartlepool, York, Bury and Carlisle. He was wanted by Hartlepool amongst others after being released from the Riverside, but chose instead to join the Conference outfit.

ORMEROD, MARK — Goalkeeper

Current Club: Dorchester Town

D o B: 05/02/1976 — Birthplace: Bournemouth

Previous clubs include: Woking - November 2000, Brighton.

O'ROURKE, JAMIE — Forward

Current Club: Havant & Waterlooville

Birthplace: Hampshire

After scoring against Havant & Waterlooville in the Hampshire Senior Cup in 1998 while playing for Cowes Sports, Jamie signed for the club in January 2000. His ability to work his way around the best defences in the league is a positive asset to the team and has in recent months scored his fair share while setting up many other goals.

OSBORNE, MATT — Defender

Current Club: Chichester City United

Birthplace: Sussex

Defender/midfielder who played a few times for Chichester City during 1999/2000: originally looked set to join Pagham from the start of 2000/01 before signing for Wick instead: switched to the Lions midway through that season and was also part of the Sussex U-18 squad: transferred to Chichester in August 2001 and called upon to make a few emergency appearances as goalkeeper during the autumn.

OSBORNE, STEVE — Midfielder

Current Club: Billingham Town

Birthplace: Cleveland

Previous clubs include: Spennymoor Utd - January 2001, Harrogate T, Billingham T, Guisborough T, Chester-le-Street, Spennymoor Utd, Chester-le-Street, Guisborough T.

OSBORNE, TOMMY — Defender

Current Club: Hastings United

D o B: 05/09/1979 — Birthplace: Dartford

Young improving defender who signed for Hastings during the 1999 close season. Previously with Gillingham.

OSBOURNE, GARY — Defender

Current Club: Stourbridge

D o B: 22/10/1969 — Birthplace: Wolverhampton

Previous clubs include: Bilston T - February 2002, Sutton Coldfield T, Redditch Utd, Tamworth, Redditch Utd, Cradley T, Colchester Utd, Stourbridge, Telford Utd, Shrewsbury T.

OSGOOD, DAVE — Midfielder

Current Club: Bracknell Town

Birthplace: Berkshire

Previous clubs include: Sandhurst T - July 1999, Aldershot T, Basingstoke T, Bracknell T, Aldershot T,m Maidenhead Utd, Burnham, Newbury T, Basingstoke T, Windsor & Eton, Maidenhead Utd, Windsor & Eton.

O'SHAUGHNESSY, STEVE — Defender

Current Club: Flexsys Cefn Druids

D o B: 13/10/1967 — Birthplace: Wrexham

Honours won: Wales Youth Int.

Previous clubs include: Oswestry T - July 2001, Bangor C, TNS Llansantffraid, Rhyl, Holywell T, Stalybridge Celtic, Barry T, Stalybridge Celtic, Darlington, Exeter C, Rochdale, Bradford C, Leeds Utd.

O'SHEA, JOE — Midfielder

Current Club: Staines Town

D o B: 22/03/1967 — Birthplace: Middlesex

Midfielder who joined Staines Town as a junior in 1982 and remained with the club until early 1988/89. He then had short spells with both Feltham and Hounslow and longer ones at Egham Town, Windsor & Eton and Walton & Hersham before returning to Staines in July 1993. Has now passed the 700-game mark for the club and won the vice-presidents player of the year award for 2001/02 - 17 years after winning the youth player of the year award!

O'SHEA, TIM — Defender

Current Club: Farnborough Town

D o B: 12/11/1966 — Birthplace: Pimlico

Honours won: Republic of Ireland u-21 Int.

Club captain and exprienced defender, Tim signed for Farnborough in August 1999 following seven successful seasons in Hong Kong with Eastern and Instant Dict. Was with Spurs for five years as a youngster and has also played for Leyton Orient and Gillingham.

OSIKOYA, MARK — Defender

Current Club: Walton Casuals

Birthplace: Surrey

Joined Casuals this season, and has now established himself as a regular 1st member, previous clubs include Bracknell, Camberley and Raynes Park Vale. Mark works for the F.A.

O'SULLIVAN, JOHN — Midfielder

Current Club: Ford United

Birthplace: Essex

Outstanding versatile player who joined newly-promoted Ryman Premier side Ford United from neighbouring Grays Athletic in July 2002. Had signed for Grays from Braintree Town in September 2000, and he has also seen service at Dagenham, Barking, Bishops Stortford and Watford.

O'SULLIVAN, VINCE — Midfielder
Current Club: Ashford Town (Middx)
Birthplace: Middlesex
Aged 18 and seen as an excellent prospect for Ashford Town (Middx). Plays in midfield or defence and has established himself in the 1st Team, playing with a maturity beyond his years. Player of the Year 2000-01.

O'TOOLE, DANNY — Forward
Current Club: Atherstone United
Birthplace: Coventry
Former Coventry City trainee forward or midfielder who signed for Dr Martens Western side Shepshed Dynamo in July 2002 from league rivals Atherstone United. Had spells with local sides Coventry Sphinx and Long Buckby after leaving the Sky Blues and then played for Rugby United before joining the Adders in the summer of 2001.

O'TOOLE, GAVIN — Midfielder
Current Club: Hinckley United
D o B: 19/09/1975   *Birthplace: Dublin*
Honours won: Republic of Ireland u-21 Int.
Gavin rejoined Hinckley United in the 2001/02 close season. In his previous spell at the club he only played 5 games, but did get a goal. Hinckley resigned him from Aberystwyth Town, where he was playing Welsh League football. Gavin started his career at Coventry City and moved to Hinckley United when he was released by them 4 years ago. He moved on to Nuneaton Borough before playing in Wales. He has also represented the Republic of Ireland at under-21 level.

OTTLEY, RICHARD — Defender
Current Club: Gorleston
Birthplace: Norfolk
From Youth team.

OUEFIA, NGIE — Midfielder
Current Club: Carshalton Athletic
Birthplace: Paris
Talented young midfielder who played at Paris St.Germains Academy with his brother Berando and then joined Ryman Division One South side Carshalton Athletic, initially for a trial, during the summer of 2002/03.

OUEFIO, BERANDO — Forward
Current Club: Carshalton Athletic
D o B: 22/05/1980   *Birthplace: Paris*
Promising young striker who played at Paris St.Germains Academy with his brother Ngie and then moved on to Le Mee Sport before joining Ryman Division One South side Carshalton Athletic, initially for a trial, during the summer of 2002/03.

OUGHAM, JAMES — Midfielder
Current Club: Arlesey Town
Birthplace: Hitchin
Hitchin-born James is a midfielder who works at a Sports Centre. Made his Arlesey Town debut vs Met Police on l6th February 2002. Former clubs include Stevenage Borough and St. Albans City, from whom he joined Arlesey in Febraury 2002.

OUTHWAITE, JOHN — Forward
Current Club: Shildon
Birthplace: Co.Durham
Previous clubs include: Peterlee Newtown - July 2001, Durham C, Peterlee Newtown, South Shields, Shildon, Guisborough T, Peterlee Newtown, Whitby T.

OVARD, JOHN — Forward
Current Club: Dover Athletic
Birthplace: Kent
From Youth team.

OVENS, STEVE — Midfielder
Current Club: Tiverton Town
D o B: 02/05/1978   *Birthplace: Trowbridge*
Formerley with Witney Town, from whom he was originally signed on a long-term loan deal, Steve signed permanently in August 1999 to become Tiverton Town's first purchase. Steve is an exceptionally quick, direct and skillful attacing midfielder, who is currently studying at Exeter University.

OVERTON, DANNY — Forward
Current Club: Swaffham Town
Birthplace: Norfolk
Clever target man who has been at Kings Lynn, Fakenham and Watton. Thoughtful player who sets up play well for Swaffham.

OVERTON, PETER — Forward
Current Club: Chatham Town
Birthplace: Kent
Previous clubs include: Welling Utd - December 2001, Fisher Ath, Sheppey Utd, Maidstone Utd, Sittingbourne, Ashford T, Sittingbourne, Tonbridge, Faversham T, Herne Bay, Dover Ath.

OVEY, SIMON — Defender
Current Club: Barnstaple Town
D o B: 28/09/1982   *Birthplace: Devon*
Previous clubs include: Exeter C - July 2000.

OWEN, ADAM — Defender
Current Club: Flexsys Cefn Druids
Birthplace: Chester
Previous clubs include: Connahs Quay Nomads - July 2001, Chester C.

OWEN, CRAIG — Midfielder
Current Club: Sheffield FC
Birthplace: Sheffield
Previous clubs include: Hallam - February 2001, Sheffield, Hallam, Maltby Main, Derby Co (Trainee).

OWEN, DAN — Forward
Current Club: Sidlesham
Birthplace: Sussex
Big forward scored once during a handful of appearances for Sidlesham during 2000/01: another reserve player to be elevated to the first-team after manager Ian Hillman quit in the summer 2001.

OWEN, DANNY — Midfielder
Current Club: Redhill
Birthplace: London
Former professional with Millwall whose full time career was cut short by a back injury. Joined Redhill early this season after playing for Herne Bay in 1999/2000. Suffered a serious injury at Shoreham early this season, which looked to have finished his playing days. Has battled back strongly and thanks to intensive physio sessions, still has hopes of a return to the game in a year or so.

OWEN, DARREN   *Defender*
Current Club: Boldmere St.Michaels
Birthplace: Birmingham
Previous clubs include: Bustleholme - August 1999.

OWEN, GARETH   *Midfielder*
Current Club: Doncaster Rovers
D o B: 21/10/1971   *Birthplace: Chester*
Honours won: Wales u-21& B Int.
Attacking midfielder who joined Wrexham as a trainee, signing professional in July 1990. Released by Wrexham at the end of 2000-01 season he joined Doncaster Rovers in July. Has won 8 under-21 and 1 B international caps for Wales.

OWEN, JASON   *Defender*
Current Club: Rushall Olympic
Birthplace: Birmingham
Previous clubs include: Halesowen T - July 2001, Stafford R, Halesowen T, West Bromwich T.

OWEN, LEE   *Midfielder*
Current Club: AFC Sudbury
Birthplace: Sudbury
Played for Sudbury Town's youth and first teams before trying his hand at a higher level of football. Very skillful, a good reader of the game and an impressive scoring record.

OWEN, MARK   *Forward*
Current Club: Worcester City
Birthplace: Birmingham
Worcester City's leading goalscorer in each of his first three seasons with the club, Mark has managed to average a goal every other game since arriving at St. Georges Lane from Willenhall Town in March 1998. Started his career as a trainee at Wolves and has also appeared for Bloxwich Strollers. Sadly, missed a good deal of the 2001/02 season through injury.

OWEN, MICHAEL   *Midfielder*
Current Club: Epsom And Ewell
Birthplace: Surrey
Played for Epsom in 2000 then he moved to Corinthian Casuals but then moved back to Epsom near the beginning of the 2001/2002 season.

OWEN, PAUL   *Defender*
Current Club: Mangotsfield United
Birthplace: Bristol
Previous clubs include: Hallen - January 2002.

OWEN, RICHARD   *Defender*
Current Club: Bangor City
Birthplace: Wales
Previous clubs include: Cemaes Bay - July 1999.

OWEN, RICHARD   *Midfielder*
Current Club: Rocester
D o B: 22/02/1968   *Birthplace: Stoke*
Previous clubs include: Armitage - July 1995, Rocester, Hatton Utd.

OWEN, ROBERT   *Midfielder*
Current Club: Gravesend & Northfleet
Birthplace: Kent
Honours won: Ryman League Premier Div.Winners
Played for Gillingham Youth as a schoolboy and eventually went on to play for the Reserve Team at Priestfield. At 18 years of age

he moved to Dr Martens League side Sittingbourne, where he spent three seasons. He had a brief spell at Tonbridge Angels before returning to Sittingbourne. He signed for Gravesend during the 2000/2001 season and quickly established himself as a regular first-team midfield player.

OWEN, VAL   *Midfielder*
Current Club: Northwich Victoria
Birthplace: Manchester
Val re-joined Northwich Victoria in October 2001 on a three-year deal. A late arrival in the senior Non-League game, Val was signed by Hyde United in the summer of 1995 after some excellent performances in the Manchester amateur football scene. His tigerish ball-winning skills and box-to-box running soon made him a regular in Hydes starting line-up and he went on to play against Northwhich in the FA Trophy semi-finals of 1996. When he became a free agent in June 1998, Val signed a two-year deal with the Greens, and he averaged a goal from every three starts. He joined Hednesford Town when his contract expired but failed to settle with the Pitmen, who were relegated from the Conference. After a brief loan spell at Southport in September 2001, the Manchester-born midfield man opted for a second spell with the Greens and was appointed club captain at the start of the 2002/03 season.

OWERS, ADRIAN   *Midfielder*
Current Club: Maldon Town
D o B: 26/02/1965   *Birthplace: Danbury*
Previous clubs include: Sudbury Wanderers - July 1999, Braintree T, Worthing, Chelmsford C, Dagenham & Redbridge, Maidstone Utd, Brighton, Chelmsford C, Southend Utd.

OWERS, GARY   *Midfielder*
Current Club: Forest Green Rovers
D o B: 03/10/1968   *Birthplace: Newcastle*
Vastly experienced midfield player who joined Conference side Forest Green Rovers in August 2002 after a long and successful professional career. Started out at Sunderland where he progressed to become a first-team regular and make more than 250 appearances, helping the club to a couple of promotions to the top division. A £250,000 move to Bristol City followed in December 1994 and he went on to play a further 150 times for the west countrymen before having a four-year stint at Notts County, from where he was released at at the end of the 2001/02 season.

OWERS, PHIL   *Goalkeeper*
Current Club: Shildon
D o B: 28/04/1955   *Birthplace: Bishop Auckland*
Previous clubs include: South Shields - December 2001, Shildon, Bishop Auckland, Shildon, Spennymoor Utd, Durham C, Bishop Auckland, Stockton, Bishop Auckland, Hartlepool Utd, Brandon Utd, Bishop Auckland, Crook T, Darlington, Gillingham, Darlington, Shildon.

OXBROW, DARREN   *Defender*
Current Club: Woodbridge Town
D o B: 01/09/1969   *Birthplace: Ipswich*
Skilfull and dominent central defender, signed from Felixstowe in July 1999, and previously with Ipswich Town, Chelmsford City, Kettering and Maidstone. Strong in the air and on the ground, he is one of the Leagues top defenders.

OXLEY, SCOTT   *Midfielder*
Current Club: Stocksbridge Park Steels
D o B: 22/11/1976   *Birthplace: Sheffield*
Previous clubs include: Alfreton T - December 2001, Hallam, Worksop T, Hallam, Stocksbridge Park Steels, York C.

PACEY, RYAN — *Defender*
Current Club: Dulwich Hamlet
Birthplace: London
Very promising 22-year-old midfielder who joined Dulwich Hamlet during the summer of 2001 after being released by Charlton Athletic. Played regularly in Charltons under-19 side and his form with Hamlet again attracted League attention.

PACHENT, MATT — *Defender*
Current Club: Whitehawk
Birthplace: Sussex
Experienced defender: previously with Seaford. Did his bit for saving Whitehawk from relegation when scoring a last minute equaliser against East Preston in May 2001.

PACK, ADRIAN — *Defender*
Current Club: Denaby United
Birthplace: Sheffield
Previous clubs include: Buxton - September 2000, Maltby Main, Parkgate, Killamarsh, Hallam, Sheffield, Gainsborough Trinity, Stocksbridge Park Steels.

PACK, LENNIE — *Forward*
Current Club: Ipswich Wanderers
D o B: 27/09/1976   *Birthplace: Salisbury*
Previous clubs include: Woodbridge T - July 2001, Diss T, Baldock T, Diss T, Woodbridge T, Kettering T, Lincoln C, Cambridge Utd.

PACKHAM, ANDY — *Defender*
Current Club: Whitehawk
Birthplace: Sussex
Defender and solid member of the Whitehawk side who progressed through the clubs youth system.

PACKHAM, MARTIN — *Defender*
Current Club: Fairford Town
Birthplace: Wiltshire
Previous clubs include: Tuffley Rovers - July 2000.

PADMORE, STEVE — *Forward*
Current Club: Rugby United
Birthplace: Leicester
A young, quick striker who joined Rugby United at the start of the 2001/02 season after impressing in pre-season. Was on the books at Leicester City before moving to Nuneaton Borough and then Bromsgrove Rovers, from whom he joined Rugby.

PAGE, GARY — *Forward*
Current Club: Glapwell
Birthplace: Doncaster
Previous clubs include: Armthorpe Welfare - July 1997, Harworth CI, Armthorpe Welfare.

PAGE, MARK — *Midfielder*
Current Club: Great Wakering Rovers
Birthplace: Southend
From Youth team.

PAGE, PAUL — *Defender*
Current Club: Kingsbury Town
Birthplace: London
Previous clubs include: Edgware T - December 2001, Kingsbury T.

PAINTER, ROBBIE — *Forward*
Current Club: Bradford Park Avenue
D o B: 26/01/1971   *Birthplace: Wigan*
Very experienced forward with over 400 League appearances to his name. Signed for UniBond Premier side Bradford Park Avenue in July 2002 after a season a rivals Gateshead. Started with Chester and then had spells with Maidstone United, Burnley, Darlington, Rochdale and Halifax.

PAISLEY, MATT — *Goalkeeper*
Current Club: Hadleigh United
Birthplace: Suffolk
Big powerful young keeper in his fifth season with Hadleigh. Confident and capable and looking for the opportunity to re-establish himself as first choice custodian.

PALMART, LEE — *Midfielder*
Current Club: Feltham
Birthplace: Feltham
Palmart joined Feltham at the beginning of the 2000/2001 season and has proved a very valuable asset to the side. Strong on the ball, an excellent passer and very strong in the tackle. Palmart tends to grab vital goals when needed.

PALMER, ADAM — *Defender*
Current Club: Arundel
Birthplace: Sussex
Defender: signed from Storrington during the 2001 close season: also played for Worthing reserves last year: long-term injury victim with a knee problem for the main part of the campaign.

PALMER, CARL — *Midfielder*
Current Club: Rushall Olympic
Birthplace: Wolverhampton
Previous clubs include: Bilston T - July 2000, Rushall Olympic, Wednesfield, Sandwell B, Wednesfield.

PALMER, JAMES — *Defender*
Current Club: Shifnal Town
Birthplace: Shropshire
From Youth team.

PALMER, JON — *Forward*
Current Club: Sutton United
Previous clubs include: Kings Lynn - July 2001, Boots Ath.

PALMER, LES — *Forward*
Current Club: Bromsgrove Rovers
D o B: 05/09/1971   *Birthplace: Quinton*
Previous clubs include: Blakenall - June 2001, Stourbridge, Kidderminster Harriers, WBA.

PALMER, NICKY — *Midfielder*
Current Club: Llanelli AFC
Birthplace: Wales
Honours won: Wales Schoolboy Int., Wales Colleges Rep.
Previous clubs include: Garden Village - July 2000, Llanelli, Hereford Utd.

PALMER, PAUL — *Forward*
Current Club: North Ferriby United
Birthplace: Hull
Previous clubs include: Hall Road Rangers - January 2002, North Ferriby Utd.

P

PALMER, RYAN — Defender

Current Club: Sutton United

D o B: 02/02/1980   Birthplace: Dulwich

Signed for Sutton United in the summer of 2000 after a season with Brighton An accomplished and versatile player who has played with success at both centre back and on the right of midfield and won the clubs Player of the Year award for 2000/01. He began his career as a trainee with Fulham.

PALMER, STEVE — Midfielder

Current Club: Telford United

Birthplace: Birmingham

A firm fans favourite due to his incredible commitment and desire to win. Tough-tackling and hard working, no-one gets a spare second in midfield with Palmer around. A goalscoring midfielder who works his socks off for Telford United FC, Steve commited himself to a new two-year deal over the summer of 2001.

PAMMENTER, MARTIN — Forward

Current Club: Ely City

Birthplace: Cambridgeshire

Previous clubs include: Watton Utd - September 1999, Soham Town R, Ely C, Cambridge C, Histon, Newmarket T.

PANNELL, WAYNE — Midfielder

Current Club: Stowmarket Town

Birthplace: Essex

Previous clubs include: Brightlingsea Utd - September 2001.

PANTER, DAMIAN — Midfielder

Current Club: Walton & Hersham

Birthplace: Surrey

Previous clubs include: Molesey - March 2002, Sutton Utd, Woking.

PAPA, BEN — Midfielder

Current Club: Leatherhead

Birthplace: Surrey

Previous clubs include: Molesey - March 2002, Leatherhead, Yeading, Leatherhead.

PAPE, STEVE — Goalkeeper

Current Club: Workington

Birthplace: Carlisle

Previous clubs include: Gretna - October 2001, St.Anns.

PARIS, ALAN — Defender

Current Club: Flackwell Heath

D o B: 15/08/1964   Birthplace: Slough

Previous clubs include: Boreham Wood - January 2002, Harrow B, Stevenage B, Sough T, Notts Co., Leicester C, Peterborough Utd, Watford, Slough T.

PARIS, ROB — Defender

Current Club: Maidenhead United

Birthplace: Berkshire

Strong central defender who signed for Ryman Premier side Maidenhead United in July 2002 after helping Aylesbury United to promotion to that division the previous season. Had joined the Ducks in October 2001 from Northwood and was previously with Slough Town, Marlow and Beaconsfield SYCOB.

PARK, ANDY — Midfielder

Current Club: Congleton Town

Birthplace: Cheshire

Midfield. Age 23. Signed in Mar 00 from local side Vale Juniors OB. Played for Cheshire Schools U/18s and represented the county at cross-country. He is now regularly available after completing a degree at Durham Univ.

PARKE, SIMON — Forward

Current Club: Halifax Town

Birthplace: Bradford

Powerful forward who joined Halifax Town from Southport in August 2002. Bradford-born, Simon started his career with home-town club Bradford Park Avenue but it was after joining Yorkshire neighbours Guiseley that he really came to notice. His form in the UniBond League earned him a move into the Conference with Southport in the summer of 2000, where he became a firm favourite prior to his move to the Shaymen.

PARKER, ADAM — Midfielder

Current Club: Aldershot Town

D o B: 14/07/1975

Previous clubs include: Hitchin T (£10,000) - September 2001, Stevenage Borough, Hatfield T.

PARKER, CHRIS — Defender

Current Club: Great Yarmouth Town

D o B: 02/10/1983   Birthplace: Norfolk

Youth team player with Yarmouth who has settled in well in the centre of the senior team defence and is a tremendous prospect, just recovering from injury.

PARKER, KEVIN — Midfielder

Current Club: Weston-Super-Mare

D o B: 20/09/1979   Birthplace: Plymouth

Signed for Weston-Super-Mare from Dr Martens League Premier Division side Weymouth in May 2002. Plymouth-born, Kevin, who is an attacking midfielder, started his career with Norwich before returning to the Wes Country with spells at Exeter and Torquay. Joined Weymouth in October 2001 following a successful loan spell.

PARKER, LEE — Midfielder

Current Club: Harrogate Railway

Birthplace: Yorkshire

Previous clubs include: Harrogate T - July 1998, Knaresborough T.

PARKER, MARTIN — Midfielder

Current Club: Bideford

Birthplace: Devon

Honours won: FA Vase Winners

Martin is an attacking mid fielder who joined us in the summer from Taunton Town, & was in their F.A. Vase winning side. He has also played for Exeter City & Torrington.

PARKER, MICKY — Midfielder

Current Club: Bracknell Town

Birthplace: Berkshire

Previous clubs include: Hungerford T - July 1993, Wokingham T.

PARKER, RICHARD — Forward

Current Club: Carmarthen Town

D o B: 06/07/1973   Birthplace: Birmingham

Striker who re-joined Carmarthen Town in August 2002 from former League of Wales rivals Rhayader Town. Started out as a trainee with Walsall and then had spells in Midlands Non-League football with Dudley Town, Wednesfield, Bilston, Willenhall and Stourbridge before heading west to Merthyr Tydfil, Rhayader Town, Cwombran and Llanelli.

PARKER, ROBBIE   Defender
Current Club: Woodbridge Town
Birthplace: Suffolk
Left-back who joined us from Grundisburgh just after the start of the season. Strong, solid defender, who passes the ball well, he has settled into the First team with the minimum of fuss.

PARKER, SIMON   Forward
Current Club: Gravesend & Northfleet
Birthplace: Essex
Previous clubs include: Heybridge Swifts - January 2002, Stowmarket T, Whitton Utd.

PARKES, MATTY   Midfielder
Current Club: Newcastle Town
Birthplace: Stoke
From Local football - July 2000.

PARKIN, GUY   Defender
Current Club: Liversedge
Birthplace: Bradford
Previous clubs include: Glasshoughton Welfare - July 1998.

PARKINS, CHRIS   Forward
Current Club: Gresley Rovers
D o B: 02/07/1974   Birthplace: Nottinghamshire
Forward who joined Gresley Rovers from Northern Counties East League neighbours Mickleover Sports in July 2002. Started out at Mansfield Town and has also seen service with Shepshed Dynamo, Eastwood Town and Alfreton Town.

PARKINSON, ANDY   Goalkeeper
Current Club: Croydon
Birthplace: Surrey
Goalkeeper who joined the club at the beginning of last season, and was a regular for the youth and reserve teams. Andy was thrust into the first team spotlight in May 2001, making his debut in a Ryman League Cup Semi-Final against Hampton, and his second appearance in the League Cup Final. His admirable performances in those two games suggest a promising future.

PARKINSON, GARY   Defender
Current Club: Stalybridge Celtic
D o B: 10/01/1968   Birthplace: Thornaby
Gary was born in Teeside has had a wide and varied career across several League clubs. He started as an Everton junior way back in 1985, before joining Middlesbrough in 1986. He made over 250 appearances in a Middlesbrough shirt between 1986 and 1993. During his seven-year spell at the Riverside he spent a couple of months of 1992 on loan to Southend. After his release from Boro, he joined Bolton Wanderers for a year, before moving on to join Burnley when he struggled to get into Wanderers first-team. Three years and over 150 appearances later, Gary moved onto Preston North End in 1997 for £50,000, where he spent four years, and made over 100 appearances. In 2001 Blackpool were in need of a quality defender, and splashed out £20,000 on the defender. He made 22 appearances for the Tangerines, but was released at the end of the 2001/02 season. Joined UniBond Premier side Stalybridge Celtic in August 2002. He made 572 league appearances in total.

PARKINSON, PHIL   Midfielder
Current Club: Newcastle Town
Birthplace: Cheshire
Previous clubs include: Nantwich T - July 2000, Crewe Alexandra (Junior).

PARKINSON, STUART   Midfielder
Current Club: Kendal Town
D o B: 18/02/1976   Birthplace: Blackpool
Previous clubs include: Fleetwood Freeport - July 2001, Morecambe, Blackpool.

PARKS, ANTHONY   Midfielder
Current Club: Witham Town
Birthplace: Essex
From Youth team.

PARKYN, ROY   Defender
Current Club: Arlesey Town
Birthplace: Islington
Islington-born Roy is very experienced defender with an educated left foot. Made his Arlesey debut on 16th February 2002 after arriving from Harlow Town. Former clubs include Spurs (Junlor), Charlton, Enfield, Gravesend, Hendon, Boreham Wood, Harlow, Kingsbury Town, Saffron Walden Town and Bishops Stortford.

PARMENTER, RUSSELL   Defender
Current Club: Evesham United
Previous clubs include: Redditch Utd - August 2000, Stourport Swifts, Redditch Utd, Stourport Swifts.

PARMENTER, STEVE   Forward
Current Club: Canvey Island
D o B: 17/01/1977   Birthplace: Chelmsford
Honours won: Wales u-21 Int., FA Trophy Winners
Signed for Cnavey Island in November 1998 from Kingstonian. Steve was a trainee with QPR before spending two years with Bristol Rovers. He made 18 Football League appearances and scored 2 gaols for Rovers and spent a period with Conference side Yeovil Town. He joined Kingstonian on a free transfer. Played for Wales U21s and has also played for Southend United as a youth trainee.

PARNELL, STEVE   Forward
Current Club: Tiptree United
Birthplace: Essex
Previous clubs include: Halstead T - July 1999, Sudbury T, Halstead T, Braintree T, Halstead T, Dagenham, Tiptree Utd.

PARR, CHRIS   Forward
Current Club: Glapwell
Birthplace: Nottingham
Previous clubs include: Dunkirk - July 2001.

PARR, KEVIN   Midfielder
Current Club: Stalybridge Celtic
Birthplace: Lancashire
Signed from Glossop, Kevin is a local lad with a great thirst for the game. He has a massive extended family, most of whom come to the home games; it is a joke that they double the attendance!

PARRAMORE, JULIAN   Forward
Current Club: Maltby Main
Birthplace: Yorkshire
Previous clubs include: Hallam - January 2002, Parkgate, Hallam.

P

PARRATT, DEAN — Midfielder

Current Club: Boreham Wood

Birthplace: Hertfordshire

Dean is the son of former Boreham Wood striker Dave Parratt, who played for the club in the early eighties. Dean joined the club in the 2001/02 season and made an impression as an attacking midfield player in the Capita League side, before making his first-team debut against Somersett Ambury V & E in the Herts Senior Challenge Cup on the 20th November 2001.

PARRATT, DEAN — Midfielder

Current Club: Braintree Town

D o B: 13/11/1970   Birthplace: London

Previous clubs include: Billericay T - July 2001, Dagenham & Redbridge, Bishops Stortford, Purfleet, Dagenham, Wimbledon (Junior), Arsenal (Junior).

PARRIS, STUART — Goalkeeper

Current Club: Frome Town

D o B: 26/06/1971   Birthplace: Somerset

Previous clubs include: Chard T - July 2001, Ottery St Mary, Wellington.

PARROTT, ANDY — Midfielder

Current Club: Brackley Town

Birthplace: Banbury

Previous clubs include: Banbury Utd - July 1999.

PARRY, DEWI — Defender

Current Club: Oswestry Town

D o B: 01/10/1972   Birthplace: Wales

Previous clubs include: Total Network Solutions - October 2001, Rhyl, Flint Town Utd, Connahs Quay Nomads.

PARRY, GILES — Defender

Current Club: Halesowen Harriers

Birthplace: Worcestershire

Previous clubs include: Lye T - July 1997, Dudley T, Lye T.

PARRY, MARK — Defender

Current Club: Atherton Laburnum Rovers

Birthplace: Bolton

Mark is a top-class defender who is very relaxed in possession. He is a superb ball-winner and very dependable in the centre of defence. Mark is a student and apart from football his main interest is cricket.

PARRY, PAUL — Defender

Current Club: Hereford United

D o B: 19/08/1980   Birthplace: Chepstow

Paul signed professional forms after completing his two-year YTS with Hereford United. He made good progress and made his first-team debut during the 1998/99 season. He looks an excellent prospect for the future and was watched by a number of Premiership clubs in recent months.

PARRY, SIMON — Defender

Current Club: Penrith

Birthplace: Cumbria

Previous clubs include: Workington - July 1999, Penrith, Cleator Moor Celtic, Stockton, Hartlepool Utd (Trainee).

PARSELLE, NORMAN — Midfielder

Current Club: Haverfordwest County

D o B: 08/01/1970   Birthplace: Wales

Previous clubs include: Bath C - December 2001, Weston-Super-Mare, Inter Cardiff, Newport AFC, Cwmbran T, Newport AFC, Forest Green R, Newport Co.

PARSLEY, DARYL — Midfielder

Current Club: Swaffham Town

Birthplace: Norfolk

Returned to Swaffham after a season at Fakenham. Highly skillful midfielder who has strength and tenacity.

PARSLEY, NEIL — Defender

Current Club: Guiseley

D o B: 25/04/1966   Birthplace: Liverpool

Previous clubs include: Witton Alb - October 1996, Exeter C, WBA, Huddersfield T, Leeds Utd, Witton Alb.

PARSONS, ANDY — Midfielder

Current Club: Brackley Town

Birthplace: Oxfordshire

Previous clubs include: Ardley Utd - July 2000.

PARSONS, DAVID — Midfielder

Current Club: Dartford

D o B: 25/02/1982   Birthplace: Greenwich

Previous clubs include: Purfleet - January 2002, Leyton Orient.

PARSONS, JOHN — Midfielder

Current Club: Northwood

Previous clubs include: Harrow Borough - July 1999, Northwood, Chelsea.

PARSONS, SPENCER — Defender

Current Club: Bedworth United

Birthplace: Bedworth

Young defender with a lot of promise. He is a product of Bedworth United's youth team and is been in the first-team squad for a couple of seasons. Has represented the County FA squad which won the County cup. Left back but can play as a centre back.

PARTINGTON, ASHLEY — Midfielder

Current Club: Woodley Sports

Birthplace: Oldham

Previous clubs include: Ashton Utd - July 2001.

PARTNER, ANDY — Defender

Current Club: Wivenhoe Town

Birthplace: Essex

Previous clubs include: Harwich & Parkeston - December 2001, Clacton T, Wivenhoe T, Heybridge Swifts, Colchester Utd.

PARTRIDGE, CHRIS — Forward

Current Club: Bedworth United

Birthplace: Coventry

Came second behind the Western Divisions top scorer in 2001/02. Chris has a great first touch, is skilful, pacey, and a handful as a predator. He has scored 100 goals for COventry Marconi in 2 seasons before joining Bedworth United in the summer of 2001. Previously with Hinckley United.

PARVIN, STEVE — *Midfielder*
Current Club: Sidlesham
Birthplace: Sussex
Experienced midfielder: has been at Sidlesham throughout their rise from the Third Division (which they won in 1996/97) of the County League, and scored the winning goal in their 2000 Division Two Cup Final victory over Hailsham: ex-Havant, Petersfield and Horndean player.

PASHLEY, STEVE — *Defender*
Current Club: Purfleet
Birthplace: Essex
Previous clubs include: Aveley - December 2001, Purfleet, Hornchurch, Purfleet.

PATCHING, MARTYN — *Goalkeeper*
Current Club: Arlesey Town
D o B: 09/12/1973   *Birthplace: Sussex*
Martyn was at Ware, Bedford, Kingstonian and Horsham before joining Arlesey Town in July 2000 and has been a terrific signing, producing some excellent display. He is a PE Teacher.

PATEL, PAUL — *Defender*
Current Club: Fairford Town
Birthplace: Wiltshire
Previous clubs include: Wootton Bassett T - July 2001.

PATERSON, GEOFF — *Midfielder*
Current Club: Gretna
D o B: 10/03/1982   *Birthplace: Dumfries*
Previous clubs include: Queen of the South - August 2001.

PATERSON, JAMIE — *Midfielder*
Current Club: Doncaster Rovers
D o B: 26/04/1973   *Birthplace: Dumfries*
Honours won: Conference Winners
Attacking midfielder who began with Halifax Town as a trainee, signing professional in July 1991. Transferred to Falkirk in December 1994 but moved back to England and Scunthorpe United in October 1995 for £18,000. He rejoined Halifax Town on a free transfer in July 1997 and helped them to win the Conference and promotion to the Football League. Doncaster Rovers signed him in July 2000.

PATES, BRADLEY — *Midfielder*
Current Club: Rossendale United
Birthplace: Manchester
Previous clubs include: Bamber Bridge - August 2002, Winsford Utd, Macclesfield T.

PATIENCE, DAVE — *Defender*
Current Club: Feltham
Birthplace: Slough
Player-manager Patience joined Feltham in 1995 along with the manager Martyn Busby from former Spartan League side, Beaconsfield SYCOB and has been a regular ever since. Dave was part of the side that beat Godalming & Guildford 5-1 in the League Cup Final during the 1996/97 season and the following year won both the Players & Managers Player of the Year Awards. A former club captain, Patience took over a joint player-management role last season and helped improved the sides league position up from 15th in 99/00 to a respectable 9th.

PATMORE, LEE — *Defender*
Current Club: St Margaretsbury
D o B: 07/01/1971   *Birthplace: Hertford*
Previous clubs include: Ware - July 2000, Hertford T, St Margaretsbury, Ware, Boreham Wood, Ware, Bishops Stortford, Ware, Hoddesdon T, Welwyn Garden C.

PATMORE, WARREN — *Forward*
Current Club: Woking
D o B: 14/08/1971   *Birthplace: Kingsbury*
Honours won: England Semi-Pro Int., Ryman League Premier Div.Winners
Warren signed for Woking from Rushden & Diamonds in September 2001 after joining them on a free transfer in June 2001 from Yeovil Town. Wazza, as he was popularly known at Huish Park, was Yeovils leading goalscorer in 1995/96 with 27 goals and again a season later with 29 goals. In the 1998/99 season Warren finished runner-up in the Conference top goalscorer list with 20 goals and then added another 22 as Yeovil finished the 2000/01 season in runners-up spot after a season-long battle with Rushden & Diamonds. Warren has won nine England semi-professiona international caps and also has a Ryman League Premier Division winners medal.

PATTEN, TONY — *Defender*
Current Club: Hamble ASSC
Birthplace: Hampshire
Previous clubs include: Gosport Borough - July 1998, BAT Sports, Romsey T.

PATTENDEN, TOMMY — *Forward*
Current Club: Peacehaven & Telscombe
Birthplace: Brighton
Forward who originally gained a reputation for being a teenage goalscoring sensation at Saltdean, and went on to be the leading marksmen for Lewes during 1999/2000. Held back by injury the following season and joined Peacehaven for the start of the 2001/02.

PATTERSON, CHRIS — *Midfielder*
Current Club: Chorley
D o B: 08/11/1977   *Birthplace: Bolton*
Experienced midfielder who followed manager Mark Molyneax to UniBond First Division side Chorley from rivals Trafford in July 2002. Began his career at Bury and then had his first spell at Chorley. Moved on to Colne Dynamoes, Atherton LR, Salford, Glossop, Fleetwood and Trafford before re-joining the Shawe View club in July 1997 from Curzon Ashton.

PATTERSON, GARY — *Midfielder*
Current Club: Farnborough Town
D o B: 27/11/1972   *Birthplace: Newcastle*
Honours won: England Semi-Pro Int., FA Trophy Winners
Left Notts County to join Shrewsbury Town, winning the 3rd Division there. A move to Wycombe Wanderers followed, again contributing well to their League campaigns. Had an excellent 98/99 with Ks, that has seen him established as one of the best midfielders in Non-League football. Voted 98/99 players and Supporters' Player of the season, and in the Conference team of the season. A regular in the England semi-pro team, Patto has also had the honour captaining the national side. Transferred to Boro in July 2001.

PATTERSON, IAN   *Defender*
Current Club: Ossett Albion
D o B: 04/04/1973
Birthplace: Chatham
Previous clubs include: Hallam - December 2001, Sheffield FC, Stocksbridge Park Steels, Stalybridge Celtic, Wigan Ath., Burnley, Sunderland.

PATTERSON, LEE   *Defender*
Current Club: Romford
Birthplace: Essex
Previous clubs include: East Thurrock Utd - March 2002, Basildon Utd, Concord Rangers, East Thurrock Utd, Hornchurch, Aveley, Hornchurch, East Thurrock Utd, Canvey Island, Tilbury, Collier Row, Witham T, East Thurrock Utd.

PATTERSON, MARK   *Midfielder*
Current Club: Bishop Auckland
Birthplace: Co.Durham
Enthusiastic all-action midfielder with a tremendous engine, who loves to get forward and score goals. Previous clubs include Middlesbrough, Durham City and South Shields. Last season Mark was voted both Player of the Year & Players' Player of the Year at Brandon United and joined Bishop Auckland in January 2002.

PATTIMORE, MICHAEL   *Midfielder*
Current Club: Cwmbran Town
Birthplace: Wales
Previous clubs include: Swindon T - July 1999, Croesyceiliog.

PATTISON, ANDY   *Midfielder*
Current Club: Thackley
D o B: 26/11/1980
Birthplace: Kirkcaldy
Previous clubs include: Bradford C - July 2000.

PATTISON, MARTIN   *Defender*
Current Club: Eccleshill United
Birthplace: Bradford
Previous clubs include: Thackley - July 2000, Eccleshill Utd, Bradford PA, Farsley Celtic, Guiseley, Bradford C.

PATTON, AARON   *Midfielder*
Current Club: Hanwell Town
D o B: 27/02/1979
Birthplace: London
Previous clubs include: Hemel Hempstead - August 2001, Slough T, Hayes, Wycombe Wanderers.

PATTON, MITCH   *Forward*
Current Club: Afan Lido
D o B: 05/10/1964
Birthplace: Wales
Lido striking legend, and probably the clubs best known player. A long-serving and loyal player who has been top-scorer in most of his time at the Lido, Mitchs greatest strength nowadays is his passing and creativity, although he's still always very close to the top of the highest scorers list.

PAUL, KINGSLEY   *Forward*
Current Club: Eastwood Town
Honours won: British Universities Rep.
Previous clubs include: Matlock T - August 2001, Stafford R, Nuneaton B, Hayes, Sheffield University.

PAUL, MARK   *Forward*
Current Club: Bedford Town
D o B: 03/01/1979
Birthplace: Peterborough
Signed for Ryman Premier side Bedford Town from Kettering Town in August 2000. Mark started his senior career at Kings Lynn after spells at Warboys Town and Peterborough and was signed by Southampton, where he spent 18 months at the Premiership club. Mark is a very skilful player with plenty of pace who can also play in midfield if required.

PAUL, MARTIN   *Forward*
Current Club: Chippenham Town
D o B: 02/02/1975
Birthplace: Whalley, Lancs
Martin joined newly-promoted Dr Martens League Premier Division side Chippenham Town from Newport County for a four-figure fee in July 2002. Had signed for County from Bath City during the summer of 2001 after being top scorer for his last two seasons at Twerton Park. He scored almost 100 goals in 200 appearances for the Romans and he formed a great link up with Garry Shephard in County's attack. A recruitment consultant, he made around 30 appearances for Bristol Rovers and also had a spell with Doncaster Rovers before joining Bath.

PAUL, TREVOR   *Forward*
Current Club: Bishops Stortford
Birthplace: Essex
Signed for Bishops Stortford midway through the 1999/2000 campaign from Romford and quickly proved to be both popular with the supporters and a great striking partner with Vinnie John. An almost ever-present figure in the first team Trevor notched up an impressive array of goals last season that took his tally over the 100-mark.

PAULING, GAVIN   *Defender*
Current Club: Wroxham
D o B: 16/12/1971
Birthplace: Norwich
Popular player returning after spending last season at Diss. Won several championship medals in previous spell at Wroxham.

PAULING, NATHAN   *Goalkeeper*
Current Club: Diss Town
Birthplace: Norwich
Previous clubs include: Watton Utd - August 2000, Blofield Utd, Diss T, Horsford Utd.

PAVER, MARK   *Defender*
Current Club: Mossley
Birthplace: Manchester
Previous clubs include: Chadderton - August 1999, Stalybridge Celtic, Chadderton.

PAY, SIMON   *Goalkeeper*
Current Club: Newcastle Town
Birthplace: Cheshire
Previous clubs include: Kidsgrove Ath - June 2001, Congleton T, Nantwich T, Witton Alb., Nantwich T, Leek T, Nantwich T.

PAYNE, ANDY   *Midfielder*
Current Club: Liversedge
Birthplace: Yorkshire
Previous clubs include: Eccleshill Utd - July 2000, Ossett Alb., Liversedge.

PAYNE, BRIAN   *Defender*
Current Club: Norwich United
D o B: 30/11/1973
Birthplace: Norfolk
Club captain at Norwich United, Mr. Reliable a strong no nonsense defender previously with Great Yarmouth Town and Diss town.

PAYNE, CHRIS — Forward
Current Club: Heybridge Swifts
Birthplace: Essex
Returned to Heybridge Swifts after a spell with Chelmsford City. Was an integral part of the teams success under previous manager Liam Cutbush. Wide man perhaps more comfortable on the left but can play either flank. Rarely wastes possession, creates countless goals from open play and deadballs, and has been known to score the odd spectacular goal or two himself. Also had spells with Canvey Island, Brentwood, Dagenham & Redbridge and Billericay. Now in his third spell with the club.

PAYNE, DEAN — Defender
Current Club: Diss Town
Birthplace: Bradford
Previous clubs include: Watton Utd - August 2000, St.Neots T, Queen of the South, St.Neots T, Bradford C (Trainee).

PAYNE, GRANT — Forward
Current Club: Woking
D o B: 25/12/1975   Birthplace: Woking
Honours won: FA Trophy Winners
Highly-rated striker who re-joined Woking in July 2002 after a three-year spell with Ryman Premier side Aldershot Town. Had signed for the Shots from Woking in November 1999 for a new club record fee of £20,000. Grant was an extremely popular player with Woking fans, netting almost 50 goals in his two-year spell at Kingfield. A former Wimbledon professional, he made history on his Shots debut by becoming the first player in 73 years to score four goals on his debut.

PAYNE, IAN — Defender
Current Club: Crawley Town
D o B: 19/01/1977   Birthplace: Crawley
Honours won: Wales Youth Int.
Defender: former Plymouth Argyle trainee (made one first-team appearance): also a one-time Welsh Youth International and has played for Vancouver 86ers in Canada.

PAYNE, KARL — Forward
Current Club: Mickleover Sports
D o B: 14/10/1974   Birthplace: Derbyshire
Previous clubs include: Belper T - July 2002, Gresley R, Belper T, Bromsgrove R, Burton Alb., Chesterfield (Junior).

PAYNE, MIKE — Goalkeeper
Current Club: Solihull Borough
Birthplace: Leicester
Previous clubs include: Highfield Rangers - July 2000, Notts Co.

PAYNE, RUSSELL — Forward
Current Club: Accrington Stanley
D o B: 08/07/1980   Birthplace: Liverpool
Moved to Accrington Stanley from Congleton in August 1999. Started at Skelmersdale where he was signed by Liverpool for £1,000. After 2 years at Anfield he joined Chorley where he was unfortunately troubled with injuries. Also played with Warrington Town.

PAYNE, STEVE — Forward
Current Club: Horsham
D o B: 12/08/1970   Birthplace: Sussex
Experienced winger: signed for Horsham from Ashford Town during the 2000 close season and scored 11 times during his first term at Horsham: previously with Hastings, Sutton and Crawley.

PAYNE, STUART — Forward
Current Club: Rushall Olympic
D o B: 10/01/1974   Birthplace: Birmingham
Previous clubs include: Bromsgrove Rovers - June 2002, Evesham Utd, Halesowen T, Kidderminster Harriers, Bromsgrove R, Halesowen Harriers, Blakenall, Stourbridge, Halesowen T, Lye T.

PAYTON, STEVE — Defender
Current Club: Beaconsfield SYCOB
Birthplace: Berkshire
Previous clubs include: Brook House - July 2000, Northwood, Brook House, Amersham T, Ruislip Manor, La Landes (France), Hanwell T, Chesham Utd.

PEACHEY, DAVE — Forward
Current Club: Herne Bay
Birthplace: Kent
Previous clubs include: Ashford T - July 2001.

PEACOCK, RICHARD — Midfielder
Current Club: Worksop Town
D o B: 29/10/1972   Birthplace: Sheffield
Vastly experienced midfielder who made over 200 League appearances for Sheffield United, Hull and Lincoln after starting out at Northern Counties East League side Sheffield. Signed for Stalybridge Celtic at the start of the 2001/02 season and then switched to Chester City in March 2002. Traneferred to UniBond Leaguers Worksop Town at the end of the 01/02 season.

PEAKE, CALLUM — Defender
Current Club: Atherstone United
D o B: 08/09/1984   Birthplace: Nuneaton
From Youth team.

PEAKE, JASON — Midfielder
Current Club: Nuneaton Borough
D o B: 29/09/1971   Birthplace: Leicester
Honours won: England Schoolboy & Youth Int.
Signed for Conference side Nuneaton Borough in March 2001 after an impressive two-month loan spell. An exerienced midfielder, he has also played for Plymouth Argyle, Leicester City, Bury and Rochdale.

PEAKE, RUSSELL — Forward
Current Club: Stafford Town
Birthplace: Staffordshire
Previous clubs include: Rushall Olympic - July 2000, Chasetown, Rocester, Shepshed Dynamo, Stafford R, Rocester.

PEAKS, ANDY — Defender
Current Club: Stamford
D o B: 25/11/1970   Birthplace: Northampton
Honours won: Dr Martens League Midland & Premier Div. Winners
Andy is an experienced utility defender who started his career with Northampton Town, before a lengthy spell at Rushden & Diamonds where he was a member of the DML winning team. He joined The Daniels, after spells with Rauds and Wealdstone, in August 2000.

PEARCE, CHRIS — Midfielder
Current Club: Willenhall Town
Birthplace: Birmingham
Signed December 2001 from Stourbridge, scored a cracker of a goal on his debut against Stapenhill.

P

PEARCE, DAREN — Midfielder
Current Club: Eastbourne Borough

Birthplace: Sussex
Club captain. Joined the club from East Preston (Sussex County League) during the 1999 close season. Also played for Colchester United, Littlehampton Town (Sussex County League), and Bognor Regis Town (Ryman League). Played for the Sussex Representative team.

PEARCE, ROBERT — Defender
Current Club: Paget Rangers

D o B: 14/01/1981   Birthplace: Birmingham
Previous clubs include: Tamworth - July 2001.

PEARCEY, JASON — Goalkeeper
Current Club: Rugby United

D o B: 23/07/1971   Birthplace: Leamington
Re-signed for Rugby United in July 2002 after a short stint in the Conference with Forest Green Rovers. An experienced goalkeeper who started his career as a YTS with Mansfield Town in 1987. Made his Football League debut the following year and spent nine years with the Stags before joining Brentford in 1997. Joined Solihull Borough in September 2001 after a spell out of the game. Leamington-born Jason then moved to Rugby in February 2002 and then on to Conference side Forest Green Rovers a month later.

PEARL, CRAIG — Midfielder
Current Club: Wingate And Finchley

Birthplace: London
Previous clubs include: Clapton - July 2001, Wingate & Finchley, Enfield, Dagenham & Redbridge, Watford.

PEARMAN, CRAIG — Forward
Current Club: North Leigh

Birthplace: Oxfordshire
Previous clubs include: Brackley T - July 2001, North Leigh.

PEARS, RICHARD — Forward
Current Club: Tiverton Town

D o B: 16/07/1976   Birthplace: London
Honours won: FA Vase Winners
Joined Tiverton Town in October 1998 from Clyst Rovers after previously making 68 appearances in six years with Exeter City, scoring eight goals. Richard, who has also played for Cullompton Rangers, has an excellent first touch and superb vision and knows how to score. He is currently working for an accountancy firm.

PEARSON, ANDY — Forward
Current Club: Afan Lido

D o B: 07/12/1980   Birthplace: Wales
A fine young forward, also used on the wing. Quick thinking and creative, Andy will be a key part of Lidos squad for many years to come.

PEARSON, CHRIS — Defender
Current Club: Guisborough Town

Birthplace: Newcastle
Previous clubs include: Jarrow Roofing - February 2002, Shotton Comrades, Easington Colliery, South Shields, Whitley Bay, Hebburn, Hartlepool Utd.

PEARSON, DAVE — Forward
Current Club: Walton Casuals

Birthplace: Surrey
Recently entered his second spell at Casuals, tireless runner with an eye for goal.

PEARSON, JAMIE — Midfielder
Current Club: Tooting & Mitcham United

Birthplace: Surrey
Jamie signed for Tooting & Mitcham United in July 2002. He was a graduate of Walton & Hershams youth side and made his senior debut in October 1996. Following a lengthy spell out with a back injury he returned to be a regular in the Suburban League side for two seasons, being voted Swans reserve Player of the Year for 1999-2000. Re-established a regular first team spot during the 2000/01 season.

PEARSON, JIMMY — Defender
Current Club: Hallam

Birthplace: Sheffield
Previous clubs include: Sheffield - July 1996.

PEARSON, JORDAN — Defender
Current Club: Port Talbot Town

Birthplace: Middlesfield
Previous clubs include: Llangeinor - July 2001, Porthcawl T.

PEARSON, LAWRIE — Defender
Current Club: Thornaby on Tees

D o B: 02/07/1965   Birthplace: Wallsend
Honours won: FA Vase Winners
Previous clubs include: South Shields - February 2002, Blyth Spartans, Bedlington Terriers, Whitby T, Blyth Spartans, Gateshead, Darlington, Chesterfield, Bristol C, Hull C, Gateshead.

PEARSON, MATT — Goalkeeper
Current Club: Guisborough Town

Previous clubs include: Hartepool Utd - July 2001.

PECK, GARY — Defender
Current Club: Sittingbourne

Birthplace: Kent
Previous clubs include: Lordswood - February 2002.

PEDDER, JOHN — Defender
Current Club: Berkhamsted Town

Birthplace: Hemel Hempstead
Previous clubs include: Hemel Hempstead - July 2001, Leighton T, Hemel Hempstead, Berkhamsted T, Hemel Hempstead.

PEDDIE, SIMON — Defender
Current Club: Enfield

From Youth team.

PEDLEY, DANIEL — Defender
Current Club: Flackwell Heath

Birthplace: Maidenhead
Previous clubs include: Marlow - January 2002, Chalfont St.Peter, Flackwell Heath, Marlow, Maidenhead Utd, Marlow.

PEDLEY, NEIL — Midfielder
Current Club: Bridgwater Town

D o B: 07/12/1983   Birthplace: Somerset
Previous clubs include: Bristol C (Trainee) - July 2000.

PEER, DEAN — *Midfielder*
Current Club: Moor Green
D o B: 08/08/1969   *Birthplace: Stourbridge*
Vastly experienced player who signed for Moor Green in July 2001 from Shrewsbury Town. Came through the Birmingham City youth team to become a first team regular at St.Andrews. Has also appeared for Walsall and Northampton Town.

PELL, ROBERT — *Forward*
Current Club: Guiseley
D o B: 05/02/1979   *Birthplace: Leeds*
Striker who switched from UniBond Premier side Droylsden to First Division Guiseley in August 2002. Born near Guiseley, he began his career with Rotherham, where he made a handful of League appearances and also had a loan spell with then Third Division Doncaster Rovers. Played in the Conference for Northwich Victoria and Southport before joining Droylsden in January 2001.

PELTON, DARYL — *Goalkeeper*
Current Club: Northwood
Previous clubs include: Uxbridge - August 2001, Northwood, Uxbridge.

PEMBERTON, STEVE — *Midfielder*
Current Club: Willenhall Town
Birthplace: Birmingham
Signed September 2001 from Boldmere. Spent 4 years at Shrewsbury Town before a serious knee injury ended his professional career.

PENBERTHY, DAVE — *Goalkeeper*
Current Club: Barnstaple Town
Birthplace: Devon
Previous clubs include: Taunton T - July 2000, Torrington.

PENDLETON, MATTY — *Defender*
Current Club: Evesham United
Previous clubs include: Racing Club Warwick - June 2000, Stourbridge, Bromsgrove R, Peterborough Utd.

PENDREY, DEAN — *Midfielder*
Current Club: Mangotsfield United
Birthplace: Bristol
Signed for Mangotsfield United from Bristol Rovers, where he had been a YTS player, in July 2000. Also played for Bitton in local football. Plays on the right side of defence or midfield, likes to get forward with his darting runs and is not afraid to take players on.

PENNEY, DAVID — *Midfielder*
Current Club: Doncaster Rovers
D o B: 17/08/1964   *Birthplace: Wakefield*
Very experienced midfielder who began his playing days with Pontefract Collieries before joining Derby in 1985. Went on to make over 300 League appearances for Derby, Oxford United, Swansea and Cardiff before returning to Yorkshire to join Doncaster in 1998.

PENNICOT-BOWEN, KEITH — *Defender*
Current Club: Bracknell Town
Birthplace: Berkshire
Previous clubs include: Hungerford T - September 1999, Bracknell T, Newbury T, Staines T, Wokingham T.

PENNINGTON, LEE — *Midfielder*
Current Club: Kendal Town
Previous clubs include: Fleetwood Freeport - August 2001, Great Harwood T, Accrington Stanley, Burnley.

PENNOCK, TONY — *Goalkeeper*
Current Club: Farnborough Town
D o B: 10/04/1971   *Birthplace: Swansea*
Honours won: Wales Semi-Pro Int., Ryman League Premier Div.Winners
Former Wales semi-professional international goalkeeper who joined Farnborough Town in July 2002 after a season with Rushden & Diamonds. Had a loan spell with Farnborough towards the end of the 2001/02 season after finding it tough displacing Billy Turley from the number one spot at Nene Park after joining from Yeovil Town shortly after Diamonds had won the Conference title. Originally with Stockport and Wigan, Tony played around 30 League games for Hereford United before moving to Yeovil in August 1998.

PENNY, ANDY — *Defender*
Current Club: Hinckley United
D o B: 24/05/1972   *Birthplace: Birmingham*
Andy joined Hinckley United from Solihull Borough in the close season of 2001. Previous clubs include Tamworth, Dudworth and Havant Town. Andy also has experience at Conference level with Stafford Rangers. Quickly gained a reputation as a no-nonsense defender.

PENNY, DANNY — *Midfielder*
Current Club: VCD Athletic
D o B: 03/07/1981   *Birthplace: Greenwich*
Previous clubs include: Slade Green - July 2001, Southall, Welling Utd.

PENNY, SHAUN — *Forward*
Current Club: Mangotsfield United
D o B: 24/09/1957   *Birthplace: Bristol*
Honours won: England Schoolboy Int.
Assistant-manager with Mangotsfield United who has enjoyed much Dr Martens League success with the likes of Clevedon Town, Bath City and Gloucester City. Former England Schoolboy International who first made his name at Bristol City, he joined Mangotsfield as assistant to Andy Black in May 2000. He's now approaching the twilight of his playing career!

PEPPER, CARL — *Midfielder*
Current Club: Blyth Spartans
D o B: 26/07/1980   *Birthplace: Darlington*
Signed for UniBond Premier side Blyth Spartans in October 2000 from Darlington. Made his debut against Droylsden on 28th October 2000 and became a fixture in the midfield for the remainder of the season. One of the more experienced players in the side, he is club captain. Received the Players' Player of the Year award for 2001/02.

PEPPER, GRAHAM — *Defender*
Current Club: Blyth Spartans
D o B: 01/01/1976   *Birthplace: Newcastle*
Signed for UniBond Premier side Blyth Spartans during the summer of 2001 from Gateshead. Has become an obvious choice for selection, following a good pre-season campaign. However Graham had suffered many injuries whilst at Gateshead, so it will be interesting to see how often he is available through fitness.

PEPPER, JULIAN — Forward
Current Club: Connahs Quay Nomads
D o B: 22/07/1979   Birthplace: Chester
Previous clubs include: Heswall - July 1999.

PEPPER, LUKE — Midfielder
Current Club: Ely City
Birthplace: Cambridge
From Youth team.

PEPPER, NIGEL — Midfielder
Current Club: Barrow
D o B: 25/04/1968   Birthplace: Rotherham
Experienced defender who joined Barrow in May 2002 after being released by Scunthorpe United Nigel started his career with his home-town club Rotherham United before joining York City in July 1990. He stayed at Bootham Crescent for seven years and made over 250 appearances for the Minstermen before leaving for Bradford City for £100,000. Scottish Premier side Aberdeen then paid three times that for him in November 1998 but he made only 14 appearances in almost two years in Scotland before joining Scunthorpe in June 2000.

PERCIVAL, JASON — Forward
Current Club: Barwell
D o B: 20/09/1973   Birthplace: Leicester
Previous clubs include: Stratford T - June 2000, VS Rugby, Racing Club Warwick, Evesham Utd, Atherstone Utd, Hinckley T, Nuneaton B, Exeter C, Stoke C.

PEREIRA, MANUEL — Midfielder
Current Club: Solihull Borough
D o B: 03/02/1975   Birthplace: Angola
Honours won: Portugal u-19 & u-21 Int.
Previous clubs include: FC Marco (Portugal) - November 2001, Belenenses (Portugal), FC Porto (Portugal), Benfica (Portugal).

PERFECT, TONY — Forward
Current Club: Leatherhead
Birthplace: Surrey
Previous clubs include: Hampton & Richmond Borough - September 2001.

PERIFIMOU, CHRIS — Midfielder
Current Club: Enfield
Previous clubs include: Chshunt - August 2001, Baldock T, Stevenage B, Barnet, Leyton Orient.

PERKINS, ANDY — Forward
Current Club: Portland United
Birthplace: Weymouth
From Youth team.

PERKINS, CHRIS — Defender
Current Club: Kettering Town
D o B: 01/03/1980   Birthplace: Stepney
Honours won: Dr Martens League Premier Div.Winners
Signed for Kettering Town at the beginning of the 2000/01 season from Southend United following a successful loan period at the end of the previous campaign which culminated in an appearance in the FA Trophy final at Wembley. A strong central defender who is also capable of doing a job as a midfielder when required.

PERKINS, CHRIS — Midfielder
Current Club: Lancaster City
D o B: 09/01/1974   Birthplace: Nottingham
Experienced defender who joined UniBond Premier side Lancaster City from rivals Stalybridge Celtic in August 2002. Began his career with Mansfield and then had spells with Hartlepool, Chesterfield and Lincoln City, making over 200 League appearances, before signing for Celtic in the summer of 2001.

PERKINS, DAVID — Defender
Current Club: Morecambe
Birthplace: Blackpool
From Youth team.

PERKINS, DECLAN — Forward
Current Club: Dulwich Hamlet
D o B: 17/10/1975   Birthplace: Ilford
Honours won: Republic of Ireland u-21 Int.
Forward who joined Dulwich Hamlet in February 2000 from Braintree Town. A regular marksman, he was Hamlets second top scorer for 2000/01 and was again amongst the goals in 2001/02 after recovering from a lengthy injury. A former Republic of Ireland under 21 International, he played League football with Southend and Peterborough, had a spell in Hong Kong with Sing Tao and has also seen service with Dagenham & Redbridge and Purfleet.

PERKINS, ROBERT — Midfielder
Current Club: Tunbridge Wells
Birthplace: Kent
Previous clubs include: Tonbridge Angels - January 2001.

PERKINS, SEAN — Midfielder
Current Club: Brodsworth Welfare
Birthplace: Yorkshire
From Youth team.

PERKINS, STEVE — Midfielder
Current Club: Dagenham & Redbridge
D o B: 05/11/1975   Birthplace: Southport
Honours won: British Universities Rep.
Steve is a very competitive and highly-rated midfielder who joined Dagenham & Redbridge in June 2002 from Conference rivals Woking. The son of Russ Perkins, a well-known manager in north-west Non-League circles, Steve started his playing days in Burscoughs youth team before joining Plymouth as a professional after impressing with Crediton United in the Western League. Made a handful of League appearances before joining Stevenage Borough in September 1997. Failed to make a real impression at Broadhall Way, however, and moved to Woking for a £10,000 fee just over a year later. Represented the British Universities and was a regular with the Cards before his switch to Dagenham.

PERNA, NANDO — Midfielder
Current Club: Oxford City
Birthplace: Aylesbury
Exciting attacking midfield player who joined Ryman Division One North side Oxford City in August 2002 from neighbours and rivals Thame United. Had re-signed for Thame in October 2001 following a short spell with Bedfprd Town. Started as a trainee with Arsenal and also had a trial period with Italian side Napoli. Turned out for Brackley Town before joining Thame for the first time in August 1999.

PERO, ADAM — Forward
Current Club: Dulwich Hamlet
Birthplace: London
Very promising 20-year-old forward who was top scorer for Dulwich Hamlets youth team in 2000/01. Netted regularly for the clubs reserve side at the start of the following campaign which earned him a call-up into the senior squad. Had trials with Brighton in 2001/02.

PERRIN, STEVE — Goalkeeper
Current Club: Forest Green Rovers
D o B: 27/10/1970   *Birthplace: Wiltshire*
Honours won: Dr Martens League Premier Div.Winners
Goalkeeper with a host of County honours in both football and cricket. His previous clubs include Trowbridge, Chippenham and Melksham Town. He is also wicket keeper and captain of Wiltshire County Cricket Club in the Minor Counties League. Joined Conference side Forest Green Rovers in July 1998 and helped the club to promotion to the Conference and to an FA Trophy final appearance.

PERRIN, STEVE — Midfielder
Current Club: North Ferriby United
D o B: 12/05/1975   *Birthplace: Yorkshire*
Midfielder who was a member of the North Ferriby United title winning squad of 1999/200. Now in his second spell with the club after rejoining from Farsley Celtic in March 2001. Previous clubs include Ossett Albion, Ashton United and Harrogate Town.

PERRY, CRAIG — Forward
Current Club: Blyth Spartans
Birthplace: Co Durham
Signed for UniBond Premier side Blyth Spartans in August 2000 having previously played for Billingham Town in the Albany Northern League. Previusly with Whitby Town and South Bank, he made his debut for Blyth against Gateshead on 28th August 2000 and scored his first goal for the club against Hucknall Town.

PERRY, GAVIN — Defender
Current Club: Rhayader Town
D o B: 21/10/1980   *Birthplace: Wales*
Talented young centre half, who has been at the club three seasons. Mostly played in the reserves, but has impressed when given the opportunity at the higher level. Strikes the ball well.

PERRY, IAN — Forward
Current Club: Ludlow Town
Birthplace: Halesowen
Previous clubs include: Bridgnorth T, Rushall Olympic, Sutton Coldfield T, Stafford R, Stourport Swifts, Willenhall T, Bilston T, Halesowen Harriers.

PERRY, JASON — Defender
Current Club: Newport County
D o B: 02/04/1970   *Birthplace: Caerphilly*
Honours won: Wales u-21, B & Full Int.
Previous clubs include: Hull C - July 2001, Lincoln C, Bristol R, Cardiff C.

PERRY, JUSTIN — Forward
Current Club: Total Network Solutions
D o B: 19/12/1972   *Birthplace: Wales*
Signed for TNS from Rhyl in November 2001 where Justin earned the reputation of a great goalscorer from long range, as well as in the 18 yard box. Works hard for the team also, and is strong on the ball. Played League football with Sunderland and Cardiff and has also turned out for Ebbw Vale, Barry Town and Methyr Tydfil.

PERRY, RICHARD — Midfielder
Current Club: Paulton Rovers
Birthplace: Bristol
Previous clubs include: Yate T - July 1999, Bristol R, Yate T, Swindon T (Trainee).

PERT, CHRIS — Midfielder
Current Club: Dereham Town
Birthplace: Norfolk
Like his brother ex-Cambridge United schoolboy, who has also spent some time with Cambridge City. Missed the past two seasons following an ankle operation.

PERT, MARTIN — Forward
Current Club: Dereham Town
Birthplace: Norfolk
Signed in pre-season having been away at University. Ex Yarmouth Town and Cambridge United schoolboy. Brother of Chris.

PETERS, BRADLEY — Midfielder
Current Club: Frome Town
D o B: 17/10/1980   *Birthplace: Somerset*
Previous clubs include: Yeovil T - July 2000, Swindon T.

PETERS, CRAIG — Midfielder
Current Club: Withdean 2000
Birthplace: Sussex
Originally a youth team player at Burgess Hill before joining East Preston (scored 3 times for them during the early part of 2000/01): signed for Southwick in March 2001 and moved to Withdean for the start of 2001/02.

PETERS, GARY — Midfielder
Current Club: Peacehaven & Telscombe
Birthplace: Sussex
Left-sided midfielder who was a squad member at Saltdean before joining Steyning in January 2000. Followed boss Glen Geard to Ringmer at the start of the following season and later moved on to Shoreham until signing for Peacehaven during the summer of 2001.

PETERS, MARK — Midfielder
Current Club: Gresley Rovers
Birthplace: Birmingham
An experienced and effective midfielder who joined Gresley Rovers during the summer of 1999 from Halesowen Town. Originally on the books at Aston Villa and Derby County, he first came to prominence with Bromsgrove Rovers, with whom he gained Conference experience.

PETERS, STEVE — Defender
Current Club: Tiverton Town
D o B: 30/11/1978   *Birthplace: Bath*
Steve signed for Tiverton Town in November 2001 for a club record fee from Clevedon Town. He had played for Clevedon Town since signing from Cinderford Town in March 1999 as a midfield player, although he made his name at the Hand Stadium as a very dominating central defender. Has also seen service with Yate Town, Trowbridge Town and Torquay.

PETERSEN, OLIVER — Midfielder
Current Club: Enfield
Previous clubs include: Harrow Borough (£2,000) - March 2001, Cheshunt, Barnet, Stevenage B.

PETHER, DAVE   *Goalkeeper*

Current Club: Brentwood

Birthplace: Essex

Dave has been with Brentwood for 17 years and spent much of that time playing as a centre back, originally in the Reserves. Returned to his original trade as keeper five seasons ago and became one of the best in the league.

PETTIFER, JON   *Defender*

Current Club: Flackwell Heath

D o B: 08/05/1972   *Birthplace: Middlesex*

Previous clubs include: Windsor & Eton - January 2002, Beaconsfield SYCOB, Chesham Utd, Northwood, Wealdstone, Ruislip Manor, Harefield Utd, Watford (JUnior), Tottenham Hotspur (Junior).

PETTY, JAMIE   *Midfielder*

Current Club: Moor Green

D o B: 06/12/1978   *Birthplace: Worcestershire*

Signed for Moor Green in the close season of 1999 from Solihull Borough. A promising young winger who had played in Bromsgrove Rovers first team before his short spell at Solihull. Brother Ben plays for Hull City.

PEVERELL, NICKY   *Forward*

Current Club: Barrow

D o B: 28/04/1973   *Birthplace: Middlesbrough*

Born in Middlesborough, Nicky is a prolific goalscorer who began his career with his home-town club as a trainee but did not make the League team before being released and joining neighbours Hartlepool United. He played 36 League games for United, scoring three times before joining York City for the first time. He was with York for 15 months before being released. He then had a spell playing in Hong Kong before joining Bishop Auckland in the UniBond League in August 1996 and finished as top scorer in the Premier Division in the 1996/97 season with 40 League and Cup goals. The majority of the following season saw Nicky play for Bishop Auckland again, although towards the end he was released on loan to Gateshead to for them in the Conference before featuring for Blyth Spartans, Whitby Town and Dunston Federation during the 1998/99 season. Nicky had a second spell in the Far East playing for Woodlands Wellington Football Club in Singapore between May and November 1998, during which he finished up as their top scorer with approximately 25 goals (League and Cup) in some 30 games. During his 15 months with York City, he played in both legs of the League Cup tie against Manchester United, the score was 3-0 to York at Old Trafford and 3-1 to Manchester United in the home leg, where Nick was the man of the match. In August 1999, he joined Barrow from Blyth Spartans and made his debut in the opening game of the season at home to Guiseley.

PEYTON, WARREN   *Forward*

Current Club: Nuneaton Borough

Birthplace: Lancashire

Warren signed for Conference side Nuneaton Borough during the close season of 2001 from Bury. A hard-working attacking player who has been impressive since joining Boro. Started his career with Rochdale.

PHELAN, LEEYON   *Forward*

Current Club: Hayes

D o B: 06/10/1982   *Birthplace: Hammersmith*

Promising young forward who signed for Ryman Premier side Hayes in July 2002 after being released by Wycombe Wanderers at the end of the 2001/02 season. Joined Wycombe as a trainee and turned professional in 2000 but failed to make the senior side at Adams Park. Had a loan spell with Dr Martens side Ashford Town during 2001/02.

PHILLIPS, DARREN   *Midfielder*

Current Club: Hall Road Rangers

Birthplace: Hull

Previous clubs include: Goole AFC - October 2001, North Ferriby Utd, Brodsworth Welfare, North Ferriby Utd, Goole T, Hall Road R, North Ferriby Utd, Winterton R, Hall Road R.

PHILLIPS, DAVID   *Forward*

Current Club: Bridgnorth Town

Birthplace: Manchester

Previous clubs include: Shifnal T - November 2001, Droylsden, Flexsys Cefn Druids, Knighton T, Manchester Utd (Trainee).

PHILLIPS, IAIN   *Goalkeeper*

Current Club: Croydon Athletic

Birthplace: Croydon

From Youth team.

PHILLIPS, IAN   *Defender*

Current Club: Selby Town

Birthplace: South Cave

Previous clubs include: Pontefract Collieries - July 1999, North Ferriby Utd, Goole T, Hull C.

PHILLIPS, IFF   *Defender*

Current Club: Barry Town

D o B: 18/03/1979   *Birthplace: Aberdare*

Honours won: Wales u-21 Int.

Previous clubs include: Cardiff C - June 2000.

PHILLIPS, LEE   *Forward*

Current Club: Weymouth

D o B: 16/09/1980   *Birthplace: Penzance*

Lee came to on-loan from Plymouth Argyle just before Christmas last season and made up part of a three-man attack that scared the daylights out of every defence. After returning to Home Park, he signed on a contract toward the end of the season. He became a hero at the Wessex Stadium by scoring the winning goal in the last couple of minutes against Dagenham and Redbridge in the FA Trophy at Dagenham.

PHILLIPS, LEIGH   *Midfielder*

Current Club: Lymington & New Milton

D o B: 29/05/1973   *Birthplace: Bournemouth*

Previous clubs include: Poole T - July 1999, Bashley, Downton, Brockenhurst, Wimborne T, Swanage & Herston.

PHILLIPS, MARK   *Defender*

Current Club: Mossley

Birthplace: Lancashire

Skilful and strong central defender who signed for North West Counties side Mossley in January 2002 from Woodley Sports. Previously with Curzon Ashton, Prescot Cables and Accrington Stanley.

PHILLIPS, MARK   *Defender*

Current Club: Caernarfon Town

D o B: 02/03/1974   *Birthplace: Liverpool*

Previous clubs include: Conwy Utd - July 2001, Caernarfon T, Conwy Utd.

PHILLIPS, MARK   *Forward*

Current Club: Letchworth

Birthplace: Herts

Previous clubs include: Biggleswade T - November 2001, Stevenage B.

PHILLIPS, MARK — Goalkeeper

Current Club: Wroxham

D o B: 17/04/1968   Birthplace: Suffolk

Experienced Jewson keeper with spells at Diss and Stowmarket.

PHILLIPS, PAUL — Goalkeeper

Current Club: Droylsden

Previous clubs include: Curzon Ashton - December 1999, Buxton, Bury.

PHILLIPS, RICHIE — Midfielder

Current Club: Littlehampton Town

Birthplace: Sussex

Quality midfielder: achieved a unique double in 1998/99, picking up championship medals with Burgess Hill (who won the County League title) and The Clifton (Sussex Sunday League winners): transferred to East Preston at the start of the following season (injured during the second half of that campaign): another EP player to join Wick for 2000/01 and scored 8 goals: previously had a spell at Crabtree Park some years ago. Joined Marigolds in January 2002.

PHILLIPS, SIMON — Defender

Current Club: Guiseley

From Youth team.

PHILLIPS, TOBY — Defender

Current Club: Whitehawk

Birthplace: Brighton

Defender and one-time youth member at Brighton & Hove Albion, who lists Loughborough as one of his previous clubs. Only made a few outings for Whitehawk during 2000/01.

PHILLIPS, TOM — Goalkeeper

Current Club: Dunston Federation Brewery

D o B: 15/03/1981   Birthplace: Newcastle

Previous clubs include: Gateshead - August 2001, Hibernian, Derby Co.

PHILPOTT, DANNY — Midfielder

Current Club: Garforth Town

D o B: 04/03/1976   Birthplace: Leeds

The play maker of the side. Full of energy and always looking for the ball. An intelligent passer of the ball either long range or short one twos. Played several games for the Reserves last season.

PHILPOTT, DEAN — Defender

Current Club: Port Talbot Town

D o B: 15/10/1971   Birthplace: Cardiff

Previous clubs include: Haverfordwest Co - February 2002, Merthyr Tydfil, Cwmbran T, Merthyr Tydfil, Aberystwyth T, Inter Cardiff, Wattstown.

PHILPOTT, KEIRAN — Forward

Current Club: Dorking

Birthplace: Surrey

Honours won: British Universities Rep.

Previous clubs include: Chertsey T - November 1999, Aldershot T.

PHILPOTT, MARK — Goalkeeper

Current Club: Kingsbury Town

Birthplace: London

Previous clubs include: Yeading - October 2001.

PHOENIX, STUART — Defender

Current Club: St.Helens Town

D o B: 03/12/1971   Birthplace: Wigan

Another long-serving player in his second spell at the club after playing for Horwich RMI and Bamber Bridge. An excellent left-sided player who started his career with Wigan Athletic.

PICK, DAVE — Defender

Current Club: Warrington Town

D o B: 24/10/1968   Birthplace: Liverpool

Previous clubs include: Rylands - August 1998.

PICKARD, OWEN — Forward

Current Club: Bideford

D o B: 18/11/1969   Birthplace: Barnstaple

Honours won: England Semi-Pro Int.

Owen joined us in the summer from Dorchester Town, he is a highly experienced striker who has also played for Plymouth Argyle, Hereford United, Rochdale, & Yeovil Town.

PICKERING, ALLY — Defender

Current Club: Mossley

D o B: 22/06/1967   Birthplace: Manchester

Previous clubs include: Gainsborough Trinity - March 2001, Hyde Utd, Altrincham, Hyde Utd, Burnley, Stoke C, Coventry C, Rotherham Utd, Buxton.

PICKERING, JAY — Defender

Current Club: Bognor Regis Town

Birthplace: Brighton

Defender who signed for Bognor Regis Town from Worthing in July 1998. Previously on Brighton books. Strong powerful player who lives in Peacehaven.

PICKERING, STEVE — Defender

Current Club: Spennymoor United

D o B: 25/09/1976   Birthplace: Sunderland

Previous clubs include: Queen of the South - August 2001, Tow Law T, Sunderland.

PICKESS, JON — Forward

Current Club: Stocksbridge Park Steels

Birthplace: Yorkshire

Previous clubs include: Emley - November 2001, Hednesford T, Sheffield, Hallam, Hucknall T, Alfreton T, Worksop T, Eastwood T, Stalybridge Celtic, Matlock T, Belper T, Rotherham Utd, Chesterfield.

PICKETT, ROSS — Forward

Current Club: Hendon

D o B: 10/02/1975   Birthplace: Middlesex

Quality goalscorer who re-joined Ryman Division One South side Walton & Hersham in the summer of 2002 from Hendon having signed for the Dons in the close season of 2000 from Swans. Ross looks to upset the oppositions defences with his pace, scoring prowess and workrate. Has previously seen service with Hayes, Slough Town and Yeading.

PICKFORD, LEE — Defender

Current Club: Abbey Hey

Birthplace: Manchester

Previous clubs include: Glossop North End - July 2001.

P

PICKFORD, STEVE — *Midfielder*
Current Club: Southport
Birthplace: Manchester
Steve signed for Southport from Stalybridge Celtic in May 2002. Originally with Glossop, Steve moved to Leigh RMI in March 1999 and developed into a highly-rated attacking midfielder. Before Glossop, he played for Leigh RMI, and had a spell at Doncaster Rovers.

PICKLES, CRAIG — *Midfielder*
Current Club: Selby Town
Birthplace: Bubworth
Previous clubs include: Glasshoughton Welfare - December 1999.

PICKNALL, GARETH — *Defender*
Current Club: Bilston Town
Previous clubs include: Hednesford T - August 2001.

PICKSTONE, DAVE — *Defender*
Current Club: Pelsall Villa
Birthplace: Birmingham
Previous clubs include: Blakenall - July 2001, Bloxwich T, Rushall Olympic, Pelsall Villa, Bloxwich Strollers, Rushall Olympic, Blakenall.

PICKUP, STEVE — *Defender*
Current Club: Great Harwood Town
Birthplace: Lancashire
Previous clubs include: Rossendale Utd - February 1999, Haslingden, Rossendale Utd, Haslingden, Accrington Stanley.

PIDCOCK, JACOB — *Forward*
Current Club: Matlock Town
Birthplace: Sheffield
Jake is a young striker who impressed new Town manager Ernie Moss in the pre-season matches. He is the nephew of the three Fenoughty brothers - Tom, Mick and Nick - who represented Matlock with such great distinction in the glory days of the 1970s.

PIEARCE, STEVE — *Forward*
Current Club: Hednesford Town
D o B: 29/09/1974   Birthplace: Sutton Coldfield
Steve joined Wolverhampton Wanderers straight from school and was a prolific scorer in youth football. After being released by Wolves he joined Doncaster Rovers and then Halesowen Town. He joined up with Hereford in July 1999 but suffered a series of injuries which restricted his appearances with the Bulls. Transferred to Hednesford Town in June 2002.

PIERCE, DAVID — *Goalkeeper*
Current Club: Ashton United
D o B: 04/10/1975   Birthplace: Manchester
Previous clubs include: Winsford Utd - November 2001, Ashton Utd, Chesterfield, Rotherham Utd, Manchester Utd (Trainee), Crewe Alexandra (Junior).

PIERCE, ROSS — *Defender*
Current Club: Halesowen Harriers
Birthplace: Worcestershire
Previous clubs include: Lye T - July 1998.

PIERCE, WESLEY — *Forward*
Current Club: Maltby Main
Birthplace: Yorkshire
Previous clubs include: Alfreton T - January 2002.

PIERCEWRIGHT, BRAD — *Defender*
Current Club: Kettering Town
Birthplace: Northampton
Honours won: Dr Martens League Premier Div.Winners
Signed for Kettering Town in July 2001 after impressing in pre-season, Brad is a good passer of the ball and comfortable in possession. Capable of playing in the centre of defence or at full back, he has previous experience at Northampton Town, Queens Park Rangers and Grimsby.

PIERPOINT, GRANT — *Forward*
Current Club: Lowestoft Town
Birthplace: Basildon
Previous clubs include: Oulton Broad - March 1996, Burnt Hill Rangers, Lowestoft T.

PIERSON, RICHARD — *Defender*
Current Club: Abingdon United
Birthplace: Oxford
Honours won: British Universities Rep.
Previous clubs include: Oxford C - July 2001, Slough T, Chesham Utd, Oxford C.

PIGGOTT, GARY — *Forward*
Current Club: Rushall Olympic
D o B: 01/04/1969   Birthplace: Birmingham
Previous clubs include: Bilston T - July 2001, Willenhall T, Halesowen T, Stafford R, Tamworth, Dudley T, Willenhall T, WBA, Dudley T, Oldswinford, Sandwell B, Princes End Utd.

PIGGOTT, PAUL — *Goalkeeper*
Current Club: Lordswood
Birthplace: Kent
Previous clubs include: Sheppey Utd - July 2000, Lordswood.

PIHAMAA, PASI — *Midfielder*
Current Club: Billericay Town
Birthplace: Helsinki (Finland)
Previous clubs include: HIFK Helsinki - November 2001, KaPa (Finland), Ponnistus (Finland), PK-35 (Finland).

PIKE, DAVID — *Goalkeeper*
Current Club: VCD Athletic
D o B: 03/02/1976   Birthplace: Dartford
Previous clubs include: Welling Utd - July 1999.

PIKE, GARY — *Midfielder*
Current Club: Molesey
Birthplace: Surrey
Previous clubs include: Aveley - February 2002.

PIKE, GREGG — *Forward*
Current Club: Arlesey Town
Birthplace: Hertfordshire
Honours won: Ryman League Div.3 Winners
Striker Gregg missed a good deal of the 2001/02 season following a nasty leg break in a pre-season friendly. He was another early Arlesey Town aquisition when manager Nicky Ironton came to the club, joining from Harlow Town, and proved his value helping the club secure promotion to Division Three of the Ryman League. Formerly with Southend and Bishops Stortford, he already has a collection of medals for promotion within the Ryman League and an Essex Senior Cup winners medal. Is a Computer Network Engineer.

PIKE, LEE   *Forward*
Current Club: Lowestoft Town
Birthplace: Great Yarmouth
From Youth team.

PIKE, RICHARD   *Midfielder*
Current Club: Newtown AFC
D o B: 30/01/1965   *Birthplace: Shrewsbury*
Assistant Manager and Coach, with vast experience in the game
and a highly popular figure with the fans. Started his career at
Shrewsbury town as a young player and is in his third spell at the
club. Is at present seeking to widen his coaching qualifications
and is well on the way to attaining his UEFA A licence.

PILER, DANNY   *Midfielder*
Current Club: Wingate And Finchley
D o B: 26/11/1968   *Birthplace: London*
From Local football - July 1997.

PILKINGTON, PAUL   *Goalkeeper*
Current Club: Great Wakering Rovers
Birthplace: Southend
Previous clubs include: Maldon T - July 2000, Chelmsford C,
Great Wakering R, Margate, Dover Ath., Southend Utd.

PILLAR, CHAD   *Midfielder*
Current Club: Great Yarmouth Town
D o B: 26/10/1982   *Birthplace: Norfolk*
Youth team player last season who broke into the first team in
January 2001 and is now a first choice up front for the senior
team. Another tremendous prospect for the club.

PINCHER, ANDY   *Defender*
Current Club: Cambridge City
Previous clubs include: Chelmsford C - March 1999, Cambridge
C, Cambridge Utd (Trainee).

PINDER, CRAIG   *Defender*
Current Club: Hallam
Birthplace: Sheffield
Previous clubs include: Alfreton T - October 1998, Maltby Main,
Kiveton Park.

PINKNEY, GRANT   *Forward*
Current Club: Evesham United
D o B: 31/01/1983   *Birthplace: Worcester*
Promising young forward who joined Dr Martens Western side
Evesham United in August 2002 after being released by Lincoln
City. Looked like heading for Premier Division Worcester City until
Evesham stepped in with their offer.

PINNOCK, JAMES   *Forward*
Current Club: Kingstonian
D o B: 01/08/1978   *Birthplace: Dartford*
Signed for Kingtonian from Gillingham in June 2001. Had on-loan
spells with Dover Athletic in 2000, scoring on his debut, and also
with Chesham United in 2001. Joined the Gills as a trainee and
made a handful of first-team appearances in attack and was a
regular scorer in their reserves.

PIPER, CHRIS   *Forward*
Current Club: Farnborough Town
Birthplace: London
Chris arrived at Farnborough Town from St. Albans City in January
2001and his making a determined effort to make a first team
berth his own. A forward who is more than capable of performing

in the midfield, he began his career at Charlton Athletic. Brother
of Lennie, who also plays for Farnborough.

PIPER, DAVID   *Defender*
Current Club: Woking
D o B: 31/10/1977   *Birthplace: Bournemouth*
Talented defender who joined Woking in the summer of 2001
from rival Conference outfit Yeovil Town. Originally a professional
with Southampton, although he failed to make the senior side at
The Dell.

PIPER, LENNIE   *Midfielder*
Current Club: Farnborough Town
D o B: 08/08/1977   *Birthplace: London*
Honours won: England Youth Int.
A former England Youth international midfielder who started his
career with Wimbledon. Failed to make the breakthrough with the
Dons and moved to Gillingham, where he made around 20
League appearances. Was released at the end of the 1997/98
season and initially joined Welling United before moving on to
St.Albans City a couple of months into the new campaign. Proved
a hit at Clarence Park, scoring a number of goals, before
switching to Boro in July 2000.

PITHER, RICKY   *Forward*
Current Club: Wealdstone
D o B: 30/04/1983   *Birthplace: Middlesex*
A young forward, Ricky signed for Wealdstone during the summer
of 2001 having formerly played for Wembley. Was a regular first-
team squad member.

PITMAN, ANDY   *Defender*
Current Club: Chippenham Town
D o B: 11/05/1974   *Birthplace: Warminster*
Utility player who prefers defence who signed for Chippenham
Town in May 2002 from League of Wales outfit Afan Lido. Signed
for Lido from Goytre United for the 1998/99 season. Agile and
versatile, Andy has played in several positions for the Lido. A
strong defender usually, he has often chipped in with a goal or
two when played as a forward. Started his career at Swindon
Town as a youngster.

PITMAN, JAMIE   *Defender*
Current Club: Hereford United
D o B: 06/01/1976   *Birthplace: Trowbridge*
Honours won: FA XI Rep.
Jamie re-signed for Hereford United in June 2002 from
Conferene rivals Woking. Had joined th Cards during the summer
of 2000 from Yeovil Town. He is a YTS graduate who made three
first-team appearances for Swindon Town before going on to play
more than 60 games for Hereford United, during which time he
gained FA XI honours. He joined Yeovil Town in July 1998 and
filled a variety of positions for them. He suffered two leg fractures
during the 1998/99 season but fought his way back into the first-
team.

PITMAN, PAUL   *Forward*
Current Club: Seaham Red Star
D o B: 13/09/1964   *Birthplace: Co.Durham*
Previous clubs include: Easington Colliery - February 2002,
Spennymoor Utd, Dunston Federation, Whitby T, North Shields,
Easington Colliery.

PITT, IAN — Forward

Current Club: Barwell

Birthplace: Burton

Honours won: Leicestershire Senior League Winners

Previous clubs include: Coalville T - June 2002, Atherstone Utd, Gresley R, Bloxwich T, Burton Alb., Gresley R, Newhall Utd, Shepshed Dynamo, Heanor T, Shepshed Dynamo, Stapenhill, Heanor T, Stapenhill, Burton Alb.

PITT, RICHIE — Midfielder

Current Club: Brandon United

Birthplace: Co.Durham

Joined the club 3 seasons ago and played a handful of games before moving to Blyth Spartans and Bedlington Terriers. Rejoined the club December 2000, and will prove to be a tremendous signing. Very strong, aggressive player with fantastic ability and great football brain.

PITTS, DANNY — Forward

Current Club: Dartford

Birthplace: Essex

Previous clubs include: Purfleet - February 2002, Southend Utd, Norwich C (Junior).

PITTS, DOUGIE — Midfielder

Current Club: Winsford United

Birthplace: Wigan

Youngster who was signed from Wigan Athletic. The Midfielder/Defender elected to stay with the Blues despite offers from Conference sides.

PITTWOOD, ADAM — Forward

Current Club: Hampton & Richmond

Birthplace: Surrey

Young striker who was with Tooting & Mitcham United's reserves during the 2001/02 season before following new Hampton & Richmond Borough assistant boss Matt Beard to the Beavers in August 2002. Has also played at Millwall, Crystal Palace, Fulham and Kingstonian.

PIZZEY, PAUL — Midfielder

Current Club: Romford

Birthplace: Essex

Previous clubs include: East Thurrock Utd - March 2002, Tilbury, Aveley, Purfleet, Concord R, Tilbury, East Thurrock Utd, Canvey Island, Purfleet, Aveley, Purfleet.

PIZZEY, TONY — Midfielder

Current Club: East Thurrock United

Birthplace: Essex

Previous clubs include: Canvey Island - December 1997, Aveley, Canvey Island, Purfleet, Heybridge Swifts, Purfleet, East Thurrock Utd.

PLACE, DAMIEN — Midfielder

Current Club: Farsley Celtic

D o B: 31/12/1978   Birthplace: Halifax

Previous clubs include: Osterholz Sharnbeck (Germany) - November 2000, Farsley Celtic, Frickley Ath., Halifax T.

PLACE, MARK — Defender

Current Club: Belper Town

D o B: 16/11/1969   Birthplace: Mansfield

Experienced defender who joined UniBond First Division Belper Town from Premier Division Frickley Athletic in July 2002. Started his career in League football with Doncaster Rovers and Mansfield but has since spent a number of years in the UniBond with Eastwood Town, Matlock Town, Hucknall Town and Frickley.

PLANCK, TOM — Forward

Current Club: Chatham Town

D o B: 15/01/1977   Birthplace: Kent

Previous clubs include: Gravesend & Northfleet - February 2002, Margate, Sittingbourne.

PLANT, DEAN — Goalkeeper

Current Club: Withdean 2000

Birthplace: Sussex

Goalkeeper, who has had links with Chelsea in the past: previously spent time at Saltdean, originally playing in their youth side (appeared in the 1999/2000 Sussex RUR Cup Final): signed by Withdean in January 2002.

PLANT, RAITH — Forward

Current Club: Newport County

D o B: 05/12/1982   Birthplace: Merthyr

Had trials with several Football League clubs, including Norwich, Luton, Coventry and Burnley and came to prominence with a goal a game average for League of Wales side Cwmbran Town for whom he has played as a substitute in European football. Joined Newport County in October 2000 but spent the vast majority of the 2001/02 season out on loan, mostly at Cirencester Town.

PLANT, ROBERT — Goalkeeper

Current Club: Stafford Town

Birthplace: Stoke

Previous clubs include: Rocester - July 2000, Chasetown, Blakenall, Newtown, Stafford R, Port Vale.

PLATT, MATTHEW — Midfielder

Current Club: Stowmarket Town

Birthplace: Suffolk

From Youth team.

PLATTEN, JAMES — Goalkeeper

Current Club: Consett

Birthplace: Co.Durham

Previous clubs include: South Moor - July 1997.

PLAYFORD, STUART — Defender

Current Club: Hastings United

Birthplace: Hastings

Defender who originally joined Hastings from Rye Utd in 1994. Spent half a season at Ashford before returning to the Arrows in January 2000. Also effective as a striker, and had scored 45 times for Hastings prior to 2001/02.

PLEDGER, IAN — Goalkeeper

Current Club: Wisbech Town

Previous clubs include: Stamford - July 2000, Blackstone, Stamford, Watford (Junior).

PLUCK, COLIN — Defender

Current Club: Yeovil Town

D o B: 06/09/1978   Birthplace: London

Honours won: FA Trophy Winners

Colin began his career at Watford under the eye of Yeovil manager Gary Johnson, who was then the Hornets Youth Academy Director. After four years at Watford, Colin moved into the Scottish League where he played for Morton. Upon his return to England, Colin had brief spells at Conference sides Stevenage Borough, Hayes and Dover Athletic between 1999 and the summer of 2001. However, in July 2001, Colin became one of three players to sign for Yeovil Town as he once again teamed up with Gary Johnson by signing a two year contract at Huish Park. Colin usually operates as a central defender, although is capable of playing as a left-back when required.

PLUCK, LEE   *Midfielder*
Current Club: Barnet
Birthplace: London
A product of Barnets Youth system. Lee has made the first-team squad and made his debut during the 2000/01 season. Now a hihgly-rated Conference midfielder.

POGLETTKE, AARON   *Defender*
Current Club: Flexsys Cefn Druids
D o B: 15/03/1983   *Birthplace: Wales*
From Youth team.

POLAND, LEE   *Forward*
Current Club: St.Helens Town
Birthplace: Cheshire
Signed originally for Northwich Victoria in August 1999 before going on-loan in March 2001 to Leek Town. Was released at the cnd of the 2000/01 season. Moved to Altrincham on trial in the summer 2001 and signed for the Robins in early August before moving on exactly a year later to North West Counties League side St Helens Town. Lees strength is on the ground where he shows good pace and skill.

POLHILL, DARREN   *Defender*
Current Club: Bideford
Birthplace: Devon
A local player who joined the club from Appledore and has developed into a quality Sweeper, having started his time with us as a wing back. Darren has now played over 100 games for us. He has also played for Holsworthy & Woolsery.

POLLARD, BEN   *Defender*
Current Club: Ossett Town
D o B: 12/11/1977   *Birthplace: Wetherby*
Talented central defender who joined Town in November 2001 after impressing in a trial. Has previously only ever played in the West Yorkshire League with local club Wetherby Athletic but made an impression on his first team debut versus Ossett Albion.

POLLARD, JOHN   *Midfielder*
Current Club: Heybridge Swifts
D o B: 17/11/1971   *Birthplace: Chelmsford*
Local Essex lad who rejoined Heybridge Swifts at the start of the 2000/01 season after a two year sojurn at St. Albans City after moving there along with ex-manager Garry Hill and a number of other Swifts players. Originally with Colchester and Bury Town, John is a dominant central defender or defensive midfielder with a great engine to get up and down the pitch. One of the fittest people in the club, he is now the record club appearance holder and first-team captain.

POLSTON, ANDY   *Defender*
Current Club: Ford United
D o B: 26/07/1970   *Birthplace: London*
Honours won: Ryman League Div.One Winners
An experienced defender who joined Ford United from Boreham Wood in November 2001 and helped the Essex side to win promotion to the Ryman League Premier Division. Originally with Spurs, where he made one first-team appearance, Andy also gained further League experience with Gillingham, Cambridge United and Brighton. He then played for Hendon and, from July 1994, St Albans City where he made almost 200 appearances.

Moves to Braintree Town and Boreham Wood followed before he joined the Motormen.

POMROY, JOHN   *Forward*
Current Club: Chertsey Town
Birthplace: London
Re-signed for Chertsey from Bognor in March 2002. A striker who was previously a YTS player at Watford. Had a short spell at Aldershot Town towards the end of last season and then swicthed to Bognor Regis Town in February 2002. Had his first spell at Chertsey before moving to the south coast.

PONSFORD, RICHARD   *Defender*
Current Club: Tonbridge Angels
D o B: 25/02/1978   *Birthplace: Kent*
Previous clubs include: Folkestone Invicta - July 1998, Margate, Sittingbourne, Charlton Ath.

POOK, ROY   *Forward*
Current Club: Withdean 2000
Birthplace: Sussex
Excellent young prospect, who was a member of Burgess Hills youth side in 1998/99: impressed for the Hillians first-team the following season, scoring 12 times: set to join Withdean at the start of 2000/01 before being diverted to Southwick (helped them towards the County League Division Two title with six goals).

POOLE, BRAD   *Defender*
Current Club: Sidley United
Birthplace: Sussex
Giant centre-back: brother of the goalkeeper: returned to the side in November 2000 after a long lay-off: also played for Sussex during 2001/02.

POOLE, BRADLEY   *Midfielder*
Current Club: Enfield Town (Essex)
Birthplace: Herts
18year-old, previously played for Brimsdown Rovers. Made his Enfield Town debut at Sawbridgeworth in September 2001. Is the grandson of ex-Enfield FC legend the late Dave Jones.

P

POOLE, DANNY   *Goalkeeper*
Current Club: Sidley United
Birthplace: Sussex
Strong goalkeeper: one-time Sussex U-18 player: returned to Sidley at the start of the 1999/2000 campaign: had a superb record in the Blues 2000/01 championship winning season, conceding just 26 goals in 37 appearances: missed the final seven matches of that campaign after injuring his shoulder in a match against Redhill during April.

POOLE, GLENN   *Midfielder*
Current Club: Ford United
D o B: 03/02/1981   *Birthplace: Essex*
Honours won: Ryman League Div.One Winners
Former Spurs YTS player, and also turned out for their under-19 academy side. A talented young midfielder, he joined Ford United in February 2002 on a permanent basis after a successful spell on loan.

POOLE, GRAHAM   *Forward*
Current Club: Buxton
Birthplace: Buxton
Previous clubs include: Matlock T - October 2000, Buxton, Leek T, Buxton.

POPE, MARK   Defender
Current Club: Corinthian Casuals
Birthplace: Surrey
Signed for Corinthian Casuals from Banstead Athletic in November 1999, Mark is a talented midfielder who has been a first team regular ever since. Started his playing days with Sutton United, for whom he appeared in the Conference as a teenager.

POPE, NEIL   Midfielder
Current Club: Mildenhall Town
D o B: 09/10/1972   Birthplace: Ashton-under-Lyne
Previous clubs include: Cambridge C - January 2002, Mildenhall T, Watton Utd, Bishops Stortford, St.Neots T, Cambridge C, Ely C, Sudbury T, Kettering T, Cambridge C, Eynesbury R, St.Neots T, Cambridge C, Peterborough Utd, Cambridge Utd.

POPE, STEVE   Defender
Current Club: Bromsgrove Rovers
D o B: 08/09/1976   Birthplace: Stoke
Previous clubs include: Evesham Utd - September 2001, Kidderminster Harriers, Crewe Alexandra.

PORTER, ALEX   Midfielder
Current Club: Bamber Bridge
Birthplace: Morecambe
A lively left sided player who stepped up from Morecambes academy. Alex played a few times for the first-team in the Conference before joining UniBond First Division Bamber Bridge in August 2002.

PORTER, BEN   Midfielder
Current Club: Kingsbury Town
Birthplace: London
Previous clubs include: Brook House - August 2000.

PORTER, CARL   Forward
Current Club: Ashington
Birthplace: Northumberland
Previous clubs include: Seaton Delaval - August 2001.

PORTER, DANNY   Defender
Current Club: Rothwell Town
D o B: 23/01/1979   Birthplace: Portsmouth
Previous clubs include: Hinckley Utd - September 2000, Derby Co., Portsmouth.

PORTER, GRAHAM   Defender
Current Club: Margate
D o B: 29/10/1974
Previous clubs include: Ashford T - July 1999, Erith & Belvedere, Horsham, Maidstone Utd (Trainee).

PORTER, JIMMY   Midfielder
Current Club: Billericay Town
Birthplace: Essex
Previous clubs include: Bowers Utd - November 2001, Romford, Maldon T, Chelmsford C, Canvey Island, Chelmsford C.

PORTER, NICK   Defender
Current Club: Telford United
Birthplace: Newport
Another product of the United youth set-up, Newport lad Nick is a talented right back. In his first season with United as a first teamer, but shows excellent pace and commitment and will surely be an asset in future. One to watch!

PORTER, STEVE   Midfielder
Current Club: Droylsden
Birthplace: Liverpool
Previous clubs include: Burscough - October 2001, Altrincham, Liverpool.

PORTREY, SIMON   Forward
Current Club: Glasshoughton Welfare
Birthplace: Leeds
Previous clubs include: Goole AFC - August 2001, Garforth T, Pontefract Collieries, Ossett T, Glasshoughton Welfare, Guiseley, Ipswich T (Trainee), Leeds Utd (Junior).

PORTWAY, STEVE   Forward
Current Club: Tonbridge Angels
Birthplace: Essex
Prolific goalscorer who has enjoyed a well-travelled career in Non-League football. Spent his early days with Dagenham, Walthamstow Avenue, Bishops Stortford, Brentwood, Witham and Boreham Wood but began to attract attention through his goals after joining Barking. He then broke all sorts of records for Gravesend which eventually earned a £17,500 transfer to rivals Gloucester City in 1994. Sadly, a career-threatening eye injury severely restricted his spell at Meadow Park. However, he made a successful comeback with Romford and has since had spells with Purfleet, Collier Row, Erith & Belvedere, Gravesend again, Billericay Town, Fisher Athletic and Chelmsford City. Re-joined Fisher at the start of the 2001/02 season and then switched to Dr Martens Eastern rivals Tonbridge Angels in August 2002.

POSKETT, BARRY   Goalkeeper
Current Club: Tow Law Town
Birthplace: Co.Durham
In his second season having signed from Crook. Has previously had a spell with Darlington and former County Junior.

POSTON, TOM   Midfielder
Current Club: Worcester City
Birthplace: Birmingham
Previous clubs include: Hednesford T - March 2002, Kidderminster Harriers.

POTBURY, WAYNE   Midfielder
Current Club: Southwick
Birthplace: Sussex
Experienced, solid midfielder/attacker: previous clubs include Lancing and Steyning: played for Southwick until joining Wick in March 2000 (also made a couple of appearances for Worthing reserves that season): returned to Old Barn Way the following autumn and scored a total of 9 goals in 2000/01: one of several Southwick players who also appeared for Withdean during the early part of 2001/02 (something that was within the rules because both clubs compete in separate leagues).

POTTER, CHRIS   Forward
Current Club: Abingdon Town
Birthplace: Oxford
Previous clubs include: Thame Utd - February 2002, Oxford C.

POTTER, DANNY   Goalkeeper
Current Club: Canvey Island
D o B: 18/03/1979   Birthplace: Ipswich
Danny switched to Ryman Premier side Canvey Island in August 2002 from Chelmsford City. He joined City from Weymouth in February 2002. Spent some time at the Wessex Stadium on-loan originally and impressed greatly. A very highly-rated goalkeeper, who has also been on the books at Chelsea, Colchester and Exeter.

POTTER, DEAN — Defender
Current Club: Horsham YMCA

Birthplace: Sussex
Big, strong tackling defender: has been at Horsham YMCA for seven years, having graduated through the youth side: has over 200 appearances to his name.

POTTER, LEE — Forward
Current Club: Radcliffe Borough

D o B: 03/09/1978   Birthplace: Salford
Previous clubs include: Bradford Park Avenue - March 2002, Atherton Collieries, Chester C, Halifax T, Bolton Wanderers.

POTTER, MATTHEW — Defender
Current Club: Burnham

From Youth team.

POTTER, WAYNE — Midfielder
Current Club: Horsham YMCA

Birthplace: Sussex
Brother of Dean Potter: spent five years at Horsham YMCA until leaving at the end of 1999/2000. had been playing for Corinthian Casuals before returning to Gorings Mead in December 2001: held back by injuries over the years.

POTTS, COLIN — Forward
Current Club: Stalybridge Celtic

D o B: 26/02/1978   Birthplace: Lancashire
Colin joined Stalybridge Celtic in May 2002 after enjoying a successful 2001/02 season with Lancaster City. He has signed for City in November 2000, and it was a testimony to his impact on the right wing that the club hardly lost a game after that. His wing play was quite exceptional in many games, and also scored some important goals. Previously with Morecambe, Bamber Bridge, Chorley and Rochdale, and he has a footballing family, as his father Eric Potts was at Preston.

POTTS, CRAIG — Midfielder
Current Club: Workington

D o B: 25/02/1974   Birthplace: Carlisle
Previous clubs include: Gretna - June 2001, Queen of the South, Gretna, Carlisle Utd.

POTTS, DANNY — Defender
Current Club: Clitheroe

Birthplace: Burnley
Young central defender who has maybe found himself in the first team earlier than expected. Will undoubtedly learn from playing alongside Lee Sculpher. Tough start for him but the lads not hiding and he's doing well.

POULTER, DANNY — Midfielder
Current Club: Peacehaven & Telscombe

Birthplace: Sussex
Midfielder who left Peacehaven for Newhaven in February 2000 before briefly returning to Piddinghoe Avenue at the start of the following season. Spent most of that campaign at Whitehawk (made his debut in November 2000) and rejoined the Tyes for 2001/02.

POULTNEY, DANNY — Midfielder
Current Club: Oadby Town

Birthplace: Leicester
Previous clubs include: Corby T - July 2000, Friar Lane OB.

POUND, MARK — Forward
Current Club: Bridgnorth Town

Birthplace: Ludlow
Previous clubs include: Wrockwardine Wood - November 2001, Chasetown, Shifnal T, Knighton T, Bridgnorth T, Oldbury Utd, Bridgnorth T, Newport T, Newtown, Ludlow T.

POUNDER, DAVID — Midfielder
Current Club: Scarborough

D o B: 03/02/1980   Birthplace: Newcastle
Signed a three year soccer scholarship for Scarborough in September 1998 and after impressing in youth matches was offered a three year professional contract at the start of season. 2000/01 He made his first team debut versus Kingstonian in August 2000 and scored his first two senior goals in the 4-0 defeat of Northwich Victoria. Very talented left sided player can also play up front or at left back if required. Has attracted a fair amount of interest from Premier League clubs.

POUNDER, TONY — Midfielder
Current Club: Frome Town

D o B: 11/03/1966   Birthplace: Yeovil
Honours won: Ishtmian League Winners
Previous clubs include: Yeovil T - July 2000, Weymouth, Bristol R, Hereford Utd.

POUNTNEY, CRAIG — Forward
Current Club: Studley

Birthplace: Birmingham
Previous clubs include: Sutton Coldfield T - August 2001, Bromsgrove R, Moor Green, Shrewsbury T.

POWELL, CHRIS — Midfielder
Current Club: Tiptree United

Birthplace: Essex
Previous clubs include: Harwich & Parkeston - September 1999, Mersea.

POWELL, DARREN — Midfielder
Current Club: Wimborne Town

Birthplace: Bournemouth
Previous clubs include: Salisbury C - October 1999, Weymouth, Bashley, Dorchester T, Poole T, AFC Bournemouth.

POWELL, DAVE — Forward
Current Club: Welling United

Birthplace: Kent
Midfielder or forward who joined Welling United during the summer of 2001 from Crawley Town. Originally with Kent League side Sheppey United before spending a number of years with Gravesend.

POWELL, DAVID — Midfielder
Current Club: Flexsys Cefn Druids

Birthplace: Wales
Previous clubs include: Glan Conwy - July 2000, Army.

POWELL, GARETH — Goalkeeper
Current Club: Bedlington Terriers

D o B: 23/03/1980   Birthplace: Newcastle
This former Tranmere Rovers keeper signed from Dunston Federation at the beginning of the season is only 21 and has already shown that he is an excellent talent. He suffered an injury in the Cleator Cup final at the start of the season but is the Terriers No.1 keeper.

P

POWELL, GARY — Forward
Current Club: Rhyl
D o B: 02/04/1969   Birthplace: Heswall
Forward who has proved an adaptable talent capable of filling virtually every position on the field. Re-joined Rhyl from TNS in July 2002 having signed from Rhyl in July 1997 after spells with League clubs Manchester City and Wigan. Also turned out for Bangor City and Conwy United.

POWELL, JAY — Defender
Current Club: Evesham United
Previous clubs include: Bilston T - June 1999, Evesham Utd, Blakenall, Bridgnorth T, Kidderminster Harriers.

POWELL, JOHN — Midfielder
Current Club: Shifnal Town
Birthplace: Shropshire
Previous clubs include: Newport T - July 1990, GKN Sankey, Tibberton.

POWELL, JOHN — Midfielder
Current Club: Cwmbran Town
D o B: 23/01/1966   Birthplace: Wales
Previous clubs include: Kungsham IF (Sweden) - July 1992, Pontllanfraith.

POWELL, LLOYD — Defender
Current Club: Egham Town
Birthplace: London
Previous clubs include: Kingsbury T - October 1998, Northwood, Wembley, Windsor & Eton, Ruislip Manor, Windsor & Eton, Wembley, Chalfont St.Peter, Harrow B, Hounslow, Belmont.

POWELL, MARK — Defender
Current Club: Rhyl
D o B: 08/05/1975   Birthplace: Chester
Previous clubs include: Total Network Solutions - June 2002, Rhyl, Winsford Utd, Stalybridge Celtic, Bolton Wanderers, Glasgow Celtic.

POWELL, RAY — Forward
Current Club: Fisher Athletic (London)
Previous clubs include: Welling Utd - October 1999, Fisher Ath.

POWELL, ROB — Defender
Current Club: Studley
Birthplace: Worcestershire
Previous clubs include: Alvechurch - July 2001.

POWELL, SHANE — Midfielder
Current Club: Bideford
Birthplace: Plymouth
Shane hails from Plymouth, & is a highly rated wingback, who also doubles up as a right-sided midfielder. He has also played for Exeter City, & Elmore. Shane has made over 50 appearances for the Club.

POWELL, STEVE — Goalkeeper
Current Club: Atherton Laburnum Rovers
Birthplace: Blackley
Signed from Atherton Collieries in March 2001, Steve is a brave and agile keeper who keeps the defenders on their toes. He is excellent in the air and a superb distributor of the ball. Steve is an insurance advisor who enjoys fishing.

POWELL, VILL — Forward
Current Club: North Ferriby United
D o B: 02/10/1979   Birthplace: Sheffield
Highly-rated forward who signed for North Ferriby United in September 2001 from UniBond First Division rivals Stocksbridge Park Steels. Started his career at Sheffield Wednesday and then had a spell in Irish football with Derry City before returning to England with Worksop Town, Denaby United and Stocksbridge.

POWER, PHIL — Forward
Current Club: Radcliffe Borough
D o B: 25/07/1967   Birthplace: Salford
Honours won: England Semi-Pro Int., Conference Winners, FA Trophy Winners, UniBond League Premier Div.Winners
Previous clubs include: Altrincham - February 2001, Macclesfield T, Stalybridge Celtic, Barrow, Chorley, Horwich RMI, Crewe Alexandra, Witton Alb., Northwich V.

POWERS, DARREN — Forward
Current Club: Chertsey Town
Birthplace: Surrey
A forward who has come through from the clubs youth set up and is still a regular goalscorer in the Under 18 side.

POXON, SIMON — Defender
Current Club: Glapwell
Birthplace: Sutton
Previous clubs include: Ashfield Utd - July 1996.

PRASHER, CHRIS — Midfielder
Current Club: Wakefield & Emley
Birthplace: Yorkshire
A midfield player who has played most of his football in Emleys reserves. He is, however, expected to push for a first team place.

PRATT, LEIGH — Defender
Current Club: Barry Town
D o B: 24/08/1982   Birthplace: Newport
Previous clubs include: Llantwit Major - August 2001, Cardiff C, Newport Co.

PRATT, SHAUN — Forward
Current Club: Evesham United
Birthplace: Worcester
From Local football - July 2000.

PREDDIE, DELROY — Goalkeeper
Current Club: Chesham United
D o B: 14/07/1976   Birthplace: Berkshire
A former Northampton Town trainee goalkeeper who, on his return to the south he played for Slough Town in the Conference before joining Walton & Hersham. Delroy joined Chesham United in July 1999 but was out of action for the end of the 2000/01 season but came back fully fit and had an excellent 2001/02 campaign.

PREDDY, MIKE — Midfielder
Current Club: Haverfordwest County
D o B: 04/11/1980   Birthplace: Wales
From Youth team.

PREECE, DAVID — Midfielder
Current Club: Enfield
D o B: 28/05/1963   Birthplace: Bridgnorth
Vastly experienced midfielder who joined Ryman Premier side Enfield in July 2002 as player-coach. Started his career with Walsall and went on to make over 550 League appearances with the Saddlers, Luton, Derby, Cambridge and Torquay.

PREECE, ROGER — *Midfielder*
Current Club: Telford United
Birthplace: Much Wenlock
Previous clubs include: Shrewsbury T - March 2000, Telford Utd, Chester C, Wrexham.

PREEDY, PHIL — *Midfielder*
Current Club: Evesham United
D o B: 20/11/1975   *Birthplace: Hereford*
Previous clubs include: Newport AFC - November 1998, Gloucester C, Hereford Utd.

PREEN, STEVE — *Forward*
Current Club: Gateshead
Birthplace: Cumbria
Previous clubs include: Queen of the South - October 2000, Gateshead, Tow Law T, Spennymoor Utd, Tow Law T, Whitley Bay, Morpeth T.

PREIDT, ROBBIE — *Forward*
Current Club: Warrington Town
D o B: 28/11/1969   *Birthplace: Warrington*
Previous clubs include: Telley Wallur September 1999, Eagle Sports.

PRENDERGAST, RORY — *Midfielder*
Current Club: Bradford Park Avenue
D o B: 06/04/1978   *Birthplace: Pontefract*
An experienced attacking midfielder who joined UniBond Premier side Bradford Park Avenue from rivals Frickley Athletic in July 2002. Made a number of League appearances through spells with Rochdale, Barnsley, York and Oldham and has also seen service with Gainsborough Trinity, Northwich Victoria, Nuneaton Borough and Emley, joining Frickley in December 2001.

PRESTAGE, ADRIAN — *Defender*
Current Club: Great Harwood Town
Birthplace: Lancashire
From Local football - July 2001.

PRESTON, LEE — *Goalkeeper*
Current Club: Chichester City United
Birthplace: Sussex
Goalkeeper: made his Chichester City debut in 1993 before going on to play for Bognor Regis, Ryde Sports and Broadbridge Heath: spent two seasons at Horsham and was their player of the year in 1998/99 (also appeared for Barnet reserves): joined Redhill at the start of 2000/01 after losing out to Burgess Hills Richard Waters in filling the vacancy at Worthing: subsequently had a short period as stand-in at Woodside Road before returning to Redhill in February 2001: signed for Chichester the following August: has attracted interest from Southampton in the past.

PRESTON, MARK — *Midfielder*
Current Club: Newport Isle Of Wight
Birthplace: London
Previous clubs include: Hayes - July 2001.

PRESTON, NICK — *Defender*
Current Club: Hinckley United
D o B: 08/07/1982   *Birthplace: Nuneaton*
Honours won: Dr Martens League Western Div.Winners
Centre back who has progressed from Hinckley United's youth team. Was previously on the books of Leicester City. Established himself in the fistt-team in season 2000/01. Plays in central defence, though can play left side. A solid defender, despite his

young physique, has earned him a fans favourite tag. Unfortunately bypassed the 200/02 season with a double fracture in his leg after only 6 games, though did return at the end of the season. Won a Dr Martens Western Division Championship Medal with Hinckley United in 2000/01.

PRESTON, RICHARD — *Defender*
Current Club: Rothwell Town
D o B: 07/05/1976   *Birthplace: Basildon*
Former Northampton Town defender who re-joined Dr Martens Eastern side Rothwell Town in July 2002 from neighbours and rivals Corby Town. After being released by the Cobblers, Richard had spells with Raunds Town and Baldock Town as well as the Bones.

PRESTRIDGE, NEIL — *Midfielder*
Current Club: Newcastle Town
D o B: 14/04/1970   *Birthplace: Stoke*
Previous clubs include: Droylsden - July 1991, Leek T, Northwich Victoria, Stoke C (Trainee).

PRICE, ALLAN — *Defender*
Current Club: Whitby Town
D o B: 24/04/1978   *Birthplace: Whitby*
A product of the Whitby Town reserve team, Allan is an outstanding young prospect at the club. He made his first team debut in the 1997/98 season away at Spennymoor United in the UniFilla Cup competition and hasn't looked back since. Making regular appearances in the team, he gains more experience with every game and slots in either in defence or in midfield. Originally with local side Fishburn Park.

PRICE, ANDY — *Forward*
Current Club: Horsham YMCA
Birthplace: Sussex
Useful striker on his day (scored 11 times during 1999/2000), but has been plagued by injuries in recent seasons: previously with Forest: scored an early goal against Ringmer in the FA Vase during September 2001 - a game that YM controversially lost thanks to a late penalty.

PRICE, BEN — *Defender*
Current Club: Havant & Waterlooville
Birthplace: Portsmouth
A Havant Town regular Ben was a founder member of the team in June 1998. Originally a Portsmouth player Bens authoritative control has seen him team Captain on numerous occasions. Making his 100th league appearance for the Hawks in the 2000/01 season, the first player to do so, Ben has been given a testimonial match to be played this year.

PRICE, CHRIS — *Defender*
Current Club: Runcorn FC Halton
D o B: 24/10/1975   *Birthplace: Liverpool*
Chris joined the Linnets from Morecambe, after previously playing his football in the Swedish First Division. Pricey never stops running throughout the match and must be one of the fittest players in the squad. Has a good shot on him, and scored several goals last season before getting off the mark this season with two against Gainsborough.

PRICE, GREG — *Goalkeeper*
Current Club: Witton Albion
Birthplace: Liverpool
Previous clubs include: Kendal T - August 2001, Burscough, Prescot Cables, Heswall, Marine.

PRICE, IAN — Defender

Current Club: Skelmersdale United

Birthplace: Cheshire
Previous clubs include: Ashton T - July 1999.

PRICE, JAMES — Defender

Current Club: Radcliffe Borough

Birthplace: Rochdale
Joined Radcliffe Borough from Chorley in January 1999, Jamie is a young player with a bright future. He plays full back or in central defence and is a very quick cover tackler. Originally on the books at Rochdale.

PRICE, JAMES — Goalkeeper

Current Club: Fairford Town

Birthplace: Wiltshire
Previous clubs include: Salisbury C - July 2001.

PRICE, JAMIE — Defender

Current Club: Doncaster Rovers

D o B: 27/10/1981   Birthplace: Normanton
Jamie was a trainee with Leeds United before joining Doncaster Rovers Youth team in the summer of 1999. As a senior player with the Youth, he has been instrumental to their success in the last two seasons. Joined the professional staff this summer.

PRICE, JASON — Defender

Current Club: Merthyr Tydfil

Birthplace: Cardiff
Uncompromising defender who joined Dr Martens Western side Merthyr Tydfil in August 2002 from Haverfordwest County where he completed the 2001/02 season after being released by Weston-Super-Mare. Has also played for Cinderford Town and Newport AFC.

PRICE, JOHN — Defender

Current Club: Eastbourne Borough

Birthplace: Brighton
Vastly experienced Non-League defender who joined Eastbourne Borough in June 2002 from Newport Isle of Wight where he had been skipper. A former Brighton junior, John went on to serve the likes of Portfield, Pagham, Bognor Regis Town, Havant Town and Newport for many years, being on the Isle of Wight since 1997.

PRICE, LEE — Forward

Current Club: Willenhall Town

Birthplace: Wolverhampton
Young, quick player recently joined from local rivals Wednesfield, eager to impress.

PRICE, MARK — Defender

Current Club: Colwyn Bay

D o B: 14/11/1969
Previous clubs include: Connahs Quay Nomads - July 1993, Holywell T, Upton AA.

PRICE, MARK — Midfielder

Current Club: Eccleshill United

Birthplace: Leeds
Previous clubs include: Ossett Alb - August 2001, Thackley, Tadcaster Alb., Ossett T.

PRICE, MARK — Midfielder

Current Club: Arundel

Birthplace: Sussex
Midfielder, built like a tank. Joined Arundel from Totton during the 1999 close season and scored 6 goals in 2000/01 but only makes limited appearances due to work commitments (only seen out during the latter stages of 2001/02).

PRICE, NEIL — Midfielder

Current Club: Oswestry Town

Birthplace: Wales
Another survivor form the double winning team of a couple of seasons ago, Neil spent some time last season with Shawbury United but returned in the spring. Always guaranteed to give 100% and has even given a competent display as a stand in goalkeeper.

PRICE, OLIVER — Defender

Current Club: Clevedon Town

D o B: 12/09/1982   Birthplace: Bristol
A former YTS player at Exeter City, Ollie joined Clevedon in July 2001 after surprisingly being released by the Grecians.

PRICE, RYAN — Goalkeeper

Current Club: Stafford Rangers

Birthplace: Birmingham
Previous clubs include: Pelsall Villa - September 2001.

PRICE, RYAN — Goalkeeper

Current Club: Rushall Olympic

D o B: 13/03/1970   Birthplace: Wolverhampton
Honours won: England Semi-Pro Int., Conference Winners
Ryan rejoined Stafford Rangers in November 2001 as both goalkeeper and Community Officer. He originally joined the club in summer 1988 from Bolton Wanderers and his debut game in August that year was the first of a club record 294 consecutive appearances. Named 1991/92 Player of the Year, Ryan moved to Birmingham City in summer 1994 having made 325 appearances for the club. After a spell at St Andrews he then joined Macclesfield Town and was a regular member of their 1996/97 Conference championship-winning side. Macclesfield moved up to the Football League and Ryan was ever-present during their first season in Division Three which the Silkmen finished as runners-up. He then joined Telford United during the 1999/00 season after a total of 100 League appearances. Capped six times as an England semi-professional international.

PRICE, SCOTT — Defender

Current Club: Guiseley

Birthplace: Yorkshire
Previous clubs include: Eccleshill Utd - November 2001.

PRICE, SCOTT — Midfielder

Current Club: Rye & Iden United

Birthplace: Hastings
Big midfielder and captain. Scored 7 goals for Rye during 2000/01.

PRICE, STEVE — Midfielder

Current Club: Goole AFC

D o B: 30/11/1974   Birthplace: Sheffield
Highly-rated and experienced midfielder who started his career with Oldham. Moved into Non-League football with Gainsborough Trinity where he enjoyed a lengthy spell of seven years before following manager Ernie Moss to Leek Town. Returned to Gainmsborough before signing for Frickley Athletic in October 2000. Switched to Northern Counties East League side Goole AFC in May 2002.

PRIDHAM, CHRIS — *Midfielder*

Current Club: Afan Lido

Birthplace: Wales

Honours won: Wales Schoolboy Int.

Competitive and skilful central midfielder brought in after the impressive Dean Johnstone left the club. Fills the role superbly - immediately becomes one of the clubs best assets.

PRIESTLEY, PHIL — *Goalkeeper*

Current Club: Bangor City

D o B: 30/03/1976   *Birthplace: Wigan*

Goalkeeper who spent three seasons with Rochdale where he gained Football League experience. Had spells at Scarborough and Chester City in the 2000/01 season before joining Bangor City in August 2001. Selected for the League of Wales Team of The Season in May 2002.

PRIESTLEY, TOM — *Defender*

Current Club: Mickleover Sports

Birthplace: Burton

From Youth team.

PRIESTNALL, SCOTT — *Midfielder*

Current Club: Eastwood Town

Birthplace: Chesterfield

Midfielder who joined UniBond First Division side Eastwood Town in August 2002 after a short return to Northern Counties East Leaguers Staveley Miners Welfare. Had spells as a junior with Chesterfield and Mansfield before joining Staveley for the first time. Then played for Dr Martens outfit Ilkeston Town before re-joining Welfare in March 2002.

PRINCE, CARL — *Goalkeeper*

Current Club: Clapton

Birthplace: Essex

Previous clubs include: Woodford T - March 2001, Grays Ath., Leyton Pennant.

PRINCE, LUKE — *Midfielder*

Current Club: Gloucester City

Previous clubs include: Forest Green Rovers - September 2001, Aston Villa.

PRINDIVILLE, STEVE — *Defender*

Current Club: Hucknall Town

D o B: 26/12/1968   *Birthplace: Harlow*

Honours won: England Semi-Pro Int., Dr Martens League Premier Div.Winners

Harlow-born Steve joined Hucknall Town as player/assistant-manager in December 2001 from Stafford Rangers. An experienced left-sided defender, he had only signed for Rangers prior to the start of the 2001/02 season. He began his career with Leicester City and made his Football League debut for the Foxes at Shrewsbury in 1987/88 before joining Chesterfield, Mansfield Town and Doncaster Rovers. Steve made a total of 131 League appearances, scoring 3 goals then played for Halifax Town, Dagenham & Redbridge and Kidderminster Harriers in the Conference. He then joined Nuneaton Borough and was an ever-present member of Nuneatons 1998/99 Dr Martens League Premier Division championship side and with it a return to Conference football. On the International scene he has one England semi-professional international cap, won against Holland in 1997.

PRINS, JASON — *Forward*

Current Club: Metropolitan Police

D o B: 01/11/1974   *Birthplace: Wisbech*

Previous clubs include: Basingstoke T - July 1996, Carlisle Utd.

PRIOR, CHRIS — *Midfielder*

Current Club: Selby Town

Birthplace: Leeds

Previous clubs include: Whitkirk Wanderers - July 2001, Yorkshire Amateurs.

PRIOR, NEIL — *Midfielder*

Current Club: Norwich United

D o B: 03/06/1977   *Birthplace: Norfolk*

Hard-working playmaker, smiler to his mates was previously with Mulbarton United and Great Yarmouth Town before joining Norwich United.

PRITCHARD, BRIAN — *Defender*

Current Club: Witton Albion

D o B: 05/11/1974

Previous clubs include: Southport - August 1995.

PRITCHARD, DANIEL — *Midfielder*

Current Club: Felixstowe & Walton United

Birthplace: Suffolk

Daniel joined the club in the close season from Hadleigh United and showed up well in pre-season , another talented and skilful player on and off the ball.

PRITCHARD, GARETH — *Forward*

Current Club: Guiseley

Birthplace: Lincolnshire

Previous clubs include: Wisbech T - March 2002, Stamford, Guiseley, Cottesmore Amateurs, Spalding Utd, Grimsby T.

PRITCHARD, JAMIE — *Midfielder*

Current Club: Maidenhead United

Birthplace: Marlow

Midfielder who returned to Ryman Premier side Maidenhead United for a third time in July 2002. Began his playing days with home-town club Marlow and then had his first spell with the Magpies. Returned to Marlow and then joined Flackwell Heath before re-joining Maidenhead and then, from Novembe 1998, Marlow again.

PRITCHARD, JUSTIN — *Forward*

Current Club: Merthyr Tydfil

Birthplace: Bristol

Joined Dr Martens Western side Merthyr Tydfil from Weston-super-Mare in the summer of 2002, following John Relishs move to the Martyrs as assistant-manager. Formerly with Yate, Bath City, Clevedon Town, Mangotsfield United and Bristol Rovers, Justin has already set up a good understanding with fellow striker Andy Mainwarring at Pennydarren Park.

PRITCHARD, KEVIN — *Midfielder*

Current Club: Ely City

Birthplace: Cambridge

Previous clubs include: Chatteris T - September 1999, Soham Town R, Newmarket T, Chester C, Wrexham, Blackburn R.

PROBERT, GARY   *Defender*
Current Club: Cirencester Town

D o B: 22/06/1983   Birthplace: Swindon
A talented young defender who came into the Cirencester Town first-team squad midway through the 2000/01 season from the academy. Was on the books at Swindon Town as a youngster.

PROBETS, CLAYTON   *Midfielder*
Current Club: Redhill

Birthplace: Kent
Powerful midfielder joined Redhill in January 2002 from VCD Athletic.

PROCTOR, ANDY   *Midfielder*
Current Club: Accrington Stanley

Birthplace: Lancashire
Previous clubs include: Great Harwood T - February 2002.

PROCTOR, IAN   *Midfielder*
Current Club: Maltby Main

Birthplace: Yorkshire
Previous clubs include: Worsbrough Bridge - October 2001.

PROKAS, RICHARD   *Midfielder*
Current Club: Workington

D o B: 20/01/1976   Birthplace: Penrith
Midfielder who returned to his native Cumbria to join UniBond First Division side Workington in July 2002 following a brief spell with Cambridge United. Spent the majority of his career with Carlisle United, making almost 200 appearances in a seven-year stint at Brunton Park.

PROTAIN, EMOND   *Defender*
Current Club: Harrow Borough

Joined Boro in the summer of 2000 from Wembley. Made his competitive debut in the Capital League victory at Croydon.

PROTHEROE, LEE   *Defender*
Current Club: Canvey Island

Birthplace: London
Highly-rated full back who played for both Walthamstow Pennant and St.Margaretsbury in the Spartan League before moving into the Ryman League with Ruislip Manor. Transferred to Yeading during the summer of 1996 and then moved to Enfield for £5,000 in July 1998. Switched to the Shots during the 2000 close season and became a firm favourite with supporters. Moved on to Canvey Island in June 2002.

PROUDFOOT, BEN   *Defender*
Current Club: Hampton & Richmond

Birthplace: Teddington
Central defender/utility player who followed assistant-manager Matt Beard from his Tooting & Mitcham United Reserve side to Ryman Premier side Hampton & Richmond Borough in August 2002. A local Teddington lad, Ben is a Sports Science graduate and is a PE teacher in Barnes.

PROUDLOCK, PAUL   *Midfielder*
Current Club: Bishop Auckland

D o B: 25/10/1965   Birthplace: Hartlepool
Arrived at Bishop Auckland following his resignation as player-manager of Gateshead in February 2002. An experienced midfielder who made over 200 Football League appearances for Middlesbrough, Hartlepool and Carlisle before joining Gateshead during the 1993/94 season. Took over as manager at the start of the 2000/01 season.

PRUTTON, ANDY   *Midfielder*
Current Club: Hertford Town

D o B: 21/02/1969   Birthplace: Hertford
Previous clubs include: Wealdstone - February 2000, Boreham Wood, Harrow B, Dartford, Cheshunt, Wormley Rovers.

PRYERS, LEE   *Defender*
Current Club: Bamber Bridge

D o B: 23/02/1980   Birthplace: Bolton
Previous clubs include: Leigh RMI - August 2000, Bolton Wanderers.

PUGH, LEE   *Defender*
Current Club: Brodsworth Welfare

Birthplace: Doncaster
From Youth team.

PUGH, MATTHEW   *Goalkeeper*
Current Club: Studley

Birthplace: Worcestershire
Previous clubs include: Burman - September 2001, Paget R, Bromsgrove R.

PULISCIANO, NATHAN   *Midfielder*
Current Club: Ludlow Town

Birthplace: Birmingham
Previous clubs include: Stourbridge - February 2002, Solihull Borough, Aston Villa (Trainee).

PULLAN, MARC   *Defender*
Current Club: Crawley Town

Birthplace: Sussex
Defender: originally played for Crawley some years ago before spending 18 months out of action: joined Wick in August 1999 until returning to the Broadfield in January that season.

PULLING, CHRIS   *Midfielder*
Current Club: Horsham

Birthplace: Sussex
From Youth team.

PUNT, DANNY   *Defender*
Current Club: Three Bridges

Birthplace: Sussex
Long serving defender: returned to the first-team in April 2001 after a long lay-off.

PURCELL, ANDY   *Midfielder*
Current Club: Arlesey Town

Birthplace: London
Previous clubs include: Bishops Stortford - January 2002, Enfield, Harlow T, Enfield.

PURCELL, STEVE   *Goalkeeper*
Current Club: Cirencester Town

Birthplace: Gloucester
Previous clubs include: Purton - November 2001.

PURDIE, ROBERT   *Midfielder*
Current Club: Hereford United

Birthplace: Leicester
Former Leicester City under-19 midfielder, who also gained experience in Leicester City's reserve team Turned out for Conference club Hereford United's reserves towards the end of the 2001/02 season before joining permanently in the close season. who has signed a season-long contract with the Bulls.

PURDY, JOHN — *Defender*
Current Club: Glapwell
Birthplace: Chesterfield
Previous clubs include: Blidworth Welfare - July 1997.

PURNELL, RHYDIAN — *Midfielder*
Current Club: Brackley Town
Birthplace: Banbury
Previous clubs include: Easington Sports - December 1999, Brackley T.

PURSER, WAYNE — *Forward*
Current Club: Barnet
D o B: 13/04/1980   Birthplace: Basildon
Signed for Barnet in the summer of 2000 after three years at QPR. A highly-impressive forward who enjoyed an exceptional 2001/02 season when he again attracted League attention.

PURVIS, ANDY — *Forward*
Current Club: Brandon United
Birthplace: Northumberland
Another all action striker who gives defences all sorts of problems. Could be seen as an old fashioned centre forward and is a firm favourite with supporters. Signed from Ashington during the 1999/2000 season. Unfortunately he is taking a year out and will be sorely missed, especially by opposing defenders.

PURVIS, LEE — *Midfielder*
Current Club: Epsom And Ewell
Birthplace: Surrey
Made his Epsom debut as a substitute against Ware in March 2000, and scored on his full debut against Clapton in December. Winner of the most improved player award in 1999-2000.

PYE, MARK — *Midfielder*
Current Club: Carshalton Athletic
D o B: 29/02/1968   Birthplace: London
Experienced midfielder who joined Carshalton Athletic from Hendon in March 2002. Began his career at West Ham. Previously with, Enfield, Aldershot, Slough Town and Harrow Borough.

PYKE, DARREN — *Midfielder*
Current Club: Consett
Birthplace: Consett
From Youth team.

QUAILEY, BRIAN — *Forward*
Current Club: Doncaster Rovers
D o B: 21/03/1978   Birthplace: Leicester
Honours won: St Kitts & Nevis Int.
Brian started his career with Deeping Rangers and then Nuneaton Borough before West Bromwich Albion gave him a chance in the Football League in September1997. He moved on to Scunthorpe United in February 2000 after spells on-loan to Blackpool and Exeter City and was a regular in the side for the rest of the 2000/01 campaign and the early part of the following season. The big, strong attacker has gained caps for the St.Kitts & Nevis international team and joined Conference side Doncaster Rovers in August 2002.

QUAILEY, DAMION — *Goalkeeper*
Current Club: Shepshed Dynamo
D o B: 31/05/1979   Birthplace: Leicester
Honours won: St Kitts & Nevis Int.
Goalkeeper whose brother Brian is with Doncaster Rovers. Like his brother, Damion is also a St Kitts & Nevis international who began his career with Notts County. Has since had spells with Easington Town, Leicestershire Senior Leaguers Highfield Rangers and two stints at Atherstone United. Joined Dr Martens Western side Shepshed Dynamo towards the end of the 2001/02 season.

QUARM, FRANCIS — *Midfielder*
Current Club: Dulwich Hamlet
Birthplace: London
Skilful and tenacious midfielder who rejoined Dulwich Hamlet in July 2001 after a short spell at Tooting & Mitcham United. Was one of the stars of Hamlets successful cup-winning youth side of 2000/01.

QUAYLE, MARK — *Forward*
Current Club: Nuneaton Borough
D o B: 02/10/1978   Birthplace: Liverpool
Former Everton striker, who signed for Nuneaton from Telford in May 2002. Released by Grimsby Town at the end of the 1999/2000 season. Started 2000/01 season with Altrincham until an injury against Lancaster City. Pllayed for Leigh RMI and then Telford before joining Boro.

QUICK, DARREN — *Defender*
Current Club: Trafford
D o B: 12/02/1970   Birthplace: Manchester
Previous clubs include: Winsford Utd - November 1999, Chorley, Accrington Stanley, Salford C. Blackpool (Trainee).

QUIGGIN, JIMMY — *Midfielder*
Current Club: Halesowen Town
D o B: 20/07/1979   Birthplace: Birmingham
Impressed as an attacking midfielder, Jimmy joined Halesown Town in May 2002 after a two-year spell with Hereford United in the Conference. Signed for the Bulls from Boldmere St Michaels in October 2000 after starting out at Burton Albion.

QUIGLEY, MICHAEL — *Midfielder*
Current Club: Bradford Park Avenue
D o B: 02/10/1970   Birthplace: Manchester
Previous clubs include: Northwich Victoria - August 2001, Hull C, Altrincham, Hull C, Wrexham, Manchester C.

QUILT, JOHN — Forward
Current Club: Wednesfield
Birthplace: Birmingham
Previous clubs include: Bloxwich Utd - December 2001, Local football.

QUINCEY, JASON — Defender
Current Club: Holmer Green
Birthplace: Bucks
From Local football - July 1992.

QUINCEY, LEE — Forward
Current Club: Shepshed Dynamo
D o B: 05/10/1977   Birthplace: Leiceser
Previous clubs include: Raunds T - July 2000, VS Rugby, Raunds T, Shepshed Dynamo, Hinckley Utd, Leicester C.

QUINLAN, JAMIE — Midfielder
Current Club: Withdean 2000
Birthplace: Sussex
Former Bognor Regis midfielder: scored 9 times whilst playing for Whitehawk during 1999/2000: another who spent the following season at Southwick and made his debut for Withdean one year late during August 2001.

QUINN, ANDY — Midfielder
Current Club: Bradford Park Avenue
D o B: 01/09/1979   Birthplace: Halifax
Honours won: FA Youth Cup Winners
A midfielder or wing-back who began his career at Sheffield Wednesday before being bought as a teenager for a fee of £75,000 by Leeds United, where he played alongside the likes of Harry Kewell and Alan Smith in Leeds all-conquering youth side, before being released in 1998. He joined Gainsborough Trinity from Scarborough in January 2000 and then signed for Bradford Park Avenue eight months later.

QUINN, JAMES — Forward
Current Club: Bishop Auckland
Birthplace: Bishop Auckland
Made the step up from the Auckland & District league and after a couple of substitute appearances made his full debut for Bishop Auckland against Accrington Stanley in March 2002.

QUINN, JIMMY — Forward
Current Club: Northwich Victoria
D o B: 18/11/1959   Birthplace: Belfast
Honours won: Northern Ireland Int.
A vastly experienced striker, Jimmy scored 210 League goals in 510 appearances during a distinguished professional career which saw spells at Swindon Town, Blackburn Rovers, Leicester City, Bradford City, West Ham, Bournemouth, Reading and Peterborough. He also won 46 caps for Northern Ireland and netted a dozen goals for his country. A fully qualified UEFA A coach, between 1994 and 1997, he acted as joint manager of Reading with Mick Gooding and took the Royals to Wembley in where only a late rally from Bolton prevented them from winning a Premiership place. His next managerial role was at SwindonTown where he almost succeeded in keeping the Robins in Division One after taking charge part way through the 1999/00 season when the Wiltshire side already deep in danger at the foot of the table. Having spent the 2000/01 season playing for a variety of Non-League clubs, including Northwich Victoria and fellow Conference clubs Hayes and Hereford, Jimmy was apppinted as player-boss at Nortwhich in the summer of 2001.

QUINN, JOE — Defender
Current Club: Trafford
D o B: 20/10/1978   Birthplace: Canada
Honours won: ISFA England Schools Rep.
Previous clubs include: Colwyn Bay December 2000, Conwy Utd, Alsager College, Nantwich T.

QUINN, STEVE — Midfielder
Current Club: Droylsden
D o B: 08/03/1978   Birthplace: Manchester
Previous clubs include: Woodley Sports - February 2002, Droylsden, Curzon Ashton, Mossley, Stalybridge Celtic, Bolton Wanderers.

QUINTON, BRADLEY — Forward
Current Club: Braintree Town
Previous clubs include: Bishops Stortford - January 2000, Romford, Aveley, Hornchurch.

QUIRK, CHRIS — Midfielder
Current Club: St.Helens Town
Birthplace: Liverpool
Mr Reliable in his ninth season with Town after spells with Witton Albion and Skelmersdale United. Exceptional competitor who never lets you down and is always first on the team sheet.

QUIRKE, FRASER — Forward
Current Club: Bashley
D o B: 08/04/1967
Honours won: Combined Services Rep.
Previous clubs include: Newport IOW - August 2001, Worthing, Bashley, Yee Hope (Hong Kong), Fareham T, Worthing, Portsmouth RN.

QUY, ANDY — Goalkeeper
Current Club: Belper Town
D o B: 04/07/1976   Birthplace: Harlow
Previous clubs include: Halesowen T - June 2001, Hereford Utd, Stevenage B, Grimsby T, Derby Co., Tottenham Hotspur.

Q

RACHEL, ADAM — Goalkeeper
Current Club: Moor Green

D o B: 10/12/1976   *Birthplace: Birmingham*
Signed for Moor Green in July 2001 from Blackpool. Came through the Aston Villa youth team and made one first team appearance.

RADCLIFFE, SIMON — Defender
Current Club: Dorchester Town

D o B: 25/02/1981   *Birthplace: Dorset*
Previous clubs include: Bridport - August 2000.

RADFORD, ALAN — Forward
Current Club: Brodsworth Welfare

Birthplace: Hull
Previous clubs include: Immingham T - July 1997, Guiseley, Brigg T, Bridlington T, Emley, Ossett T, Pontefract Collieries.

RADFORD, JOE — Goalkeeper
Current Club: Tonbridge Angels

D o B: 04/12/1963   *Birthplace: Kent*
One of the most experienced goalkeepers in Non-League football, Joe re-joined Tonbridge in July 1999. Originally with the Angels in 1996/97, he has gained vast experience with the likes of Dover, Ashford, Margate and Gillingham.

RADIGAN, NEIL — Midfielder
Current Club: Gateshead

D o B: 04/07/1980   *Birthplace: Middlesbrough*
Talented midfielder who started his career with Scarborough and also played League football with Darlington. Signed for UniBond Premier side Whitby Town in the summer of 2000 before moving to rivals Blyth Spartans in December 00. Transferred to Gateshead in August 2002.

RAE, DEREK — Midfielder
Current Club: Hednesford Town

Birthplace: Glasgow
Midfielder who joined Dr Martens Premier side Hednesford Town in February 2002. Younger brother of Wolves striker Alex, has spent his career north of the border with Albion, Stranraer, Berwick, Queens Park and Elgin City.

RAIN, STUART — Forward
Current Club: Connahs Quay Nomads

D o B: 05/06/1969   *Birthplace: Wales*
Previous clubs include: Mold Alexandra - July 1995, Everton (Junior).

RAINFORD, DAVID — Midfielder
Current Club: Heybridge Swifts

D o B: 21/04/1979   *Birthplace: Stepney*
Young midfielder who has great vision, good ball control and pace. Joined Ryman Premier side Heybridge Swifts in July 2002 from rivals Grays Athletic. Had signed for Grays at the start of the 2001/02 season from Slough Town. Originally with Colchester United.

RAISHBROOK, LEON — Forward
Current Club: Croydon Athletic

Birthplace: Surrey
Previous clubs include: Corinthian Casuals - January 2002, Banstead Ath, Sutton Utd.

RAKE, BARRY — Midfielder
Current Club: Maidenhead United

D o B: 09/04/1969
Previous clubs include: Slough T - August 2001, Maidenhead Utd, Walton & Hersham, Slough T, Chesham Utd, Slough T, Millwall.

RALPH, ANDREW — Goalkeeper
Current Club: Vauxhall Motors

Birthplace: Manchester
Highly-rated young goalkeeper who signed for UniBond Premier side Vauxhall Motors in August 2002 in a swap deal involving Chris Holmes. Had only signed for Grove a month earlier after arriving from Tranmere Rovers, where he was a member of their Youth Alliance double-winning side.

RALPH, SHAUN — Forward
Current Club: Shifnal Town

Birthplace: Shropshire
Previous clubs include: Warley Rangers - July 2001.

RAMASUT, TOM — Midfielder
Current Club: Barry Town

D o B: 30/08/1977   *Birthplace: Cardiff*
Honours won: Wales u-21 & B Int.
Previous clubs include: Merthyr Tydfil - December 2001, Llanelli, Merthyr Tydfil, Cardiff C, Bristol R, Norwich C.

RAMSAY, JAMES — Midfielder
Current Club: Flackwell Heath

Birthplace: Buckinghamshire
Previous clubs include: Chalfont St.Peter - October 2001.

RAMSAY, KEVIN — Defender
Current Club: Wealdstone

Birthplace: London
Previous clubs include: Barking & East Ham Utd - December 2001, Grays Ath, Barking, Clapton, Barking, Dorking, Hampton, Dorking, Croydon Ath., Millwall (Junior).

RAMSAY, SCOTT — Forward
Current Club: Eastbourne Borough

D o B: 16/10/1980   *Birthplace: Hastings*
Scott is a Hastings-born forward who started his football career at Brighton. Proved to be something special in his youth, turning to professional level in the 1998 season. Determined to get into the Brighton first-team he made around 10 games. However, the League was proving to be hard for Scott so he joined fellow Conference outfit Yeovil Town. His twelve-week loan with the Conference outfit saw him score four goals in 14 matches. He went on to join Dover Athletic in January 2002 and then switched to Eastbourne Borough in May.

RAMSDEN, GAVIN — Midfielder
Current Club: St.Leonards

D o B: 04/11/1977   *Birthplace: Leeds*
Gavin signed for St Leonards in December 1997 from UniBond League side Farsley Celtic, whom he had joined at the start of that season after being released following his traineeship with Oldham Athletic. A ball winner with good distribution, he is solid when defending, however his competitive style earns him more than his fair share of injuries and only returned at the end of the 2001/02 season after sustaining a broken leg which came within a year of fracturing an ankle.

RAMSHAW, JAMES   *Forward*
Current Club: Consett
Birthplace: Consett
From Youth team.

RAND, CRAIG   *Defender*
Current Club: Whitby Town
Birthplace: Bishop Auckland
Craig made his debut for UniBond Premier side Whitby Town at Colwyn Bay on March 2nd 2002 after arriving from Sheffield Wednesday. Highly-promising young central defender, originally from Bishop Auckland, who can play right-back. Excellent in the air, he looks a great prospect.

RANDALL, LEIGH   *Forward*
Current Club: Llanelli AFC
D o B: 11/07/1968   *Birthplace: Wales*
Previous clubs include: Bwlch Rangers - March 2001, Llanelli, Inter Cardiff, Aberystwyth T, Llanelli, Ammanford, Pembroke B.

RANDALL, MARTIN   *Forward*
Current Club: Hendon
D o B: 03/03/1973   *Birthplace: Pinner*
Honours won: Ryman League Premier Div.Winners
Experienced striker who joined Hendon from Woking in December 2001. Has previously played for St Albans City, Hayes and Northwood. Helped Hayes to win the Ryman League championship.

RANDALL, NICKY   *Defender*
Current Club: Letchworth
Birthplace: Herts
Previous clubs include: Braybury End - July 1998.

RANDALL, STUART   *Defender*
Current Club: Sutton Coldfield Town
Previous clubs include: Paget Rangers - July 2000, Redditch Utd, Paget R, Sutton Coldfield T, Solihull B, Bromsgrove R, Evesham Utd, Sutton Coldfield T, Redditch Utd, Coleshill T, Tamworth.

RANDELL, Sean   *Forward*
Current Club: Burgess Hill Town
Birthplace: Sussex
Forward, who really throws himself into it (sometimes oversteps the mark): previously with Whitehawk before a four year spell at Saltdean (scored 14 times during 1999/2000): struck a total of 20 goals the following season, having switched to Peacehaven (one of his old clubs) in November 2000: joined Ringmer during the summer 2001: previously renowned for his trademark long hair - but has now had a much-needed visit to the barbers: made a superb start to 2001/02, and was the leading scorer in Division One up until October when he went away to Australia for three months: returned to Sussex in January, but struggled to regain his place at Ringmer and consequently signed for Hassocks in March: Joined Hassocks local rivals Burgess Hill in the close season of 2002/2003.

RANDLE, KEVIN   *Forward*
Current Club: Ely City
Birthplace: Belper
Previous clubs include: Warboys T - August 2001, Yaxley, Warboys T, Belper T, Ilkeston T, Belper Utd.

RANDLES, GARY   *Defender*
Current Club: Marine
Birthplace: Helsby
Gary signed for Marine from Runcorn in the summer of 1999, having started his career with General Chemicals and then Avon Athletic in the Widnes League before going on to play for Warrington and Curzon Ashton. A determined left-sided defender who likes to come forward, he always gives 100 per cent.

RANKIN, DARRYL   *Defender*
Current Club: Leek Town
Birthplace: Nottingham
Defender who was a trainee with Mansfield Town before joining Alfreton Town in the summer of 1998. Switched to UniBond League side Hucknall Town in July 1999 and became a first-team regular at Watnall Road. Moved to Arnold Town during the 2001/02 season before being re-united with former Hucknall boss John Rmshaw at Leek Town in June 2002.

RANSHAW, RICK   *Forward*
Current Club: Grantham Town
Birthplace: Lincoln
Re-signed for Grantham Town late September 2001 after joining Gainsborough the previous summer. Previously had a two-season spell with the club and scored over 30 goals during the last two seasons. Has also seen service with Lincoln City, Lincoln United, Bridlington Town and Harrowby United.

RANTALA, JUHO   *Defender*
Current Club: Billericay Town
Birthplace: Finland
Honours won: Finland Int.
Previous clubs include: HIFK (Finland) - March 2002, Atliantis FC (Finland), FC Haka (Finland).

RASHBROOK, GRAHAM   *Defender*
Current Club: Three Bridges
Birthplace: Sussex
Very experienced defender, who has made some 250 appearances for Three Bridges: one-time Crawley reserve player who really blocks out the opposition: returned to the Jubilee Field for this season after a brief spell with Crawley Down: other previous clubs include Oakwood, Horsham YMCA, Horsham and Pease Pottage.

RASPIN, ROY   *Defender*
Current Club: Brigg Town
Birthplace: Scunthorpe
Previous clubs include: Gainsborough Trinity - March 1999, Scunthorpe Utd, Appleby Frodingham.

RASTALL, OLLIE   *Goalkeeper*
Current Club: Bashley
Previous clubs include: Farnborough T - July 2000.

RATCHFORD, TERRY   *Midfielder*
Current Club: Dartford
D o B: 26/08/1981   *Birthplace: Sidcup*
Tall and imposing midfield player who re-joined Dr Martens Eastern side Dartford in July 2002 from Kent Leaguers VCD Athletic. Actually began his playing days with the Darts before signing for VCD in the summer of 1999.

RATCLIFFE, CAR — Defender
Current Club: Stowmarket Town
Birthplace: Suffolk
Previous clubs include: Needham Market - February 1999.

RATTLE, JON — Defender
Current Club: Gateshead
D o B: 22/07/1976   *Birthplace: Melton*
Jon in an influential player who is capable of defensive duties as well as being a good midfield player. He joined Gateshead from St. Albans City of the Ryman League in February 2002 after re-locating to the North-East in 2002. A much-travelled player, he has also turned out for the likes of Baldock Town, Billericay Town, Cambridge United and abroad for the Sheperton club of Australia and in Finland for Aanoski.

RAVENHILL, RICKY — Midfielder
Current Club: Doncaster Rovers
D o B: 16/01/1981   *Birthplace: Doncaster*
Began with Leeds United while Mickey Walker was there, at the age of 10 and played through their acadamy until the age of 16. Realeased and joined Barnsley as a YT for two seasons and then as a pro for two season where he was a regular in the reserve team but never made the first team.

RAWLINGS, IAN — Defender
Current Club: Harlow Town
Birthplace: London
Joined Harlow Town in January 2001 from Bromley. A vastly experienced defender who made over 500 appearances for Bromley as well as playing for Leyton Wingate and Leyton Orient.

RAWLINS, MATT — Forward
Current Club: Chippenham Town
Birthplace: Gloucester
Signed for Dr Martens Premier side Chippenham Town from Gloucester City in January 2001. Matt was the top scorer at Gloucester before he decided to switch clubs. He started his career by spending five years at Arsenal, two as a schoolboy, then an apprentice before spending a year as a professional. Whilst at Arsenal he was an FA Youth cup winner and he managed to score in both legs of the final live on Sky sports against Millwall. He has also played for Clevedon Town where he was a regular scorer in their Dr Martens Western championship-winning side. He played in Chippenhams second league cup final success as well as the victory over Swindon Town in 2001/02. A great favourite with supporters, he the managers player of the year for 2001/02.

RAWLINSON, CHRIS — Forward
Current Club: Stafford Town
Birthplace: Stafford
Previous clubs include: Rocester - July 2001, Chasetown, Rocester, Stafford T, Rocester, Stafford T.

RAWLINSON, MARK — Midfielder
Current Club: Weymouth
D o B: 09/06/1975   *Birthplace: Bolton*
Mark comes to us having been released by Exeter City at the end of last season. Started his career at Manchester United in the youth team before moving on to AFC Bournemouth. Is equally comfortable in defence or midfield. Mark could be an important part of the team for some time to come.

RAY, BRIAN — Forward
Current Club: Eastbourne United
Birthplace: Sussex
Scored 12 times for Shinewater during the second-half of 2000/01. Transferred to Eastbourne United in March 2002, and instantly made an impact when scoring twice in the 4-1 victory over Hassocks - ending a goal-drought of seven consecutive matches for the club.

RAY, DAMIEN — Defender
Current Club: Croydon Athletic
Birthplace: Surrey
Previous clubs include: Banstead Ath - July 1998, Sutton Utd.

RAY, DANNY — Midfielder
Current Club: Walton & Hersham
Birthplace: Surrey
Previous clubs include: Croydon Ath - October 2001, Walton & Hersham.

RAY, SEAN — Forward
Current Club: St.Leonards
Birthplace: Hastings
Strong, fast striker who scored 9 times for Rye & Iden United during the second half of 2000/01and was in unstoppable form the following season, playing a key part in the clubs bid to reach the First Division. Transferred to Dr Martens Eastern neighbours St Leonards in July 2002.

RAY, SIMON — Forward
Current Club: Corinthian Casuals
Birthplace: Surrey
Previous clubs include: Croydon Ath - August 2000.

RAYFIELD, COURTNEY — Midfielder
Current Club: Chatham Town
From Youth team.

RAYMENT, PAT — Defender
Current Club: Diss Town
D o B: 11/04/1965   *Birthplace: Peterborough*
Previous clubs include: Gorleston - July 2000, Great Yarmouth T, Cottingham, Corby T, Chelmsford C, Stamford, Raunds T, Kettering T, Corby T, Cambridge Utd, Peterborough Utd.

RAYNER, SIMON — Goalkeeper
Current Club: Barry Town
D o B: 08/07/1983   *Birthplace: Canada*
Honours won: Canada Youth Int.
19-year old with international caps for Canada at under-18 and under-19 level. The 6ft. 5ins. goalkeeper was a non-contract player at AFC Bournemouth, and was goalkeeper for the Canadian under-19 side in a tournament in the United States before joining Barry towards the end of January 2002.

RAYNOR, PAUL — Midfielder
Current Club: Kings Lynn
D o B: 29/04/1966   *Birthplace: Nottingham*
Previous clubs include: Ossett Alb - March 2002, Gainsborough Trinity, Hednesford T, Kings Lynn, Boston Utd, Ilkeston T, Kettering T, Stevenage B, Leyton Orient, Cambridge Utd, Preston NE, Swansea C, Huddersfield T, Nottingham Forest.

RAYNOR, TERRY   *Midfielder*
Current Club: *AFC Sudbury*

Birthplace: Essex
Joined AFC Sudbury at the start of our first season from Ryman League side Heybridge Swifts. A highly gifted young player whose pace when running at players is impressive as is his ability to cross quickly and with great accuracy.

RAYSON, ANTHONY   *Midfielder*
Current Club: *Penrith*

Birthplace: Cumbria
Previous clubs include: Gillford Park - July 1999.

RAYWOOD, MATT   *Midfielder*
Current Club: *Great Harwood Town*

Birthplace: Lancashire
Previous clubs include: Rossendale Utd - July 2001, Great Harwood T, Glossop NE, Accrington Stanley, Manchester C (Trainee).

REA, GAVIN   *Defender*
Current Club: *Gloucester City*

Birthplace: Gloucester
From Youth team.

REACORD, KEVIN   *Midfielder*
Current Club: *Eastleigh*

Birthplace: Hampshire
Previous clubs include: AFC Totton - May 2002, Brockenhurst.

READ, ASHLEY   *Forward*
Current Club: *Bromsgrove Rovers*

Birthplace: Worcestershire
Highly-promising 20-year-old forward who joined Bromsgrove Rovers in May 2002. Spent the 2001/02 season with Dr Martens Western Division side Cirencester Town. Although still very raw, Bromsgrove believe he has a great deal of potential.

READ, BILLY   *Midfielder*
Current Club: *Ford United*

Birthplace: Essex
Honours won: Ryman League Div.One Winners
An experienced Non-League midfielder who has played all his football with Essex sides. Joined Ford United in July 1999 from Leyton Pennant and played a major part in helping the club to win the Ryman League Division One title. Previously with Hornchurch, Aveley, Leyton-Wingate, Walthamstow Pennant and Collier Row.

READ, DAVID   *Defender*
Current Club: *Bilston Town*

Birthplace: Birmingham
Previous clubs include: Bridgnorth T - November 2001, Bilston T, Stafford R, Telford Utd, Blakenall, VS Rugby, Cheltenham T, Atherstone Utd, Rushall Olympic, Fort Lauderdale (USA), Walsall Wood.

READ, JAMES   *Defender*
Current Club: *Brentwood*

Birthplace: Essex
An uncompromising centre back, James graduated from the youth squad making his first team debut three season ago.

READE, MATT   *Forward*
Current Club: *Great Wakering Rovers*

Birthplace: Southend
From Youth team.

READING, CHRIS   *Defender*
Current Club: *Holmer Green*

Birthplace: Bucks
Previous clubs include: Chesham Utd - July 2001, Holmer Green.

REDDINGTON, DAVE   *Defender*
Current Club: *Enfield*

Previous clubs include: Cheshunt - January 2001, Stevenage B.

REDDY, CRAIG   *Midfielder*
Current Club: *Rhayader Town*

Birthplace: Merthyr
20 years of age signed from Merthyr area. Very fit, works hard for the team and good in possession. Looking to make the step up to League of Wales.

REDFERN, JOHN   *Midfielder*
Current Club: *Glapwell*

Birthplace: Chesterfield
From Local football - July 1994.

REDGATE, CRAIG   *Forward*
Current Club: *Biddulph Victoria*

Birthplace: Stoke
Previous clubs include: Eastwood Hanley - November 1996, Milton Utd, Goldenhill Wanderers.

REDGATE, GARY   *Defender*
Current Club: *Rugby United*

D o B: 26/01/1970   *Birthplace: Coventry*
Previous clubs include: Atherstone Utd - December 2001, Rugby Utd, Hinckley Utd, Atherstone Utd, Hinckley T, VS Rugby, Burton Alb., VS Rugby, Atherstone Utd.

REDHEAD, DAVID   *Defender*
Current Club: *Newcastle Blue Star*

Birthplace: Newcastle
Previous clubs include: Ponteland Utd - July 2001.

REDKNAPP, GEORGE   *Midfielder*
Current Club: *Banbury United*

Birthplace: Oxford
Midfielder who signed for Banbury united from Witney Town at the start of the 2000/01 season. Has won Oxfordshire Youth Cup winners medals and Senior Cup finalist with North Leigh. A useful addition to the squad, is a competitive player and scorer of spectacular goals. Formerly with North Leigh, Marlow and Brackley Town.

REECE, DOMINIC   *Defender*
Current Club: *Halesowen Town*

Birthplace: Birmingham
Former Aston Villa trainee defender who signed for Dr Martens Premier side Halesowen Town in August 2002 after a spell with Conference outfit Woking. Had joined the Cards from Sutton Coldfield Town in February 2002 after spells at Atherstone United, Redditch United and Hednesford Town.

REED, IAN   *Midfielder*
Current Club: *Stafford Rangers*

D o B: 07/09/1975   *Birthplace: Birmingham*
Midfielder Ian rejoined Stafford Rangers in October 2001 from Worcester City, having previously made five appearances and scored two goals during the 1996/97 season. He began his career with Shrewsbury Town and made his League debut in April 1995 as a substitute against Brighton. Season 1996/97 was a memorable one for Ian as he was a subisute in Shrewsburys

home FA Cup Fourth Round tie against Liverpool. Has also played for Halesowen Town and Nuneaton Borough.

REED, JASON — Forward
Current Club: Selsey

Birthplace: Sussex
Excellent combative striker, who originally enjoyed success with Selsey when they were promoted from Division Two in 1995/96. Went on to play in the Ryman League for Worthing, Bognor Regis and Lewes before featuring in Langney Sports championship side for the second half of 1999/2000. Returned to Selsey in February 2001 (struck 8 times for them that season).

REED, JOHN — Midfielder
Current Club: Gainsborough Trinity

D o B: 27/08/1972   *Birthplace: Rotherham*
Previous clubs include: Ethnikos Perez (Greece) - September 1999, Gainsborough Trinity, Leek T, Gainsborough Trinity, Bury, Blackpool, Sheffield Utd.

REED, MARK — Forward
Current Club: Metropolitan Police

Birthplace: Essex
Previous clubs include: Ford Utd - February 2000, Metropolitan Police, Rainham T, Beckton Utd, Barkingside, West Ham Utd

REED, MARTIN — Defender
Current Club: Gateshead

D o B: 10/01/1978   *Birthplace: Scarborough*
Previous clubs include: Scarborough - August 2001, York C.

REED, NIGEL — Defender
Current Club: Ruislip Manor

D o B: 13/03/1975   *Birthplace: Luton*
Previous clubs include: Wealdstone - March 2002, Dunstable T.

REED, PAUL — Defender
Current Club: Slough Town

Birthplace: Swindon
Paul is a set piece specialist who can operate anywhere down the left flank. So far in his appearances for Ryman Division One North side Slough Town, whom he joined in the summer of 2002, the young full back signed from Swindon has impressed with his work rate and his delivery from dead ball situations. Always looks for the opportunity to get forward and attack down the flank and his ability to provide a telling cross will be invaluable for the Slough front line.

REEDER, MARK — Defender
Current Club: Mildenhall Town

Birthplace: Cambridge
Previous clubs include: Histon - November 2000, Cambridge C.

REES, GAVIN — Defender
Current Club: Carmarthen Town

D o B: 01/11/1978   *Birthplace: Wales*
Previous clubs include: Haverfordwest County - August 1999, Portsmouth.

REES, JASON — Midfielder
Current Club: Tiverton Town

D o B: 22/12/1969   *Birthplace: Aberdare*
Honours won: Wales u-21 & Full Int.
Very experienced midfielder who joined Tiverton Town in July 2002 and was immediately installed as club captain. He originally joined Tivvy from Exeter City in August 2000. However, he left after two months to join Torquay United, where he stayed

and played as team captain until the end of season 2001/02. This Welsh born midfielder made 43 appearances for the Grecians in 1999 scoring four goals. He started his career at Luton Town, where he won Welsh under-21 caps as well as making one appearance for the full Welsh side. Jason made over 250 League appearances playing for Exeter City, Mansfield Town, Portsmouth, Cambridge United and Torquay United.

REES, SHAUN — Defender
Current Club: Tilbury

Birthplace: Essex
From Youth team.

REESON, NICK — Midfielder
Current Club: Wisbech Town

D o B: 05/05/1980
Previous clubs include: Boston Utd - August 2000, Boston T, Lincoln C.

REEVE, ALI — Defender
Current Club: Whyteleafe

Birthplace: Surrey
Ali is a fiercely competitive central midfield player or defender, who joined Ryman Division One South side Whyteleafe in the summer of 2002 from neighbours Croydon. Had been with Croydon since July 1994 when he signed from Dulwich Hamlet. After missing much of his first season with the club through injury, Ali was a regular in the first-team ever since, making over 250 appearances for Croydon.

REEVE, CHRIS — Forward
Current Club: Thornaby on Tees

Birthplace: Cleveland
Previous clubs include: Marske Utd - November 2001.

REEVE, DANNY — Defender
Current Club: Edgware Town

D o B: 10/02/1980   *Birthplace: Essex*
Previous clubs include: Wealdstone - December 2001, Chelmsford C, Colchester Utd, Chelmsford C, Norwich C (Trainee).

REEVE, JAMIE — Midfielder
Current Club: Portland United

D o B: 26/11/1975   *Birthplace: Bournemouth*
Previous clubs include: Bridport - July 1999, Dochester T, Hereford Utd, AFC Bournemouth.

REEVE, PAUL — Midfielder
Current Club: Fakenham Town

Birthplace: Norfolk
Previous clubs include: Watton Utd - March 2000, Diss T, Fakenham T, Wroxham.

REEVE, SIMON — Goalkeeper
Current Club: Didcot Town

Birthplace: Oxfordshire
Simon has proved a more than able deputy when called into the Didcot First Team. Very popular with his colleagues, Simon will give everything for the cause. Excellent shot-stopper.

REGAN, MARTIN — Forward
Current Club: Farsley Celtic

Previous clubs include: Harrogate T - July 1999, Whitby T, Bradford PA, Harrogate T, Garforth T, Harrogate T, Garforth T.

R

REGAN, MIKE   Midfielder
Current Club: Merthyr Tydfil

Birthplace: Wales

Midfielder Mike re-joined Merthyr Tydfil in the close season of 2002 following spells at Dr Martens Western rivals Cinderford Town and League of Wales outfit Port Talbot Town. Originally joined Merthyr from Maesteg Park back in 1999 and proved popular with the fans. Will be remembered for his dazzling display in the unforgettable 4-0 win over arch-rivals Newport County and for being the man who won 15 Frozen Curries on the clubs annual golf day!

REID, ANDY   Defender
Current Club: Hamble ASSC

Birthplace: Hampshire

Previous clubs include: Gosport Borough - July 2000, Horndean, Portsmouth RN.

REID, JAMAL   Forward
Current Club: Windsor & Eton

Birthplace: Surrey

Previous clubs include: Tooting & Mitcham Utd - October 2001, Woking.

REID, JASON   Forward
Current Club: Ringmer

Birthplace: Sussex

Striker, not to be confused with the Selsey player of a similar name. Said to have once been a junior with Liverpool and in good form for Steyning before joining Ringmer during the summer 2000. Top goalscorer for the Blues last season with 19 goals, despite missing the final three months of the campaign because of a knee injury:. Marked his comeback in November 2001 by scoring in the 4-0 defeat of Saltdean Utd.

REID, JORDAN   Midfielder
Current Club: Abingdon United

Birthplace: Oxfordshire

Previous clubs include: Witney Academy - January 2002.

REID, LEWIS   Midfielder
Current Club: Edgware Town

Birthplace: London

Previous clubs include: Molesey - August 2001, Wealdstone, Slough T, Yeovil T, Watford, Millwall.

REID, PHIL   Goalkeeper
Current Club: Peacehaven & Telscombe

Birthplace: Sussex

Goalkeeper who has a wealth of experience, despite still being in his 20s. Currently in his second spell with Peacehaven, having previously played for Worthing, Lewes, Wick, Littlehampton and Burgess Hill.

REID, TOM   Defender
Current Club: Whitby Town

Birthplace: Yorkshire

Tom signed for UniBond Premier side Whitby Town from newly-promoted Harrogate Town in the summer of 2002 and has impressed with performances at right-wing back. Previously with Pickering Town in the Northern Counties East League, he is an excellent corner and free-kick specialist who gives the Seasiders a new dimension.

REID, TONY   Forward
Current Club: Fisher Athletic (London)

D o B: 06/07/1974   *Birthplace: Chelsea*

Previous clubs include: St.Leonards - January 2002, Leatherhead, Edgware T, Tooting & Mitcham Utd, Egham T, Banstead Ath., Croydon, Corinthian Casuals, Molesey, Walton & Hersham, Corinthian Casuals, Carshalton Ath., Raynes Park Vale.

REILLY, CRAIG   Midfielder
Current Club: Staines Town

D o B: 21/05/1976   *Birthplace: Middlesex*

Midfielder Craig started in Staines Town's youth side before going on to help the senior team win promotion to the Premier Division of the Isthmian League. Moved on to Hampton before returning to Staines in July 1999. Left again for Northwood during the summer of 2001 but then took the decision to retire from football before being tempted back by Staines in February 2002.

REILLY, DAVE   Defender
Current Club: Leyton

D o B: 12/07/1973   *Birthplace: Essex*

Helped Leyton to gain promotion to the Ryman League as Essex Senior League champions at the end of the 2001/02 season. An experienced defender who started out as a youngster with Brighton and Fulham but has since served a number of Essex Non-League sides, including East Ham, Fisher, Barking, Ford United and Collier Row. Joined Leyton in the summer of 2000.

REINA, RICKY   Forward
Current Club: Folkestone Invicta

D o B: 02/10/1971   *Birthplace: Folkestone*

Very popular all-action striker who rejoined Folkestone Invicta towards the end of the 2000/01 season after a short spell with Ramsgate. Ricky began his career with Invicta between 1991-95 before signing for Sing Tao in Hong Kong. He then joined Dover Athletic in the Conference before being sold to Brentford for a record £50,000. A series of knee operations took their toll and curtailed Rickys career, although he did score one Football League goal. He returned to Dover but injury forced him out of the game for a while.

REINELT, ROBBIE   Forward
Current Club: Grays Athletic

D o B: 11/03/1974   *Birthplace: Epping*

Prolific goalscorer who joined Grays Athletic from Ryman Premier Division rivals Braintree Town in May 2002 after netting 24 times for the Iron in 2001/02. Played over 150 League games for Aldershot, Colchester, Gillingham, Brighton and Leyton Orient and also had spells with Stevenage Borough and St Albans City. The Epping-born striker has always scored goals.

REIVE, JAMIE   Midfielder
Current Club: Walton Casuals

Birthplace: Surrey

A promising midfield talent, who can pass and tackle when needed, with Chipstead and Banstead at Youth Level, recently re-established a regular first team place.

RELISH, LEE   Defender
Current Club: Cinderford Town

Previous clubs include: Weston-Super-Mare - July 2001, Newport AFC, Hereford Utd, Caldicot T.

RENDALL, JOHN — Goalkeeper
Current Club: Paulton Rovers
Birthplace: Bristol
Previous clubs include: Yate T - February 2000, Keynsham T, Cinderford T, Cardiff C.

RENDALL, MARC — Midfielder
Current Club: Hassocks
Birthplace: Sussex
Dangerous midfielder: part of Hassocks Division Two promotion-winning side in 1994/95: rejoined the club from Ansty Rangers during the 2001 close season.

RENDELL, CARL — Midfielder
Current Club: Witton Albion
Previous clubs include: Winsford Utd - June 2001, Chester C.

RENFORTH, GELN — Forward
Current Club: Eastleigh
Birthplace: Newcastle
Previous clubs include: Whitley Bay - July 2001, Bedlington Terriers, Blyth Spartans, Whitley Bay, Prudhoe T, Blyth Spartans, Everton (Trainee).

RENNISON, SHAUN — Defender
Current Club: Scarborough
D o B: 23/11/1980   Birthplace: Northallerton
Shaun made his first team debut for Scarborough in December of 1998 and was immediately given a six month professional contract before his YTS course had finished. He played 14games up to the end of the season proving he was worth a further contract and signed a two year contract in the May. He is a very mature player for his age and easily copes with all the Conference strikers throw at him. This season Shaun was offered a new one year contract after turning in some excellent defensive displays last season.

RESTARICK, STEVE — Forward
Current Club: Folkestone Invicta
D o B: 28/11/1971   Birthplace: London
A well-known striker in Non-League circles, Steve joined Folkestone Invicta in July 2002. Started out as a schoolboy with Queens Park Rangers. He then moved to Colchester United, where he won both a Vauxhall Conference and FA Trophy winners medal. After moving to Chelmsford City, he then joined Dover Athletic for a five-figure fee. He subsequently played for Purfleet, Gravesend & Northfleet and Crawley, where he spent the 2001/02 season. Steve scored two goals when Gravesend beat Invicta 3-0 in the 2000 Kent Senior Cup Final.

RESTREPO, RAUL — Midfielder
Current Club: Clapton
D o B: 13/12/1983   Birthplace: London
Previous clubs include: Southend Utd - August 2001, Kingstonian.

REVILL, DOMINIC — Defender
Current Club: Lincoln United
Birthplace: Lincoln
Dominic is another player who was welcomed back to Ashby Avenue in July 2000 following spells at Spalding Town and Boston United. He is equally at home in midfield or as a left back.

REW, IAN — Defender
Current Club: Newport Isle Of Wight
D o B: 15/05/1974   Birthplace: Portsmouth
Previous clubs include: Andover - September 1998, Fareham T, Selsey, Fareham T, Gosport B.

REYNOLDS, COLIN — Defender
Current Club: Caersws
D o B: 03/10/1968   Birthplace: Wales
Honours won: Wales Semi-Pro Int.
Former Newtown club captain who leads by example, scoring important goals as well as giving towering performances at the back and in midfield. Had some particularly outstanding games in the FAW Invitation Cup. Has earned two League of Wales caps and one Welsh semi-professional Cap. He is respected by all in the League as a player of class. Switched to LoW rivals Caersws in June 2002 after over 12 years with Newtown.

REYNOLDS, CRAIG — Midfielder
Current Club: Arlesey Town
Birthplace: Stevenage
An exciting midfield prospect, Craig resides in Stevenage where he is employed by the Wine Society. Signed for Ryman Division One North side Arlesey Town in the close season of 2002 from Biggleswade Town, Craig has also turned out for Stotfold.

REYNOLDS, KARL — Defender
Current Club: Mickleover Sports
D o B: 27/02/1979   Birthplace: Derbyshire
Previous clubs include: Borrowash Victoria - January 2002, Gresley Rovers, Borrowash V, Gresley R, Mickleover RBL.

REYNOLDS, LUKE — Forward
Current Club: Willenhall Town
Birthplace: Birmingham
Signed from Tividale in February 2001, a young player with an eye for goals.

REYNOLDS, MICHAEL — Forward
Current Club: Wakefield & Emley
D o B: 19/06/1974   Birthplace: Huddersfield
Able to play on either side, and willing to take on any defence, Michael provided moments of skill to savour forever. The sort of player that gives even the most solid defence the shakes, he comes in for a lot of late tackles, often having two men on him at a time. Not that this usually stops him. Gets his fair share of goals too. Left Emley early in 1999 to join Ayr United for a reported £60,000 transfer fee. Then came back at the start of the 2001-02 season.

REYNOLDS, NEIL — Midfielder
Current Club: Clitheroe
Birthplace: Lancashire
All action battler back after a brief spell at Kendal Town. Missed everything about Shawbridge and forsake the money to come back.

REYNOLDS, TOM — Defender
Current Club: Newtown AFC
Birthplace: Wales
Promising young defender who has done really well in the reserve team and has started to impress this season. Powerful young player with pace and good vision for the game.

R

REYNOLDS, TONY — Goalkeeper
Current Club: Redhill
Birthplace: Kent
Excellent young keeper who joined from Maidstone United. Quickly established himself as a first team regular with a string of excellent performances. Commands his penalty area well and has lightning quick reflexes.

RHEAD, MIKE — Midfielder
Current Club: Atherton Laburnum Rovers
Birthplace: Billinge
A very good player who can operate in all areas of midfield, Mike joined LR from Ashton Town in December 1999. He is a good passer of the ball, always gives 100% and is frequently amongst the goals. Mike is a joiner and he likes listening to music as well as taking an interest in all sports.

RHODES, BEN — Midfielder
Current Club: Harrogate Town
D o B: 02/05/1983 *Birthplace: York*
Promising young midfielder who joined Harrogate Town in May 2002 after being released by York City. Had signed for his hometown club from school and progressed through to make his League debut against Darlington in December 2001.

RHODES, LEE — Midfielder
Current Club: Glapwell
Birthplace: Chesterfield
From Local football - July 2001.

RHODES, PHIL — Defender
Current Club: St.Leonards
Birthplace: Hastings
Former Hastings Town defender who left the Pilot Field to join Hailsham Town during the 2001 close season before moving to Rye & Iden United in the autumn. Switched to Dr Martens Eastern Division neighbours St Leonards in July 2002.

RIATT, DON — Midfielder
Current Club: Bishop Auckland
Previous clubs include: Tow Law T - February 2001, Gateshead, Spennymoor Utd, Darlington, Peterborough Utd.

RIBBENS, PAUL — Midfielder
Current Club: Maidstone United
Birthplace: Kent
Honours won: FA Vase Winners
Previous clubs include: Sittingbourne - July 2001, Ashford T, Deal T, Herne Bay, Sheppey Utd, Slade Green, Furness.

RICE, JORDAN — Midfielder
Current Club: Oldbury United
Birthplace: Birmingham
Previous clubs include: Halesowen T - July 1999.

RICE, MARC — Forward
Current Club: Lewes
Birthplace: Sussex
Forward: one-time junior at Watford who went on to play for Littlehampton, Lewes, Bognor Regis, Havant & Waterlooville and Worthing: faced with a charge of actual bodily harm after an incident during match between the Rebels and Thame Utd in September 2001 which seemed to put his future in jeopardy: followed manager Sammy Donnelly to Southwick in December before re-joining Lewes in February 2002. Also coaches the Brighton Ladies team.

RICHARDS, AARON — Defender
Current Club: Diss Town
Birthplace: Norwich
Previous clubs include: Gorleston - August 2001, Norwich Utd.

RICHARDS, ANDREW — Midfielder
Current Club: Haverfordwest County
D o B: 11/09/1980 *Birthplace: Wales*
Previous clubs include: Fishguard Sports - November 2001.

RICHARDS, DAVE — Defender
Current Club: Dulwich Hamlet
D o B: 31/12/1976 *Birthplace: Birmingham*
Central defender who rejoined Dulwich Hamlet in November 2001 after a short spell with neighbours Croydon. His consistency earned him the Hamlets player of the year award for 2000/01. Prior to moving to London he had gained experience with Walsall and Worcester City.

RICHARDS, DUNCAN — Defender
Current Club: Harrogate Town
Birthplace: Barnsley
Honours won: UniBond League Div.One Winners
Defender Duncan was at Barnsley since he was nine years old, and played for the club at all levels, up to reserve level, where he was a regular. He had joined Harrogate Town on loan for the end of the 2000/01 season, and was signed as a permanent team member in July 2001.

RICHARDS, IAN — Midfielder
Current Club: Bradford Park Avenue
D o B: 05/10/1979 *Birthplace: Barnsley*
Ian started his career at Blackburn Rovers, and then spent a number of seasons with Halifax Town. A hard-working midfield player, he signed for Bradford Park Avenue in August 2001.

RICHARDS, JAMIE — Forward
Current Club: Bridlington Town
Birthplace: Hull
Previous clubs include: Hall Road Rangers - January 2001.

RICHARDS, JAMIE — Forward
Current Club: Leyton Pennant
Birthplace: London
Previous clubs include: East Thurrock Utd - August 2001, Leyton Pennant, St.Margaretsbury, Enfield, Tottenham Hotspur (Junior).

RICHARDS, JON — Midfielder
Current Club: Fleet Town
Birthplace: London
Previous clubs include: Chertsey T - March 2000, Molesey, Chesham Utd, Molesey, Fleet T, Aldershot T, Fulham (Trainee).

RICHARDS, MARC — Midfielder
Current Club: Swindon Supermarine
Birthplace: Gloucester
Previous clubs include: Weston-Super-Mare - February 2002, Cinderford T, Cheltenham T.

RICHARDS, SIMON — Midfielder
Current Club: Colwyn Bay
Previous clubs include: Flexsys Cefn Druids - July 2001, Lex XI.

R

RICHARDSON, JAMES — *Defender*

Current Club: Bedworth United

Birthplace: Coventry

Very talented and definitely one for the future. Jamie is a strong defender and has been in the Bedworth United squad for two years. Powerfully built, he joined Bedworth in July 1999 after a spell with Rushden & Diamonds. A former Coventry City junior.

RICHARDSON, JOE — *Midfielder*

Current Club: Thackley

Birthplace: Yorkshire

Previous clubs include: Bradford Park Avenue - February 2000, Liversedge, Halifax T.

RICHARDSON, JOHN — *Midfielder*

Current Club: Berkhamsted Town

Birthplace: Berkshire

Previous clubs include: Enfield - February 1999, Crawley T, Hendon, Enfield, Slough T, Chesham Utd, Papatoetoe (New Zealand), Chalfont St.Peter, Amersham T.

RICHARDSON, JON — *Defender*

Current Club: Forest Green Rovers

D o B: 29/08/1975   Birthplace: Nottingham

Became one of Nigel Spinks last signings as manager of Conference side Forest Green Rovers when arriving from Oxford United in August 2002. An experienced defender who made over 250 League appearances for Exeter before joining Oxford in the summer of 2000. Added a further 59 games to his tally before being released.

RICHARDSON, LLOYD — *Forward*

Current Club: Droylsden

D o B: 07/10/1977   Birthplace: Dewsbury

Honours won: England Youth Int.

Previous clubs include: Salford C - August 2001, Hyde Utd, Oldham Ath.

RICHARDSON, MARTIN — *Defender*

Current Club: Hailsham Town

Birthplace: Sussex

Defender/midfielder: a product of the clubs successful youth team from 1997: son of former Hailsham manager Steve Richardson.

RICHARDSON, NICK — *Midfielder*

Current Club: Harrogate Town

D o B: 11/04/1967   Birthplace: Halifax

A vastly experienced midfielder who was signed by UniBond Premier side Harrogate Town in the close season of 2002 from York Cuty. He made over 400 League appearances for Halifax Town, Cardiff City, Wrexham, Chester, Bury and York City. Started his career with Emley.

RICHARDSON, PAUL — *Forward*

Current Club: Tow Law Town

Birthplace: Middlesbrough

Prior to joining the Lawyers last season he had been playing in Malaysia and Waterford (but not at the same time!) previously with Spennymoor and Middlesbrough.

RICHARDSON, PAUL — *Midfielder*

Current Club: Hailsham Town

Birthplace: Sussex

Left-sided midfielder (elder brother of Martin Richardson): made his first-team debut for Hailsham in 1996, when still a member of the youth team: has also played for Sussex in his time.

RICHARDSON, REECE — *Defender*

Current Club: Beaconsfield SYCOB

Birthplace: Berkshire

From Youth team.

RICHARDSON, STEVE — *Defender*

Current Club: Cirencester Town

Birthplace: Wilshire

Another player who came through Cirencester Town's successful Academy and has been a regular for the past four seasons. The defender returned to Cirencester in November 2001 after his brief spell at Dr Martens Western rivals Swindon Supermarine.

RICHARDSON, STEVE — *Midfielder*

Current Club: Pagham

Birthplace: Sussex

Made a few first-team appearances for Pagham during 1999/2000: also briefly featured for the side during the early part of 2001/02 and was virtually the only player to stay on at Nyetimber Lane after Richie Reynolds was sacked in November.

RICHENS, KRIS — *Goalkeeper*

Current Club: Clitheroe

Birthplace: Lancashire

In true supporter style, Kris dodgy football parentage, i.e., he played for Stanley, has been conveniently overlooked as he pulls off, at will, strings of top performances. Justifiably singled out as the man of the match in the Vase quarter-final, Kris will be looking to continue his unbroken sequence of appearances.

RICHES, ALEX — *Defender*

Current Club: Bishops Stortford

Birthplace: Essex

Signed by Martin Hayes from Saffron Walden in the summer of 2001. Alex is a versatile defender learning his trade quickly with The Blues and has stepped into his predecessor Gary Kimbles boots with ease. Alex likes to get forward as well, has an improving left foot and scored his senior debut goal against Northwood in the FA Cup in September 2001. One to watch.

RICHES, MARC — *Goalkeeper*

Current Club: Durham City

Birthplace: Newcastle

Previous clubs include: Crook T - September 2000.

RICHMOND, DANNY — *Midfielder*

Current Club: Whitby Town

Birthplace: Bishop Auckland

Impressive midfielder who helped Shildon to win the Albany Northern League Second Division in 2001/02 before signing for UniBond Premier side Whitby Town. Actually began at Shildon before having a spell with West Auckland Town. Returned to Shildon in the summer of 2001.

RICKARD, ANDREW — *Defender*

Current Club: Afan Lido

D o B: 09/11/1970   Birthplace: Wales
Honours won: LoW Rep.

An experienced centre-half, originally signed from Caerau. Has European experience at Lido and also at Inter Cardiff who he joined for a while. Has played for the League of Wales representative side.

RICKARD, JAMIE — *Midfielder*

Current Club: Llanelli AFC

D o B: 24/01/1976   Birthplace: Wales
Previous clubs include: Haverfordwest County - November 2001, Merthyr Tydfil, Gloucester C, Swansea C.

RICKARDS, SCOTT — *Forward*

Current Club: Tamworth

Birthplace: Derby

Local lad Scott signed for Tamworth in July 2001, having spent the previous four seasons at Derby County. He was promoted to the Rams first-team squad for the 2000/01 and also had loan spells with Oldham Athletic, Mansfield and Walsall.

RICKERS, JOHN — *Midfielder*

Current Club: Glasshoughton Welfare

Birthplace: Bradford

Previous clubs include: Guiseley - July 1997, Mansfield T, Bradford C.

RICKETTS, GARY — *Forward*

Current Club: Hucknall Town

Birthplace: Nottingham

Previous clubs include: Hinckley Utd (£1,500) - February 2001, Arnold T, Heanor T.

RICKETTS, JODY — *Midfielder*

Current Club: Clapton

Birthplace: Kent

Previous clubs include: Tonbridge Angels - July 2001, Welling Utd, Gillingham (Junior).

RIDDELL, LEE — *Forward*

Current Club: Hampton & Richmond

Birthplace: Farnborough

Promising young striker who came up through the ranks at Farnborough Town and made a number of senior appearances for the Conference club. Spent part of the 2001/02 season out on-loan with Ryman Leaguers Windsor & Eton and then signed for Premier Division Hampton & Richmond Borough in August 2002.

RIDDLE, STUART — *Forward*

Current Club: Oxford City

Birthplace: America

Previous clubs include: Des Moines Menace (USA) - August 2001.

RIDGEWAY, IAN — *Midfielder*

Current Club: Kettering Town

D o B: 28/12/1975   Birthplace: Nottingham
Previous clubs include: Notts Co - July 1998.

RIDINGS, DAVE — *Midfielder*

Current Club: Stalybridge Celtic

D o B: 27/02/1970   Birthplace: Farnworth
Experienced midfielder, formerly with Halifax Town, where he played in their last game as a Football League club, Dave moved

to Lincoln City, then to Ashton United and Crewe Alexandra before joining Leigh RMI at the beginning of the 1996/97 season. Was one of the clubs longest-serving players before departing to Stalybridge Celtic in May 2002.

RIDLEY, KAI — *Forward*

Current Club: Abingdon United

Birthplace: Buckingham

Previous clubs include: Brackley T - July 2000, Witney T, Brackley T, Buckingham T, Brackley T, Buckingham Ath.

RIDLEY, MARTIN — *Midfielder*

Current Club: Leek Town

D o B: 13/06/1975   Birthplace: Leamington Spa
Honours won: England Youth Int.

Signed for Leek Town from Rocester at the start of the 2001/02 season. Martin was an England youth international whilst with Aston Villa, where he was a professional for one season. Has also played for Leigh RMI. He is a midfielder who is deadly from free-kicks.

RIDOUT, JOHN — *Midfielder*

Current Club: Enfield Town (Essex)

Birthplace: Herts

A member of the Enfield FC Diadora League Championship winning team of 1995. Joined the Es from Harrow Borough, where he picked up both Middlesex Senior and Charity Cup winners medals in the same season. Started his career in the Southern Amateur League with Old Parmitarians. With Harlow Town last season after spells at Billericay, Purfleet and Bishops Stortford.

RIGBY, NEIL — *Defender*

Current Club: Colwyn Bay

D o B: 07/11/1971   Birthplace: Liverpool
An experienced Non-League defender who has regularly switched between the UniBond and League of Wales. Signed for UniBond Premier side Colwyn Bay in August 2002 from LoW outfit Rhyl, having only been with their north Wales coast neighbours since February 2002 after joining from Vauxhall Motors. After starting out at Tranmere and Chester, Neil has since seen service with Marine, Caernarfon Town, Southport, Droylsden, Bangor City and Trafford, and is now in his second spell at Llanellian Road.

RIGBY, PAUL — *Defender*

Current Club: Lancaster City

Birthplace: Lancaster

Paul made his full debut for Lancaster City at the age of 15 in 1992. He then left for a YTS at Dundee, only returning to City colours in 1998 for a brief spell. He then left again, Penrith being one of his clubs, but was back as a reserve team regular in 2000 when City were struck with a defensive crisis. Paul duly stepped up, and hardly put a foot wrong as he became a first-team regular.

RIGG, WAYNE — *Forward*

Current Club: Morpeth Town

Birthplace: Northumberland

Previous clubs include: Ashington - February 2002.

RIGGS, MICKY — *Defender*

Current Club: Arundel

Birthplace: Sussex

Sweeper and former Bognor youth player: featured in Arundels first-team during 1998/99 before appearing mainly for the reserves the following season: regained a regular place in the Mullets Division One line-up from October 2000 onwards.

RIGOGLIOSO, ADRIANO *Forward*
Current Club: Morecambe
D o B: 28/05/1979 *Birthplace: Liverpool*
A tall forward who can play both centre or wide. Signed on a Bosman from Marine before the start of the 2000/01 season. Other previous clubs include Liverpool where in played in the FA Youth Final 1999 against West Ham United.

RILEY, ADRIAN *Defender*
Current Club: Congleton Town
Birthplace: Liverpool
Previous clubs include: Winsford Utd - January 2002, St.Helens T, Garswood Utd, St.Helens T, Ashton T.

RILEY, JON *Forward*
Current Club: Great Harwood Town
Birthplace: Lancashire
Previous clubs include: Clitheroe - July 1999, Darwen, Clitheroe.

RILEY, KEVIN *Forward*
Current Club: Armthorpe Welfare
D o B: 04/03/1972 *Birthplace: Doncaster*
Previous clubs include: Lincoln Utd - October 2001, Gainsborough Trinity, Leek T, Gainsborough Trinity, Armthorpe Welfare, Hatfield Main

RILEY, LEE *Defender*
Current Club: Prescot Cables
Birthplace: Liverpool
Previous clubs include: St Helens T - December 1997.

RILEY, STEVE *Defender*
Current Club: Newport Isle Of Wight
Honours won: Combined Services Rep.
Previous clubs include: Bashley - March 1999, Worthing, Havant T, Basingstoke T, Fareham T.

RIMMER, STEVE *Defender*
Current Club: Marine
D o B: 23/05/1979 *Birthplace: Liverpool*
Defender who rejoined Marine in September 2001 after a short spell with UniBond Premier rivals Hyde United. Has been with Manchester City and Port Vale for whom he played a few games in League. Works for a soccer school as coach.

RINGLAND, CHRIS *Midfielder*
Current Club: Woodley Sports
Birthplace: Manchester
Previous clubs include: Glossop North End - July 2000, East Manchester.

RINSELL, CRAIG *Goalkeeper*
Current Club: Berkhamsted Town
Birthplace: Wycombe
Previous clubs include: Chesham Utd - July 1999, Berkhamsted T, Wycombe Wanderers (Junior).

RIOCH, GREG *Defender*
Current Club: Northwich Victoria
D o B: 24/06/1975 *Birthplace: Sutton Coldfield*
Signed for Conference club Northwich Victoria in the summer of 2002 after a nine-year professional career which included almost 200 League appearances. The son of former Scotland star Bruce Rioch, Greg started his career with Luton and then had spells with Peterborough, Hull, Macclesfield and Shrewsbury before joining the Vics.

RIORDAN, JAMIE *Defender*
Current Club: Ashton United
Previous clubs include: Ossett Alb - February 2000, Liversedge.

RIPLEY, ANDY *Midfielder*
Current Club: Billingham Synthonia
Birthplace: Cleveland
Previous clubs include: Billingham T - December 1999.

RISBRIDGER, GARETH *Midfielder*
Current Club: Aylesbury United
D o B: 16/04/1982 *Birthplace: Bucks*
Started his career at Marlow in the 1997/98 season playing in their under 18 team. Joined Yeovil Town in the summer of 1998 and in the three seasons he was with them, he played for the under 18 side, reserve side and the first team side. Left Yeovil Town in the summer of 2001 and joined Southend United on a full time contract. During his time at Southend, he made six appearances for them of which 5 was as a substitute. He was loaned out to Dover Athletic by Southend and made 3 appearances for them. Gareth holds a UEFA B coaching badge and is a qualified referee. Joined Salisbury in February 2002 on his release from Southend and then switched to Aylesbury a month later.

RISHMAN, BARRY *Midfielder*
Current Club: Selsey
Birthplace: Sussex
Bulky midfielder who has been around at Selsey since the 1980s (had a spell at Littlehampton about ten years ago). Inspirational member of the team.

RISHTON, GARY *Defender*
Current Club: Rossendale United
Birthplace: Lancashire
Experienced Non-League defender who has spent the majority of his playing days with North West Counties League sides Rossendale United, Bacup Borough and Clitheroe and has also had a couple of stints with Haslingden. Re-joined Rossendale in September 2000 and played a major part in the clubs promotion to the UniBond League.

RISLEY, MARK *Defender*
Current Club: Hornchurch
Birthplace: Essex
Experienced defender who signed for Ryman League Division One North club Hornchurch in June 2002 from Premier Division Grays Athletic. Had signed for Grays from Bishops Stortford in January 2002, and was a Grays player for a number of years prior to that until the mass move of players two years ago, and should be a steadying influence on the young Blues side.

RISLEY, PETER *Defender*
Current Club: Aylesbury United
D o B: 08/04/1966 *Birthplace: Hertfordshire*
Previous clubs include: St.Albans C - August 2001, Bishops Stortford, Harrow B, St.Albans C, Dagenham, Bishops Stortford, Ware, Hoddesdon T.

RITCHIE, SCOTT *Defender*
Current Club: Ashington
Birthplace: Northumberland
Previous clubs include: Seaton Delaval - July 2000.

RIVERS, MARC — Midfielder

Current Club: Hungerford Town

D o B: 17/09/1975   Birthplace: Reading

Midfielder who was club captain for Ryman Division Two side in2001/02 and is also the Football Development Officer with Reading FC. Well-travelled player who joined Hungerford at the start of the 2001/02 season from AC Newbury, having previously had spells with the likes of Tooting & Mitcham United, Wokingham Town, Thatcham Town, Andover, Kintbury Rangers and Dorking.

RIVIERE, ANTHONY — Midfielder

Current Club: Welling United

D o B: 09/11/1978   Birthplace: Kent

Highly-rated midfield player who joined Welling United from Kent League side Faversham Town in July 1999 and quickly established himself at Conference level. Strong-running and skilful, he has been the subject of frequent interest from the scouting fraternity.

ROACH, NEVILLE — Forward

Current Club: Basingstoke Town

D o B: 29/09/2001   Birthplace: Reading

Reading-born forward with plenty of League experience. Began his career with his home town club Reading and then had spells with Southend and Oldham before going Non-League with Kingstonian and St Albans City. Returned for a half a season in the League with Torquay and then had a brief stint at Conference club Stevenage Borough before joining Ryman Leaguers Slough Town in December 2001. Switched to Premier Division Basingstoke Town in the summer of 2002.

ROACH, SIMON — Defender

Current Club: Brigg Town

Birthplace: Hull

From Local football - July 1990.

ROACH, STEWART — Forward

Current Club: Lowestoft Town

Birthplace: Great Yarmouth

Previous clubs include: Great Yarmouth T - August 2001.

ROAST, PAUL — Forward

Current Club: Wimborne Town

Birthplace: Dorset

Previous clubs include: Dorchester T - July 2000, Allendale.

ROBERTS, BARRY — Forward

Current Club: Stanway Rovers

Birthplace: Essex

Previous clubs include: Wivenhoe T - July 2001, Clacton T, Sudbury W, Billericay T, Cornard Utd, Harwich & Parkeston, Grays Ath., Dagenham & Redbridge, Heybridge Swifts, Uxbridge, Harrow B, Wivenhoe T, Braintree T, Chelmsford C.

ROBERTS, DANNY — Defender

Current Club: Fleet Town

Birthplace: London

Previous clubs include: Bromley - July 2001, Leatherhead.

ROBERTS, DANNY — Forward

Current Club: Wivenhoe Town

D o B: 12/11/1975   Birthplace: Chelmsford

Right-sided wide man who can also do a job at full back. Deceptively quick and determined with a capacity for hard work. Re-joined Ryman Division One North side Wivenhoe Town in the summer of 2002 from Heybridge Swifts. Had signed for the Swifts from Wivenhoe in July 2001 after previous experience with Colchester, Sudbury Town, Harwich & Parkeston, Chelmsford City and Clacton Town.

ROBERTS, DARREN — Forward

Current Club: Worksop Town

D o B: 12/10/1969   Birthplace: Birmingham

Vastly experienced striker who started his career in Non-League football with Burton Albion before embarking on a long and successful spell as a professional with the likes of Wolves, Chesterfield, Darlington, Scarborough and Exeter. Returned to the semi-pro stage with Barrow and then helped Tamworth to the runners-up spot in the Dr martens League Premier Division in 2001/02 before switching to Worksop Town in May 2002.

ROBERTS, DAVE — Defender

Current Club: Corinthian Casuals

Birthplace: Wales

Dave is a solid and reliable defender who joined Corinthian Casuals in July 1998. Has played for Rhyl in the League of Wales. He is also a hard-working committee member with the club.

ROBERTS, DEAN — Forward

Current Club: Armthorpe Welfare

Birthplace: Sheffield

Previous clubs include: Hatfield Main - March 2001, Goole T, JI Case, Hatfield Main, Denaby Utd, Sheffield Utd.

ROBERTS, DEAN — Forward

Current Club: Evesham United

Previous clubs include: Kidderminster Harriers - August 1999, Pershore T, Evesham Utd.

ROBERTS, DUNCAN — Goalkeeper

Current Club: St.Albans City

D o B: 24/06/1979   Birthplace: Norwich

Goalkeeper who made his debut for the St Albans City at Ware in Herts Charity Cup in August 2000 shortly after arriving from Ryman Premier rivals Harrow Borough. Had spells at both Norwich City and Mansfield earlier in his career and has also turned out for Kings Lynn, Spalding United and Wisbech Town.

ROBERTS, GLYN — Midfielder

Current Club: AFC Sudbury

D o B: 19/10/1974   Birthplace: Ipswich

New signing for Clacton from Ipswich Wanderers. Ex-pro with Rotherham and plays up front or attacking midfield. Holds the ball up well, and will no doubt be scoring goals.

ROBERTS, GRAHAM — Midfielder

Current Club: Colwyn Bay

D o B: 16/09/1968   Birthplace: Wales

Honours won: Wales Semi-Pro Int.

Graham is a Welsh semi-professional International and has been at Colwyn Bay for nine years, apart from a short spell at Macclesfield Town, and regularly features among the goals. Previous clubs include British Steel, Mold Alexandra, Flint Town United and Caernarfon Town. He was originally a forward but is now playing very successfully in midfield.

ROBERTS, JAMIE — Midfielder

Current Club: Hucknall Town

Birthplace: Yorkshire

Jamie is an excellent passer of the ball, and also a penalty expert. Started his career with Doncaster Rovers before going Non-League with Bridlington Town, Worksop Town and Eastwood Town.

Signed for Hucknall Town in September 1996 and played a major role in the Nottinghamshire sides progression through the Non-League Pyramid to the UniBond Premier.

ROBERTS, MICHAEL — *Midfielder*
Current Club: Fisher Athletic (London)
Previous clubs include: Greenwich Borough - July 2001, Fisher Ath., Faversham T, Millwall (Trainee).

ROBERTS, OWAIN — *Midfielder*
Current Club: Colwyn Bay
D o B: 23/06/1979   *Birthplace: Wales*
Young midfield player who signed for UniBond Premier side Colwyn Bay from Ruthin Town in Augsut 2000. Shows great potential for the future and has firmly cemented a place for himself in the Bay side.

ROBERTS, PAUL — *Defender*
Current Club: Selby Town
Birthplace: Leeds
Honours won: FA Youth Cup Winners
Previous clubs include: Farsley Celtic - July 2000, Pontefract Collieries, Glasshoughton Welfare, Congleton T, Glasshoughton Welfare, Emley, Leeds Utd (Trainee).

ROBERTS, PAUL — *Defender*
Current Club: Walton Casuals
Birthplace: Surrey
6 3 left footed, strong defender in his third season with Casuals also possesses a massive throw, progressed through the Reserves to establish himself as a first team regular last season. Currently Club captain.

ROBERTS, PAUL — *Defender*
Current Club: Caernarfon Town
D o B: 08/08/1982   *Birthplace: Chester*
Previous clubs include: Chester C - March 2002.

ROBERTS, PAUL — *Defender*
Current Club: Erith & Belvedere
Birthplace: Kent
Honours won: FA Vase Winners
Strong reliable defender who rejoined Erith & Belvedere in July 2000 after gaining an FA Vase winners medal with Deal Town in 2000. An excellent defensive organiser.

ROBERTS, PAUL — *Forward*
Current Club: Bangor City
D o B: 29/07/1977   *Birthplace: Bangor*
Honours won: Wales u-21 Int.
League of Wales side Bangor City's longest serving player. A Welsh under-21 International, Paul was originally signed from Wrexham - whom he joined in a £15,000 transfer deal. He then returned to his original club Porthmadog for a short spell as a full-time as Football in the Community Officer before rejoining Bangor in January 1999.

ROBERTS, SEAN — *Defender*
Current Club: Harrogate Town
Birthplace: Hull
Honours won: UniBond League Div.One Winners
Sean is a defender who began his career as a trainee with Hull City. A 2001 close season signing for Harrogate Town from local football, he went on to help the club to win the UniBond Division One title.

ROBERTS, SIMON — *Midfielder*
Current Club: Clacton Town
Birthplace: Essex
New Signing for Clacton from Dartford in the new year. Very physical midfielder, capable of winning all his battles.

ROBERTS, TONY — *Goalkeeper*
Current Club: Dagenham & Redbridge
D o B: 04/08/1969   *Birthplace: Holyhead*
Honours won: Wales u-21, Full & Semi-Pro Int.
Tony joined Dagenham & Redbridge during the 2000 close season having spent the previous six months coaching in the States. He began his career as a trainee at QPR and progressed through the ranks to full professional. During his time at Loftus Road he made two under-21 appearances for Wales, both in 1991 against England and Poland. Two years later he came on as a substitute for Neville Southall to gain his first full International cap against Eire, winning a second cap in 1997. After playing 122 League games in 11 years at QPR, he moved across London to the New Den where he spent a season playing for Millwall. At the start of the 1999/2000 season, he moved into the Semi-pro game and joined St Albans where he remained until March when he crossed the Atlantic. Tony became the first Welshman to gain caps at Pro and Semi-Pro level when he played in the game against England at Rushden in February 2001.

ROBERTSON, GRAHAM — *Midfielder*
Current Club: Dartford
D o B: 02/11/1976   *Birthplace: Edinburgh*
Previous clubs include: Tonbridge Angels - February 2002, East Fife, Raith Rovers, Millwall, Raith Rovers.

ROBERTSON, JOHN — *Defender*
Current Club: Southport
D o B: 08/01/1974   *Birthplace: Liverpool*
John signed for Conference side Southport in the summer of 2001 from rivals Northwich Victoria. He is a vastly experienced centre-half who started out as a YTS player with Wigan and graduated to the Football League side, making 108 appearances between 1992 and 1995 and scoring four times. John then moved on to Lincoln City where he made an additional 38 appearances in a two-year spell.

ROBERTSON, PAUL — *Defender*
Current Club: Kidsgrove Athletic
D o B: 05/02/1972   *Birthplace: Manchester*
Honours won: NWCL Winners
Vastly experienced left-sided defender, who signed for Kidsgrove from Mossley in February 2002. Was a member of the Altrincham side that won the UniBond league in 1998/99 and has also featured with Runcorn, Hyde United, Droylsden, Accrington Stanley and Witton Albion as well as in the Football League for Stockport, Bury and Doncaster Rovers.

ROBERTSON, PAUL — *Defender*
Current Club: Washington
Birthplace: Durham
Previous clubs include: Spennymoor Utd - January 2002, Durham C, Nissan.

ROBINS, MARK — *Defender*
Current Club: Chertsey Town
Birthplace: London
Signed in the summer from Maidenhead United. A defender who originally started his career at Fulham.

R

ROBINSON, ADAM — Defender
Current Club: Saltdean United

D o B: 03/06/1981 — Birthplace: Hastings
Previous clubs include: Seaford T - July 2001, Newhaven, Brighton University.

ROBINSON, ANTHONY — Forward
Current Club: Stratford Town

D o B: 31/12/1979 — Birthplace: Birmingham
Previous clubs include: Paget Rangers - March 2002, Stourbridge, Bilston T, Bedworth Utd, Kidderminster Harriers, Coventry C, Birmingham C.

ROBINSON, COLIN — Midfielder
Current Club: Potters Bar Town

D o B: 13/11/1967 — Birthplace: Lancashire
Previous clubs include: Ruislip Manor - July 2001, Northwood, Wealdstone, Hayes, Gateshead, Burnley.

ROBINSON, DAN — Goalkeeper
Current Club: Burton Albion

D o B: 01/09/1982 — Birthplace: Derby
Dan joined Conference club Burton Albion from Blackpool in the summer of 2002 on trial and a series of impressive performances in pre-season friendlies secured a contract for the 20-year-old goalkeeper. He was at Derby County as a schoolboy before moving to the north-west coast club where he was a regular in their reserve side.

ROBINSON, DAVID — Defender
Current Club: Tamworth

Birthplace: Nottingham
Previous clubs include: Kings Lynn - March 2002, Grantham T, Gresley R, Ilkeston T, Heanor T.

ROBINSON, DAVID — Midfielder
Current Club: Accrington Stanley

D o B: 30/10/1974 — Birthplace: Wrekin
Central midfielder who signed for Accrington Stanley from Runcorn in September 2001 for £4,000. Described by Rucorns website as a tall strong midfielder who scores the odd spectacular goal. Has also played at Ashton United.

ROBINSON, GRAEME — Forward
Current Club: Whitby Town

D o B: 15/07/1974 — Birthplace: South Africa
Honours won: South Africa Youth Int., FA Vase Winners
Returned to Whitby Town in July 1998 after having played one season at Gateshead. His work rate creates numerous chances for both himself & others. Grahams a former South Africa junior International and firm favourite with the Whitby crowd. He was also a member of the Northern League Championship winning side of 1996/97 and member of the FA Carlsberg Vase-winning team at Wembley in the same season.

ROBINSON, IAN — Midfielder
Current Club: Ilkeston Town

D o B: 25/08/1978 — Birthplace: Gedling
Ian is now in his third spell at Ilkeston Town. He was born in Gedling and after shining in schools football he signed for Mansfield Town. He made a total of 17 appearances for the Stags before joining he Robins for a months loan in 1997. At the start of the next season he rejoined Ilkeston and proved to be an inspirational influence in midfield. It was no surprise when he became the target of bigger clubs and eventually he signed for Hednesford Town. During the 2000/01 season he linked up again with former boss Keith Alexander in a brief spell on loan at Northwich Victoria, and then proved to be one of Ilkestons most important signings when he returned again in July 2001.

ROBINSON, JAMES — Goalkeeper
Current Club: Hitchin Town

D o B: 12/04/1978 — Birthplace: Hitchin
Local lad who returned to first team action following Darren Bonfields move to Boreham Wood towards the end of season 2000/2001. Made his debut as a teenager before going to University in Wales where he played in the League of Wales for Inter Cardiff. Also a distinguished cricketer.

ROBINSON, KARL — Forward
Current Club: Marine

Previous clubs include: Bamber Bridge - November 2001, Marine, Caernarfon T, Swindon T.

ROBINSON, LES — Defender
Current Club: Hednesford Town

D o B: 01/03/1967 — Birthplace: Shirebrook
One of the most experienced players to have moved into Non-League football during the 2002 summer. Les signed for Dr Martens Premier side Hednesford Town after a professional career spanning almost twenty years and more than 600 League appearances. Started out at Chesterfield and then had spells with Mansfield, Stockport, Doncaster, Oxford and Mansfield again.

ROBINSON, LIAM — Forward
Current Club: Stocksbridge Park Steels

D o B: 20/12/1965 — Birthplace: Bradford
Previous clubs include: Stalybridge Celtic - February 2000, Northwich V, Scarborough, Burnley, Bristol C, Bury, Huddersfield T, Nottingham Forest.

ROBINSON, MARK — Defender
Current Club: Bedworth United

Birthplace: Coventry
Mark is a confident defender, strong on the ball and has a good mind. In his second spell as a footballer, he left the game three years ago to set up his own business. Originally with Hinckley United, he joined Bedworth United at the start of the 2001/02 season from Dr Martens rivals Rugby United.

ROBINSON, MARK — Defender
Current Club: Chippenham Town

D o B: 21/11/1968 — Birthplace: Rochdale
Honours won: Division Two Winners
Mark is a vastly experienced defender who joined Dr Martens Premier newcomers Chippenham Town in July 2002 after being forced to quit the full-time game through injury with Swindon Town. Former Swindon boss John Gorman paid £600,000 for Marks services from Newcastle United after Swindons relegation from the Premier League, and he was a regular member of the first-team squad. When his contract was up at the end of 1999/00, he was widely tipped to leave the club - but he was offered a new deal when Colin Todd arrived and he was given the captaincy by Todd, but he lost it to Alan Reeves upon Andy Kings arrival at the County Ground. Started his career with West Brom and also played for Barnsley and amassed more than 450 League appearances.

ROBINSON, MARK — Forward
Current Club: Weymouth

D o B: 09/03/1976 — Birthplace: Canterbury
Mark joined from Gravesend and Northfleet, and is now in his 5th season with the club, having just signed a new three year contract. Will look to be a major part in this side after having won last years Player of the year and Players' Player of the year.

R

ROBINSON, NEIL — Forward
Current Club: Bishop Auckland
Birthplace: Bishop Auckland
Drafted in from the Bishop Auckland under-18 team, and made his debut as a substitute in the NPL Cup game v Whitby Town in November 2000. Fast, aggressive, and a prolific scorer for the U18 team.

ROBINSON, PHIL — Defender
Current Club: Bamber Bridge
D o B: 28/09/1980   Birthplace: Manchester
Previous clubs include: Blackpool - July 2001.

ROBINSON, PHIL — Midfielder
Current Club: Stafford Rangers
D o B: 06/01/1967   Birthplace: Stratford
Appointed as player-manager at Dr Martens League Premier Division club Stafford Rangers in May 2002, Phil was Hereford United's player-coach after signing for the Bulls from Stoke City in the summer of 2000. He enjoyed a distinguished career, mainly in the lower leagues, but can count Aston Villa, Wolves, Huddersfield and Chesterfield among his former clubs.

ROBINSON, RICHARD — Defender
Current Club: Moor Green
D o B: 13/11/1979   Birthplace: Birmingham
Signed for Moor Green in the summer of 1999 from GMP Sports. Made his debut as a forward but has recently been converted into a very effective central defender.

ROBINSON, STEVE — Defender
Current Club: Grays Athletic
D o B: 31/01/1976   Birthplace: Edmonton
Joined Grays Athletic last season, he has seen service at Cheshunt, and Edgware, a strong powerfull defender who loves to come up and join in the attacks.

ROBINSON, STEVE — Defender
Current Club: Hall Road Rangers
Birthplace: Hull
Previous clubs include: Goole AFC - October 2001, Denaby Utd, Brigg T, North Ferriby Utd, Hatfield Main, Winterton R, North Ferriby Utd.

ROBINSON, STEVE — Midfielder
Current Club: Dartford
D o B: 07/09/1963   Birthplace: Kent
Previous clubs include: Maidstone Utd - January 2002, Sittingbourne, Ashford T, Dartford, Welling Utd, Dartford, Redbridge Forest, Dartford, Arsenal.

ROBINSON, TONY — Midfielder
Current Club: Coalville Town
Birthplace: Leicester
Honours won: Leicestershire Senior League Winners
Previous clubs include: Barwell - July 1999, Anstey Nomads, Barwell, Barlestone St Giles, Hinckley FC, Leicester Utd, Hinckley T, Leicester Utd, Leicester C (Trainee).

ROBISON, DARREN — Midfielder
Current Club: Newport County
D o B: 19/05/1971   Birthplace: Plymouth
Honours won: Combined Services Rep.
Signed for Newport County from Trowbridge Town in 1998 since when he has played over 150 times for the club. Darren is a particular crowd favourite and enhanced his reputation as a

competitor by playing in goal for the last two games of the 2000/01 season. Capable of playing in defence, midfield ot attack, he started his career with Millbrook in the South-Western League, moving on to Falmouth Town, Truro City, Witney Town and Weston-Super-Mare before joining Trowbridge. Is a Combined Services representative.

ROBSHAW, JAMIE — Forward
Current Club: Alfreton Town
Birthplace: Sheffield
Highly-rated forward who joined UniBond First Division side Alfreton Town in July 2002 after a spell with relegated Ossett Albion. Jamie had signed for Albion in January 2002 when the club were hoping his goals would save them from an immediate return to the NCEL. However, although he did his bit, Ossett were relegated. Originally on the books at Rotherham and Lincoln, he has also seen service with Denaby United and Emley.

ROBSON, DARREN — Midfielder
Current Club: Bashley
D o B: 18/11/1969   Birthplace: Portsmouth
Previous clubs include: Newport IOW - March 2000, Basingstoke T, Aldershot T, Farnborough T, Worthing, Southwick, Gosport B, Basingstoke T, Waterlooville.

ROBSON, DAVID — Forward
Current Club: Brandon United
Birthplace: Co.Durham
Can play in a number of positions and has electrifying pace, which always causes problems to the opposition. Now in his fourth season at the club, having signed from Annfield Plain. David has had previous Northern League experience with Consett and Seaham Red Star.

ROBSON, GLEN — Forward
Current Club: Blyth Spartans
D o B: 25/09/1977   Birthplace: Sunderland
Signed for UniBond Premier side Blyth Spartans in July 1999 from Harrogate Town. Glen was the second top scorer in the UniBond First Division during the 1998/99 season and joined the club after lengthy transfer negotiations. Took a while to score his first goal but has struck 11 times in 14 games. He then suffered a serious injury in November 1999 which saw him miss the remainder of that season. His recovery was complete in a season that saw him score a hat-full of goals. Started his career at Rochdale.

ROBSON, MARK — Midfielder
Current Club: Aveley
D o B: 22/05/1969   Birthplace: Newham
Previous clubs include: Charlton Ath - January 2001, Boreham Wood, Notts Co., Charlton Ath., West Ham Utd, Tottenham Hotspur, Exeter C.

ROBSON, MICHAEL — Midfielder
Current Club: Spennymoor United
Birthplace: Co.Durham
Previous clubs include: Marske Utd - February 2002, Whitby T, Sunderland.

ROBSON, NEIL — Defender
Current Club: Carshalton Athletic
Birthplace: Surrey
A Carshalton Athletic favourite having been voted as player of the season on a number of occasions. Has also played for Sutton United, Dorking, Epsom & Ewell and Molesey, from whom he re-joined Carshalton in August 1995.

ROBSON, STEVE — Forward
Current Club: Ashington
Birthplace: Sunderland
Previous clubs include: Consett - July 2000, Tow Law T, Sunderland.

ROBSON, TOM — Defender
Current Club: Desborough Town
Birthplace: Market Harborough
Previous clubs include: Rothwell T - August 2002.

ROCHE, LEE — Midfielder
Current Club: Paget Rangers
D o B: 25/04/1981   Birthplace: Birmingham
Previous clubs include: Tamworth - July 2001, Sutton Coldfield T.

ROCHESTER, DANNY — Forward
Current Club: Tiptree United
Birthplace: Essex
Previous clubs include: Tiptree Heath - July 1999.

ROCHESTER, DANNY — Midfielder
Current Club: Willenhall Town
Birthplace: Stoke
Signed for Willenhall in January 2002 from Stafford Town. Solid player who is a menace to defences.

RODDIS, NICK — Midfielder
Current Club: Aldershot Town
D o B: 18/02/1973   Birthplace: Rotherham
Honours won: England Semi-Pro Int., British Universities Rep.
England semi-professional international midfielder who joined Ryman Premier side Aldershot Town in August 2002 from Conference outfit Margate. Has also represented and captained Great Britain in the World University Games at the last three games. Was previously on the books at clubs such as Nottingham Forest, Aston Villa and Mansfield. But his first team break came under current Aldershot boss Terry Brown when he joined Hayes in the Conference. After a season there he moved on to Woking where he became popular as a ruthless and tenacious midfielder who adds bite to the engine room. Moved on to Margate after a public spat with Woking following his decision to travel with the GB University squad to China with two of his team mates instead of opening the 2001-02 season at Kingfield. Nicks experience adds an edge to the Shots squad and gives Terry Brown more steel at the heart of the midfield.

RODEN, CRAIG — Midfielder
Current Club: Armthorpe Welfare
Birthplace: Rotherham
Previous clubs include: Harrogate T - August 2001, Rotherham Utd.

RODGERS, ALAN — Defender
Current Club: Portland United
Birthplace: Dorset
Previous clubs include: Bridport - July 2000, Weymouth Sports, Weymouth, AFC Bournemouth (Trainee).

RODGERSON, IAN — Midfielder
Current Club: Hereford United
D o B: 09/04/1966   Birthplace: Hereford
Ian joined Hereford in the summer of 1997 from Cardiff City. Thsi is his second spell at Edgar Street, having been with the club back in the 1980s when he served his apprenticeship with the Bulls after being at neighbouring Hellenic League side Pegasus Juniors. After moving from Hereford he went to Birmingham City and then Sunderland before joining Cardiff, making over 300 League appearances in all.

RODOSTHENOUS, MIKE — Midfielder
Current Club: Enfield
D o B: 25/08/1976   Birthplace: Islington
Previous clubs include: Cheshunt - December 2000 - Plymouth Argyle, Cambridge Utd, WBA.

RODWELL, JIM — Defender
Current Club: Farnborough Town
D o B: 20/11/1970   Birthplace: Lincoln
Honours won: Conference Winners, Dr Martens League Premier Div.Winners
Towering central defender, Jim joined Conference side Farnborough Town in August 2002 after helping Boston United to win the Conference title - his second successive championship with two clubs. Had signed for Boston on a free transfer from Rushden & Diamonds in February 2002. He had been with the Diamonds since May 1996 and had made 84 appearances for them, scoring four goals. He also appeared on the TV show Britains Brainiest Footballer, finishing third! Has also seen service with Hednesford Town, Nuneaton Borough, Bedworth United and Darlington.

ROFE, DANNY — Defender
Current Club: Newport Isle Of Wight
Previous clubs include: Salisbury C - July 2000, Yate T, Bristol R (Trainee).

ROGAN, MICK — Defender
Current Club: Romford
Birthplace: Essex
Previous clubs include: Aveley - February 2001, Barking, Billericay T, Collier Row, Cheshunt, Walthamstow Ave., Southgate Ath., Enfield.

ROGAN, PAUL — Midfielder
Current Club: Barking & East Ham United
D o B: 10/02/1968   Birthplace: London
Vastly experienced midfielder who is in his third spell with Barking, having re-joined in January 2001 from Essex neighbours Romford. Formerly with Ford United, Northwood, Collier Row, Cheshunt, Boreham Wood and Enfield, Paul began a a junior with QPR and Spurs. A very popular player with both supporters and officials.

ROGERS, EAMONN — Defender
Current Club: London Colney
Birthplace: Herts
Previous clubs include: Welwyn Garden C - July 1998, Hatfield T.

ROGERS, JOEL — Forward
Current Club: Epsom And Ewell
Birthplace: Surrey
Joined Epsom in October 2001, former professional with Colchester United, has also played for Banstead Athletic, Carshalton Athletic, Heybridge Swifts and Cheirnsford City.

ROGERS, LEE — Defender
Current Club: Barrow
D o B: 28/10/1966   Birthplace: Doncaster
Born in Doncaster, Lee is an experienced defender who began his League career with Doncaster Rovers but was released without making a League appearance for the Belle Vue outfit. He joined Chesterfield and quickly established himself as a first-team regular. He made a total of 334 League appearances for the Saltergate outfit, scoring once before being released in the summer of 1998. He spent the 1998/99 season with Gainsborough Trinity but left last summer to join Grantham Town in the Dr Martens Premier Division. He joined Barrow in November 1999 and made his debut in a goalless draw at Colwyn Bay.

ROGERS, SCOTT — Midfielder

Current Club: Tiverton Town

D o B: 23/05/1979 — Birthplace: Bristol

Honours won: FA Vase Winners

Son of former Exeter City and Tiverton Town favourite Peter Rogers, Scott is cousin to manager Martyn Rogers. Scored the winning goal, after coming on as substitute, at Wembley for Tivvy to retain the FA Vase, a feat that will go down in the annals of Tivvy footballing history. Scott started his footballing career in Tiverton as a junior with Twyford Spartans. He also played for Exeter City as a schoolboy before serving an apprenticeship with Bristol City. Since joining Tivvy in 1997 he has matured and developed his game and it is surely only a matter of time before he finds himself playing in the Football League.

ROLLASON, LEE — Forward

Current Club: Stourbridge

Birthplace: Wolverhampton

Previous clubs include: Tipton T - December 2001, Bilston T, Blakenall, Bilston T, Bloxwich T, Bilston T, Paget R, Blakenall, Sutton Coldfield T, Telford Utd, Tipton T.

ROLLINS, MARK — Forward

Current Club: Windsor & Eton

D o B: 19/06/1979 — Birthplace; London

Previous clubs include: Kingstonian - August 2001.

ROLLO, JIM — Midfielder

Current Club: Bath City

D o B: 22/05/1976 — Birthplace: Birmingham

Experienced utility player, capable of performing in a variety of positions. Joined Bath City in May 2002 from Merthyr Tydfil, although it wasn't the first time hed signed for Bath as hed previously enjoyed two loan spells at Twerton Park in the past. Originally with Bristol-based side Yate Town, he made a handful of League appearances for Walsall and also had a brief spell with Cardiff before returning to Non-League football with Forest Green Rovers, Clevedon and Merthyr.

ROMUALD, BOUADJI — Defender

Current Club: Carshalton Athletic

Birthplace: France

Promising young defender who began his career at French club Saint Etienne before joining Ryman Division One South side Carshalton Athletic in the summer of 2002/03.

RONAN, KEVIN — Midfielder

Current Club: Ossett Albion

Birthplace: Sheffield

Previous clubs include: Denaby Utd - February 2002, Stocksbridge Park Steels, Denaby Utd, Maltby MW, Harworth Cl, Worksop T, Spalding Utd, Arcadia Shepherds (South Africa), Stoke C.

ROONEY, GLEN — Midfielder

Current Club: Ludlow Town

Birthplace: Shropshire

Previous clubs include: Shifnal T - July 2001, Donnington Wood.

ROONEY, MARK — Defender

Current Club: Dagenham & Redbridge

Birthplace: London

Mark joined the Daggers just before the transfer deadline in March 2001 from St Albans City for a four-figure fee. He spent two seasons at Clarence Park having signed in the summer of 1999 from Aylesbury United. Although a regular in the Watford Reserve side he never progressed through to the Hornets first team. Mark played for the Ryman League Representative side in their match against the FA XI in November 2000.

ROOTES, MICHAEL — Midfielder

Current Club: Tooting & Mitcham United

D o B: 26/01/1974 — Birthplace: Surrey

Midfielder who joined Ryman Division One North side Tooting & Mitcham United in the summer of 2000 from neighbours Leatherhead. Started out as a junior at Wimbledon and then had spell with Woking before joining Tooting for the first time. Switched to Molesey in August 1996, followed manager Mick Browne to Dulwich Hamlet in March 1997 and then moved to Leatherhead.

ROPER, ADIE — Defender

Current Club: Swindon Supermarine

Birthplace: Gloucestershire

Previous clubs include: Cirencester T - July 2000, Fairford T, Swindon Supermarine, Cirencester T, Pinehurst.

ROPKE, TONY — Midfielder

Current Club: Southwick

Birthplace: Sussex

Vastly experienced midfielder: began 2001/02 with Redhill until joining Southwick (one of his many former clubs, which also include Horsham, Ringmer, Whitehawks and Crowborough) during November.

ROSCOE, DAMIAN — Forward

Current Club: Holmer Green

Birthplace: Bucks

Previous clubs include: Penn & Tylers Green - July 1997.

ROSE, ANDY — Defender

Current Club: Maidenhead United

D o B: 09/08/1978 — Birthplace: Ascot

Previous clubs include: Harrow Borough - July 2001, Oxford Utd.

ROSE, CHRIS — Forward

Current Club: Ford United

D o B: 02/12/1975 — Birthplace: Hammersmith

Honours won: Ryman League Div.One Winners

A well-respected forward whose career began at West Ham United. After being released from Upton Park Chris embarked on a successful goalscoring career in Non-League football with the likes of Romford, Barkingside, Barking and Grays Athletic before joining Ford United in September 2001 and helping the club to promotion to the Ryman League Premier Division.

ROSE, CHRIS — Midfielder

Current Club: Hampton & Richmond

Birthplace: Surrey

Defender or midfielder who joined Hampton & Richmond Borough in the summer of 2002 from Farnborough Town, where he was a product of their youth team.

ROSE, COLIN — Midfielder

Current Club: Witton Albion

D o B: 22/01/1972 — Birthplace: Winsford

Honours won: England Semi-Pro Int.

Previous clubs include: Winsford Utd - November 2001, Hyde Utd, Runcorn, Macclesfield T, Witton Alb., Crewe Alexandra.

ROSE, DANNY — Goalkeeper

Current Club: Whyteleafe

Previous clubs include: Croydon Ath - December 1993.

ROSE, KARL
Forward

Current Club: Scarborough

D o B: 12/10/1978   Birthplace: Barnsley

Striker Karl signed for Conference side Scarborough from Barnsley during the 2001/02 season, initially on-loan. He has overcome potentially career-threatening injuries to resurrect his game. Although he only appeared 16 times for Boro during his loan spell in 2001/02 he bagged 6 goals and looks certain to make an impact this time round.

ROSE, MARCUS
Forward

Current Club: Walton & Hersham

Birthplace: Surrey

Marcus is a ball-playing, left-sided player who has progressed through the youth and reserve sides at Stompond Lane. After making his Ryman League debut for Swans in the opening game of the 1999-2000 season he has become a regular member of the senior squad.

ROSE, MATTHEW
Midfielder

Current Club: Newport County

D o B: 03/05/1976   Birthplace: Cheltenham

Matthew has made more first-team appearances than anyone else currently on Newport County's books. Originally with his home-town club Cheltenham Town, with whom he gained Gloucestershire County honours. He then spent four seasons with Cirencester Town, winning a treble including promotion from the Hellenic League. The midfielder then joined Gloucester and was signed by Newport in March 2000.

ROSE, MICHAEL
Defender

Current Club: Hereford United

D o B: 28/07/1982   Birthplace: Salford

Promising young defender who joined Conference club Hereford United in July 2002 after being released by rivals Chester City. Began his career with Manchester United where he spent a couple of years as a professional. Joined Chester at the start of the 2001/02 season and was a regular.

ROSE, STEPHEN
Defender

Current Club: Altrincham

D o B: 23/11/1980   Birthplace: Salford

Stephen was a junior with Manchester United before having a loan spell at Bournemouth and then progressing via Bristol Rovers and Chester City. Was released at the end of the 2001/02 season by Chester after spending one season at The Deva and joined UniBond Premier side Altrincham, where he has played both at centre-back and full-back.

ROSE-LAING, NATHAN
Forward

Current Club: Bilston Town

Birthplace: Wolverhampton

From Youth team.

ROSER, CRAIG
Midfielder

Current Club: Tonbridge Angels

Birthplace: Kent

Honours won: FA Vase Winners

A former FA Vase winner with Deal Town, Craig is an impressive midfielder who joined Dr Martens Eastern side Tonbridge Angels in July 2002 from neighbours and rivals Chatham Town. Started out as a trainee with Gillingham before having spells with Gravesend, Whitstable Town and Deal, re-joining Chatham for a second time in October 2000.

ROSIER, LEE
Defender

Current Club: Windsor & Eton

Birthplace: Berkshire

Signed senior forms in December 2001, Lee was previously a member of Windsor & Etons Academy side, he made his Ryman League debut during the 2001/2002 season. A highly-promising young defender.

ROSS, DAVE
Forward

Current Club: London Colney

Birthplace: Herts

Previous clubs include: Windsor & Eton - July 1998, Wealdstone, Chesham Utd, Tring T, Berkhamsted T, Hayes, St.Albans C, Wealdstone, St.Albans C.

ROSS, DAVID
Forward

Current Club: Brandon United

Birthplace: Co.Durham

Previous clubs include: Seaham Red Star - August 2001, Morpeth T.

ROSS, IAN
Defender

Current Club: Ashford Town

Birthplace: Kent

Signed for Dr Martens Eastern side Ashford Town during the 2000/01 season. Left to join Dartford, but is now back at Ashford after re-joining in the summer of 2001. Ian is popular with both players and supporters. Formerly with Wimbledon as a trainee.

ROSS, JEFF
Forward

Current Club: Ashford Town

D o B: 09/02/1966   Birthplace: Kent

Prolific striker who left Dr Martens Eastern side Ashford Town to join Folkestone Invicta but then returned in the summer of 2001for the fourth time. A great crosser of the ball, he has also played for Sittingbourne, Hythe Town, Gravesend, Tonbridge, Sittingbourne and Welling United.

ROSS, LEE
Forward

Current Club: Halesowen Town

Birthplace: Warwickshire

Honours won: Dr Martens Western Div.Winners

Signed for Halesowen Town from Bloxwich United in November 2001. Lee is still a raw striker but is very affective. His previous club was Ford Sports of the United Counties League .

ROSS, PHIL
Midfielder

Current Club: Spennymoor United

D o B: 29/07/1977   Birthplace: Cleveland

Previous clubs include: Gateshead - January 2002, Bishop Auckland, Hartlepool Utd.

ROSSITER, DEAN
Midfielder

Current Club: Carmarthen Town

Birthplace: Wales

Previous clubs include: Pembroke Borough - July 1994, Kilgetty.

ROSTRON, PAUL
Forward

Current Club: Bedworth United

Birthplace: Coventry

Promising young striker with a keen eye for goal. Paul came through the youth ranks at Bedworth United and progressed to the first-team squad during the 2001/02 season. No Phot.

ROULSTON, DARREN   *Defender*
Current Club: Thornaby on Tees
Birthplace: Hartlepool
Previous clubs include: Gretna - February 2002, Guisborough T, Barrow, Bishop Auckland, Easington Colliery, Peterlee Newtown, Guisborough T.

ROUND, PAUL   *Defender*
Current Club: Halesowen Harriers
Birthplace: Worcesteshire
From Local football - July 2000.

ROUND, STEVE   *Midfielder*
Current Club: Rushall Olympic
D o B: 08/10/1976   *Birthplace: Birmingham*
Previous clubs include: Blakenall - July 2001, Rushall Olympic, Moor Green, Stafford R, Bridgnorth T, Birmingham C.

ROWBOTHAM, DARREN   *Forward*
Current Club: Weymouth
D o B: 22/10/1966   *Birthplace: Cardiff*
Released by Exeter City, Darran joined The Terras as a proven striker and fits in well with the style of play of the present squad. His quick thinking enables others to score and Darran also scored what most people thought was a contender for goal of the season away at Cambridge.

ROWBOTTOM, MARTIN   *Defender*
Current Club: Glapwell
Birthplace: Mansfield
Previous clubs include: Shirebook T - July 2001.

ROWE, BRIAN   *Defender*
Current Club: Bishop Auckland
D o B: 24/10/1971   *Birthplace: Sunderland*
Signed for Bishop Auckland from Bedlington Terriers in July 2001. Brian is a right back, but fills into midfield when required. Started the season slowly but as the relegation scrap intensified proved to be the most committed performer on the field on numerous occasions. An experienced player who can also number Doncaster Rovers, Spennymoor United, Gateshead and Blyth Spartans amongst his former clubs.

ROWE, EZEKIEL   *Forward*
Current Club: Kings Lynn
D o B: 30/10/1973   *Birthplace: Stoke Newington*
Pacey striker who signed for Kings Lynn from Welling United in March 2001, Zeke began his career as a trainee at Chelsea before moving on to Nationwide League sides Barnet and Brighton on loan. In July 96 he signed for Peterborough United on a free transfer. Whilst at Peterborough he was loaned out to Kettering Town, Doncaster Rovers and Welling United before making the move to Park View Road permanent in June 99.

ROWE, GARETH   *Forward*
Current Club: Hyde United
D o B: 07/02/1979
Previous clubs include: Alsager T - July 2001, Port Vale (Junior).

ROWE, PHIL   *Defender*
Current Club: Oldbury United
Birthplace: Birmingham
Previous clubs include: Atherstone Utd - March 2002, Oldbury Utd, Bloxwich Utd, Solihull Borough, Bromsgrove R, Paget R, Solihull B.

ROWELL, CHRIS   *Forward*
Current Club: Stafford Rangers
Birthplace: Hereford
Teenage striker who came through Hereford United's youth ranks to the fringes of their Conference side. Rated highly, he was quickly snapped up by former Bulls player-coach Phil Robinson when he took over as manager of Dr Martens side Stafford Rangers in June 2002.

ROWLAND, JODEY   *Midfielder*
Current Club: Bognor Regis Town
Birthplace: Bognor Regis
Signed for Bognor Regis Town from Arundel in February 2001. A former member of the Bognor youth team, Jodey is a promising midfielder who lives in Bognor.

ROWLAND, OLLIE   *Forward*
Current Club: Whitehawk
Birthplace: Sussex
Honours won: England Schools Rep.
High-profile forward who played for England Schools U-18s in 1999/2000 (also had trials with Millwall that season, as well as playing for Ansty Rangers). Offered a professional contract by Crystal Palace at the beginning of 2000/01, but joined Whitehawk after being released in the Spring. Had an amazing influence on the clubs bid to avoid relegation, and fully justified the substantial weekly fee that he was reportedly paid. Scored the only goal of the game against Horsham YMCA in April (first victory for three months), and grabbed a hat-trick in the final match at Wick to ensure survival for the Hawks. Is a member of the Sussex squad for 2001/02.

ROWLAND, PHIL   *Defender*
Current Club: Brigg Town
Birthplace: Hull
Honours won: England Schoolboy Int.
Previous clubs include: North Ferriby Utd - March 2000, Brigg T, North Ferriby Utd.

ROWLAND, SIMON   *Midfielder*
Current Club: Whitehawk
D o B: 29/11/1979   *Birthplace: Brighton*
Previous clubs include: Lancing - August 2001, Burgess Hill T, Lewes.

ROWLAND, SIMON   *Midfielder*
Current Club: Saltdean United
Birthplace: Sussex
Talented midfielder who came through Burgess Hills youth ranks before moving to Lewes in December 2000. Returned to Leylands Park two months later but immediately signed up with Withdean: had a brief spell at Ringmer, prior to joining Lancing in November 2000. Scored 7 times for the Lancers before moving to Saltdean during the summer 2001. Linked up with his younger brother at Whitehawk in October (was known as Simon Chapman last season).

ROWLAND, VERNUM   *Defender*
Current Club: Altrincham
D o B: 30/03/1985   *Birthplace: Cheshire*
A very promising two-footed defender who was a key member of Altrinchams successful youth team. Vernum plays with a maturity beyond his years. He made his first-team debut in right midfield at Bishop Auckland in March 2002, but later appeared at right-back .

ROWLANDS, ALED — Defender
Current Club: Flexsys Cefn Druids
D o B: 12/07/1971   *Birthplace: Wales*
From Local football - July 1999, Holywell T.

ROWLANDS, ALED — Midfielder
Current Club: Bangor City
D o B: 09/06/1978   *Birthplace: Bangor*
Honours won: Wales u-21 Int.
As a youngster, Aled was on the books of Manchester City before joining Sligo Rovers in Ireland. An industrious midfielder who links up well with the attack and is also another former Welsh under-21 international who has played 25 times for his country at various levels. Joined League of Wales side Bangor City in July 2000.

ROWLANDS, KEITH — Forward
Current Club: Hanwell Town
D o B: 08/11/1975   *Birthplace: Perivale*
Previous clubs include: Sutton Utd - July 2000, Farnborough T, Hanwell T.

ROWLANDS, KEVIN — Forward
Current Club: Studley
Birthplace: Worcestershire
Previous clubs include: Kings Norton T - July 2000, Evesham Utd, Kings Norton T, Redditch Utd, Feckenham.

ROWLETT, LUKE — Forward
Current Club: Tamworth
Birthplace: Northampton
Luke joined Tamworth in December 2001 from Rushden & Diamonds, where he had spent the past three seasons. Made his debut in the 2 - 0 victory over Havant and Waterlooville. A very talented front-runner who came through Diamonds successful youth scheme.

ROWNTREE, PAUL — Forward
Current Club: Billingham Town
Birthplace: Newcastle
Paul has been with the club for over 10 years, having played for Gateshead, Bishop Auckland and Seaham Red Star. Paul won the Albany Northern League Player of the year award last season and also the Golden Boot winner finishing last season with 56 goals to his credit. Paul has reularly scored over 30 goals a season since he came to Town and has been rewarded with a testimonial this season.

ROXBY, LEE — Forward
Current Club: Shildon
Birthplace: Co.Durham
Previous clubs include: Willington - August 2001, Shildon, Murton, Middlesbrough.

ROYLE, CHRIS — Midfielder
Current Club: Northwich Victoria
Birthplace: Manchester
Chris is a local lad who came through the ranks at Northwich Victoria, excelling for the reserve side before playing for neighbours Congleton Town and Winsford United. Towards the end of the 2001/02 season Chris returned to Northwich and was a revelation in the Vics defence. Chris is very quick, a strong tackler and the Vics management are predicting a bright future for the 22-year-old.

ROYLE, DARREN — Defender
Current Club: Ashton United
Previous clubs include: Flixton - July 1999, Atherton LR, Altrincham.

ROYSTON, RYAN — Defender
Current Club: Tonbridge Angels
Birthplace: Manchester
Young central defender who joined Croydon at the beginning of the 2001/2002 season. A northerner, Ryan is currently studying at Greenwich University. Transferred to Tonbridge in January 2002.

RUDD, JASON — Midfielder
Current Club: Skelmersdale United
Birthplace: Liverpool
Previous clubs include: Prescot Cables - July 2000, Skelmersdale Utd.

RUDD, STUART — Forward
Current Club: Skelmersdale United
Birthplace: Wigan
Previous clubs include: Burscough - October 2001, Skelmersdale Utd (£5,000), Daisy Hill, Wigan Ath.

RUDDLE, LEE — Defender
Current Club: Fairford Town
Birthplace: Wiltshire
From Youth team.

RUDDY, PAUL — Midfielder
Current Club: Hastings United
Birthplace: Hastings
Defender or midfielder who transferred from St Leonards to neighbours Hastings during the summer of 2000.

RUDGE, NATHAN — Midfielder
Current Club: Tiverton Town
D o B: 17/06/1979   *Birthplace: Bristol*
Highly-rated midfielder or defender who joined Tiverton Town from Chippenham Town in May 2002 for an undisclosed fee. Started his career with Norwich City as a youngster before returning to his native Bristol area and having spells with Bath City, Mangotsfield United, Clevedon Town and Chippenham, whom he helped to promotion to the Premier Division of the Dr Martens League.

RUDGELEY, SIMON — Goalkeeper
Current Club: Rye & Iden United
Birthplace: Sussex
Goalkeeper and established player, who has been at the club for around eight seasons.

RUFFER, CARL — Defender
Current Club: Chester City
Birthplace: Chester
Chester-born player who can play in defence or midfield. Carl was with Everton as a junior and signed professional forms before moving away from Goodison. Joined Confrence side Chester City from Runcorn in the summer of 2000.

RUFUS, MARVIN — Midfielder
Current Club: Enfield
D o B: 11/09/1976   *Birthplace: Lewisham*
Previous clubs include: Romford - August 2001, Leyton Orient, Charlton Ath.

RUGGLES, PHIL — Forward
Current Club: Leatherhead
Birthplace: Surrey
Previous clubs include: Woking - July 2002.

RUSCOE, SCOTT — Midfielder
Current Club: Total Network Solutions
D o B: 01/06/1976 — *Birthplace: Stoke*
Attack-minded midfielder who signed for Chester from League of Wales side Newtown in the summer of 2000. Switched back to the LoW in January 2002 with TNS. Excellent as set-pieces, he links up well with whoever he plays next to in central-midfield.

RUSH, JAMES — Defender
Current Club: Hadleigh United
Birthplace: Suffolk
Tall, strong defender with good footballing skills and passing ability. Progressed with Hadleigh from the youth teams and through the Reserves. Seventh season in the First Team with nearly 230 appearances to his name.

RUSHER, VINNIE — Midfielder
Current Club: Eastleigh
Birthplace: Hampshire
Previous clubs include: Andover - May 2002, New Street, Whitchurch, Newbury T, Wokingham T, Andover, Portsmouth, Grimsby T.

RUSK, SIMON — Midfielder
Current Club: Boston United
D o B: 17/12/1981 — *Birthplace: Peterborough*
Honours won: Scottish Youth Int.
Simon was signed from the Peterborough United Academy side in March 2001 after being released by the Posh. He has played three times for the Scotland Under 18 team. Previously also had a loan spell with Cambridge City. He scored the only goal of the game on his home debut in the match against Southport, after running sixty yards to get into the right position to bundle the ball home.

RUSSELL, ADAM — Forward
Current Club: Goole AFC
Birthplace: Hull
Previous clubs include: Halifax T - November 2001.

RUSSELL, ADAM — Forward
Current Club: Frickley Athletic
Birthplace: York
Previous clubs include: Barry T - November 2001, York C.

RUSSELL, DAMON — Forward
Current Club: Caersws
D o B: 10/06/1967 — *Birthplace: Welshpool*
Previous clubs include: Rhayader T - September 2000, Bridgnorth T, Caersws, Newtown, Caersws, Welshpool T, Telford Utd, Welshpool T.

RUSSELL, DANUM — Forward
Current Club: Shepshed Dynamo
D o B: 21/07/1976 — *Birthplace: Leicester*
Previous clubs include: Barwell - December 2001, Corby T, Friar Lane OB.

RUSSELL, JAMES — Midfielder
Current Club: Eccleshill United
Birthplace: Yorkshire
Previous clubs include: Thackley - January 2002, Farsley Celtic.

RUSSELL, KEITH — Forward
Current Club: Rushall Olympic
D o B: 31/01/1974 — *Birthplace: Aldridge*
Previous clubs include: Pelsall Villa - October 2001, Hednesford T, Altrincham, Blackpool, Hednesford T, Atherstone Utd, Tamworth, Walsall.

RUSSELL, LEE — Defender
Current Club: Forest Green Rovers
D o B: 03/09/1969 — *Birthplace: Southampton*
Experienced defender who joined Forest Green Rovers in July 2002 after being released by Torquay United. Began his career with Portsmouth, where he made more than 120 League appearances. Totalled over 200 after his spell at Plainmoor.

RUSSELL, LEE — Midfielder
Current Club: Hamble ASSC
Birthplace: Hampshire
Previous clubs include: Portsmouth RN - July 2001, Bognor Regis T Gosport B.

RUSSELL, MARK — Midfielder
Current Club: Hanwell Town
D o B: 07/09/1977 — *Birthplace: Hillingdon*
Previous clubs include: Northwood - July 2001, Yeading.

RUSSELL, MATTHEW — Forward
Current Club: Bognor Regis Town
Birthplace: Rustington
Striker who signed for Bognor Regis Town at the start of the 2000/01season from Sussex County League side Horsham YMCA. Was top scorer in his first campaign at the higher level. Lives in Rustington.

RUSSELL, MATTHEW — Midfielder
Current Club: Frickley Athletic
D o B: 17/01/1978 — *Birthplace: Leeds*
Previous clubs include: Pickering T - February 2002, Frickley Ath., Scarborough, Halifax T, Scarborough.

RUSSELL-SMITH, JOHN — Defender
Current Club: Corinthian Casuals
Birthplace: Surrey
A very reliable defender who is currently in his second spell with Corinthian Casuals and is a vital part of the defence. Re-signed from Epsom & Ewell in July 1996, he has now made over 150 starts for the side.

RUST, NICKY — Goalkeeper
Current Club: Cambridge City
D o B: 25/09/1974 — *Birthplace: Ely*
Previous clubs include: Braintree T - March 2000, Cambridge C, Hendon, Barnet, Brighton, Arsenal.

RUSTELL, CHRIS — Defender
Current Club: Pagham
Birthplace: Sussex
Commanding, never-say-die defender, who was formerly with Bognor Regis: transferred from Portfield to Chichester City during the 1999 close season: held back by injury during the first-half of 2001/02 before joining Pagham in January.

RUSTON, ROBIN — Goalkeeper
Current Club: Barking & East Ham United
Birthplace: Essex
A teenage goalkeeper with great potential. Spent two years as a trainee with Barnet after being on the books at Leyton Orient as a youngster. Joined Barking in August 2001 and his performances attracted the attention of Bournemouth, Plymouth and Orient again.

RUTHERFORD, ANDY — Defender
Current Club: Atherstone United
From Youth team.

RUTHERFORD, GUY — Midfielder
Current Club: Bognor Regis Town
Birthplace: Portsmouth
Midfielder who signed for Bognor Regis Town at the start of the 2000/01 season from Worthing .Previous clubs include Fareham Town, Havant, Clanfield and is in his second spell with the Rocks. Lives in Portsmouth.

RUTHERFORD, JAMES — Forward
Current Club: Guiseley
Birthplace: Bradford
Previous clubs include: Bradford C - July 2001.

RUTHERFORD, MIKE — Midfielder
Current Club: Chelmsford City
D o B: 06/06/1972   Birthplace: Woolwich
Woolwich-born midfielder who began his career with Queens Park Rangers. Was released at the end of the 1993/94 season and joined Welling United - then members of the Nationwide Conference. Soon became a firm favourite at Park View Road and was the clubs longest-serving player with over 300 appearances before transferring to Chelmsford City in May 2002.

RUTHERFORD, MILES — Defender
Current Club: Bognor Regis Town
Birthplace: Portsmouth
Twin brother of Guy, Miles signed for Bognor Regis Town from Worthing in August 2000 . Previously with Fareham Town, Clanfield and Havant. An experienced Non-League defender who lives in Portsmouth.

RUTTER, ANDY — Forward
Current Club: Chasetown FC
Birthplace: Birmingham
Previous clubs include: Oldbury Utd - July 2001, Sandwell B, Rushall Olympic.

RUTTER, MARK — Defender
Current Club: Caernarfon Town
D o B: 15/03/1968   Birthplace: Liverpool
Previous clubs include: Rhyl - July 2000, Marine, Brymbo Steelworks, Flint Town Utd, Bangor C, Northwich V, Hyde Utd, Barrow, Macclesfield T, Winsford Utd, Chorley, Dunfermline Ath., Caernarfon T, Northwich V, Caernarfon T, Telford Utd.

RUTTER, MARK — Forward
Current Club: Shildon
Birthplace: Co. Durham
Previous clubs include: Morpeth T - March 2002.

RUTTER, NICK — Goalkeeper
Current Club: Oxford City
Previous clubs include: Oxford University - July 2000.

RYAN, DARREN — Midfielder
Current Club: Newport County
D o B: 03/07/1972   Birthplace: Oswestry
A summer 2001 signing for Newport County from Merthyr Tydfil, Darren had played six games on loan to Newport County from the Martyrs in February 2000. The midfielder was with Shrewsbury Town for two seasons before moving to Chester and Stockport taking his Football League appearance total to 57. He was with Barry Town before moving to Merthyr.

RYAN, DAVID — Midfielder
Current Club: Wealdstone
D o B: 09/07/1980   Birthplace: London
Talented midfielder who played in the Ryman League as a teenager for Kingsbury Town and became a first-team regular. Switched to Division One North neighbours Wealdstone in August 2002.

RYAN, JASON — Midfielder
Current Club: Ossett Albion
Previous clubs include: Harrogate T - March 2001, Bradford C.

RYAN, KELVIN — Forward
Current Club: Stocksbridge Park Steels
Birthplace: Sheffield
Previous clubs include: Barnsley (Junior) - July 2001, Sheffield Wednesday (Junior).

RYAN, NEIL — Defender
Current Club: Altrincham
D o B: 27/01/1975   Birthplace: Manchester
A right-back or midfielder, he signed for Altrincham from USA side Portland Timbers. Neil is the son of Jim Ryan, the Manchester United coach, and he made his Robins debut in December 2001 against Vauxhall Motors in the UniBond Cup. In the USA he also played for Boston Bulldogs and in the A-League in Richmond and Worcester, (MA). Neil is the sides regular corner-taker.

RYAN, PAUL — Defender
Current Club: Ossett Town
D o B: 28/11/1977   Birthplace: Bradford
Quick defensive player who was previously with Guiseley and Thackley before arriving at Ingfield midway though the 1999/2000 season. Came to the club as a left back, but after failing to command a regular place in the starting line up, switched to central defence where he was a revelation last season.

RYAN, PAUL — Forward
Current Club: Bamber Bridge
Birthplace: Blackpool
Previous clubs include: Blackpool (Junior) - July 1998.

RYAN, RICHARD — Forward
Current Club: Port Talbot Town
Birthplace: Neath
From Youth team.

RYAN, TIM — Defender
Current Club: Doncaster Rovers
D o B: 10/12/1974   Birthplace: Stockport
Honours won: England Semi-Pro Int.
Highly-rated defender who is also capable of doing a good job in midfield when asked. Began his career at Scunthorpe before moving into Non-League football with Buxton. Returned to the League with Doncaster before switching to Southport in July 1997. Quickly settled into the left back role and his consistency and sound performances earned him England semi-professional

international recognition. Returned to Rovers at the start of the 2000/01 season.

RYDEHEARD, CRAIG   *Midfielder*
Current Club: Hitchin Town

D o B: 07/10/1982   *Birthplace: Hitchin*

Local youngster who broke into the Hitchin Town first-team during the 2000/01 season and played on the left side of defence or midfield. Another product of the clubs highly-successful youth set-up.

RYDER, COLIN   *Goalkeeper*
Current Club: Feltham

Birthplace: Isleworth

Signed from local football in the summer of 1993 and was awarded Player of the Year for the Reserve side in the same season. Colin made the breakthrough on a regular basis to the first XI at the start of 95/96 season under Martyn Busby and remained first choice until missing most of the following season 96/97 & nearly all the 97/98 with serious knee ligament injuires. Made a full comeback in 1998/99 and has been the regular No 1 since.

RYDER, NICKY   *Forward*
Current Club: Marlow

Birthplace: London

Previous clubs include: Uxbridge - October 2000, Hayes, Farnborough T, Hounslow, Kingstonian, Brentford, Bristol R (Junior), Plymouth Argyle (Junior).

RYDER, STUART   *Defender*
Current Club: Hednesford Town

D o B: 06/11/1973   *Birthplace: Sutton Coldfield*
Honours won: England u-21 Int.

An experienced defender, Stuart joined Hednesford Town in June 2002, re-uniting with Ian Painter, who was in charge during his spell with Stafford Rangers. Had joined Rangers at the beginning of February 2000 from Nuneaton Borough and had previously played for Tamworth, Walsall, and Mansfield Town. During his spell with Walsall, Stuart made 101 League appearances and won three England under-21 caps against Brazil, Angola and France during the 1995 Toulon Tournament.

THE NON-LEAGUE PAPER

ESSENTIAL READING FOR FOLLOWERS OF THE NATIONAL GAME

SHARE THE PASSION

THE NON-LEAGUE PAPER

Issue No 136 Sunday October 27, 2002 · ESSENTIAL READING FOR FOLLOWERS OF THE NATIONAL GAME · £1.00

FA CUP SPECIAL
COVERAGE OF ALL YESTERDAY'S GAMES – INSIDE
48 PAGES OF NON-STOP SOCCER ACTION

TIVVY SEND THEM DIZZY

BBC get score wrong as Shreeves suffers

By MATTHEW DAVI

THE NON-LEAGUE PAPER

Issue No 135 Sunday October 20, 2002 · CONFERENCE & PYRAMID LEAGUES SOCCER · £1.00

EXCLUSIVE: BORG I paid £15,000 in paper bag to sign player

EXCLUSIVE: CHAPPLE Death threat to my daughter made me want to walk out

48 PAGES OF NEWS, MATCH REPORTS, RESULTS & FIXTURES

HUDSON AT HIGH-SPEED

By SAMUEL JACK

EVERY SUNDAY

SABERTON, GREGG   *Midfielder*
Current Club: Ely City
Birthplace: Cambridge
Previous clubs include: Mildenhall T - July 2001, Soham Town R.

SADDINGTON, JAMES   *Defender*
Current Club: Histon
D o B: 12/09/1972   *Birthplace: Cambridge*
Previous clubs include: Cambridge C - July 1999, Chelmsford C, Cambridge C, Kettering T, Millwall, Cambridge C, Newmarket T.

SADLER, DAVID   *Forward*
Current Club: Kingstonian
D o B: 12/09/1978   *Birthplace: Derby*
Honours won: England Schools Rep.
A former England Schools captain signed for Kingstonian from Hinckley United in August 2001. Was voted Supporters' Player of the Year 1999/00 at United. Previous clubs include Derby County, Luton Town and New York State. The striker has very good pace and first touch on the turn.

SADLER, DEAN   *Midfielder*
Current Club: Felixstowe & Walton United
Birthplace: Ipswich
Former Colchester United youth player who has also played for Division 1 side Needham Market. Joined in the close season from SIL Ipswich Athletic and is a talented and skilful player.

SAGE, KRIS   *Midfielder*
Current Club: Bilston Town
Previous clubs include: Bilston T - August 2001, Sutton Coldfield T, Stafford R, Yate T, Backwell Utd, Yate T.

SAILSMAN, NEIL   *Midfielder*
Current Club: Mickleover Sports
D o B: 01/10/1978   *Birthplace: Derby*
Previous clubs include: Shepshed Dynamo - March 2002, Rocester, Burton Alb., Manchester C (Trainee).

SAINTE, JOEL-MARIE   *Midfielder*
Current Club: Bishops Stortford
Birthplace: France
Vastly experienced Frenchman latterly with USM Senlis. Joel had trials with Stevenage before signing for the Blues in the autumn of 2001. Joel has had a leg injury that has kept him out of the senior side this season. Joel had a spell on loan with Wealdstone.

SALE, MARK   *Forward*
Current Club: Tamworth
D o B: 27/02/1972   *Birthplace: Burton*
Giant striker who signed for Dr Martens Premier side Tamworth from Conference outfit Doncaster Rovers in August 2002. Had joined Rovers from Conference champions Rushden & Diamonds in the summer of 2001. Had plenty of League experience to his name with the likes of Stoke, Cambridge United, Colchester, Preston, Mansfield and Birmingham and made a remarkable recovery from cancer.

SALES, PAUL   *Forward*
Current Club: Bashley
Birthplace: Southampton
Signed for Salisbury in August 1998 from Bashley. Former Southampton player who has been leading scorer in each of his three seasons with the club, amassing 75 goals in the process. Naturally talented player with good touch and awareness, he returned to the Bash in February 2002.

SALMON, CLIFF   *Defender*
Current Club: Barking & East Ham United
Previous clubs include: East Ham Utd - July 2001, Bishops Stortford, Braintree T, Bishops Stortford.

SALMON, GAVIN   *Forward*
Current Club: Flixton
D o B: 08/12/1977   *Birthplace: Manchester*
Previous clubs include: Hyde Utd - February 2002, Atherton LR.

SALMON, MARC   *Forward*
Current Club: Harlow Town
D o B: 10/02/1973   *Birthplace: London*
First joined Harlow Town in September 1993 from Hendon, having previously played for Enfield. Finished as the clubs top scorer in his first two seasons before embarking on a professional career with Charlton Athletic. After one year with Charlton Marc was released and re-joined Harlow in September 1996. Has had his share in injury problems in recent seasons but managed to once again top the scoring charts for the 2000/01 season. Marc has played almost 300 games for the club, scoring around 150 goals.

SALMON, MARK   *Defender*
Current Club: Bishop Auckland
Birthplace: Co Durham
Signed for Bishop Auckland from Acklam Steel Works in August 1998. A young central defender who has been in outstanding form. Players and supporters favourite, he has been one of the best players in the UniBond League over the last three seasons, winning numerous man of the match awards. A rock in the Bishops defence throughout his time with the club.

SALMON, MELFORD   *Defender*
Current Club: Wednesfield
Birthplace: Wolverhampton
Previous clubs include: Bloxwich T - July 2001, Wednesfield, Evesham Utd, Wednesfield, Bloxwich T, Bilston CC.

SALMON, MIKE   *Goalkeeper*
Current Club: Tonbridge Angels
D o B: 14/07/1964   *Birthplace: Leyland*
Vastly experienced goalkeeper who signed for Dr Martens Eastern side Tonbridge Angels in July 2002. Made over 400 League appearances during an elevn-year professional career that began at Blackburn and included spells with Stockport, Bolton, Wrexham, Charlton and Ipswich, where he was understudy to Richard Wright.

SALMON, PAUL   *Defender*
Current Club: Ford United
D o B: 14/05/1973   *Birthplace: Romford*
Honours won: Ryman League Div.One Winners
One of the most respected defenders in the Essex Non-League scene, Paul joined Ford United in the summer of 2000 from Leyton Pennant and played a major part in helping the club gain promotion to the Premier Division of the Ryman League for the first time in 2001/02. Originally on the books at Leyton Orient, spells with Leyton Pennant and Dagenham & Redbridge followed before his move to Ford.

SALMONS, ADAM   *Midfielder*
Current Club: Mildenhall Town
Birthplace: Cambridgeshire
Previous clubs include: Cambridge C - August 2001, Stockport County, Ipswich T (Junior).

SALT, DANNY — *Defender*
Current Club: St.Helens Town

D o B: 17/11/1977   Birthplace: Warrington
Right back or right midfield player arrives at Town from Runcorn were he was a regular, making over 150 First team appearances. Started his career at Wigan Athletic before moving on to Warrington Town and then Runcorn. Danny will also chip in with his fair share of goals.

SALT, PHIL — *Defender*
Current Club: Leigh RMI

D o B: 02/03/1979   Birthplace: Huddersfield
Former Oldham Athletic defender who joined Conference side Leigh RMI in August 2002 from rivals Scarborough. Had signed for Boro in February 2002.

SALTER, MARK — *Forward*
Current Club: Frome Town

D o B: 16/03/1980   Birthplace: Somerset
Previous clubs include: Stoke Hamdon - July 1998.

SALTER, STUART — *Defender*
Current Club: Eastleigh

Birthplace: Hampshire
Previous clubs include: AFC Totton - May 2002.

SAMBROOK, ANTON — *Midfielder*
Current Club: Brackley Town

Birthplace: Northamptonshire
Previous clubs include: Banbury Utd - July 1999, Woodford Utd.

SAMMONS, PAUL — *Midfielder*
Current Club: Great Wakering Rovers

Birthplace: Essex
Previous clubs include: Witham T - February 2002, Great Wakering Rovers, Stambridge, Bowers Utd.

SAMUEL, MARVIN — *Defender*
Current Club: Arlesey Town

Birthplace: London
Signed for Ryman Division One North side Arlesey Town in August 2002 from rivals Harlow Town. Had joined Harlow from Fisher Athletic in August 1997 and became a valuable member of the side. Capable of playing in most positions, including taking the keepers jersey in at match at East Thurrock. Won the Player of the Year trophy at Harlow for the first three years he was with the club.

SAMUELS, TONY — *Forward*
Current Club: Chelmsford City

Birthplace: London
Prolific goalscorer who joined Chelmsford City in mid-August 2001 from Boreham Wood. Has plenty of experience at Non-League level, particularly with Wood, where he spent many fruitful years, netting on a regular basis. Amongst his other former clubs are Leytonstone & Ilford, Leyton Wingate, Bromley and Collier Row.

SAMUELS-WILLIAMS, DARRYL — *Forward*
Current Club: Willenhall Town

Birthplace: Birmingham
Signed October 2001 from Bilston Town, young powerful striker who has impressed in his few appearances.

SAMWAYS, MARK — *Goalkeeper*
Current Club: Frickley Athletic

D o B: 11/11/1968   Birthplace: Doncaster
Previous clubs include: Glasshoughton Welfare - August 2002, Brigg T, Frickley Ath., Matlock T, Darlington, York C, Scunthorpe Utd, Doncaster R.

SAMWAYS, TERRY — *Defender*
Current Club: Hamble ASSC

Birthplace: Hampshire
Previous clubs include: Sholing Sports - July 1997, Waterlooville, Andover, Fareham T.

SANDAR, MICHAEL — *Forward*
Current Club: Borrowash Victoria

D o B: 16/04/1981   Birthplace: Derby
Previous clubs include: Gresley Rovers - August 2001, Stoke C (Junior), Derby Co (Junior).

SANDEMAN, BRADLEY — *Defender*
Current Club: Kidsgrove Athletic

D o B: 24/02/1970   Birthplace: Northampton
Honours won: NWCL Winners
Joined Kidsgrove from Hyde United at the beginning of the 2001/02 season, having previously been with Leek Town. Played for Port Vale and Maidstone in the League. Excellent crosser of the ball and a very experienced defender.

SANDERS, CHRIS — *Defender*
Current Club: Bideford

Birthplace: Devon
Chris is a promising young defender, who has progressed up through our ranks from the youth section.

SANDERS, GUY — *Defender*
Current Club: Moor Green

D o B: 01/01/1976   Birthplace: Coventry
Highly-rated defender who joined Dr Martens Premier Division Moor Green in June 2002 from Western Division Bedworth United. Had been with Bedworth since the summer of 1997 when he arrived after being on the books at Reading. Developed into a fine central defender and rated as one of the best in his position in the division.

SANDERSON, SID — *Defender*
Current Club: Chichester City United

Birthplace: Hampshire
Previous clubs include: Andover - July 2001, Havant & Waterlooville, Waterlooville, Fleetlands, Portchester.

SANDFORD, LEE — *Defender*
Current Club: Woking

D o B: 22/04/1968   Birthplace: Basingstoke
Honours won: England Youth Int., Division Two Winners
Experienced former England Youth international defender who joined Conference side Woking in August 2002 after a long and successful professional career that spanned 17 years and almost 500 League appearances. He began his career with Portsmouth and then move to Stoke in 1989, where he won a Division Two championship and an Autoglass Windows Trophy winners medal. Transferred to Sheffield United in the summer of 1996 for £500,000 and spent six years at Bramall Lane before being released at the end of the 2001/02 campaign.

SANDWITH, KEVIN — *Defender*
Current Club: Doncaster Rovers
D o B: 30/04/1978   Birthplace: Workington
Talented defender who started out as a trainee with Carlisle United, he was released at the end of season 1998/99. A spell at Barrow was followed by a move to Telford United from where Doncaster Rovers signed him in the summer of 2001.

SANGHA, DAVINDER — *Midfielder*
Current Club: Wednesfield
Birthplace: Shropshire
Previous clubs include: Shifnal T - July 1999, Telford Utd.

SANGSTER, SEAN — *Midfielder*
Current Club: Tring Town
Birthplace: Hemel Hempstead
Honours won: England Schoolboy Int.
Previous clubs include: Hemel Hempstead - August 1999.

SANSOM, RUPERT — *Forward*
Current Club: Bognor Regis Town
Birthplace: Brighton
Had spent three years on the books at Brighton & Hove Albion before being released in the summer of 2002 when he joined Ryman Division One South side Bognor Regis Town. A highly-promising teenage striker who lives in Hove.

SANTER, TOMMY — *Midfielder*
Current Club: Heybridge Swifts
Birthplace: Colchester
Young midfielder who has worked hard to develop his game after progressing through Heybridge Swifts youth and reserve sides. Versatile, but is at his best as the midfield link man pushing forward. Has an eye for goal, shows vision in his passing. Has all the attributes needed to make great progress in the game.

SAPEY, ANDY — *Midfielder*
Current Club: Stanway Rovers
Birthplace: Essex
Previous clubs include: Needham Market - July 1999.

SAPIRO, JOEL — *Forward*
Current Club: Kingsbury Town
Birthplace: Essex
Previous clubs include: Clapton - August 2001, Leyton Pennant, Clapton, Leyton Pennant, Waltham Abbey, Leyton Pennant.

SAPPLETON, PAT — *Defender*
Current Club: Hendon
Birthplace: London
Honours won: Jamaican Youth Int.
Started to make a few first team appearances for Hendon during the 2000/01season. A strong and capable defender, who has represented Jamaica at Youth international level, Pat is sure to build on his early promise.

SARGENT, ANDY — *Forward*
Current Club: Taunton Town
Birthplace: Devon
Previous clubs include: Elmore - July 2001, Weston-Super-Mare, Salisbury C, Plymouth Argyle.

SARGENT, DAVE — *Defender*
Current Club: Northwood
D o B: 22/12/1977   Birthplace: Wembley
Previous clubs include: Hayes - October 1997, Wycombe Wanderers, Watford (Junior).

SARGENT, STEVE — *Midfielder*
Current Club: Crawley Town
Birthplace: Sussex
Midfielder: one-time Portsmouth youth team player: made a few appearances for Langney Sports in 1999/2000 after joining them from Hastings: subsequently returned to the Pilot Field before becoming a Crawley reserve during 2000/01: son of former Reds player Dave Sargent.

SARGENT, WESTLEY — *Defender*
Current Club: Tiptree United
Birthplace: Essex
Previous clubs include: Dedham - August 2001.

SARGESON, CRAIG — *Forward*
Current Club: Rossendale United
Birthplace: Lancashire
Prolific striker who has been in terrific form for the past two or three seasons since making the Rossendale United senior side. Came up through the ranks with Dale and since gaining promotion to the UniBond, his goals have attracted attention from bigger clubs.

SARLL, DARREN — *Midfielder*
Current Club: Hitchin Town
D o B: 02/02/1983   Birthplace: Hitchin
A former member of Hitchin Town's youth set-up, Darren has acquitted himself well in the senior side. A foraging midfielder, he went on the youth teams tour of Brazil during June 2001.

SAROYA, NEVIN — *Midfielder*
Current Club: Yeading
D o B: 15/09/1980   Birthplace: Hillingdon
Twenty-two year old Nev made a name for himself as a Brentford trainee where he impressed boss Ron Noades enough for first team selection. At six-foot-three tall his presence at the air is immense but he is also very strong with the ball at his feet.

SAULSBURY, JAMES — *Defender*
Current Club: Thame United
D o B: 04/09/1981   Birthplace: Oxfordshire
James re-joined Thame United in July 2001 after moving to rival Ryman League club Marlow where he made an immediate impact quickly establishing himself as a first-team regular in defence. Former youth team captain at Thame, James had a brief spell in America on a soccer scholarship.

SAUNDERS, DAMIEN — *Forward*
Current Club: Molesey
D o B: 08/03/1982   Birthplace: Surrey
From Youth team.

SAUNDERS, EDDIE — *Defender*
Current Club: Bromley
D o B: 27/05/1971   Birthplace: London
Honours won: FA Trophy Winners
A powerful defender, Eddie was in his second spell at Woking before joining Ryman Division One South club Bromley in August 2002. Not perhaps the most elegant of defenders, but he is a committed player. He returned to Kingfield after manager Geoff

Chapple asked him to come back towards the end of 2001 from Kingstonian, where he won an FA Trophy winners medal. Started his career with the Civil Service side and has also been on the books at Sutton United, Yeading and Carshalton Athletic, from where he originally joined the Cards in 1997.

SAUNDERS, JAY   *Defender*
Current Club: Margate
D o B: 15/01/1979   *Birthplace: Kent*
Previous clubs include: Gravesend - August 1998, Gillingham (Trainee).

SAUNDERS, LEE   *Defender*
Current Club: Solihull Borough
D o B: 23/03/1977   *Birthplace: Nuneaton*
Signed from Shepshed Dynamo in July 2001. Nuneaton-born he played for two years with Doncaster Rovers before joining Leicester United in August 96 until they folded and then he moved to Ilkeston Town. Then he joined Shepshed in 1997.

SAUNDERS, MARK   *Defender*
Current Club: Fairford Town
Birthplace: Wiltshire
From Youth team.

SAUNDERS, NEIL   *Defender*
Current Club: Tiverton Town
D o B: 29/06/1970   *Birthplace: Reading*
Honours won: FA Vase Winners
Joined Tiverton Town back in 1988 from Crediton. He has been a superb servant to the club, always consistent and never gives less than 100%. Neil spent one season 95/96 playing for Bath City in the Conference. He returned to Ladysmead the following year an even better player. He is very proud of the fact that he is the only team member to have played in all four FA Cup First round Proper ties and is the clubs most decorated player. He works as a senior traffic technician for Devon County Council.

SAUNDERS, RICHARD   *Forward*
Current Club: Coalville Town
D o B: 04/02/1981   *Birthplace: Leicester*
Previous clubs include: St Andrews - December 2001, Downes Sports.

SAUNDERS, SAM   *Midfielder*
Current Club: Ashford Town
Birthplace: Kent
Lively young midfielder who joined Dr Martens Eastern side Ashford Town in February 2002 from Welling United. Formerly a youth team player with QPR.

SAUNDERS, SCOTT   *Defender*
Current Club: Tonbridge Angels
Birthplace: Kent
Scott signed for Dr Martens Eastern side Tonbridge Angels in July 2002 from neighours and rivals Erith & Belvedere. Had joined Erith in January 2002, after recovering from a bad injury. A quality left-sided player who lists Fisher Athletic, Sittingbourne and Dartford amongst his previous clubs.

SAVAGE, MICHAEL   *Defender*
Current Club: Peterlee Newtown
Birthplace: Co.Durham
Previous clubs include: Leicester C - July 2001.

SAVAGE, NICKY   *Defender*
Current Club: Billericay Town
Previous clubs include: Ford Utd - August 2001.

SAVAGE, WAYNE   *Midfielder*
Current Club: Port Talbot Town
Birthplace: Merthyr
Aggressive central midfielder who signed for League of Wales side Port Talbot Athletic in August 2002 from Merthyr Tydfil. Had joined Merthyr during the summer of 2000 from Welsh League side Ton Pentre. Found himself playing in the Dr Martens League 12 months on from playing in the Merthyr Simbec League. Scored on his home debut in a freindly versus a full strength Cardiff City side and netted 5 times in 22 appearances during the 2001/02 season.

SAVILLE, ANDY   *Forward*
Current Club: Goole AFC
D o B: 12/12/1964   *Birthplace: Hull*
Previous clubs include: Gainsborough Trinity - July 2000, Scarborough, Cardiff C, Wigan Ath., Preston NE, Birmingham C, Hartlepool Utd, Barnsley, Walsall, Hull C.

SAWYER, KEVIN   *Goalkeeper*
Current Club: Salisbury City
Birthplace: Swindon
A great prospect with already over 200 appearances in the Dr Martens League to his credit, and over the past five seasons had been Cirencester Town's first choice goalkeeper following promotion from the Academy side. Players' Player and Supporters' Player of the Year for 2000/01, he transferred to Eastern Division side Salisbury City in August 2002.

SAWYER, MARCUS   *Defender*
Current Club: Edgware Town
Birthplace: London
Previous clubs include: Harrow Borough - November 2001.

SAWYERS, ROBERT   *Defender*
Current Club: Hereford United
D o B: 20/11/1978   *Birthplace: Dudley*
Left back with outstanding ability who was originally with Wolverhampton Wanderers where he was surprisingly released. Made his League debut for Barnet against Rochdale in the final match of season 1997/98. Rob put in some electric performances for the club after joining in January 1998 but then lost his regular spot when the Bees signed Lee Flynn. Transferred to Conference rivals Hereford United in July 2002.

SAXBY, GAVIN   *Goalkeeper*
Current Club: Alfreton Town
Birthplace: Mansfield
Promising goalkeeper who signed for UniBond First Division side Alfreton Town from Clipstone Welfare towards the end of the 2001/02 season after previously playing for Alfreton Town's Academy side. He also had a spell with Tamworth.

SAYER, ANDY   *Forward*
Current Club: Tooting & Mitcham United
D o B: 06/06/1966   *Birthplace: Brent*
Previous clubs include: Chertsey T - August 2001, Tooting & Mitcham Utd, Egham T, Leatherhead, Walton & Hersham, Enfield, Slough T, Leyton Orient, Fulham, Wimbledon.

S

SCAIFE, NICKY — Midfielder
Current Club: Dunston Federation Brewery
D o B: 14/05/1975   Birthplace: Middlesbrough
Previous clubs include: Gateshead - September 2000, Dunston Federation, Bishop Auckland, Porsanger (Norway), Gateshead, Halifax T, York C, Whitby T, Guisborough T.

SCAINES, MARK — Forward
Current Club: Abingdon Town
Birthplace: Oxford
Previous clubs include: Oxford C - July 2001.

SCALES, JAMIE — Midfielder
Current Club: Woodbridge Town
Birthplace: Suffolk
Signed up at the beginning of September 1999, having previously been on the books of Cambridge United. Strong, pacy, left-sided midfielder or wing-back who was the overwhelming choice as the Players' Player of the Year in 1999/00.

SCANTLEBURY, GARETH — Goalkeeper
Current Club: Port Talbot Town
D o B: 03/08/1977   Birthplace: Neath
One of the most popular players at Port Talbot, Gareth made his return to the first-team and made his League of Wales debut when Simon Dyer took over as manager. A good shot stopper, he has improved on his all round game over the last two years and has seen off competition for the number one shirt. Progressed through the clubs youth system.

SCARBOROUGH, JOHN — Defender
Current Club: Eastbourne Borough
Birthplace: Gravesend
Originally from the Gravesend area, has previous experience with Gravesend & Northfleet, Ashford Town, and Herne Bay. Made his 1st team debut as a substitute at Chelmsford City last season, which he capped with a fine goal.

SCARGILL, JONATHAN — Goalkeeper
Current Club: Hallam
D o B: 09/04/1977   Birthplace: Dewsbury
Previous clubs include: Ossett T - July 2000, Oldham Ath., Hyde Utd, Chesterfield, Notts Co., Sheffield Wednesday.

SCARLETT, ANDRE — Midfielder
Current Club: Chesham United
D o B: 11/01/1980   Birthplace: Brent
A mobile central midfielder who has played for Luton Town, Stevenage Borough, Wealdstone and Hitchin Town, from whom he joined Ryman Premier rivals Chesham United in July 2002. His strengths include passing heading and is a good all-round player. He works in a sports shop in Heathrow and his footballing hero is John Barnes. His career highlight so far was staring for Luton against Sunderland and being named man of the match.

SCERRI, MILES — Forward
Current Club: Arundel
Birthplace: Sussex
Impressive, solid striker who is a former Steyning player who then played for Storrington before joining Arundel during the 1999 close season. Top scorer in the County League Division Two in his first term at Mill Road with 44 goals and was also the leading marksman for the Mullets in 2000/01, striking 19 times. Seemed to lose his zest prior to a very brief return stint at Storrington (scored once for them in March 2002). Back in action at Arundel for the final months of 2001/02 and also appeared for Sussex during that campaign.

SCHEPPEL, DANNY — Midfielder
Current Club: Moor Green
Birthplace: Birmingham
Signed for Moor Green in July 2001 from Worcester City, having previously spent three years with Birmingham City.

SCHEUBER, STUART — Midfielder
Current Club: Colwyn Bay
D o B: 03/04/1981   Birthplace: Rhuddlan
Born in Rhuddlan, this skilful midfielder started his career at Crewe Alexandra and went to Stoke City for three seasons. From there he moved to UniBond Premier side Altrincham for one season before signing for Colwyn Bay during the summer of 2001.

SCHILDER, KEVIN — Defender
Current Club: Hamble ASSC
Birthplace: Hampshire
Previous clubs include: Sholing Sports - July 1991, Netley Central.

SCHNEIDER, DAVE — Midfielder
Current Club: Wick
Birthplace: Sussex
Previous clubs include: Lancing - July 2001.

SCHOFIELD, DARREN — Defender
Current Club: Alfreton Town
Birthplace: Sheffield
Honours won: NCEL Winners
Returned to Alfreton Town in the summer of 1999 for his third spell with the Reds. Darren is an accomplished and highly-rated left back who spent a season with Denaby United where he won a League Cup winners medal. Has also seen service with Worksop Town.

SCHOLES, TIM — Midfielder
Current Club: Holmer Green
Birthplace: Bucks
From Youth team.

SCOPE, TYNAN — Goalkeeper
Current Club: Bedworth United
D o B: 30/07/1979   Birthplace: Sydney, Australia
Previous clubs include: Solihull Borough - July 2001, Bristol C, Coventry C.

SCOPES, DANNY — Midfielder
Current Club: Great Wakering Rovers
Birthplace: Southend
Previous clubs include: Southend Manor - July 1997, Great Wakering R.

SCOTCHMER, TERRY — Defender
Current Club: Barking & East Ham United
Birthplace: Essex
A young central defender who has packed in a good deal of experience into a relatively short career to date. Joined Barking in December 2001 following six months rest from the game. Has previously been on the books at Romford, Hertford Town, Leyton Pennant and Grays Athletic.

SCOTT, ANDY — Midfielder
Current Club: Southport

D o B: 27/06/1975 — Birthplace: Manchester
Honours won: England Youth Int.
Andy is another of manager Phil Wilsons signings from his former club Stalybridge Celtic and joined Southport towards the end of the 2001/02 season. Andy is a former England Youth international, who has been on the books at Blackburn, Cardiff and Rochdale, and is a utility player who can slot into a left wing-back or centre-back role. During the 2001/02 season he was selected for the North-West FA representative side.

SCOTT, CHRIS — Defender
Current Club: Rossendale United

D o B: 12/02/1980 — Birthplace: Burnley
Highly-rated 22-year-old defender whose career began at Burnley. Was released in 1999/2000 and joined Leigh RMI where he became a first-team regular. Lost his place after Leigh gained promotion to the Conference and joined UniBond First Division side Rossendale United in November 2001.

SCOTT, DANNY — Forward
Current Club: Glapwell

Birthplace: Mansfield
Previous clubs include: Worksop T - December 1997, Mansfield T (Junior).

SCOTT, DAVID — Defender
Current Club: Redhill

D o B: 15/04/1967 — Birthplace: Carlisle
Honours won: Dr Martens League Premier Div.Winners, English Universities Rep.
Previous clubs include: Dartford - January 2002, Ashford T, Dover Ath., Hastings T, Canterbury C, Hastings T, Penrith.

SCOTT, GARY — Defender
Current Club: Altrincham

D o B: 03/02/1978 — Birthplace: Liverpool
Signed for Altrincham when surprisingly released by Leigh RMIin October 2000. Started his career at Tranmere Rovers before transferring to Rotherham United in August 1997. Also had spells at Marine and Barrow.

SCOTT, IAN — Midfielder
Current Club: Hitchin Town

D o B: 25/11/1968 — Birthplace: Luton
Ian joined Hitchin Town in the summer of 1992 from St Albans City. He became a key member of the 1993 promotion-winning team as a cultured midfielder. Since then, he has been a consistent figure and has remained an integral part of the first team. Formerly with Luton Town as a youngster and Aylesbury United, he has now played around 500 games for Hitchin.

SCOTT, JOHN — Midfielder
Current Club: Fleet Town

D o B: 09/05/1967 — Birthplace: Cleveland
Previous clubs include: AFC Newbury - July 2001, Forest Green R, Andover, Wokingham T, Army, Middlesbrough.

SCOTT, KEITH — Forward
Current Club: Scarborough

D o B: 09/06/1967 — Birthplace: London
Honours won: Conference Winners, FA Trophy Winners
Signed for Conference club Scarborough in July 2002 from relegated Dover Athletic. Had joined Dover just before the start of the Conference campaign of 2001/02. Keith was a proven goalscorer, having played regularly for Lincoln, Wycombe, Swindon, Stoke, Norwich, Wycombe again, Reading, and Colchester and also had loan spells with Bournemouth and Watford. His experience has meant that he is a very dangerous player with his strength in the air, combined with his ability to hold the ball up and put others through on goal. Has Conference and FA Trophy winners medals.

SCOTT, MARTIN — Defender
Current Club: Gateshead

D o B: 07/01/1968 — Birthplace: Sheffield
Born in Sheffield, Martin played for Rotherham, Bristol City and Sunderland in most divisions of the Football League. A vastly experienced defender, he played 104 games for Sunderland before retiring because of an ankle injury and joined Gateshead in March 2002.

SCOTT, PAUL — Forward
Current Club: Dulwich Hamlet

D o B: 10/04/1979 — Birthplace: London
Striker with a good goalscoring record. Re-signed for Ryman Division One South side Dulwich Hamlet in the summer of 2002 from Premier outfit Maidenhead United. Had joined the Magpies the previous summer from Harrow Borough after serving the likes of Whyteleafe and Hendon

SCOTT, PETER — Midfielder
Current Club: Beaconsfield SYCOB

D o B: 01/10/1963 — Birthplace: Notting Hill
Previous clubs include: Aylesbury Utd - November 1998, Hayes, Barnet, AFC Bournemouth, Fulham.

SCOTT, RICHARD — Midfielder
Current Club: Telford United

D o B: 29/09/1974 — Birthplace: Dudley
Arrived on a free transfer from Peterborough, where he turned down a new contract to join United. A former Shrewsbury favourite, has plyed his trade in every division of the nationwide league. A player of considerably pedigree.

SCOTT, STEVE — Midfielder
Current Club: Ashford Town (Middx)

D o B: 08/05/1967 — Birthplace: Chiswick
Honours won: England Youth Int., Ryman League Premier Div.Winners
Previously with Chertsey Town and an experienced midfield player who came to Ashford Town (Middx) towards the end of 99-00 season. Aged 34 and player-coach, he played in the Conference with Slough Town and also appeared in the European Cup Winners Cup for Hibernians of Malta.

SCOTT, TONY — Forward
Current Club: Skelmersdale United

Birthplace: Wigan
Previous clubs include: St Helens T - November 2000, Skelmersdale Utd, Wigan Ath (Trainee).

SCOULDING, DARREN — Defender
Current Club: Stowmarket Town

Birthplace: Suffolk
Previous clubs include: Diss T - August 2000, Stowmarket T, Harwich & Parkeston, Brantham Ath., Halstead T.

SCOWEN, MICHAEL — Defender
Current Club: Fisher Athletic (London)

From Youth team.

SCROGGINS, LEE — Midfielder
Current Club: Blyth Spartans

Birthplace: Darlington

Lee had experienced the Football League during his spell with Darlington, before signing for UniBond Premier side Blyth Spartans in August 2001. A talented midfielder who made a first-team position his own during the 2001/02 season.

SCULLARD, NEIL — Defender
Current Club: Hamble ASSC

Birthplace: Hampshire

Previous clubs include: BAT Sports - July 1999.

SCULLY, MICHAEL — Defender
Current Club: Congleton Town

D o B: 26/05/1977   Birthplace: Liverpool

Previous clubs include: St.Helens T - November 2001, Winsford Utd, St.Helens T, SK Sifhalla (Sweden), Witton Alb., Holywell T, Rhyl, Flint Town Utd.

SCULPHER, LEE — Defender
Current Club: Clitheroe

Birthplace: Lancashire

Scully, not the skipper any more, but the fans acknowledged Leader. The defence is never as solid without him, and although his shooting boots are rarely tested he quite often pops up with key headed goals from set pieces.

SEABURY, KEVIN — Defender
Current Club: Welling United

D o B: 24/11/1973   Birthplace: Shrewsbury

Defender who joined Dr Martens Premier side Welling United in July 2002 from Kent neighbours Dover Athletic. A Shrewsbury player as a youth and well experienced when he left after almost ten years with the club. Kevin made almost 250 appearances for the Shrews but will be remembered by their supporters as something of a legend. After suffering from series of injuries he joined Dover in February 2002.

SEAL, DAVID — Forward
Current Club: Mangotsfield United

D o B: 26/01/1972   Birthplace: Sydney, Australia

Much travelled Australian who first arrived in Bristol several seasons ago, when Bristol City signed him from Aalst in Belgian football. He later moved on to Northampton Town for a fee of £90,000, and returned to the UK in the summer of 2000. Joined Mangotsfield United in July 2000, and although injury has hampered him, he is still renowned as being one of the top strikers in the Dr Martens Western Division.

SEALE, CHRIS — Forward
Current Club: Borrowash Victoria

Birthplace: Derbyshire

Previous clubs include: Heanor T - July 1999, Borrowash V, Stapenhill.

SEALES, STUART — Forward
Current Club: Swaffham Town

Birthplace: Norfolk

Big front-runner who always gives 100% another product of Swaffhams youth policy.

SEARLE, STEWART — Goalkeeper
Current Club: Carshalton Athletic

D o B: 27/02/1979   Birthplace: Surrey

Highly-rated goalkeeper who joined Carshalton Athletic from Aldershot for £2,500 in July 2001 for his third spell with the Robins. Previous clubs include Wimbledon, Woking, Crawley Town and Molesey.

SEARS, PAUL — Forward
Current Club: Chertsey Town

Birthplace: Surrey

Previous clubs include: Epsom & Ewell - January 2002, Dulwich Hamlet, Sutton Utd, Carshalton Ath., Crystal Palace.

SEBO, JOE — Midfielder
Current Club: Wokingham Town

Birthplace: Berkshire

Previous clubs include: Camberley T - October 2001, Fleet T, Aldershot T, Camberley T.

SEDGEMORE, JAKE — Defender
Current Club: Northwich Victoria

Birthplace: Birmingham

Honours won: British Universities Rep.

Jake is a utility player who signed for Conference side Northwich Victoria from Hednesford Town in September 2001. He began his career with West Bromwich Albion before switching to Keys Park. Competent in midfield or defence, he has also represented the British Universities.

SEDGWICK, MARTIN — Defender
Current Club: Ware

Birthplace: Bishops Stortford

Previous clubs include: Hertford T - August 2001, Bishops Stortford, Ware, St.Margaretsbury, Bishops Stortford, Harlow T, Ware, Saffron Walden T, Ware, Bishops Stortford.

SEDLAN, JASON — Midfielder
Current Club: Lincoln United

D o B: 05/08/1979   Birthplace: Peterborough

Previous clubs include: Spalding Utd - February 2001, Wisbech T, Boston Utd, Mansfield T, Notts Co.

SELBY, NEIL — Forward
Current Club: Staines Town

D o B: 12/03/1974   Birthplace: Hampshire

Free-scoring striker who joined Staines Town in September 2001 from Boreham Wood, whom he helped to promotion to the Ryman Premier. Started his career with Southampton, moving on to Havant Town, Waterlooville and Wokingham Town. Was then a regular scorer in a successful Chertsey Town side and also had spells with Aldershot Town and Aylesbury United.

SELL, RICHARD — Forward
Current Club: Epsom And Ewell

Birthplace: Surrey

Former Chelsea apprentice, in his second spell with Epsom, and recently made his 100th 1st XI appearance. In the Epsom Youth side that won the Isthmian Youth Cup in 1991 when he was named Man of the Match. Reverted back to his former striking position last season, scoring three goals in four games. Another player who constantly gives 100% every game.

SELL, STUART — *Midfielder*
Current Club: Littlehampton Town
Birthplace: Sussex
Left-sided player: won a championship medal with The Clifton (1998/99 Sussex Sunday League title winners) before rejoining Littlehampton at the start of the following season: looked to be in really good form during 2000/01, but had an unsettled period after transferring to Lancing in November and then moving onto Whitehawk after only a few games: scored a total of 6 goals last season and returned to Littlehampton in August 2001.

SELLAR, MARK — *Defender*
Current Club: St Margaretsbury
Birthplace: Hertford
Previous clubs include: Ware - July 2001.

SELLARS, PAUL — *Defender*
Current Club: Rhayader Town
Birthplace: Bangor
Bangor lad Paul, now living in Cheshire. A tall defender, has shown poise and skill in recent matches and has also fitted well in midfield. Signed for Rhayader in February 2002.

SENIOR, MARK — *Midfielder*
Current Club: Eccleshill United
Birthplace: Leeds
From Youth team.

SENIOR, RYAN — *Forward*
Current Club: Guiseley
Previous clubs include: Eccleshill Utd - July 2001.

SENK, CHRIS — *Forward*
Current Club: Clacton Town
Birthplace: Essex
Another testiment to Clacton's Youth Development. 20-year-old Chris was also second top scorer last season. Unfortunately suffered a broken leg during November 2001.

SERTORI, MARK — *Forward*
Current Club: Accrington Stanley
D o B: 01/09/1967   *Birthplace: Manchester*
Honours won: Conference Winners
A tough-tackling centre back, with a wealth of Football League experience. Effective in his customary no-nonsense style of play and a good organiser at the back. Previous clubs include Stockport County, Lincoln City, Wrexham, Bury, Scunthorpe, Halifax, York, Shrewsbury and Cheltenham. Signed for UniBond Premier side Accrington Stanley in July 2002 after spending the previous season with rivals Altrincham.

SERVICE, JOHN — *Defender*
Current Club: Metropolitan Police
Previous clubs include: Army - July 1997.

SESAY, MALIK — *Forward*
Current Club: Enfield
Birthplace: London
Previous clubs include: SISK Trelleborgs (Sweden) - December 2001.

SESTANOVICH, ASHLEY — *Midfielder*
Current Club: Hampton & Richmond
Birthplace: Croatia
Exciting young midfield of Croat descent who signed for Ryman Premier side Hampton & Richmond Borough in the summer of 2002. Played the previous season in the Eircom under-21 League for Mullingar Town in Ireland and the last few months of the campaign with Belgian club Antwerp. Started out at 17 with a professional contract at Manchester City and also had a brief spell with Millwall.

SEUKE, PAUL — *Goalkeeper*
Current Club: Chertsey Town
Birthplace: London
Goalkeeper who signed in the summer after being with Staines Town for some while where he has played first team football despite his years.

SEVERN, KEVIN — *Midfielder*
Current Club: Hatfield Main
Birthplace: Doncaster
Previous clubs include: Glasshoughton Welfare - March 2002, Harrogate T, Goole T, Hatfield Main, Brigg T, Hatfield Main, Pontefract Collieries, Hatfield Main.

SHAAPVLED, CHRIS — *Defender*
Current Club: Southwick
Birthplace: Sussex
Defender: member of Southwicks U-18 side who has also regularly appeared for the first-team during 2001/02.

SHADE, MICKY — *Defender*
Current Club: Lowestoft Town
Birthplace: Great Yarmouth
Previous clubs include: Great Yarmouth T - July 1999, Gorleston, Lowestoft T.

SHADE, NEIL — *Defender*
Current Club: AFC Sudbury
Birthplace: Essex
Recent new signing for Clacton from Witham Town. Can play at the back or in midfield. Very strong player, more than capable of scoring goals.

SHAIL, MARK — *Defender*
Current Club: Worcester City
D o B: 15/10/1966   *Birthplace: Sandviken, Sweden*
Honours won: England Semi-Pro Int.
Mark rejoined his first club Worcester City in January 2002, having been released by Kidderminster Harriers. He began at City before being sold to Yeovil Town for £8000 in 1989. A powerful central defender, he subsequently played with distinction for Bristol City for nine years before joining Harriers in 1999. Is a former England semi-professional international.

SHAKESPEARE, ADAM — *Defender*
Current Club: Newtown AFC
Birthplace: Worcestershire
Adam joined Hednesford Town from Hereford United as a youth team player and worked his way into the first team squad. A strong and versatile player in defence continued to feature regularly in the reserve team and push for a first team spot. Switched to League of Wales side Newtown in August 2002.

SHANNON, ROB — *Forward*
Current Club: Port Talbot Town
D o B: 06/01/1984   *Birthplace: Wales*
Previous clubs include: Southampton - March 2002.

SHARMAN, KEITH — *Defender*

Current Club: Chelmsford City

D o B: 06/11/1971   *Birthplace: Essex*

Big defender or midfielder who joined Chelmsford City in May 2002 from Crawley Town. Had signed for the Sussex side from Ashford Town in January 2000. Suffered with a knee injury throughout the following season but was outstanding in 2001/02. Previously with Leyton Orient and had a long seven-year spell at Bromley.

SHARP, ANDY — *Defender*

Current Club: Garforth Town

D o B: 11/07/1973   *Birthplace: Yorkshire*

Another acquisition from local football. Signed for the club at the start of last season. A battling midfield player, strong tackler and good organizer. Has developed into an excellent sweeper this season.

SHARP, ANDY — *Midfielder*

Current Club: Lincoln United

D o B: 21/06/1981   *Birthplace: Lincolnshire*

Previous clubs include: North Ferriby Utd - January 2002, Winterton Rangers.

SHARP, EDDIE — *Forward*

Current Club: Consett

Birthplace: Co.Durham

Previous clubs include: Tow Law T - August 2001.

SHARP, LEE — *Goalkeeper*

Current Club: Lincoln United

D o B: 18/12/1976   *Birthplace: Lincoln*

Previous clubs include: QPR - August 2000, Lincoln Utd.

SHARP, PAUL — *Goalkeeper*

Current Club: North Ferriby United

D o B: 09/10/1968   *Birthplace: Hull*

Goalkeeper who has made over 250 appearances for North Ferriby United since his arrival in 1996 from neighbours Goole Town, including an appearance at Wembley in the 1997 FA Vase Final. Previously with Frickley Athletic and Immingham Town.

SHARPE, PHIL — *Defender*

Current Club: Frickley Athletic

D o B: 26/01/1968   *Birthplace: Leeds*

Appointed as player-manager of UniBond League Premier Division club Frickley Athletic in July 2002 after a spell as assistant boss at First Division Guiseley. A vastly experienced player, Phil was originally a striker with Doncaster, Halifax, Farsley Celtic and abroad with Eendracht Wervik in Germany and Union de Centre in Belgium. Returned home to have spells with Gateshead, Ashton United, Bradford Park Avenue, Harrogate Town, Garforth Town and Farsley again before joining Guiseley in November 2000. Is more usually seen in central defence these days.

SHARPLING, CHRIS — *Forward*

Current Club: Woking

D o B: 21/04/1981   *Birthplace: Bromley*

Chris joined Woking on loan from Crystal Palace for the second half of the 2000/01 season and impressed everyone at Kingfield. He finally signed for the cards in October 2001 for a record £60,000 fee after months of work by former manager Colin Lippiatt and the board of Woking. A highly-promising striker who has the ability to make a return to the professional game.

SHARRATT, CHRIS — *Forward*

Current Club: Rhyl

D o B: 13/08/1970   *Birthplace: Liverpool*

Honours won: Northern Premier League Winners

Previous clubs include: Winsford Utd - October 2000, Colwyn Bay, Vauxhall Motors, Bangor C, Altrincham, Southport, Macclesfield T, Wigan Ath., Stalybridge Celtic, Caernarfon T, Bangor C.

SHARROCK, CYRIL — *Goalkeeper*

Current Club: Bamber Bridge

Birthplace: Preston

Previous clubs include: Kendal T - November 2001, Lancaster C.

SHAUGHNESSY, STEVE — *Forward*

Current Club: Winsford United

D o B: 27/04/1967   *Birthplace: Liverpool*

Experienced front-runner whose clubs include Runcorn (for whom he scored in the FA Trophy Final in 1993) Stalybridge and Chorley. Player/Manager last season and the start of this season.

SHAW, ANDREW — *Forward*

Current Club: Spennymoor United

Birthplace: Newcastle

Re-signed for Spennymoor United from UniBond First Division rivals and neighbours Bishop Auckland in July 2002. Had re-joined Bishop Auckland from Spennymoor in July 1997, having played for the Bishops for a couple of seasons in the late 80s and early 90s. A skilful goal-scoring centre forward who leads the line well.

SHAW, CHRIS — *Midfielder*

Current Club: Ossett Town

Birthplace: Grantham

From Youth team.

SHAW, CHRIS — *Midfielder*

Current Club: Grantham Town

D o B: 05/03/1971   *Birthplace: Newcastle*

Returned to Town for a third spell this summer after finishing top scorer with neighbours Ossett Albion last season. Originally came to the club from Pontefract Colls in 1994 and has now amassed over 300 appearances. Also had a spell with Emley as well as South Shields and Langley Park in his native North East.

SHAW, DARREN — *Midfielder*

Current Club: Solihull Borough

D o B: 20/12/1974   *Birthplace: Telford*

Signed for Solihull in the summer of 2001. He had a previous spell on loan at Solihull from March 2000 till the end of the season; he was signed from Stafford Rangers. He played 10 times scoring five goals. The clubs were unable to agree terms so he returned to Stafford and played for them last season in the Premier Division. Has also played for Tamworth.

SHAW, GARY — *Defender*

Current Club: Guiseley

D o B: 06/02/1974   *Birthplace: Leeds*

Defender who joined UniBond First Division side Guiseley from rivals and Yorkshire neighbours Farsley Celtic in the summer of 2002. Played Northern Counties East League football for the likes of Eccleshill United, Thackley and Garforth Town and in the UniBond with Harrogate Town before signing for Farsley in July 2001.

SHAW, JASON — Midfielder
Current Club: Aylesbury United
D o B: 04/12/1970   Birthplace: Essex
Vastly experienced midfielder who signed for Ryman Premier side Aylesbury United in July 2002 from Division One North outfit Wealdstone. Began as a junior at West Ham and then spent a number of seasons with Redbridge Forest. Moves to Dartford, Harrow Borough, Boreham Wood, Chertsey Town and Hampton & Richmond followed before he joined the Stones in August 2001.

SHAW, LEA — Midfielder
Current Club: Redditch United
Birthplace: Birmingham
Previous clubs include: Bilston T - January 2002, Stourport Swifts, Oldbury Utd, Halesowen Harriers.

SHAW, OLIVER — Midfielder
Current Club: Bashley
Previous clubs include: FC Den Haag (Denmark) (Junior) - August 2000.

SHAW, SIMON — Defender
Current Club: Barrow
D o B: 21/09/1973   Birthplace: Middlesbrough
Honours won: England Semi-Pro Int.
Middlesbrough-born full back who joined Darlington as a trainee and then turned professional in 1992. Went on to make almost 200 appearances for the Quakers before switching to Doncaster at the start of the 1998/99 season. Earned rave reviews and won caps for the England semi-professional side. Signed for Barrow in July 2001.

SHAW, STEVE — Defender
Current Club: Banstead Athletic
Birthplace: Surrey
Previous clubs include: Carshalton Ath - July 1999, Tooting & Mitcham Utd, Carshalton Ath., Molesey, Banstead Ath., Whyteleafe, Tooting & Mitcham Utd.

SHAW, STEVE — Forward
Current Club: Barking & East Ham United
Birthplace: London
27-year-old striker who joined Barking from Essex neighbours Leyton Pennant in November 2001. Played Ryman League football with Tilbury and Pennant early on and then spent a period in the Essex Senior League with Waltham Abbey.

SHEARER, ADAM — Midfielder
Current Club: Bideford
Birthplace: Devon
Adam is a classy midfielder who has also been on the Books of Exeter City, & Stoke Gabriel, he is a professional football coach. Has made over 100 first team appearances.

SHEARER, LEE — Defender
Current Club: Margate
D o B: 23/10/1977   Birthplace: Rochford
Honours won: England Schoolboy Int.
Tall and commanding central defender who joined Margate from Dover Athletic in June 2002. The former England Schoolboy international had signed for Dover from Leyton Orient in the summer of 1998 and has developed into an accomplished performer who was popular with the fans for his whole-hearted performances.

SHEFFIELD, JAMES — Defender
Current Club: Chertsey Town
Birthplace: Surrey
A defender who signed in mid-September. Has also played for Egham Town, Woking and Wycombe Wanderers.

SHEFFIELD, JON — Goalkeeper
Current Club: Yeovil Town
D o B: 01/02/1969   Birthplace: Bedworth
Jon signed for Yeovil Town in July 2001, shortly after being released by Plymouth Argyle, for whom he made 158 first team appearances as their first choice goalkeeper. Jons association with manager Gary Johnson goes back over 10 years, with the Bedworth born keeper having spent over four years at Cambridge United, where Johnson was Reserve, assistant, caretaker and first team Manager at various times. In total, Jon clocked up 319 Football League appearances and his other clubs include Norwich, Aldershot, Colchester, Swindon, Hereford and Peterborough. He lives in Saltash in Cornwall, and has recently obtained his FA Coaching badge.

SHEILS, MARK — Goalkeeper
Current Club: Gresley Rovers
D o B: 01/08/1981   Birthplace: Birmingham
Honours won: England Universities Rep.
Former English Universities representative goalkeeper, Mark was with West Brom, Hereford and Crewe as a youngster before going Non-League with Redditch United. Had a short spell with Kidderminster before joining Gresley Rovers in March 2001.

SHELTON, ANDY — Midfielder
Current Club: Ossett Albion
D o B: 19/06/1980   Birthplace: Sutton Coldfield
Previous clubs include: Harrogate T - March 2002, Chester C.

SHELTON, MATTHEW — Midfielder
Current Club: Abingdon United
Birthplace: Oxford
Previous clubs include: Brackley T - July 2001, Abingdon Utd, Abingdon T, Thame Utd, Oxford C.

SHEPHERD, DOMINIC — Forward
Current Club: Withdean 2000
Birthplace: Brighton
Former Brighton & Hove Albion apprentice who has played in the League of Ireland for Glenavon and Derry City: a prolific goalscorer for Selsey and Shoreham, but seemed to go through a dry spell when signing for Burgess Hill in 1999: spent a brief period at Southwick before joining Lewes midway through 1999/2000 (suffered with injuries): set to go to Withdean at the start of the following season, but ended up back at Southwick when that fell though (scored 22 times): has looked as good as ever since returning to all-conquering Lewes in August 2001, but joined Withdean in February 2002.

SHEPHERD, GARRY — Forward
Current Club: Newport County
D o B: 30/03/1976   Birthplace: Llwyyn-Y-Pai
Honours won: Wales Semi-Pro Int.
Garry has been Newport County's top scorer for the past two seasons and was runner-up in the Dr Martens Premier Divison scoring charts for 2000/01. Made a scoring Newport debut against Grantham Town in February 2000 having joined from Merthyr Tudfil. Initially with Ton Pentre, Garry, who is a Welsh semi-professional international, was voted Player of the Year for 2000/01.

SHEPHERD, MARK — Forward

Current Club: Solihull Borough

Birthplace: Birmingham

Prolific goalscorer who started his playing days with Kidderminster Harriers, where he made a number of Conference appearances. Joined Moor Green in October 1997. In season 1999/2000, Mark formed a lethal partnership with Derek Hall which produced over 50 goals between them as they helped the Moors to promotion to the Dr Martens Premier Division. Transferred to Worcester City in February 2001 but failed to hit it off at St Georges Lane and moved on to Solihull Borough in May 2002.

SHEPHERD, MARTIN — Forward

Current Club: Dorchester Town

Birthplace: Dorset

Martin re-joined Dorchester Town in July 2002 following three seasons with Salisbury City. A prolific scorer, he started his playing days with Westlands Sports and then had a spell with Trowbridge Town before joining Weymouth in August 1995. His form for the Terras earned him Dr Martens League representative honours before switching to neighbouring Dorchester two years later.

SHEPHERD, PAUL — Forward

Current Club: Scarborough

D o B: 17/11/1977   Birthplace: Leeds

Was another Russell Slade signing from Oldham in December 2001. The former Leeds United trainee has also played for Ayr, Tranmere, Luton and Scunthorpe. A very talented attacker.

SHEPHERD, SAM — Midfielder

Current Club: Marlow

Birthplace: Oxford

Signed for Marlow from Thame United in July 2000, Sam is a talented midfield player who started his career with Oxford United as a trainee. After being released by United he joined Ryman League neighbours Oxford City. Switched to Chesham United in March 1999 and then had a brief spell at Thame before joining Marlow. Sam is the son of a former Marlow player.

SHEPPARD, JASON — Midfielder

Current Club: Heybridge Swifts

Birthplace: Essex

Recovered well from a cruciate ligament operation and working hard as anchor man in the centre of the park. Can score spectacular goals. Also played for Maldon Town and was an inspirational skipper of the reserves before getting his senior chance.

SHEPPARD, JIMMY — Midfielder

Current Club: Brockenhurst

Birthplace: Hampshire

Previous clubs include: Lymington & New Milton - January 2002, Bashley, Poole T, Andover, Swindon T.

SHERGOLD, SIMON — Midfielder

Current Club: Corinthian Casuals

Birthplace: Surrey

Simon, a midfielder, has been a first team regular for Corinthian Casuals since joining from local football at the start of the 1995/96 season. Has now made over 350 appearances and is the club captain.

SHERIDAN, ASHLEY — Forward

Current Club: Stafford Town

Birthplace: Stafford

From Youth team.

SHERIFF, MARK — Forward

Current Club: Withdean 2000

Birthplace: Sussex

Talented forward : one-time apprentice with Brighton & Hove Albion: went on to play for Peacehaven and Burgess Hill during their successful reigns before joining Ringmer in 1998: thrown out of the side after being sent off in a match against Arundel during February 2000 (had previously served a long suspension): seemed to settle in really well at Whitehawk during 2000/01 (scored 21 goals), until a match against Littlehampton in January 2001 where he allegedly assaulted a referee who had red-carded him: subsequently awarded another lengthy ban: made his comeback for Southwick in November 2001 before signing up for Withdean shortly afterwards.

SHERLOCK, PAUL — Midfielder

Current Club: Stamford

D o B: 17/11/1973   Birthplace: Wigan

Previous clubs include: Hucknall T - January 2002, Bedford T, Mansfield T, Notts Co.

SHERRY, MICK — Forward

Current Club: Eastleigh

Birthplace: Hampshire

Previous clubs include: East Cowes Vics - May 2002.

SHERWOOD, ANDY — Defender

Current Club: Ashford Town (Middx)

Birthplace: Middlesex

From Youth team.

SHERWOOD, BEN — Midfielder

Current Club: North Ferriby United

Birthplace: Yorkshire

Previous clubs include: Scarborough - January 2002.

SHERWOOD, PAUL — Forward

Current Club: Abingdon Town

Birthplace: Oxford

Previous clubs include: Carterton T - July 2001, Thame Utd, Carterton T, Oxford C, Carterton T.

SHIELDS, ALAN — Midfielder

Current Club: Bracknell Town

Birthplace: Bracknell

From Youth team.

SHIELDS, GARY — Forward

Current Club: Chester-Le Street

Birthplace: Co.Durham

Previous clubs include: Herrington CW - July 1998.

SHIMELL, GLYN — Goalkeeper

Current Club: Banstead Athletic

Birthplace: London

Previous clubs include: Croydon Ath - February 2000, Tooting & Mitcham Utd, Croydon Ath., Netherne, Malden Vale.

SHIPP, DANNY   *Forward*
Current Club: Dagenham & Redbridge
D o B: 25/09/1976   *Birthplace: Romford*
Joined Dagenham & Redbridge from Irish side Coleraine in November 1997, he started his career at West Ham United and spent two periods on loan at the Daggers befoe being transferred to Ireland in a £150,000 deal in 1996. Within two minutes of his debut he scored a 30-yard stunner at Peterborough in the FA Cup. Has now scored over 70 goals for the club and played a major part in their Ryman League championship success.

SHIRLEY, MARK   *Midfielder*
Current Club: Accrington Stanley
Birthplace: Lancashire
Started as a trainee at Nottingham Forest, and then joined Caenarfon Town on his release, before sizeable transfer fees took him to Ashton United and then on to Lancaster City. Moved to Morecambe during the 96-97 season before joining Accrington Stanley in June 1999. Was injured for most of the 2000/01 season but was fully fit for the 2001/02 season.

SHIRTCLIFFE, SIMON   *Defender*
Current Club: Buxton
Birthplace: Buxton
From Youth team.

SHOEFIELD, ROSS   *Midfielder*
Current Club: Corinthian Casuals
Birthplace: Surrey
From Youth team.

SHORE, DANNY   *Midfielder*
Current Club: Dunston Federation Brewery
Birthplace: Newcastle
Previous clubs include: New Hartley Juniors - August 2001.

SHORT, CHRIS   *Defender*
Current Club: Bangor City
D o B: 19/12/1970   *Birthplace: Liverpool*
Experienced defender who signed for League of Wales side Bangor City from rivals Caernarfon Town in October 2001. Previous clubs include Conwy United, Fleetwood Town, Droylsden and Netherfield.

SHORT, KARL   *Midfielder*
Current Club: Jarrow Roofing & Boldon Ca
Birthplace: Newcastle
Previous clubs include: Shotton Comrades - February 2002.

SHOTTON, JOHN   *Midfielder*
Current Club: West Auckland Town
Birthplace: Co.Durham
Previous clubs include: Crook T - March 2001, West Auckland T, Manchester Utd.

SHOTTON, NEIL   *Defender*
Current Club: Dunston Federation Brewery
Birthplace: Newcastle
Previous clubs include: Spennymoor Utd - July 1999, Morpeth T, Durham C, Dunston Federation.

SHUTT, CARL   *Forward*
Current Club: Kettering Town
D o B: 10/10/1961   *Birthplace: Sheffield*
Honours won: Premiership Winners, Dr Martens League Premier Div.Winners
Carl was appointed as player-manager of Kettering Town towards the end of the 2000/01 and led the club back into the Conference in his first full season in charge. Had a notable playing career, most notably with the seasons spent at Leeds United (winning a League Championship medal), Sheffield Wednesday and Bradford City.

SHUTT, JAMES   *Goalkeeper*
Current Club: Guiseley
D o B: 27/11/1976   *Birthplace: Bradford*
Honours won: British Universities Rep.
Arrived at Ingfield in September 2001 from Guiseley, initially on loan but then permanently. Began his career as a junior with Bradford City before playing locally with Carlton Athletic and then establishing himself as Guiseleys first choice keeper. Returned to Nethermoor in the summer of 2002.

SHUTT, STEVE   *Midfielder*
Current Club: Stocksbridge Park Steels
D o B: 29/11/1964   *Birthplace: Barnsley*
Previous clubs include: Goole T - July 1995, Buxton, Goole T, Matlock T, Goole T, Scunthorpe Utd, Goole T, Barnsley.

SHUTTLEWORTH, ANDREW   *Forward*
Current Club: Guiseley
From Youth team.

SHUTTLEWORTH, BARRY   *Defender*
Current Club: Accrington Stanley
D o B: 09/07/1977   *Birthplace: Accrington*
Defender who signed for his home-town club Accrington Stanley from Third Division Macclesfield in August 2002. Began his career with Bury and then had spells with Rotherham and Blackpool, where he finally made his League debut in the 1999/2000 season. Spent a year with Scarborough in the Conference before joining the Silkmen in October 2001. Gained UniBond Premier experience whilst on-loan at Altrincham in 2001/02.

SIBANDA, ANTHONY   *Forward*
Current Club: Great Wakering Rovers
Birthplace: Zimbabwe
Previous clubs include: Ilford - August 2001, Clapton, Barking, Northwood, Hampton, Yeading, Bishops Stortford, Barking, Stansted, Saffron Walden T, Collier Row, Kingsbury T, Yeading, Hendon, Collier Row, Cobh Ramblers.

SIBSON, ANDY   *Midfielder*
Current Club: Glasshoughton Welfare
D o B: 22/11/1975   *Birthplace: Leeds*
Previous clubs include: Thackley - July 2000, Garforth T, Hucknall T, Eastwood T, Selby T, North Ferriby Utd, Leeds Utd (Junior).

SIDDALL, CHRIS   *Defender*
Current Club: Ossett Albion
D o B: 11/12/1979   *Birthplace: Sheffield*
Previous clubs include: Stocksbridge Park Steels - September 2001, Sheffield Wednesday.

SIDDALL, RICHARD   *Goalkeeper*
Current Club: Gateshead
D o B: 24/01/1982   *Birthplace: Sheffield*
Young goalkeeper who could be one for the future. Joined UniBond Premier side Gateshead in August 2002 after being released by Sheffield Wednesday. Started his career with Barnsley.

S

SIDE, CHARLEY   *Forward*
Current Club: Dulwich Hamlet

D o B: 11/02/1981   Birthplace: Kent

Talented 22-year-old forward who has scored regularly for Dulwich Hamlet since joining in October 2001 from Bromley, against whom he scored a hat-trick in the Boxing Day derby. Previously played in the Conference for Welling United as a teenager.

SIDEBOTTOM, FRASER   *Midfielder*
Current Club: Frickley Athletic

Birthplace: Barnsley

Previous clubs include: Stocksbridge Park Steels - October 2001, Barnsley.

SIDEBOTTOM, JAMIE   *Defender*
Current Club: Glasshoughton Welfare

Birthplace: Yorkshire

Previous clubs include: Denaby Utd - August 2000, Pontefract Collieries, Brodsworth Welfare, Armthorpe Welfare, Glasshoughton Welfare.

SIDWELL, TOM   *Defender*
Current Club: Racing Club Warwick

Birthplace: Coventry

Previous clubs include: Alveston - December 2000.

SIGERE, JEAN-MICHEL   *Forward*
Current Club: Stevenage Borough

D o B: 26/01/1977   Birthplace: France

Exciting striker who signed for Stevenage Borough with Simon Wormull from Rushden & Diamonds in October 2001. Originally from Bordeaux, he signed for Rushden in March 2000, and scored 11 goals in 15 starts for them. Strong and skilful runner, Siggy has already shown what he is capable of with some important and spectacular goals, and Boro have high hopes of their enigmatic Frenchman. Finished top scorer in his first season with 12 goals in only 25 starts.

SILANDER, DUNCAN   *Midfielder*
Current Club: Yeading

Birthplace: Scotland

26 year old midfielder who joined the Ding over the summer after moving down to London from Scotland. Previously played for Edinburgh University, Heriot-Watt University and Spartans FC.

SILK, ANDY   *Defender*
Current Club: Bromley

Birthplace: London

Andy played locally at St Andrews FC before joining Bromley to play in the Suburban League for the Reserve team. His goals helped him play for the first team but chances were limited at the time, and many games he was substitute. He played for Bromley from 1992-1996 and helped the Ravens to the London Challenge Cup in 1995-96. Andy then left to join Leyton Pennant in 1996 and as club captain played over 200 games for the East London side, but returned to Bromley at the start of the 2000/2001 season. Postman lives in New Eltham.

SILLS, TIM   *Forward*
Current Club: Kingstonian

D o B: 10/09/1979   Birthplace: Surrey

Fast and skilful forward who signed for Kingstonian from Basingstoke Town in early March 2002 after having impressed during a one month loan period. Scored in his first three games of his loan spell for the Ks. Joined the Stoke from Camberley Town at the end of the 1999/2000 season, scoring after just five minutes into his debut against Bishops Stortford, and racked up 19 goals in both of his seasons there.

SILSBY, LEE   *Defender*
Current Club: Southwick

Birthplace: Sussex

Promising young defender: made his debut for Burgess Hill in August 1999 and was also a member of the Sussex U-18 squad: poised to join Withdean at the start of 2000/01, but returned to Leylands Park when that fell through: signed up by Saltdean in January 2001 and switched to Southwick twelve months later.

SILVER, HADLEIGH   *Defender*
Current Club: Wingate And Finchley

Birthplace: London

Previous clubs include: Romford - March 1999, Wingate & Finchley.

SILVESTRI, ENZO   *Defender*
Current Club: Aylesbury United

Previous clubs include: Barton Rovers - August 2001, Hitchin T.

SIM, GEOFF   *Goalkeeper*
Current Club: Wimborne Town

Birthplace: Hampshire

Previous clubs include: Bashley - December 2001, Fleet T, Aerostructures, Havant T, Bognor Regis T, Andover, Chertsey T, Andover, Chertsey T, Newport IOW, Colden Common, Gosport B.

SIMBA, AMARA   *Forward*
Current Club: Billericay Town

D o B: 23/12/1961   Birthplace: Paris

Honours won: French Int.

Previous clubs include: St.Albans C - August 2001, Kettering T, St.Albans C, Kingstonian, Leyton Orient, Lille (France), Caen (France), Monaco (France), Paris St.Germain (France), AS Cannes (France), Paris St.Germain (France), Versailles (France), Houdan (France), Jeanne DArc (France).

SIMKIN, DARREN   *Defender*
Current Club: Hednesford Town

D o B: 24/03/1970   Birthplace: Walsall

Experienced defender who joined Hednesford Town in May 2002 from Dr Martens Premier Division rivals Stafford Rangers. Darren was recruited for Rangers from Blakenall during the 2000 close season and was an ever-present during both the the 2000/01 and 2001/02 seasons, a total of 103 appearances. He turned professional in November 1992 when Wolverhampton Wanderers signed him from Blakenall for a £10,000 fee and made 25 first team appearances. He moved on to Shrewsbury Town and then to Telford United before returning to Blakenall where he was team captain.

SIMMONDS, DANNY   *Midfielder*
Current Club: Hastings United

D o B: 17/12/1974   Birthplace: Eastbourne

Honours won: Bitish Universities Rep.

Midfielder, previously with Brighton & Hove Albion before making his Hastings debut at the start of 1995/96. Has helped his side to two Sussex Senior Cup Final victories as well as playing for the British Universities representative team. Leading scorer for the Arrows in 2000/01 with 21 goals.

SIMMONS, JUSTIN   *Forward*
Current Club: Withdean 2000

Birthplace: Sussex

Leading scorer for Mile Oak in 1997/98 before signing for Worthing: had spells with Saltdean and Withdean during 1999/2000, as well as playing for the County: struck 5 times for Burgess Hill the following season (often started as a substitute): returned to Withdean in the summer 2001.

SIMMONS, MICHAEL   *Defender*
Current Club: Windsor & Eton
D o B: 26/02/1982   *Birthplace: London*
Honours won: England Schooboy Int.
Previous clubs include: Margate - January 2002, Charlton Ath.

SIMMONS, MICKY   *Goalkeeper*
Current Club: Cray Wanderers
Birthplace: Kent
Previous clubs include: Dartford - July 1997, Crockenhill, Ruislip Manor, Dulwich Hamlet, Ruislip Manor.

SIMMONS, TONY   *Forward*
Current Club: Grantham Town
D o B: 09/02/1965   *Birthplace: Sheffield*
Honours won: England Youth Int.
Previous clubs include: Lincoln Utd - December 1999, Holbeach Utd, Lincoln C, Rotherham Utd, QPR, Sheffield Wednesday.

SIMMS, MARK   *Midfielder*
Current Club: Bromsgrove Rovers
Birthplace: Birmingham
Previous clubs include: Blakenall - June 2001, Solihull B, Bilston T, Bloxwich T, Tamworth.

SIMMS, MARK   *Midfielder*
Current Club: Thame United
Birthplace: Oxfordshire
Joined Thame United at the end of November 2000 from Abingdon United. Prolific goalscorer in junior football, Mark possesses a sweet left foot and is equally at home out wide or up front.

SIMPSON, ALI   *Midfielder*
Current Club: Bashley
Previous clubs include: Walton & Hersham - August 2001, Bashley.

SIMPSON, ANDY   *Defender*
Current Club: Potters Bar Town
Birthplace: Herts
Previous clubs include: Greenacres - July 2001, Hemel Hempstead.

SIMPSON, ANDY   *Midfielder*
Current Club: Matlock Town
D o B: 02/07/1976   *Birthplace: Sheffield*
Midfielder now in his third season at Causeway Lane broken only by a short spell with Rocester. He was the clubs top scorer and fans player of the year in his debut campaign, 1999/2000. Andy came on to the Non-League scene after being with Sheffield United as a youngster, and played for Gresley and Kings Lynn prior to arrival at Matlock.

SIMPSON, DEREK   *Midfielder*
Current Club: Andover
D o B: 23/12/1978   *Birthplace: Lanark*
Previous clubs include: Hampton & Richmond Borough - September 2000, Basingstoke T, Slough T, Reading.

SIMPSON, GARETH   *Midfielder*
Current Club: Diss Town
Birthplace: Norwich
Previous clubs include: Cambridge C - August 2001, Mildenhall T, Gillingham, Norwich C.

SIMPSON, JIMMY   *Midfielder*
Current Club: Banbury United
Birthplace: Kettering
Previous clubs include: Daventry T - August 2001, Raunds T, St.Neots T, Corby T, Ford Sports, Rothwell T, Raunds T, Corby T, Norwich C.

SIMPSON, LEON   *Forward*
Current Club: Yate Town
Birthplace: Bristol
Previous clubs include: Paulton Rovers - July 2000.

SIMPSON, MARK   *Midfielder*
Current Club: Whitley Bay
Birthplace: Durham
Marc was at Nottingham Forest as a junior. He then took a football scholarship in America. Recently qualified from Liverpool University with a sports degree.

SIMPSON, MATT   *Defender*
Current Club: Shepshed Dynamo
D o B: 19/12/1975   *Birthplace: Derby*
Previous clubs include: Rocester - August 2002, Ilkeston T, Stapenhill, Belper T, Burton Alb.

SIMPSON, NICKY   *Midfielder*
Current Club: Wivenhoe Town
Birthplace: Essex
Attacking midfielder who made something of a surprise move to Ryman Division One North side Wivenhoe Town in August 2002. It was a surprise as he had been hot-property after being top scorer in the Premier Division with Braintree Town in 2001/02. Began his playing days with the Iron and also had a spell with Heybridge Swifts before rejoining Braintree in November 2000.

SIMPSON, PAUL   *Goalkeeper*
Current Club: Ashington
Birthplace: Northumberland
Previous clubs include: Morpeth T - August 2001.

SIMPSON, PHIL   *Midfielder*
Current Club: Edgware Town
D o B: 18/10/1969   *Birthplace: London*
Previous clubs include: Boreham Wood - November 2001, Slough T, Yeovil T, Barnet, Stevenage B.

SIMPSON, ROBBIE   *Forward*
Current Club: Hitchin Town
D o B: 03/03/1976   *Birthplace: Luton*
Honours won: England Youth Int.
Signed for Hitchin Town in March 2001 from St.Albans City, Robbie is an experienced striker who was formerly with Tottenham Hotspur, Portsmouth and Woking. Played for Tottenham in the Inter Toto Cup - an 0-8 defeat to Cologne. A former England Youth international.

SIMPSON, RODNEY   *Forward*
Current Club: Kingsbury Town
Birthplace: London
From Youth team.

S

SIMPSON, TOM — Midfielder

Current Club: Leek Town

Birthplace: Nottingham

Signed for Leek Town in the close season of 2002 from the Hucknall Town Academy. Promising young midfield player and one to watch for the future.

SIMPSON, TONY — Midfielder

Current Club: Arnold Town

Birthplace: Nottingham

Previous clubs include: Stafford Rangers - August 2000, Ilkeston T, Nuneaton B, Tamworth, Nuneaton B, Grantham T, Nottingham Forest.

SIMPSON, WAYNE — Defender

Current Club: Hednesford Town

D o B: 19/09/1968   Birthplace: Stoke

Honours won: England Semi-Pro Int., Dr Martens League Premier Div.Winners

Signed for Hednesford Town from Nuneaton Borough during the close season of 2001, Wayne is a former Hednesford player, who was part of the very successful Pitmen side of the mid 1990s. He is a great reader of the game and rarely looks to be under pressure at the back. Wayne is already the proud holder of two DMPL Winners medals as well as caps for the England semi-professional side.

SIMPSON, WES — Defender

Current Club: Witton Albion

D o B: 29/03/1977   Birthplace: Winsford

Previous clubs include: Winsford Utd - October 2001, Northwich V, Crewe Alexandra.

SIMS, ADAM — Midfielder

Current Club: Mangotsfield United

Birthplace: Australia

Spent the early part of his career at Southampton before being released. Joined Mangotsfield in June 2000. Now an established first team player who scores plenty of goals from midfield.

SIMS, PAUL — Forward

Current Club: Lymington & New Milton

Birthplace: Hampshire

Previous clubs include: Brockenhurst - May 2002, Lymington & New Milton.

SINCLAIR, ANDY — Midfielder

Current Club: Tow Law Town

Birthplace: Co.Durham

Has played in a variety of positions over his Northern League career. His previous Clubs include Ferryhill, Consett, Whitby and Spennymoor. Joined the Lawyers from Whitby and was the Vice Captain in the League Championship winning squad of 94/95. He left the Lawyers to go to Crook and subsequently West Auckland. Rejoined us as Assistant-Manager/Player last season.

SINCLAIR, JAMIE — Midfielder

Current Club: Epsom And Ewell

Birthplace: Surrey

Joined Epsom at the start of the 2001/2002 season. Formerly with Dorking and was player of the year in 2000/2001. He is a good team player and his favourite position is left back but will play in an position that is ever short.

SINCLAIR, MARTIN — Midfielder

Current Club: Gorleston

Birthplace: Norfolk

Previous clubs include: Acle - July 2001, Gorleston.

SINCLAIR, MATTHEW — Defender

Current Club: Epsom And Ewell

Birthplace: Surrey

Joined Epsom at the start of the 2001/2002 season. Formerly with Dorking, he played soccer in America for 5 years before returning to play for Dorking.

SINCLAIR, STEVE — Midfielder

Current Club: Chesham United

D o B: 25/11/1982   Birthplace: Hertfordshire

Steve is a good dribbler and has played for Watford, Norwich and was at Ryman Premier side Boreham Wood for the 2001/02 season. His footballing hero is Pele and his best moment in football was when he became part of the YTS scheme at Watford, when he was 16 years old. He works for Thames Valley Water. Joined Chesham United in August 2002.

SINDEN, RICHARD — Forward

Current Club: Maidstone United

Birthplace: Kent

Previous clubs include: Sittingbourne - July 2001, Tonbridge, Dulwich Hamlet, Sittingbourne, Nottingham Forest (Trainee).

SINES, SAM — Midfielder

Current Club: Stanway Rovers

Birthplace: Essex

Previous clubs include: Harwich & Parkeston - February 2002.

SINFIELD, MARC — Defender

Current Club: Harlow Town

Birthplace: Essex

Vastly experienced defender who joined Harlow Town in March 2002 having previously played for Heybridge Swifts, Billericay town and Chesham United.

SINGH, JASON — Forward

Current Club: Dunston Federation Brewery

Birthplace: Newcastle

Previous clubs include: Redheugh Boys Club - July 2001.

SINGH, PAVEL — Forward

Current Club: Farsley Celtic

Previous clubs include: Harrogate T - July 2001, Farsley Celtic.

SINTON, ANDY — Midfielder

Current Club: Burton Albion

D o B: 19/03/1966   Birthplace: Newcastle

Honours won: England Schoolboy, B & Full Int.

Andy was signed on the eve of the Conference season and comes to Burton Albion with a wealth of experience. He began his career at Cambridge United before moving on to Brentford and then Queens Park Rangers. Following a very successful spell at Loftus Road he moved to Sheffield Wednesday for £2.75 million and then on to Spurs three years later for £1.75 million. During his time with QPR and Sheffield Wednesday he made 12 full international appearances for England, playing in the European Championships in Sweden in 1992. From Spurs he signed for Wolverhampton Wanderers and trained pre-season with Walsall, and with a number of other clubs after his signature, it was Brewers boss Nigel Clough who persuaded him to put pen to paper.

SIPPETTS, GARY — *Forward*
Current Club: St. Albans City
D o B: 17/07/1976   *Birthplace: London*
Striker who signed for Ryman Premier side St Albans City during the close season of 2002 from Spartan South Midlands League Premier Division champions London Colney, for whom he scored 57 goals during the 2001/02 season. Had briefly been on City's books in 1996 but returned to Colney to hone his striking skills.

SKEDD, TONY — *Midfielder*
Current Club: Bishop Auckland
D o B: 19/05/1975   *Birthplace: Hartlepool*
Previous clubs include: Spennymoor Utd - February 2002, Blyth Spartans, Whitby T, Blyth Spartans, Billingham Synthonia, Gateshead, Spennymoor Utd, Hartlepool Utd.

SKELDING, AARON — *Midfielder*
Current Club: Willenhall Town
Birthplace: Wolverhampton
Signed for Willenhall from Cradley in December 2000, very committed player who will play at a higher level, one of the Town's best assets. Returned twice this season after spells with Dilaton Town und then Atherstone United.

SKELLY, RICHARD — *Defender*
Current Club: Cambridge City
D o B: 24/03/1972   *Birthplace: Norwich*
Richard is in his second spell at Cambridge City after rejoining from Chelmsford at the end of February 2002, the club for which he left at the beginning of that season after being released by former manager Chris Tovey. Originally joined City from Sutton United at the start of the 2000/01 season. Full back whose previous clubs include Kings Lynn, Kettering Town and Northampton Town.

SKELTON, BEN — *Defender*
Current Club: Rocester
Birthplace: Stafford
Previous clubs include: Stafford T - July 2001.

SKELTON, CRAIG — *Forward*
Current Club: Whitby Town
D o B: 14/09/1980   *Birthplace: Middlesbrough*
Former Darlington professional who re-joined UniBond Premier side Whitby Town in March 2002 from rivals Blyth Spartans. Started his career with the Quakers before signing for Whitby originally in October 2000. Moved to Blyth at the start of the 2001/02 campaign.

SKELTON, GAVIN — *Midfielder*
Current Club: Gretna
D o B: 27/03/1981   *Birthplace: Carlisle*
Previous clubs include: Workington - October 2001, Carlisle Utd.

SKELTON, PHIL — *Midfielder*
Current Club: Stafford Town
Birthplace: Staffordshire
Previous clubs include: Walsall Wood - July 2001.

SKEOGH, JAMES — *Midfielder*
Current Club: Bamber Bridge
Previous clubs include: Kendal T - September 2001, Accrington Stanley, Blackpool.

SKERRITT, PETER — *Defender*
Current Club: Bracknell Town
Birthplace: Berkshire
Previous clubs include: Burnham - December 2000, Windsor & Eton, Bracknell T, Basingstoke T, Chertsey T, Egham T, Chertsey T, Slough T, Windsor & Eton.

SKIDMORE, ROB — *Defender*
Current Club: Clevedon Town
Birthplace: Bristol
Previous clubs include: Chippenham T - February 2002, Clevedon T, Bath C, Forest Green R, Clevedon T, Bristol C.

SKIDMORE, STUART — *Midfielder*
Current Club: Halesowen Town
Birthplace: Birmingham
Honours won: Dr Martens Western Div.Winners
Stuart started his career at Halesowen Town before making a switch to Causeway United in 1999. Returned to Halesowen in 2001, as Alan Moores final, and arguably best signing. Won favour with current Yeltz boss Brendan Phillips who seems to prefer him as a right back although his natural role is in the middle of the park

SKINNER, CRAIG — *Midfielder*
Current Club: Northwich Victoria
D o B: 21/10/1970   *Birthplace: Heywood*
Previous clubs include: Leigh RMI - November 2001, York C, Wrexham, Plymouth Argyle, Blackburn R.

SKINNER, DEAN — *Defender*
Current Club: Hadleigh United
Birthplace: Suffolk
Strong defender with good skills and passing ability. Huge will to win and never stops encouraging. Commanding presence. Progressed through Hadleighs Youth and Reserve sides to command a regular First Team spot.

SKINNER, JUSTIN — *Defender*
Current Club: Gravesend & Northfleet
D o B: 17/09/1972   *Birthplace: Dorking*
Justin is in his second spell with newly-promoted Conference club Gravesend & Northfleet having rejoined at the beginning of season 2001/02. A left-sided defender, he began his career at Wimbledon as a trainee before graduating to full time professional making his first-team debut in the 1992/93 season against Liverpool at Anfield. He made around 30 Football League appearances in total, some whilst on loan to AFC Bournemouth and Wycombe Wanderers. Justins consistency and high level of performance last season was rewarded with the Player of the Year Award for 2001/02.

SKINNER, PAUL — *Defender*
Current Club: Pagham
Birthplace: Sussex
Defender, originally part of the Pagham youth set-up: went on to play for Paul Gilberts Oving side, and scored twice during 1999/2000: introduced into the Lions first-team in December 2001.

SKINNER, STEVE — *Forward*
Current Club: Gretna
Birthplace: Carlisle
Previous clubs include: Queen of the South - March 2001, Carlisle Utd.

SKIVERTON, TERRY   *Defender*

Current Club: Yeovil Town

D o B: 26/06/1975   *Birthplace: Mile End*
Honours won: England Semi-Pro Int., FA Trophy Winners
Had league experience with Chelsea and Wycombe Wanderers before signing for Welling United at the beginning of 1997-98. Terry joined the full-time ranks at Yeovil Town, giving up his day job on the Sky TV football-based soap Dream Team. He is now the mainstay of the defence and was finally given a long overdue call-up to the England Semi-Professional squad and made his debut for England on February 13th 2001 at Nene Park in a home match against Wales.

SLACK, STUART   *Defender*

Current Club: Armthorpe Welfare

Birthplace: Hull
Previous clubs include: Goole AFC - November 2001, Armthorpe Welfare, Goole AFC.

SLADE, CHRISTIAN   *Forward*

Current Club: Bridgnorth Town

Birthplace: Shropshire
Previous clubs include: Ludlow T - December 2001, Shrewsbury T (Trainee).

SLADEN, STEVE   *Goalkeeper*

Current Club: Hayes

Birthplace: Middlesex
From Youth team.

SLATER, CRAIG   *Defender*

Current Club: Willenhall Town

Birthplace: Birmingham
Signed for Willenhall in 2001 from Cradley, dependable and skilful player with potentional to play in the Football League.

SLATER, KARL   *Defender*

Current Club: Glasshoughton Welfare

Birthplace: Bradford
Previous clubs include: Brodsworth Welfare - September 2000, Thackley, Ossett T, Altofts, Pontefract Collieries, Bradford PA.

SLATER, LEE   *Midfielder*

Current Club: Great Harwood Town

Birthplace: Lancashire
Previous clubs include: Clitheroe - August 2001, Darwen.

SLATER, STUART   *Midfielder*

Current Club: Weston-Super-Mare

D o B: 27/03/1969   *Birthplace: Sudbury*
Honours won: England u-21 & B Int.
Signed for Weston-super-Mare from Aberystwyth Town in December 2001. His vast professional experience includes 140 appearances for West Hame United, two seasons at Celtic (£1.5 million), three seasons at Ipswich Town (£800,000) and spells at Leicester City and Watford. Has England international caps at Under 21 level andB levels.

SLEEN, VERNON   *Midfielder*

Current Club: Racing Club Warwick

Birthplace: Coventry
Previous clubs include: Leamington Hibs - July 2001.

SLIDE, GRAHAM   *Midfielder*

Current Club: Oldbury United

Birthplace: Birmingham
Previous clubs include: Boldmere St.Michaels - July 1998, Walsall Wood.

SLINN, KEVIN   *Forward*

Current Club: Bedford Town

D o B: 02/09/1974   *Birthplace: Northampton*
Signed for Ryman Premier side Bedford Town from Eagle Bitter United Counties outfit Raunds Town in January 2000. A player well known to manager Roger Ashby who had him under his wing at Rushden & Diamonds. Kevin is a great finisher who always seems to be on the end of chances. Was the clubs leading goalscorer with 26 goals in 2001/02. Previously with Watford, Stockport, Corby Town and Cogenhoe United.

SLOANE, DARRYL   *Goalkeeper*

Current Club: Great Harwood Town

Birthplace: Lancashire
Previous clubs include: Maine Road - July 2001, Rossendale Utd, Netherfield, Accrington Stanley, Great Harwood T.

SLOUGH, CHRIS   *Forward*

Current Club: Bideford

Birthplace: Devon
Chris is a left sided attacking player who thrives on getting wide and producing quality crosses. He joined us from Dawlish Town and has also played for Minehead, Barnstaple, Clyst Rovers and Buckfastleigh.

SLOWE, ANDY   *Defender*

Current Club: Sheffield FC

Birthplace: Sheffield
Previous clubs include: Phoenix - December 1999.

SMALE, JUSTIN   *Midfielder*

Current Club: Herne Bay

Birthplace: Kent
Previous clubs include: Dartford - July 2000, Erith & Belvedere, Corinthian, Ashford T, Erith & Belvedere, Gravesend, Gillingham.

SMALL, BRYAN   *Defender*

Current Club: Kettering Town

D o B: 15/11/1971   *Birthplace: Birmingham*
Honours won: England u-21 Int.
Former England under-21 international defender who joined Kettering Town midway through the 2001/02 season. Started his career with Aston Villa, where he made around 40 first-team appearances before moving to Bolton in March 1996. Never really settled in the Bolton side and spent time out on-loan at the likes of Luton, Bradford City and Bury before moving to Stoke in the summer of 1998. Switched to Walsall three years later but suffered an injury which eventually forced his release. Tried a comeback with Forest Green Rovers and then Kettering, but only really began to find some fitness at the start of the 2002/03 campaign.

SMALLEY, DAVID   *Goalkeeper*

Current Club: Burnham

Birthplace: Hampshire
Goalkeeper signed from AFC Newbury in November 2001 and was immediately called up to replace the injured Bolger. Has had Dr Martens League experience at Fleet Town.

SMART, GARY — *Defender*
Current Club: Windsor & Eton

D o B: 29/04/1964 — *Birthplace: Totnes*
Previous clubs include: Oxford C - July 2000, Aldershot T, Slough T, Hayes, Stevenage B, Oxford Utd, Wokingham T.

SMART, GARY — *Midfielder*
Current Club: Swindon Supermarine

Birthplace: Swindon
From Youth Academy.

SMART, GARY — *Midfielder*
Current Club: Bath City

D o B: 08/12/1963 — *Birthplace: Bristol*
Gary was appointed to the position as assistant-manager of Clevedon Town in June 2001, having been signed from Paulton Rovers, where he spent the 2000-2001 season playing in the Screwfix Direct League. He is one of the most expierienced players in the area having played amongst others for Bristol Rovers, Cheltenham Town, Bath City, Mangotsfield United, Newport AFC and Forest Green Rovers. Switched back to Bath as number two in March 2002.

SMART, JOE — *Goalkeeper*
Current Club: Chertsey Town

Birthplace: Surrey
Goalkeeper who has come through the youth set up with Chertsey Juniors and is on the brink to break into senior football.

SMART, LEE — *Defender*
Current Club: Enfield Town (Essex)

Birthplace: London
An experienced competitior at Non-League level. Previous clubs include Ware, Wealdstone, Barking, Kingstonian and Dagenham & Redbridge. Spent last season with Edgware Town.

SMART, MATTHEW — *Midfielder*
Current Club: Eastbourne Borough

Birthplace: Sussex
oined from Horsham (Ryman League), where he was club captain, during the 2001 close season. Previously with Wick (Sussex County League), and has represented the County.

SMART, WARREN — *Midfielder*
Current Club: Worthing

Birthplace: Brighton
Midfielder/defender: former Brighton & Hove Albion youth, who spent a couple of years at Crawley after joining them in 1997: returned to Sussex football when signing for Worthing during the 2001 close season, having previously spent time away at university.

SMEATHERS, STUART — *Defender*
Current Club: Bedford Town

Birthplace: Northampton
22 year old defender who signed for Ryman Premier side Bedford Town in August 2002 from Eagle Bitter United Counties League outfit Raunds Town. Previously on the books at Northampton as a youngster, Stuart impressed while on trial with the Eagles in pre-season.

SMEATON, JAMES — *Defender*
Current Club: Saltdean United

Birthplace: Sussex
Played for Southwick reserves during 2000/01: gained a place in the first-team from the start of the following season: transferred to Saltdean in January 2002.

SMITH, AARON — *Forward*
Current Club: Egham Town

Birthplace: Staines
From Youth team.

SMITH, AARON — *Midfielder*
Current Club: Sutton United

Birthplace: Surrey
Promising young midfielder who has progressed through Sutton United's youth side and captained the clubsuccessful reserve side, making his first team debut in February 2001.

SMITH, ALFIE — *Defender*
Current Club: Molesey

Birthplace: London
A defender who signed in October from Molesey. Was previously with Feltham and Hampton & Richmond. Has also played for QPR and Brentford youths.

SMITH, ANDY — *Defender*
Current Club: Wivenhoe Town

Birthplace: Essex
Previous clubs include: Harwich & Parkeston - December 2001, Wivenhoe T.

SMITH, ANDY — *Defender*
Current Club: Evesham United

Previous clubs include: Solihull Borough - June 1999, Racing Club Warwick, Redditch Utd, Stratford T, Evesham Utd, Alcester T.

SMITH, ANDY — *Defender*
Current Club: Newcastle Blue Star

D o B: 11/09/1979 — *Birthplace: Wallsend*
Previous clubs include: Whitley Bay - July 1999, Hartlepool Utd, Wallsend Boys Club.

SMITH, ANDY — *Goalkeeper*
Current Club: Hamble ASSC

Birthplace: Hampshire
Previous clubs include: Gosport Borough - July 2001, Havant T, Gosport B.

SMITH, ANDY — *Midfielder*
Current Club: Haverfordwest County

D o B: 22/01/1980 — *Birthplace: Bristol*
Previous clubs include: Cinderford T - December 2001, Weston-Super-Mare, Yate T, Rhayader T, Newport Co., Hereford Utd (Trainee).

SMITH, ANDY — *Midfielder*
Current Club: Oxford City

Previous clubs include: Guisborough T - July 1995, Esh Winning, Aston Villa.

SMITH, ANDY — *Midfielder*
Current Club: Worksop Town

D o B: 13/01/1980 — *Birthplace: Blackpool*
Previous clubs include: Lincoln C - October 2001, Grimsby T.

S

SMITH, ANTHONY — Defender
Current Club: Atherton Laburnum Rovers
Birthplace: Bolton
In his second spell at LR, having rejoined from Atherton Collieries during summer 2001, Anthony is a quick and confident left back. His excellent crosses and good shooting ability make him a valuable attacking defender. He is a sales assistant for JJB Sports and likes a spot of golf.

SMITH, ANTHONY — Midfielder
Current Club: Caernarfon Town
D o B: 16/10/1973 *Birthplace: Chester*
Previous clubs include: Aberystwyth T - September 2001, Conwy Utd, Bangor C, Conwy Utd.

SMITH, BEN — Forward
Current Club: Berkhamsted Town
Birthplace: Luton
Previous clubs include: Barton Rovers - October 2000, Totternhoe.

SMITH, BEN — Midfielder
Current Club: Hereford United
D o B: 23/11/1978 *Birthplace: Chelmsford*
An apprentice at Highbury, Ben was released by Arsenal as a youngster and moved on to Reading, where he was unable to break into the senior side. In search of first-team football, he signed for Yeovil Town in March 1998 and made an immediate impact, establishing himself as a dynamic midfield player with no shortage of skill. Ben stayed at Huish Park for a further three seasons, making 143 appearances for the Glovers and scoring 17 goals. He shone during Dave Webbs spell at the club in 2000, and it was no surprise when the Southend boss came back to sign him in the summer of 2001. However, injuries affected his progress and, despite being offered another contract by the Shrimpers, he opted to return to the Conference with Hereford United in June 2002.

SMITH, CARL — Midfielder
Current Club: Worksop Town
D o B: 15/01/1979 *Birthplace: Sheffield*
Previous clubs include: Burnley - August 1999.

SMITH, CHRIS — Forward
Current Club: Solihull Borough
D o B: 03/01/1977 *Birthplace: Birmingham*
He is the current Players' Player and Supporters' Player of the Year. Chris signed from Blakenall in the summer of 2000 after spending a month on loan at Solihull in the 1999/2000 season; he scored 3 times in four games. He has also played for Bromsgrove Rovers. He was ever-present last season and finished top goalscorer with 28 goals.

SMITH, CHRIS — Midfielder
Current Club: Rothwell Town
Birthplace: Leicester
Previous clubs include: St. Andrews - October 2001, Oadby T, Rushden & Diamonds.

SMITH, CHRIS — Midfielder
Current Club: Hadleigh United
Birthplace: Suffolk
Returned to his home club Hadleigh this season after a number of years away - most recently with Needham Market. Strong and tireless, loves to get forward and score goals.

SMITH, CRAIG — Defender
Current Club: Hinckley United
D o B: 02/08/1976 *Birthplace: Mansfield*
Previous clubs include: Belper T - January 2001, Hinckley Utd, Burton Alb., Derby Co.

SMITH, CRAIG — Goalkeeper
Current Club: Brodsworth Welfare
Birthplace: Doncaster
Previous clubs include: Pontefract Collieries - July 1998, Denaby Utd, Maltby Main, Ossett T, Goole T, Bridlington T, Doncaster R.

SMITH, CRAIG — Midfielder
Current Club: Halifax Town
D o B: 08/06/1984 *Birthplace: Bradford*
Craig is definately one for the future at Halifax Town. He is a player who can play in a number of positions, in midfield and up-front and was a regular scorer for the youth and reserve teams before getting his senior chance during the 2001/02 season.

SMITH, DAMIEN — Midfielder
Current Club: Hailsham Town
Birthplace: Sussex
Midfielder/defender: a member of Hailshams cup winning youth team back in 1997, has a reputation for scoring the occasional spectacular goal, and struck a Beckham-type fifty yarder in a match against Worthing Utd in February 2001.

SMITH, DANNY — Midfielder
Current Club: Worthing
Birthplace: Sussex
Wide defender/midfielder, with some 200 Worthing appearances to his name since joining them in 1996: a former Brighton & Hove Albion trainee who has also spent time at Crawley.

SMITH, DARREN — Defender
Current Club: Eastbourne United
Birthplace: Sussex
Team captain and rock solid defender. Longest-serving member of the Eastbourne United side who has been hampered by a series of injuries in recent years.

SMITH, DARREN — Forward
Current Club: Lincoln United
Birthplace: Lincoln
Local lad who joined Lincoln United from neighbouring Lincoln Moorlands in January 2002, following manager Garry Goddard. Is quick on the ball and a proven goalscorer.

SMITH, DARREN — Goalkeeper
Current Club: Aveley
Birthplace: Gillingham
Previous clubs include: Gravesend - August 2001, Gillingham (Trainee).

SMITH, DARREN — Midfielder
Current Club: Gravesend & Northfleet
D o B: 02/11/1977 *Birthplace: Kent*
Honours won: Ryman League Premier Div.Winners
Darren began his career as a schoolboy at Dr Martens League Sittingbourne. He progressed into the first-team squad by the age of eighteen, eventually establishing himself as a regular. During season 1998/99 he was signed by Gravesend manager Andy Ford, only to return to Sittingbourne later that season. He was signed by Gravesend for the second time in March 2000 and has since established himself as a regular selection for the senior side. Darren is a skilful, hard-working, attack-minded player whos game has developed immensely.

SMITH, DARYL   *Defender*
Current Club: Brandon United
Birthplace: Co.Durham
Honours won: Player of the Year and Players' Player of the Year in 1999/2000.
A very experienced Northern League player who is in his fourth season with us. A tremendous appetite for the game and was voted Player of the Year and Players' Player of the Year in the 1999/2000 season. Previous clubs include Consett and Annfield Plain.

SMITH, DAVID   *Defender*
Current Club: Frickley Athletic
Birthplace: Yorkshire
Previous clubs include: Armthorpe Welfare - October 2001, Frickley Ath.

SMITH, DAVID   *Midfielder*
Current Club: Croydon
Birthplace: Surrey
Previous clubs include: Kingstonian - August 2002, Charlton Ath.

SMITH, ERIC   *Defender*
Current Club: Bridgnorth Town
Birthplace: Shropshire
Previous clubs include: Halesowen Harriers - February 2000, Bilston T, Evesham Utd, Bilston T, Halesowen T, Tipton T.

SMITH, GARY   *Forward*
Current Club: Sutton Coldfield Town
Birthplace: Birmingham
Honours won: St.Kitts & Nevis Full Int.
Gary, an International with St Kitts & Nevis, re-joined Dr Martens Western Division side Sutton Coldfield Town in July 2002 after helping Halesowen Town to win the title the previous season. Had signed for Halesowen from Tamworth in July 2001 and has previously been with Worcester City and Paget Rangers. A fast and direct striker.

SMITH, GAVIN   *Defender*
Current Club: Worksop Town
D o B: 24/09/1977   Birthplace: Sheffield
Previous clubs include: Sheffield Wednesday - September 1998.

SMITH, GAVIN   *Forward*
Current Club: Bracknell Town
Birthplace: Hampshire
Previous clubs include: Fleet T - July 2001.

SMITH, GAVIN   *Midfielder*
Current Club: Liversedge
Birthplace: Bradford
Previous clubs include: Ossett Alb - December 2000, Bradford PA.

SMITH, GED   *Midfielder*
Current Club: Hyde United
Birthplace: Liverpool
Signed for UniBond Premier side Hyde United in August 2002. Formerly with rivals Marine, Ged is a young, talented and skilful midfield player.

SMITH, GLEN   *Forward*
Current Club: Whitby Town
Birthplace: Brotton
Pacey young striker with bags of talent. Scored twice on his first full appearence for UniBond Premier side Whitby Town at Garforth Town in the summer of 2002. Known for his acrobatic goal celebrations and extraodinary long throws, Glen looks to have a bright future at the Turnbull Ground.

SMITH, IAN   *Defender*
Current Club: Lowestoft Town
Birthplace: Great Yarmouth
Previous clubs include: Halesworth - July 1993.

SMITH, IAN   *Forward*
Current Club: Maltby Main
Birthplace: Yorkshire
Previous clubs include: Parkgate - October 2001.

SMITH, JAMIE   *Forward*
Current Club: Gloucester City
Birthplace: Gloucester
Previous clubs include: Witney T - July 2001, Gloucester C.

SMITH, JASON   *Defender*
Current Club: Romford
D o B: 22/02/1973   Birthplace: London
Former Watford schoolboy, Jason joined Grays Athletic in 1992 where he made a handful of first team appearances. Went on to play for local rivals Tilbury. Has also had spells at Ilford, Waltham Abbey, Haringey Borough and Clapton, before joining Romford in July 2001. Has made over 200 Ryman League appearances.

SMITH, JASON   *Midfielder*
Current Club: Solihull Borough
D o B: 21/12/1975   Birthplace: Wolverhampton
Previous clubs include: Bilston T - December 2001, Stafford Rangers, Bilston T, Stourbridge, Rushall Olympic, Ettingshall HT, Wolverhampton Wanderers.

SMITH, JONATHAN   *Defender*
Current Club: Accrington Stanley
Birthplace: Lancashire
Strong defender, joined Accrington Stanley in the summer of 1999 from neighbours Great Harwood. Also played for Darwen. Signed a new two and a half year contract in February, 2001.

SMITH, KEVIN   *Defender*
Current Club: Whyteleafe
Birthplace: London
Well-travelled defender around the Ryman League scene who joined Division One South side Whyteleafe in August 2002 following a second spell with Carshalton Athletic. Played at Millwall and Ipswich as a youngster before going on to have spells with Leatherhead, Dulwich Hamlet, Croydon and Bromley. Has also played in New Zealand with Auckland.

SMITH, LEE   *Forward*
Current Club: Gloucester City
D o B: 08/09/1983   Birthplace: Gloucester
From Youth team.

SMITH, LEON — Midfielder
Current Club: Hyde United
D o B: 18/02/1980   *Birthplace: Bolton*
Signed for UniBond Premier side Hyde United in August 2002 after a spell with Altrincham. Midfielder who has Conference experience with both Stevenage Borough and Morecambe, but moved back up north to join Altrincham in November 2001.

SMITH, LUKE — Forward
Current Club: Frickley Athletic
Previous clubs include: Harrogate T - December 2000, Yeovil T.

SMITH, MARK — Defender
Current Club: Dagenham & Redbridge
Birthplace: Luton
Honours won: England Semi-Pro Int., Conference Winners, Ryman League Premier Winners
Mark joined the Daggers on the eve of the 2001/2 season from Stevenage Borough. He began his career at Woking as a centre forward and joined Borough in 1992, scoring four goals on his debut. Since switching to his more familiar centre back position he has won several England Semi-Professional caps and was named as player of the year at Broadhall Way last season. Made his Daggers debut on the opening day of the season against Southport.

SMITH, MARK — Forward
Current Club: Eastwood Town
Previous clubs include: Armthorpe Welfare - August 2000.

SMITH, MARK — Forward
Current Club: Buxton
D o B: 19/12/1961   *Birthplace: Sheffield*
Previous clubs include: Hallam - July 2000, Sheffield, Matlock T, Gainsborough Trinity, Boston Utd, Scunthorpe Utd, Grimsby T, Huddersfield T, Rochdale, Kettering T, Scunthorpe Utd, Gainsborough Trinity, Worksop T, Sheffield Utd.

SMITH, MARK — Goalkeeper
Current Club: Ilkeston Town
D o B: 02/01/1973   *Birthplace: Birmingham*
Goalkeeper who joined Dr Martens Premier side Ilkeston Town in August 2002. Began his career with Nottingham Forest and then played League football with Crewe and Walsall before having a spell with Rushden & Diamonds. Then turned out for Bedford Town, Morecambe, Eastwood Town and Scarborough, where he was released at the end of the 2001/02 season.

SMITH, MARK — Midfielder
Current Club: Hamble ASSC
Birthplace: Hampshire
Previous clubs include: Andover - July 2000, Poole T, Newport IOW, Andover, Hamble.

SMITH, MARK — Midfielder
Current Club: Royston Town
Birthplace: Herts
Previous clubs include: Ware - September 2000, Standon & Puckridge, Ware.

SMITH, MATT — Defender
Current Club: Chichester City United
Birthplace: Sussex
Previous clubs include: Hailsham T - July 2001.

SMITH, MATT — Midfielder
Current Club: Dartford
Birthplace: Kent
From Youth team.

SMITH, MATT — Midfielder
Current Club: Hailsham Town
Birthplace: Sussex
Teenage midfielder: scored against Carterton in the FA Vase (September 2000, lost 2-1 in extra time): first-team regular when Joe Stevens took charge in November 2001.

SMITH, MATTHEW — Defender
Current Club: Solihull Borough
D o B: 28/08/1973   *Birthplace: Derby*
Signed this summer from Premier Division rivals Moor Green. Started his career at Derby County before signing for Plymouth Argyle. He had a brief spell with Irish side Cork City but turned down an offer of a contract and joined Burton Albion in August 1994. He was player of the season for them in the 1995/96 season.

SMITH, MERVIN — Midfielder
Current Club: Dereham Town
Birthplace: Norfolk
Signed from Downham Town during pre-season. Strong and combative player who will provide strong competition in the midfield area.

SMITH, MIKE — Defender
Current Club: Rossendale United
Birthplace: Lancashire
Previous clubs include: Ramsbottom Utd - July 2001, Salford C, Atherton LR, Leigh RMI.

SMITH, MIKE — Midfielder
Current Club: Farsley Celtic
D o B: 19/12/1968   *Birthplace: Hull*
Previous clubs include: North Ferriby Utd - August 2001, Brodsworth Welfare, North Ferriby Utd, Brodsworth Welfare, North Ferriby Utd, Worksop T, North Ferriby Utd, Goole T, Immingham T, Harrogate T, Goole T, Brigg T, Bridlington T, Ayr Utd, Hull C.

SMITH, MIKE — Midfielder
Current Club: Hall Road Rangers
D o B: 19/12/1968   *Birthplace: Hull*
Previous clubs include: North Ferriny Utd - July 2001, Brodsworth Welfare, North Ferriby Utd, Brodsworth Welfare, North Feriby Utd, Worksop T, North Ferriby Utd, Goole T, Immingham T, Harrogate T, Goole T, Brigg T, Bridlington T, Ayr Utd, Hull C.

SMITH, NEIL — Midfielder
Current Club: Stevenage Borough
D o B: 30/09/1971   *Birthplace: Lambeth*
Made over 350 League appearances before signing for Conference side Stevenage Borough on the eve of the 2002/03 season after being released by Reading. Midfielder Neil won an FA Youth Cup winners medal with Spurs before spending six years with Gillingham. Then helped Fulham gain promotion under Kevin Keegan before switching to Reading for £100,000 in August 1999.

SMITH, NEIL — Midfielder
Current Club: Halesowen Town
D o B: 29/12/1970   *Birthplace: Cradley*
Honours won: Dr Martens League Premier & Western Div. Winners
Neil is now in his second spell at Halesowen Town, having returned from Dr Martens Premier side Stafford Rangers. Neil

started his career at Third Division Shrewsbury Town but was released by the Shropshire outfit and joined Redditch United. From Redditch he joined League side Lincoln City but found himself back in Non-League football with Cheltenham Town. Impressed Rushden & Diamonds in his spell at Whaddon Road and the Nene Park outfit made swept in to sign him. Was captain of the Diamonds when they won the Dr Martens Premier, beating Halesowen Town to the title by a couple of points. Left Rushden for a short stay with Hednesford Town before being signed by Halesowen in July 1998. Was released at the end of the 1999/00 season but within 6 months he was drafted in by Alan Moore to add some solidarity to Halesowens midfield.

SMITH, NEIL   Midfielder
Current Club: Frome Town
D o B: 16/07/1979   *Birthplace: Somerset*
Previous clubs include: Yeovil T - July 2000, Southampton (Junior).

SMITH, NICKY   Midfielder
Current Club: Maldon Town
D o B: 28/01/1969   *Birthplace: Berkley*
Previous clubs include: Braintree T - June 2000, Cambridge C, Sudbury T, Wycombe Wanderers, Colchester Utd, Southend Utd.

SMITH, NIGEL   Midfielder
Current Club: Farsley Celtic
D o B: 21/12/1969   *Birthplace: Leeds*
Previous clubs include: Eccleshill Utd - July 2001, Harrogate T, Farsley Celtic, Hatfield Main, Farsley Celtic, Guiseley, Bury, Burnley, Leeds Utd (Trainee).

SMITH, PAUL   Goalkeeper
Current Club: Rhyl
D o B: 06/12/1977   *Birthplace: Wales*
Previous clubs include: Colwyn Bay - January 2002, Total Network Solutions, Flint Town Utd, Total Network Solutions.

SMITH, PAUL   Midfielder
Current Club: Arlesey Town
Birthplace: Hertfordshire
Honours won: Ryman League Div.3 Winners
Midfielder formerly with St Margaretsbury and Langford, he joined Arlesey Town in July 1999 and he has won two championship medals with the Bedfordshire club. Damaged his crucia knee ligament and missed a good deal of the 2001/02 campaign He works in Insurance.

SMITH, PAUL   Midfielder
Current Club: Withdean 2000
Birthplace: Sussex
Payed for Alan Pook at Burgess Hill: also has past experience with Horsham: joined Withdean in September 2001.

SMITH, PAUL   Midfielder
Current Club: Redhill
Birthplace: Kent
Scholesy joined from Kent League Thamesmead and has to be one of the fittest players at this level. Boundless levels of energy and enthusiasm combined with electric pace have already made him a firm favourite with the Kiln Brow faithful. Prominent in most of Reds recent goals and has begun to find the back of the net himself.

SMITH, PAUL   Midfielder
Current Club: Arundel
Birthplace: Sussex
Versatile, experienced performer. Spent several seasons at Pagham but was held back by injuries (only made a few appearances during 2000/01). Made a comeback when signing for Arundel in March 2002.

SMITH, PETER   Defender
Current Club: Grays Athletic
D o B: 12/07/1969   *Birthplace: Cannock*
Honours won: FA Trophy Winners
Previous clubs include: Canvey Island - April 2002, Woking, Brighton, Alma Swanley.

SMITH, PETER   Forward
Current Club: Kendal Town
D o B: 22/06/1965   *Birthplace: Preston*
Previous clubs include: Fleetwood Freeport - July 2001, Bamber Bridge, Accrington Stanley, Barrow, Great Harwood T, BAC Preston, Barrow.

SMITH, PETER   Forward
Current Club: Telford United
D o B: 15/09/1978   *Birthplace: Rhuddlan*
Coming to United as something of an unkown quantity from Crewe, Telford lad Smith is possesses excellent pace and strength on the ball. Despite not breaking into the first team at Crewe last season, the former schoolboy international impressed during his time with Macclesfield Town.

SMITH, PETER   Midfielder
Current Club: Bamber Bridge
D o B: 31/10/1980   *Birthplace: Liverpool*
Previous clubs include: Exeter C - August 2001.

SMITH, PHIL   Goalkeeper
Current Club: Margate
D o B: 14/12/1979   *Birthplace: Harrow*
Joined Conference club Margate from neighbouring Dover Athletic in July 2002. Had been signed by former manager Gary Bellamy for Dover in September 2001 from Kent neighbours Folkestone Invicta. Phil is a highly-rated goalkeeper. who was originally with Millwall. Gained selection for the FA XI in 2001/02, although injury prevented him from taking part.

SMITH, RICHARD   Defender
Current Club: Eastwood Town
Previous clubs include: Notts Co (Trainee) - August 1997.

SMITH, ROB   Midfielder
Current Club: Willenhall Town
Birthplace: Birmingham
Appointed manager of Willenhall Town in December 2001, he was previously manager at Dr Martens side Redditch Utd during the past 2 seasons, leading them to 6th and 4th in the league. He also spent 8 years there as a player during which time he managed the Youth side. His other clubs include Halesowen Town, Tamworth and Stafford Rangers. Rob has registered himself as a player for the Reds.

SMITH, ROB   Midfielder
Current Club: St.Albans City
D o B: 04/11/1980   *Birthplace: Milton Keynes*
Versatile and skillful midfielder with an excellent left foot, who can also deputise in defence. Signed for Ryman Premier side

St.Albans City in June 2001after a number of other clubs were interested. Originally on the books at Norwich City and has also been at Baldock Town, from whom he joined the Saints.

SMITH, ROONEY — *Defender*
Current Club: Kidsgrove Athletic
Birthplace: Cheshire
Honours won: NWCL Winners
Previously with Nantwich Town, Rooney is a reliable defender who joined Kidsgrove at the start of the 2001/02 season. Formerly with Congleton and Trafford, he missed out on several games due to injury, but still played a key role in Groves NWCL title success.

SMITH, SCOTT — *Defender*
Current Club: Woking
D o B: 06/03/1975   Birthplace: Christchurch
Honours won: New Zealand Int.
Scott is a New Zealand-born player who has represented his country at youth and full international levels. After moving to England he played for Rotherham United where he made 55 first-team appearances. Joining Woking in July 1997 after previous Conference experience with Kettering Town, he is a regular member of the New Zealand full international side and spent the summer of 2001 playing in their World Cup qualifying group games. He was voted Woking's Player of the Year and Players' Player of the Year for 1998/99.

SMITH, SEAN — *Defender*
Current Club: Borrowash Victoria
Birthplace: Derby
Previous clubs include: Sandiacre T - December 1997.

SMITH, STEVE — *Defender*
Current Club: Eastwood Town
Birthplace: Nottingham
Previous clubs include: Notts Co (Trainee) - December 2001.

SMITH, STEVE — *Forward*
Current Club: Wakefield & Emley
Birthplace: Huddersfield
First joined Emley in 1998-99 season and a lot was expected of a played that had been released by Huddersfield Town. Steve played six league games in 1997-98. Unfortunately last season he gave up playing altogether. Still only 21 he returned to the club this season.

SMITH, STEVE — *Forward*
Current Club: Ashford Town
Previous clubs include: Sheppey Utd - February 2001, Ashford T, Gravesend, Ashford T, Gravesend.

SMITH, STUART — *Defender*
Current Club: Tiverton Town
D o B: 29/03/1971   Birthplace: London
Honours won: FA Vase Winners
Joined Tiverton Town from Chard Town in July 1998, Stuart has become a favourite with the supporters. Previously with Weymouth and Chard, Stuart is commanding in the air, quick and good with either foot and with good vision. He is a senior analyst programmer.

SMITH, TIM — *Defender*
Current Club: Epsom And Ewell
Birthplace: London
Former Charlton schoolboy and Brighton apprentice who first joined Epsom in 1993, and after missing a long spell through injury was a regular until leaving the club in 1997, played for

Redhill and other clubs before rejoining Epsom towards the end of the 1999-2000 season. Over 100 1st XI appearances.

SMITH, TOMMY — *Midfielder*
Current Club: Leatherhead
Birthplace: Surrey
Previous clubs include: Dorking - October 2001.

SMITHARD, MATTHEW — *Midfielder*
Current Club: Farsley Celtic
D o B: 13/06/1976   Birthplace: Leeds
Attacking midfield man who began his career in Leeds United's highly successful youth team winning the FA Youth Cup in 1993 against a Manchester United side that included Beckham, Scholes and the Nevilles. Injury forced him into the Non-League game where he has attracted attention from professional clubs once more. Joined Farsley Celtic and then, from July 1999, Ossett Town where he became a firm favourite, scoring a numberof important goals. Transferred back to Farsley in June 2002.

SMITHERINGALE, MARK — *Defender*
Current Club: Harrogate Railway
Birthplace: Peterborough
Previous clubs include: Harrogate T - March 1999, Droylsden, Harrogate T, Bourne T, Lincoln Utd, Radcliffe B, Bourne T, Willenhall T, Stevenage B, Willenhall T, Bilston T, Baldock T, Spalding Utd, Rushden T, Stamford, Bourne T, Kettering T, Peterborough Utd.

SMITHURST, CRAIG — *Defender*
Current Club: Belper Town
Birthplace: Derbyshire
Previous clubs include: Burton Alb - July 1999, Bromsgrove R.

SMOTHERS, NEIL — *Defender*
Current Club: Cwmbran Town
D o B: 08/12/1977   Birthplace: Wales
Previous clubs include: UWIC Inter Cardiff - July 2000, Newport AFC, Cefn Forest.

SMY, DANNY — *Forward*
Current Club: Ipswich Wanderers
Birthplace: Ipswich
From Youth team.

SMYTH, CARL — *Defender*
Current Club: Connahs Quay Nomads
D o B: 04/05/1969   Birthplace: Wales
Previous clubs include: Mold Alexandra - July 1995, Caernarfon T, Bangor C, Tranmere R.

SMYTH, PETER — *Midfielder*
Current Club: Salford City
D o B: 25/06/1973   Birthplace: Manchester
Previous clubs include: Chorley - July 2002, Leigh RMI, Curzon Ashton, Altrincham, Horwich RMI, Manchester Utd.

SMYTHE, BEN — *Midfielder*
Current Club: Ipswich Wanderers
Birthplace: Suffolk
Previous clubs include: Achilles - July 2000.

SNAPE, JOHN   *Midfielder*
Current Club: Worcester City
D o B: 05/07/1969   *Birthplace: Birmingham*
John served his apprenticeship with West Bromwich Albion. After being released by the Hawthorns club he played for several clubs, including Bromsgrove Rovers, Northfield Town and Stourbridge before joining Halesowen Town. A hard working midfield player who is an extremely good competitor, he signed for Hereford in May 1998. After four years with the Bulls, John switched to Worcester City in May 2002.

SNASHALL, SHELDON   *Defender*
Current Club: Eastbourne United
Birthplace: Sussex
Defender who emerged through Eastbourne United's junior ranks and was a regular for the reserves during 1999/2000: has also played representative youth soccer: not always available due to being at university in London.

SNELL, RICHARD   *Forward*
Current Club: Flexsys Cefn Druids
Birthplace: Wales
From Youth team.

SNOW, GARY   *Midfielder*
Current Club: Southwick
Birthplace: Sussex
Midfielder: left Sammy Donnellys Worthing at the end of 1998/99: reunited with his old boss when signing for Southwick in December 2001.

SNOWDEN, STUART   *Defender*
Current Club: Enfield Town (Essex)
Birthplace: Middlesex
Joined the club from Wisbech Town, having previously played for Bishops Stortford. Another product of the Enfield FC Youth team.

SNOWLING, LEE   *Midfielder*
Current Club: Gorleston
Birthplace: Norfolk
Previous clubs include: Wroxham - July 1999.

SOAR, DUANE   *Defender*
Current Club: Lincoln United
Birthplace: Nottingham
Previous clubs include: Eastwood T - October 2001, Dunkirk, Hucknall Rolls.

SOAR, LEE   *Defender*
Current Club: Lincoln United
Previous clubs include: Hucknall T - July 2001, Gainsborough Trinity, Hucknall T, Hucknall Rolls.

SOBIHY, SIMON   *Defender*
Current Club: Corinthian Casuals
Birthplace: Surrey
Joined Corinthian Casuals in the summer of 2000 having previously been at Kingstonian and Leatherhead. Made an immediate impact on the side in his dynamic midfield role and was voted Player of the year and Supporters' Player of the year for 2000/01.

SODJE, AKPO   *Forward*
Current Club: Margate
Birthplace: Nigeria
Previous clubs include: Hayes - September 2001, Stevenage B.

SODJE, SAM   *Defender*
Current Club: Stevenage Borough
Birthplace: Nigeria
Younger brother of former Boro favourite Efetober, Sam has shown all the signs of following in his elder brothers footsteps. He broke into the first team at the end of last season after spending much of the season out on loan, and showed great touch and tremendous determination.

SODJE, STEVE   *Midfielder*
Current Club: Whitstable Town
Birthplace: Kent
Previous clubs include: Herne Bay - July 2000, Cray Wanderers, Erith & Belvedere, Sheppey Utd, Fisher Ath.

SOFTLEY, RICHARD   *Midfielder*
Current Club: Redditch United
D o B: 28/06/1976   *Birthplace: Cambridgeshire*
Signed for Redditch United in June 2002 from Moor Green. Had joined the Moors in March 1998 from Bromsgrove Rovers where he came through the reserves to earn a first-team spot. Began his career at March Town and made a good early impression at the Moors with his tough-tackling and high work rate. Was voted both Supporters and Managers Player of the Year for 1998/99.

SOGBODJOR, PETER   *Midfielder*
Current Club: Wembley
Birthplace: London
Previous clubs include: Hillingdon Borough - August 2000, Ruislip Manor.

SOLEY, STEVE   *Midfielder*
Current Club: Southport
D o B: 22/04/1971   *Birthplace: Widnes*
Goalscoring midfielder who joined Southport from Carlisle United in June 2002. Widnes-born, he started his playing days in the Liverpool Combination with Avon Athletic and then had spells with Warrington Town and Leek Town before being snapped up by Portsmouth for a £30,000 fee in July 1998. Went on to make over 100 League appearances for Pompey and then Carlisle before re-joining manager Phil Wilson, who he had played under at Leek.

SOLOMON, MALCOLM   *Midfielder*
Current Club: Barwell
Birthplace: Burton-on-Trent
Previous clubs include: Stapenhill - June 2001, Burton Alb., Boldmere St.Michaels, Burton Alb., Boldmere St.Michaels.

SOMERS, VINNY   *Midfielder*
Current Club: Hemel Hempstead Town
D o B: 03/04/1978   *Birthplace: Hertfordshire*
Previous clubs include: Wealdstone - January 2002, Hemel Hempstead.

SOMERVILLE, ALLAN   *Midfielder*
Current Club: Kidsgrove Athletic
D o B: 01/08/1963   *Birthplace: Stafford*
Previous clubs include: Rocester - January 2002, Stafford T, Stafford R, Leek T, Rocester, Hednesford T, Stafford R.

SORBARA, GIUSEPPE   *Forward*
Current Club: Frome Town
Birthplace: Italy
Previous clubs include: Wells C - December 2001, Street, Como (Italy).

SORENSEN, KRISTIAN   *Midfielder*
Current Club: Croydon Athletic
Birthplace: Berkshire
Midfielder who signed for Ryman Division One South side Croydon Athletic in July 2002 from rivals and neighbours Banstead Athletic. Began his playing days with Aylesbury United and also had spells with Marlow and Corinthian Casual before rejoining Banstead for a second time in March 2002.

SOUTER, RYAN   *Midfielder*
Current Club: Newport County
D o B: 05/02/1978   *Birthplace: Bedford*
Midfielder who has had something of a nomadic last year or so after joining Newport County in the summer of 2001 from Bury, from whom he had spent a three-month loan period at Newport the previous season. Ryan was originally an apprentice with Swindon before joining Weston-super-Mare in 1996, spending two and a half seasons at Woodspring Park. He was then transferred to Gigg Lane for a fee of £25,000. Then had short spells away from Spytty Park at Weston and Salisbury City before returning in February 2002.

SOUTHAM, GLEN   *Midfielder*
Current Club: Bishops Stortford
Birthplace: London
Glen signed from Enfield in the summer of 2000 and was previously with Fulham. Glen instantly became a hit with the blues supporters, for his tremendous work-rate and enthusiasm. Glen was awarded the Supporters' Player of the season in 2001 but an injury near the beginning of the 2001/2 season saw Glen sidelined and a loan spell to Boreham Wood followed. Back with the Blues now and Glen is fighting for his place back in the first team.

SOUTHERN, DAVID   *Forward*
Current Club: Gateshead
D o B: 15/12/1977   *Birthplace: Gateshead*
Was pretty much an unknown quantity until he signed for Gateshead during the latter part of the 2001/02 season. He got his first man of the match award at Lancaster City and has looked very impressive since. Signed from Crook Town and previously with Birtley Town, it is rumoured that David only signed for Gateshead because he supported the club!

SOUTHERN, ROBERT   *Forward*
Current Club: Great Yarmouth Town
D o B: 22/12/1984   *Birthplace: Norfolk*
Former Norwich City youth player who joined Yarmouth Youth last term, and with his pace and crosses, he will be challenging for a first team place.

SOUTHGATE, GLENN   *Midfielder*
Current Club: Harlow Town
D o B: 01/10/1978   *Birthplace: Orsett*
Glenn joined Ryman Division One North club Harlow Town in July 2002 from Premier Division Grays Athletic. Very strong and commanding player with great vision, he likes to push up just behind the attack and scores as well. Previously played at Enfield, Spurs, St Patricks and Barking and Billericay Town, joining Grays in February 2001.

SOUTHGATE, MIKE   *Forward*
Current Club: Bideford
Birthplace: Plymouth
Mike also hails from Plymouth and is an exciting young striker, who, although he admits to be still learning his trade, is a big favourite with the supporters. He has also played for St Blazey, Saltash, & Torpoint.

SOUTHON, JAMIE   *Defender*
Current Club: Purfleet
D o B: 13/10/1974   *Birthplace: Hornchurch*
Previous clubs include: Chelmsford C - August 1997, Grays Ath., Sing Tao (Hong Kong), Purfleet, Dagenham & Redbridge, Southend Utd.

SOUTHWELL, CARL   *Midfielder*
Current Club: Withdean 2000
Birthplace: Brighton
Honours won: English Colleges Rep.
Spent four years at Saltdean (graduated through their youth team) until transferring to Withdean in March 2000: played for Southwick the next season (scored 4 times) before returning to Withdean in August 2001: a quality performer, who has represented Sussex and been selected for the English Colleges squad in the past.

SOUTHWICK, MATTY   *Midfielder*
Current Club: Bromsgrove Rovers
Birthplace: Birmingham
Highly-rated midfielder whose career began at Walsall. Moved into the Non-League game with Stourbridge and also had spells with Bilston Town and Stourport Swifts, whom he helped to promotion from the Midland Alliance. Switched to Redditch United in March 2002 and then to Bromsgrove Rovers in May 02.

SOUTHWOOD, LEE   *Defender*
Current Club: Chorley
D o B: 16/08/1975   *Birthplace: Salford*
Centre half who was spotted playing in the Manchester League for The Willows by UniBond side Trafford. Signed in February 1999, he went on to become a regular in the first-team at Shawe View before switching to Chorley in June 2002.

SOUTHWOOD, ROSS   *Midfielder*
Current Club: Rye & Iden United
Birthplace: Hastings
Utility player who switched from Hastings reserves to Hailsham during the 2000 close season (scored 11 times that year): helped a club on a Division Two promotion crusade for the second year running when joining Rye for 2001/02.

SOWDEN, MATT   *Midfielder*
Current Club: Shildon
Birthplace: Bishop Auckland
Previous clubs include: Spennymoor Utd - February 2001, West Auckland T, Shildon.

SOWERBY, PHIL   *Midfielder*
Current Club: Chester-Le Street
Birthplace: Co.Durham
Previous clubs include: Morpeth T - November 1999, Birtley T, South Shields, Gretna, Brandon Utd.

SOZZO, JOSH   *Midfielder*
Current Club: Bedford Town
D o B: 05/07/1979   *Birthplace: Bedford*
Started his senior career at Leighton Town after spells with a number of clubs as a junior, including Arsenal, Luton and Watford. Josh normally plays on the right hand side of midfield and is a very tough player who never shirks a tackle. Signed for Bedford Town in the summer of 2000 from Hemel Hempstead and helped them to win the Ryman Second Division title. Josh sustained a serious knee injury during the early part of the 2001/02 season and is now battling his way back to match fitness.

SPACEY, PETER — Defender
Current Club: Rugby United
Birthplace: Coventry
A more than useful utility player who has played in every defensive and midfield position since joining Rugby United from Bedworth United in July 1999. A strong tackler who always gives 100 per cent, Paul has also seen service with Nuneaton Borough and local side Bermuda FC.

SPARKES, LEE — Midfielder
Current Club: Feltham
Birthplace: Ashford, Middx
Another ex- Walton Casuals player, Sparkes joined Feltham in 1998 and has been a regular addition to the squad barring injury. Sparky plays most games as either a left winger or an out and out sweeper. Originally a striker during his youth days he once scored 9 in a game for Walton Casuals U18. Lee is one of Felthams many Tottenham fans and IF he can stay injury free, a valuable addition to the side.

SPARKS, CHRIS — Defender
Current Club: Yeading
Birthplace: London
Previous clubs include: Hendon - December 2001, Yeading, Hemel Hempstead, Boreham Wood, Chesham Utd, St.Albans C, Yeovil T, Hayes, Chertsey T, Brentford.

SPARROW, PAUL — Defender
Current Club: Lancaster City
D o B: 24/03/1975   *Birthplace: Wandsworth*
It was perhaps one of the clearest signs of the rising fortunes for Lancaster City when Paul decided to join them in September 1999 as he felt they would help him get back into the League. However, although that hasn't happened to date, he's got better and better, co-inciding with shifting from right-midfield to right-back and finally centre-back where he was outstanding for much of the 2001/02 season. Formerly with Preston and Rochdale.

SPEARE, JAMES — Goalkeeper
Current Club: Accrington Stanley
D o B: 05/11/1976   *Birthplace: Liverpool*
Started out as a trainee at Everton before a two year spell as a professional. He then joined Darlington. In 1997-98 he moved to Sligo Rovers, joining Accrington Stanley on his return. Players' Player of the Year 1999/2000.

SPEED, ADRIAN — Defender
Current Club: Grantham Town
D o B: 30/01/1971   *Birthplace: Peterborough*
Club captain and Grantham Town's longest-serving player with well over 400 appearances to his name. Obviously by far the clubs longest-serving player and has even managed the team for a couple of games. Signed from Holbeach United in July 1990 after previous experience with Peterborough United.

SPELLMAN, CARL — Midfielder
Current Club: Vauxhall Motors
D o B: 01/01/1972   *Birthplace: Liverpool*
Strong-tackling right-sided player, who was previously with Everton as a youngster before moving onto Witton Albion, Skelmersdale United and Bromsborough Pool. Carl is equally at home in either midfield or full back and can deliver excellent crosses. Now in his second spell with Vauxhall Motors, having re-joined in July 1997 from Curzon Ashton.

SPENCE, BRYNLEY — Defender
Current Club: Carterton Town
Birthplace: Oxford
Previous clubs include: Oxford Utd (Trainee) - July 2001.

SPENCE, RAYMOND — Forward
Current Club: Basingstoke Town
Birthplace: Hampshire
From Youth team.

SPENCER, ANDY — Forward
Current Club: Halesowen Town
Birthplace: Birmingham
Honours won: Dr Martens Western Div.Winners
A 23-year-old forward, Andy made an impressive start to his Halesowen Town career by scoring three goals in his first three games. However his impact did not amount to anything as Halesowen were relegated. Signed from Boldmere St Michaels, he has previously played with Nottingham University. A versatile player he is able to play on the wing as well as up front.

SPENCER, ANDY — Midfielder
Current Club: Boldmere St. Michaels
Birthplace: Birmingham
From Youth team.

SPENCER, JAMES — Defender
Current Club: Hayes
From Youth team.

SPENCER, NEIL — Forward
Current Club: Clitheroe
Birthplace: Lancashire
Banned by half the countrys police forces as a result of our away trips last year. Uses his strength well to engineer openings, always back him one on one with the keeper. There is no better in those positions at this level.

SPENCER, RYAN — Midfielder
Current Club: Slough Town
D o B: 03/01/1979   *Birthplace: London*
Honours won: English & British Universities Rep.
Ryan is a skilful playmaker with a flair for free kicks. He played for Hayes in the Football Conference before joining Ryman Premier side Chesham United in August 2002 but then swiftly switched to Division One North side Slough Town Ryan, previously with Tottenham and Swedish side Vasalund, has also represented England and British Universities. His footballing heros are Diego Maradona and Marco Van Basten, and his favourite moment in football was playing in the FA Cup, live on Sky television. Ryan has just graduated in business studies.

SPENCER, STEVE — Defender
Current Club: Altrincham
D o B: 06/10/1981   *Birthplace: Manchester*
Previous clubs include: Leigh RMI - December 2001, Sheffield Utd.

SPENCER, WAYNE — Forward
Current Club: Rothwell Town
D o B: 15/07/1969   *Birthplace: Milton Keynes*
Much-travelled striker who returned to Dr Martens Eastern side Rothwell Town in June 2002 from neighbours and rivals Corby Town. Had been player-manager of the Steelmen during the latter part of the 2001/02 season after re-joining the Steelmen from Barton Rovers in July 2001. Has also had spells with Milton Keynes City, VS Rugby, Baldock Town, Buckingham Town, Leighton Town, Dunstable, Hinckley United and Kings Lynn.

SPICE, BRADLEY — Forward
Current Club: Sittingbourne

D o B: 11/10/1982 — Birthplace: Kent

Very quick and with a great eye for goal, Bradley is a very promising striker who came through Sittingbournes own ranks. Had the unique distinction of finishing as leading goal scorer in the first team, reserves and the under-18 side at the end of the 2000/01 season. Could go far if he keeps developing at the present rate.

SPIKE, LEE — Forward
Current Club: Aberystwyth Town

D o B: 20/02/1980 — Birthplace: Liverpool

A tall, young striker who was acquired by League of Wales side Rhyl from Waterloo Docks in January 2002. Switched to rivals Aberystwyth Town in July 2002.

SPILLANE, PAUL — Goalkeeper
Current Club: Bashley

Birthplace: Hampshire

Previous clubs include: Lymington & New Milton - March 2002.

SPILLER, LEE — Midfielder
Current Club: Dover Athletic

Birthplace: Kent

Talented midfielder who joined Dover Athletic in May 2002 from Ryman Premier side Chesham United. Originally with Gillingham, Lee then had two spells with Gravesend with a term at Margate in between before joining Chesham.

SPINK, DEAN — Defender
Current Club: Telford United

D o B: 22/01/1967 — Birthplace: Halesowen

Vastly experienced forward who signed for Conference side Telford United in August 2002 from rivals Chester City. Had joined City from Wrexham in July 2000 after spells with Shrewsbury and Aston Villa. Started his career at Halesowen Town, Dean can play as either a centre forward or in defence and was made assistant manager to Gordon Hill in the summer of 2001.

SPOONER, DANNY — Goalkeeper
Current Club: Denaby United

Birthplace: Sheffield

Previous clubs include: Worsbrough Bridge - February 2001, Sheffield, South Normanton Ath., Sheffield, Sheffield Utd.

SPOONER, NICKY — Defender
Current Club: Leigh RMI

D o B: 05/06/1971 — Birthplace: Manchester

Honours won: England Youth Int.

As a youngster, Nicky was a youth trainee with Manchester United where he won the Youth Cup and made five appearances for the England Youth team. He began his professional career with Bolton Wanderers in 1989 and made his debut in 1992. Was a regular first-team choice until an ankle injury forced him out. He got back into the side in 1994 but broke his leg in a match against Burnley. He returned to action after 18 months as captain of the reserve team. Joined American side Charleston Battery in 1999 and captained the team last season.

SPRIGGS, KEVIN — Midfielder
Current Club: Dartford

Birthplace: Kent

Previous clubs include: Erith & Belvedere - July 2001, Dartford.

SPRINGETT, MITCHELL — Midfielder
Current Club: Stanway Rovers

D o B: 11/05/1964 — Birthplace: Colchester

Previous clubs include: Clacton T - September 2001, Cornard Utd, Clacton T, Heybridge Swifts, Dagenham & Redbridge, Heybridge Swifts, Wivenhoe T, Bury T, Chelmsford C, Braintree T, Wivenhoe T, Braintree T, Halstead T, Cambridge Utd.

SPROAT, DAVID — Goalkeeper
Current Club: Whitley Bay

Birthplace: Newcastle

Signed as cover for John Caffrey. Big keeper who dominates his box. Credited with making the save of the season at Hillheads last season to keep our FA Cup run going.

SQUIRE, KEVIN — Forward
Current Club: Barnstaple Town

D o B: 15/12/1977 — Birthplace: Devon

Previous clubs include: Combe Martin - July 1999, Ilfracombe.

SQUIRE, RORY — Midfielder
Current Club: Rugby United

Birthplace: Warwickshire

From Youth team.

SQUIRES, JAMES — Defender
Current Club: Nuneaton Borough

D o B: 15/11/1975 — Birthplace: Preston

Dominant central defender who started his career with home-town club Preston before having spells with Dunfermline and Carlisle. Joined Doncaster Rovers during the 2001/02 season and then switched to Nuneaton in May 2002.

SQUIRES, OLIVER — Midfielder
Current Club: Barking & East Ham United

D o B: 15/09/1980 — Birthplace: Harrow

Previous clubs include: Grays Ath - October 2001, St.Albans C, Aylesbury Utd, Chertsey T, Aldershot T, Watford.

ST.HILAIRE, MARTIN — Forward
Current Club: Enfield Town (Essex)

D o B: 04/04/1964 — Birthplace: Essex

A member of the Enfield FC Diadora League Championship winning team of 1995, having been signed from Harrow Borough by the then Enfield manager Graham Roberts. Won the supporters goal of the season award for season 1994-95 with his stunning strike against Wokingham Town in March 1995. Left the Es for Yeovil Town but later rejoined for a second spell. Has played for a number of clubs since then, including Dagenham & Redbridge, before joining up with Graham Roberts once more at Hertford Town. Released by East Thurrock United earlier this season, Saint made his Enfield Town debut against Bowers United in December 2001.

STABB, CHRIS — Defender
Current Club: Farsley Celtic

D o B: 12/10/1976 — Birthplace: Bradford

Right back who re-joined Farsley Celtic in July 2002 from UniBond First Division rivals Ossett Town. Was in his fourth season at Town following a move from Farsley Celtic in July 1998. Tough-tackling player, who began life at Ingfield as a midfielder before slotting into defence where he can also operate as a sweeper. Captained Bradford City Reserves as a youngster.

STACEY, DARYL — Goalkeeper
Current Club: Ramsgate
Birthplace: Kent
From Youth team.

STACK, RICHARD — Defender
Current Club: Glasshoughton Welfare
Birthplace: Yorkshire
Previous clubs include: Ossett Alb - March 2001, Glasshoughton Welfare, Tadcaster Alb., Glasshoughton Welfare.

STADHART, CHE — Forward
Current Club: Gravesend & Northfleet
Birthplace: London
Honours won: Ryman League Premier Div.Winners
An exciting and skilful player who is a handful for any defence. Joined Gravesend & Northfleet from Hampton & Richmond Borough in October 1999, scoring on his debut goal for the club against Farnborough Town in November. Previous clubs include Leyton Pennant and Chalfont St Peter. Che has been the clubs top goalscorer for the past three seasons and was selected to play for the Middlesex Wanderers Representative team on their tour to the Far East at the end of the 2001/02 season.

STAFF, DAVID — Midfielder
Current Club: Kings Lynn
Birthplace: Northampton
David is a versatile midfielder who was one of Billy Jeffreys first recruits as manager of Stamford in 1998. David can also play at right back or even as a sweeper an all round good player really. Previously with Rushden & Diamonds, he transferred to Kings Lynn in March 2002.

STAGE, MATTHEW — Midfielder
Current Club: Harwich & Parkeston
Birthplace: Essex
Local youngster who has broken into the Harwich first team from the Reserves. He has only just turned seventeen and must be one of the youngest players playing regularly at Jewson Premier level. Strong and fast, a great prospect for the future.

STAINES, GARY — Goalkeeper
Current Club: Great Wakering Rovers
Birthplace: Southend
Previous clubs include: Witham T - September 2001.

STANBOROUGH, NICK — Defender
Current Club: Barwell
Birthplace: Leicester
Previous clubs include: Atherstone Utd - July 1999, Hinckley Utd, Shepshed Dynamo, Nuneaton B, Hinckley Ath., Gresley R, Hinckley Ath., Hinckley, Earl Shilton Alb.

STANBRIDGE, NEIL — Goalkeeper
Current Club: Clacton Town
Birthplace: Essex
Rated as one of the best keepers in the Jewson Premier. Signed for Clacton this season from Felixstowe & Walton, after receiving Player of the Year .

STANBRIDGE, OLLIE — Midfielder
Current Club: Aylesbury United
Previous clubs include: Brackley T - October 2000, Aylesbury Utd, Bigbrooke St.Michaels.

STANDEN, DEAN — Midfielder
Current Club: Welling United
Birthplace: Kent
Talented midfield player who skippered Welling United's youth team before being sold to Luton Town, who paid £25,000 for his services. Returned to Park View Road just before the start of the 2001/02 season and enjoyed an excellent campaign, once again attracting attention from bigger clubs.

STANDEN, ROSS — Goalkeeper
Current Club: Lewes
Birthplace: Sussex
Joined the club in August 2001 after three seasons at Whitehawk. A good shot stopper who also kicks very well.

STANGER, RAY — Forward
Current Club: West Auckland Town
Birthplace: Co.Durham
Previous clubs include: Spennymoor Utd - July 2000, West Auckland T, Durham C, West Auckland T.

STANHOPE, ANDY — Midfielder
Current Club: Kings Lynn
Birthplace: Peterborough
Honours won: British Universities Rep., FA XI
Joined Peterborough United straight from school, making two first team appearances. Moved on to Kings Lynn before joining Boston United in December 1996. He became a regular member of the first team with some impressive performances and some important goals. He has represented the Football Association in a match against the British Universities. Switched to Gainsborough Trinity in July 2001 and then returned to Lynn in March 2002.

STANHOPE, JON — Midfielder
Current Club: Vauxhall Motors
D o B: 07/11/1980 *Birthplace: Chester*
A young forward who signed for Vauxhall Motors in the summer of 2001. Started his career with Wrexham and then spent time with Stalybridge Celtic before moving to Connahs Quay in the League of Wales. Impressed everyone in his first season at Rivacre Park.

STANLEY, DANNY — Midfielder
Current Club: Aveley
Birthplace: Essex
Previous clubs include: Witham T - March 2002, Braintree T, Maldon T, Colchester Utd (Trainee).

STANLEY, JAI — Midfielder
Current Club: Moor Green
D o B: 12/10/1978 *Birthplace: Coventry*
Signed for Moor Green in August 2000 from Bedworth United, where he came through their youth team to establish a first team place. Has also had a spell with Nuneaton Borough.

STANLEY, MARTIN — Defender
Current Club: Fairford Town
Birthplace: Wiltshire
From Youth team.

STANNARD, JAMIE — Goalkeeper
Current Club: Woodbridge Town
Birthplace: Suffolk
Previous clubs include: Felixstowe & Walton Utd - July 2000.

STANNARD, JOHN — Midfielder
Current Club: Colwyn Bay
Birthplace: Liverpool
Midfielder with experience at Conference, UniBond and League of Wales level. Signed for UniBond Premier side Colwyn Bay in August 2002 from LoW outfit Rhyl. Began as a trainee with Liverpool and then turned out for Witton Albion and Knowsley United before playing Conference football with Northwich Victoria. Joined Rhyl via Droylsden in December 2000.

STANSFIELD, ADAM — Forward
Current Club: Yeovil Town
D o B: 10/09/1978 — *Birthplace: Devon*
Honours won: England Semi-Pro Int., FA Trophy Winners
Adam signed for Yeovil in November 2001 for an undisclosed fee from Screwfix Direct Premier League side Elmore. He made his first team debut 24 hours later at Southport. Adam started his career at Cullompton Rangers before spending a season playing for Tivertons second string - returning to Cullompton when Tiverton disbanded their reserve side. Adam then transferred to Elmore, during which time he also guested for Exeter City Reserves in the Avon Combination League. As part of his time at St James Park he picked up a Combination League winners medal. Since his arrival at Huish Park, Adam has established himself as a regular first team player, scoring his debut goal against Northwich Victoria at the Drill Field on December 1st 2001. Since the turn of the year, he began to radically adjust to his three-league rise through the football hierarchy, scoring goals on a regular basis and causing opposition defences a real headache with his eye for goal. Its still early days in Adams Yeovil career, but he shows all the signs of a player who is enthusiastically learning his trade and getting better every day. His meteoric rise was capped when Adam was selected for the National Game XI (formerly England Semi-Pro Team) to play against a United States side on March 20th 2002.

STANSFIELD, JAMES — Defender
Current Club: Bradford Park Avenue
D o B: 18/09/1978 — *Birthplace: Dewsbury*
A central defender who began his career at Huddersfield Town before making over 30 League appearances for Halifax Town. He has also played for Ossett Town and Liversedge, and signed for Bradford Park Avenue shortly after the start of the 2001/2002 season.

STANT, PHIL — Forward
Current Club: Gainsborough Trinity
D o B: 13/10/1962 — *Birthplace: Bolton*
Vastly experienced centre forward who became player-manager of Gainsborough Trinity in May 2002. After starting his career with Camberley Town whilst still in the army, Phil went on to make over 450 League appearances and score over 180 goals with Reading, Hereford, Notts County, Fulham, Mansfield, Cardiff, Bury and Brighton and was also player-manager of Lincoln City. Since leaving Lincoln he has had spells in Non-League football with Worcester City, Dover Athletic, Hayes and Hinckley United before taking over at Trinity.

STANTON, LEE — Defender
Current Club: Newport County
D o B: 24/05/1983 — *Birthplace: Newport*
A former Gwent Schools defender at under-14 and under-19 level, Lee completed a two-year period at the Newport Academy before signing senior forms in the summer of 2001. Made his Dr Martens League debut at Margate in the final week of the 2000/01 season and, in doing so, became the first son of a former Exiles player to make a senior appearance, father Chris having been a regular member of the team in the clubs inaugural season.

STANWAY, TERRY — Defender
Current Club: Biddulph Victoria
Birthplace: Stoke
Previous clubs include: Goldenhill Wanderers - July 1991, Knypersley V.

STAPLES, STEVE — Goalkeeper
Current Club: Bashley
Birthplace: Dorset
Goalkeeper who was very highly-rated in the Jewson Wessex League through spells with Wimborne Town and Brockenhurst. Looked likely to join Lymington & New Milton at the end of the 2001/02 season and was also wanted by Dr Martens League side Salisbury City. In the end chose another Dr Martens Eastern side Bashley in June 2002.

STARBUCK, PHIL — Forward
Current Club: Hucknall Town
D o B: 24/11/1968 — *Birthplace: Nottingham*
Experienced forward who made over 250 League appearances for Nottingham Forest, Huddersfield, Sheffield United, Oldham and Plymouth. Had a short spell at Cambridge City before playing for Burton Albion under former Forest team-mate Nigel Clough. Embarked on his first managerial steps when he became player-manager of UniBond Premier side Hucknall Town in November 2001 and steered the club away from what was looking like a relegation season.

STARK, MARK — Forward
Current Club: Rocester
Birthplace: Stafford
Previous clubs include: Stafford T - July 2001.

STARK, PAUL — Goalkeeper
Current Club: Eastbourne Borough
D o B: 04/09/1981 — *Birthplace: Dover*
Joined the club in November 2001, having returned from a soccer scholarship in the United States. Formerly a member of the successful Eastbourne Town Youth team, and has had trials with several professional clubs, including Fulham and Charlton Athletic.

STASSINOS, DANNY — Midfielder
Current Club: Croydon Athletic
Birthplace: Surrey
Previous clubs include: Carshalton Ath - August 2001, Croydon Ath., Sutton Utd, Chelsea (Junior).

STATHAM, BRIAN — Defender
Current Club: Chelmsford City
D o B: 21/05/1969 — *Birthplace: Zimbabwe*
Honours won: England Youth & u-21 Int.
Brian has previously spent his career playing at League level. He joined Chelmsford City from Chesham United in December 2001. A stalwart in defence, his wealth of experience will help a lot of the younger players to improve.

STATHAM, MARK — Goalkeeper
Current Club: Kidsgrove Athletic
D o B: 11/11/1975 — *Birthplace: Barnsley*
Honours won: NWCL Winners
Experienced goalkeeper who joined Kidsgrove from neighbours Leek Town in August 2001. Gained plenty of League experience with the likes of Wigan and Nottingham Forest and has also seen service with Witton Albion, Stalybridge Celtic and Trafford.

STATON, LUKE   *Midfielder*

Current Club: Gainsborough Trinity

D o B: 10/03/1979   *Birthplace: Nottingham*
Honours won: England Schoolboy & Youth Int.
Luke, who hails from Nottingham, signed for UniBond Premier side Gainsborough Trinity in July 2002 after a spell with Dr Martens outfit Merthyr Tydfil. Had joined Merthyr from Barry Town in September 2001 and was installed as temporary captain. A sweet passer of the ball, who likes to get forward, he made 25 appearances in 2001/02 for the Martyrs and chipped in with three goals. Originally with Blackburn Rovers and Bolton Wanderers and is a former England Schoolboy and Youth international.

STAY, ALEX   *Forward*

Current Club: Pagham

Birthplace: Sussex
Forward: yet another ex-Oving player to be brought in when Paul Gilbert took over as Pagham boss in December 2001: suffered with injury during 1999/2000, but was in great form the following season with 19 goals for the Vikings.

STEAD, CARL   *Forward*

Current Club: North Ferriby United

D o B: 03/09/1971   *Birthplace: Hull*
Honours won: FA Vase Winners
Forward and a member of the FA Vase-winning Brigg Town side of 1996, scoring a goal in the Wembley final. Originally at Brigg, he re-joined North Ferriby United in July 2001 from the Northern Counties East Leaguers and has also seen service with Scarborough and Bridlington Town.

STEAD, MATTHEW   *Forward*

Current Club: Brigg Town

Birthplace: Hull
Previous clubs include: Hall Road Rangers - October 2001, Brigg T, Hall Road R.

STEAD, NATHAN   *Midfielder*

Current Club: North Ferriby United

D o B: 03/02/1976   *Birthplace: Hull*
Honours won: FA Vase Winners
Attacking midfielder who is capable of turning games through his own efforts. Signed for North Ferriby United in July 2001 from Brigg Town to begin his third spell at Church Road. Started his career with Hull City and also had a spell at Immingham Town, he was an FA Vase winner with Brigg where he was man of the match in the 1996 final at Wembley.

STEADMAN, DANNY   *Forward*

Current Club: Wisbech Town

D o B: 09/10/1980
Previous clubs include: Spalding Utd - July 2001, Grimsby T.

STEADMAN, DARREN   *Goalkeeper*

Current Club: Evesham United

D o B: 26/01/1970   *Birthplace: Kidderminster*
Honours won: England Schoolboy Int.
Previous clubs include: Kidderminster Harriers - August 2001.

STEADMAN, WILL   *Defender*

Current Club: Gloucester City

D o B: 21/02/1980   *Birthplace: Gloucester*
Previous clubs include: Cinderford T - March 2000, Gloucester C.

STEARNE, BEN   *Midfielder*

Current Club: Bedworth United

D o B: 17/11/1981   *Birthplace: Coventry*
Ben has been a great addition to Bedworth United after signing from Hinckley United, where he was in their Dr Martens Western Division championship-winning side, in October 2001. A midfielder who likes to get on the ball and show a few tricks. Started in Hicnkleys youth side and also had a spell on Leicester City's books.

STEDMAN, DAVE   *Defender*

Current Club: Arundel

Birthplace: Arundel
Defender: a Mullet in the true sense of the word (i.e. somebody actually born in Arundel): joined from East Preston four seasons ago.

STEELE, DAVID   *Defender*

Current Club: Tiverton Town

Birthplace: Devon
David, son of Tiverton Town legend Hedley, joined the club during the summer of 2001. He played regularly for Willand Rovers, whom he helped to win promotion to the Screwfix Western League First Division. David plays with an authority beyond his years and looks very comfortable on the ball and is an excellent crosser of the ball.

STEELE, PAUL   *Defender*

Current Club: Woking

Birthplace: Swindon
A powerful defender, Paul signed for Woking for a fee of £20,000 during the summer of 2001 from Yeovil Town where he was a member of the side that finished the 2000/01 season as Conference runners-up. He began his career with Swindon Town before moving on to Chippenham Town. He joined Yeovil in the autumn of 1998 and filled a number of positions in defence. Paul is a handful in the opposition area where he makes his presence felt, especially from set-pieces. He had an impressive loan spell with Woking towards the end of the 2000/01 season before being recalled to bolster the Yeovil title challenge.

STEELE, RICHARD   *Defender*

Current Club: Consett

Birthplace: Consett
From Local football - July 2001.

STEELE, SCOTT   *Midfielder*

Current Club: Woking

D o B: 19/09/1971   *Birthplace: Motherwell*
Honours won: Scotland Youth Int., FA Trophy Winners
Scott signed for Woking from Airdrie in 1992. He may be small in stature, but he is a tremendously hard worker with great ball skills, who doesnt even begin to know the meaning of a lost cause. He was voted Man of the Match in Wokings FA Trophy Final win over Runcorn and the following year scored one of the quickest ever goals at Wembley as Woking retained the FA Trophy against Kidderminster Harriers. Scott picked up his third FA Trophy winners medal in 1997. Sponsors Player of the Year and joint Supporters Club Player of the Year for 1998/99, his loyalty and service to the club was rewarded with a testimonial against Spurs during the summer of 2001.

S

STEELE, TIM — *Defender*
Current Club: Sutton Coldfield Town

D o B: 01/12/1967 — *Birthplace: Coventry*
Previous clubs include: Tamworth - June 2001, Exeter C, Hereford Utd, Bradford C, Wolverhampton Wanderers, Shrewsbury T.

STEER, DANNY — *Defender*
Current Club: Eastleigh

Birthplace: Hampshire
Previous clubs include: Brockenhurst - May 2002.

STEIN, MARK — *Forward*
Current Club: Dagenham & Redbridge

D o B: 29/01/1966 — *Birthplace: Cape Town*
Honours won: England Youth Int.
Joined Dagenham in August 2001 from Luton Town. Mark has been a prolific goalscorer throughout his career which has been spent in the Football League playing for Bournemouth, Stoke, Oxford, QPR, Aldershot and Ipswich. He played 50 games in the Premiership for Chelsea and has commanded just over £2 million in transfer fees. He made his debut on the opening day of the season against Southport.

STEMP, WAYNE — *Defender*
Current Club: Bracknell Town

D o B: 09/09/1970 — *Birthplace: Epsom*
Previous clubs include: Molesey - August 2001, Aylesbury Utd, Farnborough T, Bognor Regis T, Staines T, Woking, Farnborough T, Brighton.

STEPHENS, JUSTIN — *Defender*
Current Club: Fairford Town

Birthplace: Wiltshire
Previous clubs include: Swindon Supermarine - July 2001, Highworth T, Fairford T.

STEPHENS, NICK — *Goalkeeper*
Current Club: Altrincham

D o B: 30/05/1983 — *Birthplace: Plymouth*
Nick is a former YTS goalkeeper with Torquay United who appeared on the bench for the Devon sides first-team 12 times during the 2001/02 season. He left in the summer of 2002 after only being offered a three-month contract and signed for UniBond Premier side Altrincham after playing well in pre-season Hoping to establish himself at Moss Lane.

STEPHENS, PAUL — *Goalkeeper*
Current Club: Fairford Town

Birthplace: Wiltshire
Previous clubs include: Swindon Supermarine - July 1999.

STEPHENS, TONY — *Forward*
Current Club: Chichester City United

Birthplace: Hampshire
Previous clubs include: Portfield - July 2000, Newport IOW, Havant T, Bognor Regis T, Weymouth, Havant T, AFC Bournemouth.

STEPHENSON, GEOFF — *Defender*
Current Club: Consett

D o B: 28/04/1970 — *Birthplace: Durham*
Previous clubs include: White Bay - July 2001, Dunston Federation Brewery, South Shields, Morpeth T, Durham C, Harrogate T, Whitley Bay, Kings Lynn, Grantham T, Kings Lynn, Eastwood T, Boston Utd, Grimsby T.

STEPHENSON, LEE — *Forward*
Current Club: Kings Lynn

Birthplace: Lincolnshire
Prolific scorer who joined Kings Lynn from neighbours Spalding United in May 2002. Had been top scorer for the Tulips in 2001/02, despite the Lincolnshire clubs struggles. Started his career at Grimsby before going Non-League with Wisbech Town, Racing Club Warwick, Shepshed Dynamo and Winterton Rangers, from whom he joined Spalding in July 2001.

STERLING, DOMINIC — *Defender*
Current Club: Aldershot Town

Birthplace: London
Impressive central defender who signed for Ryman Premier side Aldershot Town in July 2002 from relegated Hayes. Had joined then Conference club Hayes in the summer of 2000 after some excellent performances for Wealdstone. Started out on Wimbledons books.

STEVENS, ADAM — *Defender*
Current Club: Shepshed Dynamo

D o B: 26/02/1975 — *Birthplace: Leicester*
Postman in Leicester, Adam joined Dr Martens Western side Shepshed Dynamo in the summer of 2001 from Midland Alliance outfit Barwell. Previously with Daventry Ford Sports, where he won United Counties League honours and was player of the year, Hinckley Athletic and Gresley Rovers.

STEVENS, ANDY — *Defender*
Current Club: Taunton Town

D o B: 29/01/1970 — *Birthplace: Barnstaple*
Joined Taunton Town for a second time in November 2001 from Western League rivals Barnstaple Town - his home-town club. A spolid and reliable defender, Andy has also seen service with Bideford and Torrington.

STEVENS, BARRY — *Midfielder*
Current Club: Epsom And Ewell

Birthplace: Surrey
Barry joined Epsom at the start of the 1999-2000 season from Banstead Athletic, where he had a couple of substitute 1st XI outings, after they abolished their reserve side, an exciting player with immense ability. Was voted by the players as their Player of the Year in 1999-2000.

STEVENS, DAVE — *Forward*
Current Club: Crawley Town

D o B: 29/04/1979 — *Birthplace: Ashford*
Previous clubs include: Dulwich Hamlet - March 2002, Hayes, Dulwich Hamlet (£35,000), Bromley, Crystal Palace.

STEVENS, JIM — *Midfielder*
Current Club: Aveley

Birthplace: Essex
Previous clubs include: East Thurrock Utd - March 2002.

STEVENS, LEE — *Forward*
Current Club: Selsey

Birthplace: Sussex
Small but effective striker, known as Shakey. Apparently had trials with Chelsea in his pre-teen days. Leading goalscorer for Pagham in both 1998/99 and 1999/2000 (16 goals that year) and has also made appearances for Bognor Regis, and even played for both clubs on Easter Monday April 2000. Turned down the opportunity to join the Rocks on a regular basis during 2000/01 because of work commitments. Ironically went on to score a hat-trick in Paghams amazing 6-4 Sussex Senior Cup quarter-final exit at the

hands of Bognor in February 2001. Ended up with 29 goals to his name last season. Began 2001/02 playing for the reserves at Nyetimber Lane, until signing for Selsey in September.

STEVENS, PAUL — *Midfielder*
Current Club: Belper Town

From Youth team.

STEVENS, PAUL — *Midfielder*
Current Club: Eastbourne Borough

Birthplace: Eastbourne
Well over 200 appearances for the club and now in his third spell, having rejoined from Burgess Hill Town (Sussex County League) during the1999/00 season. Peanuts has also played for Hailsham Town and Whitehawk (both Sussex County League).

STEVENS, ROBERT — *Defender*
Current Club: Dereham Town

Birthplace: Norfolk
Product of the clubs youth set-up. Skilful, dominant centre-half. Set piece expert. Played in excess of 300 First Team games.

STEVENS, SIMON — *Midfielder*
Current Club: Hailsham Town

Birthplace: Sussex
Midfielder: son of manager Joe Stevens: another product of the Hailsham Utd youth team to progress into the first-team during 2001/02.

STEVENSON, BOBBY — *Midfielder*
Current Club: Oadby Town

Birthplace: Coventry
Previous clubs include: Burton Alb - January 2002, North Ferriby Utd, Nuneaton Borough.

STEVENSON, CARL — *Midfielder*
Current Club: Fairford Town

Birthplace: Wiltshire
From Youth team.

STEVENSON, LUKE — *Defender*
Current Club: Tiptree United

Birthplace: Essex
From Youth team.

STEVENSON, MIKE — *Forward*
Current Club: Stratford Town

Birthplace: Coventry
Previous clubs include: Evesham Utd - November 2000, Shepshed Dynamo, Hannisberg Heat (USA), Moor Green, Weymouth, Hinckley Ath., Coventry C.

STEVENSON, PAUL — *Defender*
Current Club: Whitehawk

Birthplace: Brighton
Defender: one-time player for Brighton Boys and Sussex U-18s. Rejoined Whitehawk from Peacehaven during the 2000 close season. Also runs the Hawks website.

STEVENSON, PAUL — *Defender*
Current Club: Farsley Celtic

D o B: 19/05/1966   *Birthplace: Leeds*
Previous clubs include: Garforth T - August 2000, Farsley Celtic, Guiseley, Bridlington T, Farsley Celtic, Blackpool, Farsley Celtic, Harrogate T, Farsley Celtic.

STEVENSON, TOM — *Defender*
Current Club: Oldbury United

Birthplace: Birmingham
Previous clubs include: Tamworth - December 2001, Bloxwich Utd, Tamworth.

STEWARD, DONAVAN — *Midfielder*
Current Club: Woodbridge Town

Birthplace: Suffolk
Another player to have made the step up from SIL football by signing from Framlingham early last season. A predominantly left-sided player whose ability enabled him to perform well for the Reserves last season.

STEWART, ALEX — *Forward*
Current Club: Thame United

Birthplace: Oxfordshire
A product of Thame United's youth system. Alex has already shown he can make the transition to first-team football with ease. A player with a very bright future, he is tall with a great touch and an eye for goal.

STEWART, BILLY — *Goalkeeper*
Current Club: Marine

D o B: 01/01/1968   *Birthplace: Liverpool*
Vastly experienced goalkeeper who joined Marine in June 2002 following a spell in the League of Wales with Rhyl. Made over 350 League appearances with Wigan, Chester City and Northampton after starting his career with Liverpool. Since leaving the pro game he has played in the Conference with Southport and Hednesford Town and UniBond with Bamber Bridge.

STEWART, KEVIN — *Defender*
Current Club: Kingsbury Town

Birthplace: London
Previous clubs include: Leyton Pennant - January 2000, Clapton, Kingsbury T, Harefield Utd.

STEWART, MARK — *Defender*
Current Club: Clitheroe

Birthplace: Lancashire
Psycho started out as a winger, moved to full back but has now bedded in at centre back. Fearsome competitor, ought to be kept off raw meat before the game. Produced some massive performances last year. Must avoid being interviewed by local papers and giving score predictions - remember Taunton?

STEWART, MIKE — *Goalkeeper*
Current Club: Aberystwyth Town

Birthplace: Liverpool
Previous clubs include: Waterloo Dock - November 2001.

STEWART, STEVE — *Forward*
Current Club: Blyth Spartans

Birthplace: Durham
Midfielder who signed for UniBond Premier side Blyth Spartans in July 1999 from Albany Northern Leaguers Chester-le-Street. Has featured both through the middle and on the flank. Amazingly, is the clubs longest-serving player having made his debut against Leigh on 14th August 1999. Was voted both Travel Club and Supporters' Player of the Year for 2001/02.

STIFF, DARRYL   *Midfielder*
Current Club: Stowmarket Town
Birthplace: Suffolk
Previous clubs include: Sudbury Wanderers - July 2000, Stowmarket T.

STIMSON, MARK   *Midfielder*
Current Club: Grays Athletic
D o B: 27/12/1967   Birthplace: Plaistow
Honours won: FA Trophy Winners
Joined Grays Athletic at the end of April 2002 as player-coach after a successful spell with Canvey Island, whom he helped to FA Tropht success and two runners-up positions in the Ryman League. A former League player with Spurs, Newcastle, Portsmouth, Southend and Leyton Orient with over 200 appearances to his name.

STIRK, MARK   *Midfielder*
Current Club: Willenhall Town
Birthplace: Worcestershire
Signed for Willenhall from Stourbridge in February 2002. An experienced, battler who was previously with Kidderminster Harriers, Moor Green, Redditch, Halesowen Town.

STIRLING, JUDE   *Defender*
Current Club: Stevenage Borough
D o B: 29/06/1982   Birthplace: Enfield
Jude initially joined Stevenage on loan from Luton in February. Made an immediate impact on his debut against Forest Green Rovers and immediately became a firm favourite with the crowd. Possesses a long throw which opens up all sorts of attacking options. Equally comfortable in the centre of defence or in midfield, he made the move permanent in March 2002.

STITTLE, DAVE   *Forward*
Current Club: Brentwood
Birthplace: Essex
A well known figure in the Essex Senior League. The son of former manager Derrick Stittle, Dave has spent the majority of his career at Brentwood but also had spells at Grays, Aveley and Canvey Island. Top scorer last season with 19 goals.

STOCK, RUSSELL   *Forward*
Current Club: Wroxham
D o B: 25/06/1977   Birthplace: Great Yarmouth
Previous clubs include: Diss T - January 2000, Cambridge C, Kings Lynn, Kettering T, Cambridge Utd.

STODDART, LEE   *Forward*
Current Club: Fairford Town
Birthplace: Gloucestershire
Previous clubs include: Wootton Bassett T - July 2001.

STOKELD, JAMIE   *Midfielder*
Current Club: Lowestoft Town
Birthplace: Great Yarmouth
Previous clubs include: Kirkley - July 1998.

STOKER, GARETH   *Midfielder*
Current Club: Scarborough
D o B: 22/02/1973   Birthplace: Bishop Auckland
Joined Scaborough initially on loan from Rochdale in September 1999 with the move becoming permanent in December. The strong tackling and tenacious midfielder was soon made captain after turning in a number of man of the match performances. Gareth played at Leeds United as a trainee before moving to Hull

City making 30 appearances. Three seasons at Hereford followed before a move to Cardiff City. He then went to Rochdale before falling out of favour at Spotland and joining Boro.

STOKES, DEAN   *Defender*
Current Club: Newcastle Town
D o B: 23/05/1970   Birthplace: Birmingham
Previous clubs include: Leek T - September 2000, Rochdale, Port Vale, Halesowen T.

STOKES, PAUL   *Midfielder*
Current Club: Lewes
Birthplace: Sussex
The third member of the current squad who has made well over 100 appearances for the club. Paul has struggled with various injuries since the middle of last season, but on his day he is an inspirational figure in the heart for the midfield, as he proved in the Sussex Senior Cup final. A West Ham supporter and scaffolder when away from the Dripping Pan.

STONE, ADRIAN   *Forward*
Current Club: Ashford Town
Birthplace: Kent
Forward who joined Dr Martens Eastern side Ashford Town in the summer of 2001 from Ryman Leaguers Tooting & Mitcham United. Enjoyed a highly successful first season as a senior player.

STONE, DANNY   *Defender*
Current Club: Redhill
Birthplace: Sussex
Left-sided player, never one to back down in a tackle. Has been with the club for several seasons and mainly played for the reserves during 2000/01, before breaking back into the first team midway through the 2000/01 campaign. Now a regular choice for the current season.

STONE, GAVIN   *Defender*
Current Club: Ilkeston Town
D o B: 09/01/1980   Birthplace: Staffordshire
Former Tottenham Hotspur trainee defender, Gavin joined Dr Martens Premier side Ilkeston Town in July 2002. Had a lengthy spell with Stafford Rangers before joining Bilston Town in January 1999. Sadly, season 2001/02 was a troubled one for the Queen Street club and they eventually dropped out of the Dr Martens League.

STONE, PHIL   *Forward*
Current Club: Lymington & New Milton
Birthplace: Bournemouth
Previous clubs include: Brockenhurst - May 2002, Lymington & New Milton, Bashley, AFC Bournemouth (Trainee).

STONE, SCOTT   *Defender*
Current Club: Redhill
Birthplace: Sussex
Defender and brother of Danny who broke into the Redhill first team in April 2001. Has held his place and grows as a player with each game. Solid in the tackle and a good distributor of the ball.

STONEMAN, PAUL   *Defender*
Current Club: Halifax Town
D o B: 26/02/1973   Birthplace: Whitley Bay
Experienced defender who was re-signed by Conference club Halifax Town in August 2002 after originally being released by the administrators at the end of the 2001/02 season. An experienced defender who made over 140 League appearances for Blackpool, Colchester and the Shaymen.

STONER, CRAIG   *Goalkeeper*
Current Club: Bognor Regis Town

D o B: 05/11/1981   *Birthplace: Chichester*

Promising young goalkeeper who joined Ryman Division One South side Bognor Regis Town initially on loan from Portsmouth duing the 2000/01 season. Released by Portsmouth and signed permanently in the close season of 2001. Lives in Littlehampton.

STONES, ADAM   *Defender*
Current Club: Epsom And Ewell

Birthplace: Surrey

Previous clubs include: Banstead Ath - February 2001.

STONES, CRAIG   *Midfielder*
Current Club: Brigg Town

D o B: 31/05/1980   *Birthplace: Scunthorpe*

Previous clubs include: Spalding Utd - March 2001, Lincoln C.

STORE, BEN   *Forward*
Current Club: Halesowen Harriers

Birthplace: Worcestershire

Previous clubs include: Cradley T - July 2001, Halesowen Harriers.

STORER, STUART   *Midfielder*
Current Club: Hinckley United

D o B: 16/01/1967   *Birthplace: Rugby*

An experienced defender or midfielder who has 373 Football League appearances to his name, and 31 goals. Stuart signed for Hinckley United in March 2001 from Chesham United. Although the majority of his career has been spent with Bolton Wanderers and Brighton, he has also played for Wolves, Mansfield, Birmingham City, Everton, Wigan Athletic and Exeter City. More recently he has represented Atherstone and Kettering Town. Stuart scored the last ever goal at Brightons Goldstone ground.

STOREY, BRETT   *Midfielder*
Current Club: Stocksbridge Park Steels

D o B: 07/07/1977   *Birthplace: Sheffield*

Previous clubs include: Hallam - August 2001, Maltby Main, Leigh RMI, Alfreton T, Leigh RMI, Alfreton T, Matlock T, Stalybridge Celtic, Matlock T, Golden (Hong Kong), Lincoln C, Sheffield Utd.

STORR, RICHIE   *Forward*
Current Club: Billingham Town

Birthplace: Stockton

This is Richards first season with Town having signed from Guisborough. Richard is a bustling forward who scored regularly with Thornaby and Guisborough.

STOTT, STEVE   *Midfielder*
Current Club: Slough Town

D o B: 03/02/1965   *Birthplace: Leeds*

Honours won: England Semi-Pro Int., Dr Martens League Premier Div.Winners

Joined the club from Woking where he had a short spell after opening a number of games at Nationwide league hopefuls Yeovil Town. Stott was in fact captain of Yeovil before the Conference side turned full-time and Stott had to leave the club. Stotty is Sloughs player coach. He made a good impression in the early part of his Slough career before missing most of the season with injuries. This frustrated Stott as he had to watch the majority of the season from the bench. By Steves own high standards when he did return to Sloughs side he did not look the player he was when he first arrived at Slough. But this season hopefully Steve will be fitter and play a lot more games for the Rebels. His career started with Tranmere Rovers, but Steve spent a large chunk of his career in two spells at

Bromsgrove, totally nine years at the club. He then had transfers to Kettering Town (1994 for £15,000) and Rushden (for £30,000), before joining Yeovil on 17th September 1997 (£10,000). Steve was born in Leeds, but now lives in Witney. As a youngster, his dad was stationed in the army in Germany, and he played youth football for one of Werder Bremens feeder clubs. When Steve turned 16, he signed non-contract forms for Tranmere Rovers, but eventually dropped out of full time football heading to Birmingham University to study Commerce. He is now a qualified accountant. Stotty has played in many representative games. He has played six times for the England Semi-Professional side, including a goal scored against Holland. He also went on tour with the Middlesex Wanderers during the summer of 1998 to Brunei and Myanmar and has been honored with the captaincy of the same side on their tour to India.

STOTTOR, BRIAN   *Forward*
Current Club: Holmer Green

Birthplace: Bucks

Previous clubs include: Prestwood - July 1998, Southall, Chesham Utd.

STOWELL, MATTY   *Defender*
Current Club: Thame United

D o B: 01/03/1977   *Birthplace: Reading*

Previous clubs include: Bath C - March 2002, Yeovil T, Hampton & Richmond B, Rushden & Diamonds, Bristol C, Slough T, Reading.

STRANGE, GARETH   *Midfielder*
Current Club: Altrincham

D o B: 03/10/1981   *Birthplace: Bolton*

Honours won: England Schoolboy Int.

Former England Schoolboy international midfielder who started his career with Manchester United. Was released from Old Trafford at the end of the 1999/00 season and hd a spell at Accrington Stanley before switching to fellow UniBond Leaguers Alrincham in March 2002.

STRANGE, SHAUN   *Midfielder*
Current Club: Bridgwater Town

D o B: 24/01/1979   *Birthplace: Somerset*

Previous clubs include: Nether Stowey - July 1999, Blake OB.

STRANGE, STEVE   *Midfielder*
Current Club: Atherton Laburnum Rovers

Birthplace: Bury

Steve joined LR during last season and added strength and aggression to the midfield. He is an excellent tackler and is not unlikely to contribute the odd goal or two. His previous clubs include Altrincham and Ramsbottom United. Steve is a carpet fitter and is keen on swimming and tennis.

STRANGE, STUART   *Midfielder*
Current Club: Letchworth

Birthplace: Herts

Previous clubs include: Brache Sparta - July 2001, Hitchin T, Baldock T, Brache Sparta, Dunstable, Harpenden T.

STREET, KEVIN   *Forward*
Current Club: Northwich Victoria

D o B: 25/11/1977   *Birthplace: Crewe*

Talented striker who joined Conference side Northwich Victoria on the eve of the 2002/03 season from neighbouring Crewe Alexandra. Joined Alex from school and progressed to make over 100 appearances for the Gresty Road outfit and also had a spell on-loan at Luton before being one of many players to be released at the end of the 2001/02 campaign.

STREET, RENE
Defender
Current Club: Hemel Hempstead Town
Birthplace: London
Previous clubs include: Hendon - February 2002, Northwood, Army.

STREETLEY, DAVE
Midfielder
Current Club: Heybridge Swifts
Birthplace: Essex
Cultured midfielder with an eye for a goal. Joined Heybridge Swifts from Halstead Town in July 1998 and although he was unable to secure a regular spot, he has been a loyal and valued squad member. Joined as a striker under Roy McDonagh before converting to midfield, having almost signed for McDonagh during his time as boss at Colchester.

STREVENS, BEN
Forward
Current Club: Barnet
D o B: 24/05/1980   *Birthplace: Edgware*
Prolific goalscorer in Non-League football, signed for Barnet in January 1999 after an impressive record with Ryman Leaguers Wingate & Finchley. Ben is quick and skilful and is reckond to be a star of the future.

STRIBLING, GARY
Defender
Current Club: Biddulph Victoria
Birthplace: Staffordshire
Previous clubs include: Alsager T - July 2001, Knypersley V, Leek T.

STRIDE, DARREN
Midfielder
Current Club: Burton Albion
Birthplace: Burton-on-Trent
Honours won: England Semi-Pro Int.
Darren Stride was a product of Burtons highly successful youth squad. Burton-born, Darron has made nearly 300 appearances for the Brewers, scoring over 75 goals for the club. His powerful displays from the middle of the park have made him a well respected player at Non-League level. Season 1999-2000 saw Darren scoop both the Players' Player and Supporters' Player of the Year trophies and then crowned an impressive hat-trick of awards with the top goalscorer trophy. He retained the top scorer award last season too with an impressive nineteen goals from his midfield position. Darren is also club captain.

STRIDE, JASON
Defender
Current Club: Lymington & New Milton
D o B: 01/05/1969   *Birthplace: Hampshire*
Previous clubs include: Bashley - July 1996, New Milton, Thatcham T, Wimborne T, Brockenhurst.

STRINGER, DAVID
Midfielder
Current Club: Stratford Town
Birthplace: Coventry
Previous clubs include: Rugby Utd - August 2001, Barwell, Racing Club Warwick, Barwell, Ford Sports, Hinckley Ath., Bolehall Swifts, Atherstone Utd, Bedworth Utd, Atherstone Utd, Nuneaton B, Leicester C (Trainee).

STRINGFELLOW, IAN
Midfielder
Current Club: Bury Town
D o B: 08/05/1969   *Birthplace: Nottingham*
Previous clubs include: Wisbech T - November 2000, Boston Utd, Cambridge C, Boston Utd, Kings Lynn, Dagenham & Redbridge, Kettering T, Mansfield T.

STRINGFELLOW, MIKE
Midfielder
Current Club: Morecambe
D o B: 09/10/1981   *Birthplace: Lancaster*
From Youth team.

STRODDER, GARY
Defender
Current Club: Guiseley
D o B: 01/04/1965   *Birthplace: Cleckheaton*
Previous clubs include: Hartlepool Utd - August 2001, Notts Co., WBA, West Ham Utd, Lincoln C.

STRONG, DWAINE
Forward
Current Club: Didcot Town
Birthplace: Oxford
21 year old Dwaine returned to Didcot at Christmas 2001 after 3 seasons away with Oxford City. A player with blistering pace who will prove to be a handfull for defenders at this level.

STROUTS, JAMES
Midfielder
Current Club: Gravesend & Northfleet
D o B: 21/08/1971   *Birthplace: Yorkshire*
Honours won: Combined Services Rep.
Tough-tackling midfielder who has represented the Combined Services whilst serving in the army. Originally played for Harrogate Railway, Harrogate Town and Frickley before moving south where he joined Sittingbourne. Then had his firsts spell with Dover before transferring to Stevenage Borough. Returned to Dover for a £7,000 fee in February 2000 but then joined Gravesend after The Crabble outfit suffered relegation from the Conference.

STUART, MARK
Midfielder
Current Club: Guiseley
Birthplace: Chiswick
Previous clubs include: Stalybridge Celtic - July 2001, Southport, Rochdale, Huddersfield T, Bradford C, Plymouth Argyle, Charlton Ath.

STUART, MARLON
Forward
Current Club: Dulwich Hamlet
Birthplace: Essex
Previous clubs include: Chertsey T - March 2002, Egham T, Chertsey T, Hampton & Richmond B, Clapton, Tilbury, Clapton, Bishops Stortford, Clapton, Romford.

STUBBS, KEVIN
Forward
Current Club: Tilbury
Birthplace: Essex
From Youth team.

STUBLEY, PETER
Forward
Current Club: Eastwood Town
Previous clubs include: Staveley Miners Welfare - August 2001.

STURDY, SIMON
Defender
Current Club: Harrogate Town
Birthplace: Yorkshire
Tall central defender who moved up to join UniBond Premier newcomers Harrogate Town in July 2002 from Northern Counties East side Pickering Town. Had been with the Pikes since the summer of 1999 after arriving from Tadcaster Albion. Previously with Rowntrees and Glasshoughton Welfare.

STURGESS, ADAM
Defender
Current Club: Rothwell Town
Birthplace: Kettering
Previous clubs include: Wellingborough T - July 2001.

STURGESS, JAMIE — Forward
Current Club: Wimborne Town
Birthplace: Dorset
Honours won: FA Vase Winners
Previous clubs include: Bournemouth FC - July 1997, Wimborne T, Poole T, Wimborne T, Dorchester T, Hamworthy Utd.

STURGESS, PAUL — Defender
Current Club: Stevenage Borough
D o B: 04/08/1975   Birthplace: Dartford
Dartford born, Paul filled Stevenages problem area on the left side of defence admirably since his arrival in the summer of 2001. Former clubs include Hereford, Brighton, Millwall and Charlton.

STURMEY, PAUL — Defender
Current Club: Bashley
Previous clubs include: AFC Bournemouth (Junior) - August 2000.

STYLES, GRANT — Midfielder
Current Club: Tunbridge Wells
Birthplace: Kent
Previous clubs include: Sheppey Utd - July 1999, Tonbridge Angels

SUCHAREWYCZ, GARY — Defender
Current Club: Leek Town
Birthplace: Nottingham
Joined Leek Town in June 2002, defender Gary had a handful of games for Matlock in January 2000 on loan from Hucknall Town. He has since been with Spalding United and Eastwood Town and impressed after returning to Matlock in July 2001.

SUDDES, LEE — Forward
Current Club: Consett
Birthplace: Bishop Auckland
Previous clubs include: Newcastle Blue Star - January 2002, Evenwood T, West Auckland T, Consett, Tow Law T, West Auckland T.

SUDDICK, JARROD — Forward
Current Club: Spennymoor United
D o B: 06/07/1969   Birthplace: Blackpool
Jarrod is in his second spell at Spennymoor United having rejoined in July 2001 from Tow Law Town. He is an ex-Sunderland trainee who first joined the Moors shortly after being released at Roker Park. He is a striker who regularly appears on the scoresheet and has previously turned out for Workington, Ponteland United, Gretna and Queen of the South.

SUGDEN, CRAIG — Forward
Current Club: Thackley
Birthplace: Yorkshire
Previous clubs include: Eccleshill Utd - August 1999, Farsley Celtic.

SUGDEN, JEFF — Defender
Current Club: Consett
Birthplace: Consett
Signed for club in 1986.

SUGDEN, MARK — Defender
Current Club: Thackley
Birthplace: Yorkshire
Previous clubs include: Eccleshill Utd - July 1999, Farsley Celtic, Guiseley, Emley, Eccleshill Utd.

SUGDEN, RYAN — Forward
Current Club: Chester City
D o B: 26/12/1980   Birthplace: Bradford
Highly-rated young forward who joined Chester City from Conference rivals Scarborough in June 2002. Bradford-born, Ryan signed for Oldham Athletic as a trainee and went on to make around 20 first-team appearances before being released. Joined Scarborough in February 2002 and immediately impressed with his all-round ability.

SUGRUE, ANTON — Midfielder
Current Club: Corby Town
Birthplace: Peterborough
Previous clubs include: Blackstone - August 2002.

SUGRUE, JIMMY — Forward
Current Club: Billericay Town
D o B: 01/01/1974   Birthplace: Hammersmith
Previous clubs include: St Albans C - March 2002, Aldershot T, Dulwich Hamlet, Chelmsford C, Croydon, Sutton Utd, Aldershot T, Hayes, Aldershot T, Kingstonian, Fulham (Trainee).

SULLIVAN, ANDY — Forward
Current Club: Staines Town
D o B: 16/06/1979   Birthplace: Hampshire
Honours won: England Schoolboy Int.
Talented forward who joined Staines Town in the summer of 2000 from Hayes. A former England Schoolboy international, he started his career at Southampton and also had a spell with Farnborough Town, with ehom he made Conference appearances.

SULLIVAN, KIERAN — Defender
Current Club: Banbury United
Birthplace: Banbury
Returned to Banbury United in January 2000 after nearly ten years away. First made the senior squad against Aylesbury United in 1985 after an apprenticeship at Oxford United. Won a Southern League Championship medal at Buckingham and a Birmingham Senior Cup runners-up medal with VS Rugby. Banburys Player and Players' Player of the Year for the 2000/01 season, he has also seen service with Kidderminster Harriers, Aylesbury United, Worcester City and Racing Club Warwick, from whom he rejoined Banbury.

SULLIVAN, MARTYN — Midfielder
Current Club: Weston-Super-Mare
D o B: 17/02/1975   Birthplace: Plymouth
Left-sided midfielder who can also play at full back, Martyn joined Weston-super-Mare in June 2002 from Dr Martens Eastern side Dorchester Town. Was in his second spell with the Dorset outfit, rejoining in October 2000 after being released by Forest Green Rovers - then managed, ironically, by Frank Gregan who re-signed him for Weston! Started his career at Plymouth and then played for Torrington before his first spell with Dorchester.

SULLY, PAUL — Defender
Current Club: Sidley United
Birthplace: Sussex
Ultra-reliable left-back: integral part of Sidleys rise through the ranks over the past few years: played a few times as goalkeeper towards the end of 2000/01: previous experience with Bexhill and St Leonards.

SUMMERS, CHRIS — Forward
Current Club: Haverfordwest County

D o B: 06/01/1972   Birthplace: Cardiff
Previous clubs include: Carmarthen T - March 2002, Cwmbran T, Merthyr Tydfil, Cwmbran T, Merthyr Tydfil, Ton Petre, Inter Cardiff, Barry T, Hereford Utd, Cardiff C.

SUMMERS, DANNY — Midfielder
Current Club: Bideford

Birthplace: Devon
Another product of our youth section, Danny is a highly promising midfielder.

SUMMERS, MARK — Defender
Current Club: Mangotsfield United

Birthplace: Bristol
Signed for Mangotsfield United in July 2001 from local Western League side Brislington for a four figure fee despite much competetion from local rivals. Has the adaptability to play anywhere in defence or midfield and has shown the ability to play at a higher level. Has a fine scoring record from midfield.

SUMMERS, ROD — Defender
Current Club: Herne Bay

Birthplace: Kent
Previous clubs include: Ramsgate - July 2000, Folkestone Invicta, Margate.

SUMNER, TOBY — Midfielder
Current Club: Basingstoke Town

Birthplace: Reading
Signed for Basingstoke Town in December 2001 from local rivals Aldershot Town. Young midfield player with good passing capabilities and endless energy, he was originally on the books at Reading.

SUNLEY, MARK — Defender
Current Club: Gateshead

D o B: 13/10/1971   Birthplace: Stockton
Previous clubs include: Spennymoor Utd - December 2000, Stalybridge Celtic, Halifax T, Darlington, Middlesbrough.

SUPPLE, MICHAEL — Midfielder
Current Club: Diss Town

Birthplace: Ipswich
Honours won: England Youth Int.
Previous clubs include: Stowmarket T - August 2001, Ipswich T (Junior).

SURTEES, MATTHEW — Midfielder
Current Club: Thackley

Birthplace: Yorkshire
Previous clubs include: Farsley Celtic - July 2001, Thackley, Farsley Celtic, Bramley.

SUSSEX, ANDY — Defender
Current Club: Grays Athletic

D o B: 23/11/1964   Birthplace: Enfield
Powerful defender, highly thought of in Non-League circles as a solid hard-working player who likes to push up when he can. Came to Grays from Barking this season.

SUTCH, DAVID — Forward
Current Club: Bamber Bridge

Birthplace: Lancashire
Previous clubs include: Congleton T - July 2002, Chorley, Blackrod T.

SUTCLIFFE, ARREN — Midfielder
Current Club: Ashton United

From Youth team.

SUTCLIFFE, LIAM — Goalkeeper
Current Club: Farsley Celtic

Birthplace: Yorkshire
Highly-talented goalkeeper who came up through the ranks at Farsley Celtic. Has interested a number of Football League clubs.

SUTCLIFFE, STEVE — Defender
Current Club: Trafford

Birthplace: Lancashire
Full back who signed for UniBond First Division side Trafford in the close season of 2002 from North West Counties Leaguers Glossop North End. Formerly with Tranmere Rovers and Rossendale United.

SUTTON, BRIAN — Midfielder
Current Club: Felixstowe & Walton United

Birthplace: Ipswich
Signed this season and has added a touch of class to the midfield. Always comfortable on the ball, an excellent passer along with possessing a powerful shot.

SUTTON, JAMES — Defender
Current Club: Salisbury City

D o B: 12/05/1985   Birthplace: Salisbury
Local lad who has progressed from Dr Martens Eastern club Salisbury City's youth and reserve teams. Promising defender who looks comfortable on the ball for one so young.

SUTTON, PETER — Forward
Current Club: Redditch United

Birthplace: Birmingham
Signed for Solihull in the summer from Halesowen Town. Previously with Bromsgrove Rovers, Sutton Coldfield Town and Redditch United. Re-joined Redditch in February 2002.

SUTTON, WAYNE — Defender
Current Club: Mickleover Sports

D o B: 01/10/1975   Birthplace: Derby
Previous clubs include: Hinckley Utd - August 2000, Burton Alb., Woking, Derby Co.

SWAILES, MATTY — Forward
Current Club: St.Helens Town

Birthplace: Manchester
Previous clubs include: Chorley - July 2001, Workington, Chorley, Hulton, Bury (Trainee).

SWAIN, RICHARD — Forward
Current Club: Rocester

Birthplace: Stafford
Previous clubs include: Kidsgrove Ath - March 2001, Rushall Olympic, Stafford R, North Cave.

SWALES, STEVE — *Defender*
Current Club: Whitby Town
D o B: 26/12/1973   *Birthplace: Whitby*
Steve is Whitby born and bred, but has spent most of his career playing in the Football League. He transferred for £100,000 from Scarborough to Reading in 1994, where had a lot of success in the First Division, before joining Hull in 1998 for £60,000. Later he was at Halifax before being released this summer and joining UniBond Premier side Whitby ahead of local rivals Scarborough, with whom he had been training with. Steve is a no-nonsense midfielder with an excellent range of passes, he can also play on the left.

SWALLOW, SIMON — *Defender*
Current Club: Oldbury United
Birthplace: Birmingham
Previous clubs include: Sandwell Borough - July 2001, Bloxwich T, Halesowen T, Tividale, WBA (Trainee).

SWALWELL, ANDY — *Forward*
Current Club: Billingham Town
Birthplace: Newcastle
Previous clubs include: Guisborough T - February 2002, Spennymoor Utd, Ballymena Utd.

SWAN, ADRIAN — *Goalkeeper*
Current Club: Spennymoor United
D o B: 31/01/1973   *Birthplace: Middlesbrough*
Confident goalkeeper who re-joined UniBond First Division side Spennymoor United in July 2002. He started his career with Darlington and also had a loan spell with Leicester City when Brian Little switched clubs. However, he left Feethams in the summer of 1994 without managing to make a League appearance and joined Billingham Town. Transferred to Spennymoor in 1995 and then on to Gateshead at the start of the 1998/99 season.

SWAN, DAMIEN — *Midfielder*
Current Club: Hanwell Town
D o B: 25/05/1978   *Birthplace: Camden*
Previous clubs include: North Greenford Utd - July 2000, Brook House, Hayes.

SWAN, IAIN — *Defender*
Current Club: Morecambe
D o B: 16/10/1979   *Birthplace: Glasgow*
Highly-rated defender who joined Morecambe in May 2002 from Conference rivals Leigh RMI. Signed for Leigh in season 1999/00 initially on loan from Oldham Athletic before being transferred to Partick Thistle. Joined RMI on a permanent basis before the start of season 2000/01. Iain is a very reliable central defender and a young player capable of a return to a Football League club.

SWAN, PETER — *Defender*
Current Club: Ossett Town
D o B: 28/09/1966   *Birthplace: Leeds*
Newly appointed player/coach after his professional career was ended by injury whilst at York City. Began life with Leeds United and made nearly 450 football league appearances with Hull City, Port Vale, Torquay United, Bury and Burnley. Commanding central defender who can also operate up front.

SWANN, GARY — *Midfielder*
Current Club: Swindon Supermarine
Birthplace: Oxfordshire
Midfielder who started his career with Hereford United. Then played for Witney Town and, from the summer of 2001, Ryman

Leaguers Hungerford Town. Switched to Dr Martens Western outfit Swindon Supermarine in August 2002.

SWANN, MARK — *Midfielder*
Current Club: Sutton Coldfield Town
D o B: 07/07/1972   *Birthplace: Birmingham*
Previous clubs include: Redditch Utd - March 2002, Blakenall, Sutton Coldfield T, Tamworth, Armitage.

SWANN, MICHAEL — *Forward*
Current Club: Paget Rangers
Birthplace: Birmingham
Previous clubs include: Tamworth - October 2001.

SWANNICK, DAVID — *Defender*
Current Club: Hyde United
D o B: 16/05/1979   *Birthplace: Bebington*
Born in Bebington and started his career with Wrexham. Dave then joined Morecambe, developing through their youth system to the first team. He was released and joined Altrincham in August 2001 after playing well in the pre-season games. Transferred to fellow UniBond Premier side Hyde United in the summer of 2002.

SWAYSLAND, MICK — *Forward*
Current Club: Wealdstone
D o B: 21/08/1973   *Birthplace: Hertfordshire*
Having signed for Wealdstone originalyl in 1998 after spells at Aylesbury United and Chesham United. Mick joined Hemel Hempstead then later returned only to join Thame United before returning for his third spell at the Stones in Janaury 2002. Is a prolific goalscorer.

SWEENEY, GLEN — *Defender*
Current Club: Shildon
Birthplace: Newcastle
Previous clubs include: Crook T - July 2001, Spennymoor Utd, Shildon.

SWEENEY, SIMON — *Defender*
Current Club: Berkhamsted Town
Birthplace: Middlesex
Defender who moved into Division One North of the Ryman League in July 2002 by joining Berkhamsted Town. Was spotted playing for West Middlesex Colts by Beaconsfield SYCOB in the summer of 1997 and then became a regular with the Spartan South Midlands Leaguers for five seasons.

SWEET, DUANE — *Forward*
Current Club: Rye & Iden United
Birthplace: Hastings
Teenage forward who scored a stunning goal on his debut against Bosham in August 2001.

SWEET, TONY — *Defender*
Current Club: Walton & Hersham
Birthplace: Surrey
A former Crawley Town player, Tony joined Swans and made his debut at the end of January 2001, quickly securing a regular first team spot.

SWEETMAN, NICK — *Midfielder*
Current Club: London Colney
D o B: 21/10/1974   *Birthplace: Herts*
Previous clubs include: Welwyn Garden C - July 1999, Leighton T, Molesey, Leighton T, Hendon, Leyton Orient.

S

SWETMAN, BEN   *Defender*
Current Club: Withdean 2000
Birthplace: Sussex
One of many youngsters to emerge at Saltdean during 2000/01 (scored once): dogged by injuries during the second half of that season: moved in August 2001 to Southwick: switched clubs in December: left-footed, and plays as a wing-back or sweeper.

SWINSCOE, CRAIG   *Defender*
Current Club: Burton Albion
Birthplace: Mansfield
Craig started his career at Field Mill, the home of Mansfield Town, where he joined the club on a YTS scheme. He then joined Burton Albion and was a regular in their successful reserve side of 2001/02 season. His impressive displays in defence have prompted manager Nigel Clough to include him in the squad for their first Conference season, and he is reckoned to be a bright prospect for the future.

SWITZER, GEORGE   *Defender*
Current Club: Salford City
D o B: 13/10/1973   *Birthplace: Manchester*
Previous clubs include: Hyde Utd - July 2001, Darlington, Manchester Utd.

SYKES, ALEX   *Midfielder*
Current Club: Forest Green Rovers
D o B: 02/04/1974   *Birthplace: Newcastle-under-Lyme*
Honours won: British Universities Rep., Dr Martens League Premier Div.Winners
Popular attacking midfield player who was part of the Forest Green Rovers team that won the double promotion from the Southern League, Southern section through the Premier Division into the Conference and was also played in the team that took Rovers to a FA Trophy final at Wembley in 1999. The former Mansfield Town player left Rovers to join Conference rivals Nuneaton Borough in the summer of 2000 but returned to The Lawn in January 2002. Alexs first ever game for Forest Green was against Poole Town, 30th March 1996. He scored on his debut as Rovers went on to beat Poole 6-0.

SYKES, PAUL   *Defender*
Current Club: Harrogate Town
D o B: 13/01/1977   *Birthplace: Pontefract*
Left wing back or midfielder who joined UniBond First Division champions Harrogate Town in the summer of 2002 from Ossett Town. Had signed for Ossett in August 2000 after being released by Emley. Started life with Sheffield Wednesday before moving on to Glasshoughton Welfare. Extremely dangerous down the left as he loves to get forward and chips in with some crucial goals.

SYKES, PAUL   *Forward*
Current Club: Margate
D o B: 08/11/1976   *Birthplace: Kent*
Previous clubs include: Welling Utd - August 1996, Gillingham (Trainee).

SYMES, STEVE   *Defender*
Current Club: Tooting & Mitcham United
Birthplace: London
Previous clubs include: QPR (Junior) - July 1996.

SYMM, PETER   *Midfielder*
Current Club: Chester-Le Street
Birthplace: Newcastle
Previous clubs include: Dunston Federation Brewery - July 2000, RTM Newcastle.

SYMONDS, LEIGHTON   *Forward*
Current Club: Bury Town
Birthplace: Suffolk
From Youth team.

SYRETT, GARY   *Defender*
Current Club: Leatherhead
D o B: 31/03/1983   *Birthplace: Surrey*
This midfielder was on Chelseas books as a schoolboy. An IT Consultant has also been with Horsley and Dorking.

SYRETT, MATT   *Midfielder*
Current Club: Rye & Iden United
Birthplace: Sussex
Midfielder who had six goals to his name for Rye during 2000/01. Previously played for Westfield.

TAAFFE, STEVE — Forward
Current Club: Leek Town

D o B: 10/09/1979   Birthplace: Stoke
Former Stoke City striker with first-team experience. Began the 2001/02 season with Stone Dominoes before moving on to Rocester. Signed for Leek in March 2002 and made an instant impression by scoring 4 goals in his first 3 games.

TACON, MICKY — Defender
Current Club: Lowestoft Town

Birthplace: Lowestoft
Previous clubs include: Gorleston - July 1996, Lowestoft T.

TAGGERT, TONY — Defender
Current Club: Farnborough Town

Birthplace: London
Highly-rated young defender who joined Brentford from school and went through the ranks at Griffin Park, turning professional in 1999. Was released at the end of the 99/2000 season and joined Farnborough.

TAGUE, ANDY — Defender
Current Club: Warrington Town

Birthplace: Wigan
Previous clubs include: Chorley - September 1998.

TAIT, ALLAN — Forward
Current Club: Folkestone Invicta

D o B: 06/09/1981   Birthplace: London
A former junior with Tottenham Hotspur, Allan became hot property during the 2001/02 season after winning the Golden Boot in the Kent League with Deal Town, where he blossomed under manager Simon Bryant and scored 32 goals in 29 games. Good on the ball, Allan has also been with Crawley Town and has attracted the attention of Football League scouts. He joined Folkestone Invicta for a small fee during the summer of 2002.

TAKALOBOGHASI, MO — Midfielder
Current Club: Ramsgate

D o B: 15/10/1979   Birthplace: Kent
Previous clubs include: Margate - August 2002, Local football.

TALBOT, GARY — Defender
Current Club: Altrincham

D o B: 06/10/1970   Birthplace: Manchester
Now an experienced Non-League defender who re-joined UniBond Premier side Altrincham in August 2002 from Conference outfit Northwich Victoria. Had cost the Vics a £2,500 fee when signing him from Alty in January 2001. Previously with Rhyl, Wilmslow Albion, Barnton and Winsford United.

TALBOT, HASSON — Defender
Current Club: Garforth Town

Birthplace: Yorkshire
From Youth team.

TALBOT, LEE — Forward
Current Club: Potters Bar Town

Birthplace: Herts
Previous clubs include: Boreham Wood - July 1998.

TALBOT, PAUL — Defender
Current Club: Burton Albion

D o B: 11/08/1979   Birthplace: Gateshead
Previous clubs include: Gateshead - March 2002, York C, Newcastle Utd.

TALBOT, ROBBIE — Forward
Current Club: Morecambe

D o B: 31/10/1979   Birthplace: Liverpool
Signed from Burscough in February 2001 for £9,000. Previous club, Marine. Made his debut for Morecambe as a substitute against Kettering Town, away 10th February 2001, won 5-1. Appearances last season, 11 + 12, 11 goals.

TALBOT, STEVE — Defender
Current Club: Three Bridges

Birthplace: Sussex
New signing from Oakwood at the start of this season: taken to hospital after being knocked out during the game with Saltdean in August 2001.

TALBOYS, STEVE — Midfielder
Current Club: Staines Town

D o B: 18/09/1966   Birthplace: Bristol
An experienced and powerful midfielder who began at Longwell Green, Mangotsfield United, Bath City, Trowbridge Town, Cheltenham Town and Gloucester City. Then moved into the Premiership with Wimbledon where he played 31 senior games followed by 6 games with Watford. After six years in the professional game he returned to Non-League circles with Boreham Wood in 1998, going on to Kingstonian, Sutton United, Aldershot Town, Carshalton Athletic, Hampton & Richmond Borough and Gloucester again. Signed for Staines Town in the summer of 2000 and now captains the side.

TALLENTIRE, DEAN — Defender
Current Club: Arlesey Town

Birthplace: Bedford
Honours won: British Universities Rep.
Bedford born Dean is a Surveyor who signed for Ryman Division One North side Arlesey Town in the close season of 2002. Deans former clubs include Aylesbury, Corby Town and Barton Rovers. Has represented the British Universities.

TALLENTS, CARL — Midfielder
Current Club: Stamford

Previous clubs include: Rushden & Diamonds - July 1999.

TANNER, ADAM — Midfielder
Current Club: Canvey Island

D o B: 25/10/1973   Birthplace: Maldon
Honours won: FA Trophy Winners
Previous clubs include: Colchester Utd - January 2001, Peterborough Utd, Ipswich T.

TANNER, DANNY — Forward
Current Club: Carshalton Athletic

D o B: 17/12/1978
Previous clubs include: Croydon - July 2001, Carshalton Ath., Epsom & Ewell, Crystal Palace (Junior).

TANNER, RICHARD — Forward
Current Club: Barwell

D o B: 12/12/1978   Birthplace: Leicester
Previous clubs include: Shepshed Dynamo - March 2002, Belper T, Shepshed Dynamo, Corby T - March 2001, Lutterworth T.

TANNER, ROB — Goalkeeper
Current Club: Harwich & Parkeston

Birthplace: Essex
Highly-promising young keeper whose performances last season were instrumental in revitalising Harwichs Reserve side. He has

now been given the opportunity to compete at Jewson level and has grasped the opportunity eagerly. A fine future prospect.

TANNER, RUSSELL — Defender
Current Club: AFC Sudbury
Birthplace: Essex
Signed for Sudbury in October 2001 from Heybridge Swifts after having previously spent 10 seasons at Braintree. A versatile left-footed player who likes to go forward.

TANNER, RUSSELL — Goalkeeper
Current Club: Hailsham Town
Birthplace: Sussex
U-18s goalkeeper during 1999/2000 and also made several reserve and first team appearances that season: regular choice from 2000/01 onwards, although he was dropped by the manager at one point (along with two other players) after getting involved in a lager-fest over the Christmas period.

TANSLEY, DAVE — Midfielder
Current Club: Coalville Town
D o B: 18/10/1969   Birthplace: Leicestershire
Honours won: Leicestershire Senior League Winners
Previous clubs include: Kirby Muxloe - July 2001, Friar Lane OB, Anstey Nomads, Anstey T.

TAPLEY, NATHAN — Defender
Current Club: Egham Town
Birthplace: Berkshire
Previous clubs include: Wokingham T - January 2002, Egham T, Camberley T, Yeading, Aldershot T.

TAPPIN, JONATHAN — Midfielder
Current Club: Aberystwyth Town
D o B: 23/09/1980   Birthplace: Tregaron
From Youth team.

TARR, ANTHONY — Forward
Current Club: Newcastle Town
Birthplace: Stoke
Previous clubs include: Congleton T - November 2000, Port Vale.

TARR, SCOTT — Goalkeeper
Current Club: Basingstoke Town
Birthplace: Surrey
A strong, competent and experienced goalkeeper who joined Basingstoke Town from Yeading in November 1999. Previously with Leatherhead, Gravesend & Northfleet, Banstead Athletic, Egham Town and Walton & Hersham, Scott has represented the Ryman League, the Middlesex League Representative side and has a Middlesex County Cup winners medal.

TARRANT, NEIL — Forward
Current Club: Barrow
D o B: 24/06/1979   Birthplace: Darlington
Honours won: Conference Winners
Striker who signed for UniBond Premier side Barrow in August 2002 after helping Boston United to win the Conference title. Had joined the Pilgrims in January 2002 from Ross County, where he had two spells with a high-profile move to Premiership Aston Villa sandwiched between. Started his career with Darlington and has also turned out for Shamrock Rovers in Ireland.

TARRANT, ROB — Midfielder
Current Club: VCD Athletic
D o B: 29/07/1982   Birthplace: Greenwich
From Youth team.

TASKER, CARL — Goalkeeper
Current Club: Beaconsfield SYCOB
Birthplace: Berkshire
From Youth team.

TATE, NEIL — Goalkeeper
Current Club: Tooting & Mitcham United
Birthplace: Surrey
Previous clubs include: Dorking - December 2001, Tooting & Mitcham Utd.

TATE, STEVE — Forward
Current Club: Lymington & New Milton
Birthplace: Hampshire
Previous clubs include: Newport IOW - January 2002, Weymouth, Havant & Waterlooville, Waterlooville, Havant T, AFC Lymington, Bashley, Salisbury C, AFC Bournemouth (Trainee).

TATHAM, JAMES — Forward
Current Club: Bury Town
Birthplace: Bedfordshire
Previous clubs include: Leighton T - August 2001.

TAYLOR, ANDY — Defender
Current Club: Diss Town
Birthplace: Cambridgeshire
Previous clubs include: Cambridge C - January 2002, Bury T, Crawley T, Wisbech T, Boston Utd, Crawley T, Cambridge C, Sudbury T, Bury T, Long Melford.

TAYLOR, ANDY — Defender
Current Club: Clacton Town
Birthplace: Essex
Previous clubs include: Colchester Utd - October 2000.

TAYLOR, ANDY — Defender
Current Club: Bridlington Town
Birthplace: Hull
Previous clubs include: Hall Road Rangers - July 2001.

TAYLOR, ANDY — Defender
Current Club: Newcastle Blue Star
Birthplace: Newcastle
Previous clubs include: South Shields - February 2002.

TAYLOR, ANDY — Defender
Current Club: Guisborough Town
Previous clubs include: Middlesbrough - July 2001.

TAYLOR, ANDY — Midfielder
Current Club: Clitheroe
Birthplace: Lancashire
Just returned from Great Harwood. Great motor, always raises his game for the big occasion. Should slot back in well.

TAYLOR, ANDY — Midfielder
Current Club: Northwich Victoria
Birthplace: Manchester
Andy is a former Manchester United junior. He is an energetic midfielder who loves to join the attack and Conference side Northwich Victoria will be hoping his late runs into the box will prove a valuable source of goals. Andy signed for Northwich in July 2002 after some impressive displays during the pre-season programme.

TAYLOR, ASHLEY — Forward
Current Club: Whyteleafe
Birthplace: Surrey
Previous clubs include: Cobham - November 2001.

TAYLOR, BEN — Defender
Current Club: Sittingbourne
Birthplace: Kent
Highly-rated defender who re-joined Sittingbourne in June 2002 from Dr Martens Eastern Division rivals Fisher Athletic. Began his playing days in Bournes youth and reserve side before making a name for himself in the senior side as a very good defender.

TAYLOR, BILLY — Midfielder
Current Club: Tonbridge Angels
Birthplace: Kent
Previous clubs include: Millwall - March 2002.

TAYLOR, CHRIS — Defender
Current Club: Total Network Solutions
D o B: 26/11/1974   Birthplace: Birkenhead
A solid and reliable defender who is just as comfortable with the ball at his feet, as he is in the air. A handful for any forward to cope with, he joined TNS in the summer of 2001 from LoW rivals Rhyl. Originally with UniBond side Droylsden, he has also seen service with Conwy United, Bangor City, Heswall and Newtown.

TAYLOR, CHRIS — Defender
Current Club: Glapwell
Birthplace: Chesterfield
Previous clubs include: Worksop T - July 1996, Glapwell.

TAYLOR, CHRIS — Goalkeeper
Current Club: Bromsgrove Rovers
Birthplace: Bromsgrove
Experienced and highly rated goalkeeper who re-joined Dr Martens Western side Bromsgrove Rovers in August 2002 after a spell with Premier Division Hinckley United. With Rovers during their Conference days and stayed at that level after signing for Kidderminster Harriers when Rovers were relegated in 1997. Has since played for Stevenage Borough, Boreham Wood and Hinckley United before returning to the Victoria Ground.

TAYLOR, CHRIS — Midfielder
Current Club: Rugby United
Birthplace: Warwickshire
Previous clubs include: Shepshed Dynamo - March 2001, Kenilworth T.

TAYLOR, DANNY — Goalkeeper
Current Club: Bradford Park Avenue
Birthplace: Yorkshire
Previous clubs include: Farsley Celtic - October 2001.

TAYLOR, DAVID — Forward
Current Club: Shildon
D o B: 25/09/1969   Birthplace: Nottingham
Previous clubs include: Grantham T - October 2001, Hinckley Utd, Gedling T, Kings Lynn, Grantham T, Ilkeston T, Gresley R, Ilkeston T, Arnold T, Kings Lynn, GPT Plessey, Ilkeston T, Dunkirk.

TAYLOR, DAVID — Forward
Current Club: Lincoln United
Birthplace: Co.Durham
Previous clubs include: Seaham Red Star - September 2001.

TAYLOR, GEOFF — Midfielder
Current Club: Fleet Town
Birthplace: Surrey
Previous clubs include: Banstead Ath - July 2001, Molesey, Staines T, Walton & Hersham, Woking, Banstead Ath., Kingstonian, Wimbledon.

TAYLOR, JAMES — Forward
Current Club: Havant & Waterlooville
Birthplace: Hampshire
Honours won: England Semi-Pro Int.
James goalscoring ability has seen him top the Dr Martens League Eastern Division goalscoring chart for the 1998/99 season and in 1999/00 came second to Tamworths Mark Hallam in the Premier with 32 goals. Signed for Havant & Waterlooville from Bashley in August 1999, James demonstrates his ability to find the back of the net with the greatest of ease time and time again. Called into the National Game squad in April 2002 and made his debut for England in the UniBond Four Nations tournament.

TAYLOR, JAMES — Forward
Current Club: Bromley
Birthplace: London
Fringe player who joined Bromley from Kingstonian in November 2001. He scored his first Bromley goal in the 1-1 draw at Hayes Lane in the FA Umbro Trophy against local rivals Tooting & Mitcham United.

TAYLOR, JAMES — Forward
Current Club: Afan Lido
D o B: 29/09/1979   Birthplace: Wales
Up and coming striker with fantastic talent. Former trainee with Swansea City with strength and power as well as good vision, James has a big future ahead of him.

TAYLOR, JAMIE — Forward
Current Club: Aldershot Town
Birthplace: Sussex
Diminutive teenage forward: who scored 17 times for Broadbridge Heath during 2000/01. Joined Horsham at the start of the 2001/02 season, and instantly proved to be a revelation at Ryman League level. Went through a real purple patch during a 12-day spell in November 2001, striking 9 goals in three matches. Such was his form that Premier Division Aldershot Town signed him in the summer of 2002.

TAYLOR, JOHN — Midfielder
Current Club: Brentwood
Birthplace: Essex
Brentwoods longest serving player, John has been with Brentwood 25 years and been a first team squad member for virtually all that time. He retired early last season but has been called back into action recently to bolster the Blues midfield.

TAYLOR, JULIAN — Goalkeeper
Current Club: Brook House
Birthplace: Bucks
Previous clubs include: Beaconsfield SYCOB - August 2001.

TAYLOR, KEVIN — Goalkeeper
Current Club: Biddulph Victoria
Birthplace: Staffordshire
Previous clubs include: Congleton T - January 2002, Kidsgrove Ath., Leek T.

TAYLOR, LEE — Midfielder
Current Club: Chertsey Town
Birthplace: London
A summer signing for Chertsey. Played for Uxbridge last term. Plays in the midfield. Was previously with Shrewsbury Town.

TAYLOR, MARCUS — Forward
Current Club: Haverfordwest County
Birthplace: Wales
Previous clubs include: Merlins Bridge - December 2000.

TAYLOR, MARK — Defender
Current Club: Spennymoor United
D o B: 08/11/1974   *Birthplace: Saltburn*
Previous clubs include: Marske Utd - July 2001, Whitby T, Spennymoor Utd, Whitby T, Bishop Auckland, Netherfield, Northampton T, Fulham, Middlesbrough.

TAYLOR, MARK — Defender
Current Club: Whitley Bay
Birthplace: Whitley Bay
Only turned eighteen, but very highly rated. Mark was chased by a number of clubs after leaving New Hartley Juniors, but opted to sign for his home town team. He has a great future in the game.

TAYLOR, MARK — Midfielder
Current Club: Halesowen Town
D o B: 22/02/1966   *Birthplace: Birmingham*
Honours won: Dr Martens Western Div.Winners
Mark started his career at Walsall back in 1984. He stayed at Walsall for 5 years making over 130 appearances for the Saddlers. Joined Sheffield Wednesday in June 89 for £50,000 but only made a handful of appearances and joined Shrewsbury Town for £70,000 in 1991. He made over 250 appearances for the Shrews before joining Conference outfit Hereford United. In 2000 Brendan Phillips signed him for Nuneaton and in 2001 for Halesowen Town. Mark made a good start to his Yeltz career and was very able and sharp in the centre of midfield as he helped the club to the Western Division title.

TAYLOR, MATTHEW — Defender
Current Club: Peterlee Newtown
D o B: 06/03/1976   *Birthplace: Maidstone*
Previous clubs include: Burnley - July 1998.

TAYLOR, MATTY — Goalkeeper
Current Club: Burscough
Birthplace: Liverpool
Very promising young goalkeeper who graduated from UniBond Premier side Burscoughs youth team. Was with Preston North End as a junior and has also played for Evertons under-17 Academy side. Now a regular in the senior side at Burscough.

TAYLOR, MATTY — Midfielder
Current Club: Mossley
D o B: 05/12/1979   *Birthplace: Cheshire*
Honours won: Jamaican u-21 Int.
Previous clubs include: Hyde Utd - August 2002, Cheadle T, Curzon Ashton, Hyde Utd, Plymouth Argyle.

TAYLOR, MICKEY — Forward
Current Club: Durham City
Birthplace: Newcastle
Previous clubs include: Chester-le-Street - December 2000, Nissan, Bedlington Terriers, Durham C, Blyth Spartans, Durham C, Newcastle Blue Star.

TAYLOR, NICK — Forward
Current Club: Ashford Town (Middx)
Previous clubs include: St.Albans C - July 2001.

TAYLOR, PAUL — Defender
Current Club: Mossley
Birthplace: Manchester
Previous clubs include: Connollys - March 1998, Radcliffe B, Chorley, Frickley Ath., BCCI.

TAYLOR, PAUL — Defender
Current Club: Altrincham
D o B: 05/08/1977   *Birthplace: Manchester*
Tall, cultured, left-sided central defender who was signed by Altrincham from Hyde United after being surprisingly released last season. Started his career with Bury before moving on to Bamber Bridge and Castleton Gabrials. Signed close season.

TAYLOR, RAY — Defender
Current Club: Bishops Stortford
Birthplace: Essex
Signed for Blues in January 2001 from Purfleet and has forged a regular place for himself in the back four. Ray was a former captain of Essex Schools and youth teams and as a junior was on the books of Charlton Athletic. Ever present for Chelmsford City in the Southern League in season 1995/6 after spells with both Purfleet and Billericay.

TAYLOR, RICHARD — Defender
Current Club: Staines Town
Previous clubs include: Hucknall T - June 2001, Matlock T, Gainsborough Trinity, Matlock T, Frecheville Community, Scarborough.

TAYLOR, RICHARD — Defender
Current Club: Lincoln United
D o B: 24/03/1982   *Birthplace: London*
Previous clubs include: Sutton Utd - January 2002, Hampton & Richmond B, Woking, Staines T.

TAYLOR, ROSS — Midfielder
Current Club: Heybridge Swifts
D o B: 14/01/1977   *Birthplace: Rochford*
Honours won: England Schoolboy & Youth Int., FA Youth Cup Winners
Began his career at Arsenal where he was understudy to Nigel Winterburn as a left back and was a member of their FA Youth Cup-winning side. Cultured left foot, with an aggressive style, now prefers playing in midfield. Has also been with Stevenage Borough and is now in his second spell with Heybridge Swifts after spending most of the 2000/01 season with Chelmsford City. Represented England at Schoolboy and Youth international level.

TAYLOR, SCOTT — Forward
Current Club: Banbury United
Birthplace: Cambridge
Honours won: RAF Rep.
Striker who joined Dr Martens Eastern side Banbury United in July 2002 from Hellenic League side Carterton Town. Had signed for Carterton at the start of the 2000/01 season after being posted to RAF Brize Norton. Formally with Cambridge United and has represented the RAF. Was rated as one of the best strikers in the Hellenic League in 2001/02.

TAYLOR, SCOTT — Midfielder
Current Club: Hayes
Birthplace: Lincoln
Honours won: RAF Rep.
Previous clubs include: Carterton T - February 2002, Cambridge C, Grantham T, Lincoln Utd, RAF.

TAYLOR, STEVE — Defender
Current Club: Studley
Birthplace: Worcestershire
Previous clubs include: Feckenham - July 2001.

TAYLOR, STEVE — Forward
Current Club: Matlock Town
Birthplace: Mansfield
Striker who was Town's leading scorer with 29 league and cup goals, a total that was only bettered by Mark Dobie of Gretna. An aggressive and hard-working player, he took both the fans and Players' Player of the year awards in his first full campaign with Matlock. He previously represented home-town club Chesterfield, but they released him - as did Mansfield. Taylor joined Matlock from South Normanton Athletic in March 2000 and is already on the way to another prolific season.

TAYLOR, STEVE — Midfielder
Current Club: Bromsgrove Rovers
D o B: 07/01/1970   Birthplace: Stone
Honours won: England Semi-Pro Int.
Previous clubs include: Evesham Utd - February 2002, Kidderminster Harriers, Bromsgrove R, Telford Utd, Hednesford T, Northampton T, Crystal Palace, Bromsgrove R, Rushall Olympic.

TAYLOR, STUART — Defender
Current Club: Hyde United
D o B: 14/09/1981   Birthplace: Manchester
Previous clubs include: Christchurch City (New Zealand) - August 2001, Blackburn R.

TAYLOR, STUART — Forward
Current Club: Thackley
Birthplace: Yorkshire
Previous clubs include: Eccleshill Utd - July 2001, Thackley, Accrington Stanley, Guiseley, Thackley, Eccleshill Utd.

TAYLOR, TERRY — Defender
Current Club: Brodsworth Welfare
Birthplace: Yorkshire
Previous clubs include: Worsbrough Bridge - October 2001.

TAYLOR, TOMMY — Defender
Current Club: Fleet Town
Birthplace: Hampshire
Previous clubs include: Trowbridge T - September 1998, Waikato (New Zealand), Trowbridge T, Yeovil T, Mount Maunganui (New Zealand), Yeovil T, Waikato (New Zealand), AFC Bournemouth.

TEALE, SHAUN — Defender
Current Club: Burscough
D o B: 10/03/1964   Birthplace: Southport
Honours won: England Semi-Pro Int.
Southport-born Shaun returned to the Port after a long absence during which time his career peaked in the Premiership. He played with local neighbours Burscough and had a spell on the South coast with Weymouth. The highlight of his career was at Aston Villa and he followed with a spell with Tranmere Rovers and last season played for Motherwell, before finishing the season at Carlisle

United. In May 2002 Shaun embarked on his first managerial role back at Burscough.

TEARNEY, TREVOR — Forward
Current Club: Forest Green Rovers
Birthplace: Birmingham
Trevor came on-loan to Conference side Forest Green Rovers towards the end of the 2001/02 season and made such a good impression in seve games that he was offered a contract with Rovers for the 2002/03 season. A highly-rated young forward or midfielder who was previously on Birmingham City's books.

TEASDALE, DARRELL — Defender
Current Club: Tooting & Mitcham United
Birthplace: Surrey
Previous clubs include: Leatherhead - June 2001.

TEASDALE, WARREN — Defender
Current Club: Bedlington Terriers
Birthplace: Newcastle
Warren is the club captain and leads by example. An experienced player whose hard tackling and driving abilities are well suited to either a defensive or midfield slot. An apprentice at Newcastle in his younger days he has served many clubs well over the years including Whitley Bay and Blyth playing in their great FA Cup wins over Preston North End and Bury respectively. After announcing his retirement at the end of last season, he has decided to give it another season.

TEE, JASON — Forward
Current Club: Hucknall Town
D o B: 28/09/1975   Birthplace: Sheffield
Talented forward who started his career with Sheffield United. Had a spell out of the game before signing for Northern Counties East League side Sheffield FC at the start of the 2001/02 season. Joined UniBond Premier side Hucknall Town in June 2002.

TEESDALE, RICHARD — Defender
Current Club: Hereford United
Birthplace: Birmingham
A former trainee at First Division club Walsall, the young centre-half signed a years contract with Conference side Hereford United in the summer of 2002 after spending the pre-season programme at Edgar Street.

TEKELL, LEE — Midfielder
Current Club: Arlesey Town
Birthplace: London
Honours won: Ryman League Div.3 Winners
Lee joined Arlesey Town in the summer of 2000 and has earned himself the reputation of being a good goalscorer and provider from midfield, very good at supporting and supplying the forwards and gets back quick to help in defence. Has played for Gillingham, Wycombe Wanderers, Dagenham & Redbridge, Wealdstone, Ware, Boreham Wood and Egham. Has two League winners medals with Arlesey. He is a business development Manager for a Multi National Company.

TELEMAQUE, ERROL — Forward
Current Club: Yeading
Birthplace: London
Skillful forward who originally signed on loan from Conference side Hayes just before transfer deadline 2001, before making the move permanent in the close season. Scored three goals in his six appearances before the end of last season. Previously made a name for himself at Stevenage Borough.

TELFER, MARK — *Midfielder*
Current Club: Enfield Town (Essex)
Birthplace: Herts
Joined Enfield Town upon the formation of the club, previously at Harlow Town, having spent last season out of the game. Eight years experience with Enfield FC at all levels. Another player to miss a large part of the season through injury.

TELLING, MATT — *Midfielder*
Current Club: Maltby Main
Birthplace: Yorkshire
Previous clubs include: Parkgate - October 2001.

TEMPLE, CRAIG — *Defender*
Current Club: Gloucester City
Previous clubs include: Brockworth - July 2001, Gloucester C, Brockworth.

TERRINGTON, DARREN — *Midfielder*
Current Club: Wroxham
Birthplace: Norwich
From Youth team.

TERRY, PAUL — *Forward*
Current Club: Dagenham & Redbridge
Birthplace: London
A product of Dagenham & Redbridges very successful reserve side, Paul made his Ryman League debut during the 1998/99 season and scored some important goals from midfield. Now an integral part of the senior side who played a major role in the title-winning success.

TERRY, PETER — *Midfielder*
Current Club: Staines Town
D o B: 11/09/1972   Birthplace: Basingstoke
An imposing central midfiedler, Peter started with Portsmouth and gained League experience with the old Aldershot and then continued his career with Millwall, Basingstoke Town, Farnborough Town and Maidenhead United. Joined Staines Town in the summer of 2000 and has performed solidly ever since.

TERRY, STUART — *Midfielder*
Current Club: Connahs Quay Nomads
D o B: 29/10/1973   Birthplace: Liverpool
Honours won: England Semi-Pro Int.
Previous clubs include: Northwich Victoria - July 2000, Altrincham, Bangor C.

TESTER, PAUL — *Midfielder*
Current Club: Bridgnorth Town
D o B: 10/03/1959   Birthplace: Stroud
Previous clubs include: Wrockwardine Wood - November 2001, Chasetown, Bridgnorth T, Cheltenham T, Worcester C, Hereford Utd, Shrewsbury T, Cheltenham T.

THACKER, MARTIN — *Midfielder*
Current Club: Bridlington Town
Birthplace: Hull
Previous clubs include: Hall Road Rangers - July 2001, Bridlington T, Hall Road R, Denaby Utd, North Ferriby Utd, Goole T, Hull C.

THACKERAY, ANDY — *Defender*
Current Club: Nuneaton Borough
D o B: 13/02/1968   Birthplace: Huddersfield
Had been with Halifax Town for two seasons after signing from Rochdale, where he spent five years. He has also played at Manchester City, Newport, Huddersfield and Wrexham (he played in the side which beat Arsenal 2-1 in the 1994 FA Cup). Andy was a very reliable player for Halifax where he scored a number of goals. Joined Nuneaton Borough in July 1999 and was appointed player-coach in 2001/02.

THACKWRAY, BEN — *Midfielder*
Current Club: Guiseley
Previous clubs include: Farsley Celtic - August 2000, Guiseley.

THEODOSIOU, ANDY — *Defender*
Current Club: Arlesey Town
D o B: 30/10/1970   Birthplace: London
The ever-popular London-born Theo is and experienced defender and is enjoying his second spell with Ryman Division One orth side Arlesey Town, making his debut in a League Cup tie at Barking on 29th August 2000. Former clubs include Spurs, Norwich, Hereford, Brighton. Re-signed from Harlow Town in November 2001.

THICK, KEVIN — *Defender*
Current Club: Salisbury City
Birthplace: Wiltshire
Left-sided defensive player who overlaps well. A graduate of Dr Martens Eastern club Salisbury City's youth team who looks to be a great prospect.

THOMAS, ANDREW — *Defender*
Current Club: Newport County
D o B: 11/10/1982   Birthplace: Newport
Honours won: Wales Youth Int.
Capped eight times for the Welsh Schools under-18 team, Andrew is a product of the successful Newport County Football Academy. The talented young defender made a goalscoring Dr Martens League debut at Rothwell Town in April 2000 and is now very much a member of the first team squad.

THOMAS, ANDREW — *Defender*
Current Club: Caersws
D o B: 26/01/1975   Birthplace: Wales
From Youth team.

THOMAS, ANDY — *Defender*
Current Club: Newtown AFC
D o B: 14/12/1977   Birthplace: Shropshire
Previous clubs include: Halkyn Utd - January 2002.

THOMAS, BRADLEY — *Midfielder*
Current Club: Bath City
Birthplace: Gloucester
Tough-tackling midfielder, Bradley began his footballing career at Sharpness in 1991 before joining Cinderford Town in 1994. Played a large part in the clubs Hellenic League success during this period, spending 3 years at the Gloucestershire-based side, briefly punctuated by a spell in New Zealand with New Plymouth in 1995. Made the switch to Newport County to team up with his former Cinderford boss Tim Harris in November 1997, going on to be named as the Welsh sides player of the season for that campaign. His spell at the Exiles came to end in October 1999 when he moved to Conference side Forest Green Rovers but a change in management limited his first-team chances and he returned to Newport for a loan spell in December 2000. He then

answered an SOS call from Cinderford manager and close friend Chris Smith to help the side in their relegation battle. Succeeded in helping his former team to preserve the Dr Martens place but when former City player Smith moved onto Aberystwyth Town, Bradley became another new arrival at Bath City during the summer of 2001.

THOMAS, BRIAN — Goalkeeper
Current Club: Afan Lido

D o B: 07/06/1976   Birthplace: Wales
A product of the Lido youth set-up, though also spent several years in the Football League with Hereford United. Acknowledged as one of the best keepers in the League, Brian has been more or less ever-present in the team since the 94/95 season. Although he has no real weaknesses, his superb shot-stopping is a stand-out quality.

THOMAS, CARL — Goalkeeper
Current Club: Port Talbot Town

D o B: 30/01/1980   Birthplace: Swansea
Previous clubs include: Haverfordwest County - March 2001, Swansea C.

THOMAS, CERI — Midfielder
Current Club: Port Talbot Town

D o B: 02/04/1974   Birthplace: Bridgend
Previous clubs include: Maesteg Park - July 2001, Bridgend T, Llanidloes T.

THOMAS, CHRIS — Defender
Current Club: Llanelli AFC

Birthplace: Llanelli
From Youth team.

THOMAS, CLIFF — Midfielder
Current Club: Withdean 2000

Birthplace: Sussex
Previous clubs include: Redhill - October 2001, Windsor & Eton, Slough T, Horsham.

THOMAS, CRAIG — Forward
Current Club: Haverfordwest County

Birthplace: Cardiff
Previous clubs include: Cwmbran T - March 2002, Cardiff C.

THOMAS, DEAN — Forward
Current Club: Hampton & Richmond

D o B: 12/08/1979   Birthplace: Surrey
Striker Dean scored Bromleys winner in the 3-2 home win over Barking & East Ham United on the final day of the 2001/02 season. Started that season at Carshalton Athletic and went to Hayes Lane around Christmas 2001 on-loan before going back to Colston Avenue. He had a short spell at Tooting & Mitcham United before re-joining Bromley in March 2002. Dean, who has also played for Kingstonian, then switched to Hampton & Richmond Borough in August 2002.

THOMAS, DEAN — Goalkeeper
Current Club: Rugby United

D o B: 27/11/1981   Birthplace: Coventry
Previous clubs include: Shepshed Dynamo - March 2002, Burbage, Derby Co (Junior).

THOMAS, GARETH — Forward
Current Club: Metropolitan Police

Birthplace: Middlesex
Previous clubs include: Uxbridge - July 1998.

THOMAS, GARETH — Forward
Current Club: Chorley

D o B: 05/12/1978   Birthplace: Altrincham
Promising striker who followed manager Mark Molyneax from UniBond First Division side Trafford to rivals Chorley in July 2002. Molyneax had signed Gareth in the summer of 2000 after spotting him playing in the North West Counties League with Maine Road.

THOMAS, GARY — Midfielder
Current Club: Flixton

D o B: 16/12/1967   Birthplace: Manchester
Previous clubs include: Mossley - January 2002, Droylsden, Chorley, Winsford Utd, Stalybridge Celtic, Chorley, Southport, Witton Alb., Winsford Utd.

THOMAS, GRANT — Midfielder
Current Club: Merthyr Tydfil

Birthplace: Merthyr
Livewire central midfielder who is a good passer with a great engine. A Merthyr Tydfil lad who signed for this home-town club from Swansea City in the summer of 2000. Spent a fair spell of the 2001/02 season on loan in the League of Wales but did manage 17 outings in a Merthyr shirt in 2001/02 added to around 10 the year before.

THOMAS, IESTYN — Defender
Current Club: Aberystwyth Town

D o B: 25/02/1983   Birthplace: Wales
Previous clubs include: Oxford Utd - March 2002.

THOMAS, JASON — Midfielder
Current Club: Abingdon Town

Birthplace: Oxford
From Youth team.

THOMAS, JAY — Defender
Current Club: Berkhamsted Town

Birthplace: Luton
Previous clubs include: Barton Rovers - July 2001, Langford, Arlesey T, Baldock T, St.Albans C, Arlesey T, Luton T (Junior).

THOMAS, JODY — Forward
Current Club: Carmarthen Town

D o B: 13/10/1982   Birthplace: Wales
Previous clubs include: Milford Utd - September 2001.

THOMAS, LEE — Defender
Current Club: Borrowash Victoria

Birthplace: Derbyshire
Previous clubs include: Bloxwich T - October 1999, Heanor T, Mickleover Sports, Heanor T, Mickleover Sports, Burton Alb., Mickleover RBL, Stapenhill, Belper T.

THOMAS, MARK — Defender
Current Club: Newtown AFC

D o B: 03/02/1973   Birthplace: Wales
A player of great heart who has come through the ranks at Newtown. The start of many attacking moves, as well as being a dependable defender. Has done well in a mid-field role when given the responsibility. Full of enthusiasm and is still a young player of great potential.

THOMAS, NATHAN — Defender

Current Club: Haverfordwest County

D o B: 01/10/1983   Birthplace: Wales
From Youth team.

THOMAS, NATHAN — Midfielder

Current Club: Grays Athletic

Birthplace: Essex
Great forward player with a keen eye for goal, loves to race round defenders and scores goals on a regular basis. Joined Grays from Barking.

THOMAS, NEIL — Goalkeeper

Current Club: Merthyr Tydfil

Birthplace: Wales
Honours won: Wales Semi-Pro Int.
Goalkeeper who signed for Merthyr Tydfil in August 1997 from League of Wales club Ton Pentre. Also played for Cwmbran and represented The Boys Clubs of Wales at under-18 level. Won his first Welsh semi-professional cap in March 1999 against England at St Albans. Has now made almost 200 appearances for the Martyrs.

THOMAS, OWEN — Midfielder

Current Club: Carmarthen Town

Birthplace: Carmarthen
From Youth team.

THOMAS, PAUL — Midfielder

Current Club: Chichester City United

Birthplace: Hampshire
Tireless midfielder and team captain (ran the London marathon in 2001): joined Bognor Regis from Waterlooville during the 1996 close season, having previously played for Fareham and Newport IoW: went to Worthing during 1999/2000 and finished that season with a spell on-loan with Havant/Waterlooville: signed up by Chichester in August 2000 and scored 15 goals (mainly from the penalty spot) during his first year at Church Road.

THOMAS, PHIL — Defender

Current Club: Didcot Town

Birthplace: Oxfordshire
Made his Didcot debut in 1990, Phil has over 650 appearances to his name and is still as reliable as ever. Has contemplated retirement but always talked out of that by his colleagues, which is a good measure of how they rate his abilities. Works as a tubular technician.

THOMAS, RICHARD — Midfielder

Current Club: Barking & East Ham United

Birthplace: Essex
A very talented midfield player who became the youngest manager in Non-League football when he took over at Barking at the start of the 2001/02 season. A fully qualifed coach, he joined the Essex side from Enfield in July 2000.

THOMAS, WAYNE — Midfielder

Current Club: Hednesford Town

D o B: 28/08/1978   Birthplace: Walsall
Previous clubs include: Shrewsbury T - March 2002, Walsall.

THOMAS, WYN — Defender

Current Club: Carmarthen Town

D o B: 11/01/1979   Birthplace: Wales
Honours won: Wales Schoolboy Int., Wales Colleges Rep.
Previous clubs include: Aberystwyth T - July 1998.

THOMPSON, ALEX — Midfielder

Current Club: Chertsey Town

Birthplace: Surrey
Signed for the senior side in the close season after progressing through the Chertsey Juniors youth sides over many years.

THOMPSON, ANDY — Forward

Current Club: North Ferriby United

D o B: 14/01/1978   Birthplace: Hull
Midfielder or forward who signed for North Ferrby United from Northern Counties East League side Hall Road Rangers in February 2001 season. Andy signed schoolboy forms with Hull City and represented Hull Schools and the East Riding of Yorkshire under-18s.

THOMPSON, ANDY — Midfielder

Current Club: Herne Bay

Birthplace: Kent
From Youth team.

THOMPSON, BENN — Forward

Current Club: Marske United

Birthplace: Cleveland
Previous clubs include: Billingham Synthonia - July 1997, Nunthorpe.

THOMPSON, CHRIS — Defender

Current Club: Gloucester City

D o B: 15/08/1982   Birthplace: Swindon
Previous clubs include: Northampton T - March 2002.

THOMPSON, CHRIS — Forward

Current Club: Arnold Town

Birthplace: Nottingham
Previous clubs include: Eastwood T - November 2000, Ilkeston T.

THOMPSON, COLIN — Defender

Current Club: Bury Town

Birthplace: Suffolk
Previous clubs include: Newmarket T - November 2000, Sudbury T, Castle Camps, Haverhill R.

THOMPSON, DARREN — Midfielder

Current Club: Newcastle Blue Star

D o B: 01/01/1972   Birthplace: Newcastle
Previous clubs include: Whitley Bay - July 1998, South Shields, Whitley Bay, Morpeth T, Millwall (Trainee).

THOMPSON, DAVID — Defender

Current Club: Soham Town Rangers

D o B: 20/11/1968   Birthplace: Ashington
Previous clubs include: Cambridge C - March 2001, Chesham Utd, Yeovil T, Cambridge Utd, Blackpool, Brentford, Bristol C, Millwall.

THOMPSON, DAVID — Forward

Current Club: Marine

D o B: 27/05/1962   Birthplace: Manchester
Player with vast experience in Football Leauge with Notts County, Wigan and Rochdale. Moved into the Conference with Southport before linking up with Marine in August 1999. Midfielder or forward.

THOMPSON, GARY   *Forward*
Current Club: Morecambe

D o B: 24/11/1980   Birthplace: Kendal
A fast forceful young winger with growing first-team presence. Another player who has come up the ranks from the Academy. Joined the club July 1999, previous club Wrexham. Also scored in the first minute of his 1st team debut.

THOMPSON, GRAEME   *Defender*
Current Club: Metropolitan Police

Birthplace: Cleveland
Previous clubs include: Gretna - July 2000, Blyth Spartans, Murton, Norton, Hartlepool Utd.

THOMPSON, GRAHAM   *Defender*
Current Club: Brigg Town

Birthplace: Lincoln
Previous clubs include: Bourne T - July 1995, Brigg T, Grantham T, Boston T, Kings Lynn, Boston Utd.

THOMPSON, IAN   *Forward*
Current Club: Oadby Town

D o B: 17/02/1975   Birthplace: Leicester
Honours won: England Schoolboy Int.
Previous clubs include: Highfield Rangers - January 2002, Shepshed Dynamo, Hinckley Utd, Corby T, Shepshed Dynamo, VS Rugby, Rothwell T, Spalding Utd, Leicester C.

THOMPSON, IAN   *Midfielder*
Current Club: Canvey Island

D o B: 28/09/1981   Birthplace: Rochford
Honours won: FA Trophy Winners
Pacey winger who signed for Canvey Island from Norwich City's Academy in February 2001. Spent a month on loan at both Great Wakering Rovers and Bishops Stortford during the 2001/02 season to gain further experience.

THOMPSON, KEVIN   *Defender*
Current Club: Chasetown FC

Birthplace: Shropshire
Previous clubs include: Ludlow T - June 2002, Bilston T, Bridgnorth T, Stourbridge, Willenhall T, Halesowen Harriers, Telford Utd.

THOMPSON, KEVIN   *Defender*
Current Club: Vauxhall Motors

D o B: 14/12/1974   Birthplace: Cheshire
Spent eight seasons with West Cheshire club Heswall before joining Vauxhall Motors three years ago as an attacking left sided player. Kevin quickly became a firm favourite on the back of his goals when he first joined the Motormen but he has now settled into a deeper role on the left side of defence.

THOMPSON, LEE   *Goalkeeper*
Current Club: Metropolitan Police

Birthplace: London
From Local football - July 1995.

THOMPSON, LIAM   *Forward*
Current Club: Swindon Supermarine

Birthplace: Swindon
From Youth Academy.

THOMPSON, MARC   *Midfielder*
Current Club: Harrogate Town

Birthplace: York
Signed for UniBond Premier side Harrogate Town in August 2002 from York City, where he made 24 appearances. A highly-promising young midfielder who hasn't given up hope of making a return to the full-time game.

THOMPSON, MARK   *Defender*
Current Club: Wisbech Town

D o B: 28/04/1982
Previous clubs include: Boston T - November 2000, Grimsby T.

THOMPSON, MIKE   *Defender*
Current Club: Bradford Park Avenue

Birthplace: Yorkshire
Powerful centre back who signed for Bradford Park Avenue from Frickley Athletic at the start of the 2000/01 season. Started his career at Scunthorpe and in between spells at Frickley has also played for Goole Town, Emley and Ashfield United.

THOMPSON, NATHAN   *Defender*
Current Club: Atherstone United

Previous clubs include: Bedworth Utd - October 2001, Rugby Utd, Rothwell T, Nuneaton B.

THOMPSON, NEIL   *Defender*
Current Club: Boston United

D o B: 02/10/1963   Birthplace: Beverley
Honours won: Conference Winners
Joined Boston United from Scarborough to help with the coaching. Was drafted into the Boston first team after all the regular defenders were ruled out due to injury or suspension.

THOMPSON, PAUL   *Forward*
Current Club: Boldmere St. Michaels

Birthplace: Birmingham
Previous clubs include: Paget Rangers - July 2001, Boldmere St.Michaels, Pelsall Villa, Rushall Olympic.

THOMPSON, PAUL   *Forward*
Current Club: Lowestoft Town

Birthplace: Great Yarmouth
Previous clubs include: Gorleston - July 1999.

THOMPSON, PAUL   *Forward*
Current Club: Jarrow Roofing & Boldon Ca

Birthplace: South Shields
Previous clubs include: Whitley Bay - November 1996, Boldon CA, Jarrow Roofing, South Shields.

THOMPSON, PAUL   *Goalkeeper*
Current Club: Chippenham Town

Birthplace: Swindon
Honours won: Dr Martens League Western Div.Winners
An experienced and well-respected goalkeeper who was signed by Chippenham Town for a £2,500 fee from Western League neighbours Devizes Town. Originally on the books at Swindon, he won a Dr Martens championship medal with Farnborough Town and has also had spells with Oxford City, Hungerford Town, Westbury United, Salisbury City and Melksham Town.

THOMPSON, PAUL   *Goalkeeper*
Current Club: Oxford City

Honours won: Dr Martens League Premier Div.Winners
Previous clubs include: Mangotsfield Utd - August 2001, Devizes T, Hungerford T, Oxford C, Hungerford T, Westbury Utd,

Melksham T, Salisbury C, Farnborough T, Swindon T.

THOMPSON, PAUL — Midfielder
Current Club: Gateshead

D o B: 17/04/1973 — Birthplace: Newcastle
Previous clubs include: Stevenage Borough - June 1999, Gateshead, Hartlepool Utd.

THOMPSON, PHIL — Midfielder
Current Club: Swaffham Town

Birthplace: Norfolk
Honours won: RAF Rep.
Great character and a key element in the last seasons rebuilding of the Swaffham midfield. Has played for the full RAF side.

THOMPSON, RICHARD — Defender
Current Club: Yate Town

D o B: 11/04/1969 — Birthplace: Bristol
Previous clubs include: Taunton T - July 2000, Tiverton T, Taunton T, Mangotsfield Utd, Forest Green R, Yate T, Salisbury C, Trowbridge T, Yeovil T, Torquay Utd, Newport Co., Yate T.

THOMPSON, RICHARD — Forward
Current Club: Croydon

D o B: 02/04/1974 — Birthplace: Lambeth
28-year-old striker who joined Croydon in March 2001 from Carshalton Athletic, and who played an important part in Croydons storming end to the season, scoring 10 goals in 17 appearances. Richard had spent the previous two seasons at Wycombe Wanderers, where his chances were limited by injuries. Has also played for Crawley, Kingstonian, Sutton United and Dulwich.

THOMPSON, SEAN — Forward
Current Club: Gorleston

Birthplace: Norfolk
Previous clubs include: Local football - July 1997, Gorleston.

THOMPSON, STEVE — Midfielder
Current Club: Banbury United

Birthplace: Middleton Cheney
Having played for Banbury United's reserves for two seasons, this midfielder progressed to the first-team during the 2000/01 season. Has represented Northamptonshire Under-16s and also the Oxfordshire Senior League Representative XI. Also won that Leagues Division One title with Middleton Cheney before joining United in July 1999. Has a tremendous attitude, and is a good squad member.

THOMPSON, STEVE — Midfielder
Current Club: Yeovil Town

D o B: 12/01/1963 — Birthplace: Plymouth
Honours won: England Semi-Pro Int.
Joined Yeovil in March 1998 from Woking. England semi-pro international who has also played for Saltash United, Bristol City, Torquay United, Slough Town, RAF, Combined Services and Wycombe Wanderers. He was a member of the Wycombe team that won the Conference and Trophy double. Steve was part of the clear-out of older players from Kingfield by John McGovern, and came to Yeovil along with Kevan Brown. Steve had always kept himself fit and continued to play at an older age than many others. However, he spent much of the 1999/2000 season out injured. Steve took over from Colin Lippiatt as Head Coach and now works as assistant to Gary Johnson.

THOMPSON, TONY — Forward
Current Club: Burnham

D o B: 11/12/1971 — Birthplace: Berkshire
Previous clubs include: Egham T - December 2001, Windsor & Eton, Slough T, Beaconsfield SYCOB, Staines T.

THOMSETT, PAUL — Midfielder
Current Club: Lewes

Birthplace: Sussex
Signed in September 2000 from Burgess Hill, Paul belied his veteran status last season with some excellent performances, indeed he hardly had a bad game. Neither it seems could most of the supporters, who made him their Player of the Season.

THOMSON, BEN — Forward
Current Club: Bashley

Birthplace: Bournemouth
Highly-rated forward who re-joined Dr Martens Eastern side Bashley in July 2002 from Newport Isle of Wight. Started his career on the books at AFC Bournemouth before signing for Bashley for the first time in 2000. Newport beat several other clubs to his signature in March 2001 but he returned to The Dell after the Islanders relegation from the Premier Division.

THOMSON, PETER — Forward
Current Club: Southport

D o B: 30/06/1977 — Birthplace: Bury
Tall striker who was signed by Conference side Southport in the summer of 2002 after being released by Luton. Bury-born, he started his career with his home-town club before playing Non-League football with Chorley and Lancaster City. Impressed whilst with the Dollies and earned himself a £10,000 move to Dutch side NAC Breda before joining the Hatters.

THORNE, GARY — Defender
Current Club: Bath City

D o B: 22/03/1977 — Birthplace: Swindon
Vastly experienced central defender, Gary joined Bath City in the summer of 2001 from Dr Martens Premier Division rivals Newport County. Formally with Swindon Town, he made his way up through the ranks at the County Ground before signing a professional contract in 1995. However, costing-cutting at the Wiltshire side saw him released in March 1996 and he made the switch to Non-League football with Gloucester City. Ironically, Swindon-born Gary had a trial with his home club as his performances at the Tigers made a move back into the full-time game a possibilty. In the end he remained at Meadow Park and went on to made over 200 appearances for City before moving on to Newport in March 1999. Another 100-plus appearances for the Welsh side meant that, despite only being 25, he has now made over 300 outings at the Dr Martens level. Hardman Gary is excellent in the air despite his lack of inches and also had a huge long throw that has added another dimension to City's attacks.

THORNE, WAYNE — Midfielder
Current Club: Chippenham Town

D o B: 28/07/1980 — Birthplace: Reading
Wayne is a strong midfielder who joined Chippenham Town in May 2002 from Clevedon Town. Had signed for Clevedon from Gloucester City in January 2001, where he had been player of the year the previous season. A big crowd favourite, Wayne began his career at Swindon Town as a YTS player before being released and joining Gloucester City.

THORNHILL, WAYNE — Defender

Current Club: Barwell

Birthplace: Derby
Previous clubs include: Borrowash Victoria - July 2002, Gresley R, Derby Co (Trainee).

THORNLEY, MARK — Goalkeeper

Current Club: Lancaster City

D o B: 26/07/1965   Birthplace: Derbyshire
An exprienced goalkeeper, Mark re-joined Lancaster City from Barrow and was in fine form during the 2001/02 season. Originally signed in January 1995 from Morecambe, having formerly been with Fleetwood, Stafford, Worksop, and Alfreton, he is renowned for his loud goalkeeping shirts.

THORNLEY, ROD — Forward

Current Club: Altrincham

D o B: 02/04/1977   Birthplace: Bury
Deadline day signing for Altrincham in March 2001 from Congleton Town. Rod finished that season with 9 goals in 9 games. Brother of ex-Manchester United and Huddersfield Town player, Ben, Rod works for Manchester United and England as a masseur. Previous clubs include Warrington Town, Doncaster Rovers and Salford City.

THORNLEY, STUART — Defender

Current Club: Flexsys Cefn Druids

Birthplace: Wales
Previous clubs include: Aston Villa - February 2001.

THORNTON, ANDY — Midfielder

Current Club: Pickering Town

Birthplace: Malton
Previous clubs include: Westlers Utd - July 1996, Pickering T, Malton, Norton Utd.

THORNTON, JAMES — Forward

Current Club: Littlehampton Town

Birthplace: Sussex
Useful forward, who has only been available to play for Littlehampton in the summer and christmas holidays during the last two years: scored 7 goals in 1999/2000 and 2 during 2000/01: first-team regular this season.

THORNTON, PETER — Defender

Current Club: Penrith

Birthplace: Cumbria
Previous clubs include: Kirkby Stephen - July 1998, Milnthorpe Corinthians.

THORP, MICHAEL — Defender

Current Club: Oxford City

D o B: 05/12/1975   Birthplace: Wallingford
Previous clubs include: Basingstoke T - July 1999, Slough T, Reading.

THORPE, ADRIAN — Midfielder

Current Club: Arnold Town

D o B: 25/11/1963   Birthplace: Chesterfield
Previous clubs include: Grantham T - July 1998, Arnold T, Kettering T, Instant Dict (Hong Kong), Northampton T, Walsall, Notts Co., Bradford C, Heanor T, Mansfield T.

THORPE, ALEX — Goalkeeper

Current Club: Mildenhall Town

Birthplace: Norfolk
Previous clubs include: Downham T - July 1999.

THORPE, DANNY — Goalkeeper

Current Club: Accrington Stanley

Birthplace: Lancashire
Previous clubs include: Daisy Hill - August 2001.

THORPE, GARY — Midfielder

Current Club: Alfreton Town

Birthplace: Sheffield
Previous clubs include: Worksop T - January 2000, Denaby Utd.

THORPE, MILES — Midfielder

Current Club: Wakefield & Emley

Birthplace: Yorkshire
Another player to follow manager Ronnie Glavin from Frickley Athletic. Now in his third season at Emley, Miler is a firm favourite with both playing colleagues and spectators alike. Prior to joining Frickley, he played for Parkgate and Worsborough Bridge.

THORPE, PAUL — Defender

Current Club: Frome Town

D o B: 15/06/1964   Birthplace: Somerset
Previous clubs include: Barnstaple T - July 2000, Taunton T, Cinderford T, Trowbridge T, Newport AFC, Dorchester T, Trowbridge T, Dorchester T, Yeovil T, Torquay Utd, Bristol C, Newport Co.

THORPE, STEVE — Midfielder

Current Club: Eastleigh

Birthplace: Sheffield
Previous clubs include: Sheffield Wednesday - May 2002.

THRELFALL, DEAN — Forward

Current Club: Port Talbot Town

D o B: 15/07/1970   Birthplace: Wales
Previous clubs include: Maesteg Park - January 2002, Inter Cardiff, Rhayader T, Cinderford T, Inter Cardiff, Cwmbran T, Inter Cardiff, Barry T, Inter Cardiff, Ton Pentre.

THRELFALL, MARK — Midfielder

Current Club: Carterton Town

Birthplace: Oxfordshire
Previous clubs include: Cirencester Academy - July 2001, Carterton T.

THROWER, IAN — Forward

Current Club: Sidlesham

Birthplace: Nottingham
Forward, brought into the side during the latest season: scored twice on his debut against Shinewater in October: a student from the Midlands, who was sourced from University College Chichester.

THURGOOD, SEAN — Defender

Current Club: Kingstonian

D o B: 11/02/1980   Birthplace: London
Young defender who has progressed into the first-team squad at Kingstonian from the clubs Suburban League side during the 2001/02 season.

TIBBENHAM, ANDY — Midfielder
Current Club: Buxton
Birthplace: Sheffield
Previous clubs include: Hallam - September 2000, Stocksbridge Park Steels, Alfreton T, Stocksbridge Park Steels, Exeter C, Denaby Utd, Hallam, Ashfield Utd.

TICKLE, DAVE — Midfielder
Current Club: Warrington Town
Birthplace: Wigan
From Youth team.

TICKNER, SIMON — Defender
Current Club: Leyton Pennant
Birthplace: Essex
Previous clubs include: Waltham Abbey - July 2000.

TIDAY, ANDY — Forward
Current Club: Oadby Town
Birthplace: Market Harborough
Previous clubs include: Rothwell T - February 2000, Oadby T, Rothwell T, Rushden & Diamonds, Aston Villa (Junior).

TIDSWELL, MALLY — Defender
Current Club: Caernarfon Town
D o B: 12/02/1973   Birthplace: Wales
Previous clubs include: Colwyn Bay - July 2001, Conwy Utd, Holywell T, Conwy Utd, Prestatyn, Landudno.

TIERNEY, FRANCIS — Forward
Current Club: Doncaster Rovers
D o B: 09/10/1975   Birthplace: Liverpool
Honours won: England Youth Int.
Came through the youth system at Crewe Alexandra, signing pro in March 1993. Moved on a free transfer to Notts.County in July 1998 and was released by the club at the end of season 1999/00. Had a spell with Witton Albion before Doncaster Rovers signed him in March 2001. An England Youth international.

TIERNEY, STEVE — Goalkeeper
Current Club: Peterlee Newtown
Birthplace: Co.Durham
Previous clubs include: Washington - July 2001.

TIGHE, JASON — Defender
Current Club: Southwick
Birthplace: Sussex
Defender, who has plenty of miles on the clock: originally played for Southwick several years ago, before spending time at Shoreham and Newhaven: also made a few appearances for Lewes during 1999/2000: looked set to become manager at troubled Newhaven for the start of the following season, but the job fell through and he consequently returned to Old Barn Way: didnt feature in the side during the second half of the 2000/01 season.

TILBURY, DANIEL — Midfielder
Current Club: Hayes
From Youth team.

TILBURY, DANNY — Forward
Current Club: Wealdstone
D o B: 22/06/1978   Birthplace: Middlesex
Midfielder or forward, Danny joined Wealdstone from Hayes during the summer of 2000 and established himself quickly in the first team Now in his third aseason at the club.

TILBURY, DAVE — Defender
Current Club: Windsor & Eton
Birthplace: London
Defender who signed for Windsor & Eton in December 2001from fellow Ryman League side Kingsbury Town. Started out as a youngster on the books at QPR and also had a spell with Conference club Hayes. Previously with Yeading, Edgware Town, Wealdstone, Molesey and Boreham Wood.

TILLEY, ANTHONY — Midfielder
Current Club: Bashley
D o B: 11/02/1977   Birthplace: Zambia
Previous clubs include: Weymouth - June 2001, Wimborne T, Super Sport Utd (South Africa), Southampton, Portsmouth, Brighton.

TILLEY, GARY — Midfielder
Current Club: Chatham Town
From Youth team.

TILLEY, NEIL — Midfielder
Current Club: Leyton Pennant
Previous clubs include: Waltham Abbey - February 2000, Potters Bar T, Waltham Abbey, Redbridge Forest, Enfield.

TILLEY, PAUL — Midfielder
Current Club: Trafford
Birthplace: Lancashire
Young midfield player who signed for UniBond First Division side Altrincham in close season of 2002 from Altrincham. His other clubs were Runcorn and Wigan Athletic.

TILLSON, DANIEL — Goalkeeper
Current Club: Burnham
Birthplace: Berkshire
Young keeper signed from Sandhurst Town. Made debut 2 seasons ago in the FA Trophy at Oxford City. Suffered a bad leg break last September playing for the reserves and is not expected back until around Christmas 2001.

TILLY, NICKY — Midfielder
Current Club: Matlock Town
D o B: 14/05/1968   Birthplace: Sheffield
Popular winger Nick is Town's current longest-serving player and is the club captain. He reached 500 games earlier this season and sits second in the all-time appearance list, having scored over 120 goals in his time at Causeway Lane. Nick joined the Gladiators at the start of the 1989/90 season and just an eighteen-month spell at Gainsborough following relegation in 1996 interrupting his time here.

TILSTON, MARK — Midfielder
Current Club: Stafford Town
Birthplace: Stafford
From Youth team.

TIMMS, DAVE — Defender
Current Club: Oswestry Town
D o B: 18/08/1980   Birthplace: Shrewsbury
Transferred from Newtown last season and has proved his consistencey for the club.

TIMONS, CHRIS — Defender
Current Club: Stalybridge Celtic
D o B: 08/12/1974   Birthplace: Old Langworth
Joined Stalybridge Celtic in May 2002 from Dr Martens Leaguers Ilkeston Town. Had been with the Robins since June 2000, signing from Altrincham who in turn had paid Gainsborough Trinity £20,000 for his services. A tall and commanding central defender, Chris worked his way through the ranks at Mansfield Town and made over 40 league appearances for the Stags before joining Gainsborough. His outstanding form earned him a short spell at Leyton Orient where he scored two goals in three starts before returning to Gainsborough. He performed heroics as Ilkestons captain saw him deservedly voted Supporters and Players' Player Of the Year.

TIMOTHY, BILLY — Midfielder
Current Club: Port Talbot Town
D o B: 30/01/1978   Birthplace: Swansea
Previous clubs include: Haverfordwest County - February 2001, Llandarcy.

TIMOTHY, DAVID — Midfielder
Current Club: Sutton United
Birthplace: Surrey
A right-sided midfielder or wing back who was a 2001 close season signing for Sutton United after spending two seasons with Slough Town He began his career with Reading as a junior and has also played for Woking and Hampton.

TINGLEY, DANNY — Defender
Current Club: Tonbridge Angels
D o B: 11/04/1968   Birthplace: Kent
Previous clubs include: Sittingbourne - July 1992, Sheppey Utd, Gravesend, Sheppey Utd, Gillingham (Junior).

TINKLER, GARY — Defender
Current Club: Stafford Town
Birthplace: Stafford
From Youth team.

TITTERTON, DAVID — Defender
Current Club: Ludlow Town
D o B: 25/09/1971   Birthplace: Hatton
Previous clubs include: Racing Club Warwick - November 2001, Bridgnorth T, Oldbury Utd, Stourport Swifts, Bloxwich T, Stourbridge, Burton Alb., Hednesford T, Wycombe Wanderers, Hereford Utd, Coventry C.

TITTERTON, MORETON — Midfielder
Current Club: Hinckley United
D o B: 20/12/1969   Birthplace: Warwick
Honours won: Dr Martens League Western Div.Winners
Club captain and record appearance holder. Midfielder Morton joined Hinckley United from Bedworth United and made his debut in United's first ever match after the amalgamation in 1997. Previous clubs include Wolverhampton Wanderers and Stratford Town. Often plays in the central midfield role, holding and releasing the ball, although he can get forward and score goals. A firm fans favourite and in the 2001/02 season Morton passed the double century for appearances and also won a Dr Martens Western Division championship medal with Hinckley United.

TITTLEY, PHIL — Midfielder
Current Club: Frickley Athletic
Birthplace: Yorkshire
Previous clubs include: Gainsborough Trinity - October 2001.

TIVEY, MARK — Midfielder
Current Club: Bromley
D o B: 10/02/1971   Birthplace: London
Honours won: FA Youth Cup Winners
Colourful character who played for Charlton Athletic from the age of 8 to 22 and spent 8 years playing in Sweden where he won 6 league titles in Sweden. He has played on every Premier League ground and has won the FA Youth Cup and League Cup final for Charlton Youth. Has Non-League experience with Dulwich Hamlet and had a spell with Harlow Town earlier this season before re-joining Bromley after a pre-season period with the Ravens.

TOBIN, DANNY — Defender
Current Club: Newcastle Blue Star
D o B: 07/11/1973   Birthplace: Gosforth
Previous clubs include: Gosforth Bohemians - August 1995.

TOBIN, STEVE — Midfielder
Current Club: Kidsgrove Athletic
Birthplace: Manchester
Honours won: NWCL Winners
Joined on loan from Hyde United at the end of last season, and obviously liked it at Kidsgrove as he signed permanently in August 2001. Scored several important goals in the run-in to the NWCL title. Previous clubs include Leeds United, Altrincham and Leek Town.

TOBOLEWSKI, ROSS — Midfielder
Current Club: Barking & East Ham United
Birthplace: Essex
Very talented and promising 21-year-old midfielder who was a trainee with West Ham United. Joined Barking upon his release in November 2001 and shows great promise for the future.

TODD, ANDY — Midfielder
Current Club: Worksop Town
D o B: 22/02/1979   Birthplace: Nottingham
Previous clubs include: Eastwood T - October 2001, Ilkeston T, Eastwood T, Scarborough, Nottingham Forest, Eastwood T.

TODD, DARREN — Midfielder
Current Club: Holmer Green
Birthplace: Bucks
Previous clubs include: Penn & Tylers Green - July 2000, Holmer Green.

TODD, PAUL — Midfielder
Current Club: Gorleston
Birthplace: Norfolk
From Youth team.

TODD, SCOTT — Forward
Current Club: Carshalton Athletic
D o B: 10/04/1983   Birthplace: Middlesex
Teenage striker who progressed through the Ashford Town (Middx) youth squad. Established himself in the first-team at the start of the 2000/01 season and ended up as top scorer with 26 goals. Had opportunities to play the following season, but now has the responsibility of carrying Carshalton Athletic's Graham Roberts praise as ....the best signing Ive made in my time as a Manager, after signing for the Division One South side in the summer of 2002.

TODHUNTER, STUART — *Midfielder*
Current Club: Clitheroe

D o B: 05/03/1970   *Birthplace: Preston*
Ex-Fleetwood who bedded in well into the midfield last year. Has the pedigree and could put in a massive year this season.

TOLAN, JORDAN — *Forward*
Current Club: Tilbury

Birthplace: Essex
From Youth team.

TOLHURST, JAMIE — *Midfielder*
Current Club: Witham Town

Birthplace: Essex
Previous clubs include: Great Wakering Rovers - July 2001, Bowers Utd, Burnham Ramblers, Southend Manor, Basildon Utd.

TOLSON, CORD — *Midfielder*
Current Club: Tonbridge Angels

D o B: 29/12/1978   *Birthplace: Australia*
Previous clubs include: Kenblawarra (Australia) - January 2002.

TOMKINS, LYNDON — *Midfielder*
Current Club: Gloucester City

Birthplace: Gloucester
Started his playing days with Gloucester City's youth side before gaining Southern League experience with Witney Town and Trowbridge Town. Lyndon is a highly-regarded midfielder who re-signed for Gloucester in July 2002 after spending four seasons with Cinderford Town.

TOMLIN, GAVIN — *Forward*
Current Club: Ashford Town

Birthplace: Kent
Previous clubs include: Tooting & Mitcham Utd - January 2002.

TOMLINSON, ANDY — *Midfielder*
Current Club: Heybridge Swifts

Birthplace: Essex
Young midfield playmaker who returned for a second spell with Heybridge Swifts in February 2002 after begining the 2001/02 season at Billericay Town following a loan spell from Swifts at the end of the previous campaign. Skilful and a sweet left foot, can pass well short and long. Aggressive and competitive player who has the capacity to boss the game when in the mood. Previously with Brentwood and Enfield.

TOMLINSON, GRAEME — *Forward*
Current Club: Stevenage Borough

D o B: 10/12/1975   *Birthplace: Watford*
Respected forward who started his career with Bradford City. Made only 17 first-team appearances for the Bantams before being signed by Alex Ferguson for Manchester United for £100,000 in July 1994. Soent four years at Old Trafford without managing to break into their star-studded senior side and moved onto Macclesfield in the summer of 1998. Had a two-year spell with Exeter before joining Conference side Stevenage Borough on the eve of the 2002/03 season.

TOMLINSON, MIKE — *Defender*
Current Club: Runcorn FC Halton

Birthplace: Liverpool
Currently in his fourth season with the Linnets after progressing from the reserve team during the 1997/98 season. Originally brought into the team as a right back, but has now established himself as Runcorns first choice centre half. Tommo is also vice-captain for the Linnets, and his no nonsense attitude in defence has led to him being man of the match on numerous occasions. Tommo is also good going forward, and is an excellent crosser of the ball, which had led to several League Scouts taking a look at him this season.

TOMLINSON, MIKE — *Midfielder*
Current Club: Burnham

Birthplace: Buckinghamshire
Honours won: British Universities Rep.
Signed 8 years ago from Aylesbury United. Equally at home in midfield or defence Tommo has played at Banbury United, Bedworth Town and Tring Town and also represented British Universities.

TOMLINSON, PAUL — *Forward*
Current Club: Ossett Town

D o B: 23/12/1969   *Birthplace: Brierley Hill*
Signed in December 2001 from Hucknall Town and scored on his debut. Powerful, strong centre forward who has also played for Grantham Town and Lincoln United.

TOMLINSON, RICHARD — *Defender*
Current Club: Selby Town

Birthplace: North Cave
Previous clubs include: Ponterfract Collieries - July 1998, Selby T, Pickering T, North Cave.

TOMPKINS, STEVE — *Midfielder*
Current Club: Feltham

Birthplace: Feltham
Last seasons Reserve Player of the Year Tommo joined Feltham during the summer of 2000 and capped a fine season with the afore mentioned trophy. Made his debut for the first team against Viking Greenford and promptly scrambled home a goal to earn the blues a point. Tommo or Jody (Jody Morris) as he is often referred to (I think its a height thing), supports Chelsea and aims to grab a regular place in the first XI this season.

TOMS, FRASER — *Midfielder*
Current Club: Barnet

D o B: 13/09/1979   *Birthplace: Ealing*
Dynamic left-sided midfielder with an excellent turn of pace. Joined Barnet on a free transfer from Charlton Athletic and quickly impressed the fans with his skill and quality sideburns, has made the left midfield spot his own.

TONER, JOHN — *Forward*
Current Club: Total Network Solutions

D o B: 09/09/1977   *Birthplace: Montreal, Canada*
Renowned goalscorer in the League of Wales, his pace and shooting accuracy are his best assetts. Joined TNS from Conwy United in November 1999, he began his career as a trainee with Liverpool and then had spells with Colwyn Bay, Warrington Town, Altrincham and Cemaes Bay.

TONGE, DAVID — *Midfielder*
Current Club: Coalville Town

Birthplace: Leicester
Honours won: Leicestershire Senior League Winners
Previous clubs include: Thringstone - July 2001, Friar Lane OB, Shepshed Dynamo, Hinckley T, VS Rugby, Grantham T, Leicester Utd, Corby T, Leicester Utd, Hinckley T, Oadby T, Leicester Utd, St Andrews.

TONKIN, ANTHONY — *Defender*
Current Club: Yeovil Town
Birthplace: Plymouth
Honours won: Engand Semi-Pro Int., FA Trophy Winners, British Universities Rep.
Can play at centre back or full back, and is a very athletic player who says his main hobby is keeping fit. Anthony has represented British Universities and gained England semi-pro caps in 2002. A young player who broke through into the Yeovil Town first team from the reserves, and has kept his regular place at left back.

TONKIN, KELLY — *Defender*
Current Club: Barking & East Ham United
Previous clubs include: Barkingside - July 1999.

TONKS, ROBERT — *Midfielder*
Current Club: Wakefield & Emley
Birthplace: Leeds
In his third season at Emley, he was signed from local football. Able to play in several positions, while always liable to score a vital goal.

TOOMEY, DAVE — *Forward*
Current Club: Barry Town
D o B: 12/05/1971   Birthplace: Swindon
Previous clubs include: Tiverton T - November 2001, Cinderford T, Hungerford T, Fairford T, Witney T, Swindon Supermarine.

TOONE, LEIGH — *Midfielder*
Current Club: Stocksbridge Park Steels
Previous clubs include: Scarborough - August 2001.

TOPPIN, ADRIAN — *Defender*
Current Club: Epsom And Ewell
Birthplace: Surrey
Defender/midfielder reviously with Molesey and Wealdstone, joined Epsom in January 2001. Scored on his debut against Hornchurch on 20th January last season.

TORONCZAK, DANNY — *Forward*
Current Club: Thackley
Birthplace: Yorkshire
Previous clubs include: Ossett Alb - February 2002, Guiseley, Ashton Utd, Liversedge, Frickley Ath., Liversedge, Littletown.

TORPEY, NICK — *Midfielder*
Current Club: Dorking
Birthplace: Surrey
Previous clubs include: Bognor Regis T - July 1995, Charlton Ath.

TORRES, MICK — *Goalkeeper*
Current Club: Abingdon Town
Birthplace: Oxford
Previous clubs include: Oxford C - July 2001, Abingdon Utd, Oxford C, Banbury Utd, Bicester T.

TORSON, SOLOMON — *Midfielder*
Current Club: Cheshunt
D o B: 28/07/1973   Birthplace: Berkshire
Previous clubs include: Windsor & Eton - January 2002, Slough T, Wokingham T.

TORTO, GODFREY — *Forward*
Current Club: Harrow Borough
Birthplace: London
Striker or attacking midfielder who rejoined Ryman Premier side Harrow Borough during the 2001/02 season after a spell with Arlesey Town. Previously with Kingstonian, Southend United and Chelsea. A Market Research Supervisor.

TOTTON, CRAIG — *Forward*
Current Club: Beaconsfield SYCOB
Birthplace: Berkshire
Previous clubs include: Edgware T - December 2000, Wealdstone, Cheshunt, Hemel Hempstead, Chalfont St.Peter, Chesham Utd.

TOVEY, CHRIS — *Midfielder*
Current Club: Histon
Birthplace: Cambridge
Experienced midfielder who has spent the majority of his career with Cambridge City with four separate spells with the latter being as player-manager before he returned to Chelmsford in December 2001. His initial stay with the Clarets saw him take on the role of player-coach. Chriss other clubs have been Letchworth Garden City, Royston and Great Shelford. Signed for Histon in May 2002.

TOVEY, LUKE — *Midfielder*
Current Club: Gloucester City
Birthplace: Cheltenham
Previous clubs include: Cheltenham Saracens - March 2001, Cheltenham T.

TOVEY, PAUL — *Midfielder*
Current Club: Paulton Rovers
Birthplace: Bristol
Previous clubs include: Yate T - August 1999, Clevedon T, Yate T, Bath C, Bristol R.

TOWERS, DAVE — *Midfielder*
Current Club: Sidlesham
Birthplace: Sussex
Young midfielder: son of the manager and originally a product of Chichester City's youth team: joined Sidlesham at the start of 1999/2000: restricted by injury during 2000/01 (scored 4 times): made a terrible start to the latest season with two red cards in the opening month: subsequently spent time recovering from a wrist operation before returning to action in December 2001.

TOWERS, SEAN — *Defender*
Current Club: Sidlesham
Birthplace: Sussex
Defender: another one of the managers sons: also played for Chichester U-18s during 2000/01.

TOWLER, COLIN — *Defender*
Current Club: Chippenham Town
Birthplace: Bristol
Commanding central defender whose playing days began at Mangotsfield United. Moved on to Yate Town and then joined Bath City, then members of the Conference, in January 1997. Became skipper at Twerton Park and was one of the longest-serving players on their books when he switched to newly-promoted neighbours Chippenham Town in May 2002.

TOWLER, PAUL — Defender

Current Club: Hendon

D o B: 01/02/1972 — Birthplace: London
Honours won: England Schoolboy & Youth Int., FA Youth Cup Winners

Summer 1999 signing for Hendon from Metropolitan Police where he had played for six years. Having previously played for Newport County, Paul earlier graduated from the FA School of Excellence before going on to become England Youth Captain and also winning the FA Youth Cup whilst with Watford. The management team certainly made an astute choice when he brought this capable defender to Claremont Road. Paul is a serving Police Officer.

TOWN, DAVID — Forward

Current Club: Boston United

D o B: 09/12/1976 — Birthplace: Bournemouth
Joined Rushden & Diamonds in the summer of 1999 for £35,000 from Bournemouth, his home-town club. Notched up some 56 League games for the Cherries but had struggled to hold down a place befoe joining the Diamonds. Spent a frustrating 1999/2000 season at Nene Park when injuries affected his appearances. Transferred to Boston in March 2001.

TOWNLEY, LEON — Defender

Current Club: St.Albans City

D o B: 16/02/1976 — Birthplace: Loughton
Centre-back who signed for Ryman Premier side St Albans City in the summer of 2002 from rivals Aldershot Town. Spent his early days at Tottenham Hotspur before gaining Football League experience with Brentford. Also had a spell with Slough Town before joining the Shots in July 2001.

TOWN'S, MATTHEW — Goalkeeper

Current Club: Congleton Town

Birthplace: Macclesfield
Goalkeeper. Aged 18 and lives in Macclesfield. Played for the District FA side and both Cheshire FA and Cheshire Schools FA in 2000/01. Played for Macclesfield Town Youth side. Enjoyed a trip to France to represent the Stockport Metro League.

TOWN'S, RYAN — Goalkeeper

Current Club: Hamble ASSC

Birthplace: Hampshire
Previous clubs include: BAT Sports - July 2001.

TOWN'SEND, GARY — Forward

Current Club: Worksop Town

From Youth team.

TOWN'SEND, KEVIN — Midfielder

Current Club: Ringmer

Birthplace: Sussex
Stylish midfielder who spent three highly successful years at Saltdean, which culminated in victory over Burgess Hill in the John OHara League Cup Final in May 2000. Joined Ringmer midway through last season and is also a regular player for Sussex. Previous clubs include Worthing, Peacehaven and Whitehawk.

TOWN'SEND, MARK — Defender

Current Club: Walton Casuals

Birthplace: Surrey
Mark has recently re-joined Casuals following a season with Hersham RBL. Previosly had 2 seasons at Franklyn Road.

TOWN'SEND, QUENTIN — Defender

Current Club: Redditch United

D o B: 13/02/1977 — Birthplace: Worcester
Previous clubs include: Bilston T - January 2002, Stourport Swifts, Bromsgrove Rovers, Stourbridge, Racing Club Warwick, Evesham Utd, Worcester C, Hereford Utd, Wolverhampton Wanderers.

TOWN'SEND, RITCHIE — Forward

Current Club: Marine

D o B: 01/01/1976 — Birthplace: Liverpool
Striker who signed for Marine in March 1998 from League of Wales side Cwmbran Town. Began as a schoolboy with Marine before moving on to Everton for whom he played in the reserves. A prolific scorer, he returned to the Mariners squad in 2001/02 after missing almost a season and a half with a cruciate injury.

TOWN'SEND, RYAN — Forward

Current Club: Broxbourne Borough V&E

Birthplace: Enfield
Previous clubs include: Potters Bar T - July 1999, Cheshunt, Colchester Utd (Junior).

TOWSE, MARK — Defender

Current Club: Folkestone Invicta

D o B: 02/06/1984 — Birthplace: Kent
Tall teenager who has forced his way into the Folkestone Invicta first-team squad after joining the club from Kent League neighbours Hythe United. Marks first starting appearance for the first-team was certainly eventful as he headed the side into an early lead at Newport County but then headed into his own goal during the second half.

TRACEY, CHRIS — Defender

Current Club: AFC Sudbury

Birthplace: Suffolk
Was awarded a testimonial against West Ham United after 10 loyal years service with both Sudbury Town and AFC Sudbury. Commanding in the area and a rock at the heart of the defence. A real winner.

TRACEY, SEAN — Defender

Current Club: Maldon Town

Birthplace: Essex
Previous clubs include: Burnham Ramblers - July 2000.

TRAFFORD, ANDY — Defender

Current Club: Dereham Town

Birthplace: Norfolk
Previous Jewson experience with Swaffham Town. Quality act whose ability is only matched by his outstanding attitude.

TRAINOR, ROBERT — Midfielder

Current Club: Tow Law Town

Birthplace: Co.Durham
Also signed from Morpeth having previously been with South Shields. Has also been with Whitley Bay, Blue Star and Whickham.

TRANTER, CARL — Forward

Current Club: Bromsgrove Rovers

D o B: 04/10/1978 — Birthplace: Birmingham
Highly-rated striker whose career began at West Bromwich Albion. Had spells at Bridgnorth, Kingstonian, Grantham, Stafford Rangers, Worcester and Halesowen Town before resurrecting his career at Bridgnorth Town in the Midland Alliance. Became one of the top scorers in the league for 2001/02 and moved to newly-promoted Bromsgrove Rovers in May 2002.

TRANTER, WILLIE _Defender_
Current Club: Chasetown FC
Birthplace: Staffordshire
Previous clubs include: Bilston T - January 1999, Stourbridge, Blakenall, Ebbw Vale, Stapenhill, Bilston CC.

TRAVERS, LEWIS _Midfielder_
Current Club: Banbury United
Birthplace: Banbury
Teenage midfield product of the Banbury United youth team. Lewis has played for United's junior teams from a very young age, and has also spent two years with Peterborough United. Possesses tremendous skill for someone so young, and could prove to be a very exciting member of the squad. Very popular with the supporters.

TRAVERS, MATTHEW _Midfielder_
Current Club: Banbury United
Birthplace: Banbury
A former member of Banbury United's successful Oxfordshire Youth Cup-winning team. A highly-promising midfielder who became a regular first-team squad member during the 2001/02 season.

TRAVIS, SIMON _Defender_
Current Club: Stevenage Borough
D o B: 22/03/1977   Birthplace: Preston
Honours won: England Semi-Pro Int., British Universities Rep.
Simon is a highly-rated defender who joined Stevenage Borough from Forest Green Rovers in May 2002. Signed for Forest Green from Telford United during the close season of 2001, he was chosen to represent the British Students at the World Student Games in China at the start of that season. An accomplished right-sided player, he earned his first England semi-professional international caps during 2002.

TREADWELL, DAVE _Goalkeeper_
Current Club: Southwick
Birthplace: Sussex
Former Sussex goalkeeper, who Carl Stabler signed from Shoreham when he took over at East Preston for the start of the 1999/2000 campaign: followed Stabler to Wick for the beginning of the following season: disappeared, under somewhat mysterious circumstances, around Christmas that year before returning to action in March: stopped playing again in September 2001, apparently due to work commitments, before resuming at Southwick (one of his old clubs) in January.

TREBBLE, NEIL _Forward_
Current Club: Arlesey Town
D o B: 16/02/1969   Birthplace: Hitchin
Honours won: Conference Winners
Neil proved to a magnificent signing for Arlesey Town after arriving in February 2001 from Molesey. A centre forward who shields the ball well and has a good turn of speed. Very hard to get off the ball and causes all sorts of trouble for defences. Has been with Steveange, Preston North End, Scunthorpe, Scarborough, St Albans and Hayes. Has a Conference championship medal under his belt as well as promotion from Nationwide Division 3. Is a Director of an Education Company.

TREES, ROBERT _Midfielder_
Current Club: Mossley
D o B: 18/12/1977   Birthplace: Manchester
Previous clubs include: Droylsden - August 2002, Leigh RMI, Bristol R, Manchester Utd.

TREGURTHA, DAVE _Defender_
Current Club: Abingdon Town
Birthplace: Oxfordshire
Previous clubs include: Aylesbury Utd - January 2002, Thame Utd, Oxford Utd (Junior), Chelsea (Junior).

TREHARNE, JASON _Forward_
Current Club: Shifnal Town
D o B: 15/09/1970   Birthplace: Shropshire
Previous clubs include: Bridgnorth T - July 2001, Shifnal T, Rhayader T, Bridgnorth T, Shifnal T, Oakengates, Shifnal T, Bridgnorth T, Redditch Utd, Worcester C, Bilston T, Alvechurch, Bridgnorth T, Stafford R, Oakengates.

TRENKLE, DANNY _Forward_
Current Club: Great Wakering Rovers
Birthplace: Southend
From Youth team.

TRESADERN, PAUL _Midfielder_
Current Club: Leyton Pennant
Birthplace: Essex
Previous clubs include: Barkinside - August 2001, Burnham Ramblers, Eton Manor.

TRETTON, ANDREW _Defender_
Current Club: Hereford United
D o B: 09/10/1976   Birthplace: Derby
Joined Conference club Hereford United from Third Division Shrewsbury Town in July 2002. Originally a trainee with his home-town club Derbu County, he signed for Shrewsbury in December 1997 and became a main stay in the Shrews defence. Renowned for his simplicity in defence, he became a firm favourite with supporters at Gay Meadow.

TREVITT, SIMON _Defender_
Current Club: Guiseley
D o B: 20/12/1967   Birthplace: Dewsbury
Previous clubs include: Ossett Alb - January 2000, Guiseley, Hull C, Huddersfield T.

TRICKER, SIMON _Goalkeeper_
Current Club: Banbury United
Birthplace: Oxford
Signed for Banbury United from Abingdon United in October 2000 and made his debut at Wisbech Town. Was previously with Burnham before spending 5 years at Abingdon. He was always one of the best Hellenic League keepers but is now playing at a higher level and looking as though he has been there all of his career. Has had two Berks & Bucks Senior Cup winners medals. Good shot stopper and was player of the year for 2000/01.

TROTT, ROBIN _Defender_
Current Club: Stevenage Borough
D o B: 17/08/1974   Birthplace: Orpington
Robin joined Stevenage from Welling in August 1997 where he was voted player of the year, and went on to take the same accolade in his first season at Boro. Rob was captain in the games against Newcastle, and has gained League experience at Gillingham. Spent much of last season filling in on the left side of defence. Boros longest-serving player with well over 150 appearances for the club.

TROTTER, MIKE — *Defender*
Current Club: Goole AFC
D o B: 26/09/1967   *Birthplace: Hull*
Previous clubs include: North Ferriby Utd - October 2001, Lincoln Utd, North Ferriby Utd, Goole T, North Ferriby Utd, Brigg T, Bridlington T, Sheffield Utd.

TROUGHT, MICHAEL — *Defender*
Current Club: Bath City
D o B: 19/10/1980   *Birthplace: Bristol*
Powerful central defender who joined Dr Martens Premier side Bath City in July 2002 after being released by Bristol Rovers. Played around 30 times for Rovers after coming up through the ranks.

TRUMAN, SIMON — *Forward*
Current Club: Cinderford Town
Previous clubs include: Barry T - August 2001, Newport Co., Caldicot T, Llanwern, Bristol R (Junior).

TUACH, GAVIN — *Goalkeeper*
Current Club: Bideford
Birthplace: Devon
A local teenage, who has also developed up through the youth section. Gavin is a goalkeeper that we have high hopes for, and last season, he appeared for the first, second & third teams.

TUCK, STUART — *Defender*
Current Club: Eastbourne Borough
D o B: 01/10/1974   *Birthplace: Brighton*
Signed in October 2001 from Worthing, where he was club captain. Previously at Brighton and Hove Albion, for whom he made 93 appearances, some as captain.

TUCKER, ADRIAN — *Goalkeeper*
Current Club: Port Talbot Town
D o B: 26/09/1976   *Birthplace: Wales*
Previous clubs include: Maesteg Park - November 2001, Aberystwyth T, Ebbw Vale, Inter Cardiff, Ton Pentre.

TUCKER, ANTHONY — *Goalkeeper*
Current Club: Woking
Birthplace: London
Highly-regarded goalkeeper who joined Woking in the summer of 2001 after being released by Fulham. Didnt make the senior side at Craven Cottage but did have a spell on loan to League of Wales champions Barry Town beftween December 2000 and March 2001. Now firmly established as one of the most promising keepers in the Conference.

TUCKER, CRAIG — *Goalkeeper*
Current Club: Dartford
D o B: 07/10/1962   *Birthplace: Essex*
Honours won: FA Vase Winners
Veteran goalkeeper with bags of experience and a good number of honours to his name, including an FA Vase winners medal and Ryman League champiionship successes. Re-joined Dr Martens Eastern side Dartford towards the end of the 2001/02 season, teaming up again with manager Tommy Sampson, who was in charge of the Deal Town side that won the Vase. Amongst Craigs numerous previous clubs are Haringey Borough, Boreham Wood, Ashford Town, Erith & Belvedere, Purfleet, Leyton-Wingate and Grays Athletic.

TUCKER, JASON — *Midfielder*
Current Club: Yeading
D o B: 03/02/1973   *Birthplace: Isleworth*
Creative midfielder who came back for his third spell at The Warren in October 2000. Previous clubs also include Hayes, Boreham Wood, Chertsey and Aldershot, for whom he played in the Football League. Scored ten goals in all competitions last season, including two from the penalty spot.

TUCKER, JON — *Defender*
Current Club: Bognor Regis Town
Birthplace: Sussex
Aggressive centre-back, who originally played in the Bognor Regis Town youth team. Signed by Sussex County Leaguers Arundel from rivalsPagham during 1998/99 and was the Mullets player of the year that season. Played for Sussex during 2001/02 and then returned to Bognor, this time as a first-team squad member.

TUCKER, MARK — *Defender*
Current Club: Bedford Town
D o B: 27/04/1972   *Birthplace: Woking*
Honours won: England Semi-Pro Int., FA Trophy Winners
Previous clubs include: Worcester C - August 2001, Kettering T, Rushden & Diamonds, Woking, Fulham.

TUCKER, MATTHEW — *Goalkeeper*
Current Club: Racing Club Warwick
Honours won: British Universities Rep.
Previous clubs include: Crewe Alexandra - July 2001.

TUCKER, ROBIN — *Defender*
Current Club: Wealdstone
D o B: 05/05/1976   *Birthplace: Buckinghamshire*
Robin played against Wealdstone during the pre-season of 2000/01 for Arlesey Town, and joined shortly afterwards. He was previously at Buckingham Town and Newport Pangell Town. He has been a regular in defence in the senior side ever since.

TUCKER, SIMON — *Forward*
Current Club: Gresley Rovers
Birthplace: Carlisle
Very talented goalscorer who has been in prolific form in recent seasons. Had a peculiar start to his career in that he began at home-town club Carlisle United but then drifted into local football before having a short spell with Barrow in the UniBond League. Decided to take a university degree and moved to Loughborough, where his talents as a striker began to take shape. Originally joined Gresley Rovers in October 2000 but his goalscoring exploits saw him being snapped up by Leek Town in the summer of 2001. However, things didnt quite work out at Harrison Park and he returned to Gresley in February 2002.

TUDOR JONES, OWAIN — *Midfielder*
Current Club: Bangor City
D o B: 15/10/1984   *Birthplace: Bangor*
Teenage local midfielder who impressed for League of Wales side Bangor City's reserves to be given a first-team place. A tall, gifted player with a great deal of promise. Has become a regular member of the first team squad since October 2001 and attracted the attention of Premiership scouts.

TUFFEY, RICHARD — *Defender*
Current Club: Oadby Town
Birthplace: Leicester
Previous clubs include: Friar Lane OB - July 2001, Corby T, Friar Lane OB.

TUFT, DEAN — *Defender*
Current Club: Connahs Quay Nomads
Birthplace: Wales
From Youth team.

TULLOCH, STUART — *Midfielder*
Current Club: Shifnal Town
Birthplace: Shropshire
Previous clubs include: Bridgnorth T - July 2002, Shifnal T, Chasetown, Shifnal T, Bridgnorth T, Shifnal T, Wednesfield, Shifnal T, Llansantffraid, GKN Sankey.

TULLY, STEVE — *Defender*
Current Club: Weymouth
D o B: 10/02/1980   *Birthplace: Paignton*
Defender for whom Dr Martens Premier side Weymouth won a race for his signature ahead of a number of other interested parties, including Oldham in August 2002. Devon-born, Steve joined Torquat as a trainee and spent five years at Plainmoor, making over 100 League appearances before being released at the end of the 2001/02 season.

TUNNELL, LEE — *Forward*
Current Club: Aylesbury United
Birthplace: Middlesex
Prolific goalscorer ho joined Aylesbury United from fellow Ryman League side Uxbridge in May 2002. Started his playing days as a junior with Brentford before joining Chertsey Town. However, it wasn't until after arriving at Uxbridge in August 1999 that his goalscoring abilities came to the fore. Top scored for the Middlesex outfit for three successive seasons prior to his move to the Ducks.

TUNNICLIFFE, ANDY — *Forward*
Current Club: Altrincham
D o B: 24/05/1983   *Birthplace: Stockport*
Talented young midfielder who joined UniBond Premier side Altrincham in last August 2002 after being released by Manchester City. Had played for the Robins on-loan during the 2001/02 season but unfortunately suffered a broken leg in March.

TUNSTALL, JAMIE — *Defender*
Current Club: Ossett Albion
Birthplace: Derbyshire
Previous clubs include: Parkgate - February 2002, Buxton, Selston, Alfreton T, Hallam, Denaby Utd, Matlock T, Worksop T, Denaby Utd, Sheffield, Denaby Utd, Worksop T, Chesterfield, Derby Co (Trainee).

TUPPENNEY, PAUL — *Defender*
Current Club: Rye & Iden United
Birthplace: Hastings
Defender who returned to Hastings from Ashford during the 2000 close season, but only scored once for them early on. Scored five more times during that campaign after joining Rye, and also played once for Eastbourne Borough in April 2001.

TURBOTT, SCOTT — *Goalkeeper*
Current Club: Shifnal Town
Birthplace: Shropshire
Previous clubs include: Willenhall T - July 2001, Bloxwich T, Pelsall Villa, Bloxwich Strollers.

TURK, WAYNE — *Midfielder*
Current Club: Salisbury City
D o B: 21/01/1981   *Birthplace: Gloucestershire*
Signed for Dr Martens Eastern side Salisbury City in July 2000 from Cirencester Town. Highly-rated product of the Cirencester Academy whom he joined on his release from Oxford United. Hard-working midfield player who has adapted well to the higher league.

TURNBULL, IAIN — *Defender*
Current Club: Shifnal Town
Birthplace: Stafford
Previous clubs include: Warley Rangers - July 2001, Chasetown, Pelsall Villa, Stafford T.

TURNBULL, LEE — *Defender*
Current Club: Barrow
D o B: 27/09/1967   *Birthplace: Stockton*
Lee is a utility player who is very quick and skilful on the left side of midfield. He is a great crosser of the ball who has the knack for getting the ball over from seemingly impossible angles. Signed for Barrow from Halifax in September 1999, he made over 300 League appearances with Middlesbrough, Aston Villa, Doncaster Rovers, Chesterfield, Wycombe, Darlington, Halifax and SCunthorpe when he was also in charge of the clubs Youth Academy. An accredited UEFA coach he was signed as player/assistant-manger in September 1999. Lee was born in Stockton.

TURNBULL, MATT — *Midfielder*
Current Club: Arlesey Town
Birthplace: Hertfordshire
Matt is a firm favorite with Arlesey Town supporters with his dynamic midfield play. Has previosuly been with Welwyn Garden City and Hatfield and spent a while at Harrow Borough during the 2000/01 season. Rejoined Arlesey in August 2001.

TURNER, AARON — *Forward*
Current Club: Wimborne Town
Birthplace: Dorset
Previous clubs include: Hamworthy Engineering - July 2001.

TURNER, ANDY — *Midfielder*
Current Club: Frome Town
D o B: 21/05/1983   *Birthplace: Wincanton*
Previous clubs include: Yeovil T - March 2002, Westlands Sports, Bristol R (Junior).

TURNER, ANDY — *Midfielder*
Current Club: Tamworth
D o B: 23/03/1975   *Birthplace: Woolwich*
Honours won: England Schoolboy & Republic of Ireland u-21 Int.
Left winger Andy signed for Dr Martens League Tamworth in June 2002 almost exactly a year after arriving at Yeovil Town, following his release from Rotherham United, who had just been promoted to Division One. Turner, who can also operate as a striker, was born in Woolwich and joined Tottenham Hotspur as an apprentice in 1992, making 20 league appearances, scoring three goals in eight starts for the Premiership side. During his four-year spell at White Hart Lane, Turner also saw loan spells at Wycombe Wanderers, Doncaster Rovers, Huddersfield Town and Southend United. Whilst at White Hart Lane he played under managers such as former England manager Terry Venables, Ossie Ardiles and Gerry Francis. In 1996, Terry Venables - who was by then managing Portsmouth - signed him up for £250,000 and the former England Schoolboy and England Youth player made 40 league appearances at Fratton Park over the course of two seasons. He was re-united for a third time with Venables in

October 1998, when a £75,000 move saw him leave the South Coast for Crystal Palace. Following a loan spell at Wolverhampton Wanderers, Turner joined Rotherham United in the summer of 1999 where he made a further 36 league appearances along with further loan spells at Rochdale and Boston United. With Rotherham United preparing for life in Nationwide Division One next season, Turner was one of five players released in mid-May by the Yorkshire side and so moved to Somerset to become Gary Johnsons first signing as Yeovil Town manager.

TURNER, DALE — Midfielder
Current Club: Atherstone United
Birthplace: Leicester
Previous clubs include: St.Andrews - August 2001.

TURNER, DANNY — Defender
Current Club: Hemel Hempstead Town
Birthplace: Luton
Previous clubs include: Barton Rovers - October 2001, Shillington, Vauxhall Motors, Shillington.

TURNER, DARREN — Midfielder
Current Club: Leek Town
D o B: 23/12/1977   Birthplace: Nottingham
Midfielder who moved to Leek Town in June 2002 from UniBond rivals Belper Town. Darren began his career as a winger at Nottingham Forest and has also played for Dr Martens Western Division outfit Gresley Rovers.

TURNER, DAVID — Midfielder
Current Club: Chester-le-Street
Birthplace: Co. Durham
Previous clubs include: Birtley T - August 2001.

TURNER, DAVID — Midfielder
Current Club: Billingham Town
Birthplace: Stockton
Previous clubs include: Thornaby - February 2002.

TURNER, GLENN — Midfielder
Current Club: Gorleston
Birthplace: Norfolk
Previous clubs include: Great Yarmouth T - July 2001, Gorleston.

TURNER, JAMIE — Goalkeeper
Current Club: Gravesend & Northfleet
Birthplace: Kent
Honours won: Ryman League Premier Div.Winners
Signed for Gravesend at the beginning of the 2000/01 season from Kent League side Deal Town. Previously with Welling United, Horsham and Greenwich Borough, Jamie claimed the number one shirt at the club with some imposing performances in the early part of the season. It is reckoned that Jamie has a big future in the game.

TURNER, JASON — Forward
Current Club: Rothwell Town
Birthplace: Kettering
Previous clubs include: Rothwell Corinthians - July 1999.

TURNER, JOHN — Midfielder
Current Club: Nuneaton Borough
D o B: 22/01/1980   Birthplace: Blackburn
Originally from Blackburn and currently studying at Loughborough University. A former Lancashire Schools representative, John is a talented midfielder who was on the books at Blakburn Rovers and Preston as a youngster and then played in the UniBond League with Bamber Bridge before moving to Loughborough. Had short

spells with Shepshed Dynamo and Loughborough Dynamo before attracting the attention of Nuneaton Borough whilst with Coalville Town, and he moved into the Conference in March 2002.

TURNER, LEE — Goalkeeper
Current Club: Margate
D o B: 04/03/1965
Previous clubs include: Gravesend - January 1997, Bury T, Corinthian, Sittingbourne, Corinthian, Leyton Orient.

TURNER, MARK — Defender
Current Club: Wimborne Town
Birthplace: Bournemouth
Previous clubs include: Bournemouth FC - July 1997.

TURNER, MARK — Defender
Current Club: Selby Town
Birthplace: Goole
Previous clubs include: Immingham T - July 1999, Goole T.

TURNER, MARK — Defender
Current Club: Edgware Town
Birthplace: London
Previous clubs include: Hendon - December 2001, Reading, Hemel Hempstead, Chertsey T, Hendon, Chesham Utd, Staines T, Hayes, Walton & Hersham, Chertsey T, Slough T, Brentford (Trainee).

TURNER, MARK — Midfielder
Current Club: Tamworth
D o B: 04/10/1972   Birthplace: Bebbington
Mark joined Tamworth in June 2000 from Kings Lynn. A strong player he likes to get forward and add his firepower to the attack. Mark previously played for Telford United, whom he left in 1998 to join the Linnets, and had League experience with Wolves and Northampton and also turned out in the Conference with Hereford United.

TURNER, MARTIN — Defender
Current Club: Armthorpe Welfare
Birthplace: Mansfield
Previous clubs include: Brodsworth Welfare - December 1999, Alfreton T, Armthorpe Welfare, Stocksbridge Park Steels, Goole T, Glasshoughton Welfare, Armthorpe Welfare, Hatfield Main, Worksop T, Chesterfield, Mansfield T (Trainee).

TURNER, MICKEY — Midfielder
Current Club: Hassocks
Birthplace: Sussex
Hard working utility man who looks more like accountant than a footballer!: main claim to fame was scoring for the county within twenty seconds of his debut some years back: proved to be effective as a makeshift striker for a large part of 2000/01, scoring 10 times.

TURNER, MIKE — Forward
Current Club: Altrincham
Birthplace: Manchester
A tall striker, who was released by North West Counties side Mossley at the end of 2001/02 and joined UniBond Premier outfit Altrincham. His previous clubs include Maine Road, Witton Albion, Mossley, Winsford United, Trafford, Hyde United, Witton Albion, Ashton United and Wythenshawe Amateurs.

TURNER, PAUL — Midfielder
Current Club: Egham Town
Birthplace: Slough
From Youth team.

TURNER, PAUL — Midfielder
Current Club: Bedford Town
D o B: 13/11/1968
Birthplace: Cheshunt
Previous clubs include: St.Albans C - August 2000, Yeovil T, Enfield, Farnborough T, Cambridge Utd, Arsenal.

TURNER, PHIL — Defender
Current Club: Farsley Celtic
From Youth team.

TURNER, ROSS — Goalkeeper
Current Club: Worksop Town
Birthplace: Sheffield
Honours won: NCEL & Cup Winners
Highly-rated goalkeeper who signed for Worksop Town in May 2002 after helping Alfreton Town to win the Northern Counties East League title. Had joined Alfreton in November 2001 from Stocksbridge Park Steels where he had played at both youth and reserve team level. Had a spell with Worsborough Bridge before joining Scunthorpe United halfway through season 1999/00, where he made one Football League appearance and several for their reserve side. Ross has attracting interest from clubs within the Football League and has undertaken trials with Mansfield Town.

TURNER, SIMON — Defender
Current Club: Bracknell Town
Birthplace: Berkshire
Previous clubs include: Wokingham T - December 2001, Aldershot T, Oxford Utd.

TURNILL, JUSTIN — Forward
Current Club: Pagham
Birthplace: Sussex
Forward: leading scorer for Oving in 1999/2000 with 20 goals: previously had Pagham, Bosham, Arundel: had been playing for South Bersted in the West Sussex League until returning to Nyetimber Lane in December 2001.

TURPIN, JAMIE — Defender
Current Club: Bilston Town
Previous clubs include: Bromsgrove Rovers - August 2001, Wolverhampton Wanderers.

TUTTON, ALAN — Defender
Current Club: Dartford
D o B: 23/02/1973
Birthplace: Kent
Experienced Non-League defender who re-joined Dr Martens Eastern side Dartford in the summer of 2002 from rivals and Kent neighbours Ashford Town. Started out at Erith & Belvedere and then had spells with the likes of Alma Swanley, Maidstone United, Margate, Tonbridge and Gravesend, once even straying out of Kent to play for Boreham Wood.

TWEDDLE, STEVE — Forward
Current Club: Chippenham Town
Birthplace: Wiltshire
Signed for Chippenham Town from Melksham Town in July 1999, Steve is excellent at holding the ball up and was a great signing for our club. Played centre forward at Wembley. Is a Safety Officer outside football.

TWIDELL, DARREN — Midfielder
Current Club: Great Wakering Rovers
Birthplace: Essex
Previous clubs include: Grays Ath - August 2000, Billericay T.

TWIGG, DARREN — Forward
Current Club: Kidsgrove Athletic
Birthplace: Stoke
Honours won: NWCL Winners
Top scorer for the last two seasons, after joining Kidsgrove in January 2001 from Leek Town. Has previously played for Newcastle Town, Witton Albion, Ashton United and Eastwood Hanley amongst others and has always been a prolific scorer.

TWIN, DANNY — Defender
Current Club: Welling United
D o B: 19/12/1980
Birthplace: Kent
From Youth team.

TWISS, MICHAEL — Midfielder
Current Club: Chester City
D o B: 26/12/1977
Birthplace: Salford
Highly-rated Salford-born attacking midfielder who began his career on the books at Manchester United. Went on to play League football with Sheffield United and Port Vale before joining Leigh RMI in September 2001. Enjoyed an excellent 2001/02 season with the Railwaymen before switching to Chester in May 2002.

TWOSE, GERAINT — Defender
Current Club: Llanelli AFC
Birthplace: Wales
Previous clubs include: Rhayader T - July 2001, Bridgend T, Cwmbran T.

TWYNHAM, GARY — Forward
Current Club: Port Talbot Town
D o B: 08/02/1976
Birthplace: Manchester
Previous clubs include: Haverfordwest County - February 2002, Macclesfield T, Hednesford T, Bangor C, Grantham T, Gateshead, Darlington, Manchester Utd.

TYDEMAN, GRAHAM — Midfielder
Current Club: Sutton United
Birthplace: Surrey
From Youth team.

TYDEMAN, SAM — Midfielder
Current Club: Fisher Athletic (London)
D o B: 14/12/1978
Birthplace: Chatham
Previous clubs include: Sittingbourne - July 1999, Gravesend, Gillingham.

TYE, ADAM — Defender
Current Club: Harrogate Railway
Birthplace: Yorkshire
Previous clubs include: Yorkshire Amateur - July 2000, Farsley Celtic.

TYE, KEVIN — Goalkeeper
Current Club: Matlock Town
Birthplace: Mansfield
Talented young goalkeeper who joined Matlock from Whitby Town in October 2000. Kevin was with Mansfield as a youngster and a return to the full-time game cannot be ruled out if he continues to improve at Causeway Lane.

TYNE, TOMMY — Forward
Current Club: Dover Athletic
D o B: 02/03/1981
Birthplace: Lambeth
Prolific marksman who joined Dover Athletic at the start of the 2001/02 season from Millwall. Had begun his career in Non-League football with Catford Wanderers and then Kent Leaguers Slade Green, where his potential started to come to the fore. Spent a period on loan at Welling United in 01/02.

UBERSCHAR, NEIL   *Defender*
Current Club: Morecambe
D o B: 16/02/1981   *Birthplace: Morecambe*
From Youth team.

UDALL, JAMIE   *Defender*
Current Club: Leigh RMI
D o B: 12/06/1975   *Birthplace: Lancaster*
Signed for Leigh RMI at the beginning of season 2000/1 from
UniBond League side Lancaster City. Previously with Morecambe
in the Nationwide Conference. Another of RMIs young players
who has quickly established himself as a regular member of the
team.

UGBAH, JOHN   *Defender*
Current Club: Crawley Town
D o B: 12/08/1972   *Birthplace: Nigeria*
Defender: joined Crawley from Carshalton in October 1999:
previous experience in the Conference with Welling and
Stevenage: on the long-term injury list during the current season.

ULASI, OBINNA   *Defender*
Current Club: Maidenhead United
D o B: 06/08/1973   *Birthplace: Hammersmith*
Previous clubs include: Hayes - October 1996, Feltham &
Hounslow.

ULATOWSKI, PETER   *Midfielder*
Current Club: Broxbourne Borough V&E
D o B: 03/01/1979   *Birthplace: Middlesex*
Previous clubs include: Brimsdown Rovers - July 2000.

ULFIG, STEVE   *Defender*
Current Club: Stourport Swifts
Previous clubs include: Bromsgrove Rovers - March 2001,
Halesowen T, Walsall (Trainee).

ULLATHORNE, ANDY   *Midfielder*
Current Club: Farsley Celtic
Previous clubs include: Harrogate T - August 2001, Harrogate
RA, Selby T, Harrogate RA, Hatfield Main, Goole T.

ULLATHORNE, SIMON   *Forward*
Current Club: Slough Town
Birthplace: Cumbria
Recent signing from Dover Athletic.Simon has acquitted himself
very well since joining the Rebels. He is not an out and out
forward player but plays in a role just behind the strikers and links
up extremely well with the Rebels midfield. Simon is a very
intelligent player who creates space for himself well. He had a
very impressive debut for the Rebels against Uxbridge. Former
Slough manager Graham Roberts once tried to sign Simon
Ullathorne from Crawley Town after we played the Reds in an FA
Cup match. Simon has played for many different clubs in his
career. His former clubs include Hastings, Sittingbourne,
Kingstonian, Aldershot and Purfleet. In Simon Ullathorne Slough
looked to have picked up a very astute signing and hopefully
Ullers can produce a good partnership with fellow new striker
Michael Bartley which can fire the Rebels towards the top half of
the table.

UMEH, EMMANUEL   *Forward*
Current Club: Windsor & Eton
D o B: 08/12/1982   *Birthplace: London*
Honours won: England Schoolboy Int.
Previous clubs include: Leyton Orient - January 2002.

UNDERHAY, MARTIN   *Forward*
Current Club: Weymouth
D o B: 04/10/1970   *Birthplace: Paignton*
Martin previously played for Wimborne Town, and is a very
enthusiastic and energetic player who always gives you 100%.
Suffered a broken ankle during last season, but not before
winning the hearts of the Terras' fans with his performances,
coming on from the bench and scoring some tremendous goals.
Known for being, 'The Supersub', Martin scored the goal
culminating from a 28-pass move against Kings Lynn at the
Wessex Stadium.

UNDERHILL, SAM   *Defender*
Current Club: Cheshunt
Birthplace: London
Previous clubs include: Leyton Pennant - August 2002, Waltham
Abbey, St.Margaretsbury, Enfield.

UNDERWOOD, ANTONY   *Midfielder*
Current Club: Selby Town
Birthplace: Yorkshire
Previous clubs include: North Cave - July 2001,

UNDERWOOD, JEFF   *Defender*
Current Club: Burscough
Birthplace: Liverpool
Formerly with Preston North End, young defender Jeff was signed
by UniBond Premier side Burscough in August 2002 after being
on Conference forms with Southport. Also had a short spell with
North West Counties outfit Skelmersdale United during the
2001/02 season.

UNDERWOOD, JON   *Midfielder*
Current Club: Bracknell Town
Birthplace: Berkshire
Previous clubs include: Staines T - January 2002, Aylesbury Utd,
Farnborough T, Wokingham T.

UNDERWOOD, MARK   *Defender*
Current Club: Leighton Town
Birthplace: Herts
Well-travelled midfielder who followed manager Paul Burgess and
returned to Ryman Division Two side Leighton Town in July 2002
from Tring Town. Had been in his second spell with Tring after re-
joining from Leighton in July 1999 and has also worn the colours
of Northwood, Hemel Hempstead and Harpenden Town.

UNDERWOOD, STEVE   *Midfielder*
Current Club: Goole AFC
Birthplace: Halifax
Previous clubs include: North Ferriby Utd - October 2001,
Harrogate T, Halifax T.

UNITT, DAVE   *Defender*
Current Club: Paget Rangers
Birthplace: Coventry
Previous clubs include: Stourbridge - January 2002, Bedworth
Utd.

UPTON, DAVID   *Defender*
Current Club: Norwich United
D o B: 03/11/1974   *Birthplace: Norfolk*
A reliable defender for Norwich United who always gives his best,
unfortunately his season has been disrupted by illness.

U

URE, LEE — Forward

Current Club: Whitby Town

D o B: 17/11/1979   *Birthplace: Newcastle*
Exciting young player who was signed by Whitby Town from local league side Norton. He's exceptionally quick and skilful and came highly recommended to the club. Another promising signing for the Blues.

USHERWOOD, RICHARD — Forward

Current Club: Dartford

Birthplace: Kent
From Youth team.

UTLEY, DARREN — Defender

Current Club: Denaby United

Birthplace: Sheffield
Previous clubs include: Sheffield - July 2001, Stocksbridge Park Steels, Emley, Doncaster R.

UTTERSON, JOHN — Midfielder

Current Club: Ramsgate

Birthplace: Kent
Previous clubs include: Margate - July 2000, Gillingham (Trainee).

VAHID, ED — Midfielder

Current Club: Ramsgate

Birthplace: Kent
From Youth team.

VAHID, STUART — Forward

Current Club: Ramsgate

Birthplace: Kent
From Youth team.

VALE, CRAIG — Midfielder

Current Club: Boldmere St.Michaels

Birthplace: Birmingham
Previous clubs include: Chasetown - October 2001, Boldmere St.Michaels.

VALENTI, FABIO — Midfielder

Current Club: Harrow Borough

Joined Ryman Premier side Harrow Borough in March 2001 from Edgware Town. Previously with Wealdstone, St Albans City and Hertford Town. At youth level played for Slough Town, Barnet, Charlton Athletic and Swansea City.

VALENTINE, JASON — Forward

Current Club: London Colney

Birthplace: Herts
Previous clubs include: Potters Bar T - July 2000, London Colney, Potters Bar T, Langford, Welwyn Garden C, Hatfield T, Codicote.

VALLENCE, LEE — Midfielder

Current Club: Corby Town

Birthplace: Corby
Previous clubs include: Rothwell T - July 2001, Stewarts & Lloyds.

VALLI, GARRY — Defender

Current Club: Tunbridge Wells

Birthplace: Kent
Previous clubs include: Tonbridge Angels - July 1998.

VAN HUGH, WAYNE — Midfielder

Current Club: Seaham Red Star

Birthplace: Co.Durham
Previous clubs include: Easington Colliery - February 2002, Spennymoor Utd, Tottenham Hotspur, Northallerton T, Hartlepool Utd (Junior), Middlesbrough (Junior).

VANDEPEER, DANNY — Defender

Current Club: Broxbourne Borough V&E

D o B: 25/05/1982   *Birthplace: Edmonton*
From Local football - July 1999.

VANSITTART, JOFF — Forward

Current Club: Farnborough Town

D o B: 12/09/1974   *Birthplace: Sussex*
Joff signed for Farnborough Town for a £12,000 fee from fellow Conference club Dover Athletic during the 2001 close season. Previously with Sutton United, Crawley Town and Brighton, the big striker has become a firm favourite at the Aimita Stadium.

VANSON, GRANT — Defender

Current Club: Littlehampton Town

Birthplace: Sussex
Defender: previously on the books of Brighton & Hove Albion and played several times for Worthing reserves during 2000/01: current member of the Sussex under-18 squad and made his Littlehampton debut in August 2001.

VARGAS, CRAIG — Defender
Current Club: Yeading
Birthplace: Middlesex
Twenty year old left-sided player who impressed pre-season after arriving in at The Warren during the summer. Previously with Hampton & Richmond Borough.

VARLEY, PAUL — Defender
Current Club: Chorley
D o B: 27/01/1975   *Birthplace: Salford*
Previous clubs include: Trafford - March 2002, Salford C, Woodley Sports, Trafford, Salford C.

VARLEY, PETER — Forward
Current Club: Bideford
D o B: 06/03/1974   *Birthplace: London*
Honours won: FA Vase Winners
Peter is a P.E teacher in North Devon and he joined us in the close season from Ilfracombe. He has also played for Norwich City, Kingstonian, Trowbridge Town, & Tiverton Town (4 Seasons), for whom he scored the winning goal in their 1998 F.A Vase win over Tow Law at Wembley.

VARNEY, PAUL — Goalkeeper
Current Club: Alfreton Town
Birthplace: Sheffield
Previous clubs include: Hallam - November 2000, Denaby Utd, Maltby Main, Sheffield, Hallam, Matlock T, Buxton, Rotherham Utd.

VARTY, WILL — Defender
Current Club: Workington
D o B: 01/10/1976   *Birthplace: Workington*
Workington-born defender who finally signed for his home-town club on a permanent basis in June 2002 after being released by Carlisle United. Started his career with Carlisle and also had a spell with Rotherham befor returning to the Cumbrian outfit. Played over 60 times in the League and had two stints on loan at Workington in the past.

VASEY, MICHAEL — Defender
Current Club: Tow Law Town
Birthplace: Newcastle
Previous clubs include: Durham C - December 2001, Crook T, Blyth Spartans, Tow Law T, Crook T, Newcastle Blue Star, Ferryhill Ath.

VASSELL, ROB — Defender
Current Club: Rushall Olympic
Birthplace: Worcestershire
Previous clubs include: Wednesfield - July 2001, Halesowen Harriers, Bilston T, Gloucester C, Dudley T, Moor GReen, Stafford R, Oldswinford, Redditch Utd, Worcester C, Leicester C (Trainee).

VAUGHAN, FRANCIS — Defender
Current Club: Salford City
Birthplace: Manchester
Previous clubs include: Ramsbottom Utd - July 2001, Salford C.

VAUGHAN, GARRY — Midfielder
Current Club: Salford City
Birthplace: Lancashire
Previous clubs include: Trafford - July 2000, Hyde Utd, Trafford, Hyde Utd, Northwich V, Port Vale, Burnley (Junior).

VAUGHAN, IAN — Defender
Current Club: Port Talbot Town
Birthplace: Neath
Previous clubs include: Llanelli - July 2001, Afan Lido, Yeovil T.

VAUGHAN, NATHAN — Goalkeeper
Current Club: Willenhall Town
Birthplace: Birmingham
Young keeper in his 2nd season, progressed from the reserves. A former Plymouth Argyle YTS player who attracted several league scouts last season.

VAUGHAN, STEVE — Midfielder
Current Club: Dagenham & Redbridge
Birthplace: London
Steve progressed to the first team from Dagenham & Redbridges School of Excellence. He played in the Charity Shield against Farnborough Town last season and in three County Cup ties. Will be pushing for a first team place.

VAUGHAN, STEWART — Goalkeeper
Current Club: Corinthian Casuals
D o B: 07/11/1978   *Birthplace: Surrey*
Previous clubs include: Leatherhead - December 2001, Croydon Ath, Banstead Ath., Chelsea.

VAUGHAN, WAYNE — Forward
Current Club: Purfleet
D o B: 15/02/1980   *Birthplace: Dagenham*
Honours won: England Schoolboy Int., FA Trophy Winners
Highly-rated striker who joined Ryman Premier side Purfleet from rivals Canvey Island in August 2002. Had been with the Islanders since July 2000 when he signed after being released by Spurs. Was a regular scorer for the Gulls and helped the club to win the FA Trophy in 2001. A former England Schoolboy international.

VEART, CRAIG — Midfielder
Current Club: Whitby Town
D o B: 18/11/1970   *Birthplace: Co Durham*
Craig signed for UniBond Premier side Whitby Town in the pre-season of 2001 from rivals Spennymoor United. He is a very skilful midfield player with extensive experience at this level. During the 2001/02 season Craig scored from the halfway line at the Turnbull Ground against the Blues for The Moors! Was on loan at Northallerton Town but is now back to his best in Whitby colours. Has also had spells with Gateshead, Ferryhill Athletic and Bishop Auckland.

VECCHIO, DANNI — Midfielder
Current Club: Lordswood
Birthplace: Kent
From Youth team.

VEIGA, PAUL — Forward
Current Club: Hailsham Town
Birthplace: Sussex
Striker: previously left Hailsham to join Eastbourne Utd during 1999/2000: generally plays for the reserves, but came on as a substitute and scored the consolation goal in Hailshams 3-1 defeat against Corinthian Casuals in the FA Vase (September 2001).

V

VENABLES, ROSS — Midfielder
Current Club: Lewes
D o B: 22/03/1979 — Birthplace: Dartford
Arrived at the Dripping Pan from St Leonards at the beginning of October 2001, having previously been at Millwall and Raith.

VENTON, DEAN — Defender
Current Club: Whitehawk
Birthplace: Sussex
Defender who originally emerged through Burgess Hills youth side, and was a member of the Sussex U-18 squad in 1999/2000. Finished that season at Withdean and spent the first half of last season with struggling East Preston, before moving to Saltdean in January. Began the latest campaign back at Burgess Hill before snapped up by Whitehawk in October.

VERCESI, MARK — Midfielder
Current Club: Tonbridge Angels
Birthplace: Cornwall
Previous clubs include: Erith & Belvedere - March 2002, St.Blazey.

VERCESI, RICHARD — Forward
Current Club: Croydon Athletic
Birthplace: Surrey
Talented forward who signed for Ryman Division One South side Croydon Athletic in July 2002 from Dr Martens Eastern outfit Erith & Belvedere. Has switched regularly between the Dr Martens and Ryman leagues through spells with Banstead Athletic, Erith, Welling United, Hampton, Ashford Town, Leatherhead and Croydon. Re-joined Erith in February 2001.

VERITY, DANNY — Defender
Current Club: Eccleshill United
D o B: 19/04/1980 — Birthplace: Bradford
Previous clubs include: Gresley Rovers - July 2001, Bradford PA, Harrogate T, Bradford C.

VERNON, LEE — Defender
Current Club: Sheffield FC
Birthplace: Nottinghamshire
Previous clubs include: Staveley Miners Welfare - July 2000, Matlock T, Staveley MW, Oakham Utd, Staveley MW.

VEROW, IAN — Midfielder
Current Club: Eastbourne Borough
Birthplace: Eastbourne
Previous clubs include: Eastbourne T - July 2001.

VERTANNES, DES — Midfielder
Current Club: Ashford Town (Middx)
D o B: 25/04/1972 — Birthplace: Hounslow
Signed for Ashford Town (Middx) from Bracknell Town in 1997. Made an immediate impact on the left hand side of midfield and was a vital cog in Ashfords run-in to the Combined Counties championship in 96/97. Started his career with Fulham for whom he made 2 appearances in the Football League. Has now made over 150 appearances for Ashford.

VICARY, DARREN — Forward
Current Club: Vauxhall Motors
Birthplace: Liverpool
Previous clubs include: Stalybridge Celtic - July 2001, Northwich V, Cammell Lairds, Vauxhall GM.

VICKERAGE, MARK — Forward
Current Club: Brodsworth Welfare
Birthplace: Yorkshire
From Youth team.

VICKERMAN, LEE — Defender
Current Club: Clevedon Town
D o B: 24/08/1980 — Birthplace: Bristol
Former Cheltenham Town midfielder or defender who joined Bath City in August 1998. Didnt make the senior side at Cheltenham but became a regular at Bath in the Dr Martens Premier Division before transferring to Chippenham Town at the start of the 2001/02 season. Switched to Clevedon Town in May 2002.

VICKERS, ASHLEY — Defender
Current Club: Dagenham & Redbridge
D o B: 14/06/1972 — Birthplace: Sheffield
One of manager Garry Hills last signings of the 1999/2000 season, joining from St.Albans City in March. A tall and commanding central defender who began his playing days as a trainee at Sheffield United. Decided to study at university and turned out for Worcester City, Malvern Town, The 61 Club (Luton) and Heybridge Swifts, where he first played under Garry Hill. Showed such good form for Heybridge that Barry Fry took him to Peterborough in 1997/98 for £5,000. However, he failed to settle at London Road and re-joined Hill at his new club, St.Albans City, in exchange for a £10,000 fee. Hill was delighted to be re-united with the giant centre half when the Saints surprisingly made him available.

VICKERS, IAN — Forward
Current Club: Kendal Town
Birthplace: Blackpool
Previous clubs include: Fleetwood Freeport - July 2001, Bamber Bridge, Southport, Blackpool,

VICKERS, RYAN — Midfielder
Current Club: North Ferriby United
D o B: 22/12/1978
Honours won: England Schoolboy Int.
Previous clubs include: Raunds T - October 2000, Whitby T, Hucknall T, Worsbrough Bridge, Liversedge, Brigg T, Lincoln C, Scunthorpe Utd, Leeds Utd (Trainee).

VICKERS, SIMON — Forward
Current Club: Windsor & Eton
Birthplace: Canada
Previous clubs include: Hendon - March 2002, Oxford C, Barking & East Ham Utd, Grays Ath., Chester C, Clyde, Partick Thistle.

VINCE, DALE — Midfielder
Current Club: Woodbridge Town
Birthplace: Suffolk
One of two signings in August 2001 from Bury Town, for whom he gave tremendous service for a number of seasons. A skilful and consistent performer whose ability is well respected throughout the Jewson League.

VINCE, NIGEL — Defender
Current Club: Wisbech Town
D o B: 05/04/1971
Previous clubs include: Spalding Utd - July 2001, Boston T, Blackstone, Boston T, Grantham T, Cambridge Utd.

VINCENT, ALAN   *Midfielder*
Current Club: Witham Town
Birthplace: Essex
Previous clubs include: Chelmsford C - January 2000, Braintree T, Witham T, Braintree T, Bramston CML, Witham T.

VINH NGUYEN, THE   *Forward*
Current Club: Bromley
Birthplace: London
Previous clubs include: Osakta (Japan) - February 2002, Charlton Ath.

VINNICOMBE, LUKE   *Defender*
Current Club: Tiverton Town
D o B: 07/03/1980   *Birthplace: Paignton*
Joined Clevedon Town in November 2001 from Tiverton Town, having previously been released by Exeter City. Switched back to Tivvy in March 2002. Luke is a very good defender, good in the air, who likes to get forward and deliver quality crosses.

VINTON, PAUL   *Defender*
Current Club: Hamble ASSC
Birthplace: Hampshire
From Youth team

VIRGO, JAMES   *Defender*
Current Club: Folkestone Invicta
D o B: 21/12/1976   *Birthplace: Brighton*
A left wing back, James started his career with Brighton & Hove Albion, for whom he made one first team appearance. He joined Conference club Dover Athletic from Sutton United in 1998 and spent the second half of the season on loan with Folkestone Invicta after recovering from heart surgery during that summer. A set piece specialist, James joined Invicta on a permanent basis in August 2001.

VITALE, GIORGIO   *Forward*
Current Club: Arnold Town
Birthplace: Nottingham
Previous clubs include: Ilkeston T - July 2000.

VIZCAINO, MIGUEL-ANGEL   *Forward*
Current Club: Flexsys Cefn Druids
Birthplace: Spain
Previous clubs include: Real Zaragoza (Spain) - February 2001.

VOICE, SCOTT   *Forward*
Current Club: Hereford United
D o B: 12/08/1974   *Birthplace: Birmingham*
A former Wolves trainee who has built a reputation for goals in the lower leagues. Much is expected of the man who scored 46 goals for Bilston Town last season.

VOUT, SCOTT   *Defender*
Current Club: Swaffham Town
Birthplace: Norfolk
A product of the Swaffhams youth system, Scott has developed into an outstanding defender.

VOWDEN, COLIN   *Defender*
Current Club: Cambridge City
D o B: 13/09/1971   *Birthplace: Newmarket*
Colin is now in his second spell at Cambridge City. He originally joined the club from neighbours Cambridge United via a short stint with Newmarket Town in October 1994 before moving back across the river in a £15,000 deal at the end of the 94/95

season. A move to Kettering followed where he scored for the Poppies in the FA Trophy final a couple of years ago. Dover Athletic was his next stop as he became former Chelmsford manager Gary Bellamys first signing for the Kent club. A towering central defender.

VRHOVSKI, MARTIN   *Midfielder*
Current Club: Burnham
Birthplace: Berkshire
Midfielder who joined from Wingate & Finchley. Previously at Beaconsfield SYCOB. Martin, whose career has been interrupted in the past by injuries made his debut midway through last season.

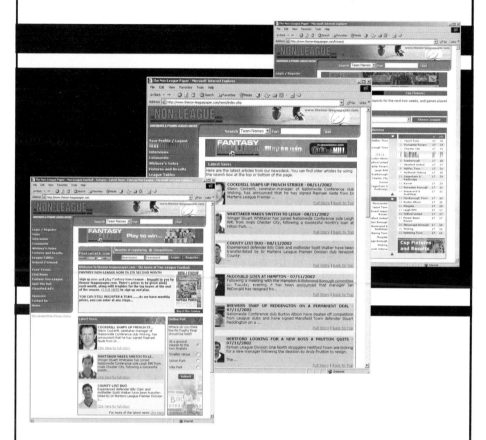

www.thenon-leaguepaper.com

WADDLE, CHRIS — Forward
Current Club: Newcastle Blue Star
Birthplace: Newcastle
From Local football - July 2001.

WADDLE, CHRIS — Midfielder
Current Club: Gedling Town
D o B: 14/12/1960 — Birthplace: Hedworth
Honours won: England u-21 & Full Int.
Well-known former England winger who joined Northern Counties East League side Gedling Town in the summer of 2002 after spending a couple of seasons on Worksop Town's books. His appearances are restricted now because of his media commitments, but he is still a joy to watch on his day. Made his name at Newcastle United and Spurs, won 62 full caps for England and also managed Burnley.

WAGER, GARY — Goalkeeper
Current Club: Cwmbran Town
D o B: 21/05/1962 — Birthplace: Bridgend
Honours won: Wales Semi-Pro Int., Southern League Premier Div.Winners
Previous clubs include: Inter Cardiff - January 2000, Ebbw Vale, Merthyr Tydfil, Bridgend I.

WAGHORN, IAN — Forward
Current Club: Corinthian Casuals
Birthplace: Surrey
Iain has been with Camberley Town for over ten years, graduating from the youth team. He has a great goalscoring record and has scored over eighty goals for the club.

WAIN, MATTHEW — Forward
Current Club: Selby Town
Birthplace: Strensall
Previous clubs include: Rowntrees - July 2001, Pickering T, Selby T, York RI.

WAINMAN, LEON — Forward
Current Club: Hallam
Birthplace: Sheffield
Previous clubs include: Matlock T - July 2001, Emley, Alfreton T, Emley, Denaby Utd.

WAINWRIGHT, LEE — Defender
Current Club: Stocksbridge Park Steels
Previous clubs include: Alfreton T - July 1999, Matlock T, Ashfield Utd, Buxton, Sheffield Utd (Trainee).

WAITON, STEVE — Midfielder
Current Club: Spalding United
Birthplace: Lincolnshire
Previous clubs include: Wisbech T - January 2001, Winterton R.

WAKE, BRIAN — Forward
Current Club: Tow Law Town
Birthplace: Co.Durham
Signed from Wolviston last season after a very successful season scoring over 50 goals. Last season had trials with Norwich and Grimsby.

WAKE, COLIN — Defender
Current Club: Chester-Le Street
Birthplace: Co.Durham
Previous clubs include: Ferryhill Ath - July 1995.

WAKEFIELD, DAVE — Midfielder
Current Club: Bashley
Birthplace: Portsmouth
An attacking midfield player who joined Bashley in June 2002 from Newport Isle of Wight. Started his career with Portsmouth where he progressed through to become a professional. Left to join Havant Town in July 1994 and spent seven years at Westleigh Park before switching to Newport in the summer of 2001.

WALDOCK, JOHN — Defender
Current Club: Weymouth
D o B: 27/11/1975 — Birthplace: Newcastle
John is now in his 7th season, having joined us from Sunderland F.C. and has established himself as a first class defender. Took over as team captain during the Alex Browne's injury period and having impressed, has held on to it. Player of the year in 1998/99.

WALDRON, MATT — Defender
Current Club: Leyton Pennant
Birthplace: Bishops Stortford
Previous clubs include: Ware - August 2001, Bishops Stortford, Cambridge Utd (Junior).

WALES, MARK — Midfielder
Current Club: Soham Town Rangers
Birthplace: Cambridgeshire
Previous clubs include: Wisbech T - July 1999, Bury T, Wisbech T, Kings Lynn, March Town Utd, Wisbech T.

WALES, RICHARD — Defender
Current Club: Garforth Town
Birthplace: Leeds
From Youth team.

WALES, STEVE — Midfielder
Current Club: Cheshunt
D o B: 05/08/1982 — Birthplace: Paddington
Previous clubs include: Broxbourne Borough V&E - August 2002, Cockfosters.

WALKER, ANDY — Goalkeeper
Current Club: Tonbridge Angels
D o B: 30/09/1981 — Birthplace: Sidcup
Previous clubs include: Exeter C - November 2001, Colchester Utd.

WALKER, ANDY — Midfielder
Current Club: Radcliffe Borough
Birthplace: Lancashire
From Youth team.

WALKER, CLIVE — Midfielder
Current Club: Sutton Coldfield Town
Birthplace: Birmingham
Previous clubs include: Rushall Olympic - February 2001, Bilston T, Tamworth, Evesham Utd, Racing Club Warwick, Hinckley Utd, Nuneaton B, Stourbridge, Oldbury Utd, Shifnal T, Brierley Hill, Bilston T.

WALKER, DEAN — Midfielder
Current Club: Letchworth
Birthplace: Beds
Previous clubs include: Brache Sparta - July 2001, Toddington R, Brache Sparta, Toddington R.

WALKER, GARETH — Goalkeeper
Current Club: Didcot Town
Birthplace: Oxfordshire
20 year-old keeper who moved to Didcot from near neighbours Milton United in the summer of 2001. With age on his side, and an abundance of ability, Gareth has an exciting future in the game.

WALKER, GARY — Forward
Current Club: Histon
Previous clubs include: Baldock T - June 2001, St.Neots T, Eynesbury R.

WALKER, JOSH — Midfielder
Current Club: Moor Green
D o B: 20/12/1981   Birthplace: Birmingham
Young midfielder with an excellent pedigree. Started his career as a junior with Aston Villa before going on to spend four years with Manchester United. Transferred to Shrewsbury Town in 2001 and played a handful of League games before being released at the end of the 2001/02 season. Signed for Dr Martens Premier side Moor Green in July 2002.

WALKER, KEITH — Midfielder
Current Club: Fairford Town
Birthplace: Wiltshire
Previous clubs include: Highworth T - July 2001.

WALKER, LEE — Forward
Current Club: Wealdstone
D o B: 02/11/1972
Previous clubs include: Molesey - November 1995, Chesham Utd, Bashley, Slough T, Millwall.

WALKER, LEIGH — Goalkeeper
Current Club: Scarborough
D o B: 27/02/1981   Birthplace: Sheffield
Talented goalkeeper who joined Conference club Scarorough in June 2002 from relegated Stalybridge Celtic. Started his career with Sheffield United before being released and then turning out for Barnsley and Central Midlands side South Normanton Athletic. Moved to UniBond Premier side Emley at the start of the 2001/02 season and soon caught the attention of Stalybridge, who snapped him up in December 2001. Despite Celtics relegation, Leigh performed well and it came as little surprise when he was given the opportunity to remain in the Conference with Scarborough.

WALKER, MARVIN — Midfielder
Current Club: Boreham Wood
Birthplace: London
Attacking midfielder who joined Ryman Premier side Boreham Wood in August 2002 from rivals Enfield. Actually started out with the Es as a youngster and then had spells with Harlow Town, Haringey Borough, Leyton Pennant, Harrow Borough, Billericay Town, Edgware Town and Yeading, re-joining Enfield in October 2001.

WALKER, PAUL — Forward
Current Club: Great Harwood Town
Birthplace: Lancashire
From Youth team.

WALKER, PAUL — Midfielder
Current Club: Llanelli AFC
D o B: 23/06/1967   Birthplace: Wales
Previous clubs include: Haverfordwest County -December 2001, Carmarthen T, Haverfordwest Co., Cwmbran T, Briton Ferry Ath.

WALKER, PHIL — Defender
Current Club: Harrogate Railway
Birthplace: Yorkshire
Previous clubs include: Knaresborough T - July 1999.

WALKER, RAY — Midfielder
Current Club: Rocester
D o B: 28/09/1963   Birthplace: North Shields
Honours won: England Youth Int.
Previous clubs include: Newcastle T - August 2001, Leek T, Port Vale, Aston Villa.

WALKER, RICHARD — Defender
Current Club: Liversedge
Birthplace: Yorkshire
Previous clubs include: Emley - November 2001.

WALKER, RICHARD — Defender
Current Club: Wakefield & Emley
Birthplace: Leeds
Young defender. He has been at Emley for several years graduating from their junior sides. He is expected to become a regular member of the Emley first team squad.

WALKER, RICHARD — Defender
Current Club: Haverhill Rovers
Birthplace: Suffolk
Tight-marking defender with Haverhill who has a knack of quickly overlapping and sending over accurate crosses. Almost always seems to be in the right place at the right time.

WALKER, ROB — Midfielder
Current Club: Heybridge Swifts
Birthplace: Essex
Made a fleeting appearance for Heybridge Swifts two seasons ago in a Full Members Cup tie and scored a goal, whilst on-loan from Chelmsford City. Right-sided defender or midfielder who started with Hornchurch, he is now looking to make his mark after making the move a permanent one at the start of the 2001/02 season.

WALKER, RONNIE — Midfielder
Current Club: Wednesfield
Birthplace: Wolverhampton
Previous clubs include: Blakenall - July 2001, Redditch Utd, Stafford R, Evesham Utd, Bloxwich T, Stourbridge, Bilston CC, Worcester C, Matlock T, Worcester C, Malvern T, Worcester C, Wolverhampton Utd.

WALKER, SCOTT — Midfielder
Current Club: Newport County
D o B: 17/03/1980   Birthplace: Exeter
Highly-rated young defender or midfielder who was with Exeter City as a schoolboy, YTS trainee and first year professional without making a senior appearance. Moved to Bath City in 1999 and was an automatic choice at Twerton Park before moving to Newport County on a Bosman-type international transfer in July 2001.

W

WALKER, STEVE — Midfielder

Current Club: Tow Law Town

Birthplace: Co.Durham

Joined last season from Whitley Bay. His previous clubs include and Blyth and Bedlington where he was part of the League Championship squad.

WALKER, STUART — Midfielder

Current Club: Kidsgrove Athletic

Birthplace: Cheshire

Honours won: NWCL Winners

Was originally on loan from Hyde at the end of the 2000/01 season, and joined permanently at the start of the following campaing. Contributed several important goals from midfield during Groves title success. Previously with Altrincham and Knutsford.

WALKINGTON, JASON — Midfielder

Current Club: Wokingham Town

Birthplace: Reading

Previous clubs include: Fleet T - February 1999, Wokingham T, Hayes, Wokingham T, Basingstoke T, Windsor & Eton, Reading, Southampton,

WALKLATE, STEVE — Midfielder

Current Club: Durham City

D o B: 27/09/1979   Birthplace: Durham

Previous clubs include: Queen of the South - July 2001, Blyth Spartans, Darlington, Newcastle Utd.

WALKLETT, CRAIG — Midfielder

Current Club: Kidsgrove Athletic

Birthplace: Stoke

Wogger enjoyed a new lease of life last year, after the signing of Twiggy. A member of the 1997/8 squad, he scored in both the quarter and semi-finals of the Vase. His nickname has caused problems with certain visiting teams.

WALKLETT, CRAIG — Midfielder

Current Club: Rocester

Birthplace: Staffordshire

Previous clubs include: Kidsgrove Ath - November 2001, Knypersley V.

WALL, COLIN — Defender

Current Club: Boreham Wood

D o B: 14/05/1976   Birthplace: Essex

Giant, well-travelled central defender who returned to the Ryman Premier with Boreham Wood in July 2002 after a brief spell with Jewson Eastern Leaguers Tiptree United, with whom he appeared in the 2002 FA Vase final at Villa Park. Had previously spent the majority of his playing days in the Ryman with the likes of Canvey Island, Heybridge Swifts, Billericay Town, Gravesend and also had a couple of spells with Chelmsford City.

WALL, JAMES — Defender

Current Club: Burton Albion

D o B: 21/03/1980   Birthplace: Carshalton

James Wall has rejoined the Brewers after a summer plying his trade in the American Soccer League. He has also played for Hereford United in the Conference and was formerly with Derby County. James came to the Brewers and had a successful spell at Eton Park, his last match being in the Dr. Martens League Cup final against Hastings Town which the Brewers won on aggregate.

WALL, STUART — Forward

Current Club: Diss Town

Birthplace: Norwich

Previous clubs include: Norwich Utd - July 2001, Scole, Diss T.

WALL, STUART — Midfielder

Current Club: Glapwell

Birthplace: Chesterfield

From Local football - July 1996.

WALLACE, ADAM — Forward

Current Club: Salisbury City

Birthplace: Witshire

Joined Dr Martens Eastern side Salisbury City in August 2002, having made a couple of appearances for the club the previous season following his release from Southampton. Had a short spell with Southend United at the end of the 2001/02 season, making two Football League appearances.

WALLACE, CARL — Forward

Current Club: Stafford Town

Birthplace: Stoke

Previous clubs include: Newcastle T - July 2000, Port Vale.

WALLACE, JAMIE — Forward

Current Club: Billericay Town

Birthplace: Essex

Jamie is a tall striker, the archetypal target man. He signed for Billericay before the start of the 2001/02 season, making his debut as a substitute in the second game of the season at Hendon. His previous clubs include Grays, Ford United and Dagenham.

WALLACE, NATHAN — Defender

Current Club: Basingstoke Town

D o B: 15/07/1981   Birthplace: Hampshire

Young utility player who rejoined Basingstoke Town in November 2001 after a short spell with Staines Town. Started his playing days in Basingstokes youth side before moving to Staines at the start of the 2001/02 season.

WALLBRIDGE, ANDY — Defender

Current Club: Banbury United

Birthplace: Oxford

Top of the managers shopping list when he signed for Banbury in the summer of 1999, and the faith played off when he played in all 62 games in Banburys promotion season. Capped a brilliant season when he one the hat-trick of Managers, Players and clubs Player of the Year during the 2000/01 season. Mr Consistent, he has also seen service with Oxford United, Fulham, Worcester City, Abingdon Town, Marlow and Oxford City, from whom he joined Banbury.

WALLER, MICKEY — Defender

Current Club: Guisborough Town

Birthplace: Middlesbrough

Previous clubs include: Gretna - July 2001, Barrow, Whitby T, Morecambe, Bishop Auckland, Northallerton T, Bishop Auckland, Northallerton T, South Bank, Middlesbrough.

WALLING, DEAN — Defender

Current Club: Gainsborough Trinity

D o B: 17/04/1969   Birthplace: Leeds

An experienced and commanding centre-half who joined Gainsborough Trinity in June 2002 after being released by Third Division Cambridge United. Had signed for Cambridge on the eve of the 2001/02 season after a successful pre-season trial. Dean has enjoyed promotion three times with Carlisle United (twice) and Lincoln City. John Beck worked with the former Carlisle captain before, having signed him for Lincoln, and brought him back to League football after spells with Doncaster Rovers and Northwich Victoria in the Conference. Made over 400 League appearances and has also had spells in Canada with Franklin and Kitchener Spirit.

WALLSGROVE, JON — *Forward*
Current Club: Hamble ASSC
Birthplace: Hampshire
Previous clubs include: Chichester City Utd - September 2001, Hamble.

WALMSLEY, BILLY — *Midfielder*
Current Club: Hall Road Rangers
Birthplace: Hull
Previous clubs include: Goole AFC - December 2001, Bridlington T.

WALMSLEY, DARREN — *Forward*
Current Club: Tunbridge Wells
Birthplace: Kent
Previous clubs include: Tonbridge Angels - July 1998, Margate, Folkestone Invicta, New Romney.

WALMSLEY, DAVE — *Forward*
Current Club: Hall Road Rangers
Birthplace: Hull
Previous clubs include: Pontefract Collieries - July 2000, Harrogate T, North Ferriby Utd, Immingham T, Harrogate T, Goole T, Guiseley, Hull C.

WALMSLEY, JIMMY — *Defender*
Current Club: Goole AFC
Birthplace: Hull
Previous clubs include: Denaby Utd - November 2000, Pontefract Collieries, North Ferriby Utd, Hall Road R, North Ferriby Utd, Goole T, Winterton R.

WALMSLEY, MARC — *Defender*
Current Club: Whitley Bay
Birthplace: Newcastle
Marc is a local lad in his third season at the club. Signed from New Hartley Juniors. He is a good strong tackler with a liking to get up with forwards. Recently played his 100th game for the club. The first time this has been achieved by a player not yet 21. Voted Player of the Year last season.

WALSH, DANNY — *Midfielder*
Current Club: Ossett Town
D o B: 16/09/1978   Birthplace: Manchester
A midfielder who was released by Oldham Athletic in the summer of 2001, Danny joined Chesterfield and uniquely had his wages sponsored by his Uncle, hence making him a no-cost to the club player He suffered with illness in recent times but he's fully fit now. Joined Ossett Town in March 2002.

WALSH, DANNY — *Midfielder*
Current Club: Kettering Town
D o B: 16/09/1978   Birthplace: Manchester
Talented wide midfielder who joined Conference side Kettering Town in July 2002 after impressing in pre-season trials. Manchester-born, he began his career with Oldham and made a couple of League appearances for the Latics before switching to Chesterfield in December 2001. Made just one first-team appearance for the Spireites and also spent time on-loan at Ossett Albion before being released at the end of the 2001/02 season.

WALSH, GED — *Midfielder*
Current Club: Rossendale United
D o B: 28/04/1968   Birthplace: Rossendale
Vastly experienced and well-respected midfielder who has graced the north-west Non-League scene for many years. Capable of playing in midfield or at centre back, he was originally with Bacup Borough and then turned out for his home-town club Rossendale United before moving into the UniBond with Accrington Stanley via a second spell at Bacup in 1995. Switched to Bamber Bridge in July 1997 and spells with Radcliffe Borough, Great Harwood Town and Stanley again followed befor he returned home to Rossendale in October 1999.

WALSH, LEE — *Midfielder*
Current Club: Eastbourne United
Birthplace: Sussex
Consistent midfielder or attacker who was previously with Eastbourne Town (graduated from their youth team in 1998/99): scored 9 times in 1999/2000, and was Town's leading marksman with a tally of 11 in 2000/01: joined Eastbourne United at the start of the latest season.

WALSH, MARC — *Defender*
Current Club: Arlesey Town
Birthplace: Hertfordshire
Marc joined Arlesey Town during the 2001/02 season and has proven to be a great asset, forging a good partnership with Dave Hatchett in the centre of defence. His previous clubs have been Colchester, Welwyn Garden City, London Colney and Harrow Borough. He is a postman.

WALSH, RONNIE — *Defender*
Current Club: Croydon
Birthplace: Surrey
22-year-old right back who joined Croydon this summer from Crystal Palace.

WALSH, STEVE — *Defender*
Current Club: Tamworth
D o B: 03/11/1964   Birthplace: Fulwood
Honours won: League Cup Winners, Freight Rover Trophy Winners
Hugely experienced central defender who started his career at Wigan and then went on to make over 400 appearances for Leicester City, captaining them for the majority of his time at Filbert Street. Had a short spell at Norwich before joining his ex-Leicester team-mate Gary Mills at Tamworth in November 2001.

WALSH, STEVE — *Defender*
Current Club: Northwich Victoria
Birthplace: Warrington
A product of Northwich Victorias reserve team, Warrington-based Steve grabbed the opportunity to impress at senior level with both hands. He is an assured defender with a good turn of speed, who seldom looks fazed, whoever the opposition.

WALSHE, LIAM — *Midfielder*
Current Club: Belper Town
Birthplace: Derby
Previous clubs include: Burton Albion - November 2001, Gresley Rovers, Lincoln C.

WALTERS, DAME — *Forward*
Current Club: Clapton
Birthplace: Jamaica
Honours won: Jamaica u-21 Int.
From Local football - July 2001.

WALTERS, DEREK — *Defender*
Current Club: Staines Town
D o B: 29/09/1965 — Birthplace: Middlesex
A very experienced defender who began in Staines Town's youth side back in 1984, playing just three games before moving on to Egham Town and Windsor & Eton. Joined Farnborough Town in 1994/95, helping them to regain their Conference place and then returned to Staines in January 1995. Left the club again in the summer of 1997, spending the following season at Wokingham Town, followed by a few injury-troubled months with Maidenhead United before returning to Wheatsheaf Lane in October 1998.

WALTERS, GARY — *Midfielder*
Current Club: Lincoln United
Birthplace: Lincoln
Skilful winger who came to Lincoln from local rivals Boston United in December 2000. Played for Holbeach United before signing for Boston United. He is a player with a tremendous amount of pace.

WALTERS, MARK — *Midfielder*
Current Club: Ilkeston Town
D o B: 02/06/1964 — Birthplace: Birmingham
Honours won: England Schoolboy, Youth, u-21, B & Full Int., FA Cup Winners, European Super Cup Winners, Scottish Premier League Winners, Scottish League Cup Winners,
One of the best-known players to join the Non-League circuit during the summer of 2002. Mark has won a whole host of honours during an illustrious professional career that took in more than 600 games, 160-plus goals, caps for England at Schoolboy, Youth, under-21, B and full international level and spells at the top level in both England and Scotland, winning FA Cup, Scottish Premier League and European Super Cup medals. Began his career with Aston Villa and then moved to Glasgow Rangers for £550,000 in 1987 and then cost Liverpool £1,250,000 when joining them in 1991. Spells with Southampton, Swindon and Bristol Rovers followed before he was released at the end of the 2001/02 season and eventually joined Ilkeston Town in August 2002, scoring on his debut.

WALTERS, SASHA — *Midfielder*
Current Club: Afan Lido
D o B: 20/06/1984 — Birthplace: Wales
From Youth team.

WALTERS, SCOTT — *Forward*
Current Club: Leighton Town
Birthplace: Hemel Hempstead
Much-travelled and experienced striker who re-joined Ryman Division Two side Leighton Town in July 2002 following a second spell with Tring Town. Originally on the books at Colchester, he has since seen service with Hitchin Town, Hemel Hempstead, St Albans City and Berkhamsted Town, re-joining Tring from Leighton in October 1999.

WALTERS, STEVE — *Midfielder*
Current Club: Rhyl
D o B: 09/01/1972 — Birthplace: Plymouth
Honours won: England Youth & Semi-Pro Int., NWCL Winners
Became a real coup for League of Wales outfit Rhyl when they signed Steve from Kidsgrove Athletic in August 2002. Former Crewe Alexandra midfielder, he signed for Kidsgrove from Stevenage Borough for £10,000 in November 2001. Scored after just 7 minutes of his debut at Ramsbottom. A former England Youth and semi-professional international, he also served Northwich Victoria and Morecambe in the Conference.

WALTERS, WAYNE — *Defender*
Current Club: Harrow Borough
Birthplace: London
Joined Ryman Premier side Harrow Borough in the summer of 2001 from Wembley where he had been a first team regular for a number of years. A TV and satellite engineer.

WALTON, ANDY — *Defender*
Current Club: Witham Town
Birthplace: Essex
From Youth team.

WALTON, CHARLIE — *Midfielder*
Current Club: Shildon
Birthplace: Bishop Auckland
Previous clubs include: Hartlepool Utd (Junior) - August 1992.

WALTON, DAVID — *Goalkeeper*
Current Club: Haverhill Rovers
Birthplace: Essex
24 years old, in his second season with Haverhill after joining from AFC Sudbury. Has a wealth of experience at Jewson League and Dr Martens League levels. Previously with West Ham United, Southend United, Watford and Baldock Town.

WALTON, KEVIN — *Midfielder*
Current Club: Whitley Bay
D o B: 02/05/1975 — Birthplace: Durham
Recently signed from Berwick Rangers, but previously was with UniBond League outfit North Ferriby United, where he enjoyed 5 successful seasons. Has great ball control and passing skills.

WALTON, SCOTT — *Defender*
Current Club: Edgware Town
Birthplace: Hertfordshire
Previous clubs include: Potters Bar T - July 2001, Cockfosters, Potters Bar T.

WARBURTON, RAY — *Defender*
Current Club: Boston United
D o B: 07/10/1967 — Birthplace: Rotherham
Honours won: Conference Winners
Previous clubs include: Rushden & Diamonds - March 2002, Northampton T, York C, Rotherham Utd.

WARD, ADIE — *Midfielder*
Current Club: Racing Club Warwick
Birthplace: Birmingham
Previous clubs include: Mile Oak - November 2001.

WARD, DAVID — *Defender*
Current Club: Pagham
Birthplace: Sussex
Defender: joined Pagham from Oving in December 2001: also plays for University College Chichester.

WARD, DAVID — *Midfielder*
Current Club: Sidley United
Birthplace: Sussex
Midfielder, now in his fifth season at the club: scored six times during 2000/01: previously with Bexhill.

WARD, DEREK   *Defender*
Current Club: Vauxhall Motors
D o B: 17/05/1972   Birthplace: Birkenhead
Honours won: UniBond League Premier Div. Winners
Good with both feet, so is adaptable at the back on both flanks.
Useful going forward, as well as providing good cover as sweeper
when required. Derek joined UniBond Premier side Vauxhall
Motors in August 2002 from League of Wales club Total Network
Solutions. Had signed for TNS in October 2001from Stalybridge
Celtic, whom he had helped to win the UniBond title. Previously
with Bury, Southport and Northwich Victoria, with whom he
appeared in the 1996 FA Trophy final at Wembley.

WARD, GAVIN   *Forward*
Current Club: Wokingham Town
Birthplace: Hampshire
Previous clubs include: Chalfont St.Peter - September 1999,
Camberley T, Cove, Westfield.

WARD, GEOFF   *Defender*
Current Club: Littlehampton Town
Birthplace: Sussex
Classy defender: joined East Preston from Wick at the start of
1999/2000: spent the following season with Horsham (one of his
old clubs) and Worthing: signed for Littlehampton in August 2001.

WARD, KARL   *Goalkeeper*
Current Club: Stafford Rangers
D o B: 23/03/1984   Birthplace: Stafford
A former Stafford Rangers youth team goalkeeper, Karl made his
first-team debut at the end of March 2001 against Havant &
Waterlooville, a few days after his seventeenth birthday. He has
enjoyed an extended run in the first-team during the following
campaign and attracted the attention of numerous scouts.

WARD, KEITH   *Midfielder*
Current Club: Carshalton Athletic
Birthplace: Surrey
Previous clubs include: Banstead Ath - December 2001, Tooting
& Mitcham Utd, Dulwich Hamlet.

WARD, KEVIN   *Midfielder*
Current Club: Spalding United
Birthplace: Yorkshire
Previous clubs include: Lincoln Utd - December 2001, Grantham
T, Lincoln Utd, Harrogate T, Goole T, Gainsborough Trinity, BK IFK
(Sweden), Halifax T, BK IFK (Sweden), Var TP (Sweden), MP IFK
(Sweden), Cove Rangers, Barnsley.

WARD, LEE   *Goalkeeper*
Current Club: Arlesey Town
Birthplace: London
Lee was a real star in Arlesey Town's championship-winning
season in the Spartan Premier League. Missed the entire
2000/01 season through injury but recovered to stake his claim
in Town's goal again. In his travels he has been with Watford,
Hayes, Hemel Hempstead, Wembley, Hillingdon Borough and
Ruislip. Works as a recruitment consultant.

WARD, MARK   *Forward*
Current Club: Stocksbridge Park Steels
D o B: 27/01/1982   Birthplace: Sheffield
Promising young striker who joined UniBond First Division side
Stocksbridge Park Steels in August 2002 after being released by
Sheffield United. Trialled with a number of clubs in the summer of
2002 before chosing Steels. Made 2 League appearances for
United.

WARD, MICKEY   *Forward*
Current Club: Marske United
Birthplace: Northallerton
Previous clubs include: Guisborough T - July 2001, Marske Utd,
Billingham Synthonia, Bishop Auckland, Billingham Synthonia,
North Ormesby, Northallerton T.

WARD, NICKY   *Forward*
Current Club: Total Network Solutions
D o B: 30/11/1977   Birthplace: Wrexham
Skilful winger or hard-working midfielder, Nicky runs well with the
ball as well as providing his fellow strikers good ammunition with
crosses from all over the pitch. Joined TNS in November 1999
from LoW rivals Newtown after spells with League clubs Wrexham
and Shrewsbury.

WARD, NICKY   *Midfielder*
Current Club: Marske United
Birthplace: Middlesbrough
Nickys previous clubs were Guisborough Town and New Marske.
He has progressed through the junior side at Marske United. A
strong, hard-working midfielder with an eye for goal.

WARD, PAUL   *Defender*
Current Club: Lincoln United
Previous clubs include: Sleaford T - December 2000, Lincoln Utd.

WARD, RUSS   *Forward*
Current Club: Maltby Main
Birthplace: Yorkshire
Previous clubs include: Denaby Utd - October 2001, Maltby
Main. Alfreton T, NCB Maltby, Maltby Main.

WARD, SCOTT   *Goalkeeper*
Current Club: Chesham United
D o B: 05/10/1981   Birthplace: Luton
Scott is an agile, aggresive keeper who is a great shot-stopper.
He has previously played for Luton for four years and his hero is
Peter Shilton. His most memorable moment in football was
making his debut for Luton against Brentford. Signed for Ryman
Premier side Chesham United in August 2002.

WARD, SIMON   *Goalkeeper*
Current Club: Kettering Town
Birthplace: Peterborough
Previous clubs include: Yaxley - August 2002.

WARD, STEVE   *Defender*
Current Club: Canvey Island
Birthplace: Essex
Honours won: FA Trophy Winners
Central defender who spent many years with Essex neighbours
and rivals, Grays Athletic, progressing from the youth and reserve
teams to make over 400 appearances for the first-team. Steve
transferred to Canvey Island in October 1996 for a £3000 fee.
He is currently a P.E. teacher in Gravesend.

WARD, TONY   *Defender*
Current Club: Runcorn FC Halton
D o B: 04/04/1970   Birthplace: Liverpool
Previous clubs include: Chorley - May 1997, Marine, Chorley,
Wigan Ath., Everton.

WARD, TONY — Midfielder

Current Club: Arlesey Town

Birthplace: Stevenage
Honours won: FA Vase Winners, Ryman League Div.3 Winners

Tony is an inspirational midfielder who never knows when to stop, he's not satisfied until he has covered every blade of grass. An Inspiration to his team mates as he was at his former clubs, Stevenage, Hitchin, Hertford and Stotfold. Has collected Isthmian Division 2 North, South Midlands Premier (2), FA Vase 1995, Spartan South Midlands League and Ryman Division 3 winners medals.

WARDEN, JON — Midfielder

Current Club: Herne Bay

Birthplace: Kent
Honours won: FA Vase Winners

Previous clubs include: Ashford T - July 2001, Deal T, Ashford T, Crawley T, Bromley, Kingstonian, Carshalton Ath., Tooting & Mitcham Utd, Croydon.

WARDER, AIDEN — Midfielder

Current Club: Warrington Town

Birthplace: Liverpool

Previous clubs include: Prescot Cables - August 2001, Accrington Stanley, Runcorn, Curzon Ashton, Runcorn, Warrington T, South Liverpool.

WARDLE, DARREN — Forward

Current Club: Mossley

Birthplace: Bury

Previous clubs include: Oldham Ath - August 2000, Bury.

WARDLE, RICHARD — Midfielder

Current Club: Gresley Rovers

D o B: 16/01/1971 *Birthplace: Staffs*

Vastly experienced midfielder who is Gresley Rovvers longest-serving player and enjoyed a testomonial during the 2001/02 season. Has been voted as player of the year at Gresley three times since joining from Tamworth in the summer of 1991.

WARDLEY, SHANE — Defender

Current Club: Cambridge City

D o B: 26/02/1980 *Birthplace: Ipswich*

Ipswich-born attacking full back who joined Dr Martens Premier Cambridge City in June 2002 from Ryman Premier side Enfield. Started his career as a trainee with his home-town club and then had spells with Rushden & Diamonds and Chelmsford City before returning to the full-time game with Cambridge United in August 2000. Switched to Southend for £5,000 in December 2000 but made only a handful of League appearances before having brief spells with Windsor & Eton and Enfield towards the end of the 2001/02 season.

WARE, PAUL — Midfielder

Current Club: Hednesford Town

D o B: 07/11/1970 *Birthplace: Congleton*

Re-signed for Dr Martens Premier side Hednesford Town in July 2002 after spells back in the League with Macclesfield and Rochdale. Originally joined the Pitmen in August 1997 after being at Stockport and Stoke. Totalled over 200 League appearances.

WAREHAM, STEVE — Midfielder

Current Club: Tiptree United

Birthplace: Essex

Previous clubs include: Halstead T - August 2000, Saffron Walden T.

WAREING, JON — Defender

Current Club: Marine

Birthplace: Merseyside

Talented defender who joined Marine in the summer of 2000. A student, who was on Wigan Athletic's books and came through Marine Reserves to become a first-team regular in 2001/02.

WARNER, ADAM — Defender

Current Club: Hertford Town

Birthplace: Herts

Adam joined Ryman Division One North side Hertford Town during the 2001/02 season from Edgware Town and towards the end of the season was a defensive mainstay. Unfortunately, Adam suffered a serious road traffic accident injury and is not yet fit to return to playing.

WARNER, ASHLEY — Forward

Current Club: Rugby United

D o B: 15/09/1971 *Birthplace: Leicester*

Previous clubs include: Rothwell T - March 2002, Corby T, Barwell, VS Rugby, Atherstone Utd, Rothwell T, Corby T, VS Rugby, Gloucester C, Peterborough Utd, VS Rugby, Hinckley T, VS Rugby, Friar Lane OB, Hillcroft, Anstey T, Coventry C (Junior).

WARNER, DANNY — Defender

Current Club: Droylsden

Previous clubs include: Curzon Ashton - February 2000, Buxton, Oldham T, Bury (Junior).

WARNER, DAVID — Forward

Current Club: Hayes

D o B: 27/04/1981 *Birthplace: Hillingdon*

Previous clubs include: Watford - October 2001, Brook House, Uxbridge.

WARNER, KEVIN — Forward

Current Club: Hayes

Birthplace: Middlesex

Previous clubs include: Brook House - August 2001, Uxbridge, Yeading.

WARNER, MICHAEL — Defender

Current Club: Farnborough Town

D o B: 17/01/1974 *Birthplace: Harrogate*

Micky was Farnborough Town's chairman/manager Graham Westleys first signing in 1999, from Northampton, and couples his playing duties with that of Club Commercial Executive. Quickly made himself a favourite with Boro fans with his eager displays on the right side of midfield. Started his playing days with Midlands Non-League sides Tamworth and Redditch United.

WARNER, ROB — Defender

Current Club: Tamworth

D o B: 20/04/1977 *Birthplace: Stratford*

An accomplished full back, Rob joined Tamworth in August 1998. He had previously been with Hereford United on a YTS scheme before becoming a full-time professional making several appearances in the Football League and the Conference. Player of the Year for both players and supporters in the 1998/99 season, he was chosen for the Dr Martens League representative team in the 1999/2000 season.

WARNER, TIM — Midfielder
Current Club: Shepshed Dynamo

D o B: 16/03/1976   *Birthplace: Leicester*
Experienced Non-League midfielder who re-joined Dr Martens Western side Shepshed Dynamo in July 2002 from Midland Alliance neighbours Barwell. Began his career as a trainee with Leicester City and then had spells with Barwell, Bedworth United, Hinckley United, Racing Club Warwick and Shepshed before returning to Barwell in September 1999.

WARNES, BILLY — Midfielder
Current Club: Rye & Iden United

Birthplace: Sussex
Left-sided player. Scored six goals for Rye during 2000/01.

WARREN, KEVIN — Forward
Current Club: Enfield

Birthplace: Essex
Previous clubs include: Barking & East Ham Utd - February 2002, Romford - November 2001.

WARREN, LEE — Defender
Current Club: Barrow

D o B: 28/02/1969   *Birthplace: Manchester*
Born in Manchester, Lee is an experienced defender who began his career as a trainee with Leeds United but did not make the first-team before being released. He then joined Rochdale and made 31 appearances for the Spotland outfit, scoring once before moving on to Hull City. He enjoyed a lengthy spell with the Tigers making 153 League appearances for them, scoring once. He also made three appearances on loan for Lincoln City, scoring once. He joined Doncaster Rovers whilst they were still in the Football League and made 125 appearances for them, scoring three times before they lost their League status in the summer of 1998. He remained with them during their first two seasons in the Conference before being released in the summer. He joined Barrow in July 2000 and made his debut on the opening day of the season at home to Emley.

WARREN, MATT — Defender
Current Club: Mickleover Sports

D o B: 14/02/1976   *Birthplace: Derby*
Previous clubs include: Gresley Rovers - August 2001, Moor Green, Alfreton T, Gresley R, Derby Co.

WARRILOW, IAN — Midfielder
Current Club: Skelmersdale United

Birthplace: Liverpool
From Local football - July 1999.

WARRILOW, TOMMY — Defender
Current Club: Horsham

D o B: 26/07/1964   *Birthplace: London*
Veteran defender who was originally a Millwall reserve and then signed for Crawley from Torquay in the 1980s: subsequently sold to Hythe for £15,000 and later became the manager at Leatherhead: brought into the Horsham side during 2000/01.

WARRINGTON, ANDY — Goalkeeper
Current Club: Doncaster Rovers

D o B: 06/10/1976   *Birthplace: Sheffield*
Talented goalkeeper who started his career as a trainee with York City. Turned professional and made over 70 League appearances before being somewhat surprisingly released at the end of the 1998/99 season. Moved to Doncaster and soon earned a reputation as being amongst the best in the Conference.

WARWICK, TERRY — Forward
Current Club: Maldon Town

Birthplace: Essex
Previous clubs include: Heybridge Swifts - July 2001, Tiptree Utd.

WASDEN, BRETT — Defender
Current Club: Maltby Main

Birthplace: Yorkshire
Previous clubs include: Parkgate - October 2001, Hallam.

WASSALL, DARREN — Defender
Current Club: Burton Albion

D o B: 27/06/1968   *Birthplace: Edgbaston*
Darren Wassall was signed prior to the start of the 2000/2001 campaign; the Brewers manager snapping up the highly-rated defender after injury forced Darren to take early retirement from the pro game. Darren started his career at Nottingham Forest, before he made the short trip up the A52 to Derby County. He enjoyed four successful years at the Baseball Ground, which included loan spells at Hereford and Bury, Birmingham City then paid £100,000 for his signature, but his career at St. Andrews was cut short by injury. His first season at Eton Park saw many outstanding displays that resulted in him picking up both the Supporters and Players' Player of the Year trophies.

WASTELL, JAMES — Goalkeeper
Current Club: Banstead Athletic

Birthplace: Surrey
Goalkeeper who re-joined Ryman Division One South side Banstead Athletic during the summer of 2002 from Worthing. Had signed for Worthing during the 2001 close season of 2001 after being released by Croydon. Previous experience with Horsham, Chipstead, Welling United, Molesey and Redhill.

WATERMAN, LEE — Defender
Current Club: Bashley

Birthplace: Hampshire
Previous clubs include: Havant & Waterlooville - November 2001.

WATERS, CARL — Forward
Current Club: Barrow

Birthplace: Barrow
Carl is a very promising striker who began playing soccer at local level and first sprung to prominence when he finished second top scorer in the North West Counties Second Division during the 1999/00 for Holker OB with 26 goals. He joined Barrow in February 2001 and has now become a first-team regular at Holker Street.

WATERS, GARY — Defender
Current Club: Braintree Town

Previous clubs include: Heybridge Swifts - July 2001, Canvey Island, Billericay T, Barking, Grays Ath., Aveley, West Ham Utd.

WATERS, MATT — Forward
Current Club: Clacton Town

Birthplace: Clacton
A product of Clacton's Youth development, young Matt is a dedicated player with superb ability on the ball. Very fit and very fast. One to look out for in the future.

WATKIN, DANNY — Forward
Current Club: Newtown AFC

D o B: 09/01/1983   *Birthplace: Wales*
Previous clubs include: Wrexham - March 2002.

WATKINS, CHRIS — *Forward*
Current Club: Cwmbran Town

Birthplace: Wales

Honours won: Wales Schoolboy Int.

Previous clubs include: Llanelli - March 2001, Rhayader T, Cwmbran T, Croeseceilog, Swansea C.

WATKINS, DALE — *Forward*
Current Club: Kettering Town

D o B: 04/11/1971   Birthplace: Sheffield

Honours won: England Semi-Pro Int., Nationwide Conference Winners, Dr Martens League Premier Div.Winners

Signed for Kettering Town in December 1999 for a £22,000 fee from Cheltenham Town after a successful loan spell at Rockingham Road. Has represented England at semi-professional level and struck up an impressive partnership with another ex-England player in Darren Collins in the Poppies attack. Formerly with Grimsby, Rotherham, Peterborough, Grantham Town, Rushden & Diamonds and Gloucester City, Dale started his career with his home-town club Sheffield United.

WATKINS, DAVE — *Midfielder*
Current Club: Newtown AFC

Birthplace: Wales

Honours won: Wales Schoolboy Int.

Previous clubs include: Presteigne - January 2000.

WATKINS, NEIL — *Defender*
Current Club: Boldmere St.Michaels

Birthplace: Birmingham

From Youth team.

WATKINS, PAUL — *Defender*
Current Club: Northwood

Previous clubs include: Southall - July 1999, Hayes, Harefield Utd.

WATKINS, RICHARD — *Forward*
Current Club: Fairford Town

Birthplace: Wiltshire

Previous clubs include: Purton - December 2000.

WATNEY, CHRIS — *Forward*
Current Club: Corinthian Casuals

Birthplace: Surrey

Chris signed for Corinthian Casuals from Banstead in 1999 and scored on his full debut. He won the most improved player award in 2000 and has come on a lot since joining and has been in good scoring form. He is a versatile character who has turned his public school educated hand to bar work and scaffolding in the Casuals cause. Currently working on Eagle FM as a member of the breakfast show posse.

WATSON, ANDY — *Midfielder*
Current Club: Doncaster Rovers

D o B: 13/11/1978   Birthplace: Leeds

Flying and skilful wide midfielder who played for Yorkshire Amateur and Farsley Celtic before joining Garforth Town. Had trials with Huddersfield Town before Doncaster Rovers snapped him up from Garforth for around £25,000 in March 1999. His form for the past season or so has attracted numerous attentions from Premiership and Football League clubs.

WATSON, DANNY — *Goalkeeper*
Current Club: Evesham United

Previous clubs include: Bilston T - September 2001, Worcester C, Bridgnorth T, Willenhall T, Kidderminster Harriers.

WATSON, IAN — *Defender*
Current Club: Felixstowe & Walton United

Birthplace: Suffolk

Local based player who joined the newly merged club in the close season last season from Bury Town having previously played for Walton United. Now a senior member of the squad, a strong and powerful defender.

WATSON, JIMMY — *Midfielder*
Current Club: Sidley United

Birthplace: Sussex

Strong midfielder: has been at Sidley for six seasons, having previously played for Stamco and Bexhill: brother of Brighton & Hove Albion player Paul Watson: scored five times during 2000/01, including the winning goal against Sidlesham in the John OHara Cup Final.

WATSON, LEE — *Forward*
Current Club: Chalfont St.Peter

Birthplace: Wycombe

Previous clubs include: Bracknell T - February 2002, Chalfont St.Peter, Flackwell Heath, Croydon Ath., Flackwell Heath, Chalfont St.Peter.

WATSON, LIAM — *Forward*
Current Club: Runcorn FC Halton

D o B: 21/05/1970   Birthplace: Liverpool

Honours won: England Semi-Pro Int.

Liam is a frustrating player who plays along the line, and gets caught offside countless times during the game. However given that one chance, he normally punishes teams and is now established as one of the clubs leading scorers having scored over 100 goals for the club. Liam was tempted back to the club in September last year from Accrington Stanley with the Player Managers role, succeeding Mark Carter. After a disappointing end to his first season, finishing 12th, the fans hope that he can turn the tide and lead us back to the Conference.

WATSON, MARK — *Forward*
Current Club: Sutton United

D o B: 28/12/1973   Birthplace: Birmingham

Highly-rated striker who re-joined Ryman Premier side Sutton United from rivals Aldershot Town in August 2002. Actually began his career with the Us before being transferred to West Ham. Made League appearances for Bournemouth before returning to Non-League with Welling United, Sutton again and Chesham United, joining Aldershot in May 2001.

WATSON, MARK — *Goalkeeper*
Current Club: Wokingham Town

D o B: 23/08/1967   Birthplace: Berkshire

Previous clubs include: Fleet T - September 2001, Banstead Ath., Walton & Hersham, Banstead Ath., Fleet T, Basingstoke T, Aldershot T, Camberley T, Newbury T, Plymouth Argyle, Reading, Southampton.

WATSON, MELVYN — *Goalkeeper*
Current Club: Studley

Birthplace: Worcestershire

Previous clubs include: Pershore T - July 2001, Evesham Utd, Worcester C, Upton T, Crewe Alexandra (Trainee).

WATSON, RICHIE — Defender

Current Club: Spennymoor United

Birthplace: Newcastle

Previous clubs include: Gateshead - January 2002, Spennymoor Utd, Billingham T, Bishop Auckland, Billingham T, Whitley Bay, Billingham T.

WATSON, RONNIE — Midfielder

Current Club: Enfield Town (Essex)

Birthplace: Herts

Another product of the Enfield FC Youth team, going on to make 36 first team appearances. Joined the Enfield Town when it was formed. Has also represented Middlesex. Missed several weeks of the current season through injury.

WATSON, SIMON — Midfielder

Current Club: Harrogate Town

D o B: 22/09/1980   Birthplace: Strabane

Honours won: UniBond League Div.One Winners

Simon is a midfielder and another ex-Leeds United player currently on Harrogate Town's books. He signed for Town from Doncaster Rovers in July 2001 and helped the club to win the UniBond Division One title.

WATSON, STEVE — Midfielder

Current Club: Farnborough Town

Birthplace: Surrey

Honours won: England Semi-Pro Int.

Started his career as a schoolboy at Crystal Palace before having spells with Whyteleafe and Croydon. Then spent four years at Sutton United where, from midfield, he scored 14 goals in their 1998/99 Ryman League title-winning side before being snapped up by Farnborough Town in the summer of 1999. Won his first England semi-professional international caps in May 2002.

WATT, CRAIG — Forward

Current Club: Hallam

Birthplace: Sheffield

Previous clubs include: Denaby Utd - March 2000, Phoenix, Alfreton T, Scarborough (Trainee).

WATTERS, CHRIS — Forward

Current Club: Hemel Hempstead Town

Birthplace: Hertfordshire

Previous clubs include: Cheshunt - October 2001.

WATTS, DAVID — Forward

Current Club: Ossett Albion

Previous clubs include: Thackley - February 2000, Ossett T.

WATTS, DAVID — Midfielder

Current Club: Clevedon Town

Birthplace: Bristol

Honours won: Wales Youth Int.

Former Wales Youth international midfielder who signed for Dr Martens Western side Clevedon Town in July 2002 after a spell in the League of Wales with Haverfordwest County. Had joined County in February 2002 from Bath City following periods at Newport County, Inter Cardiff and Weston-super-Mare. Had started his career as a trainee with Bristol Rovers.

WATTS, GARRY — Defender

Current Club: Barton Rovers

Birthplace: Bedford

Honours won: Ryman League Div.3 Winners

Previous clubs include: Arlesey T - January 2002, Stotfold, Biggleswade Utd, Bedford T.

WATTS, GRANT — Forward

Current Club: Bromley

D o B: 05/11/1973   Birthplace: London

Brother of Kirk. Joined Bromley after playing for Egham Town, Crystal Palace (where he broke his leg), Croydon and Banstead Athletic. Has given Bromley a new dimension in play, and links well with his brother Kirk in attack.

WATTS, KIRK — Forward

Current Club: Bromley

Birthplace: Kent

Re-joined Bromley in the summer of 2001 for his second spell at Hayes Lane, having left to join Ashford Town in November 2000. Previously joined Bromley in 1999 from Egham Town. Other clubs include Gravesend & Northfleet, Croydon and Thamesmead Town. Has now made 100 appearances for Bromley.

WATTS, LEW — Defender

Current Club: Gravesend & Northfleet

D o B: 14/09/1974   Birthplace: Maidstone

Talented defender who was one of Welling United's longest-serving players before switching to newly-promoted Conference side Gravesend & Northfleet in June 2002. Had joined the Wings in July 1995 from Fisher Athletic. Started out with Gravesend, Lew represented Welling in both the Conference and Dr Martens Leagues.

WATTS, MATT — Defender

Current Club: Redhill

Birthplace: Sussex

Starting to become a regular at left back for Redhill despite being only 15 years old. Has already generated interest from several clubs and been on trial at Charlton Athletic.

WATTS, PAUL — Forward

Current Club: Kings Lynn

Birthplace: Boston

Previous clubs include: Gainsborough Trinity - February 2002, Boston Utd, Grantham T.

WATTS, SHAUN — Midfielder

Current Club: Barnstaple Town

D o B: 11/11/1980   Birthplace: Devon

Previous clubs include: Exeter C - July 2000.

WATTS, STEWART — Midfielder

Current Club: Cray Wanderers

Birthplace: Kent

Previous clubs include: Erith & Belvedere - July 2001, Gravesend, Welling Utd.

WAUGH, WARREN — Forward

Current Club: Enfield

D o B: 09/10/1980   Birthplace: Harlesden

Big, strong attacker who joined Enfield in June 2002 from Crawley Town. Had signed for the Dr Martens Leaguers at the start of the 2001/02 season from rivals Cambridge City. Although born in London, Warren started his career with Exeter City, where he made 10 League appearances before joining Cambridge in July 2000. Crawley from Cambridge City during the 2001 close season: previously with Exeter.

W

WAY, DARREN — *Midfielder*

Current Club: Yeovil Town

D o B: 21/11/1979　　　*Birthplace: Plymouth*
Honours won: England Schoolboy Int., FA Trophy Winners

Former Norwich City midfielder who joined Yeovil a day or two before the start of the 2000/1 season. He did well in the reserves set-up at Carrow Road, having joined the club initially as a 14-year-old. He went on to skipper the reserve side, and made one first team appearance. He also has 20 England under-16 caps. The term terrier-like is a bit overused for small midfielders, but itd be pretty appropriate for Darren. He's quite prepared to get involved in the physical side of the game when required, but still has good ball skills.

WAY, MARK — *Forward*

Current Club: Dereham Town

Birthplace: Norfolk

Excellent pacey striker who has been brought into this level by Dereham from their Anglian Combination. Superb on the ball with an eye for goal.

WEAFER, JASON — *Midfielder*

Current Club: Barwell

Birthplace: Leicester

Previous clubs include: Ford Sports - July 1998, Shepshed Dynamo, Nuneaton B, Corby T, Rothwell T, Leicester Utd, VS Rugby, Leicester Utd.

WEALE, CHRIS — *Goalkeeper*

Current Club: Yeovil Town

D o B: 09/02/1982　　　*Birthplace: Yeovil*
Honours won: FA Trophy Winners

Chris lives at East Coker, and has previously represented Chard Town. He became first-choice goalkeeper for Yeovil Town's 1999/00 youth team that won the SWEB South-West Counties under-18s League title, and during the latter half of that season broke into the Screwfix League Reserve side. Chris made his first team debut coming on as a substitute against Southampton in Tony Pennocks testimonial game in July 2000 and followed that up with his competitive debut against Wellington in the Somerset Premier Cup in October of the same year. The 2000/01 season gradually saw Chris gain more and more experience as injury and suspension gave him his chance with him definitely looking the part. He looks to be an excellent prospect and was outstanding as Yeovil won the 2002 FA Umbro Trophy at Villa Park.

WEALE, RICHARD — *Defender*

Current Club: Rothwell Town

Birthplace: Leicester

Previous clubs include: Blackstone - July 2002, Stamford, Kettering T, Leicester C (Trainee).

WEARDEN, ANDY — *Midfielder*

Current Club: Curzon Ashton

Previous clubs include: Woodley Sports - July 2000, Glossop NE.

WEARDEN, MATTY — *Defender*

Current Club: Curzon Ashton

Previous clubs include: Woodlsey Sports - July 2000, Glossop NE.

WEATHERSTONE, ROSS — *Defender*

Current Club: Boston United

D o B: 16/05/1981　　　*Birthplace: Reading*

A young defender who was signed by Boston United from Oxford United, along with his brother Simon, on a free transfer in February 2001. Like his brother, he came through the youth scheme at Oxford. An instant hit with the Boston supporters. A fearless tackler, he was knocked unconscious and picked up a large gash across his forehead following a challenge in his debut match, at home to Northwich Victoria. A knee injury picked up in the home game against Southport in March 2001 ruled him out for the rest of the season. At Oxford, he made his League debut in a match against his home town club Reading, which Oxford won 2-1. He made three League appearances for Oxford, before picking up a knee injury that kept him sidelined.

WEATHERSTONE, SIMON — *Forward*

Current Club: Boston United

D o B: 26/01/1980　　　*Birthplace: Reading*

A young striker signed for Boston United from Oxford United on a free transfer in February 2001. He settled well into the side and soon got on the scoresheet, producing five goals in his thirteen starts. He came through the youth scheme at Oxford, and was offered a professional contract at the club when just seventeen years old. He scored his first League goal in the dying seconds of a match against Nottingham Forest, after coming on as a substitute. Overall he made 56 League appearances, scoring 4 goals. He is the brother of defender Ross Weatherstone.

WEAVER, STEVE — *Goalkeeper*

Current Club: Clevedon Town

D o B: 05/05/1972　　　*Birthplace: Bristol*

Reliable and experienced goalkeeper who re-joined Dr Martens Western side Clevedon Town from Chippenham Town in July 2002. Started his career with Bristol City and then had spells with Weymouth, Salisbury City, Clevedon, Mangotsfield United and Weston-super-Mare before joining Chippenham in November 2001 and helped them gain a place in the Premier Division.

WEBB, CHRIS — *Goalkeeper*

Current Club: Swindon Supermarine

D o B: 30/11/1976　　　*Birthplace: Swindon*

Chris joined the club in July 1999 from WantageTown and after demonstrating what a good keeper he was with two solid performances against us the previous season we had no hesitation in making him the clubs number 1. After an unsteady start he had a marvellousfirst season conceding only 23 league goals and playing a major part in our two-cup successes. Last season was similar, his overall contribution was immense, onlymissing one game and gave some outstanding performances that help secure the Championship. Over the two seasons at the club he has grown in stature and is now regarded as one of the best keepers around. He commands his area with great assurance and confidence.

WEBB, GARY — *Defender*

Current Club: Brentwood

Birthplace: Essex

Gary joined Brentwood as a 16 year old and although he has rarely threatened to win a regular first team place he has given ten years loyal service mostly in the 2nd and 3rd teams. Has earned himself a number 1st team outings early this season.

WEBB, GRAHAM — *Forward*

Current Club: St.Leonards

Birthplace: Hastings
Previous clubs include: Hastings T - February 2002.

WEBB, KEVIN — *Forward*

Current Club: Epsom And Ewell

Birthplace: Surrey
Previous clubs include: Banstead Ath - March 2002, Dulwich Hamlet, Banstead Ath., Epsom & Ewell, Sutton Utd.

WEBB, KIERON — *Forward*
Current Club: Berkhamsted Town
Birthplace: Berkshire
Forward who joined Ryman Division One North side Berkhamsted Town in July 2002 after a two-year spell with Spartan South Midlands outfit Beaconsfield SYCB. Began his playing days with Aylesbury United and then signed for SYCOB from Chalfont St Peter in the summer of 2000.

WEBB, MATTHEW — *Forward*
Current Club: Halesowen Harriers
Birthplace: Worcestershire
Previous clubs include: Cradley T - July 2001, Halesowen Harriers.

WEBB, MICHAEL — *Midfielder*
Current Club: Leatherhead
D o B: 10/10/1980   Birthplace: Surrey
The former Horsley Youth captain is now a first-year at Kingston University. Formerly with Woking, the midfielder also captained Surrey Youth.

WEBB, NICK — *Goalkeeper*
Current Club: Berkhamsted Town
D o B: 23/02/1979   Birthplace: Luton
Competent goalkeeper who re-signed for Ryman Division One North side Berkhamsted Town in July 2002 from Premier Division Hitchin Town. Had joined Hitchin exactly a year earlier 2001 from Berkhamsted, and with the departure of Darren Bonfield and Richard Wilmot, competed for the first-team place. Previously with LutonTown, Harlow Town and Barton Rovers.

WEBB, NIGEL — *Forward*
Current Club: Carshalton Athletic
D o B: 22/07/1973   Birthplace: Surrey
Prolific striker who has mainly plied his trade in the lower divisions of the Ryman League, but in recent seasons has proved that he can score goals at Division On level. Signed for Carshalton Athletic in July 2002 from rivals Tooting & Mitcham United, where he had been since the start of the 2000/01 campaign. Formerly with Banstead Athletic, Epsom, Leathrhead, Yeading and Whyteleafe.

WEBB, TOM — *Midfielder*
Current Club: Gloucester City
Birthplace: Gloucestershire
Creative midfield player who linked up with City's youth set-up having been released from schoolboy forms with Luton Town. Having done well in the Midland Floodlit Youth League he became one of three players from the u-18s to sign DML registration forms in February 2001. Began to break into the first team in April 2001 and can expect to be a regular squad player again in the 2001/2 season. Will need to be used sparingly but has shown real touches of class that suggest a great deal of promise for the years to come.

WEBB, TONY — *Goalkeeper*
Current Club: Tooting & Mitcham United
Birthplace: Surrey
Previous clubs include: Croydon Ath - July 2000, Aveley, Yeading, Leatherhead, Banstead Ath., Leatherhead, Eposm & Ewell, Banstead Ath.

WEBBER, DAMIAN — *Defender*
Current Club: Worthing
D o B: 08/10/1968   Birthplace: Rustington
Defender: former Millwall professional who originally played for Worthing some 12 years ago: other previous clubs include Brighton & Hove Albion, Bognor Regis and Crawley before returning to Woodside Road in October 1999: released during the autumn 2001.

WEBBER, DAMIEN — *Defender*
Current Club: Burgess Hill Town
Defender: former Millwall professional who played for Worthing some 12 years ago: other previous clubs include Brighton & Hove Albion, Bognor Regis and Crawley before returning to Woodside Road in October 1999: left the club midway through 2001/02 and re-surfaced at Southwick during the closing stages of the campaign: signed for Burgess Hill Town in the 2002/2003 close season as a Player and as Assistant Manager.

WEBSTER, AARON — *Midfielder*
Current Club: Burton Albion
Birthplace: Burton
Honours won: England Semi-Pro Int., UniBond League Premier Div.Winners
Aarons natural skill and talent has really blossomed under Nigel Cloughs tutorship at Burton Albion. He progressed through youth and reserve football and the left-sided midfielder has attracted many football league scouts to Eton Park. His coolness under pressure was demonstrated last season with a series of crucial goals from the penalty spot. Aaron is the clubs dead ball expert and his free kicks and corners have created many problems for opposing defences. Won his first England semi-professional international caps during the UniBond Four Nations tournament in May 2002.

WEBSTER, ADAM — *Forward*
Current Club: Worcester City
D o B: 03/07/1980   Birthplace: Leicester
A December 2001 £August 20000 signing for Worcester City from Dr Martens Western Division outfit Bedworth United, Adam is a very highly-rated forward who began his career at Notts County before joining the Greenbacks two seasons ago.

WEBSTER, ADRIAN — *Midfielder*
Current Club: Maidstone United
Birthplace: Australia
Previous clubs include: Ashford T - July 2001, Folkestone Invicta, Ashford T, Charlton Ath.

WEBSTER, COLIN — *Defender*
Current Club: Colwyn Bay
Birthplace: Wales
Previous clubs include: Rhyl - August 2002, Total Network Solutions, Newtown.

WEBSTER, CRAIG — *Defender*
Current Club: Maidenhead United
D o B: 04/12/1979   Birthplace: Taplow
From Youth team.

WEBSTER, DANNY — *Defender*
Current Club: Hyde United
Birthplace: Liverpool
Young central defender signed by UniBond Premier side Hyde United from rivals Vauxhall Motors in August 2002. Had come up through the ranks at Rivacre Road to become a regular in their first-team squad.

WEBSTER, IAN — Defender

Current Club: Warrington Town

Birthplace: Warrington

Previous clubs include: Tetley Walker - July 2001.

WEEDON, MARK — Defender

Current Club: Uxbridge

D o B: 14/02/1978   Birthplace: Middlesex

Mark is a stylish but powerful central defender who signed for Uxbridge in August 1997 from Wealdstone. Previously with Nationwide League neighbours Brentford, he has also appeared for Harrow Borough and Watford. Mark has made almost 200 appearances.

WEEKS-PEARSON, JON — Midfielder

Current Club: Abingdon Town

Birthplace: Oxford

Previous clubs include: Quarry Nomads - August 2001, Thame Utd, Oxford C, Burnham, Oxford C.

WEIR, MARTIN — Defender

Current Club: Worcester City

D o B: 04/07/1968   Birthplace: Birmingham

Honours won: Conference Winners, FA XI, Middx Wanderers

Previous clubs include: Kidderminster Harriers - September 1999, Birmingham C.

WEIR, TONY — Midfielder

Current Club: Guisborough Town

From Local footbvall - July 2001.

WELCH, BRIAN — Forward

Current Club: Lancaster City

D o B: 17/07/1973   Birthplace: South Shields

Gained national fame through being a centrefold in the Non-League Magazine, Brian is a striker who typifies the word bustling. He signed for Lancaster City in August 2000 from Clitheroe and had a successful first season. Good at holding the play up as well as finishing, he combines football with his job as a fireman. Hails from the north-east and numbers Hebburn, Burnley, Barrow, Accrington Stanley, Droyslden and Netherfield amongst his former clubs.

WELCH, DANNY — Midfielder

Current Club: Glapwell

Birthplace: Chesterfield

Previous clubs include: Alfreton T - August 2001, Glapwell, Matlock T, Staveley MW.

WELLS, CARL — Midfielder

Current Club: Tunbridge Wells

Birthplace: Kent

From Local football - July 1996.

WELLS, COLIN — Defender

Current Club: Racing Club Warwick

Birthplace: Stratford

Solid and reliable defender who joined Racing Club Warwick from Midland Alliance side Stratford Town in July 1999. Had two spells with Stratford with time at Sutton Coldfield Town sandwiched between.

WELLS, DAVID — Midfielder

Current Club: Billingham Synthonia

D o B: 19/02/1981   Birthplace: Cleveland

Previous clubs include: Whitby T - July 2001, Spennymoor Utd, Bishop Auckland, Darlington.

WELLS, MICKEY — Defender

Current Club: Ramsgate

Birthplace: Kent

Previous clubs include: Sheppey Utd - July 2000, Chatham T, Margate, Tonbridge, Sittingbourne, Canterbury C, Folkestone, Chatham T, Maidstone Utd.

WELLS, TONY — Goalkeeper

Current Club: Uxbridge

Previous clubs include: Chertsey T - July 2001, Staines T, Leighton T, Hendon, Walton & Hersham, Windsor & Eton, Staines T.

WELSBY, KEVIN — Goalkeeper

Current Club: Southport

D o B: 10/07/1979   Birthplace: Crewe

A talented goalkeeper who signed for Conference side Southport in July 2002 from UniBond First Division Leek Town. Had joined Leek in August 2001 following his release by Crewe Alexandra. Had a short spell on loan at Leek during the 2000/01 season.

WELSH, DANIEL — Defender

Current Club: Thame United

Birthplace: Oxfordshire

Dan was still a member of Thame United's successful youth side in 2001/02 but has already gained considerable experience at first-team level. A talented left-sided defender who should develop into a good all round player.

WELSH, STEVE — Defender

Current Club: Lincoln United

D o B: 19/04/1968   Birthplace: Glasgow

Steve is a vastly experienced central defender who has over 300 Scottish and Football League games under his belt. Joined UniBond First Division side Lincoln United in the summer of 2002 as player-coach after a season at Kings Lynn. Lynn beat several Conference clubs, including Nuneaton Borough and Telford United for his signature from Lincoln City in July 2001. Formerly with Cambridge United, Preston, Partick, Peterborough, Dunfermline and Ayr.

WELTON, NICK — Forward

Current Club: Vauxhall Motors

D o B: 10/09/1975   Birthplace: Wirral

Tall and powerful attacker who re-joined UniBond Premier side Vauxhall Motors from League of Wales outfit Rhyl in July 2002. Had spent a couple of seasons in the LoW with TNS and Rhyl after beginning at Ashville prior to his first stint at Motors.

WELTON, SCOTT — Midfielder

Current Club: Hadleigh United

Birthplace: Suffolk

Forced his way into the reckoning for a First Team spot after excellent pre-season performances - having not had even a competitive Reserve team game under his belt. Terrier-like midfielder, with legs and lungs that never seem to tire. Good vision and passing ability. Progressed through the Hadleigh youth set up.

WENLOCK, STEVE — Defender
Current Club: Grantham Town

D o B: 11/03/1978   *Birthplace: Peterborough*
Former Leicester City trainee who had a couple of years as a professional before being released at the end of the 1998/99 season. The talented defender then joined Cambridge City where he enjoyed three good seasons before switching to Grantham Town in May 2002.

WEST, MARK — Forward
Current Club: Thame United

D o B: 12/02/1966   *Birthplace: Wycombe*
Honours won: England Semi-Pro & England Schoolboy Int., Conference Winners, FA Trophy Winners, Isthmian League Premier Div.Winners
Joined Thame United from Farnborough Town in September 1999. Mark has gained vast experience at Conference level with Wycombe Wanderers and Slough Town and has represented England at both Schoolboy and Non-League internatioanl level. Has a proven goalscoring record including the Wembley winner in the Trophy Final for Wycombe.

WEST, MARTIN — Defender
Current Club: Ashford Town

Previous clubs include: Ramsgate - July 2001.

WEST, NEIL — Defender
Current Club: Eastwood Town

Previous clubs include: Welbeck Welfare - July 2001.

WEST, NICK — Defender
Current Club: Arundel

Birthplace: Sussex
Big centre-half: left East Preston to join Littlehampton in October 1998, before returning to The Lashmar during the 2000 close season. Had a particularly bad month during January - sent off in the match against Redhill and a week later scored the winning own goal in the 3-2 defeat at Saltdean: signed for Arundel (one of his old clubs) during the autumn 2001.

WEST, PAUL — Defender
Current Club: Taunton Town

D o B: 20/10/1970   *Birthplace: Taunton*
Honours won: FA Vase Winners
Taunton Town's club captain and a product of the clubs youth policy having played in the Western League since he was sixteen years of age. Apart from short spells away with the likes of Weston-Super- Mare, Elmore and Wellington to gain experience, Paul has remained loyal to the club and is worshipped by the fans. Strong, pacy defender who played in both of Tauntons FA Vase Final teams.

WEST, PAUL — Defender
Current Club: Redditch United

D o B: 22/06/1970   *Birthplace: Birmingham*
Previous clubs include: Evesham Utd - September 2001, Bradford PA, Morecambe, Wigan Ath., Bradford C, Port Vale, Alcester T.

WEST, SIMON — Midfielder
Current Club: Willenhall Town

Birthplace: Birmimgham
Former WBA apprentice who has spent five years playing for Ashland University in America before joining Willenhall in 2001/2002.

WEST, STEVE — Defender
Current Club: Dagenham & Redbridge

D o B: 15/11/1972   *Birthplace: Essex*
Honours won: England Semi-Pro Int.
Steve arrived at Victoria Road from Woking on a two-year contract in February 2002. He joined the Cards as a powerful centre-forward, for a club record fee of £35,000 from Enfield in September 1997 where he had been the leading scorer. Prior to that he was playing junior league football in Essex. Woking converted him into a commanding defender and team captain where he won their player of the year award. He made his England semi-professional international debut against Wales last season.

WEST, STEVE — Defender
Current Club: Bishop Auckland

Birthplace: Bishop Auckland
Re-signed for Bishop Auckland from neighbours West Auckland Town at the start of the 2001/02 season. A long-serving player with Bishops until his release in the late 90s. At his best a very capable defender at this standard.

WESTCOTT, JOHN — Forward
Current Club: Eastbourne Borough

D o B; 31/05/1979   *Birthplace: Eastbourne*
Initially joined on loan from Sutton United during the 2000/01 season and later made his move permanent. Began his career with Brighton and Hove Albion (over 40 appearances), and also had a loan spell with Newport IOW.

WESTCOTT, MARTIN — Forward
Current Club: Mildenhall Town

Birthplace: Cambridgeshire
Previous clubs include: Chatteris T - August 2001, Ely C, Royston T.

WESTHEAD, MARK — Goalkeeper
Current Club: Stevenage Borough

D o B: 19/07/1975   *Birthplace: Blackpool*
Experienced and highly-rated goalkeeper who began his playing days in the North West Counties League with Blackpool Mechanics. Was signed by Bolton in 1996 but didnt make the senior side and, after short spells with Telford United and Kidderminster in the Conference, joined Wycombe where he finally made his League debut. Signed for Leigh RMI at the start of the 2001/02 season and made the first-team place his own. Was snapped up by Stevenage Borough in May 2002.

WESTON, ADAM — Forward
Current Club: Kings Lynn

Birthplace: Lincolnshire
Previous clubs include: Wisbech T - June 2002, Spalding Utd.

WESTON, CRAIG — Midfielder
Current Club: Leek Town

D o B: 04/09/1969   *Birthplace: Burton*
Joined Leek Town during the close season of 2002 from Belper Town. He managed the Derbyshire outfit in a caretaker capacity from January 2002 and steered them clear of the relegation zone but was replaced at the end of the campaign. Appeared in an FA Vase Final whilst with Gresley Rovers and has also played for Alfreton Town, Burton Albion and Grantham.

WESTON, LEE — Midfielder
Current Club: Worthing

Birthplace: Sussex
Midfielder, who graduated through the reserve team in 1999: had short spells on-loan at Wick during both 2000/01 and 2001/02.

WESTON, PETER — *Midfielder*
Current Club: Chorley
D o B: 13/02/1974   Birthplace: Cheshire
Well-travelled attacking midfielder who re-joined manager Mark Molyneux at UniBond First Division side Chorley from rivals Trafford in July 2002. Started out at Derby and Crewe and has also seen service with Leek Town, Fleetwood Town, Buxton, Bamber Bridge, Caernarfon Town, Knypersley Victoria, Newcastle Town and Congleton, returning to Trafford for a second time in August 2001.

WESTON, TOM — *Midfielder*
Current Club: Banstead Athletic
Birthplace: Surrey
Previous clubs include: Crystal Palace - August 2002.

WESTWOOD, JAY — *Defender*
Current Club: Ashford Town
Highly-promising defender or midfielder. Young player who signed for Dr Martens Eastern side Ashford Town from Kent Leaguers Greenwich Borough in January 2001.

WESTWOOD, LEE — *Defender*
Current Club: Mickleover Sports
Birthplace: Derby
Previous clubs include: Gresley Rovers - February 2002, Bamber Bridge, Crewe Alexandra.

WESTWOOD, SCOTT — *Midfielder*
Current Club: Stalybridge Celtic
Birthplace: Sheffield
Started with Sheffield United reserves, but most recently played for Leigh RMI. Midfielder with bags of talent and commitment who joined UniBond Premier side Stalybridge Celtic in July 2002.

WETHERLEY, ANDY — *Midfielder*
Current Club: Ramsgate
Birthplace: Kent
From Youth team.

WEYMAN, DARREN — *Defender*
Current Club: Cinderford Town
Birthplace: Gloucester
Highly-promising young defender who is a former youth team captain of Cinderford Town. Played local football with Lydbrook Athletic during the 2000/01 season, but was a first-team regular upon his return to Cinderford.

WHALLEY, DAVE — *Midfielder*
Current Club: Portland United
Birthplace: Weymouth
Previous clubs include: Bridport - July 2001, Weymouth, Wimborne T, Dorchester T, Weymouth, WBA (Trainee).

WHALLEY, NEIL — *Midfielder*
Current Club: Runcorn FC Halton
D o B: 29/10/1965   Birthplace: Liverpool
Neil is one of the most commanding defenders in the team when he plays, and must win half of the headers he goes for during a game thanks to his frightening Whalleeeeeessssss shout when the ball is coming down. Neil is also Runcorns assistant manager alongside Liam Watson, and the experience gained during his time at Preston North End - where he was captain on 75 occasions - is now showing.

WHALLEY, PAUL — *Defender*
Current Club: Great Harwood Town
Birthplace: Lancashire
Previous clubs include: Clitheroe - July 2001, Accrington Stanley, Clitheroe, Great Harwood T, Accrington Stanley, Great Harwood T, Bacup Borough, Rossendale Utd, Bacup Borough.

WHALLEY, RUSSELL — *Defender*
Current Club: Great Harwood Town
Birthplace: Lancashire
Previous clubs include: Accrington Stanley - July 1999, Clitheroe, Accrington Stanley, Bacup Borough, Great Harwood T, Bury.

WHARTON, GARETH — *Defender*
Current Club: Llanelli AFC
Birthplace: Wales
Previous clubs include: Rhayader T - July 2001.

WHARTON, JOHN — *Defender*
Current Club: Workington
Previous clubs include: Penrith - January 2001, Gillford Park.

WHARTON, NATHAN — *Midfielder*
Current Club: Stalybridge Celtic
Birthplace: Manchester
Nathan started playing for the Oldham Youth team, being one of the few that actually progressed into the senior side. After an injury hit season, the change of management decided to cut back on the wage bill, and released him. A midfield player, who is quite adept up front, he had trials for Burnley, but instead went onto Manchester City to play in the reserves during 1998. At the end of 1999, Nathan joined Radcliffe Borough.

WHARTON, PAUL — *Midfielder*
Current Club: Ossett Town
D o B: 26/06/1977   Birthplace: Newcastle
Midfielder Paul was a trainee at Leeds United, and then spent two seasons at Hull City. Signed initially for Bradford Park Avenue on loan from Farsley Celtic towards the end of the 2000/01 season, and was a key member of the UniBond League Division One championship-winning side. Signed permanently for Bradford Park Avenue in August 2001 and then moved onto First Division Ossett Town exactly a year later.

WHARTON, SEAN — *Forward*
Current Club: Cwmbran Town
D o B: 31/10/1968   Birthplace: Newport
Previous clubs include: Weston-Super-Mare - July 2001, Inter Cardiff, Cwmbran T, Sunderland.

WHATLING, ADRIAN — *Midfielder*
Current Club: Stowmarket Town
Birthplace: Essex
Previous clubs include: Woodbridge T - March 2001, Framlingham T.

WHEALING, TONY — *Defender*
Current Club: Radcliffe Borough
D o B: 03/09/1976   Birthplace: Manchester
A former trainee at Blackburn Rovers who appeared for them in the European Champions League, Tony is a classy defender who joined Radcliffe Borough from Leigh RMI in August 1999. A dead-ball specialist who has scored many important goals.

WHEELER, ADAM — Goalkeeper
Current Club: Aylesbury United
D o B: 29/11/1977   *Birthplace: Sheffield*
Previous clubs include: Baldock T - July 2001, Stocksbridge Park Steels, Hong Kong Rangers (Hong Kong), Doncaster R, Newcastle Utd.

WHEELER, PAUL — Defender
Current Club: Woodley Sports
D o B: 03/01/1965   *Birthplace: Caerphilly*
Previous clubs include: Winsford Utd - December 1999, Leigh RMI, Stalybridge Celtic, Chester C, Stockport Co., Hereford Utd, Hull C, Cardiff C, Aberaman, Bristol R.

WHEELER, PAUL — Midfielder
Current Club: Great Wakering Rovers
Birthplace: Essex
Previous clubs include: Burnham Ramblers - July 1998, Stambridge.

WHEELER, PAUL — Midfielder
Current Club: Kingsbury Town
Birthplace: London
Previous clubs include: Brook House - August 2001.

WHELAN, CHRIS — Defender
Current Club: Walton & Hersham
Birthplace: Wales
Honours won: British Universities Rep., Welsh Cup Winners
Chris won Welsh Cup winners medals with Llansantffraid, for whom he also played in the European Cup Winners Cup, and his last club, Bangor City. He has also represented British Universities, playing in the World Student Games in Sicily in 1997. Joined Swans at the beginning of 1998-99 and was voted Player of the Year by both supporters and players at the end of that season. Club skipper who has now played well over 100 appearances for Swans.

WHELAN, DANNY — Midfielder
Current Club: Dartford
D o B: 24/06/1977   *Birthplace: Cheltenham*
Honours won: English Universities Rep.
Highly-rated midfield player who joined Dr Martens Eastern side Dartford in July 2002 from Kent League neighbours VCD Athletic. Started his career as a junior with Oxford United before enjoying a soccer scholarship in America at California State University, returning to England to sign for VCD in the summer of 1999.

WHELAN, GARY — Defender
Current Club: Banstead Athletic
Birthplace: London
Previous clubs include: Croydon Ath - September 2000, Tooting & Mitcham Utd, Banstead Ath., Croydon, Dulwich Hamlet, Malden Vale, Dulwich Hamlet, Sutton Utd, Fulham (Junior).

WHELDON, MARK — Forward
Current Club: Thornaby on Tees
Birthplace: Co.Durham
Previous clubs include: West Auckland T - December 2001, Spennymoor Utd, West Auckland T, Cleveland Bridge, Bishop Auckland, Shildon.

WHELLANS, ROBBIE — Forward
Current Club: Harrogate Town
D o B: 14/02/1969   *Birthplace: Harrogate*
Honours won: UniBond Div.One Winners
Prolific goalscorer at Non-League level, Robbie began his career at Bradford City before signing for Harrogate Town. He then moved to Frickley Athletic, Harrogate Railway and then Farsley Celtic, where he made almost 400 appearances and scoring almost 200 goals for the club. He then re-joined Harrogate via a spell at Guiseley and another at Farsley in the summer of 2001. Robbie has been the UniBond Leagues leading goalscorer on two occasions.

WHITE, BARRY — Forward
Current Club: St Margaretsbury
D o B: 06/03/1973   *Birthplace: Hertford*
Previous clubs include: Hoddesdon T - July 2000, Ware, Cheshunt, St Margaretsbury.

WHITE, CHRIS — Defender
Current Club: Eastleigh
D o B: 11/10/1970   *Birthplace: Portsmouth*
Was one of the longest serving players at Ryman Leaguers Slough Town, having signed from Farnborough Town for a small fee, before switching to Jewson Wessex League side Easleigh as player-coach in April 2002. He made his Slough debut away at Aylesbury that year. Chris is capable of playing in a number of positions. He is a centre back by trade and that is where he prefers to play, but he is also been used in a right back role, which is the position he started his career playing and a central midfield role for the club as he did to good effect sometimes last season. White started his career at Portsmouth where he failed to break into the first team and moved on. He then made many appearances for Exeter, before signing for Yeovil Town where he spent most of his career. Last year Whites season was hampered by injuries and did not make many starts for the Rebels, but this year he hopes to make himself a permanent fixture in the Slough side. This year is set to be Chris last season at the club before retiring at the end of the season.

WHITE, CHRIS — Forward
Current Club: Gresley Rovers
D o B: 08/04/1981   *Birthplace: Leicester*
Highly-promising young striker who was a junior at Leicester City before joining Hinckley United. Failed to gain a regular place with United and moved to Gresley Rovers in December 2001 where, under the guidance of former boss John McGinlay, he blossomed and scored a number of important goals.

WHITE, CHRIS — Midfielder
Current Club: Leek Town
Birthplace: Nottingham
Experienced midfielder who joined Leek Town in July 2002 from Lincoln United where he was skipper for the 2001/02 season. Played in the Football League with Peterborough United, he has also been on the books at Farnborough Town, Yeovil, Hucknall Town, Hinckley Utd, Long Eaton, Ashfield United, Oakham United, Arnold Town and GPT Plessey.

WHITE, DALE — Midfielder
Current Club: Shildon
Birthplace: Billingham
Previous clubs include: Billingham T - October 1997.

WHITE, DANNY — Defender

Current Club: Ashton United

Birthplace: Buxton

Talented young defender who was signed by Ashton United from Northern Counties East League side Buxton in the summer of 2002 upon their promotion to the UniBond Premier Division. Came up through Buxtons youth and reserve ranks to become recognised as one of the most promising young back four players in the NCEL.

WHITE, DANNY — Midfielder

Current Club: Diss Town

Birthplace: Norwich

Previous clubs include: Cambridge Utd (Trainee) - July 2000.

WHITE, JAMIE — Midfielder

Current Club: Corinthian Casuals

Birthplace: Surrey

Jamie is a talented midfielder who signed for Corinthian Casuals from Banstead Athletic in July 1998. Enjoyed his new free role during 2001/02 which saw him hit double figures in goals.

WHITE, JASON — Goalkeeper

Current Club: East Thurrock United

D o B: 05/05/1966 Birthplace: Nottingham
Honours won: Combined Services Rep.

Previous clubs include: Barking & East Ham Utd - November 2001, Leyton Pennant, Romford, Aveley, Bishops Stortford, Enfield, Romford, Portsmouth RN, Worthing, Portsmouth RN.

WHITE, JON — Midfielder

Current Club: Gorleston

Birthplace: Norfolk

Previous clubs include: Great Yarmouth T - December 1998.

WHITE, KARL — Defender

Current Club: Peterlee Newtown

Birthplace: Co.Durham

Previous clubs include: Shotton Comrades - August 2000.

WHITE, KEIRON — Defender

Current Club: Frome Town

D o B: 21/01/1978 Birthplace: Somerset
Previous clubs include: Wells C - July 2001, Street.

WHITE, LEE — Defender

Current Club: Hertford Town

Birthplace: London

Defender Lee joined Ryman Division One Noth side Hertford Town in January 2002 from Yeading and made a very promising start. However, he then got badly injured in a holiday accident. Now fully fit and captaining the side at only 21 years old. Originally with Leyton Orient, he has also had a stint at Chesham United.

WHITE, LEIGH — Midfielder

Current Club: Swindon Supermarine

D o B: 09/08/1976 Birthplace: Bristol
Signed for Swindon Supermarine in July 2002 from fellow Dr Martens Western side Weston-super-mare. Had joined Weston from Cheltenham Town during the 95/96 season. Was previously a member of Bristol City youth team and has captained his county youth representative side.

WHITE, LEON — Defender

Current Club: Chesham United

Birthplace: London

Leon is a good all round footballer who has played for Kingstonian, Wimbledon and Sutton United and signed for Ryman Premier side Chesham United in August 2002. He is a claims handler for an insurance company.

WHITE, MARTIN — Goalkeeper

Current Club: Witton Albion

Birthplace: Manchester

Previous clubs include: Flixton - January 2002, Curzon Ashton, Mossley, Cheadle Heath Nomads, Flixton, Curzon Ashton, Stalybridge Celtic, Ashton Utd, Mossley, Accrington Stanley, Hyde Utd, Manchester C (Trainee).

WHITE, MICHAEL — Defender

Current Club: Dorchester Town

Birthplace: Dorset

Previous clubs include: Wimborne T - August 2000.

WHITE, REECE — Midfielder

Current Club: Egham Town

D o B: 21/12/1980 Birthplace: Surrey
Midfielder who spent a year at Aldershot Town as a youth then spent two seasons at Woking, playing several games in the Conference. Played for Surrey at County Youth level. Joined Windsor & Eton in August 2000 and then made the switch to neighbours at Ryman Division One South rivals Egham Town in August 2002.

WHITE, ROCKY — Forward

Current Club: Eastwood Town

Previous clubs include: Staveley Miners Welfare - July 2001, Chesterfield.

WHITE, ROSS — Midfielder

Current Club: Cheshunt

Birthplace: Herts

Previous clubs include: Grays Ath - August 2002, Cheshunt, Chesham Utd, Barnet.

WHITE, STEVE — Forward

Current Club: Erith & Belvedere

Birthplace: Kent

Joined Erith & Belvedere from Bromley in 1999. A very quick and sharp striker who finished the 1999/2000 and 2000/2001 seasons as the Deres leading goalscorer.

WHITE, STUART — Forward

Current Club: Dorking

Birthplace: Reading

Previous clubs include: Peppard - July 1998.

WHITE, STUART — Midfielder

Current Club: Ashford Town

D o B: 30/11/1963 Birthplace: Ashford
Now at the veteran stage of his playing career, Stuart is a former Ashford Town favourite who left with manager Neil Cugley for Folkestone Invicta but then returned in September 2001after two years away. Vastly experienced midfielder who spent a number of years with Welling United and has also seen service with Charlton, Gillingham and Brighton.

WHITE, TOM — Defender

Current Club: Yeovil Town

D o B: 26/01/1976   Birthplace: Bristol

Honours won: FA Trophy Winners

central defender who joined Yeovil Town at the start of the 2000/01 season from Bristol Rovers, where he made over 50 League appearances. Had previous Conference experience on loan at Hereford United.

WHITE, TONY — Defender

Current Club: Wimborne Town

D o B: 03/11/1966   Birthplace: Bournemouth

Previous clubs include: Newport IOW - July 2001, Havant T, Dorchester T, AFC Bournemouth, Dorchester T.

WHITEHALL, STEVE — Forward

Current Club: Southport

D o B: 08/12/1966   Birthplace: Bromborough

Previous clubs include: Nuneaton Borough - October 2001, Chester C, Oldham Ath, Mansfield, Rochdale, Southport.

WHITEHEAD, DAMIEN — Forward

Current Club: Leigh RMI

D o B: 24/04/1979   Birthplace: Whiston

Damien is a striker who joined Conference side Leigh RMI in June 2002 after being released by Macclesfield. Was signed by the Silkmen in the summer of 1999 from Warrington Town after a prolific run in Non-League football. Damien had a tremendous scoring record whilst at Warrington Town - 58 goals in 43 starts. In the season 1999/00 Damien broke into the Macclesfield side, scoring 6 goals in 7 games.

WHITEHEAD, JAMES — Defender

Current Club: Ilkeston Town

Birthplace: Nottingham

James joined Ilkeston in 1996 starting at youth level before being the captain of the successfull reserve team and gained a first team place under Ex-manager Chris Marples. James can play anywhere along the back four or midfield and is an excellent crosser of the ball.

WHITEHEAD, KEVIN — Goalkeeper

Current Club: Witton Albion

Birthplace: Manchester

Previous clubs include: Manchester C - August 2001.

WHITEHEAD, LINDEN — Midfielder

Current Club: Worksop Town

Previous clubs include: Alfreton T - July 1992, Worksop T.

WHITEHEAD, MATTHEW — Midfielder

Current Club: Oxford City

Previous clubs include: Abingdon T - July 1998, Reading (Junior), Oxford Utd (Junior).

WHITEHEAD, SHAUN — Forward

Current Club: Chorley

D o B: 15/10/1981   Birthplace: Salford

Highly-promising young striker who re-joined manager Mark Molyneux at UniBond First Division side Chorley from rivals Trafford in July 2002. Started out as a trainee with Oldham and then drifted into local football with The Willows before joining Trafford in September 2000. Soon rediscovered the form that made him so highly-rated as a junior and Molyneux was quick to take him to Chorley shortly after taking over.

WHITEHOUSE, ADAM — Midfielder

Current Club: Sutton Coldfield Town

D o B: 19/11/1968   Birthplace: Birmingham

Previous clubs include: Paget Rangers - June 2000, Bilston T, Sutton Coldfield T, Tamworth, Hednesford T, Tamworth, Sutton Coldfield T, Bilston T, Sutton Coldfield T.

WHITEHOUSE, CHRIS — Defender

Current Club: Erith & Belvedere

Birthplace: Kent

Signed for Erith & Belvedere in August 1999 from Gravesend & Northfleet. A promising young defender.

WHITEHOUSE, JOHN — Goalkeeper

Current Club: Ashford Town

Goalkeeper who signed for Dr Martens Eastern side Ashford Town from Kent Leaguers Greenwich Borough in the summer of 2001. A very confident and strong shot stopper who has also served Corinthian, Fisher Athletic and Erith & Belvedere.

WHITEHOUSE, TOM — Midfielder

Current Club: Oxford City

Previous clubs include: Oxford Utd (Junior) - July 2000.

WHITELEY, MARK — Defender

Current Club: Ossett Albion

Birthplace: Huddersfield

Previous clubs include: Bradley Rangers - July 1993.

WHITEMAN, MARC — Midfielder

Current Club: Altrincham

D o B: 01/10/1982   Birthplace: St.Hellier, Jersey

Previous clubs include: Bury - March 2002, Manchester Utd.

WHITMAN, TRISTAM — Forward

Current Club: Doncaster Rovers

Birthplace: Nottingham

A February 2000, £10,000 signing from Northern Counties East League side Arnold Town. Tristam is a very promising young striker who progressed through the Nottinghamshire clubs youth and reserve team ranks to become a first-team regular. Became a regular goalscorer which attracted a number of scouts, eventually chosing Rovers ahead of a number of other offers.

WHITMORE, CRAIG — Midfielder

Current Club: Bedworth United

Birthplace: Coventry

Bedworth United's player of the season for 2001/02, Craig is 100% committed and played every gameof that season. Solid, tough-tackling midfielder who can play either on the left side but prefers to slot in the hole in the middle of the park. Signed for the Greenbacks from Nuneaton Griff in September 2000.

WHITTAKER, ANDY — Forward

Current Club: Lancaster City

D o B: 29/01/1968   Birthplace: Preston

First came to Lancaster City's attention in 1992, when as a striker with then North West Counties League Bamber Bridge he scored a hat-trick against them in a friendly. The clubs manager at the time didnt rate him however, and Andy went off to Netherfield, then Ashton United, Barrow, Southport and Bamber Bridge again, scoring goals for virtually all of them, and often being transferred for four-figure fees. Finally joined City in the summer of 2001, and scored a bucketful of goals, even though he missed a good chunk of the season through injury and suspension.

WHITTAKER, DAVE — Forward
Current Club: Leek Town

D o B: 13/08/1978   Birthplace: Stockport
Former Crewe Alexandra striker who originally moved to Leek Town in July 1999. Became a regular at Harrison Park and was the clubs leading goalscorer for 2001/02 with 17 goals before switching to Gresley Rovers in February 02. Returned to Leek just over a month later. Is something of an expert from the penalty spot.

WHITTAKER, STUART — Forward
Current Club: Chester City

D o B: 02/01/1975   Birthplace: Liverpool
Stuart is a left winger who has had a successful spell with Macclesfield. This Liverpool born 27-year-old started his career with Liverpool Juniors from where he joined Bolton. He them moved on to Wigan before his spell with the Silkmen. Transferred from Southport to Chester in january 2002.

WHITTAMORE, MARK — Goalkeeper
Current Club; Enfield

Birthplace: Stevenage
Promising goalkeeper who re-joined Ryman Premier side Enfield in July 2002 after a spell with Hemel Hempstead Town. Had signed for Hemel in November 2001 from the Es after previously seeing service with Stevenage Borough and Edgware Town.

WHITTINGHAM, GUY — Forward
Current Club: Newport Isle Of Wight

D o B: 10/11/1964   Birthplace: Evesham
Previous clubs include: Wycombe Wanderers - August 2001, Portsmouth, Sheffield Wednesday, Aston Villa, Portsmouth, Yeovil T, Army.

WHITTINGTON, RICHARD — Goalkeeper
Current Club: Southwick

Birthplace: Sussex
Experienced goalkeeper previously played for Shoreham and Mile Oak: made over 150 appearances for Lancing until returning to Southwick during the summer 2001.

WHITTINGTON, TREVOR — Defender
Current Club: Studley

D o B: 20/06/1968   Birthplace: Worcestershire
Previous clubs include: Evesham Utd - July 2000, Redditch Utd, Worcester C, Redditch Utd, Solihull B, Evesham Utd, Telford Utd, Redditch Utd, Northfield T.

WHITTLE, CLAYTON — Forward
Current Club: Egham Town

Birthplace: Surrey
Previous clubs include: Netherne - September 1998.

WHITTON, STEVE — Midfielder
Current Club: Lordswood

Birthplace: Kent
Previous clubs include: Chatham T - July 2001.

WHYTE, ANDY — Defender
Current Club: Metropolitan Police

Birthplace: Lincoln
Previous clubs include: Lincoln Utd - July 1999.

WICKENS, ADAM — Defender
Current Club: Metropolitan Police

Birthplace: Middlesex
Previous clubs include: Southall - July 1995, Chertsey T, Windsor & Eton, Chertsey T, Yeading, Uxbridge, Hounslow.

WICKETTS, DALE — Defender
Current Club: Whitstable Town

Birthplace: Kent
Previous clubs include: Sheppey Utd - July 2000, Gillingham (Junior).

WICKHAM, JUSTIN — Forward
Current Club: Newtown AFC

D o B: 21/11/1975   Birthplace: Shropshire
Previous clubs include: Ludlow T - July 1996.

WIETECHA, DAVE — Goalkeeper
Current Club: Folkestone Invicta

D o B: 01/11/1974   Birthplace: Colchester
Big goalkeeper who joined Folkestone Invicta from Bromley during the 1998/99 season and has now made well over 150 appearances for the club. He had joined Bromley from Millwall, where he spent four years, during which he had loan spells at both Crewe Alexandra and Rotherham United. Spent the summer of 2001 playing for Manawatu in New Zealand.

WIGG, NATHAN — Midfielder
Current Club: Cwmbran Town

D o B: 27/09/1974   Birthplace: Newport
Previous clubs include: Gloucester C - July 2000, Forest Green R, Dundalk, Cardiff C.

WIGGS, ROBERT — Defender
Current Club: Leyton

D o B: 07/06/1974   Birthplace: Essex
Defender who joined Leyton in the summer of 2000 and helped them to gain promotion to the Ryman League in 2001/02. Joined from Ilford and has also seen service with Hornchurch, Saffron Walden Town and Tilbury.

WIGLEY, RUSSELL — Midfielder
Current Club: Port Talbot Town

D o B: 09/01/1972   Birthplace: Cardiff
Highly experienced and respected League of Wales campaigner who brings much needed experience to the young Port Talbot Team. A Cardiff based Policeman, Russell is one of the main players in the team due to his intelligent play and strong tackling.

WIGNALL, JACK — Defender
Current Club: Cambridge City

Birthplace: Essex
Signed for Cambridge City at the start of the 2001/02 season from Conference side Dagenham & Redbridge. Son of former Colchester manager Steve Wignall. Jack is a defender who was previously with Colchester United.

WILBY, CRAIG — Midfielder
Current Club: Brigg Town

Birthplace: Hull
From Local football - July 2001.

WILCOX, BRETT — Midfielder
Current Club: Rushall Olympic
D o B: 27/12/1968   Birthplace: Sutton Coldfield
Previous clubs include: Bilston T - January 2002, Bridgnorth T, Bilston T, Blakenall, Bilston T, Bromsgrove R, Stafford R, Bromsgrove R, Telford Utd, Shifnal T, Bridgnorth T, Kidderminster Harriers.

WILDE, ADAM — Midfielder
Current Club: Cambridge City
D o B: 22/05/1979   Birthplace: Southampton
Adam joined Cambridge City during August 1999 after surprisingly being released by neighbours Cambridge United. He made a few first-team appearances for United in the Football League. Several clubs have shown an interest in Adam and the club turned down a five-figure fee for the attacking midfielder during the 2000/01 season.

WILDE, MARK — Forward
Current Club: St.Helens Town
Birthplace: Liverpool
Centre forward who became Town's record signing when he joined from Burscough during the summer. Vastly experienced striker who creates as well as scores goals. Previous clubs include Witton Albion, Marine and Bootle.

WILDER, CHRIS — Defender
Current Club: Halifax Town
D o B: 23/09/1967   Birthplace: Wortley
Honours won: NCEL & Cup Winners
Vastly experienced full back who joined Alfreton Town at the beginning of September 2001 from Halifax Town, where he had sustained a knee injury which ended his League career in a game at Blackpool on Boxing Day 2000. After starting his career as an apprentice at Southampton, he played for several league clubs including Bradford City, Rotherham United and Sheffield United, making a total of 463 Football League appearances. Took on the player-managers role in October 2001 with great success, guiding the team back to the UniBond League and with two cups to boot. Then, in June 2002, Halifax tempted Chris back to The Shay as their new manager.

WILE, JOHN — Defender
Current Club: Llanelli AFC
Birthplace: Cardiff
Previous clubs include: Cwmbran T - September 2001, Haverfordwest Co., Inter Cardiff, Merthyr Tydfil, Inter Cardiff, Ton Pentre, Cardiff C.

WILES, IAN — Defender
Current Club: Chelmsford City
D o B: 24/08/1980   Birthplace: Epping
Versatile defender who moved from Heybridge Swifts to Chelmsford in June 2001. Was with Colchester United during his teenage years and earned a good reputation at City's neighbours following a succession of classy displays.

WILFORD, AARON — Defender
Current Club: Whitby Town
Birthplace: Yorkshire
Aaron signed for UniBond Premier side Whitby Town in March 2002, where he originally played up front but has since found his niche in central defence. Strong but skilful and still only 19, Aaron has a big future in the game.

WILFORT, JOHN — Midfielder
Current Club: Bromley
Birthplace: London
Joined Bromley from Ryman League Second Division outfit Molesey in January 2001. Previous clubs include Charlton Athletic, Carshalton Athletic and Tooting & Mitcham United.

WILKERSON, PAUL — Goalkeeper
Current Club: Gravesend & Northfleet
D o B: 11/12/1974   Birthplace: Hertford
Tall and reliable goalkeeper who joined Conference newcomers Gravesend & Northfleet in August 2002 from rivals Stevenage Borough. Paul had signed for Stevenage in June 2000, after a spell at Welling United. Formerly with Watford, Slough Town and Hayes, he was well-known to Boro fans as he once played a game whilst on-loan to Boro and went on to save a penalty, denying Boro in the quarter-finals of the FA Trophy whilst playing for Slough. At 6'3 he is an imposing figure between the posts.

WILKES, DARYL — Midfielder
Current Club: Stafford Rangers
D o B: 07/10/1979   Birthplace: Newcastle-under-Lyme
A highly-rated midfielder, Daryl joined Stafford Rangers the 2001 close season from Kidsgrove Athletic. Started his playing days with Nantwich Town and had two spells at Kidsgrove with a stint at Leek Town sandwiched between.

WILKES, TIM — Midfielder
Current Club: Hinckley United
D o B: 07/11/1977   Birthplace: Nottingham
Tim joined Hinckley United from Grantham Town in the 2001/02 close season. Started his career as a striker, but moved to midfield while playing for Grantham. He has tended to play between the midfield and strikers for Hinckley. His previous clubs include Notts County, Kettering Town, Telford United and Gainsborough Trinity.

WILKIE, GLEN — Midfielder
Current Club: Enfield
Previous clubs include: Cheshunt - August 2001, IFK Mariehamn (Finland), Cheshunt, Leyton Orient, Tottenham Hotspur (Junior).

WILKIN, KEVIN — Forward
Current Club: Cambridge City
D o B: 01/10/1967   Birthplace: Cambridge
Kevin is in his second spell at Cambridge City. He spent two seasons with the club before being sold to Northampton Town for a then club record fee of £15,000. A serious knee injury restricted his appearances before moving to Rushden & Diamonds and then Nuneaton Borough. He was leading goalscorer for the 2001/02 season.

WILKINS, CHRIS — Forward
Current Club: Pelsall Villa
Birthplace: Birmingham
Previous clubs include: Blakenall - October 2000, Pelsall Villa, Bromsgrove R, Rushall Olympic, Blakenall, Mansfield T.

WILKINS, CRAIG — Defender
Current Club: Gravesend & Northfleet
Birthplace: Kent
Honours won: Ryman League Premier Div.Winners
Craig started his playing career as a striker in Maidstone United's youth team and then in the Kent League for Maidstone Invicta. He joined Tonbridge at the start of the 1995/96 season, scoring goals regularly in the Dr Martens League. He then joined Gravesend during the 1997/98 season and has since converted

to a central defensive role where he has proved highly successful with his pace and aerial power. In recent seasons Craig has won the Supporters and Players' Player of the Year Awards and is a big favourite with Fleet supporters.

WILKINS, DAVID — *Forward*
Current Club: Arnold Town
Birthplace: Nottingham
From Youth team.

WILKINS, IAN — *Defender*
Current Club: Grantham Town
D o B: 03/04/1980 — *Birthplace: Lincoln*
Voted managers player of the year for 2001/02, Ian was a regular choice by the manager in Grantham Town's promotion challenge. Signed from Spalding United in February 2001, the defender was originally on the books at Scunthorpe.

WILKINS, RICHARD — *Midfielder*
Current Club: Bury Town
D o B: 28/05/1965 — *Birthplace: Lambeth*
Previous clubs include: Colchester Utd - July 2000, Hereford Utd, Cambridge Utd, Colchester Utd, Haverhill R.

WILKINS, STEVE — *Forward*
Current Club: Hassocks
Birthplace: Sussex
Young left-winger: has developed into a regular member of the Hassocks side over the last year and scored three times during 2000/01: also part of the Sussex U-21 squad this season.

WILKINSON, ALAN — *Defender*
Current Club: St Margaretsbury
Birthplace: Barnsley
Previous clubs include: Potters Bar T - July 2001, Ware, Hertford T, Baldock T, Boreham Wood, Stevenage B, Boston Utd, Barnsley.

WILKINSON, BOBBY — *Midfielder*
Current Club: Burnham
Birthplace: Berkshire
A midfield player now in his second spell at the club. Last season played for Reading Town and has also played for Thame United.

WILKINSON, DAMIEN — *Midfielder*
Current Club: Mossley
Birthplace: Manchester
Previous clubs include: Abbey Hey - November 2001.

WILKINSON, DARRON — *Midfielder*
Current Club: Slough Town
D o B: 24/11/1969 — *Birthplace: Reading*
Signed on a free transfer from local rivals Woking in the 2000/01 season. Since Darrons signing he has made himself a firm favorite with the fans. He is a very hard working midfield player who gives the opposition no time on the ball at all. He is also a good passer of the football. Made his Slough debut at Home to Croydon and impressed whenever he pulled on a Slough shirt. But injuries forced him to miss a large chunk of the Rebels season and he was sorely missed in the Slough midfield. In the 2000/01 season Darron had to perform as a emergency goalkeeper for the Rebels after Steve Mautone was sent off against Harrow and despite the Rebels losing 1-0, you would not have known Steve was not in goal as Darron played really well. Wilkinsons former clubs include Wokingham where he was managed by Slough secretary Roy Merryweather, before joining Hayes where he was club captain under Terry Brown. He then was snapped up by former Rebels boss Brian McDermott at Woking. If Darron can stay free from injuries in the coming season, he will be a huge asset to the Slough side.

WILKINSON, DAVE — *Midfielder*
Current Club: Gloucester City
Previous clubs include: Brockworth - July 2001.

WILKINSON, JAMES — *Defender*
Current Club: Altrincham
Birthplace: Cheshire
James is a young ex-Macclesfield Town defender, who joined Altrincham in November 2001. Made his first-team debut for the Robins against Spalding in the FA Umbro Trophy replay on 6th November 2001.

WILKINSON, JEFF — *Midfielder*
Current Club: Corinthian Casuals
Birthplace: Surrey
Previous clubs include: Croydon Ath - December 2001, Leatherhead, Croydon Ath., Banstead Ath., Sutton Utd, Chelsea (Trainee).

WILKINSON, JOHN — *Midfielder*
Current Club: Tiverton Town
D o B: 24/08/1979 — *Birthplace: Exeter*
Previous clubs include: Exeter C - December 2001.

WILKINSON, KRAIG — *Forward*
Current Club: Bishop Auckland
Birthplace: Co.Durham
Signed for Tow Law from Billingham Synthonia at the beginning of this season. Previous clubs include Gateshead and was at one stage signed as a professional with Sheffield Wednesday. Returned to play for Billingham Synthonia at the end of last season after recovering from a broken leg earlier that season. Switched to Bishop Auckland in February 2002.

WILKINSON, LEE — *Forward*
Current Club: Trafford
D o B: 05/01/1975 — *Birthplace: Littleborough*
Previous clubs include: Hyde Utd - September 2000, Mossley, Castleton Gabriels, Bury.

WILKINSON, MARK — *Goalkeeper*
Current Club: Frickley Athletic
Birthplace: Sheffield
Previous clubs include: Stocksbridge Park Steels - January 2002, Frickley Ath, Sheffield, Worsbrough Bridge MW, Grimethorpe MW, Worsbrough Bridge MW.

WILKINSON, MATTHEW — *Defender*
Current Club: Frickley Athletic
Previous clubs include: Selby T - August 2000.

WILKINSON, PAUL — *Midfielder*
Current Club: Basingstoke Town
D o B: 22/06/1972 — *Birthplace: Reading*
Honours won: England Schools Rep.
Hard-working and skilled midfielder who signed for Basingstoke Town from Dorchester Town in September 1997. Represented Reading and District Schools and England at under 18 level, was awarded a Scholarship in the USA. Played in the sweeper position during 2001 - a posistion which earned him player of the year. Paul recently won FA XI representative honours and has also played for England Schools. Also played for Bashley, Wokingham Town and Reading, where he was a trainee.

WILKINSON, ROB — Midfielder
Current Club: Oxford City
Birthplace: Oxford
Previous clubs include: Carterton T - July 2001, Quarry Nomads, Oxford C, Northampton T (Trainee).

WILKINSON, STUART — Goalkeeper
Current Club: Eccleshill United
Birthplace: Yorkshire
Previous clubs include: Ossett T - July 1999, Eccleshill Utd, Burnley (Junior).

WILKINSON, TONY — Midfielder
Current Club: Swindon Supermarine
D o B: 07/07/1972   Birthplace: Cirencester
A tireless worker in midfield who always gives 100%. 'Wilko', who returned for a second spell with the club in the summer of 1999. Having suffered a bad ankle injury that plagued him all the previous season he quickly returned to fitness to secure a first team place. Another bout of injuries limited his appearance last season but when fit a great asset to the squad. He will always pop up with the odd goal or two and usually important goals at that.

WILKINSON, TREVOR — Forward
Current Club: Arlesey Town
Birthplace: London
Honours won: Ryman League Div.3 Winners
Trevor is a strong forward who can trouble defences by just being there and has proved to be a good provider and ball winner. A much-travelled player, he has had spells with Tottenham, Enfield, Hendonm Cheshunt, Ware, Harrow Borough, St Albans City and Harlow Town amongst others. He is an Interbranch Driver.

WILLARD, CRAIG — Midfielder
Current Club: Rye & Iden United
Birthplace: Hastings
Assisted St Leonards Stamcrofts climb into the Southern League after joining them from Bexhill in 1994: signed for Langney Sports in 1998 and once again helped a County League side gain promotion when captaining them to a title success in 1999/2000 (also played for Sussex that year): made a few appearances for Sidley Utd early in 2000/01 before returning to St Leonards midway through that campaign: joined Rye at the start of the latest season: has had trials with Watford in his time.

WILLARD, STEVE — Defender
Current Club: Rye & Iden United
Birthplace: Hastings
Defender, known as Sticky (no relation to Craig Willard): one-time trialist with Coventry City: previously with Sidley Utd before spending eleven years at Hastings: joined Eastbourne Borough from St Leonards during 1999: retired from Southern League football in October 2001 and consequently signed for Rye.

WILLCOCK, CHRIS — Forward
Current Club: Rossendale United
Birthplace: Manchester
Well-travelled forward who joined Rossendale United at the start of the 2001/02 season from North West Counties League neighbours Ramsbottom United. Spent the majority of his playing days swapping between the NWCL and UniBond through spells with Flixton, Warrington Town, Curzon Ashton, Netherfield, Leigh RMI, Mossley and Salford City.

WILLETTS, HARVEY — Goalkeeper
Current Club: Redditch United
Birthplace: Birmingham
Honours won: England Youth Int.
Experienced goalkeeper who joined Redditch United from Dr Martens Premier side Tamworth in Match 2001. A former England Youth international who started his career with Leeds, he also had a spell as a professional with Stockport and played in America for Cape Cod Crusaders. Since returning to England he has turned out for Stalybridge Celtic, Cheltenam, Evesham United, Trowbridge Town abd Bloxwich .

WILLGOOSE, MARK — Forward
Current Club: Matlock Town
Previous clubs include: Alfreton T - September 2001, Hallam, Staveley MW, Worksop T, Barnsley (Junior).

WILLGRASS, ALEX — Midfielder
Current Club: Pickering Town
D o B: 08/04/1976   Birthplace: Scarborough
Previous clubs include: Harrogate T - July 2000, Kingstonian, Harrogate T, Gateshead, Bromsgrove R, Scarborough.

WILLIAMS, ALAN — Defender
Current Club: Flexsys Cefn Druids
Birthplace: Wales
Previous clubs include: Ruthin T - July 1996.

WILLIAMS, ANDY — Defender
Current Club: Bath City
D o B: 08/10/1977   Birthplace: Bristol
Honours won: Wales u-21 Int.
Former Welsh Under-21 international, where he played against Brazil in Sao Paolos Maracana Stadium, Andy moved to Bath City from Swindon Town in September 2001. An extremely versatile player capable of playing on either flank from a defensive of attacking position, Bristol-born Andy began his career as a trainee at Premiership side Southampton in 1997. He went on to make over 20 appearances at this level, although mainly from the bench, before a loan spell at Swindon lead to a permanent transfer in October 1999 for the sum of £65,000. Injury restricted his progress at the County Ground, he made around 40 appearances in his two seasons there, and Andy decided to give up full-time football in the summer of 2001 to pursue a career in the police force.

WILLIAMS, ANDY — Defender
Current Club: Thame United
D o B: 26/08/1979   Birthplace: Oxfordshire
Joined Thame United in March 1999 from Witney Town. A central defender who has developed into an integral part of the side. Composed and confident defender with a great future.

WILLIAMS, ASHLEY — Defender
Current Club: Hednesford Town
Birthplace: Birmingham
Teenage defender who has come up through the ranks at Dr Martens Premier side Hednesford Town. Made his first-team debut during the 2001/02 season and looks to have a very bright future.

WILLIAMS, BARRY — Defender
Current Club: Nuneaton Borough
D o B: 06/05/1973   Birthplace: Birmingham
Honours won: England Semi-Pro Int.
A very highly-rated central defender, Barry started his career with Cambridge United (whilst playing for United he also made a few loan appearances from Ely City). After his stay with Cambridge he moved back to the Midlands and enjoyed spells with Alvechurch and Redditch United. Nuneaton Borough signed him from Redditch

United in June 1995 and he has became one of the most reliable players in the team and possibly the fans favourite player.

WILLIAMS, BEN   *Defender*
Current Club: Berkhamsted Town
Birthplace: Luton
Previous clubs include: Southall - December 2000, Tring T, Leighton T.

WILLIAMS, BEN   *Forward*
Current Club: Llanelli AFC
D o B: 28/02/1984   *Birthplace: Wales*
From Youth team.

WILLIAMS, BRETT   *Defender*
Current Club: Arnold Town
D o B: 19/03/1968   *Birthplace: Nottingham*
Previous clubs include: Nottingham Forest - August 1996.

WILLIAMS, CARL   *Midfielder*
Current Club: Bedford Town
D o B: 14/01/1977   *Birthplace: Cambridge*
Highly-rated attacking midfielder who joined Bedford Town in May 2002 after spending almost six years with Hitchin Town. Started his career as a trainee with Queens Park Rangers and then made a handful of League appearances for Fulham before going Non-League with Collier Row, Carshalton Athletic and then the Canaries, whom he joined in October 1996.

WILLIAMS, CRAIG   *Defender*
Current Club: Rhayader Town
Birthplace: Rhayader
Local lad starting his fifth season at the club. Versatile player who last season became a regular in the side. Current first team player of the year.

WILLIAMS, CRAIG   *Forward*
Current Club: Sidlesham
Birthplace: Hampshire
Scored five times for Oving after joining them for Gosport Borough (Wessex League) during the autumn 2001: signed for Sidlesham in January 2002.

WILLIAMS, DANNY   *Midfielder*
Current Club: Stourbridge
D o B: 29/10/1968   *Birthplace: Wolverhampton*
Previous clubs include: Bilston T - December 2001, Worcester C, Stafford R, Bilston T, Blakenall, North Park, Harrisons, Bloxwich T, Wolverhampton Utd.

WILLIAMS, DANNY   *Midfielder*
Current Club: Hereford United
D o B: 02/03/1981   *Birthplace: Sheffield*
Young attacking midfielder who joined Conference club Hereford United in August 2002 after impressing in pre-season trials. Sheffield-born, he started his career with Chesterfield and progressed to make over 30 League appearances before being released at the end of the 2001/02 season.

WILLIAMS, DAVID   *Midfielder*
Current Club: Bedworth United
Birthplace: Coventry
Key figure in Bedworth United's reserve side that enjoyed a superb 2001/02 season. Very unfortunate not to be given a run in the first-team but will be knocking on the door for his deserved chance. An attacking midfielder who is dangerous from set pieces. Was previously on Atherstone United's books as a youth teamer.

WILLIAMS, DEAN   *Defender*
Current Club: Colwyn Bay
D o B: 25/09/1980   *Birthplace: Worcester*
From the Worcester area, Dean is currently a student at Preston University. A midfielder who previously played for Malvern Town in the West Midlands League. Signed for UniBond Premier side Colwyn Bay in August 2001.

WILLIAMS, EMRYS   *Defender*
Current Club: Caernarfon Town
D o B: 03/06/1975   *Birthplace: Wales*
Previous clubs include: Banor C - October 2001, Caernarfon T, Porthmadog, Caernarfon T, Tranmere R.

WILLIAMS, GABBY   *Forward*
Current Club: Hertford Town
Birthplace: London
New signing for Ryman Division One North side Hertford Town for the 2002/03 season. Previously with Harrow Borough, Yeading and Wealdstone, he is already notching goals for his new club.

WILLIAMS, GARETH   *Forward*
Current Club: Bangor City
D o B: 30/03/1983   *Birthplace: Wales*
Young winger who joined League of Wales side Bangor City in July 2002 after a season with Wrexham. Previously appeared for Gresford Athletic.

WILLIAMS, GARETH   *Midfielder*
Current Club: Blyth Spartans
D o B: 12/03/1967   *Birthplace: Newport IOW*
Gareth can play as a wing back midfielder or as a forward and spent a season and a half at Scarborough in the Nationwide Conference before joining Ilkeston Town at the start of the 2001/02 season and then on to Gainsborough Trinity in November 2001. He started his career at Gosport Borough in the Southern League and signed for Aston Villa in 1988 for a £30,000 fee. He made twelve appearances for the Villians before joining Barnsley for £200,000 in August 1991. After two brief loan spells at Hull City he signed for Woverhampton Wanderers, Bournemouth and Northampton all within the space of a month or so in 1994. His next stop was Scarborough where he made over a hundred League appearances before returning to Hull City. In December 1998 he made his last move this time back to the North Yorkshire coast with Scarborough before going back to the Non-League scene. Switched to UniBond First Division side Matlock Town in August 2002.

WILLIAMS, GARETH   *Midfielder*
Current Club: Matlock Town
Birthplace: Co Durham
Midfielder who signed for Blyth Spartans in August 2000 having had previous UniBond experience with Whitley Bay. Made his debut against Hyde United on 26th August 2000 and scored his first goal for the club against Bishop Auckland.

WILLIAMS, GARY   *Defender*
Current Club: Northwood
Previous clubs include: Uxbridge - December 1997, Southall, Uxbridge.

WILLIAMS, GARY   *Defender*
Current Club: Bedford Town
D o B: 19/06/1969   *Birthplace: Adelaide*
Signed for Ryman Premier side Bedford Town during December 1998 and has since become a great success for the Eagles. He is an absolute brick at the back. and can also play up front if

required and was given the captains armband during the 2001/02 season. Started his career at Luton Town as a midfielder and his previous clubs include Vauxhall Motors, Stevenage Borough and Baldock Town before spending many seasons at Hitchin Town. Joined Hayes in 1996 and his goals played a major part in their Isthmian title success.

WILLIAMS, GARY — *Forward*
Current Club: Rossendale United
Birthplace: Lancashire
Previous clubs include: Accrington Stanley - August 2002, Doncaster R, Accrington Stanley, Ashton Utd, Morecambe.

WILLIAMS, GAVIN — *Midfielder*
Current Club: Yeovil Town
D o B: 20/07/1980   *Birthplace: Merthyr Tydfil*
Honours won: Wales Semi-Pro Int.
Gavin served a two-year YTS apprenticeship with Hereford United before being offered a professional contract in the summer of 1998. Featured in the first-team during the 1998/99 season and began to establish himself. A midfielder or striker who has represented Wales at semi-professional level, he transferred to Yeovil Town in May 2002.

WILLIAMS, GRAEME — *Defender*
Current Club: Whitby Town
D o B: 07/01/1975   *Birthplace: Yorkshire*
Honours won: FA Vase Winners
Re-signed for Whitby Town in August 98 after a brief spell in America. First signed in 1996 from neighbours Guisborough Town, Graeme is a former Aston Villa youth player who excels going forward with his speedy running. He scored the second goal at Wembley for the Blues against North Ferriby United in the FA Vase Final of 1996/97 and was also a valued member of the 97/98 UniBond First Division Championship winning team,

WILLIAMS, GREG — *Defender*
Current Club: Aylesbury United
Previous clubs include: Thame Utd - July 2001.

WILLIAMS, IAN — *Defender*
Current Club: Woodbridge Town
Birthplace: Wales
Honours won: Wales Schoolboy Int.
Rejoined in July 1999 from Felixstowe, having enjoyed a consistent season for us three seasons ago. Former Welsh Schoolboy international who has played for Harwich and Sudbury, he is equally at home right-back or in central defence.

WILLIAMS, IAN — *Forward*
Current Club: Lincoln United
Birthplace: Lincoln
Rejoined Lincoln United in July 2000 from Spalding United after originally leaving Ashby Avenue for Wisbech Town. Began his football career as a trainee at Leicester City and Ian has also played for Holbeach United, Grantham and Stamford.

WILLIAMS, JAMIE — *Midfielder*
Current Club: Hinckley United
D o B: 03/01/1980   *Birthplace: Bedworth*
Jamie rejoined Hinckley United midway trough the 2001/02 season, for a reported 4-figure sum, from Conference side Nuneaton Borough. He had left Hinckley to join the Borough during season 2000/01. Jamie started at Coventry City, but an injury put paid to his professional career. He plays left back or left wing back and was a firm favourite before leaving for Nuneaton.

WILLIAMS, JARED — *Midfielder*
Current Club: Harrogate Railway
Birthplace: Yorkshire
Previous clubs include: Farsley Celtic - July 2000.

WILLIAMS, JOHN IDAN — *Forward*
Current Club: Bangor City
D o B: 05/12/1983   *Birthplace: Wales*
From Youth team.

WILLIAMS, JUSTIN — *Defender*
Current Club: Afan Lido
D o B: 30/09/1981   *Birthplace: Wales*
Another former youth team player. Making a fine impression in the centre of defence in his first full season in the first-team.

WILLIAMS, LEE — *Defender*
Current Club: Margate
Previous clubs include: Gillingham (Trainee).

WILLIAMS, LEE — *Forward*
Current Club: Billericay Town
D o B: 13/03/1977   *Birthplace: London*
Lee joined Billericay Town in the summer of 1999 from Enfield. He is another of Town's ex-Leyton Orient players, having played 16 games for them earlier in his career. Before joining Enfield, he played for Grays. A versatile player, Lee has played in almost all outfield positions during his time at Billericay. He played his 100th game in the early part of the 2001/02 season and has also made a respectable goalscoring contribution.

WILLIAMS, MARK — *Defender*
Current Club: Chester City
D o B: 10/11/1978   *Birthplace: Liverpool*
Signed for Hereford from Rotherham at the start of the 2001/2002 season. Was a squad member in the Millers two successive promotions. Switched to Chester in February 2002.

WILLIAMS, MARK — *Forward*
Current Club: Newtown AFC
Birthplace: Worcestershire
Previous clubs include: Causeway Utd - July 2001.

WILLIAMS, MARK — *Forward*
Current Club: Halesowen Harriers
D o B: 10/12/1973   *Birthplace: Bangor*
Previous clubs include: Shelbourne - December 1999, Shrewsbury T, Newtown.

WILLIAMS, MARTIN — *Forward*
Current Club: Stevenage Borough
D o B: 12/07/1973   *Birthplace: Luton*
Released by Swindon in the summer of 2001, former Stevenage boss Paul Fairclough was quick to swoop for the pacy frontman. He was rewarded with a goal in his first game, and a Man of the Match award, making him instantly popular with the home faithful. Former clubs include Leicester, Luton, Colchester and Reading. Can play either up front, or on the wing.

WILLIAMS, MATTHEW — *Midfielder*
Current Club: Rhayader Town
Birthplace: Wales
Recent addition to the squad who has League of Wales experience with UWIC. Strong player who puts himself about.

W

WILLIAMS, NEIL — Defender
Current Club: Rhayader Town
Birthplace: Wales
Recent acquisition from Merthyr Tydfil. Centre half who is very composed on the ball.

WILLIAMS, PAUL — Defender
Current Club: Leigh RMI
D o B: 11/09/1969   *Birthplace: Leicester*
Very experienced defender who made over 270 League appearances after starting his career with his home-town club Leicester City. Spells with Stockport, Coventry, Plymouth, Gillingham and Bury followed before he had a brief time in the Dr Martens League with Ilkeston Town. Signed for Leigh RMI in June 2002.

WILLIAMS, PAUL — Midfielder
Current Club: Burgess Hill Town
Birthplace: Sussex
Evergreen midfielder: has been around the County League for some time, having rejoined Burgess Hill from Wick in 1998 (previously with Peacehaven): a Sussex representative player and has a knack of scoring vital goals from dead ball situations.

WILLIAMS, RICHARD — Goalkeeper
Current Club: Bedworth United
D o B: 13/03/1973   *Birthplace: Birmingham*
Honours won: Dr Martens League Premier & Western Div. Winners
Experienced goalkeeper who joined Bedworth United from Stafford Rangers in January 2002. Richard signed for Rangers at the end of October 1999 from Nuneaton Borough, coinciding with the clubs record breaking unbeaten run. He began his career with Birmingham City before moving to Atherstone United. Richard them joined Hednesford Town in 1996 for a four-figure fee, playing a few games at the end of their Beazer Homes League Premier Division title season. He returned to Atherstone then moved to Nuneaton Borough where he was a regular member of their Dr Martens League title side of 1998/99. Richard was a regular members of Rangers 1999/00 Western Division Championship side.

WILLIAMS, ROBBIE — Defender
Current Club: Accrington Stanley
Birthplace: Liverpool
Signed for Accrington Stanley, his first senior Non-League side, in July 1999 from St Dominics who the previous season had won the Liverpool Combination Championship and the Lancashire Amateur Cup. Unfortunately he was injured in the second league game and he was unable to play until the following January, though happily he is now fully recovered. Early in his career he had played in Southports Youth Team, representing the Liverpool FA during his time there.

WILLIAMS, ROBBIE — Forward
Current Club: Spalding United
Birthplace: Lincolnshire
Previous clubs include: Deeping Rangers - June 2001.

WILLIAMS, SCOTT — Defender
Current Club: Witton Albion
Birthplace: Wales
Honours won: Wales u-21 Int.
Previous clubs include: Bangor C - October 2001, Rochdale, Wrexham.

WILLIAMS, SCOTT — Defender
Current Club: Newtown AFC
D o B: 07/08/1974   *Birthplace: Bangor*
Honours won: Wales u-21 Int.
Previous clubs include: Leek T - October 2001, Chester C, Rotherham Utd, Rochdale, Wrexham.

WILLIAMS, SCOTT — Midfielder
Current Club: Billericay Town
Previous clubs include: Hertford T - August 2001, Leyton Pennant, Bishops Stortford, Hornchurch.

WILLIAMS, SHANE — Forward
Current Club: Cinderford Town
Birthplace: Wales
Previous clubs include: Cwmbran Celtic - September 2001.

WILLIAMS, SHAUN — Midfielder
Current Club: Bilston Town
Birthplace: Wolverhampton
From Youth team.

WILLIAMS, STEVE — Midfielder
Current Club: Llanelli AFC
D o B: 04/02/1985   *Birthplace: Wales*
From Academy.

WILLIAMS, STUART — Defender
Current Club: Fakenham Town
Birthplace: Norfolk
Previous clubs include: Diss T - July 1997, Cambridge Utd.

WILLIAMS, TOM — Forward
Current Club: Ilkeston Town
Birthplace: Ilkeston
Originally on the books as a youngster at Nottingham Forest and Notts County,Tom was snapped up after a trial match with Dr Martens Premier side Ilkeston Town from Ripley Town in May 2002. He is a quality striker with bags of pace and skill despite his young age. Tom has lived in Ilkeston all his life and will be looking to brake into The Robins starting eleven. He was set to join Conference outfit Doncaster Rovers at the start of the season which fell through.

WILLIAMS, TOMMY — Midfielder
Current Club: Carshalton Athletic
D o B: 30/06/1979   *Birthplace: Surrey*
Attacking midfielder who originally came to Staines Town's notice while playing against the juniors for Barnes Eagles. Tommy then signed for Staines from Hayes in September 1997 and quickly stepped up into the first-team, spending two years with the club before a brief return to Hayes followed by a spell at Leatherhead. Returned again to Staines in August 2001 before switching to Division One South rivals Carshalton Athletic in the summer of 2002.

WILLIAMS, WARREN — Midfielder
Current Club: Gravesend & Northfleet
Birthplace: Middlesex
Previous clubs include: Hampton & Richmond Borough - January 2002, Hanwell T, Viking Greenford.

WILLIAMSON, COLIN — Midfielder
Current Club: Ossett Albion
Previous clubs include: Liversedge - July 2000, Nostell MW.

WILLIAMSON, GARY — Midfielder
Current Club: Spennymoor United
Birthplace: Cleveland
Previous clubs include: Darlington - January 2002.

WILLIAMSON, RUSSELL — Midfielder
Current Club: Chelmsford City
D o B: 17/03/1980   *Birthplace: Epping*
Speedy forward or midfielder who was surprisingly freed by Southend United after making nearly 30 senior appearances at Roots Hall last season. Went to Dagenham & Redbridge during the 2001 pre-season but Chelmsford City quickly stepped in to secure his services after his impressive displays in the warm-up matches.

WILLIAMSON, STUART — Defender
Current Club: Workington
Birthplace: Carlisle
Long serving player and a one-club-man who made the Workington first-team in the mid-nineties and has now made over 250 appearances. Has captained the side in the past and a vital part of the championship team three seasons ago.

WILLINGHAM, BARRY — Forward
Current Club: Hadleigh United
Birthplace: Suffolk
Powerfully built, front runner. Tireless worker who loves to unsettle defenders with his pace and control. Sixth season with Hadleigh.

WILLIS, BEN — Defender
Current Club: Ford United
Birthplace: Essex
Honours won: Ryman League Div.One Winners
Reliable defender who came through the youth and reserve ranks at Ford United. Has been a first-team regular now for a few seasons and played a major part in the clubs promotion to the Ryman League Premier Divsion in 2001/02.

WILLIS, RICHARD — Defender
Current Club: Fairford Town
Birthplace: Wiltshire
Previous clubs include: Brockenhurst - July 2001.

WILLIS, STEVE — Defender
Current Club: Soham Town Rangers
Birthplace: Cambridge
Previous clubs include: Cambridge C - January 2002.

WILLIS, TIM — Defender
Current Club: Hallam
Birthplace: Sheffield
Previous clubs include: Alfreton T - October 1998, Maltby Main, Parramore Sports.

WILLMOTT, JAMIE — Midfielder
Current Club: Yeovil Town
Birthplace: Bristol
Previous clubs include: Bristol R - July 1999.

WILLS, DAVID — Forward
Current Club: Abbey Hey
D o B: 09/03/1979   *Birthplace: Manchester*
Previous clubs include: Altrincham - March 2002, Trafford, Hyde Utd, Halifax T, Manchester Utd.

WILMOT, RICHARD — Goalkeeper
Current Club: St.Albans City
D o B: 29/08/1969   *Birthplace: Hitchin*
Experienced goalkeeper who joined Ryman Premier side St Albans City in the summer of 2001. Gained Football League experience at Scunthorpe United and numbers Stevenage Borough, Hitchin Town and Hendon amongst his Non-League clubs.

WILSON, ANDY — Midfielder
Current Club: Wakefield & Emley
Birthplace: Huddersfield
Young midfield player who signed for Emley in July 1999 from Ossett Albion. Andy was not a regular last season but more is expected from him this season.

WILSON, CLIVE — Defender
Current Club: Wingate And Finchley
D o B: 13/11/1961   *Birthplace: Manchester*
Previous clubs include: Tottenham Hotspur - July 2000, QPR, Chelsea, Manchester C.

WILSON, CRAIG — Midfielder
Current Club: Eastwood Town
Previous clubs include: Spalding Utd - August 2001, Worksop T, Barnsley (Junior).

WILSON, DARREN — Forward
Current Club: Workington
Has finished as the clubs top scorer in two of the past three seasons, collecting championship and county Cup medals in the process. Previously with Carlisle United and Lancaster City.

WILSON, DAVE — Defender
Current Club: Newport Isle Of Wight
Honours won: Scottish Youth Int., Combined Services Rep.
Previous clubs include: Bashley - August 1998, Portsmouth RN, Havant T, Worthing, Royal Navy, Kilmarnock.

WILSON, GUS — Defender
Current Club: Radcliffe Borough
D o B: 11/04/1963   *Birthplace: Manchester*
Previous clubs include: Hyde Utd - February 2001, Crewe Alexandra, Runcorn, Accrington Stanley, Droylsden, Flixton, Northwich V.

WILSON, KEITH — Defender
Current Club: East Thurrock United
Birthplace: Essex
Previous clubs include: Hornchurch - July 1999.

WILSON, LEE — Forward
Current Club: Tamworth
D o B: 23/05/1972   *Birthplace: Mansfield*
Lee is in his second spell at Tamworth and also the seoond time he has played under the management of Gary Mills. A consistent goalscorer, he joined the club in the close season of 2001. He has played for Kings Lynn, Solihull, Ilkeston, Grantham, Telford, Dagenham and Halifax.

WILSON, MARK — Goalkeeper
Current Club: Mickleover Sports
Birthplace: Derby
Previous clubs include: Lincoln Utd - December 2000, Shepshed Dynamo, Matlock T, Racing Club Warwick, Spalding Utd, Belper T, Ilkeston T, Chesterfield, Derby Co (Trainee).

WILSON, MARK — Midfielder
Current Club: Ossett Albion

D o B: 12/10/1971 — Birthplace: Yorkshire
Previous clubs include: Emley - January 2002, Ossett T, Bradford PA, Harrogate T, Emley, Bradford PA, Farsley Celtic, Shepshed Alb., Frickley Ath., Huddersfield T, Rotherham Utd.

WILSON, PAUL — Midfielder
Current Club: Bridlington Town

Birthplace: Hull
Former Hull City youngster who will be a fine addition to the club. Despite only being 20 he will provide craft and mobility in midfield and should be able to command a regular place.

WILSON, PHIL — Goalkeeper
Current Club: Stevenage Borough

D o B: 17/10/1982 — Birthplace: Oxford
Highly-promising young goalkeeper who started his career with home-town club Oxford United. Moved to neighbouing Ryman Leaguers Oxford City in March 2002 and created quite an interest with some excellent performances. Transferred to Stevenage Borough in May 2002.

WILSON, RICHARD — Defender
Current Club: Eccleshill United

Birthplace: Bradford
Previous clubs include: Thackley - July 1999, Accrington Stanley, Bradford C.

WILSON, ROBBIE — Forward
Current Club: Wednesfield

Birthplace: Wolverhampton
Previous clubs include: Bloxwich T - November 2000, Wednesfield, Rushall Olympic, Bloxwich T, Ettingshall HT, Wolverhampton Utd.

WILSON, ROSS — Defender
Current Club: Halesowen Harriers

Birthplace: Worcestershire
Previous clubs include: Cradley T - July 2001.

WILSON, RUSSELL — Midfielder
Current Club: Ramsgate

Birthplace: Kent
Previous clubs include: Margate - July 1995.

WILSON, SCOTT — Midfielder
Current Club: Radcliffe Borough

Birthplace: Rochdale
An all-action midfielder, known as Scholesy because of his resemblance to the Manchester United and England star. Joined Radcliffe Borough in September 2000 after a short spell with Altrincham and was originally with Rochdale.

WILSON, STEVE — Goalkeeper
Current Club: Bedford Town

D o B: 29/11/1978 — Birthplace: Leicester
Goalkeeper Steve signed for Bedford Town from Dr Martens side Kings Lynn in June 2002. Had joined Lynn from Kettering Town in May 2001. He was formerly with Leicester City under both Mark McGhee and Martin ONeil and made 15 Reserve team appearances in four years before moving on to Rockingham Road in August 1998.

WILSON, STUART — Forward
Current Club: Grantham Town

D o B: 16/09/1977 — Birthplace: Leicester
Signed for Grantham Town on a two-year contact from Shepshed Dynamo late September 2001. First came to the clubs notice when he score goals against Grantham in a pre-season friendly against Leicester City. Stuart made a number of appearances on loan with Sheffield United before being released towards the end of last season. Also had short spells with Cambridge City and Anstey Nomads.

WILSON-CUNNINGHAM, DEAN — Forward
Current Club: Kidsgrove Athletic

D o B: 28/05/1977 — Birthplace: Stoke
Honours won: NWCL Winners
Signed for Kidsgrove from Newcastle Town, where he had been top scorer, at the beginning of the 2001/02 season. Like most of the rest of the Kidsgrove squad, he used to play for Leek after starting his career with Port Vale.

WILTSHIRE, GARY — Forward
Current Club: Flackwell Heath

D o B: 11/02/1975 — Birthplace: Maidenhead
Previous clubs include: Windsor & Eton - January 2002, Marlow, Flackwell Heath, Marlow, Chalfont St.Peter, Marlow, Flackwell Heath, Marlow, Maidenhead Utd., Marlow.

WIMBLE, SHAUN — Midfielder
Current Club: Oxford City

Honours won: England Schoolboy Int.

Previous clubs include: Witney T - July 1999, Yeovil T, Fulham, Woking, Swindon T.

WIMBLETON, JASON — Midfielder
Current Club: Arundel

Birthplace: Sussex
Midfielder: returned to Arundel from Littlehampton in September 2000: proved to be a major asset to the side with his aerial strength, and rounded off the 2000/01 season by scoring a superb solo-run decisive goal in the Brighton Charity Cup Final victory over Whitehawk.

WINCELL, SAM — Forward
Current Club: Arundel

Birthplace: Sussex
Hard-working forward who really shuts out the opposition: previously with Lancing and Wick until signed by Arundel during 1998/99: second highest scorer in Division Two for 1999/2000 (behind team-mate Miles Scerri) with 25 strikes, including both goals in the come-from-behind 2-1 victory over Worthing Utd in April 2000 which sealed promotion for the Mullets: had 17 goals to his name in 2000/01.

WINCHCOMBE, KEVIN — Defender
Current Club: VCD Athletic

D o B: 13/11/1979 — Birthplace: Greenwich
Previous clubs include: Thamesmead T - July 2000, West Ham Utd (Junior).

WINCHCOMBE, STEVE — Forward
Current Club: Swindon Supermarine

Birthplace: Swindon
From Youth Academy.

WINDOWS, JAMIE — Forward
Current Club: Heybridge Swifts
Birthplace: Colchester
Three years on the books of Southend United gave this young striker an impressive pedigree. Released by Southend, he is now looking to make his mark in the Non-League game.

WINFIELD, DARREN — Midfielder
Current Club: Folkestone Invicta
D o B: 13/12/1981   Birthplace: Kent
Left-sided youngster who made a rapid rise from the Folkestone Invicta youth team to the first team. Made his Premier Division debut as a substitute at Cambridge City and his full debut in an FA Trophy replay away to Oxford City.

WINGER, NICKY — Midfielder
Current Club: St Margaretsbury
D o B: 11/11/1979   Birthplace: Hoddesdon
Previous clubs include: Bishops Stortford - July 2001.

WINGFIELD, PHIL — Midfielder
Current Club: Kingstonian
D o B: 11/00/1000   Birthplace: London
Experienced midfielder with many honours in the Non-League game, including Ryman League Premier Division winners medals. Rejoined Kingstonian for the fourth time in July 2002 after a spell with Sutton United. Had signed for the Us in December 2001 from the Ks and has also turned out for Hayes, Farnborough Town and Walton & Hersham.

WINKS, GARY — Midfielder
Current Club: Hemel Hempstead Town
Birthplace: Watford
Previous clubs include: Tring T - January 2002, Hemel Hempstead, Berkhamsted T, Hemel Hempstead.

WINNETT, STEVE — Midfielder
Current Club: Corinthian Casuals
Birthplace: Surrey
Steve joined Corinthian Casuals from Epsom & Ewell in December 1999. A hard-working and energetic midfielder.

WINSHIP, DAVE — Midfielder
Current Club: Felixstowe & Walton United
Birthplace: Suffolk
Former Walton United player who had occasional games for the Seasiders last season while playing for Grundisburgh. Has committed himself to Jewson League football this season and is proving to be a vital member of the squad.

WINSLADE, GLENN — Midfielder
Current Club: Bashley
Previous clubs include: Aldershot T - July 2000, AFC Bournemouth (Junior).

WINSTANLEY, MARK — Defender
Current Club: Southport
D o B: 22/01/1968   Birthplace: St Helens
Vastly experienced defender who joined Southport in May 2002 after being released by Carlisle United. Started his career with Bolton where he stayed for eight years and played over 200 times before moving to Burnley in August 1994. Made a further 150 appearances for the Clarets before transferring to Shrewsbury in July 1999. Added another 100-plus games to his tally with the Shrews and Carlisle before joining Port.

WINSTANLEY, MARK — Goalkeeper
Current Club: Runcorn FC Halton
Birthplace: Liverpool
Established himself this season as Runcorn's Number One goalkeeper with some fantastic displays between the sticks. Signed for Runcorn during the 2000/2001 season from Prescot Cables originally as cover. Mark is one of the best goalkeepers around in one-on-one situations, and although prone to the odd error, gives confidence to the defence with his presence in goal.

WINSTON, SAMMY — Forward
Current Club: Slough Town
D o B: 06/08/1978   Birthplace: London
Previous clubs include: Kingstonian - November 2001, Sutton Utd, Chesham Utd, Yeovil T, Leyton Orient, Norwich C.

WINSTONE, SIMON — Defender
Current Club: Paulton Rovers
D o B: 04/10/1974   Birthplace: Bristol
Previous clubs include: Mangotsfield Utd - July 1999, Clevedon T, Mangotsfield Utd, Telford Utd, Torquay Utd, Stoke C.

WINTER, DARRYL — Defender
Current Club: Maltby Main
Birthplace: Yorkshire
Previous clubs include: Alfreton T - December 2000, Parkgate, Maltby Main.

WINTER, HADLEIGH — Defender
Current Club: Mangotsfield United
Birthplace: Bristol
A youngster who has progressed through Mangotsfield United youth and reserve ranks. Can play in defence or midfield and is rated as one for the future.

WINTER, STEVE — Midfielder
Current Club: Tiverton Town
D o B: 26/10/1973   Birthplace: Bristol
Steve was signed for Tiverton Town from Ryman Premier Division side Basingstoke Town in the summer of 2001. He is a player with excellent vision and passing skills with an eye for goal and became an instant hit with the supporters. Previously played 18 games for Walsall as well as spending two seasons at Torquay United. He played in the 1999 FA Trophy final at Wembley for Forest Green Rovers and has also had spells with Yeovil Town, Dorchester Town and Salisbury City.

WISE, DANNY — Midfielder
Current Club: Banstead Athletic
Birthplace: Surrey
Previous clubs include: Whyteleafe - August 2001, Croydon.

WISEMAN, JUSTIN — Midfielder
Current Club: Racing Club Warwick
Birthplace: Warwick
Talented midfielder who came through VS Rugbys youth ranks to become a regular in their Dr Martens League side. Also gained experience with Coleshill Town and then joined Racing Club Warwick at the start of the 2000/01 season.

WISEMAN, PAUL — Forward
Current Club: Port Talbot Town
D o B: 22/04/1973   Birthplace: Neath
Previous clubs include: Goytre Utd - December 1999, Afan Lido, Goytre Utd, BP Llandarcy.

W

WITCOMBE, KRISTIAN — *Midfielder*
Current Club: Merthyr Tydfil

Birthplace: Wales
Joined Dr Martens Western side Merthyr Tydfil in the close-season of 2002 from Welsh League side Caerleon AFC where he was also under the guidance of new Martyrs boss Andy Beattie. Known to everyone as Ginge, can play full back on either side. A strong defender who likes to get forward.

WITNEY, SCOTT — *Forward*
Current Club: Maldon Town

Birthplace: Essex
Previous clubs include: Tilbury - July 2000, Bishops Stortford, Maldon T, Bowers Utd, Heybridge Swifts.

WITT, STEVE — *Forward*
Current Club: Salisbury City

Birthplace: Salisbury
A product of Dr Martens Eastern club Salisbury City's youth and reserve teams, this young midfielder or forward likes to go forward and score goals. Finished top goalscorer for the reserve side for the 2000/01 season and then netted a number of senior goals the following campaign.

WITTINGHAM, CHRIS — *Defender*
Current Club: Clitheroe

Birthplace: Lancashire
Bags of pace, enormous will to win, exciting on the ball. A favourite with the fans.

WOJTOWICZ, MATTHEW — *Defender*
Current Club: Egham Town

D o B: 10/04/1975   *Birthplace: Berkshire*
Previous clubs include: Flackwell Heath - March 2002, Windsor & Eton, Flackwell Heath, Marlow, Flackwell Heath, Slough T, Marlow.

WOLF, DANNY — *Defender*
Current Club: Bishops Stortford

Birthplace: Essex
Talented youngster previously with Aveley and Leyton Pennant. Had a spell on loan with Barking & East Ham Utd.

WOLFE, KEVIN — *Goalkeeper*
Current Club: Workington

Birthplace: Newcastle
Previous clubs include: Durham C - August 2001, Harrogate T, Durham C, Chester-le-Street, Bedlington Terriers, Dunston Federation Brewery, Bishop Auckland, Blyth Spartans, Workington, Seaham Red Star, Durham C, Newcastle Blue Star, Durham C, Darlington, Newcastle Utd.

WOLLEN, ANDY — *Defender*
Current Club: Cirencester Town

D o B: 14/11/1966   *Birthplace: Swindon*
An vastly experienced defender who can command and help the younger players. Andy started his career with Swindon Town but has since played Non-League football for many years with the likes of Newbury Town, Hungerford Town, Newport Isle of Wight, Gloucester City and Swindon Supermarine. Signed for Cirencester Town in July 2001, he ended the campaign as the clubs player of the year.

WOLSEY, MARK — *Midfielder*
Current Club: Evesham United

D o B: 27/12/1973   *Birthplace: Birmingham*
Previous clubs include: Tamworth - June 2000, Kidderminster Harriers, Solihull B, Redditch Utd, Nuneaton B, Moor Green, Kidderminster Harriers.

WOMBLE, ANDY — *Forward*
Current Club: Worksop Town

Previous clubs include: Belper T - July 1997, Lincoln Utd, Gainsborough Trinity, Belper T, Glapwell.

WOOD, BEN — *Defender*
Current Club: Ford United

Birthplace: Essex
Honours won: Ryman League Div.One Winners
A fireman by trade and returning from an injury which made him miss the run-in to the end of last season as Ford United won the Ryman League Division One title. Signed from Avley in July 2000 and his other previous clubs include Clapton, Woking and Leyton Pennant. A reliable young defender.

WOOD, CARL — *Midfielder*
Current Club: North Ferriby United

Birthplace: Hull
Defensive midfield player who joined North Ferriby United in the summer of 2001 from Northern Counties East League neighbours Hall Road Rangers. Had made his debut for Rangers as a teenager.

WOOD, GRAHAM — *Defender*
Current Club: Brentwood

Birthplace: Essex
Spent much of his early career at Brentwood and has also had spells at Canvey Island, Ford United and Bowers. Has often been plagued by injury during his career but when fully fit Woody is still a great asset at the back.

WOOD, JASON — *Midfielder*
Current Club: Chippenham Town

Previous clubs include: Brislington - August 2001.

WOOD, JEFF — *Forward*
Current Club: Leyton

D o B: 08/03/1964   *Birthplace: Essex*
Prolific Non-League marksman whose goals helped Leyton to win the Essex Senior League title in 2001/02 and promotion to the Ryman League. Started as a junior with West Ham and then served the likes of Greenwich Borough, Crawley Town, Dartford, Bishops Stortford, Harlow, Purfleet, Barking, Aldershot Town, where he was highly-successful, Ford United and Leyton, whom he joined in the summer of 2001.

WOOD, JONATHAN — *Defender*
Current Club: Buxton

Birthplace: Derbyshire
From Local football - July 2000, Matlock T, Buxton.

WOOD, MARCUS — *Midfielder*
Current Club: Parkgate

Birthplace: Sheffield
Previous clubs include: Goole AFC - November 2001, Denaby Utd, Alfreton T, Denaby Utd, Glapwell, Alfreton T, Matlock T, Rotherham Utd (Trainee).

WOOD, MARK — Defender
Current Club: Mickleover Sports
Birthplace: Derby
Previous clubs include: Belper T - July 2002, Stafford R, Gresley R, Burton Alb., Mansfield T, Derby Co (Trainee).

WOOD, MARK — Forward
Current Club: Pickering Town
Birthplace: York
Previous clubs include: Goole T - July 1996, York C.

WOOD, MARTIN — Midfielder
Current Club: Hall Road Rangers
Birthplace: Hull
From Youth team.

WOOD, NICKY — Defender
Current Club: Wakefield & Emley
Birthplace: Huddersfield
Now in his fifth season at Emley, joining after being released by Huddersfield Town. A university graduate, he took time to establish himself but is now a valued member of the fist team squad. Spent some time on trial at Ayr United during pre season in 1999.

WOOD, PAUL — Forward
Current Club: Hallam
D o B: 01/11/1964   Birthplace: Middlesbrough
Joined Havant & Waterlooville in September 1998 from Hong Kong team Happy Valley. In his career he has made over 350 league appearances for Portsmouth, Brighton, Bournemouth and Sheffield United. His experience and dazzling ball skills frequently lead to some spectacular goals, his long range strike against Burton Albion in 1999 at Westleigh Park is widely regarded by fans as one of the greatest goals the club has seen. Paul was last seasons Player of the Year and over his first three seasons with the club has scored an incredible 57 goals. He chalked up his 100th league appearance for the team after returning from lengthy injury in February 2002.

WOOD, PAUL — Forward
Current Club: Wingate And Finchley
D o B: 14/10/1977   Birthplace: Sheffield
Previous clubs include: Denaby Utd - August 2000, Alfreton T, Worksop T, Sheffield Utd.

WOOD, PAUL — Forward
Current Club: Havant & Waterlooville
D o B: 17/02/1983   Birthplace: London
Previous clubs include: Potters Bar T - July 2000.

WOOD, PETER — Defender
Current Club: Carshalton Athletic
D o B: 05/10/1973   Birthplace: Surrey
Signed for Carshalton Athletic from Hampton & Richmond Borough in December 2000. Previous clubs include Malden Vale, Molesey, Kingstonian and Sutton United. A solid a reliable defender.

WOOD, PHIL — Defender
Current Club: Stourbridge
Birthplace: Wolverhampton
Previous clubs include: Bilston T - November 2001, Halesowen T, Pelsall Villa, Bilston T, Dudley T, Bilston T, Rushall Olympic, Bilston T.

WOOD, PHIL — Goalkeeper
Current Club: St.Helens Town
Birthplace: Liverpool
Goalkeeper purchased from neighbours Prescot Cables in summer 2000. Excellent handling skills and good distributor of the ball. His efforts earned him a Safe Hands Award from ICIS during last season.

WOOD, ROBBIE — Defender
Current Club: Total Network Solutions
D o B: 26/11/1977   Birthplace: Chester
One of the best wing-backs in the League of Wales, Robbie can provide telling crosses as well as crunching tackles. Has also made a couple of appearances as emergency goalkeeper when needed. Joined TNS after returning to Britain after a spell with Swedish side IF Fuglafjardar, he also had experience with Altrincham.

WOOD, SIMON — Midfielder
Current Club: North Ferriby United
D o B: 24/09/1976   Birthplace: Hull
Honours won: England Youth Int.
Previous clubs include: Brigg T - October 1998, North Ferriby Utd, Mansfield T, Coventry C.

WOOD, STEVE — Midfielder
Current Club: Stalybridge Celtic
D o B: 23/06/1963   Birthplace: Oldham
Honours won: Conference Winners, FA Trophy Winners
Previous clubs include: Macclesfield T - July 2001, Stalybridge Celtic, Droylsden, Mossley, Chadderton.

WOODARDS, BRADLEY — Midfielder
Current Club: Ford United
Birthplace: Essex
A player who has come through Ryman Premier side Ford United's youth ranks. A very capable, reliable and solid player in all positions ask to play. A Business Consultant by trade.

WOODCOCK, ANDY — Forward
Current Club: Hucknall Town
Birthplace: Nottingham
Andy is a promising young striker who is a product of Hucknall Town's youth system. Made a number of first-team appearances during the 2000/01 season and then became a regular member of the senior squad.

WOODCOCK, ROBERT — Goalkeeper
Current Club: Norwich United
D o B: 15/04/1974   Birthplace: Norfolk
Honours won: FA Vase Winners
New signing for Norwich United in the summer of 2001 from Attleborough Town. Played for Diss Town in their FA Vase-winning side.

WOODFIELD, CRAIG — Forward
Current Club: Stratford Town
D o B: 04/09/1979   Birthplace: Coventry
Previous clubs include: Bedworth Utd - August 2001, Solihull B, Shepshed Dynamo, Blackburn R.

WOODFORD, SIMON — Midfielder
Current Club: Altrincham
Birthplace: Lancashire
Simon is a young right-sided midfield player who impressed during the 2002 pre-season friendlies for UniBond Premier side Altrincham and was signed shortly before the start of the

W

2002/03 campaign. He was formerly at North West Counties outfits Ramsbottom United and Cheadle Town.

WOODHOUSE, CARL — Goalkeeper
Current Club: Haverfordwest County
D o B: 08/03/1978   Birthplace: Chester
Previous clubs include: Fishguard Sports - March 2002.

WOODHOUSE, GEORGE — Forward
Current Club: Billingham Town
Birthplace: Stockton
Previous clubs include: Thornaby - December 2001, Dunston Federation, Gateshead, Billingham T, Netherfield, Billingham T, Bishop Auckland, Guisborough T, Stockton.

WOODHOUSE, PAUL — Defender
Current Club: Oxford City
D o B: 08/01/1982   Birthplace: Taplow
Previous clubs include: Maidenhead Utd - October 2001, Brentford.

WOODING, TIM — Defender
Current Club: Cambridge City
D o B: 05/07/1973   Birthplace: Wellingborough
Honours won: Dr Martens Premier Div. Winners
Tim signed or Cambridge City from Conference side Boston United during February 2001. Previously with Rushden & Diamonds, whom he helped to promotion to the Conference. The attacking full back started his career with Norwich and Bournemouth.

WOODLEY, CRAIG — Midfielder
Current Club: Nuneaton Borough
D o B: 04/12/1975   Birthplace: Worcestershire
Signed for Nuneaton Borough in May 2002 from Dr Martens League Premier Division side Moor Green, whom he had joined in August 1999. Lively midfielder who came through the Burton Albion youth team before joining Bromsgrove Rovers. He then had spells at Solihull, Paget and Redditch before moving to the Moorlands, where he was voted as Supporters' Player of the Year for 2000/01.

WOODLEY, JASON — Defender
Current Club: Rugby United
Birthplace: Coventry
A tall and very strong defender, Jason joined Rugby United at the start of the 1999/00 season from Racing Club Warwick. Was voted a player of the year in his first season with the club, although injury prevented him from performing consistently after that. Started his playing days with Stratford Town and has also had spells with Tamworth, Bedowrth United, Bolehall Swifts, Hinckley United and Shepshed Dynamo.

WOODLEY, NATHAN — Defender
Current Club: Carterton Town
Birthplace: Berkshire
Previous clubs include: Abingdon T - July 2000, Reading T, Reading (Junior).

WOODLEY, RICHARD — Midfielder
Current Club: Great Wakering Rovers
Birthplace: Essex
Previous clubs include: East Thurrock Utd - July 1996, Basildon Utd, Great Wakering R.

WOODMAN, SCOTT — Midfielder
Current Club: Paulton Rovers
Birthplace: Bristol
Previous clubs include: Clevedon T - July 1999, Oldland, Norwich C, Swindon T (Trainee).

WOODRAY, MIKE — Forward
Current Club: Winsford United
Birthplace: Cheshire
Bustling centre forward who was playing for Leek Town last season.

WOODRUFFE, LEON — Midfielder
Current Club: Hendon
Birthplace: London
Signed for Hendon in December 2001 from local rivals Harrow Borough, having previously appeared for Yeading, Hampton & Richmond Borough and Wembley. Leon is a talented midfielder who can also play in defence.

WOODS, ANDY — Goalkeeper
Current Club: Scarborough
D o B: 15/01/1976   Birthplace: Colchester
Honours won: England Semi-Pro Int.
Andy signed for Scarborough in 1999 after making an impact in a pre season friendly match against Huddersfield Town, single handily keeping the score line blank. During his first season the former Doncaster Rovers player kept long serving keeper Kevin Martin on the side lines with his impressive form. After starting his career at Oldham Athletic as a trainee Andy played 124 games for Halifax Town in the Conference before joining Doncaster and then Boro. He broke the clubs consecutive clean sheet record after going eight games (862 minutes) unbeaten setting a new Conference record of six games without conceding.

WOODS, DANNY — Midfielder
Current Club: Eastleigh
Birthplace: Bournemouth
Previous clubs include: Bournemouth FC - May 2002.

WOODS, DERREN — Forward
Current Club: Littlehampton Town
Birthplace: Sussex
Big centre-forward and seasoned campaigner: had previously scored 64 goals in 200+ appearances for Lancing and was one of the leading Division Two marksmen when playing for Southwick in 1998/99: signed for Littlehampton midway through 1999/2000 and scored 17 times last season: returned to Southwick at the start of the latest term, but reportedly was considering retirement after only a few games: turned up at Littlehampton again in October.

WOODS, JOHN — Midfielder
Current Club: Marske United
Birthplace: Cleveland
Previous clubs include: Northallerton T - July 1998, Whiby T, Northallerton T, Bridlington T, Northallerton T, Guisborough T.

WOODS, MARK — Defender
Current Club: Colwyn Bay
D o B: 26/07/1965
Previous clubs include: Pieksamaki (Finland) - July 1990, Colwyn Bay, Flint Town Utd, United Services.

W

WOODS, MATT — *Defender*

Current Club: Rossendale United

D o B: 09/09/1976 — *Birthplace: Gosport*

Talented defender whose career began at Everton. Joined Chester City in 1996 and played over 100 times in the League for the club prior to their relegation to the Conference.

WOODS, RAY — *Midfielder*

Current Club: Worcester City

D o B: 07/06/1965 — *Birthplace: Birkenhead*

Vastly experienced winger who is also Worcester City's Youth Development Officer. Played at Tranmere Rovers, Wigan Athletic, Coventry City and Shrewsbury Town, then Telford and Nuneaton, before joining Worcester in 1997.

WOODS, TRISTAN — *Midfielder*

Current Club: Molesey

Birthplace: Surrey

Previous clubs include: Croydon Ath - February 2002, Egham T, Wokingham T, Carshalton Ath., Croydon Ath., Sutton Utd.

WOODTHORPE, COLIN — *Defender*

Current Club: Morecambe

D o B: 13/01/1969 — *Birthplace: Liverpool*

An experienced defender who made over 250 League appearances both in England and Scotland. Started his career with Chester City and then joined Norwich for £175,000 in July 1990. A £400,000 move north of the border to Aberdeen then followed four years later before he returned to England with Stockport in the summer of 1997. Played for Bury in 2001/02 and then signed for Conference side Morecambe in August 2002.

WOODVINE, DAVE — *Defender*

Current Club: Newcastle Town

D o B: 12/07/1979 — *Birthplace: Stafford*

Previous clubs include: Stafford T - June 1999, Eccleshall, Stafford T.

WOODWARD, ANDY — *Defender*

Current Club: Northwich Victoria

D o B: 23/09/1973 — *Birthplace: Stockport*

Andy is an experienced defender who joined Conference side Northwich Victoria on the eve of the 2002/03 season after being released by Halifax Town. Made over 160 League appearances with Bury, Sheffield United and Halifax after starting his career with Crewe Alexandra.

WOODWARD, CHRIS — *Defender*

Current Club: Leatherhead

Birthplace: Surrey

20-year old player who can play in defence or midfield. Made his full debut for Leatherhead during the 2000/01 season, and was a product of the clubs youth team. Is a full-time student.

WOODWARD, SIMON — *Defender*

Current Club: Bamber Bridge

Birthplace: Preston

Previous clubs include: Kendal T - March 2002, Bamber Bridge, Kendal T, Bamber Bridge, Local football.

WOODYATT, LEE — *Defender*

Current Club: Chester City

Birthplace: Chester

Honours won: Wales u-21 Int.

A young defender who graduated from Conference club Chester City's youth team into the first-team squad in 2001. His progress was rewarded with a call-up to play for the Welsh under-21 squad.

WOOLDRIDGE, PHIL — *Forward*

Current Club: Gorleston

Birthplace: Norfolk

Previous clubs include: Great Yarmouth T - July 2000.

WOOLF, MATTHEW — *Midfielder*

Current Club: Harlow Town

Birthplace: London

Attacking midfield player who joined Harlow Town in December 2001 from Crawley Town. Previously with Bromley, Greenwich Borough and Fisher Athletic.

WOOLGER, GRANT — *Defender*

Current Club: Walton Casuals

Birthplace: Surrey

Tall central defender in his second spell with us, signed last season from Camberley Town.

WOOLISCROFT, ASHLEY — *Defender*

Current Club: Telford United

D o B: 28/12/1979 — *Birthplace: Stoke*

Previous clubs include: Stoke C - August 2001.

WOOLLEY, BARRY — *Defender*

Current Club: Ilkeston Town

D o B: 06/09/1978 — *Birthplace: Staffs*

Versatile performer who became a much sought-after commodity after enjoying an excellent 2001/02 season with Gresley Rovers, scoring a number of important goals after being thrust into a more forward role. Spent his early days as a defender with Stoke as a youngster and then in Burton Albions second string. Moved to Rocester in July 1999 and became a regular in their Dr Martens League side. Transferred to Gresley in February 2001 and then eventually followed former manager John McGinlay to Ilkeston Town in July 2002.

WOOLNER, MICHAEL — *Midfielder*

Current Club: Hendon

Birthplace: Middlesex

Young and highly-promising midfiedler who joined Hendon at the beginning of the 2001/02 season and made his debut in the first game of the season against Purfleet at the Thurrock Hotel. Previously with Ruislip Manor of the Spartan South Midlands League.

WOOLSEY, JEFF — *Defender*

Current Club: Grays Athletic

D o B: 08/11/1977 — *Birthplace: Upminster*

Previous clubs include: Billericay T - March 2002, Dagenham & Redbridge, Brighton, QPR, Arsenal.

WOOZLEY, BEN — *Forward*

Current Club: Wokingham Town

Birthplace: Berkshire

Previous clubs include: Bracknell T - March 2002, Windsor & Eton.

WORBOYS, GAVIN   Forward

Current Club: Armthorpe Welfare

D o B: 14/07/1974   Birthplace: Doncaster
Previous clubs include: Hucknall T - October 2001, Eastwood T, Armthorpe Welfare, Hatfield Main, Bradford PA, Northampton T, Darlington, Notts Co., Doncaster R.

WORDSWORTH, DEAN   Midfielder

Current Club: Windsor & Eton

D o B: 02/07/1972   Birthplace: London
Previous clubs include: Uxbridge - February 2002, Crawley T, Ashford T, Bromley, Stevenage B, Bromley, Crystal Palace, Bromley, Welling Utd, Dagenham & Redbridge, Greenwich B.

WORMULL, SIMON   Midfielder

Current Club: Stevenage Borough

D o B: 01/12/1976   Birthplace: Crawley
Honours won: England Semi-Pro Int., Conference Winners
Signed for Stevenage from Rushden & Diamonds in October 2001, and immediately went straight into the side for a debut against Woking. Simon has long been regarded an outstanding midfielder and has been rewarded with England Semi-Pro honours, despite limited chances at Nene Park. He started his career at Dover.

WORNHAM, DAN   Defender

Current Club: Great Wakering Rovers

Birthplace: Essex
Previous clubs include: Witham T - March 2002, Boston Utd.

WORSEY, JON   Midfielder

Current Club: Rushall Olympic

Birthplace: Birmingham
Previous clubs include: Blakenall - July 2001, Evesham Utd, Rushall Olympic, Bloxwich T, Blakenall, Tamworth.

WORSFOLD, DEAN   Midfielder

Current Club: Leatherhead

D o B: 09/11/1982   Birthplace: Brussels, Belgium
Previous clubs include: Millwall - March 2001, Leatherhead.

WORSFOLD, PAUL   Midfielder

Current Club: Egham Town

Birthplace: Berkshire
Previous clubs include: Wokingham T - August 2002, Fleet T, Thatcham T.

WORTHINGTON, DANNY   Forward

Current Club: Winsford United

Birthplace: Liverpool
Signed from Marine in 1999, Danny has used his exceptional speed and skill to put defences under pressure. Scored 23 goals last season.

WOSAHLO, BRADLEY   Forward

Current Club: Mossley

D o B: 14/02/1975   Birthplace: Ipswich
Previous clubs include: Ashton Utd - November 2000, Ipswich Wanderers, Sudbury T, Diss T, Cambridge Utd, Sudbury T, Woodbridge T, Brighton, Ipswich Wanderers.

WOTTON, GARY   Defender

Current Club: Boreham Wood

Birthplace: Plymouth
Honours won: Combined Services Rep.
Garry is a commanding central defender who joined Boreham Wood from Aylesbury United and made his debut against Leatherhead on the 11 November 2000. He previously gained experience whilst playing for Plymouth Argyle, Reading, Yeovil Town, Dorchester Town, Liskeard Athletic, Weston-Super-Mare, Cheltenham Town, Hayes, Bath City, Chesham United and the Combined Services Representative X1. Garry was appointed club captain, during the 2000/01 season, but was transferred to Chesham United in November 2001. He re-joined Boreham Wood for a second spell in mid-January 2002.

WOZNIAK, MARK   Midfielder

Current Club: Sidlesham

Birthplace: Sussex
Midfielder: played a few times for Chichester City in 1997/98 and 1998/99: joined Sidlesham from Petersfield (Hampshire League) during November 2001.

WRAIGHT, GARY   Midfielder

Current Club: Harlow Town

D o B: 05/03/1979   Birthplace: Epping
Midfielder who joined Ryman Division One North side Harlow Town in August 2002 from Premier Division neighbours St Albans City. Began his career with Wycombe and then played Conference football for Stevenage Borough before signing for the Saints in November 2000.

WRAITH, PAUL   Midfielder

Current Club: Burton Albion

Paul Wraith is another product of the successful Albion youth set up at Eton Park. He began his career at Derby County at the age of 11 and progressed through the junior ranks before joining The Brewers. One season in Albions Youth side was quickly followed by promotion to the reserves where his impressive displays last season persuaded Nigel Clough to offer Paul and extension to his current contract. A true testimony of how highly the manager rates this skilful midfield player.

WRAY, MATT   Midfielder

Current Club: Ware

Previous clubs include: Canvey Island - March 2001.

WRAY, SHAUN   Midfielder

Current Club: Hednesford Town

D o B: 14/03/1978   Birthplace: Ludlow
Honours won: Dr Martens League Premier Div.Winners
A tall, rangy striker, Shaun joined Dr Martens Premier side Hednesford Town in July 2002 following a second spell with Stafford Rangers. Had re-signed for the Rangers just prior to the start of the 2001/02 season and spending three years at Nuneaton where he was a member of their 1998/99 Dr Martens League championship side. He began his career with Shrewsbury Town, making his League debut at Oxford United in April 1996 and then made 32 appearances for Rangers during the 1997/98 season.

W

WRIGHT, ANDY   Forward

Current Club: Workington

D o B: 12/09/1979   Birthplace: Bristol
Previous clubs include: Gateshead - July 2001, Macclesfield T.

WRIGHT, ANDY   *Midfielder*

Current Club: Scarborough

D o B: 21/10/1978   *Birthplace: Leeds*

Andy was plucked from Dutch league football at Fortuna Sittard by Scarborough boss Russell Slade in March 2002. The Leeds-born midfielder was a trainee at Elland Road and also had a spell at Reading before moving abroad.

WRIGHT, ANTHONY   *Midfielder*

Current Club: Cwmbran Town

D o B: 01/09/1979   *Birthplace: Swansea*

Honours won: Wales u-21 Int.

Previous clubs include: Llanelli - July 2001 Port Talbot T - October 2001, Llanelli, Oxford Utd.

WRIGHT, ARRON   *Forward*

Current Club: Aveley

Birthplace: Essex

Previous clubs include: Grays Ath - January 2001, East Thurrock Utd, Barking, Hornchurch, Eton Manor, Purfleet, Hornchurch.

WRIGHT, ASHLEY   *Forward*

Current Club: Newport Isle Of Wight

Birthplace: Isle of Wight

Previous clubs include: Cowes Sports - July 1998.

WRIGHT, CARL   *Forward*

Current Club: Ilkeston Town

Birthplace: Derbyshire

A highly-promising young forward who has proved to be player with pace and tenacity. Carl showed his undoubted potential, scoring a number of improtant goals for Ilkeston Town in the 2001/02 season. Joined the Robins in March 2000 after being on Ipswich Town's books as a youngster,

WRIGHT, DALE   *Midfielder*

Current Club: Hucknall Town

D o B: 21/12/1974   *Birthplace: Middlesbrough*

Dale signed for UniBond Premier side Hucknall Town in August 2000, after playing for Ilkeston Town in the Dr Martens League. A former professional at Nottingham Forest, he has become an integral part of the team who has also pitched in with more than his fair share of goals. Tough-tackling and good distribution is his trademark at the hub of the midfield.

WRIGHT, DARREN   *Forward*

Current Club: Droylsden

D o B: 07/09/1979   *Birthplace: Warrington*

Pacy forward who was a product of Chester City's youth set-up. Powerful header of the ball. Recalled by manager Mark Wright from a loan period at Droylsden befor making the move permanent in February 2002.

WRIGHT, DARREN   *Goalkeeper*

Current Club: Arnold Town

Birthplace: Nottingham

Previous clubs include: Alfreton T - September 2000.

WRIGHT, DAVID   *Midfielder*

Current Club: Bognor Regis Town

D o B: 24/11/1979   *Birthplace: Portsmouth*

The Bognor Regis Town's Supporters' Player of the year for 2000/01. Midfielder David joined Bognor from Dorchester Town in October 1999 after previous experience with Portsmouth and Crystal Palace. Lives in Portsmouth.

WRIGHT, DEAN   *Forward*

Current Club: Paget Rangers

Birthplace: Birmingham

Previous clubs include: Bromsgrove Rovers - September 2001, Paget R, Rushall Olmypic, Bloxwich T, Blakenall, Paget R, David Lloyd, Sutton Coldfield T, Bilston T, Tamworth, Redditch Utd, Sutton Coldfield T.

WRIGHT, DOMINIC   *Midfielder*

Current Club: Broxbourne Borough V&E

D o B: 17/09/1974   *Birthplace: London*

Previous clubs include: Cockfosters - July 2001, Potters Bar T.

WRIGHT, EVRAN   *Forward*

Current Club: Rushall Olympic

D o B: 17/01/1964   *Birthplace: Birmingham*

Previous clubs include: Sutton Coldfield T - February 2002, Rushall Olympic, Halesowen T, Worcester C, Halesowen T, Telford Utd, Halesowen T, Bilston T, Stafford R, Barry T, Walsall, Halesowen T, Stourbridge, Oldbury Utd, Stourbridge, Spingvale-Tranco.

WRIGHT, GARETH   *Midfielder*

Current Club: Frome Town

Birthplace: Bristol

Previous clubs include: Welton Rovers - February 2002.

WRIGHT, GARY   *Defender*

Current Club: North Leigh

Birthplace: Oxfordshire

Previous clubs include: Witney Academy - January 2002.

WRIGHT, IAN   *Defender*

Current Club: Hereford United

D o B: 10/03/1972   *Birthplace: Lichfield*

United's skipper and defensive king-pin. Formerly with Stoke, Bristol Rovers and Hull, Ian has forged a strong defensive partnership with Tony James.

WRIGHT, MARK   *Defender*

Current Club: Morecambe

Birthplace: Manchester

Honours won: Scottish Youth Int.

Manchester-born deefnder, who previous club was Droylsden. Also played for Everton, Huddersfield and Wigan Athletic before moving into semi-professional football. Has had schoolboy honours for Scotland at u-16 and u-18 levels.

WRIGHT, MARK   *Midfielder*

Current Club: North Leigh

Birthplace: Oxfordshire

Previous clubs include: Witney Academy - January 2002.

WRIGHT, MATT   *Defender*

Current Club: Trafford

D o B: 18/09/1971   *Birthplace: Wolverhampton*

Previous clubs include: Ashton Utd - September 2000, PGS (Holland), Tooting & Mitcham Utd, Fisher Ath., Wrexham.

WRIGHT, MATTHEW   *Defender*

Current Club: Diss Town

D o B: 06/01/1978   *Birthplace: Norwich*

Previous clubs include: Kings Lynn - October 1998, Galway Utd, Torquay Utd, Great Yarmouth T.

W

WRIGHT, PETER — Midfielder
Current Club: Burscough

Birthplace: Liverpool
Talented young midfielder who joined UniBond Premier side Burscough in August 2002 after being released by Halifax Town upon its relegation to the Conference at the end of the 2001/02 season. Began his career as a trainee with Newcastle United before joining the Shaymen in the summer of 2001, where he made 14 League appearances.

WRIGHT, RICK — Defender
Current Club: Grantham Town

Birthplace: Lincoln
Previous clubs include: Lincoln Utd - December 1999, Lincoln C (Junior).

WRIGHT, ROBBIE — Defender
Current Club: Shildon

Birthplace: Newcastle
Previous clubs include: Esh Winning - July 2001.

WRIGHT, STUART — Midfielder
Current Club: Vauxhall Motors

D o B: 01/03/1978   *Birthplace: Cheshire*
Grown in stature over the last few months to become a very capable regular on the left side of midfield. Originally signed or Vauxhall Motors from West Cheshire side Shell in July 2000 as cover, he soon made a senior spot his own and contributed a number of goals to the cause.

WRIGHT, TOMMY — Forward
Current Club: Kings Lynn

D o B: 10/01/1966   *Birthplace: Dunfermline*
Signed for Kings Lynn in May 2000 from Doncaster Rovers and was appointed as player-coach in January 2001. Tommy has played at the highest level having played for Leeds United, Oldham, Leicester City, Middlesborough, Bradford and St. Johnstone, making close to 400 League appearances in total. He also made one appearance for Scotland U-21s. Tommy is winger who has a wealth of experience.

WRIGHT, TONY — Forward
Current Club: Total Network Solutions

D o B: 06/03/1978   *Birthplace: Liverpool*
Previous clubs include: Droylsden - March 2000, Barrow, Wrexham.

WRIGLEY, PETER — Forward
Current Club: Harrogate Railway

Birthplace: Harrogate
Previous clubs include: Harrogate T - January 2001 Harrogate CSC.

WYATT, MIKE — Forward
Current Club: Clevedon Town

D o B: 12/09/1974   *Birthplace: Bristol*
Signed form Bath City in October 2001, Mike started his career at Bristol City , before moving on to neighbours Bristol Rovers, Bath City, Gloucester City, Worcester City and then returning to Bath City for a second spell. Mike appeared in the Football League for both Bristol clubs before moving to the Non-League game.

WYATT, NICKY — Forward
Current Club: Bognor Regis Town

D o B: 22/10/1979   *Birthplace: Portsmouth*
Fast, skilful forward player who was previously with Portsmouth. Signed for Bognor Regis Town at the start of the 2000/01 season from Havant & Waterlooville. Lives in Portsmouth and has also played for Newport IOW.

WYATT, PAUL — Goalkeeper
Current Club: Worcester City

Birthplace: Worcester
Proved himself to be an able goalkeeping deputy for Danny McDonnell at Worcester City on a number of occasions, having made his full debut in the final game of the 1999/00 season. A product of the Youth and Reserve Teams at St. Georges Lane, although he did have a spell away at Rushden & Diamonds before returning in March 2000.

WYKE, TONY — Forward
Current Club: Guisborough Town

Previous clubs include: Billingham T - July 2001, Guisborough T, Marske Utd.

WYLIE, DAVID — Goalkeeper
Current Club: Gretna

D o B: 04/04/1966   *Birthplace: Johnstone*
Previous clubs include: Clydebank - February 2002, Clyde, Greenock Morton.

WYNNE, DARREN — Midfielder
Current Club: Caernarfon Town

Birthplace: Wales
Previous clubs include: Rhyl - July 2000, Connahs Quay Nomads, Chester C, Connahs Quay Nomads.

XAVIER, MARK — Forward
Current Club: Molesey

Birthplace: London
Vastly experienced Non-League forward who joined Ryman Division One South side Molesey in July 2002 from Premier Division outfit Harrow Borough. Has scored goals for all of his former clubs, which include Hampton, Dulwich Hamlet, Basingstoke Town, Boreham Wood, Hendon and Ruislip Manor.

YAKU, LAWRENCE — Forward
Current Club: Maidenhead United
Birthplace: Nigeria
Nigerian-born striker who has been one of the most prolific scorers in Division One of the Ryman League for two or three seasons with Northwood. Joined the Wood from Ruislip Manor in July 1999 after starting out at Wealdstone. Switched to Maidenhead United in May 2002.

YATES, BRENDAN — Forward
Current Club: Glapwell
Birthplace: Derbyshire
Previous clubs include: Gedling T - July 2000, Eastwood T, Gedling T, Oakham Utd, Belper T, Oakham Utd, Shirebrook T, Glapwell.

YATES, DAVID — Midfielder
Current Club: Rushall Olympic
Birthplace: Worcestershire
Previous clubs include: Stapenhill - February 2000, Chasetown, Boldmere St.Michaels, Chasetown, Shifnal T, Willnehall T, Armitage, Stourbridge, Chasetown

YATES, IAN — Midfielder
Current Club: Ashford Town (Middx)
Birthplace: Middlesex
Midfielder, aged 24 and another player from the Ashford Town (MIddx) youth set up who has remained loyal to the club. Determined in the tackle.

YATES, JASON — Forward
Current Club: Bridgnorth Town
Birthplace: Shrewsbury
Previous clubs include: Oswestry T - November 2001, Newtown, Stafford R, Clevdon T, Bridgnorth T, Shrewsbury T.

YATES, LUKE — Midfielder
Current Club: Racing Club Warwick
D o B: 19/03/1974   Birthplace: Birmingham
Much-travelled and experienced midfielder who rejoined Racing Club Warwick in December 2001 following the demise of Bloxwich Town. A former Nottingham Forest trainee, Luke has since turned out for Halesowen Town, Sandwell Borough, Bilston Town, Hednesford Town, Nuneaton Borough, Stourbridge, Blakenall, Paget Rangers and Bromsgrove Rovers - with some of those clubs on more than one occasion!

YATES, MICHAEL — Forward
Current Club: Lancaster City
Birthplace: Liverpool
Former Liverpool trainee. Michael came to the fore after joining Burscough. The young striker immediately attracted attention through hus goalscoring ability and eventually moved to Scottish side Dundee for a £12,000 fee in 1999/00. Things didnt quite work out, however, and he joined Lancaster City in January 2002 and scored two goals on his debut.

YATES, NEIL — Midfielder
Current Club: Berkhamsted Town
Birthplace: Hertfordshire
Previous clubs include: Barton Rovers - October 2000, Berkhamsted T, Barton R, Wealdstone, Barton R, Hemel Hempstead, St.Albans C.

YATES, PAUL — Defender
Current Club: Brook House
Birthplace: London
Previous clubs include: Burnham - July 1998, Fisher Ath., Yeading, Chelsea (Trainee).

YATES, PAUL — Midfielder
Current Club: Hendon
Birthplace: Middlesex
Young midfielder who joined Hendon at the beginning of 2001/02 from Spartan South Midlands League side Brook House. Hendon had been keeping watch on Paul since the previous season after attracting interest from a number of clubs.

YATES, STEVE — Midfielder
Current Club: Hastings United
Birthplace: Hastings
Hastings stalwart with 200+ appearances to his name. Originally played in the youth and reserve sides before making his first-team debut in November 1996. Had a fairly frustrating inconsistent season during 2000/01.

YEARDLEY, CHRIS — Forward
Current Club: Brook House
Birthplace: Middlesex
Previous clubs include: Beaconsfield SYCOB - July 1999, Southall, Uxbridge, Wycombe Wanderers.

YEBOAH, YADAM — Defender
Current Club: Brook House
Birthplace: Middlesex
Previous clubs include: Hillingdon Borough - December 2001.

YEE, JUDY — Forward
Current Club: Bracknell Town
Birthplace: Berkshire
Previous clubs include: Wokingham T - March 2002, Camberley T.

YEMBE, PATRICK — Midfielder
Current Club: Cheshunt
Birthplace: France
Previous clubs include: Enfield - January 2002, US Cagnes Sur Mer (France), ES La Ciotat (France), Marvejols Sports (France), St Cyr Sur Mer (France), Sporting Club De Toulon (France), AS Cannes (France), AS Vauzelle (France).

YEOMAN, DANNY — Forward
Current Club: Uxbridge
Birthplace: Middlesex
Previous clubs include: Northwood - February 2002, Farnborough T, Northwood, Southall, Brook House, Yeading.

YEOMANS, CARL — Midfielder
Current Club: Mickleover Sports
Birthplace: Burton
Previous clubs include: Burton Alb - July 1999.

YEOMANS, COLIN — Forward
Current Club: Stowmarket Town
Birthplace: Essex
Previous clubs include: Framlingham T - July 1999, Maldon T.

Y

YEOMANS, MARK — *Defender*
Current Club: Borrowash Victoria

Birthplace: Derbyshire
Previous clubs include: Gresley Rovers - July 1999, Borrowash V,
Stapenhill, Heanor T, Stapenhill, Burton Alb., Shepshed Alb.,
Gresley R.

YEOMANSON, CARL — *Goalkeeper*
Current Club: Barton Rovers

Birthplace: Buckingham
Previous clubs include: Buckingham T - August 2001.

YHDEGO, ESYAS — *Forward*
Current Club: Hampton & Richmond

Birthplace: London
Left-sided forward or midfielder who made a handful of
appearances for Ryman Premier side Hampton & Richmond
Borough during the 2001/02 season. Also played at QPR,
Fulham and Farnborough Town.

YORATH, DEAN — *Midfielder*
Current Club: Tonbridge Angels

D o B: 18/12/1979   Birthplace: Kent
Impressive midfielder who joined Dr Martens Eastern side
Tonbridge Angels in July 2002 from Conference neighbours
Margate. Had progressed through the Gates youth set-up to
become a first-team squad regular and played a big part in
helping the club to gain their place in the Conference.

YORK, ANDREW — *Defender*
Current Club: Barry Town

D o B: 28/05/1968   Birthplace: Wales
Previous clubs include: Merthyr Tydfil - July 1996, Chesham Utd,
Merthyr Tydfil, Ebbw Vale, Exeter C.

YORK, MATT — *Forward*
Current Club: Carshalton Athletic

Birthplace: Surrey
Signed for Carshalton Athletic from Banstead Athletic in March
2001. A pacey striker who has previously been with Sutton
United.

YOUNG, BARRY — *Defender*
Current Club: Oldbury United

Birthplace: Birmingham
Previous clubs include: Sandwell Borough - July 2001, Redditch
Utd, Odbury Utd, Willenhall T.

YOUNG, CHRIS — *Forward*
Current Club: Altrincham

Birthplace: Manchester
Chris had a spell with UniBond Premier side Altrincham as a
youngster but only ever got to be an unused substitute for the
first team. The young striker has now re-joined the Robins after
playing at Flixton, Droylsden, Curzon Ashton and most recently
Hyde United.

YOUNG, DARREN — *Defender*
Current Club: Ossett Albion

Birthplace: Barnsley
Previous clubs include: Barnsley - September 2001.

YOUNG, GARY — *Defender*
Current Club: Pagham

Birthplace: Sussex
Experienced defender/midfielder: former Pagham player who also
spent time at Worthing, Lewes, Horsham and Bognor Regis
before joining East Preston in August 1999: followed manager
Carl Stabler to Wick twelve months later (scored 11 times that
season): took charge at Crabtree Park for one game after Stabler
quit in January 2002, but then immediately switched to Pagham:
a Sussex representative player over the last two seasons.

YOUNG, GEOFF — *Midfielder*
Current Club: Tow Law Town

Birthplace: Co.Durham
Signed from Willington at the beginning of the season. Has a
reputation as a good Northern League player. Previous Clubs
include Durham City and Workington and was a member of
Durham City's Championship side.

YOUNG, JAMES — *Midfielder*
Current Club: North Ferriby United

Previous clubs include: Louth Utd - August 2001, Grimsby T
(trainee).

YOUNG, KANE — *Midfielder*
Current Club: Gretna

Birthplace: Dumfries
Previous clubs include: Queen of the South - January 2001.

YOUNG, LEE — *Midfielder*
Current Club: Rushall Olympic

Birthplace: Wolverhampton
Previous clubs include: Stourport Swifts - November 2000,
Oldbury Utd, Dudley T, Bromsgrove R, Stourbridge, Dudley T,
Halesowen T, Lye T, Oldbury Utd.

YOUNG, MARTIN — *Midfielder*
Current Club: Harlow Town

Birthplace: Hertfordshire
Joined Harlow Town in March 2000 from Barton Rovers. Still only
22, the midfielder has also played for Stevenage Borough and
Welwyn Garden City.

YOUNG, NICKY — *Forward*
Current Club: Vauxhall Motors

D o B: 24/04/1973   Birthplace: Liverpool
Very skilful front player who has come into his own in the last few
seasons. Previously with Bromborough Pool and with experience
at Everton and Bury, Nicky joined Vauxhall Motors in July 1996,
but only blossomed into the renowned striker he is today after an
uneasy start. He is now the envy of many Non-League managers
and the scorer of 30 goals in seasons 1998/99, 99/00, and
2000/01, with almost as many coming the following campaign.

YOUNG, RICHARD — *Forward*
Current Club: Eastbourne United

Birthplace: Sussex
Striker, who has been on the books of Conference side Hayes:
signed up for Eastbourne United in February 2002.

YOUNG, RYAN — *Goalkeeper*
Current Club: Hucknall Town

Birthplace: Birmingham
One of the most promising shot-stoppers in Midlands Non-
League football. He joined Nuneaton for a small fee from
Chasetown and was mainly understudy to Chris MacKenzie last
season. He made his debut at Hayes on the final day of the
1999/2000 . Transferred to Hucknall in February 2002.

ZABEK, JAMES — *Midfielder*

Current Club: Clevedon Town

Birthplace: Bristol

Previous clubs include: Bath C - January 2002, Clevedon T.

ZAHANA-ONI, LANDRY — *Forward*

Current Club: Hastings United

D o B: 08/08/1976   *Birthplace: Ivory Coast*

Honours won: French Youth Int.

One-time French Youth International striker, who originally played for George Wakeling at Bromley before going on to make nine appearances for Luton. Joined Hastings on trial from Dulwich Hamlet in November and became an instant hit when scoring a hat-trick against Lancing in the Sussex Senior Cup during November.

ZAMRUTEL, SONER — *Forward*

Current Club: Harlow Town

D o B: 06/10/1974   *Birthplace: Islington*

Striker who signed for Harlow Town in March 2002 from Ryman Premier Division side Hampton & Richmond Borough. Has had something of a nomadic career to date, having begun at Arsenal and Cambridge United. He then had spells with Altrincham, Aydinspor in Turkey, Kettering Town, Frickley Athletic, Dover Athletic, Bedford and Hampton, the latter five all during the 2001/02 season!

ZDRENKA, MATTHEW — *Midfielder*

Current Club: Bury Town

Birthplace: Suffolk

From Youth team.

ZICCARDI, MARIANNO — *Goalkeeper*

Current Club: Grantham Town

D o B: 01/12/1977   *Birthplace: Aylesbury*

Signed for Grantham Town from Lincoln United for £3000 in January 2000. A keeper that has generated interest from a number of League clubs during his time with Grantham. During 2000/01 had the misfortune to be sent off three times. Did not miss a match during the promotion campaign of 2001/02. Formerly on the books at Oxford United and Scunthorpe.

ZOBBO, TIM — *Defender*

Current Club: Leatherhead

Birthplace: Surrey

From Youth team.

ZOLL, STEFAN — *Forward*

Current Club: Whitby Town

Birthplace: Bradford

Striker who has been in prolific form in recent seasons in the Northern Counties East League with Yorkshire Amateurs and, most recently, Pickering Town. Switched to UniBond Premier side Whitby Town in July 2002 and can count Bradford City, Guiseley and French side Dunkerque amongst his previous clubs.